# Jimmy Swaggart Bible Commentary

# I Corinthians

# JIMMY SWAGGART BIBLE COMMENTARY

- Genesis [656 pages 11-201]
- Exodus [656 pages 11-202]
- Leviticus [448 pages 11-203]
- Numbers
  Deuteronomy [512 pages 11-204]
- Joshua
  Judges
  Ruth [336 pages 11-205]
- I Samuel
  II Samuel [528 pages 11-206]
- I Kings
  II Kings [560 pages 11-207]
- I Chronicles
  II Chronicles [528 pages 11-226]
- Ezra
  Nehemiah
  Esther [288 pages 11-208]
- Job [320 pages 11-225]
- Psalms [688 pages 11-216]
- Proverbs [320 pages 11-227]
- Ecclesiastes
  Song Of Solomon [288 pages 11-228]
- Isaiah [688 pages 11-220]
- Jeremiah
  Lamentations [688 pages 11-070]
- Ezekiel [528 pages 11-223]
- Daniel [416 pages 11-224]
- Hosea
  Joel
  Amos [496 Pages 11-229]
- Obadiah
  Jonah
  Micah
  Nahum
  Habakkuk
  Zephaniah [544 pages 11-230]
- Haggai
  Zechariah
  Malachi [448 pages 11-231]
- Matthew [888 pages 11-073]
- Mark [624 pages 11-074]
- Luke [736 pages 11-075]
- John [736 pages 11-076]
- Acts [832 pages 11-077]
- Romans [704 pages 11-078]
- I Corinthians [656 pages 11-079]
- II Corinthians [608 pages 11-080]
- Galatians [496 pages 11-081]
- Ephesians [576 pages 11-082]
- Philippians [496 pages 11-083]
- Colossians [384 pages 11-084]
- I Thessalonians
  II Thessalonians [512 pages 11-085]
- I Timothy
  II Timothy
  Titus
  Philemon [704 pages 11-086]
- Hebrews [848 pages 11-087]
- James
  I Peter
  II Peter [736 pages 11-088]
- I John
  II John
  III John
  Jude [384 pages 11-089]
- Revelation [592 pages 11-090]

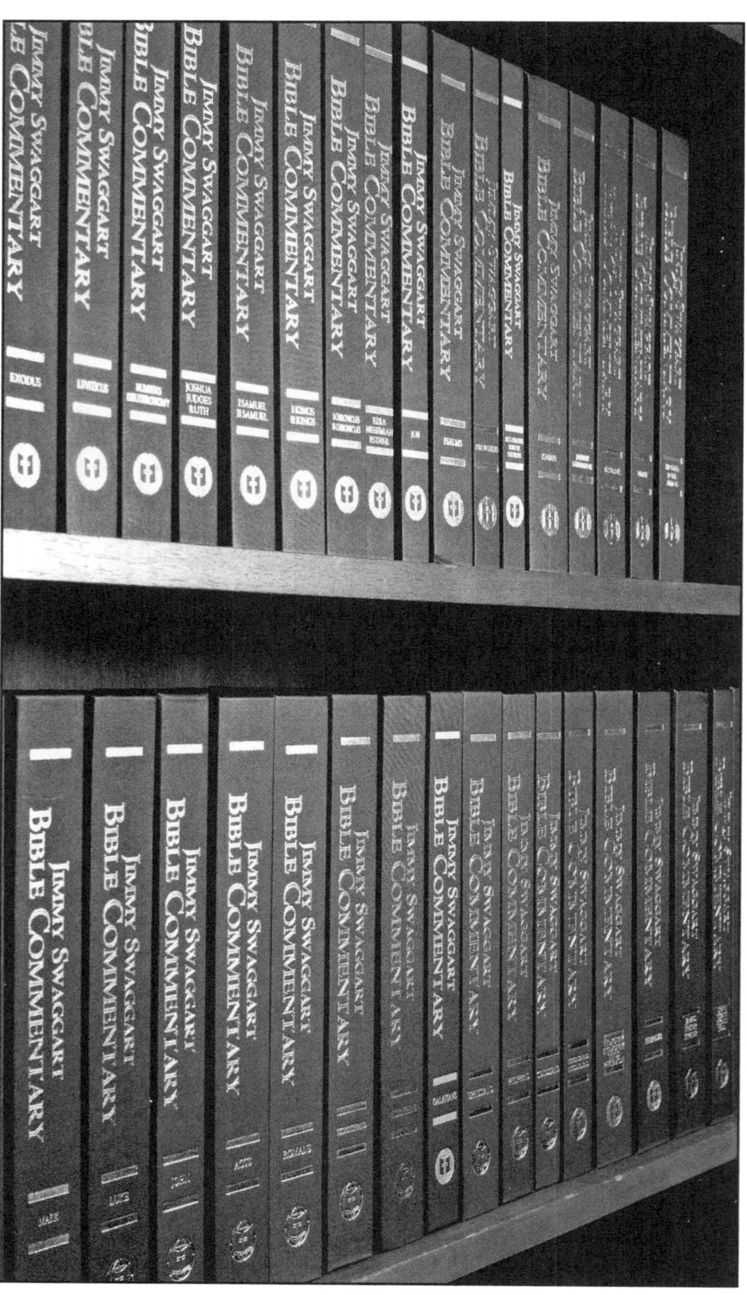


---

For prices and information please call: 1-800-288-8350
Baton Rouge residents please call: (225) 768-7000
Website: www.jsm.org • E-mail: info@jsm.org

# JIMMY SWAGGART BIBLE COMMENTARY

# I Corinthians

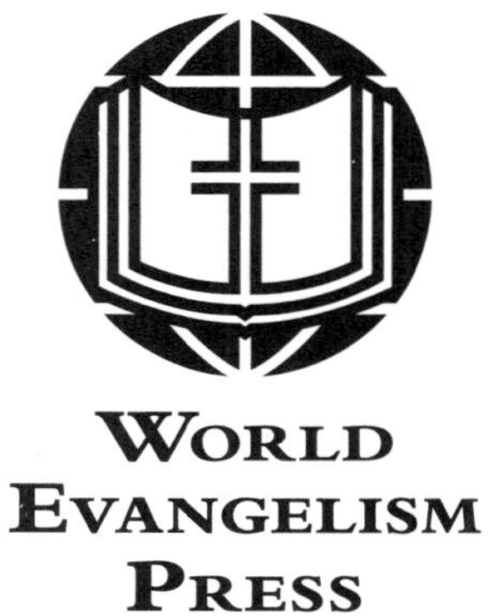

WORLD
EVANGELISM
PRESS

ISBN 978-1-934655-10-8


P.O. Box 262550 • Baton Rouge, Louisiana 70826-2550
Website: www.jsm.org • E-mail: info@jsm.org
(225) 768-8300
20 21 22 23 24 25 26 27 28 29 / Sheridan / 14 13 12 11 10 9 8 7 6 5

# TABLE OF CONTENTS

# INTRODUCTION

It was a beautiful, sunshiny day, but yet bitter cold in the first part of December, 1985 (if I remember the year correctly), when Frances and I were driven by car from Athens, Greece to the ruins of Corinth. It was a distance of approximately 70 miles.

As we walked among the ruins, looking at the fabled spot where presided the Court of Marcus Annaeus Novatus Gallio, and before whom Paul had appeared, it is very difficult to describe my feelings. With my back to the Inlet, the looming Acrocorinthus stood in the background, not tall as mountains go, but yet making its presence felt, and that upon which the Apostle Paul had looked many times. This was the site of the Corinthian Church, the Church in fact, to which Paul had written First and Second Corinthians.

## PAUL'S ENTRANCE

When Paul left Athens, after his memorable address in the Areopagus, and sailed to Corinth, it would have taken about five hours before his vessel dropped anchor in the bright waters of the Saronic Bay at Cenchreae. From there to Corinth was a walk of about eight miles, over which the Apostle probably traveled alone, to be joined a little later by Silas and Timothy (Acts 18:5; II Cor. 1:19). He said that he entered Corinth *"... in weakness, and in fear, and in much trembling"* (I Cor. 2:3). In this city he spent over 18 months of his life, and built a great Church.

## THE CITY OF CORINTH

The ancient city of Corinth had been utterly laid in ruins when Rome subjugated Greece in the middle of the Second Century B.C. But in the year 46 B.C. Caesar had caused it to be rebuilt and colonized in the Roman manner, and during the century that had elapsed it had prospered and grown enormously. The city into which Paul entered, had a population at that particular time estimated between 600,000 and 700,000, by far, the larger portion of whom were slaves.

Its magnificent harbors, Cenchreae and Lechaeum, opening to the commerce of East and West, were crowded with ships, and its streets with travelers and merchants from almost every country under Heaven. Even in that old Pagan world the reputation of Corinth was bad; it was compared with the worst.

At night it was made hideous by the brawls, lewd songs and drunken revelry. In the daytime its markets and squares swarmed with Jewish peddlers, foreign traders, sailors, soldiers, athletes in training, boxers, wrestlers, charioteers, racing men, betting men, courtesans, slaves, idlers, and parasites of every description, feeding off its licentiousness.

The corrupting worship of Aphrodite, with its hoards of prostitutes (over a thousand), was dominant, and all over the Greek-Roman world, *"to behave as a Corinthian"* was a proverbial synonym for leading a low, shameless, and immoral life. However, by the Grace of God, and through the Ministry of the Apostle, the very name *"Corinthian"* was to change, which was a perfect example of what the Gospel of Jesus Christ could do.

## THE GOSPEL

Having been led to this city by the Holy Spirit, he enters it no doubt with anxiety, and yet with almost audacious hopefulness. He determined to know nothing among its people save Jesus Christ and Him Crucified (I Cor. 2:2).

Undoubtedly he was conscious that the Mission of the Cross approached its crisis here. If it could abide here, it could abide anywhere.

The worse moral sins of the city were dishonesty, drunkenness, and above all, sensuality, which was directly due to the worship, as stated, of Aphrodite. Against these sins again and again the Apostle lifted up his voice (I Cor. 5:10; 6:9-20; 10:7-8; 11:21; II Cor. 6:14; 7:1; 12:21, etc.).

Along with its moral vices, its chief intellectual faults were a litigious spirit, restless speculation, eager facetiousness, and inflated vanity. To these the Apostle would not pander for a moment.

Perhaps he had learned from his experience at Athens, that he should discard all appeal to human wisdom and eloquence, and rather preach the Gospel in its uttermost and humblest simplicity, knowing nothing among them but Christ Jesus, yes and Christ Crucified.

## PAUL'S EXAMPLE

The volatile suspicious character of the people made the Apostle feel the necessity for being most carefully on his guard. He was determined to set an example of the most lofty and disinterested self-denial. He had been trained for a trade, like every other Jewish boy, in accordance with a wise rule of the Rabbis. His trade was the humble and mechanical business of tent-making. In this manner he would make his living, in order that he would be the very opposite of the Priests of the Pagan Temples, who were constantly demanding sums of money, etc.

Finding a Jewish compatriot named Aquila, who worked at this same trade, with his wife Priscilla, Paul entered into partnership with them. They had been expelled from Rome by a decree of Claudius in A.D. 52, and had probably been converted to Christianity by the unknown Disciples who had founded the Roman Church. With them Paul formed a happy and lifelong friendship, and by toiling with them, he was able to earn a living, which was, however, so scanty that it often barely sufficed even for his simple needs (Acts 20:34; I Cor. 4:11-12; 9:4, 12; II Cor. 7:2; 11:9).

After a time he was joined by Silas and Timothy, who not only aided him effectually in his mission work, but also brought a welcome supply for his needs from the Church at Philippi.

## THE CHURCH IS PLANTED

Paul's mission was successful, but as usual, not without opposition.

Crispus the Ruler of the Jewish Synagogue accepted Christ and was Baptized, with all his house. The Jews, however, as a body, showed such determined opposition, that Paul had to leave their Synagogue altogether and turn to the Gentiles. He went with his converts to a room near the Synagogue, which was placed at his disposal by a proselyte named Justus, and there preached for many months. His labors brought about the Conversion of many Gentiles (Acts 18:8), and the founding of Churches, not only in Corinth, but also in Cenchreae and other towns of Achaia (Rom. 16:1; II Cor. 1:1).

It was here, and to which we have alluded, that the Jews filled with bitter hatred against him, seized the opportunity offered them by the arrival of a new Governor (Gallio), to accuse him of acting contrary to Mosaic Law. Gallio, dismissed their accusation with true Roman contempt but the strong indignation of the Apostle against his obstinate and infatuated fellow-countrymen breaks out in his First Epistle to the Thessalonians (I Thess. 2:14-16), believed to be his First Epistle, which, like the Second, was written from Corinth.

## THE GREATEST FEATURE OF I CORINTHIANS

Although addressing the many and varied questions respecting moral conduct and practical Christianity, the most notable feature of this Epistle is its exaltation of the Cross of Christ as the Power and Wisdom of God unto Salvation.

This was the force that began to move and unsettle, to lift and change from its base, the life of the old heathen world. It was neither Paul, nor Apollos, nor Cephas who accomplished that colossal task, but rather the preaching of the Crucified Christ.

The Christianity of Corinth and of Europe began with the Gospel of Calvary and the open tomb. It can never with impunity draw away from these central facts. The river may broaden and it may deepen as it flows, but it is never possible for it to sever itself from the living fountain from which it springs, the Cross of Christ.

If I Corinthians taught us nothing but this, it would still be priceless, in effect laying the Foundation for *"Victory over sin, and purity within."* It was the Cross, ever the Cross, and more importantly, what Jesus did on that Cross, in effecting the double cure for the double curse — the debt of sin forever paid and the grip of sin forever broken for all who would believe.

## THE REASON FOR THIS EPISTLE

Questions had been asked of Paul by the Corinthians, concerning particular practices in the Church, or else the correct manner of those practices.

For instance, they had questions about marriage and celibacy; about second marriages or mixed marriages, etc. As well, there had been disputes on the question of *"meats offered to idols."* They also had a serious lack of understanding respecting the operation of Spiritual Gifts. The Resurrection was another big question.

Even though the following was not mentioned in their appeal to Paul, still, the bearer of the Letter to the Apostle informed him of other problems in the Church at Corinth which were far worse than those things of which they desired answers (I Cor. 1:11).

For instance, the Church was splintered into factions which represented a party spirit. One part adhered to Paul and another to Peter, etc. Paul would address this.

And even worse, no doubt the worst of all, moral uncleanness was being condoned in the Church, concerning a case of incest so flagrant that the very heathen cried shame upon it.

It was under these almost heartrending circumstances

that Paul wrote his First Epistle to the Corinthians. It was probably written from Ephesus.

## APPRECIATION

Once again I must express appreciation to Frances and Donnie for attending to many duties which I once attended, in order that I may have more time to devote to the very enjoyable task of these Commentaries.

There are many who help make these Commentaries possible. My secretary, Nikki Tracy, who goes far beyond the position of secretary in attending to duties, which alleviates my responsibilities, giving me more time to work on these Volumes. I owe a debt of gratitude to Barbara Eversburg, who transcribes all of my dictation, as well as checking for punctuation and grammar, which takes a great load of responsibility, as well, off of me. In fact, her expertise in the area is of such quality, that it also saves several steps in the final proof of the material. And then we must express deep and abiding appreciation to Donna Simpson, who heads up the Art Department, which actually constitutes the final draft of each Volume. As well, Sharon Whitelaw, formats and also edits the material, making it ready for the publisher.

I personally think that of all of our years of efforts regarding publications, we have the best team ever. We give the Lord the praise and glory for that.

During the latter part of 1996 I felt led of the Lord to postpone all of our Crusades for a period of time, which has actually lasted all of 1997. We postponed meetings in the States, Mexico, Central and South America, along with Africa, etc. The Lord has been doing great things at Family Worship Center at Baton Rouge, and I felt that He would have us devote our full time and attention to this particular move. Consequently, I have been able to spend a little more time writing than normal.

However, after much prayer, it is almost certain that we will begin Crusades once more in foreign countries. So, I would implore you to pray for us that God will give us many souls.

## AS WELL . . .

I also wish to express my deepest appreciation to the many and varied Scholars from whom I have been able to glean, and which have made my task easier. To attempt to relate all their names would not be productive at this time, but in no way diminishes my thankfulness regarding their Scholarship and Spirituality. To them, and as varied as they may be, with many already with the Lord, I am indebted.

As usual, our Commentaries, and especially these later Volumes, are a mix of several things, which makes them somewhat different than most efforts of this nature. For instance, along with the Commentary on the subject at hand, oftentimes there are word studies, topical headings which at times go into great detail respecting varied subjects, with at least the shadow of a Bible Dictionary. Our intent is, and hopefully obvious, that we want you to understand what the Word of God says about any given subject. We also desire that your Christian Growth be enhanced, which is a given providing there is a greater understanding of the Word of God. If we succeed in this, even in the slightest, all of our labors and efforts will have been worthwhile.

Jesus Christ is the Head of the Church. If somehow in the midst of the instruction and the helps, we are able to lift Him up, our goal will have been realized. Time and time again in the writing of these Volumes, the Spirit of God will at times become so real that on my part the tears will begin to come. If that of which I often feel is translated into the Text, even in a small way, I then know it will be a blessing to you, the Reader. Even though men were instruments, the Holy Spirit was the Author of the Bible. As such, we implore the Lord daily that we would be led and guided by the Holy Spirit, in other words controlled by Him. Actually, this is absolutely imperative if we are to properly and rightly divide the Word of Truth.

A long time ago Solomon wrote, *"He that walketh with wise men shall be wise: but a companion of fools shall be destroyed"* (Prov. 13:20).

THE

# BOOK OF I CORINTHIANS

(1) "PAUL, CALLED TO BE AN APOSTLE OF JESUS CHRIST THROUGH THE WILL OF GOD, AND SOSTHENES OUR BROTHER,"

The phrase, *"Paul, called to be an Apostle of Jesus Christ,"* is used more or less by Paul in this manner as a salutation in all of his Epistles with the exception of Philemon, Philippians, and the two to the Thessalonians, which were written before the Judaizers had challenged his claim to this title in its more special sense. In fact, there were many in the Early Church who claimed otherwise respecting the Apostleship of Paul.

WHY?

Paul was a very controversial figure, not because he desired to be, but simply because the role and mission which the Lord carved out for him, were in effect a lightening rod.

As is understood, the beginning stages of the Early Church were made up entirely of Jews, with the exception of possibly a few Gentile proselytes. Jerusalem being the first Church, and being very large (possibly as many as 50,000 people), it pretty well set the stage. This particular stage consisted of accepting, believing, and following Christ, but as well continuing in the Law of Moses. The Law was the distinguishing characteristic of the Jews, which actually set them apart from all the other people in the world. In fact, they were different and decidedly so. They were the people who had given the world the Word of God and the Messiah, even though the greater State of Israel did not accept Jesus as the Messiah, rather branding Him as an imposter, crucifying Him.

PAUL

Immediately upon Paul's Conversion (Acts Chpt. 9), the Message was given to him by the Lord that he was to be *"a chosen vessel unto Me* (Jesus), *to bear My Name before the Gentiles, and Kings, and the Children of Israel"* (Acts 9:15). Paul immediately set about to his task.

NOTES

However, very soon after his Conversion, the Lord gave him the Great Covenant of Grace, which Paul always looked at as an extension, or rather a fulfillment of Biblical Judaism. He never looked at the two as such, but as one.

In the Epistle to the Romans and other Epistles as well, Paul graphically outlined that the Law was fulfilled in Christ. Due to the fact that the Reality had now come, namely Jesus, the symbolism of the Law, for other than its moral content that's what it was, was now no longer needed. With many Christian Jews this did not set well at all. They saw it as a threat to their identity as the Children of Israel. For them to give up the Law and look solely to Christ, was too much for many of them. Consequently, they looked at the Apostle as a threat, and maybe even a traitor to Judaism.

While Christian Jews (sounds like a misnomer, doesn't it!) finally accepted Gentiles coming in, many of them from Jerusalem insisted upon the Gentiles being forced to keep the Law of Moses along with their acceptance of Christ. They even argued that such had to be done in order for one to be Saved (Acts Chpt. 15).

Despite the fact that the Council at Jerusalem ruled that out, still, the old habits died hard, with many continuing to look at Paul in a jaundiced way.

UNYIELDING

While the Apostle did everything he could to keep harmony and peace, even bending over backwards in order that the Church not be split over this issue, and I speak of the Law/Grace controversy, still, he would not yield at all when it came to the purity of the Gospel. He even went so far as to say, and approved by the Holy Spirit I might quickly add, *"But though we, or an Angel from Heaven, preach any other Gospel unto you than that which we have preached unto you, let him be accursed"* (Gal. 1:8).

However, in all of this, there is no record that the original Twelve opposed him in any way. Every example proves their total dedication to the Gospel of Grace. And yet it was Paul who the Lord called for this momentous task, and what a task it was! (The little problem with Peter was quickly settled, Gal. Chpt. 2.)

*"Call"* in the Greek is *"kletos,"* and means *"appointed."* It carries the sense of predestination, at least as far as the calling itself is concerned, and no doubt was. Predestination in this sense does not mean that Paul was forced to do such a thing, but that his calling was definitely predestined; however, the foreknowledge of God knew that he would accept this responsibility and call.

*"Apostle"* in the Greek is *"Apostolos,"* and means *"he that is sent, but with a special message or work, officially a Commissioner of Christ."*

## THE OFFICE OF THE APOSTLE

The Office of the Apostle is the highest of the Fivefold Callings (Rom. 11:13; Eph. 4:11). In fact, an Apostle can function in all of the Fivefold Callings of, *"Apostles, Prophets, Evangelists, Pastors and Teachers"* (Eph. 4:11).

All Preachers of the Gospel, or Ministers in any capacity, can be said to be *"sent"*; however, the word *"sent"* as it applies to Apostles, takes on an entirely different perspective. Whatever the Message or Work of the Apostle, it will affect, I think, the Body of Christ in a positive way, all over the world. That does not mean at all that the Apostle is known all over the world, but that his Message or Work will definitely in some way have an affect over the entirety of the Body of Christ.

In fact, there is evidence in the Text that *"Sosthenes"* as named by Paul, also functioned in the Office of the Apostle. What his contribution was, or others named in the Book of Acts or the Epistles, we are not told, at least to any degree; however, whatever it was, one can be certain that it was of great advantage in some manner to the Work of God and the Body of Christ as a whole.

NOTES

As well, there are still Apostles in the Church presently as then, and in fact, always has been since the Day of Pentecost. Some disagree with that, because they think only of the original Twelve as Apostles. While it was true that there will never be any more like the original Twelve, and for the obvious reasons, still, there are some 24 listed in the New Testament, that is if Sosthenes is to be concluded as an Apostle. Actually, there are 25 if one includes Jesus Who is called such in Hebrews 3:1. So, there were more than the original Twelve, and today around the world, there are no doubt many more than that, even though the title *"Apostle"* is seldom used, or wrongly used, as it is in many cases.

As well, Paul was called to be an Apostle, not by man, but by *"Jesus Christ."* This is very important, because there are some presently, who use such a designation, but solely because it has been ascribed to them by men. Such has no spiritual worth or value, at least in the Eyes of God, Whose Eyes Alone matter.

## JESUS CHRIST

In the Gospels the word *"Christ"* is all but invariably *"The Christ,"* i.e., *"The Anointed,"* actually *"The Messiah."*

It is the designation of the Office of Jesus as the Promised Deliverer. We trace in the New Testament the gradual transition of the word from a title into a proper name. In the two names together our Lord is represented as *"The Saviour,"* and *"The Anointed Prophet, Priest, and King,"* first of the chosen people, Israel, and then of all mankind (Farrar).

Jesus Christ is the *"Head"* of the Church, and as such, calls those whom He desires to serve in His Work, and any capacity which He chooses (Eph. 1:20-23; 4:11-12). In fact, Paul using this statement as he did, concerning being called by Jesus Christ, has far greater significance than meets the eye. In this area is the greatest danger of the Church.

## ABROGATION OF HEADSHIP

Religious men, not satisfied with Christ being the *"Head"* desire that position themselves. In abrogating the Headship of Christ they gradually take over this position, with the Church then being run by men instead of God. Almost without exception, and I think one can say without exception, apostasy always leads in that direction. It is what ultimately destroyed the Early Church, although it took several centuries to do so.

However, when Satan completed his effort in this direction, the Early Church as recorded in the Book of Acts ceased to be, becoming what became known as the Catholic Church. Consequently, the world was plunged into the Dark Ages, where it remained for about one thousand years. Only with the Advent of the Reformation did men begin to climb out of this morass of religious evil. However, even now, this problem is rife in the Church, with men usurping authority over Christ, which automatically abrogates the Work and Ministry of the Holy Spirit.

In fact, if present so-called Spiritual Leadership had been in authority during the time of Paul, I think it would not have been possible for Paul's Ministry to have existed, which for all practical purposes, had that been so, would have shut down the Work of God, or else caused it to be seriously hindered.

So, when we read the words, *"Paul, called to be an Apostle of Jesus Christ,"* we must not take them lightly, but must attempt to grasp the true meaning behind the statement, as it pertains to Christ as the Head of the Church and not man.

The phrase, *"Through the Will of God,"* means *"by God's Own Appointment and Will."*

The vindication of the Divine and independent claim was essential to Paul's work. It was not due to any personal considerations, but to the necessity of proving that no human authority could be quoted to overthrow the Gospel which was peculiarly *"His Gospel"* (Gal. 1:11; Eph 3:8), or rather that given to him by the Lord, of which one main feature was the freedom of the Gentiles from the yoke of Judaic bondage (Farrar).

The phrase, *"And Sosthenes our brother,"* probably refers to the man mentioned in Acts 18:17.

If this is the same man, he was once a ruler of the Synagogue in Corinth, and was converted under Paul's Ministry. If in fact this was the same man, Paul could have added him in the Salutation, simply because he was well known among the Believers in Corinth.

However, whoever he was, he is only mentioned by Paul in the realm of courtesy, and probably for other reasons of which we are not now aware, but to be sure, in no way is he responsible for the contents of this Epistle, that being solely of Paul.

NOTES

(2) "UNTO THE CHURCH OF GOD WHICH IS AT CORINTH, TO THEM THAT ARE SANCTIFIED IN CHRIST JESUS, CALLED TO BE SAINTS, WITH ALL THAT IN EVERY PLACE CALL UPON THE NAME OF JESUS CHRIST OUR LORD, BOTH THEIRS AND OURS:"

The phrase, *"Unto the Church of God which is at Corinth,"* presents the form of address used in First and Second Thessalonians, First and Second Corinthians, and Galatians. In Paul's later Epistles, for some reason, he prefers the address *"To the Saints."* These forms of address show the absence of any fixed Ecclesiastical Government. As well, when Jesus addressed Himself to the Seven Churches of Asia, He too addressed the Pastor of each Church, and not any Ecclesiastical Government or Body. This should tell us something.

## THE LOCAL CHURCH

In today's Church climate, Paul would have been forced to address his Letter (Epistle) to Jerusalem, and so would Christ for that matter. However, Paul never looked at Jerusalem, or any other particular city, as the Headquarters of the Church, and neither did Jesus. In fact, the Local Church is the Highest Spiritual Authority there is, and proclaims so in the Book of Acts and the Epistles, even as we are addressing here.

By the Highest Spiritual Authority, we mean that all decisions for the Local Church, must be made by the Local Church and enforced by the Local Church. This means that it is *not* Scriptural for any outside Ecclesiastical Body to interfere with the Local Church in any manner. By that I mean this:

## RELIGIOUS DENOMINATIONS

There is nothing Scripturally wrong with a Religious Denomination being formed or joined. In an organizational and administrative capacity, such can be a great help to the Work of God all over the world. A group banded together in like Faith and like Work, can be used greatly by the Lord. So, within itself there is no inherent wrong or evil, in Denominational Structures, as long as they remain in an administrative capacity. However, the moment these Denominational Headquarters exert authority over the Local Church, which most all do, it then becomes unscriptural, because in reality, such have abrogated the Headship of Christ. While such can certainly serve in the capacity of advice or counsel, Scripturally, that is as far as it should go. Whatever decision the Local Church makes, whether guided by the Lord or not, should be the final authority in all things. To be frank, that is not too difficult to understand.

Whatever problems that may be in a Local Church, even as Paul is addressing here, are best known by the Local Church. While they needed the advice and counsel of Paul, and which he does give such counsel even in the form of this First Epistle to the Corinthians, still, he cannot force them to carry out what he pronounces in the Lord. It is up to them to walk therein, even as it should be.

## A VERY SERIOUS THING

Church Government, even to which we have already alluded, is probably the area in which Satan works the hardest and causes greater problems. His purpose is to sidestep or abrogate altogether the Leadership of Christ through the Holy Spirit, and to replace such by man, which he has been very successful in doing.

The Bible is to always be the Pattern for all things. If it is not Scriptural, it is not right, and if continued will always lead to Spiritual catastrophe. A little leaven always leavens the entirety of the lump, if it is not ultimately removed (I Cor. 5:6).

If one is to notice, the manner in which Paul addressed the Church at Corinth, makes it very clear and visible that the Church belongs to God and not man. Jesus said, *"Upon this Rock I will build My Church"* (Mat. 16:18).

The phrase, *"That are Sanctified in Christ Jesus,"* tells us much about the Work and Plan of Redemption.

As we shall see, as we go deeper into this Epistle, the Corinthians had all types of spiritual problems, even to the sordid sin of incest. So how could Paul refer to these people as *"Sanctified"*?

## SANCTIFICATION

He referred to them in this manner because they were Sanctified. Actually, it is impossible for a person to be Saved without being Sanctified. This is a Work of Grace which takes place at Conversion, and refers to one's *"Standing"* in Christ Jesus, which cannot be moved or altered.

As Paul will later say (I Cor. 6:11), when the believing sinner comes to Christ:

1. First of all he is *"washed."* Of course, this is a spiritual term and refers to being washed in the Blood of the Lamb (Jesus). Upon Faith in what Christ did at Calvary, the believing sinner is granted the results of what Jesus did in the shedding of His Life's Blood.

2. Second, the believing sinner is instantly *"Sanctified,"* which means *"to be made clean,"* thereby, *"set apart unto God."*

3. The next step is *"Justification,"* which means that the sinner is now *"declared not guilty or clean,"* which cannot be done until the sinner is first *"Sanctified,"* i.e., *"made clean."*

As stated, all of this happens instantly upon Faith, and is totally a Work of the Spirit. At the moment of Conversion, the believing sinner has a *"Standing"* with Christ, even as we have stated, which cannot be changed. This is that of which Paul spoke.

Even though some of the Corinthians were now in a bad state spiritually, their *"Standing"* in Christ had not changed, in fact, because it could not change. Consequently, Paul could refer to all of those in the Church who were truly Saved as *"Sanctified."*

If one is to notice, he also used the words *"in Christ."* This means that as long as a person is *"in Christ,"* which means that person is trusting Christ, irrespective of circumstances or even failures, the *"Sanctification"* process does not change.

(There is another part to the Sanctification process which we have not addressed, but will do so later in this Volume, which refers to our *"State"* in Christ, even as we have just referred to our *"Standing."*)

## SAINTS

The phrase, *"Called to be Saints,"* means that everyone who is *"in Christ,"* is a *"Saint,"* and in fact, is a Saint from the moment of Conversion.

The word *"called"* here is the same as used concerning the Apostle Paul. Therefore, it means that it was predestined by God in eternity past, that all who accept Christ are Saints, and are so immediately at Conversion.

NOTES

Inasmuch as it is all in Christ, it is absolutely necessary that it be in this manner, otherwise it is by works which has no place in the Gospel. Consequently, all those who are referred to as *"Saints"* by the Catholic Church, which has to involve its long, tedious procedure, in fact, has no bearing on anything. In other words, whatever the Catholic Church does, or any other man-devised institution for that matter, may sound good in the ears of men, but is not recognized at all by God. Either these people called Saints by the Catholic Church have always been Saints from Conversion as all are, or else they are not Saints at all, for such is impossible after death.

The phrase, *"With all that in every place call upon the Name of Jesus Christ our Lord,"* refers to the fact that this Epistle of I Corinthians, is meant not only for the Church at Corinth, but for all other Churches and for all time. In other words, Paul knew that this which he was writing, was and is the Word of God, and as such, is applicable to all, timeless and changeless. If the individual is *"in Christ,"* and irrespective as to whom he may be or where he may be, this Epistle is for him.

IN CHRIST

The phrase, *"Both theirs and ours,"* deals a death blow to Christians who claim a monopoly of Christ for themselves and their own sects, etc.

As stated, if a person is *"in Christ,"* which means and means only, that he has accepted Christ by Faith, and with no addendum, that person is a Brother or Sister in the Lord, and must be treated accordingly.

Too many Christians believe their Church is the only Church, and all who do not belong to their Church are not Saved, or else are looked at as second-class Christians, etc. However, Christ cannot be parcelled into fragments, nor has any party or Religious Denomination the right to boast exclusively, *"I am of Christ,"* thereby insinuating that others are not, simply because they do not belong to their particular group or Church.

This problem is far more acute than one realizes. Men love to make up rules which have no foundation in the Word of God, and then demand that others keep those rules, and if not, automatically brand them as no longer Saved, or else inferior in some respect. In the Denomination with which I was once associated, I often heard Preachers say, *"If they are right with God, they will be with us, and of they're not with us, that means that something is wrong with them,"* or words to that effect. Other Denominations say and think the same thing.

NOTES

How utterly crass!

Any time this is done, individuals are adding something to the Word of God, and in effect saying, that what Christ did at Calvary is not enough, and needs something added, namely their own contrived foolishness — for that's what it is!

Jesus Christ must ever be the Center, the Circumference and the Focal Point. Nothing must be added or taken away. That which is all important is to be *"in Christ,"* and not a particular Church. Church of course is very important, which means that where one attends Church is very important and for the obvious reasons. However, Salvation is exclusively in Christ and only Christ.

(3) "GRACE BE UNTO YOU, AND PEACE, FROM GOD OUR FATHER, AND FROM THE LORD JESUS CHRIST."

The phrase, *"Grace be unto you, and Peace,"* is used by Paul in every salutation of his Epistles, with the exception of those to Timothy and Titus. In those three Epistles he adds the word *"Mercy."*

Farrar says, *"Grace is the beginning of all Blessings, while Peace is the end of all Blessings."*

What makes this so amazing is, that it is independent of external circumstances, in other words, the Lord has not promised Believers a tranquil journey; however, He has promised a tranquility of heart, which is unlike anything else in the world. This is what sets Christianity apart from the religions of the world and every other philosophy of the world, for that matter.

*"Peace"* in the Greek is *"eirene,"* and means *"prosperity, quietness, rest, to set at one again."* In simple terms, it means that there is Peace with God, tranquility having been restored at Conversion and the result being, *"prosperity of spirit."*

*"Grace"* in the Greek is *"charis,"* and means *"the Divine influence upon the heart, and its reflection in the life, translating into unmerited favor."*

The phrase, *"From God our Father, and from the Lord Jesus Christ,"* places the *"Father"* first, and in this paternal role, as the Source of *"every good gift and every perfect gift."*

The Resurrection Name of our Saviour is, *"The Lord Jesus Christ."* Christ, in His mediatorial Kingdom, is especially and immediately *"our Lord."* One of Paul's peculiarities of style is the constant reiteration of one dominant word. In the first nine verses of this Epistle, the Name *"Jesus Christ"* is repeated no less than nine times (Farrar).

Chrysostom said, *"How he nails them down to the Name of Christ, not mentioning any man, either Apostle or Teacher, but continually mentioning Him for Whom they yearn, as men preparing to awaken those who are drowsy after sleep. For nowhere in any other Epistle is the Name of Christ so continually introduced . . . by means of it he weaves together almost his whole exhortation."*

In attempting to explain God the Father and The Lord Jesus Christ, one is tempted to succumb to long exhortations, which even then would not even begin to do justice to the Creator of the Ages. So, understanding that no grand eloquence of words would ever begin to suffice, simply due to the lack of proper adjectives and superlatives, one is reduced to the simplicity of saying, and perhaps it explains it better than all, *"God is good!"*

(4) "I THANK MY GOD ALWAYS ON YOUR BEHALF, FOR THE GRACE OF GOD WHICH IS GIVEN YOU BY JESUS CHRIST."

The phrase, *"I thank my God always on your behalf,"* was not meant as mere flattery, as was the case in some many letters of that particular day, but rather thanksgiving which was the natural overflow of a full heart. In other words, Paul was writing exactly what he was and felt.

The word *"always"* spoke of constant prayer on their behalf. He could still thank God for them, though his Letter was written *"with many tears"* (II Cor. 2:4).

PAUL THE SHEPHERD, i.e., PASTOR

In Paul the Apostle, as in all Apostles, one sees the entirety of the Fivefold Callings.

In the role of the *"Apostle,"* Paul was always a Prophet. So many of his statements are prophetic in that they speak of the coming Rapture, Great Tribulation, Rise of the Antichrist, Second Coming of the Lord, and the Coming Kingdom Age. As well, he was the consummate Evangelist. I think few have ever had a burden for souls as Paul.

NOTES

And now, as statement after statement shows, he was also the consummate Pastor, with care and concern constantly expressed, regarding his sheep. Without comment, I think it is obvious as to his ability to fill the Office of the Teacher.

If one is to notice, despite the problems which were obvious in the Church at Corinth, Paul addressed these people as Believers, and as well, spoke so highly of them in his Salutation. This is the heart of a True Shepherd. All efforts, even those of correction, are presented with the idea of solving the problem instead of otherwise.

The phrase, *"For the Grace of God which is given you by Jesus Christ,"* refers to several things:

1. The Corinthians were given the Grace of God, which refers to all Believers as well and for all time; consequently, this *"Grace"* was and is sufficient for victory in all things (II Cor. 12:7-10).

2. Grace must be freely *"given,"* or it is not Grace, and must be freely received, or it is not Grace. Any intrusion of works of any nature, nullifies the Grace of God (Gal. 2:21; 5:4).

3. The Grace of God must come through Jesus Christ, for there is no other way. This means that Mohammed, nor Buddha, nor Confucius, nor any other fake luminary will suffice. It is only Jesus.

John the Baptist said, *"For the Law was given by Moses, but Grace and Truth came by Jesus Christ"* (Jn. 1:17).

Among other things, this means that even though the Law was from God and of God, and as such was great; it was not great enough to be brought Personally by the Lord, therefore, it was brought by Moses.

Conversely, *"Grace and Truth"* were of such magnitude, that the Lord delivered it Himself, but better said, He was and is *"Grace and Truth."* In other words, He does not merely contain such, but in fact, is Such!

4. Even though it was *"given"* by Jesus Christ, nevertheless, though free to Believers, it was in fact, of great Price to Him, i.e., the Price being that of His Own Life.

What a Price and what a Gift!

(5) "THAT IN EVERY THING YE ARE ENRICHED BY HIM, IN ALL UTTERANCE, AND IN ALL KNOWLEDGE;"

The phrase, *"That in every thing ye are enriched by Him,"* is not so much specifically directed toward the Corinthians, but is more so meant to exclaim the Source of *"every good thing"* Who is Christ Jesus.

When Paul said *"everything,"* he meant *"everything."* This means that all Life is found in Christ, all fulfillment, all development, all true pleasure, all strength, all guidance, all leading, and all direction. He Alone is the Source of all things which are good, helpful, and beneficial.

*"Enriched"* in the Greek is *"ploutizo,"* and means *"to make wealthy, to make rich."* It carries the idea of the Things of God, which are far higher than mere material possessions, and which alone can satisfy. This speaks of that which makes life worthwhile, such as Peace, Love, Fulfillment (in Christ), Grace, Joy, True Happiness, and are actually spelled out in what Jesus said, *"The thief* (Satan) *cometh not, but for to steal, and to kill, and to destroy: I am come that they might have Life, and that they might have it more abundantly"* (Jn. 10:10).

The phrase, *"In all utterance,"* is not speaking of the Gift of Tongues as some think, but rather all the Promises of God, which He has uttered or given since the beginning of time.

*"Utterance"* in the Greek is *"Logos,"* but in its conclusive meaning as given here, it is *"Rhema,"* which denotes that which is spoken, what is uttered in speech or writing.

The significance of *"Rhema"* (as distinct from *"Logos"*) is exemplified in the injunction to take *"the Sword of the Spirit, which is the Word of God"* (Eph. 6:17); here the reference is not to the whole Bible as such, but to the individual Scripture which the Spirit brings to our remembrance for use in time of need, or else in our study of the Word of God, the Lord will make real a particular Passage which meets a need in our life at that time. It is as if the Lord takes that particular Scripture out of its setting, places it into our problem, which instantly meets our need. In fact, the actual results may not be forthcoming immediately, but we are given direction, and we know the need is going to be met whether now or later.

## AN EXAMPLE

I suppose I could fill this book with examples, should I take the time, but this which I will give, I think will suffice. I want to go back to the very beginning of my Ministry, and then come up to as late as this morning (1-31-98).

Frances and I began in Evangelistic Work in 1956. Just beginning and considering that we were virtually unknown, meetings were few and far between. As well, I held down a full-time job, but with allowable time for the meetings when we were invited. This particular routine lasted for about two years, with the Lord impressing upon me, I strongly felt, to give up my job and depend totally upon Him. This we did.

We had two Meetings scheduled, the first in Arkansas and the second in Louisiana. That of which I wish to relate took place in the second Meeting. After about three or four nights, I came down with pneumonia, which meant the Meeting was over.

Since the Lord healed me as a child I have rarely been sick, actually, if I remember correctly, this was the only occasion.

I was taken to a hospital close to home, where I remained for some two or three days. I then went home, but was unable to get out of the bed, actually still retaining the pneumonia.

## SATAN'S METHODS

The Evil One organizes particular situations against the Child of God, and then takes advantage of the situation to peddle his wares. However, we have the assurance and knowledge that he can only do what the Lord allows him to do (Job Chpt. 1); however, at times, especially in the very midst of the crisis, we forget that this mortal enemy of our soul is on a leash. But thank God, nevertheless, he is.

At that time I had three cousins in Entertainment who were quite well known. Jerry Lee Lewis, who was then vying with Elvis Presley for the number one spot in Rock'n'roll. Mickey Gilley was also making his debut, with a song, if I remember correctly, at that time in the Top 40. Another cousin, Carl Glasscock was playing with the Bill Black Combo, also with a song in the Top 40 over the Nation.

This was before Television, and Frances having the Radio on at different times of the day, it seemed like almost every few minutes they would air a song by one of my cousins. As stated, Jerry Lee and Elvis were at that particular time fighting for the top spot, with Jerry Lee's song being Number One in the Nation one week and then that of Elvis the next, etc.

The particular night in question was Wednesday. Frances had just left for Prayer Meeting and I was alone. That which I wish to relate took place, I suppose about 15 minutes after she left.

THE ATTACK

Still so sick I could hardly get out of bed, all of a sudden, the most evil presence I think I have ever felt in my life filled the room. To fully describe it, would be hard to do so. Satan (or else one of his demon spirits) began to speak to me, at the beginning in the form of a taunt.

*"You are a fool. You call yourself an Evangelist, and you have no Meetings to preach, no money to live on, and you are sick."*

He then said, *"Where is your God, and why isn't He taking better care of you?"*

Even more forceful he said, *"Jerry Lee is making millions of dollars, you don't even have enough money to buy groceries."* And then, *"Your cousins are smart, but you are the dumbest of the lot. You chose the Lord, and it was the biggest mistake you ever made."*

Up to that time, and as stated, I don't think I had ever felt the Powers of Darkness to such an extent. I began to weep, literally to sob, crying to the Lord to help me. My Bible which I had been trying to study, at least when I was not too sick to do so, was laying beside my pillow. I literally grabbed for it like a drowning man clutching at anything that would give help, pulling it to me. As I did so, and without me attempting to open it to any degree, it actually seemed to open of its own accord.

I looked down at the pages, and a particular Scripture seemed to be capitalized, and leaping off the page. It was Joshua 1:9. It read, *"Have not I commanded thee? Be strong and of a good courage; be not afraid, neither be thou dismayed: for the Lord thy God is with thee whithersoever thou goest."*

A RHEMA WORD

The moment I read this Passage, I knew it was a Rhema Word to me, even though at that particular time I had never heard the word *"Rhema"* in all my life. However, this one thing I do know, the powers of Satan left that room immediately, and it was filled instantly with the Power of God.

The Spirit of God instantly began to cover me like a cloud. I began to quote this Passage over and over, shouting the Praises of God all at the same time. Immediately, strength began to fill my body, and I slowly got out of the bed, gaining strength even as I began to stand. In a few moments' time I was shouting all over the house, going from room to room (such as they were) shouting the Praises of God.

I was healed immediately. When Frances came home about two hours later, I was a different man than when she had left. Actually, I was still shouting the Praises of God. As well, I knew that whatever the future would hold, that the Lord would take care of us, and meet our needs.

And that He did!

Untold numbers of times, and in untold ways, the Lord has done the same thing over and over again from then until now.

THE HOLY SPIRIT CONTINUES

As stated, just this morning, even after seeking the Lord all week for the Message concerning the Sunday Morning Service at Family Worship Center, I did not have a Word from the Lord. As well, tremendous problems were plaguing the Ministry, the least not being the tremendous financial difficulties we were facing. To be sure, we had faced them for some ten years, with the Lord literally having to perform a Miracle a day to keep us going. But yet, the present crisis always seems like the worst, and seems to dim the great things God has done in the past.

It is Saturday, January 31st, 1998, as I write these words. Coming to the Office this morning, I was playing one of the tapes of one of our Radio Programs which we had aired a few weeks earlier. All of a sudden it happened. The Spirit of the Lord filled the car, and the Lord gave me His Word which He wanted me to give to the people. However, it was much greater than that.

The Word He gave me, not only pertained to the Sunday Morning Service, but as well addressed itself to our particular needs for the Ministry. I knew it was God! It was His Rhema Word to me.

Without going into detail as to what it was, He will do the same thing for anyone who will believe Him, and do so often, even as He did those Corinthians of whom Paul spoke so long ago. This *"utterance"* is for every Believer, not just a select few.

Sometimes this Word is for Leading, sometimes for Direction, sometimes for Comfort. Sometimes it is for Strength, and at other times it can be a rebuke. However, if it is from the Lord, it will always, and without exception, turn out to our good.

The phrase, *"And in all knowledge,"* completely refutes the foolishness of some Preachers in claiming that the Church at Corinth was weak, etc. Most of those who say such a thing, do so because it is in this Epistle that Paul explains the Gifts of the Spirit, and gives direction concerning speaking with Tongues and Prophesying. Therefore, not believing in these things for today, they attempt to demean or belittle the Corinthian Church.

The *"knowledge"* addressed here is *"gnosis"* in the Greek, and denotes as given here, knowledge, especially of Spiritual Truth.

In fact, these Corinthian Christians were so knowledgeable in the Word of God that many of them were tempted to pride themselves on purely intellectual attainments, which were valueless for Spiritual Life. St. Clement of Rome also, in writing to them, speaks of their *"mature and established knowledge"* (Farrar).

(6) "EVEN AS THE TESTIMONY OF CHRIST WAS CONFIRMED IN YOU:"

*"Testimony"* in the Greek is *"marturion,"* and means *"evidence given or witness."*

*"Confirmed"* in the Greek is *"bebaioo,"* and means *"to establish,"* in that the Corinthians were a living confirmation of the Apostolic Testimony.

The idea of the 6th Verse is that as the Witness of Christ was confirmed in the Corinthian Believers, at the same time they were enriched by Him. Even though this enrichment affected every single thing in their lives, it particularly spoke of *"leading"* (special Words from the Lord), and a knowledge of Jesus. Knowledge of Him speaks to His Word, *"Come unto Me, all ye that labour and are heavy laden, and I will give you rest. Take My yoke upon you, and learn of Me . . ."* (Mat. 11:28-30).

The Holy Spirit is the One Who reveals knowledge of Jesus. The idea is, that if we will make room for the Holy Spirit to have total control within our lives, His primary objective and focus is to reveal Jesus unto us, which means all that pertains to Jesus. Likewise, the more that we give Jesus access in our lives, the more the Holy Spirit can work.

NOTES

(7) "SO THAT YE COME BEHIND IN NO GIFT; WAITING FOR THE COMING OF OUR LORD JESUS CHRIST:"

The phrase, *"So that ye come behind in no gift,"* is not limited to the Nine Gifts of the Spirit which Paul lists in Chapter 12 as some teach, but rather every single thing given by the Lord which He paid for at Calvary and the Resurrection.

*"Gift"* in the Greek is *"charis,"* and means *"the Divine influence upon the heart, and its reflection in the life."*

The implication of the thrust of Paul's Salutation is actually threefold:

1. These Corinthians knew all about the Grace of God and what Jesus had done for them in the Atonement. Actually, they had been taught by the greatest Teacher of all, the Holy Spirit through the Apostle Paul. So, they had the *"knowledge."*

2. Many had availed themselves of what Paul had taught, consequently, had made, and were making great strides in Christ.

3. Some had made few strides at all, with Paul in effect, telling them that they can have these wonderful things in the Lord (Gifts) if they will consecrate their lives.

The Corinthian Church was like most Churches, there were some in the Church who were on fire for God and others who were not. However, for those who were not, it was not because of a lack of proper teaching, but rather that they had not availed themselves of what was taught.

The phrase, *"Waiting for the Coming of our Lord Jesus Christ,"* pertains here to the Rapture of the Church (I Thess. 4:13-18).

*"Waiting"* is *"apekdechomai,"* and means *"eagerly expecting or to expect fully."*

*"Coming"* is *"apokalupsis,"* which means *"that which is revealed or manifested."* It refers to something which has been confusing in the past, but which now has the mystery removed so that all can see what is manifested. When it is used of a person, it pertains to a visible manifestation.

Four Greek words are used of Christ's Coming:

1. *"Apokalupsis"*: As we have just stated, this means to reveal or to manifest something (I Pet. 1:7, 13).

2. *"Epiphaneia"*: This word is used of both the Rapture and the Second Coming of Christ;

it means *"appearing"* (II Thess. 2:8; I Tim. 6:14; II Tim. 4:1, 8; Titus 2:13).

3. *"Phaneros"*: This word also means for something to be manifested (Col. 3:4; I Pet. 5:4; I Jn. 2:28; 3:2).

4. *"Parousia"*: This word also speaks of both the Rapture of the Church and the Second Coming of Christ. It pertains to a personal appearance and presence.

As it refers to the Rapture, it is found in I Corinthians 15:20-23; I Thessalonians 2:19, 3:13, 4:15, and 5:23; II Thessalonians 2:1; James 5:7-8; and I John 2:28. Regarding the Second Coming of Christ, it is found in Matthew 24:3, 27, 37, 39; II Thessalonians 2:8; and, II Peter 1:16; 3:4.

The idea is that every single Believer should be earnestly expectant of the Lord's Return at any moment. Expecting His Return (Rapture) we should live accordingly.

## MORE ABOUT THE *"PAROUSIA"* OR THE COMING OF THE LORD

The Greek inscriptions throw a flood of light upon the New Testament. One of the current expressions in the First Century was the word *"parousia,"* used in the East as a technical expression for the royal visit of a King or Emperor. The word means literally *"the being beside,"* thus, *"the personal presence."*

In that culture, whenever it was known that the King was coming, those who had the knowledge were to inform all the people, for there were certain things which must be done. There were special payments and taxes to defray the cost of the festivities on that occasion. In many cases, advent-coins were struck in order to raise money for this event. As well, advent-sacrifices were offered at the time of the coming. A particular manuscript of that time speaks of contributions given for a crown of gold to be presented to the King at his coming.

## THE ACTUAL EVENT

These *"comings"* were noted for their special brilliance. New eras in the history of mankind were proclaimed at the parousia of a sovereign. At times, after the event, more advent-coins were struck and became official coinage of the Empire. (The word *"advent"* is the Latin equivalent of the Greek for parousia.) Monuments were erected. The day of the visit was designated *"a holy day."*

As the Pagan world designated the *"parousia"* of its sovereigns by their number (the times he came), so the Christian system has its three *"parousia* (comings)*"* of the Kings of kings and Lord of lords, twice to the Earth, and once between these events, into the air (Rapture or Resurrection).

## TRANSLATED *"COMING"*

As we have already stated, the word *"parousia"* is translated *"coming"* in our English Text, in relation to the Coming of our Lord in the air to catch out His Body the Church, and the Second Coming, when He will come back to the Earth with the Saints to set up His Millennial Kingdom, when Israel will at that time, be restored.

It also refers to the coming of the Antichrist to attempt to establish his worldwide kingdom during the Tribulation (II Thess. 2:1, 8-9).

## THE PARALLELS

The Christians of the First Century felt the parallelism between the *"parousia"* of the reigning Emperor and the *"Parousia"* of Christ. In the case of the Rapture (Resurrection), it will be the royal visit of the Lord Jesus Christ into the atmosphere of the Earth to receive His Body, the Church, to Himself and to take the Church with Him to Heaven. (At this time He will not actually come back to the Earth, but into the atmosphere.)

In the case of the return of the Lord to this Earth at the Second Coming, such will be the royal visit of the King of kings and Lord of lords Who comes from the Royal Line of David, Who will dethrone the Antichrist and set up the Throne of David which has been in ruins, even now for approximately 2600 years (Acts 15:15-17).

In the case of the Antichrist, it will be the coming of the Wild Beast (Greek) of Revelation 13:1-8 as a King, to assume absolute authority (or attempt to do so) as world dictator, occupying Satan's throne for a brief space of some seven years, or more particularly, three and one half years.

Note again, if you will, the parallelism which exists. As the royal visit of a Roman Emperor

NOTES

was marked by elaborate and brilliant festivities, so our Blessed Lord's Parousia, both when He comes *for* His Body (the Church), and when He comes to the Earth *with* His Body to reign as King of kings, will be accompanied by a heavenly splendor that will far outshine the displays of earthly sovereigns.

At the Rapture or Resurrection (both mean the same), the display will be for the most part spiritual, especially considering the instant disappearance of many millions of people. However, at the Second Coming when the Lord actually comes back to this Earth, that Coming will be accompanied by a heavenly display, even as Jesus said, as the world has never seen in all of its history. It is described in Matthew 24:27-31.

## A NEW ERA

As the parousia of a Roman Emperor brought in a new era, so the First Advent (His Birth) of our Lord ushered in a new era, both dispensationally, and for the world at large. As advent-coins were struck at the parousia of a Roman Emperor, so our money is dated as well, according to our Lord's First Advent.

But note the contrast. Solemn sacrifices were offered before earthly sovereigns who were worshiped as gods, whereas our Lord in His First Advent was Himself the Sacrifice that paid for sin.

## JESUS IS LORD AND KING

Such was the imperialism of Christianity in the First Century that it clearly saw the parallel between the parousia of an earthly sovereign and the parousia of the Lord Jesus, and at the same time, the rival claims of each.

These Christians were not afraid to give allegiance to the lowly Carpenter from Nazareth, the travel-worn itinerant Teacher Who was rejected by His Own people and nailed to a Roman Cross. They were convinced that He was what He claimed to be, God the Son, Incarnate in humanity.

They were not intrigued by the Roman purple, the armies of the Empire, the far-flung colonies. Their hearts responded rather to the unique beauty of the meek and lowly Jesus, and to the fragrance of His Person. He was the King of Glory, and they would rejoice in His Coming.

So must our anticipation be as well!

NOTES

(8) "WHO SHALL ALSO CONFIRM YOU UNTO THE END, THAT YE MAY BE BLAMELESS IN THE DAY OF OUR LORD JESUS CHRIST."

The phrase, *"Who shall also confirm you unto the end,"* refers to the keeping power of *"our Lord Jesus Christ."*

The word *"confirm"* reaches back to *"confirmed"* in Verse 6. As the Witness of Christ is brought about in the heart and life of the Believer, such will also confirm the Believer *"unto the end,"* i.e., the Rapture and Resurrection.

This natural expression of the Apostle's yearning hope for them must not be overpressed into any such Doctrine as *"Unconditional Eternal Security."* In fact, some of these Believers at Corinth were in dire straits spiritually, even as Paul will later address, and stood in danger of losing their souls.

All honest and earnest students must resist the tendency to strain the meaning of Scripture Texts into endless logical inferences which were never intended to be deduced from them (Farrar).

The phrase, *"That ye may be blameless,"* refers back to Verse 2, where Paul said *"That are Sanctified in Christ Jesus."*

*"Blameless"* in the Greek is *"anegkletos,"* and means *"unaccused,"* and, therefore, by implication *"irreproachable — blameless."*

As far as practice is concerned, no Christian can claim to be *"sinless."* However, he *can* claim to be forgiven, renewed, and Sanctified, which speaks of trust in the Finished Work of Christ. The idea is not in sinless perfection for such does not exist in the Believer, but rather trust in the sinless perfection of Christ, which by Faith such perfection is granted to the Believer.

The phrase, *"In the day of our Lord Jesus Christ,"* in this case refers to the Rapture of the Church (I Cor. 5:5; II Cor. 1:14; Phil. 1:6, 19; 2:16).

## THE RAPTURE AND THE RESURRECTION

Regrettably there are many in the Modern Church who claim not to believe in the Rapture of the Body of Christ. Most, probably the majority of these people, have been influenced by modern Kingdom Teaching, which is extremely varied, but by and large teaches that the coming Kingdom Age when Christ will rule Personally on the Earth, will be ushered in by political means, etc. In other words, Christianity, they say, will overtake the world, coming to terms with various religions, with more and more Godly men elected to High Political Office, and this as the Church exerts its influence, etc. However, nothing of this nature is taught in the Bible, but actually the very opposite.

In Matthew Chapter 24, Jesus proclaims to us in glaring detail as to how His Second Coming is going to be cataclysmic, in other words with great power and even with great violence. Daniel featured the Second Coming in the ushering in of the Kingdom as a very violent measure, with Jesus being likened as *"a Stone* (Who) *was cut out without hands, which smote the image upon his feet* (Nations of the world) *that were of iron and clay, and brake them to pieces."*

He then said, *"And the Stone* (Jesus) *that smote the image became a great mountain, and filled the whole Earth"* (Dan. 2:31-35).

The Scripture teaches that the Church is going to be raptured out of this world, with it (the world) then being plunged into great tribulation which John proclaims in the Book of Revelation Chapters 6-19.

Actually, the Rapture as proclaimed here by Paul in I Corinthians Chapter 1 and I Thessalonians Chapter 4, is the same as the Resurrection explained in I Corinthians Chapter 15. They are one and the same.

## THE NEXT GREAT EVENT

Looking over the Prophetic horizon, the next great event on the Prophetic Calendar in the Bible, is the Coming of Jesus of Nazareth for His Church. The event is imminent.

There are no Prophecies unfulfilled which could withhold His Coming. Briefly, its purpose is to raise the Righteous Dead from Adam to the time of this Coming, and to translate Believers who are on Earth at that time. This will involve the bringing of the former with Him from Heaven, referring to their souls and spirits (I Thess. 4:13-18) who are now with Him in Heaven, the transforming of their dead bodies, which have molded into dust, into Perfect Glorified Bodies, the transformation of the Bodies of Believers then on Earth into like perfect, Glorified Bodies, and the transportation of both classes to Heaven.

This event is called in theological circles, the Rapture of the Church, in that the Church of Jesus Christ will be joined forever to her Great Redeemer, Jesus of Nazareth.

NOTES

## THAT WHICH JESUS SAID

Our Lord speaks of His Coming for His Own in John 14:1-3, where He tells His Disciples that He is going to His Father's House to prepare a place for them, and that He will come again and receive them unto Himself. In other words, He is coming from Heaven into the atmosphere of this Earth to take the Church with Him back to Heaven.

This event may take place at any moment. Believers will be taken to Heaven, and unbelievers will be left on Earth to undergo the terrible times of the Great Tribulation proclaimed by John in Revelation Chapters 6-19.

## WHAT IS EXACTLY INVOLVED IN THIS GREAT EVENT?

First of all, where is Heaven? how far is it from the Earth? how long will it take the Lord Jesus to traverse that distance? and just how close to the Earth will He come?

## THE LOCALITY OF HEAVEN

As to the locality of Heaven, Isaiah gives us some hints. He reports the words of Lucifer, the mightiest Angel God created, who was His regent on the perfect Earth of Genesis 1:1 (Isa. 14:12-14).

Lucifer said, *"I will ascend into Heaven."* This means that he was not in Heaven when he rebelled against God.

He then said, *"I will exalt my throne above the stars of God."* This tells us that Lucifer had a throne below the stars of God, on this Earth, and having a throne, he reigned over a pre-Adamic race of beings, directing their worship to the God of Heaven. In fact, Jeremiah mentions this as well (Jer. 4:23-26), and so did Peter (II Pet 3:5-8). This last utterance of Lucifer also teaches that God's Throne is beyond the stars of the Universe.

God's Throne, the place of His centralized authority, is in Heaven.

Heaven is outside of the Universe. Lucifer speaks again: *"I will sit also upon the Mount of the Congregation, in the sides of the North."* This localizes Heaven as above the Earth in a line with the axis of the Earth, above the North Pole, and in a place beyond the farthest Star.

Heaven is not above the Earth in all directions. The inhabitants at the equator look up and see blue sky. But Heaven is not above them as they look directly up from where they stand. As well, the explorers of Antarctica looked up and saw blue sky. But Heaven was not above them. Heaven has a fixed location above the North Pole, in a line with the axis of the Earth.

HOW FAR IS HEAVEN FROM THE EARTH?

By new and more powerful telescopes, astronomers have discovered stars that are over 500,000,000 light years from the Earth. That means that it has taken light from these stars, travelling at the speed of light (186,000 miles per second), 500,000,000 years to reach this Earth. But how far are these stars from the Earth?

Multiply 500,000,000 by 60 seconds, that number by 60 minutes, that number by 24 hours, that number by 365 days, and that number by 186,000, and you will have the number of miles which the stars are from the Earth.

The number is 2,932,848,000,000,000,000,000.

Ever how much that is, Heaven is at least that many miles from the Earth.

Astronomers say that beyond these stars, there is a thinning out of stars, indicating either that the material Universe ends here, or that there may be a relatively empty space, after which stars may again appear. In fact, if my information is correct, recent discoveries have found exactly that. Such figures stagger one's imagination. Think of the Magnificence and the Greatness of God Who could speak such a Universe or even Universes into existence by Divine fiat (Heb. 11:3).

THE CREATIVE POWER OF GOD

The Lord spoke the Word, and a Universe sprang into existence. Job says that the Sons of God (Angels) shouted for joy when they saw the Universe come into existence (Job 38:7). And we should be careful to note that they did not exclaim with joy over a chaos, as Genesis 1:2 portrays, but rather, a cosmos, a perfect ordered creation, even as outlined in Genesis 1:1. The chaos came about as the result of Lucifer's Fall.

GOD'S MANNER OF TRAVEL

Of course, in trying to portray the Lord in human terms, one falls far short, in fact not even coming close.

NOTES

For instance, when the Lord comes to take His Church out of this world, even as the Word says He will do (I Thess. 4:13-18), exactly how will He traverse this great distance — a distance of 2,932,848,000,000,000,000,000 miles, and most likely, even much more?

If He traveled through space at the speed of light, 186,000 miles per second, it would take Him 500,000,000 years to reach the Earth. However, we know that Bible History and Prophecy show that the Divine Program for the human race on Earth previous to the New Creation is only about 7,000 years, about 6,000 of which have already rolled around. So we know that Jesus will not use any type of travel or transportation of which man can comprehend.

The answer is simple, Jesus of Nazareth Who is Very God of Very God, will come with the speed of *thought.* One moment He will be in Heaven, and the next, in the atmosphere of this Earth. In fact, the speed of thought is the manner of travel for God, and will be the manner of travel for the Glorified Saints after the Resurrection.

HOW CLOSE TO THE EARTH WILL HE COME?

Paul in his classic account of the Rapture (Resurrection) (I Thess. 4:13-18) says that we will *"meet the Lord in the air."*

The Greeks have two words for *"air* (aer)*"*, referring to the lower, denser atmosphere, and *"aither,"* which speaks of the rarefied, thinner atmosphere.

A Greek would stand on the summit of Mt. Olympus which is 6,403 feet high, and pointing downward would say *"aer,"* and pointing upward, would say *"aither."*

Which word did Paul use?

A glance at the Greek Text shows *"aer."* Considering that the Holy Spirit told him to use this word, it means that the Lord Jesus, when He comes for His Body, the Church, will descend to a distance not too much above a mile from the Earth.

THE THESSALONIANS

The great Apostle was writing to the Thessalonian Christians who were sorrowing over the loss of loved ones who had died. He tells them not to sorrow as others who have no hope.

In fact, some of the tombstones in the cemeteries of Thessalonica were inscribed with the words *"No Hope."* The Pagan Greeks, striving to pierce the future through their philosophies, could never arrive at any positive assurance of a reunion with loved ones in the after life. Consequently, they had no hope.

To these Christian Greeks, Paul holds out the assured hope of reunion with loved ones who were Believers, a reunion in the air, when Jesus comes for His Church. He says that since we believe that Jesus died and rose again, God will bring with Jesus from Heaven (in their soul and spirit form), our loved ones who have fallen asleep (Christian word for death) in Jesus.

He also states that we who are alive when Jesus comes, will not prevent (old English for *"precede"*) the dead in the order in which we will receive our Glorified Bodies. In fact, the Christian dead will receive their new bodies first.

## CLOUDS

After receiving our new bodies, we who are alive when Jesus comes, will be caught up together with the dead who have been raised. We will be caught up in the clouds.

Actually, there is no definite article in the Greek Text before the word *"clouds,"* i.e., *"the clouds."* Consequently, the word *"the"* should not be in the translation as well.

The idea is, we shall be caught up in clouds, clouds of Believers. That is, the great masses of Glorified Saints going up to Heaven, will have the appearance of clouds.

The Greek word for *"clouds"* here is used in Hebrews 12:1 in the clause, *"Wherefore seeing we also are compassed about with so great a cloud of witnesses,"* Paul wrote, probably visualizing a Greek stadium with its thousands of onlookers occupying the tiers upon tiers of seats. The same word is used in the Greek classics of a large army of foot soldiers.

## CAUGHT UP

Paul says that we will be *"caught up."* The Greek word translated *"caught up"* has a number of meanings which give us some important information regarding the Rapture. The Greek word is *"harpazo,"* and has some five parts to its meaning:

1. TO CARRY OFF BY FORCE

NOTES

First of all it means *"to carry off by force,"* and this gives us the reason why the Lord Jesus will descend to very near the Earth at this particular time.

Satan and his kingdom of demons occupy this lower atmosphere. Paul speaks of him as *"the Prince of the power of the air"* (Eph. 2:2), and uses the Greek word *"aer"* of which we have already noticed, which speaks of the lower, denser atmosphere in which we live.

Demon spirits inhabit this portion of the atmosphere around the Earth in order that they may prey upon Christian Believers. They attempt to disrupt the workings of the Church, spoil the testimony and service of Christians, and prevent the unsaved from receiving the Lord Jesus as Saviour. In fact, they are trying to insulate the Church from Heaven.

At the time of the Rapture, they will attempt to keep the Church from going up to Heaven with the Lord Jesus. Jesus of Nazareth will exert His Omnipotent Power in taking the Saints with Him to Heaven through the kingdoms of Satan, and against his power and that of his demons.

2. TO RESCUE FROM THE DANGER OF DESTRUCTION

The Greek word *"harpazo,"* also means *"to rescue from the danger of destruction."* That means that the Church will be caught up to Heaven before the seven-year period of Great Tribulation occurs on Earth.

By the Church here we do not mean the visible organized present-day Church composed of both Believers and unbelievers, but only those in the visible Church whose Christian profession will stand the test of actual possession of Salvation.

The nominal Christian, that person merely identified with the visible Church, and not actually possessing a Living Faith in the Lord Jesus as Saviour, will be left on Earth to go through the terrible times of the Great Tribulation.

## A PRE-TRIBULATION RAPTURE

We believe and teach from the Word of God that the Rapture of the Church will take place before the Great Tribulation. A Divine analysis of the Book of Revelation proclaims first of all *"the things seen"* (the Patmos Vision of the Lord Jesus), which is portrayed in Revelation Chapter 1; *"the things that are"* (the Church Age), which include Chapters 2-3; *"the things which shall be after these things"* (events happening after the Church Age, which include the Great Tribulation, Second Coming of the Lord, the Kingdom Age and the Coming Perfect Age), all found in Chapters 4-22. This outline is found in Revelation 1:19, and indicates that the Church will be caught up before the Tribulation Period begins.

Revelation Chapters 6-19 describe that period. These events take place after the Church Age.

### ISRAEL YES, THE CHURCH NO!

Again, there is nothing in Scripture which indicates that the Church will either enter or pass through the Great Tribulation. Israel is given many signs which will warn her of the near approach of that period (Mat. Chpt. 24), but the Gospels and Epistles are entirely devoid of any sign given to the Church.

The Epistles speak of the Day of Christ Jesus, even as we are now discussing (I Cor. 1:8; Phil. 1:6), an expression not found in the Old Testament or the Gospels. This is a day to which the Church is to look forward with joy. It is the end of the pathway of the Christian Church.

If this day does not occur before the Tribulation, then there is no place for it in the Prophetic calendar of events which will take place during or after that period.

### DIVINE WRATH

The Great Tribulation Period is a time when the Divine Wrath is to be visited upon Earth-dwellers, particularly upon Israel. In fact, one of the major reasons for the coming Great Tribulation is that Israel may be brought to a place to where she will cry to God for deliverance, which will take place in the Battle of Armageddon (Zech. Chpts. 12-14; Mat. Chpt. 24). But the Promise to the Church is that it has been delivered from the Wrath to come (Rom. 5:9; I Thess. 1:9-10; 5:8).

The Bible expressly states who will be the objects of the Divine Wrath during the Tribulation Period, namely, Israel and the ungodly of the Gentile Nations. If the Church were destined to suffer, surely, the Bible would make note of that fact along with the mention of the above two companies of individuals.

The Biblical attitude of the Believer is one of waiting for the Glorification of his body (Rom. 8:23), and of looking for the Saviour (Phil. 3:20-21; I Thess. 1:9-10), not of looking for the Antichrist, etc.

The language is clear that the Believer is to expect the Lord at any moment, not look for Him in connection with some predicted event for which signs have been given regarding Israel and not to the Church.

### WHAT THE BIBLE TEACHES

In fact, many are presently teaching that there is no coming Great Tribulation, that having passed away with the destruction of Jerusalem in A.D. 70, etc. Of course, to believe such foolishness, one has to believe that the Book of Revelation was all fulfilled at that time as well. Jesus has not yet come, even as Revelation Chapter 19 proclaims; therefore, Revelation Chapters 6 through the conclusion of the Book have not yet been fulfilled as should be obvious.

On the other hand, some teach the very opposite, believing correctly that there is coming a Great Tribulation, even as the Bible teaches, but going into error when they teach that the Church must go through this terrible time. To teach such nullifies the Biblical Teaching of the *imminent* Coming of the Lord Jesus for the Church.

Even though events on Earth are presently closer to this coming time of the Great Tribulation than ever, still, that period has not yet arrived. However, certain events tell us that in fact, it is close.

But the Lord may return for His Church at any moment. Paul (Phil. 4:5), Peter (I Pet. 1:13-15), and John (I Jn. 3:2-3), all make the *imminent* Coming of the Lord for the Church a ground of appeal for holy living and diligent service.

### THE BIBLE TEACHES THAT THE CHURCH MUST BE TAKEN FIRST

Paul in II Thessalonians 2:1-12, states that the Day of the Lord (the Great Tribulation), cannot come unless the departure of the Church from the Earth comes first.

Actually, there are four days in Scripture:

A. The day of man which actually speaks of Gentile dominion, which will conclude at the Second Coming (Lk. 21:24; I Cor. 4:3).

B. The Day of Christ: This pertains to the time of the Resurrection, when Christ has His Day, when He comes for His Body (Phil. 1:6; I Thess. 4:13-18) (Rapture).

NOTES

C. The Day of the Lord: This is given in II Thessalonians 2:2, and should have been translated *"Day of the Lord,"* instead of *"The Day of Christ."* The best Greek Texts portray this.

This is when the Lord has His Day of Judgment, which includes the Tribulation Period and the Millennium.

D. The Day of God: This is given in II Peter 3:12, and speaks of the Millennium merging into Eternity.

THE FALSE LETTER

In our II Thessalonians Passage (2:2), Paul is speaking of the Great Tribulation.

Someone had written a letter to the Thessalonian Church, stating that the period of the Great Tribulation was then present, and had forged Paul's name to the document. The great Apostle calms their fears by saying that Day cannot come until *"a falling away"* comes first (II Thess. 2:3).

The Greek word translated *"falling away"* has as one of its meanings, *"a departure."* Actually, the definite article appears before it in the original Text, *"the departure."* This word is used in other places in the New Testament, and in these places the context indicates that from which the departure is made.

But here there is no such information. It follows that this particular departure must have been in the teaching of Paul to the Thessalonian Saints at a previous time, and was known by them and him.

Actually Paul had already taught them about the Rapture in I Thessalonians 4:13-18.

The context speaks of the True Church which restrains iniquity on Earth, leaving the Earth for Heaven (II Thess. 2:7). (The word *"letteth"* should have been translated *"restrains."*)

The words *"falling away"* in II Thessalonians 2:3, are an interpretation of the Greek word, not a translation. Furthermore, no apostasy would withhold the coming of the Antichrist and the Great Tribulation, but on the other hand, would prepare for the coming of both.

Thus, the departure of the Church precedes the Great Tribulation. The Church will thus be rescued from the danger of destruction.

3. TRANSFERRING A PERSON FROM ONE PLACE TO ANOTHER

The third meaning of the word *"harpazo,"* refers to the use of Divine Power in transferring a person marvelously and swiftly from one place to another.

NOTES

It refers here to the act of the Lord Jesus taking with Him to Heaven all Believers from Adam's time to the Rapture. Concerning the time it will take to do this, once again, it will happen with the speed of thought.

4. TO CLAIM FOR ONESELF EAGERLY

The fourth meaning of the word *"harpazo,"* means, *"to claim for oneself eagerly."*

Here, the Lord, the Great Head of the Church, will come from Heaven to claim that which is His, and for which He died, and to take the Church to Himself.

He has the right to claim the Church, simply because He paid the price for the Redemption of mankind.

Again, we are speaking of the True Body of Christ, and not all who claim to be a part of this Church.

5. TO SNATCH OUT AND TAKE AWAY

Last of all, the fifth meaning of the word *"harpazo,"* means as our heading states, *"to snatch out and take away."*

This tells us that the Rapture will occur so suddenly that it will take the Church by surprise.

As we have already stated, there are no Signs or Prophecies to be fulfilled before the Rapture can occur. However, there are many Prophecies to be fulfilled before the Second Coming of the Lord, but none respecting the Rapture. In other words, it could take place at any moment, and will do so without warning.

WHEN WILL IT BE?

First of all, it cannot be far off. Glance down Bible History for a moment.

It is significant that God has been in the habit of doing some great things with reference to Salvation, at the turn of a Millennium or of two Millenniums.

According to Bible History, the date of Adam was approximately 6,000 years ago.

The Plan of Salvation in which God the Judge was to step down from His Judgment Throne to take upon Himself the guilt and penalty of human sin in order that He might satisfy His Justice, maintain His Government, and at the same time open the flood-gates of Mercy to lost sinners, was prefigured in the Sacrifices which He instituted at the time of Adam, when

He made coats of skins and clothed Adam and Eve (Gen. 3:21).

The initial step in the fulfillment of this Plan took place in 2,000 B.C., when He called Abraham to be the Progenitor of the Jewish Nation from which would come the Saviour who would die and pay for sin.

The next step He took was in 1,000 B.C., when He began the Dynasty of David, from which line of Kings the Messiah and Saviour would come.

## THE GREAT STEP

The next step, which was the great step, took place a thousand years after David, when God, in the Person of His Son came to Earth, became Incarnate in the human race by Virgin Birth, and died on Calvary's Cross, the Substitutionary Atonement for sin. This was His First Advent.

The Second Advent of the Son of God is predicted in Scripture, even as we have been studying here. All indications point to the fact that it is very near at hand.

The Church has been in existence almost 2,000 years. It would seem logical that the Lord would repeat His custom of doing something of great importance at or near the turn of this coming Millennium. This pertains to His Coming to Earth a second time.

However, the Rapture must take place before the Second Advent, which means it must be very close.

## CHURCH HISTORY

The Second and Third Chapters of the Book of Revelation contain the History of the Church. It has often been asked if the Message of Christ to the Seven Churches of Asia, pertain only to warnings, or does it speak of particular times with each Church representing a particular age in Church History this past 2,000 years?

It is definite, that these are warnings given by Christ to the Church. In other words, whatever warning is given for one Church can apply to all, and is meant to apply to all, even presently.

However, there is an excellent possibility that these Seven Churches definitely do contain the history of the Church, divided into seven periods or ages. Again, the Holy Spirit could definitely have intended that, and probably did. If so, they are as follows (it should be noted that all dates have a lappage time):

NOTES

1. The Apostolic Church: This period began in A.D. 33, and continued to A.D. 96, or approximately so, when it is thought that the last of the original Twelve of the Apostles died, John the Beloved. In fact, the fervor of this period began to die along the last years, with Jesus saying, *"I have somewhat against thee, because thou hast left thy first love.*

*"Remember therefore from whence thou art fallen, and repent, and do the first works; or else I will come unto thee quickly, and will remove thy candlestick out of his place, except thou repent"* (Rev. 2:4-5). It is the Message to the Church of Ephesus.

2. The Martyr Church: This began in A.D. 96 and continued to A.D. 313, when Constantine who had become sole ruler of the Western leg of the Roman Empire, and, in conjunction with his Eastern colleague Licinius, issued the famous edict of toleration from Milan, on March 30th, 313. In this edict, all religions were granted equal tolerance, and Christianity was thus placed on an equal footing with heathenism.

Before then, Rome had sought to check Christianity by extreme persecution, in which thousands paid with their lives. This was the Message to the Church in Smyrna, when Jesus said, *"Fear none of those things which thou shalt suffer: behold, the Devil shall cast some of you into prison, that ye may be tried; and ye shall have tribulation ten days: be thou faithful unto death, and I will give thee a Crown of Life"* (Rev. 2:10).

The number *"ten"* as in *"ten days,"* and referring to tribulation, could refer to one of two things, or even both.

It could refer to some ten periods of extreme persecution during this somewhat over 200-year period of time.

As well, some believe that the number ten at certain times in the Bible (not always), refers to *"ordinal perfection."* This refers to a series of events, in this case persecutions, which lead to a particular conclusion, in this case a particular place of consecration in Christ. It is the Smyrna Message.

3. The State Church: This period lasted from about A.D. 313 to approximately A.D. 500.

After making Christianity equal with Paganism, Constantine began to be inclined more

NOTES

and more toward Christianity. His dream was to weld Pagan and Christian into one society under the same laws. However, with the founding of Constantinople, Christianity became practically the State Religion — an alliance with baneful consequences for Christianity.

This was the Message of Jesus to the Church in Pergamos. He said of this Church and time, *"I know thy works, and where thou dwellest, even where Satan's seat is"* (Rev. 2:13). He demanded repentance of this Church even as He did that of Ephesus.

4. The Papal Church: This began approximately in the year 500, and lasted to approximately 1500, a period of about a thousand years. The Early Church had finally apostatized to such an extent, that it was now the Catholic Church, which bears absolutely no resemblance whatsoever to the Church of the Book of Acts. It was rightly called *"The Dark Ages."* Worship had degenerated into pure formalism and ceremony, which brought no comfort to the heart.

During this time, untold thousands went to their death, simply because they would not swear allegiance to the Pope. The Catholic Church became a State within a State, thereby ruling particular States from within.

This is the time of the Church of Thyatira. He said of this Church, *"Thou sufferest that woman Jezebel, which calleth herself a prophetess, to teach and to seduce my servants to commit fornication, and to eat things sacrificed unto idols."*

He then said, *"Behold, I will cast her into a bed, and them that commit adultery with her into great tribulation, except they repent of their deeds"* (Rev. 2:20, 22).

The words *"fornication"* and *"adultery,"* here refer to spiritual fornication and spiritual adultery, and not the literal sins as commonly thought.

If this time period does reflect the Catholic Church as some teach, and which probably is correct, we now know what Jesus thinks of such. Anyone who associates with it, is branded as a spiritual fornicator and spiritual adulterer. Of the Church Jesus demanded Repentance.

5. The Reformation Church: This began in about the year 1500, and continued until about the year 1800. Martin Luther, a Catholic Priest, helped bring about this Reformation, along with many others, with their motto being *"The Just shall live by Faith,"* which meant, that Salvation was not by works as taught by the Catholic Church.

The world now began to be pulled out of the Dark Ages, with the Protestant Church coming into being, although at the beginning at great price. As well, the invention of the printing press made it possible for Bibles to be printed in large numbers, actually the Words of Scripture being the very first thing that was printed on the first crude press.

With the Word of God in the hands of the common people, once again great Moves of God took place, with literally hundreds of thousands coming to a Saving Knowledge of Jesus Christ.

This period is said to be the time of the Message of Jesus to the Church in Sardis. He said to them of this time period, *"Remember therefore how thou hast received and heard, and hold fast, and repent"* (Rev. 3:3).

6. The Missionary Church: This period began in about 1800, and continued to about 1988. During this time, the world was touched with the Gospel, and especially after the turn of the century when the mighty Baptism with the Holy Spirit began to be poured out all over the Earth. Men and women, full of the Spirit, and called by the Spirit, began to do great and mighty things, even in fulfillment of Joel's Prophecy concerning the Latter Rain (Joel 2:23).

This is the Message of Jesus to the Church in Philadelphia. Concerning Missionary activity and regarding this particular Church and time, Jesus said, *"Behold, I have set before thee an open door, and no man can shut it"* (Rev. 3:8). No Repentance was demanded.

7. The Apostate Church: If these time periods are correct, we are now living in the seventh and last age of Church History. It is the time of Apostasy, which perfectly defines the Modern Church. The word *"apostasy"* means *"a departure from Truth."*

Regrettably, almost all of the old-line Churches have denied the Baptism with the Holy Spirit, and vigorously so, and tragically, the Modern Pentecostal Church has for the most part, forsaken the Holy Spirit. The Charismatic Church World, which is quite large, is beset with all types of false doctrines, i.e., *"The Prosperity Message," "The Kingdom Now Message,"* etc., with almost all embracing Humanistic Psychology.

This is the Message of Jesus to the Church of the Laodiceans.

To this Church He said, *"I know thy works, that thou art neither cold nor hot: I would thou wert cold or hot.*

*"So then because thou art lukewarm, and neither cold nor hot, I will spue thee out of My Mouth."*

He then said, *"Because thou sayest, I am rich, and increased with goods, and have need of nothing; and knowest not that thou art wretched, and miserable, and poor, and blind, and naked"* (Rev. 3:15-17).

Of this Church, Jesus demanded repentance, even as He did of Sardis, Thyatira, Pergamos, and Ephesus. The only two of which repentance was not demanded, was Smyrna and Philadelphia. The former was the Martyr Church, with the latter being the Missionary Church.

The Rapture will close the Church Age. So near are we to that great event.

(9) "GOD IS FAITHFUL, BY WHOM YE WERE CALLED UNTO THE FELLOWSHIP OF HIS SON JESUS CHRIST OUR LORD."

The phrase, *"God is faithful,"* was a favorite expression among Jews of the integrity of God (II Cor. 1:18; I Thess. 5:24; II Thess. 3:3). It simply means, that He will not leave His Promises unfulfilled or His Work unfinished.

## THE FAITHFULNESS OF GOD

All of Paul's thoughts respecting the Faithfulness of God would have been derived from the Old Testament.

In the Old Testament this attribute of God's Faithfulness is ascribed to Him in Passages where the Hebrew words denoting faithfulness do not actually occur. It is implied in the Covenant Name Jehovah as unfolded in Exodus 3:13-15, which not only expresses God's self-existence and unchangeableness, but, as the context indicates, puts God's immutability (will not change) in special relation to His Gracious Promises, thus denoting God's unchangeable Faithfulness which is emphasized in the Old Testament to awaken trust in God (Deut. 7:9; Ps. 36:5; Isa. 11:5; Hos. 12:6-9).

God's Faithfulness as well as His Immutability is also implied in those Passages where God is called a *"Rock,"* meaning that He is the secure object of Spiritual Truth (Deut. 32:4-15; Ps. 18:2; 42:9; Isa. 17:10).

NOTES

## CONCERNING THE PATRIARCHS

This same attribute is also implied where God reveals Himself to Moses and to Israel as the God of Abraham, Isaac, and Jacob (Ex. 3:6, 15-16).

The Truth taught here concerning God is not simply that He stood in a gracious relation to the Patriarchs, but that He is faithful to His Gracious Promises to their fathers, and that what He was to them He will continue to be to Moses and to Israel. This is the fundamental idea in the Old Testament concerning the Faithfulness of God.

## COVERS MANY AREAS

The Hebrew words used in this respect, which we will not go into now, express the idea that God is always faithful to His Covenant Promises. It is this attribute of God which the Psalmist declares (Ps. 40:10), and the greatness of which he affirms by saying that God's Faithfulness reacheth to the clouds (Ps. 36:5).

It is this which he makes the object of Praise (Ps. 89:1-2; 92:2), and which he says should be praised and reverenced by all men (Ps. 89:5-8).

And even this Faithfulness is itself characterized by constancy, if we may so speak, for the Psalmist says that it endures to all generations (Ps. 100:5).

Being thus a characteristic of God, it also characterizes His Salvation, and becomes the basis of confidence that God will hear Prayer (Ps. 143:1). It thus becomes the security of those who put their trust in Him (Ps. 91:4); and the Source of God's Help to His people (Ps. 31:5).

## FAITHFULNESS IN MERCY AND GRACE

Accordingly in the teaching of Prophecy, the Salvation of the Covenant People rests upon no claim or merit of their own, but solely upon God's Mercy, Grace, and Faithfulness. When Israel incurred God's Judgments, it might have appeared as if His Promise was to fail, but, so far from this being true, as Jehovah He is faithful to His Word of Promise which stands forever (Isa. 40:8).

Even from Eternity His Counsels are characterized by Faithfulness and Truth (Isa. 25:1); and this is not because of Israel's Faithfulness, but it is for His Own Sake that He blots out their transgressions (Isa. 43:22-25; Micah 7:18-20). As well, this constancy is from generation to generation.

Since the Covenant-keeping Jehovah is faithful, Faithfulness comes also to be a characteristic of the New Covenant which is everlasting (Ps. 89:28; Isa. 54:8; Jer. 31:35; Ezek. 16:60; Hos. 2:19).

The phrase, *"By Whom ye were called unto the fellowship of His Son Jesus Christ our Lord,"* presents several things:

1. This was the Plan of God, Salvation through Jesus Christ, even *"before the foundation of the world"* (I Pet. 1:20).

God Who is Omniscient, knew through foreknowledge that man would Fall, and that he must be Redeemed. That Redemption would come through God becoming Man, i.e., *"The Lord Jesus Christ."*

2. *"Were called"* refers to predestination, but of the Plan and not of the person. In fact, the invitation is extended to all (Jn. 3:16; Rev. 22:17). Those who accept are predestined to have certain things in Jesus Christ.

3. *"Fellowship"* in the Greek is *"koinania,"* and means *"Communion with Christ as the sole means of Spiritual Life"* (Jn. 15:4; Gal. 2:20).

As well, through the Son, and only through the Son, we also have fellowship with the Father (I Jn. 1:3).

All of this pertains to Christ and our Fellowship with Him. This is done through the Holy Spirit in this life, and pertains to the Kingdom Age in the next life (II Cor. 13:14; Phil. 3:10; I Jn. 1:3).

4. There is only one *"Lord"* in this world, and to the hearts of men, and that is The Lord Jesus Christ. It is this allegiance and supremacy which Satan fights constantly, attempting to usurp Lordship over Christ in one's heart.

Six titles are given to the Lord Jesus Christ in Verses 1-10. These reveal His Glory, and rebuked the narrow and bigoted attitude of some of the Corinthian Believers who were failing to give Christ His proper place, by placing too much confidence in men as we shall see in Verses 12-13. It is a problem no less real at this present hour.

(10) "NOW I BESEECH YOU, BRETHREN, BY THE NAME OF OUR LORD JESUS CHRIST, THAT YE ALL SPEAK THE SAME THING, AND THAT THERE BE NO DIVISIONS AMONG YOU; BUT THAT YE BE PERFECTLY JOINED TOGETHER IN THE SAME MIND AND IN THE SAME JUDGMENT."

NOTES

The phrase, *"Now I beseech you, Brethren,"* presents an oft used expression by the Apostle. However, the word *"now"* implies the transition from thanksgiving to reproof (Farrar).

*"Beseech"* in the Greek is *"parakaleo,"* and means *"to call near, to call to one's side, hence, to call to one's aid."* This Greek word is the basic term from which we get one of the titles for the Holy Spirit (Rossier). Consequently, when Paul used this term, as he often did, he is in effect saying, *"Let me help you with this question or problem,"* in essence, the same manner in which the Holy Spirit appeals to us as Believers.

In using the word *"Brethren,"* Paul appeals to them to aim at unity among themselves, and as well uses the word to soften any austerity which might seem to exist in his reproof (Farrar).

The phrase, *"By the Name of our Lord Jesus Christ,"* proclaims the Lord as the Head of the Church, and that all must answer to Him. Paul is projecting Jesus Christ as the Bond of Union between True Christians, meaning that it is not our will which should be brought forth but rather His Will.

Actually, the Name *"Lord Jesus Christ,"* is the Resurrection Name of the Lord, and the Highest Authority among men.

## LET'S LOOK AT THE NAME *"LORD JESUS CHRIST."*

Immediately after Paul's Conversion, the Scripture says, *"And straightway he preached Christ in the Synagogues, that He is the Son of God"* (Acts 9:20).

Paul's Synagogue audiences were amazed at Paul's theology. However, what I want to know is, *"Why were they amazed?"* Surely, a Jewish audience would find nothing surprising in the fact that Christ is the Son of God, for that was clearly taught in the Old Testament and believed by all Orthodox Jews. However, they wanted to kill Paul for having made that statement.

## THE ANOINTED

The word *"Christ"* is a transliteration of a Greek word which means *"Anointed."* By transliteration we mean the act of bringing a word from one language into another in its *spelling,* whereas by translation we refer to the *meaning* of the word being taken over into another language.

The Greek word *"Anointed"* is a translation from a Hebrew word which means *"The Anointed"* and which later is brought over into English by transliteration in the word *"Messiah."* Consequently, the Messiah of Israel, Who is Christ, is the Anointed of God. Thus, when the Name *"Christ"* is found in connection with Israel, either in the Old or New Testament, it refers to Israel's Messiah.

JESUS OF NAZARETH

Now if Paul had preached *"Christ"* in the Synagogue in Damascus, the Jews would have welcomed him with open arms, for they were accustomed to hearing such constantly. However, there is a reason they grew so angry.

It is said that the best Greek Texts have the word *"Jesus"* not *"Christ,"* respecting Acts 9:20. Either that is correct and should have been translated accordingly, or else Paul grandly explained, which he no doubt did, that *"Christ,"* the Anointed of Israel, is Jesus of Nazareth. Now, to announce Jesus of Nazareth, the One Whom the highest Court of Israel condemned as a blasphemer, as the Son of God, therefore, Messiah, was quite another thing. No wonder that the hatred and antagonism of the Jews were aroused, and that they were amazed at the fact that one who had so recently persecuted those who were preaching the same Message which he was now presenting, should have turned so suddenly. Paul was announcing Jesus of Nazareth as Deity.

The Jews had tried to stone our Lord for claiming to be the Unique Son of God. *"Therefore the Jews sought the more to kill Him, because He not only had broken the Sabbath, but said also that God was His Father, making Himself equal with God"* (Jn. 5:18).

HIS

The key to the interpretation of this Passage is in the Greek word translated *"His."* Had our Lord used the ordinary pronoun showing possession, the Jews would have taken no exception to His Words. But He used a word which in the Greek speaks of uniqueness. Our Lord was the Son of God in a way different from that of any other person.

A Believer is a Son of God like all other Believers. But our Lord's Sonship was unique.

It was not only different from that of others, but it was the only one of its kind. The Jews at once recognized it as a claim to joint participation in the Divine Essence of the Father. Thus, Jesus of Nazareth is the Messiah of Israel.

NOTES

SAVIOUR

The Name Jesus is also a transliteration from the Hebrew. The Angel said to Mary (Mat. 1:21), *"Thou shalt call His Name JESUS: for He shall save His people from their sins."*

Matthew reports the Angel's words in Greek. Being a Jew, Matthew of course knew Hebrew and transliterated the Hebrew word which means *"Saviour,"* into Greek, from which language we brought the Name over into English in the Name Jesus.

The Hebrew word is in English *"Yeshua,"* or *"Joshua."* Thus, the Name *"Jesus"* speaks of our Lord as the Saviour, the One Who shed His Precious Blood on Calvary's Cross for lost sinners, while the Name *"Christ"* speaks of Him in a context of Israel as Israel's Messiah.

Where the two Names, Jesus Christ, appear together, they refer to Him as The Anointed of God, the Saviour. The Name *"Lord,"* refers to Him in His relation to the Church, its Head.

LORD

This significant word occurs again and again in the Old Testament and the New Testament. What does it mean when the Old Testament identifies God as Lord? And what does it mean when this Name is ascribed to Jesus Christ? The answer to these questions initiates us into some of the wonders of our Faith.

OLD TESTAMENT WORDS IN THE HEBREW

Two Hebrew words are translated *"Lord"* in the Old Testament. *"Adon"* means *"Lord"* in the sense of a superior, master, or owner. It is also used as a term of respect. It is generally found in the Old Testament in reference to human beings (Gen. 18:12; 19:2; 24; I Sam. 16:16). But at times, especially in a series of names such as *"The Lord, The God of Israel"* it is used of God.

A special intensified form, *"donay,"* is found over 300 times in the Old Testament, and this plural form refers only to God. Where *"adon"* or *"donay"* refers to God, the English Versions of the Bible show it by capitalizing the first letter *"Lord."*

NOTES

## YAHWEH

The other Hebrew word translated *"Lord"* is *"Yahweh,"* which is God's Revealed Personal Name. This Name occurs 5,321 times in the Old Testament in this form, and 50 more times in the poetic form *"Yah." "Yahweh"* is particularly significant, and when it occurs, most English Versions indicate this by the form *"Lord."*

## MEANING OF THE NAME YAHWEH

Most Scholars believe that the Name is derived from an old form of the Hebrew verb meaning *"to be"* or *"to become."* The word stresses existence, with the meaning being that expressed in Exodus 3:14: *"I AM."* This has been taken to emphasize the unchanging nature of God, particularly His changeless commitment to His people.

But the Name suggests more, especially in the context of its introduction to Israel. This came as Moses, standing before the Burning Bush, hesitated to accept God's Commission.

*"Moses said to God, 'Suppose I go to the Israelites and say to them, "The God of your fathers has sent me to you," and they ask me, "What is His Name?" Then what shall I tell them?'*

*"God said to Moses, 'I Am Who I Am. This is what you are to say to the Israelites: "I AM has sent Me to you."'*

*"God also said to Moses, 'Say to the Israelites, "The Lord, the God of your fathers — the God of Abraham, the God of Isaac and the God of Jacob — has sent Me to you." This is My Name forever, the Name by which I am to be remembered from generation to generation'"* (Ex. 3:13-15).

## THE GOD WHO IS ALWAYS PRESENT

Later God revealed more to Moses. He told of His appearances to Abraham, Isaac, and Jacob as God Almighty, but said *"By My Name the Lord I did not make Myself known to them"* (Ex. 6:3). It was in the Exodus that God unveiled His Character as Yahweh. It was in His action bringing Israel out of Egypt and accompanying them to the Land of Canaan (Ex. 3:12) that His Nature was unveiled.

The Exodus generation, which had only heard of God through stories passed on by their ancestors, would suddenly experience God as the One Who Is — One Who was present with them.

It is in this way, by this Name, that God is *"to be remembered from generation to generation"* (Ex. 3:15). What is the meaning of the Name Yahweh?

It is God's affirmation that He is *"The God Who is always present."* He is not simply a God afar off, or a God of past history, or a God Who will appear in that future the Prophets foretell. He is a God Who is present and Who acts at every point of the history and experience of His people.

He is such a God for us as well. And we are to remember Him by this Name. For whatever our situation, whatever our need, our God is One Who is always present. He is with us now — now and evermore.

## THE NEW TESTAMENT WORD, *"LORD."*

The word translated *"Lord"* in the English Versions is *"Kyrios."* In ordinary speech it may simply have been a term of respect or a form of address that emphasized superior position, as that of the master of a slave. When the word is used in reference to people, it is translated by an appropriate English equivalent, such as *"Master," "Owner,"* or even *"Sir."*

When *"Kyrios"* designates God or Jesus, it is rendered *"Lord."*

In the Gospels, however, this should not be taken to mean that the speaker acknowledges Jesus as God (Mat. 8:2, 21; Lk. 9:59). However, since the Greek Version of the Old Testament uses *"Kyrios"* for *"Yahweh,"* it is clear that in many of its uses in the Gospels, the title Lord is equivalent to The Divine Name.

It seems certain that when Jesus spoke of Himself — the time He called Himself *"Lord of the Sabbath"* (Mat. 12:8) — He was ascribing Deity to Himself (Lk. 20:42-44).

Some uses of the title *"Lord"* by the Disciples may also reflect the growing awareness that Jesus truly was Divine, as Thomas finally confessed when he exclaimed, *"My Lord and My God!"* (Jn. 20:28).

It is after the Resurrection, and in the Epistles, that we discover the significance of *"Kyrios* (Lord)*"* as applied to Jesus.

## JESUS IS LORD

The earliest Chapters of Acts testify to the fact that after the Resurrection, the Church immediately confessed *"Jesus is Lord"*; and the rest of the New Testament constantly affirms Jesus' Lordship.

In Philippians, Paul traces the process of Jesus' self-emptying, the Crucifixion, and His subsequent exaltation, Jesus, *". . . being in very nature God, did not consider equality with God something to be grasped, but made Himself nothing, taking the very nature of a servant, being made in human likeness.*

*"And being found in appearance as a Man, He humbled Himself and became obedient to death — even death on the Cross!*

*"Therefore God exalted Him to the highest place and gave Him the Name that is above every Name, that at the Name of Jesus every knee should bow, in Heaven and on Earth and under the Earth, and every tongue confess that Jesus Christ is Lord, to the Glory of God the Father"* (Phil. 2:6-11).

To recognize Jesus as Lord is to acknowledge His Deity. And this is evidence that God the Spirit has accomplished His Saving Work within (I Cor. 12:3).

THE IMPLICATIONS OF JESUS' LORDSHIP

Jesus is Lord. What does this mean and imply? It implies that He has authority of various kinds, and it is to this authority that we should now look.

UNIVERSAL AUTHORITY

The New Testament teaches us that the Risen Christ is seated at God's Right Hand, the place of authority. His authority is universal, *"far above all rule and authority, power and dominion, and every title that can be given, not only in the present age but also in the one to come"* (Eph. 1:21). All *"Angels, authorities and powers"* are *"in submission to Him"* (I Pet. 3:22).

SOVEREIGN AUTHORITY

The Lordship of Jesus is worked out in this present world. Peter explores the situation in which a Believer does what is right but still endures suffering. He reminds us that the *"Eyes of the Lord are on the Righteous"* (I Pet. 3:12).

Even if we suffer for what is right, we can *"set apart Christ as Lord"* in our hearts (I Pet. 3:15); that is, we can remain confident that Christ, as Lord, is superintending events.

NOTES

PERSONAL AUTHORITY

In Romans Chapter 14, Paul looks into the freedom of the Christian person. In matters of conviction each Believer is to *"be fully convinced in his own mind"* and then must act on his convictions.

It is not the Christian community but Jesus Who is Lord, for this is the *"very reason"* that *"Christ died and rose again,"* that is, *"so that He might be the Lord of both the dead and the living"* (Rom. 14:5, 9).

Jesus' Authority as Lord extends to the personal relationship that He has with each believing individual.

PERVASIVE AUTHORITY

Both the Church and the individual Believer live *"in," "under,"* and *"through"* the Lord. These recurring prepositions in reference to one's relationship to the Lord remind us that it is only by the Presence and Power of Jesus, Who is Lord, that present and future victories are made possible.

The very fact of our existence is determined by the reality of Jesus as Lord.

ULTIMATE AUTHORITY

The New Testament speaks of a Coming Day of the Lord. Jesus will appear again, and then His ultimate Lordship over all Creation will be demonstrated.

The title *"Lord"* affirms the Deity of Christ and His Authority over every power — natural and supernatural. As Lord, Jesus governs the sweep of history and guards each individual's step.

One practical implication of Jesus' Lordship is seen in Scripture's call to us to abandon judging or attempting to control others. Jesus died and rose again that He might actually be Lord in the life of each person who trusts in Him. Consequently, He is the only One qualified to judge others, because He Alone is *"Lord."*

(The material on the Name *"The Lord Jesus Christ"* was derived from Kenneth Wuest and Lawrence O. Richards.)

The phrase, *"That ye all speak the same thing,"* does not imply that we should agree on every minor point; therefore, it must relate to the necessity of our maintaining unity with respect to the Person of Christ. We can afford to differ on minor points, but not on those relating to Christ's position in the Body, the New Testament Church (Rossier).

The phrase, *"And that there be no divisions among you,"* speaks of those within the Church and not separatists from it.

*"Divisions"* in the Greek are *"schisms,"* and mean *"a rent, something that is torn."*

God gives a Preacher a *"Vision,"* and then provides for the Vision, i.e., *"provision."* Then Satan attempts to come in with *"division."*

Even though the word *"division"* can refer to minor differences, the manner in which it is used here, however, denotes far more than that. Many in the Church had been reduced to quarrelling and what one might refer to as a *"Church fight."*

The inhabitants of Corinth in general had a high opinion of themselves intellectually. Perhaps this had rubbed off on some in the Church, hence the preference of certain Preachers, etc.

One could probably say without fear of contradiction, that the cause of all *"divisions"* in the Church, can be traced in some way back to self-will. When gossip is added, one has a perfect recipe for a Church fight.

What were they fighting about?

The next few verses will reveal their contentions.

The phrase, *"But that ye be perfectly joined together in the same mind and in the same judgment,"* presents that which can only be done, when one focuses totally and completely on The Lord Jesus Christ.

*"Perfectly joined"* in the Greek is *"katartizo,"* and means *"to complete thoroughly, repair, perfectly mend,"* as one would mend a torn fishnet.

First of all, if one has the *"Mind of Christ,"* which is humility, then the *"judgment will be correct"* (Mat. 11:28-30; Phil. 2:5-8).

*"Judgment"* in the Greek is *"gnome,"* and means *"resolve, counsel, consent, advice, purpose or will."*

## UNITY

The theme of Christian Unity fascinates many. Yet there is little agreement about the nature of that Unity or about the way Unity is best expressed. A literal translation of Jesus' Prayer for Unity among His followers is *"that they may be having been brought to the goal into one"* (Jn. 17:23).

NOTES

One might argue from context that this is a Unity found in a relationship marked by commitment to one another and to common goals; but the Greek wording itself provides no clue.

## LOVE

What of other Passages on Unity? Romans 15:5 translates *"phronein"* (*"the same mind,"* i.e., *"setting one's mind on"*) as a *"spirit of Unity."* Again, context is instructive.

Unity is seen when *"with one heart and mouth you . . . glorify God"* (Rom. 15:6).

In Colossians 3:14 Love is portrayed as the bonding which glues virtues together which brings Unity. Undoubtedly, Love is the absolute requirement.

## TOGETHER

While none of these Passages or words do more than give us clues to the nature of Christian Unity, there is another Greek word that may help. It is *"homothymadon,"* sometimes meaning little more than *"together,"* but capable of expressing unanimity and concerted action. It occurs 12 times in the New Testament (Acts 1:14; 2:1, 46; 4:24; 5:12; 7:57; 8:6; 12:20; 15:25; 18:12; 19:29; Rom. 15:6).

Tracing through these verses, we find additional clues to Unity — vital images of the Church praying, worshiping, and reaching decisions together. In these activities we have more than togetherness; in *"homothymadon"* there is an intimation of the harmony of shared lives.

A great orchestra gathers. The different instruments express their own individuality. But under the baton of a great conductor, the orchestra is capable of blending different sounds to produce the greatest symphonies.

Perhaps the Unity of the Church is like that. It is not found in uniformity or in organizations. It is found, however, wherever Believers focus together on the Lord, expressing their common commitment in Prayer and Worship. It is in and through our union with Jesus that Unity exists, and it is in our common commitment to Jesus that He shapes us to live in harmony with others in the community of Faith (Richards).

(11) "FOR IT HATH BEEN DECLARED UNTO ME OF YOU, MY BRETHREN, BY THEM WHICH ARE OF THE HOUSE OF

CHLOE, THAT THERE ARE CONTENTIONS AMONG YOU."

The phrase, *"For it hath been declared unto me of you, my Brethren,"* once again proclaims the tactfulness of the Apostle. He uses the word *"Brethren"* in order to hopefully register upon them the fact that they should act like they are *"Brethren."* They were quarrelling with each other when they should have been doing the opposite.

The phrase, *"By them which are of the house of Chloe,"* actually gives us little clue as to who this is. The Greek says *"By them of Chloe."* Farrar says, *"Paul wisely and kindly mentions his authority for these reports."*

Nothing is known of this woman or her household. It has even been conjectured that Stephanas, Fortunatus, and Achaicus, Corinthians who were now with Paul at Ephesus (I Cor. 16:16), may have been slaves of Chloe or even freedmen. It is not even certain whether this woman lived in Corinth or in Ephesus, or even if she was a Believer.

(It has been suggested by some that those of I Cor. 16:17 may have even been the sons of Chloe, and that she was a very prominent person in Corinth.)

The phrase, *"That there are contentions among you,"* proclaims as we shall see, that these strifes were obvious.

*"Contentions"* in the Greek is *"eris,"* and means *"strife, debate, and variance."* The contentions were caused by the divisions of verse 10.

As we can see here, the disclosure of this information about the Corinthian Church truly troubled Paul (Rossier).

(12) "NOW THIS I SAY, THAT EVERY ONE OF YOU SAITH, I AM OF PAUL; AND I OF APOLLOS; AND I OF CEPHAS; AND I OF CHRIST."

The phrase, *"Now this I say, that every one of you saith,"* refers to a self-assertive manner, which is proved by the use of the word *"saith."* In other words, Paul is placing heavy emphasis on the error of the party spirit at Corinth which had divided the Church into quarrelling factions. It was over Preachers, but not in this particular instance caused by Preachers. One might quickly add though, just how evil it would have been for a Preacher to have taken advantage of this situation, which untold numbers have down through the centuries.

NOTES

## THE BEGINNING OF DIFFERENT CHURCH DENOMINATIONS OR BELIEF SYSTEMS

Regrettably and sadly, the admonition of the Holy Spirit through the Apostle that all *"be perfectly joined together in the same mind and in the same judgment,"* of the 10th verse, was not heeded in its ultimate authority, even though it does seem that the Corinthian Church did come into line. One could say, that these words of which we read in the 12th Verse of this First Chapter of I Corinthians are the beginning of various Church Denominations which presently make up modern Christianity. And yet, there is a positive as well as a negative side to this situation.

Sometimes, something new is begun simply because the old no longer functions in its intended Biblical purpose. Even though it is extremely regrettable regarding the old, it becomes absolutely necessary respecting the New. So, as long as the Church is in the world, these situations which bring division, sometimes good and sometimes bad, which in its original form are negative, due to the human component, find it necessary at times to embark upon the New. I am saying that the Church will not be *"one"* as it ought to be, until the return of The Lord Jesus Christ. That is regrettable, but at the same time it is a fact.

## WHAT TYPE OF UNITY?

Repeatedly, men have attempted to unify the Church under human banners and by human ingenuity. Such can never work, for the simple reason that such are man-instituted and directed. Only the Holy Spirit can unify the Church. Any effort made outside of that perspective is doomed to failure.

The efforts of men to create Unity by ignoring the Word of God is bound to fail, and at the outset proclaims that which the Holy Spirit cannot condone. Everything of the Spirit always coincides perfectly with the Word of God. Unfortunately, men have different viewpoints respecting the Scripture. Some of those viewpoints are minor but some are major, and some extremely so!

## THE FUNDAMENTALS OF THE FAITH

To be brief, the great Fundamentals of Salvation are the belief in Jesus Christ that He is the Son of God, and died on Calvary that man might be Saved, and rose from the dead on the third day. It is that man is a sinner, and as such, cannot save himself, with Salvation coming only through Christ, and by the believing sinner having Faith in what Christ did at Calvary and the Resurrection (Jn. 3:16; Rom. 10:9-10, 13; Eph. 2:8-9).

In an oversimplified manner that which we have just said, constitutes the Fundamentals of the Faith. For those who do not believe this, even though they may claim Salvation, with those people there can be no unity or fellowship. The Prophet Amos said, *"Can two walk together, except they be agreed?"* (Amos 3:3). As well, Jesus had no fellowship with the Pharisees, and for the obvious reasons.

However, having said that, if we agree upon the Fundamentals, we should not allow peripheral doctrines to drive a wedge between us.

## PAUL

The phrase, *"I am of Paul,"* shows the indignation of the Apostle at the partisanship of these people by rebuking those who had used his own name as a party watchword. He disliked Paulinism as much as Petrinism (Peter) (Bengel).

## CONTENTIONS

Their *"contentions"* are defined to be equivalent to *"religious partisanships,"* which were antagonistic adoption of the names and views of special teachers, and even taking it to the extreme. This party spirit ran so high that they were all listed on one side or the other. Actually, it seems that none, or at least very few, were wise enough and spiritual-minded enough to hold aloof from parties altogether. They prided themselves on being *"uncompromising"* and *"party men"* (Farrar).

What did it mean for these people to say *"I am of Paul,"* or whoever for that matter, in effect, what was the wrong? Inasmuch as Paul had founded this Church, and almost all the people were his converts, had it not been for the visit of other particular Preachers and Teachers, all would have been Paulinists.

Continuing to use Paul, this party in the Church probably consisted of those who adhered to his teaching about Gentile freedom, and who liked the simple spirituality of his teaching. So what was wrong with that, considering that Paul wrote almost half the New Testament, and was in effect, the Moses of the New Covenant?

NOTES

Nothing as far as that went. Actually, it was right.

It was the spirit of this position which was held that was wrong. What was believed was right, but the manner in which it was believed was wrong. What was that spirit and manner?

## SPIRIT OF EXCLUSIVITY

That which seemed to characterize all of these parties, was first of all, a spirit of exclusivity. In other words, all others in every other group (whatever group it was) were wrong, they thought, and, consequently, nothing in the sight of God. As well, there was a *"holier-than-thou"* attitude respecting the spirit of each party, it seems. The idea was, *"We know the way and you don't, consequently, you have little standing with the Lord."*

A person can be right about what he believes, but wrong in the manner in which it is believed. In other words, he has a contentious, unteachable, strident, harsh spirit. To be truly Christlike is to be the very opposite of these things.

This does not at all mean that Believers are not to hold and hold firmly for Sound Doctrine. It just means that it should be done in the right manner, with the right attitude, which is a gracious, kind, and forgiving spirit.

The idea is, that all of us have been wrong about some things at one time or the other. How grateful we were when we finally saw the light on the subject. However, for those who truly knew the right way, but treated us disdainfully, did not help our situation, but only exacerbated the problem, even delaying the entrance of the Light as intended by the Lord. It is one thing to disagree, but something else altogether to disagree disagreeably. This is the spirit that Paul is attacking.

## APOLLOS

The phrase, *"And I of Apollos,"* probably consisted of those who had been greatly impressed by the Ministry of Paul's friend, even carried away with his polished oratory and obvious intellectual manner. It seemed that these were puffed up with the conceit of knowledge.

This could well have been the reason for Apollos refusing to visit Corinth at this time, even though Paul greatly desired that he do so, inasmuch as he was indignant even as Paul himself at the perversion of his name into an engine of party warfare (Farrar). This no doubt was embarrassing to Apollos that these people would pit him against Paul, with whom he differed not at all. In fact, he no doubt considered Paul as his mentor.

PETER

The phrase, *"And I of Cephas,"* speaks of Simon Peter.

As with Paul and Apollos, Peter is not to be personally blamed for the situation. In fact, there is no record that Peter ever visited Corinth.

This party, assuming things about the noted Apostle that they should not have assumed, were probably Judaizers, or else leaning in that direction. As such they personally disliked Paul, and, as well, questioned his Apostolic authority. So they seized on Peter as their champion, even though most probably, most, or maybe none, had ever met him.

CHRIST

The phrase, *"And I of Christ,"* would at first glance seem to be proper. But yet Paul condemns this action as well and for proper reason.

As someone has said, it is the privilege of every Believer to say *"I am a Christian;"* but if he says it in a haughty, loveless, and exclusive spirit, he forfeits his own claim to the title. In fact, this exclusive Christ party is, perhaps, addressed by Paul in II Corinthians 10:7-11.

So why was it wrong for one to claim to be of the party of Christ?

This party, as many others, was not ashamed to degrade into a party watchword even the Sacred Name of Christ, in effect, claiming for a miserable clique an exclusive interest in the Lord of the whole Church. Once again, it is this exclusivity which is wrong. Such takes one into self-righteousness, holier-than-thou attitudes, and spiritual eliteness, which are abhorrent to the True Christlike Spirit, which is humility.

As well, and certainly not least, these people were in effect saying, that they had no need of *"Apostles, Prophets, Evangelists, Pastors, and Teachers,"* who are given by the Lord and empowered by the Holy Spirit, *"For the perfecting of the Saints, for the work of the Ministry, for the edifying of the Body of Christ"* (Eph. 4:11-12).

NOTES

Bringing this last thought up to modern times, the Full Gospel Businessmen's Organization was greatly used of God, and in fact, is still being used in some parts of the world. However, I personally think that they did not give proper place to *"Apostles, Prophets, Evangelists, Pastors, and Teachers,"* the idea being projected that successful Christian Businessmen know more about the Work of God than God-called Preachers. If in fact this was the idea in the minds of some, whether they realized it or not, they were setting aside God's prescribed order, and in its place inserting their own man-devised order. Just because a Christian Businessman is successful in his endeavors, in no way means that he is called of God in the realm of Ministry, or that the techniques of business can also be applied to the Work of God.

In fact, the Work of God is not a business, but rather a Calling. It is not carried out by techniques, methods, or the ways of the world, but rather by the Leading, Guidance, and Empowerment of the Holy Spirit (Acts 1:4, 8).

At the same time, that in no way means that Godly Businessmen cannot be used in the Kingdom of God, rather the very opposite. In fact, they can be used greatly and are used greatly, but in the proper Scriptural manner.

Once again, it was not so much the statements made by the Full Gospel Businessmen's Association, but rather the spirit that was projected. In fact, this is exactly what Paul is addressing.

(13) "IS CHRIST DIVIDED? WAS PAUL CRUCIFIED FOR YOU? OR WERE YE BAPTIZED IN THE NAME OF PAUL?"

The question, *"Is Christ divided?"*, has to be answered with a solid *"no,"* but at the same time, with the reality being, as wrong as it may be, *"yes,"* He is divided all over the landscape.

Farrar asked the question, *"Is there a Pauline, a Petrine, an Apollonian, a Christian Christ?"* Paul is saying, *"Your party spirit is a sin, and all the worse a sin because it pranks itself out in the guise of pure religious zeal."*

*"Divided"* in the Greek is *"merizo,"* and means *"to part, to apportion, disunite, difference between, divide."*

The question, *"Was Paul Crucified for you?"*, presents him using himself as an example, but which refers to all other Preachers as well, etc. He again rebukes the partisanship which attached itself to his own name. In fact, the introduction of the question as it is given in the original Greek expresses astonished indignation.

The idea is, *"Can you possibly make a watchword of the name of a mere man, as though he had been crucified for you?"* (Farrar).

If it is to be noticed, Paul did not enter into the discussion or thought as to which of these parties were right, or which Doctrines were correct or incorrect, but rather denounced them all, because of the sectarian spirit which controlled them, irrespective of their Doctrine.

The question, *"Or were ye Baptized in the name of Paul?"*, proclaims the idea that he had never attempted to draw away Disciples after himself, but rather to Christ.

He uses this question concerning Water Baptism in this manner, not because anyone at the time of the Early Church were Baptizing people after themselves or in their own name, but to show the utter absurdity of the party spirit concerning Preachers, evidenced in the Church. He wanted his question to shock the Corinthians, which it no doubt did.

They had been Baptized in the Name of the Lord because He was and is the Redeemer, the Son of God, Who had died on Calvary and risen from the dead on the third day. To compare some mere man with Him, or Him with some mere man, borders on insanity, for Jesus is God. Paul is attempting to shock them back to their proper place in Christ, of Christ, and through Christ, which evidently succeeded. How so greatly we sin, when Christ is relegated to a secondary position, or no position at all. Entire Denominations do this, when they abrogate the position of Christ as the Head of the Church. As well, it is easy to do such individually, by the route of self-will.

(14) "I THANK GOD THAT I BAPTIZED NONE OF YOU, BUT CRISPUS AND GAIUS;"

If Water Baptism were essential to Salvation, as some claim, I hardly think that Paul would have blatantly announced as he did here, that he had only Baptized two converts.

Let's look at the Ordinance of Water Baptism as it is taught in the Word of God.

## WATER BAPTISM

The two words *"Baptize,"* or *"Baptism,"* are not native to the English language. Therefore, they do not have any intrinsic meaning of their own. The only rightful meaning they can have is the one that is derived from the Greek word of which they are the spelling.

The Greek verb is spelled *"Baptizo,"* from which with a slight change in spelling we get our word *"Baptize."* The Greek noun is *"Baptisma,"* and taking off the last letter, we have *"Baptism."*

## A STUDY OF THESE GREEK WORDS

We will study these words first in their classical usage. The word *"Baptizo"* is related to another Greek word *"Bapto."* The latter means *"to dip, dip under."* It was used of the Smith tempering the red-hot steel. It was used also in the sense of *"to dip in dye, to color, to steep."* It was used of the act of dying the hair, and of glazing earthen vessels. It was used as a proverb in the sense of *"steeping someone in crimson,"* that is, to beat him until he is covered with blood.

It meant also *"to fill by dipping in, to draw."* It was used of a ship that dipped, that is, sank.

*"Baptizo,"* the related word means *"to dip repeatedly."* It was used of the act of sinking ships. It meant also, *"to bathe."* It was used in the phrase *"soaked in wine,"* where the word *"soaked"* is the meaning of *"Baptizo."*

It is also found in the phrase *"overhead and ears in debt,"* where the words *"overhead and ears"* are the graphic picture of what the word meant. In other words, *"completely submerged."* Our present-day English equivalent would be *"sunk."*

A *"Baptes"* is one who dips or dyes. A *"Baptisis"* is a dipping, bathing, a washing, a drawing of water. A *"Baptisma"* is that which is dipped. A *"Baptisterion"* is a bathing place, a swimming bath. A *"Baptistes"* is one that dips, a dyer. *"Baptos"* means *"dipped, dyed, bright colored, drawn like water."*

In these examples of the various uses of the words *"Bapto"* and *"Baptizo"* we discover three distinct usages, mechanical, ceremonial, and metaphorical.

## THE MECHANICAL USAGE

The mechanical usage can be illustrated by the action of a Blacksmith dipping the hot iron in water, tempering it, or the dyer dipping the cloth in the dye for the purpose of dying it. These instances of the use of the Greek word *"Baptizo"* give us the following definition of the word in its mechanical usage.

The word refers to the introduction or placing of a person or thing into a new environment or into union with something else so as to alter its condition or its relationship to its previous environment or condition. While the word, we found, has other uses, yet the one that predominated above the others was the illustration of the Blacksmith dipping the hot iron in water, etc., or the dyer dipping the cloth in the dye, etc.

## BAPTISM INTO CHRIST

Observe how perfectly this meaning is in accord with the usage of the word in Romans 6:3-4 where the believing sinner is Baptized into vital union with Jesus Christ. The believing sinner is introduced or placed in Christ, thus coming into union with Him. All of this is done by Faith on the part of the believing sinner, and that is the reason we refer to this action as *"mechanical."*

By that action he is taken out of his old environment and condition in which he had lived, the First Adam, and is placed into a new environment and condition, the Last Adam, The Lord Jesus Christ. By this action his condition is changed from that of a lost sinner with a totally depraved nature to that of a Saint with a Divine Nature.

His relationship to the Law of God is changed from that of a guilty sinner to that of a Justified Saint. All this is accomplished by the act of the Holy Spirit introducing or placing him into vital union with Jesus Christ. No ceremony of Water Baptism ever did that, nor could it do that. The entire context is supernatural in its character. Unfortunately, many Believers confuse the Baptism into Christ which takes place at Conversion, with Water Baptism, when the two are not related at all.

It is because we so often associate the English word *"Baptism"* with the rite of Water Baptism, that we read that particular ceremony into Romans Chapter 6, when it has no reference to Water Baptism at all, but rather into Christ.

The purely mechanical usage of the word is seen in the following places: (Mat. 3:11; Mk. 1:8; Lk. 3:16; 16:24; Jn. 1:33; 13:26; Acts 1:5; 11:16; Rom. 6:3-4; I Cor. 12:13; Gal. 3:27; Eph. 4:5; Col. 2:12; Rev. 19:13).

## ITS CEREMONIAL USAGE

The Levitical Washings of the Mosaic Law pertain to the Ceremonial Usage, and are found in the following places: (Lev. 14:8-9; 15:5-8, 10-11, 16, 18, 21-22, 27; 16:4, 24, 28; 17:15).

NOTES

Expressions like those in Isaiah 1:16, and the Prophecies like those in Ezekiel 36:25; 37:23, and Zechariah 13:1, are connected with the Levitical Washings. These Washings and the Prophecies are connected with the purification which followed the act of expiation or cleansing from sin (Ex. 19:14; Lev. 13:14; Heb. 10:22-23).

Thus, that which the word *"Baptizo"* stood for was not unknown to the Jews; however, they would not have been familiar with the manner in which John the Baptist performed these Baptisms.

Actually, the Ceremonial Washings of Leviticus were performed by the person himself, instead of by the Priests.

## WATER BAPTISM IN THE MINISTRY OF JESUS AND JOHN

All Water Baptism whether by Jesus, John, or presently, are exactly like the Theocratic Washings and Purifications of the Old Testament, Ceremonial in nature, a symbol whose design was to point to the purging away of sin on whom the rite was performed (Mat. 3:6; Jn. 3:22-25). In other words, John's Baptism was in response to the repentance of the individual, a spiritual experience already performed (Mat. 3:11). It was connected with his Message of an Atonement for sin that was to be offered in the future, and the necessity of Faith in that Atonement (Acts 19:4).

Whereas John's Baptism looked ahead to a Coming Saviour, Christian Baptism, identical in ceremonial nature, now looks back to a Saviour Who has died and Who has arisen again (Acts 19:5).

That the rite of Water Baptism is the outward testimony of the inward fact of a person's Salvation, and that it *follows* his act of receiving Christ as Saviour and is not a prerequisite to his receiving Salvation, is seen in the use of the Greek proposition *"eis"* in Matthew 3:11. It was translated in the King James, *"I indeed Baptize you with water unto repentance,"* but should have been translated, *"I indeed Baptize you with water because of repentance."* In other words, they translated the Greek word *"eis"* as *"unto"* when they should have translated it as *"because."*

While the act of Christian Baptism is a testimony of the person that his sins have been (already done) washed away, it also pictures and symbolizes the fact of the believing sinner's identification with Christ in His Death, Burial, and Resurrection (Rom. Chpt. 6), for *"Baptizo"* means, *"to dip, to immerse."* It never means *"to sprinkle,"* which should be obvious, because such would not symbolize the Death, Burial, and Resurrection of Christ, and in a sense, the same respecting the Believer.

THE METAPHORICAL USAGE

A metaphor is the use of a word or phrase literally denoting one kind of object or idea in place of another by way of suggesting a likeness or analogy between them, for example, *"The ship plows the sea."* Actually, the ship is not plowing, at least as one thinks of plowing, but the phrase is used as a metaphor, which hopefully describes the manner of the ship going through the sea.

We find the metaphorical use of *"Baptizo"* in Matthew 20:22-23; Mark 10:38-39; and Luke 12:50.

In these Passages, our Lord is speaking of His Sufferings in connection with the Cross. He speaks of them as a Baptism, thereby using a metaphor. The words were uttered while He was on His way to Jerusalem to be Crucified.

John the Baptist had announced His Coming and had Baptized the multitudes. As well, our Lord's Disciples had been Baptizing during the approximate three and one half years of His Ministry.

The word *"Baptizo"* which is used by Matthew, Mark, and Luke had by that time become the technical and common Greek word used to describe the Water Baptism Ceremony administered by John and our Lord's Disciples. Jesus then used the Rite of Water Baptism as a metaphor to speak of His Coming Sufferings.

Just as a Convert was plunged into the Baptismal waters, He was about to be plunged into His Sufferings. Just as the person would be immersed in the water, so He would be overwhelmed (completely covered) by His Sufferings. Just as the person would come up out of the water, so He would be freed from His Sufferings and arise from the dead, hence Him using the word *"Baptizo* (Baptism)*"* in this fashion.

Actually there are two other uses of the Greek word *"Baptizo* (Baptism)*"* which we have not addressed, which is the *"Baptism with the Holy Spirit"* (Acts 1:5), and the *"Baptism unto Moses"* (I Cor. 10:2).

NOTES

Both could be said to be both mechanical and metaphorical.

The phrase, *"But Crispus and Gaius,"* probably referred first of all to the ruler of the Synagogue who gave his heart to Christ (Acts 18:8), with the latter referring to the one mentioned by Paul in Romans 16:23.

Doubtless there were some strong special reasons why, in these instances, that Paul departed from his general rule of not personally Baptizing his Converts (Farrar).

(15) "LEST ANY SHOULD SAY THAT I HAD BAPTIZED IN MINE OWN NAME."

The idea was in the mind of Paul, that he should do nothing that would even remotely have a tendency to pull away allegiance from Christ to himself. One might possibly think from Paul's statement, that others were possibly doing just that, Baptizing in their own name, etc. However, I do not think that was the idea at all relative to his statement.

Inasmuch as Paul had been given the great New Covenant of Grace and was strongly promoting this Message, and as well loudly saying that one could not mix Judaism with Christianity, Paul quickly developed enemies. Had he Baptized many people, it is quite possible that he would have been accused of Baptizing in his name, claiming he was building a religion upon himself, etc. So, he let others do the Baptizing.

(16) "AND I BAPTIZED ALSO THE HOUSEHOLD OF STEPHANAS: BESIDES, I KNOW NOT WHETHER I BAPTIZED ANY OTHER."

The phrase, *"And I Baptized also the household of Stephanas,"* seems from I Corinthians 16:15 to have been those among the first converts in Corinth.

The phrase, *"Besides, I know not whether I Baptized any other,"* informs us, that the inspiration of the Apostles involved none of the mechanical infallibility ascribed to them by popular dogma. He forgot whether he had Baptized anyone else or not, but this made no difference as regards his main argument (Farrar).

(17) "FOR CHRIST SENT ME NOT TO BAPTIZE, BUT TO PREACH THE GOSPEL: NOT WITH WISDOM OF WORDS, LEST THE CROSS OF CHRIST SHOULD BE MADE OF NONE EFFECT."

The phrase, *"For Christ sent me not to Baptize,"* presents to us a Cardinal Truth.

Paul is not minimizing Water Baptism, for it has its place in the Gospel of Jesus Christ. However, Water Baptism does not save anyone, does not add anything to one's Salvation, and is not necessary in the Salvation process. Unfortunately, much of our contemporary religious world has exalted the external ceremony to the extent that the Truth behind it has been lost (Rossier).

WATER BAPTISM

Water Baptism is to the New Covenant what Circumcision was to the Old Covenant. Both were symbols of that particular Covenant. To be sure, the symbol did not save, as the symbol cannot save. Unfortunately, the Jews came to the place that they believed the rite of Circumcision saved them, even as many Christians believe that the ordinance of Water Baptism saves. It doesn't!

We must never confuse the symbol with the substance. The symbol was meant, and is meant, to portray the substance, and that alone.

As it regards Water Baptism, the person going down into the water symbolizes the Death of Christ, and, in effect, the death of the one being baptized – death of the old man. Being under the water symbolizes the Burial of Christ, and symbolizes the Burial of all the sins of Believers. Coming up out of the water symbolizes the Resurrection of Christ, and also symbolizes our new life in Christ (Rom. 6:3-5).

The phrase, *"But to preach the Gospel,"* simply means the manner in which one may be Saved from sin, which is totally by Faith in what Christ did at Calvary and the Resurrection, and which Water Baptism has absolutely no part.

WHAT IS THE GOSPEL OF JESUS CHRIST?

Paul said, *"I am not ashamed of the Gospel of Christ: for it is the Power of God unto Salvation to every one that believeth"* (Rom. 1:16).

Man is afflicted with the terrible malady called *"sin."* To be sure, sin is not merely a philosophical question, nor is it a slight error. In other words, man is not slightly maladjusted as the philosophy of psychology would have us believe. He is altogether going in the wrong direction, actually bound by the powers of darkness, a slave to sin. Sin is a spirit of such magnitude, that it affects the character, nature, bent, and direction of the human being, beyond his own power to correct. In fact, it is of such terrible consequence, that even though God could speak worlds into existence, He could not speak Redemption into existence, i.e., speak sin out of man, but rather had to come down to this world and become man, and die on a Cross thereby paying the price for man's Redemption, by offering up the Perfect Sacrifice of His Own Body. This is why the Power is in the Cross, for it was there that Jesus paid the sin debt and as well, broke the grip of sin on the human family. However, the price was high even as should be obvious. Nevertheless, as horrible as that price was, the giving of God's Only Son, it had to be paid, that is if man was to be Redeemed.

So I am saying that the Gospel of Jesus Christ has Power, and far beyond anything that we could think, which alone can set the captive free. That's the reason it is so foolish for Preachers, or anyone for that matter, to resort to Humanistic Psychology. It is not only wrong, but has no power to do anything, much less break the bonds and shackles that bind humanity.

TWO GREEK WORDS TRANSLATED *"POWER"*

This first word is found in John 1:12, the other in Romans 1:16. John said, *"To as many as received Him, to them gave He the Power to become the sons of God."*

The word here is from a Greek word which was used in the First Century to refer to a legal right, that is a person was given the legal right to do or be something. A sinner who appropriates Jesus Christ as Saviour, is given the legal right to become a Child of God. He becomes a Child of God through Regeneration. But his legal right to Regeneration is procured by his action by trusting the Lord Jesus as Saviour.

REGENERATION

In Regeneration, God is extending Mercy to a sinner who has violated His Laws. Violation of Laws incurs a penalty. Justice demands that the penalty be paid. Until the penalty is paid no Mercy can be given. But if one bears the penalty himself, no Mercy can be shown. Therefore, Jesus Christ paid the penalty of the broken Law in the sinner's stead. Justice is satisfied.

If the sinner desires Mercy from God, he must recognize the payment of the penalty by Jesus Christ before he can be a recipient of that Mercy.

NOTES

When he does that, he has the legal right to accept that Mercy.

Therefore, Regeneration must first be preceded by Justification, not in point of time, but in the Divine Economy. In other words, all of this happens at the moment of Salvation. Therefore, *"To as many as received Him, to them gave He the legal right to become Children of God."*

The word in the Greek translated *"sons"* is from a word whose root comes from a verb which means *"to give birth to."* Thus, the word means, *"born once."* The New Birth is in view here.

The word *"receive"* here implies an active appropriation, not a passive acceptance. It is used synonymously for the word *"believe"* which in a context like this one refers to a definite act of the will entrusting oneself into the keeping of another.

The same word for *"believe"* is used in John 2:24, where Jesus did not commit Himself or entrust Himself to men. The whole translation can read, *"To as many as appropriated Him, to them gave He the legal right to become born ones of God, to them who are trusting in His Name."*

GOD'S SPIRITUAL DYNAMITE

The other word for *"Power"* is in Romans 1:16, *"I am not ashamed of the Gospel of Christ: for it is the Power of God unto Salvation to every one that believeth."*

The word in the Greek means *"Power,"* in the sense of that which overcomes resistance. Our English word *"dynamite,"* comes from this Greek word. The Gospel is God's Spiritual Dynamite which breaks the granite-like heart of the sinner into rock dust, pulverizing it so that it becomes rich soil in which the Seed of the Word finds root and grows.

The Gospel is the most powerful thing in all the world. When it is unloosed in the Spirit-empowering preaching of the Word, souls are Saved.

THE GOSPEL

The word *"Gospel"* is from a Greek word which means *"Good News."* The Good News is that God has wrought out a Salvation through the Blood of the Cross for needy sinners who may by pure Faith without the addition of good works, appropriate that Salvation as a free unmerited gift. Anything else than that is not Gospel, for it is not Good News.

NOTES

The phrase, *"Not with wisdom of words,"* proclaims to us the fact that intellectualism or even philosophic intellectualism is not the Gospel. Regrettably, it is the *"Wisdom of words"* which characterizes most modern pulpits. Consequently, no one will be Saved, nor can they be Saved, under such preaching.

PREACHING

For the Preaching of the Gospel to be effective, it must do one thing and have one thing.

First of all, one must *"Preach the Word"* (II Tim. 4:1-2). That speaks of Preaching Christ and Him Crucified, and all that which accompanies the great Work of Atonement carried out by Christ at Calvary and the Resurrection. In other words, everything that Calvary affords, should be Preached.

THE ANOINTING

Not only must one Preach the Word, but the Word which He Preaches must be Anointed by the Holy Spirit (Lk. 4:18-19).

Paul told the Thessalonians, *"For our Gospel came not unto you in word only, but also in Power, and in the Holy Spirit"* (I Thess. 1:5).

To be honest, not many Preachers preach the Truth. However, there are some who do preach the Truth, but still see very few results, and because there is no Anointing of the Holy Spirit on that particular Truth. This can only come about by the Preacher *"giving themselves continually to prayer, and to the Ministry of the Word"* (Acts 6:4).

THREEFOLD

The Preaching of the Gospel, at least to be effective, must embody a threefold application. It is as follows:

1. As we have stated, the Preacher must Preach the Truth.

2. The Word must be Anointed by the Holy Spirit, which is not automatic, even though it is the Truth. That comes about only by the Moving and Operation of the Holy Spirit on the Word.

3. The personal preparation of the Preacher is of utmost importance and an absolute necessity. To the degree that the Holy Spirit controls the Preacher, to that degree can he or she be Anointed, with the Truth of the Word then becoming effective. This is brought about only

by prayer, fasting, the study of the Word, in other words, a consecrated life.

It is not that one earns anything by doing these things, but that the Holy Spirit has an opportunity to perform His Work in the heart of the Preacher. This is absolutely imperative!

The phrase, *"Lest the Cross of Christ should be made of none effect,"* proclaims the Truth that it is what Jesus did at Calvary which alone effects one's Salvation.

Perhaps the better translation would read, *"Lest the Cross of Christ should be emptied."* It is not possible to actually make the Cross of none effect.

The idea is, that the insertion of man's wisdom makes void its special and independent power (Farrar).

If the Message of the Preacher does not lead the person to the Cross in some manner, then he is really not Preaching the Gospel.

This means that not only is Salvation found in the Price that Jesus paid at Calvary, but as well, Divine Healing is centered up in the Cross, and also, the Baptism with the Holy Spirit is predicated totally upon the Cross of Christ. If Jesus had not paid the sin debt, the Holy Spirit could not have come to live within the hearts and lives of men and women as He now does regarding Believers. That's why Jesus said concerning the Holy Spirit and this very thing, *"For He* (the Holy Spirit) *dwelleth with you* (before Calvary), *and shall be in you* (after Calvary)*"* (Jn. 14:17).

All victory over sin after Salvation is found in the Cross, exactly as Paul explained in Romans Chapter 6. That means our Sanctification is in the Cross, our Victory is in the Cross, our Power is in the Cross, our Prosperity is in the Cross, etc.

(18) "FOR THE PREACHING OF THE CROSS IS TO THEM THAT PERISH FOOLISHNESS; BUT UNTO US WHICH ARE SAVED IT IS THE POWER OF GOD."

The phrase, *"For the Preaching of the Cross is to them that perish foolishness,"* proclaims such in this manner, and continues to be, because it requires spiritual discernment, which the unsaved (perishing) do not have.

## HOW IS THE CROSS THOUGHT OF AS FOOLISHNESS BY THE UNCONVERTED?

To the Jews *"The Cross"* was the tree of shame and horror; and a crucified person was *"accursed of God"* (Deut. 21:23; Gal. 3:13).

NOTES

(In fact, Jesus was *"accursed of God,"* but not for sins He had committed, for He committed none, but for sins we had committed. In other words, He was *"accursed of God"* in our place, which was necessary if we were to be Saved. The *"Curse of the Law"* was death; consequently, Jesus died. However, due to the fact that Satan had no claim on Him, because He had never sinned even though He did bear our sin, which was necessary for our Salvation, death and the grave could not hold Him, therefore, He rose from the dead.)

To the Greeks the Cross was the gibbet on a slave's infamy and a murderer's punishment. There was not a single association connected with it except those of shame and agony.

The thought of *"a Crucified Messiah"* seemed to the Jews a revolting folly; the worship of a Crucified malefactor seemed to the Greeks *"a ridiculous superstition"* (Farrar).

## THE PREACHING OF THE APOSTLE PAUL

Yet so little did Paul seek for popularity or immediate success, that this was the very Doctrine which he put in the forefront, even at a city so refined and so voluptuous as Corinth.

He deliberately Preached the Doctrine of the Cross because he knew that therein lay the Conversion and Salvation of the world, although he was well aware that he could Preach no Truth so certain at first to revolt the unregenerate hearts of his hearers.

*"Preaching"* in the Greek is *"logos,"* and means *"something said,"* i.e., *"the Word of God."*

*"Perish"* in the Greek is *"apollumi,"* and means *"to destroy fully."*

*"Foolishness"* is *"moria,"* and means *"silly, absurd, foolish."*

The phrase, *"But unto us which are Saved it is the Power of God,"* actually should have been translated, *"But unto us who are being Saved."*

This refers to the fact that Salvation has a past effect, a present effect, and a future effect (Rom. 13:11; Phil. 2:12; I Thess. 5:8-9; II Tim. 1:9; 3:15; 4:18; I Pet. 1:5).

More than all, it refers to the Truth that as it was by the Cross that the believing sinner came to Christ, it is by the Cross that the Saint of God stays in Christ. In other words, not only was the sin debt paid at Calvary by Jesus, but the grip of sin was broken as well. It is through a proper understanding of the Cross, which speaks of Jesus dying for mankind, and, as well, the believing sinner understanding that he literally died in Him, was buried with Him, and rose with Him in newness of life; consequently, the Believer's Victory over sin is maintained in this fashion, by constantly remembering this, and acting upon it in Faith. Once again, it all centers up on Calvary.

The phrase, *"It is the Power of God,"* which is the very opposite as thought of by the world.

## HOW COULD THE CROSS BE THE POWER OF GOD?

First of all, it is this manner chosen by God, in which man could be Redeemed. Actually, it is the only manner in which man can be Redeemed. The Cross was that of which the Lord was speaking, when He addressed the serpent (Satan) in the Garden of Eden, and said, *"And I will put enmity* (hatred) *between thee* (Satan) *and the woman* (female gender of the race), *and between thy seed* (those who serve Satan) *and her Seed* (Jesus born of the Virgin Mary)*; It* (Jesus) *shall bruise thy head* (what Jesus did at Calvary), *and thou* (Satan) *shall bruise His Heel"* (the Crucifixion) (Gen. 3:15).

The Power of God was manifested at Calvary in a very peculiar way. In a sense it was demonstrated through weakness. For Paul also wrote, *"For though He was crucified through weakness, yet He liveth by the Power of God"* (II Cor. 13:4).

In fact, in weakness He died, but His Death, which was the death of a Perfect Sacrifice, paid the terrible sin debt owed by man, which man could not pay, and as stated, also broke the grip of sin on the human family. However, even though that was carried out in *"weakness,"* the fact of it being carried out, provides Salvation for all sinners, even the worst, which translates into the Power of God. The Power was actually manifested in the Resurrection of Christ.

## HOW MUCH DID SATAN KNOW ABOUT CALVARY?

I cannot see how that Satan was not well versed in Calvary. In fact, even as we have just stated, from the very beginning the Lord had said what He would do, with further Prophecies making it more and more evident. Even though Satan is not Omniscient as God, still, he is extremely intelligent and wise, even though it is a perverted wisdom because of sin (Ezek. 28:12, 17). However, Satan is not only the great deceiver of the ages, he is in fact, deceived himself.

In other words, he has believed, and in fact still believes, that he will ultimately win out over God. He knows what the Bible says, but he does not believe the Bible. That's the reason his dupes do not believe the Bible as well.

Understanding Calvary and what it would do to him if it succeeded, he had deceived himself into believing it would not succeed, because he felt he could keep Christ from being raised from the dead. However, the Evil One did not succeed, and he will not succeed, because he cannot succeed.

(19) "FOR IT IS WRITTEN, I WILL DESTROY THE WISDOM OF THE WISE, AND WILL BRING TO NOTHING THE UNDERSTANDING OF THE PRUDENT."

The phrase, *"For it is written,"* is found in Isaiah 29:14.

Once again, Paul undergirds his statements, which in effect are the Word of God, with the Word taken from the Old Testament. In effect, we have the Word upon the Word, which in effect interprets itself.

The phrase, *"I will destroy the wisdom of the wise, and will bring to nothing the understanding of the prudent,"* speaks to those who are wise in their own eyes, in effect having forsaken the Ways of the Lord.

Going back to the original statement in Isaiah, the Leaders of Judah planned to counter the threat of the Assyrian Sennacherib by depending on their own power and ability, i.e., wisdom.

The Lord made it clear, though, that deliverance would come as a result of God's Work and not their own efforts. He was not at all dependent on their wisdom.

The same principle holds true regarding Salvation from sin. The Doctrine here is extremely concise and cogent: God does not deliver people from the bondage of sin because of any *"wisdom of the wise"* or *"understanding of the prudent."* In fact, God literally said, *"I will set aside"* these human attempts to gain Salvation (Rossier).

One of the greatest means of Satan to hinder the Church, is to insert the wisdom of man. Because it seems to be wise, and in fact, is wise to the carnal minded, it seems to be the right way. Consequently, Churches or even entire

NOTES

Denominations tend to opt for man's ways instead of God's Ways.

THE HEAD OF THE CHURCH

I think it is obvious here that the Lord is saying that man must follow Him, and that He will not follow man. In fact, He plainly tells us here that He will not use the *"wisdom of the wise,"* and as well, says, *"And will bring to nothing the understanding of the prudent."*

So this means that He is the Head of the Church (Eph. 5:23). However, He is no longer the operating Head of many Church Bodies; He has been relegated to the position of Figure-Head.

The following is given by Dr. Bernard Rossier, and is a description of what occurs in a Church, Fellowship or Denomination that ceases to permit Christ to be its operating Head.

HIERARCHY?

The pattern for Church Government is given in the Book of Acts and the Epistles. This, as is obvious, is the Word of God, and is meant to be followed.

It shows clearly the pattern for Government.

In looking at this pattern, one would be hard-pressed to prove that any official Hierarchy existed outside the local Assemblies. True, they did recognize Apostles like Peter and Paul whose Ministries were much broader than the Local Churches.

However, the acquiescence was purely voluntary. It related primarily to the issues of giving recommendations and beginning new Churches in areas that were being Evangelized; therefore, the development of an Ecclesiastical Hierarchy normally ensues when Christ is not respected as the operating Head.

ORDINATION

Proponents of Ecclesiastical Hierarchies try to prove from such Passages as I Timothy 3:1-7; 5:17-22; II Timothy 1:6, and Titus 1:5-9 that Pastors were ordained to the Ministry by a Church Hierarchy. In other words, the individual is not a recognized Minister unless ordained by such a Hierarchy. However, there is no way that such can be proven by the Passages given.

The Truth is, *"Ordination"* to the Ministry is from God Himself. People or Preachers are simply to recognize that Ordination, not to approve it. Paul made it very clear that Christ appoints the fivefold Ministry (Eph. 4:11) to His Body. Therefore, in order for a group of individuals to gain control of a Church Body, the first logical step would be to gain control of the Ordination process.

NOTES

THE PROPAGATION OF THE GOSPEL

As these Church Structures become more and more Hierarchical, they gradually set aside their reason for existence, which should be the propagation of the Gospel.

A *"Hierarchy"* is a ruling body of Clergy organized into orders or ranks each subordinate to the one above it. As stated, such does not exist in the Book of Acts, which is the account of how the Holy Spirit works respecting the Church, or the Epistles.

BUREAUCRACY

The more that the Church organization loses sight of its real purpose, the spread of the Gospel, the more the system will become bureaucratic and will concentrate on perpetuating itself. In other words, that becomes the chief end of the organization. The Gospel becomes secondary, if given much of any place at all.

CHARISMATIC LEADERS

In the process of doing so (becoming more bureaucratic) the system will gradually eliminate all Charismatic Leaders who generally are independent enough to oppose the self-perpetuating Hierarchy. They will do this, using any means at their disposal.

It doesn't really matter how many people are Saved under the Ministry of such an individual, how many lives are changed, etc., in fact, rather than that being a plus it is actually a minus, at least in their eyes. Anyone they cannot totally control, they must eliminate. As well, their methods are not limited, feeling that the end justifies the means.

EDUCATIONAL INSTITUTIONS

Although it uses other ways, the Organization will concentrate on its educational institutions where its Pastors and other Leaders are trained. For example, it will require that all of the teachers of those individuals be educated in the official graduate institutions or institutions of the Denomination.

It will also establish an official index of all textbooks to be permitted for educational courses. In conjunction with the index, it will institute an official procedure for the approval of textbooks.

### MACHIAVELLIANISM

Machiavellianism will become prevalent as members of the Official Hierarchy become more loyal to one another than they are to the Teachings of Scripture. Because politics allegedly are amoral, these Bureaucrats have no problem justifying the use of unscrupulous means to accomplish their purposes. This especially occurs with reference to their dealings with individuals who attempt to speak out against the ensconced system.

Machiavelli projected the view that politics are amoral, which means that it lies outside the sphere to which moral judgments apply, and that any means, however unscrupulous, can justifiably be used in achieving political power.

In fact, whenever the Hierarchy gradually begins to be formed, of necessity, and because it is unscriptural, it must begin to abandon the Scriptural direction, instead, adopting the ways of the world. Consequently, it becomes political.

### CHURCH GROWTH

Gradually abandoning the Ways of the Lord, the Salvation of souls becomes secondary and in time, has no place at all. Consequently, Church growth, if there is any, will result more from members transferring from one Church to another than it does from actual Conversions to Christ.

### PROGRAMS

Programs will replace prayer, and *"How To"* Seminars will replace Crusades and Campmeetings that concentrate on worship and winning souls.

Endless committees will be formed, concentrating more and more on particular programs which create much religious machinery, stirring up more and more activity; however, in Truth, very little, if anything, is actually done for the Lord.

### GREATER AND GREATER HIERARCHIES

National Officials will countermand the decisions made at State/District/Conference levels. Consequently, the secondary authorities will tend to check with the primary ones before making major decisions, because this is the way Hierarchies work.

The idea that God speaks to individuals other than the Hierarchy is frowned upon, and then finally completely denied. It is not possible to control individuals who claim to be led by the Holy Spirit. In effect, these people take the place of the Holy Spirit.

### A MANIFEST DESTINY MIND-SET

These Organizations often develop a *"manifest destiny mind-set"* in which they equate the particular Denomination with the Kingdom of God. Sometimes they honestly believe that God Personally appoints each incumbent, especially the ones who occupy upper-level positions. (They want to appoint all other positions themselves.)

Terminology then begins to float about which hints or outright says, that if the Preacher is truly of God, He will be a part of their Organization. While they may admit that others might also know the Lord, the attitude is, that if so they are secondary Christians, if Saved at all. If one is not a part of that particular Organization, so they think, then something must be wrong with the individual. Spiritual elitism becomes more and more pronounced.

### QUESTIONING GOD!

This, in turn, implies that anyone who questions these incumbents also questions God.

Never mind that they were elected to this position on a political ballot which in no way is Scriptural, they consider themselves without question to be the *"Spiritual Authority."* Consequently, if one does not obey them, irrespective as to what is demanded, one is rebelling against Scriptural Authority, they say!

### EX CATHEDRA PRONOUNCEMENTS

Once these Organizations have placed Jesus into the position of Figurehead, they will discourage people from thinking that the Holy Spirit speaks individually to Believers. When this matter is taken to its ultimate, the expression of God's Will is reserved to one person or to an oligarchy (Government in which a small group exercises control for corrupt and selfish purposes) supposedly qualified to make *"ex cathedra pronouncements."*

NOTES

When these Leaders speak to other Preachers in their Denomination, they demand total obedience, irrespective as to whether the demand is Scriptural or not. They take the position that Spiritual Authority is speaking, and if what they are saying is wrong, they will be responsible and not the Preacher, etc. Consequently, the Word of God and the Spirit of God are no longer the Spiritual Guides of the people, but rather the Hierarchy.

## PRONOUNCEMENTS

These pronouncements, written or oral, gradually will become the official interpretation of Scripture for the Denomination. In other words, the Word of God is no longer the Standard or the Pattern for what is done, but rather their own pronouncements.

As well, they make no attempt to make their pronouncements Scriptural, but rather political. As stated, the Word of God now has no place in their decision making.

## GROUPS BREAK OFF

Surprisingly, many Preachers are pleased at such an arrangement, because this absolves them of any type of Spiritual or Scriptural responsibility. In other words, someone else is doing the thinking for them.

However, almost always, all are not happy with such an arrangement, with some finally breaking away.

## BRANDED

When this happens, the breaking away of certain groups, the Denomination will brand these break-offs as *"cults."*

These people, whomever they may be, are automatically denied any type of spiritual status by the Parent Denomination. As well, almost all the time, measures will be taken, even after the Preacher or Preachers are no longer part of the particular Organization, to hinder them and cause as much difficulties as possible. They seem to feel they have the right to destroy, and to use any means at their disposal to do so, all who separate themselves. They are not content with just simply allowing these individuals to go their way, while the Parent Organization goes its way, they feel their mission is not complete until they have succeeded in completely destroying the individual, or at least denying the person any type of Ministry.

NOTES

What I am about to say most will not believe, even though I know it to be true.

Were it not for the Laws of the Land, in many cases, these types of Organizations would actually kill the individual who has incurred their displeasure. To be frank, history is replete with untold thousands who have paid with their lives in this very fashion. The only thing that stops such now, is, as stated, the Law of the Land. However, not able to carry out that extreme, they will resort to the next best measure of destroying the person reputation wise.

## PROPERTY REVISION CLAUSES

To keep Local Churches from leaving the Denomination, they will require property reversion clauses in the Constitutions of these Churches. Even then, these types of Organizations are normally engaged in several law suits at any given time.

As well, they will gradually require all Churches to insert the Denominational name into the Local Church name.

As stated, the more the system becomes bureaucratic and, therefore, political, it will forget its chief purpose of Preaching the Gospel, and will concentrate more and more on perpetuating itself.

Inasmuch as we are living in the last years of the Church Age, an Age which will be characterized and is characterized by apostasy, that which we have addressed is rampant in the land presently. Regrettably, the situation will not get better but rather worse. In fact, and regarding Biblical Spirituality and Authority, the age of Denominations has ended. While they may continue to get larger and larger and even richer and richer, as far as a Work for God is concerned, such is becoming less and less. In fact, the spiritual slide downward for most Denominations is so swift as to be almost unbelievable. Pentecostal Denominations which once touched the world for Christ, now for the most part, touch nothing at all, at least for the Lord.

These things are not said out of rancor, but because of a deep-seated concern for the Word of God, and because the Call of God on my life demands such an evaluation.

(20) "WHERE IS THE WISE? WHERE IS THE SCRIBE? WHERE IS THE DISPUTER

OF THIS WORLD? HATH NOT GOD MADE FOOLISH THE WISDOM OF THIS WORLD?"

Paul draws these questions from combining Isaiah 19:12 and 33:18.

The question, *"Where is the wise?"*, presents the first of three classes of learned people who lived in that day.

Concerning Salvation for the lost, a solution for the human problem, Paul implies by this question that no human exists who is capable of thinking up a Plan of Salvation that will work.

This question would come home to the Jews, who regarded their Rabbis and the *"people of the wise"* as exalted beings who could look down on all poor ignorant persons, or people of the land. In fact, Paul before his Conversion was in this very class.

He was probably looked at as the great hope of Pharisaism. His Scholarship in the Scriptures (Old Testament) would have been profound, but yet without their true meaning, simply because for all his learning, he did not truly know God. Consequently, he did not truly understand the Scriptures, and in fact, could not understand them until he was converted on the road to Damascus.

So, when he asked this question, it is a question that is very close to home and one in which he understands, possibly as few other men.

As well, this question would have been aimed at the Greeks, who regarded none but the Philosophers as *"wise."*

The question, *"Where is the Scribe?"*, pertained to the Jewish Theologians of that day. They were the ideal of dignified learning and orthodoxy, though for the most part mistook elaborate ignorance for profound knowledge.

Paul is saying that no human exists, even the Scribes, who is capable of writing up a workable Plan of Salvation (Rossier).

The question, *"Where is the disputer of this world?"*, covers the waterfront.

The word *"disputer"* would especially suit the disputatious Greeks, who constantly were putting forth great (or so they thought) questions, which instigated all type of disputations. As stated, they relished these type of things.

The Holy Spirit through Paul, shows that no human exists who is capable of defending a Plan of Salvation, even if humans could devise one, which they cannot.

NOTES

These questions are meant to put to rest any and all Philosophy, Body of Learning, Psychology, Psychological Concepts, Religion, Secular Education, Political Promises, or anything else for that matter, which claim to address the human problem.

The question, *"Hath not God made foolish the wisdom of this world?"*, proclaims that what God did in the sending of His Son to Redeem humanity, was all totally of God and none of man. In other words, the Lord insulted the wisdom of this world and its claims in the most graphic, open, and obvious way possible. He did so purposely because of the conceit of man. This included both Jews and Gentiles.

(21) "FOR AFTER THAT IN THE WISDOM OF GOD THE WORLD BY WISDOM KNEW NOT GOD, IT PLEASED GOD BY THE FOOLISHNESS OF PREACHING TO SAVE THEM THAT BELIEVE."

The phrase, *"For after that in the Wisdom of God the world by wisdom knew not God,"* means that the *"Wisdom of God"* is so profound and so above that of man, that man's puny wisdom, even the best he has to offer, cannot come to know God in any manner. In other words, God considers the intellect of man so nothing, especially considering that it is warped and twisted by sin, that to such God will not even respond.

These words might be written as a epitaph on the tomb of ancient Philosophy, and of modern Philosophy and Science so far as it assumes an anti-Biblical form (Lk. 10:21). Human wisdom, when it relies solely on itself may *"feel after God,"* but hardly find Him (Acts 17:26-27) (Farrar).

The phrase, *"It pleased God by the foolishness of preaching to save them that believe,"* should have been translated, *"It pleased God by the foolishness of the thing preached* (as men esteemed it) *to save them that believe."*

God by leaving man to his own wisdom demonstrated man's folly; for he not only was incapable of knowing God, but he degraded Him to the level of a *"creeping thing"* (Rom. Chpt. 1) in ancient times, and in modern days to a piece of bread which he first adores and then devours (the Catholic Mass); and, further, by offering him life on the principle of believing in opposition to the principle of merit, God demonstrated man's moral and intellectual corruption (Williams).

As we have stated, Paul is dealing here with that preached, which is the Cross, rather than the art of Preaching itself. The Cross of Christ is not palatable to the world, or acceptable by the world.

(22) "FOR THE JEWS REQUIRE A SIGN, AND THE GREEKS SEEK AFTER WISDOM:"

The phrase, *"For the Jews require a sign,"* presents a strange contrast. In fact, the Jews had been given the most far reaching, powerful display of miraculous signs, and by the thousands at that, regarding the Ministry of Christ in healing the sick and casting our devils, etc. However, these were signs the Jews would not accept, instead demanding rather some type of stunt (Mat. 12:38; 16:1; Jn. 2:18; 4:48). The Truth is, they would not have accepted anything that Jesus did, irrespective as to how grand or glorious it may have been.

The phrase, *"And the Greeks seek after wisdom,"* means that they thought that such solved the human problem. However, if it did, why were they ever seeking after more wisdom?

The Jews demanded that the claims of Jesus Christ should be accredited by some type of physical wonders, and the Greeks, that it should be demonstrated by commanding arguments presented with intellectual splendor. Both found it difficult to accept as God a dead Man hanging on a Cross, for such Christ was to them (Williams).

In fact, the Greeks were seekers, not doers. They actually did not know what they were seeking, but they gloried in the very fact that they were zealous seekers. They even thought of God as Wisdom or Truth. Their great heros, Socrates, Plato, and Aristotle were thinkers. Therefore, they were ever seeking but never finding, because they were looking in all the wrong places — basically within their own minds. So what they produced, was no greater than themselves, because the creature cannot be greater than the Creator. Consequently, they were imprisoned in their own philosophy, as the Jews were imprisoned in their own self-righteousness.

(23) "BUT WE PREACH CHRIST CRUCIFIED, UNTO THE JEWS A STUMBLINGBLOCK, AND UNTO THE GREEKS FOOLISHNESS;"

NOTES

The phrase, *"But we preach Christ Crucified,"* even though short, is actually the basic Foundation of Salvation.

Even though it was necessary that Jesus be born of the Virgin Mary, be a Miracle-Worker, and the greatest Preacher and Teacher of all, those things within themselves could not Redeem anyone. Jesus as a Good Man, as a Wise Man, even as the Messiah, even as the Son of God, could not save anyone. It is only through the Crucified Christ, with all its attendant horror, attendant humiliation, shame, and spectacle, in which men can be Saved. In other words, Calvary was not something which just happened, but was a determined necessity. Jesus came to this world to die on Calvary. It took that, the offering up of His Own Perfect Body as a Sacrifice, which alone God would accept, that the terrible sin debt may be paid.

The offering up of literally hundreds of millions of lambs in the previous centuries as Sacrifices, all prefigured Christ. As well, all the Ceremonial aspect of the Mosaic Law regarding the Sacrifices, Sacred Vessels in the Tabernacle and then the Temple, the Feast Days, Sabbath-keeping, Circumcision, etc., all pointed to the expiatory, vicarious, Offering of the Son of God.

## CALVARY

Satan attacks this Message as he attacks no other. He has done it through Modernism, through Intellectualism, through Psychology, and he has attacked it severely in the Charismatic Community in what is known as the Faith Message, etc.

Many Churches in this particular belief system, will not sing any songs about Calvary, about the Shed Blood of Jesus Christ, etc., referring to those things as *"past miseries."* While they admit that such is necessary for one to be Saved, thereafter, they teach, such is a detriment to the Believer. To make the long story brief, they claim their Victory is in Faith and Confession and not the Cross. In fact, it is a misplaced Faith and a misrepresented Confession. In other words, their Faith is not really in Christ, but rather in themselves, and their Confession is really not in what Christ did for them at Calvary and the Resurrection, but rather in their own Faith.

Even though they would pay lip service to what Paul says here about Preaching Christ Crucified, because it is the Word of God; however, they would explain it away by claiming it refers only to Salvation with no bearing on one's Sanctification. In fact, they have a basic misunderstanding respecting the Atonement, which is serious indeed!

The Truth is, everything hinges on Calvary, one's Salvation, one's Sanctification, one's constant Victory in Christ, Divine Healing, Answered Prayer, the Baptism with the Holy Spirit, etc. In other words, the effect of Calvary does not stop with Salvation, but continues just as important in one's everyday walk before God (Rom. Chpt. 6).

STUMBLINGBLOCK

The phrase, *"Unto the Jews a stumblingblock,"* speaks of the reason for Israel's rejection of Jesus.

They had for centuries been looking for a regal and victorious Messiah, Who should exalt their special privileges. The notion of a Suffering and Humiliated Messiah, Who reduced them to the level even of the Gentiles, was to them *"a stone of stumbling and a rock of offence"* (Isa. 8:14; Rom. 9:33).

*"Stumblingblock"* in the Greek is *"skantalon,"* and means *"scandal, offense, or the thing that offends."*

Why was the Crucifixion a scandal or an offense to the Jews?

In the eyes of the Jewish Leadership, Jesus was wrong on all counts, despite the fact that He was actually right on all counts. He fulfilled the Scriptural demands to the letter.

First of all, He was of the lineage of David which the Prophecies had said must be (II Sam. Chpt. 7), going back to that Monarch through Solomon on the side of Joseph His Foster Father, and through Nathan another of David's sons, through Mary. In effect, Jesus being the Firstborn, had the Davidic Dynasty continued, would have been the King of Israel, and in fact will be, at the Second Coming (Rev. Chpt. 19).

He fulfilled all the Prophecies concerning His humiliation, even as Isaiah had prophesied graphically so (Isa. Chpt. 53). So, the Crucifixion should not have been a surprise to Israel, especially considering that the offering up of every lamb, which they had done hundreds of millions of times in the past 15 centuries, was a direct symbolism and representation of that horrible event.

NOTES

As well, if a Jew committed a death penalty sin, and in fact was executed (stoned to death), and then as a further humiliation to his family, his body hanged on a tree, he shall be judged as *"accursed of God,"* i.e., doomed to eternal darkness without God (Deut. 21:21-23).

Inasmuch as Jesus was Crucified, in their minds, even though they were the ones who demanded this execution by the Roman Authorities, this meant that Jesus was *"cursed by God."* The idea that someone like this could be the Messiah of Israel, was unthinkable, i.e., a stumblingblock.

The Truth is, Jesus was cursed by God, but not for any sins He had committed, for He had committed none, but for the sin of the world (Jn. 1:29). As stated, Isaiah spelled this out in detail (Isa. Chpt. 53), so there was no excuse for Israel not knowing what the Messiah would be like and what the Messiah would do.

In fact, the very reason that Jesus was a *"stumblingblock"* to Israel, is first of all because of their turning away from the Word of God. They simply did not know the Scriptures, even though they trumpeted them loudly each and every day. Lest we point a finger at them, that is our very problem presently as well.

FOOLISHNESS?

The phrase, *"And unto the Greeks foolishness,"* actually refers to the Gentiles. However, Paul refers to the Greeks for the simple reason, that they were the Philosophers of the world, claiming to hold the answers for the dilemma of mankind, or at least sincerely seeking those answers.

Both alike, the Jews and the Greeks, had failed. The Jew had not attained ease of conscience or moral perfectness; the Greek had not unraveled the secret of Philosophy; yet both alike rejected the Peace and the enlightenment which they had professed to seek.

*"Foolishness"* in the Greek is *"moria,"* and means *"silliness and absurdity,"* in other words, not worthy of any serious consideration.

The accent of profound contempt is discernable in all the early allusions of Greeks and Romans to Christianity. The only epithets which they could find for it were *"execrable," "malefic," "depraved," "damnable"* (Tacitus, Suetonius, Pliny, etc.). The milder term is *"excessive superstition."*

The word used to express the scorn of the Athenian Philosophers for Paul's *"strange Doctrine"* is one of the coarsest disdain, calling him *"a seed-pecker."* It referred to birds that picked seeds out of manure (Farrar).

Regrettably and sadly, the Crucified Christ still remains a *"stumblingblock"* or *"foolishness"* to the majority of the world.

WHY WAS AND IS THE CROSS OF CHRIST AN OFFENSE TO MANKIND?

The problem stems from two directions: A. First, man's proposed self-sufficiency; and, B. Second, the humiliation and shame of the Cross.

SELF-SUFFICIENCY

Man's problem of self-sufficiency stems from the Fall. Man fell because of disobeying God in the realm of not believing God's Word, thereby going in a direction which was not of God, i.e., the Way of God. Consequently, man has been going his way ever since, thinking that he holds the answer or the solution to his problems. It is a rebellion of the creature against the Creator, in effect claiming self-sufficiency, no need of God.

So, in man's fallen condition, he doesn't think or realize his need for Salvation or Redemption. He realizes that he has problems, even terrible problems, but he keeps thinking he can solve these problems by education, better environment, money, brute force, or Psychology, i.e., Psychotherapy. The idea that he can't, even as the Bible graphically declares, offends him.

Throwing oneself on a Crucified Christ, albeit Risen from the dead, is that which he does not desire to do, and basically because he will not admit that he needs such.

THE HUMILIATION OF THE CROSS

The Humiliation of the Cross is still present in the world even after some 2,000 years of Ministry by the Holy Spirit; however, it is somewhat a different type of humiliation.

After some 2,000 years, and the work done by the Holy Spirit, the fact of Jesus, the Son of God coming from Heaven and dying on a Cross, is not so much at the present time a source of contention. People either believe it or they do not. In other words, the Holy Spirit has somewhat softened the blow of the humiliation of the Person of Jesus and the ignominy of His cruel Death.

NOTES

By and large, the humiliation rests upon the act of the person accepting Christ. Satan, who is the god of this world, opposes greatly that of which we speak, the acceptance of Christ. So, the sinner in most cases who accepts Christ, is held up to ridicule. Many if not most, simply cannot bear such ridicule; therefore, they refuse to accept the King of kings and Lord of lords.

However, I remind one and all, that what is a stumblingblock or foolishness today, will not be such tomorrow.

(24) "BUT UNTO THEM WHICH ARE CALLED, BOTH JEWS AND GREEKS, CHRIST THE POWER OF GOD, AND THE WISDOM OF GOD."

The phrase, *"But unto them which are called,"* actually refers to those who accept the Call, for the entirety of mankind is invited (Jn. 3:16; Rev. 22:17).

*"Called"* in the Greek is *"kletos,"* and means *"an invitation extended, invited."*

The phrase, *"Both Jews and Greeks,"* actually stands for *"both Jews and Gentiles."* The idea is, that the Call is extended equally to all. Henceforth, the middle wall of partition between them is thrown down, and there is no difference (Rom. 9:24).

In fact, this is at least one of the reasons that the Jews hated Paul. Being the people of the Book and the Prophets, which meant they were the only people on Earth who were privileged to have the Word of God, they considered themselves above the Gentiles. The idea that they had to come on exactly the same basis as Gentiles, which meant admitting that they were sinners and needed a Redeemer, infuriated them. As someone has said, all ground is level at the foot of the Cross.

The phrase, *"Christ the Power of God, and the Wisdom of God,"* sums up Christianity.

To those who accept God's Great Offer of Salvation through Jesus Christ, whether Jews or Gentiles, Christ is the Great Miracle of God and the Great Philosophy of God, one might say.

The Power of God in destroying sin and death, man's greatest foes, constituted the answer to man's dilemma.

As well, the Wisdom of God in devising such a Plan of Salvation which pardoned guilty men and at the same time vindicated and glorified the Justice of God, stands out as the wisest and most remarkable Plan of all time (Williams).

However, it is only the *"Called ones"* that is, those who accept the Call, who are privileged to know this *"Power,"* and be the beneficiary of this *"Wisdom."*

This is what Jesus was talking about when He said, *"I thank Thee, O Father, Lord of Heaven and Earth, that Thou hast hid these things from the wise and prudent, and hast revealed them unto babes: even so, Father; for so it seemed good in Thy Sight"* (Lk. 10:21).

(25) "BECAUSE THE FOOLISHNESS OF GOD IS WISER THAN MEN; AND THE WEAKNESS OF GOD IS STRONGER THAN MEN."

The phrase, *"Because the foolishness of God is wiser than men,"* actually means that which men take to be foolish and weak, because with arrogant presumption they look upon themselves as the measure of all things.

God achieves the mightiest ends by the humblest means, and the Gospel of Christ allied itself from the first, not with the world's strength and splendor, but with all which the world despised as mean and feeble — with fishermen and tax-gatherers, with slaves, and women, and common laborers (Farrar).

The Text does not mean that God is foolish, but rather refers to that which men think of as *"foolishness,"* but which is rather the *"Wisdom of God."*

The phrase, *"And the weakness of God is stronger than men,"* once again refers to that which men take to be weak, but actually is not.

The idea is, that God infuses with the Holy Spirit, those who actually are foolish and weak, and then they attempt and carry out great things for the Lord. Regrettably, and for the greater part, only the broken and humble are willing to allow the Lord such access to their lives.

(26) "FOR YE SEE YOUR CALLING, BRETHREN, HOW THAT NOT MANY WISE MEN AFTER THE FLESH, NOT MANY MIGHTY, NOT MANY NOBLE, ARE CALLED:"

The phrase, *"For ye see your Calling, Brethren,"* refers to the nature and method of their Heavenly Calling.

The fact that the group of Christians at Corinth was composed mostly of poor men, and that they were *"Called"* to the Gospel by men who as well were not noble, was a further

NOTES

demonstration of God's Judgment of man's assumed importance and wisdom (Williams).

The phrase, *"How that not many wise men after the flesh, not many mighty, not many noble, are called,"* does not say not *any,* but rather, *"not many."* There are a few of the worldly wise, mighty, or noble, who do accept the Lord, but most think of serving Christ as foolishness, or else they feel the price is too high to pay. In the New Testament, at least as far as it is known, of such rank we have only Joseph of Arimathaea, Nicodemus, Sergius Paulus, and Dionysius the Areopagite (Acts 13:7; 17:34).

If one is to notice, Paul mentioned *"Wise men after the flesh,"* which means they were wise in the things of the world but not in the things of God.

Those who hear the Calling are alone the truly wise; but they are not wise with a carnal wisdom, not wise as men count wisdom; they have but little of the wisdom of the serpent and the wisdom of *"this age."*

The Sanhedrin looked down on the Apostles as *"unlearned and ignorant men"* (Acts 4:13). *"God"* says Augustine, *"caught orators by fishermen, not fishermen by orators."*

All this was a frequent taunt against Christians, but they made it their boast. Christianity came to Redeem and elevate, not the few, but the many, and the many must ever be the weak and the humble. Hence, Christ called fishermen as His Apostles, and was known as *"the Friend of Publicans and sinners."* In fact, very few of the Rulers believed on Him (Jn. 7:48).

Once again I emphasize, that the strength of the Text proclaims the fact that *all* are *"Called,"* i.e., are extended an invitation, but only a few accept. In fact, in comparison to the whole, only a few of the poor truly accept, and as stated here, only a tiny, tiny few of the mighty and the noble, etc.

(27) "BUT GOD HATH CHOSEN THE FOOLISH THINGS OF THE WORLD TO CONFOUND THE WISE; AND GOD HATH CHOSEN THE WEAK THINGS OF THE WORLD TO CONFOUND THE THINGS WHICH ARE MIGHTY;"

The phrase, *"But God hath chosen the foolish things of the world to confound the wise,"* tells us some things about how God works in this Great Plan of Salvation.

First of all it tells us that God deliberately and with forethought chose this particular Plan, which means it will carry through to Victory without fail.

## WHY DID GOD CHOOSE THIS TYPE OF PLAN?

First of all, the system which produces the *"wise, mighty and noble,"* is not of God. It is rather, and as stated, the *"wisdom of the serpent,"* and *"the wisdom of this age."* It portrays the very finest that Satan has to offer. As a result, not only does it deceive those few who are in this category, but it deceives the masses as well, because they aspire to be like their heros, or idols, etc.

Consequently, it is common to hear various people refer to the rich and the famous by saying, *"He made it,"* or *"She has reached the top."*

One longs to ask, *"Made what?"* Or *"Reached the top of what?"*

While it is not true that all would have to give up their place and position if they found Christ, still, many would. The manner in which some make their money or gain their place and position, is contrary to the Word of God; therefore, even though at times God deals with these people greatly, most, in fact virtually all, refuse that Call. Pontius Pilate is a perfect example, along with Felix and King Agrippa (Acts 24:25; 26:27-28).

The terrible bane is, that the Modern Church has so compromised the Message, pretty much telling any and all they can live any way they desire, remaining in any type of environment, and still be a Christian. Consequently, the name *"Christian,"* means very little anymore!

While a person definitely can be a Christian in any environment, if in fact that environment is ungodly, it is almost impossible for one to not allow the environment to get into him. It is similar to a ship that is on the water. As long as the water doesn't get in the ship, it remains a valuable piece of equipment bringing sustenance and life to those in need. However, if the water gets into the ship, things are going to be damaged, and if enough water gets in the ship, it will sink. So it is with the Christian!

The Christian is *in* the world, but he must not be *of* the world. To the degree the world is in the Christian, to that degree will there be damage. If there is enough of the world in the Christian, the Christian can *"sink,"* lose his way, and, consequently, his soul.

NOTES

The phrase, *"And God hath chosen the weak things of the world to confound the things which are mighty,"* is once again done for purpose.

God calls all, and accepts all who come to Him, irrespective as to how foolish, sinful, wicked, or weak they may be. All are accepted on the same basis, that of Faith in Christ. As well, this alone hinders many of the *"noble,"* for the simple reason, that most balk at the idea of having to humble themselves even as the low and lowly. God doesn't have a first-class section, business-class section, or tourist-class section, as do most airplanes. All come on the same basis, and all are treated in the same manner.

## THE SYSTEM OF THE WORLD

The system of the world is the *"survival of the fittest."* That holds true not only in the animal kingdom, which suffered a change as a result of the Fall, through no fault of their own, but as well in the human race. In much of the world, the high and mighty take advantage of the weak and helpless, and there is nothing they can do. One of the things that has made America great, is that our system of Government which is based at least partly on the Bible, has attempted to address these issues in a fair and equitable way. In other words, justice for all!

But still, even in America, too oftentimes, the poor get poorer and the rich get richer.

## GOD'S PLAN

As stated, the Lord receives all who come to Him. At the outset He makes new creatures of all, never attempting to rehabilitate what is there, for that is man's way, incidentally a way which cannot work. At the moment of the New Birth, the Holy Spirit comes into the heart and the life of the new Believer. Irrespective of what that person has been in the past, or the previous deficiencies, the potential for great things now resides in the heart and the life of that person, irrespective as to whom he may be. As stated, God caught orators by fishermen, not fishermen by orators.

Men are ever attempting to *"make themselves over,"* or *"find themselves,"* or *"find their niche in life,"* but never seem to succeed irrespective as to what they do. The Truth is, self-motivation is not the answer. Man's problem cannot be fixed by a three-hour Seminar. All of these things for which men seek, can be found, but not in the world or the ways of the world, but only in Jesus.

He makes giants out of pygmies, winners out of losers, champions out of the weak and masters out of slaves. In fact, He is the only One Who can do such a thing, and has done it in untold millions of lives, and can do it for you if you have not already allowed Him to do so.

(28) "AND BASE THINGS OF THE WORLD, AND THINGS WHICH ARE DESPISED, HATH GOD CHOSEN, YEA, AND THINGS WHICH ARE NOT, TO BRING TO NOUGHT THINGS THAT ARE:"

The phrase, *"And base things of the world, and things which are despised, hath God chosen,"* must be met with a shout of *"Hallelujah,"* for were this not so, I would not be Saved, and most probably neither would you.

Once again, the Holy Spirit calls to the attention of all concerned, that God has purposely chosen this Way of Salvation. He needs nothing man has, irrespective as to how wise or strong it may seem to be.

The phrase, *"Yea, and things which are not, to bring to nought things that are,"* refers to that which is accounted by the world as nothing, and in fact, is nothing! Actually that's all that God can really use. He is little interested in our talent, ability, wisdom, money, success, place, or position. He is interested only, in an empty vessel desiring to be filled with His Love and Grace.

## WHAT HATH GOD WROUGHT!

Every iota of freedom, prosperity, equality, advancement, true education, fair treatment, in other words all that is good in this world, can be laid at the feet of Bible Christianity.

Understanding that Bible Christianity is made up of the *"poor who heard Him gladly,"* we now realize, or at least certainly should, that the Lord has taken *"things which are not, to bring to nought things that are,"* i.e., bring to nought ignorance, poverty, hate, prejudice, etc., in many parts of the world. Whatever freedoms or prosperity are in the world presently, were not brought about by the *"wise men after the flesh, the mighty, the noble,"* but rather, by the *"foolish things, base things, and despised things,"* i.e., those whom God has touched!

NOTES

(29) "THAT NO FLESH SHOULD GLORY IN HIS PRESENCE."

*"Flesh"* here refers to human effort.

By *"human effort"* we mean the effort of man to save himself, to effect his own Salvation, to make himself Righteous. On the contrary, these things actually prevent the Grace of God from working.

For the weak instruments of God's triumphs are so weak, that it is impossible for them to ascribe any power or merit to themselves. In contemplating the Victory of the Cross, the world can only exclaim, *"This hath God wrought." "It is the Lord's doing, and it is marvelous in our eyes."*

## THE IMPERIALISM OF CHRISTIANITY

Christianity came into a world dominated by the Cult of the Caesar, a religious system if you will, in which the Roman Emperor was worshiped as a god. The Empire, made up of many widely different peoples with their own distinctive languages, customs, and religions, was held together not merely by one central ruling power at Rome which was supported by the military power of its legions, but also, and more probably, more efficiently so, by the universal religion of Emperor-worship.

Political and military ties are strong, but religious ties are stronger. Rome knew this and guarded jealously its Cult of the Caesar.

## VARIOUS RELIGIONS

Its policy was to allow its subjects to retain their own religions as long as they accepted Emperor-worship in addition to their own system of belief. But Rome would not countenance a religion that set itself up as unique and as taking that place in the hearts of men which was occupied by the Cult of the Caesar.

Into this atmosphere Christianity came with its unique and imperialistic claims. It was inevitable that there would be a clash between these two imperialisms, that of Heaven and that of Rome.

It came in the form of the bloody persecutions hurled against the Christian Church by Rome during the first 300 years of its existence. What an unanswerable proof of the Divine origin of Christianity we have in the fact that by A.D. 316, Christianity had displaced Emperor-worship as the predominating system of belief in the Roman world and that the Emperor Constantine at that time made it the State religion.

While this bode no good at all for Christianity, still, it is an example as to what God could do with *"base things and despised things."* He took things which were not, and brought to nought things that are.

THE CULT OF THE CAESAR

The inscriptions which Archaeologists have unearthed give us some information regarding the Cult of the Caesar which throws an abundance of light upon some Passages in the New Testament. They reveal a parallelism between Christianity and the Imperial Cult with reference to the position of the Lord Jesus in the system called Christianity and that of the Roman Emperor in the system called the Cult of Caesar, and the official titles held by each.

LORD

For instance, the term *"kurios"* meaning *"Lord"* was used as a Divine title of the Emperor. It was also an official title of our Lord Jesus.

This Greek word *"kurios"* is the translation in the Septuagint (Greek translation of the Old Testament) of the august title of God in the Old Testament, *"Jehovah."* The term *"Lord"* was understood to be a title which included within its meaning of *"Master"* the idea of Divinity. It was a Divine title.

These facts throw a flood of light on Paul's assertion (I Cor. 8:5-6), *"For though there be that are called gods, whether in Heaven or in Earth (as there be gods many, and lords many),*

*"But to us there is but one God, the Father, of Whom are all things, and we in Him; and One Lord Jesus Christ, by Whom are all things, and we by Him."*

These words are set in a context in which Paul is pleading for separation from the Pagan Greek Mystery Religions. He cites the example of the Christian's separation from the Cult of Caesar, arguing that if the Corinthian Christians have thrown off their allegiance to the Caesar so far as worshiping him is concerned, they ought also to separate themselves from any participation in the Greek religious practices.

Here the chief exponent of Christianity is throwing out into the arena of the imperialistic contest the imperialistic challenge of Christianity, namely, that while the Greeks may people the heavens with deities (supposed deities), and the Romans may worship the Emperor on Earth, yet so far as Christians are concerned, they do not recognize these, for they are monotheists, worshiping the Absolute God, and His Son Jesus Christ Who Himself is God.

NOTES

LORDSHIP

Our Lord referred to this practice of the deification of the Emperor when He said, *"The kings of the Gentiles exercise lordship over them"* (Lk. 22:25). The meaning of the word *"lordship"* here is not merely that the Emperor rules as an absolute autocrat (one ruling with unlimited authority), but that he rules as an Emperor-god. In answer to the question of the Herodians (Mat. 22:15-22), *"Is it lawful to pay taxes to Caesar, or not?"* He said, *"Render therefore to Caesar the things that are Caesar's."*

The question was fully answered. The words, *"And unto God the things that are God's,"* is a protest against Emperor-worship. Taxes should be paid to Caesar, but no worship should be accorded him. To be worshiped is the prerogative of God Alone.

*"There went out a decree from Caesar Augustus that the whole inhabited Earth,"* i.e., the Roman Empire, *"should be enrolled"* (Lk. 2:1). The Greek word is not *"taxed,"* but *"enrolled."*

Taxation was probably one of the purposes of this enrollment, but it was the imperial census that was being taken. The inscriptions furnished instances of other enrollments, showing that such a thing was neither unreasonable nor impossible, the destructive critics notwithstanding.

Joseph and Mary in obedience to the imperial decree go to Bethlehem where the Prophecy of Micah (5:2) is fulfilled. Now comes the imperialistic announcement, brought by an Angel from Heaven.

*"Fear not: for, behold, I bring you good tidings of great joy, which shall be to all people.*

*"For unto you is born this day in the city of David a Saviour, which is Christ the Lord"* (Lk. 2:10-11).

Here was Heaven's King coming to dispute the claims and position of the Caesar who arrogated to himself the title of *"Lord,"* and who was worshiped as a god. No wonder that Herod and the Jews were agitated at this news

(Mat. 2:1-8), the former because of the imperialistic challenge which would present new problems of administration to him in addition to the ones he already had in connection with troublesome Israel, the latter because, entrenched in their ecclesiastical sin, they did not want to be deprived of their lucrative positions.

Once again, it is hard for the high and mighty, to accept the Lord Jesus Christ, because it threatens their position in one way or the other.

## HUMILIATION

While Heaven's King came in humiliation the first time and did not displace the world empire of the ruling Caesar, but only found a place in a few hearts, He will someday come in exaltation to dethrone the Antichrist, the then ruling Caesar, and, occupying the Throne of David, will rule over a world-empire as King of kings, and Lord of lords.

It was Thomas who exclaimed, *"My LORD and my God"* (Jn. 20:28). This was enough to involve him in serious trouble with the Roman Authorities had they known of it, for he was acknowledging Jesus of Nazareth as his Lord and his God instead of Caesar.

Polycarp, who lived A.D. 156, was confronted with the question by the Roman Official, *"What is the harm in saying 'Lord Caesar'?"* He refused to acknowledge Caesar as Lord, and was martyred.

Festus said regarding Paul, *"Of whom I have no certain thing to write unto my Lord"* (Acts 25:26). His Lord was Caesar, *"Lord"* in the sense that Festus recognized Nero, who was then Caesar, as the Emperor-god to whom worship was due.

## THE IMPERIALISTIC CHALLENGE OF CHRISTIANITY

But see the imperialistic challenge of Christianity in the words of the Apostle Paul (Phil. 2:9-11), *"Wherefore God also hath highly exalted Him, and given Him a Name which is above every name:*

*"That at the Name of Jesus every knee should bow, of things in Heaven, and things in Earth, and things under the Earth;*

*"And that every tongue should confess that Jesus Christ is Lord, to the Glory of God the Father."*

NOTES

The terms *"theos"* (*"god"*), and *"huios theou"* (*"son of god"*), were both used in the Cult of the Caesar and were titles of the Emperor. Our Lord claimed Oneness in essence with the Father (Jn. 10:30), He said (Jn. 8:58), *"Before Abraham came into existence, I am."* He claimed to be the Son of God (Jn. 9:35-38) and accepted worship as the Son of God, thus demonstrating the fact that His position as Son of God made Him a Co-participant in the essence of Deity. All this was in startling contrast to the claims of the then ruling Emperor, and our Blessed Lord knew it.

Luke 22:25 shows His accurate knowledge of the customs, political practices, and happenings of His day, when He speaks of those who exercise authority over the people as being called *"Benefactors."* The term *"Benefactor"* was an honorable title given to Princes and other imminent men for valuable services rendered to the State.

The Emperor was also given the title *"Overseer."* He was the *"Overseer"* of his subjects in that he was charged with the responsibility of caring for their welfare. The same term *"Overseer"* is given God the Father in I Peter 2:25 where the word meaning *"Overseer"* is translated *"Bishop."*

Peter, in writing his Epistle, must have been conscious of the imperialistic challenge of Christianity when presenting the God of Christians as the Overseer of their souls, refusing to acknowledge the overseeing care of the Emperor-god.

## KING

Another title given the Emperor was *"basileus"* (*"king"*). Some Monarchs used the title *"King of kings."* Our Lord claimed this title in relation to His distinctive position as the Messiah of Israel. The Jews recognized this as directly opposed to the imperial position of Caesar as King.

Not that there were no kings in the Empire ruling under the authority of the world-Caesar. But the Jewish Leaders understood Old Testament Truth well enough to know that our Lord's claim to the position of King over Israel involved world-dominion, which at once struck at the throne of Caesar.

They tried to use this as a means of involving Him in difficulties with Rome, for they said to Pilate (Jn. 19:12), *"If thou let this man go, thou art not Caesar's friend: whosoever maketh himself a king speaketh against Caesar."* They had accused him of forbidding them to pay taxes to Caesar, which was a lie, and of claiming to be the Anointed of God, which was the Truth (Lk. 23:2).

Upon our Lord's acknowledging the fact that He was a King, Pilate turned to the Jews and said, *"I find no fault in this Man"* (Lk. 23:3-4). One look at Jesus was enough to convince Pilate that he was not a dangerous character and he dismissed from his mind any disposition to treat our Lord's claim seriously.

Had Pilate taken our Lord's claims at their face value, his position as a representative of Caesar would have demanded that he deal with the case before him in no hesitant manner. When Pilate said to them (Jn. 19:14-15), *"Behold your King,"* the Jews who hated and despised the Roman yoke and the Emperor who ruled them, cried in a false patriotism, *"We have no King but Caesar."*

KING OF KINGS AND LORD OF LORDS

Paul, after he had faced Nero as the prisoner of the Roman Empire and had been liberated, wrote the following to Timothy, *"Now unto the King Eternal, Immortal, Invisible, the only Wise God, be Honour and Glory for ever and ever. Amen.*

*"Which in His times He shall shew, Who is the Blessed and only Potentate, the King of kings, and Lord of lords;*

*"Who only hath immortality, dwelling in the Light which no man can approach unto; Whom no man hath seen, nor can see: to Whom be honour and power everlasting. Amen"* (I Tim. 1:17; 6:15-16).

Again the Great Apostle having been snatched from the jaws of death at the hands of Rome, puts himself within reach of the long arm of the Empire when he denies the supremacy of the Emperor in things spiritual.

SAVIOUR

But not only did the Emperor have the titles of lord, son of god, god overseer, and king, all of which were titles of our Lord also, but he was also given the title *"soter"* (*"savior"*).

At least eight of the Emperors carried the title *"savior of the world."* They were hailed as the saviors of the people.

NOTES

For the most part, the Roman world was well governed and policed, Roman Law was administered in equity, the Roman roads caused travel and commerce to flourish, and the Roman peace made living conditions bearable and in some places pleasant.

Thus, the Emperors were the world-saviors. Now comes Christianity with its imperialistic announcement (Lk. 2:11), *"For unto you is born this day in the city of David a Saviour, which is Christ the Lord."*

But this Saviour's Name was Jesus, One Who would save them from the sins which they loved and from which they did not want to be separated.

What motive would they have in transferring their allegiance from a world-savior who gave them the comforts of life and at the same time allowed them to go on in their sin, to the Lord Jesus, especially when allegiance to this New Saviour could very well result in their crucifixion by Rome?

And yet for the first 300 years of the Church's history, tens of thousands willingly embraced this New Saviour and went to a horrible death. How is this explained?

The only answer is that the supernatural Power of God was operative in their hearts. The Samaritans said (Jn. 4:42), *"We have heard Him ourselves, and know that This is indeed the Christ, the Saviour of the world."* It took grace to say that, for they realized that should this come to the ears of Rome, they could be charged with treason.

GOD AND SAVIOUR

In I Timothy 1:1, Paul refers to *"The Commandment of our God and Saviour Jesus Christ,"* coupling the titles *"God"* and *"Saviour"* together as they are in the Cult of the Caesar. In the same Epistle (4:10), he speaks of God as the Saviour of all men.

The context, which brings in the idea of Faith, seems to indicate that the idea of Salvation from sin and the impartation of Eternal Life is the function here of God as Saviour. He is Saviour of all men in the sense that our Lord is *"The Saviour of the world"* (Jn. 4:42). He is the actual Saviour of those who believe, and the potential Saviour of the unbeliever in the sense that He has provided a Salvation at the Cross for the sinner, and stands ready to save that sinner when the latter places his Faith in the Lord Jesus.

The Emperor claimed to be Saviour of the world. No wonder that Rome recognized in Christianity a formidable rival. No wonder the Roman Writer Tacitus says of Christianity, *"This destructive superstition, repressed for awhile, again broke out, and spread not only through Judaea where it originated, but reached this city also (Rome), into which flow all things that are vile and abominable, and where they are encouraged."*

Paul uses the words *"God our Saviour"* in Titus 1:3, here the Saviour of believers in a spiritual sense. Peter applies the title *"Saviour"* to our Lord in His Second Epistle (II Pet. 1:11), adding the title *"Lord,"* which also was claimed by the Emperor.

Jude closes his Book with the words, *"To the only wise God our Saviour,"* (Jude vs. 25) again a conscious assertion of the preeminence of God over all the claims of earthly sovereigns.

## HIGH PRIEST

Another term found in the Christian system and which was used by Roman Emperors was *"archiereus"* (*"high priest"*). The Emperors were called *"Pontifex Maximus"* in the East, the name being the Latin translation of the Greek *"archiereus"* (*"high priest"*).

In contrast to the arrogancy, cruelty, and wickedness of the Roman Emperor who was recognized not only as lord, son of god, god savior, but also as high priest, we have the words of Paul, *"Seeing then that we have a Great High Priest, that is passed through the Heavens, Jesus the Son of God, let us hold fast our profession,*

*"For we have not an High Priest which cannot be touched with the feeling of our infirmities; but was in all points tempted like as we are, yet without sin.*

*"Let us therefore come boldly into the Throne of Grace, that we may obtain Mercy, and find Grace to help in time of need"* (Heb. 4:14-16).

The primary contrast here is undoubtedly between the Aaronic High Priest and our Lord as High Priest, but the background of Roman Imperialism seems to be in the picture also. The Roman Emperor was Pontifex Maximus, a High Priest upon the throne of the Caesars.

But our Lord Jesus as a High Priest Who, now seated upon a Throne of Grace, will someday as High Priest in the Messianic Kingdom occupy the Throne of David in Jerusalem, as Zechariah says, *"He shall be a Priest upon His Throne"* (Zech. 6:13).

NOTES

## FRIEND

Turning now to words used in a technical sense in the Cult of the Caesar with reference to the people instead of the Emperor, we have the expression, *"Friend* (philos) *of the Emperor,"* which was an official title in the imperial period. What a flood of light this throws upon our Lord's Words. *"Ye are My Friends, if ye do whatsoever I command you.*

*"Henceforth I call you not bondslaves; for a bondslave knoweth not what his lord doeth; but I have called you Friends"* (Jn. 15:14-15).

As our Lord knew of the Roman custom of calling a servant of the State a Benefactor (Lk. 22:25), so He knew of this custom of certain ones being called *"Friends of the Emperor."* There was a real point to His Words and they were not lost upon His Disciples.

Think of what Faith this involved on His part and theirs. The King of kings was on His way from the Upper Room where they had celebrated the Passover together for the last time, to His Crucifixion and Death, the rejected King of Israel.

Yet in all the dignity of His royal position as King of the Jews in the Davidic Dynasty, He said, *"I have called you Friends."* Yes, they were Friends of the Emperor who would be raised from the dead, ascend to Heaven, and someday come back to this Earth to reign as King of kings and Lord of lords (Rev. Chpt. 19).

## BONDSLAVE

Another official title was *"Bondslave* (doulos) *of the Emperor."* There were imperial slaves all over the Roman world. There was an honor in even being a Bondslave of Caesar. Paul must have been conscious of the analogy when he wrote, *"Paul, a Bondslave of Christ Jesus"* (Rom. 1:1).

If it was an honor in the Roman world to be a Bondslave of the Emperor, what an exalted privilege it was to be a Bondslave of the King of kings.

## AMBASSADOR

In II Corinthians 5:20, Paul calls himself an *"Ambassador for Christ."* The Greek word is

*"Presbeuo,"* a technical term used of the Emperor's legate, namely, the one who speaks for the Emperor. Paul was a spokesman on behalf of Christ.

The word is used also in Ephesians 6:20 and in Luke 14:32, in the latter text appearing in the translation as *"Ambassage."* The word clearly refers to the imperial service of Caesar, and in the Scriptures to the imperial service of Christ in which the Saints are engaged. Thus did Christianity parallel the imperialism of Rome.

The imperial secretary used the technical expression *"pepisteumai,"* which means *"I am entrusted,"* the qualifying word being added which would designate the matter with which he was entrusted.

Paul as an imperial secretary of the Lord Jesus entrusted with the writings of the Epistles which bear his name, uses the same technical phrase current in the Roman world at that time. The word is used in Galatians 2:7, *"committed"*; in I Corinthians 9:17, *"committed"*; in I Thessalonians 2:4, *"put in trust"*; I Timothy 1:11, *"committed to my trust"*; and in Titus 1:3, *"committed."*

The correspondence of the imperial secretary was designated by the technical expression, *"hiera grammata," "sacred writings."* It was used of imperial letters and decrees.

The expression *"theia grammata," "divine writings"* was used of imperial letters. Imperial ordinances were referred to as *"divine commandments."*

This shows clearly how completely the religious or ecclesiastical position of the Emperor made its influence felt throughout the affairs of State.

Alongside of all this we have Paul using the same expression, *"hieras grammata,"* in II Timothy 3:15 and the words *"Holy Scriptures."* Here the writings of the Old Testament are put over against the imperial decrees of Caesar, which later had not only governmental but also religious significance. New Testament writings were looked upon by the early Christians in the same way.

## GOOD NEWS

Finally, the word *"euaggelion"* (*"good news"* or *"good tidings"*) was used in a profane sense of any piece of good news. But it also had a sacred connection as when it was used to refer to the good news of the birthday of the Emperor-god. At the accession of a Caesar to the Throne, the account of this event was spoken of as *"euaggelion"* (*"good tidings"*).

See the parallel in the imperialistic announcement by the Angels, *"Fear not: for, behold, I bring you good tidings of great joy, which shall be to all people.*

*"For unto you is born this day in the city of David, a Saviour, which is Christ the Lord"* (Lk. 2:10-11).

How all of this gives further point to Paul's words, *"I am ready to preach the Good News to you that are at Rome also.*

*"For I am not ashamed of the Good News: for it is the Power of God resulting in Salvation to every one that believeth"* (Rom. 1:15-16).

Paul was expecting to come to Rome where the real *"Good News"* of the True Emperor found its reality, that Emperor Who was called Lord, Son of God, God, King, Saviour, and High Priest, and he was to announce the True Lord from Heaven Who was the Son of the Eternal God, yes, Very God Himself, Coming King of kings, Saviour of the Believer, and High Priest Who by His Atoning Death on Calvary's Cross paid for sin and put it away.

He was to announce this *"Good News,"* this *"Gospel,"* for that is what the word *"Gospel"* means, right in the stronghold of Emperor-worship.

But he was not afraid to do so, for he knew that it was of Divine and Supernatural origin and would accomplish that whereunto it was sent.

(The material on the imperialism of Christianity was derived from Kenneth Wuest.)

(30) "BUT OF HIM ARE YE IN CHRIST JESUS, WHO OF GOD IS MADE UNTO US WISDOM, AND RIGHTEOUSNESS, AND SANCTIFICATION, AND REDEMPTION:"

The phrase, *"But of Him are ye in Christ Jesus,"* pertains to this great Plan of God which is far beyond all wisdom of the world. It is as follows:

1. God is the Author Alone of this great Plan of Salvation, with man making no contribution whatsoever.
2. Upon Faith, God placed us in Jesus Christ, that which we could not do ourselves.
3. Our strength consists in acknowledged weakness, meaning there was no way we could

save ourselves, for it is solely derived from our fellowship with God by our unity with Christ.

4. In the Mind of God, we are literally *"in"* Christ Jesus, this greatest Gift of God awarded strictly on the merit of Faith and Faith alone. Believing on Christ, awards the sinner all that which Christ has done.

5. The Believer, therefore, cannot boast of anything in himself, but he can glory of all that he possesses in the Lord Jesus (Williams).

WISDOM

The phrase, *"Who of God is made unto us Wisdom,"* should have been translated, *"Who of God is made unto us Wisdom from God."*

The idea is, that this *"Wisdom"* is not from the world, not of the world, and in fact has nothing to do with the world, being solely of God and from God, all centered up in Jesus.

So, the One Who the Jews called a Blasphemer, and to Whom the Greeks referred to as Foolishness, is instead, the Wisdom of the Ages.

This should have been obvious when Jesus faced the most brilliant of Jewish Scholars, and bested them so completely that the Scripture says, *"Neither durst any man from that day forth ask Him any more questions"* (Mat. 22:46). Even though that was relatively insignificant in comparison to His Creation of all things (Jn. 1:1-4), still, it should have told them something at least!

RIGHTEOUSNESS

The phrase, *"And Righteousness,"* presents a forensic term which means to be declared Righteous in a legal and positional sense. Upon exhibiting Faith in Christ, the believing sinner instantly has all charges dropped against him, because the Righteousness of Christ has been freely imputed to him by God. God can accept us as not guilty because Christ met all the demands of the Old Testament Law in our place. In other words, He did for us what we could not do for ourselves.

Jesus literally becomes to us Jehovah-Tsidkenu — *"The Lord our Righteousness"* (Jer. 23:6). This is the theme of Chapters 3-7 of Romans.

SANCTIFICATION

The phrase, *"And Sanctification,"* refers to the Believer, once again upon Faith, being given a *"Standing"* of Holiness, which is the basic meaning of Sanctification. It relates to the New Believer being set apart for a particular purpose (Rossier).

NOTES

REDEMPTION

The phrase, *"And Redemption,"* actually refers to a ransom being paid.

To be frank, the meaning and nature of the act, as regards God, lie in regions upon our comprehension, but the meaning and nature of it, as it regards man, is our deliverance from bondage, and the payment of the debt which we had incurred (Mat. 20:28; Rom. 8:21-23; Titus 2:14; I Pet. 1:18). As someone has well said, all four of these Salvation Words have a double meaning — both of an inward act and of an outward result (Farrar).

(31) "THAT, ACCORDING AS IT IS WRITTEN, HE THAT GLORIETH, LET HIM GLORY IN THE LORD."

The phrase, *"That, according as it is written,"* is derived from Jeremiah 9:23-24.

The phrase, *"He that Glorieth, let him Glory in the Lord,"* is meant to address the Corinthians who were boasting of particular Preachers.

The word rendered *"Glory"* is more literally, *"boast."*

The prevalence of *"boasting"* among the Corinthians and their teachers, drove Paul to dwell much on this word — from which he so greatly shrinks. Please note II Corinthians Chapters 10-12, where the word occurs 20 times.

Paul insists that the only True object in which a Christian can properly Glory or boast is the Cross of Jesus Christ (Gal. 6:14), not in himself, or in the world, or in men.

*"In the Cross of Christ I Glory,*
*"Towering o'r the wrecks of time;*
*"All the light of sacred story gathers*
*round its head sublime."*

*"When the woes of life o'r - take me,*
*"Hopes deceive, and fears annoy,*
*"Never shall the Cross forsake me; lo! it*
*glows with peace and joy."*

*"When the sun of bliss is beaming,*
*"Light and love upon my way,*
*"From the Cross the radiant streaming*
*adds more luster to the day."*

*"Bane and Blessing, pain and pleasure,*
*"By the Cross are Sanctified;*

*"Peace is there, that knows no measure,*
*joys that through all time abide."*

CHAPTER 2

(1) "AND I, BRETHREN, WHEN I CAME TO YOU, CAME NOT WITH EXCELLENCY OF SPEECH OR OF WISDOM, DECLARING UNTO YOU THE TESTIMONY OF GOD."

The phrase, *"And I, Brethren, when I came to you,"* speaks, of course, of Corinth, and probably was in the year A.D. 52 or even as late as A.D. 54. He stayed there for about one year and a half (Acts 18:11). He had now been in Ephesus about three years, actually writing this Epistle from that City.

The phrase, *"Came not with excellency of speech or of wisdom,"* means that he depended not upon oratorical abilities, nor did he delve into philosophy, which was all the rage of that particular day.

Is it possible that those who were impressed by the polished rhetoric of Apollos were the ones who spoke of Paul's speech as *"contemptible"*? (II Cor. 10:10). However, if it was, Apollos had nothing to do with that, being a Godly man, and not at all holding himself in the same place or position as Paul his mentor.

Throughout this Letter, even as we have seen and shall continue to see, the Apostle keeps emphasizing the key to unity — permitting Christ His rightful place in the Church (Rossier).

In these first five verses of the Second Chapter of I Corinthians, Paul deals with the Preaching of the Gospel and its manner. As we shall see in Verse 2, *"Jesus Christ and Him Crucified,"* must always in some way be the central core and the foundation on which everything else builds. If not, it is simply not the Gospel.

The phrase, *"Declaring unto you the Testimony of God,"* which is Christ and Him Crucified.

THE PURPOSE OF PREACHING THE GOSPEL

The purpose is the Preaching of Christ through which only the Holy Spirit can work.

One could say, that the purpose of Preaching is that the Holy Spirit may function according to His desires, appealing to the hearts of the people relative to the particular need in each life. He can only do that if the proper Message is presented, and as stated, that Message is Christ and Him Crucified.

NOTES

While there are many peripheral Doctrines relating to this great Message, such as the Baptism with the Holy Spirit, Divine Healing, the Gifts of the Spirit, the Fruit of the Spirit, Prophecy, Consecration and Victory over Sin, etc., nevertheless, Christ is the Central Core of all things and must never under any circumstances be placed in a peripheral position.

It is our business to preach Jesus, and Jesus in every aspect of His Life and Ministry, in essence, the purpose of His Coming, which was to die on Calvary and be raised from the dead. Of course, it was the Crucifixion which carried out all of this of which we know as Salvation, but had the Resurrection not occurred, which in effect ratified Calvary, all that Calvary accomplished, would have been in vain. But thank God, there was a Resurrection. That is the *"Testimony of God,"* and it must be our Testimony as well!

THE MANNER OF PAUL'S PREACHING

Business, Government, Warfare, Athletics, Labor — Paul draws from them all as he seeks to make clear the Message of God. In Business it may be a title deed, the credit and debit side of a ledger, the forfeiture of what was thought to be a gain, the earnest money paid down in the transference of property, the receipt *"paid in full,"* a last will or testament, a broken contract.

In Warfare, it is the soldier, his weapons, his armor, his shield, his wages, even as he outlined in Ephesians Chapter 6. In Government, the Commonwealth, its citizens, their responsibilities and privileges appear in the Apostle's writings (Rom. Chpt. 13). In the world of Labor, the slave and the skilled artisan, the finished product, the possibility that a piece of work may be returned by the employer, rejected because of failure to meet specifications, all become illustrations which Paul uses (I Cor. Chpt. 3).

In Athletics, the racecourse down which the runners speed, the crown of oak leaves that graces the brow of the winner, the desperate agonizing efforts of two wrestlers, the concerted teamwork of one group of Athletes against another group, the Greek Stadium with the watchers intent upon the outcome, the Judge's stand, all become for Paul illustrations familiar to the public of the Roman world, and because familiar, an ideal medium by which to Preach the Gospel.

Paul, the Scholar, the man of books, trained in the Greek Schools, yet spoke and wrote the language of the average man when he preached the Word of God (I Cor. Chpt. 9; Phil. Chpt. 3; Heb. Chpt. 12, etc.).

## JESUS CHRIST AND HIM CRUCIFIED

Writing to the Corinthians he says in his first Epistle (I Cor. 2:1-5), *"And I having come to you, Brethren, came, not having my message dominated by transcendent rhetorical display or by philosophical subtlety when I was announcing authoritatively to you the Testimony of God, for after weighing the issues, I did not decide but to know any thing among you except Jesus Christ and Him Crucified. And when I faced you, I fell into a state of weakness and fear and much trembling. And my Message and my Preaching were not couched in specious words of philosophy, but were dependent for their effectiveness upon a demonstration of the Spirit and of Power, in order that your Faith should not be resting in human philosophy but in God's Power."*

The words, *"I did not decide"* are a literal rendering from the Greek, possibly a bit cumbersome in English, but nevertheless a true representation of what Paul wrote.

The tendency in the First Century was that of a blending of religions. If someone embraced a new Faith, his desire would be to bring over into its system some of the elements of the old. We see that in the case of Judaism.

Another tendency was that of the new convert explaining his new-found Faith in terms of the old, or harmonizing, or attempting to do so, the new with the old. This we observe in instances where Greeks embraced Christianity.

## PAUL KNEW BY THE SPIRIT OF GOD

Paul was faced with this situation when he was Saved, and with respect to both Judaism and the Greek Philosophies, for he was probably well trained in both. Consequently when he said, *"I did not decide but to know anything among you except Jesus Christ and Him Crucified,"* he meant that he, after weighing the issues after reflecting on the matter of presenting the Gospel to the Greeks in terms of their philosophies (for he said he wanted to become all things to all men, that is, adapt himself and his methods to their needs), knew by the impression of the Holy Spirit that he was not to address the Greeks in this manner, but to preach Christ, and not to do so *"with wisdom of words"* (I Cor. 1:17), that is, not in specious words of a false philosophy, but in the everyday language of the people.

Thus, we see him drawing from contemporary life, from the Greek games, the Roman Armies, the language of Government, the business world, and the life of the laboring classes, in other words in the words and ways of the common people, but yet not identifying whatsoever with even the smallest measure of Greek Philosophy. That should be a lesson for us presently.

## HIS MANNER

He uses a business term when he speaks of Faith as the title deed of things hoped for (Heb. 11:1), the word *"substance"* being translated from a Greek word used in legal practice for a title deed. When he warns the Hebrews against the act of renouncing their professed Faith in the Messiah and going back to the Old Testament Sacrifices after having been led along by the Holy Spirit in His pre-Salvation work, up to and including Repentance, he says that the renunciation would be like the act of a man breaking a contract which he had made (Heb. 6:6), for they would be breaking the contract which they had made with the Holy Spirit in allowing Him to lead them on towards Christ, the words *"fall away"* being the ones referred to here.

When he desires to explain the necessity of the Death of Christ in order that the New Testament might become effective, he uses the illustration of a will not being effective until the death of the testator (Heb. 9:16-17).

When he tells us (Rom. 8:17) that as *"heirs of God,"* we are also *"joint-heirs with Christ,"* he draws from Roman Law which made all children, including adopted ones, equal heirs. Think of it, equal heirs with Jesus Christ!

Should he wish to assure Believers that they will receive their Glorification, he uses the business term *"earnest"* which refers to a down-payment in kind, guaranteeing the full payment of the rest (Eph. 1:14). The Spirit is the down-payment in kind, His indwelling being part of our Salvation.

NOTES

## WHAT HE SAID TO THE PHILIPPIANS

He explains to the Philippians (Phil. 3:8) that when he trusted Christ as his Saviour, he *"suffered the loss of all things."* He uses a business term which meant *"to punish by exacting a forfeit."* The Greek actually says, *"I have been caused to forfeit."*

Paul took punishment in the business sense when he put his trust in Christ. It meant the forfeiture of all that he counted dear. That means Crucifixion of self, and self dies hard.

He thanks the Philippians (Phil. 4:15) for the gift which they had sent, and reminds them that when he left Macedonia, no Church but theirs *"communicated,"* that is, *"had partnership"* with him *"as concerning giving and receiving,"* meaning that they supported him financially.

After the words *"had partnership,"* the Greek has *"with respect to an account of giving and receiving"* the ledger with a credit and debit page. The Philippians kept a ledger in which they recorded the good things received from Paul on the credit page and the debt they owed Paul on the debit side, so to speak.

He acknowledged the receipt of their gift in the words, *"I have all,"* using a business term meaning, *"I have received in full"* (Phil. 4:18).

The word *"abound"* in Philippians 4:17, is taken from the money market. It was used of the accumulation of interest. The word *"account"* is used here much as we would use the term *"bank account."*

The fruit concerning which Paul is speaking is the reward accumulating to the bank account of the Philippian Saints in the Bank of Heaven, reward given for the generosity of these Believers in their support of Paul the Missionary.

## THE VOCABULARY OF THE LABORING MAN

When he desired a word that would give to the ordinary Reader of the First Century, what the Christian system of teaching included with respect to the individual Believer's relation to his Lord as a servant, he searched the vocabulary of the laboring man for the proper term.

In the Greek, the language he spoke and the language in which he wrote, he had a choice of six words, all speaking of one who serves. One referred to a person captured in war or kidnapped, and sold as a slave. Another spoke of a household servant, as in Romans 14:4 and I Peter 2:18. Another was used as a designation of a servant in official capacity, with emphasis upon his activity and service, as in John 2:5; 12:26; Rom. 13:4; 15:8; 16:1; I Cor. 3:5; Phil. 1:1 (Deacon).

Still another referred to servants who were Court Officers as in Matthew 26:58.

Yet another word (Heb. 3:5) spoke of a servant who was an attendant upon someone, the emphasis being upon the fact that his services are voluntary, whether as a freeman or as a slave. But he chose none of these.

The word which the Holy Spirit led him to use is found in Philemon Verse 16.

## SLAVE

Onesimus was the slave of Philemon, one bound to him, one born into slavery, one bound to his master in a permanent relationship which only death could break, one whose will is swallowed up in the will of his master, one who is devoted to his master even to the disregard of his own interests.

Onesimus did not before his Salvation live up to the last two specifications, but the Greek word which Paul used to speak of the place he occupied among the various classes of slaves in the Roman world, included the above details. This was the word known to the average man of the First Century, whose content of meaning as given above, would exactly fit Paul's teaching regarding the Believer's relationship to the Lord Jesus, and the unbeliever's relationship to Satan as well.

The word was used as the exact opposite of the word for *"freeman,"* thus emphasizing the fact that the Christian is *not* his own, but is bought with a price. Again, the servile relationship is emphasized.

These two conceptions were part of that *"offence of the Cross"* which confronted the First Century sinner, and continues to do so unto this hour. The word meant *"a slave."*

Other words for the idea of one who serves were more noble and tender. But this word *"servant"* referred to a common slave. This was the word the Holy Spirit had Paul to choose.

To translate this word by *"servant"* in such Passages as Romans 1:1 or 6:16-17, is to miss the point in Paul's teaching. The word should be rendered either *"slave"* or *"bondman."*

NOTES

Of course, to be a slave of a Pagan master, with all which that implied of misery, cruelty, abject servitude, was one thing. However, to be a *"slave"* of the Lord Jesus, with all which that implies of wonderful fellowship with one's Master, and the high privilege of serving the Lord of Glory, is quite another.

Nevertheless, the term *"slave"* or *"bondman"* is the idea presented. The First Century world so understood Paul's use of the word. And that is the way in which we of the 20th Century should use it as well!

TO LABOR

Again, Paul speaks to the laboring classes in his use of the Greek word which means *"to labor to the point of exhaustion,"* which experience was a very common thing among the downtrodden masses of the Roman world.

He speaks of a certain Mary *"who was of such a nature as to have labored to the point of exhaustion with reference to many things for us"* (Rom. 16:6). He speaks of himself in the words, *"I laboured more abundantly than they all"* (I Cor. 15:10).

Thus, they understood Paul's language. He spoke and wrote the tongue of the working man. He kept in mind that *"... not many wise men after the flesh, not many mighty, not many noble, are called:*

*"But God hath chosen the foolish things of the world ... the weak things of the world ...*

*"And base things, and things ... which are not ..."* (I Cor. 1:26-28).

WEAPONS

Paul also borrows from the language of the soldier and the war. The instruments we are to put at the Service of God in Ephesians 6:13 are referred to by the Greek word as *"weapons."* The word was used of implements of war, either offensive or defensive, harness, armor, the heavy shield used by the Greek foot-soldiers, etc.

Its use here gives one the idea of two armies, Satan's and God's with the Believer in God's Army. The word *"wages"* in Romans 6:23 is from a Greek word which means *"cooked meat."* At Athens it meant *"fish."* It came to mean the *"provision-money"* which Rome gave its soldiers.

The same word is used in I Corinthians 9:7, *"Who goeth a warfare any time at his own charges?"*

NOTES

As the Roman Soldier received provision-money with which to sustain life so that he could fight and die for Caesar, so the unsaved receive provision-money from sin, spiritual death, so that they can serve it, then physical death, and finally, final banishment from the Presence of God for all eternity. Neither receives wages, only enough sustenance to enable him to serve his master.

WARFARE

In Ephesians Chapter 6 we have accoutrements of warfare, armor, breastplate, shield, arrows, illustrations which Paul took from the marching legions of Rome. See his reference to the expected endurance of a soldier in II Timothy 2:3, and to the man in Verse 4, who raises an army for military purposes.

In II Corinthians 2:14 in the words *"causeth us to triumph,"* and in Colossians 2:15, in the word *"triumphing"* we have another instance where Paul draws from First Century life.

The translation should read, *"leadeth us in triumph,"* and *"leading them in triumph."* The word referred to a victorious General, home from the wars, leading a triumphal procession through the streets of Rome. The captives and spoils of war would precede him, and he would follow in a chariot, a slave holding over his head a jewelled crown. Then would come his victorious army.

Paul's Readers were conversant with all this. They would understand his illustrations as well. In II Corinthians 2:14, it is God Who leads Paul in a triumphal procession as His captive, by means of whom the knowledge and fame of the Victor is made manifest. He rejoices that he has been so used of God.

In Colossians 2:15, our Lord through His Victory over the hosts of evil is enabled to lead them in a triumphal procession as His captives. In II Corinthians 10:4, Paul again uses the illustration of war and of a fortress.

THE LANGUAGE OF GOVERNMENT

As to his use of terms taken from the language of Government, we have Philippians 1:27, and 3:20. In the first Passage, the words *"let your conversation be,"* are from a word which refers to the duty of citizens to the commonwealth in which they live, and in the second, *"conversation"* is translated from a Greek word meaning *"commonwealth."*

The illustration is taken from the fact that the City of Philippi was a Roman Colony. Its citizens possessing Roman Citizenship with its privileges and responsibilities. So the Philippian Saints as citizens of Heaven, are to live a heavenly life in that colony of Heaven far from their commonwealth itself. Translate, *"Only conduct yourselves as citizens as it becometh the Gospel of Christ. For the commonwealth of which we are citizens has its fixed abode in Heaven."*

## THE GREEK GAMES

The frequency with which Paul refers to the Greek athletic games far surpasses his illustrations for many other single aspect of First Century life. The Greeks were an athletic-minded people. Paul himself, though a son of Hebrew parents who maintained their Jewish separation even to the point of refusing to read their Scriptures in the Septuagint (Greek) translation (Acts 6:1; Phil. 3:5), yet did not wash his hands of his hellenistic training before his fellow-countrymen when he admitted that he was a native of the Greek City of Tarsus, for he used the milder of two Greek adversatives (two words opposing each other) (Acts 22:3).

He was influenced greatly by his Greek training, and he could not deny it. Part of that Greek culture included a familiarity with an interest in athletics. It is significant that when writing to the Romans, he uses terms borrowed from warfare, but his Epistles to the Corinthians and Philippians, which were to Churches composed of Greek Christians, and those to Timothy whose father was a Greek (Acts 16:1), these abound with illustrations from the Greek games.

The Great Apostle was chosen by God for his Greek background as well as for his Jewish training. Truly, he was the Apostle to the Gentiles. And his Greek training paid no little part in his ministry to them.

As to his references to the Greek athletic games so well known even in the Roman period, having such a background of history in the time when Greece was at the height of its glory, we have the following:

Both the Christian life (Phil. 3:7-16), and Christian service (I Cor. 9:24-27) are illustrated by the stadium games and the desperate agonizing efforts put forth by the Greek Athletes in their endeavor to win. He visualizes the stadium crowds intently watching the contest. He speaks of the garland or crown of oak leaves placed upon the winner's brow.

NOTES

## THE FIGURE OF A RACE

One of the classic Passages in which Paul refers to the Greek games is I Corinthians 9:24-27. The Isthmus of Corinth was the scene of the Isthmian games, one of the four great national festivals of the Greeks.

During the period of the writing of the Pauline Epistles, these games were still being celebrated. He was familiar with similar scenes in Tarsus and in all of the great cities of Asia Minor, especially at Ephesus.

The word *"race"* in this Passage is from a Greek word which comes over into our language in the word *"Stadium"* and *"stade."* The stade was a race course about 607 feet long, and the word came to mean a *"race"* because the track at Olympia was exactly that number of feet in length.

Here Paul uses the figure of a race to illustrate the life of Christian service. *"Striveth for the masteries"* is from a Greek word which refers to an Athlete contending or striving in the games.

*"Temperate"* is from a word occurring only in I Corinthians 9:25. Here it refers to the ten months preparatory training, and the practice in the gymnasium immediately before the Games under the direction of the Judges who had themselves been instructed for ten months in the details of the Games.

The training was largely dietary.

Epictetus says, *"Thou must be orderly, living on spare food; abstain from confections; make a point of exercising at the appointed time, in heat or in cold; nor drink cold water or wine at hazard."*

Horace says, *"The youth who would win in the race hath borne and done much, he hath sweat and hath been cold: he hath abstained from love and wine."*

Tertullian, commending the example of the Athletes to the persecuted Christians says, *"They are constrained, harassed, wearied."*

## TO SERVE JESUS

If an Athlete goes through ten months of rigorous training which involves rigid self-denial and much hardship in order that he might compete in a contest that may last a few minutes or a few hours at the most, and for a prize, a chaplet of oak leaves, should not a Christian be willing to subject himself to just as rigid a discipline and self-denial in order that he might serve the Lord Jesus in an acceptable manner?

What soft flabby lives we Christians live. How little of stern soul-discipline do we know. The training period of a Greek Athlete was a time of separation for him, separation from things which might in their place be perfectly proper, but which would prevent him from running his best race, and separation most certainly from things that were of a harmful nature. If we Christians would exercise as much care and self-denial, and rigidly hold to a life of separation as did the Greek Athlete, what powerful, successful, God-glorifying lives we would live. Illustrations such as these were not lost upon Paul's Greek Readers.

## THE VICTOR'S CROWN

Paul uses the chaplet or crown of oak leaves which fades, as an illustration of the unfading Victory's Crown which the Christian will wear someday, given him for the service he rendered in the Power of the Holy Spirit.

He speaks of the Greek Runner who speeds down the racecourse not uncertainly, but straight as an arrow for the goal. So should a Christian run his race, refusing to allow anyone or anything to turn him from the consuming desire that the Lord Jesus be preeminent in his life.

## THE PROPER TECHNIQUE

In Philippians 3:13-14, we catch a glimpse of Paul's knowledge of racing technique.

He uses the illustration of a Runner *"pressing toward the mark for the prize,"* that is, literally, *"pursuing down toward the mark for the prize."* See him flashing down the racecourse. He forgets the things which are behind.

The word is a strong one, *"completely forgetting."* Paul knew that the moment a Greek Runner would think of the men behind him, the thud, thud of their pounding feet, his speed would be slackened. So he presses home the lesson that when a Child of God thinks of his past failures, the things he should have done and failed to do, the things he did which he should not have done, his onward progress in the Christian Life is hindered.

NOTES

When a Christian has made things right with God and his fellowman, the proper technique is to completely forget them.

## LOOKING TO JESUS

A similar idea is presented in Hebrews 12:1-2, where Paul visualizes the Stadium crowds, and the Runners setting themselves for a race which they know will be a long grind and a real test of endurance. But they run entirely oblivious of the thousands of onlookers, their attention diverted from every consideration except that of running the best possible race.

We get that from the words *"looking unto."* The word, *"looking,"* has a prefixed preposition which implies abstraction. That is, the person's attention is concentrated upon one thing to the total exclusion of everything else. It is, *"looking off or away to Jesus,"* as the Greek Runner looks away from everything else and with eyes fixed upon the goal sees not the cheering crowds or even his own opponents.

To turn his head ever so slightly toward the tiers upon tiers of spectators, means that his speed will be lessened, and he himself will be just that much behind.

What a lesson for the Christian. The minute we turn our eyes toward our fellowmen and take them from our Lord, our pace is slackened. Pride, discouragement, envy, the desire for praise, these and other evils incapacitate the Christian Runner as he looks at men instead of keeping his eyes fixed upon Jesus.

The word *"fight"* (I Cor. 9:26-27) is from a Greek word which means *"to fight with the fist."* He speaks of the Greek Boxer who beats the air, that is, practices without an adversary. This is called shadowboxing.

Or, he might purposely strike into the air in order to spare his adversary, or the adversary might evade his blow, and thus cause him to spend his strength on the air uselessly.

But Paul says that he is not like the Greek Boxer in these respects. In his conflict with evil, he strikes straight and does not spare.

## THE BOXER

The words *"keep under"* are from a word which means *"to strike under the eye,"* or *"to give one a black eye."*

When we think that the Greek Boxer wore a pair of fur-lined gloves covered with cowhide which was loaded with lead and iron, one can imagine the punishment to which the recipient of the blows is subjected.

If a Christian would be as energetic against and unsparing of evil in his life as the Greek Boxer was of his opponent, and would strike with the same devastating force, sin would soon be cleared out of his life and would stay out. What *"softies"* we Christians are with regard to sin in our lives. How we sometimes cherish it, pamper it, play with it, instead of striking it with a mailed fist of a Holy Spirit-inspired hatred of sin and a refusal to allow it to reign as king in our lives.

As we consider this illustration of a Boxer which Paul uses, we must remember that boxing among the Greeks was not the degraded form of pugilism such as we have today with all of its attendant evils and associations, but was part of the great program of the Stadium Athletic Games which included foot races, discus throwing, wrestling, and other forms of athletics, engaged in by Athletes of splendid physique, expending their last ounce of energy, not for a money price, but for a simple garland of oak leaves which would fade in a few days.

Thus, this form of Athletic Competition while extremely brutal among the Greeks, and, therefore, to be condemned as a sin against the human body, yet was devoid of much of what is associated with pugilism today.

## BARRED FROM COMPETITION

Finally the word *"castaway"* is from a technical word used in the Greek Games, referring to the disqualifying of a Runner because he broke the training rules. He was barred from competing for the prize.

Paul was apprehensive, that, if he did not live a life of separation from the world, if he did not live a victorious life over sin, God would disqualify him, that is, take away from him his position as Apostle to the Gentiles. A Christian sometimes wonders, after years of fruitful service, why he should so suddenly see his usefulness gone, and his life powerless and without the Joy of the Lord.

The answer lies in the words, *"disqualified, broke training rules."* Paul refers to this same manner of obeying training rules in I Timothy 4:7-8 and II Timothy 2:5, where he says that if a Greek Athlete is to be awarded the victor's garland he must strive lawfully, that is, live up to the requirements prescribed for the preparation which the Athlete makes and the life which he lives while engaged in Athletic Competition.

He warns Timothy regarding this, and then in II Timothy 4:8, uses the illustration borrowed from the act of the Judges at the goal awarding the victor's crown to the winning Athlete.

So will Timothy someday, like Paul, receive a Crown of Righteousness from the Lord Jesus.

## AGAINST EVIL INSTEAD OF EACH OTHER

Then, there are Passages where the background of the Greek Games is not so evident in the English translation.

For instance, in Philippians 1:27, *"striving together,"* and Philippians 4:3, *"laboured with"* are from a Greek word used of Athletes contending in concert with one another against the opposition, for the prize offered at the Athletic Games.

The root of the word comes into English in our word *"Athlete."* In Romans 15:30 *"strive together,"* is from a Greek word which refers to the concerted action of a group of Athletes working in harmony against opposition. The root of the word comes into our language in the word *"agony."* What a plea this is for unity among the Saints and the expenditure of agonizing effort in concert against evil rather than the use of that energy in contention against one another.

In Philippians 1:30, *"conflict,"* Colossians 2:1, *"conflict,"* I Thessalonians 2:2, *"contention,"* II Timothy 4:7, *"fight,"* and Hebrews 12:1, *"race,"* are all from the noun whose root gives us the word *"agony,"* referring in the Greek to the contests in the Greek Athletic Games.

In Colossians 1:29, *"striving,"* 4:12, *"labouring,"* I Timothy 6:12, *"fight,"* II Timothy 4:7, *"fought,"* are all from the verb whose root comes into English in the word *"agony,"* and the meaning of which is *"to contend in the Greek Games for a prize."*

Here we have instances where First-Century Christians were striving in concert for the Faith of the Gospel; where some had labored with Paul in the extension of the Gospel; where others were exhorted to strive in concert with Paul in prayer; where still others were having conflict, that is, were enduring persecution; and in the case of Paul, where he fought the good fight;

NOTES

all these varied activities of the Christian Life being referred to by the two Greek words used of an Athlete engaged in the intense competition of the Games even to the point of physical agony.

What a commentary this is upon First-Century Christianity. What intense lives these early Christians must have lived. With what desperate earnestness that they must have worked for the Lord. What fervor and intensity there must have been in their prayers.

## THE FULLNESS OF THE HOLY SPIRIT

These Christians did not have a long line of Christian ancestry back of them, nor centuries of Christian practice and tradition to encourage them. In fact, they were Saved out of rank Paganism. Yet they lived their Christian lives with an intensity of purpose which puts us of the 20th Century to shame.

The secret of all this is the Fullness of the Holy Spirit, which results in a conscience sensitive to the slightest sin, the enthronement of Jesus as Lord of the life, and a love for Him that finds expression in a life of intense and purposeful service in His Name.

If there were more Believers filled moment by moment with the Holy Spirit, controlled by Him in thought, word, and deed, there would be more First-Century Christianity in the present-day Church. The secret of that Fullness is in a desire for His Control and a Trust in the Lord Jesus for the same (Jn. 7:37-38).

## ALL THINGS TO ALL MEN

Paul, who seeks to become all things to all men that he might by all means save some, sets aside the language of the schools, the highly-polished rhetoric, the philosophical subtleties which he learned in the Greek Schools at Tarsus, and instead uses the everyday words of the common people.

He neither wrote above the understanding nor talked above the heads of those to whom he ministered. What an admonition this is to us who have the high privilege and great responsibility of ministering the Word.

With us let utter simplicity be the watchword, *"not with wisdom of words, lest the Cross of Christ should be made of none effect"* (I Cor. 1:17).

(The above material on Paul and his manner of Preaching, was derived from the Scholarship of Kenneth Wuest.)

NOTES

(2) "FOR I DETERMINED NOT TO KNOW ANY THING AMONG YOU, SAVE JESUS CHRIST, AND HIM CRUCIFIED."

The phrase, *"For I determined not to know any thing among you,"* refers to Paul purposely and with design, not resorting at all to any knowledge or philosophy of the world regarding the Preaching of the Gospel, other than Christ.

*"Determined"* in the Greek is *"krino,"* and means *"to conclude, determine, judge, call in question."* The idea is, that Paul would not depend on any human knowledge.

Paul neither means to set aside all human knowledge nor to disparage other Christian Doctrines. His words must not be pressed out of their due context and proportion.

His dependence was totally upon his Message of Jesus Christ and Him Crucified, and the Anointing of the Holy Spirit on that Message. In essence, this is what he is saying.

The phrase, *"Save Jesus Christ, and Him Crucified,"* presents Christ, in the lowest depth of His abasement and self-sacrifice.

Paul would *"know"* nothing else; that is, he would make this the central point and essence of all his knowledge, because he knew the *"excellency"* of this knowledge (Phil. 3:8) — knew it as the only knowledge which rose to the height of wisdom. Christ Alone is the Foundation (I Cor. 3:11).

In the Person and the Work of Christ is involved the whole Gospel (Farrar).

## WHY WAS THIS MESSAGE CENTRAL IN PAUL'S PREACHING?

This Message alone is the answer to man's dilemma.

Man is a sinner in desperate need of a Saviour, and that Saviour is The Lord Jesus Christ. There is no other. This means that all the religions of the world are insufficient to meet the needs of man, and, therefore, false. This speaks of Islam, Buddhism, Shintoism, Confucianism, Mormonism, Catholicism, Humanism, or even the part of Christianity which is corrupt.

(I do not consider Catholicism to be Christian, for the simple reason that it bears no resemblance whatsoever to the Book of Acts and the Epistles. It holds up the Church as the Saviour and Mary as the way into that Church. While Jesus is mentioned, it is only in an auxiliary manner.)

WHY THE CRUCIFIXION WAS NECESSARY

Man as a sinner had and has a terrible debt of sin upon him, and no way to pay or atone for that sin. If God demanded payment of any nature from man, man would be and is unable to pay.

The Crucifixion of Christ in the Offering up of His Perfect Body, was the only Sacrifice which God would accept as payment for the sin of man. Upon simple Faith in that Sacrifice, God counts the sin debt as completely paid, and, thereby, stricken from the ledger (Jn. 3:16; Rom. 6:23; I Jn. 1:7).

WHY CRUCIFIXION?

Paul said, *"But this Man* (Jesus), *after He had offered one Sacrifice* (the Crucifixion) *for sins for ever, sat down on the Right Hand of God; . . . for by one Offering* (the Crucifixion) *He hath perfected for ever them that are Sanctified* (Saved)*"* (Heb. 10:12-14).

The only Sacrifice for sin which God would accept, was the Sacred Body of our Lord Jesus Christ offered at Calvary.

This was necessary because the Eternal Life of God in Adam and Eve had been forfeited because of their disobedience which instantly resulted in the Fall. Payment for that forfeited Life had to be another Life, albeit a Perfect Life. This was impossible for man to do, simply because his life as a result of the Fall, is now polluted, sinful, wicked, in other words, a life which God will not accept.

WHY JESUS?

As we have already stated, Adam and Eve due to the Fall were corrupted, and as a result all of their offspring would be corrupted as well. It is what is referred to as original sin, meaning that every baby that is born is born in the likeness of the First Adam, the Representative Man. So, there was no way that man could save himself.

The only answer is that God would become Man, pay the price for man, in effect becoming the Second or Last Adam, Who we know, as The Lord Jesus Christ. This was the only way that man could be Saved, which portrayed an act of Love so absolutely overwhelming, that it is impossible to comprehend or to even fully grasp. So, God *"gave His Only Begotten Son, that whosoever believeth in Him should not perish, but have Everlasting Life"* (Jn. 3:16).

NOTES

FROM THE BEGINNING . . .

At the very outset of the Fall, the Lord told Satan in effect how that He would Redeem man (Gen. 3:15). As well, until that time would come, the Lord instituted the Sacrificial System which would be a type of the Coming Redeemer, and would enable man to have his sins covered and give him the privilege of worship, until that Coming.

The Old Testament, in careful detail, gives complex instructions for worshiping God with Sacrifices and Offerings. Later, the Prophets scathingly condemned their people for mere ritualism — a condemnation repeated by Jesus.

But in the New Testament we discover the true meaning of Sacrifice and realize how God through the centuries clearly communicated His Message of Salvation; He did it by the Sacrifice of particular living animals referred to as *"clean,"* which prefigured the ultimate Sacrifice — that of God's Son.

IN THE OLD TESTAMENT

The Old Testament contains an extensive and technical vocabulary dealing with its various Sacrifices and Offerings. The prescribed rituals were a major means of expressing the Worshipers' Faith. They were also one of God's means for illustrating the nature of their relationship with Him.

Often our words *"Offering"* and *"Sacrifice"* are used interchangeably. Old Testament ritual involved Offerings, in that everything brought for use in worship was viewed as being offered to God and thus, as set apart and holy (Ex. 28:38).

The ritual system also featured Sacrifice. The most significant Offerings called for the Sacrifice of a living animal. Other ancient cultures also had clearly defined and complex rituals, including Sacrifice. But these cultures tended to view the Sacrifice as food for the gods, and their Priests used the entrails of the animals for occult divination.

In Israel the Sacrifice, while pleasing to God, was not His food (Ex. 29:38-41; Ps. 50:8-15). And only in Israel was the Blood of the Sacrificial Animal central in the worship. In fact, in the Old Testament the Blood was crucial: it defined the significance of Sacrifice itself. *"For the life of a creature is in the Blood,"* God says in Leviticus 17:11, *"and I have given it to you to make Atonement for yourselves on the Altar; it is the Blood that makes Atonement for one's life."*

Thus, the Worshiper, who with hands placed on the head of the living animal saw it killed and its Blood sprinkled on the Altar, was being graphically shown that sin called for the surrender of a life and was also made poignantly aware that God would accept a Substitute, in effect, a Type of the Great Substitute Who would ultimately come, Jesus Christ our Lord.

In fact, throughout sacred history, Sacrifice has been the avenue by which a sinning humanity has approached a Holy God.

## HISTORIC ROOTS OF SACRIFICE

The practice of Sacrifice precedes the Mosaic Law. Many believe that the First Sacrifice was God's killing of an animal to provide skin coverings for Adam and Eve after the Fall (Gen. 3:21). The story of Cain and Abel (Gen. Chpt. 4) seems to show that the way to approach God with Sacrifice was evidently made clear to the first family.

Genesis tells us that Cain *"brought some of the fruits of the soil as an Offering to the Lord.*

*"But Abel brought fat portions from some of the firstborn of his flock. The Lord looked with favour on Abel and his Offering, but on Cain and his Offering He did not look with favour"* (Gen. 4:3-4). God's rebuke to an angry Cain, *"If you do what is right, will you not be accepted?"* (Gen. 4:7), obviously suggests that Cain's Offering was made in conscious violation of God's known Will.

Animal Sacrifices continued to be the norm. They were made by Noah after the Flood (Gen. 8:20-21). In fact, Abraham was known as an Altar-builder, with all the Patriarchs calling on the Name of the Lord at Altars they constructed (Gen. 12:8; 13:4; 26:25).

## ABRAHAM'S SACRIFICES

History's most symbolic Sacrifice is reported in Genesis Chapter 22. To test Abraham, God sent him to a distant mountain, where he was to sacrifice his son Isaac. There, as Abraham was about to kill Isaac, God called out to him and stopped him.

NOTES

Abraham substituted a Ram, which had been caught by its horns in a thicket, and he named the place *"The Lord will provide."* Abraham was not, after all, called on to surrender the life of his only son. That kind of surrender would be reserved for God Himself.

Following their deliverance from slavery in Egypt, the Israelites were provided a Law that established moral, social, civil, and other standards for them. That Law clearly defined the way in which Israel was to worship. It set up a complex, but well-defined, system of Sacrifice.

During the age of the Judges and the reigns of Saul and David, Sacrifices were offered at a number of locations, particularly where the Tabernacle was set up.

## DAVID

The era of David introduced dramatic changes in all of Israel. Jerusalem was established as a political and worship center. There David reorganized the ritual responsibilities of the Priests and Levites (I Chron. Chpts. 22-23). After David's death, his son Solomon built the magnificent Temple in Jerusalem.

This was to be the site at which required Festivals would be held and the only site at which it was legitimate to offer Sacrifices. The command to worship and sacrifice only at the place where God had put His Name is strongly stated: *"To that place you must go; there bring your Burnt Offerings and Sacrifices, your Tithes and special Gifts"* (Deut. 12:5-6).

After this injunction is repeated, the Passage goes on: *"Be careful not to sacrifice your Burnt Offerings anywhere you please. Offer them only at the place the Lord will choose"* (Deut. 12:13-14).

## THE FAITHLESSNESS OF GOD'S PEOPLE

This injunction was later ignored. Many in Israel established their own local *"high places"* to worship Jehovah or some god or goddess of the Canaanites. The faithlessness of God's people, who ignored His guidelines for worship, contributed to their being ultimately exiled from the land.

The Temple in Jerusalem was destroyed when Judah was taken captive to Babylon. It was rebuilt after their return. The Sacrifices were still offered in Jesus' day — at the magnificent Temple reconstructed by Herod. But that Temple later was destroyed by Rome in A.D. 70, and the place ordained for Sacrifice was lost to the Jewish people. But of course, God intended for the Sacrifices then to stop, for the simple reason that Jesus, Who the Sacrifices had represented all along, had now come. Consequently, in view of His Great Sacrifice, there was no need for more Animal Sacrifices.

## FUTURE

However, Daniel prophesied that in the coming Great Tribulation which is soon to break upon the world, Israel will once again reinstitute the Sacrifices, which will be on the occasion of the rebuilding of the Temple (Dan. 9:27). Nevertheless, that will not last long, with the Antichrist taking over the Temple himself.

But yet, a far more positive Prophecy was given by Ezekiel concerning the yet future rebuilding of Jerusalem's Temple at the beginning of the coming Kingdom Age (Ezek. Chpts. 40-48).

There the Prophet pictures the Offering of perpetual Memorial Sacrifices and Burnt Offerings.

It seems these will be carried forever as memorials of Christ's Great Sacrifice, in order that men may never forget the price that He paid for our Redemption.

## PROPHETIC CONDEMNATION

Sacred history records the failure of generation after generation to keep the Mosaic Law. It is not surprising to find the Prophets condemning Israel's approach to worship, as they condemn their other failures.

At the division of Solomon's Kingdom, Jeroboam, who became ruler of Israel's Ten Tribes, set up his own worship system. He feared that if Israel looked to Jerusalem as the spiritual center, they might reunite politically with the Two Tribes that composed the Southern Kingdom, Judah. Jeroboam established worship centers at Bethel and Dan, set up a non-Aaronic Priesthood, and established new festival dates, thus counterfeiting the system established in the Mosaic Law.

Despite the system's violation of every point of the Divine Command, Israel continued this supposed worship of Jehovah until the Assyrians destroyed the Kingdom and dispersed the people in 722 B.C.

NOTES

No wonder Prophets thundered forth in words such as these: *"Go to Bethel and sin; go to Gilgal and sin yet more"* (Amos 4:4). God hardly could be pleased with Sacrifices and Offerings that were supposed to honor Him, but ignored and violated His Commands.

## EVEN IN JUDAH

There were other breakdowns as well. Not only did the Northern Kingdom of Israel rebel against God, setting up their own system in violation of the plain commands of Jehovah, even in Judah, where the form was maintained, the people's worship was contaminated by foreign elements.

*"High places"* (local worship centers) continued to be used for Sacrifice despite God's Command that worship must take place only at Jerusalem. Isaiah reports God's reaction:

*"These people come near to Me with their mouth and honour Me with their lips, but their hearts are far from Me. Their worship of Me is made up only of rules taught by men"* (Isa. 29:13).

For insight into how corrupt Judah finally became, read Ezekiel's description of what happened in the Temple itself in the days just before the Babylonian captivity (Ezek. Chpt. 8).

## NO CONCERN FOR HOLINESS

But perhaps most serious of all, worship of the Lord was to be offered by a Holy people, and the people of Judah had little concern, it seems, for Holiness. The Sacrifices of expiation were ordained for those who fell into inadvertent sin and later discovered their failure (Lev. 4:2). Sacrifice was to be the expressions of a repentant heart, and Offerings were supposed to overflow out of an ever-deepening love for the Lord.

The Prophet's primary thunder was directed against those who supposed that God was concerned only with the form of worship, not with the heart of the Worshiper.

So Isaiah and the other Prophets sought to reestablish the link between Sacrifice and social concern, between worship and morality. Through Isaiah, the Lord cried out: *"Stop bringing meaningless Offerings! Your incense is detestable to Me . . . Your New Moon Festivals and your appointed Feasts My Soul hates. They have become a burden to Me; I am weary of bearing them.*

*"When you spread out your hands in prayer, I will hide My Eyes from you; even if you offer many prayers, I will not listen. Your hands are full of blood; wash and make yourselves clean. Take your evil deeds out of My sight! Stop doing wrong, learn to do right! Seek justice, encourage the oppressed. Defend the cause of the fatherless, plead the case of the widow"* (Isa. 1:13-17; Jer. 7:20-23; Amos 5:21-27; Micah 6:6-8).

In other words, the Sacrificial Ceremonies were not merely to be rituals, but were supposed to represent a devotion to the Lord made evident by the right treatment of others, etc.

THE LESSON FOR TODAY

Thus, the Prophets taught Israel, and thus they are still teaching us today.

The Worship of God is not a matter of ritual or form. Worship must be an expression of commitment to the Lord. In fact, Worship is what we are, while Praise is what we do.

But True Commitment also finds expression in a lifestyle marked by Justice and Mercy. Worship is never acceptable if the Worshiper has wandered from God's Way of morality.

SACRIFICE IN THE GOSPELS

In Jesus' day, the prescribed Sacrifices were being offered at the magnificent Jerusalem Temple, which had just undergone a 40-year reconstruction and beautification process. Nowhere does Jesus condemn the practice of making Sacrifices and Offerings. In fact, He told those He had healed to make the Offerings required by Law (Mat. 8:4; Mk. 1:44; Lk. 5:14).

And He angrily cleansed the Temple Court of profiteers so that God's House might be treated as a place of Prayer and Worship (Mat. 21:12-13; Mk. 11:15-17; Lk. 19:45; Jn. 2:13-17).

WHAT JESUS SAID

But Jesus also reestablished priorities. Among a people whose Leaders put ritual first, Jesus agreed with the Prophets. Twice He alluded to Micah 6:6-8, which reads: *"With what shall I come before the Lord and bow down before the exalted God? Shall I come before Him with Burnt Offerings, with Calves a year old?*

*"Will the Lord be pleased with thousands of Rams, with ten thousand Rivers of Oil? Shall I offer my firstborn for my transgression, the fruit of my body for the sin of my soul?*

NOTES

*"He has showed you, O man, what is good. And what does the Lord require of you? To act justly and to love Mercy and to walk humbly with your God."*

Thus, Jesus challenged His critics and told them to *"Go and learn what this means: 'I desire Mercy, not Sacrifice'"* (Mat. 9:13; 12:7).

And He said that if one who is approaching the Altar harbors anger against a Brother, he must leave his Gift (the Sacrifice he is about to offer) and be reconciled (first) with his Brother. Then he can return to the Altar and offer his Gift to God (Mat. 5:23-24).

Jesus agreed with the Teacher of the Law who said that to Love God and Neighbor *"is more important than all Burnt Offerings and Sacrifices"* (Mk. 12:33-34).

But humanity failed in its Calling to Love. And so the Great Sacrifice that the Old Testament System prefigured lay ahead, as Jesus knew, and actually for the very reason that He had come (Mat. 20:28; 26:28; Mk. 10:45; 14:24; Lk. 22:20).

Jesus Himself would soon be shown to be the Sacrificial Lamb of God (Jn. 1:29, 36).

THAT WHICH WAS GIVEN TO PAUL

The Apostle Paul uses the language of Sacrifice in two contexts:

1. First, and most important, Jesus' Death is understood as a Sacrifice. Jesus is our Passover Lamb, Who has been sacrificed for us (I Cor. 5:7).

God has provided Redemption and Justification for us in Christ Jesus, for *"God presented Him as a Sacrifice of Atonement, through Faith in His Blood"* (Rom. 3:25).

Jesus died *"for us,"* and He justified us by *"His Blood"* (Rom. 5:8-9).

ATONEMENT

Often the Epistles state and assume that Salvation has been won for mankind through God's Great Act of Self-giving on Calvary, where the Sacrifice of Christ is to be understood as fully efficacious (having the power to produce a desired effect). Thus, the Death of Jesus is seen, as symbolized in the Great Sacrifice of the Day of Atonement, as the Ultimate Sacrifice of expiation (to extinguish the guilt incurred, to pay the penalty for, to make amends for).

## CHRISTIAN LIFESTYLE

2. Second, Paul adopts the language of Sacrifice to speak of the Christian lifestyle. Believers are to present themselves to God as Living Sacrifices (Rom. 12:1). This *"Spiritual Worship"* corresponds to the Old Testament whole Burnt Offering of consecration.

Like the Old Testament, our spiritual commitment can come only after the Sacrifice of expiation has been offered for us.

Using the same symbolism, Paul sees his approaching death as a libation (to pour out as an Offering), added to enrich the full commitment to service demonstrated by the Philippians (Phil. 2:17). Paul also uses the analogy of the *"Sacrifice"* in speaking of the Philippians' gifts to him: such are fragrant Offerings, acceptable Sacrifices that please God (Phil. 4:18),

Thus, Paul uses the Sacrificial System of the Old Testament in a literal way to interpret the meaning of the Death of Jesus and in a symbolic way to emphasize the significance of Christian commitment and service (Eph. 5:1-2).

## THE BOOK OF HEBREWS

This notable Book in the New Testament offers the Bible's definitive statement concerning Sacrifice and Offerings. Written I think by the Apostle Paul to those who look back nostalgically to Old Testament Faith, Hebrews seeks to demonstrate just how the Gospel of Jesus Christ is superior.

The Passage that explores Sacrifice is Hebrews Chapters 8-10. Paul begins in Chapter 8 by affirming that the Old Testament Sanctuary where Gifts and Sacrifices were offered is simply *"a copy and shadow of what is in Heaven"* (Heb. 8:5).

In fact, the whole Mosaic Covenant under which the Old Testament Sacrifices were ordained has been replaced by a superior Covenant, under which God will be able to work a full transformation of Believers and so perfectly forgive that He *"will remember their sins no more"* (Heb. 8:12).

## ILLUSTRATIONS FOR THE PRESENT TIME

Hebrews Chapter 9 affirms the elements of the earthly Tabernacle and its worship regulations served as illustrations for the present time. They applied only until Christ established the New Order, for *"The Gifts and Sacrifices being offered were not able to clear the conscience of the Worshiper"* (Heb. 9:9). They were only *"external regulations"* that could not touch the inner person, where the real need was (Heb. 9:10).

But Christ entered the Most Holy Place in Heaven. *"He did not enter by means of the blood of goats and calves; but He entered the Most Holy Place once for all by His Own Blood, having obtained Eternal Redemption"* (Heb. 9:12).

The Old Testament Sacrifices made a person *"outwardly clean"* (Heb. 9:13). However, the Blood of Christ, Who offered Himself, works within to *"cleanse our consciences from acts that lead to death, so that we may serve the Living God"* (Heb. 9:14).

## THE NEW COVENANT HAS REPLACED THE OLD SYSTEM

Paul goes on to show that the New Covenant that has replaced the Mosaic was instituted by Jesus' Sacrifice of Himself (Heb. 9:15-22). That Sacrifice was so effective that *"once for all at the end of the ages"* Jesus was able to *"do away with sin by the Sacrifice of Himself"* (Heb. 9:26).

This one Sacrifice was enough to *"take away the sins of many people"* (all who will believe) (Heb. 9:28).

In Hebrews Chapter 10 Paul returns to his theme: the Old Testament patterns are *"only a shadow of the good things that are coming — not the realities themselves"* (Heb. 10:1). Thus, the repeated Sacrifices could not cleanse the worshipers from sins, or they would not have needed to be repeated.

But now *"We have been made holy through the Sacrifice of the Body of Jesus Christ once for all"* (Heb. 10:10).

His one Sacrifice perfects Believers and provides a perfect forgiveness (Heb. 10:11-18).

*"And where these* (sins) *have been forgiven, there is no longer any* (need for further) *Sacrifice for sin"* (Heb. 10:18).

## THE GREAT PLAN OF GOD

The Old Testament shows that Sacrifice has always been an element in the sinners' approach to God. Sacrifice was institutionalized, as stated, in the Mosaic Law and was an essential aspect of Old Testament Worship.

But the ritual itself was actually not important to God, but only what it represented, and more particularly, Who it represented — The Lord Jesus Christ.

The Prophets reminded Israel that God was concerned with the attitude of people's hearts. This attitude had to be revealed in a concern for Justice and Mercy as well as in faithfulness to ritual requirements.

The New Testament points out those aspects of Old Testament Worship, like other aspects of the Mosaic System, which mirrored heavenly realities. They were important as illustrations, foreshadowing the present age and helping us see the significance of Jesus' Death.

## THE DEATH OF JESUS

The New Testament consistently presents Jesus' Death as a Sacrifice — the Ultimate Sacrifice. His Blood won forgiveness for human beings and laid the foundation for transformation. There is no more (need for) Sacrifice for sin: *"By one Sacrifice He has made perfect forever those who are being made holy"* (Heb. 10:14).

The Bible's Teaching on Sacrifice gives insight into the true nature of sin. Sin can never be viewed lightly by God. He must call for the death of the sinner as the necessary penalty.

But God is rich in Love and Mercy. And that Love impelled Him to an act of deliverance. The Son of God became a Man and offered up His Own Life as a Substitute for sinners.

All the blood spilled on Jewish Altars over the centuries testifies to the necessity and the meaning of Calvary.

(Most of the material on Sacrifices, typifying the Great Sacrifice of The Lord Jesus Christ, was supplied by Lawrence O. Richards.)

(3) "AND I WAS WITH YOU IN WEAKNESS, AND IN FEAR, AND IN MUCH TREMBLING."

The phrase, *"And I was with you in weakness,"* no doubt applies to an utter dependence on the Lord.

*"Weakness"* in the Greek is *"asthenia,"* and means *"feebleness of body or mind, by implication, infirmity or sickness."*

If it pertained to the physical, I think that the record will bear out that it was only temporary. Considering the mode of transportation in those days, and the rigorous schedule normally kept by Paul, I think one would have to conclude that he was physically strong.

NOTES

If Paul was speaking in the spiritual sense, referring to his utter dependence on God, and not at all on the flesh, which I think is the case presented here, the other two words he used (fear and trembling), would be apropos as well.

The phrase, *"And in fear,"* points to the terrible problems he had upon first coming to Corinth (Acts Chpt. 18).

## FEAR

*"Fear"* in the Greek Text is *"phobos,"* and means *"alarm or fright, even to be exceedingly afraid."*

This was not the type of fear which speaks of a lack of Faith, but rather that which is from the mind which signals impending danger, etc. In fact, when Paul first came to Corinth and began ministering in the Synagogue, the situation soon became so volatile that he even feared for his life. The account says that the Lord spoke to Paul *"in the night by a Vision* (saying), *'Be not afraid, but speak, and hold not thy peace:*

*"For I am with thee, and no man shall set on thee to hurt thee: for I have much people in this City'"* (Acts 18:9-10).

The phrase, *"And in much trembling,"* has to do with the fear.

*"Trembling"* in the Greek is *"tromos,"* and means *"quaking with fear."*

Some might presently claim that Paul was not exhibiting Faith. However, those who would claim such, little know or understand the circumstances at times under which he ministered. In fact, his life was in danger constantly and at times, as would be obvious, more so than others.

As well, I think Paul labored constantly under several tremendous burdens. First of all, he knew what God had called him to do respecting the Gentiles. He also knew how this would impact the Jews, for he had once been on that side of the fence. The hatred and animosity toward him by the Jews was intense to say the least. To be frank, even Christian Jews were not too very sympathetic toward him.

Knowing how important all of this was, I think he labored constantly, or at least at times, under the fear of not being in the Will of God. Knowing the constant danger to his life which he all the time faced, he knew that if God did not see him through, he simply could not survive. Consequently, it was absolutely imperative that he be in the Will of God at all times, and I think at times he feared that he may have missed it. In fact, Acts 18:9-11, I think, and to which we have already alluded, bears this out.

Few men in history have been used by God as Paul, and yet he was human just like everyone else.

## FAITH

No, I do not feel that Paul was exhibiting a lack of Faith in the slightest. To be frank, Faith is not necessarily the absence of these things mentioned by Paul, such as *"weakness, fear, and trembling,"* but rather, the persistence and continuing despite these liabilities. Some people erroneously think that Faith is the absence of all difficulties, problems, hindrances, weaknesses, etc. Not at all!

Faith is continuing to believe despite everything saying the opposite. Faith is refusing to quit, when you have failed. Faith is getting up when you have fallen down. Faith is pressing on despite the obstacles, difficulties, and circumstances.

We are too prone to think of Faith only when the sickness is healed. However, it is also Faith when the sickness is not healed, but the person continues anyway to say *"I believe."*

We make a big mistake when we equate Faith with a lack of hindrances, difficulties or problems. To be frank, most of the time such is not Faith, but rather the Lord knowing that actually the person is so lacking in Faith, that if He (the Lord) allowed Satan any latitude at all, the individual simply could not stand. As someone has well said, even though one's action is very important, still, it is his reaction that is the most important.

(4) "AND MY SPEECH AND MY PREACHING WAS NOT WITH ENTICING WORDS OF MAN'S WISDOM, BUT IN DEMONSTRATION OF THE SPIRIT AND OF POWER:"

The phrase, *"And my speech and my preaching was not with enticing words of man's wisdom,"* no doubt, presents the very opposite of what could be thought that would attract the Corinthians.

As today so in Paul's day, people demanded that the Gospel should be preached in *"terms of modern thought,"* embellished with scholastic learning, convincing logic, forensic reasoning, and cultured eloquence.

The Apostle refused, declared such culture to be the wisdom of this world, and said that Preaching according to the Divine Wisdom was Preaching in the Power of the Holy Spirit, and that such was the only Power which effected the moral result of the New Birth — Jesus and Him Crucified (Williams).

Actually, the theme of Apostolic Preaching was the Divine Person and Atoning Work of the Great God and Saviour Jesus Christ.

What a rebuke to much of the Modern Church! What a rebuke to the foray into Modern Psychology!

Paul is saying that he would not attempt to use the keen sword of philosophical dialectics or human eloquence, but would only use the weapon of the Cross — but what a weapon!

This simplicity of the Apostle was the more remarkable because *"Corinthian words"* was a proverb for choice, elaborate, and glittering phrases (Wetstein). Even though Corinth was the vice capital of the world of that day, still, strangely enough, the Corinthians also considered themselves to be intellectuals in the philosophical sense.

## THE HOLY SPIRIT

The phrase, *"But in demonstration of the Spirit and of Power,"* speaks of the Work of the Holy Spirit respecting the Anointing upon Paul and his Message, which penetrated deep into the hearts of his Corinthian converts.

In a similar statement, Paul had said to the Thessalonians, *"Our Gospel came not to you in Word only, but also in Power, and in the Holy Spirit, and in much assurance"* (I Thess. 1:5).

As we have said previously, to preach the Truth, as necessary as that is, is within itself not enough to break the stranglehold of the Powers of Darkness upon humanity. Truth to be effective, must be exactly as Paul says here, Anointed and Empowered by the Holy Spirit, which to be frank is very, very scarce.

This is what makes Christianity different than the religions of the world. Those are mere philosophy, whereas Bible Christianity is with power and as Paul said *"demonstration."* By demonstration we mean several things:

## DEMONSTRATION

Just yesterday morning at Family Worship Center here in Baton Rouge, I had all the people to come forward who had been delivered from Alcoholism or Drugs or both. The line reached almost from one side of the Church to the other.

NOTES

A wave of Praise filled the Auditorium as these people stood there, symbolic of the Grace of God and the Power of God. It takes the Power of God to set the captive free. Regrettably, the Church little more believes in deliverance, which is actually a part of the foundation of Christianity, but rather refers the *"hard cases"* to psychological counseling, etc. As such, not only are these people not helped, but are actually harmed. As I have said many times, were it possible to *talk* these problems out of people, and that's all that Psychology can do, why did Jesus have to come from Heaven and die on a Cross in order that the power of sin may be broken?

The answer is simple. These problems are too severe to be talked out of anybody. Bondages can be broken only by the Power of God, of which Paul speaks here, and which is just as available today as it was then, at least for those who believe.

The tragedy is, most Preachers do not believe the Bible. It is just that simple, they do not believe the Word of God. Consequently, they resort to humanistic wisdom, the very thing which Paul speaks against (vs. 4).

(5) "THAT YOUR FAITH SHOULD NOT STAND IN THE WISDOM OF MEN, BUT IN THE POWER OF GOD."

The phrase, *"That your Faith should not stand in the wisdom of men,"* sadly and regrettably, is exactly the place where the Faith of most professing Christians does actually stand. The facts are *"the wisdom of men"* is the bane of the Church.

### WHAT DID PAUL MEAN BY THE WISDOM OF MEN?

Paul meant anything which deviates from the Word of God.

Millions today belong to and attend Churches, where the Gospel is not preached, the Power of God is not evident, and in fact, the entirety of the effort is made up of humanistic philosophy of one description or the other. To be frank, the philosophy of Christianity is probably the greatest deceiver of all.

Let me explain!

The philosophy of Christianity is Christianity without Christ, except in some elementary role. In other words, Jesus is lifted up as a *"Good Man,"* or a *"Miracle-Worker,"* etc., but not as the Son of God Who died on Calvary and rose from the dead.

NOTES

And then again, there are some who do believe that Jesus is the Son of God, died on Calvary and rose from the dead, which is all correct, but deny the Baptism with the Holy Spirit, which basically leaves them with a form of Godliness, but denying the Power thereof. Paul said of these, *"From such turn away"* (II Tim. 3:5).

### THE GOLDEN RULE

The philosophy of Christianity claims to accept the *"Golden Rule,"* but with its adherents not truly *"Born Again"* (Jn. 3:3). To be frank, most, if not all, the old-line Denominations fall into this category, with some of the Pentecostal following suit.

Actually, there was a day, not too many years ago, when one could tell what a Church taught or believed, by whatever particular Religious Denomination with which they were associated. However, that day has long since gone, at least for so-called Pentecostal Denominations. When one opens the door to any Church anymore, one never knows what one will find. So much of that which calls itself *"Church,"* has been riddled with the *"wisdom of men."*

### THE LORD JESUS CHRIST

To truly know Salvation, one must have a personal experience with Jesus Christ, exactly as Paul did on the road to Damascus. No, it may not be that outwardly demonstrative or dramatic, but in its own way, it will be just as life-changing. Jesus is Christianity. Jesus is Salvation. Jesus is the Deliverer from the bondages of darkness. Jesus is the Healer. Jesus is the Baptizer with the Holy Spirit. Jesus is Victory. Jesus is Power, and that Power is ensconced in what He did at Calvary and the Resurrection.

The phrase, *"But in the Power of God,"* refers to the Power of the Holy Spirit which works from the premise of the Crucified, Risen Christ, making Jesus real in one's heart and life. In other words, the Lord does not save in sin, but from sin. That means, when a person comes to Christ, if they have been an Alcoholic, the bondage of alcohol is broken, or drugs, etc. It means that jealousy, envy, malice, and greed are addressed. In fact, the Divine Nature of the Lord is implanted in the Believer's heart, which in effect, makes a *"new creature"* out of the person, irrespective of what he or she has previously been (II Cor. 5:17).

Sometimes the individual may have a struggle with some of the things which had been a bondage before Conversion, but Trust and Faith in Christ will ultimately handle the situation, irrespective as to what it is. This means that Jesus Christ is the Answer for all sin, aberrations, wickedness, and bondage. In fact, He is the only Answer.

*"Power"* in the Greek is *"dunamis,"* and means *"miraculous power."* In fact, the Miracle-working Power of God, is the only miraculous content in the world. Irrespective of unbelieving Preachers attempting to take the *"Miracle"* out of Bible Christianity, the Power of God is just as efficient, workable, ever present, and mighty as it ever has been, and will bring forth the intended results, if men will only believe (Mk. 9:23; 11:24).

(6) "HOWBEIT WE SPEAK WISDOM AMONG THEM THAT ARE PERFECT: YET NOT THE WISDOM OF THIS WORLD, NOR OF THE PRINCES OF THIS WORLD, THAT COME TO NOUGHT:"

The phrase, *"Howbeit we speak wisdom among them that are perfect,"* refers to the fact that only the spiritually mature would be able to fully understand the *"wisdom"* of which he spoke. Actually, as he will say in the first verse of the Third Chapter, the Corinthians were not mature, but rather *"babes in Christ."*

## WHAT DID PAUL MEAN BY THE WORD *"PERFECT?"*

Paul writes to the Corinthians that he speaks wisdom among those who are perfect. The Greek word for *"perfect"* is *"teleios,"* and means *"full-growth, maturity, workability, soundness, and completeness,"* in this case *"spiritual maturity."* In the Pagan Greek mystery religions, the word referred to those devotees who were fully instructed as opposed to those who were novices.

As well, we can get a fuller meaning of the word by contrasting it with another word. For instance, the words *"full age"* (Heb. 5:14) are from *"teleios,"* which is said in contrast to the word *"babe"* (Heb. 5:13).

The word *"babe"* is from *"nepios,"* a Greek word meaning *"an infant, a little child, a minor, not of age,"* and refers to one who is *"untaught, unskilled."* The idea of immaturity is in the word, and according to the context in which it is found, it could refer to either mental or spiritual immaturity.

## THE CORINTHIANS

Paul says in I Corinthians 3:1, that he could not speak to the Corinthians as to spiritual Christians, but as to carnal ones, namely, babes in Christ. In passing, it might be well to note that the phrase *"babes in Christ"* as Paul uses it in the Greek, does not mean *"young converts,"* but *"Christians who have not attained to a mature Christian experience,"* even though they have had the opportunity to do so.

It is a sad thing to see one who has been a Christian for many years and who still is spiritually immature, in other words, a *"babe in Christ,"* which sadly, characterizes all too many. Here we have the contrast spoken between *"teleios"* which means *"perfect,"* that is mature, and *"nepios,"* which means *"babe,"* that is, *"immature."* Paul makes it clear that he is speaking of maturity and immaturity in spiritual things when he uses the word *"spiritual"* in I Corinthians 3:1 by comparison to the person in I Corinthians 2:6 who was spoken of as *"perfect."* Thus, the word *"perfect"* when used to describe a Christian means *"spiritually mature."*

## COMPLETENESS

In Ephesians 4:13-14, we have the same contrast between a perfect (teleios) man and children (nepios). But *"teleios"* has an added shade of meaning here.

Not only does it refer to spiritual maturity by its contrast to *"nepios"* which speaks of spiritual immaturity, but it speaks also of *"completeness."* This latter shade of meaning comes from the words in the context, *"the measure of the stature of the fullness of Christ."*

The word *"completeness"* speaks of a well-rounded Christian character, where the Christian Graces are kept in proper balance. For instance, a Christian who has much zeal but little wisdom to guide that zeal into its proper channels and restrain it when necessary, is not a well-balanced Christian, and is not spiritually mature, in other words, not complete.

## WHAT DID PAUL MEAN CONCERNING HIMSELF IN THIS REGARD?

We come now to Paul's use of the *"teleios"* and the verb from the same root *"teleioo"* in

NOTES

Philippians 3:12-15, which Passage in the English translation seems to involve a contradiction, because the meaning of the Greek word cannot be fully and clearly brought out in a translation which is held down to a minimum of words.

In Philippians 3:12, Paul states that he is not yet perfect. In Philippians 3:15 he urges those of the Philippian Saints who are perfect to be *"thus minded,"* namely, to account themselves as not yet perfect. How are we to understand this? Surely, the inspired Apostle does not ask them to deny the reality of something which they know to be a fact, namely their spiritual maturity. The following hopefully will solve this difficulty.

THE MEANING OF WORDS

As most know, the New Testament was originally written in Greek, hence the necessity, if possible, to attempt to understand particular Greek words. Languages are different, and the same word in one language may not mean exactly the same in another. As well, some languages, even as Greek, have far more words for a particular subject than other languages.

The Greek language was a very full and descriptive language, at least as far as words are concerned. Consequently, to fully understand certain things which are said in the New Testament, it is necessary to go back to the original Greek. However, in no way does that mean that a person has to be a Greek Scholar in order to understand the New Testament. Not at all! In fact, even though there are many Biblical Translations, some few good and most, I think, not so good; nevertheless, I personally think the King James is an excellent Translation, in my opinion the best. They did an excellent job in bringing the Text over from the original Hebrew and Greek to English.

Of course, as most understand, this Translation was finished in the very early 1600's. Consequently, a few words have changed their meaning in the meantime. However, having said that, the King James Translation I continue to believe is still the best in the world.

PERFECTION?

When Paul says, *"Not as though I . . . were already perfect"* (Phil. 3:12), he means that the Holy Spirit had not yet brought him to the place in his Christian life where His Sanctifying Work was no longer needed, in other words, to the place of absolute spiritual maturity from which place there was no possibility of slipping back to a condition of spiritual immaturity, and beyond which there was no more room for growth.

Then he exhorts those among the Philippian Saints who were spiritually mature, to take the same attitude toward their own growth in Grace. That is, a Christian is spiritually mature if he is not a *"nepios,"* a *"babe."* Just as an adult becomes more mature as he grows older and wiser, so a Child of God grows in degrees of spiritual maturity. But he must ever realize that he will never be spiritually mature in an absolute sense, that is, come to the place where he cannot grow in the Christian Life, because he has already reached perfection, etc.

He must always realize how far short he comes of absolute Christlikeness, what an infinite distance there is between the most Christlike Saint and the Lord Jesus.

NO CONTRADICTION

Thus, the contradiction in the English Translation, or that which seems to be a contradiction, is cleared up by the Greek Text. In Philippians 3:12, Paul is speaking of absolute spiritual maturity, in 3:15, of relative spiritual maturity.

In Philippians 3:12, he is speaking of a process that has reached a state of completion, which he says he has not yet attained, and to be frank neither has anyone else.

In Philippians 3:15, he refers to a process that was still going on. In 3:12, he denies having reached the place in his Christian Life where there was no more improvement possible. In 3:15, he speaks of the constant need of growth in the Christian Life.

In Philippians 3:12 he denies being spiritually mature in an absolute sense. In 3:15, he asserts that as a spiritually mature Christian, there is always a need for more maturity in one's spiritual experience.

OTHER EXAMPLES

It remains for us to trace briefly the use of *"teleios"* in the other Passages where it occurs (spiritual maturity). In Matthew 5:48, the word implies growth into maturity of Godliness on the part of the Believer. The word when used here of God the Father does not refer to his sinlessness, which He certainly is, but rather to His Kindness, as the context points out, thus to His Character.

In Matthew 19:21, that spiritual maturity meant is the result and accompaniment of a self-sacrificial character.

In Romans 12:2, it describes the Will of God as a Will that lacks nothing necessary to completeness.

In I Corinthians 13:10, the word means *"complete,"* and is contrasted to that which is incomplete.

In I Corinthians 14:20, *"Be ye children,"* is from our word *"nepios"* which means *"immaturity,"* while *"men"* is our word *"telios,"* which speaks here of spiritual maturity.

In Colossians 1:28, Paul's desire is to present the Saints to whom he ministers as spiritually mature Believers. Epaphras (Col. 4:12) prays that the Colossian Saints might be spiritually mature Believers.

In Hebrews 9:11, the Tabernacle of the New Testament in Heaven is said to be more complete than the Tabernacle which Moses built, for the latter lacked what the former has, the out-poured Blood of Christ.

## PERFECT

It remains for us to look at the places where the word *"perfect"* appears in the translation of the Greek verb *"teleioo,"* as it relates to *"teleios,"* i.e., *"spiritual maturity."*

In Luke 13:32, *"Today, tomorrow and the third day"* is an expression used to designate a short while. *"Perfected"* here is used in the same sense as in Hebrews 2:10.

In His Death on the Cross, Jesus was made complete as the Saviour. In John 17:23, *"made perfect"* is to be understood in the sense of *"brought to a state of completeness."*

The word *"one"* refers to the unity into which Believers are brought by the fact that the Lord Jesus is in each Saint. In being united together by the indwelling Christ, Believers are in that state of completeness with reference to their Salvation which would not be true of them if Christ were not in them. In other words, the perfection is in Christ, and not the individual per se.

In II Corinthians 12:9, Paul's strength is brought to such a state by the Power of the Holy Spirit in that it is lacking nothing necessary to completeness.

NOTES

In Hebrews 2:10 and 5:9, the Lord Jesus through His Death on the Cross was *"made perfect"* in that He was made complete as a Saviour; in 7:19 the Mosaic Economy brought nothing to completeness in that it could not offer a Sacrifice that could pay for sin.

In Hebrews 9:9 and 10:1, we are told that the Levitical Sacrifices could not make Believers perfect, while in 10:14 and 12:23, we find that the New Testament sealed in Jesus' Blood does.

## A PERFECT SALVATION

In Hebrews 9:9, *"Make perfect as pertaining to the conscience,"* refers to the inability of the typical Sacrifices themselves to bring the Believer's conscience to a state of completeness in the sense that they could not *"put his moral religious consciousness and its inward feeling into a state of entire and joyful looking for of Salvation so that his conscience should be an onward-waxing consciousness of perfect restoration, of entire cleaning up, of total emancipation, of his relation to God"* (Alford). In other words, the Old Testament Sacrifices could not bring peace of mind and heart.

The words *"make perfect as pertaining to the conscience,"* therefore, refer to that Work of God in Salvation that is a complete Work in the Believer's conscience.

*"Abraham rejoiced to see My day,"* means that he rejoiced to see in the future of God's Prophetic Program, the Death and Resurrection of the Messiah. The very fact of the constant repetition of Sacrifices showed him that sin had not yet been actually paid for. Thus, Believers under the First Testament Sacrifices never had that sense of completeness in which there was nothing lacking that was necessary (Heb. 10:1).

But our Lord on the Cross cried, *"It is finished,"* i.e., *"It stands completed,"* using the word *"telioo,"* referring to His Work of Salvation wrought out on the Cross, in other words complete (Jn. 19:30).

Thus, Believers today have that complete sense of forgiveness which was lacking in the Old Testament Saints (Heb. 10:14). Abraham had Righteousness reckoned to him, that is, put to his account. But he did not possess it as the Believer does today.

Therefore, he was not as complete in Salvation as we are, and we are not as complete today as we shall be in the Resurrection, when at that time we as Saints will be Glorified (I Cor. 15:52).

IN HEAVEN

In Hebrews 12:23 we have *"the spirits of just men made perfect."* The Greek shows that it is the men who are made perfect. These are Saints in Heaven, made perfect in the sense that they have been brought to that spiritual maturity which is the result of sufferings, trials, of having run and ended their race.

*"All is accomplished, their probation, their Righteousness, God's Purposes respecting them."* There is a completeness about them in Heaven that is now lacking in the Saints yet on Earth, as should be obvious. In fact, total perfection will not come until the Resurrection.

(The material on perfection was derived from the Scholarship of Kenneth Wuest.)

The phrase, *"Yet not the wisdom of this world,"* relates to the fact that the Wisdom of God which pertains to Salvation, has absolutely no relationship whatsoever to the *"wisdom of this world."*

It is ironical, in the Apostle's description of the Gospel as being, in the world's judgment, *"weak"* and *"foolish,"* that in fact, it is the highest Wisdom of all, but can only be understood by the spiritually mature.

The *"wisdom of the world"* as it is given here, refers to its moral and intellectual aspect. Such is foolishness with God (I Cor. 3:19).

The *"wisdom"* spoken of here, does not pertain to education as one thinks of such, relative to the sciences, etc., but rather, that which pertains to spiritual things, i.e., Salvation as given by God.

The phrase, *"Nor of the Princes of this world, that come to nought,"* in its strict sense referred to the Roman Governors and Jewish Sanhedrin, who treated the Divine Wisdom of the Gospel, i.e., The Lord Jesus Christ, with sovereign contempt (Acts 4:27).

However, in its broader aspect, Paul's statement impacts the religions of the world, as well as the Rulers of the world who do not recognize the Lord of Glory or His Word, i.e., *"Salvation."* As we shall see, it all centers up in Christ Jesus, meaning, that one cannot truly understand or know God to any degree whatsoever, without first accepting Christ Jesus as one's Saviour and Lord.

NOTES

Paul sees mighty Empires vanishing before the Gospel of Jesus Christ, and that is exactly what has happened. Even though it has seen some hard days in the past, this Gospel, i.e., the True Church of Jesus Christ, reigns supreme today as the mightiest Government on the face of the Earth. However, this Government is not political or even material, but rather spiritual. As well, it is only here in part, and will be here in totality only upon the return of Jesus Christ, the King of this Kingdom.

PAUL AND KNOWLEDGE

Some may think from these Passages, that Paul is denigrating knowledge. Not at all! He is opposed to knowledge which is false, as anyone should be. And it should be quickly stated, that all knowledge of the world as it relates to Salvation is false. Paul portrays this by strongly contrasting the Wisdom of God with the wisdom of this age.

God's Wisdom sets up the Sacrifice of Christ on the Cross as the most important fact of history. On the other hand, the wisdom of this age completely rejects the Sacrifice of Christ and considers it meaningless and foolish.

Paul deals quite thoroughly with this contrast between God's Wisdom and the wisdom of this age. The wisdom of this age is false because it does not allow for the Sacrifice of Christ, and as stated, considers it as nothing. As such it is blatantly false, and leads men astray, as actually it is designed by Satan to do. God's Wisdom leads sinful men to the great Sacrifice of history, the offering up of Jesus on the Cross of Calvary, which paid the terrible sin debt of man, at least for all who will believe (Rossier).

(7) "BUT WE SPEAK THE WISDOM OF GOD IN A MYSTERY, EVEN THE HIDDEN WISDOM, WHICH GOD ORDAINED BEFORE THE WORLD UNTO OUR GLORY:"

The phrase, *"But we speak the wisdom of God in a mystery,"* pertains to the Gospel of Jesus Christ, which was not understood up to the time of its Revelation. None of the great Princes of the world knew of this Revelation; if they had fully known and understood it, they certainly would not have crucified the Lord.

As the Prophets of old uttered their great Prophecies, they searched greatly in an attempt to understand what they had prophesied regarding Christ; even Angels sought to comprehend its greatness and glory (I Pet. 1:10-13).

The Mystery is now made clear, with much of the understanding of the New Covenant given to the Apostle Paul (Rom. 1:1-15; 16:25-26; I Cor. 2:9-16; Gal. 1:12, 16; Eph. 3:1-8; Heb. 8:6; II Pet. 3:16).

*"Mystery"* in the Greek is *"musterio,"* and means *"a Truth, once hidden, now revealed."*

The word *"Mystery"* as it is now used, pertains to that which is dark and incomprehensible, but it has no such meaning in the New Testament, where it means *"what was once secret has now been made manifest."*

In discussing the Wisdom of God, Paul is not discussing one wisdom among many, but God's Wisdom which stands alone. He states four major facts about this Wisdom:

1. God is its Source.
2. It is a mystery, at least to those who do not know the Lord.
3. God determined this system of Truth before Creation.
4. He ordained it for our Glory, and that we might participate in the provisions He has prepared for them who love Him (Rossier).

The phrase, *"Even the hidden wisdom,"* refers to the fact that a person cannot come to this Knowledge of God through the normal ways of learning. God has to reveal Himself to people before they can be lifted out of their lost, natural condition. Without God's assistance, human reasoning cannot fathom the Mystery of God (Rossier).

It refers as well to the fact that even the Prophets of old could little understand their Prophecies relative to the Gentiles and the Sacrifice of Christ. They knew what was said, and had some small Revelation, but the majority remained a mystery.

Maybe Abraham came closer to seeing this great *"Mystery"* than any of the Patriarchs or Prophets of old. Jesus said of him, *"Your father Abraham rejoiced to see My day: and he saw it, and was glad"* (Jn. 8:56). But yet, except here and there, and even then in small degrees, it was a *"mystery."*

The phrase, *"Which God ordained before the world unto our glory,"* means that God determined to bring about His Plan for the good of all who would believe.

NOTES

*"Ordained"* in the Greek is *"proorizo,"* and means *"pre-determined."*

## PREDESTINATION AS IT OCCURS HERE

The word *"predestinate"* as well comes under the translation of *"proorizo,"* from which is also derived the word *"ordained."*

*"Proorizo"* comes from the Greek word *"horizo,"* which means *"to divide or separate from as a border or boundary, to mark out boundaries, to mark out, to determine, appoint."* Thus, the compound word means *"to divide or separate from a border or boundary beforehand, to determine or appoint beforehand."*

The genius of the word is that of placing limitations upon someone or something beforehand, these limitations bringing that person or thing within the sphere of a certain future or destiny. These meanings are carried over into the New Testament usage of the word. Thus, the *"chosen-out"* ones, have had limitations put around them which bring them within the sphere of becoming God's Children by adoption (Eph. 1:5), and of being conformed to the Image of the Lord Jesus (Rom. 8:29), and of the Sacrifice of Christ, which we are now studying.

As well, by Paul using the words *"our glory,"* as it refers to man, and more particularly, believing man, such clearly tells us that *"the future age"* is in God's Counsels subjected, not to the Angels, but to man. But *"our glory"* is that we are *"called to His Eternal Glory by Christ Jesus"* (I Pet. 5:10).

(8) "WHICH NONE OF THE PRINCES OF THIS WORLD KNEW: FOR HAD THEY KNOWN IT, THEY WOULD NOT HAVE CRUCIFIED THE LORD OF GLORY."

The phrase, *"Which none of the Princes of this world knew,"* pertains to their ignorance being a willful ignorance, which was their judgment for rejecting Christ (Acts 3:17; 13:27).

Jews and Romans, Emperors, Procurators, High Priests, Pharisees, had in their ignorance conspired in vain to prevent what God had foreordained even before there was a world. Consequently, they had about as much chance at success, to be crude, as a snowball does in Hades.

The phrase, *"For had they known it,"* speaks of a willful ignorance. In other words, had they desired to have known, they could have known. They did not want to *"know"*; therefore, God saw to it that they would not know, and in fact, could not *"know."*

For instance, lack of knowledge concerning the Gospel in the United States, and many other countries of the world for that matter, is for the most part a *"willful ignorance."* If one desires to know, one can know. Unfortunately, that is not the case in some places.

IGNORANCE

The Greek word *"agnoeo"* and its derivatives are used to express the idea of ignorance. While some argue that in a few instances *"agnoeo"* implies an ignorance that comes from lack of knowledge, all agree that human ignorance in spiritual affairs cannot be corrected simply by learning unknown facts.

The problem in spiritual ignorance is a misunderstanding that comes from a wrong perception of available data. For instance, Jesus' listeners heard what He told them, but they could not understand its meaning for them (Mk. 9:32; Lk. 9:45). They could not understand, because they did not desire to understand.

Ignorance lies at the core of Pagan Worship (Acts 13:27) and explains the failure of all the lost to realize that it is God's kindness only, designed to lead them to repentance, that delays God's Judgment (Rom. 2:1-4).

GREEK WORDS

The significant Greek words that express the concept of ignorance as misperception are as follows: *"agnoeo,"* which means *"to be ignorant"* (Mk. 9:32; Lk. 9:45; Acts 13:27; 17:23; Rom. 1:13; 2:4; 6:3; 7:1; 10:3; 11:25; I Cor. 10:1; 12:1; 14:38; II Cor. 1:8; 2:11; 6:9; Gal. 1:22; I Thess. 4:13; I Tim. 1:13; Heb. 5:2; II Pet. 2:12), *"agnoeoma,"* which means *"a sin of ignorance"* (Heb. 9:7), *"agnoia,"* which means *"ignorance"* (Acts 3:17; 17:30; Eph. 4:18; I Pet. 1:14), and *"agnosia,"* which means *"lack of knowledge"* (I Cor. 15:34; I Pet. 2:15).

THE MIND

What is the Bible's antidote to an ignorance that comes from failure to perceive spiritual realities? Romans 12:2 says, *"Be transformed by the renewing of your mind."* The Greek word for *"mind"* is *"nous,"* which refers to the mind as the organ of perception.

It is by listening to God's Will expressed in His Word and putting that Will into practice that we will have a totally new outlook on life's issues. But inner transformation requires both a grasp of what the Word says and an obedient response to the Word.

NOTES

Only by a commitment to obedience to God can our ignorance be replaced by firm knowledge based on the Word of God.

The phrase, *"They would not have crucified the Lord of Glory,"* presents a powerful statement. This is not a mere equivalent of *"The Glorious Lord"* (Ps. 24:10).

It is *"The Lord of the Glory,"* i.e., *"The Lord of the Shechinah."* The Shechinah was the name given by the Jews to the Cloud of Light which symbolized God's Presence.

Actually, the Cherubim are called, in Hebrews 9:5, *"Cherubims of Glory,"* because the Shechinah was borne on their outspread wings.

There would have been to ancient ears, and should be to ours as well, a startling and awful paradox in the words *"Crucified the Lord of Glory."* The words brought into juxtaposition the lowest ignominy and the most splendid Exaltation (Farrar).

(9) "BUT AS IT IS WRITTEN, EYE HATH NOT SEEN, NOR EAR HEARD, NEITHER HAVE ENTERED INTO THE HEART OF MAN, THE THINGS WHICH GOD HATH PREPARED FOR THEM THAT LOVE HIM."

The phrase, *"But as it is written,"* primarily comes from Isaiah 64:4 but as well has some structure from Isaiah 52:15 and 65:17.

To be frank, the whole sentence in the Greek is unfinished. The thought seems to be, *"But God has revealed to us things which eye hath not seen, etc., though the Princes of this world were in ignorance of them"* (Farrar).

The phrase, *"Eye hath not seen, nor ear heard, neither have entered into the heart of man,"* basically employs three means of natural knowledge, *"to see," "to hear," "to understand."* The purpose is to show that we cannot come to a knowledge of God through these normal ways of learning (Rossier).

The phrase, *"The things which God hath prepared for them that love Him,"* refers to the Lord revealing these wonderful secrets to those who love Him, and hiding them from the curious and skeptical, irrespective of their educational or intellectual abilities. In other words, the key is *"Love,"* and more particularly, that of loving God, which refers to serving Him and giving

Him His rightful due regarding Worship and Service. Scientific quest or intellectual pursuit meet a closed door.

Why should it not be thus so? God's creative abilities and intellectual honesty is so far above the prattle of even the most brightest or educated of human beings, as to have no comparison. In other words, even if one leaves out the spiritual completely, still, there remains no common ground whatsoever respecting these other pursuits.

As well, as an aside, this verse has nothing to do with Heaven as many have been taught, but rather concerns God's Present Salvation Plan.

(10) "BUT GOD HATH REVEALED THEM UNTO US BY HIS SPIRIT: FOR THE SPIRIT SEARCHETH ALL THINGS, YEA, THE DEEP THINGS OF GOD."

The phrase, *"But God hath revealed them unto us by His Spirit,"* plainly tells us the manner of the impartation of spiritual knowledge, which is by Revelation. What is undiscoverable by human reasoning God makes known to us by the Holy Spirit (Rossier). The only requirement on the part of Believers is some knowledge of the Word, even as little as that may be, and Faith in God. The Holy Spirit then begins His Revelation, which actually never stops, and will not stop until the Resurrection.

The phrase, *"For the Spirit searcheth all things, yea, the deep things of God,"* means that the Holy Spirit is the only One amply qualified to reveal God. The Personality and Godhead of the Holy Spirit are declared in verses 10-13; for Godhead cannot be separated from the Spirit of God as manhood cannot be separated from the spirit of man (Williams).

## WHO IS THE HOLY SPIRIT?

Of course, we know the Holy Spirit to be God. As one example, Jesus referred to Him by the use of personal pronouns (Jn. 16:7-15), and as well, distinct from the Father and the Son. He is the Third Person of the Triune Godhead. There is One God manifest in Three Persons, God the Father, God the Son, and God the Holy Spirit (Mat. 28:19).

The expression *"Spirit"* or *"Spirit of God,"* or *"Holy Spirit,"* is found in the great majority of the Books of the Bible.

In the Old Testament the Hebrew Word uniformly employed for the Spirit as referring to God's Spirit is *"Ruah,"* and means *"Breath, Wind, or Breeze."*

The Greek word used in the New Testament is *"Pneuma,"* and means the same as in the Hebrew.

## GOD THE HOLY SPIRIT

In considering the Spirit of God there are several points to be noted. The first is that there is no indication of a belief that the Spirit of God is a material particle or emanation from God the Father.

(Many have attempted to claim that God the Father and God the Holy Spirit are One and the Same, the Holy Spirit merely being the Presence of God. However, that is incorrect, inasmuch as the Holy Spirit is always referred to separate and distinct from the Father, i.e., a Person within His Own right.)

The point of view of Biblical Writers is nearly always practical concerning the Holy Spirit rather than speculative. They did not philosophize about the Divine Nature. In other words, the identification of God the Father and the Spirit of God present a clear distinction between them. The identification is seen in Psalm 139:7 where the Omnipresence of the Spirit is declared, and in Isaiah 63:10; Jeremiah 31:33; Ezekiel 36:27, etc.

## THE HOLY SPIRIT AS HE WORKED IN ISRAEL OF OLD

The greater part of the Old Testament Passages which refer to the Spirit of God deal with the subject from the point of view of the Covenant relations between Jehovah and Israel. And the greater portion of these, in turn, have to do with Gifts and Powers conferred by the Spirit for service in the ongoing of the Kingdom of God.

We fail to grasp the full meaning of many statements in the Old Testament unless we keep constantly in mind the fundamental assumption of all the Old Testament, unless we understand it in relationship to the Covenant Relations between God and Israel. This was always paramount.

Extraordinary powers exhibited by Israelites of whatever kind were usually attributed to the Spirit. These are so numerous that our limits of space forbid an exhaustive presentation. However, we will touch on one or two.

The Children of Israel cried unto the Lord and He raised up a Saviour for them, Othniel the son

NOTES

of Kenaz: *"And the Spirit of the Lord came upon him, and he judged Israel"* (Judg. 3:10).

Another example among many pertains to Bezaleel who was filled *"with the Spirit of God, in wisdom, and in understanding, and in knowledge, and in all manner of workmanship,"* etc. respecting the building of the Tabernacle (Ex. 31:2-4; 35:31).

Joshua was qualified for leadership by the Spirit (Num. 27:18).

## OTHER ACTIVITY OF THE HOLY SPIRIT IN THE OLD TESTAMENT

The activity of the Spirit in the Old Testament is not limited to Gifts for service. Moral and spiritual character is traced to the Spirit's operations as well (Neh. 9:20; Ps. 51:11; 143:10; Isa. 63:10; etc).

Another example is David's Prayer in Psalm 51:11, where there was an intense sense of guilt and sin, with David praying *"Take not thy Holy Spirit from me."* Thus, we see that the Old Testament in numerous ways recognizes the Holy Spirit as the Source of inward moral purity, although the thought is not so developed as in the New Testament.

## THE HOLY SPIRIT IN THE LIFE AND MINISTRY OF JESUS

The Anointing of Jesus with the Holy Spirit qualified Him in two particulars for His Messianic Office:

1. First of all, it was the Source of His Own Enduement of Power for the Endurance of Temptation, for Teaching, for Casting out Demons, and Healing the Sick, for His Sufferings and Death, for His Resurrection and Ascension.

The question is often raised, why Jesus, the Divine One, should have needed the Holy Spirit for His Messianic Vocation? The reply is that His Human Nature, which was real, required the Spirit's Presence. Man, made in God's Image, is constituted in dependence upon the Spirit of God. Apart from God's Spirit man fails of his true destiny, simply because of our nature is constituted as dependent upon the indwelling Spirit of God for the performance of our true functions.

Jesus as Human, therefore, and as the Second Adam, required the Presence of God's Spirit, notwithstanding His Divine-Human Consciousness, simply because He was fully Man.

NOTES

2. However, Jesus had a qualification of the Spirit, that is not really given to anyone else. The Holy Spirit's coming upon Him in fullness, due to His Divinity, also qualified Him to bestow the Holy Spirit on His Disciples, which He did, giving them Power to do great things (Mat. 10:1). The *"Power"* is vested in Jesus, but He dispenses it through the Person, Office, and Ministry of the Holy Spirit (Mat. 28:18). He is also the Baptizer with the Holy Spirit regarding all His Followers, and for all time (Mat. 3:11; Lk. 4:18).

## THE HOLY SPIRIT IN THE EARLY CHURCH

Due to what Jesus did at Calvary and the Resurrection, in paying the sin debt, the Holy Spirit could now come into the hearts and lives of Believers, whereas before Calvary He could not do so, at least in this fashion (Jn. 14:17). The Day of Pentecost was the time and beginning of this great event (Acts Chpt. 2).

The activity of the Holy Spirit in the Early Church is so pronounced, that He is mentioned by Name over 50 times in that one Book alone. He was truly the One who set the Pattern for the Church, respecting its Direction, Government, Activity, and Mission.

Such must be identical in the Modern Church, that is if we are to have what the Lord wants and desires. The Holy Spirit is to be no less the Empowering Agent now than He was then.

## THE HOLY SPIRIT IN THE HEART AND LIFE OF THE BELIEVER

In John Chapter 16, the Lord graphically outlines the Work and Ministry of the Holy Spirit in the lives of Believers.

He reproves or convicts *"the world of Sin, and of Righteousness, and of Judgment"* (Jn. 16:8), not only regarding unbelievers, but Believers as well.

He also does the following:

1. He guides into all Truth: This speaks of His Overseership of the Word of God which is Truth.
2. He will show you things to come: This speaks of Revelation respecting futuristic events, but it also speaks of Guidance, Leading, and Direction.
3. He shall glorify Me: This speaks of the Holy Spirit making Jesus real in our hearts and lives, and revealing as to Who exactly Jesus rightly is.

4. He shall receive of Mine, and shall shew it unto you: This speaks of Revelation, which means that the Believer is the only one who is the recipient of such, which the world cannot receive. This speaks of Leading, respecting what the Child of God is to do respecting all things.

5. All things that the Father hath are Mine: This speaks of the Will of the Father being carried out in the life of the Believer, which can only come about by the Administration of the Holy Spirit in the life of the Believer (Jn. 16:8-15).

The material we are about to give has to do totally with the Work and Ministry of the Holy Spirit respecting the Word of God. It will help us to understand the manner in which the Word of God was originally given to the Prophets of old, as well as the Apostles respecting the New Testament. It is as follows:

## PAUL'S DOCTRINE OF VERBAL INSPIRATION

The classic Passage on this subject is found in that which we are now studying, I Corinthians 2:9-16, and was written for all men and for all time, but particularly to a racial group in Paul's day who stands out in history as the most intellectual of all people, the Greeks. They were a race of creative thinkers. The sole instrument which they used in their attempt to pierce through the mysteries of existence was human reason. This they sharpened to a keen edge. However, it was inadequate to solve the great mysteries of origins, of the wherefore of human existence, of God, and of evil.

Plato, one of their great Philosophers, said, *"We must lay hold of the best human opinion in order that borne by it as on a raft, we may sail over the dangerous sea of life, unless we can find a stronger boat, or some sure Word of God, which will more surely and safely carry us."*

This great Philosopher acknowledged that mere human reason was not sufficient to answer the riddles with which man is confronted, and that the only sure foundation for a system of Truth was, not even the best of human opinions, but a Revelation from God. But sadly, there is no record that Plato ever had such a Revelation.

## PAUL OF TARSUS

Paul who was inspired by the Holy Spirit to write these Passages in I Corinthians Chapter 2, declared to these Intellectuals that the Bible had come, not from human reason, but by Divine Revelation, and was himself trained in their schools. He was a native of Tarsus, a City where Greek Culture predominated. The University of Tarsus was known all over the world. Strabo placed it ahead of the Universities of Athens and Alexandria in its zeal for learning.

Paul's people were Roman citizens, and also citizens of Tarsus, which the latter fact tells us that his family was one of wealth and standing, for during the time of Paul, only people of wealth and class in the community were allowed to possess Tarsian citizenship. This explains Paul's statement, *"I have suffered the loss of all things"* (Phil. 3:8).

## ACTIVITY AND ATMOSPHERE

The City of Tarsus was noted for its intense activity, its atmosphere of what we today call *"drive."* Paul was not reared in the lassitude and ease of an oriental City, but in an atmosphere of physical and mental achievement. That he had a thorough training in the University of Tarsus is evident from his words to the Corinthians: *"And I having come to you, Brethren, came, not having my Message dominated by a transcendent rhetorical display or by philosophical subtlety . . . and my Message and my Preaching were not couched in specious words of philosophy"* (I Cor. 2:1-4).

To be sure, he could have used these had he wanted to. He was schooled in Greek rhetoric, philosophy, and sophistry (an argument apparently correct in form but actually invalid, used to deceive, in effect, a philosophy that will not work despite it being correct in form), also in Greek literature. Consequently, in giving the Greeks his teaching of Verbal Inspiration (how the Holy Spirit inspired him and all other Prophets and Apostles to write the Holy Scriptures), Paul was not looking at the subject from only one angle, that of someone who knew what fellowship with God was, and who had received communications from God, but he had also heard the other side of the problem in the Greek University, where he was brought into contact with human reason at its best.

## THIS OF WHICH HUMAN KNOWLEDGE COULD NOT LEARN ON ITS OWN

He begins the treatment of his subject by telling the Greeks that neither scientific

NOTES

investigation nor human reason has ever been able to discover a sure foundation upon which a True spiritual system could be built. He says, *"Eye hath not seen, nor ear heard, . . . the things which God hath prepared for them that love Him"* (I Cor. 2:9).

The context makes it clear that these *"things"* consist of the Revelation of Truth, the Holy Scriptures.

But not only has scientific investigation never discovered this Truth, but this Truth as well, has not been produced by the activity of man's reason, for he said, *"Neither have entered into the heart of man"* (I Cor. 2:9).

The Greek word translated *"entered,"* does not refer to something entering the mind from the outside, but was used of things that come up in one's mind, in other words berthed in one's mind. We use the expression today, *"It never entered my mind,"* meaning that the things never occurred to us.

Thus, we have the statement of Paul that the Truth of Scripture never arose in the consciousness of man, never found its source in the reason of man.

## THE ERRONEOUS DIRECTION OF HUMAN REASONING

Observe the bearing this has upon teaching that finds its basis in the theory of Evolution, teaching to the effect that all that the human race knows is the result of some type of Divinity resident in man, which in some way, they say, makes man god, and that, therefore, all knowledge has come from within the race, none from without.

After asserting the fact of the final inadequacy of reason in solving the riddle of existence, Paul proceeds to describe the three successive steps in the transmission of Truth from the Heart of God to the heart of man.

These are, *"Revelation,"* the Act of God the Holy Spirit imparting to the Bible Writers Truth incapable of being discovered by man's unaided reason (I Cor. 2:10-12): *"Inspiration,"* the Act of God the Holy Spirit enabling the Bible Writers to write down in God-chosen words, infallibly (without error), the Truth revealed (I Cor. 2:13): and *"Illumination,"* the Act of God the Holy Spirit enabling Believers to understand the Truth given by Revelation and written down by Inspiration (I Cor. 2:14-16).

NOTES

## REVELATION

We will deal first with *"Revelation."*

Paul wrote, *"But as it is written, Eye hath not seen . . . , with the first word being but."* However, the Translators should have translated it *"for,"* since the Greek word here originally used is an explanatory word.

Paul explains that the Bible did not come by the way of scientific investigation and human reason, but that it came in another way, by *"Revelation."* Then he shows that the very fact that God gave this Truth by Revelation proves that in the nature of things it could not have been given in any other way, and proceeds in verse 11 to show that this is true.

The word *"revealed"* is the translation of a Greek word which means *"to uncover, to lay open what has been veiled or covered up."* Consequently, the pronoun *"us,"* in the 10th Verse, refers to the Bible Writers, for Paul is explaining to the Greeks his knowledge of the Truth.

The Holy Spirit Who searches the deep things of God, uncovered this Truth to the vision of these men who wrote in the Old Testament, and the New as well!

## HUMAN REASON IS OUT

Then Paul by the use of pure logic proves to these Greeks the impossibility of discovering God's Word through scientific investigation or human reason. The word *"man"* in the Greek as used in Verse 9 (I Cor. 2:9) is not the word which refers to an individual male member of the human race, but is the generic term for man, which includes individuals of both genders.

The second use of the word *"man"* (vs. 11) is accompanied by the definite article (the man) which in Greek points out individuality. Thus, the Translation could read, *"For who is there of men who knows the things of the* (individual) *man."* That is, no individual knows the inner thoughts and heart-life of another person. Man is inscrutable (hard to grasp) to his fellowman.

## THE SPIRIT OF MAN

The word *"spirit"* as used by Paul in Verse 11, in the Greek refers to the rational spirit of man, the power by which a human being reasons, thinks, wills, and decides. Again, the word *"man"* in the phrase *"save the spirit of man,"* is preceded by the article, i.e., *"the man."*

Therefore, it can be translated, *"For who is there of men who knows the things of the* (individual) *man except the spirit of* (that) *man which is in him."* Only the individual knows what is in his heart of hearts. To his fellowman he is inscrutable.

## PAUL'S LOGIC

Just so, Paul says, logic will lead us to the conclusion that if a man is inscrutable to his fellowman, so God must be inscrutable to man as well. And just as only the individual person knows what is in his own heart, so only God knows what is in His Own Heart.

Therefore, if man finds it impossible through scientific investigation and human reason to discover the inner secrets of his fellowman, it is clear that he cannot find out the Mind of God by the same methods. The only way in which a person can come to know the inner heart-life of another person is to have that person uncover the secrets of his inner life to him.

It likewise follows that the only way in which a person can know the Mind of God is to have God uncover His Thoughts to man. Thus, Paul has demonstrated to these Greeks the absolute need of a Revelation from God if we are to know what is in God's Heart.

The first step, therefore, in the transmission of Truth from the Heart of God to the heart of the Believer is *"Revelation,"* the Act of God the Holy Spirit uncovering the things in the Heart of God to the Bible Writers, thus imparting the Truth of Scripture to them.

## VERBAL INSPIRATION

This brings us to the Doctrine of *"Verbal Inspiration"* which Paul states in Verse 13.

After the Bible Writers had been given the Truth by means of the Act of the Holy Spirit in uncovering it to them, the Apostle says that they were not left to themselves to make a record of it. It is one thing to know a certain fact. It is quite another altogether to find the exact words which will give someone else an adequate understanding of that fact.

And right here is where the need of Verbal Inspiration comes in. Paul first makes the negative statement, *"Which things we speak, not in words taught by human wisdom."* That is, the words which the Bible Writers used were not dictated by their human reason or wisdom.

NOTES

## TAUGHT BY THE SPIRIT

Then the Apostle makes the positive statement, *"But which the Holy Spirit teacheth"* (I Cor. 2:13). He says that the words which the Bible Writers use were taught them by the Holy Spirit. That is, as they wrote the Scriptures, the Holy Spirit who had revealed the Truth to them, now chooses the correct word out of the Writer's vocabulary, whose content of meaning will give to the Believer the exact Truth God desires him to have.

This, however, does not imply mechanical dictation nor the changing of the Writer's own personality. The Holy Spirit took the Writers as He found them and used them infallibly.

Luke's Greek is the purest and most beautiful. Paul's Greek is far more involved and difficult than, for instance, that of John's, for Paul had university training, while John's knowledge of Greek was that of the average man of the First Century who knew Greek as his second language but never had any formal training in it.

However, whether it is the pure Greek of Luke, the difficult Greek of Paul, or the simple Greek of John, it is all correct as to grammar and syntax, i.e., *"the way in which words are put together to form phrases, clauses, or sentences."* In other words, the Holy Spirit observed the rules of Greek grammar (for that was the language then used) as they existed in the common Greek of that time. And the wonder of it all is seen in the fact that John brings to his readers, in his simple Greek, truth just as precious and just as deep, as Paul does in his intricate constructions and involved sentences.

In fact, God the Holy Spirit is above language. Thus, we have in the original Hebrew and Greek Texts of the Bible Manuscripts, the very Words that God taught the Writers to use as they recorded the Truth which they had received by Revelation. This is what is meant by *"Verbal Inspiration."*

## CHOOSING THE RIGHT WORD

Then Paul in the words *"comparing spiritual things with spiritual"* (vs. 13), explains this process of choosing the right word in each case.

We will look carefully at the Greek word translated *"comparing,"* for it throws a flood of light on Paul's teaching of Verbal Inspiration.

The word *"comparing"* as Paul used it, is a compound of the verb meaning *"to judge,"* and a preposition meaning *"with,"* thus *"to judge with."*

It speaks of the action of judging something with something else. For instance, a Milliner wishes to trim a red hat with ribbon of the same color. She takes the hat over to the spools of ribbon and *"judges"* the various shades or red ribbon *"with"* the hat.

She compares the hat with ribbon after ribbon in an attempt to find one which will exactly match the color of the hat. She rejects one after another until she finally finds one ribbon that exactly matches the hat. And that is exactly what the word means, *"to join fitly together, to combine, to compound,"* i.e., *"comparing."*

That is just the procedure which the Bible Writers went through in writing their Books. As led by the Holy Spirit, they searched their vocabularies for the exact word which would adequately express the Truth they wished to record. By the process of comparing the word with the Truth they wished to write down, they rejected all those words which the Holy Spirit showed them would not correctly express the thought, and finally chose the word to which the Holy Spirit had led them, and upon which the Holy Spirit had put His Stamp of Approval.

Thus, the Holy Spirit allowed the Writers the free play of their personalities, vocabulary, and training, while at the same time guiding them to make an infallible record of Truth infallibly revealed.

Consequently, Paul's statement, *"Comparing spiritual things with spiritual"* (vs. 13), to help us understand it even better, could be translated, *"combining spiritual things with spiritual words,"* or *"putting together spiritual words to spiritual things."*

## ILLUMINATION

We now come to the Doctrine of *"Illumination,"* namely, the Act of God the Holy Spirit enabling the Believer to *understand* the Truth given by Revelation, and by Inspiration written down.

Paul says, *"The natural man receiveth not the things of the Spirit of God"* (vs. 14). The word *"natural"* is the translation of a Greek word which Paul uses to describe to the Corinthian Greeks the unregenerate man at his best, the man whom Greek Philosophy commended, the man actuated by the higher thoughts and aims of the natural life.

NOTES

The word used here is not the Greek word which speaks of the sensual man. It is the word coined by Aristotle to distinguish the pleasures of the soul, such as ambition and the desire for knowledge, from those of the body. The natural man spoken of here is the educated man at the height of his intellectual powers, but devoid of the Spirit of God.

The word translated *"receiveth"* does not imply an active appropriation, but a certain attitude of passive acceptance when favorable, and of rejection if unfavorable.

This man, whose powers of apprehension are limited to the exercise of his reason, does not admit these spiritual things into his heart. The reason for this rejection is that they are foolishness to him.

## THE SPIRIT OF GOD AND THE BELIEVER

Then Paul states the impossibility of man by natural reason knowing and understanding the Scriptures, and the reason being, because they are spiritually discerned.

The Greek word translated *"discern"* means *"to investigate, inquire into, scrutinize, sift, or to question."* Thus, the investigation of, inquiry into, scrutinizing, and sifting of Scripture Truth is done in the energy of the Holy Spirit Who illuminates the Sacred Page of Scripture to the Believer.

It is *"he that is spiritual who judgeth all things"* (vs. 15).

The word *"judgeth"* is the translation of the same Greek word rendered *"discerneth."* The Spirit-controlled Christian investigates, inquires into, and scrutinizes the Bible, and comes to an appreciation and understanding of its contents, as he is guided and helped by the Holy Spirit.

(The material on Verbal Inspiration was supplied by Kenneth S. Wuest.)

(11) "FOR WHAT MAN KNOWETH THE THINGS OF A MAN, SAVE THE SPIRIT OF MAN WHICH IS IN HIM? EVEN SO THE THINGS OF GOD KNOWETH NO MAN, BUT THE SPIRIT OF GOD."

The question, *"For what man knoweth the things of a man, save the spirit of man which is in him?"*, means as we have stated, that a man does not even know what is in the heart of another man, much less what is in the Heart of God, unless the Lord reveals such to man. Man can only know what is in his own mind and heart, which speaks of his spirit, which is the part of man that knows, i.e., the will, the ability to reason, the intellect.

Men may be able to discern some things about another man, by testing the spirit of that particular individual; however, even then, it is more guesswork than anything else.

## THE SPIRIT OF MAN

The spirit and the soul of man are two different things, but yet are very similar. Actually, this Eleventh Verse tells us that the spirit is the part of man which *"knows."* Consequently, it pertains to the will, the intellect, the mind, etc.

The soul of man is the part of man which *"feels,"* in other words, his passions, etc. As stated, the soul and spirit of man are indivisible, meaning they cannot be separated. They leave the human being only at death, meaning it is the body which dies, and not the soul and spirit.

## THE INNER MAN

Peter said, *"But let it be the hidden man of the heart, in that which is not corruptible"* (I Pet. 3:4). *"Incorruptible"* in the Greek is *"aphtharsia,"* which means *"unending existence, immortality, incorruption."* The idea is, as stated, that the soul and the spirit of man cannot die or be destroyed. They are the parts of man which are eternal. That is why the soul and the spirit are of such consequence, hence Jesus saying that a man is profited nothing if he gain the world, the whole world, and lose his own soul (Mat. 16:26).

The soul and the spirit of man are so important, so valuable, and because they are eternal, that God would become man and die on a Cross, in order that the soul might be saved. Considering the great price paid, this should give us an idea as to the value of the eternal soul of man.

A simple *"yes"* to the Lord Jesus Christ, will guarantee the salvation of the soul. Today is the day of Salvation.

The phrase, *"Even so the things of God knoweth no man, but the Spirit of God,"* refers to the fact, that men cannot learn about God through scientific investigation or human reasoning, but only as the Spirit of God reveals such to the Believer. Without Spirit-directed Revelation, which is always based on the Word of God, it is impossible for man to know anything about God.

NOTES

## THE SPIRIT WORLD

If one is to notice, at times Psychics and Fortunetellers, etc., claim that their revelations are from the Lord. I suppose they think such claims will make their services more desirable, or it may be, that some of them are deceived by Satan, which they no doubt are.

Inasmuch as their manner of operation is unscriptural, and that God does not appear to people through crystal balls, tarot cards, or through the voices of dead people, etc., we know that what they are receiving is not from God, but rather from Satan, i.e., the world of spiritual darkness. In other words, they are trafficking with demon spirits.

However, Satan not only traffics in the world of fortunetelling or psychic phenomenon, but traffics often in the realm of familiar spirits (Lev. 19:31; 20:6; Deut. 18:11; I Sam. 28:3, etc.).

These spirits imitate dead people, and in many cases the *"Virgin Mary."* Actually, if it is not something made up out of thin air, this is what is being seen by many Catholics respecting the sightings of who they think is the Virgin Mary. It is a familiar spirit imitating her, consequently, from the Devil.

Pope John Paul II claims to have been visited by the Virgin Mary many years ago, telling him that he would be Pope. Consequently, since his appointment to that position (not by God), Mary-worship has increased at least fourfold, if not up to tenfold. In 1997, this Pope even suggested that Mary be made into co-Redemptress with the Lord Jesus Christ. Of course, such is rank blasphemy.

So, who actually appeared to Pope John Paul II those years ago?

To be sure, it was not the Virgin Mary, because such is unscriptural. Without a doubt, it was a familiar spirit, which means the man was and is guided by Satan.

Unfortunately, Catholics are not the only ones deceived by that which claims to be of God, but is really of the spirit world of darkness. Millions of Protestants (a word we do not hear much anymore), are exactly as the woman at Jacob's Well, when Jesus said unto her concerning worship, *"Ye worship ye know not what"* (Jn. 4:22). In other words, your worship is not of the Spirit of God, but rather of self or either from the Powers of Darkness.

So we have two situations respecting Revelation given by the Spirit of God:

1. First of all, any and all Revelation from God will always come through the Person, Office and Ministry of the Holy Spirit.

2. Second, the individual must really know the Word of God, in order to know if what is being received is actually from the Spirit of God, or spirits of darkness. That is why John the Beloved said, *"Believe not every spirit, but try the spirits whether they are of God: because many False Prophets are gone out into the world"* (I Jn. 4:1).

(12) "NOW WE HAVE RECEIVED, NOT THE SPIRIT OF THE WORLD, BUT THE SPIRIT WHICH IS OF GOD; THAT WE MIGHT KNOW THE THINGS THAT ARE FREELY GIVEN TO US OF GOD."

The phrase, *"Now we have received, not the spirit of the world,"* refers to the power of Satan, who is the *"god of this present world"* (II Cor. 4:4). One of the reasons that intellectual man cannot understand God, is because he has *"the spirit of the world,"* and not the *"Spirit of God."* As we have repeatedly stated, it is literally impossible for anyone with this *"spirit"* to know anything about God, to understand anything about God, or to come to any correct conclusion about God. In fact, a little six-year-old girl who truly knows Jesus as her Saviour, knows more about God, than the most educated Professor in the most prestigious schools of the world who is not Born Again.

The phrase, *"But the Spirit which is of God,"* means simply that when the believing sinner came to Christ, he did not receive more of the *"spirit of the world,"* which he already had, but rather the *"Spirit of God,"* which now makes it possible for him to understand the things of God. The Divine Nature is imparted to the Believer, which changes him completely, all done by the Holy Spirit.

The phrase, *"That we might know the things that are freely given to us of God,"* means that this is the only way one can truly know.

*"Freely"* in the Greek is *"dorean,"* and means *"graciously bestowed."* In fact, all of God's Gifts are *"without money and without price"* (Isa. 55:1), and not *"to be bought with money"* (Acts 8:20).

NOTES

The only thing that is required is consecration to the Lord, and Faith in His Promises (Jn. 3:16; Eph. 2:8-9).

(13) "WHICH THINGS ALSO WE SPEAK, NOT IN THE WORDS WHICH MAN'S WISDOM TEACHETH, BUT WHICH THE HOLY SPIRIT TEACHETH; COMPARING SPIRITUAL THINGS WITH SPIRITUAL."

The phrase, *"Which things also we speak,"* means that Paul was speaking only that which God had given him to speak. He is in effect saying, that what he is writing is from the Lord, therefore, inspired by the Holy Spirit, therefore, not only revealed but illuminated as well, which means that it can be understood by all Believers. Paul is speaking here of Verbal Inspiration, which pertained to all the Bible Writers, and to which we have alluded.

The phrase, *"Not in the words which man's wisdom teacheth,"* refers to corrupted wisdom, which is of the *"spirit of the world."* Consequently, and as stated, it cannot know anything about God, but yet, that is what comes from behind many if not most modern pulpits.

The phrase, *"But which the Holy Spirit teacheth,"* pertains to the Word of God, and means that the Bible is not the words of men, even though written by men, but rather of God, therefore, error-free.

The phrase, *"Comparing spiritual things with spiritual,"* means as previously stated, that the Bible Writers were inspired by the Holy Spirit to write what they did, even with the Holy Spirit helping them to find exactly the right word to express what He (the Spirit of God) wanted said. Please allow me to say it again. The Holy Spirit allowed the Writers the free play of their personalities, vocabulary, and training, while at the same time guiding them to make an infallible record of Truth infallibly revealed.

## THE WISDOM OF GOD

Inasmuch as Paul mentioned man's wisdom and the Wisdom of the Holy Spirit, Who in fact is Wisdom, perhaps a fuller treatment would be helpful.

The concept of wisdom is of course, an important one. It may be particularly important for us in our technological society, where we place a strong emphasis on knowledge.

However, the type of wisdom of which we wish to address, is not that of the world but rather of God.

THE HEBREW WORDS

The basic word group expressing the idea of wisdom in the Old Testament includes *"hakam"* and its sister word *"hokmah."* Together they occur in the Old Testament over 300 times.

This word (hakam-wisdom) expresses a person's approach to life. Wisdom to master life's challenges can be found only in one's relationship with God. The Hebrew view is practical in focus. Wisdom is expressed in Godly living, *"For the Lord gives wisdom, and from His Mouth come knowledge and understanding.*

*"Then you will understand what is right and just and fair every good path.*

*"For wisdom will enter your heart, and knowledge will be pleasant to your soul.*

*"Wisdom will save you from the ways of wicked men, from men whose words are perverse"* (Prov. 2:6, 9-10, 12).

WISDOM AND THE WORD OF THE LORD

The wise person, then, is one who is sensitive to God and who willingly subjects himself to Him. The wise person is one who goes on to apply Divine Guidelines in everyday situations and, guided by God's Will, makes daily choices.

It is only in wedding the Lord's Words to experience that Wisdom can be found or demonstrated.

The wedding of knowledge and experience so that one gains skill and becomes wise is seen in other uses of the word *"Wisdom."* A person can be wise (skilled) in Arts (Ex. 36:1-4), in Government (Prov. 8:15), in making money (Prov. 8:18).

Combining knowledge and experience to successfully meet moral or other challenges in daily life is what demonstrates the possession of wisdom.

WISDOM LITERATURE

In the Old Testament the Books of Proverbs, Ecclesiastes, and Job, are looked at and referred to as *"Wisdom Literature."* Actually, several Psalms fall into this category as well (Ps. 19, 37, 104, 107, 147, 148).

Wisdom Literature does not express itself in terms of Prescriptive Law, nor even in exposition of the Mosaic Law. Rather, Wisdom Literature describes a lifestyle, contrasting the wise and foolish choices that individuals make.

Only one who approaches life with a deep awe and fear of the Lord will discover and apply wisdom.

NOTES

THE NEW TESTAMENT

The concept of Wisdom in the New Testament is expressed by the Greek word *"sophia."* In Greek culture, *"Wisdom"* represented an unusual ability, an attribute. By New Testament times the subject of *"Wisdom"* was philosophic or speculative knowledge, at least as it referred to the world.

Words in this group appear seldom in the Gospels, but when they do appear, they are used in the Old Testament sense. Actually, the greatest number of uses of *"wise"* and *"wisdom"* are clustered in I Corinthians Chapters 1-3, even as we are now studying. In the balance of the New Testament, *"Wisdom"* focuses on that same practice of the Godly life that is the concern of the Old Testament.

I CORINTHIANS

The Book of I Corinthians is a Book of problems. Paul focuses on issue after issue that tore at the unity of the Church in Corinth. Again and again he guided his Readers to an understanding of how to deal effectively with each.

The first problem Paul touched in this Epistle was the divisions that developed at Corinth as little groups formed, claiming allegiance to this or that leader. Paul invited the Corinthians to think about the nature of wisdom, for he believed their division was caused by the application of a merely human wisdom to spiritual issues, which continues to plague the Church even today.

THE WORLD AND THE KNOWLEDGE OF GOD

In I Corinthians 1:18-31, even as we have already studied, Paul notes that the world's wisdom did not bring it a knowledge of God. This is because the Jews and the Greeks approached God on their own terms. Their basic orientation to life left no room to recognize Christ as the Power and Wisdom of God (I Cor. 1:24). Here Christ is presented as God's practical solution to the problem of man's alienation from God the One Who Himself is *"our Righteousness, Holiness, and Redemption."*

HUMAN WISDOM

Human wisdom — man's approach to the problem of relationship with God — is thus demonstrated to be foolishness, though God's approach is viewed as foolishness by the world.

Paul shows that for a correct perspective, one must gain access to the very thought processes of God (I Cor. Chpt. 2). These thought processes have been revealed to us in words taught by the Holy Spirit (I Cor. 2:13-16; II Tim. 3:15; II Pet. 3:15).

In I Corinthians Chapter 3, Paul returns to the problem of divisions. The Corinthians had been acting and thinking as mere human beings, not applying the Revealed Words of God nor seeking to discern their implications.

Paul then applies several basic Truths to show the error in the debate over leaders (I Cor. Chpt. 4).

In this extended Passage *"wisdom"* represents the perspective or orientation that one brings to dealing with the issues of life. Human beings are foolish, because they fail to recognize the fact that their notions must be subject to Divine evaluations.

Only when one abandons what seems wise by human standards to accept without hesitation the Divine viewpoint as revealed in Scripture can he claim true wisdom.

WISDOM AS THE HOLY SPIRIT INTENDS

This theme — that Christ is God's Wisdom, applied to resolve the problems caused by human sin (I Cor. 1:3) — is picked up in Ephesians 3:10, which expresses God's intention to make known to spiritual (Angelic) powers *"the manifold Wisdom of God"* as His Purposes are worked out in history *"through the Church."*

In most places, however, *"Wisdom"* is the Divine perspective available to and applied by Believers to the issues of their lives. Thus, Paul prayed that God would fill the Ephesians with *"the Spirit of Wisdom and Revelation"* so they might grasp and experience the power available in Christ (Eph. 1:17).

The same theme is addressed in a prayer in Colossians Chapter 1. Paul yearned for these Believers to be filled with a knowledge of *"what God has willed"* (Col. 1:9). He qualified his

NOTES

prayer by adding that the knowledge must be treated with Spiritual Wisdom and insight, so that the Believers might *"live a life worthy of the Lord and . . . please Him in every way . . ."* (Col. 1:10). It is Wisdom that guides the application of what is known.

RELIGIOUS NOTIONS WHICH HAVE THE APPEARANCE OF WISDOM

Paul turned again to human notions in Colossians 2:23, speaking of religious approaches that *"have an appearance of Wisdom,"* that is, approaches that seem to be practical, effective ways to spiritual growth. But again Paul turned his readers to Jesus.

The Word of Christ, dwelling in us, alone enables us to teach and admonish each other in Wisdom (Col. 3:16).

James, reflecting the Old Testament's convictions, said that one who lacks Wisdom should appeal to God and expect God to provide it (James 1:5-7).

Later (James 3:13-18) he carefully defined the characteristics of the Wisdom that comes from above.

It is *"pure, . . . peace-loving, considerate, submissive, full of Mercy and good fruit, impartial and sincere."* A character that displays envy, selfish ambition, and similar destructive traits is not from God.

Wisdom, then, is a critical concept in both Testaments: Wisdom is concerned with how one lives his or her life. Both the Old Testament and the New Testament make it clear that only when our life is oriented to God, and His Revealed Viewpoint is applied to our daily experience can we become truly wise (Richards).

Inasmuch as Paul addressed himself to teaching, both that which comes from the world and that which comes from God, I think it would be wise to also look at this very important subject, which affects every single Believer.

TEACHING

It is never easy for a person to divorce himself from his experiences in his own age and society. We carry into our reading and study of Scripture assumptions that color perceptions of meaning without even being aware of all that we import.

This is particularly true in the area of Teaching and Learning, for assumptions about the nature and goal of education vary dramatically from culture to culture. Thus, one of our major concerns in looking at words associated with education and Scripture, and particularly words translated *"teach"* and *"learn,"* is to recapture the community and interpersonal context in which they functioned and to understand the goal as well as the process of Teaching as outlined in the Scriptures.

## THE BIBLICAL CONCEPT OF TEACHING AND LEARNING

The Hebrew words for Teaching and Learning given in the Old Testament, give us insight into several aspects of the Biblical concept. Teaching and Learning involve hearing a word addressed from outside — from the older and wiser person or, most often, from God Himself.

The word heard is an instruction, designed to shape the Learner's moral perceptions and so to lead to Godly living. The focus on shaping life's choices is significant. In the Old Testament, the goal of education is a Godly life, one that expresses the Believer's loving fear of the Lord.

## PROVERBS

The famous opening lines of Proverbs explain the purpose not only of those recorded sayings but also of education itself as understood in the Old Testament:

*"For attaining wisdom and discipline; for understanding words of insight; for acquiring a disciplined and prudent life, doing what is right and just and fair; for giving prudence to the simple, knowledge and discretion to the young — let the wise listen and add to their learning, and let the discerning get guidance"* (Prov. 1:2-7).

Thus, while teaching and learning involve the Word coming from outside, that Word is sharply focused on the moral life. To learn is to attain wisdom, discipline, and insight, and to acquire prudence so that one does what is right and just and fair.

## THE MANNER OF THE SPIRIT

Teaching and Learning involve the Divine Word, as we have stated, from *"outside"* that must be *"heard."*

So there is unquestionably a *"content"* in Old Testament education. But because learning is viewed as shaping values, character, and lifestyle itself, the content must be processed in a life-transforming way. It is not enough to gain mental mastery of Biblical information. The Divine Word must be taken into the very heart of the learner and expressed in his every choice and act.

It is important, therefore, to note the context in which the Word from outside is heard and processed. Moreover, unlike teaching in our culture, teaching as envisioned in the Old Testament does not presuppose a classroom. Rather, the Old Testament presupposes a distinctive community and a distinctive interpersonal setting for teaching and learning — meaning that the entire community is supposed to learn the Word of God.

## THE COMMUNITY CONTEXT OF THE OLD TESTAMENT

The Bible Student in Old Testament times was viewed as living in a Faith Community that itself was to be shaped by the Words of God. The *"Torah* (Law),*"* the Divine Instruction, patterned the society, and the whole community was to be guided by God's Word. Thus, the content to be taught and learned was to be practiced by members of the community with whom the Student lived; modeling was a basic aspect of the process by which the Divine Word was taught.

In fact, Old Testament Law established annual worship Festivals in which the entire community was to participate. Some of these Festivals involved reenactment of the great historic events in which God had acted for the benefit of His People Israel.

## PARTICIPATION

Participation by all members of the family in such events was another vital aspect of Old Testament Bible Education, which in essence was the entirety of education.

Each celebration was designed to help the Student participate in and identify with God's Acts and capture personally the identity shared by all Israel as God's Special People.

The Sacrificial System symbolically communicated the great themes taught formerly in the Scripture. The reality of sin, the necessity of Atonement, and the willingness of God to accept the sinner who came to him were

NOTES

constantly acted out as persons brought the required Sacrifices to the Priests.

These elements are only a few of the aspects of the Old Testament lifestyle through which the community itself provided a unique context for teaching and learning God's Word. But it is important for anyone who thinks seriously about education in Faith to consider community relations along with the content to be taught.

To teach God's Word-from-outside with life-changing impact, modeling and example, participation and identification, and symbolic rehearsal, remain highly important.

## FAMILY

The lifestyle of the Community of Faith as laid out in the Mosaic Law is itself a vital context for teaching. But so are the more intimate relationships that the Student has with his Teachers. Deuteronomy 6:4-9 is the definitive Old Testament Passage. Israel is called on to love the Lord wholly. Only by Leaders who love God can the Words of God be truly heard.

The family is envisioned in this Passage as the Teaching unit, but it is in a broader, extended-family sense that we need to understand what we mean by the word *"family."*

The Words of God are to be in the heart of those Elders of the family who will be the Teachers (Deut. 6:6). The Words are to be spoken and impressed on the children. This is done, God told the Fathers, by talking *"about them* (Scriptures) *when you sit at home and when you walk along the road, when you lie down and when you get up"* (Deut. 6:7).

That is, as life is lived by adult and child, the recurrent experiences they share are to be constantly interpreted by the Divine Word. Thus, learning does not take place in classrooms but in the cycle of ordinary events, as everything is brought under the Light of the Word of God.

## THE TEACHING METHOD

One refers to God's Word in order to explain the *"why"* of life's choices as they are made. In this way, content and practical implication are always linked in the experience of the Learner.

This stands in contrast to much modern educational process, which is so designed that the Learner is expected to master content apart from his or her present experience.

NOTES

While we rightly focus on *what* is to be taught to build a Biblical understanding of life and to develop Christian Character, we all too often miss the process of the Teaching that enables us to impress God's Word from *"outside."*

The Old Testament shows us that teaching Faith and learning it are intended to take place in the context of a community that lives according to Scripture and in intimate personal relationship with those who share our lives and can help us sense what God's Word means for the reality of daily experience.

Bringing it up to modern times, if the Word of God is applicable only during the times we attend Church, we are missing the entirety of the import of what the Word is all about. It is actually meant to mold and shape our lives, and that means in every capacity. Consequently, as Israel of old, we are to apply the Word to everything we do, everywhere we go, everything we say, and all personal relationships.

## THE GREEK WORDS TRANSLATED *"TEACH"* AND *"LEARN"*

Although the vocabulary of Teaching and Learning shifts in the New Testament from Hebrew to Greek, basic assumptions about Faith do not change. There is still a Word from outside (the Word of God), intended to shape the Believer toward Holiness; and there is still a necessary process by which that Word is to be impressed upon the human heart.

So while the Greek vocabulary is significant in any study of teaching and learning respecting the New Testament, we must again be concerned about Scripture's assumptions concerning the context in which they function.

## TO TEACH

The Greek word *"Tidasko,"* which means *"To Teach,"* has broad application. It suggests a relationship between a Teacher and a Student or between an Instructor and an Apprentice. Teaching can involve informing, instructing, and demonstrating. The content may be knowledge or skills. In the Septuagint (the translation of the Old Testament from Hebrew to Greek), this word is commonly chosen to translate the Hebrew word *"lamad."*

In the New Testament, Jesus' Teaching as identified by this root included His Public Preaching and Instruction. It involved the use of illustrations and parables, as well as a direct statement of concepts. The most impressive aspect of Jesus as a Teacher, as far as His hearers were concerned, was apparently the complete authority with which He spoke of God (Mk. 1:22).

Because this Greek word has so many shades of meaning, the specific meaning must be determined from each context in which it appears.

## INSTRUCTION

Another Greek word for Teaching is *"Katecheo,"* and means *"instruction,"* which focuses on giving information or reporting. It is found only eight times in the New Testament (Lk. 1:4; Acts 18:25; 21:21, 24; Rom. 2:18; I Cor. 14:19; Gal. 6:6) and is not used in the Septuagint to translate any Hebrew term.

## TO EDUCATE

Another Greek word for Teaching is *"Paideuo,"* and means *"to instruct, train, and educate."* The Septuagint is most likely to use this word when translating the Hebrew *"yasar,"* which means *"to chastise, or correct."*

*"Paideuo"* often suggests discipline in the New Testament, not simply as chastisement but as the whole process by which God trains His People and testifies through a chastening experience to the Believer's sonship.

## TO LEARN

Another Greek word for Teaching is *"Manthano"* and means *"to learn,"* but in its most recognizable form, it means *"Disciple."*

In other words, a *"Disciple"* is a Learner.

## JESUS AS THE TEACHER

Jesus was not only recognized as a Miracle-Worker and Healer, but as well as a Teacher. Actually, the Gospels portray Him often addressed as *"Teacher."* As other Teachers in that day in Judea, Jesus' Teaching focused on shaping the Hearer's perception of God and God's Kingdom, and thus it dealt with the implications of a personal relationship with God.

In John's Gospel, much of Jesus' Public Instruction focused on Himself and His Own Place as Son of God.

Teaching situations are varied and complex. Jesus taught great crowds from a mountain or a boat anchored by the seashore. He dialogued as well. He illustrated Truth by pointing to the commonplace and by telling obscure Parables.

He answered questions and asked questions. Over and over again, events like the healing of a man with a paralyzed hand led to discussion in which the Character and Purposes of God were more sharply unveiled.

## JESUS AND HIS DISCIPLES

Jesus maintained an intimate Teaching Ministry with His Disciples. He answered their questions about a day's events and questioned them in turn.

The Disciples observed Jesus' Life while traveling with Him, and Jesus gave them life assignments, as when He sent them out two by two. This powerful, intimate form of instruction is best understood as Discipline, and it is significant that Jesus' Instructions to the Disciples after His Resurrection were that they should *"Go and make Disciples of all Nations,"* Teaching them to obey everything He had commanded them (Mat. 28:19-20).

Just as in the Old Testament era, the Teaching that Scripture finds significant is not that which provides information alone but also the Teaching that creates Disciples who live in responsive obedience to God's Will.

## TEACHING AND LEARNING IN THE EPISTLES

In the Epistles, the emphasis in contexts where words linked with Teaching and Learning are found rests squarely on content. The Doctrine of Christ is derived from outside of space and time, communicated in words *"taught by the Spirit"* (I Cor. 2:13).

Those who are skillful Teachers are charged with the task of maintaining the pattern of Doctrine delivered them by the Apostles (II Tim. 1:13). But in these same contexts we make surprising discoveries.

Teaching is to be not only of *"Sound Doctrine"* but of *"what is in accord with"* Sound Doctrine (Titus 2:1). Reverence, love for husbands, wives and children, self-control, doing what is good, subjection of slaves to masters, trustworthiness — all these things in Titus Chapter 2 are the object of Christian Teaching.

The pursuit of *"Righteousness, Faith, Love and Peace"* with those who *"call on the Lord out of a pure heart"* (II Tim. 2:22) is the product of a gentle instruction that relies on God to enlighten and transform (II Tim. 2:23-26).

FAIRLY EQUIPPED

Like the Old Testament, the New Testament places emphasis on a Word from outside; and like the Old Testament, that Word from outside is focused on transformation of the Believer. So the God-breathed Scripture (Word from outside), *"is useful for Teaching, Rebuking, Correcting and Training in Righteousness, so that the man of God may be thoroughly equipped for every good work"* (II Tim. 3:16).

Although the Teaching is not as clearly institutionalized in the New Testament, the parallelism between the Old Testament and the New Testament contexts for Teaching is also maintained.

THE CHURCH

Again like the Old Testament, the New Testament presupposes community as the context for Teaching and Learning. The Church as the Body of Christ is an extended family, in which the Believer, *"rooted and grounded in Love"* (Eph. 3:17), has the power to grasp the reality of Christ's Love and be filled with all the fullness of God.

Even Paul, struggling to describe the relationship with others to whom he so successfully taught the Word, could only turn to the image of the family (I Thess. 2:7-12).

Even the *"daily life"* emphasis of Deuteronomy Chapter 6 finds clear expression as Paul reminds Timothy, *"You . . . know all about my teaching, my way of life, my purpose, Faith, patience, Love, endurance, persecutions, sufferings . . ."* (II Tim. 3:10-11).

We cannot understand the Teaching of Faith in the Early Church simply by studying the Greek vocabulary. Understanding comes only by seeing how Teaching actually took place in the context of that first Christian Community.

TEACHERS OF CHRISTIAN FAITH

An understanding of how Faith was taught in the Early Church helps us toward a deeper understanding of the Teacher role. There had to be a mastery of the Word from outside, committed *"to reliable men who* (would) *also be qualified to teach others"* (II Tim. 2:2).

The phrase, *"Qualified to teach,"* should be understood in the context of qualifications for leadership laid down in the Pastoral Epistles, from which this *"comes."* Later in this same Chapter, Paul gives specific instructions for Timothy, one of which is that *"The Lord's servant . . . must be . . . able to teach"* (II Tim. 2:24).

In a previous Letter, Paul had said that a Bishop had to be *"able to teach"* (I Tim. 3:2). Of course, that means that he must be grounded in the Word of God. Both Passages use the same Greek word for this English phrase; it is *"didaktos,"* found only in these two Passages in the New Testament. Thus, skill in teaching is important for Church Leadership.

As was true in Deuteronomy's early prescription, so it remains true in the Church: to be a Teacher one must have taken the external Word into the heart, so that it finds expression in a Godly life.

MODERN CELL GROUPS

One of the modern methods of Evangelism presently, is the Cell Groups instituted by many Churches.

The community is broken up into particular areas, with a person assigned to that particular area, having a social/teaching session one night a week in their respective homes.

The idea is, that acquaintances or neighbors can be invited to these social gatherings where the Bible is discussed, and will probably feel more comfortable coming in that type of setting, than they would in many Churches. If they are not Saved, hopefully they will accept the Lord, and then begin to attend Church. In simplistic form this is the modern Cell Group.

Whatever problems there may be in such an effort, the major difficulty is going to center up in the very purpose for which the Cell Group is intended, the Teaching of the Word. Whatever the size of the Church instituting such a program, there simply aren't an abundance of God-called Teachers available for such a task. Consequently, for every one or two Teachers who truly are called by the Lord for this purpose, and are thoroughly grounded in the Word, consequently able to be a blessing to whoever sits under them, there are several more who are attempting to teach, and are really not qualified.

Many attempt to remedy this situation by proper instruction to these particular so-called Teachers. However, proper instruction

NOTES

(properly prepared lessons to teach) are only a part of Teaching, with the Call of God being the great part. The Truth is, there simply aren't that many who are truly called of the Lord to Teach, at least to attempt to care for 50 to 100 Cell Groups relative to a Local Church. Consequently, the far greater majority of people who sit under these folk, will not only not be helped regarding the Word of God, but oftentimes will be led astray, in other words, they are worse after they come than before they came.

Qualified Pastors can give proper instructions to Teachers, carefully preparing the lessons, but they cannot call men and women to Teach the Gospel, that being the work solely of the Holy Spirit. Furthermore, attempting to make Teachers out of those whom God has not called for that purpose, is contradicting the instructions given by Paul to Timothy when he said, *"The Lord's servant . . . must be . . . able to Teach,"* which means, called by the Lord and prepared for that purpose (II Tim. 2:24).

## THE BOOK OF ACTS

In the Book of Acts, which is the story of the Early Church and the way the Holy Spirit moved and operated in that sphere, we do not find anything of this nature. In fact, we find the opposite.

While it is true that most of the Churches of that time were in fact in houses (Acts 5:42; 16:40; 18:7; 20:20; Rom. 16:5; I Cor. 16:19; Col. 4:15; Phile. vs. 2), that was done out of necessity, Rome not allowing buildings of other nature, etc. And yet Paul was constantly attempting to get qualified Preachers and Teachers to visit the Churches, which he did as often as possible, knowing the necessity of proper Teaching (I Cor. 16:7, 10, 12; Eph. 6:21-22, etc.).

The Word of God must be the criteria for all things, and above all the Book of Acts and the Epistles must be the criteria for the Church. The Holy Spirit laid down the pattern in these Books and Epistles, and He intended that it be followed. Of course, we are speaking of Government, procedure, methods, etc.

The modern Cell Group effort, while creating much activity, will in the long run, probably not create very much proper Fruit for the Lord. While some few single Cells will probably accomplish an excellent work because of having a God-called Teacher in charge, for the most part, such will not be the case.

NOTES

## COMPLEX

Teaching and Learning are complex processes, whatever is being taught. The Teaching and Learning of Faith is even more complex.

Both Testaments agree that our Teaching is a Truth from God, which comes from outside the realm of human experience. Both agree that this Truth focuses on a personal relationship with God and on how the relationship is expressed in a Godly lifestyle.

To understand the process by which the external Word is translated into personal Faith and Godliness we need to examine, not just the terms used for Teaching and Learning in Hebrew and Greek, but also the contexts in which they were expected to function.

When we examine contexts, we see that response to the external Word and effective Teaching of it calls for participation in a Church, at least as it is addressed presently, in which that Word is put into practice, and it calls for intimate, ongoing relationships with those who model and explain the Word in life situations to which it applies.

(Much of the material on Teaching and Learning was derived from Lawrence O. Richards.)

(14) "BUT THE NATURAL MAN RECEIVETH NOT THE THINGS OF THE SPIRIT OF GOD: FOR THEY ARE FOOLISHNESS UNTO HIM: NEITHER CAN HE KNOW THEM, BECAUSE THEY ARE SPIRITUALLY DISCERNED."

The phrase, *"But the natural man receiveth not the things of the Spirit of God,"* presents the man who does not know God relative to the Born-Again experience. *"Natural"* in the Greek is *"psuchikos,"* and means *"the lower or bestial* (animal) *nature."*

This Passage presents man living under the control of fleshly passions, in other words, governed by the sin nature. Regrettably, this is not only the case with those who do not know Christ, but also with many Christians, who, although saved, still are being controlled by the sin nature.

Why?

How?

One can only be controlled by the Divine Nature, which every true Believer has as such a Believer places his faith entirely in Christ and the Cross, which then gives the Holy Spirit latitude to work in his heart and life, bringing about the desired results.

This is one of the reasons that the Teaching of Evolution is popular, in that man acts far more like an animal than he does the Image of God. In fact, without being Born Again, he only exhibits minute traces of that Image.

MAN'S INABILITY

This is the reason that it is impossible for man within his own capabilities to solve the crime problem, the drug problem, the sin problem, or man's aberrations in any capacity. Outside of God, and irrespective of education, environment, money, law, etc., man is helpless. To be frank, it would be easier to get a Sabertoothed tiger to act like a poodle dog, than to get man to conduct himself right outside of God. Due to the Fall the capabilities simply are not there. That is the reason a spiritual transformation which alone can be carried out by the Lord, and is referred to as the Born-Again experience, is absolutely necessary, if man is to actually change.

NATURE/NATURAL

The concepts expressed by these terms are reflected in the New Testament but not in the Old Testament. In Old Testament thought, all is related directly to God and to His Ordering. Actually, it was the Greeks who developed the categories by which the nature and origin of things in themselves might be explored. Consequently, the New Testament uses the vocabulary of the Philosopher in some places where English Versions read *"nature"* and *"natural."* But this is not always the case. For instance, the Holy Spirit through Paul recognizes the tripartite nature of man — spirit, soul, body (I Thess. 5:23).

SOULISH

The term *"phychikos,"* which means *"soulish,"* is found six times in the New Testament. Four times it is rendered *"natural"* (I Cor. 15:44, 46; Jude vs. 19), three of those being in contexts where the Resurrection Bodies are contrasted with the present bodies of Believers. In the other two instances it is rendered *"without the Spirit"* (I Cor. 2:14), which we are now studying, and *"unspiritual"* (James 3:15).

NOTES

The word describes a person who acts in or is controlled by his old human nature, or that which is of that old nature.

PROPER MEANING

What does the New Testament mean to express by the words *"nature"* and the *"natural"*? Romans 1:26-27 affirms heterosexual union as being according to nature, whereas homosexuality is *"unnatural."*

A significant statement is made in Romans 2:14, which teaches that human beings have a moral sense implanted within human nature, due to being created in the Image of God, despite the Fall. However, this capacity does not Save, but it does prove human moral responsibility.

Human beings are spoken of as *"by nature the children of wrath"* (Eph. 2:3) but are promised through Jesus a share in the *"Divine Nature"* respecting the New Birth (II Pet. 1:4).

CREATION AND THE FALL

The Pagans of course, did not believe in Creation as taught by the Bible, therefore, had no prescribed order on which to build anything. The Greeks attributed man's fallen nature to whim or blind chance. In fact, they knew things were wrong, terribly wrong, even as advanced by Socrates, Plato, and Aristotle; however, they had absolutely no idea as to how to address that wrong. They could see the good that should be, but had no way to cross the chasm to that good.

As Believers in the Word of God, we know that the world exhibits order and structure because that order was imposed by a Personal Being, namely the Lord, to Whom all the Creation testifies.

We also know that man is in the condition he is in, due to the Fall. Modern Science, falsely called, claims that man through Evolution is getting better and better, while the Bible teaches the very opposite.

*"Things"* in the Greek in Verse 14 is *"agathos,"* and means *"good things, or that which is beneficial."*

First of all, the Spirit of God has nothing but good things for man, but which the unregenerate man cannot perceive or receive.

The phrase, *"For they are foolishness unto him,"* refers to a lack of understanding.

*"Foolishness"* in the Greek is *"moria,"* and means *"silliness, absurdity."* It is this way because

the spiritual capacity of unregenerate man is dead, and, therefore, the things of the Lord are shut up to him. He has no capacity to grasp, understand, comprehend, or to know these *"good things."* Consequently, his depraved, lower nature, refers to that of the Lord which he does see, which he in no way understands, as silly or foolish.

That is why Jesus referred to this miraculous change which must be brought about in man, as the *"Born-Again"* experience (Jn. 3:3). As fallen man was born physically, he has to as well be born spiritually. This tells us how lost that man actually is, and how absolutely ridiculous it is for man to think that his problems can be changed by the foolishness of psychological counseling. Anyone who knows anything about the Bible knows better than that. Man's problem is not slight, small, or minor. In other words, he is not just slightly maladjusted, but actually going totally in the opposite and wrong direction. Consequently, he has to be totally turned around in a spiritual sense, which can only be done by Faith in what Jesus did at Calvary and the Resurrection, and by the Power of the Holy Spirit.

The phrase, *"Neither can he know them,"* means that the organ for the recognition of such Truths — namely, man's spirit — has become paralyzed or fallen into atrophy, from neglect; therefore, fallen man has lost the faculty whereby alone Spiritual Truth is discernable. It becomes to him what painting is to the blind, or music to the deaf.

This elementary Truth is again and again insisted on in Scripture, but ignored by skeptics (Jn. 3:3; 6:44-45; 14:17; Rom. 8:6-7; II Cor. 4:3-6).

Consequently, it is, perhaps, sufficient to say that if God has no need of perverted human knowledge, He as well, has still less need of human ignorance (Farrar).

NOTES

## THE FALL OF MAN

The Fall of man forms the whole of the Biblical Doctrine of sin and Redemption. To be sure, it does not rest only on a few vague Passages, but forms an indispensable element in the Revelation of Salvation. The whole contemplation of man and humanity, of nature and history, of ethical and physical evil, of Redemption and the way in which to obtain it, is connected in Scripture with a Fall, such as Genesis Chapter 3 relates to us.

Sin is a result of the Fall, and is common to all men (I Ki. 8:46; Ps. 14:3; 130:3; 143:2), and to every man from his conception (Gen. 6:5; 8:21; Job 14:4; Ps. 51:7).

Sin arouses God's anger, and because of its destructive nature, deserves all kinds of punishment, not only of an ethical but of a physical nature as well (Gen. 3:14-19; 4:14; 6:7-13; 11:8; Lev. 26:14; Deut. 28:15; Ps. 90:7).

The whole of Scripture proceeds from the thought that sin and death, which incapacitates man, are connected in the closest degree.

## THE CREATION OF GOD

The first man was created by God after His Own Image, not, therefore, in brutish unconsciousness or childlike innocence, but in a state of bodily and spiritual maturity, with understanding and reason, with knowledge and speech, with knowledge of God and His Law — actually, an intelligence that far exceeds anything we presently know.

## THE FIRST COMMAND

There was given to Adam and Eve a Command not to eat of the Tree of Knowledge of Good and Evil. This Command was not contained in the Moral Law as such; it was not a natural but a positive Commandment; it rested entirely and only on God's Will and must be obeyed exclusively for this reason.

In other words, God did not go into much explanation respecting the reason that man was not to eat of this particular Tree (Gen. 2:15-17), the idea being that God had given the Command, and it must be obeyed simply because this was God's Will. It placed before man the choice, whether he would be faithful and obedient to God's Word and would leave to Him Alone the decision as to what is good or evil, or whether man would reserve to himself the right arbitrarily to decide what is good or evil.

## THEOLOGY OR AUTONOMY?

Thus, the question was: Shall *"theonomy* (Government by God)*"* or *"autonomy* (self-government)*"* be the way to happiness and fulfillment of life? On this account also the Tree was called *"The Tree of Knowledge of Good and Evil."*

NOTES

It did not bear this name in the sense that man might obtain from it the knowledge of good and evil, for by his transgression he in Truth lost the knowledge of good. But the Tree was so named, because man, by eating of it and so transgressing God's Commandment, arrogated to himself (claimed or seized without justification) the capacity of independent choice of the means by which he would attain his happiness and fullness of life.

So, the Fall of man in the Garden of Eden, presents man now attempting to find his way without the aid of his Creator, because he has denounced his Creator Who is God. The stupidity of such an act knows no bounds, and presents the reason that man is ever casting about attempting to *"find himself."*

The world of Psychology would attempt to make man believe that those who are so lost, are only isolated cases, and are that way because of the foul deeds of others, etc. The Bible teaches the very opposite.

All men are lost, and, consequently, attempting to *"find themselves,"* but always in the wrong manner and the wrong way. Man cannot find himself, until he comes back to his Creator, and makes amends. Then and then alone, does he *"find himself"* and then and then alone does he know true fulfillment, life, and happiness.

## FALSE WAYS

In the meantime, he attempts to find such in money, immorality, drugs, power, education, scientific investigation, etc. All are bound to failure, because man's fulfillment lies only in his Creator, and that Way is Jesus and only Jesus (Jn. 10:10).

When man fell he spiritually died, which means that he was separated from God. To be sure his spirit did not die, because it is impossible for the spirit of man to die at least as we think of death. However, it did die to all things spiritual and because the link to the Creator was severed. In this state, dead in trespasses and sins, man has no contact with anything truly spiritual which is of God. However, being a creature who was originally made to worship God, man, irrespective of his fallen condition, casts about for something to worship.

In this false worship, for all men worship constantly, it is quite common to hear men speak of having a spiritual experience, which might pertain to any type of thing such as sporting events, transcendental meditation, or whatever. However, in Truth, what they are having is not a Biblical spiritual experience, but rather something engineered by Satan, which he does constantly with all who do not know the Lord.

## THE AWAKENING

On his own, at least within his own abilities, man cannot reach God in any capacity. When the Lord told Adam and Eve if they partook of *"The Tree of the Knowledge of Good and Evil"* that they would die, He meant exactly what He said. He was speaking of spiritual death which is separation from God, but this death in every form was complete at least as far as the spirit of man can die. However, it dies only to God, but not to evil or Satanic spirits, which are the cause of all the trouble, heartache, poverty, sickness, war, hatred, prejudice, etc. which are in the world today.

The only way that the fallen, depraved spirit of man can be awakened to God, is for the Word of God in some manner to be preached or given to him, which is then energized by the Holy Spirit. Man is then awakened to his terrible lost condition, placed under conviction, which is the Purpose and Work of the Holy Spirit (Jn. 16:7-11), with man then given the opportunity to accept or reject the Lord. If he accepts, he is instantly regenerated by the Power of the Holy Spirit, with the Divine Nature of God instantly imparted to him, which Jesus called *"Born Again"* (Jn. 3:3). Now he can respond to God!

The phrase, *"Because they are spiritually discerned,"* gives us the key to the Things of God. This means they are not scientifically discerned, not psychologically discerned, not intellectually discerned. In fact, they are not religiously discerned either, religion being the effort of man and not God.

*"Spiritually"* in the Greek is *"pneumatikos,"* and means *"that which is not physical but rather Divine."*

When the believing sinner comes to Christ, he is transformed by the Power of God, and as stated, the Divine Nature of God is implanted within his heart and life. Now he can understand the Things of God, which means he can discern or understand spiritual things.

## KNOWLEDGE OF GOD

Each of you holding this book in your hands, can remember back to before you were Saved, and recall that there was absolutely no knowledge of God in your heart at that particular time. In fact, some of you may have been raised in Church, but did not give your heart to God until your late teens or later. During your unconverted state, although in Church and hearing spiritual terminology constantly, still, if you will think back, you had little or no knowledge whatsoever of what that terminology actually meant.

That is the reason to an unsaved man or woman, Church is about as boring as anything could ever be, or anything which pertains to God for that matter. They do not understand what is happening or being said, until the Word of God begins to penetrate their heart, with the Holy Spirit placing them under conviction. Even then, the only understanding of spiritual things that they presently have, at least in that state, is the knowledge they are a sinner, and, consequently, dying lost without God. The Holy Spirit convicts them of sin by letting them know they are a sinner, and of Righteousness, by letting them know they do not have any, and of Judgment, by letting them know that there is a Judgment coming, unless they get right with God (Jn. 16:7-11).

(15) "BUT HE THAT IS SPIRITUAL JUDGETH ALL THINGS, YET HE HIMSELF IS JUDGED OF NO MAN."

The phrase, *"But he that is spiritual judgeth all things,"* portrays the spiritual person only as being capable of judgment.

## WHAT DOES IT MEAN TO BE SPIRITUAL?

The spiritual man has placed his faith in Christ and the Cross, and has done so exclusively. This means that he is now controlled by the Holy Spirit, and not by passions of the flesh (Rom. 8:1-2, 11). Most Christians have no understanding of the Cross regarding Sanctification; therefore they are governed by the sin nature, which causes all type of problems.

## HOW DOES THE SPIRITUAL MAN JUDGE ALL THINGS?

*"Judge"* in the Greek is *"anakrinei,"* and means *"to discern, examine, inquire, investigate, and scrutinize."* The term refers to a sifting process to get to the Truth by investigating, much as a Judge would do before making a decision. It means to know and understand the Word of God, and to be able to judge everything according to the Word of God.

NOTES

This term was used by Luke to describe the manner in which the Bereans examined the Scriptures to see if what Paul and Silas said was true (Acts 17:11). Therefore, the spiritual person is the person in whom the Holy Spirit rules, and does so by the Word of God (Rossier).

If one is to notice, the Scripture says *"all things,"* and not *"all people."* In fact, we are forbidden to judge the hearts or motives of other people, which only God is qualified to do (Mat. 7:1-2).

Because the Holy Spirit rules within the truly spiritual person, this individual is able to judge or scrutinize every situation as God Himself would judge or scrutinize it. In other words, this person sees things as God sees them. That is the idea as the Holy Spirit through Paul presents this Truth. Actually, the equipment of the spiritual person to investigate all things rests in the fact that he has the Mind of Christ (Phil. 2:5-8) (Rossier).

The phrase, *"Yet he himself is judged of no man,"* refers at least to judgment which God will accept.

In fact, he may be judged, condemned, depreciated or slandered every day of his life, and most probably is, but the arrow-flights of human judgment fall far short of him.

In fact, the Corinthians were judging and comparing Paul and Apollos and Peter; but their judgments were false and worthless, and Paul told them that it was less than nothing to him to be judged by them or by man's feeble transitory day (I Cor. 4:3) (Farrar).

One who criticizes a spiritual person who is doing all within his power to bring about God's Will is in danger of criticizing God Himself. In fact I know it can be said, that to oppose that which belongs to God, is to oppose God.

(16) "FOR WHO HATH KNOWN THE MIND OF THE LORD, THAT HE MAY INSTRUCT HIM? BUT WE HAVE THE MIND OF CHRIST."

The question, *"For who hath known the Mind of the Lord, that he may instruct Him?"*, is taken from Isaiah 40:14.

The idea is, that the Mind of the Lord as should be obvious, is the highest authority. God knows all and that means all in every sense. So, anyone who would question God is foolish to say the least.

The phrase, *"But we have the Mind of Christ,"* means that Paul and all spiritually mature people for that matter, have the correct information on the subject relative to the Word of God.

Incidentally, having the *"Mind of Christ"* as Paul uses the phrase here, means to think like Christ, rather than the way it is used in Philippians 2:5, which has to do with *"attitude."*

People who possess the Mind of Christ judge every situation as God would judge it, and they see things as God sees them, which is the intention of the Holy Spirit in the heart and life of the Believer.

And yet, in I Corinthians 14:37, Paul speaks of the spiritual person as one who is able to receive admonition. Consequently, one of the marks of true spirituality, is the recognition that one does not know it all. In his writings, Paul makes it clear, that spiritual people still can grow spiritually, still need admonition, and still need to be careful to avoid falling into sin.

Spiritual individuals have no right to be boastful about their relationship with Christ, nor to consider themselves on a higher spiritual level than other people. On the other hand, their chief characteristic is that they know and do God's Will. Always, spiritual Christians will have a keen interest in the Bible because God's Word expresses God's Will for His People. In other words, they measure everything by the Word of God, but always with a kind, gracious, forgiving and humble spirit (Rossier).

*"I have found His Grace is all complete,*
*He supplieth every need.*
*"While I sit and learn at Jesus' Feet,*
*I am free, yes, free indeed."*

*"I have found the pleasure I once craved,*
*it is joy and peace within;*
*"What a wondrous blessing! I am Saved*
*from the awful gulf of sin."*

*"I have found that hope so bright and clear,*
*living in the realm of Grace;*
*"Oh, the Saviour's Presence is so near,*
*I can see His smiling Face."*

*"I have found the joy no tongue can tell,*
*how its waves of glory roll!*
*"It is like a great o'er-flowing well,*
*springing up within my soul."*

*"It is joy unspeakable and full of glory,*
*full of glory, full of glory;*
*"It is joy unspeakable and full of glory,*
*Oh, the half has never yet been told."*

NOTES

## CHAPTER 3

(1) "AND I, BRETHREN, COULD NOT SPEAK UNTO YOU AS UNTO SPIRITUAL, BUT AS UNTO CARNAL, EVEN AS UNTO BABES IN CHRIST."

The phrase, *"And I, Brethren, could not speak unto you as unto spiritual, but as unto carnal,"* presents a solemn rebuke, and tells us several things:

1. First of all, it is possible as noted here, that Christians can be either carnal or spiritual, or somewhere in between. In fact, some of the Believers at Corinth were no doubt spiritual, but many of them were *"carnal,"* even as Paul relates here. Irrespective, we know that all were Saved, because Paul speaks of them as *"Brethren."*

2. *"Carnal"* in the Greek as used here is *"sarkikos,"* and means *"thinking and acting in the flesh and therefore not spiritual."* In other words, this type of Christian thinks and acts somewhat as an unsaved person, which is quite an indictment.

3. A particular segment of Believers in the Church in Corinth had begun to fight and squabble referring to a preference in Preachers, but it could refer to anything.

In this case, having a preference in Preachers is not necessarily wrong; however, when such a preference degenerates to the point of ending in strife, which causes division, it then is carnal and thereby sinful.

The words *"carnal"* and *"carnality"* are not, within themselves, sinful. As human beings, we eat, sleep, and do other such like things, which could be labeled as carnal; however, things become sinful when carried to the point of envying and strife, etc.

## INCONCEIVABLE!

For some in Corinth to criticize Paul, claiming that his teaching was elementary and that they preferred that of others, was spiritual ignorance at its highest. In effect, Paul is saying to them, *"You thought yourselves quite above the need of my simple teaching. You were looking down on me from the whole height of your spiritual inferiority. The elementary character of my Doctrine was after all the necessary consequence of your own incapacity for anything more profound."*

The phrase, *"Even as unto babes in Christ,"* ironically enough, is spoken to people who considered themselves to be spiritual giants. Actually, that is the entirety of the gist of this situation.

The idea is, that if people are truly spiritual, they will know what the Lord is doing, and will be in line with that which He is doing. If they are not truly spiritual, irrespective of their claims, they will do exactly as those at Corinth did, find fault with God's Program.

## AN EXAMPLE . . .

In the early Spring of 1997, the Lord began to move beautifully at Family Worship Center here in Baton Rouge. The Spirit of God would begin to move in the Services to such an extent, that oftentimes the entirety of the congregation was swept up in that which the Lord was doing. There was no fanaticism, only worship.

Unbidden and uncalled, at least by man, people would simply get out of their seats and begin to come down the Aisles, throwing themselves on the Altars, broken before the Lord. It was, I think, to date, the deepest and most spiritual Move regarding worship, we had ever had. How so thankful we were to the Lord. How so grateful we were to Him for touching and stirring us, for which we so desperately needed.

However, I noticed something that was completely shocking to me. Some of the people in the Church who I thought to be very spiritual, I found not to be so spiritual after all. In fact, some few of them began to severely criticize this which the Lord was doing. As stated, it came as a shock to me, because I felt these should have been the very ones who would have understood and known exactly what the Lord was doing.

NOTES

The Truth is, they did not know, because they actually were not spiritual but rather carnal.

And then again, some few to whom I would not have attributed a very high degree of spirituality, I found to the contrary.

I also learned, that when the Spirit of God really begins to move, even as it did in our Church, and even as I think it must have been doing somewhat at Corinth, such a Move will always draw out that which is genuine and that which is not, i.e., *"spiritual or carnal."* It may be relatively easy to fool other people for a while, but one cannot fool the Lord. He knows what is in the heart, and the Moving of His Spirit will generally bring it out.

The word *"babes"* as used here by Paul has a good and a bad sense. In its good sense it implies humility and teachableness, as in I Corinthians 14:20, *"In malice be ye babes"*; and in I Peter 2:2, *"As newborn babes, desire the sincere milk of the Word"*; and in Matthew 11:25. Here it is used in its bad sense of spiritual childishness (Farrar).

(2) "I HAVE FED YOU WITH MILK, AND NOT WITH MEAT: FOR HITHERTO YE WERE NOT ABLE TO BEAR IT, NEITHER YET NOW ARE YE ABLE."

The phrase, *"I have fed you with milk, and not with meat,"* means simply that he could not give them 12th grade material when they in fact, were still in the first grade, spiritually speaking. In fact, they were still in kindergarten, while all the time thinking of themselves as college graduates.

The word *"milk,"* as here used, is merely a symbolism, or figurative statement, regarding the elementary principles of Christianity (Heb. 5:11-14; 6:1). The word *"meat"* is another such example, as used by Paul, which denotes the opposite of *"milk,"* i.e., the great Doctrines of the Bible.

The phrase, *"For hitherto ye were not able to bear it,"* evidently has reference to the time that Paul planted this Church some few years earlier.

The record shows that Paul stayed at Corinth about two years. During this time he had the opportunity, as should be obvious, to observe the spiritual progress of all the people who had come to Christ. Evidently he saw the spiritual deficiency of some even then, in other words, that they were not growing in Christ as they should.

However, let it be quickly known, that this was not the fault of the Apostle or his teaching. Pure and simple, it was the fault of these Believers. It is hard to imagine people not growing spiritually under the Ministry of Paul, but it is plainly evident here that these did not experience proper spiritual growth.

Why?

## WHAT IS THE KEY TO PROPER SPIRITUAL GROWTH?

First of all there must be consecration and dedication to the Lord, which involves a proper prayer life and devotion to the study of the Word of God. These things must be habitual if there is to be proper spiritual growth.

Three key terms are associated in the New Testament with the ideas of growth or increase, and are expressed by three Greek words: *"pleonazo," "plethyno,"* and *"auxino."*

*"Pleonazo"* suggests an abundance, an increase in number; the New Testament uses it nine times (Rom. 5:20; 6:1; II Cor. 4:15; 8:15; Phil. 4:17; I Thess. 3:12; II Thess. 1:3; II Pet. 1:8).

*"Plethyno"* means *"to multiply, to abound,"* and it occurs 12 times in the New Testament (Mat. 24:12; Acts 6:1, 7; 7:17; 9:31; 12:24; II Cor. 9:10; Heb. 6:14; I Pet. 1:2; II Pet. 1:2; Jude vs. 2).

## GROWTH

The most fascinating of the terms is *"auxano,"* which, together with its related term *"auxo,"* means *"to grow."* These words (occurring 22 times in the New Testament) suggest the natural process that God has structured into His Universe. In the Gospels, they are used of the growth of lilies, trees, and the Child Jesus (Mat. 6:28; 13:32; Mk. 4:8; Lk. 1:80; 2:40; 12:27; 13:19).

In recording the response of John the Baptist to his Disciples, the Apostle John includes the fact that Jesus must increase, but John the Baptist must decrease (Jn. 3:30). These words are also used of the growth of the Church, spoken of as the increase of the Word of God, of which we are given a great clue respecting proper spiritual growth (Acts 6:7; 12:24; 19:20) and also the increase of the number of people (Acts 7:17).

In the Epistles we see another dimension of this concept. Believers, and the Church as an entity, are also involved in a growth process, superintended by God Himself (I Cor. 3:6-7; Eph. 2:21; 4:15). Individually, we grow in Faith (II Cor. 10:15), in knowledge of God (Col. 1:10), and in Grace (II Pet. 3:18).

Corporately, we grow up into a Holy Temple (Eph. 2:21), and we mature as the Body of Christ (Eph. 4:15-16).

## HIS SPECIFICATIONS

The suggestion of growth as a natural and a supernatural process is exciting. In the natural world the shape of the mature plant or animal is stamped with its genetic code. Each seed and each infant grow in an ordered way toward a maturity appropriate to its nature. The use of the Greek word *"auxano,"* which emphasizes the growth process, to speak of spiritual development is exciting.

God has designed the individual and the Church according to His Perfect Specifications. As we grow, we move toward a Perfection that He has planned for us.

## NOT AUTOMATIC

But Christian growth is not automatic. The New Testament makes it clear that we need to feed on the Word of God (Heb. 5:11-14; I Pet. 2:2). Consequently, this tells us that these who Paul is addressing in the Corinthian Church had not made the Word of God their Standard and Foundation. They were operating according to self-will, etc. In other words, they did not pass everything under the Light of the Word.

As well, we need to root ourselves deeply in the shared life of the believing community, which refers to Church (Eph. 3:17-19; 4:13-16).

In other words, it is very important as to where we attend Church. While Church has absolutely nothing to do with one's Salvation, it has very much to do with one's spiritual growth. If one is not receiving the proper teaching from behind the pulpit, proper growth cannot be insured or guaranteed, as should be obvious. So, if one attends Church for any reason except the following: A. The Word of God is preached in totality and without compromise; and, B. The Holy Spirit has freedom to move and operate in that Local Church. Unless that is the case, one is going to be greatly shortchanged in the spiritual sense.

## CHURCH?

Regrettably, most people attend Church for all the wrong reasons, love of Denomination,

NOTES

social activities, near one's home, a good sports program, where friends attend, etc., and a hundred and one other things that one could name. This means that which is referred to as Church, oftentimes in the Eyes of God is not Church at all, but some type of religious social center, etc.

The Believer is also called on to make personal choices that will facilitate his growth (II Cor. 9:6-11; Heb. 5:14). The Lord is deeply involved in the process of our growth, and He has ordained its direction.

Moreover, He has given us the privilege of cooperating with Him as He works within us. I speak primarily of control by the Holy Spirit.

Actually, the *"control"* the Holy Spirit has in our lives, determines our spiritual growth, but yet it is *"control"* which we must give Him, for He will never take it by force. We must be ever conscious of His Presence, and work with Him as He carries out the Will of God in our lives. Tragically, He is not given too very much control in the lives of most Christians, even as was the case at Corinth.

The phrase, *"Neither yet now are ye able,"* means that during this intervening three to five years, for that's how long most Scholars believe it was since Paul had planted this Church, there had been no spiritual advancement at all, at least for this particular group. What a tragedy! All of this time wasted on a spiritual treadmill.

And yet, I wonder how many of us fall into the same category?

## SPIRITUALLY ELITE?

What we are reading here is that which the Holy Spirit desired that Paul would say, which means that this was not merely Paul's assumption, but actually the way it was. And yet, this particular group in the Corinthian Church actually felt that they were the spiritual elite, in other words, spiritually mature, far advanced over all others. The Truth is that they were spiritual babies, the very opposite of their own thinking.

I wonder what their reaction was when they read Paul's Letter? The Holy Spirit designed these Words, and as such did so in order to bring these people to Repentance. To be sure, Repentance is not a place to which the spiritual elite are easily brought. Most do not even remotely see their need for such. And yet, there is evidence in Paul's Second Epistle to this Church, that they actually did repent (II Cor. Chpt. 7).

NOTES

Sometimes it takes hard preaching as Paul is doing here. In fact, this was not really the time for teaching, but rather preaching, and hard preaching at that! As is obvious, he pulled no punches, played no favorites, and spared no Scriptural ammunition.

(3) "FOR YE ARE YET CARNAL: FOR WHEREAS THERE IS AMONG YOU ENVYING, AND STRIFE, AND DIVISIONS, ARE YE NOT CARNAL, AND WALK AS MEN?"

The phrase, *"For ye are yet carnal,"* presents that which is even more blunt.

*"Carnal"* as used here, is different than the word *"carnal"* used in Verse 1. Carnal as used at the first, simply means *"of the flesh, resulting in weakness and the absence of spirituality."* Even though *"carnal"* as used here is also *"sarkikos,"* and involves all the meaning of the first word, it also pertains to the dominance of the lower nature and antagonism to the spiritual.

So, Paul is saying, *"You are not only operating in the flesh rather than the spiritual, you are also antagonistic to things which are truly spiritual."*

What an indictment!

The phrase, *"For whereas there is among you envying, and strife, and divisions,"* presents cravings of the sinful nature, i.e., *"works of the flesh"* (Gal. 5:20).

Partisanship (siding with a certain party in the Church) and discord, the sins of the Corinthians — sins which have disgraced so many ages of Church history — are *"works of the flesh"* (Gal. 5:19), and involve many other sins (James 3:16), and are, therefore, sure proof of the carnal mind, though they are usually accompanied by a boast of superior spiritual enlightenment (Farrar).

Jealousy is resentment which one feels concerning something possessed by another. Envy is the same, but with an added thrust. The one who envies desires that which the person has, whatever it might be, or else desires to destroy the person, so that his advantage is no longer possible. One can quickly see how evil that these things actually are.

*"Strife"* in the Greek is *"eris,"* and means *"a quarrel, wrangling, contention, debate,"* in other words, a running fight.

*"Division"* is *"dichostasia,"* and means *"disunion, dissension and sedition."*

It is a shame that such would be at work in a Local Church, which should be the very opposite, but regrettably, such is all too often the case.

The question, *"Are ye not carnal, and walk as men?"*, tells us why.

They were acting like unconverted people instead of acting like Christians. Once again, what an indictment!

(4) "FOR WHILE ONE SAITH, I AM OF PAUL; AND ANOTHER, I AM OF APOLLOS; ARE YE NOT CARNAL?"

The phrase, *"For while one saith, I am of Paul,"* once again portrays the Apostle rebuking first those adherents who turned his own name into a party watchword.

The phrase, *"And another, I am of Apollos,"* portrays as well, no doubt, the grief of Apollos that his name and Ministry were linked to such.

The Truth was, there was no difference in the Doctrine of Paul and Apollos. Both taught the same thing. As well, I am sure the same thing could be said of Simon Peter (Cephas). But yet, some of the Believers at Corinth had made more out of each of these men than they should have made and as a result, greatly hurt their own spiritual growth, and as well, hindered the Church.

The question, *"Are ye not carnal?"*, is meant to elicit a *"yes"* response, because the evidence is undeniable, *"envying, strife, and divisions."*

(5) "WHO THEN IS PAUL, AND WHO IS APOLLOS, BUT MINISTERS BY WHOM YE BELIEVED, EVEN AS THE LORD GAVE TO EVERY MAN?"

The beginning of the question, *"Who then is Paul, and who is Apollos . . . ?"*, would have been better translated *"What then is Paul . . . ?"*

The word *"what"* which is greater implied in the Greek Text, also implies a still greater depreciation of the importance of human Ministers.

The idea is, that these men, though used greatly by God, were still mere men. They were not the author of the Salvation of these people, nor any people for that matter, and neither is any other Preacher. To those of us who have become large in our own eyes, such terminology as used by the Holy Spirit through the Apostle, should take us down a notch or two.

The phrase, *"But Ministers by whom ye believed,"* could probably be better translated *"Through whom ye believed."* As well, if one is to notice, the word is *"Through whom"* and not *"In whom"* (Bengal). The idea is, that the Apostles were merely the instruments of Conversion, and not the cause, that being Christ and Christ Alone.

*"Ministers"* here in the Greek is *"diakonoi,"* and is the same word as that rendered *"deacons,"* and actually means *"to serve, or act as a servant."*

The conclusion of the question, *". . . even as the Lord gave to every man?"*, simply means that whatever gifts each Preacher had, they came from the Lord, and not due to their own abilities or merit (Rom. 12:6).

(6) "I HAVE PLANTED, APOLLOS WATERED; BUT GOD GAVE THE INCREASE."

The phrase, *"I have planted,"* presents Paul recognizing that his gift lay preeminently in the ability to found (plant) Churches (Acts 18:1-11; I Cor. 4:15; 9:1; 15:1), but more particularly it referred to him being the founder of the Church per se under Christ.

Paul was also a great Teacher which of course should be obvious; however, he had a special Calling by the Holy Spirit concerning the taking of the Gospel to virgin territory, and among rank heathen, establishing Churches.

The phrase, *"Apollos watered,"* portrays it seems, how striking was his power of strengthening the Faith of wavering Churches. Deep insight into the Scriptures, seems to have been his special endowment (Acts 18:24-27).

The phrase, *"But God gave the increase,"* presents God's method of operation. In fact, we learn several things from this statement as given by Paul:

1. It is beautiful the manner in which God allows poor mortals to work with Him in the furtherance of His Work. To be frank, God does not need man in any capacity, but honors us by allowing us to have a part in this great and wonderful thing in which He is doing.

2. The *"increase"* as spoken here, is not in man or his efforts, but entirely in God. If He does not give the increase, it simply is not true increase, but rather a work of the flesh.

3. The *"increase"* of which He speaks, pertains to souls, and their spiritual growth. It does not pertain to money, place, position, or people referring to favor, although these things may possibly be the by-products of an ancillary position.

4. In all of this, it is beautiful to observe the humble figure of speech used by Paul referring to his own work in founding the Corinthian Assembly (Acts 18:1-17) and to the Ministry of Apollos in helping these Believers to mature in the Lord (Acts 18:27; 19:1). It shows that in comparison to God's part, their part was momentary and minuscule. Consequently, their position as *"servants"* did not in any manner denote an official ministerial position.

In fact, the literal word *"ministers"* or *"servants"* refers to floor-sweepers. It was used commonly in that period for day-laborers who were at the mercy of landowners who would hire them and compensate them one day at a time. Jesus used this same term when He told His Disciples to view themselves as servants (Mat. 20:26; Mk. 10:43), rather than as people who lorded it over other individuals (Rossier).

Paul's opinion of himself is a far cry from the hierarchical domination of many modern so-called Pentecostal Leaders. That of which Paul illustrates, as certainly should be obvious, is the Biblical example, consequently of the Spirit, while much of the modern example is of man.

5. Referring to the *"increase"* as spiritual growth, according to Romans 8:29, God predestined Christians to be conformed to the Image of Jesus. The more we grow spiritually the more we will be like our Lord.

Spiritual maturity is a process that never is complete in this earthly life. Hence, becoming mature Christians involves knowing and doing God's Will. If God has planned to make us like Christ, then we cannot go wrong if we allow the Holy Spirit to do what He wants to do with us.

Spiritual maturity does not belong exclusively to an elite group of Christians. It is available and intended for all Believers who are willing to obey the Teachings of God's Word, especially those Teachings which relate to allowing the Grace of God to surface in the Believer (Rossier).

(7) "SO THEN NEITHER IS HE THAT PLANTETH ANY THING, NEITHER HE THAT WATERETH; BUT GOD THAT GIVETH THE INCREASE."

The phrase, *"So then neither is he that planteth any thing, neither he that watereth,"* presents Paul answering his own question of Verse 5. In other words, the Planter and the Waterer are nothing by comparison to the Lord.

NOTES

The phrase, *"But God that giveth the increase,"* if we add Verse 5, makes it three times that this statement is made in one form or the other. Consequently, the Holy Spirit is telling us something.

It is not only God Who gives the increase, but God Alone from Whom the increase comes, but as well Who must help the Planter and Waterer. Considering this, no individual has any right to boast.

(8) "NOW HE THAT PLANTETH AND HE THAT WATERETH ARE ONE: AND EVERY MAN SHALL RECEIVE HIS OWN REWARD ACCORDING TO HIS OWN LABOUR."

The phrase, *"Now he that planteth and he that watereth are one,"* literally means in the Greek, *"one thing,"* which should be obvious.

The one who plants the garden is dependent upon the one who waters it, and the one who waters would have nothing to water if someone had not planted. Considering this, it becomes somewhat silly doesn't it, for these two to oppose each other, seeing that they are attempting to bring about the same end, and that both are dependent on each other. But yet, mutual dependence and help are not the criteria for the far greater majority of the Modern Church, and in fact, little has been. In the Eyes of God, how stupid our actions must be, at least if we fall into the category of opposing each other.

I thank God for all people who come to Christ, irrespective of where they are Saved, or under whose Ministry. Whoever is having success at getting people to God, I pray such success will quadruple and even greater.

As well, all who properly *"water* (teach)*"* these people the Word of God, are to be helped in every way possible. Thank God for those Ministries, and pray they will multiply.

However, the criteria should be that the *"watering* (teaching)*"* would be as that of Apollos. By that I mean this:

## APOLLOS!

If one is to notice, Paul said, *"I have planted, Apollos watered."* Apollos believed and taught the same thing as the Apostle Paul; consequently, the *"watering"* was done proper and right. However, when Judaizers later came in, attempting to *"water"* in an improper way, i.e., teaching False Doctrine, Paul opposed this type

NOTES

of *"watering"* very strongly, as he should have done. The analogy is obvious.

If someone properly plants, which occasions the birth of the seed, and then someone comes along and applies the wrong type of *"watering* (teaching)*"* which is actually done constantly, even as it was in Paul's day, such efforts must be opposed, because as should be obvious, the very existence of the plant (souls) is jeopardized.

As an example, Paul greatly opposed the type of watering done by the Judaizers, simply because their Doctrine was wrong, and would jeopardize the souls of those who had truly been brought into the Kingdom. They were teaching that which was unscriptural, and which Paul would address to a much greater extent in his Second Letter to the Corinthians, as well as other Epistles. Consequently, I think that Paul, if ministering presently, would greatly oppose much of the *"watering*(teaching)*"* of this modern era. I firmly believe he would oppose the Prosperity Teaching, Works Religion, Kingdom Now Teaching, the Psychological Way, much of the so-called modern Christian music, and a lack of dependence on the Holy Spirit. I think he would have been just as vocal against these things as he was against the Judaizers. To be frank, he had no choice then, and those Preachers who truly follow the Lord presently have no choice as well. *"He that planteth and he that watereth are one,"* only so long as they are both Teaching and Preaching the same thing. By that I am not meaning that everything is agreed upon in every single point of detail, but that the general thrust is the same.

## LABOUR

The phrase, *"And every man shall receive his own reward according to his own labour,"* presents a very interesting statement.

If one is to notice, Paul did not say *"according to his own success,"* but rather *"labour."*

God has not called us to be successful, but rather to be faithful (Mat. 25:21). In fact, Paul will address this in Verses 12-15 of this Chapter.

*"Reward"* in the Greek is *"misthos,"* and means *"pay for service whether good or bad."* If one is to notice, Salvation is not being addressed here, but rather *"reward."* In fact, Paul is speaking about the coming Judgment Seat of Christ, before which every Believer will appear. However, that Judgment will not be regarding sins, for that has already been handled at Calvary, but rather, and as stated, the reward for labor expended. As we shall see, much reward will be lost, and because of wrong motivation, etc., which carries in its penalty eternal loss, because Judgment rendered there (the Judgment Seat of Christ) will have eternal consequences.

*"Labor"* in the Greek is *"kopos,"* and refers to *"toil, or by implication pains, trouble, and weariness."* To be sure, labor for the Lord at times, involves all of this and even more.

Paul is the perfect example. He suffered beatings, imprisonment, shipwreck, and every type of opposition one could think. Considering these situations, this evidently is the reason Jesus said, *"The harvest truly is plenteous, but the labourers are few;*

*"Pray ye therefore the Lord of the harvest, that He will send forth labourers into His harvest"* (Mat. 9:37-38).

In other words, the Lord is looking for laborers and not loafers.

(9) "FOR WE ARE LABOURERS TOGETHER WITH GOD: YE ARE GOD'S HUSBANDRY, YE ARE GOD'S BUILDING."

The phrase, *"For we are labourers together with God,"* pertains to labor in the harvest.

Throughout the Bible we are taught that God requires the work of man, and that He will not help those who will do nothing for themselves or for Him. The world was to be Evangelized, not by sudden miracle, but by faithful human labor (Mk. 16:20) (Farrar).

The phrase, *"Labourers together with God,"* does not so much mean that we are workers together *with* God as it implies we are workers together *for* God. The manner in which it is given in the Greek, does not so much speak of cooperation with God, which of course is demanded, but rather cooperation with one another because we all belong to God.

Paul was speaking in this manner because the Corinthians seemed to be acting as if these Preachers belonged to them, rather than to God. If that attitude is brought into play, people who have that mind-set will soon feel justified in exalting or demeaning Preachers at will. This is a dangerous thing to do with God's Servants. It is sad when the members of a congregation act as if they own their Pastor. If so, they are conducting themselves as spiritual babies, exactly as these Corinthians did (Rossier).

The phrase, *"Ye are God's husbandry,"* literally means in the Greek, *"God's field, God's tilled land."*

The thought which Paul desires again and again to enforce is that they (the Preachers, and all for that matter) belong to God, not to particular parties of human teachers, etc. (The word *"husbandry"* can also mean vineyard and is used as such in Isa. 5:1; 27:2; Mat. 13:3-30; Lk. 13:6-9; Jn. 15:1; Rom. 11:16-24.)

The phrase, *"Ye are God's building,"* presents one of Paul's favorite metaphors (Rom. 15:20; I Cor. 3:16-17; II Cor. 6:16; Eph. 2:20-22; II Tim. 2:19).

In a sense, Paul separates the *"labourers"* from the *"building."* Even though all, both Preachers and the laity fall into both categories in the final analogy, still, the Holy Spirit through the Apostle spells out the practical difference.

Even though all are *"labourers"* in a sense, still, it is the fivefold calling (Eph. 4:11), which the Lord has placed in charge of the Vineyard or Building. The Vineyard or Building, pertains to the Saints of God (Laity), or the *"Church"* as we would refer to such.

The idea is, at least as given here, that Ministers of the Gospel are to work in unity with the Lord. In truth, Believers are the Building of God (Eph. 2:19-22).

(10) "ACCORDING TO THE GRACE OF GOD WHICH IS GIVEN UNTO ME, AS A WISE MASTERBUILDER, I HAVE LAID THE FOUNDATION, AND ANOTHER BUILDETH THEREON. BUT LET EVERY MAN TAKE HEED HOW HE BUILDETH THEREUPON."

The phrase, *"According to the Grace of God which is given unto me, as a wise Masterbuilder,"* tells us several things:

1. God is actually the Architect of the Plan. And yet, the Plan was entrusted to the Apostle Paul as the *"Masterbuilder."*

2. This responsibility was given to the Apostle, *"according to the Grace of God,"* which meant that Paul on his own did not merit such. In fact, everything given to anyone is *"according to the Grace of God."*

3. Paul was *"wise"* in the sense of subordinating every pretense of human wisdom to the Will of God. Here the Greek Text brings it out that this applies only to the wisdom required by a builder. In other words, *"wise"* is here equivalent to *"skilful."* Since Paul had received the Grace of God for this very purpose, the establishment of the Church, he was made *"wise"* by the Knowledge of Christ (Farrar).

NOTES

The phrase, *"I have laid the Foundation,"* refers to Paul as much more than just a Planter or Builder of Churches, but rather that he was given the very *"Foundation"* of the Church, which is the New Covenant. As he will say in the next verse, that *"Foundation"* is *"Jesus Christ."*

Whenever one reads the Book of Acts, one is reading the story, among other things, of how the Holy Spirit through the Apostle laid the Foundation of the Church. When one reads the Epistles, one is reading the instructions as to how Believers should live as the Church.

The phrase, *"And another buildeth thereon,"* speaks of all the Preachers who have followed thereafter, even unto this very moment, and have built upon this Foundation.

The phrase, *"But let every man take heed how he builds thereupon,"* refers to the fact that whatever doctrine is preached and practiced must not be contrary to Paul.

(11) "FOR OTHER FOUNDATION CAN NO MAN LAY THAN THAT IS LAID, WHICH IS JESUS CHRIST."

The phrase, *"For other foundation can no man lay than that is laid,"* by its very implication informs us that any Doctrine presented which is other than that preached by the Apostle Paul, is in fact, *"another foundation,"* which will not, and in fact, cannot be recognized by God. Let us say it again and because of its great significance. If it is not exactly according to the Book of Acts, and the Epistles, it is an improper foundation. Consequently, that means that Catholicism is another foundation, and to be frank, much of that which is Protestant as well! It also means that Mormonism, Hinduism, Islam, Buddhism, Shintoism, etc., are all other foundations, which in fact, is no foundation at all, and because it is not built on Jesus Christ.

## FOUNDATION

The idea is, that there can be no other foundation laid alongside this Foundation laid by Paul under the auspices of the Holy Spirit. So, when the Mormons say they have another revelation along with the Bible, to put it pure and simple they are lying.

The phrase, *"Which is Jesus Christ,"* tells us that the Church is not merely built on a Doctrine about Christ, but actually on Christ Himself. Whenever people accept Him as their own personal Saviour, they become members of His predestined Body.

The Doctrine of Jesus Christ is the Foundation of all Theology; His Person is the Foundation of all Life. This is again and again inculcated in Scripture. The Prophet said, *"Behold, I lay in Zion for a Foundation a Stone, a Tried Stone, a Precious Corner Stone, a sure Foundation"* (Isa. 28:16).

On this Rock, Jesus Christ, the Church is built (Mat. 16:18; Acts 4:11-12; Eph. 2:20).

## WHO IS JESUS CHRIST?

We shall begin with the Testimony of John the Evangelist, and look first at the Gospel that bears his name.

John begins his Testimony regarding Jesus of Nazareth with the statement, *"In the beginning was the Word, and the Word was in fellowship with God and the Word was as to its essence, Deity"* (Jn. 1:1). John uses the Greek word *"Logos"* as a designation of Jesus of Nazareth.

Logos is from the Greek word *"Leg,"* which means *"to pick out, to gather or put words together."* Hence, *"Logos"* is first of all, a collecting or collection both of things in the mind, and of words by which they are expressed. It, therefore, signifies both the outward form by which the inward thought is expressed, and the inward thought itself.

As signifying the outward form, it is never used as simply the name of a thing or act, but means a word as the thing referred to, the material, a word as embodying a conception or idea.

## WHAT JOHN SAID

Jesus of Nazareth, according to that which the Holy Spirit gave to John, is related to God as the Word to the idea, the Word being not merely a name for the idea, but the idea itself expressed.

The Logos of John is the Real, Personal God, the Word, Who was originally before the Creation with God, and was God, One in essence and nature, yet Personally distinct; the Revealer and Interpreter of the hidden Being of God; the Reflection and Visible Image of God, and the organ of all His Manifestations in the world.

He made all things, proceeding Personally from God for the accomplishment of the act of Creation, and became Man in the Person of Jesus of Nazareth, accomplishing the Redemption of the world.

NOTES

## JESUS AS THE VOICE OF GOD

The writer to the Hebrews says, *"God, Who in many parts and in many ways spoke in time past to the Fathers by means of the Prophets, has in these last days spoken to us in the Person of His Son"* (Heb. 1:1-2). In Old Testament times, God spoke through the Prophets by means of spoken Words. Now, He speaks to us in the Person of His Son, Jesus of Nazareth, not only in the Words He (Jesus) spoke, but in the kind of Person He was, in the kind of life He lived on Earth, in the vicarious death He died on the Cross, and in the victorious Resurrection He Himself accomplished.

Jesus of Nazareth is the Word of God in that He is Deity told out. He said, *"He that hath seen Me hath seen the Father"* (Jn. 14:9).

That is, He is the visible Revelation of what invisible Deity is like. And only Deity could clearly manifest forth Deity. This Manifestation was through a human medium in order that it might be perceptible to human intelligences. And that is one reason among many for the Incarnation.

## THE BEGINNING OF CREATION

This Person John says, was in the beginning. That does *not* mean that Jesus as God had a beginning, for He did not. The context, speaks of the act of creating the Universe, indicating that this beginning refers to the beginning of the created Universe. Jesus said of Himself, *"Before Abraham came into existence, I am"* (Jn. 8:58). Since Jesus existed before all created things were brought into existence, He is uncreated. Since He is uncreated, He is Eternal. Since He is Eternal, He is God.

He is the Person of the Godhead Who is the Revealer of what Deity is like, God the Son proceeding by eternal generation from God the Father in a birth that never took place because it always was. Thus, in John's first five words, we have the Deity of Jesus of Nazareth.

### FELLOWSHIP

John goes on to say, *"And the Word was in active communion with God."* In the Greek that which is referred to as the definite article precedes the Word *"God"* here, in essence saying *"The God"* pointing out the fact that it is God the Father to Whom reference is made.

Here we have brought to our attention a fellowship which never had a beginning, but always was, which was broken for those six awful hours in which Jesus hung on the Cross, and which was resumed after the debt of human sin was paid, never to be broken again. The picture in the Greek Text is that of God the Son facing God the Father in a fellowship between two persons of the Godhead.

### DEITY

But John is not satisfied to let the matter of the Deity of Jesus of Nazareth rest there. He says, *"And the Word was as to its essence, Deity"* (Jn. 1:1). The definite article in the Greek is absent before the word *"God"* in this instance. However, the absence of the definite article qualifies rather than nullifies. In this instance it shows essence. Jesus of Nazareth possesses the same essence (the properties or attributes by means of which something can be placed in its proper class or identified as being what it is) that God the Father and God the Spirit possess, and that, eternally.

He is Absolute God, Very God of Very God. Such is John's opening Testimony to the identity of Jesus of Nazareth.

### JESUS THE CREATOR

After informing his readers Who Jesus of Nazareth is, John tells them what He did.

He says, *"All things through His intermediate agency came into existence, and without Him, there came into existence not even one thing that stands existed"* (Jn. 1:3).

The inspired Writer teaches us three things here:

1. Matter is not eternal, but was brought into existence.
2. Jesus of Nazareth was the Intermediate Agent in the Godhead Who brought matter into existence.
3. Matter is indestructible. That is, the existence of matter today, depends upon the original act of Creation.

NOTES

Jesus was the Intermediate Agent of Creation. God the Father is the Ultimate Source, Jesus, the Son, is the Person of the Godhead charged with the work of bringing into existence a Universe (or Universes) which had no existence before.

### HE IS LIFE

Not only is Jesus of Nazareth the Creator, John says, but *"In Him is Life, and this Life is the Light of men"* (Jn. 1:4). The particular Greek word used for Life here is *"zoe,"* speaking of the Life Principle. Life begets life. All that has life in the Universe, receives its life from One Source, Jesus of Nazareth. But here is Life which had no antecedent source. It always was.

When one pushes the idea of an Absolute, Eternal God as far as a finite mind can reach, one is staggered at the immensity of the thought.

The little boy asks, *"Who made God?"* One cannot hold one's mind very long on the thought of the Eternal Being of God. Here is a Wonderful Being, Omnipotent, Omnipresent, and Omniscient, Who always was. This God is Jesus of Nazareth.

We are accustomed to looking at Him as the Carpenter of Nazareth, the Man Christ Jesus, the Teacher, the Healer, the traveled-stained, weary, itinerant Preacher. But that takes into consideration only 33 years of His Life on Earth.

He had an eternal existence before the Shepherds found Him as a little helpless Baby in a manger in Bethlehem. John, the Seer, is looking before that to His Preincarnate Work of Creation.

### HE IS LIGHT

This Light, John says, *"Was the Light of men. And the Light is shining in the darkness, and the darkness did not overcome it"* (Jn. 1:4-5).

The Light that Jesus is, was shining in the midst of the darkness of human sin. It is the Preincarnate Light of Jesus, seen through the created Universe, to which John refers here.

It is the Light which God gave of Himself to man before the Incarnation of Deity in human flesh as seen in Jesus of Nazareth. The King James says: *"And the darkness comprehended it not."* That is, the human race, its reasoning faculties darkened by sin, did not comprehend or understand the Revelation of God through the created Universe. But that is far from all the Truth.

The word John uses is *"katalambano,"* and means *"to take hold of so as to make one's own, to seize, to take possession of, to apprehend."*

The idea is, that the human race *did* comprehend the Revelation of Deity seen through the created Universe, and, antagonistic to it, attempted to overcome it in the sense of barring it from its spiritual consciousness, substituting for it, gods of man's own creation.

A WILLFUL IGNORANCE

Paul gives us this information in the words: *"The Wrath of God is revealed from Heaven against all ungodliness and unrighteousness of men, who are holding down* (suppressing) *the Truth in unrighteousness;*

*"Because that which may be known of God is plainly evident among them; for God made it clear to them,*

*"For the invisible things of Him since the creation of the Universe are clearly seen, being understood by means of the things which are made, namely, His Eternal Power and His Divinity, resulting in their being without a defense,*

*"Because knowing God, they did not glorify Him as God, neither were they thankful; but became futile in their reasoning, and their foolish heart was darkened.*

*"Professing themselves to be wise, they became fools,*

*"And exchanged the glory of the uncorruptible God for an image made like corruptible man, and birds, and fourfooted beasts, and creeping things"* (Rom. 1:18-23).

Paul is saying that man suppressed the Truth. That means that the human race was in possession of the Truth. The Truth here is that of a Divine Creator to Whom worship and obedience should be given, this Truth is seen through the created Universe.

Man, reasoning from the law of cause and effect, which Law requires an adequate cause for every effect, must reason, that is if he is honest, that such a tremendous and wonderful effect which the Universe is, demands a Divine Being for its Creator. This is the Light which both John and Paul state, was shining in the midst of the darkness of human sin.

John says that mankind did not extinguish it, in fact, because they could not. However, Paul says that the race did suppress it. This was the Light of Creation which pointed to Jesus of Nazareth, its Creator.

NOTES

THE INCARNATION

After speaking of Jesus of Nazareth in His Preexistence with reference to the created Universe and, therefore, His Eternal Existence with the correlative of the possession of Absolute Deity, of His Act of speaking a Universe into existence, and of the Light which that Universe gave to the human race concerning His Eternal Power and Divinity, John enters upon a discussion of His Incarnation.

He presents His forerunner John the Baptist. As Kings of the Orient had Heralds who preceded them as they journeyed through their domains, so Jesus of Nazareth, The King from the Royal Line of David, had a Herald who announced His Coming.

He introduces Him in the words, *"There came upon the scene a man, sent as an Ambassador from the Presence of God, his name, John"* (Jn. 1:6).

Actually, this just given, is the English Translation from the eight words which John originally used in his fisherman's Greek. Where did he learn to write in such a succinct style? Actually, he never saw the inside of a higher school of learning.

After a brief education such as was given to Hebrew boys, he went into business with his Father catching and selling fish. The only answer to this question is that his literary style was given him by the Holy Spirit as he was guided in the writing of the Gospel attributed to him.

First, John notes the historical manifestation, the emergence of John the Baptist into the economy of the Revelation of this Light. It was first, the Light which the created Universe gave concerning the Creatorship and Deity of Jesus of Nazareth. But now, a personal Revelation is to be made in the form of an Incarnation, Deity taking upon itself through Virgin Birth, a human body and putting itself under human limitations.

But this coming of God the Son upon the human scene, was to be announced by a Herald, a forerunner.

The Greek verb translated *"sent"* was used of a King sending a personal Representative,

NOTES

an Ambassador, on a commission to do something for him. John the Baptist was the envoy of the King from Heaven. He was sent literally *"from beside God,"* that is, from His Presence.

This gives the Messenger of Jesus more dignity and significance than if John had written merely *"Sent by God."*

The Baptist came preaching to Israel from the Presence of God. He was a rugged, heroic man's man. He had been living in the deserted regions about Jerusalem, along with God, his food and clothing of the simplest kind. He came from the Presence of God with the Touch of God upon him, and the Power of God in His Message.

A WITNESS

John states his mission in the words: *"This one came as a witness, in order that he may bear Testimony concerning the Light, in order that all might believe through him. That one was not the Light, but he came in order to bear Testimony concerning the Light"* (Jn. 1:7-8).

Then John introduces the One concerning Whom the Baptist bears Testimony, in the words: *"He was the Light, the Genuine Light which illuminates every man, as it comes into the world."*

LIGHT

John's use of the word *"genuine"* indicates that whereas there is a Light that is genuine, namely, real, perfect, substantial, there is also one that is counterfeit, false. Satan, a fallen angel, as an angel of light. He is a God-aping Devil, copying everything that God is and does, within the reach of his ability.

He has, Paul says, disguised himself as an angel of light, assuming a light covering which does not come, nor does it represent what he is in his inner being. He thus masquerades as an angel of light, impersonating the Absolute God against Whom he has sinned.

Jesus of Nazareth was the genuine Light previous to His Incarnation, Who through His creative Work, illuminated every man, as that Light was shed abroad in the Universe, teaching every person that there was a God in Heaven Who created the Universe and who should be worshiped.

John gives his position as such in the Universe, in the words: *"In the Universe He was, and the Universe through His Intermediate Agency came into existence, and the world of lost humanity did not know Him."*

The heathen know that there is a Supreme Being, and they know this by means of the Light which the created Universe affords. But they worship demons through fear, and do not know the Living God, at least in a personal way. The Greek word John uses means just that.

RECEPTION

But not only does the world of sinners fail to know the Preincarnate Logos at least in a personal way, but it fails to receive Him when He becomes Incarnate. John says: *"He came into the midst of His Own Things, and His Own People did not take Him to their hearts"* (Jn. 1:11).

Jesus of Nazareth, the Omnipresent God in the Universe, yet centralized as to His Throne and Authority in Heaven, is the Performer of and the Participant in a stupendous Miracle, so stupendous that no human mind would naturally think of such a thing or of its possibility. He wraps about Himself the physical body of an infant and puts Himself under human limitations, in other words, the Creator becoming the Creation.

He comes from outside of the Universe, yet all the while imminent in it, and through the womb of a Virgin, is born, and then laid in a manger in the Town of Bethlehem in Judaea. He lives as a Peasant in the Town of Nazareth and works as a day laborer in the Carpenter Shop of Joseph, His legal, but not His actual Father.

He has come to His Own Things, His Own Land of Israel, His Own Capital City, His Own Davidic Throne. He offers Himself as Messiah to His Own People, the Jews. And His Own People do not reach out and take Him to themselves.

Instead, they reject Him, and hand Him over to the Roman Authorities in order that He might be Crucified.

ALL THAT HE IS

*"But"* John says, *"As many as did appropriate Him, He gave to them a legal right to become born-ones of God, to those who place their trust in His Name"* (Jn. 1:12).

To appropriate Jesus of Nazareth and to put one's trust in His Name, are one and the same thing. The expression *"The Name"* is an Old Testament expression speaking of all that God

NOTES

is in His Majesty, Glory, and Power. *"The Name"* as it applies to Jesus of Nazareth includes all that He is in His Glorious Person.

The Sinner is given a legal right to receive the Mercy of God as he recognizes Jesus of Nazareth as the One Who procured that legal right for him at the Cross. The Sinner has no legal right or standing regarding the Mercy of God. The Law which he broke is against him. But Jesus satisfied the just demands of that Law which you and I violated, and thus makes it possible for us to receive God's Mercy in Salvation.

One of these Mercies, Regeneration, John mentions here. The words *"born ones"* are the translation of a Greek word whose root has in it the idea of birth.

Justification, namely, the removal of the guilt and penalty of sin, and the bestowal of a positive Righteousness, comes first, that is after Sanctification (I Cor. 6:11). This is the legal right to which reference is made.

Regeneration, or the impartation of Divine Life, is second in the economy of Salvation. Thus, Jesus of Nazareth, is not only the Creator of the Universe, but also the Source of Salvation.

## THE INCARNATION AGAIN

And then John speaks of the Incarnation again in the beautiful words, *"And the Word became flesh and lived in a tent among us"* (Jn. 1:14). The King James says, *"The Word was made flesh."*

To make something is to take something and mold it into a new form, changing its shape. The first form disappears to have something that has different form take its place. However, nothing like that happened to Jesus of Nazareth.

Absolute God in His Preincarnate State, He remained such in His Incarnation. He did not relinquish His Deity upon becoming Man. He was not made flesh. He became flesh. The Greek word is *"ginomai,"* and it is in a tense and a classification of that tense which speaks of entrance into a new condition. By becoming flesh John means that the Invisible, Eternal, Omnipresent, Omnipotent, and Omniscient God added to Himself a Human Body and put Himself under human limitations, yet without human sin. While still Deity and Omnipresent, He became localized in a human body.

While still Deity and, therefore, Omniscient, He lived the life of a human being on Earth. He thought with a human brain. He became exhausted. He broke into tears. He needed food, clothing, and shelter.

He gave us a picture of what Deity is like through the medium of a human life. He lived in a tent in the midst of humanity. That tent was His Human Body.

Thus, Jesus of Nazareth is a Person having two Natures. He is Absolute Deity. He is True Man. His Deity did not add to His Humanity. His Humanity did not detract from His Deity. Consequently, the King James Version should have translated John's statement, *"The Word became flesh."*

## GOD ONLY BEGOTTEN

This combination of Deity and Humanity in One Person, Jesus of Nazareth, John speaks of again in the words: *"Deity in its invisible essence no one has ever yet seen. God only begotten, the One Who is constantly in the bosom of the Father, that One has fully explained God"* (Jn. 1:18).

The words *"God only begotten"* refer to Jesus of Nazareth. He is God only begotten, proceeding by Eternal Generation as the Son of God from the Father in a Birth that never took place because it always was. This One, John says, fully explained Deity.

The Greek word translated *"fully explained"* means literally *"to lead out."* Jesus in the Incarnation led Deity out from back of the curtain of its invisibility, showing the human race in and through a human life, what God was like. Our word *"exegesis"* is the transliteration of the Greek word here.

The Science of Exegesis is that of fully explaining in detail the meaning of a Passage of Scripture. In the Incarnation, Jesus of Nazareth fully explained God so far as a human medium could explain the Infinite, and human minds and hearts could receive that Revelation. And He could do that only because He was God Himself.

John has answered our question, *"Jesus of Nazareth, Who is He?"*

## THE WORDS OF PAUL

We turn to Paul for an answer to the same question. He calls Jesus of Nazareth *"God"* in Titus 2:13. The King James says, *"The Glorious Appearing of the Great God and our Saviour Jesus Christ."*

One could gather from this wording that Paul is speaking of two individuals, God and Jesus of Nazareth, and one could maintain that the former was Deity and the latter a Man. But an examination of the Greek Text discloses the fact that we have the Deity of our Lord brought out in the translation, *"The appearing of the Glory of our Great God and Saviour Jesus Christ."* The Greek Text brings it out.

Paul, the Scholar, probably educated in the foremost Greek University of his time, the University of Tarsus, where he received his Greek training, and in the Theological School in Jerusalem headed up by Gamaliel, where he received his training in the Old Testament, teaches that Jesus of Nazareth is Deity.

Peter, the fisherman, in his Second Epistle (II Pet. 1:1) has the same expression in his Greek Text, *"Through the Righteousness of our God and Saviour Jesus Christ."* It is clear that Jesus of Nazareth was worshiped as God by the First Century Church. The use of the pronoun *"our"* is polemic (beyond question).

The citizens of the Roman Empire looked upon Caesar as their god. There were two cults in the Empire at that time, that which we have previously explained in other Commentary, the Cult of the Caesar, which was the State Religion of the Roman Empire, in which the Emperor was worshiped as a god, and the Cult of Christ, Christianity, in which Jesus of Nazareth was worshiped as God.

The people of Syrian Antioch, who had a reputation for coining nicknames, gave the name *"Christian"* to the Disciples of Jesus of Nazareth. To these people (nonbelievers) it was a term of derision and contempt. They were proud worshipers of Caesar. Agrippa said to Paul, *"With but little persuasion, you would make me a Christian"* (Acts 26:28).

## ONE FOR WHOM ONE WOULD DIE

It was a common practice in the Roman world to deify rulers. But Jesus of Nazareth must have been something more than a man, and His followers must have been convinced of that fact, for untold numbers willingly suffered a horrible martyrdom for their Testimony to His Deity. Thousands upon thousands of people do not go to a violent death for something they know is a fraud.

NOTES

One cannot explain the willing acceptance of Jesus of Nazareth as Saviour by a sin-loving Pagan who accepted with Him that which he formerly hated, namely, Righteousness, and by that forsook his sin which he loved, knowing that by so doing he would be liable to capital punishment for his act, except upon the basis of a supernatural working in his heart, providing for the willing acceptance of that which he formerly hated, Righteousness.

Jesus of Nazareth, therefore, stands as history's outstanding Enigma, unless He is accorded the place which the Bible gives Him, Very God of Very God. One cannot explain Him without this fact of His Deity. One can dismiss Him with an *"I do not believe that,"* but that does not solve the problem nor blot Him from the pages of history.

He stands there, astride the world of mankind, a unique individual, God and Man in One Person.

## GODHEAD

The Great Apostle in Colossians 2:9 recognizes these two Natures, Deity and Humanity, residing in the Person of Jesus of Nazareth.

He says, *"In Him dwelleth all the fullness of the Godhead Bodily."* The Greek word which Paul uses and which is translated *"Godhead,"* needs some study.

The word *"Godhead"* is found three times in the above mentioned Version, Acts 17:29; Romans 1:20; and, Colossians 2:9. However, to arrive at that word, the King James translated it from two different Greek words.

In the first two instances, Paul uses the Greek word *"theiotes,"* and in the last, named *"theotes."* In *"theiotes,"* Paul is declaring how much of God may be known from the Revelation of Himself which He has made in nature . . . yet it is not the Personal God Whom any man may learn to know by these aids: He can only be known by the Revelation of Himself in His Son; but in nature only His Divine Attributes, His Majesty and Glory.

However, when Paul is speaking personally of Jesus of Nazareth, he uses the Greek word *"theotes."* This takes on a much more personal direction, with Paul declaring that in the Son there dwells all the fullness of Absolute Godhead: they were no mere rays of Divine Glory which guided Him, lighting up His Person for a season and with splendor not His Own; but He was, and is, Absolute and Perfect God.

Paul speaking of Jesus of Nazareth in His Incarnation says: *"In Him there is at home, permanently, all the fullness of absolute Deity in bodily fashion. That is, in the human Body of Jesus of Nazareth, there resided permanently at home, all that goes to make Deity what it is. He was Absolute Deity clothed with a human body."*

### THE GREAT STATEMENT

Finally, we will look at Paul's great, classic Christological Passage in Philippians 2:5-11. The Greek Text literally leaps at one in the words:

*"Let this mind be in you which was also in Christ Jesus, Who subsisting permanently in that state of Being in which He gives outward expression of the essence of Deity, that outward expression coming from and being truly representative of His Inner Being, did not consider it a prize to be clutched, the being on an equality with Deity* (in the expression of the Divine Essence)*, but emptied Himself, having taken the outward expression of a bondslave, that expression coming from and being truly representative of His Inner Being, having become in the likeness of man. And having been found in outward guise as Man, He humbled Himself, having become obedient to the extent of death, even such a death as that upon a Cross: on which account also God supereminently exalted Him, and in Grace gave Him the Name which is above every Name, to the end that in the Name which Jesus possesses, every knee should bow, of those in Heaven and those upon the Earth, and those under the Earth, and that every tongue should openly confess that Jesus Christ is Lord to the Glory of God the Father."*

See the statements Paul makes here concerning Jesus of Nazareth. Jesus gives outward expression in His Preincarnate state of the Essence of Deity, that expression necessitating the possession of Deity. He claims equality with Deity in the expression of the Divine Essence. He empties Himself of Self, setting aside His desire to be worshiped, the legitimate desire of Deity, in order to come to Earth, take upon Himself the outward expression of a bondslave, and go to the Cross for guilty sinners, paying the penalty for their sins, satisfying the just demands of God's Law, thus making a way whereby a Righteous God can bestow His Grace upon believing sinners, yet on the basis of Justice satisfied.

So we now see, why Paul said, *"For other foundation can no man lay than that is laid, which is Jesus Christ."*

(The statement on Jesus Christ was derived from material furnished by the Greek Scholar, Kenneth Wuest.)

(12) "NOW IF ANY MAN BUILD UPON THIS FOUNDATION GOLD, SILVER, PRECIOUS STONES, WOOD, HAY, STUBBLE;"

The phrase, *"Now if any man build upon this foundation gold, silver, precious stones,"* presents Paul using symbols. The first three are materials which will stand the test of fire, for fire, again symbolic of the Word of God, will be the standard.

The idea seems to be concerning these durable materials, of proper Doctrine, the right motivation and faithfulness.

The phrase, *"Wood, hay, stubble,"* once again is used symbolically of that which will not stand the test of fire.

These words could definitely symbolize erroneous or imperfect Doctrines which will not stand the Bible test, and which lead to evil practices. Such were the *"philosophy and vain deceit,"* the *"weak and beggarly elements,"* the *"rudiments of the world,"* of which Paul speaks in Galatians 4:9 and Colossians 2:8.

The Doctrines to which he alludes are not so much anti-Christian, but rather imperfect and human — from a human source. Such will not stand the test of fire, because it does not coincide with the Word of God.

As well, motivation and faithfulness, or the wrong type of motivation and faithfulness, play a great part also. So, one could probably sum up this of which Paul speaks in three words, *"Doctrine, Motivation, and Faithfulness,"* and not be very far off base.

(13) "EVERY MAN'S WORK SHALL BE MADE MANIFEST: FOR THE DAY SHALL DECLARE IT, BECAUSE IT SHALL BE REVEALED BY FIRE; AND THE FIRE SHALL TRY EVERY MAN'S WORK OF WHAT SORT IT IS."

The phrase, *"Every man's work shall be made manifest,"* refers to that of every Believer.

*"Manifest"* in the Greek is *"phaneron,"* and means *"to open up, to reveal."*

NOTES

The *"Foundation"* of Verse 12 is not being discussed here, because it is unquestionably durable and valuable because God Himself laid it. Hence, because it cannot be destroyed there will be no need to test it.

However, each superstructure built upon the Foundation, will be examined to manifest its durability and value (Rossier). So, whatever the nature of our work here on Earth, at that particular time, *"The Judgment Seat of Christ,"* it will be opened up to all and tested before all regarding its real nature — the worth or worthlessness — made clear.

The phrase, *"For the day shall declare it,"* refers as stated, to *"The Judgment Seat of Christ."*

## THE JUDGMENT SEAT OF CHRIST

1. *What is the Judgment Seat of Christ?* It is the place and time of Judgment, when Christ as the Head of the Church, will judge all Believers.
2. *Who will be at this Judgment?* It will be a Judgment for Believers only, with no unbelievers present.
3. *What type of Judgment will it be?* It will be the time when the *"works"* of all Believers are judged. It will not be a Judgment for Believers' sins, for that was handled at Calvary. It will pertain only to the person's service for the Lord, and the manner in which it was conducted and carried out. At this time, Believers can lose their reward, as many will, but not their souls.
4. *Where will this Judgment occur?* It will take place in Heaven.
5. *When will this Judgment occur?* The Scripture does not plainly say, but it will probably be brought about immediately before the Second Coming. At that time, Believers will come back with Christ, and with duties and station no doubt already assigned, which could hardly be done until this Judgment is concluded (Rev. Chpt. 19).
6. *Who will be the Judge?* Jesus.

The phrase, *"Because it shall be revealed by fire,"* actually refers to the fire of God's Word, which must be the Standard for all that is done. As it always has been, it always shall be. That which does not measure up, shall be consumed by the pronouncements of the Word.

The phrase, *"And the fire shall try every man's work of what sort it is,"* pertains to the Holy Spirit Who is the Superintendent of the Word, but yet under the direction of the Lord Jesus Christ. Hence, John said, *"He* (Jesus) *shall Baptize you with the Holy Spirit, and with fire:*

*"Whose fan is in His* (Jesus') *Hand, and He will throughly purge His floor, and gather His wheat into the garner; but He will burn up the chaff* (all that is of the flesh) *with unquenchable fire"* (Mat. 3:11-12).

The idea is, that all the *"works"* of the Child of God must have as their origination the instigation of the Holy Spirit. Unless the Holy Spirit is the One Who works through us, the results will not be durable because the material will not be durable. He Alone can produce works through us that will stand the examination of God.

Actually, the work of Christians sometimes cannot be detected as worthless, for outwardly the results may look similar to those which are of great worth. However, the fire of that coming day will reveal the purity or impurity of such works.

*"Fire"* in the Greek is *"puri,"* and speaks of the ability of Christ to see through everything we do (Rev. 2:18). He Alone knows our very motives! (Rossier).

## TWO KINDS OF TESTINGS

That to which we will address ourselves, concerns not only the Judgment Seat of Christ, but, as well, testings which are carried out by the Lord in this present life, which should be an indication to us of the spiritual state of affairs.

There are two words in the Greek both meaning *"to test."* It is important in the interests of accurate interpretation, to distinguish between them, since they refer to different kinds of testings.

## PASSED THE EXAMINATION

The first Greek word is *"dokimazo."*

We will look at some instances of its use in the early Manuscripts. These are of great help in the forming of an accurate Judgment as to the usages of New Testament words, since an illustration is often clearer than a definition.

The word is used in a Manuscript of A.D. 140 which contains a plea for the exemption of physicians, and especially of those who have passed the examination. The words *"passed the examination"* are the translation of *"dokimazo."* From this we arrive at the definition.

The word refers to the act of testing someone or something for the purpose of approving it. These Physicians had passed their examinations for the Degree of Doctor of Medicine. In the inscriptions, the word is almost a technical term for passing as fit for a public office. It is found in the sentence, *"Whichever way, then, you also approve of, so it shall be,"* and in the phrase, *"To instruct, if you will, any Magistrate whom you may sanction."*

The words *"approve"* and *"sanction"* are the translations of *"dokimazo."*

The word has in it the idea of proving a thing whether it be worthy to be received or not. It implies that the trial itself was made in the expectation and hope that the issue would be such, that of approval. At all events, there was no contrary hope or expectation.

## TO BREAK DOWN UNDER THE TEST

The other Greek word is *"peirazo."* It means in the first place *"to pierce, search, attempt."* Then it came to mean *"to try or test intentionally, and with the purpose of discovering what good or evil, what power or weakness, was in a person or thing."*

But the fact that men so often break down under this test, gave this Greek word (peirazo) a predominant sense of putting to the proof with the intention and the hope that the one put to the test may break down under the test. Thus, the word is used constantly of the solicitations and suggestions of Satan.

Consequently, the Greek word *"dokimazo"* is used generally of God, but never of Satan, for Satan never puts to the test in order that he may approve.

*"Peirazo"* is used at times of God, but only in the sense of testing in order to discover what evil or good may be in a person.

Consequently, we can see from this study that it is important that one recognize the difference in these words which both mean *"to test,"* especially when one learns that they have the same translation in some parts of the New Testament.

For instance, *"dokimazo"* occurs in Luke 14:19 and *"peirazo"* in John 6:6, and yet the one English word *"prove"* is the translation.

The man who bought the oxen went to examine them, not for the purpose of discovering what their good points might be or whether they had any defects. He bought them for sound, healthy stock, and fully expecting that they were what the Seller represented them to do, he merely went to put his approval upon what he had bought. That is, *"dokimazo."*

When our Lord posed the question to Philip, *"Whence shall we buy bread, that these may eat?",* He was testing him to discover what Faith or lack of Faith, what clear spiritual insight or lack of it, what natural or supernatural view, that Apostle might have. The test brought out what was in Philip's thinking. He was reasoning along a natural line. That is *"peirazo."*

These two words are translated by the one English word *"try"* in Revelation 2:2 and I Corinthians 3:13, which we are now studying.

## TESTING AT THE JUDGMENT SEAT OF CHRIST

At the Judgment Seat of Christ, the Believer's service will be tested, not for the purpose of finding out what good or evil there was in it, but to put God's Approval upon that part of it which was the Work of the Holy Spirit and the Holy Spirit Alone.

A *"Well done, thou good and faithful servant . . . enter thou into the joy of thy lord"* (Mat. 25:23), and a reward in addition to those blessed words, are awaiting every Believer in the Lord Jesus, for God will put His Approval upon this Spirit-wrought works of the Saints and reward them.

It is precious to note that *"dokimazo"* is used here, not *"peirazo."* The Believer's works are not up for Judgment with a penalty attached for those works not done in the Power of the Holy Spirit. These latter works, however, will be burned up, and the Believer will lose the reward he would have received had they been done in the Power of the Spirit. The Judgment Seat of Christ is not for the Judgment of the Believer himself, and certainly not for his retention or loss of Salvation. It is not *"peirazo,"* to discover what evil or good there may be. It is *"dokimazo,"* to examine in order to approve.

God expects to find, that in the service of the Saint upon which He can put His Approval, for the Holy Spirit produces good works in all the Saints (Eph. 2:10), more in those who are definitely subjected to His Control.

So the great loss at this time, at least for those whose works or part of their works, are

NOTES

not proper (Spirit-instituted), will be the loss of reward, which in itself, is serious enough. Therefore, we should not take it lightly.

TRYING THEM

In the case of the Church at Ephesus (Rev. 2:2) *"trying"* those who came to it representing themselves as Apostles, we have the Greek word *"peirazo,"* which means *"to try or test intentionally, and with the purpose of discovering what good or evil, what power or weakness, is in a person or thing."*

The Church was suspicious of these strangers. It had no reason to believe that it would find in these men that upon which it could put its approval. Thus, the Greek word *"dokimazo,"* which means *"the testing of someone or something for the purpose of approving it,"* is not used here. The Church put these men to the test, that is, examined them to see what good or evil there was in them, intending to accept them if good, but to reject them if evil. They found them to be liars.

EXAMINE

Both words (*"doximazo"* and *"peirazo"*) are translated *"examine"* in I Corinthians 11:28 and II Corinthians 13:5. In the first Passage, it is expected that the Believer partake of the Bread and Wine at the Lord's Table only when he can approve his life after having examined himself. If he finds nothing between him and his Saviour, then he is in an approved state, eligible to observe the Lord's Supper. This is *"dokimazo."*

In the second Passage, the members of the Corinthian Assembly are exhorted to examine themselves to see whether they are True Believers or not. This is in accord with the meaning of *"peirazo,"* namely, that of finding out what there is of good or evil in a person.

If the examination showed that they were True Believers (peirazo), then they could *"prove"* themselves, that is, put their approval upon that fact, the word *"prove"* being the translation of *"dokimazo."*

We will now list the places where each word is found, and study a few representative Passages, leaving for the Reader the delightful task of looking into the other instances of their use in the light of the distinctive meanings of each word.

NOTES

WHERE *"DOKIMAZO"* IS FOUND

Dokimazo is found in the following places and is translated by the words *"discern, prove, did like, approve, try, examine, allow"*; Lk. 12:56; 14:19; Rom. 1:28; 2:18; 12:2; 14:22; I Cor. 3:13; 11:28; 16:3; II Cor. 8:8, 22; 13:5 (*"prove"*), Gal. 6:4; Eph. 5:10; Phil. 1:10; I Thess. 2:4; 5:21; I Tim. 3:10; Heb. 3:9; I Pet. 1:7; I Jn. 4:1.

THE MANNER IN WHICH THE WORD *"DOKIMAZO"* IS USED

In Luke 12:56, the hypocrites could examine the weather conditions and put their approval upon them, but they were unable to understand the character of the coming of the Messiah to Israel, and then put their approval upon it.

In Romans 1:28, lost humanity after scanning Deity for the purpose of putting its approval upon Him, did not find anything in or about Him that met with its approval, a sad commentary upon the total depravity of the human heart.

As well, in Romans 14:22 we have, *"Spiritually prosperous is he who does not condemn himself in the thing which after being examined, he has put his approval upon."*

In I Thessalonians 2:4, Paul says that after God examined him, He put His approval upon him as one worthy to be entrusted with the Gospel, the words *"allowed"* and *"trieth"* both being from the Greek word *"dokimazo."* The other occurrences of *"dokimazo"* are translated by the words *"prove, try, and examine,"* and the English Reader should have no difficulty with them.

*"PEIRAZO"* IS USED IN THE FOLLOWING . . .

We come now to the places where the Greek word *"peirazo"* is used, and where it is translated by the words *"tempt, try, hath gone about, assayed."*

The word is found in Matthew 4:1, 3, 7; 16:1; 19:3; 22:18, 35; Mark 1:13; 8:11; 10:2; 12:15; Luke 4:2; 11:16; 20:23; John 6:6; 8:6; Acts 5:9; 15:10; 16:7; 24:6; I Corinthians 7:5; 10:9, 13; II Corinthians 13:5; Galatians 6:1; I Thessalonians 3:5; Hebrews 2:18; 3:9; 4:15; 11:17, 37; James 1:13-14; Revelation 2:2, 10; 3:10.

We will look at representative Passages.

THE MANNER IN WHICH IT IS USED

In Matthew 4:1, our Lord was led by the Holy Spirit into the wilderness to be tested by the Devil, the test being in the form of solicitations to do evil. In Matthew 4:7 our Lord said to Satan, *"It stands written, thou shalt not put the Lord thy God to the test* (to see what good or evil there may be in Him)*."*

In Matthew 22:18, our Lord asks the hypocrites why they are putting Him to the test. Such an action on the part of man with relation to God always shows a state of unbelief.

The words *"Hath gone about"* in Acts 24:6 are from *"peirazo."* Paul was charged with bringing Greeks into the Temple at Jerusalem, making a test-case of his action, possibly to show that Gentiles in this Age of Grace were not only admitted into Salvation along with Israel, and were members of the same Body, but that they also had equal access to the Jewish Temple along with the Jews. The charges of course were totally false, but they show the Jewish attitude towards Paul's Ministry to the Gentiles.

In I Corinthians 10:13, the word *"tempted"* refers to any test which Satan may put before us, the purpose of which is, of course, to bring out evil in our lives if he can, as in the case of Job, or a direct solicitation to do evil, as in the case of Israel as seen in the context.

In Hebrews 11:17, *"Abraham, when he was tried,"* that is, put to the test by God to see whether his Faith would surmount the obstacle of the loss of his son, met the test, thus demonstrating his Faith.

The word *"peirazo"* is found in the Septuagint translation of the Old Testament Passage reporting this incident, and is translated *"tempted."*

In James 1:13-14, the word *"tempted"* is to be understood as *"solicit to do evil."* God at times does test man in order to show man his sinfulness and, consequently, to develop his character (James 1:2, 12), but He *never* solicits man to do evil.

(14) "IF ANY MAN'S WORK ABIDE WHICH HE HATH BUILT THEREUPON, HE SHALL RECEIVE A REWARD."

The phrase, *"If any man's work abide,"* presents the stress placed on the word *"if."* Actually, Paul uses this word not only here but as well in Verses 15, 17, and 18.

NOTES

*"If"* in the Greek is *"ei,"* and *"normally assumes something to be true."* In other words, the Holy Spirit is having the Apostle to use this word in this fashion indicating, that the Believer knows his own motives, and knows whether his work will abide or not.

The Judgment Seat of Christ will not be for the purpose of the Lord embarrassing us publicly. In effect, the Lord will pronounce that which we already know to be true.

Again, the idea is, that we know our own motives. We know if we truly are exalting God or exalting self (Rossier). So, there will be no exclamated surprise at that time by the Saint, as the Lord announces the result. Each and every Believer knows at this moment, his true purpose, motives, or reason. The idea is that we shape up, if in fact, our motives are wrong, or what we are doing is not instituted by the Holy Spirit.

The phrase, *"Which he hath built thereupon,"* concerns the manner in which it is built.

Is what we are doing of self, or of the Holy Spirit? The sad fact is, most of what is presently done in the Name of the Lord is in fact, instituted and engineered by man, and not the Holy Spirit. In fact, being led by the Holy Spirit is something which the far greater majority of the Church knows absolutely nothing about.

Actually, several of the major Old-Line Denominations do not even believe in the leading of the Holy Spirit, so that door is permanently closed. This means that for all practical purposes, at least as a whole, these Denominations are doing absolutely nothing for the Lord, all of their efforts being in the realm of man-birthed, man-instituted, man-directed, etc. Regrettably, many of the Pentecostal Denominations are following suit, even though the very purpose and thrust of their being is supposed to be the leading of the Holy Spirit. However, in these circles (Pentecostal Denominations), men have abrogated, at least for the most part, the Headship of Christ in the Church respecting Government, which automatically abrogates or stops the leading of the Holy Spirit in this capacity.

While some Preachers and Laity in these particular Denominations may continue to be led by the Spirit despite the spiritual disobedience of its Leadership, such will actually become less and less.

The following is an example, although drastic! While the Holy Spirit rarely works in this manner, still, it is His prerogative if He so desires.

## THE LEADING OF THE SPIRIT

A. N. Trotter, who is now with the Lord, but was one of the great Pentecostal Lights of this century, related this illustration.

If I remember correctly, the time setting was in the 1930's. The Great-Grandson, if I remember the relationship correctly, of General William Booth, Founder of the great Salvation Army, was wondrously Baptized with the Holy Spirit, with the evidence of speaking with other Tongues. It is said that the man had an IQ rating of genius. As well, he spoke several languages, and had one or two earned Doctorates.

He was a tremendous Preacher of the Gospel, said to have had the eloquence of an Apollos of the Book of Acts (Acts 18:24).

Having been recently Baptized with the Holy Spirit, he was much in demand for Camp-meetings, Conventions, etc. in Pentecostal circles. As a shock to most, he then stated that the Lord had called him to Africa.

There was a tremendous hew and cry respecting his claims, with most saying that the Lord would not waste the talents and abilities of this man in Africa. In other words, they were questioning what he had said.

Of course, it was not improper or wrong for the man to be encouraged respecting assurance concerning the Will of God, for many people claim things which God really has not called them to do. Nevertheless, he maintained that this is what the Lord wanted. Most never did agree with him, claiming that his great talents and abilities would be wasted in Africa.

Some months later he went. He had not been there three days (if I remember the time correctly), when he contracted Blackwater Fever, and in less than ten days was dead. In fact, he never preached a sermon in that country.

Of course, when the news reached America, almost all stated that this proved that he had missed God, for such a thing would not have happened had he been in the Will of the Lord.

## A GREAT MOVE OF GOD

His funeral was delayed for some days, as the news spread throughout the African Bush concerning this man who had come from America, and in effect given his life for Africans. When they finally conducted the funeral, it is said that thousands of natives were there, some from many miles distant.

At the funeral it is said, the Spirit of God fell on the proceedings, in effect, proclaiming by God's Presence that what had been done, was in fact, the Will of God. Many Africans were Saved that day, but that was only the beginning.

Brother Trotter, who incidentally spent some years in Africa himself, went on to relate how that a fire began to burn that day in that part of Africa, that resulted in the greatest Move of God that had ever been seen in that part of the world. Over a period of time, which actually continues unto this hour, many, many souls were Saved, with many Believers being Baptized with the Holy Spirit. Churches were founded, which are thriving to this hour, in that land. He went on to relate as to how he had participated in that great move, seeing God do great things, but he attributed it to this man, the Great Grandson of William Booth, who gave up his life in order that the Spirit of God may work.

As stated, this is a drastic illustration, with the Lord not working in this manner too very often. But at times He does. As well, He must always have this prerogative. We are not our own, but in fact, are bought with a price, a great price at that, the Death and Resurrection of our Lord and Saviour Jesus Christ.

## WHY WOULD THE LORD MOVE THIS WAY?

I do not have the answer to that, and neither does any other human being. The Lord is not required to explain to us all that He does. It is our business as Believers to be followers, to hear from Heaven, and to obey what the Lord has told us to do. This we do know, whatever He says, is always right.

In the natural, no one wants to see someone cut down in the very prime of life, even as was the man we have just mentioned. But yet, the Lord knew the future. He acted accordingly, in that this man giving his life without even preaching one Message in Africa, would in effect, win more souls to Christ, than if he had lived. The key is, that he heard from the Lord and followed the Lord, and when he stands at the Judgment Seat of Christ, his reward will be great.

We must always remember, this life is merely a dress rehearsal for Eternity. While it is true that what we do here is very important, as should be obvious, still, the only truly important thing is that we have the leading of the Holy Spirit and follow accordingly. Perhaps this is what Jesus meant in His description of the faithfulness of the Holy Spirit to prune our lives so that our fruit will remain and even bear much more fruit (Jn. 15:16).

The phrase, *"He shall receive a reward,"* pertains to that which will be eternal. However, we are not told exactly what the *"reward"* will be. Nevertheless, this we do know:

Whatever the Lord does is always on a grand and glorious scale. Consequently, we can be certain that whatever the reward is, it will be wonderful, glorious, and of supreme worth.

## REWARDS AS EXPRESSED IN THE BIBLE

Thirteen Hebrew root words of which *"saker"* and *"sohad"* are the chief, lie behind Old Testament expressions of *"reward."*

In the Greek Text, from which the New Testament is written, the verb *"apodidomi"* and noun *"misthos"* are used. All convey the meaning of payment, hire or wages. There are instances of *"reward"* as pay for honest work done (I Tim. 5:18), and it can refer to dishonest gain, i.e., bribes (Micah 3:11).

## THE CHARACTER OF ITS BESTOWER

Any reward depends for its significance upon the character of its Bestower, and God's Rewards, with which the Biblical Writers are chiefly concerned, both as Blessings and as Punishments, are manifestations of His Justice, i.e., of Himself (Ps. 58:11) and inseparable from the Covenant (Deut. 7:10) to which His Commands are annexed.

Thus, the Second Commandment in the Old Testament relates the penalty of disobedience to the jealousy of God, and the reward of obedience to His Mercy (Ex. 20:5).

Deuteronomy Chapter 28 explains Israel's well-being in terms of submission to the Covenant, a theme developed by the later Prophets (Isa. 65:6-7; 66:6). That obedience to God will bring visible temporal rewards as rightly expected throughout the Bible, but two false conclusions were also drawn from such teaching as in Deuteronomy Chapter 28, namely:

1. That Righteousness is automatically rewarded materially.
2. That suffering is a certain sign of sin.

Both of these assumptions are wrong, with both Job and the Psalmist reflecting the tension created by these False Doctrines (Ps. 37 and 73).

Yet it must be noted that in the Old Testament God Himself and His Salvation are already known to be the supreme reward rather than His Gifts (Ps. 63:3; Isa. 62:10-12).

## THE NEW TESTAMENT

Jesus promised rewards to His Disciples (Mat. 5:3-12; Mk. 9:41; 10:29), so coupled with self-denial and suffering for the Gospel's sake as to prevent a mercenary attitude. Actually, He slew the Pharisaic notion of meritorious service (Lk. 17:10) and discouraged desire for human reward (Mat. 6:1), since the Father is the Disciple's best reward.

Jesus shows that reward is inseparable from Himself and from God, and the Apostles labored to establish the complete dependence of man's Obedience and Faith upon Mercy and Grace (Rom. 4:4; 6:23). Work and, therefore, reward, is certainly looked for, but simply as an index of living Faith (Jn. 6:28; James 2:14-16), not as a basis of claim upon God.

The reward of Salvation in Christ begins in time (II Cor. 5:5) and its fulfillment is looked for after the Resurrection, when God's Covenant People enter into full enjoyment of the Vision of God which is their enduring reward (Rev. 21:3).

Actually, just to be with Christ, and to be with Him forever, will be reward enough. Anything else that He may give the Saints, as wonderful and gracious as it may be, will pale into insignificance by comparison to His Glorious Presence. The sight of Him, and most of all to be with Him forever, will be the reward of all the ages.

(15) "IF ANY MAN'S WORK SHALL BE BURNED, HE SHALL SUFFER LOSS: BUT HE HIMSELF SHALL BE SAVED; YET SO AS BY FIRE."

The phrase, *"If any man's work shall be burned, he shall suffer loss,"* refers to the loss of rewards but not Salvation. Most importantly,

NOTES

this is a judgment of works, not a judgment of persons (Rossier).

I am positive that this is understandable; however, to make certain of the clarity, no sins of any Believer will ever be brought up again, not even here at the Judgment Seat of Christ. All sins at the time of Conversion have been washed and taken away, and every sin committed since Conversion falls into the same category. Therefore, at this Judgment, no one has to be concerned about past failures, sins, or wrongdoing of any nature, for the simple reason that all were judged at Calvary, and the Believer's Faith in what Christ did at that momentous time in history, totally and completely handled the sin problem. One can only say, *"Thank you Lord!"*

The phrase, *"But he himself shall be Saved; yet so as by fire,"* actually means, that the person is Saved *"despite the fire."*

This *"fire"* of the Spirit and of the Word of God will address itself to the works of every Believer, and that which is of *"wood, hay and stubble,"* will be instantly consumed (figuratively speaking), but such cannot touch the soul, as the Lord Jesus Christ has already taken that fire of Judgment on Calvary's Cross.

Some use this Verse attempting to teach the Doctrine of Purgatory; however, that idea is totally foreign to this Verse.

First, the Verse does not deal with Salvation, but rather the works of Believers. As well, the language is metaphorical as should be obvious.

The fire is *"probatory,"* not *"purgatorial,"* and it is not in itself a fire of wrath, for it tests the gold and silver as well as the inferior elements of the structure. It is the fire of the refiner, not of the avenger (Farrar).

(For a complete treatment on the Doctrine of Purgatory, please see our Commentary on the Gospel of Luke.)

(16) "KNOW YE NOT THAT YE ARE THE TEMPLE OF GOD, AND THAT THE SPIRIT OF GOD DWELLETH IN YOU?"

The beginning of the question, *"Know ye not that ye are the Temple of God,"* presents to this point, a long succession of miraculous wonders, as the Plan of God step by step has brought man to this wonderful place.

## FROM THE BEGINNING

After the Fall in the Garden of Eden, God was forced to drive man out of that sacred place in order *"to keep the way of the Tree of Life"* (Gen. 3:23-24). In fact, it was an act of Mercy instead of Judgment.

Had fallen man eaten of the Tree of Life, he would have lived forever in this fallen, horrible state, which would have been a catastrophe of unprecedented proportions. Think of an Adolph Hitler, or a Joseph Stalin living forever! (Gen. 3:22).

Nevertheless, when the Lord drove Adam and Eve out of the Garden, He went with them, and in essence, promised that He would bring man back.

From the very beginning the Lord established a means by which He could communicate with fallen man, which was by the slaying of an innocent victim, actually a clean animal, which would symbolize the coming Redeemer, The Lord Jesus Christ (Gen. 3:21; 4:4). God Who is Thrice Holy could not approach man or have man approach Him in the normal sense of the word, due to the fact that the Holiness of God would have slain sinful man on the spot. Therefore, He communed with man by way of the Altar, which was actually carried through until Jesus came, for it was a Type of Christ. In fact, all the Patriarchs were Altar-Builders, for the simple reason that Calvary has always been the way to approach God, whether before the fact, or now after the fact. In fact, Calvary is the most graphic, striking, pivot point in all of history. In other words, everything revolves around the Death of Jesus, the Son of God, on the Cross, and His Glorious Resurrection.

## THE TABERNACLE

Salvation has always been none of man and all of God. As such, all the plans, efforts, design, expense, and price, have always been afforded by God. His unending Love for man is the reason (Jn. 3:16). Step by step He has continued to come closer to man, all because of the price He has paid.

The Sacrifices which began in the Garden, continued for about 2400 years, offered up by individual Patriarchs, etc. (Gen. 8:20; 12:7; 13:4; 22:8-9; 26:25; 35:1; 46:1).

After God called Abraham and from his loins and Sarah's womb, Isaac was born, the Child of Promise, from this couple came the great Nation of Israel, raised up for the expressed purpose of being a Holy People, in order that

NOTES

the Messiah, the Redeemer of mankind through them, could be brought into the world.

After delivering the Children of Israel from Egyptian bondage, God gave Moses the Law on Mount Sinai. In fact, this was the only Law of God in the entirety of the Earth, which made Israel far and away superior to all other people.

In this Law, were the plans for the Tabernacle with the Lord saying, *"And let them make Me a Sanctuary; that I may dwell among them"* (Ex. 25:8-9). This would be a great improvement over the individual Sacrifices, with a system of Worship elaborately set up by God, even as He would dwell between the Mercy Seat and the Cherubim. He said, *"And there I will meet with thee, and I will commune with thee from above the Mercy Seat, from between the two Cherubims which are upon the Ark of the Testimony, of all things which I will give thee in Commandment unto the Children of Israel"* (Ex. 25:22).

So, the Lord has now come closer, in that He actually lives among His People. But still, He can only be approached in a certain manner, and only by the Priests at that, and more particularly, by the High Priest, who was a Type of Christ. But still, this was a vast improvement over the previous Altars, in that God now resided with His People constantly.

## SINFUL MAN AND A THRICE HOLY GOD

Despite the elaborate system of worship devised by the Lord respecting the Sacrifices, the Law and the Feast Days, etc., God still could not draw near to man for the simple reason that the blood of bulls and goats could not take away sin (Heb. 10:4). While the Blood of the Sacrifices did cover the confessed sin of man, it did not take it away. Consequently, even though these who truly believe were definitely Saved, and because Salvation has always been by Faith (Gen. 15:6), still, the Sacrifice of animals, could not remove the terrible sin debt of man.

As a result, several things remained pertinent:

1. The sin debt still unremoved, provided a barrier between God and believing man. Because of this sin debt, a Thrice Holy God could not approach man, or man would have died. Therefore, a total sense of forgiveness which is enjoyed at present by Believers, was not the privilege of those before Calvary.

NOTES

2. Due to the remaining of the sin debt against man, when Believers died before Calvary, they were actually taken captive by Satan into the nether world of the lost. Admittedly, they enjoyed the place called Paradise, but still, the only thing that separated Paradise from the burning side of Hell, was a great gulf (Lk. 16:19-31; Eph. 4:8-10).

3. As well, due to the sin debt, the Holy Spirit, even though able to provide help, could not indwell Believers before Calvary (Jn. 14:16-17).

## THE TEMPLE

During the nearly one thousand years from the time of Solomon to the time of Christ, three Temples existed in Israel: A. Solomon's Temple; B. Zerubbabel's Temple, erected after the dispersion; and, C. Herod's Temple which was in existence during the Life and Ministry of Christ.

Theologically the Tabernacle as a dwelling-place of God on Earth is of immense importance, as being the first in the series: Tabernacle, Temple, the Incarnation of Christ, and now the body of the individual Believer, even as we are presently studying.

It follows from the fact that the Tabernacle was built to God's design as *"a copy and shadow of heavenly things"* (Heb. 8:5) that its symbols conveyed spiritual meaning to the Israelites of the time. What that meaning was is often stated explicitly, as with the Ark and Mercy Seat (Ex. 25:16, 22; Lev. 16:15-16) etc.

The Tabernacle was constructed during the Exodus, and though it was maintained for some centuries, after that era, it was eventually lost to history.

The construction of Solomon's Temple in Jerusalem provided a great improvement over the Tabernacle. In the first place, it served as a gathering-point for all the people, a symbol of their unity in the worship of God.

Even though the Temple procedure established form and ceremony, still, God was still no closer to man than He had been in the Tabernacle. Buildings, be they crude or ornate, and the Temple was without a doubt the most expensive building ever constructed, in 1998 currency costing approximately a trillion dollars; nevertheless, those things did not address man's real problem, which was sin. That problem could be eradicated in only one way, to which all of this pointed, God becoming Man, in order to pay the supreme price of Redemption (Isa. 7:14).

## THE INCARNATION

For the first time God now dwelt in a man, and I speak of the Incarnation of Christ. He is now a giant step closer, which will ultimately deal with the terrible problem of sin.

In effect, we now have two Temples of God on Earth at the same time, the Physical Body of Jesus, and Herod's Temple. However, the Truth was, that the Lord no longer resided in the Holy of Holies in this particular Temple. In fact, there was no Ark of the Covenant left or Mercy Seat, that having been lost when Nebuchadnezzar invaded Jerusalem, destroying Solomon's Temple.

## JESUS AND THE TEMPLE

The attitude of Jesus to the Temple of Jerusalem contains two opposing features. On the one hand, Jesus greatly respected it; on the other hand, He attached relatively little importance to it. Thus, He called it the *"House of God"* (Mat. 12:4; Jn. 2:16).

Everything in it was Holy, He taught, because it was Sanctified by God Who was supposed to have dwelt in it. Zeal for His Father's House inspired Him to cleanse it (Jn. 2:17), and thought of the impending doom of the Holy City caused Him to weep (Lk. 19:41).

In contrast are those Passages in which Jesus relegated the Temple to a very subordinate position. He was greater than the Temple, and for all the obvious reasons (Mat. 12:6). Actually, it had become a cover for the spiritual barrenness of Israel (Mk. 11:12-26). Soon the Temple would perish, because He had fulfilled all its Types and Shadows.

When Jesus died on Calvary and was raised from the dead, this One Great Sacrifice laid forever to rest, the necessity of further Animal Sacrifices. Consequently, no Lamb would need ever again to be offered up. As well, the Priests could fold their robes, and bank the Altar fires. As far as God was concerned, there would never again be the need of the body of a little animal to be laid upon the burning pyre. All of it, from the very beginning in the Garden of Eden, with the Sacrifice of every animal, the poured-out blood of untold numbers of bleating lambs, the One Sacrifice of Jesus made it all unnecessary anymore, and forever.

NOTES

## THE SIN DEBT IS FOREVER PAID

As a result of the sin debt being forever canceled out by the Sacrifice of Christ, Satan now has no more hold on believing sinners. The debt is gone, with no more sin hanging over the head of believing man. It is all by Faith in what Christ did at Calvary (Eph. 2:8-9).

Consequently, since Calvary, when the Believer dies, Satan can no longer take him down into Paradise as a captive, but rather, he instantly goes to be with Jesus (Phil. 1:21-24). So, Paradise is now empty, vacated by Jesus Christ when He rose from the dead.

Now as well, due to the sin debt being paid, the Holy Spirit can now come into the heart and life of the Believer as He does at Conversion, actually making the spirit, soul, and body of believing man His House or Temple.

As the dwelling place of God among men, the living personality of the Believer replaces the beautiful but cold stone of the Temple. Moreover, the Church, the Body of Christ itself, united by the Bond of Peace, *"is growing into a Holy Temple for the Lord"* (Eph. 2:21).

The Tabernacle and the Temple of old did have contemporary significance for God's Old Testament People. They were, each in its turn, the place of meeting, the place where God's Presence dwelt. However, because of Christ, all now is fresh and new. Today God dwells within us, for Christ has offered the Perfect Sacrifice and provides perpetual access to the Father.

By virtue of God's Presence, you and I become the place of meeting Jesus for all who stumble in darkness through our lost world.

## ONE LAST STEP

Even though nothing can bring man closer to God than Calvary, still, there is one final step to this Holy Union.

After the Millennial Reign and the cleansing of the Heavens and the Earth by fire at the end of that period, God is going to transfer His Headquarters from Heaven to Earth. John wrote about it in the last two Chapters of the Book of Revelation. He said:

*"And I saw a new Heaven and a new Earth: for the first Heaven and the first Earth were passed away; and there was no more sea.*

NOTES

*"And I John saw the Holy City, New Jerusalem, coming down from God out of Heaven, prepared as a Bride adorned for her husband.*

*"And I heard a great voice out of Heaven saying, Behold, the Tabernacle of God is with men, and He will dwell with them, and they shall be His People, and God Himself shall be with them, and be their God"* (Rev. 21:1-3).

Paul then closed it out in effect saying, *"And when all things shall be subdued unto Him, then shall the Son also Himself be subject unto Him that put all things under Him, that God may be all in all"* (I Cor. 15:28).

The conclusion of the question . . . *"And that the Spirit of God dwelleth in you?"*, tells us of something beautiful.

*"Dwelleth"* in the Greek is *"oikeo,"* and means *"to occupy a house and to remain."* In other words, the Holy Spirit comes in to stay and in effect will abide forever.

In fact, when the going gets rough He will not leave. He has come to abide. Actually, the only way that He will leave, is that the Believer no longer believes, and, consequently, no longer desires Him. He will not stay where He is not wanted (Heb. 6:4-6; 10:26-31).

There is absolutely no greater privilege on the face of the Earth than to serve as a House or Temple for the Spirit of God. As well, to know that all of this is made possible by the Great Sacrifice of Christ at Calvary, makes us realize how much that God must love us.

So much has gone before us in order that we might have this privilege and what a privilege it is, even as stated, to serve as a House of God.

(17) "IF ANY MAN DEFILE THE TEMPLE OF GOD, HIM SHALL GOD DESTROY; FOR THE TEMPLE OF GOD IS HOLY, WHICH TEMPLE YE ARE."

The phrase, *"If any man defile the Temple of God, him shall God destroy,"* could be translated, *"God shall ruin the ruiner of His Temple."*

*"Defile"* in the Greek is *"bhtheriro,"* and means *"to corrupt, spoil, ruin, waste, destroy"* (I Cor. 15:33; II Cor. 7:2; 11:3; Eph. 4:22; Jude vs. 10; Rev. 19:2).

This is a solemn warning against all sins of the flesh, which have a tendency to destroy the body.

It should be obvious, that inasmuch as the Lord now occupies the spirit, soul, and body of the Believer, that such is His Temple. As a result, we should be very careful about where we take His Temple, in other words places to which we go which may not be proper, things which we look at, listen to, or in which we participate.

Including the sins we have just mentioned, one can also add to that gossip and slander, or any sin for that matter such as jealousy, envy, malice, greed, pride, bias, prejudice, lust, etc.

THE CLEANSING OF THE TEMPLE

The Temple of which we will now speak, is the material Temple in Jerusalem, of such, which of course, is no longer in use. However, the principle of what Jesus did in cleansing that Temple, holds true for the present residence of the Holy Spirit, our physical bodies, etc.

The first thing he did was to cleanse the Temple of the moneychangers (Mk. 11:15-17).

Before we look at that, please allow me to say at the outset that the Temple of old, has absolutely nothing to do with modern Churches. In other words, God does not dwell in Church Buildings, so even though they should be dedicated to the Lord, still, there is nothing Sacred or Holy about a Church Building, irrespective of what type it may be. Consequently, there is nothing sinful or wrong about having a kitchen in a Church Structure or a Bookstore, etc.

In the Temple at the time of Christ, the Religious Leaders of Israel had set up in the Court of the Gentiles, stalls for moneychangers and for the sale of sacrificial animals such as lambs, etc. To be sure, the profit was huge. No Roman money was allowed to be used in the Temple because of the likeness of Caesar which was on the coins. So, to exchange these coins for Jewish coins of silver or gold, a hefty fee was charged, etc.

The Court of the Gentiles was supposed to be reserved for Gentiles exclusively in their worship of God. However, with the traffic of merchandise taking place in their very area of worship, there was little way at all that they could worship the Lord as should be obvious. So Jesus ran out the moneychangers and cleansed this area.

As well, we learn from this that the chief end of man, and of course I speak of Believers, should be to use his body, mind, and faculties, to Glorify God, rather than the sole interest being that of the things of this world. In Jesus cleansing this Temple, we are warned against worldliness, worldly attractions, the ways of the world, and the world in general. While the Believer is in the world, and as such must traffic with the world, still, we are not of the world or its system, and must not allow its system to come into our lives or thinking.

PRAYER

Jesus said that His House should be called *"The House of Prayer"* (Mk. 11:17). In glaring overtones, this tells us that the Believer should have a strong prayer life. But yet, the sad fact is, most Believers do not. Consequently, True worship and praise are foreign to most Believers, and for the simple reason that such are virtually impossible without a proper prayer life.

OF ALL NATIONS

As we have just stated, Jesus cleansed the Court of the Gentiles, because this was where Gentiles were supposed to come and worship God. However, the Jews cared little anymore if any Gentiles ever heard of the Lord, much less come to worship Him. Therefore, they had turned this area into a *"den of thieves"* (Mk. 11:17).

Jesus referring to *"all Nations,"* tells us that the chief obligation and duty of each and every Believer, is the propagation of the Gospel to the entirety of the world. Someone brought the Gospel to us, and we are to do all within our power to take the Gospel to others.

This should be the effort of every Believer respecting our prayer life and our giving. For those who do not know of Jesus and His Power to Save, as far as that person is concerned, Jesus died in vain.

JESUS, THE HEAD OF THE BODY

Jesus is the One Who cleansed the Temple then, and He is the One Who cleanses the Temple presently, albeit through the Person and Ministry of the Holy Spirit. It is His Church, i.e., *"Body,"* which translates into each particular individual. In other words, the word *"Body"* is used collectively for the entirety of the Church, and used individually and literally for each Believer.

THE DAY THE HOLY SPIRIT LEFT THE TEMPLE

During the time of Jeremiah and Ezekiel, the Lord was dealing greatly so with Judah through these Prophets, with Jeremiah being in Judah Proper and Ezekiel in Babylonia. Regrettably, Judah would not heed and went to her doom.

The Lord showed Ezekiel the terrible abominations of Judah which were taking place at that time, and He pictured them as happening in the Temple, even though it spoke of the entirety of Judah. The Temple was where the Lord dwelt between the Mercy Seat and the Cherubim, therefore, it was at the Temple where Ezekiel was taken in a vision (Ezek. Chpt. 8).

In the 11th Chapter of this Prophet's Book, the Lord showed Ezekiel the Holy Spirit leaving the Temple. It says, *"Then did the Cherubims lift up their wings, and the wheels beside them; and the Glory of the God of Israel was over them above.*

*"And the Glory of the Lord went up from the midst of the City, and stood upon the mountain which is on the East side of the City"* (Ezek. 11:22-23).

This was a vision of the Holy Spirit leaving out of the Holy of Holies of the Temple because He was no longer desired. As stated, Judah went to her doom.

So, the Holy Spirit can leave out of a Temple, whether a material Temple of old, or present Believers speaking of their Body, Soul, and Spirit. He does so if He is not wanted.

Consequently, this shatters the unscriptural Doctrine of Unconditional Eternal Security. The Believer cannot have both God and sin at the same time. Ultimately, one or the other has to go.

THAT WHICH GOD DEMANDS

The phrase, *"For the Temple of God is Holy, which Temple ye are,"* refers here to the physical body of the Believer as well as the soul and the spirit (Rom. 12:1; II Cor. 7:1).

The idea is, as should be obvious, that God demands that His Temple be *"Holy."* However, the Holiness He demands, is not that which is contrived by man, but that which is given totally and completely by the Lord Jesus Christ, actually given at Conversion. In other words, it is not something that someone works into, but is a Gift from the Lord (I Cor. 6:11).

While *"Holy"* or *"Holiness"* is a *Standing* which does not vary or change, and as stated, is given freely by the Lord, and comes by Faith, that does not mean that sin is allowable. As stated, while no Believer is perfect, the idea is, that the Believer work in cooperation with the Holy Spirit, that He be allowed to get everything out of our lives which is not pleasing to the Lord. God will have patience in this process, in order that our *"State"* be brought up to our *"Standing"*; however, the Grace of God is never a license to sin, but rather liberty to live a holy life before God. While there is nothing the Saint can do which would earn anything from God, there are many things the Saint can do which will drive the Lord away. As stated, even though the Lord will forgive times without number, ultimately, the sin is going to have to go, and of course, the sooner the better.

## THE HOLINESS OF GOD IN RELATION TO HIS PEOPLE

The Old Testament applies the word *"Holy"* to human beings in virtue of their consecration to the Lord. This applied to the Priests who were consecrated by special ceremonies, and even to the whole Nation of Israel as a people separated from other Nations and consecrated to God. Thus, it was relationship to God that constituted Israel a Holy People, and in this sense it was the highest expression of the Covenant Relationship.

Due to Jesus not yet having come, therefore, the price at Calvary not yet being paid, the Holy Spirit could not literally come into Believers, even though He did help them. Consequently, Holiness was more ritualistic and ceremonial than anything else.

However, upon the Advent of Christ and the price He paid at Calvary and the Resurrection, the conception of Holiness greatly advanced, even as the Revelation of God advanced. From the outside to the inside, from ceremonial to reality, it took on a strong ethical significance, and this is the main, and practically its exclusive, connotation in the New Testament. The Holy Spirit could now live in the hearts and lives of Believers, thereby, perfecting Holiness.

## THAT WHICH THE PROPHETS OF OLD TAUGHT

The Old Testament Prophets proclaimed Holiness as preeminently God's Self-Disclosure, the Testimony He bears to Himself and the aspect under which He wills His creatures to know Him.

NOTES

Moreover, the Prophets declared that God willed to communicate His Holiness to His Creatures, and that, in turn, He claims Holiness from them. If *"I am Holy"* is the Divine Self-assertion, lifting God immeasurably above His Creatures, so *"Be Holy"* is the Divine Call to His Creatures to *"share in His Holiness"* (Heb. 12:10).

It is this imparting of the Divine Holiness which automatically takes place in the soul of man in Regeneration and becomes the spring and foundation of Holy Character.

## THE LORD JESUS CHRIST

Christ in His Life and Character is the Supreme Example of the Divine Holiness. In Him it consisted in more than mere sinlessness: it was His entire consecration to the Will and Purpose of God, and to this end Jesus Sanctified Himself (Jn. 17:19). The Holiness of Christ is both the Standard of the Christian Character and its guarantee: *"He Who Sanctifies and those who are Sanctified have all one origin"* (Heb. 2:11).

## SAINTS

In the New Testament the Apostolic designation for Christians is *"Saints,"* and it continued to be used as a general designation at least up to the days of Irenaeus and Tertullian, though after that it degenerated in ecclesiastical usage into an honorific title. Actually, this took place as the Church began to apostatize, in other words, attempting to earn particular things by *"works,"* etc. One is made a Saint by one's Faith in Christ, which actually takes place instantly at Conversion.

Though the primary significance of Holiness is relationship, it is also descriptive of character, and more especially of Christlike Character. The New Testament everywhere emphasizes the ethical nature of Holiness in contrast to all moral uncleanness.

It is represented as the supreme vocation of Christians and the goal of their living. In the final assessment of human destiny, the two categories known to Scripture are the Righteous (Holy) and the wicked (unholy).

## THE ESCHATOLOGICAL OR FUTURISTIC SIGNIFICANCE OF HOLINESS

Scripture emphasizes the permanence of moral character (Rev. 22:11). It also emphasizes the retributive aspect of the Divine Holiness. It involves the world in Judgment.

From a moral necessity in God, life is so ordered that in Holiness is spiritual welfare and blessing, and in sin is doom. Since the Divine Holiness could not make a Universe in which sin would ultimately prosper, the retributive quality in the Divine Government becomes perfectly plain. But retribution is not the end; the Holiness of God ensures that there will be a final restoration, a bringing to pass of the Regeneration of the moral Universe.

The eschatology (future events) of the Bible holds out the Promise that the Holiness of God will ultimately sweep the Universe clean and create *"New Heavens and a New Earth, in which Righteousness will dwell"* (II Pet. 3:13).

The Holiness of God demands such!

## THE HOLINESS OF GOD'S CHARACTER

From what has already been said it becomes clear that Holiness is not so much a relation of the creature to the Creator as of the Creator to the creature. In other words, it is the Holiness of God that underlies that separation of life and distinctiveness of Character that belong to God's People. This gives point to the distinction that different terms are applied to the Holiness of God and that of His People.

Holiness belongs to God as Divine, and He would not be God without it. In that respect, *"There is none Holy like the Lord"* (I Sam. 2:2). The ethical quality in Holiness is the aspect most commonly brought to the fore when the word is applied to God. It is basically a term for the moral excellence of God and His freedom from all limitations in His Moral Perfection (Hab. 1:13).

It is in this respect that God Alone is Holy and the Standard of ethical purity in His Creatures.

## HOLINESS AND THE GODHEAD

Since Holiness embraces every distinctive attribute of the Godhead, it may be conceived of as the outshining of all that God is. As the Sun's rays, combining all the colors of the spectrum, come together in the Sun's shining and blend into light, so in His Self-manifestation all the attributes of God come together and blend into Holiness. Holiness has, for that reason, been called *"An attribute of attributes,"* that which lends unity to all the attributes of God.

NOTES

To conceive of God's Being and Character as merely a synthesis of abstract perfection is to deprive God of all reality. In the God of the Bible these perfections live and function in Holiness.

For these reasons we can understand why Holiness is expressly attributed in Scripture to each Person in the Godhead, to the Father (Jn. 17:11), to the Son (Acts 4:30), and especially to the Spirit as the One Who manifests and communicates the Holiness of God to His people.

(18) "LET NO MAN DECEIVE HIMSELF. IF ANY MAN AMONG YOU SEEMETH TO BE WISE IN THIS WORLD, LET HIM BECOME A FOOL, THAT HE MAY BE WISE."

The phrase, *"Let no man deceive himself,"* proclaims that which is possible, or the admonition would not have been given. Paul also said, *"Be not deceived"* (I Cor. 6:9; 15:33; Gal. 6:7).

Jeremiah said, *"Deceive not yourselves"* (Jer. 37:9); Jesus said, *"Let no man deceive you"* (Mat. 24:4; Lk. 21:8).

In fact, Believers are very liable to self-deception (Gal. 6:3; I Jn. 1:8), as well as being deceived by others (II Tim. 3:13). Consequently, there is a need as should by now be obvious, to repeat this warning incessantly.

## DECEPTION AS IT IS TAUGHT IN THE BIBLE

There is more than a *"lie"* involved in the complex web of ideas expressed by *"deceit"* or *"falsehood"* in the Bible. The deceitful and the false are always wrong. But they are not always the same thing.

## DECEPTION AS EXPLAINED IN THE OLD TESTAMENT

The best way to build our understanding of the Old Testament concept of deception is to note that the same Hebrew words are translated by the English words *"false," "falsehood," "deceit,"* and *"deception"* and to realize that the Hebrew words often more clearly define shades of meaning only implied in English.

*"Ramah"* is a Hebrew word and it has several derivatives. The root means *"to mislead"* or *"to deceive,"* and is used of misleading speech and of shady business practices (Gen. 34:13; Ps. 10:7; Amos 8:5; Zeph. 3:13).

Another Hebrew word *"Saqar,"* means *"to deceive"* or *"to tell a falsehood."* It implies the breaking of a promise or a commitment. It is found six times in the Old Testament (Gen. 21:23; Lev. 19:11; I Sam. 15:29; Ps. 44:17; 89:33; Isa. 63:8).

It also refers to groundless words or actions. Such things are deceiving because they have no basis in fact. This particular word (Saqar, or its derivatives) occurs often in Psalms, Proverbs, and Jeremiah, and is frequently used to identify a false accusation or a false Prophecy.

*"Saw"* another Hebrew word appears 53 times in the Old Testament, and is usually translated *"vain, or empty."* It actually means *"emptiness and deceit,"* in the sense of presenting as real something that is unsubstantial and unreal.

*"Nasa"* another Hebrew word, indicates deceptions that lead a person astray. This is the word used in Eve's excuse: *"The Serpent deceived me"* (Gen. 3:13).

*"Kahas"* is another word, and indicates deceit or falsehood, the word suggesting undependable behavior in a given relationship. The person who thus deals falsely causes harm to others.

The portrait of falsehood and deceit suggested by the Hebrew words is far from pretty. Action and words designed to deceive are not supported by reality. Worse, they violate the basic relationship of trust and honesty that are to exist between human beings, and they are often intended to mislead and so to harm another person.

## THE NEW TESTAMENT

There are several different Greek terms associated with the idea of deceit. The most common is *"planao,"* which means *"to lead astray or deceive by words or behavior."*

The New Testament almost always uses this word when speaking of the influence of false teachers. It is also the word chosen to speak of Satan's final effort to deceive at history's end.

When the New Testament warns, *"Don't be deceived,"* this statement expresses the Writer's concern that we might be led away from the Biblical Message and lifestyle.

There are other Greek words, *"Apatao," "Dolos,"* with their derivatives and have different shades of meaning. However, they all ultimately mean *"to deceive."*

Deception sometimes comes from within, as our desires impel us to deceive. But more often in the New Testament, deceit is error urged by external evil powers or by those locked into the world's way of thinking, even as Paul is addressing in I Corinthians 3:18.

NOTES

## SUBJECTIVE TRUTH AND OBJECTIVE TRUTH

The concept underlying the truth/falsehood dichotomy in Scripture is important relative to deception, particularly to those who live in a relativistic world that can speak of something as being *"true for you"* (Subjective Truth which changes according to the experience) while denying Absolute (Objective) Truth.

The Bible clearly affirms Objective Truth, and it grounds that belief in the Biblical concept of God. God is Truth. In other words, He will never change, and, accordingly, Truth cannot change.

Therefore, even though Subjective Truth can be real according to the reality of one's experience, that is if it lines up with the Word of God, still, most of the time Subjective Truth is really no Truth at all, simply because it does not base its direction on the Word of God, but rather on experience.

## REALITY

All that God says is in strict accord with reality. His Words are, therefore, firm and trustworthy. The word *"reality"* is very important, in that this describes the Biblical concept of Truth.

By contrast, we human beings are trapped in illusion. We struggle to understand the meaning of the world around us and of our experiences. However, unaided, we cannot distinguish between the real and the counterfeit, the Truth and the lie.

Only reliance on God's Word, which is Truth, enables us to build our lives on a firm foundation. Consequently, if one truly follows the Lord, there is absolutely no place or reason for deception. In fact, in the Lord is the only place where there is no deception, otherwise all is deception in one way or the other.

The phrase, *"If any man among you seemeth to be wise in this world,"* is not meant to denigrate education, but rather to portray the Truth that God or His Ways, cannot be found out relative to the wisdom of this world, i.e., higher education, etc.

The Reader is not to think that Paul is denigrating higher learning, for he is not. In fact, higher learning in many areas is very valuable. When I ride in an airplane, I want the pilot of that airplane to be fully educated respecting his profession, and such could be said for a myriad of other things as well.

The idea is, as stated, that men cannot use the ways of the world, i.e., the wisdom of the world, and thereby learn about God, as they learn about airplanes, and many other things.

The phrase, *"Let him become a fool,"* means that any person who wants to know about the Lord, must first accept the Lord as his Saviour, and then go to the Word of God to learn about God — that which the world thinks is foolish. So, in the eyes of the world, anyone who serves God and reveres the Word of God is a *"fool."*

The phrase, *"That he may be wise,"* concerns itself with true wisdom.

While this person may be a *"fool"* in the eyes of the world for trusting and serving God, and adhering to His Word, in the Eyes of God, Whose Eyes alone matter, *"he is wise"*

NOTES

## THE EVANGELIST

Paul of course was an Apostle; however, he was also the consummate Evangelist. The manner in which he describes things, left absolutely no room for doubt respecting what he was Teaching or Preaching. Even as here, oftentimes his statements would have a tendency to anger people, that is, if they were not sincere in what they were doing. In fact, even though everything he says is Rock-solid Truth, and inspired by the Holy Spirit, which means the Holy Spirit gave him these words, or rather allowed him to use them, still, there is even a touch of sarcasm in some of the things he says. And rightly so, we might quickly add.

The mistake that foolish men make is to not take the Gospel seriously. When they did such with Paul, it was not exactly the right thing to do. They were dealing with one who knew both sides of the fence. To be frank, had he chosen the ways of the world, he would have been classed as an intellectual. But yet he used that not at all in his approach and Ministry for the Lord. He purposely said, *"My speech and my Preaching was not with enticing words of man's wisdom,"* etc. However, even though he did not use this manner of approach, which he certainly should not have, still, that did not mean that he was not very well aware of such direction, and had once been very prolific in this particular genre.

When the Evangelist is truly Anointed by the Holy Spirit, his Message, or apology, or even argument as the world would classify such, not only presents the right way, but as well, cuts the props out from under all that is false. There is no Truth other than God's Truth. As such, it stands on a solid Rock-hard base, unmovable, because it is based, as stated, on reality.

(19) "FOR THE WISDOM OF THIS WORLD IS FOOLISHNESS WITH GOD. FOR IT IS WRITTEN, HE TAKETH THE WISE IN THEIR OWN CRAFTINESS."

The phrase, *"For the wisdom of this world is foolishness with God,"* speaks of wisdom in totality and in any capacity. The idea is, that God is so far above the rambling and prattle of man, that to Him the efforts of the most brilliant in this world, constitute no more than *"foolishness."* Let it be understood, that the word *"foolishness"* used by Paul, was actually chosen by the Holy Spirit.

Even more importantly, the efforts of men to know about God, or the Ways of God, respecting their own intellect and scientific investigation, are *"foolishness"* as well, because God cannot be realized or known in this manner. In fact, and even as we have stated, the only way that God can be understood in any capacity, is for Him to reveal Himself to man, which He has done in the form of His Word and His Son, The Lord Jesus Christ. Even then, one must be *"Born Again"* before one can even begin to learn about the Creator and His Ways.

The phrase, *"For it is written, He taketh the wise in their own craftiness,"* is taken from Job 5:13, one of the few times that the Book of Job is quoted in the New Testament. It comes from the speech of Eliphaz, and is quoted verbatim by Paul, at least in the English translation.

*"Craftiness"* in the Greek is *"panougia,"* and means *"the cleverness of selfish people to attempt to enhance their own positions by deceiving or trapping other people."* God promises to trip these crafty people with their own craftiness. In other words, they will be trapped in the traps they set for other people (Rossier).

The idea is, that men who attempt to outwit God, and this is what the world does, can make no headway with such an effort, even though they are deceived into thinking they can.

A perfect Example is Jesus Who faced all the *"craftiness"* of the Pharisees and Sanhedrin, who thought surely they could trap or snare Him. They had no success, in fact, the Scriptures said, *"Neither durst any man from that day forth ask Him any more questions"* (Mat. 22:46).

(20) "AND AGAIN, THE LORD KNOWETH THE THOUGHTS OF THE WISE, THAT THEY ARE VAIN."

This Passage is taken from Psalm 94:11.

*"Vain"* in the Greek is *"mataios,"* and means *"empty, profitless, in effect empty nothings."*

Why?

They concentrate on accumulating that which is transitory and that which will disappear totally after this earthly life is over. Conversely, truly wise people, those who serve the Lord, invest in that which is eternal, consequently, permanent (Rossier).

These obscure Scriptures used by Paul show as to the degree in which he knew the Word of God. This portrays a familiarity with the Scriptures which is absolutely phenomenal. I realize, considering this is Paul, that one may not be surprised. Nevertheless, please believe me, the knowledge this man had of the Word of God just may have been unexcelled in human history.

(21) "THEREFORE LET NO MAN GLORY IN MEN. FOR ALL THINGS ARE YOURS;"

The phrase, *"Therefore let no man glory in men,"* harks back to I Corinthians 1:12, where it had been called to the attention of Paul that some in the Church at Corinth had formed particular Preacher parties, saying, *"I am of Paul; and I of Apollos; and I of Cephas; and I of Christ."* Consequently, several very important things are said here:

1. The Holy Spirit is directing Paul in these statements; consequently, they should be well heeded by all.

2. The Holy Spirit is saying that Believers should not get their eyes on men, even someone of the caliber of Paul, etc.

3. While it is true that God-called Preachers are used by the Lord, still, such shows no special ability on their part, the fact being that God gave them whatever it is they have.

4. Even though Preachers are given to the Church *"For the perfecting of the Saints, for the work of the Ministry, for the edifying of the Body of Christ"* (Eph. 4:12), still, Preachers are little more than pipelines, with the Source being the Lord. Consequently, the Church should certainly benefit from these particular Ministries, for that is their very purpose; however, at the same time the Believer must never take his eyes off of Christ.

NOTES

The phrase, *"For all things are yours,"* means that everything that God has given to the Church, is available to every single Believer, if that Believer will conduct himself right, and keep his eyes on the Lord. The Truth is this:

Paul had a Ministry which was desperately needed by the Body of Christ, which should be overly obvious, that is if anything in the world is obvious. To have the opportunity to glean from that Ministry, and not do so because of foolish pride, or any other reason for that matter, is like the man who cuts off his nose to spite his face.

Likewise, Apollos had a Ministry which was desperately needed by the Body, as well as Simon Peter, and any God-called Preacher for that matter. The Holy Spirit desired that these Corinthians, as well as all others, glean from all. How foolish we are, when we do not take advantage of that which the Holy Spirit has provided, and instead allow ourselves to be suckered in by Satan to just one room in the house, when the entirety of the house is available to us.

And probably one could say that those who were a part of the *"Christ"* party, were worse off than any. In effect, they were saying they did not need any Preachers, in effect, receiving everything directly from Christ, they claimed. Such an attitude sets aside the Work and Plan of God, which the Lord cannot bless. Consequently, they received nothing. And as well, those who had sectioned themselves off to one particular Preacher, were not really even receiving what he was capable of giving, for the simple reason that their spirit was wrong. Consequently, the very thing they thought they were getting in their elitism, they were not getting, and in fact, were getting nothing.

Receiving from the Lord, is not just a matter of being a Christian, but it pertains to the open heart of a person to the Spirit of God. To be sure, one who is involved in strife and contention, as some of these Corinthians were, is in no spiritual condition to receive anything, which sadly, is the shape of many in the Church presently.

(22) "WHETHER PAUL, OR APOLLOS, OR CEPHAS, OR THE WORLD, OR LIFE, OR DEATH, OR THINGS PRESENT, OR THINGS TO COME; ALL ARE YOURS;"

The phrase, *"Whether Paul, or Apollos, or Cephas,"* portrays exactly what I have just said. The Ministries of each of these men were given by the Holy Spirit for all the Believers at Corinth, etc. As stated, it is the same presently.

The phrase, *"Or the world, or life, or death, or things present, or things to come,"* pertains to the fact that the Lord is over all, and can do, and will do, whatever one needs in any capacity, according to His Providence.

When people serve men, they get only what the man can give, which is precious little. When people truly serve the Lord, they get what He can give, which is everything.

It means that not a single thing can happen to the Child of God unless the Lord permits it or causes it. We can be sure, that He will never permit anything that will fall out to our harm. When we use the word *"permit,"* we are speaking of the latitude in which the Lord allows Satan. Satan of course, would destroy every Believer if he could, but the fact is, he cannot.

However, if a Believer through his own free moral agency, desires to do stupid things, even as these Corinthians were doing, the Lord will allow such; however, we will suffer the consequences. The Lord has the Power to do anything, but He will never override the free moral agency of His Children. He will respect that privilege, even if what we are doing is to our own detriment.

So, the One Who the Believer serves, controls the world, controls life, controls death, as well as things present and things to come.

If we faithfully serve the Lord, such totality is of great comfort, strength, and courage to the Believer.

The phrase, *"All are yours,"* presents the idea that if trust is placed solely in the Lord, He will cause *"all things to work together for good to them who love Him, and are the called according to His Purpose"* (Rom. 8:28). However, it must be remembered that it's only for those who truly love Him, and who truly have His Purpose in mind.

(23) "AND YE ARE CHRIST'S; AND CHRIST IS GOD'S."

The phrase, *"And ye are Christ's,"* presents the greatest privilege on the part of the Believer that he could ever have. To belong to Jesus is the greatest honor, the greatest privilege, the most wonderful opportunity, the greatest move that one could ever begin to make.

NOTES

As well, there is a veiled reminder in this Verse that this privilege is not open just to a select group of super-spiritual individuals. It is available to all Believers who will humbly submit to the Lordship of Christ (Rossier).

The phrase, *"And Christ is God's,"* pertains to the following:

Christ is equal to the Father as touching His Godhead, but inferior to the Father as touching His Manhood, hence in I Corinthians 11:3 Paul says, *"The Head of Christ is God"*; and in I Corinthians 15:28, we read of Christ resigning His Mediatorial Kingdom, that God may be All in All (Farrar). However, the *"All in All"* speaks more so of the fulfillment and completion of the great Plan of God in Redemption, than anything else. Christ will always retain His Place of honor and splendor, because *"God also hath highly exalted Him, and given Him a Name which is above every name"* (Phil. 2:9).

*"O boundless Salvation, deep ocean of Love;*
*"O fullness of Mercy Christ brought from above,*
*"The whole world redeeming, so rich and so free,*
*"Now flowing for all men, come flow over me."*

*"My sins, they are many, their stains are so deep,*
*"And bitter the tears of remorse that I've weeped;*
*"But weeping is useless thou great crimson sea,*
*"Thy waters can cleanse me, come flow over me!"*

*"The tide now is flowing; I'm touching the wave,*
*"I hear the loud call of the Mighty to save.*
*"My Faith's growing bold ere-delivered I'll be!*
*"I plunge 'neath the waters, they flow over me!"*

*"And now, Hallelujah! the rest of my days*
*"Shall gladly be spent in promoting His Praise,*

*"Who opened His Bosom to pour out this sea,*
*"Of boundless Salvation, for you and for me!"*

CHAPTER 4

(1) "LET A MAN SO ACCOUNT OF US, AS OF THE MINISTERS OF CHRIST, AND STEWARDS OF THE MYSTERIES OF GOD."

The phrase, *"Let a man so account of us,"* proclaims the fact that it is inevitable that Christians should form some estimate of the position of Ministers of the Gospel, and Paul proceeds to tell the people at Corinth, and all others for that matter, what that estimate should be.

Ministers are not to be unduly magnified, for their position is subordinate to Christ, and neither are they to be unduly depreciated, for if so, the people will answer to their Master, The Lord Jesus Christ.

The phrase, *"As of the Ministers of Christ,"* first of all proclaims that Preachers of the Gospel are not Ministers of the people, i.e., called by the people and answerable to the people, but rather Ministers of Christ, thereby, answerable to Him.

In fact, Federal Judges in the United States are appointed in essence by the President and Congress for life. It is done in this manner so they will not be dependent on people for reelection, etc. Ideally, they are then free to render judgments of an unbiased opinion.

Ministers of the Gospel are supposed to function in the same manner. They are answerable first of all to Christ, because they are *"Ministers of Christ."*

*"Ministers"* in the Greek is *"huperitas,"* and means *"servants or under-rowers."* However, all of this is in relation to Christ and not to men.

As such, the Preacher of the Gospel is to conduct himself toward his fellowmen as a servant, which was what Jesus taught in St. John Chapter 13.

However, inasmuch as the Preacher of the Gospel is a servant of none other than Christ, he should be accorded all respect and honor (Rom. 13:7; I Tim. 5:17).

NOTES

HOUSE-MANAGERS

The phrase, *"And Stewards of the Mysteries of God,"* literally means a house-manager.

Property owners of that day often would turn over the management of their houses to trusted servants (Lk. 12:32; 16:1) and even make them responsible for other servants (Mat. 20:8). This particular person was not responsible to his fellows but to his Master.

Consequently, Preachers of the Gospel are actually house-managers of the Kingdom of God on Earth. As such, and as should be obvious, they hold a tremendous responsibility. Consequently, the people should pray for Preachers constantly, even as Paul constantly requested (I Thess. 5:25; II Thess. 3:1; Heb. 13:18).

*"Mysteries"* in the Greek is *"musterion,"* and means *"truths once hidden but now revealed."* Jesus said to His Disciples, *"Unto you it is given to know the mysteries of the Kingdom of God"* (Lk. 8:10).

This refers to the fact that during Old Testament times, certain parts of the Plan of God were hidden from all, even the Prophets, even though they prophesied respecting these coming Blessings. However, according to the fullness of time, these *"Mysteries"* were opened, and their contents revealed, which had to do with the Church and the great Gospel of Grace, etc. Consequently, all Preachers of the Gospel, are administrators or house-managers of these great Revealed Truths which were once a *"Mystery."*

I think it should be obvious as to what the Holy Spirit through the Apostle is here doing. He is admonishing Preachers, as stated, to be humble servants of the Lord, and to ever conduct themselves accordingly. But at the same time, realizing who Preachers represent, and that they as *"servants"* are not servants of just anyone, but actually of The Lord Jesus Christ, and as such, hold in fact, the most responsible positions on the face of the Earth.

By the Holy Spirit using the word *"Stewards"* we are here given the terrible responsibility borne by Preachers of the Gospel. He has made us answerable to Himself for what we do with these Great Revelational Truths. As well, we are not ultimately accountable to ecclesiastical authorities (people appointed Church Leaders), but to Christ Himself. Once again, this gets into Church Government, and is perhaps the most volatile area of the Church, actually, the area where Satan desires to seize control, and has in most cases.

## SPIRITUAL AUTHORITY

I do not want the Reader to think that we are opposed to Church Administration for we are not. As well, we are not opposed to administrative authority, for such is necessary in the operation and management of anything, whether of the Lord or otherwise. In fact, it is very proper for there to be administrative management concerning Religious Denominations, Churches, etc. It is not wrong for men to occupy these administrative positions, doing all they can to properly administer the Work of God.

However, it must always be remembered, that these are administrative offices, and not Spiritual Offices. As such, those who occupy such offices, must always remember that they have no spiritual authority over anyone for that matter.

The difficulty in Religious Denominations arises, when these men who are elected by popular ballot, therefore, occupying offices which are administrative only, but yet, conclude to be spiritual. As such, they demand obedience in spiritual matters, which is the prerogative of Christ Alone. In other words, whatever they demand, and irrespective of its unscripturality, obedience is required. Such is the ruination of entire Denominations and Preachers, for any Preacher who yields to such, has just abrogated the Headship of Christ, subordinating His Position as the Head of the Church to mere men.

## THE CATHOLIC CHURCH!

The Pope of the Catholic Church claims to be the Vicar of Christ on Earth, and, consequently, demands obedience. Because of this apostasy, the world went through an approximate thousand years of dark ages. Only with the Reformation was this yoke thrown off, but at great price. However, sadly and regrettably, there are many so-called Religious Leaders (not Leaders appointed by Christ), in Protestant Churches, although not referring to themselves as *"Pope,"* nevertheless, demand the same obedience.

Some even go so far as to say to Preachers, *"You are to obey me irrespective of what I say, and if what I say is unscriptural, that will be my responsibility and not yours."*

First of all, such is rank blasphemy, and to be sure, if any Preacher who is truly Called of God is so foolish to obey such prattle, he can be certain that he will be held responsible by God, irrespective as to what the unscriptural Pope has demanded.

Once again, the Holy Spirit plainly tells us that Preachers of the Gospel are *"Ministers of Christ,"* and not Ministers of the Baptist Church, Assemblies of God, Nazarene, Church of God, etc.

While it is not wrong to be associated with these groups, it is very wrong when the Headship of Christ is subordinated to the headship of these religious groups, if in fact that does happen.

(2) "MOREOVER IT IS REQUIRED IN STEWARDS, THAT MAN BE FOUND FAITHFUL."

Several powerful things are said in this particular statement:

1. What is required of Ministers is neither brilliancy, nor eloquence, nor profound knowledge, nor success, but only faithfulness.

2. That faithfulness is to Christ and not man. It is the business of the Preacher of the Gospel to know what his Master wants and desires, and we speak of The Lord Jesus Christ, and then do what he is told to do. We are given the Holy Spirit Who conveys the Will of the Lord to us; therefore, we have no excuse not to know that particular *"Will,"* nor any excuse in not carrying it out (Rom. 8:27-28).

3. *"Required"* in the Greek is *"zeteo,"* and means *"a demand of something due."* So, faithfulness is demanded and faithfulness to Christ.

4. *"Faithful"* in the Greek is *"pistos,"* and means *"trustworthy, trustful, sure and true."*

5. *"Found"* in the Greek is *"heurisko,"* and means *"to find, get, obtain, perceive and see."* The idea is, that the Preacher of the Gospel is going to be judged according to his faithfulness at the Judgment Seat of Christ. It pertains to faithfulness to the Call, and faithfulness to our Master, The Lord of Glory.

That is the reason I have dogmatically stated, that we are going to have to answer for ourselves, and will not be able to place the responsibility on others, even ecclesiastical authorities, irrespective as to what their demands may have been.

NOTES

The Call of God upon a Preacher's life is an awesome thing, and as well carries an awesome responsibility.

(3) "BUT WITH ME IT IS A VERY SMALL THING THAT I SHOULD BE JUDGED OF YOU, OR OF MAN'S JUDGMENT: YEA, I JUDGE NOT MINE OWN SELF."

The phrase, *"But with me it is a very small thing that I should be judged of you,"* opens up to us all manner of things which ought to be examined.

TO JUDGE PAUL?

1. In retrospect, how foolish were these Corinthians who thought they had the maturity and qualifications to judge the Apostle Paul. Think about that for a moment.

Every iota of what anyone in the world knew about the great Gospel of Grace, in effect, the Gospel of Jesus Christ, they learned it from the Revelation given by the Lord to the Apostle Paul (Gal. 1:11-12). As we have previously stated, he was the Moses of the New Testament. As Moses wrote the Pentateuch (the Law), Paul wrote the Covenant of Grace, of course both, that of Moses and Paul, were from the Lord. And yet these Corinthians who thought they were so mature in spiritual matters, mature enough that they could judge Paul, were in reality so spiritually ignorant and immature, that it would be difficult to find the proper adjectives to describe their situation.

How many presently fall into the same category, thinking they are mature enough to pass judgment upon those who God is obviously using?

INDIFFERENCE

2. Even though Paul did warn them of their precarious situation, doing such for their sakes, but respecting his own person, he expressed complete indifference to their shallow, unfair, and even ignorant estimate of his Ministry. In other words, he brushed it aside as if the prattle of small children. In fact, he had already referred to them as babies in Christ. However, the sad fact, they were babies not because of having lived for the Lord only a short period of time, but rather because they simply had not grown in the Lord, despite the fact of having lived for Him now for several years.

NOTES

3. Paul took the position as someone has said; *"The Devil says things about me, people say things about me, and God says things about me." "It is only what God says that matters."*

4. *"Judged"* in the Greek is *"anakrino,"* and means *"to interrogate, question or examine."* Technically it means *"an examination preliminary to trial."*

These people were not judging Paul's Doctrine, which every man has the right to do according to the Word of God, but rather his person, motives, and actions, in other words, judging the man himself. No Believer is allowed to do that to another Believer. In fact, Jesus plainly warned against such (Mat. 7:1-5). The Believer would do well to read this warning given by Christ very carefully.

TO JUDGE?

The phrase, *"Or of man's judgment,"* refers to any man. It literally says in the Greek, *"man's day."*

The idea is, that man is so absolutely unqualified to judge anyone else, that when he does so, he only portrays his ignorance, at least in the Eyes of God. James addressed this when he said, *"There is One Lawgiver* (God), *Who is able to save and to destroy* (to properly judge)*: who art thou that judgest another?"* (James 4:12).

In other words, James is saying, *"Who do you think you are, thinking you are qualified to judge someone else?"* The fact is, no one, not even the Godliest Believer on Earth, is morally qualified to judge anyone else. Only God can do that.

The idea is, that all Believers should judge all Doctrine that is preached by the Word of God, and never attempt to judge the person themselves regarding motive, etc. And yet in a sense, the Believer is called upon to inspect or even judge the Fruit of a Ministry (Mat. 7:15-23). However, judging the Fruit of a Ministry, is not the same thing at all as judging the motives and actions of a person's heart. In fact, Believers are obligated to judge the Fruit, which in effect, is the same as judging what one preaches, i.e., *"Doctrine."*

LET OTHERS DO THE THINKING

Unfortunately, most Believers do not check the Fruit or the Doctrine themselves, but let others such as Denominational Heads, or even their Pastor do the thinking for them. In other words, if the Pastor, or other Preachers, disapprove of someone, too oftentimes, the Believer automatically accepts their judgment without checking the situation themselves. That is exactly what Satan wants the person to do. In fact, that is what Israel did with Jesus.

The first two years of Jesus' Ministry, the crowds were huge, with the entirety of Israel shaken by the Mighty Power of God, in fact, as it had never been shaken before. However, the last year of His Public Ministry, the crowds thinned out considerably, despite the fact that Miracles were being performed in a manner that the world had never seen, or even remotely so. In fact, it no doubt can be said that Jesus performed more Miracles in His Ministry, than had been performed in the entirety of history past.

The Religious Leaders of Israel railed out against Christ, refusing to accept His Ministry, and above all refusing to accept Him as the Messiah, which He actually was, and many of the people accepted their false judgment. Admittedly, many during this last year held back from Jesus' Ministry for fear of excommunication from the Synagogue, but still, the results were the same. Out of fear or ignorance, they let others do the thinking for them, and Israel went to her doom.

## IS PERCEPTION REALITY?

Unfortunately, for most of the world perception is reality.

That means that people judge circumstances, or what they can see with their eyes, or else think they see, or they listen to what others say, and without really knowing the Truth themselves, perception to them becomes reality, when oftentimes it is the very opposite.

While it is understandable that unbelievers would conduct themselves in this fashion, it is not understandable or excusable at all for Christians to do so. Christians are to have spiritual discernment. First of all, they are to seek God and His Word, asking Him to show them what is right or wrong about a particular person or situation. Every Christian definitely ought to be led by the Lord before they support any Preacher, but sadly, most are not led by the Lord, but rather by man. Paul warns, that the Judgment Seat of Christ is going to expose all

NOTES

of this, so we had best get our act together now, instead of suffering the loss of reward then.

The phrase, *"Yea, I judge not mine own self,"* in effect means, that a Believer is not actually even qualified to properly judge himself, much less others.

Most certainly we would know our own heart and motives, but yet the Scripture plainly warns us that the heart is liable to self-deceit (Jer. 17:9-10). Consequently, no man is able to pronounce a judgment regarding even his own actions with unerring accuracy. In view of that, and as stated, how in the world does he think he can judge someone else when he is not even qualified to judge himself?

(4) "FOR I KNOW NOTHING BY MYSELF; YET AM I NOT HEREBY JUSTIFIED: BUT HE THAT JUDGETH ME IS THE LORD."

The phrase, *"For I know nothing by myself,"* in effect says, *"The verdict of my own conscience acquits me of all intentional unfaithfulness, but this is insufficient, because God sees with clearer eyes than ours."* In fact, the Psalmist said, *"Who can understand his errors? Cleanse thou me from secret faults"* (Ps. 19:12). The *"secret faults"* against which the Psalmist prays, are not hidden vices, but sins of which he was himself unconscious. It must be remembered that Paul is here only speaking with conscious integrity of his ministerial work (Farrar). Nothing could have been further from his mind than to claim an absolute immunity from every form of self-reproach. Those who attempt to claim immaculate holiness can little do so from the sanction of Paul (I Cor. 9:27; 15:9; Eph. 3:8; Phil. 3:13). In fact, the confessions of the holiest must ever be the most humble.

The phrase, *"Yet am I not hereby justified,"* in effect says, *"Even though I know of nothing in my life or Ministry that is contrary to the Lord, still it is not my judgment that counts in this case, but rather that of the Lord."* The idea is this:

Every man is apt to be right in his own eyes, at least respecting the judgment of himself, but it is God Who pondereth the hearts and, therefore, in God's Sight *"no man living is justified."*

As stated, Paul knew that he did not know enough about himself to be able to judge himself in the final sense, and if he were not capable of doing so, then certainly these immature Corinthians were not able to judge him.

The phrase, *"But He that judgeth me is the Lord,"* refers to the Lord as the final and in fact, only True Judge. In fact, the Scripture says of Him:

*"And He shall not judge after the sight of His Eyes, neither reprove after the hearing of His Ears:*

*"But with Righteousness shall He judge the poor, and reprove with equity* (that which is totally fair) *for the meek of the Earth"* (Isa. 11:3-4).

(5) "THEREFORE JUDGE NOTHING BEFORE THE TIME, UNTIL THE LORD COME, WHO BOTH WILL BRING TO LIGHT THE HIDDEN THINGS OF DARKNESS, AND WILL MAKE MANIFEST THE COUNSELS OF THE HEARTS: AND THEN SHALL EVERY MAN HAVE PRAISE OF GOD."

The phrase, *"Therefore judge nothing before the time, until the Lord come,"* in effect, refers to the coming *"Judgment Seat of Christ."*

This reference points to the Rapture of the Church, and not to the Second Coming of the Lord (Jn. 14:1-13; I Cor. 15:23, 51-58; Phil. 3:20-21; I Thess. 4:13-15; II Thess. 2:7).

What did Paul mean by the two words *"judge nothing?"*

We have already stated, that the Lord actually commands us to judge the *"Fruit"* of a Ministry. In fact, Believers are called on to make judgments constantly. The idea is this:

If something is judged to be obviously unscriptural, it is to be set aside and refused. In other words, everything is to be judged according to the Word of God. However, if it is not obviously unscriptural, and yet there are some things which we do not understand, this means we should *not* pass judgment. We should leave those things to the Lord Who will judge all accordingly at the coming time.

*"Until"* in the Greek is *"heos an,"* and means *"a time entirely indefinite."* In other words, Paul did not know when the Rapture would take place, and neither do we, but when it does happen, very shortly thereafter will commence the *"Judgment Seat of Christ."*

The phrase, *"Who both will bring to light the hidden things of darkness,"* refers to the fact that *"All things are naked and opened unto the Eyes of Him with Whom we hath to do"* (Heb. 4:13; Eccl. 12:14).

*"Darkness"* in the Greek is *"skotos,"* and means *"shadiness or obscurity."* With the exception of the significance of secrecy (God dwelling in secrecy) and the night, darkness is always used in a bad sense.

NOTES

### A MORAL METAPHOR

Darkness (spiritual darkness) is a powerful New Testament image. As a moral metaphor, it describes sinful acts and a sinful lifestyle. Believers are to put aside *"deeds of darkness"* (Rom. 13:12; Eph. 5:11). We do not *"belong to the night* (spiritual night) *or to the darkness* (spiritual darkness)*"* (I Thess. 5:5).

### AN EVIL POWER

But spiritual darkness is more than a lifestyle. It is an evil power, holding people in its dominion (Col. 1:13). We sense the restless activity of sin within our personality, even the best of us.

All people were once impelled by inner evil (Eph. 5:8) and so chose to turn their backs on God's Light and to embrace the darkness, which in fact, almost all the world has done (Jn. 3:19). It may be this of which Jesus warned, when He pointed out that if one's eye (the organ that directs and guides the body) is darkness, the whole body (life) will be full of darkness (Mat. 6:23; Lk. 11:34-35).

### JESUS IS THE ONLY LIGHT

There is only one hope for those in the grip of darkness: the Light provided by Jesus (Jn. 1:5). In God there is *"no darkness at all"* (I Jn. 1:5). He can release us from sin's power and illumine us, so that the person who follows Jesus *"will never walk in darkness"* (Jn. 8:12). And how vital it is that we be drawn *"out of darkness into His wonderful Light"* (I Pet. 2:9).

### LIGHT

In the New Testament, Light is an image of both holiness and illumination. But most significantly, Light characterizes Jesus. He is *the "Light of the world"* (Jn. 8:12); He is the Light that shines in the darkness, bringing Life (Jn. 1:4-5).

People who are in the grip of darkness may scurry away from His Light (Jn. 3:19-20). But only the Good News of Jesus can provide perspective on reality. Only through Jesus can people recognize their lost state, come to God (Jn. 14:1; II Cor. 4:4), and find their way to a Righteous Life (Eph. 5:8-9).

Believers, who respond to Jesus, are rescued from the realm of darkness to become children of the Light (Eph. 5:8). They share a place in God's Kingdom of Light (Col. 1:12) and are even Lights in this dark world (Mat. 5:14-16). Believers are to reflect Jesus and declare His Praises (I Pet. 2:9).

LIGHT AND DARKNESS

The theological significance of Light and Darkness is shown in a number of New Testament Passages, especially in the writings of John.

John 1:4-9: Jesus is the *"True Light,"* Whose Coming into the world puts the whole Creation in proper perspective. In Jesus we discover Who God is, and we are given the vital Divine Life that can overcome our darkness.

John 3:19-21: Despite the demonstration of God's Love in the Coming of Jesus, humanity scurries deeper and deeper into darkness. Man's Love of darkness rather than light demonstrates the reality of human sinfulness: *"Everyone who does evil hates the Light, and will not come into the Light for fear that his deeds will be exposed"* (Jn. 3:20).

But one who is willing to face reality comes to the Light. Only Believers, whose trust in Jesus has carried them beyond condemnation will come (Jn. 3:16-18).

John 8:12: Only through Jesus, *"the Light of the world,"* are people released from darkness and given the *"Light of Life"* — that is, Eternal Life.

II Corinthians 4:4-6: Satan blinds the lost so *"they cannot see the Light of the Gospel of the Glory of Christ,"* and so they fail to recognize Jesus *"Who is the Image of God."*

For a person to respond to Jesus and be enlightened by *"the knowledge of the Glory of God in the Face of Christ"* (II Cor. 4:6), calls for a Divine Created Act parallel to the original Creation when God saith, *"Let Light shine out of darkness"* (II Cor. 4:6).

Ephesians 5:8-9: Those who have been translated from darkness to Light are expected to live *"as children of Light."* This means bringing forth in one's life the Fruit of the Light — *"all Goodness, Righteousness and Truth"* — and having nothing to do with *"the fruitless deeds of darkness"* (Eph. 5:11).

I John 1:5-7: Maintaining fellowship with God calls for us to walk in the Light and not in darkness, for God is unshadowed Light. Walking in the Light is not sinlessness, however; for as we walk in the Light, *"the Blood of Jesus, His Son, purifies us from all sin."*

Because this Passage associates Light with Truth, it seems best to take *"walking in the Light"* in the sense suggested in John 3:19-21.

NOTES

TRUTH

To walk in the Light is to accept God's Verdict on our actions and to come to Him for cleansing and forgiveness when we fall short (I Jn. 1:9).

I John 2:8-10: John makes it clear that any Believer who hates other Believers is not living according to God's Way and is actually showing behavior typical of the moral realm of darkness.

Christians can test their fellowship with the Lord by observing their relationship with other Believers. Any Believer who loves other Christians *"lives in the Light, and there is nothing in him to make him stumble"* (Rom. 13:8-10) (Richards).

The *"Hidden things of darkness"* of which Paul here speaks, concerns any and all things in the life of the Believer which can be referred to as sin, unholy motives, in other words, anything which is not according to the Word of God, and has not been repented of and forsaken. It does *not* refer to sins or any wrong thing for that matter, which have been properly taken to the Lord and forsaken. Things which are properly handled with Christ (I Jn. 1:9), will never again be brought up before the Child of God. However, anything and everything which has not been properly handled, will be brought to light, i.e., revealed before all.

That should make the Believer strongly desire to handle everything here and now, in order that we not be embarrassed then.

WILL MAKE MANIFEST

The phrase, *"And will make manifest the counsels of the hearts,"* means that the Lord will reveal the True Motives behind the actions of His People (Rossier).

The phrase, *"And then shall every man have Praise of God,"* actually means *"such Praise as He deserves."*

In that day, the *"Praise from God"* — the *"Well done, good and faithful servant"* (Mat. 25:21) —

will be so infinitely precious that it reduces to insignificance the comparative value of human praise or blame (Farrar).

In essence, Paul is saying that he is not looking for the praise of the Corinthians, or anyone else for that matter. Praise from man means nothing. Too oftentimes it is based on impure motives respecting the one doing the praising. In other words, he wants something from the individual, or to be made to look good in that person's sight, etc., so he praises him, etc. Consequently, praise from man is of no value. It is only Praise from God which really matters, and which will come at the Judgment Seat of Christ, that is, and as stated, if we deserve such.

The entire gist of all of this is that Christian people should regard themselves and regard each other as simply servants and stewards.

As to stewards, what is most required by a master is faithfulness. Servants are not to judge one another, nor to judge themselves respecting approval, for though a servant may know nothing against himself, yet that does not prove him to be without blame. The Master only is entitled to judge.

Servants, therefore, must not exercise premature judgment upon each other but wait until the Master comes, and He will bring to light hidden actions and secret motives, and then every servant shall receive the praise due to him (Williams).

(6) "AND THESE THINGS, BRETHREN, I HAVE IN A FIGURE TRANSFERRED TO MYSELF AND TO APOLLOS FOR YOUR SAKES; THAT YE MIGHT LEARN IN US NOT TO THINK OF MEN ABOVE THAT WHICH IS WRITTEN, THAT NO ONE OF YOU BE PUFFED UP FOR ONE AGAINST ANOTHER."

The phrase, *"And these things, Brethren,"* is presented by Paul to soften his statements. He is not insinuating that these Brethren by their actions, as wrong as they may be, are not Saved. He is strongly warning them that such attitude will stunt their spiritual growth, even as it already has.

The phrase, *"I have in a figure transferred to myself and to Apollos for your sakes,"* means that he has used himself and Apollos as examples. By rebuking this party spirit in those who were his followers and those of Apollos, he robbed his remarks of all semblance of personality or bitterness. It showed his generous attitude of not alluding to the adherents of Peter or anyone else for that matter.

NOTES

The phrase, *"That ye might learn in us,"* makes Apollos and himself the instances of the undesirability of over-exalting human teachers.

The phrase, *"Not to think of men above that which is written,"* refers to the Scriptures. In other words, what Paul was telling them was Scriptural, which they should have known themselves. In fact, all the Old Testament quotations he had used in this admonition, had referred to humility. In I Corinthians 1:19 he referred to Isaiah 29:14. In I Corinthians 1:31 he referred to Jeremiah 9:23-24. In I Corinthians 3:19 he referred to Job 5:13. As stated, all of these Passages in one way or the other, deal with the attitude of the Lord respecting pride.

This is the age-old problem of mankind — going beyond what the Scriptures tell us.

The phrase, *"That no one of you be puffed up for one against another,"* tells us the results of going beyond the Scriptures which always results in a puffed-up inflation of pride.

## PRIDE IS THE ROOT SIN OF ALL SINS

Arrogance and pride describe an attitude that Scripture carefully analyzes — and condemns. Both the Old Testament and New Testament add to our understanding of the nature of the self-exalting traits, which draw us away from Godliness.

### THE OLD TESTAMENT

There are several Hebrew words which deal with this extremely sinful problem. The first word is *"zid,"* and is usually translated *"arrogance."* This word or one of its derivatives is used 34 times in the Old Testament, and conveys the broad idea of a self-important pride, which leads to acts of rebellion and willful disobedience.

Another Hebrew word *"Ga'ah,"* or one of its derivatives, is usually translated *"pride"* or *"proud."*

Used at times of Israel or of God, such words express excellence or majesty. But these words are usually applied to persons and are used then in a negative sense. This word *"Ga'ah,"* or one of its derivatives is used most often by Isaiah, Jeremiah, and Ezekiel and in the Psalms, Proverbs, and Job. The words imply an arrogant insensitivity to others, matched with overwhelming self-confidence.

This attitude leads to conduct that in turn brings destruction, for only God can rightly be the Source and Object of our pride, never ourselves.

## THE NATURE OF PRIDE

We sense the basic nature of these traits in Deuteronomy 1:42. There God warned a disobedient Israel not to attack those in Canaan at that particular time, *"Because,"* He said, *"I will not be with you."* Moses recalls Israel's sin:

*"You would not listen. You rebelled against the Lord's Command and in your arrogance you marched up into the hill country"* (Deut. 1:43).

The same theme is often found elsewhere in the Old Testament: *"In his arrogance* (pride) *the wicked man hunts down the weak... in his pride the wicked does not seek the Lord; in all his thoughts there is no room for God"* (Ps. 10:2-4).

The actual root of arrogance and pride is refusal to consider God or respond to Him. Instead, the arrogant supposes that human beings can live successfully apart from an obedient relationship with the Lord.

## THE SIN

The dangers of arrogance and pride are well documented. Even the Godly can be drawn away from God when success stimulates pride (II Chron. 26:16-17). According to Proverbs, pride is an evil to be hated (Prov. 8:13), leads to disgrace (Prov. 11:2; 29:23), breeds quarrels (Prov. 13:10), and goes before destruction (Prov. 16:18).

But pride is not only dangerous; it is sin. Pride and arrogance involve a denial of our place as creatures, living in a world shaped and governed by the Creator, Who has given a Word that is to govern our lives. Thus, the Old Testament makes it clear: God is committed to punish pride and arrogance.

In almost identical phraseology, Isaiah twice declared: *"The eyes of the arrogant man will be humbled and the pride of men brought low; the Lord Alone will be exalted in that day"* (Isa. 2:11, 17).

The theme of judgment is often associated with this sin, which involves not only a basic denial of the significance of God but also the foolish exaltation of the individual or the human race, even as Paul is addressing in I Corinthians Chapters 1-4 (Lev. 26:19; Dan. 5:20).

NOTES

## THE CAUSE OF SATAN'S FALL

There are two Old Testament Passages which describe the Fall of Satan. Each Passage refers to a *"King,"* who is the unseen spiritual power behind the Pagan Ruler (Dan. 10:12-15).

The first of those Passages is found in Ezekiel 28:11-19. This King (Lucifer) is described as a Guardian Cherub who was created blameless but sinned and was expelled from the Presence of God. The cause?

*"Your heart became proud on account of your beauty, and you corrupted your wisdom because of your splendor"* (Ezek. 28:17).

The second example is found in Isaiah. The Prophet describes a Morning Star fallen from Heaven and points out the swelling pride that led to his downfall: *"You said in your heart, 'I will ascend to Heaven; I will raise my throne above the stars of God; I will sit enthroned on the mount of assembly, on the utmost heights of the sacred mountain.*

*"I will ascend above the tops of the clouds; I will make myself like the Most High'"* (Isa. 14:13-14).

The pride of the creature who seeks to displace God as the Center of the Universe and denies the Lord the Glory due Him as Creator, is the root cause of all the evil that mars the Universe and, specifically, of man's original sin (Gen. 3:4-5).

This problem continues to be paramount in the world — the displacement of God as the Center of all things, and denying Him the Glory due Him as Creator, in effect, replacing Him with self.

## THE NEW TESTAMENT

A number of Greek words are translated *"arrogance"* or *"pride."*

*"Hyperephania"* is translated *"arrogance"* in Mark 7:22 (its only New Testament occurrence), and *"hyperephanos"* (appearing five times in the New Testament) is translated four times *"pride"* or *"proud"* (Lk. 1:51; II Tim. 3:2; James 4:6; I Pet. 5:5) and once *"arrogant"* (Rom. 1:30).

Another Greek word *"hypselophroneo"* also means *"proud"* or *"haughty."* It is used in Romans 11:20 and in I Timothy 6:17 of those who presumptuously rest their confidence in something other than God Himself.

Another Greek word *"physioo"* is found only in I Corinthians 4:6, 18-19; 5:2; 8:1; 13:4; in Colossians 2:18, and *"physiosis,"* found only in II Corinthians 12:20. These words direct our attention to the inner impact of pride.

PRIDE PUFFS UP

Even as Paul mentions in I Corinthians 4:6, pride puffs us up, making us arrogant and conceited. Believers are warned against becoming puffed up about following one leader over another, or for belonging to one particular group rather than another.

The Corinthian Church was warned against being puffed up while sin was permitted in the fellowship. In other words, they did not have anything to be puffed up about.

Paul goes on to teach that Love never puffs up (I Cor. 13:4). The seriousness of being puffed up is seen by its association in Scripture with quarreling, jealousy, anger, factions, slander, and gossip (II Cor. 12:20).

Another Greek word *"authades"* is found only in Titus 1:7 and II Peter 2:10, and means *"self-willed," "stubborn,"* and, in that sense, *"arrogant."*

IS ALL PRIDE WRONG?

No! All pride is not wrong.

Two Greek words *"kauchesis"* and *"kauchema"* stress, not the individual's attitude, but the object or thing in which a person takes pride. Such pride can be good or bad, depending on its object.

Paul wants the Believer to take pride, not in externals, but in what God is doing in men's hearts (II Cor. 5:12). Paul himself takes pride in the progress of the Corinthians in the Faith (II Cor. 7:4; 8:24).

We Believers can all take pride in the Grace of God ourselves without comparing ourselves with others, when we lovingly support one another (Gal. 6:4). Both poor and rich Believers — for very different reasons — can take pride in their new position in the Faith, providing it is in a Christlike humility (James 1:9-10).

Such may seem to be a contradiction in terms, associating pride with humility, and it always is if the object of pride is wrong. However, if the pride is in Christ, with a correct understanding of who we are, which means sinners who were and are Saved by Grace, then such adoration is not only not wrong, but is actually commanded (Lk. 10:27) (Richards).

NOTES

(7) "FOR WHO MAKETH THEE TO DIFFER FROM ANOTHER? AND WHAT HAST THOU THAT THOU DIDST NOT RECEIVE? NOW IF THOU DIDST RECEIVE IT, WHY DOST THOU GLORY, AS IF THOU HADST NOT RECEIVED IT?"

The question, *"For who maketh thee to differ from another?"*, means that all human beings are on the same level, sinners in desperate need of God. Paul's question means that this glorification of some and depreciation of others, sprang from unwarrantable arrogance. It involved a claim to superiority, and a right to sit in judgment, which they did not possess (Farrar). Actually, this unscriptural mind-set is the cause of all racial, religious, cultural, and social bias (Col. 3:11), and is the basic problem of the human race. It is based on a false notion of being separate from or better than other people (Rossier).

The question, *"And what hast thou that thou didst not receive?"*, refers to the fact, that whatever special gift a particular person might have, it is just that, a gift, and not a merit, and, therefore, something for which to be thankful, but never to boast. As one can see, this is hitting at the very heart of pride.

SELF AND GOD

The question, *"Now if thou didst receive it, why dost thou glory, as if thou hadst not received it?"*, actually is asking the following:

Considering that every Gift given to men is from God, and given not because of any merit on the part of the individual, but rather because of the Grace of God, why would anyone want to act as if the Gift originated within themselves?

In fact, the world, and I speak of those who do not know God, does actually believe that whatever gifts they may have, in fact, originate with themselves. As stated, this is the cause of all racism, prejudice, bias, etc. However, there is no excuse for the Believer, who should know better.

And yet many Believers have it in their mind that if they are blessed by the Lord, that it is because of their consecration, or great Faith, in other words, merit. In fact, none of that is so.

From studying the Scriptures for over a half century, I have come to believe, that the most consecrated Christians, even the most Faith-filled, cannot stand many Blessings. I think Paul is a perfect example of this, even as we will study in II Corinthians. He needed the thorn in the flesh to keep him humble (II Cor. 12:7-12).

I have also come to believe that most things we think of as Blessings, such as financial prosperity, or a lack of problems, etc., are mostly extended by the Lord to new Converts, or those who we would refer to as spiritually immature. It seems that their Faith needs such, etc.

However, the more spiritually mature one becomes, it is my feeling that the Lord withdraws many of these things we consider as *"Blessings,"* and primarily because of two reasons:

1. The Believer's Faith has reached such a stage of maturity that it no longer requires a lot of tangible things. Christ Alone becomes enough (Phil. 3:9-10).

2. As a result of the Fall, pride is such an ever constant problem, even in the lives of Godly Believers, that many things which are grossly distasteful, we find are necessary. I speak of *"infirmities, reproaches, necessities, persecutions, distresses,"* etc. (II Cor. 12:10).

A prideful attitude and spirit had caused some in the Corinthian Church to begin favoring Preachers, even in a way that was contradictory to their Christian experience. That which they were supposed to have, a Christlike attitude, had deteriorated to such a degree because of this prideful arrogance, that in their exaltation of one set of Teachers, it was invariably accompanied by a mean and unjust depreciation of any who could be supposed to be their rivals. In other words, the Corinthian who was *"for Cephas* (Peter)*"* would be almost certain to be, to some extent, *"against Paul."* In fact, this is how this spirit always works, and because it is the spirit of the world.

They were not satisfied to merely exalt one Preacher over another, as bad as that would be, but felt they must denigrate all others as well, which is generally, if not always, the case.

(8) "NOW YE ARE FULL, NOW YE ARE RICH, YE HAVE REIGNED AS KINGS WITHOUT US: AND I WOULD TO GOD YE DID REIGN, THAT WE ALSO MIGHT REIGN WITH YOU."

NOTES

The phrase, *"Now ye are full, now ye are rich,"* presents the Apostle using irony. (The use of words or expressions to denote the opposite of the literal meaning. In other words, *"You look beautiful,"* when in reality, the person is the very opposite.)

Using irony, Paul in effect is saying, *"You have reached perfection very quickly, far outstripping any of us."* In other words, they already were confident that they had no further need to *"hunger and thirst after Righteousness"* (Mat. 5:6). They had arrived!

Furthermore, Paul, using the words *"Ye are rich,"* pronounces language very similar to Jesus' rebuke of the Laodicean Church, *"Thou sayest, I am rich, and increased with goods, and have need of nothing; and knowest not that thou art wretched, and miserable, and poor, and blind, and naked"* (Rev. 3:17).

The phrase, *"Ye have reigned as kings without us,"* proclaims the idea that they were acting as if the Millennium had already come, and they were reigning accordingly. The words *"Without us"* refer to the Apostles, and in effect said, that these Corinthians had reached such a state in Christ, that they had no more need of what Paul or other Apostles could teach. Again, they were lauding some particular Preacher or Teacher, while at the same time, denigrating others. Seemingly, they did not have sense enough to know or understand, even as many today, that they desperately needed the Teaching of all the Apostles, and not just one or two.

The phrase, *"And I would to God ye did reign, that we also might reign with you,"* in effect says that he wished they were actually in the Millennium. They were conducting themselves as if they were spiritual giants, when in effect, Paul had already referred to them as carnal babes in Christ (I Cor. 3:1-4). In fact, that was their actual condition (Rossier).

This of which Paul states in the 8th Verse regarding these Corinthians, is remarkably similar to many in the so-called modern-day Faith Ministry.

How so subtle is Satan, and how so quick we are to follow him, all the time thinking it is a path of great spirituality, when in Truth, it is the very opposite.

(9) "FOR I THINK THAT GOD HATH SET FORTH US THE APOSTLES LAST, AS IT

WERE APPOINTED TO DEATH: FOR WE ARE MADE A SPECTACLE UNTO THE WORLD, AND TO ANGELS, AND TO MEN."

The phrase, *"For I think that God hath set forth us the Apostles last, as it were appointed to death,"* refers it seems, to be that of gladiators in the arena.

Paul is referring here to the gladiators who fought in the Roman arenas. The ones who came out in the morning and fought were given armor and weapons with which to defend themselves. The ones who were brought out in the afternoon were given no armor and no weapons. In other words, they were consigned to death. They made their appearance last and actually were called *"the last."*

Paul compares the suffering of the Apostles to that of these particular individuals.

A SPECTACLE!

The phrase, *"For we are made a spectacle unto the world, and to Angels, and to men,"* refers to those who are truly called of God.

*"Spectacle"* in the Greek is *"theatron,"* and means *"theatre"* (Acts 19:29-31).

It means that God-called men and women are presented before the spirit world as a spectacle. The idea is that we properly hold up the Name of Christ, irrespective of the cost. The word *"Angels"* when used in this manner, always means good Angels, who are here to look down in sympathy (Heb. 12:22).

This which is presented concerning the humiliation of those who are truly called of God, in no way is appealing to the flesh. In fact, it is the very opposite of much of that which passes for Gospel presently.

The present cry is, *"Come to Jesus and get rich!"* Or, come to Jesus and you will never have another problem! Such may be tantalizing and appealing to the carnal man, but it is not the Gospel of Jesus Christ.

While living for God is the most wonderful and glorious thing that could ever be, still, the Believer is in a hostile environment, and the closer to God one is, and the more the Call of God rests upon one's life, the greater that hostility will be.

When it comes to this *"spectacle"* I personally know of that of which Paul speaks. I realize that almost all the Church world would claim that such is my own fault. However, while all wrongdoing of any nature is definitely the fault of the individual, still, that was only the excuse and not the reason. It is the Call of God upon my heart and life, and that alone, which has made me a *"spectacle"* to the world and even to the Church. I am not alone, it has been that way from the very beginning, even as Paul says here, and it will not stop until Jesus comes to reign Personally upon this Earth, which He shall!

(10) "WE ARE FOOLS FOR CHRIST'S SAKE, BUT YE ARE WISE IN CHRIST; WE ARE WEAK, BUT YE ARE STRONG; YE ARE HONOURABLE, BUT WE ARE DESPISED."

The phrase, *"We are fools for Christ's sake, but ye are wise in Christ,"* once again portrays the use of irony.

Paul is actually telling the Corinthians, and all others as well, that if they *truly* walk close to the Lord Jesus Christ as they should, they will meet with the same contempt and hatred which men showed to Christ, even as the Apostles were then suffering, and, in fact, all will suffer (II Tim. 3:12).

The phrase, *"We are weak, but ye are strong,"* refers to that which is extremely important.

Paul, of all people, knew how weak the flesh is, and to be frank, the closer one gets to the Lord, the more one realizes this fact. Whereas this *"weakness"* is definitely a negative, still, the knowledge of such weakness is extremely positive. When one truly realizes how weak one actually is, at least within oneself, then one is fully more liable to depend completely on Christ.

By contrast, the Corinthians were busy telling all and sundry just how *"strong"* they were in the Faith, etc. Once again please forgive my comparison, but Paul's statements cause one to be reminded of the modern-day Faith Teaching, which in reality, is not much Faith at all.

Almost all the genre of that Teaching is in the very category in which Paul is here so severely criticizing. In essence, he is saying that their constant reminder as to how strong they are in the Faith and in Christ, is more than anything, an exclamation of the very opposite.

The phrase, *"Ye are honourable, but we are despised,"* portrays another great Truth.

The more popular the Church actually is, one has to wonder whose side they are actually on. In fact, the more that the Preacher preaches the

NOTES

Gospel, and I mean without fear, or compromise, the Truth is going to be, that he will be *"despised,"* and so will all those who follow Christ through him.

On one of the major Television Christian Networks, so-called, no one is allowed to mention anything about erroneous Doctrines, and especially Catholicism. Catholics contribute quite heavily to their coffers, so nothing must be said to upset that. In fact, they try to become all things to all men, but not in the sense which Paul said, but rather that nothing be said which will offend.

To be frank, the Gospel of Jesus Christ, that is if it is properly preached under the Anointing of the Holy Spirit, is automatically an offense (Rom. 9:33; Gal. 5:11; I Pet. 2:8).

(11) "EVEN UNTO THIS PRESENT HOUR WE BOTH HUNGER, AND THIRST, AND ARE NAKED, AND ARE BUFFETED, AND HAVE NO CERTAIN DWELLINGPLACE;"

The phrase, *"Even unto this present hour,"* speaks of the moment to which he was writing this particular Epistle. At this time he was in Ephesus, where he had endured much difficulties and trials (Acts 20:31). In fact, his situation really never did change, even until he was called home to Glory.

## PAUL AS THE EXAMPLE

There are few men, if any, who have furthered the Work of God as the Apostle Paul. The debt of gratitude owed him by the world is of untold proportions. As no other man, this Apostle is responsible for what we refer to as *"Western Civilization,"* which of course, is structured on the Message and the Redemptive Power of the Lord Jesus Christ.

I think one could say without any fear of exaggeration, that very few, if any, in history, labored as this man to further the Cause of Christ. As a result, countless millions have found the Lord Jesus Christ as their Saviour.

My intention, is not to give Glory to Paul for that would not be proper at all. It is the Lord Himself Who must receive the Glory, and yet, even as Paul himself wrote, we are to *"Give honour to whom honour is due"* (Rom. 13:7).

## THE CHURCH

Not meaning at all to take away from the original Twelve, nor the work and labor of other Apostles and all used by the Lord during the time of the Early Church, still, I think it must be said, that the Holy Spirit used Paul to found or plant the Church. In fact, he referred to himself as the *"Masterbuilder,"* and as well said concerning the Church, *"I have laid the foundation"* (I Cor. 3:10). As well, we must remember that it is the Holy Spirit Who caused Paul to make these statements, and for a reason.

In fact, all that we presently enjoy, and all before us for that matter, respecting this great Covenant of Grace, we owe first and most of all to The Lord Jesus Christ, and then to His instrument, the Apostle Paul.

Satan did all within his power to subvert, compromise, or to dilute this Message of Grace with the Law. But it was Paul who stood his ground, and brooked no tolerance respecting this great Message of Grace.

## THE MOSES OF THE NEW TESTAMENT

I think one can say, and in fact must say, that as was Moses to the Old Covenant of the Law, likewise, was Paul to the New Covenant of Grace. So, one could call him the Moses of the New Testament.

This is remarkable, especially when one considers that Paul began his ministerial journey as perhaps the greatest opposer of Christ on the face of the Earth of that time. And yet, God would take this firebrand of hate, save his soul, instantly change his life and direction, fill him with the Holy Spirit, and almost in a moment's time, turn him into the greatest Champion for Christ in the world of that day.

This Miracle of Conversion was not brought about by theological argument or by religious pressure, but rather by a Personal Appearance of The Lord Jesus Christ. One moment of that Glorious Face, one sound of that Eternal Voice, and Paul would never be the same again. He would say in his Second Epistle to the Corinthians, *"For God, Who commanded the Light to shine out of darkness, hath shined in our hearts, to give the Light of the knowledge of the Glory of God in the Face of Jesus Christ"* (II Cor. 4:6).

Knowing and understanding, that Paul in this particular statement was referring to far more than his own personal experience, still, I cannot help but believe that the *"Light"* of which he mentioned, at least in part spoke of

NOTES

the Light he saw that day on the Road to Damascus, and as well, the Personal Appearance of Christ to him, i.e., *"the Face of Jesus Christ."*

## TERRIBLE TROUBLES AND DIFFICULTIES

One would think that an Apostle of the caliber of Paul would have very few difficulties, especially considering his great Faith. But yet, the troubles and problems were so severe, that at times Paul even despaired of his life. In fact, it was an unending situation of beatings, stonings, shipwrecks, imprisonments, humiliation, privations, wants, etc., which continued to the moment of his death — his execution by Nero.

And yet, regarding these things, Paul stated, *"Yet of myself I will not glory, but in mine infirmities"* (II Cor. 12:5).

Again referring to these things, he referred to them as *"light afflictions"* (II Cor. 4:17).

Paul's life and Ministry were a far cry from much of that which passes for *"gospel"* presently. Then, it was come to Jesus and suffer; now, it is come to Jesus and get rich.

I realize, that speaking of suffering is not exactly palatable or appetizing. In other words, it is not something a public relations man desires to turn into a positive. But it happens to be the Truth.

And yet, despite the *"suffering,"* untold thousands came to Christ during the times of the Early Church, even realizing they risked their lives in doing so, with many actually paying with their lives.

What was it that drew them?

It was the fulfillment of the Salvation experience, in making Christ their Saviour that gave them a purpose and reason for living. The suffering came about then, even as it comes about now, because of the hostility of the spirit of the world against Christ. Satan as the god of this present world hates Christ, as should be obvious, and his children, which make up most of the planet, follow accordingly. However, despite the opposition, i.e., even suffering, living for Jesus is still hands-down the greatest life, in fact, the only life that one can live, in which one will truly find fulfillment. Jesus Alone can provide that.

That was the Jesus Paul served and preached.

The phrase, *"We both hunger, and thirst,"* speaks of the many times in Paul's travels, when money was in short supply in order to purchase food, or else there was little or no food to purchase.

NOTES

## CONDITIONS

As I am certain the Reader understands, conditions in those days respecting travelers, were a far cry from the present. There were not that many places where people could stay for the night, or where prepared food was readily available. And then, in many places where Paul built Churches, being in rank heathen territory virtually all of the time, his income was meager to say the least.

The phrase, *"And are naked,"* actually refers to not having enough money to buy proper clothing.

The phrase, *"And are buffeted,"* literally means *"to be slapped in the face."* Such insults, together with scourgings, fell to the lot of Paul and other Apostles (Acts 16:23; 23:2; I Pet. 2:20).

It showed the utter contempt with which they were treated; for though Paul ought to have been exempt from such violence, both as a freeman and a Roman Citizen, he was treated many times as vilely as if he had been a mere foreign slave (Farrar).

The phrase, *"And have no certain dwellingplace,"* refers to being itinerant Preachers, not knowing where they would live. Perhaps this homelessness was among the severest of all trials.

## A PERSONAL EXAMPLE

In this short statement, I in no way mean to imply that our efforts for Christ have any resemblance whatsoever to that of which Paul speaks, but yet, in a way I do know of that of which he speaks, even as do some of you.

Frances and I began in Evangelistic Work in 1956. For about the first 12 or 13 years, we did not have a home, in effect living out of a suitcase. Our home was Church basements, Church apartments, inexpensive motel rooms, or staying with the Pastor or someone in the Church, etc. It is not a very easy life.

On top of that, for the first four years of Donnie's education, Frances homeschooled him, using the Calvert School Course. In fact, this Course was excellent, but required several hours of teaching and instruction each day which fell to her lot. After four years of that, Donnie enrolled in the Public School wherever we were at the time, actually attending some 32 schools before he entered High School in Baton Rouge.

As stated, it was not an easy life. When the Lord enabled us to build a home in 1969, I don't even have the words to express how I felt respecting having a *"certain dwelling-place,"* irrespective of the fact that we still were not there very much. At least it was some place we could call home.

As stated, these are minor things in comparison to that of which Paul speaks, hardly worth mentioning, but most people do not know what it is like to live in this manner, even as the Apostle mentions. But yet, that is what the Lord called us to do, and we were honored to serve in any capacity. And what few hardships we suffered, were as Paul stated, *"light afflictions."*

FOOLISH STATEMENTS

It is unfortunate, that some in the last few years have even claimed that Paul's sufferings were because of his lack of Faith. Some have actually stated, that if Paul had had their Faith, he could have foregone all of these problems, etc.

To be frank, I do not actually have the proper vocabulary and neither does anyone else I think, to do justice in addressing such Scriptural and Spiritual ignorance. No, Paul did not suffer these things because of a lack of Faith, but rather because of great Faith.

Many who are no more than babies in Christ (carnal), judge Faith by the trinkets or toys it can bring about (supposedly so), or the so-called life of ease it can afford. If in fact, that is the end of one's Faith, it is a poor substitute.

The Truth is, that the ultimate goal of the Holy Spirit respecting our Faith, is that we become more and more like Christ. In other words, Christlikeness is the objective (Mat. 11:28-30).

In this Faith journey, Satan throws everything he can at us to hinder this progress, and does so in every way possible, whether physical, spiritual, mental, financial, domestical, etc. As well, the Lord allows Satan certain latitude respecting these things of which Paul mentions. Of course, it is Satan's objective to destroy our Faith, or at least to cause it to be seriously weakened. In fact, every attack by Satan, and in whatever capacity, is always against the Faith of the Believer. In other words, he wants the Believer to quit, and sadly, millions have.

NOTES

However, the intention and direction of the Lord is, as should be obvious, the exact opposite of Satan; He strongly desires to strengthen our Faith, hence Him allowing certain difficulties and problems, etc.

(12) "AND LABOUR, WORKING WITH OUR OWN HANDS: BEING REVILED, WE BLESS; BEING PERSECUTED, WE SUFFER IT:"

The phrase, *"And labour, working with our own hands,"* spoke of the manner in which Paul attempted to meet his personal needs.

Almost, if not all of his efforts for Christ, were in the midst of rank Pagans to whom he preached the Gospel and raised up Churches. The heathen religions of these people, which varied with the area, nevertheless, demanded substantial monetary offerings. The Priests of these false religions resorted to every means at their disposal to extract funds from their devotees, etc. In fact, it was a great burden on the people, exactly as Satan's wares are always a great burden.

So, Paul knowing these things, made little or no demands whatsoever on the people respecting money so as to be totally different than these heathen Priests. In these areas, in fact wherever he was raising up a Church, he supported himself by the dreary toil and scant earnings of a tentmaker, in the expressed determination to be no burden upon his converts (Acts 18:3; 20:34; I Cor. 9:6; II Cor. 11:7; I Thess. 2:9; II Thess. 3:8).

Such conduct was the more noble, especially considering that all mechanical trades, of which tent-making certainly came under, were looked down upon by the Greeks as a sort of task of ignorance. In other words, when people did these type of things, it meant they were not intelligent enough to do more intelligent things, etc. In this we cannot help but see the humility of this Apostle.

However, after the Churches were established, he did receive Offerings, in fact making extensive efforts in this realm for the Work of God. Actually, his teaching respecting *"giving,"* as outlined in Chapters 8 and 9 of II Corinthians, is the most extensive found in the entirety of the Word of God.

The phrase, *"Being reviled, we bless,"* presents the correct spiritual stance for the Child of God.

NOTES

Only the Grace of God, which comes to us by the means of the Cross, and which demands that our faith be placed in the Cross, can enable a Believer to do what he must do in order to serve Christ. Whatever is done to us in the negative sense, we as Believers, with Christ as our example, are not to retaliate (Mat. 5:38-48; Rom. 12:17-21).

The phrase, *"Being persecuted, we suffer it,"* had to do primarily, even as the previous phrase, with the very fact of one being a Christian.

The early Christians were falsely accused of the most terrible crimes, so that the very name *"Christian"* was regarded as equivalent to *"malefactor"* (I Pet. 4:14-16). Herein, Paul addressing himself to these indignities as he did, and as well which all Believers must, obeyed the direct precept of our Lord (Mat. 5:44), as well as His example (Lk. 23:44; I Pet. 2:23; 3:9) (Farrar).

(13) "BEING DEFAMED, WE INTREAT: WE ARE MADE AS THE FILTH OF THE WORLD, AND ARE THE OFFSCOURING OF ALL THINGS UNTO THIS DAY."

The phrase, *"Being defamed, we intreat,"* pertains basically to the response regarding the Message preached.

*"Defamed"* in the Greek is, *"blasphemeo,"* and means *"to rail on, revile, to speak evil of, against God or man."* In this case it was against Paul, and all other true Apostles as well.

*"Entreat"* in the Greek is *"parakaleo,"* and means *"to call near, to invite, to invoke, in order to comfort and console."*

The idea is, that irrespective as to how evil was the response to the Message, the Apostle would not allow his spirit to be affected by the opposition, but would continue to appeal tenderly to the sinner to give his heart to God.

When Paul preached, it was, I think, under a heavy Anointing of the Holy Spirit. This means that sinners were greatly moved to make a decision. Some of them accepted the Lord, but some fought against this call and urging by the Holy Spirit, turning on the one who had delivered the Message, even as many do.

While it is definitely the Message that is opposed, still, more particularly it is the Anointing of the Holy Spirit on the Message, Who convicts of *"Sin, Righteousness, and Judgment"* (Jn. 16:8-11).

## THE HOLY SPIRIT

In fact, most Preachers preach a compromised Message which engenders no opposition whatsoever. And then others do preach the Truth, but without the Anointing of the Holy Spirit, for such Anointing is never automatic. As well, they will receive little opposition. However, there are some few who not only preach the Truth, but do so by the Power and Anointing of the Holy Spirit, which most always results in a favorable or unfavorable response. In these cases, neutrality seldom happens. However, irrespective of the anger or hostility of the response, the *"entreaty"* is to continue, ever attempting to bring the sinner to Christ.

The phrase, *"We are made as the filth of the world,"* could be translated, *"We are treated as the filth of the world."*

*"Filth"* in the Greek is *"perikatharma,"* and means *"the sweepings of a dirty room."*

The phrase, *"And are the offscouring of all things unto this day,"* shoots down the idea of popularity, doesn't it?

*"Offscouring"* in the Greek is *"peripsema,"* and means *"an unwanted wretch whose body was cast into the Sea to try to appease the so-called angry gods."* In other words, the person was good for nothing, etc.

Christianity is popular only when it is compromised. This means if a person truly tries to live and preach the Gospel exactly as the Word of God gives it, which is what we are supposed to do, and does so by the Power and Help of the Holy Spirit, which in fact is the only way it can be done, irrespective of how nice, kind, gracious, or diplomatic one may attempt to be, the very fact of what he is and what he preaches, will effect a very hostile response.

## WHY?

The negative response of the individual is actually not toward the Believer, even though it may seem to be, but rather the Spirit of God which is in the Believer. Unregenerate man is totally without God, and will mostly respond with hostility toward the Holy Spirit, at least in some fashion. The reason is obvious, one is holy and the other unholy. One is Righteous and the other unrighteous. One is of Light and the other is of darkness. Satan hates God and all that pertains to God, and his children likewise hate God and all that pertains to God, i.e., God's Children.

In fact, there is no opposition in the world against Islam, Buddhism, Confucianism, Spiritism, Mormonism, Catholicism, etc., unless someone of one of these particular religions commits a personal offense against the person in question. Then the opposition would be because of the offense, and not because of their religion. There is no opposition as there is with Bible Christianity, simply because it is all of the same spirit. In other words, the spirit of Islam, etc., is the same as the spirit of the world in every capacity, and in fact all of these religions are of the spirit of the world, i.e., *"Satan."* That is the reason they looked at Believers in the Early Church as *"filth"* or *"offscouring,"* and in fact, it is somewhat the same presently and for the obvious reasons.

A DIFFERENCE?

However, there is a difference now than then, in that the Gospel has made tremendous inroads into the entirety of the world, which has somewhat ameliorated the hostility, but definitely not altogether. At least one of the reasons for the lessening of hostility, is that there are simply more Believers now than then, considerably more. As *"Light"* and *"Salt,"* that carries tremendous weight, and a tremendous influence for good.

However, the Believer must ever understand, that as far as the core of hostility is concerned, that has not lessened at all, and in fact, cannot lessen. It is just as hostile presently toward the Gospel and those who bear the Gospel, as it always was. The Devil has not gotten Saved or better, but is rather, of the same evil and wickedness that he always was, and so are his children. Consequently, there is no way to come to terms with evil. If such is done, it is never evil that is compromised, but always the Gospel.

(14) "I WRITE NOT THESE THINGS TO SHAME YOU, BUT AS MY BELOVED SONS I WARN YOU."

The phrase, *"I write not these things to shame you,"* carries the meaning that he is not merely venting his spleen, so to speak, but that there is a lesson, an important lesson at that, which the Holy Spirit desires that he teach. Consequently, he has used some strong words and strong analogies. He does not write angrily or bitterly, even though he has used strong expostulation and keen irony.

The phrase, *"But as my beloved sons I warn you,"* carries in its structure a very strong statement.

NOTES

Let not the Reader think that these first Four Chapters are merely the hurt feelings of a Preacher who has been rejected, consequently, replaced by someone else. If that is all the Reader sees, then the Reader is missing entirely that which the Holy Spirit is teaching, which is of extreme significance, especially considering the amount of space devoted to this particular subject. It was far more than merely preferring one Preacher over another. What was being done was engineered by Satan, and was meant to completely set aside God's Plan for spiritual growth. In a sense it was the Garden of Eden all over again.

THE PLAN OF GOD

The matter of the Gospel is really very simple. God has a Way and man must follow that Way. However, this is where the rub comes in. Satan connives and schemes attempting to change that *"Way"* which of course is the Scripture, and devises his own plans. He does so very subtlety and very religiously, so much so in fact, that many are fooled, which in fact, is his intention all along.

So, the Believer must know what the Plan of God is, which is always according to the Word of God, and follow that Plan without fail.

GOD'S ORDER

*"For the perfecting of the Saints, for the Work of the Ministry, for the edifying of the Body of Christ,"* (Eph. 4:12) the Lord has set in the Church, *"Apostles; and some, Prophets; and some, Evangelists; and some, Pastors and Teachers"* (Eph. 4:11).

This is God's Order for the Church, and of course Satan tries to change that Order.

All Spiritual Authority is ensconced in this Order, and not in any other manner. That means that men elected by popular ballot to a religious office, or appointed, may in fact serve the Lord well in that capacity; however, that particular religious office, no matter how high it is looked at by the world or even the Church for that matter, carries no Spiritual Authority, at least that given in the Word of God and superintended by the Holy Spirit. Actually, this has been one of Satan's greatest efforts to destroy God-appointed Authority, by substituting His Own.

No, that does not mean that all men who are in religious offices respecting Denominations are favoring the work of Satan. In fact, some are Godly, and are definitely doing the Work of the Lord. Nevertheless, if they at any time think that such a position is Scriptural and thereby Spiritual, they have then abrogated what good they can do, rendering themselves ineffective as far as the Cause of Christ is concerned, and are rather a hindrance, and sometimes greatly so! The Word of God must be adhered to strictly, and even the Spirit of the Word of God. To do otherwise, always leads the Church astray.

ACCEPTANCE OR REJECTION

Some of the people at Corinth were in effect picking and choosing who they liked among the Apostles and denigrating the rest. In other words, they were refusing to accept the Order laid down by the Lord, in effect devising their own order, which is why I said it was the Garden of Eden situation all over again, which in fact, plays out constantly all over the world.

There was nothing inherently wrong with the Tree of the Knowledge of Good and Evil. The wrong came respecting obedience or disobedience concerning the Word of God. As previously stated, Adam and Eve were faced with the decision of *"Theonomy or Autonomy."*

Theonomy says that we look to God our Creator for all things, thereby, doing what He tells us to do, and, thereby, reaping the results of obedience which is abundant life, and which can only be found in the Creator.

Autonomy ignores God, looking to self, in other words, devising its own strategy.

As Adam and Eve faced that question in the Garden, men continue to face it each and every day, and even Believers, and especially Believers!

God the Holy Spirit had called certain men to serve as Apostles, or Prophets, etc., but some of the people at Corinth were saying that they did not want or desire the Ministry of these particular people, whomever they may have been. In other words, God's Choice was not sufficient for them, in effect, demanding their own choice.

The modern situation is identical! Too oftentimes the Church refuses to accept those whom God has called and set in the Church for the very purpose and thing needed; many do not like God's Choices, and in effect, choose their own. Consequently, there are no *"Perfecting of the Saints,"* or *"Work of the Ministry,"* or *"Edifying of the Body of Christ."* In effect, when one rejects the one sent by God, one rejects God.

NOTES

THE WORST PROBLEM IN THE CHURCH?

Paul had received a letter from the Church at Corinth asking about particular situations. There were questions about marriage and celibacy; about second marriages; about mixed marriages, etc. They had questions as well concerning *"meats offered to idols."* Also, they had questions about Spiritual Gifts, and about the Resurrection. Of course, Paul addressed himself to all of these questions.

However, there were two grave matters of which they did not mention in their Letter: A. First of all the deplorable party spirit, which we are now discussing; and, B. The case of incest so flagrant that the very heathen cried shame upon it (I Cor. Chpt. 5). The information concerning these two very weighty problems was probably given to Paul by the very ones who brought the Letter, *"By them which are of the house of Chloe"* (I Cor. 1:11).

The point I want to make is this:

As deplorable, evil, and ungodly as was the problem of incest, the Holy Spirit deemed the *"party spirit"* in the Church of far greater magnitude. It was addressed first, and given the space of four Chapters, with the other problem addressed second, and given the space of only one Chapter. The idea is this:

Sins of vice are very wicked, as are obvious. However, it is not too difficult to get a Believer to repent of such sins, because they automatically know it is wrong, despite whatever excuses they attempt to make at the outset. In fact, most all sins of passion fall into this category.

Sins of pride, which this party spirit was, are not so easy to address. To be frank, most people do not even think of such as sin, with the people in the Church at Corinth who were involved, actually feeling and thinking they were spiritually elite. In fact, spiritual pride pretty well always functions in this capacity — spiritual elitism, self-righteousness, etc.

But yet, and as stated, the Holy Spirit knew this sin to be so deplorable and destructive to the Cause of Christ, that He had the Apostle to address it first, and to devote an extraordinary deal of space to the situation.

Unfortunately, the Church continues to fall into this trap of Satan, of not recognizing the true culprits in the Church, but rather causing more time and energy to be spent on that which is not nearly as significant.

That which is destroying the Church presently, and in fact always has, is not sins of passion, as evil and wicked as they may be, but rather sins of pride, which refers to so-called Religious Leaders leading the Church astray.

(15) "FOR THOUGH YE HAVE TEN THOUSAND INSTRUCTORS IN CHRIST, YET HAVE YE NOT MANY FATHERS: FOR IN CHRIST JESUS I HAVE BEGOTTEN YOU THROUGH THE GOSPEL."

The phrase, *"For though ye have ten thousand instructors in Christ,"* refers to Teachers.

*"Instructors"* in the Greek is *"paidagogos,"* and means *"a schoolmaster."*

## THE OFFICE OF THE TEACHER

The Office of the *"Teacher"* is of course, extremely important, being one of the Fivefold Callings (Eph. 4:11).

To these individuals, be they man or woman, the Lord gives a special Anointing that they may open up the Scripture. Two things are said here:

1. The Teacher must know and understand the Word of God, in fact, be a master of the Word.
2. If he (or she) feels the Lord has set him in this Office, he must seek the Lord constantly, that the Power of the Holy Spirit may rest upon him in order that he may have a continued Anointing to open up the Word of Life. While the Prophet and the Evangelist may teach, even as they should, for all good Preaching has an element of Teaching, still, they will not experience the same Anointing to Teach as that of the *"Teacher"* who stands in that particular Office (Rom. 11:13; 12:4; I Tim. 3:1, 10, 13).

The Apostle is Called of God respecting a particular Message, which is always for the good of the entirety of the Body of Christ all over the world. In other words, the Apostle is in the forefront, actually setting the Standard for the Church according to the Moving and Operation of the Holy Spirit, which is always according to the Word of God. As a result, the Apostle can fill, and in fact does fill, all five of the Ministerial Callings or Offices (Eph. 4:11).

As well, it is believed, and probably correctly, that *"Pastors"* and *"Teachers"* are supposed to be connected, i.e., *"Teaching Pastors."*

NOTES

## FALSE TEACHERS

The Church was plagued in Paul's day by false teachers, has continued to be plagued, and greatly suffers this problem even unto this present hour.

The manner in which Paul used the phrase or number *"ten thousand,"* and speaking of Teachers or Instructors, implies a touch of impatience at the itch of Teaching which seems to have prevailed at Corinth (Farrar).

What do we mean by false teachers?

We speak of those who deviate from the Word of God. In other words, whenever false teachers came into the Churches in Paul's day, telling the people that they must keep the Law of Moses in order to be Saved, as well as accepting Christ, this was false and they were false. It caused great problems in the Early Church as should be obvious, and it continues to cause great problems presently.

The problem of false teachers, at least at this time, did not seem to be the difficulty at Corinth (but very soon would be), but rather the attitude of certain people in making more out of particular Preachers than they should have. So the Devil works both ways.

If he cannot get the man or woman to teach that which is false, he will attempt to get the people to make more out of God-called Preachers than they should, even to the point of contention and serious contention at that.

As well, we must remember, that Satan in using false teachers to teach a false gospel, will most of the time do it in such a subtle way, that many Believers will not be able to tell the difference in the true and the false. In fact, many Believers are so little versed in the Word of God, that the Evil One has little difficulty in leading them down a wrong path. What they hear is cleverly disguised, and almost always contains some Truth, even at times, much Truth. In fact, it is the Truth that is the snare and not the lie. Because there is some Truth, then it is easy to slip in the false and have it eagerly accepted.

## FALSE TEACHING

Almost always, false teaching appeals to particular, selfish, base motives in Believers. In other words, the Prosperity Message, which papers itself with Scriptures, and contains some Truth as we have stated, appeals to greed and pride. In fact, the party spirit at Corinth appealed to pride. They imagined themselves to be spiritually elite, and all who were not following their particular Preacher, they roundly condemned, as stated even to the point of contention.

In fact, I think one can always say that teaching that is not according to the Word of God, even though it may seem to be at first, in some way, always appeals to *"self."* That which is truly of the Word, and Anointed by the Holy Spirit always lifts up Christ, making Him the Object, actually the Object of all things. The Holy Spirit *never* glorifies self, but always the Lord of Glory (Jn. 16:13-15).

The phrase, *"Yet have ye not many fathers,"* speaks of one who has brought the Gospel to the sinner in order that he might be Saved. Paul presents a yearning desire that his unique claim as the founder of the Church at Corinth should not be so ungratefully overlooked, as though it were of no importance (Acts 18:11; I Cor. 3:6; 9:1-2).

The phrase, *"For in Christ Jesus I have begotten you through the Gospel,"* speaks of more than a mere presentation of the Gospel.

## THE CALL

It speaks of the Call which was on Paul's life, which consumed him day and night, in a sense, making him a driven person, which is perfectly proper. The idea is, that the Salvation of these Corinthians, and all others who had come to Christ under Paul's Ministry for that matter, or any Preacher who falls into this category, does not come about easily, but rather through much Burden and Intercession before God. In other words, the burden for these particular souls lay heavy on Paul's heart, long before he ever came to Corinth, or even knew these people in a personal way. This is a very high and holy thing before God, and one of the reasons that not a lot of Preachers truly win souls. While the Gospel must be preached, and preached under the Anointing of the Holy Spirit, still, it is far more involved even than that.

Every tear shed by the Apostle, every moment of Intercessory Prayer, every ounce of the Burden that was incumbent upon him day and night, all went into the Salvation of these souls, even though the final work is always done by Christ.

NOTES

*"Begotten"* in the Greek is *"gennao,"* and means *"to procreate, to regenerate, beget, bring forth, conceive, be delivered of."*

Actually, Paul was using the word *"begotten"* in a secondary and metaphoric sense, because in the highest sense sinners are only begotten by the Will of God, by that Word of Truth (James 1:18), to which he alludes in the words *"through the Gospel"* (Farrar).

However, even though Paul's use of the word was secondary or metaphorical, still, it is much closer to the true and higher sense than one may realize. We must remember, that the Holy Spirit had him to use this word and for purpose. The reason is to proclaim to Believers the part that they play (if in fact they do) in the Salvation of souls. Regrettably, many today are merely attempting to confess souls into the Kingdom, but, unfortunately, such is not Biblical. Even Jesus Christ could not *"confess"* Salvation or Redemption into existence, but had to instead come down here and pay the price, in order that man might be Saved. There is a price to pay, even as Paul here speaks, concerning souls being brought from darkness to Light.

## THAT WHICH THE HOLY SPIRIT IS SAYING

Even though we have touched on this previously, it is so important that I feel it would be very difficult to overstate the case.

How was it possible for these Believers at Corinth who had been brought out of paganistic darkness into Light by the Burden and Ministry of the Apostle Paul, to turn on him, even as some of them did?

This goes to show us how subtle Satan is, and how easy it is for people to get off track. The fault was not that of Paul, but rather these particular people, and because they were glorifying self instead of Christ.

In our own personal Ministry, the Lord has helped us to see many souls brought to Christ, for which we give Him all the Praise and Glory. If the Lord had not helped us to take the Telecast into their particular part of the world, one must wonder if the Lord would have helped them find Salvation in another way?

One could ask the same question respecting the building of these Churches by Paul? If Paul had not obeyed the Lord, would they have been brought in by other means?

Of course, only the Lord knows the answer to those questions, but at the same time, we must never take lightly the burden, care, and concern that it took to get the Gospel to Corinth and other cities, or to the parts of the world where the Lord has helped us, as well as every other Preacher of the Gospel who falls into this category.

And yet, even as Paul, I have seen some turn against us, in effect, their Father in Christ. Consequently, I know a little bit of the pain that the Apostle suffered.

Incidentally, Paul did not disobey Jesus' prohibition against calling earthly leaders *"Father* (Patera)*"* (Mat. 23:9) because he was using the term only in the sense of leading them to accept the Gospel of Christ (Rossier).

(16) "WHEREFORE I BESEECH YOU, BE YE FOLLOWERS OF ME."

The phrase, *"Wherefore I beseech you,"* in effect says, *"I plead with you."*

The phrase, *"Be ye followers of me,"* should have been translated, *"Be ye imitators of me."*

Paul was not pleading with the Corinthians to become his followers in the modern usage of this word. We do Christian Leaders a real disservice when we call ourselves their followers. We follow only One — Christ!

We need to realize that when the King James Version was translated, the term *"followers"* then meant what *"imitators"* means today. Unfortunately, the word *"followers"* has taken on a cultic meaning in our contemporary society.

In effect, the Greek basically means to *"keep on becoming imitators"* (Rossier).

And now after looking at the word *"followers,"* we should also look at the pronoun *"me."* Paul was telling these people to be imitators of him and not other Preachers or Teachers. This did not mean that he lacked respect for other Preachers, for the Text indicates the very opposite. In fact, he will mention Timothy in the very next Verse and his Ministry at Corinth.

THE FOLLOWING IS WHAT PAUL DESIRED:

He wanted the people at Corinth as well as all the other Churches to be blessed by any and all Ministries truly given by the Lord, and which functioned in the Will of God, but there were things which Paul knew that the people did not know. It is as follows:

NOTES

1. Being their *"Father"* in the Lord, he knew that his burden for them was sincere, and that he had only their highest spiritual good at heart. In other words, there was no ulterior motive in his demeanor or Ministry respecting the people. Consequently, he wanted his Converts to imitate him, and rightly so.

2. He wanted and desired that these people, whomever they may be, to be exposed to other Ministries as well; nevertheless, he wanted the people to judge what was taught or preached by what he taught and preached, i.e., *"imitators of him."*

3. Paul knew that there were many parasites at large, who really did not have the spiritual growth of the people at heart, but rather their own selfish desires. In other words, they used people to get what they wanted, instead of being a servant to the people as the Lord demanded. As well, Paul knew how slick, sophisticated, coy, and confidential these false teachers could be, in other words, con artists. So, he is telling the people, measure everything you hear by what you have heard from me, and if it does not match up with what I have taught and preached, do not accept what you have heard, in fact reject what you have heard and as well, reject the false teacher.

4. Paul grieved over these people, realizing how subtle Satan is, so able to present his wares in such a way, that at times even the strongest are deceived.

Some may think it egotistical of Paul, holding himself up in this fashion, but that was not the idea at all. Paul was not promoting himself whatsoever. He was promoting the Gospel he preached, and the veracity of that Gospel was obvious to all because of the fruit it had borne, i.e., *"Souls Saved."*

5. Some may say that Paul only urged this direction to those who had been Saved under his Ministry. However, that is false.

While he definitely did direct attention to these individuals, inasmuch as he was their *"Father"* in Christ, still, his Epistles were to be read in all the Churches, and whatever he intended, we know that the Holy Spirit intended for this Word to go to all, irrespective as to whether they had been Saved under Paul or not, and for all time, as should be obvious.

(17) "FOR THIS CAUSE HAVE I SENT UNTO YOU TIMOTHEUS, WHO IS MY

BELOVED SON, AND FAITHFUL IN THE LORD, WHO SHALL BRING YOU INTO REMEMBRANCE OF MY WAYS WHICH BE IN CHRIST, AS I TEACH EVERY WHERE IN EVERY CHURCH."

The phrase, *"For this cause,"* means that Paul had a deep interest in their spiritual well-being, hence his admonition to them.

One must remember, that he was only using himself as a human example to guide them in the special virtues of humility, self-denial, and faithfulness (Heb. 13:7; I Pet. 5:3). In the highest sense we can only be *"imitators of God"* (Eph. 5:1).

The phrase, *"Have I sent unto you Timotheus,"* refers to Timothy who had been brought to Christ on Paul's first Missionary journey (Acts 14:6-7; 16:1-2). Timothy's home it seems had been *"Lystra,"* a small city very near Derbe to the East, and Iconium to the North. In fact, Lystra was probably about 175 miles West of Paul's hometown of Tarsus, both in modern-day Turkey.

Timothy had started before this Letter was sent (Acts 19:22), but did not reach Corinth until after its arrival, it seems because he had been unable to go by Sea, and had to travel around by Macedonia. As well, it seems that Paul knew that his Epistle would reach Corinth before Timothy arrived (I Cor. 16:10).

The phrase, *"Who is my beloved son, and faithful in the Lord,"* referred to Timothy being his son in the Lord. As stated, Paul had won him to Christ some years before.

Timothy had been faithful all of this time respecting his help to Paul, and service for the Lord.

The phrase, *"Who shall bring you into remembrance of my ways which be in Christ, as I teach every where in every Church,"* tells us several things.

Paul is not sending the youthful Timothy as an authoritative Teacher, since the Corinthians, fond of high pretention and soaring oratory, might scorn to show any submission to a shy and shrinking youth; but he is only sending him because, as his closest companion, Timothy would be best able to explain to them *"Paul's ways which be in Christ,"* in the Organization of Churches (Farrar).

(18) "NOW SOME ARE PUFFED UP, AS THOUGH I WOULD NOT COME TO YOU."

NOTES

The phrase, *"Now some are puffed up,"* speaks of prideful attitudes.

*"Puffed"* in the Greek is *"phusioo,"* and means *"to make proud or be haughty."*

The Apostle is speaking of the disparaging comparisons that some at Corinth had made of him with others.

Once again, it is very difficult to understand how that anyone, much less the Converts of the Great Apostle, could stoop to the level of disparaging one of the greatest men of God who has ever lived! And yet, it is not so difficult to understand after all. Satan is a master at deception, and as such, inflates the *"self"* of the one he is seeking to destroy, or else to use to hurt the Work of God, with many falling for his ploys.

The phrase, *"As though I would not come to you,"* could have been translated, *"As though they would not eventually have to face me in person."*

Actually, Paul was on the eve of starting from Macedonia on his way to visit them (I Cor. 16:5), but, owing to the grievous state of the Church, he subsequently changed his purpose (II Cor. 1:15, 23). In other words, he delayed his visit to them, despite the fact that his many enemies and critics were likely to say, *"He is afraid to come himself, and so he sends Timothy."* They evidently flattered themselves that he was alarmed by their culture and intellectualism.

No doubt, Paul earnestly sought the Lord about this situation, and the Lord evidently gave him directions respecting the delay of this visit, which would prove to be right. How close to the Lord the Apostle was, and what an example he is to us.

(19) "BUT I WILL COME TO YOU SHORTLY, IF THE LORD WILL, AND WILL KNOW, NOT THE SPEECH OF THEM WHICH ARE PUFFED UP, BUT THE POWER."

The phrase, *"But I will come to you shortly, if the Lord will,"* presents something more than mere form as it is used by the Apostle (Rom. 15:32; Heb. 6:3; James 4:15). The Will of the Lord meant everything to Paul, as it should mean to us; consequently, his use of the term *"If the Lord will,"* expressed a real and humble spirit of dependence. In other words, he was seeking to be led by the Holy Spirit in all that he did, and that means all!

Paul did go to Corinth soon after writing his Second Epistle to them, which is recorded in Acts 20:1-2.

NOTES

The phrase, *"And will know, not the speech of them which are puffed up, but the power,"* in effect says, if the Corinthians did not heed Timothy's appeal, they would have to face the Apostle himself. By using the words *"puffed up,"* he is speaking of the prideful attitude of these particular Corinthians, who in effect thought their spirituality was greater than that of Paul. Once again, even though I may be overly repetitive, the significance of this is of such magnitude that it defies description.

## OPPOSING PAUL?

First of all, considering the degree to which the Holy Spirit addressed this situation through the Apostle, we know that what was taking place at Corinth was not merely the prattle of one or two misguided souls, which most every Church seems to have, but rather a spirit that was about to sweep the entirety of the Church, if it had not already done so. To which we have previously alluded, with Paul speaking of many instructors (I Cor. 4:15), the manner in which he used this phrase could very well indicate, that unnamed outside Teachers had in fact come into the Assembly with their false message, whatever it may have been. In their presentation, they flattered the people with some falling for the appeal, and then they set about to denigrate the person of Paul. If in fact such a thing did happen, which it probably did, they felt they had to denigrate the Apostle, tearing him down in the eyes of the people in order to promote their false gospel of self-esteem, etc. It is unthinkable that anyone could turn the heads of anybody against the Apostle Paul, especially considering that these people had been Saved under Paul's Ministry; nevertheless, they had done exactly that, or would do so shortly, which threatened the entirety of the Church. In fact, this was one of the reasons for Paul's great distress as is recorded in II Corinthians 2:12-13.

It is virtually impossible for Satan to denigrate the Message unless he can as well denigrate the Messenger.

*"Power"* in the Greek as here used is *"dunamis,"* and means *"inherent power; the power of reproducing itself like a dynamo."* It speaks of the Holy Spirit within Paul.

The insinuation is, that this false direction at Corinth was fueled only by words, for the simple reason that the Holy Spirit cannot bless, help, or anoint that which is false. By contrast, the Holy Spirit was with Paul and with him in a grand and powerful way, which would be evident if he came to Corinth. In fact, the only defense against false doctrine, is the Truth, but the Truth empowered by the Holy Spirit, which is never automatic. For the Truth to be presented with Power, requires Jesus being large in one's life. The ideal is according to the following:

If Jesus is big in one's life, the Holy Spirit will always be big as well. In other words, according to the degree that Christ has a person, to that degree can the Holy Spirit use that person.

As well, wherever and whenever the Holy Spirit is given complete latitude in one's life, He will always glorify Christ, in effect making Christ bigger and bigger in one's life (Jn. 16:13-15).

## THE TWO PROBLEMS WITH THE MODERN CHURCH

1. The first problem pertains to the lack of Truth in the Churches. By that I mean that the Word of God is not adhered to at all, or else only in a partial sense.

Most of the old-line Religious Denominations, irrespective as to what their Constitution and Bylaws may say, for the most part, do not even believe anymore that the Bible is the Word of God. In fact, they little believe in the Virgin Birth of Christ, that Jesus was and is the Son of God, or in His vicarious, atoning Work at Calvary. Neither do they believe in the Resurrection.

So, with almost no Truth at all going out from behind most of those pulpits, Church for the most part is little more than a social center in those circles.

2. And then there is an element in the old-line Churches which claims to believe and preach all the Bible, but in fact denies the Veracity and Power of the Holy Spirit. They claim that the Acts Chapter 2 experience passed away with the Apostles, or they attempt to explain it away in other directions, etc. Irrespective, they deny the Baptism with the Holy Spirit with the evidence of speaking with other Tongues as a viable modern-day Biblical experience. As such, and even though some Truth is preached from behind those pulpits, there is no power to back it up because the One Who has and gives the Power, the Holy Spirit, is looked at and

thought of as some type of silent partner, which is the second problem.

Regrettably, some Pentecostal Denominations which were built on the very premise of the Baptism with the Holy Spirit, are following suit, denying His Power, casting about for other means of approach for the human dilemma, such as Humanistic Psychology, etc.

So the problem with the Modern Church is: A. A lack of Truth; and, B. A lack of Power. It is truly the time of Apostasy, the time of the Laodicean Church, as it proclaims that it is *"rich and increased with goods, and has need of nothing."* And yet Jesus says, *"And knowest not that thou art wretched, and miserable, and poor, and blind, and naked"* (Rev. 3:17).

Regrettably, because we are living in the last of the last days, the situation is not going to improve but rather worsen (II Tim. 3:1-5; 4:3-4).

(20) "FOR THE KINGDOM OF GOD IS NOT IN WORD, BUT IN POWER."

The phrase, *"For the Kingdom of God,"* is an expression which was used constantly by Christ Himself in His earthly Ministry. It relates to two basic matters:

1. That one day He will physically and literally reign over this Earth.
2. And that He now reigns in the hearts of people who acquiesce to His Lordship (Rossier).

THE KINGDOM OF GOD AND THE KINGDOM OF HEAVEN

Both John the Baptist and our Lord came offering the *"Kingdom of Heaven"* to Israel (Mat. 3:2; 4:17). Regrettably, Israel rejected the Kingdom. As a result of the Kingdom being rejected, the world has been submitted, now presently some 2,000 years, to continued war, famine, starvation, etc. Had Israel then accepted Christ, and thereby the Kingdom, all of this suffering and heartache could have been avoided.

*"The Kingdom of Heaven"* could actually be translated *"The Kingdom from the Heavens."* It was, and is, headed up by Jesus Christ, and presents that which we now have in our hearts, but which one day will be visible over the entirety of the Earth. This will be at the Second Coming, when Christ will rule and reign Personally from Jerusalem (Mat. 11:12, 20-24; 27:22-25; Lk. 19:11-27; Acts 1:6-7; 3:19-26).

*"The Kingdom of God"* pertains to the entirety of God's creation, even that which is now in rebellion against Him. *"The Kingdom of Heaven"* can be said to be the Earthly aspect of the Kingdom of God; however, it is only when the Earthly aspect of the Kingdom is brought into line that the Kingdom of God and the Kingdom of Heaven will then be one and the same.

As stated, the *"Kingdom"* will commence when Jesus comes back, which will be the beginning of that which is commonly referred to as the *"Kingdom Age."* It is impossible to have a *"Kingdom"* unless you have a king. Jesus Christ will be, and is, that *"King."*

Inasmuch as Christ will rule Personally at that time, the entirety of the complexion of the Earth will totally change. Sickness will be completely eliminated, as well as all poverty; consequently, the change will be so dramatic as to be miraculous.

THE DIFFERENCE IN THE TWO KINGDOMS

While the Kingdom of Heaven is only a part of the Kingdom of God, being the part which will ultimately come from Heaven to Earth at the Second Coming, even as we have already said, the Kingdom of God actually encompasses everything.

The Kingdom of God refers to the entirety of God's Creation, which includes all Angels, be they fallen or Righteous, all men, be they Believers or unbelievers, even including Satan and demon spirits.

The Lord did not create Satan as Satan nor fallen angels in that manner, for that matter. They were originally created by God in Righteousness, Purity, and Holiness. Their Fall does not make them any less a part of the original Creation.

To which we have already alluded, a part of that Kingdom is in rebellion against God, which comprises most of this Earth, Satan and his followers. However, one day soon, at least compared to Eternity, this rebellion is going to be completely put down, with the entirety of the Kingdom of God then being in harmony with its Creator. Paul referred to that as *"God . . . All in All"* (I Cor. 15:28).

The phrase, *"Is not in Word, but in Power,"* places Bible Christianity in a class all its own.

POWER

The religions of the world have only *"words,"* and words made up by man at that. Bible

Christianity is totally different in that if the Lord is properly followed, the Truth (the Word) will always be accompanied by *"Power."* This speaks of Power to live a Holy Life, to overcome sin, to become Christlike. However, in effect, the *"Power"* is resident in the Holy Spirit (Acts 1:8).

If the Holy Spirit is rejected in any fashion, even though the part of the Word of God which is preached may be Truth, still, it will bring forth few results, even as we have previously stated, without the Power of the Holy Spirit.

The bane of much of modern Christianity is Churches without power, Preachers without power, and Believers without power. We are speaking of those who have never been Baptized with the Holy Spirit (Acts 1:4), either because they do not believe in the Baptism with the Holy Spirit, or through neglect have never received, or else no longer depend on the Holy Spirit even though they are presently filled. These people will see nothing done for the Lord in their lives, simply because the door which admits all of these great things from God, they have closed. In fact, all is resident in Jesus as our Saviour, but it is Jesus Who Baptizes with the Holy Spirit (Mat. 3:11).

The word *"Power"* as Paul uses it here, and to which we alluded in Commentary on the last Verse, actually means inherent Power, that which reproduces itself like a dynamo.

It refers to the Holy Spirit residing in the Believer, with the Believer then not having to look to an outside source.

## AN EXPLANATION

The best way to explain this would be in the form of a perpetual motion machine. Such a machine, which of course does not exist, if in fact it did exist, would have to run perpetually without any outside source of power being applied such as electricity, gasoline, diesel fuel, or Atomic Energy, etc. In other words, in some manner, the machine produces its own power as it operates and, therefore, does not have to have any outside source of energy or power. As stated, such a machine in reality does not exist.

However, when the Holy Spirit comes into the heart and life of a Believer, it is in effect, the Lord in one sense, moving His Headquarters from Heaven to Earth, and more particularly into the heart and life of the Believer (I Cor. 3:16).

NOTES

The Holy Spirit reproduces His Own Power on a constant basis, in effect, perpetually or into perpetuity. Actually, Jesus said of the Holy Spirit, *"And I will pray the Father, and He shall give you another Comforter, that He may abide with you forever"* (Jn. 14:16). In other words, the Holy Spirit came to stay and stay He does.

In fact, He will remain in the Believer until the Resurrection, when He will effect that glorious change, and then continue in the Glorified Body of the Saint of God forever, in effect becoming the total life system of the Resurrected Saints.

It actually seems as if in the Resurrection, even though the Glorified Body will be of flesh and bone, there is thought that it will not contain blood. When Jesus referred to His Glorified Body after the Resurrection, He said, *"Behold My Hands and My Feet, that it is I Myself: handle Me, and see; for a spirit hath not flesh and bones, as ye see Me have"* (Lk. 24:39).

Knowing that the life of the flesh is in the blood (Lev. 17:14), and if in fact the Glorified Body will contain no blood, the generating force of life in the Resurrected Body will have to be the Holy Spirit, Who as stated, will remain forever. He is and ever shall be, the Reproducing Dynamo.

(21) "WHAT WILL YE? SHALL I COME UNTO YOU WITH A ROD, OR IN LOVE, AND IN THE SPIRIT OF MEEKNESS?"

The question, *"What will ye?"*, is actually in the form of an ultimatum! The state of puffed-up pride in these Corinthians, which was threatening to destroy the Church and their soul's Salvation as well, either had to go, or Judgment from God would be the next offing. We must remember that this is actually coming from the Holy Spirit. Paul was the instrument, but the Holy Spirit was and is the Author.

In fact, the Church at this present hour is in a far worse shape than it was then. So, I wonder if we are not hearing the same Words of the Holy Spirit, and coming like an arrow to our souls! *"What will ye?"*

I believe the Church is very near the Rapture, in fact, it could happen at any moment. That being the case, the Holy Spirit at the same time is getting the Church ready for the Rapture. In fact, some few are ready, but the Truth is, that most are in a terrible spiritual condition. To these, and most likely to us all, the Holy

Spirit is issuing an ultimatum. Those who reject His Ultimatum, will apostatize and lose their souls.

So, in effect, He is saying to all of us, *"What will ye?"*

The beginning of the question, *"Shall I come unto you with a rod . . . ?"*, speaks of authority and chastisement.

*"Rod"* in the Greek is *"rhabdos,"* and means *"a cane, a cudgel, or a baton of royalty."*

The word actually has a variety of meanings, but in this case, Paul is speaking of it as an instrument of punishment.

What type of punishment is the Holy Spirit here intending through the Apostle?

I think it would be helpful if we would look at the word *"rod"* as it applies to discipline, for that actually is what we are addressing.

## DISCIPLINE

Often when we think of discipline we mean punishment. But Biblically, Discipline is much more than mere painful correction, but rather an effort to pull the individual back to the rightful path or way, even as Paul is attempting to do here.

Let us look at this subject from both the Old and New Testaments, and perhaps it will give us some insight.

## HEBREW WORDS

The key Hebrew word for Discipline is *"yasar,"* which means *"to discipline," "to chastise,"* or *"to instruct."*

A derivative, *"musar,"* means *"discipline."* These Hebrew words are translated both *"discipline"* and *"chastisement."* The root denotes correction that contributes to education. Consequently, Biblical Discipline (chastisement) is goal oriented: it seeks to develop a Godly person who is responsive to the Lord and who walks in His Ways.

## THE MANNER OR CHARACTER OF OLD TESTAMENT DISCIPLINE

Discipline (chastisement) involves correction that contributes to one's education and training in Righteousness. As stated, this is exactly what Paul was attempting to do.

The goal of Old Testament Discipline is well expressed in the stated purpose of Proverbs: *"For attaining wisdom and discipline, for understanding words of insight; for acquiring a disciplined and prudent life, doing what is right and just and fair"* (Prov. 1:2-3).

NOTES

Old Testament Discipline is exercised in the context of close family relationships. God urged Israel to view His Own Discipline of them in a family framework: *"Know then in your heart that as a man disciplines his son, so the Lord your God disciplines you"* (Deut. 8:5).

## NOT PRIMARILY FOR PUNISHMENT

The Deuteronomy context makes it very clear that discipline is not primarily punishment. Deuteronomy 8:1-5 reminds Israel of how God cared for His People in the Exodus years. God caused them to hunger — but then He gave them Manna, *"to teach* (them) *that man does not live on bread alone, but by every Word that comes from the Mouth of the Lord"* (Deut. 8:3; 11:1-7).

This illustrates a major aspect of Old Testament Discipline. God provided instructive experiences for His People. Throughout Scripture, Israel is called to look back into their history and to learn not only from God's Punishments but also from His Provisions.

## CORRECTION

Both Biblical History and the Proverbs make the point that even though discipline is not primarily punishment, still, there is an element of punishment in God's Discipline of His People — when this is required. God corrected with punishment (Lev. 26:18, 28; Isa. 8:11; Hos. 5:2; 7:12). And Proverbs recommends the rod of correction to parents with unresponsive youngsters (Prov. 22:15; 29:15, 17).

But the rod is reserved for those who will not respond to verbal lessons. And verbal instruction remains the primary resource for discipline and correction.

This is exactly what Paul is doing regarding the Corinthians. He is using verbal correction first, but if that is not heeded, the rod of correction will follow.

## IN LOVE

Proverbs also identifies another vital element in discipline. It must be administered in Love. In his relationship with Israel, God has set an example for us to follow:

*"My Son, do not despise the Lord's Discipline and do not resent His rebuke, because the Lord*

*disciplines those He loves, as a Father the son he delights in"* (Prov. 3:11-12).

## GREEK WORDS

The Greek word that most closely corresponds with the Hebrew *"yasar"* is *"paideuo."* This Greek word means *"to bring up, or train,"* and in this sense *"to discipline."*

The other times it is used, it is used in the Old Testament sense of corrective guidance as a means of training or education.

## THE CHARACTER AND MANNER OF NEW TESTAMENT DISCIPLINE

The key New Testament Passage on discipline is Hebrews 12:4-13. In the context of the Christian's struggle against sin, Paul quotes Proverbs 3:11-12. God's rebuke, and even His punishments, flow from Love. God accepts the parent's responsibility: He will discipline (train) His sons.

The suggestion in Verse 7 in Hebrews Chapter 12 that God's Discipline is often experienced as hardship harks back to the Old Testament. God continues to use circumstances that cause us pain in a positive way, even as He used a variety of hardships to correct Israel.

The Writer tells us that we should submit to the Father. He *"disciplines us for our good, that we may share in His Holiness"* (Heb. 12:10). The painful experiences of today are intended to produce *"a harvest of Righteousness and Peace for those who have been trained by it"* (Heb. 12:11).

Because of this, we are not to become discouraged in our difficulties, but are to *"strengthen... feeble arms and weak knees"* (Heb. 12:12).

## SAME ELEMENTS AS IN THE OLD TESTAMENT

The Hebrews Chapter 12 picture of discipline emphasizes the same elements that are so prominent in the Old Testament. There is a special family relationship from which discipline flows. There is a distinctive goal. Discipline is guidance toward Holiness. Discipline uses circumstances and experiences as well as verbal instruction to correct. Evidence of God's Love helps us respond appropriately when hard times come.

Both the verbal and historic elements that we see so prominently in the Old Testament are also presented in the New Testament. Scripture is given by God for *"teaching, rebuking, correcting and training* (discipline) *in Righteousness"* (II Tim. 3:16).

NOTES

We need the Guiding Words of the Bible to correct us and to point us toward Holiness.

Titus 2:11-13 points back to Jesus, as Deuteronomy Chapter 8 points back to the God of the Exodus. Paul writes that *"The Grace of God that brings Salvation has appeared to all men. It teaches* (disciplines, guides) *us to deny all ungodliness... to live self-controlled, upright and Godly lives in this present age."*

Knowledge of God's Love in Christ creates the climate of Love in which we can accept discipline experiences. We are brought to the Path of Righteousness by consideration of God's Grace as well as by the pain of His Punishments when necessary.

## GUIDELINES FOR FAMILY DISCIPLINE

Little is said in either Testament of specific child-rearing practices or of parental discipline. But much is implied.

God's relationship with His Children provides a model for our relationship with our own children. In general, the guiding principles are:

1. Be sure children have many experiences that prove parental love and commitment.
2. Be sure children have clear verbal guidance.
3. Be sure to provide corrective experiences when children need help to apply verbal instructions or when they resist them. This speaks of corporal punishment if necessary.
4. Be sure discipline used is in harmony with the long-range goal of developing Godly character, rather than with short-ranged goals or for our own convenience.

It is important to remember that no discipline can be effective out of the context of loving relationships and that caring enough to let each child know that he or she is truly important is essential.

## CHURCH DISCIPLINE

Church discipline is in the same corrective tradition as that characterized in the Old Testament and in Hebrews Chapter 12. But Church discipline is the responsibility of the Christian community.

It too involves words and actions designed to correct a straying brother or sister, even as Paul is doing here in I Corinthians.

The purpose of Church discipline is to restore rather than to condemn. Church discipline is exercised only in matters that the Scriptures clearly identify as sin, and only when the sin is continuously practiced and the individual rebelliously refuses to respond when verbally confronted.

In fact, Paul gives guidance as to what to do in such cases, which he outlines in I Corinthians, Chapter 5. He also tells us what to do when the individual responds favorably, which is outlined in II Corinthians, Chapter 2.

The conclusion of the question, *"Or in Love, and in the spirit of meekness?"*, specifies the other manner in which the Lord can deal with us respecting our spiritual declension and wrong direction.

The *"spirit of meekness"* which pertains to gentleness, is the very opposite of the *"Rod."*

If the Believer will hear the Voice of the Lord, and in whatever manner the Lord chooses to send that Voice, corrections can be made without difficulty. However, the problem oftentimes is, that the wayward Believer does not like the instrument used by the Lord, i.e., the Preacher God sends, etc. As well, the problem is compounded when the sin is spiritual elitism. In the first place, as ridiculous as it sounds, this particular group in the Church in Corinth actually thought they knew more about God and His Work than even the Apostle Paul. So it makes it hard for any Preacher to reach people of this spirit.

However, if the Lord cannot reach them with Love and Meekness, He will always then resort to the *"Rod."* He does such, because He loves these Believers, even as erring as they may be.

## IN WHAT MANNER DOES HE USE THE ROD?

Of course, that prerogative belongs to the Lord. But yet, He can do so in a physical, domestical, financial, or spiritual way.

Even though this certainly would not apply to all, I do believe that some Christians are physically ill and cannot seemingly improve, and for this very reason. The Rod has been applied, and until they repent before the Lord of their wayward direction, the situation will not improve. As stated, this is definitely not the case in all, but I definitely feel it is in the case in some.

NOTES

The same holds true in the financial sense, and in any other way. God Who knows all things, can apply the Rod any way He so desires.

## THE ROLE OF THE GOD-CALLED PREACHER

The only manner in which Paul, or any Preacher for that matter, can be used of the Lord in this fashion, is *"to deliver such an one unto Satan for the destruction of the flesh, that the spirit may be saved in the Day of the Lord Jesus"* (I Cor. 5:5).

Other than that, no Believer, Preacher, Spiritual Leader, or otherwise, can take any steps toward punishment. In the first place, even as James said, no Believer, irrespective as to how close to God he or she may be, is morally qualified to do so (James 4:12).

## WHAT DOES IT MEAN TO DELIVER SUCH A ONE UNTO SATAN?

The purpose of delivering a rebellious individual to Satan is to destroy the flesh. This requires the Church to withdraw all fellowship and spiritual influence from him, in effect, to quit praying for him, so as to permit Satan to afflict his body, thus, perhaps bringing him to repentance.

In the first place, if a Believer is going wrong, he does not really have the help of the Lord, and especially if he is of a rebellious spirit, even as were these people at Corinth. In that state, the Lord cannot really answer prayer, or work on behalf of the person in any capacity. Nevertheless, there is still an aura of protection about that individual because of his Salvation experience.

Then when fellow Believers quit praying for the individual in a positive sense, and begin to pray that the Lord will stop the person, using whatever tactics that need to be used, the Lord will oftentimes then take measures to allow Satan certain latitude, with the purpose in mind of course, to bring the individual to repentance. In this, one can see the tremendous weight and authority carried by True and Faithful Believers.

Believers doing such a thing presently, should be carried out only when every effort to bring the person to their spiritual senses has been expended. This is a serious thing as should be obvious, and should be applied only as a matter of last resort.

In fact, this is exactly what Paul was doing. He was appealing to these people to repent of this party spirit which was threatening the very existence of the Church at Corinth. If so, Judgment would not be necessary, and there is evidence in the Second Chapter of II Corinthians, that Paul's admonition in fact was heeded.

*"Christ has for sin Atonement made,*
*what a wonderful Saviour!*
*"We are redeemed! The price is paid!*
*What a wonderful Saviour!"*

*"I praise Him for the cleansing Blood,*
*what a wonderful Saviour!*
*"That reconciled my soul to God; what a*
*wonderful Saviour!"*

*"He cleansed my heart from all its sin,*
*what a wonderful Saviour!*
*"And now He reigns and rules therein;*
*what a wonderful Saviour!"*

*"He walks beside me all the way, what a*
*wonderful Saviour!*
*"And keeps me faithful day by day; what*
*a wonderful Saviour!"*

*"He gives me overcoming power, what a*
*wonderful Saviour!*
*"And triumph in each trying hour; what*
*a wonderful Saviour!"*

*"To Him I've given all my heart, what a*
*wonderful Saviour!*
*"The world shall never share a part; what*
*a wonderful Saviour!"*

## CHAPTER 5

(1) "IT IS REPORTED COMMONLY THAT THERE IS FORNICATION AMONG YOU, AND SUCH FORNICATION AS IS NOT SO MUCH AS NAMED AMONG THE GENTILES, THAT ONE SHOULD HAVE HIS FATHER'S WIFE."

The phrase, *"It is reported commonly,"* tells us three things:

1. In all the questions which the Believers at Corinth had for Paul to address, they had not mentioned, at least in their Letter, the problem of the party spirit or this problem of immorality. These two things were related to Paul by those *"of the house of Chloe,"* quite possibly those who had brought the Letter to Paul from Corinth (I Cor. 1:11).

2. The word *"commonly"* insinuates that the immorality was more widespread than just the problem addressed.

3. Paul selects the worst case of the lot, that being a situation involving incest.

The phrase, *"That there is fornication among you,"* speaks of all kinds of impurity, perversion, and immorality. As stated, immorality, and of all types, seemingly was widespread in the Church at this time.

### WHAT IS FORNICATION?

The Greek word is *"porneia,"* and as stated, means all kinds of impurity, perversion, and immorality. However, it is somewhat different than adultery.

For instance, it is commonly thought that adultery refers to those who are married, with fornication referring to those who are single. That is incorrect. Fornication or adultery has nothing to do with one's marital or single status. The meaning of fornication is as follows:

1. First of all it means repeated adultery, going from one partner to the next (Mat. 5:32; 19:9; I Cor. 7:2; 10:8; I Thess. 4:3; Rev. 9:21).

All fornicators are adulterers, but all adulterers are not fornicators.

As bad as either sin is, an individual who has an affair with someone other than his or her wife or husband, is not a fornicator, but is definitely an adulterer.

For instance, David was an adulterer, but he was not a fornicator. By contrast, Esau was a fornicator (Heb. 12:16).

2. Incest is fornication (I Cor. 5:1; 10:8). Incest is sexual intercourse between persons so closely related that they are forbidden by law to marry. So, this man living with his Stepmother even while his Father was alive (II Cor. 7:12) constituted incest.

3. Idolatry and adultery in honor of idol gods is fornication (II Chron. 21:11; Isa. 23:17; Ezek. 16:15, 26, 29; Acts 15:20, 29; 21:25; Rev. 2:14-21; 14:8; 17:2-4; 18:3-9; 19:2).

Temple prostitution in honor of idol gods was a common thing in Paul's day and before.

In fact, Corinth was filled with this vice, which in fact, made it one of the most debauched places in the world of that time.

4. Natural harlotry (prostitution) is fornication (Jn. 8:41; I Cor. 6:13-18).

5. Spiritual harlotry is also called fornication (Ezek. 16:15, 26, 29; Rev. 17:2-4; 18:3-9; 19:2).

This speaks of Believers, or those who are supposed to be Believers, forsaking the Lord and going after idols or false Doctrine. The Holy Spirit likens these to spiritual fornicators.

6. Sodomy (male homosexuality) and male prostitution come under the heading of fornication (Rom. 1:24-29; I Cor. 6:9-11; II Cor. 12:21; Gal. 5:19; Eph. 5:3; Col. 3:5; Heb. 12:16; Jude 6-7).

Adultery does not merely pertain to those who are married, but rather to any type of unlawful relationship between men and women, whether single or married. However, the term does not cover the wide scope as does fornication.

The phrase, *"And such fornication as is not so much as named among the Gentiles,"* simply means that it was not common among the Gentiles, even though it definitely was at times committed. The idea is, that even the Gentiles who looked at most immorality with indifference, in fact, frowned severely on this particular sin.

The phrase, *"That one should have his Father's wife,"* refers to his Stepmother. As stated, it seems from II Corinthians 7:12 that the Father was alive for it refers there to the one *"that suffered wrong"* as well as the one who had *"done the wrong."*

Evidently, this man was ignoring what had been said regarding this sin in Leviticus 18:17 and Deuteronomy 27:20. As well, from the complete silence regarding the woman, it may be inferred that she was not a Believer.

In fact, Mosaic Law demanded death for such an act, and even Roman Law prohibited it.

(2) "AND YE ARE PUFFED UP, AND HAVE NOT RATHER MOURNED, THAT HE THAT HATH DONE THIS DEED MIGHT BE TAKEN AWAY FROM AMONG YOU."

The phrase, *"And ye are puffed up,"* tells us that this action was not, on the surface, motivated by animal passion but by false religious philosophy; but this only made this conduct, example, and teaching the more deadly to the spiritual life and the more destructive to the Gospel.

NOTES

This Chapter, therefore, uncovers something of the evil and folly of the natural heart even in a Christian; and also illustrates the depths of Satan in cunningly persuading Believers that grossly immoral conduct can be misconstrued as exalted Christian liberty (Williams).

## A LEADER IN THE CHURCH?

There is some evidence in Paul's statement, that this man was not merely a member of the Corinthian Church, but was rather one of its Leaders. The idea seems to be that the people in the Church seemed to think little about this situation, and if we are to interpret Verse 6 literally, were actually glorying in what was being done. In fact, and as stated, it seems that other types of immorality were taking place as well.

Unless they met in a cave or some such like place, the Churches in Paul's day were normally made up of several groups, each group meeting in a house with its particular Leader. As stated, this man could have been one of those Leaders.

## HOW COULD THE CHURCH COME TO THIS ERRONEOUS CONCLUSION?

Whatever the thinking in their minds, the real reason was that they had left the Word of God as is blatantly obvious, had become puffed up in their spiritual pride thinking they were spiritual giants, so much so they were denigrating Paul, all which made them easy targets for Satan.

A broken and contrite spirit, which speaks of humility, and which is actually a Christlike spirit, closes the door to Satan and keeps it open to the Holy Spirit. This is the reason that over and over again in the Bible, we are warned that brokenness and contrition are the spiritual qualities looked for by the Spirit of God, and in fact, the only qualities which God can bless (Ps. 51:17; Isa. 66:2; Mat. 5:3-5; Lk. 18:14).

Some Expositors claim that Paul using the words *"puffed up"* only pertains to the Church not taking action concerning this matter. While it is certainly true, that they did not take action, the entirety of the situation was of far greater magnitude than that.

As we have previously stated, this matter was not merely a sin of animal passion, as bad as that would have been, but was rather far deeper and of far greater consequence, in that it was motivated by false religious philosophy. In fact, this is why the Holy Spirit took up so much space respecting the first Four Chapters of this Epistle, in dealing with this problem. It was not a matter of merely preferring one Preacher over the other, or even exalting one out of proportion to reality. Again, it was deeper and of greater magnitude than that.

NOTES

## SPIRITUAL ELITISM

Once again, it was the sin of spiritual elitism, which makes one unteachable except by some designated individual. Consequently, they make up their own rules as they go along.

Through the years, I have seen people in my Church do the same thing, as I suppose has every other Pastor, etc. Exactly as they did Paul, they would begin to insinuate that I was not deep enough for their spiritual intelligence. Oftentimes, I would watch them attach themselves to a Preacher who I knew was not living right, or else was conducting himself improperly in other ways.

The Truth is, that these people whomever they may have been, even as those at Corinth, were spiritual babies regarding the Word and its understanding, even though they considered themselves to be spiritual giants.

This type of people become very big in their own eyes, spiritually speaking, and then begin to cast about for clever things which they are deluded into believing are the *"deep things of God."* When they come to this stage, even as at Corinth, and sadly there are many in modern Churches, the Salvation of lost souls is now of little significance. Believers being Baptized with the Holy Spirit is not worth their attention. People being delivered from the powers of darkness do not raise an eyebrow in their thinking. They are looking for something *"deep,"* and these things mentioned, which is what Calvary is all about, are simply not deep enough in their thinking.

## FOOLISHNESS!

Just today (2-27-98) I was told of a Bible Teacher, so-called, who said over Television that the sightings (so-called) of aliens (so-called) were probably real, and in fact, these *"aliens"* were probably fallen Angels, etc.

Now, if in fact that is what the man said, those of which I speak would conclude such to be *"spiritually deep,"* when in reality, it is *"foolishness!"* There is nothing in the Word of God which even remotely hints at such. And if it is not in the Word, then it simply is not real, but merely someone's imagination, outright lies, or even demon spirits impersonating whomever and whatever. There is no Biblical evidence of any fallen Angel conducting himself in that type of fashion.

The Truth is, there are Christians in this *"spiritual elitism"* who have by and large abandoned the True Ways of God, and are constantly casting about for these spiritual tidbits. As well, there are Bible Teachers, so-called, who are ready and willing to supply all of the so-called clever insights. In fact, the land is full of them.

Even as Paul said, despite their claims, these people are by and large babies respecting spiritual maturity, in other words, they do not have any maturity. As well, their spiritual growth has come to a grinding halt, at least as long as they remain in this posture, with regression actually the case.

Such is Satan and such is deception!

The phrase, *"And have not rather mourned,"* presents that which should have been the attitude of the Corinthian Believers respecting what was taking place all around them and especially the situation addressed by Paul.

## SPIRITUAL CONDITION!

The fact is, these people did *"mourn,"* at least in a sense. One could say that they were *"mourning"* in that Paul was too shallow now for their spiritual maturity. Oh yes, they were greatly saddened, and in their thinking how pitiful it was, that Paul simply had not matured in the Lord as they had. I would hope that my irony is at least somewhat as pointed as that of Paul when he said, *"We are fools for Christ's sake, but ye are wise in Christ; we are weak, but ye are strong; ye are honourable, but we are despised"* (I Cor. 4:10).

Once again it is ironical. Paul was crying to God on their behalf, while at the same time they were demeaning him. That is the reason the Spirit of God took so much time in dealing with this particular subject. It was and is of extreme significance.

The phrase, *"That he that hath done this deed might be taken away from among you,"* carries with it several powerful statements:

First of all, the idea is presented in the Text that such an individual should be immediately told to repent and cease such activity, and if not, he must be disfellowshiped. However, not only was there no demand for Repentance, there was seemingly no understanding as to how bad the situation really was. In fact, Verse 2 proclaims the thought that the perpetrator was *"glorying"* in his situation instead of seeing it for what it really was (vs. 6).

In this Chapter (vs. 5), the Holy Spirit through the Apostle informs us, that those who are involved in something of this nature must be given an opportunity to repent. If they in fact, humble themselves before the Lord in True Biblical Repentance, the matter should end there. True Repentance before God always stops Judgment of any nature. However, sin always brings negative consequences, irrespective as to what the sin may be. So, if anyone thinks that Repentance means that someone is getting by, that person is engaging in fantasy. The simple reason being, that all sin, irrespective of how much that Repentance is engaged, always exacts a terrible toll. However, that toll must be confined to the act itself, and must never be the result of fellow Believers. Always remember, that *"with what measure you mete, it shall be measured to you again"* (Mat. 7:1-2).

## SOME MATTERS MAY HAVE TO BE LOOKED AT DIFFERENTLY

If the sin is child molestation, or homosexuality, and even possibly other things one could name, even though Biblical Repentance may be truly enjoined, the individual who has repented, as sincere as it may be, should not desire to be placed in a position to where the same thing could easily happen again. Neither should Church Leaders desire to place one in such a position.

In other words, if a man was teaching a class of boys in the Church, and was found to be molesting one of these boys, even though he may sincerely repent of the action, he should not immediately be placed in this position again, nor should he desire to be. Notwithstanding the crime that has been committed other than the sin, such action should not at all be forthcoming.

However, there definitely can come a time, that is if the individual walks closely to the Lord and such is obvious, that he could be trusted again in whatever capacity. However, special care and wisdom would have to be exercised in such a case.

NOTES

If we truly believe that Jesus Christ delivers, and we certainly do, if in fact such a person is truly delivered, they must be treated as such. As well, such will be obvious.

## IF NO REPENTANCE IS FORTHCOMING . . .

This 5th Chapter makes it very clear, if the individual refuses to repent and line up with the Word of God, then that person, as stated, is to be disfellowshiped.

Once again, we are speaking of scandalous sins, and not all types of wrongs which, in fact, every Church has.

All people must be dealt with patiently and kindly, showing great compassion, for this is the Way of the Lord. But a situation such as Paul addresses here, which is an extreme violation of the Word of God in just about every capacity, and being carried out openly, must be dealt with, or else it will destroy the Church.

## LET ME GIVE AN EXAMPLE

A young man and a young lady who were members of our Church, Family Worship Center, were seeing each other, with both of them of course professing Salvation, etc. To make the story very brief, the young lady became pregnant.

As the Senior Pastor of the Church, I met with one of my Associate Pastors who was more acquainted with the situation than anyone else, and we discussed as to what should be done, in other words how we should handle the situation.

First of all, there was never a thought which entered our minds, that we should make these young people leave the Church, because they might be an embarrassment to the Church, etc. Those things were never even once thought of or spoken. Our every action was to salvage this young man and young lady, getting them back on track with God, putting this thing, as serious as it was, behind them.

My Associate went to them and addressed the problem. They immediately told him that they were going to be married, which was the right course in this situation.

This was done, with a beautiful little baby boy born to them a short time later, and now they have a second child. They are both in the Church serving God, closer to the Lord I think than they have ever been before, and to be frank with you, I personally am very proud of both of them.

Of course it was not right what they did. It was sin, and in a sense despite the Love of God and the Grace of God, there will always be some hurt between both of them because of this sin.

But yet, as the Pastor of this Church, it was my responsibility to love them, to help them, to pray with them, to get them back on track according to the Word of God, which we did, and thankfully to which they both acquiesced, and they were both beautifully and wondrously salvaged. That is True Bible Christianity.

## HOWEVER!

To be kind and loving, even as Christ demands, does not mean that one condones the sin or the failure. It merely means that one knows and understands, that one is not morally qualified to point a finger at others. Knowing that all of us, even the best of us whomever that may be, are in constant need of the Grace of God, and knowing that, we should be very quick to judge ourselves harshly, but others very leniently.

However, if that young man and young lady had refused to do the right thing which was to marry, which in this case was possible, in other words if they had flagrantly ignored the Word of God and charted their own course whatever that may have been, I would have continued to love them and try to help them, but I would have told them to leave the Church, just as Paul here speaks. However, that would be done only as a matter of last resort, and only after we had exhausted every means to try to get them back on track. As stated, it is not the business of the Preacher or anyone else for that matter, to purify the Church, that being solely the Business of the Holy Spirit, and because He Alone is qualified to do so. But when people, purposely set themselves against the Word of God, refuse to repent, and, as stated, chart their own course which is in opposition to the Word, and blatantly so, even as Paul here addresses, there is no alternative but to disfellowship these individuals, which the Apostle here plainly proclaims.

## ARE SOME SINS WORSE THAN OTHERS?

Yes, some sins are worse than others. Jesus said to Pilate, *"Thou couldest have no power at all against Me, except it were given thee from above: therefore he that delivered Me unto thee hath the greater sin"* (Jn. 19:11).

NOTES

The criteria is the amount of *"Light"* which has been given to an individual. Even though Pilate was committing sin, even grievous sin in crucifying Christ, the Religious Leaders of Israel who had delivered Jesus to the Governor, were guilty of far greater sin, simply because they of all people should have known better.

Jesus also said, *"And that servant, which knew his Lord's Will, and prepared not himself, neither did according to His Will, shall be beaten with many stripes."*

He then said, *"But he that knew not, and did commit things worthy of stripes, shall be beaten with few stripes. For unto whomsoever much is given, of him shall be much required"* (Lk. 12:47-48).

So it is very obvious, that some sins are definitely worse than other sins, and have to be dealt with accordingly. However, in no way does that mean we are to be lax concerning things in our lives which one may consider to be small. Wrongdoing is wrongdoing, and should be dealt with. Little things lead to larger things. In fact, Solomon said, *"The little foxes, that spoil the vines"* (Song of Solomon 2:15).

## WHY DID THE HOLY SPIRIT TREAT THIS SIN OF INCEST DIFFERENT THAN THE SIN DEALT WITH IN THE FIRST FOUR CHAPTERS?

It was the sin of pride which Paul dealt with in the first Four Chapters of this Book, and which was so severe that it threatened to destroy the Church. But yet, even though Paul did demand repentance (4:17-21), at no time did he speak of these being disfellowshiped as he did the one guilty of incest, as recorded in this 5th Chapter.

Why?

Some may answer that I Corinthians, Chapter 5 pertained to morals, while I Corinthians, Chapters 1 through 4 did not. However, that is incorrect.

The prideful factor of I Corinthians, Chapters 1 through 4 was moral in nature as was that in I Corinthians, Chapter 5. Actually, the word *"moral"* or *"morals"* simply means *"principles of right and wrong pertaining to behavior."*

Consequently, the behavior of those in Chapters 1 through 4 was morally wrong as was the one in Chapter 5. Actually, this is one of the problems of the Church.

It considers sins such as the incest of I Corinthians, Chapter 5 to be immoral, which it definitely is, but does not think of slander as immoral, or gossip, or a prideful attitude for that matter. However, they are all immoral in the Eyes of God, and should be in the eyes of all others as well.

The reason that the Holy Spirit did not instruct Paul to threaten disfellowship for those of I Corinthians, Chapters 1 through 4, is because in a sense this situation was a matter of Doctrine. Their Doctrine was terribly wrong, and the Holy Spirit through the Apostle called attention to this fact. Actually, had they continued in this vein, they stood in great danger of losing their souls. If error is not corrected, it only gets worse. But yet, to call attention to this situation and demand repentance was all that the Holy Spirit did. He did not demand disfellowship, as He did in I Corinthians, Chapter 5. The sin of Chapter 5 was a direct and flagrant breaking of the Fifth Commandment, *"Honour thy Father and thy Mother,"* of the Seventh Commandment, *"Thou shalt not commit adultery,"* and the Tenth Commandment, *"Thou shalt not covet thy . . . neighbour's wife"* (Ex. Chpt. 20). Of course all sin, and irrespective of its nature, is a breaking of the Ten Commandments in some manner. But yet, some are far more obvious, even as this sin of Chapter 5, and, consequently, must be dealt with accordingly.

## THE TEN COMMANDMENTS

Even though I will not go into a long dialogue on the Ten Commandments, except to say that these Commandments given by God are the undergirding and foundation of all Moral and Civil Law in the world today, and in fact have been since they were given. Regarding the foundation of all Civil Law, the closer to these Commandments they are, the more freedom is guaranteed the people of that particular country, etc. The more they are disregarded, the less freedom and prosperity the people have.

Even though all Ten of the Commandments were given by God, and are still relative to this hour, and all affect Him if broken, still, the first Four pertain directly to Him, while the remaining Six pertain directly to man's dealings with his fellowman.

Inasmuch as the first Four deal primarily with man's relationship with God, they are difficult to police, at least by man. Consequently, man is not wise when he attempts to judge accordingly.

However, the remaining Six which deal, as stated, with man's relationship to his fellowman, can be policed very easily, as should be obvious. In fact, some of these Six require retribution such as *"Thou shalt not kill,"* and *"Thou shalt not steal,"* etc. Irrespective, if the Believer breaks these Commandments, he must repent, thereby ceasing such action, and which the Lord will instantly forgive. However, if he will not discontinue the adultery, or stealing, or lying, etc., he must be disfellowshiped, even as Paul says here.

In fact, many Believers break one or more of the first Four Commandments, which is what Paul is addressing in the first Four Chapters of I Corinthians. Nevertheless, inasmuch as that is a matter of the heart, and between the individual and the Lord on a personal basis, even though the wrongdoing may be pointed out even as it was by Paul, no disfellowship is recommended, and for the obvious reasons. Regarding Doctrine and motives, only God is qualified to judge (James 4:12).

## THE AUTHORITY OF BELIEVERS OVER OTHER BELIEVERS

The Scriptures teach and assume that in a world warped by sin, governing authorities are a necessity.

But a vital question for Christians has to do with the nature of authority within the Body of Christ. In its philosophical and theological sense as freedom of action to control or limit the freedom of action of others, do Christian Leaders really have authority within the Church?

The issue is an important one and deserves much study and debate. But a number of observations should be made to help us think about this issue.

For instance, Jesus delegated authority to His Disciples (Mk. 3:15; 6:7; Lk. 9:1; 10:19), but this was authority over demons and diseases. No Passage suggests freedom to exercise control

NOTES

over other human beings. In fact, the freedom of choice of those to whom these Disciples came is clearly protected (Mk. 6:11; Lk. 10:8-12).

## AUTHORITY?

One incident reported in the Synoptics is especially significant. Matthew Chapter 20, Mark Chapter 10, and Luke Chapter 22 all tell of a heated debate among the Disciples over which of them would be greatest. Jesus took that opportunity to instruct them on Leadership and its character within the Church.

Each Passage reports that Jesus said, *"You know that the rulers of the Gentiles lord it over them, and their high officials exercise authority over them."* In each Passage Jesus bluntly rules out this kind of Leadership Authority for His Disciples and Followers. He said, *"Not so with you!"*

The alternative that Jesus spells out is a *"Servant Leadership."* And a servant is a far cry from a ruler!

These Passages suggest strongly that whatever authority Christian Leaders may have, their freedom of action does not include the right to control the actions and choices of their Brothers and Sisters in the Lord.

## THE APOSTLE PAUL

The Apostle Paul is deeply aware of the fact that as an Apostle he does have authority. He speaks of it in II Corinthians, Chapters 10 and 13. He told the Corinthians that the Lord gave him authority with a specific purpose: *"For building you up, not for tearing you down"* (II Cor. 10:8; 13:10). In II Corinthians, Chapter 13 Paul speaks of his concern not to be *"harsh in the use of* (his) *authority"* (I Cor. 13:10). The context shows that the Christians in Corinth refused to admit that Christ was speaking through this servant Leader.

Paul did not respond by threatening. He did not try to manipulate or to coerce. He simply reminded them, "(Christ) *is not weak in dealing with you, but is powerful among you"* (II Cor. 13:3). By that he meant the following:

Paul had no need to resort to manipulation or to coercion, because Jesus was alive and acting as Head of His Church. Jesus remained powerful among His People and was free as the Head of the Church to exercise His Authority in disciplining ways. Paul relied on Jesus to bring about a response to the Words that He, Jesus, had given to Paul to speak to the Corinthians.

NOTES

## LIMITATION OF AUTHORITY GIVEN TO LEADERS

These Passages, and studies of Paul's style of Leadership, suggest strongly that in the Church God limits the authority given to Leaders.

The Leader's authority is not an authority to control, but an authority to help the Believer to use his or her freedom to respond willingly to Jesus as the Head of the Church.

Using Paul as an example, which is what the Holy Spirit intended, it becomes easy to observe how wrong it is for so-called Church Leaders to attempt to exercise dictatorial control over others, even going so far as to demand that they do things which are unscriptural. As should be obvious, this is not according to the Word of God, and must be rejected hands down, irrespective of the cost.

## THE LOCAL CHURCH

Even though Paul as an Apostle definitely had Spiritual Authority, still, he could not force the Church at Corinth to do what the Holy Spirit through him had stated concerning this matter. He could only point out the correct direction, and it was up to them to follow it to its conclusion.

When one considers that Paul had planted this Church, and that many, if not most, of the Converts there had been brought to Christ under his Ministry, one would think that he had the authority to say and do whatever. However, the Holy Spirit as is here obvious, limits that authority to pointing out direction.

This means that it is terribly wrong for any outside influence to exercise dictatorial control over the Local Church. While they might advise and counsel, even as Paul did here, which is the pattern given by the Holy Spirit we are to follow, that is as far as it should go. When Religious Leaders, so-called, who have been elected by popular ballot, and in no way are Apostles, etc., exercise dictatorial control over the Local Church, they are in fact abrogating the Headship of Christ, which causes the Holy Spirit to cease and desist all operations. Consequently, some Pentecostal Denominations are all but totally bereft of the Working and Moving of the Holy Spirit, and for this very reason. They have instigated a secular type Government in the Church, which the Holy Spirit cannot condone, because it is not Biblical.

IN SUMMARY

The Biblical pattern for dealing with such matters in the Church are clearly outlined in this Fifth Chapter. Sins of such nature by a member or members of the Local Body, are to be addressed in the following fashion:

1. The guilty party is to repent. As well, if one has truly repented, such is not difficult to ascertain.

2. If one truly repents, one is to be instantly restored to full fellowship in the Church (II Cor. 2:6-11; Gal. 6:1; I Jn. 1:9).

3. There is no such thing in Christ as probation. Such is an insult to the Integrity and Atonement of Christ. When God forgives, all is forgiven, and the person must be treated accordingly.

There is no such thing as a partial forgiveness by God, or a probationary forgiveness, or forgiveness which is consummated at a later time. As stated, such is an insult to God.

4. In some cases, as previously stated, proper discretion should be used regarding full restoration to a particular position. To which we have already addressed, if a child molester or something similar should truly repent, due to the nature of the situation, the individual in question should not desire to instantly begin serving once again in the same position. Where safety, protection, and responsibility of helpless victims are at stake, such as children, all precaution should be taken, and should desire to be taken.

However, even in the worst type of cases such as we have just mentioned, the Lord is able to completely deliver, and if such is proven, as it certainly can be, such an individual can be ultimately restored to whatever position they once held.

5. Irrespective of the situation, the guilty party must always be dealt with in Compassion, Love, and Understanding. Spiritual Leaders in the Local Church must always understand, that within themselves, and irrespective of their consecration, they have no moral right to point a finger at anyone. In other words, all of us, even the best among us whomever that may be, have had to go to the Lord time and time again seeking His Mercy, Grace, and Forgiveness.

NOTES

Always remembering this and understanding it accordingly, should cause us to deal with others in the same way the Lord has dealt with us.

Instead of harshness, if the Believer errs in dealing with those who have sinned, he should always err on the side of Mercy and Grace. As stated, that is the manner in which the Lord has always dealt with us, and that is the manner in which we should deal with others.

(3) "FOR I VERILY, AS ABSENT IN BODY, BUT PRESENT IN SPIRIT, HAVE JUDGED ALREADY, AS THOUGH I WERE PRESENT, CONCERNING HIM THAT HATH SO DONE THIS DEED."

The phrase, *"For I verily,"* is meant to convey the significance of the statement about to be rendered. As well, in a sense, it denotes the broken heart of Paul, in other words saying, *"You should have known this, without me having to give any instructions at all."*

The phrase, *"As absent in body, but present in spirit,"* means that even though he is not present personally in Corinth, still, the direction he will now give, is to be taken just as seriously as if he were there personally. In other words, what he is about to say, is the Word of God, and not for the Corinthians only, but for all men and for all time.

However, notice that he did not step in from the outside, as some ecclesiastical potentate, and take action, as many do presently. He did not even command the congregation to act. He did state what was right and what was wrong, but it was up to the congregation to carry out what was stated.

THE LOCAL CHURCH

As we have already addressed, it is never proper for any outside Religious Authorities (outside of the Local Church), to exercise authority over the Local Church, for in doing so, the correct form of Church Government given by the Holy Spirit, and outlined in the Book of Acts and the Epistles, is always abrogated. The Leadership of the Local Church is to exercise the highest Spiritual Authority even as outlined here, and for the obvious reasons.

First of all, the Leadership of the Local Church knows the present situation better than any other, and is more qualified to deal with whatever problems there may be. If one is to notice, Jesus when addressing the Churches of

Asia, did not address a single Letter to the Church at Jerusalem, or Antioch, but rather to each individual Church (Rev. Chpts. 2-3). More particularly, He addressed each Letter to each particular Pastor, even referring to them as *"And unto the Angel of the Church of. . . ."*

As well, all directions given for the Church by the Holy Spirit, were always given through an Apostle, in this case, the Apostle Paul, with one exception. There was one Letter which came from Jerusalem, which was to be addressed to all the Churches, and for the obvious reason (Acts 15:23).

As we have already stated, outside Leadership, even as Paul, can advise and counsel, but that is as far as it should go. To do otherwise, sets aside the Government or Rule of God which places Jesus as the Head of the Church.

## WHAT DO WE MEAN BY THE WORD *"HEAD"*?

To begin with, the word *"head"* may be a sensitive word for some women, who have often heard the phrase *"head of the house"* used in a rigid, Hierarchical way. Too often a claim of headship has been used to justify domineering attitudes by so-called Religious Leaders, or selfish behavior by men regarding their wives or to deny women their full partnership in Church or home.

So it is important that we look at the concept of *"head"* in both the Old Testament and the New Testament. Only in this manner can we affirm what Scripture teaches and avoid the tragedies that are associated with selfish misinterpretation.

## *"HEAD"* IN THE OLD TESTAMENT

The word that means *"head"* in the Hebrew is *"ro's."* Other words are at times translated *"head,"* but these are specific terms, meaning *"skull"* or *"scalp."*

Although *"ro's"* also denotes the head of a person (Gen. 3:15), the idea is extended in many ways, making *"headship"* a complex idea indeed.

For instance, *"ro's"* can mean the first in a series. Or it can mean the beginning, the source. It is often used to indicate the top of a mountain or building (Ex. 17:9). It is as well used to indicate the chief of a family or clan (Num. 1:4). This may be the current living head or it may refer to the ancestor of the group.

NOTES

*"Ro's"* can suggest priority, as in God's Promise to make Israel *"the head and not the tail"* among the Nations (Deut. 28:13; Isa. 9:14). In the Old Testament, the word is also used to indicate bureaucratic rank or position. This is found in the organization of ancient Israel for judicial, military, and religious matters (Ex. 18:25; II Ki. 25:18).

Thus our image of a Hierarchical Order is justified, as far as the Old Testament is concerned.

## HEADSHIP IN THE NEW TESTAMENT

The Greek word for head is *"kephale."* It is used much like the Hebrew word *"ro's,"* which refers to the head of a person, the beginning of a month, the source or mouth of a river, etc. The Greeks viewed the head as the superior member of the body, the seat of reason and authority.

*"Kephale"* appears over 75 times in the New Testament, usually to designate the literal head of a person or animal. In certain Passages, we need to know the background of certain New Testament sayings before we can understand them.

For example, *"Do not swear by your head"* (Mat. 5:36) is a reference to a Rabbinical Judgment that one who makes an oath *"by his head"* (by his very life) cannot be released from the oath under any circumstances.

Other sayings, such as Jesus' assurance of God's Care as expressed in the statement, *"The very hairs of your head are all numbered"* (Lk. 12:7), are easily understood.

There are, however, three theologically significant uses of *"head"* to which we need to pay careful attention. They help us gain insight into issues of great concern for Christians today.

## CHRIST, THE HEAD OF THE CHURCH

The New Testament pictures the Church as a living organism, a Body of which Jesus is the Head (Eph. 1:22; 4:15; 5:23; Col. 1:18; 2:10, 19).

A review of these Passages suggests that Christ's Headship emphasizes His role as Sustainer, Protector, Organizing Principal, and Source of the Church's life. The Passages emphasize Jesus' exalted position so that we may have complete confidence in Him. We respond to Him because He is Lord and the only One with wisdom and motive to direct us into God's Perfect Will.

## AN ORGANISM, NOT AN INSTITUTION

On the other hand, the New Testament pictures the Church not as an institution but as an organism (something which is alive — a complex structure of interdependent and subordinate elements whose relations and properties are largely determined by their function in the whole).

In the place of institutional principles of organization, the New Testament advances organic principles of organization for the Church (Rom. Chpt. 12; I Cor. Chpt. 12). In fact, Jesus stressed the importance of rejecting all thought of rank in relating to fellow Believers (Mat. 20:25-28; 23:8-12; Rom. 12:3-8), which means that even though all Preachers of the Gospel should be respected as should be obvious, however, all man-instituted Religious Offices, are to be looked at as administrative only and never in the position of Spiritual Leadership.

In thinking about Leadership in the Church it is important to recognize the fact that Jesus is the Sole Head of the Church, the only Lord. Whatever Leaders are within the Body of Christ, they are not superior persons of higher rank whose office gives them a right to direct and control other Believers.

## A PERSONAL EXAMPLE

Relative to one particular Pentecostal Denomination, I was made aware after speaking to one of its Administrative Leaders, who had been elected to his particular man-instituted office by popular ballot, that he concluded his office to be a Spiritual Office thereby having Spiritual Authority. In fact, all the others in his particular Denomination, as far as I know, felt the same way. In fact, that would go for most Pentecostal Denominations.

In believing that these positions are Spiritual and Scriptural, which they are not, these men also believed that whatever they said must be obeyed without question. To which we have already related in previous Volumes, they actually believed that Preachers were supposed to obey them, even if what they demanded was unscriptural. The idea was and I suppose still is, that if it is not Scriptural the responsibility will be on the head of this particular Leader and not the Preacher who carries out such an unscriptural directive. Of course, such is so off base Scripturally, that it is not worthy of serious comment. But yet that is what these men believed, and that is why the Holy Spirit has pretty much abandoned this particular organization, as least as far as its so-called Leadership is concerned.

NOTES

## SPIRITUAL OFFICES

There are only five Scriptural Offices of Leadership which carry any authority. Those Offices are, *"Apostles, Prophets, Evangelists, Pastors and Teachers"*(Eph. 4:11). Of course, the greater authority would rest with the Apostle.

However, even with this God-given Authority, such only applies to authority over demon spirits, etc., and never over other people.

(The words *"Pastor, Shepherd, Overseer, Presbyter, Bishop, or Elder,"* are all used interchangeably, and always refer to the Pastor of a Local Church. This means that the title *"Bishop"* as it is presently used, or Presbyter, or Overseer, referring to the head over many Churches, or a given area, is all man-devised and not Scriptural. In other words, there is no such thing in the New Testament as a man being called a *"Bishop"* and being in charge of many Churches, etc. Such simply does not exist. As stated, it always refers to the Pastor of a Local Assembly.)

This means that offices or positions such as Superintendent, District Superintendent, Overseer, State Overseer, General Overseer, Bishop, President, Moderator, etc., are in fact not Scriptural Offices, and, consequently, carry no Spiritual Authority, at least according to that which is God-given. While men may unscripturally take such to themselves, thereby demanding obedience, their authority is strictly man-devised, and is no way authority which is recognized by the Holy Spirit.

And yet, these offices or positions are not unscriptural if they are addressed correctly. In other words, if they are administrative and organizational only, and looked at in that manner, there is nothing Scripturally wrong with such positions. It is only when men attach a phony authority to these offices, which brings about the wrong, and a serious wrong at that. Then, the Headship of Christ, which we are here studying, is abrogated. Unfortunately, many if not most of those occupying these particular man-devised positions, have a wrong conception of those particular positions.

### FURTHER SCRIPTURAL ADMONITIONS REGARDING *"HEAD"* OR *"HEADSHIP"*

In I Corinthians, Chapter 11, Paul explores what is proper in worship respecting the covering of the *"head."*

He argues that the women in the Church at Corinth should have a proper covering of hair on their head, in other words they should not cut their hair in the fashion of a man (I Cor. 11:6).

(The Greek word for *"covered"* is *"katakalupto,"* and means *"veiled."* From this, some have concluded that women who are Christians should be veiled like a Moslem or wear a hat, etc. However, the Greek word here given simply refers to hair, because the two words *"shorn"* or *"shaven"* are used.)

In this Passage, Paul protects the freedom of women, but he clearly does not approve of their symbolizing their liberation by praying and prophesying with their heads shaved or with hair cut short like a man. It is in effect a denial of their femininity.

He refers to Creation and shows that there is a Creation Order that includes both men and women (I Cor. 11:3, 7-10). Men and women are interdependent in God's Design for the Universe (I Cor. 11:11-12). It is the Glory of each being within Creation to proudly take the place God has assigned.

### MEN AND WOMEN

Paul writes that *"The Head of every man is Christ, and the head of the woman is man; and the Head of Christ is God"* (I Cor. 11:3). This defines the flow of the Creation Order:

Christ flowed from God the Father, man came into being by Christ's activity as Creator, and woman was taken from the side of man. In this verse, then, the Order of Creation is established. There is no suggestion here of inferiority, for Jesus is and always was the complete Equal of the Father.

Thus, Paul's appeal is not that women take a subordinate place in the Church. His appeal is that they recognize the fact of an order in Creation that is unchanged by the wonderful Message that in Christ all are equal (Gal. 3:26-28).

What is a woman to do? Simply this:

She must live within the culture as a woman rather than deny her womanhood by conducting herself as a man.

NOTES

A woman in the Corinthian Church, and all Churches for that matter, was to pray and prophesy with a proper complement of hair on her head, because of the Order of Creation. To the contrary, men were not to have long hair. This signified that Christ was his Covering instead, whereas the man is the covering for the woman (I Cor. 11:3).

Neither need deny his or her identity within the Creation Order to affirm significance in the Body of Christ. A man can be proud of his place as a man. And a woman can be equally proud of her place as a woman.

However, the modern feminism movement has attempted to abrogate this position in Creation. But in doing so it has only succeeded in destroying the identity of womanhood.

### THE HEADSHIP AND MARRIAGE

In Ephesians, Chapter 5 Paul continues his instruction on how to be *"imitators of God"* and live a life of Love (Eph. 5:1). There is to be harmony and mutual submission in the Church (Eph. 5:15-21). Then Paul shows how to maintain harmony within marriage (Eph. 5:22-33). Each partner in a marriage is to seek to imitate Jesus. The wife takes the lead in imitating the virtue of submission (I Pet. 2:21; 3:6), responding to the husband as the Church does to Jesus (Eph. 5:22-23).

The husband has the challenging task of imitating Christ in His Headship.

It is very critical here not to read into this Passage Hierarchical notions. In other words, the wife is to submit to the husband only as he follows the Lord, and not in whims of dictatorial fancy, etc.

Instead, it would appear that *"head"* is used in its well-established sense of source and nourisher of life. Rather than demand from the Church, Christ *"gave Himself up for her* (the Church)*"* (Eph. 5:25).

His Purpose is not to rob the Church of her identity but to help her achieve her full potential: *"To make her holy, cleansing her by the washing with water through the Word, and to present her to Himself as a radiant Church, without stain or wrinkle or any other blemish, but holy and blameless"* (Eph. 5:26-27).

The husband imitates Christ by loving his wife — *"feeds and cares for her"* (again in the sense of head as source and nourisher) — *"just as Christ does the Church"* (Eph. 5:29).

As should be understood, this is a far cry from the husband demanding foolish things in a dictatorial spirit, which is not at all characterized in this given by the Holy Spirit through the Apostle.

TO JUDGE THE FRUIT

The phrase, *"Have judged already, as though I were present, concerning him that hath so done this deed,"* does not as some think, contradict Jesus' instructions not to judge (Mat. 7:1-5).

Paul is here judging an action, as all Believers are called upon to do, i.e., *"Fruit"* (Mat. 7:15-20). As stated, it is the responsibility to evaluate or to judge the obvious external Fruit of individuals, even as Paul is here doing. While it is not our place to judge motives, we can, and we should, judge external Fruit. In the Corinthian Assembly, this man's evil Fruit was so blatantly obvious that something had to be done immediately (Rossier).

This Chapter, therefore, uncovers something of the evil and folly of the natural heart even in a Christian; and also illustrates the depths of Satan in cunningly persuading Christians that grossly immoral conduct can somehow be claimed as a Christian liberty.

The Apostle sternly reproves this man, and as we will see, commands that he should be handed over to Satan for the destruction of his flesh (Williams).

(4) "IN THE NAME OF OUR LORD JESUS CHRIST, WHEN YE ARE GATHERED TOGETHER, AND MY SPIRIT, WITH THE POWER OF OUR LORD JESUS CHRIST,"

The phrase, *"In the Name of our Lord Jesus Christ,"* refers to Christ here as the Head of the Church, and not some outside ecclesiastical body. This means that what is to be done, is by His Divine Authority.

There is no hint here of any Monarchical Episcopacy, or any other type of Ecclesiastical Hierarchy, being the authority for this step to be taken.

As we have stated, and will continue to state, it is never right for any outside Religious Authority to abrogate the authority of the Local Church, that being the highest Scriptural Authority given in the Word of God.

The phrase, *"When ye are gathered together,"* presents the authority of the Local Church.

The Church is to come together in order to disfellowship this person, but it is to be done only when all efforts and appeals for repentance have been spurned. As we have stated, if repentance is enjoined, no action of this sort is to be taken, nor does it need to be taken, and for the obvious reasons. When sin is washed away by the Blood of Jesus, all penalty against the guilty party is removed (I Jn. 1:9).

NOTES

MATTHEW CHAPTER 18

This procedure is also in conjunction with Jesus' Instructions concerning discipline (Mat. 18:15-20). The Lord specified three distinct layers with respect to this matter:

1. If a person sins against another individual, the issue should be handled between those two.

2. If the one sinning will not accept that step, then the offended one should take two or three others to help rectify matters.

3. If that does not work, there is no choice but to take the issue before the entire congregation; however, this refers only to the Leadership of the Church, and not the entirety of the Church Body.

If it is then ascertained, that the person is truly in the wrong, and refuses to repent, the Assembly has no alternative but to consider the individual as unsaved.

Again, notice that our Lord did not give any higher level than the Local Assembly. He even added in Matthew 18:18 that whatever we bind on Earth *"shall be bound in Heaven,"* and whatever we loose on Earth *"shall have been loosed in Heaven."*

We must remember, that this statement relates primarily to the context of discipline, and not in other areas as commonly taught. However, it definitely can apply to anything in the spirit world, at least under certain guidelines.

The key idea in the entire Epistle to the Corinthians is that when Jesus is allowed to govern His Church, unity will exist (Rossier).

APOSTLES

The phrase, *"And my spirit,"* refers to Paul being there in spirit, even though he could not be there in the flesh. This tells us several things:

1. Spiritual Authority in the Church is invested in *"Apostles, Prophets, Evangelists, Pastors and Teachers."* However, this Authority as stated, is not over people but rather evil spirits, etc.

2. Even though authority over the Church is not given to Apostles, direction definitely is given. Actually, this is mainly the thrust of the statement as given by the Holy Spirit through the Apostle. However, it is through the Apostle only as it addresses the New Testament Church, which does *not* include authority over *"Prophets, Evangelists, Pastors and Teachers."*

In other words, the leading and guidance of the Church is always in the Hands of Christ, Who directs through the Ministry and Office of the Holy Spirit, Who uses Apostles as instruments.

(Direction was vested in Prophets in the Old Testament Economy.)

If one will carefully analyze the Book of Acts and the Epistles, one will quickly come to the conclusion, that it is always through Apostles that direction for the Church is given. In fact, such has always held true from then until now.

This means that direction for the Church, is not vested by the Holy Spirit in so-called Church Leaders, who are elected by popular ballot, etc. However, this is the area of the great struggle in the Church. Religious man does all within his power to overthrow the Government of God, thereby establishing his own government. Consequently, Apostles (truly God-called as such, though not so named), are generally ignored, or else strongly opposed. This was the downfall ultimately of the Early Church, has remained the crisis center ever since, and continues unto this present hour.

THE MANNER

The manner in which this is done (direction as given by the Holy Spirit through Apostles), is never by the meeting of Committees, Boards, Denominational Heads, etc., but rather by the Preaching of the Word, and the Operation of the Holy Spirit in certain directions.

As an example, when the Holy Spirit began to fall at the turn of the century, fulfilling Joel's Prophecy of the Latter Rain, it did not come through any Denominational Hierarchy, or any Denominational Heads of any nature, but rather through Apostles, even though they may not have been referred to as such. In other words, the Lord began to Baptize hungry hearts with the Holy Spirit, with the evidence of speaking with other Tongues, and then Apostles, newly filled themselves, begin to proclaim the Message, and to do so with strength and authority.

NOTES

There were no Board Meetings or Committee Meetings, with one exception — and that was to deny the Moving and Operation of the Holy Spirit in many Church circles.

When the great Healing Move took place in the 1950's and 60's, it was the same thing. God began to move upon Apostles who heralded this great Message. Once again, it did not come from Denominational Leaders, who for the most part, sadly and regrettably, opposed this which the Lord was doing.

In the 1980's, the Lord used this Preacher in the same capacity regarding World Evangelism. If I did not say so I would be dishonest. The same could be said for Church Direction respecting Doctrine. Of course, this did not and does not set well with many Religious Leaders who in fact, have embraced Humanistic Psychology (Psychotherapy), the Prosperity Message, the Political Message, Unscriptural Unity, etc.

3. Disfellowshiping a fellow Christian, is of such magnitude that the Holy Spirit will not allow it to be done without the gathering of the entirety of the Church (the Leadership of the Local Church). This means that even the word of an Apostle is not sufficient in these particular matters, without the agreement of the Local Body. Consequently, one can easily see the checks and balances provided by the Holy Spirit in such cases.

THE LORD JESUS CHRIST

The phrase, *"With the Power of our Lord Jesus Christ,"* pertains to the wherewithal that is needed respecting the authority ensconced in the *"Name of our Lord Jesus Christ."* The authority is in the Name, and the Power is in the Person of Christ. This recognizes Him totally as the Head of the Church.

The Lord in effect is saying, *"Inasmuch as this man will not repent, your responsibility to disfellowship him will be upheld and backed up by My Power."*

Again, this total Passage indicates that the Local Congregation possesses the competence and the power to execute correct measures respecting excommunication if such is demanded. This is *not* the prerogative of some external body! (Rossier).

As a matter of clarification, this does not mean that an Apostle has to preside over, or give directions to every Local Church Body. In fact, this direction has already been given by the Apostle Paul nearly 2,000 years ago, and stands unto this hour, because it is the Word of God. However, even though this direction as given by the Apostle need never be changed and, therefore, needs no further word, the Lord is still calling men to be Apostles, and these men will continue to give direction to the Church in various ways, even as the Lord leads, but regrettably, will be most of the time rejected.

(5) "TO DELIVER SUCH AN ONE UNTO SATAN FOR THE DESTRUCTION OF THE FLESH, THAT THE SPIRIT MAY BE SAVED IN THE DAY OF THE LORD JESUS."

The phrase, *"To deliver such an one unto Satan for the destruction of the flesh,"* pertains to the following:

1. This does not refer merely to excommunication from the Church. There is no proof in Church History that such a formula existed for ejection. Besides, how could excommunication have taught Hymenaeus and Alexander, two opposers of Paul, not to blaspheme (I Tim. 1:20)?

2. It means to release the power of Satan to punish for the purpose of discipline. Of course, Satan means to destroy, but the Purpose of the Lord, and which should be of the congregation as well, is to Save. Oftentimes, affliction will drive a man to his knees, which is what this is designed to do.

3. God's aim in discipline is not only to preserve the purity of the Church, but to save the person who sins. Sometimes Believers forget this latter purpose.

4. Even though the Church can do such a thing as here suggested, still, it is God Who ultimately Alone can turn a person over to Satan. This is another check and balance of the Holy Spirit.

While this situation at Corinth was definitely right respecting turning this man over to Satan, as would be obvious, some situations are not right, even with the Church at fault. So, God only sanctions and upholds that which is right in *His* Sight, not the sight of others.

The phrase, *"That the spirit may be Saved in the day of the Lord Jesus,"* refers to the purpose of such an act, which of course is a very serious thing.

As stated, the purpose of the Lord is to bring the individual to repentance. Consequently, the Church in doing such a thing, must have the same end result in mind, that is if it is to be sanctioned by the Lord.

NOTES

When religious men deviate at all from God's prescribed direction as here portrayed, one can always be certain that personal vendettas, vengeance, or scores to settle are in the offing. The Lord can never sanction such actions, as should be overly obvious. In the first place, such is evil; and, in the second place, to do such in the Name of the Lord (under Church rules and authority), only exacerbates the sin of those who engage in such. Most of the time, such sin is in fact worse, than that which is being addressed.

## THE PRESENT SITUATION

I do not personally know of any modern situation where the Biblical condition of repentance is accepted. In fact, repentance presently is given little acknowledgement, if any at all.

Instead, these situations are too often used to wreak vengance on someone who is disliked, etc.

Regarding Preachers, all types of stipulations are added such as not preaching for a year, or two years, or some such time. As well, it is demanded at times that Preachers move away from their particular City to some other location. Almost always, Psychologists are brought in, with psychological counseling demanded, which is totally unscriptural.

The hypocrisy of such action literally defies description. Once again, as the Holy Spirit through James said, *"There is One Lawgiver* (God), *Who is able to save and to destroy: Who art thou that judgest another?"* (James 4:12).

In other words, *"Who do you think you are, thinking you have the right to judge someone else, thereby pronouncing punishment, when you are in serious spiritual condition yourself, having to depend as well on the Mercy and Grace of God?"*

Anytime men leave the Word of God, devising their own rules and regulations, they always do so with ulterior motives in mind. Such is always the end of man's government in the Church which replaces the Government of God.

(6) "YOUR GLORYING IS NOT GOOD. KNOW YE NOT THAT A LITTLE LEAVEN LEAVENETH THE WHOLE LUMP?"

The phrase, *"Your glorying is not good,"* can be taken in two ways:

1. The boasting over gifts, privileges, or particular Preachers, etc.

2. The *"glorying"* of some of the Corinthians in what they considered to be liberty respecting this man living with his Father's wife. (*"Glorying"* in the Greek means *"boasting."*)

Due to the last phrase of this verse, and in fact, the entirety of this Fifth Chapter, it is without doubt the second situation which Paul addresses here.

In fact, the Greek word used here, does not mean merely the act of boasting, but the thing of which we boast, which undoubtedly was what this man was doing. Instead of responsible Leaders in the Church strongly censuring this vile act, they were instead *"glorying"* over this man's freedom to do such a thing, and still at the same time remain in Christ. Evidently the *"glorying"* was led by the guilty party himself. In other words, he was his own cheerleader.

When Paul uses the words *"not good,"* in this particular sentence, he uses a Greek word *"kalon,"* which is almost untranslatable. It implies all moral beauty, and resembles the English word *"fair"* or *"noble."*

As well, in the two words *"not good,"* Paul uses the Greek figure called *"litotes,"* which means that he has intentionally expressed himself weakly, in order that it may be corrected in a stronger way by the involuntary indignation of the Reader.

In other words, the way it is expressed in the Greek, the Reader is meant to say, *"What do you mean 'not good,' in fact, it is awful!"*

It is amazing the manner in which Paul uses irony and particular Greek idioms to emphasize his point. Unfortunately, such does not always come out in the translation, as is the problem with all translations.

The question, *"Know ye not that a little leaven leaveneth the whole lump?"*, does not here represent the sinning person as is commonly believed, but the presence and approval of the sin.

Leaven is figurative of something minuscule in quantity, but extremely pervasive in its penetrating force (Mat. 13:33). In this particular Passage in I Corinthians, leaven stands more for the arrogant boasting than even for the sin committed by this particular member.

The adage holds true in our own particular lives on a personal basis. Anything which is wrong must be eradicated, or else it will ultimately grow until it incorporates the whole.

NOTES

## LEAVEN

The earliest Mosaic Legislation (Ex. 23:18; 34:25) prohibited the use of leaven during the *"Passover"* and the *"Feast of Unleavened Bread"* (Ex. 23:15; Mat. 26:17).

This was because both of these Feasts represented Christ Who was perfect; consequently, leaven which represents fermentation and corruption could not be used.

Two exceptions to this rule should, however, be noted (Lev. 7:13; Amos 4:5). *"Leavened Bread"* was an accompaniment of the Thank-Offering, which pertained to the Peace-Offering and leavened loaves were also used in the Wave-Offering, which was a part of the Feast of Pentecost.

However, leaven was demanded in these two particular examples for the simple reason that both represented the worshiper, who of course is always tainted by sin, and totally dependent on the Grace of God.

## THE WORD LEAVEN AS USED BY JESUS

The figurative uses of leaven in the New Testament to a large extent reflect the former view of the Old Testament as *"corrupt and corrupting."* Jesus utters warnings against the leaven of the Pharisees, Sadducees, and Herodians (Mat. 16:6; Mk. 8:15):

The Pharisees' hypocrisy and preoccupation with outward show (Mat. 23:14, 16; Lk. 12:1);

The Sadducees' skepticism and culpable ignorance (Mat. 22:23, 29);

The Herodians' malice and political guile (Mat. 22:16-21; Mk. 3:6).

## AS PAUL USES THE WORD

The two Pauline Passages in which the word occurs support this view (I Cor. 5:6; Gal. 5:9), with the former going on to contrast *"the leaven of malice and evil"* with *"the unleavened bread of sincerity and truth,"* remembering the new significance of the Old Feast: that *"Christ, our Paschal Lamb, has been sacrificed."*

(7) "PURGE OUT THEREFORE THE OLD LEAVEN, THAT YE MAY BE A NEW LUMP, AS YE ARE UNLEAVENED. FOR EVEN CHRIST OUR PASSOVER IS SACRIFICED FOR US:"

The phrase, *"Purge out therefore the old leaven,"* is spoken in Old Covenant terminology, but with the same meaning carried over in the hearts and lives of New Testament Believers.

Paul is speaking of the Jewish Passover which in Christ was totally fulfilled, but yet its Type presents a tremendous lesson for us presently, even as Paul is here admonishing.

The *"Passover,"* which commemorated the deliverance of Jews from Egyptian captivity (Ex. 12:29-51), was the first of seven Feasts of the Jews' religious year. It was held on the 14th day of the first month, Abib. Immediately following came the seven-day Feast of Unleavened Bread during which the Israelites had to remove all leaven from their dwellings and eat only unleavened bread as a reminder of God's Deliverance from the sins and bondage of Egypt. On the eve of the Feast each household kneaded a fresh lump of dough with pure water and prepared the unleavened cakes that they ingested during the seven days (Rossier).

Even though the Passover commemorated, as stated, deliverance from Egypt, it had a more perfect application in that it represented Christ Who would give His Life on Calvary's Cross for the Redemption of all humanity.

THE PERFECTION OF CHRIST

The fact that there was to be no leaven, spoke of the absolutely spotless, pure, unsullied Life and physical Body of the Lord Jesus Christ. It was necessary that He walk perfect and be perfect as the Last Adam, despite Satan's constant attacks, in order that His perfection be given to us, which is done through Faith in Him (Jn. 3:16). As well, He had to be perfect (no corrupting sin or influence) in order to provide a Sacrifice which God would accept, which He did!

Consequently, on the day preceding the Passover, which the Jews kept for nearly 1600 years (or were supposed to keep), the most essential requisite of the Jewish regulations, with which their whole training had made them so familiar, was the absolute putting away, and even destruction of every trace of leaven.

The putting away or the *"purging"* as Paul says, has nothing to do with leaven in the modern sense, but actually speaks of the Sanctification process in the heart and life of the Believer. In other words, the Believer is to purge himself of all sin, faults, spiritual weights, or anything that is displeasing to the Lord.

NOTES

*"Purge"* in the Greek is *"ekkathairo,"* and means *"to cleanse thoroughly and do it now. It speaks of urgency of the matter and the need for decisiveness."*

The word *"old"* speaks of the sinful activity of the former life before Christ came into our heart. All Believers are to rid themselves of any residue (even scraps) of their former lifestyle that gloried ungodliness.

If it is to be noticed, the manner of the sentence structure is that the Believer himself is to rid himself of the old influences. Of course, the Lord helps the Believer, but the initiative lies with the Believer.

The phrase, *"That ye may be a new lump, as ye are unleavened,"* presents a startling and wonderful Truth.

The idea is, that the Believer conduct himself according to who and what he actually is in Christ Jesus, *"a new creature"* (II Cor. 5:17).

Ideally, Christians can only be addressed as *"unleavened,"* i.e., as *"purged from their old sins"* (II Pet. 1:9); and it is the method of Scripture (indeed, it is the only possible method) to address Christians as being Christians indeed and, therefore, in their ideal rather than their actual character (Farrar). Once again it speaks of Sanctification, and the following will hopefully portray it more clearly:

1. The moment the believing sinner comes to Christ he is instantly, *"Washed, Sanctified, and Justified"* (I Cor. 6:11). That is his *"Standing"* in Christ, is imputed upon Faith, and cannot change. In other words, from henceforth, and irrespective of the Believer's actions whether good or bad, the Lord looks at the Believer as Sanctified, which means *"set apart for the Lord exclusively, made holy."*

2. The actual *"State"* of the Believer's Sanctification, however, is not up to his *"Standing"*; therefore, it is the business of the Holy Spirit to deal with the *"State,"* bringing it up to the *"Standing,"* which in fact, begins immediately at Conversion, and continues through the entirety of the life of the Believer, as long as that may be. This is what Paul meant when he said, *"And the Very God of Peace sanctify you wholly"* (I Thess. 5:23).

In effect one can say, that we are Sanctified, are being Sanctified, and shall be Sanctified.

If one is to notice, Paul called these Believers at Corinth *"unleavened,"* which means without taint of sin or spiritual corruption, even though they were anything but that. In fact, as is glaringly obvious, he is now addressing hideous sins present in the Corinthian Church. And yet he could address them as unleavened because in fact, in Christ, that is what they actually were. In other words, whenever the Lord looked at these Corinthians, even as He looks at us, He did not see them according to their present *"State,"* but rather according to their *"Standing"* in His Son Jesus Christ. In fact, He sees Jesus, for that is the only way He can look at us. He treats us according to our legal Standing in Christ, even while the Holy Spirit, as stated, is attempting to bring our *"State"* up to our *"Standing."*

### WAS THIS MAN GUILTY OF THE SIN OF INCEST AT THIS TIME SAVED?

This is the question that must be asked regarding this scenario.

Only God truly knows the answer to this question. It is quite possible that the man had never truly been Saved, only making a profession which actually did not come from his heart. In fact, Churches are filled with people of this nature. They claim Salvation, and say all the right words, but they have actually never truly made Jesus their Lord and Saviour. So, even though they are religious, they are not Saved.

However, the weight of the Text lends credence to the thought that the man indeed had truly been Saved, and, consequently, was Saved, even in the midst of this terrible sin.

The spirit of the Text is that every effort should be made to get this man to repent, which is the language of a Believer, but if repentance was rejected on the grounds that he thought he was not doing anything wrong, as seemed to have been the case, he was then to be turned over to *"Satan for the destruction of the flesh, that the spirit may be Saved in the day of the Lord Jesus."* Once again, this is terminology that applies to a Believer and not an unbeliever.

However, the very idea of the Text is, that if repentance was not forthcoming, the man's soul would ultimately be lost. No Believer can habitually practice sin and continue in Christ. Even as Paul is here discussing, one or the other must eventually cease.

NOTES

That does not mean that the Believer becomes perfect, for none are. But it does mean that the Believer must ultimately have victory over the Sin Nature in his or her life, even though at times there may be inadvertent failure. In fact, it is not possible for a Believer to continue in the state this man was in, or any similar situation, for the very reason that the Believer has a new nature in Christ Jesus. In other words, the Divine Nature, i.e., the Holy Spirit, now lives in the heart and life of the Believer, which cries out against any wrongdoing. Admittedly, the Believer can stifle the checks of the Holy Spirit within him, to where the voice becomes less and less, which is what we are discussing here.

Sin is a powerful factor, which has a tendency to deaden Divine impulses in the heart and life of the Believer, and if left unchecked will deceive the individual into thinking that both can be enjoyed — sin and Salvation. However, such is an oxymoron, which means that it is impossible.

### THE BELIEVER AND SALVATION

The Believer does not drift in and out of Salvation as some people think. In other words, if the Believer loses his temper, conducting himself in a wrong manner which is sin, he does not at that time lose his Salvation, and then have to get Saved all over again a short time later. In fact, that would hold true for any type of sin, whatever it may be. One's Salvation is according to one's Faith in Christ, and not according to one's conduct. That is the reason there could be no Salvation in the Law, because it demanded a perfect conduct, which was not possible for any person (Rom. 5:19-21).

In fact, God does demand perfect conduct, which demands were met in Christ Jesus. Consequently, the Believer's Faith in Christ, gives the Believer, even as we are here studying, the perfect conduct of Christ. Actually, that is what Salvation is all about — Faith in Christ as our Substitute, with Whom we identify.

### THE BELIEVER AND SINS

It seems clear, both through experience and through Scripture, that Christians at times, regrettably, do sin. When the Christian does sin, his recourse is forgiveness through Christ. As stated, the Believer does not wander in and out of Salvation. Such is not possible. Our Lord sits continually at the Right Hand of the Father, making Intercession for us (Rom. 8:34; I Jn. 1:8-9; 2:1-2).

There is a great difference, however, between inadvertent sin and consciously choosing a sinful lifestyle. Actually, it is un-Biblical, un-Christlike, and unnatural for a Born-Again Believer to sin habitually. Whenever the sinner comes to Christ, as we have stated, the Divine Nature is imparted to him, which makes him *"a new creature"* in Christ Jesus (II Cor. 5:17). Whereas sin was a natural thing before Conversion, now it is foreign to the new Believer, actually repugnant. This is all because of the new nature of the Believer.

THE PRACTICING OF SIN

We are told in God's Word that *"He who practices sin is of the Devil, and whosoever is born of God does not practice sin"* (I Jn. 3:5-9). In other words, a Christian neither embraces situations that lead to sin nor feels comfortable in situations conducive to sin.

The Apostle Paul, speaking under the Anointing and Inspiration of the Holy Spirit, states in Romans 8:1 that the Child of God is free from condemnation. Therefore, God does not demand that a person become free of sin before he seeks Salvation, nor perfect afterward. We all have flaws and shortcomings of one kind or another. Once we become Christians, though, we begin to be conscious of our shortcomings as we seek the Face of God and the Holy Spirit begins to work toward the goal of improving our State, through the Grace of God.

Without question, we do not lose all of our worldly tendencies and inclinations the instant we become Christians. But we do suddenly recognize these old leanings for what they are and we are repulsed by them. Sin, as stated, is foreign to the new nature, so when the old nature occasionally reappears, as it sometimes does, the new nature recognizes the situation and reacts to it. Now we are repelled by sin and its temptations, rather than being drawn to them.

When we encounter these unexpected incursions of sin in our lives, we as Christians should turn immediately to Jesus Christ as our Propitiation (Atoning Sacrifice) for sin, but not as we did as unbelievers seeking Salvation.

NOTES

The lost sinner turning to God does so as an *"outsider"* seeking a new status within the Family of God. We, with occasional failings, come before Christ knowing we are Children of the Most High God, with Christ as our Advocate before the Father.

We do not have to question our Standing, as stated, that never changes. We know God is not going to suddenly change His Mind about our Salvation. The critical question is, do we want to live for God and walk in the Light? If the answer is yes, there can be no question as to our Salvation — even with occasional failings as repugnant and distasteful as those failings may be.

However, the idea of the Work of the Holy Spirit within our lives, is not that we live with these occasional failings, but that ultimately we rid ourselves of them totally and completely.

SALVATION CAN BE FORFEITED

A Believer can be lost if he disregards the continued checks of the Holy Spirit and can even reach the point where he rejects Jesus as his Saviour and no longer believes. It is possible to come to belief — and then to draw back when temptation intervenes and ultimately lose both belief and Salvation. It is not possible for a person to lose their Salvation as long as they continue to trust Christ. However, habitual sin in the life of the Believer will ultimately affect that trust, and if not purged out, even as Paul here commands, will ultimately cause one to lose Faith (Lk. 8:13).

The idea is not that God ultimately loses patience with the Believer, for He never loses patience. In fact, He will forgive as many times as the Believer earnestly and sincerely comes before Him seeking forgiveness. He places no time limit or restrictions on His Grace (I Jn. 1:9).

However, sin always has a negative effect on the Believer even though forgiven, and continued sin has an even greater continued negative effect. It tends to deceive the Believer. Paul said, *"Take heed, Brethren, lest there be in any of you an evil heart of unbelief, in departing from the Living God.*

*"But exhort one another daily while it is called To day; lest any of you be hardened through the deceitfulness of sin"* (Heb. 3:12-13).

If it was not possible for a Believer to quit believing, and then to depart from God, and all because of the deceitfulness of sin, then Paul would not have said such a thing.

FREE WILL

The Believer has a free will (Rev. 22:17). It is through such a will that the sinner comes to God, and through the same free will he can reject God after coming to Him.

That does not mean that it is the *"free will"* which saves the sinner, for Salvation is solely of Christ. It does mean that the sinner after being convicted by the Holy Spirit, has to will to be Saved. In fact, that is all that is actually required of the sinner, which in effect is tantamount to Faith.

Likewise, if the Believer ceases to believe, and many have, with his will he can elect to turn away from God, which is tantamount to the loss of Faith, and then according to Scripture, will be eternally lost. That is the reason Jesus said, *"If ye continue in My Word, then are ye My Disciples indeed"* (Jn. 8:31; Heb. 6:4-6; 10:26-29).

God always responds favorably to Faith, but unfavorably to sin, as should be obvious. Let not the Believer think that he can have both sin and Salvation at the same time, in other words, to live a sinful lifestyle and at the same time be Saved.

There is some evidence that the Brother mentioned in this Fifth Chapter of I Corinthians ultimately repented (II Cor. 2:6-7). To be sure this was the effort of the Holy Spirit with him as it is with us all. Nevertheless, if the man had continued to rebel against the Truth, maintaining his incestuous lifestyle, refusing to repent, his rebellion would have ultimately taken him into unbelief, and thereby, the loss of his soul. As stated, were this not the case, Verse Five would have made little sense. Him being turned over to Satan for the destruction of the flesh constitutes drastic measures; however, if those measures had failed, the person would have been lost.

The phrase, *"For even Christ our Passover is sacrificed for us,"* presents Jesus as the Paschal Victim (Passover Lamb) Who has been offered, Whose Sacrificial Blood has been shed for Redemption (Jn. 1:29; 19:36; I Pet. 1:19).

The idea of Paul's statement is, that Christ, our Passover Lamb, has been sacrificed, yet we have allowed the leaven of sin to remain in our hearts and lives. It would be the same, as a Jew of old upon approaching Passover, to ignore the demand to rid his house of all leaven. Such would have been looked at as a terrible breach of the Word of God, as extremely sinful and wicked. It is the same as the modern Believer rejoicing in Jesus as his Saviour, but at the same time allowing sin to remain in his life.

NOTES

Jesus died to take away sin, not to allow it to remain within us with all of its destructive force. He did not save us in sin but rather *"from sin"* (I Jn. 1:7).

(8) "THEREFORE LET US KEEP THE FEAST, NOT WITH OLD LEAVEN, NEITHER WITH THE LEAVEN OF MALICE AND WICKEDNESS; BUT WITH THE UNLEAVENED BREAD OF SINCERITY AND TRUTH."

The phrase, *"Therefore let us keep the Feast,"* is meant to serve as a symbolism, and not to Believers actually keeping the old Jewish Passover. He wants us to understand what the Passover represented, which was the Death of Christ on the Cross, which paid the terrible sin debt of man, and as well, broke the grip of sin in the human heart and life; however, whereas the actual keeping of the old Jewish Passover was only seven days, that which we now have is constant and everlasting.

THE PASSOVER

Assuming that most Believers know what the old Jewish Passover was, but at the same time realizing that some do not, please allow me to give a brief synopsis of this extremely important portrayal of Redemption, for that is what it is.

The historic roots of the Passover are found in Exodus Chapter 12. When the destroying Angel swept through Egypt, he *"passed over"* (for that is what Passover means) the homes of the Israelites, which were identified by the Blood of a Lamb sprinkled on the doorposts. The homes of the Egyptians did not have the applied Blood, which was a Type of the Shed Blood of Jesus Christ, therefore, the firstborn died in all of those particular homes, whereas the firstborn was spared in the homes of the Israelites who had the applied Blood.

Israel was given explicit instructions on how to keep the Passover so it would be an annual reminder of God's Deliverance (Lev. 23:5-8; Num. 28:16-25; Deut. 16:1-8). This ritual was a reenactment of Israel's preparations for leaving Egypt and focused on killing the Paschal Lamb.

It was to take place in the month of Abib, which incorporated the latter half of March and the first part of April. Regrettably, God's people were not very much faithful to this instruction, though the Old Testament tells us of several specific times when the Passover was in fact observed; these were often linked with Revivals (Num. 9:1-14; Josh. 5:10-12; II Ki. 23:21-23; II Chron. 30:1; 35:1-19; Ezra 6:19-22).

## SIGNIFICANT TO CHRISTIANS AS WELL

The Passover is theologically significant to Christians as well as to Jews, although it is no longer kept. In fact, there is no need for it to be kept any longer, for the simple reason that Jesus came, fulfilling its Type, which made the symbol unnecessary.

To God's Old Testament people, the Passover recalled a Redemption linked with death and the shedding of Blood. To the Christian, the Passover speaks of Jesus. Christ is our Passover Lamb, Who has been sacrificed for us (I Cor. 5:7).

Our Redemption is linked to His Shed Blood, which the Passover symbolized, as it protects us from the ultimate destroyer, Satan himself.

## WHAT DO WE MEAN BY *"TYPE"* OR *"TYPES"*?

When the word *"type"* is used in this sense, it is merely referring to an Old Testament happening which is a Symbol or Type of Christ.

For instance, the Passover which we are now addressing, was a Type of Christ, and meant to be that way by the Holy Spirit. The Sacrifices as well, were Types of Christ. The Lamb on the Altar signified Christ, with the Altar symbolizing the Cross. The Fire symbolized the Judgment of God which would come upon Jesus (the Lamb) rather than upon the sinner. The poured-out Blood of the slain Lamb was a Type of the Blood shed by Christ on the Cross at Calvary.

Along with that which we have stated, all the Feasts of the Jews were Types of Christ, and meant to be so by the Holy Spirit. In fact, that was the major reason for their origination.

For instance, as stated, the Passover was a Type of Calvary. The Feast of Unleavened Bread was a Type of the Perfect Life and Body of Christ, symbolized by the lack of leaven. The Feast of Firstfruits was a Type of the Resurrection of Christ.

NOTES

The Feast of Pentecost was a Type of Jesus as the Baptizer with the Holy Spirit. The Feast of Trumpets is a Type of the Second Coming of the Lord when Israel at long last accepts her Messiah.

The Great Day of Atonement, is a Type of Israel's cleansing upon her acceptance of Christ at the Second Coming. The Feast of Tabernacles is a Type of Christ ruling and reigning in the coming Kingdom Age.

In fact, the entirety of the Tabernacle, the Temple, and all the Sacred Vessels, were all Types of Christ in various parts of His Atoning Work and Sacrificial Offering.

The phrase, *"Not with old leaven,"* refers to the fact that old sins should be laid aside. For a Believer to have old sins still clinging to him, is a shame indeed.

The phrase, *"Neither with the leaven of malice and wickedness,"* refers to the ways of the world from which the Child of God has been delivered.

This tells us that even after Conversion, as should be obvious, the ways of the world continue to cling to the Child of God. It is the business then, or rather should be, that the Believer set about to work with the Holy Spirit in ridding oneself of all semblance of the former life. As we have previously stated, that is one of the great Office Works of the Holy Spirit. He is there to rid the Temple of all that is unholy, impure and un-Christlike.

## MALICE

A range of ideas is suggested in the Old Testament words translated *"malice,"* including the ideas of hatred and violence.

The basic Greek word for *"malice"* in the New Testament is *"kakia"*; the word occurs 11 times.

The word actually means *"wickedness,"* but in these contexts it is a wickedness that manifests itself in a hard and vicious disposition toward others. In Romans 1:29 the word is *"kakoetheia,"* and is translated *"maliciousness."* It tends to put the worst possible construction on others' words and actions. It suggests slander.

By Paul using this word, we know that some in the Church at Corinth were denigrating others, especially those who did not belong to their particular party or follow their particular Preacher. Regrettably, this problem of speaking negatively (maliciously) of others, is a tremendous problem presently in the Church, and in fact always has been. It is without a doubt one of the grievous sins prevalent at this present time, and yet most do not even think of it as sin.

WHAT CHRIST COMMANDED

Jesus said, *"But I say unto you, Love your enemies, bless them that curse you, do good to them that hate you, and pray for them which despitefully use you, and persecute you"* (Mat. 5:44).

Of course, it takes the Love of God in one's heart to be able to do such a thing, *"Love your enemies,"* etc.; therefore, it tells us that there isn't much of the Love of God in the hearts of many Christians.

WICKEDNESS

Wickedness is the fruit of sin, but it has distinctive aspects that set it apart from other words that portray our human condition.

AS USED IN THE OLD TESTAMENT

The Hebrew words *"ra'"* and *"ra'ah"* are sometimes translated *"wicked."* The basic meaning of this word group is *"evil"* or *"bad."*

When used to describe a person, these words focus on those moral deficiencies that move one to injure others. Such wickedness may be descriptive of the deeds done or of persons who are characterized by wicked attitudes and actions.

The Old Testament word most commonly translated *"wickedness"* is *"rasa."* The word is used over 250 times in the Old Testament and is found in tandem with the entire Hebrew vocabulary of sin.

A SIN AGAINST OTHERS

Wicked acts violate God's Standards for life with other people and thus stand in sharp contrast to the Divine Character. But wickedness is not necessarily committed against God (as for instance, is iniquity).

Wickedness is sin against others and one's community. Wicked acts are criminal in character, violating the rights of individuals and threatening the pattern of reciprocity that holds the Church together.

NOTES

One finds that where wickedness is present, dishonesty, violence, oppression, extortion, fraud, and other sins are also present, with the perpetrator being proud and vicious.

Wickedness as it is used in the Old Testament, speaks of attempting to damage others.

THE MANNER IN WHICH IT IS USED IN THE NEW TESTAMENT

Several different Greek words are translated *"wicked"* and *"wickedness"* in the New Testament; however, two of these words *"poneria"* and *"poneros,"* are most used.

The concept is a strong one, focusing on actions that are dangerous because they are destructive to others. In other words, it means the same in the New Testament as it does in the Old.

It indicates the idea of committing an injustice toward others, which is what Paul here is addressing.

Once again we emphasize the fact, that infighting and slander had become part of the Church at Corinth, which regrettably, characterizes so many in the modern Church as well.

The phrase, *"But with the unleavened bread of Sincerity and Truth,"* speaks of all that corresponds to an unsullied, uncontaminated, and genuine Christian Character, which the Holy Spirit is constantly working toward.

SINCERITY

A number of Greek words are translated *"sincere"* or *"sincerity"* in the New Testament.

*"Anypokrites"* means *"without hypocrisy."* It indicates that a person acts or speaks out of genuine motives, without deceit or wavering. It is used some six times (Rom. 12:9; II Cor. 6:6; I Tim. 1:5; II Tim. 1:5; James 3:17; I Pet. 1:22).

*"Eilikrinea"* means *"simplicity"* or *"sincerity,"* and also means *"freedom from all admixture."* Actually, this is the word used here by Paul, and is found also in II Corinthians 1:12; 2:17.

*"Gnesios"* is another Greek word, and means *"sincere."* It is used in II Corinthians 8:8.

In its only New Testament appearance, a fascinating word, *"dilogos,"* is used by Paul in I Timothy 3:8, and means *"not double-tongued."* It is taken here in the sense of an honest expression of what one really thinks rather than the alternate possibility — that is, gossip.

These words portray to us that God places a high value on the undivided heart and on the honest expression of what is in the heart via words and actions.

### TRUTH

The word *"Truth"* as used here by Paul in the Greek is *"aletheuo,"* and means *"to be true, speak the Truth, as not concealing the Truth."* In other words, it is very similar to the word *"sincerity."*

The person does not flatter and neither does he speak evil of another person. By speaking evil, we refer to gossip, slander, etc.

In fact, there may be times one has to say something very negative, but one will do so without adding to the situation, and with the idea in mind of restoration rather than destruction.

(9) "I WROTE UNTO YOU IN AN EPISTLE NOT TO COMPANY WITH FORNICATORS:"

The phrase, *"I wrote unto you in an Epistle,"* refers to a previous letter written to the Church at Corinth, of which has been lost. This does away with the idea, as proposed by some, that every line which the Apostle wrote, or any Apostle for that matter, must necessarily have been inspired and infallible. Such is unscriptural and grossly superstitious.

In fact, Paul no doubt wrote many letters which no doubt contained excellent advice, counsel, and instruction, but was not inspired by the Holy Spirit, and, consequently, was not intended by the Holy Spirit to be a part of the Word of God.

The phrase, *"Not to company with fornicators,"* actually means *"not to be mingled up among."*

The spirit of the injunction is repeated in Ephesians 5:11, *"Have no fellowship with the unfruitful works of darkness, but rather reprove them."*

As we have already stated, the individual in the Church in Corinth who was committing the sin of fornication (incest) was doing so evidently claiming that Christianity gave him license. Of course, such was rank blasphemy, as True Christian liberty is liberty to live a life of Holiness, and that liberty was purchased at the expense of Christ's priceless Life.

From the way Paul writes, this was not the only incident of *"fornication"* in the Church. This ungodly idea of *"Christian license,"* seemingly had made deep inroads into the thinking of many. Inasmuch as the Church seemingly had not too much heeded his former admonition, he now comes down even harder.

NOTES

(10) "YET NOT ALTOGETHER WITH THE FORNICATORS OF THIS WORLD, OR WITH THE COVETOUS, OR EXTORTIONERS, OR WITH IDOLATERS; FOR THEN MUST YE NEEDS GO OUT OF THE WORLD."

The phrase, *"Yet not altogether with the fornicators of this world,"* places a difference respecting those in the world and those in the Church.

If all communication with fornicators in the world (not in the Church) was to be forbidden, the sin was so universal, especially at Corinth, that all dialogue with sinners would have then become impossible, as should be obvious.

The phrase, *"Or with the covetous, or extortioners, or with idolaters,"* pretty well describes virtually all of mankind outside of the Saving Grace of Jesus Christ.

In other words, if the Christian is going to refuse to have any association whatsoever, even in a business sense, with those of this stripe, which as stated, makes up the world system, the Christian then would not even be able to attend to the basic necessities of life.

The phrase, *"For then must ye needs go out of the world,"* refers to normal commerce and activity.

Paul is saying that Christians should not be pharisaical exclusivists who have no contact with outsiders. This would be absurd and could happen only if Christians could leave the Earth totally. Besides, we cannot help the unsaved by taking this stance. We are to be a light to the world, and if a light is hidden, it in fact is no light (Mat. 5:13-16).

This is exactly what the Pharisees did in Jesus' day. They had become so self-righteous, that if a Gentile had asked one of them something about the Lord, they would have immediately insulted the person, with the idea that they (the Pharisees) were so good and holy that they would not sully themselves by even speaking with a Gentile. In fact, they held themselves aloof even from other Jews who did not meet their particular criteria.

The Truth was, that the ones on whom they looked down so insultingly, in the Eyes of God, Whose Eyes Alone matter, were in far better shape morally even than these Pharisees. Such is self-righteousness!

(11) "BUT NOW I HAVE WRITTEN UNTO YOU NOT TO KEEP COMPANY, IF ANY MAN THAT IS CALLED A BROTHER BE A FORNICATOR, OR COVETOUS, OR AN IDOLATER, OR A RAILER, OR A DRUNKARD, OR AN EXTORTIONER; WITH SUCH AN ONE NO NOT TO EAT."

The phrase, *"But now I have written unto you not to keep company,"* in effect says, *"I am adding to that which I wrote to you in my last Epistle."*

## WHAT DOES PAUL MEAN BY *"KEEPING COMPANY"*

The Reader needs to realize that the Apostle was writing about people who constantly practiced these sins, not to people who fail momentarily, then repent.

The idea is, that the Leadership of the Church proclaim the Gospel in such a way, that all will know that Jesus does not save in sin, but from sin. As well, and as stated, it must be ever related that Christianity contains great freedom, but freedom to live a holy life and not to sin.

The problem with most Churches, is that individuals who practice these things, are made to feel comfortable in these sins. God forbid!

While everyone should be treated with love and kindness and patience, still, no person must ever be made to feel comfortable in continued sin.

Regrettably, many so-called Believers especially seek out Churches where the Holy Spirit is little present respecting His Convicting Power, so they will not feel uncomfortable in that which they are doing. In other words, they do not desire to attend a Church where the Holy Spirit is truly present, Who will always convict them of that which is wrong. Consequently, they are made to feel uncomfortable, and so they seek places where such is not prevalent. In fact, the Nation is filled with *"feel good"* Churches. In other words, nothing is ever said that will make anyone feel uncomfortable in their sin, etc.

The Truth is, that the Holy Spirit when truly active, will definitely at times make a person feel good. However, at other times, He will convict so strongly, that the Believer is made to feel like he is hanging over Hell on a rotten stick. As stated, many Believers do not enjoy the latter; consequently, they seek the Church, of which there are many, where such is not present.

NOTES

The phrase, *"If any man that is called a Brother be a fornicator, or covetous, or an idolater, or a railer, or a drunkard, or an extortioner,"* plainly tells us that many will call themselves *"Christian"* or *"Brother,"* who practice these type of sins.

In fact, in America alone at this time, over 100,000,000 people claim to be Born-again. Even though the Lord Alone knows the true number, I think it should be obvious that the true number, whatever it is, is far, far smaller. Regrettably, the Church as a whole, even as stated, is filled with these of which Paul mentions.

Once again, we emphasize that the Apostle is not speaking of those who may momentarily fail in one of these particular sins, and then repent. He is speaking of those who practice these things, and plan to continue. Any Believer who momentarily falls into such, or even one who is having a problem with repeated offenses in one of these areas, but is diligently seeking victory, should be dealt with in all kindness and patience.

## THE PROBLEM IN THE CHURCH

The Church has a tendency to go in one of two erroneous directions:

1. Those who practice such things are made to feel welcome, and because they give a lot of money or for whatever reason. The Preacher does not preach against sin. In other words, he does not preach as Paul here preaches. Consequently, many are made to feel comfortable in their sin.

In February of 1998, Donnie was in Australia in a series of Meetings. Actually, that was his fifth or sixth trip to that great country.

In one of the Services he happened to mention something about the imbibing of strong drink, i.e., alcohol, and how wrong it was. In the next service he did the same thing, even though he really was not preaching on that particular subject.

The Pastor called him aside the next morning (Sunday Morning) before Service began, and revealed something which was extremely interesting.

He told Donnie that the Holy Spirit had been dealing with him all night, and that he had been unable to sleep. In other words, he was under great conviction.

He related as to how he was a social drinker, and that many in his Church were as well. He went on to relate how that many Preachers in his particular Denomination were drinkers. In fact, he stood before his Church that Sunday Morning and confessed this thing, and repented before them, which was an extremely admirable thing to do, but yet that which should have been done.

After Service, a goodly number of the people came up to Donnie, relating to him how that they had never heard any Preacher say that it was wrong for a Christian to drink alcoholic beverage. In other words, they were grateful to him for saying these things.

Sadly, many Churches fall into the same category, and because the pulpit is silent. So, many Churches are filled with *"fornicators, covetous, idolaters, railers, drunkards, and extortioners."*

2. Many Churches, and the number is higher than one realizes, take the exact opposite direction. They are very self-righteous, and if an individual in their congregation does something that does not meet with their approval, they show little or no patience at all, in fact, demanding that they leave the Church, etc.

While sin should never be approved, as should be obvious, still, we are always to show kindness and patience to those who may be weak, or for whatever reason have fallen into sin, but sincerely want victory over the situation. Such a person is to be dealt with in tenderness and compassion, just as the Lord has dealt with us. Their repentance is always to be accepted, and to be sure, it is not difficult at all to tell if one is truly sincere or not.

There are many people in the Church who are truly Saved, and love the Lord with all of their heart, but are struggling with sin in their lives. The Gospel should be preached to these people in such a way, that they will know that they can have victory. They are not to be made to feel comfortable in that sin, but neither are they to be made to feel put down either.

## AN EXAMPLE

Without going into great detail, many years ago a dear Brother had given his heart and life to Jesus Christ, but found himself still addicted to alcohol. In other words, even though trying to serve Jesus, he was having a terrible time overcoming this thing, in fact, having yielded several times and gotten drunk.

NOTES

Thankfully, the Pastor of the Church dealt with him very patiently and with kindness, noting that the Brother wanted victory. To make the story short, even after many months or even two or three years, the Brother in question did gain total victory over this dread malady.

God called him to Preach, and Tommy Anderson was the first Preacher of the Gospel to open up the country of Venezuela to the great Pentecostal Message. In fact, literally tens of thousands of people were brought to Christ as a result of this man's life and Ministry.

But what if this Pastor had been unkind to this man in the times of his struggle, which as stated went on for some time? What if he had told him to go somewhere else to Church or to quit entirely? When he actually did gain victory, what would have happened had this Pastor treated him as some type of second-class Christian?

In fact, the questions are almost endless. But thank God this Pastor was a Godly man, and did not conduct himself in that fashion. The results were glorious to see, a life changed, a Ministry born, and untold numbers of people brought to a Saving Knowledge of Jesus Christ.

Tommy Anderson, as stated, opened up Venezuela to the great Pentecostal Message, with the results being that that great country has been almost entirely touched with the Gospel of Jesus Christ.

The phrase, *"With such an one no not to eat,"* speaks more so of the Lord's Supper than it does anything else.

In fact, Paul will address this very thing in the Eleventh Chapter of this Epistle. We will save Commentary until then.

To sum up, the entire gist of Paul's statements is, that Preachers plainly and clearly present to their congregations the Truth that these things are wrong and terribly wrong at that. As well, even though dealing with people in kindness and patience, if individuals attempt to delude themselves, attempting to make themselves believe that such conduct is satisfactory, and make no efforts to cease such activity, they should be ultimately told to go elsewhere.

However, irrespective of the number of times a person may fail, if they are sincerely trying to obtain victory, we are to deal with that person, as stated, in continued kindness and patience, believing that ultimately victory will be theirs.

(12) "FOR WHAT HAVE I TO DO TO JUDGE THEM ALSO THAT ARE WITHOUT? DO NOT YE JUDGE THEM THAT ARE WITHIN?"

The question, *"For what have I to do to judge them also that are without?"*, speaks of those who are unsaved, in other words outside the Church.

The translation is rather clumsy. The idea is, that we have no right to apply these standards to people who have not professed Christ as Saviour. They will be judged also, but not by the Church, but at the appointed time, i.e., the Great White Throne Judgment (Rom. 2:5; Heb. 13:14; I Pet. 4:17; Rev. 20:11-15) (Rossier).

The question, *"Do not ye judge them that are within?"*, tells us several things:

1. As Believers are not to judge the world, likewise the world is not to judge Believers. While the world, however, definitely will judge Believers, and in fact does so constantly, the Church in no way is to accept such judgment. The reasons should be obvious, the world knows nothing of the Grace of God, and nothing of the Word of God. So why would Believers desire to accept their judgment?

We have little information as to how such was done during Paul's day, but we do know it must have happened or else the Apostle would not have mentioned this. However, this problem is rampant today respecting the modern Media.

So-called Investigative Reporters, who work for large news organizations, are quite adept at portraying Preachers over Television as charlatans, crooks, scoundrels, etc. Having had much experience with this type of effort, I have some knowledge as to the inner workings of such. I will deal with it more directly momentarily.

2. It is the business of the Leadership of each Church to judge the Fruit of all the people who attend that Church (Mat. 7:15-20).

The idea of Paul's question is, that God is the Ruler of the Universe and is the final moral Arbiter. He, the Judge, had already announced His verdict on the practices of which Paul has mentioned. He has identified these practices as sin.

NOTES

What the Church is called on to do is to agree with God in the Divine assessment of the actions of this *"one"* or *"ones"* who *"calls himself* (or themselves) *a Brother or Sister."* As a Church Body, it is to *"expel the wicked"* from its fellowship if they refuse to repent.

Condemning someone by calling into question that person's motives, actions, or personal convictions, is vastly different from accepting God's Verdict that certain actions are sins and that those who practice them and refuse to repent, must be ostracized.

## DISCIPLINE

What necessitates discipline is an individual's choice to practice what the Bible identifies as sin. In fact, all of us may fail at times, or even often, and have to come to God in confession. For *this* there is no call for discipline. Discipline is applied only when a person refuses to acknowledge that his practices are sin and refuses to change his ways.

## RESTORATION

As we have already stated, the goal of Church discipline must always be toward restoration and never destruction. In the case mentioned by Paul, the *"punishment inflicted on* (the offender) *by the majority in the Church"* (II Cor. 2:6) was sufficient, and the guilty man repented. Paul then called on the Corinthians to accept him back and *"to reaffirm"* their love for him (II Cor. 2:8).

(Once again as stated, some claim that this man was not the same as the one in I Corinthians, Chapter 5. Nevertheless, the principle is the same.)

## THE OCCASION FOR DISCIPLINE

The occasion for Church discipline is moral fault: the practice of sin. The Church is not permitted to discipline for other deviations. Difference in convictions or even Doctrinal differences do not call for Church discipline.

It is only the consistent practice of sin, sin which is already identified and condemned in the Bible, in which the person will not acknowledge the fault or show any desire to quit, that occasions discipline.

Exercising Church discipline is very different from adopting the judgmental and condemning attitude against which Scripture speaks. In Church discipline we see the loving action of the Christian community, committed to obedience, intending through the discipline to help the Brother or Sister turn from sin and find renewed fellowship with the Lord.

Let's look again at the Church accepting the verdict of the world, and especially that of the modern News Media.

## EXPERIENCE

Being on Radio or Television since 1969, and conducting Citywide Crusades over many parts of the world, I have had much experience with the News Media. Consequently, I hope you will read the following, and perhaps there may be some things said that would be useful to you.

When Frances and I first began, I had the foolish notion that if I would be perfectly open with the News Media, then they would portray, whether by Television or in print, a fair, unbiased report. How foolish and how wrong I was!

Consequently, during those times of years ago, we opened up everything we had to these people; in other words, we let them see anything they asked for and provided them with any information they sought, even from our accounting records. I found to my dismay, and shockingly so, that most of them had absolutely no desire whatsoever to know the Truth. In other words, their minds were already made up.

## THE PREACHER OF THE GOSPEL

To them, anybody who preached the Gospel of Jesus Christ, and especially those who used the Media such as Radio and Television to do so, were crooks in their sight. Nothing that one said could change their minds. Consequently, it is impossible for anyone of that nature to give a fair, unbiased report on anything.

If one answers *"yes"* to a question, they will make something sinister out of it. To the same question, if one answers *"no,"* they will do the same thing. They have no desire for the Truth; actually, they would not recognize it if they saw it, at least when it regards the Gospel of Jesus Christ.

## AN EXAMPLE

Back in the 1980's, Jimmy Swaggart Ministries built approximately 30 Schools for children in Haiti. (Actually, we built 176 Schools in Third-World Countries.)

NOTES

These Schools were very elementary affairs, costing approximately $50,000 per School. Most of them only went through the sixth grade, with some doing double-duty, operating approximately ten or more hours a day teaching two different groups of children, etc. These were the poorest of the poor and so thankful for the opportunity to attend school. And we were thrilled and thankful that we had the opportunity to help them, such as it was.

In most of these Schools we provided a hot meal each day at noon, which at times was the only meal these children would get.

## AN INVESTIGATIVE REPORTER

A very prominent Newswoman who is presently seen daily on one of the major Television Networks, did a story on these Schools. As stated, this was in the 1980's.

I say she did a story on *"Schools"*; actually she claimed that we had only built one School and that it was for rich children, etc.

Please understand, the existence of our Schools was widely known. She did not find them because she did not look for them. She did not go down there to tell the Truth. She went down there to portray a story which was totally false.

Her program aired over a major Television Station in a major American City, with the intention of ultimately airing it Nationwide. We immediately contacted the Station when we found out what had happened, demanding that they run a retraction. The Manager was indignant, stating primarily, *"These people are with one of the major Networks in America; they would not dare air something that is not true."*

We furnished him documentation concerning the Schools and where they were built, and to his credit he ran a retraction, actually tendering an apology which we very much appreciated. However, that should give you an example of what I am talking about.

## WHETHER HONEST OR DISHONEST . . .

What I want you, the Reader, to understand is that the News Media for the most part have little regard or concern whether the Preacher is honest or not. While we all know there are some dishonest Preachers, in the minds of these people almost all are dishonest, that is

NOTES

if they truly preach the Gospel. In other words, they treat almost everyone identically, making every attempt to destroy. Here is the way they work:

They look for Preachers who are obviously dishonest. Sad to say there are some! They enjoy doing stories on this kind because it paints the picture they desire to paint. However, their ultimate purpose is to tar all, both honest and dishonest with the same brush. They set about with just as much determination to destroy the Godly Preacher as they do the other.

Of course, their purpose is to destroy the confidence that the Christian public or anyone else may have. They know their business well, and as I said to one not so long ago, *"You could take the Sermon on the Mount and make it seem like a plot to overthrow the Government."*

Regarding an evil mind of this disposition, that is no exaggeration!

### ANOTHER EXAMPLE, AMONG MANY WE COULD GIVE

Late in 1997, a major Television Network did a program on us, actually airing it several times.

To be sure, I could deal with the entire program, but I think to do so would dignify their fabrication.

Always remember this: *"Whenever the Media sets out to twist and pervert the Truth, even if they do happen to tell something at times that is in fact True, that within itself becomes a lie because of the intention of perversion of the entire program."* In other words, their intention is to pervert everything, and they work diligently to bring that conclusion about.

This manner should be obvious, especially considering that it is one of Satan's favorite ploys. He is a liar and the father of lies and he knows how to make his lies seem like Truth. Consequently, his children follow in his footsteps, and the *"lie"* is their major weapon.

However, they do it very subtly, and as I have suggested, they take the Truth and twist it in whatever direction they desire, making it appear what they want it to be. Inasmuch as there is some Truth in what is being said, it makes the entire lie seem plausible.

In fact, the Pharisees and the Sadducees did the same with Jesus when they accused Him of saying that He was going to destroy the Temple and raise it up in three days. He did say something to this effect, but He was speaking of His Own Body which would be killed and the Resurrection which would take place three days later.

The news report of which I have just mentioned (news!), claimed that Jimmy Swaggart Ministries in 1995 gave $396 to something they called *"benevolence."* In this totally fabricated statement they were insinuating that even though we spoke of Missions constantly and of taking the Gospel to the world, in reality we had only spent $396 in the entire year.

### WHAT IS THE TRUTH?

Our total giving between the years 1992 and 1996 concerning taking the Gospel of Jesus Christ to the world (not counting the U.S.A. and Canada) was $1,768,000. However, this only referred to cash dollars going out of this Office all over the world and does not count at all any type of overhead, production costs for Television, etc.

As this Reporter's statement concerning the money we spent to take the Gospel to the world was untruthful, to put it mildly, just as untruthful was all else that he portrayed which again contained either no Truth whatsoever, or else perverted Truth.

The sadness is that many Christians believe what they see and hear, even coming from a source of this nature.

### WHY WOULD CHRISTIANS BELIEVE SUCH REPORTS?

I can understand the world being titillated by such, but I can little understand Believers who would want to watch such perversion over Television, much less believe what they see.

In all of these years if I remember correctly, I have only watched a part of one of these type of programs, and that was many years ago. Irrespective as to whom the Preacher may be, who the News Media have targeted, I know it is Satan's effort to steal, kill, and destroy, in other words, to hurt the entirety of the Work of God. Consequently, I will not be a party in any measure to his efforts.

### THE SPIRIT OF WHAT IS BEING DONE

It is virtually impossible for any Believer to watch such an effort over Television, which we know, as stated, is Satan's effort to hurt the entirety of the Work of God, without being affected by the spirit of what is being projected. It is the spirit of darkness that is propelling the Media and helping them do the things they are doing. Consequently, whenever a Believer views a carefully prepared lie, irrespective of whether the Preacher being portrayed is Godly or ungodly, the viewer will not come away unaffected.

By that statement, I am not meaning only that they will believe something which is untrue, which definitely will happen. It goes far deeper than that. The minds of all are so adversely affected by viewing such that their picture of the Gospel is warped and twisted from then on, which is exactly what Satan desires.

IT WILL NOT STOP . . .

We are living in the last days, actually the time of spiritual apostasy. Regrettably, this situation concerning the Media is not going to stop but rather grow worse. Satan is going to increase his all-out attack against the Work of God. He wants Godly Preachers off Television, at least what few there are. To accomplish this task, he will use any tactic at his disposal. The Media have plenty of money, and they have plenty of Television airtime or newspaper space.

In this effort, and sadly so, the so-called *"Church,"* will aid and abet Satan in these tactics, and in fact has long since begun to do so. So the attack is increasingly going to be double-barreled.

HOWEVER . . .

In the midst of all this and irrespective of what Satan will attempt to do, and he is going to use every method at his disposal, I believe the Holy Spirit is going to be poured out in a way the world has never known before. As far as my own particular Ministry is concerned, I am expecting the greatest Move of God that I have ever seen. I am expecting to see more people Saved, more lives changed, more Believers Baptized with the Holy Spirit, more sick bodies healed and more bondages broken than ever before. Let me tell you why:

He said that in the last days He would pour out of His Spirit upon all flesh. That is the Promise of the Lord, and it will be done exactly as He has said (Joel 2:28-29; Acts 2:17-18).

NOTES

He also said, *". . . When the enemy shall come in like a flood, the Spirit of the Lord shall lift up a Standard against him"* (Isa. 59:19).

That *"Standard"* is Jesus Christ!

(13) "BUT THEM THAT ARE WITHOUT GOD JUDGETH. THEREFORE PUT AWAY FROM AMONG YOURSELVES THAT WICKED PERSON."

The phrase, *"But them that are without God judgeth,"* proclaims again what Paul said in the first part of Verse 12. God will ultimately judge the world. Our responsibility relates to discipline within the Assembly (Rossier).

EXACTLY HOW DOES GOD JUDGE THE WORLD OF UNBELIEVERS?

He does so in a twofold manner:

1. Even as we have already stated, the Final Judgment of all unbelievers will take place at the Great White Throne Judgment (Rev. 20:11-15). This will take place at the conclusion of the Kingdom Age and immediately prior to the New Jerusalem transferring from Heaven to Earth (Rev. 20:4-9; 21:1-3).

2. However, the second method of Judgment is that which has been going on constantly from the time of the Fall, and continues unto this hour, and will continue until the Second Coming.

This Judgment consists of war, disease, plagues, adverse weather elements, etc.

Some may argue that it is Satan who does these things and not God. However, while the direct instrument is most of the time Satan, the Author of such is God, because Satan cannot do anything but that it is allowed by the Lord (Job Chpts. 1-2). To claim differently, puts God in a subservient position to Satan, which of course is absurd. Even a cursory examination of the Word of God presents this even in a glaring way. God is extremely involved in all the activities of this world, even to the point of numbering the very hairs of each person's head and noting each sparrow's fall (Mat. 10:29-30). In fact, as should be obvious, that is involvement to a degree that is incomprehensible to the human mind.

Paul said, *"For the Wrath of God is revealed from Heaven against all ungodliness and unrighteousness of men, who hold the Truth in unrighteousness"* (Rom. 1:18).

The *"Wrath"* of which Paul speaks, portrays itself in the things mentioned, such as adverse elements, etc.

### ARE THE PEOPLE OF GOD AFFECTED IN THESE JUDGMENTS?

Yes, they are, and at times, adversely so.

Jesus said, *"For He* (God) *maketh His Sun to rise on the evil and on the good, and sendeth rain on the just and on the unjust"* (Mat. 5:45). And yet in the midst of difficult times, the Lord has promised that He would protect His Children.

The Psalmist said a long time ago, *"He* (the Believer) *that dwelleth in the Secret Place of the Most High shall abide under the shadow* (protection) *of the Almighty.*

*"I will say of the Lord, He is my Refuge and my Fortress: my God; in Him will I trust."*

He then said, *"Surely He* (the Lord) *shall deliver thee from the snare of the fowler, and from the noisome pestilence.*

*"He shall cover thee with his feathers, and under his wings shalt thou trust: his truth shall be thy shield and buckler."*

He then went on to say, *"Thou shalt not be afraid for the terror by night; nor for the arrow that flieth by day;*

*"Nor for the pestilence that walketh in darkness; nor for the destruction that wasteth at noonday."*

And then with a shout of Hallelujah we continue to quote the Psalmist, *"A thousand shall fall at thy side, and ten thousand at thy right hand; but it shall not come nigh thee"* (Ps. 91:1-7).

Of course we know that the Psalmist is primarily speaking of God's Protection of His Son The Lord Jesus Christ; however, Paul also said, *"For ye have not received the spirit of bondage again to fear,"* and because, we are *"joint-heirs with Christ"* (Rom. 8:15, 17).

### ISN'T THERE LESS JUDGMENT NOW UNDER GRACE THAN WHEN THE WORLD WAS UNDER LAW?

No!

In fact, there is far more Judgment now under Grace than there was under Law.

The reason is simple, the more Light that is given, the more that is expected. Jesus said of the cities where He ministered the most and *"Because they repented not, Woe unto thee. . . ."* (Mat. 11:20-24). The Judgment leveled at these Cities by Christ, fell out to them exactly as He said, in that none of these Cities exist at this time.

NOTES

In fact, under Law, Israel lasted for about 1500 years. Under Grace she lasted only about 70 years and was destroyed.

Paul plainly addressed this situation when he said, *"And the times of this ignorance* (before Jesus) *God winked at* (held back Judgment)*; but now* (under Grace) *commandeth all men everywhere to repent"* (will not withhold Judgment) (Acts 17:30).

So, God is constantly judging!

As another example, the former mighty Soviet Union persecuted the people of God, blasphemed God, with her Cosmonauts boasting that they did not see God anywhere in outer space, etc. The Soviet Union is no more, brought down from within.

Some time ago, I stood in Rome observing the ancient Coliseum where untold numbers of Christians went to their death, torn by wild beasts or dispatched in other ways. Where is the mighty Roman Empire today?

Believers around the world number in the hundreds of millions, but the mighty Roman Caesars are no more. When men pit themselves against God, it is a battle they cannot hope to win, irrespective as to their present power or position. Regrettably, most learn that fact too late.

The phrase, *"Therefore put away from among yourselves that wicked person,"* is derived from Deuteronomy 17:7 and 24:7.

This speaks of the so-called Christian who persists in sin without repentance.

It is important, of course, to remember that God is concerned about restoring the sinning person, not destroying the individual. That is one reason Christ established the Church discipline procedure in Matthew 18:15-20.

From these Passages, it is quite obvious that the Lord wants us to take care of matters at the lowest possible level. In other words, if a man sins against his wife or a woman against her husband, there is no need to make the issue a public situation. Ask God for forgiveness and ask the spouse for forgiveness. However, if a Believer sins against an entire Assembly, then God and the total Body should be addressed respecting forgiveness.

Sometimes we forget the other side of the coin. God always forgives and forgets, but sometimes people fail to do so. Paul had to deal with these same Corinthians about this issue

(II Cor. 2:5-11). In fact, he basically told them that if they did not forgive the offender, they would destroy themselves.

Why?

God's Forgiving Power cannot continue to cleanse us from sin if we refuse to forgive others, especially when they seek such forgiveness (Mat. 6:14-15). We must never forget that forgiveness is not optional! Once discipline has resulted in repentance, we are obligated by God to forgive and forget, just as God does.

The idea of punishment after repentance is totally contrary to the fact that God forgives and forgets totally (Col. 2:13-14) (Rossier).

*"Sons of God, beloved in Jesus!*
*"Oh the wondrous Word of Grace;*
*"In His Son the Father sees us,*
*"And as sons He gives us place."*

*"Blessed hope now brightly beaming,*
*"On our God we soon shall gaze;*
*"And in light celestial gleaming,*
*"We shall see our Saviour's Face."*

*"By the Power of Grace transforming,*
*"We shall then His Image bear;*
*"Christ His Promised Word performing,*
*"We shall then His Glory share."*

## CHAPTER 6

(1) "DARE ANY OF YOU, HAVING A MATTER AGAINST ANOTHER, GO TO LAW BEFORE THE UNJUST, AND NOT BEFORE THE SAINTS?"

The beginning of the question, *"Dare any of you, having a matter against another . . . ?"*, pertained to Believers suing Believers in Courts of Law. This situation had evidently been brought to his attention by the House of Chloe (I Cor. 1:11).

Apparently, Paul was not addressing a hypothetical situation, but something which was actually occurring at that present time. In fact, it seems that the situation of suing in Public Court was beginning to be common, hence Paul using the word *"matter"* which means *"disputes."* He did not say *"the matter,"* but rather *"a matter,"* which speaks of more than one.

The ironic thing is that while the Corinthians were extremely careless about immorality, they were very quick to take one another to Pagan Courts over petty differences (Rossier).

NOTES

Continuing the question, *"Go to Law before the unjust,"* is not meant to leave the impression that the Apostle is totally opposed to the concept of secular jurisprudence. On the contrary, he clearly taught that Christians should respect and submit themselves, at least when possible, to Civil Authorities (Rom. 13:1-7). In fact, he himself appealed to Caesar's Court for justice (Acts 25:10-12).

Consequently, his statement here given, should not be interpreted to mean that Believers should never go to court. These verses do not warrant such an extreme approach. There are times when Christians have no other recourse, even as Paul himself resorted to Caesar, to which we have already alluded.

Paul's point of concern was that the Corinthians had become litigation prone and were taking one another to Pagan Courts over minor disputes that they should have handled among themselves (Rossier).

The major point is that the *"unjust"* or *"ungodly"* cannot possibly understand disputes that might arise between Christians over spiritual matters. The wrongdoing or impropriety comes from taking what should relate exclusively to *"the Saints"* to those people who understand nothing about being consecrated to God's Service. Such brings reproach on the Cause of Christ.

The conclusion of the question, *"And not before the Saints?"*, portrays that which our Lord had proclaimed, as He laid down the rule how that *"Brothers"* ought to settle their quarrels among themselves (Mat. 18:15-17). The idea of taking disputes between Saints to a secular court is nothing less than preposterous to say the least. And yet, the courts regrettably, are full of such cases. What does that say about the modern Church?

Paul will now tell us exactly what it says.

(2) "DO YE NOT KNOW THAT THE SAINTS SHALL JUDGE THE WORLD? AND IF THE WORLD SHALL BE JUDGED BY YOU, ARE YE UNWORTHY TO JUDGE THE SMALLEST MATTERS?"

The question, *"Do ye not know that the Saints shall judge the world?"*, should be addressed in two directions.

First of all, it should be pointed out that this emphatic question *"Do ye not know?"*, occurs in one form or the other ten times in this one Epistle (I Cor. 3:16; 5:6; 6:2-3, 9, 15-16, 19; 9:13, 24). It occurs only twice in all of Paul's other Epistles (Rom. 6:16; 11:2).

It was a fitting rebuke to those who took for knowledge their obvious Spiritual and Scriptural ignorance. It resembles the *"Have ye not so much as read?"*, as posed by Jesus to the Pharisees who professed such profound familiarity with the Scriptures (Farrar).

By the Saints judging the world, this refers to the coming Kingdom Age when Christ will then rule the world with the help of all His Saints. His Headquarters will be in Jerusalem (Isa. 9:6-7; Dan. 2:44-45; 7:13-14, 27; Zech., Chpt. 14; Mat. 19:28; Lk. 2:31-32; Rev. 1:6; 5:10; 11:15; 20:4; 22:5).

The question, *"And if the world shall be judged by you, are ye unworthy to judge the smallest matters?"*, presents a fitting rebuke.

The situations over which the Corinthian Believers were going to court evidently were trivial. Consequently, two things are said here:

1. First of all, going to court over such matters was ridiculous.

2. Second, falling out with each other, especially considering that all were Christians, over such trivial things as they evidently were, does not speak very well of their walk with the Lord.

(3) "KNOW YE NOT THAT WE SHALL JUDGE ANGELS? HOW MUCH MORE THINGS THAT PERTAIN TO THIS LIFE?"

The question, *"Know ye not that we shall judge Angels?"*, pertains only to the Angels who fell with Lucifer (himself an Angel) in his revolution against God, some time in eternity past (II Pet. 2:4; Jude vs. 6; Rev. 20:10). The Bible does not say what form this participation will take, but it affirms that the Saints will somehow be involved (Rossier). Nowhere does the Bible speak of Christians judging the Angels who have stayed obedient to God. In fact, the Bible portrays the Righteous Angels as effecting a division between Godly and ungodly people (Mat. 13:36-43).

The question, *"How much more things that pertain to this life?"*, regards the situations in this present life as being elementary in comparison to that which is to come.

In other words, the Apostle is telling the Corinthians, and all other Believers for that matter who fall into the same category, that they should grow up and conduct themselves in a mature way.

NOTES

### A WORLD VIEW

In fact, Believers are the only ones on the Earth who have a proper understanding of events. This speaks of the past, present, and future.

Believers interpret the past (history) in the realm of the Word of God, which of course outlines the Purpose of God in the redemptive process of man. Only then can history be properly understood which, as well, throws great light on the present and the future. In fact, those who do not know the Lord, and, consequently, do not know the Bible, have absolutely no idea whatsoever regarding the future. To them it is a blank, a void, the great unknown!

From the Word of God, the Believer knows and understands, or at least he should, what the future holds. I speak of the overall Plan of God, concerning the Rapture of the Church, the coming Great Tribulation, the rise of the Antichrist, and above all, the Second Coming of the Lord.

### THE WORD OF GOD

If one is to notice, in the Old Testament it is only the Nations of the world that impact Israel in some way, that are mentioned. Otherwise, they are ignored!

Why?

In fact, there were mighty Nations in the world engaging tremendous enterprises, during Old Testament times which should be obvious. But yet they are not addressed at all, simply because they had no bearing on the people of God, the Israelites.

As well, if one is to notice, the mighty Roman Empire is mentioned in the New Testament, only as it impacted the Church. Even though the Roman Empire was certainly important in the Eyes of God, as well as the other Nations of the world before Christ, still, the central thrust was always the Plan of God relative to Redemption, and that of necessity dealt with Israel in the Old Economy and the Church in the New. So, the Believer is to have a world view as God sees the world, not as the world sees itself.

In essence, Paul is chastising the Church at Corinth for involving themselves in pettiness, when of all the people in Corinth, they were the only ones who had a correct view of things, or at least should have had.

(4) "IF THEN YE HAVE JUDGMENTS OF THINGS PERTAINING TO THIS LIFE, SET THEM TO JUDGE WHO ARE LEAST ESTEEMED IN THE CHURCH."

The phrase, *"If then ye have judgments of things pertaining to this life,"* is addressing the constant litigation in which they seemingly were constantly engaged.

The phrase is somewhat of a question statement. In other words, he is in a sense asking them as to how they could have so many problems between themselves that would require legal action?

The phrase, *"Set them to judge who are least esteemed in the Church,"* presents Paul again using irony. In essence, he is saying that the least esteemed members of the Church would be more qualified to judge than the most esteemed Pagan Judge, or at least certainly should be (Rossier).

(5) "I SPEAK TO YOUR SHAME. IS IT SO, THAT THERE IS NOT A WISE MAN AMONG YOU? NO, NOT ONE THAT SHALL BE ABLE TO JUDGE BETWEEN HIS BRETHREN?"

The phrase, *"I speak to your shame,"* presents Paul addressing the irony he has just used in the last verse.

The question, *"Is it so, that there is not a wise man among you?"*, drips with sarcasm. In fact, the Corinthians concluded themselves to be intellectuals. So, Paul cuts deep with this question.

Notice how the Apostle shows up the conceit of these people, which in effect cuts to pieces their ridiculous claims of Scriptural maturity — in the thinking of some, even greater than that of Paul. When people are deceived, and they were, they come up with ridiculous conclusions. As well, anyone who gets at cross purposes with the Word of God does not think right, even as these Corinthians.

The question, *"No, not one that shall be able to judge between his brethren?"*, is asked in the Greek in a manner which demands an affirmative answer. *"Of course there is!"* (Rossier).

(6) "BUT BROTHER GOETH TO LAW WITH BROTHER, AND THAT BEFORE THE UNBELIEVERS."

The word *"but"* in the Greek is *"alla,"* and means in this instance, *"strong emphasis."*

Instead of settling the issue between themselves, whatever the problem may have been, Brother was taking Brother to Pagan Courts to settle these issues before unbelievers who could not possibly understand spiritual things.

NOTES

(7) "NOW THEREFORE THERE IS UTTERLY A FAULT AMONG YOU, BECAUSE YE GO TO LAW ONE WITH ANOTHER. WHY DO YE NOT RATHER TAKE WRONG? WHY DO YE NOT RATHER SUFFER YOURSELVES TO BE DEFRAUDED?"

The phrase, *"Now therefore there is utterly a fault among you, because ye go to Law one with another,"* presents that which would be bad enough even if Believers lived in different cities. However, considering that these were all from the same Church made the situation extremely grievous. If people who are sitting on the same pew cannot solve their own problems without going to court, their Christianity to be sure, is not much.

*"Fault"* in the Greek is *"hettema,"* and means *"a failure."* In effect the word *"fault"* or *"failure"* means that Christianity has failed with these people, or such as they are doing would not be done. Of course, we know that Christianity has not failed, but rather the individuals responsible. Nevertheless, to the unbelievers in the city of Corinth, or anywhere and at any time for that matter, Christianity has failed, i.e., Christ has failed. This is the main theme of Paul's dissertation.

The situation was bad enough among the individuals involved, but the picture that this action portrayed to the general unbelieving public, was grievous indeed!

The question, *"Why do ye not rather take wrong?"*, portrays the perfect example of uncrucified self.

Regrettably, many in the modern Church are so busy demanding their personal rights, that they totally forget the One Who they are representing, The Lord Jesus Christ. The Truth is, that when we properly understand our position in Christ, we learn that we actually have no personal rights. It is all in Christ and Christ is in all. In this manner the offender is attacking Christ, which is an unenviable position for anyone to find himself (Acts 9:4).

The idea is, that the person would be so in love with Christ, so filled with Christ, that he would rather take wrong than to bring a reproach on that Wondrous Name.

The question, *"Why do ye not rather suffer yourselves to be defrauded?"*, actually means to suffer material loss than to suffer spiritual loss.

Again we emphasize, that Paul is not saying that it is always wrong for Christians to go to court in order to rectify injustices. Sometimes it is the only recourse; however, the reason must never be that of the sole purpose of oneself. I think the Scripture is clear on this.

(8) "NAY, YE DO WRONG, AND DEFRAUD, AND THAT YOUR BRETHREN."

To defraud anyone is bad enough, but to defraud one's own *"Brethren"* in the Lord, is worse still.

Paul had previously written, *"That no man go beyond and defraud his Brother in any matter: because that the Lord is the Avenger of all such, as we also have forewarned you and testified"* (I Thess. 4:6).

To incur the Anger of God is a very serious matter. And whenever we defraud, harm, slander, or hurt a Brother in the Lord in any fashion, as the Holy Spirit through the Apostle has written, we have in fact, incurred God's Anger.

## HOW DOES THE LORD AVENGE SUCH?

The words *"vengeance"* and *"revenge"* occur only a few times in the Bible. Yet the concept is unmistakably there, boldly affirmed in both the Old Testament and the New Testament.

The idea that God is a *"God Who avenges"* (Ps. 94:1) troubles some. Is not vengeance evil? How can a trait that we deplore in human beings be appreciated in God?

## WHAT THE OLD TESTAMENT SAYS ABOUT VENGEANCE

In God's Revelation of Himself to Israel, the Hebrew word *"naqam"* is definitely applied. Moses' early Psalm celebrating God focuses several times on vengeance (Deut. Chpt. 32).

Speaking of the enemies of Israel, who are devoted to Pagan gods, this Psalm portrays God crying out, *"Have I not kept this in reserve and sealed it in My vaults? It is Mine to avenge; I will repay. In due time their foot will slip; their day of disaster is near and their doom rushes upon them"* (Deut. 32:34-35).

The Lord then reveals His Compassion for those who trust Him (Deut. 32:36-38). After recording God's Declaration that He is the One with ultimate Power to bring to life and put to death, the Psalm returns to the Judgment theme: *"I will take vengeance on My adversaries and repay those who hate Me . . . Rejoice, O Nations, with His people, for He will avenge the Blood of His Servants; He will take vengeance on His enemies and make Atonement for His land and people"* (Deut. 32:41-43).

## SELDOM BY HUMAN BEINGS

At times the Old Testament speaks of God acting to punish His people when they break the Covenant (Lev. 26:24-25). But normally vengeance is focused on those who reject God and actively persecute His people.

Only a few times is vengeance executed through or by human beings (Num. 31:2-3; Josh. 10:13). Even then it is understood that they act as God's Agents, and unwitting Agents at that.

The Old Testament makes it clear that individuals are not to act to take vengeance on their own. *"Do not seek revenge or bear a grudge against one of your people, but love your neighbour as yourself"* is God's Word to the individual (Lev. 19:18; Deut. 32:35).

Personal vengeance is ruled out; but judicial vengeance is not.

It is significant that in the Prophet's view of the future, vengeance is most often reserved for history's end (Isa. 34:8; 61:2; 63:1-6; Ezek. Chpt. 25).

## EXAMINATION OF OUR GOD-CONCEPT

One of the reasons we hesitate to accept the Old Testament's presentation of a God-vengeance is our failure to develop a balanced God-concept.

We have tried to measure God by ourselves, and we cannot. Because vengeance is associated with attitudes and emotions that distort the human personality, robbing us of compassion and infusing a bitter vindictiveness, we mistakenly export these human characteristics to God. Yet God is at once and always a God of Love and Compassion. No emotion or decision can rob any act — even acts of Judgment — of those qualities.

Only in God is it possible for Love, Compassion, and Vengeance to be exhibited, along with Holiness, in the same act.

It is also important to remember that the Old Testament maintains a distinction between personal and judicial acts of vengeance. Infrequently, human beings may be agents of God's Vengeance, but taking personal revenge or even bearing a grudge is forbidden in God's Law.

NOTES

Thus, it follows that the Law, an expression of God's moral Standards, unveils an important fact about His Vengeance. When God takes vengeance, He does not act merely out of outraged feelings. He acts as the Moral Judge of the Universe, responsible to punish sin as well as to reward Righteousness.

WHAT THE NEW TESTAMENT TEACHES ON VENGEANCE

The Greek words *"dike"* and *"ekdikesis"* mean *"vengeance"* or *"punishment,"* with *"dike"* having the primary meaning of *"justice."* In those Passages in which this word group is translated *"avenge"* or *"vengeance"* we see a clear expression of the basic position of the Old Testament in regard to justice. Vengeance is God's prerogative Alone (Rom. 12:19; Heb. 10:10).

JUSTICE

The future perspective is also clear in the New Testament. The day of vengeance (graphically described in II Thessalonians 1:5-10) is delayed because in the *"riches of His Kindness, Tolerance and Patience"* (Rom. 2:4) God has chosen to make this present time the day of opportunity and Salvation.

As the One responsible Moral Agent in the Universe, God can do no less than punish. As the One Who truly loves a lost humanity, God chose to delay punishment to provide the human race with an era of opportunity.

In reality, God's Anger, His Vengeance, fell on Christ when He became a Sin Offering for sinful humanity (II Cor. 5:17-21).

However, we must never forget what Nahum the Prophet said: *"The Lord is slow to anger and great in Power; the Lord will not leave the guilty unpunished"* (Nahum 1:2-3).

For fellow Believers who are guilty of such action, the punishment can be stopped immediately upon proper repentance, which means repenting before the Lord, and seeking forgiveness from the offended party. Otherwise, the Lord will level punishment at the offending Believer, even in a greater manner than He would an unbeliever. The reason being that the Believer should know better.

ON A PERSONAL BASIS

There are many Believers who think if their Denominational Leaders lead the way by attacking a fellow Believer, that this gives them license to do such as well, with no fear of retribution. Nothing could be further from the Truth.

As we have already stated, the Lord seldom uses human beings to punish fellow human beings, and the times in which He does, most always these people are unwitting agents. In other words, they do not know they are being used in this capacity.

So, it is never proper for Believers to take it upon themselves to punish fellow Believers. The Lord takes matters such as this very seriously and to be sure, will repay.

That is the reason, I believe, that many Christians are sick, or suffer other difficulties, with some even dying prematurely. While such situations would certainly not be the case at all times, it is definitely the case, I think, many times.

When we attack one who belongs to God, we in effect, attack God.

(9-10) "KNOW YE NOT THAT THE UNRIGHTEOUS SHALL NOT INHERIT THE KINGDOM OF GOD? BE NOT DECEIVED: NEITHER FORNICATORS, NOR IDOLATERS, NOR ADULTERERS, NOR EFFEMINATE, NOR ABUSERS OF THEMSELVES WITH MANKIND,

"NOR THIEVES, NOR COVETEOUS, NOR DRUNKARDS, NOR REVILERS, NOR EXTORTIONERS, SHALL INHERIT THE KINGDOM OF GOD."

The question, *"Know ye not that the unrighteous shall not inherit the Kingdom of God?"*, refers to that which is of God, which includes the *"Born-again"* experience, as well as the Baptism with the Holy Spirit, in other words, Eternal Life and all that goes with this great Gift of God. To be frank, it is impossible to even begin to grasp the beginning stages of that which is the Kingdom of God. The Holy Spirit through Paul compares what we know now which compares to the understanding of a child, to that which we will know then which compares to the knowledge of an adult (I Cor. 13:9-12). If one contemplates that for a few moments, one quickly comes to the understanding that the gap is very wide.

When one realizes the absolute wonder of that which the Lord has prepared for them who love Him, which can only be understood by the

NOTES

converted mind, then the thought of not inheriting the Kingdom of God presents a tragedy of unprecedented proportions. First of all, one must wonder why the Lord would want to do such for the human family, and especially to pay the price that He paid in order that we might have this *"Kingdom."* That means the Love of God is beyond the ability of anyone to grasp, even those closest to Him.

*"Inherit"* in the Greek is *"kleronomeo,"* and means *"an heir to, a sharer by lot, a possessor."* In fact, the only way that the Believer can inherit anything respecting the Lord, is that we become *"joint-heirs with Christ"* at Conversion, and by that *"heirs of God"* (Rom. 8:17).

In other words, we inherit the Kingdom of God only because of Jesus Christ. Within ourselves we have no merit and in fact, can inherit nothing.

*"Unrighteous"* in the Greek is *"adikos,"* and means *"unjust, wicked, treacherous."*

This shoots down the unscriptural Doctrine of Unconditional Eternal Security.

CHANGED LIVES!

Some claim that the only difference in the Believer and the unbeliever is that the Believer trusts Christ while the unbeliever does not. Nothing could be further from the Truth.

The Gospel of Jesus Christ is a Gospel which produces changed lives, and for the better we might quickly add. The Lord does not save one in sin but from sin. While the Bible does not teach sinless perfection, it does teach that the dominion of sin is broken in the heart and life of the Believer (Rom. 6:11, 14).

When the sinner comes to Christ, the change in the individual is of such dramatic form, that Jesus referred to it as *"Born-again"* (Jn. 3:3). At that time, the Divine Nature comes into the Believer, which effects a powerful change in one's heart and life (II Cor. 5:17-21).

Whereas sin was once part and parcel of the sinner, now due to the Divine Nature imparted in the Believer's heart and life, sin is now repugnant. So, while the Believer definitely does trust Christ, that trust is not the only difference in his life and that of the unsaved. The Truth is, proper trust brings about a change of astounding proportions. In fact, the change never stops from the moment the sinner comes to Christ, and continues to the moment of death.

NOTES

The phrase, *"Be not deceived,"* presents the same words of our Lord, *"Let no man deceive you"* (Mk. 13:5). In fact, Paul uses the warning very solemnly again in I Corinthians 15:33 and Galatians 6:7.

WHAT DOES PAUL MEAN BY DECEPTION?

The self-deception of merely verbal orthodoxy is the most dangerous of all, and because it is religious. Such refers to subscribing to something with one's mouth, but in reality having nothing in the heart. As well, Jesus said, *"Take heed lest any man deceive you"* (Mk. 13:5). So, if such were of little moment, Jesus would not have been so plain in His Warning.

Paul lays down, as distinctly as does James, that Faith without works is dead, and privileges without Holiness are abrogated. The spirit of his warning is the same as that of Jeremiah 7:4, *"Trust ye not in lying words, saying, The Temple of the Lord . . . are these"*; or that of John the Baptist, *"Say not unto yourselves, We be Abraham's sons."*

Christians have often been liable to the temptation of underrating the peril which results from the falling asunder for lack of knowledge of the Word of God. One must ever understand, that Salvation is not an outward service, but a spiritual life manifested by holy living (Farrar).

CEREMONY AND RITUAL

Untold millions even at this present hour, are deceived into believing they are Saved because they are a member in good standing with some particular Church. Untold numbers of others think that ritual and ceremony institute their Salvation, and I speak of Water Baptism, the Lord's Supper, the Mass, etc.

A NARCOTIC

The narcotic of the doing of religion is the most damnable curse of all. Notice what I said, *"the doing of religion!"*

Men do religious things and they think somehow this constitutes Salvation. Such is a narcotic, and actually, the greatest narcotic of all.

These people have no relationship with Christ, other than some type of mental confession. In other words, their heart has never been changed, i.e., they have never been Born-again.

Very plainly and clearly Paul will now name sins, which is almost unknown in modern religious circles. However, the Preacher had better understand that it is not merely Paul saying these things, but the Holy Spirit through him, which are meant for our edification and instruction. In other words, Paul is preaching against sin. The sins named are as follows:

1. *"Neither fornicators"*: As we have previously explained in Commentary on Chapter Five, fornication covers a wide range of sexual immorality. This sin is no doubt one of the most committed sins in the world at present, and in fact, always has been. The Bible says, *"Lest there be any fornicator, or profane person, as Esau"* (Heb. 12:16).

2. *"Nor idolaters"*: This sin pertains to anything that is placed ahead of Jesus Christ. God as our Creator is to be worshiped exclusively. But yet, most of the human race worships a god of their own making.

Because of the Gospel the world is more enlightened presently than previously, and as a consequence, the worshiping of idols made of gold or silver, or whatever, is not nearly as pronounced as it once was. However, this sin is just as rampant presently, for the simple reason that untold millions make gods out of sports figures, Hollywood actors, business tycoons, and even Preachers, even as Paul addressed in the first Four Chapters of this Epistle. To be frank, one of America's many gods is sports. It worships at the shrine of football, baseball, or basketball, etc.

My statement is not meant to imply that sports themselves are sinful, for they are not. However, the sin comes in, when men deify the game and its participants. The same can be said for rock stars, etc.

So, the sin of idolatry is committed today just as much, if not more than in ages past.

## JESUS ALONE

Jesus Christ Alone is to be the object of our worship, which at the same time speaks of God the Father. Jesus said, *"Thou shalt worship the Lord thy God, and Him only shalt thou serve"* (Mat. 4:10).

As well, one must quickly add that many Believers worship God, but at the same time worship other things as well. By that I mean the following:

NOTES

In the early days of Israel's history, Samuel admonished them by saying, *"If ye do return unto the Lord with all your hearts, then put away the strange gods and Ashtaroth from among you, and prepare your hearts unto the Lord, and serve Him only"* (I Sam. 7:3).

Notice that he said, *"Serve Him* (the Lord) *only."* In other words, while Israel was serving the Lord, they were also serving these *"strange gods,"* just exactly as are many Believers presently.

To these people, and they number into the untold millions, Jesus is just a part of the mix. He is not in all their thoughts, neither is He the core and circumference of all they are and do. In fact, most Believers, and I think I can say most without exaggeration, know far more about other things than they do about Christ. They know more about sports figures than they do about Jesus Christ. They know more about the Stock Market and world events of every description than they do Jesus Christ. And yet, they still claim Him to be Lord!

3. *"Nor adulterers"*: If one is to notice, Paul lists both *"fornicators"* and *"adulterers."* In fact, all *"fornicators"* are *"adulterers,"* but all *"adulterers"* are not *"fornicators."*

David was an *"adulterer"* but not a *"fornicator,"* as Esau. David had a problem as was graphically described in the Word of God, but repented of the situation (Ps. 51). By contrast, Esau was a predator going from one sexual partner to the next, and refusing to repent (Gen. 25:34). Consequently, the Scripture says that *"God hated Esau"* (Mal. 1:3; Rom. 9:13).

4. *"Nor effeminate"*: The Greek word for *"effeminate"* is *"malakos,"* and means a *"male who submits his body to unnatural lewdness"* (Joel 3:3).

This man is known as a *"catamite,"* which refers to a boy or man who sells himself to a homosexual, even though he is not himself a homosexual.

5. *"Nor abusers of themselves with mankind"*: The Greek word for *"abusers"* is *"arsenokoites,"* and means *"one guilty of unnatural sex offenses; a sodomite; a homosexual"* (I Tim. 1:10; Rom. 1:27).

This sin is rampant in the world, with the Homosexual Lobby in America attempting to force Congress to recognize same sex marriages, which is presently being done in some States. Homosexuality is a grievous sin, mocking all that God has done and created, and in its perversion attempts to force its ungodly way of life on others.

Secret homosexuality is bad enough, but attempting to flaunt this perversion (the most gross of all perversions), is the worst insult to God and His Creation that there is.

6. *"Nor thieves"*: God demands total honesty on the part of His people. And that means in every capacity.

As grievous as may be the modern Income Tax System, it is wrong, and actually stealing, for any Believer to evade taxes. It is perfectly proper and Scriptural to avoid paying taxes by legal means, but never to evade the paying of taxes, which is stealing. Of course, stealing applies to many and varied things, which in brief means *"to take something which belongs to someone else."*

7. *"Nor covetous"*: This refers to wanting something which belongs to someone else with an attempt to secure it by unlawful means. It refers to desire which goes beyond the normal, and most of the time for that which the person should not have.

The idea is, that a person is to be led by the Lord, thereby looking to Him to supply our needs, and not to desire anything which He does not want for us. In other words, He charts our course, and not we ourselves. If He leads us, there is no place for covetousness.

8. *"Nor drunkards"*: There are about 20,000,000 Alcoholics in America, and as well about 20,000,000 problem drinkers we are told. The Greek word for *"drunkard"* is *"methusos,"* and means *"tipsy, a sot, to drink to intoxication."*

## SOCIAL DRINKING

Some Believers have attempted to use the word *"drunkards,"* as an excuse for social drinking. In other words, as long as one does not become drunk, one has not violated the Word of God. Such is not true.

First of all, every single Alcoholic who has ever lived, started out by taking his first drink, with most all of them thinking they could handle the situation.

As well, it is a scientific fact, if it takes, for instance, ten beers to make one drunk, that one beer makes one one-tenth drunk. In other words, the vision and reflexes are impaired to that degree, which is a major cause of automobile wrecks, etc.

NOTES

Does any Believer desire to justify his social drinking, by claiming that he is only one-half drunk, or one-fourth drunk, or one-tenth drunk?

I think we make our point!

9. *"Nor revilers"*: The Greek word for *"revilers"* is *"loidoros,"* and means *"abusive, a railer."* This speaks of an attitude that is not Christlike, in a word, one with an abusive spirit. The manner of a Believer should be one of composure, kindness, and gentleness, which pertains to the Fruit of the Spirit (Gal. 5:22-23).

10. *"Nor extortioners"*: The Greek word is *"harpax,"* and means *"rapacious, excessively grasping, unscrupulous plundering."* The idea speaks of one who sets out to obtain what he desires, and to do so by hook or by crook.

## SAVED?

The phrase, *"Shall* (not) *inherit the Kingdom of God,"* refers to those who call themselves Believers, and yet continue to practice the sins mentioned, who the Holy Spirit says, irrespective of their claims, are not Saved, and are headed for eternal separation from God in the Lake of Fire.

This role call of the eternally damned contains language similar to what is in Romans 1:24-32; I Corinthians 5:9-10; and, Revelation 21:8.

The Truth is, I think I can say, that every Believer at one time or the other, has committed regrettably and sadly so, at least one of these sins or more. However, the Believer has the privilege of taking such situations to the Lord, asking His forgiveness and cleansing, and strength not to commit any of these acts again. The Lord has promised that He would always forgive and cleanse respecting an honest, seeking heart (I Jn. 1:9). However, the Believer, unlike the *"ways of Pagans"* does not practice these sins or any sin for that matter. In fact, it is impossible for him to do so, even though with some there may in fact be repeated failures. To be sure, the Lord will always forgive, as He puts no time frame or limitation on His Mercy and Grace, as long as the Believer earnestly and sincerely seeks such forgiveness. However, any Believer who purposely sets out to commit these sins, in fact to live a life of such sins, will soon cease to be a Believer, and thereby will lose his soul.

To be sure, even though the Lord readily and quickly forgives upon sincere repentance, still, sin always takes a deadly toll, even though washed, cleansed, and forgiven. The Believer is to never look at sin lightly, but always as to the deadly force and power that it is.

Jesus Christ Alone is the Answer for sin, and more particularly what He did at Calvary and the Resurrection. As we have previously stated, He saves from sin and not in sin. The very purpose of the Gospel is its power to change lives. And that the Holy Spirit does instantly upon Conversion even as He imparts the Divine Nature into the believing sinner, and then thereafter as He makes the Believer into the Image of the Heavenly; however, He can only do such, as the Believer cooperates with Him.

So, Paul named sin, spoke against it vehemently, and said in no uncertain terms, that Believers who think they can practice sin and still be Saved are in for a rude awakening. Emphatically, *"They shall not inherit the Kingdom of God."*

All other Preachers should understand that this is the pattern of Ministry laid down by the Holy Spirit, and should at least be a part of the Message proclaimed by the Preacher.

(11) "AND SUCH WERE SOME OF YOU: BUT YE ARE WASHED, BUT YE ARE SANCTIFIED, BUT YE ARE JUSTIFIED IN THE NAME OF THE LORD JESUS, AND BY THE SPIRIT OF OUR GOD."

The phrase, *"And such were some of you,"* speaks of the terrible sinners mentioned in Verses 9 and 10. In fact, such describes all of humanity in one way or the other, before coming to Christ. This is the reason the world is in the condition it is in, with all the murder, rape, bias, prejudice, war, evil, and wickedness of every sort.

## WASHED

The phrase, *"But ye are washed,"* refers to the Blood of Jesus cleansing from all sin. The Greek word for *"washed"* is *"apolouo,"* and means *"to wash the whole being, not a part of it."* The first part of the word *"apo,"* means *"away from,"* and in this case, means to wash the sins away from the individual. Of course all of this is done by Faith, meaning that the believing sinner proclaims his Faith in Christ and what He did at Calvary and the Resurrection. Upon the evidence of Faith, which is a state of the heart moved upon by the Holy Spirit, the Lord awards the believing sinner that which was paid for at Calvary by the shedding of the innocent Blood of Christ.

NOTES

Actually, in the Mind of God, when Jesus died on the Cross, the payment of the Shed Blood sufficed for all of humanity and for all time. Of course, those who had died without Faith in that Atoning Sacrifice, will never have an opportunity to accept its benefits. In fact, that is the same for all who die. First, second, and third opportunities are on this side of the grave. However, all who accept that Atoning Sacrifice, which as stated is done exclusively by Faith, instantly are changed from the debit side to the credit side. In other words their terrible debt of sin is instantly accounted as paid, and that which Jesus did is accredited to them. As we have stated, it is something that is already done, but cannot accrue to the benefit of the sinner until Faith is evidenced in Christ (Gen. 15:6; Jn. 3:16; Rom. 10:9-10, 13; Eph. 2:8-9; Rev. 22:17).

Incidently, Jesus giving His spotless Life as a payment for the sin debt, which demanded the pouring out of His Innocent Blood, for the Life is in the Blood, is the only Sacrifice that God would accept, and because it was the only Sacrifice which was acceptable. This and this alone settled the terrible sin debt, a debt incidentally, which man in no way could pay.

The Songwriter said:

*"Have you been to Jesus for the*
*cleansing power?*
*"Are you washed in the Blood of*
*the Lamb?*
*"Are you fully trusting in His Grace*
*this hour?*
*"Are you washed in the Blood of*
*the Lamb?"*

*"Are you walking daily by the*
*Saviour's Side?*
*"Are you washed in the Blood of*
*the Lamb?*
*"Do you rest each moment in the*
*Crucified?*
*"Are you washed in the Blood of*
*the Lamb?"*

*"When the Bridegroom cometh, will*
*your robes be white,*
*"Pure and white in the Blood of the Lamb?*

*"Will your soul be ready for the mansions bright,*
*"And be washed in the Blood of the Lamb."*

*"Lay aside the garments that are stained with sin,*
*"And be washed in the Blood of the Lamb;*
*"There's a fountain flowing for the soul unclean;*
*"Oh, be washed in the Blood of the Lamb."*

*"Are you washed in the Blood, in the soul-cleansing Blood of the Lamb?*
*"Are your garments spotless? Are they white as snow?*
*"Are you washed in the Blood of the Lamb?"*

## SANCTIFIED

The phrase, *"But ye are Sanctified,"* refers to the fact that one is *"washed."* In other words, by the process of Faith in the Shed Blood of the Lamb, the believing sinner is *"made clean."*

Sanctified in the Greek is *"hagiazo,"* and means *"to make holy, purify or consecrate."* In other words, the individual through Faith is set apart from something to something, in this case, from darkness to Light, from Satan to God.

As we have previously explained, this Sanctification presents the Believer's *"Standing,"* and never changes. It is a Work of Grace, and is imputed to the believing sinner upon Faith.

## JUSTIFIED

The phrase, *"But ye are Justified,"* actually refers to a legal work.

The Sanctification process *"makes one clean,"* while the Justification process *"declares one clean."* In other words, because of Faith in Christ, God can be just in declaring the person *"not guilty,"* even though he in fact is guilty. He does this on the premise of Jesus having taken the sinner's place. Therefore, God can be *"Just"* and the *"Justifier"* at the same time.

*"Justified"* in the Greek is *"dikaioo,"* and means *"to render one just or innocent."*

## SANCTIFICATION AND JUSTIFICATION

If one is to notice, the Work of Sanctification takes place before the Work of Justification. That is understandable when one considers that God cannot *declare* one Righteous which Justification is, until that person is first *made* Righteous, which is Sanctification. Sanctification makes the believing sinner ready for the legal process of Justification. Of course, all of this takes place upon one's Faith in Christ, and is done instantly. Actually, and as stated, it is a work that has really already been done, which awaits only the acceptance of the sinner, which must be done by Faith.

Some people, even as we have already explained in other Commentary, get the Work of Sanctification confused. They confuse the *"Standing"* of Sanctification which is what is being described here, with the *"State"* of Sanctification, which is actually an ongoing, progressive process. That which the believing sinner receives at Conversion is his *"Standing"* in Christ, and as stated, never changes, irrespective of the actual condition or situation of the Believer.

However, Sanctification as a progressive Work which it actually is, is an ongoing situation in the life of the Believer and deals with the Believer's State, which unfortunately, changes constantly. While the believing sinner is awarded a *"Standing"* because of his Faith, this in no way means that the actual *"State"* is as it ought to be. In fact, it never is. Consequently, the Holy Spirit sets about immediately, which in effect is a lifelong process, to bring the Believer's *"State"* up to his *"Standing."*

## THE NAME OF JESUS

The phrase, *"In the Name of the Lord Jesus,"* refers to the only manner in which one can be Saved.

It is The Lord Jesus Christ Who is God, but became Man in order to pay the terrible price for Redemption. Consequently, Salvation and anything else from God for that matter, is always *"In the Name of the Lord Jesus,"* for the simple reason, that He is the One Who paid the price for all that man has. In other words, He is *"The Man!"*

That is why Peter said, *"Neither is there Salvation in any other: for there is none other Name under Heaven given among men, whereby we must be Saved"* (Acts 4:12). That means there is no Salvation in Buddha, Confucius, Mohammed, Joseph Smith, Mary Baker Eddy, Mary Ellen White, or the Virgin Mary, or anyone else who might be named. Jesus is the Way to the Father, Jesus is the Way to Salvation, Jesus is the Way to Divine Healing, Jesus is the

NOTES

Way to the Baptism with the Holy Spirit, Jesus is the Way to Eternal Life, Jesus is the Way to More Abundant Life, Jesus is the Way to Heaven, and Jesus is the Only Way.

THE SPIRIT OF GOD

The phrase, *"And by the Spirit of our God,"* proclaims the Third Person of the Triune Godhead as the Mechanic in this great Work of Grace.

The Holy Spirit is the One Who superintends the Work of God in every capacity. Whenever the Word of God is preached to the lost sinner, it is the Holy Spirit Who anoints the Preacher to preach the Truth, and as well, convicts the sinner upon hearing the Word. In other words, He makes the sinner aware of his lost condition, and need for Redemption, found only in Jesus Christ. If the sinner is favorable toward the Word of God, even as the Holy Spirit convicts him, the Spirit of God as well grants to the sinner *"the measure of Faith,"* in order that he may have the capacity to believe and be Saved (Rom. 12:3).

From then on out in the Believer's life, it is the Holy Spirit Who makes real all that Jesus has done for the Believer. His Work at Salvation only begins. Taking up abode in the Life of the Believer, He then begins to work with the Believer, making him into the Image of the Heavenly, and does so according to cooperation by the Believer with Him. He is a Perfect Gentleman at all times, and will never violate the person's free moral agency, although He does impress, convict, seize, stir, and move upon. As well, another part of His Great Office Work, is to Glorify Christ, which He constantly does (Jn. 16:12-14).

(12) "ALL THINGS ARE LAWFUL UNTO ME, BUT ALL THINGS ARE NOT EXPEDIENT: ALL THINGS ARE LAWFUL FOR ME, BUT I WILL NOT BE BROUGHT UNDER THE POWER OF ANY."

The phrase, *"All things are lawful unto me,"* simply refers to the fact that Christianity is not a religion. Religion has all types of rules and regulations, while Christianity has none. Christianity is not a system of do's and don'ts, but rather, freedom and relationship in Christ.

Judaism was fraught with all types of laws and regulations, which were necessary for the obvious reason that men were being shown

NOTES

through the Law of Moses how to live, in other words, what was right and what was wrong. That having been established, and serving its purpose, is now no longer needed.

*"Lawful"* in the Greek is *"exesti,"* and means *"it is permitted."*

What does Paul mean by this statement other than what we have said, especially considering that he has just now listed particular sins which in fact, are not permitted respecting the Believer?

LED BY THE SPIRIT

The phrase, *"But all things are not expedient,"* explains what Paul means.

Upon coming to Christ the Divine Nature is implanted in the heart and life of the Believer by the Holy Spirit. Consequently, this New Nature completely changes the heart, life, and desires of the individual, in effect, making the person a *"New Creature in Christ Jesus"* (II Cor. 5:17-18). As well, the Holy Spirit comes in to abide in the heart and life of the Believer, giving the Believer whatever help is needed to live a life of Holiness and Godliness (I Cor. 3:16-17).

So now, the Believer is Spirit led, whereas before Conversion he was led by animal passions. As a result of the Divine Nature now implanted, the Believer's likes and dislikes instantly change. So, it is not a question of can or can't regarding the doing of certain things, but rather a question of following the Holy Spirit, Who is duty bound to lead the Child of God on the Path of Righteousness (Rom. 8:14).

The word *"expedient"* in the Greek is *"sumphero,"* and means *"profitable."* So, Paul is saying, that while these things mentioned, even as evil as they may be, are not unlawful to me as a Christian, still, they are in fact, very unprofitable. Knowing such, the Believer wants no part of these things of the world.

The phrase, *"All things are lawful for me, but I will not be brought under the power of any,"* tells us several things:

SIN AND GRACE

1. First of all, the abruptness with which the phrase, *"All things are lawful unto me,"* is introduced perhaps shows that, in the Letter of the Corinthians to Paul, they had used some such expression themselves, attempting to justify their ungodly actions. In other words, they

had taken Paul's Teaching on Grace, and had enlarged it to the place of including anything. They could sin all they wanted to and Grace covered it, and in fact, the more they sinned the more that Grace abounded, or so they thought.

It is not certain if I Corinthians or Romans was written first. However, if Paul wrote Romans first, he had just addressed this subject by asking the question, *"What shall we say then? Shall we continue in sin, that Grace may abound?"*

His answer to that was short and to the point, *"God forbid. How shall we, that are dead to sin, live any longer therein?"* (Rom. 6:1-2).

If he had not already written Romans, it would be written very shortly, in that both I Corinthians and Romans were written very close together.

It is sad when Believers attempt to twist the Word in order to provide them license to sin, when the intention of the Holy Spirit is the very opposite, liberty to live a Holy Life.

2. To the Believer it is not whether something is lawful or not, but rather whether it is profitable or right.

3. By Paul using the word *"power,"* we are told that sin is not something to be trifled with, even by Believers. If in fact, the Believer allows himself to engage in these sins, he will soon find himself bound by their power, and even though a Believer, he will find himself imprisoned just as quickly as the unbeliever. The Lord has promised to protect and keep us in all things, but not in a willful disregard for His Word, which has already pronounced what is right and what is wrong, i.e., *"The Ten Commandments."*

4. The freedom given and guaranteed in Christ, which in fact is its great strength, is not freedom to violate moral Truths. Using America as an example, its citizens are free, but not free to disregard its laws, and for all the obvious reasons.

5. The unbeliever has no choice in his direction, being a sinner he sins, consequently, led into all types of vices and passions. However, the Believer is not controlled by sin or the things of this world. Being a New Creature in Christ Jesus, he now has the power and liberty to chart a course which is the opposite of the old life once lived, and now which brings a satisfaction, fulfillment, and joy that defies all description. Previously, he was under the power of sin, but upon coming to Christ that power has been broken. Consequently, for one to come back under that power is stupidity of the highest order (Rom. Chpt. 6).

NOTES

(13) "MEATS FOR THE BELLY, AND THE BELLY FOR MEATS: BUT GOD SHALL DESTROY BOTH IT AND THEM. NOW THE BODY IS NOT FOR FORNICATION, BUT FOR THE LORD; AND THE LORD FOR THE BODY."

The phrase, *"Meats for the belly, and the belly for meats,"* was a statement the Corinthians had no doubt previously heard Paul use. In using the statement, Paul had directed attention no doubt to the Levitical ban regarding certain meats, etc.

The idea was and is, inasmuch as the Levitical Law had served its purpose respecting reasons which we will now not examine, with the Advent of Christ, these rulings were no longer applicable to Believers. In other words, what one ate was merely physical, with no spiritual content. Jesus Himself taught that it is not what people ingest that defiles them, but what comes from the heart that defiles them (Mk. 7:15-23).

However, some of the Corinthians were concluding all matters pertaining to the physical body as being in the same category as the eating of food. In other words, they were claiming that sexual relationships were no more immoral than eating because both were natural bodily functions. As stated, they had also apparently twisted Paul's emphasis on Grace to bolster this same kind of unscriptural mentality (Rossier).

## GREEK PHILOSOPHY

In fact, this dangerous mind-set was also a part of the Greek Philosophy of the day, which lumped all natural drives together; hence, prostitution was looked at as no more serious than eating. That is one reason for the degradation of the women of that day and one reason for the downfall of the Grecian Empire. The Greeks so dichotomized the body and the soul (separated the two) that they believed the natural functions of the body had no impact on the spiritual part of a person. Actually, the gnostics taught the same basic fallacy. So, these *"Doctrines of Devils"* had made their way into the Christian thinking of some in the Church in Corinth.

The phrase, *"But God shall destroy both it and them,"* refers to the digestive system of human beings which will be changed for Believers at

NOTES

the Resurrection. The Resurrection will make the physical body into a spiritual body, like that of the Angels of God (I Cor. 15:44, 51-52). How vile, then, is it to make a god out of the belly — only to sleep and feed! — in other words, like an animal?

THE PHYSICAL BODY AND FORNICATION

The phrase, *"Now the body is not for fornication, but for the Lord,"* refers to our bodily members which ought to be used *"as instruments of Righteousness unto God"* (Rom. 5:13). As well, our bodies are to be presented as a living, holy, reasonable, acceptable Sacrifice to God (Rom. 12:1). The end of our existence is *"to serve God here and enjoy Him forever hereafter"* (Farrar).

Consequently, the argument, which would class this sin (fornication) as a matter of indifference, as was the Levitical distinction between different kinds of food, at once fell to the ground. Food was a necessity, and the stomach was formed for its assimilation. However, fornication is not a necessity, but actually a perversion of the intention of God respecting the human body, and in fact, *"a deadly sin."* It is not a natural necessity, but a consuming evil. In fact, the body was created for higher ends — namely, to be a Temple of God.

Consequently, *"God hath not called us unto uncleanness, but unto Holiness"* (I Thess. 4:7) (Farrar).

The phrase, *"And the Lord for the body,"* in essence says that He will one day (at the Resurrection) change this vile body into a spiritual body. The idea is, that if we do not use our physical body for the Lord, actually making it a Living Sacrifice unto Him, He in turn will not resurrect it at the time to come, and for the simple reason that it is spiritually filthy. Paul said as much when he spoke of our bodies being Temples of the Holy Spirit, and that the person who *"defiled the Temple of God, him shall God destroy"* (I Cor. 3:16-17).

(14) "AND GOD HATH BOTH RAISED UP THE LORD, AND WILL ALSO RAISE UP US BY HIS OWN POWER."

The phrase, *"And God hath both raised up the Lord,"* proclaims the fact of the Coming Resurrection, by the fact of the Resurrection of Jesus Christ which has already occurred.

The phrase, *"And will also raise up us by His Own Power,"* carries the idea that the human body, not just the soul and spirit, belongs to God because it will also participate in the physical Resurrection of Believers. We will see many details about this Glorious Event in Chapter 15 of this Epistle.

This Chapter completely refutes the idea held by some, that when the Believer sins, it is only his physical body that sins, and not his soul and spirit. Others claim that it is the body and the soul but not the spirit. However, both arguments are baseless.

To attempt to separate the body from the soul and the spirit respecting right and wrong, is the same trap the Greeks fell into respecting their warped philosophy. Where their warped ideas may be somewhat forgivable respecting their ignorance, Believers are not ignorant, unless they choose to be, even as these Corinthians. Once again, the Holy Spirit is attempting to draw us toward Holiness, while all too often, we are attempting to go in the very opposite direction.

(15) "KNOW YE NOT THAT YOUR BODIES ARE THE MEMBERS OF CHRIST? SHALL I THEN TAKE THE MEMBERS OF CHRIST, AND MAKE THEM THE MEMBERS OF AN HARLOT? GOD FORBID."

The question, *"Know ye not that your bodies are the members of Christ?",* is rhetorical, in other words, demanding an affirmative answer. It could be translated, *"You do know, don't you, that your bodies are the members of Christ?"*

Elsewhere the union between Christ and Christians is described by the metaphor of a tree and its branches; a building and the stones of which it is composed (Eph. 2:21-22). In fact, Paul will say in Verse 20, *"For ye are bought with a price,"* which means we are not our own but in reality, belong to Him.

The question, *"Shall I then take the members of Christ, and make them the members of an harlot?",* constitutes every part of the physical body, which includes the sex organs, as belonging to the Lord Jesus Christ.

The phrase, *"God forbid,"* presents an admirable idiom to express the real force of the original, which means, *"May it never be!"* (Farrar).

WHAT THE BIBLE SAYS ABOUT IMMORALITY

The Bible is serious about sex sins. Adultery and its companion, fornication (sometimes translated *"prostitution"* or *"sexual immorality"*) are

NOTES

forbidden to God's people. Our Loving God rules out these practices for us. And in Scripture both *"adultery"* and *"prostitution"* sometime represent spiritual unfaithfulness to the Lord, which further emphasizes the perversion and wrong of these acts.

## THE NATURE OF ADULTERY AND PROSTITUTION

Two Hebrew words introduce us to God's view of heterosexual (a man and a woman) relationships outside of marriage.

*"Na'ap* (adultery)*"* is intercourse with one to whom one is not married. The Old Testament prohibition here is unequivocal: the Sixth Commandment states, *"You shall not commit adultery"* (Ex. 20:14; Deut. 5:18). Actually, the Law of Moses instructed Israel to put adulterers and adulteresses to death (Lev. 20:10). Both the inclusion of this prohibition among the Ten Commandments and the severity of the penalty, underline the importance of sexual faithfulness as a foundation to a healthy marriage and society.

*"Zanah"* is another Hebrew word which is translated *"fornication"* in some versions, and *"prostitution"* in others, or *"marital unfaithfulness"* in some modern versions. It occurs some 93 times in the Old Testament and refers not only to adultery, but as well to other elicit sexual practices such as homosexuality, incest, etc.

## ISRAEL AND THE SURROUNDING NATIONS

The Biblical commitment to sexual purity, which was so integral a part of God's Will for Israel, is striking in view of the role of sexuality in the other religions of the time and area. Those religions stressed fertility, and their rites often called for sexual orgies to stimulate the gods and goddesses and thus, ensure bountiful harvests, etc.

Consequently, ritual prostitution by men and women was also part of these religions, and the role of a religious prostitute was viewed as honorable, to be accepted by the respectable of society.

Pagan attitudes toward sexuality reflected the beliefs of the people about their gods and goddesses. The attitude of the Old Testament toward sexuality reveals the nature of God and the nature of God's relationship with His people. Pagan gods and goddesses were selfish and capricious, ruled by the passions that rule humans.

By contrast, the God portrayed in the Bible is not selfish nor untrustworthy: He is ruled by the Covenant Relationship He committed Himself to with Abraham.

Because sexual relationships between a man and a woman are intended to reflect the intimate relationship between God and His people, a Covenant of faithfulness between marriage partners is absolutely essential. Adultery and other sex relations outside of marriage violate something basic to the very nature of God and to our own nature as beings created in His Image.

Marriage, as an exclusive commitment, is the necessary context for sexual expression for God's people. Our faithfulness to that relationship is critical.

## SPIRITUAL ADULTERY OR PROSTITUTION

Regrettably, ancient Israel fell short of God's Call to sexual purity. The Israelites found the Pagan religions, with their open sensuality, all too attractive. The symbolic linkage of idolatry with the sexual sins that idolatry encouraged is found early — in Leviticus 17:7. There God warns the people that they *"must no longer offer any of their Sacrifices to the idols to whom they prostitute themselves."*

The later Prophets picked up the thought. Over and over the Prophets represented Israel's unfaithfulness to God in turning to idolatry as an act of spiritual adultery or prostitution (Jer. 3:1-9; Ezek. 23:1-45; Hos. Chpt. 4).

These terms are used in the same way in Revelation 2:20-22; 17:1-16. Consequently, the association of *"na'ap"* and *"zanah"* with idolatry, the most detestable of religious sins, shows how seriously God considers sex sins to be.

## THE MESSAGE OF HOSEA

The Prophet Hosea preached to Israel in the decades just before that Northern Kingdom was taken captive by Assyria (722 B.C.).

The people in the northern part of that divided land had been unfaithful to God for some 250 years and during that time had been led by 18 evil kings, many of whom imported Pagan religions and morals. In the first Three Chapters of his Book, Hosea tells his own story to Israel.

The Prophet was commanded by God to marry *"an adulterous wife"* (Hos. 1:2). The couple had children, but then the wife, Gomer, left home to live with a series of lovers. Hosea was called to bear the pain of this betrayal and finally was told: *"Go, show your love to your wife again, though she is loved by another and is an adulteress. Love her as the Lord loves the Israelites"* (Hos. 3:1).

To restore the shattered relationship, Hosea actually purchased his prostitute wife from the one who then owned her.

PARALLELS

The rest of the Book draws parallels between Hosea and Gomer's relationship and that of God and faithless Israel. Prostitute Israel had abandoned God and hurt Him deeply. But God continued to love them anyway. Israel's coming defeat by Assyria and subsequent exile would be a severe discipline for them, but God said, *"They will seek My Face; in their misery they will earnestly seek Me"* (Hos. 5:15). They were told to pray for restoration through forgiveness (Hos. 14:2). God promised to heal their waywardness (Hos. 14:4), and they would again become a faithful and fruitful people (Hos. 14:5-8).

THE MESSAGE

The Message of Hosea is a Message of pain and of healing. It is a triumphant affirmation of the Faithfulness of God.

Both sexual unfaithfulness and spiritual unfaithfulness tear at the basis of intimate interpersonal relationships and bring deep suffering. But God remains faithful to His wandering people, and He acts to restore.

The forgiveness and the inner transformation God offers all who will respond to Him is the key that makes all things possible — even the restoration of a shattered marriage and home.

ATTITUDES TOWARD IMMORALITY

The New Testament speaks just as strongly as the Old Testament against adultery and prostitution, i.e., immorality in any fashion. However, there is an important shift of rationale. There is a powerful new reason why sex outside of marriage is repugnant to the Lord. But some New Testament statements on adultery have often been misunderstood. The New Testament never suggests that adultery (moicheia) or prostitution (porneia) is acceptable. But it makes clear how we should deal with individuals who fall short.

NOTES

THOSE WHO ARE UNBELIEVERS

We must not avoid such persons who are outside the Christian fellowship. Paul told the Corinthians not to associate with *"sexually immoral people* (pornos)." Later he had to write and explain, even as we have been studying, that he did *"not at all mean"* to suggest withdrawal from *"the people of this world"* (I Cor. 5:10).

That would mean isolation from the very people Christians are called to lead to Jesus! Certainly Jesus did not avoid such persons; and as the story of the woman caught in the act of adultery illustrates, Jesus' first concern was to bring forgiveness and then, with it, release from the power of every kind of sin (Jn. 8:1-11).

AMONG BELIEVERS

There must be discipline respecting those who are Believers. Thus, sexual immorality in the fellowship is to be dealt with decisively by the Christian community, if repentance is refused (I Cor. 5:1-12).

The rationale is explained in I Corinthians 6:12-20, even as we are now studying. In a Christian's relationship with Jesus, the Believer is actually an organic part of the Lord's Body (a part of a living organism, in this case, Christ).

It is unthinkable that Christ would be involved with immorality. Thus, our bodies, linked with Jesus and being the Temples of the Holy Spirit, must be kept holy. We are to treat ourselves as holy instruments, to be used in God's Service and not involved in sexual sins.

Finally, Paul reminds us, *"You are not your own: you were bought with a price. Therefore honour God with your body"* (I Cor. 6:20).

THOSE WHO REJECT GOD

Judgment is coming, irrespective that the world does not believe it.

Sexual immorality is characteristic of those who reject God and the lifestyle of His Kingdom (II Pet. 2:14).

Those who practice immorality will be judged and excluded from the Eternal Kingdom, which is the Word of the Lord (I Tim. 1:10; Heb. 13:4; Rev. 21:8; 22:15).

## ADULTERY AND LUST OF THE HEART

Matthew quotes Jesus as saying, *"You have heard that it was said, 'Do not commit adultery.' But I tell you that anyone who looks at a woman lustfully has already committed adultery with her in his heart"* (Mat. 5:27-28).

What does this mean?

Is an appreciative glance at a member of the opposite sex a sin? Even the original words for *"longing look"* are not decisive in helping us interpret Jesus' meaning.

But the context is decisive. Jesus had just told His listeners that He came to *"fulfill"* (express the true meaning of) the Divine Law (Mat. 5:17). He warned that to come near Heaven's Kingdom one must have a Righteousness exceeding the Righteousness of the Pharisees. Jesus then explained by providing a series of illustrations.

The Law on which the Pharisees penned their hope of Heaven forbade murder, but Jesus shows that anger is the source of murderous intent (Mat. 5:21-22). The Law forbade adultery, but Jesus shows that adultery grows out of lust located in the heart (Mat. 5:27-28).

In His illustrations, Jesus shows that while Law is able only to help regulate behavior, God is concerned with the human heart. To live as members of the Heavenly Kingdom, something must be done about the anger that produces murder and the lust that leads to adultery.

## RIGHTEOUSNESS

Righteousness for Jesus' people is not simply a matter of what a person does or does not do. Righteousness is a matter of what a person is within. God's Kingdom can be entered and enjoyed only by those whose hearts are pure; the Pharisees' legalistic approach stressed actions but ignored the human heart.

In this context, then, Jesus is not speaking of appreciating beauty, nor even of momentary desire. Jesus is teaching us that we need to become the kind of individuals who do not perceive others as objects to be used but see them as persons to be respected and valued, even as they were originally created in the Image of God.

To fix our attention on another person and indulge in sexual fantasies about him or her (other than one's spouse) shows that God must still do much purifying work within our hearts.

NOTES

## GROUNDS FOR DIVORCE

It is commonly accepted in the Christian community, but wrongly we might add, that adultery provides Biblical grounds for divorce and subsequent remarriage.

Jesus said, *"But I say unto you, that whosoever shall put away his wife, saving for the cause of fornication, causeth her to commit adultery: and whosoever shall marry her that is divorced committeth adultery"* (Mat. 5:32; 19:9).

In His Statement, Jesus used the Greek *"porneia"* which means *"fornication,"* and then in the latter part of the verse He used the Greek word *"moicheia,"* which means *"adultery."* As we have already explained, fornication is different than adultery, including all types of sexual immorality such as prostitution (adultery committed over and over), forbidden marriages such as between relatives, incest, and all kinds of unnatural intercourse.

One must remember, that Jesus could have used the word *"moicheia"* in both cases, but He did not do so, instead using that word for fornication (the Hebrew equivalent).

The idea is this: Adultery is a hideous sin that can devastate a marriage, the most intimate of personal relationships. But adultery should not be viewed as grounds for an automatic termination of the relationship, but rather every effort should be made to bring the offending party to forgiveness and, thereby, reconciliation.

This Divine model is supported by the argument of two Chapters of Matthew's Gospel (Mat. 18 and 19). The sequence begins with a definition of greatness in God's Kingdom. We are to remember that all Christians who fall into sin are, like straying sheep, to be restored with joy, at least wherever and whenever possible.

We are to realize that we are like quarrelling children, and we must cover hurts with forgiveness. When it is hard to forgive, we are to remember that we ourselves have been forgiven an incalculable debt.

In fact, fornication is the only grounds for divorce other than desertion by an unbelieving husband or wife (I Cor. 7:12-15).

Fornication carries in its meaning all types of immorality such as homosexuality, incest, child molestation, continued adultery over and over, etc. As should be obvious, it is difficult, if not impossible, for someone to remain in such a relationship. Hence, Jesus said that fornication is grounds for divorce. However even then, every effort should be made to restore the marriage if at all possible. *"Grounds"* means only the pain of necessity.

As well, in Jewish thought and rightly so, Scriptural grounds for divorce always gave the right to remarry if so desired.

## THE COMMANDMENTS

Sexual intercourse of any nature outside of marriage is sin for both the married and the unmarried. God forbids it, for our good. The Commandments against adultery and sexual immorality are rooted deep in the Character of God. As a faithful and loyal person, we are to mirror His Faithfulness and show the same kind of loyalty in our relationships.

The serious nature of adultery is seen in references to it in the Old Testament and in Revelation as an illustration of the ultimate unfaithfulness, apostasy, and idolatry. The New Testament reinforces the serious nature of sex sins for Believers by reminding us that we are linked forever with Jesus and indwelt by the Holy Spirit.

Jesus has paid the ultimate price for us, and, as His Own people now, we are to commit our bodies to the Lord's service, not to serve sinful passions.

## THE WAY TO LIFE

As sexual beings we will experience the pull of temptation toward fornication or adultery. To surrender is not only wrong but also foolish. Like other sins, adultery erodes our character and brings guilt and suffering. As the Biblical Proverbs remind us, we need to be guided by the traditions of the Godly and the Commands of the Scripture, for they are *"the Way to Life, keeping you from the immoral woman, from the smooth tongue of the wayward wife. Do not lust in your heart after her beauty or let her captivate you with her eyes, for the prostitute reduces you to a loaf of bread, and the adulteress preys upon your very life"* (Prov. 6:23-26).

(The material on sexual immorality was derived from Lawrence O. Richards.)

(16) "WHAT? KNOW YE NOT THAT HE WHICH IS JOINED TO AN HARLOT IS ONE BODY? FOR TWO, SAITH HE, SHALL BE ONE FLESH."

NOTES

The one word question, *"What?"*, is meant to be given in exclamated surprise. In other words, how could anyone, especially a Believer, think that the Holy Spirit would sanction the terrible sin of fornication! But yet, this is exactly what some of the Believers, Spirit-filled Believers at that, were thinking at Corinth.

Considering that Paul was their Father in Christ, hence their Teacher, and that they were Spirit-filled as stated, this tells us something about human nature.

First of all, this tells us that the Believer cannot live off the consecration of someone else, which regrettably, millions attempt to do. Paul had remained at Corinth nearly two years, *"Teaching the Word of God among them"* (Acts 18:11). So, these new converts had been blessed with having the greatest instruction from the Word of God that anyone could have, as well as a Moving and Operation of the Holy Spirit which, no doubt, were absolutely unexcelled. And yet some of them drifted off into spiritual elitism and immorality.

How did they do this? Why did they do this?

## PERSONAL RELATIONSHIP WITH CHRIST

As we have already stated, the personal dedication and consecration of a Preacher, or anyone for that matter, will suffice only for that person, and cannot be extended to another. A perfect example is Judas.

This man had the privilege of walking side by side with Jesus for approximately three and one half years. He was privileged to observe the greatest panoply of Miracles the world has ever known. He experienced the Power of God as few human beings on Earth have ever experienced such Power. And yet, in the midst of the greatest Move of God the world had ever known, Judas lost his way, and regrettably and sadly, died lost.

First of all, a personal relationship with Christ is absolutely necessary if the person is to be what he ought to be in the spiritual sense. As well, it is absolutely impossible to have such a relationship without the individual having a concerted prayer life which includes the study of the Word of God. Those two necessities, the Bible and Prayer, are absolutely necessary, in other words, without such, the Believer becomes spiritually anemic and ultimately dies in a spiritual sense. As stated, most do not have that, which regrettably is by their own choice, and, consequently, they are sucker bait for whatever Satan is dishing up at the moment. That is the reason I plead with Believers to get these Commentaries and study them. I know that the information contained therein, will challenge one, spur one, and might even make one angry. Nevertheless, if the Believer keeps studying these, the Word of God will begin to take effect and in a positive sense.

The question, *"Know ye not that he which is joined to an harlot is one body?"*, involves an argument against this sin which is the most original and impressive that could have been used. To this Passage especially is due the tone taken by Christians as to these sins, at least the tone they certainly should take, which differed so totally from that taken by the heathen (Farrar).

The phrase, *"For two, saith He, shall be one flesh,"* is quoted from Genesis 2:24. This appeal, also offered by Jesus in Matthew 19:5, reaches back to the earliest admonition in the Garden of Eden, and, consequently, is equivalent to the rule that no intercourse between the sexes is free from sin except under the sanction of marriage. Incidentally, that speaks of marriage between a man and a woman.

It would seem that it would be unnecessary to make that stipulation, but America has gone so deep into sin, and because the Church has lost its way, that now even some Preachers are performing same sex marriages. Even as I dictate these notes (3-14-98), the Methodist Church has just given its sanction to one of its Preachers who performed a wedding ceremony a short time ago between two lesbians. To be frank, it would be difficult to imagine a more abominable sin — that of the homosexuals or that of the Preacher (Preacher?) who would officiate at such an abominable union.

(17) "BUT HE THAT IS JOINED UNTO THE LORD IS ONE SPIRIT."

The phrase, *"But he that is joined unto the Lord,"* indicates the closest possible union, which is symbolized by the sexual union of a Christian husband and wife.

As a husband and wife are joined together in holy matrimony, God intended from the beginning that sexual intercourse would effect the consummation of the marital bond (Gen. 2:24; Mat. 19:5-6). Just as a husband and wife become one flesh through this consummation, a person becomes one spirit with the Lord when that person experiences the New Birth (Rossier).

The phrase, *"Is one spirit,"* reflects in a sense, the same union with Christ, albeit in a spiritual sense, as a husband and wife have in a physical sense. As well, the Greek Text speaks of a continuous relationship with Jesus, even as a husband and wife should have a continuous relationship, at least until death.

(18) "FLEE FORNICATION. EVERY SIN THAT A MAN DOETH IS WITHOUT THE BODY; BUT HE THAT COMMITTETH FORNICATION SINNETH AGAINST HIS OWN BODY."

The phrase, *"Flee fornication,"* we must remember is an admonition, even a command, given by the Holy Spirit through the Apostle. There is no mistaking what is being said.

In the battle against sensual sins, there is no victory except in absolute flight, for the reason which immediately follows, namely, that these sins have their dwelling in that body which is a part or our being, and which yet they tend to destroy. In other words, they make a man his own deadliest enemy.

Is this sin worse than some other sins?

Sin is sin, but yes, some sins are worse than others, and the sin of fornication is one of those sins (Jn. 19:11). The idea is, that some sins have greater consequences than other sins. Having sexual intercourse outside of marriage joins one total being, not just the body, with another total being. The ultimate result is that a person becomes a bondslave to that which he joins himself. Bondage results from sexual impurity, and that bondage enslaves a person (Rossier).

## THE BODY

The phrase, *"Every sin that a man doeth is without the body,"* speaks of all sins other than fornication.

Some would argue that gluttony or drunkenness, or even drug addiction, is not without the body; however, that is incorrect. Even though they certainly affect the body, the cause and incentive to these sins are external, whereas the source of uncleanness is in the heart and in the thoughts which come from within, and so defile the man. Other sins may be with and by means of the body, and may injure the body, even as these we have mentioned, but none are so directly against the sanctity of the whole bodily being, spirit, soul and body, as fornication. In other words, fornication affects the entirety of the person's being.

It is so wicked because it perverts the type. And what do we mean by that?

As stated, God intends for the sexual union of husband and wife to be a type in the physical sense, of the spiritual union between Christ and the Believer. As should be obvious, the sexual union of a husband and wife is as close as one can possibly get, actually with both becoming one — joined together. In its purest form, which speaks of Love between a Christian husband and wife, it typifies the spiritual union with Christ as nothing else, hence the terrible degree of this sin.

The phrase, *"But he that committeth fornication sinneth against his own body,"* presents in the physical sense a type of the spiritual union of man with devils. That's the reason that God referred to Israel worshiping idols as *"spiritual adultery or fornication"* (Jer. 3:1-9; Ezek. 23:1-45; Hos. Chpt. 4). In fact, that is what John the Beloved was talking about in Revelation 17:1-2.

## SIN

Inasmuch as Paul has mentioned the word *"sin,"* and in one of its most wicked forms, perhaps it would be good if we could deal with this word as it is given in the New Testament.

There are nine different Greek words in the New Testament which present sin and its various aspects. They are, *"hamartia, hamartema, parakoe, anomia, paranomia, parabasis, paraptoma, agnoema, and hettema."*

### *"HAMARTIA"*

The word used most frequently in the New Testament, is *"hamartia."* This word in classical Greek never approaches the depth of meaning it has in the Bible. The Pagan Greeks used it of a warrior who hurls his spear and fails to strike his foe. It is used of one who misses his way.

*"Hamartia"* is used of a poet who selects a subject which is impossible to treat poetically, or who seeks to obtain results which lie beyond the limits of his art. The *"hamartia"* is a fearful and embarrassing mistake.

NOTES

It sometimes is employed in an ethical sense where the ideas of right and wrong are discussed, but it does not have the full significance of the Biblical content of the word. In the moral sphere, it had the idea of missing the right, of going wrong. In the classics, its predominating significance was that of the failure to attain in any field of endeavor.

Brought over into the New Testament, this idea of failing to attain an end, gives it the idea of missing the Divinely-appointed goal, a deviation from what is pleasing to God, doing what is opposed to God's Will, perversion of what is upright, a misdeed. Thus, the word *"hamartia"* means a *"missing of the goal conformable to and fixed by God."*

It is interesting to note that in Romans the word *"dikaiosune"* which means *"conformity to the standard"* appears as the opposite of *"hamartia,"* a missing of the Standard set by God (Rom. 6:16-18).

The noun *"hamartia"* is everywhere translated in the New Testament by the word *"sin"* except in II Corinthians 11:7, where it is rendered *"offence,"* since the context speaks of Paul's relations to the Corinthians.

### *"HAMARTEMA"*

The second word is *"hamartema."* This word differs from *"hamartia"* in that it *"is never sin regarded as sinfulness, or as the act of sinning, but only sin contemplated in its separate outcomings and deeds of disobedience to a Divine Law."* It is found in Mark 3:28; 4:12; Rom. 3:25; I Cor. 6:18.

### *"PARAKOE"*

The third word is *"parakoe."* It means *"a failing to hear, a hearing amiss,"* the idea of active disobedience which follows on this inattentive or careless hearing, being superinduced upon the Word.

The sin is regarded as already committed in the failing to listen when God is speaking. In the Old Testament, the act of refusing to listen to God is described as disobedience (Jer. 11:10; 35:17). In Acts 7:57 this is seen very clearly.

*"Parakoe"* is found in Romans 5:19; II Corinthians 10:6, and Hebrews 2:2, where it is translated by the word *"disobedience"* in each case.

What a flood of light is thrown upon Adam's original sin. He was careless about listening to the Commands of God, inattentive when God was speaking. Then followed the act of disobedience to the Divine Command. The lack of an earnest and honest attempt to know God's Will in any instance, is sin.

This carelessness or inattentiveness with respect to the Will of God, has its roots in the desire to have one's own way, and to cover up that desire and the consequent wrongdoing by the excuse that one did not know His Will in the particular instance.

### *"ANOMIA"*

The fourth word is *"anomia."* The word is a compound with the word *"nomos* (law)*"* and the letter Alpha which make the whole word mean literally *"no law."* The word means *"contempt or violation of law, lawlessness."* It refers to the condition or deed of one who is acting contrary to the Law.

It is set over against the Greek word *"dikaiosune* (Righteousness)*"* in II Corinthians 6:14. That is, *"What things does Righteousness have in common with 'anomia'* (lawlessness)*?"* The word *"dikaiosune"* refers to a fixed and objective Standard of life set up by God.

Any deviation from that Standard is an act contrary to Law, the Law of God. The word is used in classical Greek writings, joined with *"anarchia,"* which is defined as *"the state of a people without Government, without lawful Government, lawlessness, anarchy."*

The word is made up of *"archos," "a leader, a chief, a commander"* and *"alpha,"* the compound word meaning *"without a leader or commander."* Thus, anyone in a regularly constituted Government who does not recognize and obey that Government is *"anarchos,"* without Law, anarchist, thus, *"anomia,"* lawless.

The word is used in the New Testament, of one who acts contrary to Law. The word *"paranomia"* refers to the act of one going beyond the limits which the Law lays down. It is used only in II Peter 2:16. *"Anomia"* is found in the following places where it is translated either *"iniquity"* or *"the transgression of the Law"* (Mat. 7:23; 13:41; 23:28; 24:12; Rom. 4:7; 6:19; II Cor. 6:14; II Thess. 2:7; Titus 2:14; Heb. 1:9; 8:12; 10:17; I Jn. 3:4).

### *"PARABASIS"*

The next word is *"parabasis."* It comes from *"parabaino"* which means *"to step on one side"* thus, *"to transgress, violate."* It is translated by the word *"transgression"* in the New Testament, except in Romans 2:23 where one version has *"breaking the Law."*

Trench says of this word; *"There must be something to transgress before there can be a transgression. There was sin committed between the time of Adam and Moses, as was attested by the fact that there was death; but those between the Law given in Paradise (Gen. 2:16-17) and the Law given from Sinai, sinning indeed, yet did not sin 'after the similitude of Adam's transgression' (Rom. 5:14).*

*"With the Law of Moses came for the first time the possibility of the transgression of Law (Rom. 4:15)."*

This word is found in Romans 2:23; 4:15; 5:14; Gal. 3:19; I Tim. 2:14; Heb. 2:2; 9:15.

### *"PARAPTOMA"*

*"Paraptoma"* is our next word. This word comes from *"parapipto"* which means *"to fall beside"* a person or thing. Thus, *"paraptoma"* means *"a fall beside, a lapse or deviation from Truth and uprightness."*

Cremer defines the word as follows: *"A fault, a mistake, an offense, neglect, error."* He says that *"paraptoma"* does not in Scripture, as in profane Greek, imply palliation or excuse, . . . it denotes sin as a missing and violation of right . . . it may, therefore, be regarded as synonymous with *"parabasis,"* which designates sin as a transgression of a known and rule of life, and as involving guilt . . . still the word is not quite as strong as *"parabasis,"* . . . See for instance Galatians 6:1 . . . where, though a sin involving guilt is clearly meant, a missing of the mark, rather than a transgression of the Law, is the form of sin referred to there.

We must accordingly affirm that *"parabasis"* denotes sin objectively viewed, as a violation of a known rule of life, but that in *"paraptoma"* reference is specially made to the subjective passivity and suffering of him who misses or falls short of the enjoined command; and the word has come to be used both of great and serious guilt, . . . and generally of all sin, even though unknown and unintentional (Ps. 19:13; Gal. 6:1), so far as this is simply a missing of the right, and involves but little guilt, therefore, a missing or failure including the activity and passivity of the acting subject.

In Galatians 6:1 we have the case of Christians who, having been the subjects of the Ministry of the Holy Spirit, had in following the Teaching of the Judaizers, put themselves, thereby, under Law, and thus, had deprived themselves of the victory over sin which the Spirit had been giving them. They were trying their best in their own strength to live a life of victory over sin, and sin had taken them unawares.

Sin had entered their experience before they knew it, for they were shorn of the victorious power which they previously had.

This is *"paraptoma,"* a sin which was not on their part a deliberate or desirable disobedience of the Will of God, but an unintentional one committed through the inability to prevent it entering the life, due to attempting to overcome by means of the Law instead of Grace.

The word is found in the following places where it is translated *"trespass, offense, fall, fault"* (Mat. 6:14-15; 18:35; Mk. 11:25-26; Rom. 4:25; 5:15-18, 20; 11:11-12; II Cor. 5:19; Gal. 6:1; Eph. 1:7; 2:1, 5; Col. 2:13; James 5:16).

*"AGENOEMA"*

The next word is *"agenoema."* This word comes from *"agnoeo,"* a verb meaning *"to be ignorant, not to understand, to sin through ignorance."* Trench says of this word, *"Sin is designated as an 'agnoema' when it is desired to make excuses for it, so far as there is room for such, to regard it in the mildest possible light (Acts 3:17)."*

There is always an element of ignorance in every human transgression, which constitutes it human and not devilish; and which, while it does not take away, yet so far mitigates the sinfulness of it, as to render its forgiveness not in the necessary, but possible. Thus, compare the Words of the Lord, *"Father, forgive them, for they know not what they do"* (Lk. 23:34), with those of Paul. *"I obtained Mercy because I did it ignorantly, in unbelief"* (I Tim. 1:13).

Commenting on the usage of this word in Hebrews 10:26, the only place where it is used in the New Testament, Trench says, *"There is therefore an eminent fitness in the employment of the word on the one occasion referred to already where it appears in the New Testament. The 'agnoemata' or 'errors' of the people, for which the High Priest offered Sacrifice on the Great Day of Atonement, were not willful transgressions, 'presumptuous sins' (Ps. 19:13), committed against . . . conscience and with a high hand against God; those who committed such were cut off from the congregation; no provision having been made in the Levitical Constitution for the forgiveness of such (Num. 15:30-31), but they were sins growing out of the weakness of the flesh, out of an imperfect insight into God's Law, out of heedlessness and lack of due circumspection (. . . Lev. 4:13; compare 5:15-19; Num. 15:22-29), and afterwards looked back on with shame and regret."*

NOTES

*"HETTEMA"*

Our last word is *"hettema."* This word does not appear in classical Greek. A briefer form of the word, *"hetta,"* is used, and is opposed to *"nika* (victory)."

It means *"a discomfiture, a failure of victory."* It is used twice in the New Testament, in Romans 11:12 where it has the nonethical sense of diminution, decrease, and in I Corinthians 6:7 where it has the ethical sense of coming short of duty, a fault.

TO SUMMARIZE

Sin in the New Testament, is regarded as the missing of a mark or aim (hamartia or hamartema); the overpassing or transgressing of a line (parabasis); the inattentiveness or disobedience to a voice (parakoe); the falling alongside where one should have stood upright (paraptoma); the doing through ignorance of something wrong which one should have known about (agnoema); the coming short of one's duty (hettema); and the nonobservance of the Law of God (anomia).

(The statement on sin was derived from Kenneth Wuest.)

(19) "WHAT? KNOW YE NOT THAT YOUR BODY IS THE TEMPLE OF THE HOLY SPIRIT WHICH IS IN YOU, WHICH YE HAVE OF GOD, AND YE ARE NOT YOUR OWN?"

The question, summed up in one word, *"What?",* once again exclaims shocked surprise, but this time in the very opposite direction.

The first time this word is used by Paul in Verse 16, it speaks of the terrible sin of fornication, and how that the Believers at Corinth should have known how bad it actually is. Now he says they certainly should have known how holy their physical body actually is, inasmuch as it is now a Temple of the Holy Spirit. The word *"what"* in the Greek actually means *"by this time,"* in other words, you have been living for God long enough, that by this time you ought to know these things.

The beginning of the question, *"Know ye not that your body is the Temple of the Holy Spirit which is in you, . . . ?"*, actually refers to the human body of the one Born-again as being a Sanctuary of the Holy Spirit.

Without a doubt, this, the Holy Spirit making His home in the heart and life of the Believer, is the deepest and newest Truth of Christianity.

## TEMPLE

Three great Epochs are marked by the use of the word *"Temple"*:

1. In the Old Testament it means the material Temple, the sign of localized worship and a separated people, i.e., Israel.

2. In the Gospels our Lord uses it of His Own Mortal Body (Lk. 4:18-19; Jn. 1:33-34).

3. In the Epistles it is used (as here) of the physical body of every Born-again Believer, who is washed in the Blood, and Sanctified by the Indwelling Spirit of God.

As in the prior rebuke, so here two amazing statements are made: A. That the Lord exists for the Believer's body (vs. 13) — He ministers to it, He cherishes it, and He will raise it from the grave (vs. 14); and, B. That the Believer's body is a Sanctuary of the Holy Spirit. In fact, there is a tacit inference here in the Greek, that the human body was created for the purpose of being indwelt by the Holy Spirit. Therefore, a person does not have the right to defile that body in any way. That would speak of nicotine, alcohol, and other types of drugs, gluttony, as well as sexual impurity.

To understand the situation in a greater sense, Greek Philosophy which had been carried over into Roman practice, made sexual intercourse a part of the consecration to their so-called gods and goddesses. Great Temples were built for this very purpose, employing literally thousands of young men and young ladies as Temple prostitutes. In fact, as we have previously stated, it was an honor in those days, or so they thought, for a young lady or young man to be dedicated to this purpose.

As well, I might quickly add, that this evil debauchery did not begin with the Greeks, they only defined it more particularly, but actually began almost at the dawn of time. In fact, the Old Testament is full of references to this gross abomination, which also included human Sacrifice.

In effect, the Believers at Corinth, or at least some of the Believers, were succumbing to the same demonic activity as that practiced in the Temples at Corinth, and which had been a staple since the Fall. Consequently, the Apostle is showing them, which they should have known even as he said, the correct function of the human body — a Sanctuary for the Holy Spirit with all His attendant Holiness and Righteousness.

As well, the Apostle uses the emphatic *"in you,"* actually meaning that the physical body, which includes the soul and the spirit, becomes the domicile of the Holy Spirit. Nothing could be more holy, more wonderful, more gracious, more righteous, more sacred, and no one could be more privileged to have such than this of which we speak.

## OUR OTHER COMFORTER . . .

Due to the great significance of this vast subject, perhaps it would be helpful to give a little more instruction respecting that of which Paul speaks.

Our Lord was about to return to Heaven. The Disciples were troubled because the One Who had been their Guardian, Helper, Adviser, Strength-giver, was now leaving them. They thought that Jesus would leave them alone. But He told them that *"Another Comforter"* would come to their aid, even the Holy Spirit (Jn. 14:16-17).

The word *"Comforter"* is from a Greek word which means literally *"to call alongside."* It was used in the First Century of one called in to support another or give him aid. It was also a technical term to describe a Lawyer in the Greek Law Courts, one who was called in to aid the accused.

But in this case, we are not really dealing with Law, even the Law of Moses, for a Christian is not under the Law but under Grace. Therefore, the word here merely means *"one called in to help another."*

## ONE WHO COMES WITH STRENGTH

The word *"Comforter"* is a good translation if rightly understood. It comes from the Latin and means *"one who comes with strength."* To comfort in the sense of consoling one, is just one of the many Ministries of the Holy Spirit to the Believer. His many-sided Work can be summed up in the phrase, *"one called in to stand by and give aid."* The idea *"to stand by"* comes from the preposition which is part of this Greek word.

ANOTHER

The word *"another"* as in *"another Comforter"* is significant. There are two words in Greek which mean *"another,"* one referring to another of a different kind, and the other meaning *"another of the same kind."* Jesus uses this latter word.

The Holy Spirit is a Helper of the same kind as Jesus. The Holy Spirit is a Divine Person just like our Lord and has the same attributes and qualities.

TEMPLE

Paul says in this very verse we are now studying, *"What? know ye not that your body is an Inner Sanctuary of the Holy Spirit Who is in you, Whom ye have from God, and that ye are not your own?"*

There are two words in Greek translated *"Temple,"* one referring to the Temple in its entirety, the other speaking of the Inner Sanctuary. The latter is used here.

The physical body of each Saint is an Inner Sanctuary in which the Holy Spirit has come to take up His permanent abode. In fact, it is actually the same as the *"Holy of Holies"* in the Tabernacle and Temple of the Old Economy of God.

The Truth of the fact that the Holy Spirit resides permanently in the body of the Believer is from the word translated *"dwelleth"* in James 4:5. Thus, our Great Helper, the One Jesus called to the aid of the Believer when He left this Earth, has taken up His permanent residence in our hearts to stand by, ready to render instant help at any time.

WILLING COOPERATION

But He comes to the help of the Saint when that Saint expresses a desire for that help and trusts Him to render that help. Our Lord says (Jn. 7:37-38), *"If any man thirst, let him come unto Me and drink. He that believeth on Me, as the Scripture hath said, out from his inmost being shall flow rivers of Living Water."* John says that the Living Water refers to the Holy Spirit.

NOTES

Our Lord sent the Holy Spirit to come to our aid. Now He lays down the necessary procedure for the Believer to follow in order to avail himself of that aid.

DEPENDENCE ON THE HOLY SPIRIT

The Christian life is not a life of self-effort but of dependence upon the Holy Spirit to put sin out of our life and to produce His Fruit in us. He does that as we desire Him to do that and trust Him to do that.

As we fulfill these two requirements, dependence on Him and the producing of His Fruit in us, we are then literally filled with the Spirit in every sense.

The Holy Spirit is constantly working in and for the Believer who is filled with the Spirit. Only in that way can He give us aid. The Holy Spirit is God's Provision for living a life pleasing to Him.

Of course, the Holy Spirit has many other Ministries which He carries out in the heart and life of the Believer, but this for now is that of which Paul speaks.

The phrase, *"Which ye have of God,"* means that this astounding Work of the Holy Spirit living and abiding within our hearts and lives, is totally of God and none of man. Actually, it was all made possible by what Jesus did at Calvary and the Resurrection. He paid the terrible sin debt owed by man, a debt incidentally which man could not pay, and by Faith in that, the believing sinner removes all negative claims of God (the debt rightly owed to God), which also gave Satan a claim as well. With the sin debt hanging over man, Satan had the legal right to hold man in bondage. However, when Jesus removed that debt, not only were the Claims of God satisfied, but the claims of Satan were also made completely ineffective. As a result of the believing sinner now being sin free (debt free), the Holy Spirit can now come and abide permanently within the heart and life of the Believer.

As stated, and as should be obvious, it is all of God.

The conclusion of the question, *"And ye are not your own?"*, refers to the fact that the Believer has not been bought with a price such as silver or gold, but with the Precious Blood of

Christ; he is, therefore, a slave, but a slave in a totally different sense of the word than he had been previously to Satan. Consequently, his physical body has been redeemed, along with his soul and spirit, not for the purpose of practicing impurity, but by saintly conduct for Glorifying God.

Inasmuch as we are not our own, and because Jesus purchased us, we cannot, therefore, use our bodies as though they were absolutely under our own control. They belong to God, and, *"whether we live or die, we are the Lord's"* (Rom. 14:8).

(20) "FOR YE ARE BOUGHT WITH A PRICE: THEREFORE GLORIFY GOD IN YOUR BODY, AND IN YOUR SPIRIT, WHICH ARE GOD'S."

The phrase, *"For ye are bought with a price,"* refers as is obvious to the price paid by Christ at Calvary and the Resurrection (Acts 20:28; Heb. 9:12; I Pet. 1:18-19; Rev. 5:9).

The word *"price"* as it is used here in the Greek is *"time,"* and means *"a value of something paid, something very precious, to pay a ransom."*

The word *"price"* carries with it the idea of something so valuable, in this case the Shed Blood of Jesus Christ at Calvary, that it is absolutely impossible for mere mortals to comprehend or grasp the significance of the worth of such. When we consider that this *"price"* included God literally becoming Man, in a sense the Creator becoming the Creation, which within itself is incomprehensible, we then at least begin to grasp, at least in some small measure, the absolute infinitude of such a price. As well, this great price paid, has its full and absolute applicability to man, in other words it was all done for man and sinful man at that.

EFFECT!

The effect of Christ's Death for us is that we are redeemed from slavery and prison, and, consequently, the right of our possession is with Christ.

Actually, the price was paid to God, for it was to God that the debt was owed. Man had sinned against God, in his disobedience to God, in effect the creature joining with Satan in his rebellion against God.

Some Christians erroneously think that Jesus paid a debt owed to Satan, but that is not correct. The terrible debt was owed to God, and Jesus by His Death paid that debt.

NOTES

However, even though the debt was paid to God to Whom it was rightly owed, the believing sinner was purchased from Satan. As we have already stated, due to this sin debt, Satan could legally lay a claim on all of mankind, which he did.

One would think that due to the fact that this debt was owed to God, that the one who owed the debt, namely man, would also belong to God. In a sense, that is true; however, God could not accept man even though in a sense he belonged to Him, because man was sinful and polluted. Due to this fact, Satan had the legal right to imprison man, which he did.

AN EXAMPLE

An analogy would be of a great debt owed to a Bank, with a great building put up as collateral. When the owners of the building through bankruptcy were unable to meet the notes, the Bank then stepped in to take possession. However, they found that the structure was worthless due to termites having eaten into its very foundation.

Due to this condition, the City condemns the building, it then being vacated by all tenants, in effect abandoned. As a result, many undesirables begin to take up abode in the structure, winos, drug addicts, etc. In effect, they lay a pseudo claim to the building because it has been abandoned, and because of its detestable condition.

The Bank can now do one of two things: A. It can give up the project, and write it off as a total loss; or, B. It can spend whatever amount of money is necessary to make the building livable once again. It elects to do the latter.

At great price, the Bank completely guts the structure, making it completely new inside, even into its very foundation, which of necessity drives out the winos, drug addicts, etc. It can now be occupied by worthwhile tenants.

The illustration is crude, but perhaps applicable to the situation. Satan, as the winos and drug addicts, has no real claim on the building, i.e., *"man."* He can only take up abode in this *"building"* (our physical bodies, hearts, and lives), due to the infestation of sin which has made this building unlivable for the Lord. Once the price has been paid to restore the project, and it was paid by Jesus Christ, the Holy Spirit can now make His abode in this building, i.e., Temple called *"man."*

The phrase, *"Therefore Glorify God in your body,"* continuing to use the metaphor of the building, refers to the structure. As such a building would certainly not allow winos and drug addicts to inhabit the place, now that it has been completely refurbished by its owners, we are not to allow anything in our physical bodies which would defile. Once again, we speak of nicotine, alcohol, drugs which bring on addiction, sexual immorality, etc.

## YOUR SPIRIT

The phrase, *"And in your spirit,"* refers to the use of the building. In other words, for what is the building being used?

Even though such a structure may not allow in its confines the like of winos or derelicts, but still if the building was used for unlawful transactions in whatever capacity, its use certainly would not be proper. It is the same with Believers.

To Glorify God in our spirit, refers to the use being that which is Holy and Righteous.

When Jesus cleansed the Temple in Jerusalem, He was able to deal with it as a *"Body,"* i.e., the driving out of the moneychangers, etc., but He was not able to deal with the spirit of the Temple, for the simple reason that it was controlled by the Jewish Sanhedrin, which was evil. For the Temple to be put to proper use, it would in effect, have to change ownership. That it refused, and, consequently, it was destroyed in A.D. 70. In effect, that is exactly what the Lord said He would do to the Temple of our bodies, if they are unrighteously used (I Cor. 3:16-17).

If one is to notice, many religions attempt to clean up the body, concerning dress, rituals, ceremonies, etc. However, they are unable to do anything with the *"spirit of man,"* their efforts applying only to the externals. So, even though they may look as if to be righteous on the outside, due to that alone being addressed, there is really no change within their lives, due to the heart not being changed.

God first of all deals with the spirit of man, which in effect changes the outward, i.e., *"body."* That is the reason, if the Church attempts to effect Holiness from the outside in, it always fails, as fail it must. Holiness can only be perfected, as it comes from within (the spirit of man), and then works its way outward.

NOTES

If one is to notice, the Holy Spirit through the Apostle deals with matters which come from the spirit, and not the externals only. That's the reason that Churches are foolish attempting to define Holiness by not wearing jewelry, or the wearing of certain types of clothing, or participation in certain types of religious rituals and ceremonies, etc. For the *"body"* of man to take its proper place and to conduct itself properly, the spirit of man must be addressed first of all. If we Glorify God inwardly (the spirit), we will Glorify God outwardly, i.e., *"the physical body."*

The phrase, *"Which are God's,"* refers to man belonging to Him, first of all because God is the Creator of man, but in the sense of which Paul here speaks, Jesus has paid a great price for man. Consequently, we now belong to God, and should conduct ourselves accordingly. Everything we think, do, or say, should be done with the attitude of pleasing Him, and in effect, seeking His Leading and Guidance as to what we should do in all things. Inasmuch as the Holy Spirit now lives within us, there is no excuse for us going off track, as He is there to lead and guide (Jn. 16:7-15). As stated, He is our Helper, Leader, Guide, Guardian, Sustainer, Strength-giver and Power. How so much we are honored and privileged to have Him. God help us to conduct ourselves accordingly!

*"Holy Spirit, Faithful Guide, ever near the Christian's side,*
*"Gently lead us by Thy Hand — pilgrims in a desert land;*
*"Weary souls forever rejoice, while they hear that sweetest Voice*
*"Whispering softly 'Wanderer, come; follow Me, I'll guide thee home.'"*

*"Ever present, truest friend, ever near Thine aid to lend,*
*"Leave us not to doubt and fear, groping on in darkness drear;*
*"When the storms are raging sore, Hearts grow faint and hopes give o'er,*
*"Whisper softly, 'Wanderer, come; follow Me, I'll guide thee home.'"*

*"When our days of toil shall cease, waiting still for sweet release,*
*"Nothing left but Heaven and Prayer, trusting that our names are there;*
*"Waiting deep the dismal flood, pleading naught but Jesus' Blood,*

*"Whisper softly, 'Wanderer, come! Follow Me, I'll guide thee home.'"*

## CHAPTER 7

(1) "NOW CONCERNING THE THINGS WHEREOF YE WROTE UNTO ME: IT IS GOOD FOR A MAN NOT TO TOUCH A WOMAN."

The phrase, *"Now concerning the things whereof ye wrote unto me,"* presents Paul now addressing himself to the questions which had been asked in the letter sent to him concerning certain particulars. In this Chapter he will deal with questions respecting marriage and divorce, etc.

He has spent six Chapters in dealing with situations which were very serious, but yet had not been mentioned in the letter. Such is the natural heart! It eagerly discusses social, ecclesiastical, and even doctrinal questions, but it is blind to personal moral faults (Williams).

The phrase, *"It is good for a man not to touch a woman,"* needs background in order to understand where the Apostle is coming from.

Considering the party spirit which prevailed at Corinth, and which Paul has amply addressed, there were diversities of opinion concerning marriage.

Looking at his statements in I Corinthians 9:1-6, it is deducible that Paul's opponents at Corinth argued that he could not be an Apostle because he was unmarried. They evidently argued that to be celibate was to be a rebel against God's Marriage Laws (Gen. 2:23-24). Therefore, they concluded Paul was a rebel, and celibacy was an unholy and immoral condition.

The Apostle replies that such is not sinful, as some of these Corinthians were concluding, but in fact, under certain situations which certainly applied to him, the unmarried state could even be good.

Others evidently were going in the opposite direction, disparaging matrimony as involving an inevitable moral stain.

### THE SPIRIT OF GNOSTICISM

Man has two problems: A. First of all, he finds it easy to believe a lie; and, B. Second, he has a tendency to pervert Truth in either direction until it becomes heresy. No doubt, some of the Corinthians had perverted Paul's Teaching on Grace, making liberty a cloak for lasciviousness. Others, as stated, went overboard in the other direction.

Gnosticism, and the spirit which led to it, oscillated between the two extremes of asceticism on one hand (practicing strict self-denial as a measure of personal and especially spiritual discipline), and uncleanness (sexual immorality).

Both extremes were grounded on the assertion that matter (the flesh) is inherently evil. Ascetic Gnostics, therefore, strove to destroy by severity every carnal impulse. In other words, all sexual activity even between a husband and wife was evil, etc.

On the other hand, a certain type of Gnostic Teaching, argued that the life of the spirit was so utterly independent of the flesh that what the flesh did was of no consequence. In other words, they taught that it didn't matter what a person did, whether adultery, fornication, drunkenness, etc., that it was only the flesh that did these things, which consequently did not touch the spirit of man. They argued that whereas matter (the flesh) was already evil, any particular acts of immorality committed, did not make it more evil, etc. So they concluded that these things were not sinful to the spirit of man.

### THIS SAME SPIRIT PRESENTLY

Some presently, not understanding the sin nature in man, even Believers, in a similar manner teach the same thing.

They claim that the Born-Again experience only involves the soul, and the spirit and not the body. In other words, the soul and the spirit are Saved but the body isn't. Even though most of those who teach this erroneous Doctrine, do not condone immorality, still, they claim that the body is being Saved, but will not know full Redemption until the Resurrection.

Others teach that while the spirit is Saved, the soul and the body are not, or at least they are being Saved. They are actually, as is obvious, separating one from the other.

### THE TRUTH

Even though the spirit, soul, and body of man, which actually constitute man, are definitely different in their functions, still, what happens

NOTES

to one happens to all three. Paul said as much in I Thessalonians 5:23, *"And the Very God of Peace Sanctify you wholly; and I pray God your whole spirit and soul and body be preserved blameless unto the coming of our Lord Jesus Christ."* As is obvious here, he places no difference in the three respecting the Salvation experience.

The only time the Bible teaches a separation of the body from the soul and the spirit, is at death. At that time the body remains on Earth, going back to dust, while the soul and the spirit, at least of the Redeemed, go to be with the Lord (Gen. 3:19; Ps. 103:14; 104:29; Eccl. 3:21; I Cor. 15:35, 38; Phil. 1:23).

Whenever a person sins, whether Believer or unbeliever, it affects the spirit, soul, and body of man alike. There is no such thing as the body sinning and the soul and the spirit not sinning.

As stated, this false Teaching springs from a misunderstanding respecting the sin nature. In fact, the people who teach that the body sins and not the soul and the spirit, pretty well deny the existence of a sin nature; therefore, denying this Truth, they cast about for other explanations respecting the spiritual frailty of the human body.

WHAT IS THE SIN NATURE?

The answer is found in Romans, Chapters 6, 7, and 8.

In brief, the sin nature or evil nature of man is the result of the Fall of man in the Garden of Eden. This is the driving force of evil in man which makes him what he is in the realm of sinfulness, wickedness, and iniquity. Romans, Chapters 1 and 3 grandly describe this nature. It is not a very pretty sight. It is the cause of all wars, murders, man's inhumanity to man, etc.

Upon Redemption, the believing sinner is *"Born Again,"* in effect, becoming a *"New Creature in Christ Jesus"* (II Cor. 5:17). But yet, the Lord allows the sin nature to remain in the Believer, although isolated. In other words, it no longer controls the Believer as it once did before Conversion. In fact, in its isolation it need not cause the Believer any problem; however, all of us have found that sometimes it does not remain in isolation and for varied reasons.

As an example, if the Believer begins to rely on the flesh, in other words his own self-will or strength, invariably he will fail God, in other words, sin. When this happens, the sin nature springs to life, even as it was before Conversion, and if not handled according to the Word of God, the Believer can find himself being dominated by sin exactly as he was before Conversion. Were this not so, why would Paul have said, *"For sin shall not have dominion over you: for you are not under the Law (Law of Moses), but under Grace"* (Rom. 6:14).

Were it not possible for sin to have dominion over a Believer, for Paul is speaking of Believers, then his statement makes little sense.

As well, he also said, *"Let not sin* (sin nature) *therefore reign in your mortal body, that ye should obey it in the lusts thereof"* (Rom. 6:12).

In this statement he tells us that the *"sin nature"* while remaining in the Believer, is not to *"reign"* or *"dominate"* the Believer. In fact, Paul is not speaking here of acts of sin, but actually the *"sin nature."*

Paul knew exactly what he was talking about, having learned the answer to this problem the hard way. This is the reason that he said in the 24th Verse of the Seventh Chapter of Romans, *"O wretched man that I am! Who shall deliver me from the body of this death?"*

After being Saved and Baptized with the Holy Spirit, Paul thought surely that he could live the perfect life. He then found himself doing the very opposite, even as Romans, Chapter 7 proclaims, hence, his startling exclamation in Verse 24.

However, the Lord showed him how to have victory over the flesh, which he gives to us in Romans, Chapters 6 and 8. Consequently, he said, *"I thank God through Jesus Christ our Lord"* (Rom. 7:25).

No, Romans, Chapter 7 is not a description of Paul before Conversion as many teach, but rather his struggle after Conversion to find the answer to this perplexing problem.

WHY DID THE LORD LEAVE THE SIN NATURE IN THE BELIEVER?

Knowing and understanding that it is the human body through which the sin nature works, some have come to the erroneous conclusion, even as we are here studying, that the body must be evil. No, within itself, the body is not evil. It is merely an instrument, which can be used for either Righteousness or unrighteousness, hence Paul saying, *"Neither yield ye your members* (the members of your physical body) *as instruments of unrighteousness unto sin: but yield yourselves* (your physical members) *unto God, as those that are alive from the dead, and your members as instruments of Righteousness unto God"* (Rom. 6:13).

So, as stated, the physical body is not evil within itself, refuting the contention of the Gnostics that all matter is evil, but rather neutral. In other words, it can be used for bad things or good things, i.e., *"unrighteousness or Righteousness."*

## DISCIPLINE

The Lord allows the sin nature to remain in the life of the Believer as a discipline measure. In other words, when the Believer finds that through his own self-efforts he cannot overcome sin, but that his own efforts only make matters worse (activates the sin nature), he then turns to the Lord throwing himself on God's Mercy and Grace. To be frank, were it not for this ever-present discipline in the Believer, man would easily become so puffed up thinking it is his own strength bringing about his victory, that he would soon be telling the Lord how to operate His Kingdom. Consequently, man must be constantly reminded of his personal weakness, and how that within himself he cannot hope to overcome the Evil One, and must depend totally and completely on the Lord at all times, in other words depending on the Grace of God, which to be frank he would not do, were it not for the constant reminder of the sin nature. Of course, we are speaking totally of Believers and not unbelievers.

So it is for our discipline that the Lord allows this thing to remain and in a sense, keeps us depending totally upon Him for the maintenance of victory.

Getting back to Paul's original statement of it being good for a man not to touch a woman, Paul is using the word *"touch"* as a euphemism for sexual intercourse. Actually we will see the adjective *"good"* used a number of times in this Passage. It does not mean morally superior, but it does mean commendable in certain situations.

## THE CATHOLIC CHURCH

The Catholic Church claims from this Passage, their Doctrine of the celibacy of their Priests. However, what they fail to see, is that in Verse 26, Paul limits what he says concerning

NOTES

this particular situation by the clause, *"Good for the present necessity."* He was speaking of the Roman oppression, which would only grow more severe in the coming days.

Actually there are two specific areas that cause tremendous difficulty in the personal lives of Catholic Priests: A. The first is the consumption of alcoholic beverage (wine) that is required during the performance of the Mass. This has resulted in a tragic rate of alcoholism among Priests; and, B. The second is the matter of mandatory celibacy.

Former Priest Bartholomew F. Brewer tells of one of his first experiences in hearing confession. He says:

*"When I slid back the door covering the opaque screen between the penitent and me, a man's voice on the other side gave the standard opening: 'Bless me, Father, it has been two weeks since my last confession. I confess to Almighty God, to the Blessed Virgin Mary, to Blessed Michael the Archangel, to Blessed John the Baptist, to the Holy Apostles Peter and Paul, to all the Saints and to you, Father, that I have sinned exceedingly in word, thought, and deed, through my fault, through my fault, through my most grievous fault.' He then went on to say, 'I am a Catholic Priest and here are my sins.'"*

What followed was a lengthy and graphic description of one sexual affair after another. His confession was a detailed account of a series of seductions and conquests in rapid succession.

## THE REAL REASON

The Catholic Church demands that the Office of Priest not be consistent with sexual relationships. It should be pointed out, however, that celibacy is not supported by any Scripture. It is against nature, and the Apostle Peter (who is supposedly the role model for all Popes) was definitely married. Over the centuries a number of Popes, in fact, have been married.

The actual purpose for the imposition of celibacy on the Priesthood is that Rome wishes to have total control of the labor, money, property, and actions of every Catholic Priest, Monk, and Nun. All the arguments in the world will not dispel this one simple fact alone.

Bartholomew Brewer continues:

*"The system of celibacy is utterly mischievous and the cause of much immorality and aberrant behavior — including homosexuality."*

It is certainly to be admitted and regrettably so, that drunkenness and immorality have their place as well, in the Ministry of Protestantism; however, I think if the Truth be known, it is not even remotely as widespread as among the Catholic Priesthood, and for the obvious reasons.

(2) "NEVERTHELESS, TO AVOID FORNICATION, LET EVERY MAN HAVE HIS OWN WIFE, AND LET EVERY WOMAN HAVE HER OWN HUSBAND."

The phrase, *"Nevertheless, to avoid fornication,"* presents Paul by this one statement refuting all the dangerous and unwarrantable inferences drawn by some.

For instance, Jerome who lived not so long after the Early Church (during the time of Augustine) concluded from Paul's statement, *"If it is good for a man not to touch a woman, it must be bad to do so, and therefore celibacy is a holier state than marriage."* Such reasoning shows:

1. The danger of pressing words to the full extent of the logical inferences which may be deduced from them.

2. The errors which always arise from arguing upon isolated texts dissevered from their context, and from all consideration of the circumstances under which they were written.

3. The necessity of following the guidance of the Holy Spirit when He shows, by history and experience, the need for properly interpreting such statements as may be given, even as here, with reference to altered conditions.

There is in celibacy a moral beauty, that is if it is called for by the Holy Spirit. But in most cases marriage, being no less a duty, even as Paul proceeds to show, is even fairer and more excellent. Neither state, the wedded or the unwedded is in itself more holy than the other. It is rather what the Holy Spirit wants and desires in certain cases.

For the far greater majority, and in fact almost all, marriage will be that which is the Plan of God; however, with some few, even as with Paul, the Holy Spirit may desire the opposite. It is following Him in obedience which provides the Blessing, in other words, the Will of God.

Those who make Paul judge slightingly of marriage contradict his own express rules and statements as given by the Holy Spirit through him (Eph. 5:24, 31-32; I Tim. 2:15). As well, the following contributes to this direction:

NOTES

1. Jesus beautified with His Presence the marriage at Cana of Galilee. Actually, it was here where He performed His first Miracle (Jn. 2:1-2).

2. We go back to the primary Law which is said by the Lord, *"It is not good for man to be alone"* (Gen. 2:18).

3. The fact of marriage is chosen by the Holy Spirit to serve as a symbolism of the relation between Christ and His Church.

## FORNICATION?

Some have argued that Paul takes a *"low"* and *"poor"* view of marriage by regarding it only in the light of a remedy against fornication. However, Paul is not here addressing himself to the idealized and spiritual aspect of marriage, which is a very precious and special thing, but only of large practical necessities. Actually, when he speaks of marriage as a high Christian mystery as in II Corinthians 11:2 and Ephesians 5:22-33, he adopts a very different tone.

He is actually speaking of the masses of mankind without God, in which without the benefit of marriage, fornication would be even worse than it presently is, even on a pandemic scale.

The phrase, *"Let every man have his own wife, and let every woman have her own husband,"* is here given as a rule, and not a mere permission.

As stated, he is here addressing himself to the entirety of humanity and not just to the Church.

(3) "LET THE HUSBAND RENDER UNTO THE WIFE DUE BENEVOLENCE: AND LIKEWISE ALSO THE WIFE UNTO THE HUSBAND."

The phrase, *"Let the husband render unto the wife due benevolence,"* presents something revolutionary for that particular day. Females generally had no rights of their own, but the Holy Spirit through the Apostle guarantees these rights.

The word *"benevolence"* in the Greek is *"eumoia,"* and means *"good will and kindnesses."* As it is used here, it refers to the husband respecting the sexual needs of his wife, and to meet them accordingly. In other words, he is Scripturally obligated to do so, that is if he desires to please the Lord.

The phrase, *"And likewise also the wife unto the husband,"* proclaims the same duty imposed upon the wife regarding the husband.

Both men and women have sexual needs, which means that the husband and the wife are to satisfy each other, at least as it regards that which is lawful. If this is ignored, one may be responsible for the infidelity of the other, but this does not excuse the infidelity.

## AS THE BIBLE ADDRESSES SEX

In the following statement we will look specifically at the sexual nature of human beings and how this nature is to find expression.

Both Testaments tend to speak indirectly about sex. This does not suggest a negative attitude or an attitude of shame toward sexuality. It simply means that the sexually implicit speech of our day and of other cultures in Bible times was not used in the Scriptures.

Sexual matters are dealt with openly but in a vocabulary that honors the privacy of the male and the female. The Bible does not trivialize sex.

## A EUPHEMISM

A euphemism is the substitution of an agreeable or inoffensive expression for one that may offend or suggest something unpleasant.

For instance, the euphemism in the Bible for having sexual intercourse is *"to know."* The Hebrew reads, *"Adam knew his wife"* (Gen. 4:1). *"To know"* is *"yada"* in the Hebrew.

The Hebrew word *"sakab"* which means *"to lie down"* is also used to describe sexual intercourse (Gen. 34:7; Num. 31:17-18). References to illicit sexual activity are often expressed as to *"uncover* (galah) *the nakedness"* of someone. This Hebrew expression is found in Leviticus, Chapters 18 and 20. The phrase *"Become one flesh"* also implies intercourse, though the phrase suggests much more.

As well, the Bible does not refer directly to genital areas. While specific terms are used in speaking of the female breast (Song of Sol. 1:13; 4:5; 7:3, 7-8; 8:1, 8, 10), no specific terms are used for the male or female members otherwise.

The restraint of Scripture is striking in view of the explicit nature of the poetry and religious verse of surrounding Pagan Nations of Bible times. There is an affirmation in the Bible of the sexual nature of human beings and a deep appreciation for sexuality.

But the whole subject is carefully guarded, lest the mystery be lost and the special nature of sexual relationships be made to seem commonplace or unholy.

NOTES

## SEX OUTSIDE OF MARRIAGE

Sexual expression outside of marriage — both adultery and fornication — is forbidden.

Homosexuality and intercourse with animals are strictly forbidden (Lev. 18:22-23). Prostitution is also forbidden.

Although polygamy (more than one wife) was practiced in Old Testament times, the Divine ideal remained the one provided in the Creation model: a husband joined to one wife for life.

The Bible does not deal with masturbation; however, inasmuch as masturbation is almost impossible without immoral fantasizing, the nature of that practice is sinful as well.

## SEX WITHIN MARRIAGE

When we turn to questions of sex within marriage, we find, not restriction, but freedom. Sexual activity outside of marriage is tightly regulated, in other words forbidden. There is no such regulation of sexual practices of married couples within bounds of decency. By that we refer to oral sex.

Oral sex even between a husband and his wife tends toward uncleanliness and perversion. Even though not specifically dealt with in Scripture, propriety (the standard of what is principally acceptable in conduct or speech) mitigates against the practice. As well, the employ of pornography in any capacity, whether in print or by film or tape, even between a husband wife is wrong, and for the obvious reasons. To provide the material, whether on paper or the screen, other parties have had to engage in that which is ungodly.

We are living in a sensual age with unlawful conduct (unlawful according to the Scriptures) becoming more and more acceptable. As a result, the Christian must set himself and herself apart from the ways of the world, attempting to follow the Scriptures with all diligence by the help of the Holy Spirit.

Those who would deny the rightness of marriage are condemned for following *"things taught by demons"* (I Tim. 4:1), for what God has created . . . to be received with thanksgiving (I Tim. 4:4) is consecrated by the Word of God itself (I Tim. 4:5). It is clear from the Creation Story that God is the One Who, when He created human beings, *"Created them male and female"* (Gen. 1:27).

THE UNION

The Genesis account immediately announces that *"For this reason a man will leave his Father and Mother and be united to his wife, and they will become one flesh"* (Gen. 2:24).

The lifelong unity of husband and wife in marriage is symbolized by their physical union, and sexual bonding is vital in creating the lifelong unity that God intends. It is because of the sacramental impact of sexual bonding that Paul reacted so strongly when asceticism was introduced in Corinth.

Some Believers there held that Believers should not marry, or if they did marry, they were to withdraw from sex in order to have a pure, *"spiritual"* union.

Paul responds, *"The husband shall fulfill his marital duty to his wife, and likewise the wife to the husband. The wife's body does not belong to her alone, but also to her husband. In the same way, the husband's body does not belong to him alone but also to his wife. Do not deprive each other except by mutual consent and for a time, so that you may devote yourselves to prayer"* (I Cor. 7:3-5).

PROCREATION ONLY?

Although it is clear that marriage is definitely designed for procreation (the bringing of offspring into the world) (Gen. 1:28), procreation is not the sole reason for sexual relations. Again, although it is also clear that human beings have sexual drives, and marriage is God's provision for the satisfaction of these drives (I Cor. 7:9), these drives should not be the sole reason for engaging in sexual relations. Rather, the basic reason for sex within marriage is sacramental (that which is sacred as a sign or symbol of a spiritual reality, in this case the spiritual union of the Believer and Christ) (I Cor. 6:17). In that context, sex is intended to affirm and express the intimate bonding and unity of the married. Sexual relations are the sign and seal of marital commitment and are vital to maintaining that commitment.

THE INTIMACY OF MARRIED LOVE

In the context of sacrament, God expects sex to be enjoyed. This is testified first of all by human nature; all our pleasurable sensations came from God in the original Creation and are not wrong, unless perverted. It is also testified to in the spontaneously joyful *"Song of Solomon"* which celebrates married love. It is further testified to by the separation in Scripture of the concept of shame which is not attached to married sex. Sex outside of marriage is identified as wrong and shameful, but within marriage there is no such shame.

While Scripture may not deal with sex explicitly, the Bible does speak openly about the intimacy of married love. Scripture gives detailed lists of sexually wrong attitudes and acts outside of marriage but frees us within marriage to enjoy His Gift to the fullest.

Within the context of marriage, each sensation offered by the couple to one another is a fresh joy, a recognition that it is God, Who created us male and female, and it is God Who blesses our union. Moreover, it is God Who frees us to enjoy His Gifts to the fullest, but in the context of His boundaries.

(4) "THE WIFE HATH NOT POWER OF HER OWN BODY, BUT THE HUSBAND: AND LIKEWISE ALSO THE HUSBAND HATH NOT POWER OF HIS OWN BODY, BUT THE WIFE."

The phrase, *"The wife has not power of her own body, but the husband,"* refers to the fact that the husband and wife belong to each other. This means that the husband must satisfy the needs of the wife, and the wife, the husband; however, those *"needs"* must all come under the heading of that which is normal. All perversion or unnatural affection must be rejected.

The phrase, *"And likewise also the husband hath not power of his own body, but the wife,"* proclaims the same rights and privileges of the wife as enjoyed by the husband.

Marriage is not a capricious union, but a holy bond. *"They two"* become *"one flesh"* (Farrar).

(5) "DEFRAUD YE NOT ONE THE OTHER, EXCEPT IT BE WITH CONSENT FOR A TIME, THAT YE MAY GIVE YOURSELVES TO FASTING AND PRAYER; AND COME TOGETHER AGAIN, THAT SATAN TEMPT YOU NOT FOR YOUR INCONTINENCY."

The phrase, *"Defraud ye not one the other,"* in the Greek actually says, *"Stop defrauding each other."* It seems that some married couples in that day were refraining from sexual activity, which they erroneously thought enabled them to live more spiritual lives.

The phrase, *"Except it be with consent for a time, that ye may give yourselves to fasting and prayer,"* in effect says that abstinence from sexual activity between a husband and wife may be engaged for a short period of time, as one gives oneself over to fasting and prayer. Even then, such is not mandatory, but is given only in the realm of suggestion.

The phrase, *"And come together again, that Satan tempt you not for your incontinency,"* actually says, *"And be together again."*

The idea is, that the Believer not unnecessarily places himself or herself into a self-tormenting, repression beyond what God demands.

At times, Believers attempt to arrive at Sanctification and Holiness by means which are not actually of the Spirit, but really of the flesh. As such, they are doomed to failure, only increasing unnecessary hardships.

Jesus said, *"For My yoke is easy, and My burden is light"* (Mat. 11:30). Unfortunately, religious men tend to attempt to make the yoke harder and the burden heavier. Such is never pleasing to God, and in effect, a direct violation of His Word.

(6) "BUT I SPEAK THIS BY PERMISSION, AND NOT BY COMMANDMENT."

This verifies what I have just said.

*"This"* applies to his advice in general, but especially to Verse 5.

The phrase, *"By permission"* is generally misunderstood. It does not mean that Paul was permitted though not commanded to give this advice, but that his gentle advice was given *"by way of permission"* to Christians, not *"by way of injunction."*

He means to say that he leaves the details of their lives, whether celibate or married, to their individual consciences, though with large-hearted wisdom and charity he would emancipate them from human and unauthorized restrictions (Farrar).

(7) "FOR I WOULD THAT ALL MEN WERE EVEN AS I MYSELF. BUT EVERY MAN HATH HIS PROPER GIFT OF GOD, ONE AFTER THIS MANNER, AND ANOTHER AFTER THAT."

The phrase, *"For I would that all men were even as I myself,"* is not meant by Paul to denigrate marriage as some have supposed. In effect he is saying that he wished for the Coming Resurrection, when all will then be as he was then. Then the condition of man will be like that of the Angels in Heaven, who neither marry nor are given in marriage. Among the Resurrected Saints there will be no death, therefore, no reason for procreation. As well, the sex drives of the physical body, which will then be Glorified, will be gone.

NOTES

Paul is also stating that the Lord had helped him with this problem, in that his sex drive was held in control, or else taken away altogether, which it may well have been.

The phrase, *"But every man hath his proper Gift of God, one after this manner, and another after that,"* in effect speaks of his particular type of Ministry. Others would have another type of Ministry, and would be equipped by the Holy Spirit accordingly.

Due to Paul traveling almost constantly, and the hardships which accompanied traveling in those days, and as well the terrible opposition which he constantly faced, he evidently had settled the marriage problem with the Lord years before. He had reasoned in his heart that such a life would be very difficult for a wife and family, and he evidently felt that the Lord would desire that he maintain his particular lifestyle. However, this pertained only to him and not others. Others must receive direction from the Lord concerning His Will for their lives, which the Holy Spirit would give them upon request.

## WAS PAUL EVER MARRIED?

There has been much conjecture concerning this question.

Some claim he was married at the time of his Conversion, with his wife then deserting him. Some even claim that he had been a member of the vaunted Jewish Sanhedrin, which required that its members be married and have at least one son. However, I personally do not think there is enough evidence for one to properly arrive at that conclusion. In fact, I think there is some small evidence that mitigates against that position.

Again, others think that Paul had been married, with his wife dying either sometime before his Conversion, or immediately after.

In Church History, Clemens of Alexandria, Grotius, Luther, and Ewald, claim that Paul was a widower. On the other hand, Tertullian and Jerome, both who lived not long after Paul, say that the Apostle was never married.

The Scripture is silent either way, so it is best I think, not to conjecture.

(8) "I SAY THEREFORE TO THE UNMARRIED AND WIDOWS, IT IS GOOD FOR THEM IF THEY ABIDE EVEN AS I."

The phrase, *"I say therefore to the unmarried and widows,"* is evidently given in response to a question asked in the letter written from the Church in Corinth to him. They were evidently wanting to know if it was proper for the unmarried to marry, or for the widows to remarry. If it is to be noticed, widowers who are men, are not mentioned.

The reason is, that men at that time had certain rights which were not accorded to women. I speak mostly of the world and not the Church. In other words, men whose wives had died were free to remarry, but the people at Corinth were not so sure about the women whose husbands had died. Once again, the Holy Spirit through the Apostle puts all on equal footing.

The phrase, *"It is good for them if they abide even as I,"* is explained in Verse 26, where he says *"For the present distress."*

What did he mean by that?

The Apostle no doubt sensed in his spirit that hostility by Rome toward Believers was already in the making, at least in the spirit world. In fact, in a short time it would come into full blossom, with untold thousands of Believers having to pay with their lives. The persecutions began in earnest under Nero, and continued for over a hundred years.

(9) "BUT IF THEY CANNOT CONTAIN, LET THEM MARRY: FOR IT IS BETTER TO MARRY THAN TO BURN."

The phrase, *"But if they cannot contain, let them marry,"* refers to the sex drive.

*"Contain"* in the Greek is *"engkrateuomai,"* and means *"self control, to have command of the passions and appetites."*

The phrase, *"For it is better to marry than to burn,"* refers to burning with passion. Paul's statement refers to difficulty in controlling passions.

In attempting to look at the situation as it then was in the Church at Corinth, the Holy Spirit used the occasion to present Teaching, which of course is extremely valuable, respecting spiritual, domestic, and social situations. Evidently, because of false Teaching or because of erroneous thinking, one or more young people in the Church had determined they would not marry, but rather give their life unto the Lord in totality. If in fact this was the case, it evidently was not something the Lord had required, but rather a position generated by self-will. As a result, this young person, or possibly several, were finding it difficult to control their desires. In other words, this which they in their minds had reasoned would be so holy, they were finding to be the very opposite. So Paul addressed the situation by simply saying, *"It is better to marry than to burn."*

NOTES

## DESIRE AND PASSION

Looking over the Biblical Passages that contain the word *"desire"* raises a number of questions. Is it the object of desire that makes desire good or bad?

Is there something suspicious about the very act of desiring?

Are our desires intrinsically evil? The original languages, especially the Greek, help us find important answers.

## DESIRE AS PORTRAYED IN THE OLD TESTAMENT

The two basic Hebrew words for *"desire"* are *"awah"* and *"hamad." "Awah"* means *"to desire," "to long for," "to want," "to wish."* It is used with both good and bad objects of desire.

*"Hamad"* emphasizes the desirability of the object as a source of delight, but is used often in a strongly negative sense. It is this word that is translated *"covetousness"*: desire running riot, trapping the subject in an evil passion. In fact, it is the Tenth Commandment, *"Thou shalt not covet thy neighbour's house, thou shalt not covet thy neighbour's wife, . . ."* (Ex. 20:17).

The actual Hebrew word used here for *"covet"* is *"chamad,"* which is a derivative of *"hamad."*

The use of these words makes it clear that human desires are often twisted out of the pattern God established. But the words themselves make no statement about fallen human nature.

There are other, special words that are also translated *"desire"* in the Old Testament. *"T'suqah"* means *"desire or longing."* It appears only in Genesis 3:16; 4:7; and Song of Solomon 7:10. In Genesis 3:16 it describes the changed relationship that sin introduced in husband-and-wife relationships. A hierarchy is imposed where none existed; it is expressed in the phrase

*"Your desire will be for your husband, and he will rule over you."*

In Genesis 4:7 sin is portrayed as a wild beast gazing hungrily at Cain, desiring to devour him if he fails to respond to God's Instructions.

*"Mis'alah"* another Hebrew word, is a petition. It is found only in Psalm 20:5 and 37:4, in which God grants the desires and petitions of those who love Him.

Another major term is *"rason."* It has three basic meanings:

1. It represents God's favor.
2. It expresses His acceptance of a Sacrifice or a person in a ritual sense.
3. It means *"desire,"* in the sense of that which motivates a choice of one's will. It is used in one or more of these sense in Genesis 49:6; Leviticus 1:3; 19:5; 22:19, 29; II Chronicles 15:15; Ezra 10:11; Nehemiah 9:27-37; Esther 9:5; Psalms 40:8; 51:18; 143:10; 145:16, 19; and, Daniel 8:4; 11:3, 16, 36.

### DESIRE AS A CHOICE AS EXPRESSED IN THE NEW TESTAMENT

The Greek word *"thelo"* is translated *"desire"* in some Versions but not the King James (Mat. 9:13; 12:7; Jn. 8:44; Rom. 7:18; 9:16; II Cor. 8:10; Gal. 5:17; I Tim. 5:11; Heb. 13:18). The word actually means *"to want"* or *"to will."*

There is a strong dimension of choice in *"thelo."* When Jesus quoted the Old Testament in saying, *"I will* (desire) *Mercy, not Sacrifice"* (Mat. 9:13; 12:7), He was not speaking of God's feelings but of the Father's conscious choice of what is truly important in a relationship with Him (Heb. 10:5, 8).

### DESIRE AS AN EXPRESSION OF THE SIN NATURE

The Greek word *"epithymeo,"* which means *"to desire"* came to be used in an ethically bad sense, even long before the time of Christ. It suggested dangerous passions growing out of one's false evaluation of the world and its contents.

In the New Testament, the two Greek words *"epithymia"* and *"epithymeo,"* are used in a positive or neutral sense only in Luke 15:16; Philippians 1:23; I Thessalonians 2:17; I Timothy 3:1; Hebrews 6:11. In other Passages, the words are used in its ethically bad sense. Furthermore, the Passages where they are used develop a picture of human nature that reveals a Truth the Greeks sensed when they used this word to mark their suspicion of their own passions.

NOTES

### HUMAN PASSIONS AND SIN'S POWER

The New Testament reveals that the desires that drive human beings lie deep within sinful human nature (Gal. 5:16; Eph. 2:3; 4:22). Driven by passions, human beings fall under sin's power (Rom. 6:12; Eph. 2:3).

What is more, human beings create a world (society) that institutionalizes as values the tragic misinterpretations of what is truly important, for these values are derived from the passions of our twisted nature (Mk. 4:19; I Jn. 2:16). Thus, temptation does not come from the things that attract us: it is found in our response to them (James 1:14-15).

Only by turning to God and learning to rely on the Holy Spirit can we resist our warped passions and develop a new system of values (Rom. 8:9; Gal. 5:16; Eph. 4:23).

The Biblical Teaching that the Fall warped and twisted human nature is underlined by the treatment given *"epithymia"* in the New Testament. Human personality, which of course includes the sex drive, is wholly infected by sin. Mind, heart, and will are all corrupt: even the desires that motivate us are twisted by our inability to evaluate what is truly good for us.

### THE HOLY SPIRIT CAN SHAPE OUR DESIRES

It is not wrong for us to have desires. The capacity to feel pleasure and delight has been given to us by God, a reflection of His Own rich emotional capacity. But both Testaments indicate that we may desire the wrong things.

The New Testament helps us realize that we cannot explain away our actions by an appeal to the desirability of the thing that motivated them. Our desire for what is desirable is often tainted, for we are flawed by sin. The flaw includes those desires that lead us to many wrong evaluations. Thus, the desires of sinful human beings are shaped by the sin nature and all too often impel us toward what is both evil and bad for us.

But there is release for those who are in Christ. We can let the Holy Spirit shape our desires. We can reject the old and choose those things that God holds to be of value, and so we ourselves may in this way be purified and cleansed (Richards).

(10) "AND UNTO THE MARRIED I COMMAND, YET NOT I, BUT THE LORD, LET NOT THE WIFE DEPART FROM HER HUSBAND:"

The phrase, *"And unto the married I command, yet not I, but the Lord,"* means that it is not mere permission as in Verse 6, but rather an injunction, i.e., *"a Commandment."* This had already been laid down by Christ Himself (Mat. 5:32; 19:6; Mk. 10:11-12; Lk. 16:18).

The phrase, *"Let not the wife depart from her husband,"* pertains to departing on grounds which were not Scriptural. The scenario as Paul addresses it here could have involved several situations.

It, no doubt, involved marriages where the husband or wife was unsaved. Some had evidently got it in their minds, that being the case, that the marriage should be dissolved. Actually, and as we shall see, the Text bears that out, with Paul giving instructions as to what should be done.

In such a situation, on those grounds alone, the wife was not to *"depart from her husband."*

(11) "BUT AND IF SHE DEPART, LET HER REMAIN UNMARRIED, OR BE RECONCILED TO HER HUSBAND: AND LET NOT THE HUSBAND PUT AWAY HIS WIFE."

The phrase, *"But and if she departs, let her remain unmarried,"* refers to divorce. Paul restricted such a one to stay single, unless she remarried her former husband.

The idea is, as stated, that the rupture of this marriage was on grounds other than that which was Scriptural, which we will discuss momentarily.

The phrase, *"Or be reconciled to her husband,"* refers to the fact that every effort must be made to salvage the marriage where it is at all possible.

The phrase, *"And let not the husband put away his wife,"* places the same restriction on the husband as it does the wife. Once again, the Holy Spirit through the Apostle gives women the same rights as men, which was not the case in the Grecian culture of that time.

Some have argued that through verse 11, Paul is speaking exclusively to Christians. In other words, both the husband and wife are Believers. However, the Text does not seem to bear that out, the weight of the evidence seemingly pointing toward one of the mates who was unsaved.

NOTES

Others claim that Paul is not speaking in Verses 10 and 11 of divorce, but rather separation, etc. However, I seriously doubt that the Holy Spirit would have given such Commandment merely on that premise. Once again, I think the weight of the evidence lends toward divorce.

If the wife felt she could not live with her husband due to incompatibility, she was free to leave and get a divorce, but she could not remarry, unless she remarried her former husband. Not having Scriptural grounds, she was not free to marry another man. The same could be said for the husband, the situation being reversed.

## INCOMPATIBILITY AND OTHER PROBLEMS

Concerning causes for divorce, the Pharisees asked Jesus this question, *"Is it lawful for a man to put away his wife for every cause?"* (Mat. 19:3).

Actually, this was the great controversy among the Jews at this particular time. The Rabbis had made void Deuteronomy 24:1-4. As well, the wife in effect had few, if any, rights at all, with the husband given pretty much every latitude. Of course, this was not the Law of God, but rather the manner in which the Pharisees had twisted the Law of Moses.

Some now permitted divorce on many frivolous grounds, such as the wife carelessly seasoning the food, causing the husband to eat food which had not been tithed, going into the street with loose or uncombed hair, loud talk or constant talking in the home, etc.

Jesus took His detractors back to the original Law of God found in Genesis 1:26-28; 2:21-25. He then said, *"Moses because of the hardness of your hearts suffered you to put away your wives: but from the beginning it was not so"* (Mat. 19:8).

He then said, *"But I say unto you, That whosoever shall put away his wife, saving for the cause of fornication, causeth her to commit adultery: and whosoever shall marry her that is divorced committeth adultery"* (Mat. 5:31-32).

In His statement, He gave the Scriptural grounds for divorce which is *"fornication,"* which we have explained in other Commentary. Paul will now give one further Scriptural ground for divorce, which means that divorce is not allowed for incompatibility or other such things.

(12) "BUT TO THE REST SPEAK I, NOT THE LORD: IF ANY BROTHER HATH A

WIFE THAT BELIEVETH NOT, AND SHE BE PLEASED TO DWELL WITH HIM, LET HIM NOT PUT HER AWAY."

The phrase, *"But to the rest speak I, not the Lord,"* does not mean that what Paul is about to say is any less inspired by the Holy Spirit than the other remarks. The Apostle is merely saying that Jesus did not teach anything about what to do with mixed marriages. The Lord had made no express reference to such cases, since it had been no part of His Mission to lay down minute details which would be duly settled from age to age by the wisdom taught by the Holy Spirit (Farrar).

The Lord inspired Paul to write extensively about this situation even as we now see.

The phrase, *"If any Brother hath a wife that believeth not, and she be pleased to dwell with him, let him not put her away,"* proclaims the problem of a marriage lacking unity as a result of the husband being Saved and the wife remaining unsaved. Evidently, this had come about after the marriage ceremony had been performed. Regrettably, it typifies many cases of this nature.

The Holy Spirit through Paul here plainly says that such a situation does not provide Scriptural grounds for divorce. If the unsaved wife elects to maintain the marriage, which is far, far better, the husband who is Born Again, should not think of divorce. In fact, in countless situations of this nature the unsaved member has ultimately given his or her heart to Christ.

(13) "AND THE WOMAN WHICH HATH AN HUSBAND THAT BELIEVETH NOT, AND IF HE BE PLEASED TO DWELL WITH HER, LET HER NOT LEAVE HIM."

This is the same as the previous verse, yet in reverse.

Once again, the Holy Spirit proclaims here in the giving of these instructions, that men and women have complete equal rights in Scripture (Gal. 3:28; Col. 3:11).

This presents a change from Old Testament instruction which required Jews to separate from Pagan spouses who had not converted to Judaism (Ezra Chpts. 9-10).

## WHY DID THE HOLY SPIRIT MAKE THIS CHANGE?

The Old Testament injunction presented a totally different situation than this presented in the New Testament.

NOTES

The purpose for the Old Testament injunction pertained to keeping the Jewish lineage pure, in respect to the coming Redeemer, namely, The Lord Jesus Christ. In fact, the Lord had raised up the Jews from the loins of Abraham and the womb of Sarah for this very reason. The Law of Moses had been given to them which contained strict dietary regulations, as well as a host of other things, all for the purpose of the coming Redeemer.

The Gentiles of those times, for the most part, were so polluted by sexual immorality and perversion, which had taken such a toll mentally and physically, that to mix such with the Jews would have defeated the very Purpose of God.

In fact, during those times, each City had one or several Temples dedicated to particular heathen deities, so-called, which were filled with Temple prostitutes, both male and female, and which polluted the entirety of the population. The initiation ritual in this heathen worship was marked by sexual intercourse with one or more of these prostitutes, and as should be obvious, caused disease to be rampant.

Inasmuch as Jesus has now already come, this particular purpose of the Jews had now come to an end. As well, the union of a husband and wife did not now pose the same problems as under the Old Economy of God. Consequently, the requirements were different.

(14) "FOR THE UNBELIEVING HUSBAND IS SANCTIFIED BY THE WIFE, AND THE UNBELIEVING WIFE IS SANCTIFIED BY THE HUSBAND: ELSE WERE YOUR CHILDREN UNCLEAN; BUT NOW ARE THEY HOLY."

The phrase, *"For the unbelieving husband is sanctified by the wife, and the unbelieving wife is sanctified by the husband,"* refers to the fact that if either the husband or wife is unsaved, such a relationship is not considered unlawful. The phrase, as given by Paul, also refers to the spiritual influence of the one who is saved over the marriage and home.

The word *"sanctified"* of course refers to the believing spouse, and simply means that God looks at such a home and the marriage, as a Christian home and marriage, even though one or the other partner is unsaved. *"Sanctified"* simply means *"set apart,"* or *"dedicated to,"* and in this case, has nothing to do with Salvation. In other words, the Salvation of the believing spouse, although sanctifying the home, does not serve as Salvation for the unbelieving mate. Each person must make his own decision for Christ. It means that God will not withhold blessings from the home because of the unbelieving spouse, so the unbelieving mate owes everything to the believing partner.

The phrase, *"Else were your children unclean; but now are they holy,"* went back to the Jewish thinking of the Old Covenant.

## HEATHEN

The Jews considered any child born to Gentiles, with the exception of certain Gentile proselytes to Judaism, as being unclean. There were several reasons for this; one was the fact that Gentile mothers consecrated their children to particular idols.

In fact, Corinth was a hot bed of all types of heathenistic, debauched, impure, ungodly forms of immortal worship. In fact, one could probably say that most all of these people in the Church at Corinth had lived very licentious lives before Conversion. With all of this fresh in their minds, they were no doubt wondering if an unsaved spouse would keep the Blessings of God from a home and marriage, and especially to what status would children born to such a wedlock occupy? Paul assures them that the innocent children would not be penalized because of the unsaved member, but rather blessed by the Lord.

However, once again, the word *"Holy"* as it is here applied, pertains only to the marriage and what it produces, and has nothing to do with the Salvation of the children. Upon reaching the age of accountability, whatever that may be, they must give their hearts to Christ, just like all others, or else they will be lost.

## THE STATE OF CHILDREN

Some have attempted to use this 14th Verse as a Standard for Righteousness or unrighteousness respecting children below the age of accountability. By that I mean this:

They claim that if the parents of the child who is born are Saved, or at least one parent is Saved, the child is protected by God until it reaches the age of accountability when it can accept Christ on its own. In other words, if it should die before the age of accountability, it is Saved, i.e., *"Sanctified, Holy."*

Conversely, they teach that if both parents are unsaved, and the child should die in infancy or before it reaches the age of accountability, in other words while innocent, it will die eternally lost.

## NOT SCRIPTURAL!

To attempt to stretch this statement as given by Paul into such far-reached meanings, is not warranted in the Text. Actually, I think the evidence in Scripture is clear, that every single baby or child below the age of accountability (and that varies with children) who dies during that particular time, all without exception go to Heaven, irrespective as to whether their parents were Saved or not. The following are the reasons why:

1. Jesus said, *"Verily I say unto you, Except you be converted, and become as little children you shall not enter into the Kingdom of Heaven"* (Mat. 18:3).

If one is to notice, Jesus did not distinguish between children, He just simply said *"children."*

As well, I hardly think He would have used a child as an example regarding Salvation, if in fact, almost all the children of the world who had died, had died lost.

Also, He did not distinguish between the children of Gentile or Jewish parents. The Truth was, that the far greater majority of Jews during Jesus' day were not Believers, even though they professed much.

2. Jesus also said, *"Suffer* (permit) *the little children to come unto Me, and forbid them not: for of such is the Kingdom of God"* (Mk. 10:14).

Once again, He did not distinguish between children. Also, if the majority of the children who have ever lived and died below the age of accountability, in fact died lost, it would have made little sense for Jesus to use a child as an example of *"the Kingdom of God."*

3. Jesus also said, *"Take heed that ye despise not one of these little ones; for I say unto you, That in Heaven their Angels do always behold the Face of My Father which is in Heaven"* (Mat. 18:10).

While this statement applies to all Believers, still, Jesus was using a little child as an example (Mat. 18:2-4), as He presented this Message.

NOTES

I hardly think if children are spiritually lost, at least those of unsaved parents which in fact make up most of the population of the world and for all time, that their *"Angels"* would be beholding the Face of God.

No, I think the Scriptural record is clear, that *all* babies and little children who die below the age of accountability, are protected by the Lord in their innocency and in fact go to Heaven. That would mean as well, that there is not a single child below the age of accountability that is in Hell.

WHAT IS THE AGE OF ACCOUNTABILITY?

That would vary with children, and the environment in which they are raised.

If the child is raised in a Christian home, brought up by parents dedicated to the Lord, the age of accountability for a child could be reached as young as six years old. With others who are raised in homes that do not know the Lord, it would of necessity be a little older. Basically we are speaking of the ability of the child to reason and to understand. As well, it is surprising as to how much a child can grasp and understand concerning the Lord, especially considering that the Lord being Omniscient, can easily address a child on the child's level without any difficulty.

I was Saved when I was eight years old. When the Lord spoke to my heart, I knew it was God, and I knew exactly what He said to me. Thankfully, I obeyed Him. From that moment I was accountable.

Regarding each child, the Lord is the One Who determines the accountability of the child, and not man. In accordance with that, I will say as Abraham said so long ago, *"Shall not the Judge of all the Earth do right?"* (Gen. 18:25).

(15) "BUT IF THE UNBELIEVING DEPART, LET HIM DEPART. A BROTHER OR A SISTER IS NOT UNDER BONDAGE IN SUCH CASES: BUT GOD HATH CALLED US TO PEACE."

The phrase, *"But if the unbelieving depart, let him depart,"* speaks of desertion, and desertion for the sole purpose of the Cause of Christ. In other words, the unbelieving spouse simply does not want to keep the marriage together because of the believing spouse living for God. In fact, this has happened untold numbers of times down through the centuries, and continues unto this hour.

NOTES

The phrase, *"A Brother or a Sister is not under bondage in such cases,"* means there was nothing that the Believer could do to stop the unbelieving spouse from departing, and in that case, the Believer is free to remarry.

Paul here gives us a second legal and scriptural reason for divorce and remarriage. The first is fornication (Mat. 5:32).

At times, in such a marriage, a husband or a wife doesn't want to live for God, and thereby breaks up the marriage on this account. If this is the case, the Christian is not responsible for the situation and is not required to remain single the rest of his or her life. In other words, such a one is free to remarry, basically for the reason that there is no choice in the matter.

Of course, everything should be done by the Believer to keep the marriage together, but as Paul said, *"If the unbelieving depart, let him depart."*

Some would argue against what we have just stated, pointing to what Jesus said in Matthew 5:31-32 and 19:3-9, giving *"fornication"* as the only Scriptural reason for divorce and remarriage. However, Jesus did not mention that which Paul brought out, simply because the Church was not then in existence. In Israel there was no such thing as an unbeliever departing, etc. That only came about after the Gospel began to go to the entirety of the world. So, had He used Paul's words, even as the Holy Spirit gave them to Paul, they simply would not have made sense in the climate in which He was speaking.

The word *"bondage"* as Paul uses it here, in the Greek is *"douloo,"* and means *"to enslave or to be in subjection or subserviency."* This speaks of the marriage vows.

In fact, in a situation of this nature, and there have been untold thousands, there is actually nothing that the believing spouse can do. They cannot force the unbelieving partner to remain in the marriage or to do much of anything for that matter. So in a sense, it is a situation out of the control of the believing partner.

As well, divorce on Scriptural grounds, of which this is one, means that a person is free to remarry, providing it is to another Christian.

## QUESTIONS CONCERNING DIVORCE AND REMARRIAGE

Particular Religious Denominations hold all type of rulings respecting this very important question. Many rulings contradict each other from one Denomination to the next. However, what a Denomination says is one thing, while what the Bible says is something else altogether. In other words, it is what the Word of God says that counts.

Regarding some Religious Denominations, anyone who has a divorce in their background is not allowed to hold credentials in those particular organizations. In other words, they are not allowed to preach the Gospel, at least in that Denomination.

In other Churches, those who have a divorce in their background are treated somewhat as second-class Christians, etc. And then there are others, which have no restrictions whatsoever.

The following is taken from a paper written on this subject by Dr. Bernard Rossier, who is a friend, and once served as an Associate at Jimmy Swaggart Ministries. I feel his statement is very helpful, and I am giving it verbatim. It is as follows:

## SHOULD A DIVORCED PERSON BE ALLOWED TO PREACH THE GOSPEL?

Here is a question that has plagued the Christian Church for centuries. Should a divorced person be allowed to preach the Gospel of Jesus Christ? Many ecclesiastical organizations say no while other ones say yes.

I once believed the former approach, but I later began to realize that my opinion was based merely on the stance of the Denomination to which I once belonged.

What changed my opinion? About two years before I resigned from this particular organization, I was asked by the General Overseer of a small Pentecostal Denomination if I would help him in a study concerning whether or not divorced people should be credentialed. He asked me to study the New Testament, and he said he was going to ask someone else to study the matter in the Old Testament and a third person to study the issue from still another perspective.

I felt impressed by the Holy Spirit to look at my responsibility by doing a survey of New Testament Passages that had even the most remote connection to the question. I purposely did not resort to Commentaries in this study. I have listed the Passages, as well as my responses.

NOTES

## MATTHEW

Matthew 5:31-32 — In the Sermon on the Mount Jesus definitely taught His opposition to divorce. His statements were directed toward His Disciples and not toward the unconverted. He permitted His followers to divorce their partners only under one condition: fornication or consistent marital unfaithfulness.

Matthew 9:1-8 (Parallel Passages Mark 2:1-12; Luke 5:17-26) — In connection with the healing of the Paralytic, Jesus established His Authority to forgive sins. He did not make a distinction between forgiving some kinds of sin and not forgiving other kinds. The emphasis seems to be on all types.

Matthew 12:22-37 (Parallel Passage Mark 3:20-30) — Jesus definitely stated that all sins (vs. 31) except blaspheming the Holy Spirit would be forgiven. He did not make preconversion marital infractions an exception.

Matthew 18:21-35 — After Peter asked if he should forgive a sinning Brother seven times, Jesus said seventy times seven, an obvious reference to the fact that we must forgive as often as a person who sins against us asks to be forgiven. Would God establish a lower standard for Himself?

Matthew 19:1-12 — Again, we see that God is not in favor of divorce. Jesus explained, however, that Moses permitted it because of the hardness of people's hearts, the obvious result of sin. The Lord added that divorce is permitted now only for marital unfaithfulness that continues on a regular basis.

## MARK

Mark 1:4-8 (Parallel Passages Matthew 3:11; Luke 3:3) — John the Baptist preached repentance, a term which refers to a complete about-face, a definite severance with the past life, and a determination to live a new life by God's Grace. If repentance implies the complete break with the past, why should we insist on connecting a person to his past mistakes?

Mark 10:1-12 — Here we see God's displeasure over divorce, but we also see that it was permitted because of the sins of the people.

LUKE

Luke 4:16-21 — In the Synagogue in Nazareth, Jesus said He came *"To preach deliverance to the captives."* Why then do we continue to make people captives to their past lives in sin?

Luke 7:36-50 — After the woman anointed the Feet of Jesus with expensive perfume, He stated literally, *"Her many sins have been forgiven"*(vs. 47). This is a perfect tense verb which indicates the initial forgiveness must have taken place at an earlier time, but the results were continuing. Jesus did not attach any conditions to this forgiveness.

Luke 11:1-4 — In the *"Disciples' Prayer,"* Jesus said we are to forgive everyone who sins against us. Does God do any less than He requires us to do?

Luke 11:29-32 — Jesus reminded the crowd of the repentance of Nineveh and the important fact that a greater than Jonah was speaking to them. Certainly, He forgives completely when a person truly repents.

Luke 13:1-5 — In fact, if we do not repent we will face the Wrath of God. That must mean that if we do repent, we will not.

Luke 15:1-7 — The Parable of the lost sheep centers around repentance.

Luke 15:8-10 — The Parable of the Lost Coin also focuses on repentance.

Luke 15:11-31 — The famous story of the Prodigal Son continues the same theme as well. There is no hint in these three Passages of punishing the repentant ones for their past sins.

Luke 17:3-4 — Jesus again said we should forgive a person as often as that person asks for forgiveness. Would God do any less for us?

JOHN

John 3:3 — Jesus literally told Nicodemus he had to be *"born from above,"* a perfect description of God reaching down and starting a person's life over. Why, then, do we punish that person for some aspect of the old life?

John 5:24 — Jesus very clearly stated that the person who has Eternal Life will not be condemned. Why, then, do we condemn the person with respect to marital infractions before Conversion or those foisted on a person by an unconverted spouse?

John 8:1-11 — Jesus did not condemn the woman taken in adultery. Instead, He warned her not to sin any longer.

NOTES

John 9:1-34 — Jesus would not get entangled in a discussion concerning why this man was born blind (vs. 3). Instead, He healed him, and God was Glorified. It was the Pharisees who tried to pin the sins of the past on this man (vs. 34).

ACTS

Acts 2:38 — In his famous sermon on the Day of Pentecost, Peter emphasized repentance as a requisite for receiving the Baptism with the Holy Spirit.

Acts 17:30 — Paul also made the same requirement of the Athenians. Neither he nor Peter made any requirements concerning suffering for sins committed before repentance.

Acts 26:19-20 — Paul even preached repentance to King Agrippa by reminding him of the Apostle's own faithfulness to preach repentance. He did not preach it with strings attached.

ROMANS

Romans 5:6-11 — Paul told the Romans that Christ's Sacrifice saved them from the Wrath of God. Verse 9 should be compared with Romans 1:18.

Romans 6:1-4 — Water Baptism is an external sign of a new life. Why strap a person with something that relates to the old life?

Romans 6:20-23 — Before Conversion, we were slaves to sin; but Conversion sets us free from it. Why should we bind people to their former sins?

Romans 7:1-4 — We should remember that Paul used this reference from the Mosaic Law only as an illustration within the center of his own struggle, not with the intent of establishing a Doctrine. This Passage should be compared with Hebrews 13:4 which reminds us of the Judgment of God on adulterers. Is a person who was divorced before Conversion living in a continuous state of adultery and under the continuous Wrath of God, even though that person is forgiven?

Romans 8:1-4 — Paul reminded his readers that they were not under condemnation. Surely, some of these readers must have had preconversion marital entanglements.

Romans 10:6-13 — This Passage reminds us that Salvation comes through Faith and public confession to that Faith, not from a life free from preconversion marital entanglements.

### I CORINTHIANS

I Corinthians 7:12-16 — If a Christian's companion leaves, the Christian is not under obligation any longer to that person.

I Corinthians 7:39 — Marrying in the Lord definitely is God's Plan for the Believer, but this verse does not bring up preconversion problems.

### II CORINTHIANS

II Corinthians 5:16-21 — Verse 19 definitely states that God does not count reconciled people's sins against them. Also Verse 17 states that *"Old things are passed away."* This comes from an aorist verb which depicts the decisiveness of Conversion.

### GALATIANS

Galatians 3:24-25 — The Mosaic Law served as a trainer to point us to Christ or to show us our lost condition. Once we have accepted Christ, we are no longer under its supervision. Why, then, do we bind Christians to its regulations?

### EPHESIANS

Ephesians 2:1-6 — These verses show the decisive break with the past (vss. 1-3), and a reminder of the present new life in Christ (vss. 4-6), especially with the words *"but God"* in Verse 4. God does not hold the past over our heads.

### PHILIPPIANS

Philippians 3:7-14 — In his own experience, Paul made it clear that he made a complete break with the past and exchanged it for the Knowledge of Christ.

### COLOSSIANS

Colossians 2:9-15 — This Passage reminds us of our completeness in Christ (vs. 10). Due to that, we have True Circumcision (vs. 11), true Baptism (vs. 12), true Resurrection (vs. 12), true Forgiveness (vs. 13), true Forgetting (vs. 14), and true Freedom (vs. 15). Verse 14 is extremely clear in showing that God removed all the charges against us when we accepted Christ. If God does that, why do we hold the past over people's heads?

### I TIMOTHY

I Timothy 1:12-16 — Paul never could get over the fact God had mercy on him in spite of the way he persecuted the Church before his Conversion. He used this as an example for others to follow. Aren't we failing to do this when we hold the past sins of people over their heads?

I Timothy 3:1-7 — The statement in Verse 2 could refer to polygamy. Many people, however, dogmatically interpret it to mean that a divorced and remarried man actually has two wives. I remind you that this view is only an interpretation.

I Timothy 3:8-13 — Paul could have meant the same thing in Verse 12. Polygamy was very common in that day.

### TITUS

Titus 1:5-9 — Verse 6 could also have the same meaning, which seems to be more consistent with the prevalence of polygamy that existed at that time.

### HEBREWS

Hebrews 10:15-18 — This Passage contains a beautiful promise that God does not remember the sins of a person who accepts Christ (vs. 17). Why do we do what God does not do?

### I JOHN

I John 2:2 — The Apostle John wrote that Jesus is the Atoning Sacrifice for all sin. If He atoned for all sin, why do we hold one particular sin against some of our brothers and sisters in Christ?

It seems quite clear that the New Testament makes a very definite break with the old life. Moreover, it seems to delineate a distinct difference between preconversion and post-conversion marital infractions.

Therefore, why should we punish people who feel called into the Preaching Ministry just because they experienced marital infractions before Conversion? Furthermore, why should we punish people for infractions foisted on them by unconverted partners? Obviously, every case should be examined individually.

(16) "FOR WHAT KNOWEST THOU, O WIFE, WHETHER THOU SHALT SAVE THY HUSBAND? OR HOW KNOWEST THOU, O MAN, WHETHER THOU SHALT SAVE THY WIFE?"

The question, *"For what knowest thou, O wife, whether thou shalt save thy husband?"*, pertains to an unsaved husband. This speaks of a believing wife who should do everything she can to keep the marriage together, even though her husband is unsaved. Of course, this speaks of the wife being Saved after the marriage. It does *not* pertain to a believing woman marrying an unbelieving man. That should never be the case. To do so, is actually a violation of the Word of God, which can bring great difficulties (II Cor. 6:14-18).

After the marriage, at a point in time the wife comes to Christ, with the husband continuing to resist, the situation as should be obvious, is not as it ought to be. However, if the unbelieving husband does not desire to break up the marriage, which it is certainly hoped that he would not, the wife is to then believe God that her husband is going to be Saved. Peter addressed this by saying, *"That, if any obey not the Word* (speaking of unsaved husbands), *they also may be won . . . by the conversation* (Godly behavior) *of the wives"* (I Pet. 3:1).

## A BEAUTIFUL EXAMPLE

My Grandmother's Sister was one of the Godliest women I ever had the privilege to know. But yet her husband, exactly as Paul here describes, was not Saved.

Even though he did not desire to break up the marriage, if she had so desired she had Scriptural grounds for a divorce. His life was filled with fornication, and about every other sin that one could imagine. But still, she continued to hold onto God for his Salvation, even though at times other Believers encouraged her to get a divorce. In fact, she had to make the living most of the time for the family.

Nevertheless, she refused to even consider divorce, which was the right decision for her to make, believing God that he ultimately would be Saved.

## THE PART THE LORD ALLOWED ME TO PLAY IN THIS

If I remember correctly, it was about 1972 or 73. I had a dream about my Uncle (he was my Great Uncle). I dreamed that he died, but before he died, he gave his heart and life to the Lord Jesus Christ. I felt in my heart that the Lord was telling me to speak to him about his soul, which I did.

The following Saturday, Frances and I went to their home, which was actually my hometown, about a hundred miles from Baton Rouge. My Uncle at this time must have been about 75.

NOTES

When we arrived at their home, thankfully he was there and of course my Aunt, and my Dad was there as well.

We walked into the kitchen, with all of us sitting around the table, as my Aunt had served a piece of cake or something like that if I remember correctly.

All the time I was praying that the Lord would give me the favorable opening, and finally He did.

*"Uncle Arthur,"* I said to him, addressing him by name. He looked up at me.

*"I had a dream about you the other night,"* I said to him. *"Part of it was good, and part was bad."*

Without pausing, I said, *"I dreamed that you died."*

I remember, he looked up at me and said, *"Well that's not good."*

I then said, *"No it isn't, but what I'm about to say now is good."*

I paused for a few moments and then said, *"I dreamed that you gave your heart and life to the Lord."*

The room grew very quiet. My Aunt was standing near the table. I noticed that she bowed her head, and I knew she was praying. Actually, she had been praying for over 40 years — years of sorrow, heartache, and about every other type of difficulty that one could begin to imagine. But still she had held on faithful, believing God that the Lord was ultimately going to save her husband. And now the time had come.

## THE GREAT DECISION

*"Uncle Arthur, don't you think it's about time?"*

Once again, the room grew very quiet, and I'll never forget then what happened.

He looked up at me and without another word said, *"Yes, I think it's time."*

It was that quick, as the Spirit of God began to move on his heart.

Everyone around the table bowed their heads, and I led my Uncle in the Sinner's Prayer, and when he finished, there was no doubt that he was Saved.

The Presence of God filled that room, and my Aunt stood there with tears rolling down her face, knowing that the Lord had answered her prayers after all of these years.

Was it worth the wait?

Well of course it was. If I remember correctly, my Uncle lived about another ten years, and walked very close to God. During that time, the Lord gave my Aunt the happy home that she really had never had. Yes, it was worth the wait in more ways than one. To be frank, I seriously doubt that my Uncle would have been Saved, if she had not held on to God as she did. But she did, and thank God, he was Saved.

The question, *"Or how knowest thou, O man, whether thou shalt save thy wife?"*, presents the same scenario as the first question, but this time points to the unsaved wife.

(17) "BUT AS GOD HATH DISTRIBUTED TO EVERY MAN, AS THE LORD HATH CALLED EVERY ONE, SO LET HIM WALK. AND SO ORDAIN I IN ALL CHURCHES."

The phrase, *"But as God hath distributed to every man,"* refers to the rule that the circumstances of our lives are regulated by the Providence of God, and must not be arbitrarily altered at our own caprice.

This refers to the fact that God has a particular Plan or Rule of Life for each Believer. The Believer is to find what that Rule or Plan is, and walk therein.

The phrase, *"As the Lord hath called every one, so let him walk,"* means that Christ has allotted His portion to each Christian, in effect, calling each man and woman for a particular Work and Ministry. That Lot and that Call are to guide his life.

The phrase, *"And so ordain I in all Churches,"* refers to the fact that the instructions given are applicable to all Believers everywhere and for all time.

NOTES

## ASSIGNED

Going to the Old Testament from which Paul would have received his instructions, we find various Hebrew words expressing the idea of *"give"* or *"assign."* When God is the Actor, *"assign"* carries the binding force of Law or, in Prophecy, conveys the certainty that what has been announced will happen (Isa. 53:9).

Psalm 16:5 shifts our attention to the fact that God assigns individuals their place in life. David realized what is also taught in the New Testament: God, he said, has *"assigned me my portion and my cup."*

The New Testament expresses this thought with the Greek word *"merizo,"* which means *"to divide"* and, at times, *"to assign."* The most significant Passage where the word is used is that of which we are now studying (I Cor. 7:17-23), which suggests that all the circumstances of our lives are assigned by God. Consequently, we are not to be troubled by our lot, for whatever our circumstances, they provide us with opportunities to serve God and others.

## ASSIGN RATHER THAN WINNING IT

In the same way, even the most respected leaders of the Church (II Cor. 10:13) are simply servants who have been assigned their place rather than winning it. We are hardly to view them with awe.

Two other New Testament Passages that speak of assigning are significant: Matthew 24:51 and Luke 12:46. Both use the word *"tithemi,"* which means *"to place or put."*

These Passages speak of individuals who are *"assigned a place"* with the hypocrites and unbelievers respectively. But the context makes it clear that this is not predestination to eternal judgment. In the stories Jesus told, each individual made the choices and took the actions that led to this final assignment.

In effect, these individuals addressed by Jesus, were those who would not follow *"the assignment"* laid out for them by the Lord, but rather chose their own direction. It led, as always, to destruction and judgment. Refusing the original assignment, they were then assigned to perdition.

## GOD'S WAY OR . . .

Every Believer, as stated, is assigned a place and position in the great Work and Plan of God. This is the place selected by the Lord and for obvious purposes and reasons. Consequently, the Believer will not be happy, fulfilled, or satisfied any other place. The idea is to find what that place is, which can be found easily, and walk therein, thereby making the most of what God has called us to do, irrespective as to what it might be.

However, if the Believer, or anyone for that matter, rebels against this which is selected by the Lord, in effect going his own way, the end result can be nothing but destruction.

## TWO PROBLEMS . . .

The latter of which we have spoken, refers to sinners who will not come to their assigned place of Salvation, and, correspondingly, die eternally lost. In other words, all sinners are *"assigned"* to Salvation, but if they refuse and rebel, they are then *"assigned"* to eternal perdition.

Believers as well, even as we are here studying, are assigned particular places in the Plan of God. It is in that place only that the Believer can grow in Grace and the Knowledge of the Lord.

Regrettably, many Believers attempt to carve out their own place, ignoring that which the Lord has assigned for them, which stops all spiritual growth, by and large making the Believer ineffective for the Cause of Christ. Regrettably, that's where many Believers are.

(18) "IS ANY MAN CALLED BEING CIRCUMCISED? LET HIM NOT BECOME UNCIRCUMCISED. IS ANY CALLED IN UNCIRCUMCISION? LET HIM NOT BE CIRCUMCISED."

The question, *"Is any man called being circumcised?"*, presents Paul using an illustration which dealt with both Jews and Gentiles. The first question pertains to the Jew.

The phrase, *"Let him not become uncircumcised,"* in effect says, *"Forget the Circumcision, it has already served its purpose, and is of no more consequence, at least as far as having a spiritual meaning is concerned."*

The question, *"Is any called in uncircumcision?"*, refers to Gentiles.

The phrase, *"Let him not be circumcised,"* refers to Circumcision for spiritual reasons. In effect, the Holy Spirit through the Apostle is saying that both, Jews and Gentiles, enjoy parity in God's Church (Gal. 3:28), which means that the symbolism of the past, as important as it then was, has all been fulfilled in Christ, and, consequently, should not now be given any spiritual weight.

## EARLY CHRISTIANITY

The early fortunes of Christianity had been almost shipwrecked by the attempt of Jewish rigorists to enforce this odious bondage on the Gentiles, and their deliverance from it had been due almost solely to the Apostle Paul.

It was inspired insight which had swayed the decision of the Council at Jerusalem (Acts Chpt. 15); and at a later period Paul's Epistle to the Galatians was the manifesto of Gentile Emancipation. He proved that after Christ's Death *"Circumcision"* was of no more spiritual value (Phil. 3:3).

NOTES

## WHAT ACTUALLY DID CIRCUMCISION MEAN?

On the eighth day of life, a Hebrew boy was to have the fold of skin covering the end of his penis cut off. This rite was called *"Circumcision."*

After God reconfirmed His Covenant Promise to Abraham for the third and last time, the Lord said to his descendants: *"Any uncircumcised male, who has not been circumcised in the flesh, will be cut off from his people; he has broken My Covenant"* (Gen. 17:14).

This meant that the uncircumcised Israelite was not covered by the Covenant Promise given to Abraham. Circumcision was the symbol of that Covenant.

## SUBMISSION TO GOD

The rite symbolized submission to God and belief in His Covenant Promise, that He would send a Redeemer. But God also required a *"Circumcision of the heart"* (Deut. 10:16; 30:6; Jer. 4:4), which of course was spiritual, and explained as a Faith-rooted, heart-and-soul Love for God that issues in obedience.

The New Testament argues that Abraham was Justified by Faith even while he was uncircumcised, years before the rite was actually given. Circumcision was a sign: *"A seal of the Righteousness that he had by Faith while he was still uncircumcised"* (Rom. 4:11; Gen. 15:6; 17:10-27).

## THE CHURCH

When Jesus came, the sign of Circumcision was no longer needed, because the Covenant was now fulfilled. Consequently, the sign of Circumcision was not carried over into the Church. However, many Hebrew Christians struggled to impose Circumcision, and the Mosaic Law as well, on Gentile Christians (Acts 15:1). As stated, this was rejected at the Jerusalem Council (Acts 15:1-29).

Paul, as stated, vigorously opposed the efforts of some to bring the old Jewish customs into the Church, especially considering that all of it had been fulfilled in Christ. His point was that God has never been concerned for the symbol as a thing in itself. God cares about the reality.

It is our heart response to Him that counts. Thus, looking into hearts and examining those who have responded to Christ's Gospel, the Bible says, *"It is we who are the* (true) *Circumcision, we who worship by the Spirit of God, who Glory in Christ Jesus, and who put no confidence in the flesh"* (Phil. 3:3).

(19) "CIRCUMCISION IS NOTHING, AND UNCIRCUMCISION IS NOTHING, BUT THE KEEPING OF THE COMMANDMENTS OF GOD."

The phrase, *"Circumcision is nothing, and uncircumcision is nothing,"* presents in fact, an inflammatory statement.

In fact, the Jews, even most Christian Jews, regarded it as everything. For Paul to make this assertion so grandly and boldly required courage to say the least. However, what he said was right, and the Holy Spirit, Who inspired him to say these words, desired that he say it just as boldly as he did.

Jewish Christians (sounds like a misnomer, doesn't it!), for the most part, were still trying to hold on to the Mosaic Law, as well as accepting Jesus as Lord and Saviour. In other words, they were attempting to wed the two.

Paul was given the New Covenant by a Revelation from Jesus Christ. Of course, with the New Covenant given, there was no more need for the Old Covenant, it being fulfilled in Christ. So, the Ceremonial part of the Law, which was fulfilled in Christ, and which included Circumcision, was no more needed. Why would one need the symbol, when the reality was now present!

Irrespective, it was very difficult for many Jews to lay the old garment aside even though it was now old and worn. They kept trying to attach the new cloth to the old, and it simply would not work (Mat. 9:16).

The phrase, *"But the keeping of the Commandments of God,"* would have seemed like a contradiction to many Jewish Christians. They would have argued, that the rite of Circumcision was a *"Commandment of God."*

While of course, that had been correct in the past, it was no longer correct at present, and because that which Circumcision symbolized and represented, namely The Lord Jesus Christ, had now come, making all the symbolism invalid. Many Christian Jews were attempting to make the keeping of the Law of Moses a part of one's Salvation (Acts 15:1). Paul combatted this endlessly, in that Salvation was strictly by Faith and Faith alone (Eph. 2:8-9).

NOTES

### WHAT ARE THE COMMANDMENTS OF GOD OF WHICH PAUL SPEAKS?

The Commandments in the Words of Jesus, can be summed up in their entirety, and covering both Testaments, in the Great Commandment of Loving the Lord with all of one's heart, etc., and one's neighbor as oneself (Mat. 22:36-40).

However, it would be profitable to look at the entirety of *"Commandments"* relative to both, the Old and New Testaments.

### COMMANDMENTS

To some people the word *"command"* evokes quick resentment. To them, even God's Commandments seem restrictive, as if they are barriers that limit freedom. But such persons are unaware — or have forgotten — that God's Commands were given to Israel for her own good (Deut. 10:13).

### HEBREW WORDS

Many different Hebrew words are translated *"command"* or *"order."* Some are ordinary words meaning *"to speak or utter"* (such as *"dabar"* and *"amar"*). With such words, context determines whether the utterance is a Command, a Revelation, a Statement, a Message, or some other entity.

Three Hebrew words are found most often when English Versions speak of God's Commands and Commandments.

*"Peh"* means *"mouth."* Found some 500 times in the Old Testament, this Hebrew word in 50 or so occurrences refers to God's Mouth. In nearly every context in which God is speaking with His Mouth, He is portrayed as Lord. Twenty-four times the phrase *"according to the Mouth of the Lord"* is used as a formula to indicate the Divine origin of a statement.

Where *"peh"* is found, the emphasis is on the fact that God speaks clearly and with authority. Whether an utterance is a Prophecy (Isa. 40:5; 62:2) or a Command (Ex. 7:1; 38:21; Num. 3:39; 14:41; Deut. 1:26, 43), the Message comes from the Creator and Lord of the Universe.

The use of the word *"mouth"* does not imply an anthropomorphic view of God. The mouth is the organ of speech. Used in relationship to God, *"peh"* affirms that God can and does communicate with His People.

GOD'S COMMANDS

*"Sawah"* means *"to command"* or *"to charge."* What God *"commands"* is always significant. God commanded the world into existence (Ps. 33:9; Isa. 45:12). He commanded the Covenant (Ps. 105:8; 111:9). He commands Blessing to those who are faithful to Him (Deut. 28:8; Ps. 133:3).

God's Commands give structure to our Universe. In commanding Creation, God established regularity and stability in the material realm. In commanding the Covenant, He gave regularity and stability to His relationship with His People. In commanding human beings, God gives regularity and stability in the moral realm.

Thus, the Old Testament warns Israel, *"Be careful to do what the Lord your God has commanded you; do not turn aside to the right or to the left. Walk in all the way that the Lord your God has commanded you, so that you may live and prosper and prolong your days in the land that you will possess"* (Deut. 5:32-33).

RELATIONSHIP WITH GOD

The Hebrew word *"miswah"* is found in nearly all instances where the English Texts read *"Commandment."* It is used almost exclusively in a spiritual way.

Specifically, *"miswah"* spells out the responsibilities of human beings who live in Covenant Relationship with the Lord. Thus, the Commandments, though they unveil those moral principles on which the social Universe is established, are ultimately rooted in relationship with God.

Keeping the *"miswah"* is a personal response to God, for the Commandments show how His People must live to remain in harmony with One Who is Holy.

THE COMMANDMENTS OF GOD

God's Commandments reveal the moral structure of our Universe. More significantly, the *"miswah"* defined how Israel was to live in Covenant Relationship with God.

The Old Testament provides a number of important insights that shape our view of the Commands and Commandments of God.

NOTES

THE MORAL CHARACTER OF GOD

The Commandments express the Moral Character of God, consequently telling us Who and What He is. As such, they are pure (Ps. 19:8), true (119:151), reliable (119:86), and righteous (119:172).

The person in right relationship with God delights in the Commandments (119:47, 143), loves them (119:48), and finds comfort in them (119:52). Our conviction concerning God, that declares to Him, *"You are good, and what you do is good"* (Ps. 119:68) helps the Believer realize that God's Commands are intended to define for us what is morally good and thus, to reveal the Character of our Lord.

GOD'S MOTIVE IN GIVING THE COMMANDMENTS

His Motive is explained in the Old Testament. The Commands given to Israel *"set before* (them) *life and death, blessings and curses"* (Deut. 30:19).

God's Own Moral Character demands that He punish evil and bless good. Thus, making the good clear to humanity is a distinct Blessing: the Commandments that express the good are clearly a rich gift.

So God's Love for Israel was not only expressed in His Sovereign choice of this family and in their Redemption from Egypt (Deut. 4:37). It was also seen in the Mosaic Law.

Moses told Israel to keep God's *"Decrees and Commands . . . I am giving you today, so that it may go well with you and your children after you"* (Deut. 4:40).

THE FREE MORAL AGENCY OF HUMAN BEINGS

Human beings can choose to respond obediently to or to reject God's Commandments. The context in which the Commandments are found promises Blessing for obedience and warns against disasters which follow disobedience.

But no individual is forced against his or her will to choose to live by the Commandments.

CONSEQUENCES

Moral choices have consequences. The warnings and the promises provided with the *"miswah* (Commandment)*"* make it plain that a Moral Law operates in the Universe. In addition, God is Personally involved in supervision of the consequences of moral choices.

No wonder, then, that Moses warns, *"Know therefore that the Lord your God is God; He is the faithful God, keeping His Covenant of Love to a thousand generations of those who love Him and keep His Commandments.*

*"But those who hate Him He will repay to their face by destruction; He will not be slow to repay to their face those who hate Him"* (Deut. 7:9-10).

More seriously, violation of the Commandments is sin and requires Atonement.

## MOTIVATION

Love alone is able to motivate a keeping of God's Commandments. God's Call to Israel through Moses is: *"Hear O Israel: The Lord our God, the Lord is One. Love the Lord your God with all your heart and with all your soul and with all your strength. These Commandments that I give you today are to be upon your hearts"* (Deut. 6:4-6). Love for God must be in our hearts before His Commandments will be taken to heart (Deut. 10:12-13; 11:1).

Because God is a Moral Person and the Universe He structured is intended to express His Character, humanity needed a Revelation of the good. Old Testament Commandments served as that Revelation, setting before God's People the way of goodness and making possible intelligent personal moral choices.

The giving of the Commandments was motivated by Divine Love: keeping them is also motivated by the Believer's Love for God.

## THE TEN COMMANDMENTS

After Israel left Egypt and came to Mount Sinai, God gave the people His Law.

First, the Lord said to Moses, *"Come up to Me on the mountain and stay here, and I will give you the Tablets of Stone, with the Law and Commands I have written for their* (Israel's) *instruction"* (Ex. 24:12).

Those stone-etched Commandments are recorded in Exodus, Chapter 20 and Deuteronomy, Chapter 5. Although the Old Testament contains many Commandments in similar form (*"You shall not . . ."*), these Ten Commandments from Sinai are set apart as special. They were written by the Finger of God and later enshrined in the Ark of the Covenant (II Chron. 5:10; Heb. 9:4).

NOTES

## RELATIONSHIPS

The Ten Commandments deal with relationships — with God and with other members of God's Covenant Community. Commandments 1 through 5 have to do with our relationship with God.

The First: God Alone is to be recognized as God (Ex. 20:3).

The Second: No idol is to be made, to represent either God or any other supernatural power (Ex. 20:4).

The Third: The Name of God is not to be considered an empty symbol, as though God were not real and powerful (Ex. 20:7). God is to be honored as Creator.

The Fourth: The seventh day is to be set apart for rest. Israel's life is patterned by the rhythm of a seven-day week (Ex. 20:8-11).

The Fifth: Parents are to be honored by their children. This is often considered a Command for the Second Tablet, which deals with relationships within the community. But the Command adds the formula *"so that you may live long in the land the Lord your God is giving you,"* a Blessing that is associated with obedience to the Lord (Deut. 4:40; 6:2; 11:9; 22:7; 25:15; 30:18; 32:47).

It seems better to consider this Fifth Command as part of the First Tablet linked to our relationship with God. Briefly, children must be obedient to the authority of parents so they will learn to submit and later obey God's Ultimate Authority (Ex. 20:12).

## INTERPERSONAL RELATIONSHIPS

The next Five Commands governed interpersonal relationships in Israel.

The Sixth: God's People are to guard one another's lives (*"You shall not murder,"* Ex. 20:13).

The Seventh: God's People are to be faithful to Covenant commitments (*"You shall not commit adultery,"* Ex. 20:14).

The Eighth: God's People are to respect others' property (*"You shall not steal,"* Ex. 20:15).

The Ninth: God's People are to guard one another's reputations (*"You shall not give false testimony,"* Ex. 20:16).

The Tenth: God's People are not to envy other people for their possessions (Ex. 20:17).

This final Command defines the heart attitude that releases us to keep the other Four in the Second Tablet.

There are several things to notice about the relationship of these Ten Commandments with the other Old Testament Commandments.

## COMMUNICATION

Most Commandments are given as negatives: *"You shall not"* (Lev. Chpts. 18-19). The negatives describe a specific action rather than a general principle. In a list given in Leviticus, Chapter 19 we are likely to find *"Do not steal"* (Lev. 19:11) and also *"Do not defraud your neighbor or rob him"* (Lev. 19:13) and *"Do not hold back the wages of a hired man overnight."*

The list also contains *"Do not lie"* and *"Do not show partiality . . . but judge your neighbor fairly"* (Lev. 19:15).

Why these multiplied examples rather than a simple general statement of principle?

Probably because there are different ways of communicating meaning. A dictionary defines words by the use of other words, relying on concepts to communicate meaning. An operational or behavioral definition takes a different approach. It defines by providing a number of examples or illustrations, thus giving a feeling for, or a sensitivity to, meaning.

The Old Testament chooses to use the second approach to help God's People grasp the Path of Righteousness.

## ILLUSTRATIONS

Some view the Ten Commandments, and rightly so, as the essence of the Commandments and believe that all the others can be derived logically from them. In a sense, then, the other Commandments are illustrations of how God's People are to go about building moral sensibilities.

It has been noted in support of this that the Chapters immediately following the giving of the Ten Commandments (Ex. 21-24) present case Laws: they give illustrations of how principles expressed in the Stone Code can be applied to the daily life of God's Old Testament People.

## POSITIVE GENERAL STATEMENTS

Within the Leviticus, Chapter 19 list of *"Do nots"* are two strong positive general statements: *"Fear your God"* (Lev. 19:14) and *"Love your neighbour as yourself"* (Lev. 19:18).

These two statements express the core principles of Love for God and for neighbor that find expression in the Tablets of the Ten Commandments and the other Commandments of the Old Testament.

NOTES

## THE NEW TESTAMENT

A number of Greek words are found where various Translations read *"Command"* and *"Commandment."* Some, like the Hebrew words, simply mean *"to speak"* or *"to transmit a message."*

The nature of the Message is determined by the contexts. Several other terms mean *"to charge," "to command,"* or *"to give orders"* (entellomai, epitasso, prostasso, keleuo). But the word group that is particularly important to us is that of *"entellomai"* (verb) and *"entole"* (noun).

These Greek words were used in the Septuagint to translate most Hebrew words rendered *"command,"* and especially for the critical *"miswah."* As is so often the case, the Biblical meaning of God's *"entole* (Command)*"* is defined within the Scriptures and is not derived from the cultural meaning of the term.

## JESUS AND THE COMMANDMENTS

In Jesus' time there was debate about Commandments. Some Rabbis attempted to distinguish between the vital and the less significant Commandments of the Law.

Other Rabbis sought to formulate foundational principles that would express the heart and soul of the Law. Jesus' Teachings take on special meaning against the background of these controversies.

## THE MOTIVES OF ONE'S HEART

On the one hand, Jesus warned that *"Anyone who breaks one of the least of these Commandments and teaches others to do the same will be called least in the Kingdom of Heaven"* (Mat. 5:19). No Commandment of God is irrelevant or to be ignored. But immediately Jesus went on to point out that an individual's righteousness must surpass that of the Pharisees and the Teachers of the Law, who took pride in keeping all the Commandments.

Jesus then gave illustrations (Mat. 5:21-24) that show that while the Commandments deal with behavior, God looks within at the motives of one's heart. The Commandments must not be ignored, but neither should they be understood as God's last Word on Righteousness.

NOTES

### THE GREATEST COMMANDMENT?

When Jesus was asked, *"Teacher, which is the greatest Commandment in the Law,"* He responded: *"Love the Lord your God with all your heart and with all your soul and with all your mind. This is the First and Greatest Commandment. And the Second is like it: 'Love your neighbour as yourself.' All the Law and the Prophets hang on these Two Commandments"* (Mat. 22:36-40).

All the Commandments are important, for each Commandment is an expression of God's basic concern: Love for God and Love for others.

### MAN'S INVENTIONS

The Pharisees misunderstood the unitary nature of the Commandments. They invented one interpretation that permitted them to will property or income to the Temple after their death. They then used the excuse *"It is dedicated to God"* to withhold help from their needy parents. By this traditional interpretation the Pharisees placed the Commandments in a hierarchy and in effect argued that keeping a greater Commandment (to honor God) made breaking of a lesser one (to honor parents) acceptable (Mat. 15:1-9).

This hypocritical tradition denied the unity of God's Commandments — a unity that rests on the fact that the Commandments show man how to Love God and how to Love others. No Israelite who followed God's Old Testament Commands would ever be required to break one to obey another.

The Commandments were woven together into a unified whole, revealing to Israel Love's lifestyle.

### THE NEW COVENANT

In view of this, Jesus' Words at the Last Supper are uniquely significant. At this meal the evening before the Crucifixion, Jesus introduced God's New Covenant, about to be instituted in His Death (Mat. 26:17-30; Mk. 14:22-25; Lk. 22:17-20).

John takes us into the Upper Room with the Lord and records the conversation that took place. What is important to us is to remember that the Commandments showed Israel how to live in Covenant Relationship with God. Now that a New Covenant was to be instituted to replace the old Mosaic Covenant, there had also to be New Commandments to guide the Believer.

Jesus stated the Believer's ultimate guideline with utter simplicity. *"A New Command I give you: Love one another. As I have loved you, so you must Love one another"* (Jn. 13:34).

### GENERAL PRINCIPLES

What is significant here is not that the Old Commandments are set aside with the Old Covenant but that now Believers are guided more by general principles and less by detailed instructions.

Paul comments on this New Commandment and on Jesus' remark that the Law and the Prophets hang on the Command to Love God and others: *"Let no debt remain outstanding, except the continuing debt to Love one another, for he who loves his fellowman has fulfilled the Law."*

The Commandments, *"Do not commit adultery," "Do not murder," "Do not steal," "Do not covet,"* and whatever other Commandment there may be, are summed up in this one rule: *"Love your neighbour as yourself. Love does no harm to its neighbour. Therefore Love is the fulfillment of the Law"* (Rom. 13:8-10).

### PAUL

Paul's attitude toward the Commandments in Old Testament Law is expressed in Romans, Chapter 7. Viewed in themselves, the Commandments are *"Holy, Righteous and Good."* But when the system as a whole is examined, linking Commandment, humanity and sin, Law itself is seen to be ineffectual.

*"We know that the Law is spiritual,"* Paul says, *"But I am unspiritual"* (Rom. 7:14). Law with its Commandments is powerless to release the individual from the principle of sin and debt, *"In that it* (Law) *was weakened by the sinful nature"* (Rom. 8:2-3).

The Rabbis held that the Law with its Commands was a tool to subdue evil inclinations. Paul argues the opposite.

Evil is in human nature. The Commandment energizes that sinful nature rather than subdues it (Rom. 7:5, 8:11). Just as a Mother's warning to a small boy not to touch the cookies makes his mouth water, so God's *"You shall not covet"* provokes human desire.

### THE SOLUTION?

The solution is not to deny the goodness of the Commandments. The solution for Paul is to realize that the external expression of God's Moral Nature found in the Written Commandments is no longer relevant to Faith. Jesus has abolished, Paul says, *"In His Flesh the Law with its Commandments and Regulations"* (Eph. 2:15).

Rather than relating to Written Commandments, the Believer now lives in relationship to the Spirit of God, Who Personally guides him along the path the Commandments also mark out (Rom. 8:4-9).

Given a new nature and being supernaturally enabled by the Spirit, we today are to live a life of Love, for *"Love does no harm to its neighbour"* and thus, *"Love is the fulfillment of the Law"* (Rom. 13:10).

## HEBREWS

The writer of Hebrews makes the same points. The Old Covenant has been replaced, the *"Former Regulation* (Commandment) *is set aside because it was weak and useless"* (Heb. 7:18). It is replaced with a better hope, linked to the Priesthood of Jesus, Who offered Himself up as a Sacrifice that God might keep His Promise: *"I will put My Laws in their minds and write them on their hearts"* (Heb. 8:10; Jer. 31:31-34).

What no external Commandments could accomplish, God has now made possible by planting Love for Him and for others deep within our renewed hearts.

## JOHN THE BELOVED

In the Gospel of John, unlike the Synoptics, *"Commandments"* usually refer to an utterance of Jesus rather than to an Old Testament Commandment. Jesus is the Revealer of the Will of God and speaks with Divine Authority.

Not only does Jesus' New Commandment lay the basis for our understanding of all Commandments, but Jesus Himself demonstrated what He meant. He loved us unselfishly, to the death (Jn. 13:33-34).

## FELLOWSHIP

John's First Letter focuses on fellowship with God. In a sense it is the New Testament's Answer to Leviticus. That Old Testament Book explained how a person maintained fellowship with God under the Mosaic Covenant.

John explains how we live in fellowship with God under the New Covenant. John emphasizes: A. Jesus' continual purification of our sins (I Jn. 1:5-2:2); B. Response to God that is demonstrated in keeping His Commandments/Word (I Jn. 2:3-8); and, C. Response to God that is demonstrated in Love for our brothers (I Jn. 2:9-11). These last two themes are repeated again and again in John's Epistles.

## LOVING JESUS

Unlike Moses in Leviticus, John does not detail numerous Commandments that Believers are to keep. John deals with principles, holding that Believers know the Truth, for they have been Anointed by the Holy Spirit and thus given spiritual insight into all things (I Jn. 2:20-27).

The specific Commandments are of value, in that one who is unresponsive to God's inner Voice can look to the Old Testament Code and in the Commandments imbedded in Law, have an objective criterion against which to measure his or her actions (I Jn. 3:4).

The Christian, however, develops a righteous life not by studying the Commandments but by loving Jesus. We are Children of God and have been given New Birth by Him. God's Seed is within us, so we will not *"go on sinning"* but will do what is right (I Jn. 3:1-10).

Like Paul, John places no trust in the Old Testament System, which had to rely on a righteousness expressed in external Commandments. John relies instead on the Work of God within the heart of the Believer.

The Old Testament Code demanded performance, which man was helpless to provide. To the contrary the New Covenant is based on *"Promise,"* which pertains to The Lord Jesus Christ.

In other words, He promised as the Representative Man, to do for us what we could not do for ourselves. That He did and in every capacity.

As well, He lived up totally to the Old Testament demand for *"performance,"* satisfying the Law in every respect, and then turned around as a result of our Faith, and gave the performance (Perfect Law Keeping) to Believers.

## RIGHTEOUSNESS AND HUMANITY

God's Commandments express His Moral Character and thus reveal Righteousness to humanity. The Old Testament Commandments express the moral responsibilities of those living in Covenant Relationship with God.

NOTES

Although the Commandments were in themselves holy, just, and good, they were unable to produce Righteousness in members of the Old Testament Community because of human weakness.

Jesus affirmed the Commandments. He taught that not one of them could be ignored. But He also taught that God is concerned with more than the behavior that the Commandments regulated.

God is concerned with our inner desires and motives. Moreover, Jesus showed that the specific regulations imbedded as Commandments in Old Testament Law actually expressed two principles. God wants us to Love Him and to Love one another. The Old Testament Commandments were pointers along the pathway of life and were designed to show Israel how to Love.

## A NEW COMMANDMENT

When Jesus instituted His New Covenant, He stated a New Commandment. Believers are to Love one another as Jesus has loved them. Paul points out that the one who loves in this way will fulfill the Commandments.

More importantly, Paul argues that the Old Testament System, which relied on Commandments to control human inclination to evil, was bound to fail. As long as the human heart is in bondage to sin, the Commandments can only stimulate it to evil. God's Solution has been to give human beings a new heart.

He now writes His Own Morality, once expressed in Stone, in the Living Person. As a Believer lives in fellowship with Jesus, his actions flow from his New Birth and he spontaneously fulfills the requirements expressed in the Commandments.

## WHAT THEY TEACH

We should study God's Old Testament Commands. They teach us about God and help us develop sensitivity to His Will.

And when our hearts wander from the Lord, the Commandments give us objective evidence that we are not walking in fellowship with Jesus. Yet it is not the Commandments but the New Birth and a Living Relationship with Jesus that will transform us from within, which the Commandments could never do.

Jesus Alone will enable us to live the life that is truly good.

NOTES

(The statement on Commandments provided by Lawrence O. Richards.)

(20) "LET EVERY MAN ABIDE IN THE SAME CALLING WHEREIN HE WAS CALLED."

The idea of this Verse pertains to the state or position in which one is, when one comes to Christ. Hence, John the Baptist had not bidden Publicans (Tax-collectors) or soldiers to abandon their callings, but to do their duty in that state of life to which God had called them, or in which they found themselves (Lk. 3:12-14).

Of course this pertains to positions or particular jobs which are honorable. It does not mean that the bartender is to continue tending bar, or the dope pusher is to continue in his wicked trade, etc.

*"Calling"* in the Greek is *"klesis"* and means *"an invitation."* In other words, the *"Calling"* alluded to is not what is described as a *"vocation,"* a calling in life, but the condition in which we are when we are Called by God (Eph. 1:18; 4:1).

*"Called"* in the Greek is *"kaleo,"* and means *"an order or command,"* in other words, one's occupation.

This illustrates the distinction between Christianity and violent social revolutions. As well, Christians place little stock even in peaceful political revolutions. The Child of God, with Jesus in his heart, knows that conditions cannot really be changed, until the hearts of wicked men are changed. Consequently, Christians are to attempt to live a life which portrays what the Lord can do, and that men may see the changed life, and desire what the individual has in Christ. This is the ideal of Christianity, and actually its driving force. Untold numbers have come to Christ, and been remarkably changed, simply because they saw what Jesus had done in the lives of others. Remarkably, this works in any and all walks of life, from the lowest to the highest, and is what makes Biblical Christianity the most effective change agent on the face of the Earth.

(21) "ART THOU CALLED BEING A SERVANT? CARE NOT FOR IT: BUT IF THOU MAYEST BE MADE FREE, USE IT RATHER."

The question, *"Art thou called being a servant? Care not for it,"* strikes at the very heart of most modern social and political programs.

The word *"servant"* as used here, actually refers to being a slave. Paul is saying that being a slave will not hinder one from being a Christian. In other words, the Holy Spirit can make His Home in the heart of a slave just as much as He can anyone else, and as well, use that person for the Glory of God.

## A PRESENT DILEMMA

The other day while listening to my car radio on the way to the Church, I overheard for a few minutes a round-table discussion, I suppose it was, by several African Americans. One made the statement:

*"We all felt that when President Johnson instituted the most sweeping Civil Rights Legislation in American history, that that would solve our problems; however,"* the man went on to say, *"we find ourselves little better off than before."*

Another asked, *"Well, what is the answer?"*

There was a moment of silence, and then another member of the discussion said, *"It is education that the Nation needs respecting the race problem."* He then said, *"If that could be brought about, our problems will be solved."*

Regrettably, this man is dead wrong! The problem is not legislation nor education, but rather spiritual. In other words, man does not treat his fellowman right, until his wicked heart is changed. Regrettably, that cannot be done by legislation or education, or anything else for that matter, except Jesus Christ. To be frank, man is not free, until he is free spiritually, and he can only be free spiritually, when he is set free by his Faith in Jesus Christ, The Lord of Glory. When he experiences that freedom, there is nothing that man can do to him thereafter, that will ever truly enslave him again.

## SLAVES UNDER THE MOSAIC LAW

While there were slaves under Old Testament Law, which meant this was Law given by God, the fact is, the situation was mostly subject to economic conditions and had nothing to do with race or status. But yet, Gentiles who were taken in battle could be used as slaves.

The Law sought to avoid the risk of wholesale population-drift into slavery and serfdom under economic pressure on the unfortunate, by limiting the length of service that insolvent debtors had to serve. Six years was the limit, and their release had to be accompanied by the provision of sufficient assets to make a new start (Ex. 21:2-6; Deut. 15:12-18).

NOTES

A man already married when thus enslaved took his wife with him at release, but if he was formerly single and was given a wife by his master, that wife and any children remained the master's. Hence, those who wished to stay in service and keep their family could do so permanently (Ex. 21:6; Deut. 15:16).

However, at Jubilee (every fiftieth year), he would be released in any case (Lev. 25:40), along with the restoration of all his inheritance previously lost (Lev. 25:28).

## VOLUNTARY SLAVERY

At times, Hebrews would voluntarily sell themselves into slavery to escape from poverty and would serve their master until Jubilee year, when they would go free (Lev. 25:39-43) and receive back their inheritance at that time (Lev. 25:28).

However, if their master was a foreigner (and foreigners were allowed to own Hebrew slaves in Israel), they had the option of purchasing their freedom or being redeemed by a relative at any time before Jubilee (Lev. 25:47-55).

## CONDITIONS

As we can see, even though the Law of Moses did allow slavery, it was under very stringent conditions and was tied mostly to economic situations. To be frank, it was not so much different than an employer and employee relationship. While that term may not be quite strong enough, in no way did *"slavery"* under the Old Testament Economy resemble anything as to what is known as slavery elsewhere in the world.

To be sure, at times the Law of Moses was greatly abrogated by the Leadership of Israel, with such men and women being treated harshly. However, it was greatly rebuked by the Holy Spirit through the Prophet (Jer. 34:8-17).

## PAUL AND SLAVERY

The word *"emancipation"* sometimes seems (as in the Letter to Philemon) to be *"trembling on Paul's lips,"* but he never utters it, because to do so would have been to kindle a social revolt, and lead to the very thing Christianity was attempting to avoid.

Our Lord had taught the Apostles to adapt means to ends; and the method of Christianity was to inculcate great principles, the acceptance of which involved, with all the certainty of a Law, the ultimate regeneration of the world.

In other words, it was not the purpose of Christianity to change political situations, but rather to preach Jesus, and, therefore, to change the hearts of men. Then, and only then, can satisfactory political situations change. In fact, that is what has changed much of the world today from the time of the Roman Empire when most of humanity were slaves and in the most servile sense. To be sure, it has not been the foray of the Church into the political arena, as it is now attempting to do, but rather the very opposite. In fact, situations can little be changed by political means. They can only be changed in an absolute sense, by the preaching of the Gospel of Jesus Christ, with the Holy Spirit doing His Office Work in the hearts of men regarding the New Birth, changing them for the better, which then brings about political, economic, and social changes.

To be sure, in Paul's day, or any other time for that matter, slavery was and is wrong, at least in the sense that it was being carried on in the Roman Empire, and had been in most of the world since the dawn of time. Nevertheless, slavery was not the real problem of humanity, but rather the result of an evil heart. As stated, there is only One Who can change that, and that is The Lord Jesus Christ.

## AS THE DAWN, NOT AS THE NOON

Christianity came into the world as the dawn, not as the noon, a shining light, which brightened more and more unto the perfect day.

In other words, Judaism, at least in its purest form, prepared the world for the Advent of the Messiah, even though in its corrupted form, it did not even recognize Him when He came. Nevertheless, the founding of the Church by Christ, due to the fact of Israel's rejection of the Kingdom and the King, actually characterized the beginning, even though society had been in existence for approximately four thousand years.

All wrongs, all grievances, all of man's inhumanity to man, all unfairness, all iniquities, have been addressed alone by Biblical Christianity, i.e., *"The Lord Jesus Christ."*

The phrase, *"But if thou mayest be made free, use it rather,"* refers to freedom as a preference, if such can be obtained, which of course would be obvious. Nevertheless, the idea of the Text is that it doesn't make a great deal of difference either way. A person's life is not in that type of freedom or the lack of such.

NOTES

I think it should be obvious at the indifference which Paul felt and expressed towards mere earthly conditions (Gal. 3:28), as things of no real significance (Col. 3:22). The idea in this life is service to Christ. In whatever place we find ourselves, and the Apostle means whatever place, we can be of service to the Lord, which is all that really matters.

(22) "FOR HE THAT IS CALLED IN THE LORD, BEING A SERVANT, IS THE LORD'S FREEMAN: LIKEWISE ALSO HE THAT IS CALLED, BEING FREE, IS CHRIST'S SERVANT."

The phrase, *"For he that is called in the Lord, being a servant* (though he be a slave), *is the Lord's freeman,"* is all that really matters.

A slave was to live in the power of being Christ's freedman; and that power would deliver him from depression of heart because he was a slave. But if he could obtain his freedom he should do so, for thus, he would be liberated from the capricious government of a heathen master and be free to wholly serve the Lord. But all, whether bond or free, were to be most concerned with their relation toward the Lord.

## THE MANNER OF THE HOLY SPIRIT

It is beautiful the way the Holy Spirit uses the Apostle to drive home the fact that right relationship with the Lord, can make pleasant even the most servile life of an individual, even a slave.

The idea is, that the bondage of Satan is so crushing that mere earthly bondage is in comparison, as nothing; and that the liberty wherewith Christ has made us free, though it might seem to take the form of service, is in fact, the greatest freedom of all. Those in sin are the most hopeless slaves irrespective of their status in the world; the servants of God alone are free (Rom. 6:22; II Tim. 2:26; I Pet. 2:16) (Farrar).

## A BONDSLAVE OF JESUS CHRIST

The phrase, *"Likewise also he that is called* (Saved), *being free, is Christ's servant,"* makes us bondslaves of Jesus Christ.

The use of these terms, such as a *"bondslave of Jesus Christ,"* may seem somewhat strange. Actually, the Greek inscriptions show that many technical terms in Pagan religions and in Governmental circles of the First Century A.D., are also found in the terminology of Christianity, even as it is used here by Paul.

For instance, the expression, *"Slave of the Emperor,"* was in current use in Paul's day. There were imperial slaves all over the Roman world. This throws light upon Paul's claim to be a *"bondslave of Jesus Christ"* (Rom. 1:1), the word *"servant"* coming from a Greek word literally meaning *"bondslave,"* the same Greek word being used in the inscriptions.

Paul knew of this custom. The Lord Emperor was not only revered as a human ruler but also worshiped as a god. When Paul wrote these words to the Christians in Rome, he must have been conscious of the Imperialistic challenge of Christianity proclaiming a Saviour Whose bondslave He was, and Who someday would come to displace the Imperialism of Rome.

Paul was someday to stand before Nero, not as a bondslave of the Lord Emperor, but as a bondslave of the King of kings, the One Who came from the Royal Line of David.

## THE LORD'S FREEMAN

The title, *"Freedman of the Emperor,"* is found frequently in the Greek inscriptions of the First Century.

To be a bondslave of the Emperor was a position of servitude with a certain degree of honor attached to it, but to be the Emperor's freeman, meant that the bondslave was liberated from that servitude and promoted to a position of a free man, which was a higher station. Paul in this Verse we are now studying (I Cor. 7:22) says that the Christian is both the bondslave and the freeman of the Lord.

How can he be both at the same time? The beautiful story can be told in three Greek words translated *"bought"* and *"redeem."*

## *"BOUGHT"*

The first word *"bought"* means *"to buy in the marketplace."* It was used of the purchase of slaves. Sinners were bondslaves of Satan and sin (Rom. 6:17-18; Eph. 2:2).

We were purchased in the slave market, the price paid, the Precious Blood of Jesus. I Corinthians 6:20 uses this word. We were bondslaves of Satan, and we became bondslaves of Jesus Christ.

NOTES

A slave cannot say that he belongs to himself, but to his master. We belong to Christ. The word is also used in II Peter 2:1, where false teachers who deny the Lord who purchased them in the slave market refuse to avail themselves of the high privilege of becoming His bondslaves.

In Revelation 5:9, the Saints in Heaven are singing a song which speaks of the Lamb Who bought them in the slave market to become His Own bondslaves. Thus, Paul tells his readers that those who have put their trust in Jesus as Saviour, were purchased in the slave market, and are bondslaves of the coming King of kings (I Cor. 7:22-23).

## *"REDEEMED"*

We are told in the same Passage (I Cor. 7:22) that we are also the Lord's freemen. This brings us to the other words translated *"redeemed."*

One of those words means *"to buy out of the marketplace."* Galatians 3:13, which uses this word, tells us that we were purchased in the slave market, but in such a way that while we are bondslaves of the Purchaser, the Lord Jesus, we are never again to be put up for sale in any slave market. We have been bought out of the slave market. This means that we are bondslaves of the Lord Jesus forever.

He will never sell us or permit us to be sold as slaves to anyone else. A bondslave of Jesus Christ never becomes a bondslave of Satan again.

## THE PAYMENT OF A RANSOM

The other word translated *"redeemed"* means *"to release or liberate by payment of a ransom,"* and is used in Titus 2:14 and I Peter 1:18. The noun having the same root means *"ransom money used to liberate a slave."*

After our Blessed Lord buys us in the slave market, the ransom money being His Own Precious Blood, we become His private property. We are His bondslaves. Then He so arranges the details of the purchase that we will never be put up for sale in any slave market. He buys us out of the slave market. Then He sets us free.

We are freemen, freed from the guilt, penalty, and power of sin, someday to be freed even from the presence of sin, which will come about at the Resurrection.

We are liberated from all that, so that we might realize in our lives that for which we were created, namely to Glorify God.

## HOW CAN WE BE HIS BONDSLAVES AND HIS FREEMEN AT THE SAME TIME?

After we have been purchased as His bondslaves, and have been liberated from our old master Satan, out of pure gratefulness of heart we say to our Lord, *"Lord Jesus, we want to serve Thee as Thy bondslaves forever."*

Our position as His bondslaves is not one of compulsion, but of free will energized by an imparted Divine Nature and a supernaturally imparted Love. Therefore, we are His bondslaves and His freemen at the same time, a thing impossible in the case of earthly slaves. Thus is solved one of the delightful paradoxes of Holy Scripture (Wuest).

(23) "YE ARE BOUGHT WITH A PRICE; BE NOT YE THE SERVANTS OF MEN."

The phrase, *"Ye are bought with a price,"* refers to the ransom price of which we have just mentioned, which was the Precious Shed Blood of Jesus Christ at Calvary's Cross.

The phrase, *"Be not ye the servants of men,"* seems like a contradiction relative to Verse 21; however, it is not a contradiction at all.

Paul is saying that liberation by Jesus Christ not only frees us from sin, but also from the fear of man and what man can do to us. That's the reason Paul referred to himself while in prison as a *"prisoner of Jesus Christ,"* and not a prisoner of Nero (Philemon 1:1).

Even though Paul's statement, *"Be not ye the servants of men,"* is very short, still, it carries a wealth of meaning.

Most of humanity serves other men, and regrettably, does so out of fear. So, in a sense, they are slaves to that man or woman. Most of the world does not know the Lord, so they fear what men can do to them. Therefore, they serve them in one way or the other.

Without a doubt, one could say that religion is the greatest slave master of them all. Untold hundreds of millions serve a religious system out of fear, in essence, slaves of sorts. As well, the religion, whatever it might be, centered up in a man or men. Consequently, these men must be obeyed and pleased.

Even though religion is the greatest slave master of all, economics enter into the picture as well. Inasmuch as the welfare of unsaved people is decided by other men or women, in a sense, these individuals, whomever they may be, are served by those who look to them.

NOTES

## WHAT JESUS SAID

Speaking of this very thing, Jesus said, *"And fear not them* (men) *which kill the body, but are not able to kill the soul: but rather fear Him* (God) *which is able to destroy both soul and body in Hell"* (Mat. 10:28).

So, the Lord tells us that we do not have to fear other men, and uses the most graphic illustration to do so. In effect He is saying, that the worst that man can do to you is to take your life. He cannot take your soul.

When a person comes to Christ, Jesus then becomes the Lord of his life. At that moment, they enter into the Economy of God. Consequently, from then on Believers look to Him, and not to men. As a result the hold of fear held over them formerly is now gone, whatever the situation might have been, or whatever the situation may presently be. That's what Paul means by his statement.

Now that the sinner has come to Christ, he is no longer a slave of men, does not look to men, but rather places all his trust and confidence in the Lord. Consequently, man's hold over him is broken, irrespective as to what that hold may have previously been.

## DESPOT GOVERNMENTS

That's the reason that Communist Governments, and such like, consider the Bible and Christianity as an enemy. While in fact, Christianity is no real threat to them, still, they know and realize, that those who serve The Lord Jesus Christ cannot be intimidated, at least if they truly have Faith in the Lord.

While the Christian may in fact be the best citizen of all, even in a Totalitarian Regime, still, the Communist masters or such like, do not have his loyalty, and neither can they have his loyalty. It belongs to Christ and Christ Alone. Consequently, that's the reason that they oppose the Bible and Christianity to such a degree.

While Christians will respect all men, irrespective of their station in life, and while they will conduct themselves with a kind and gracious spirit and attitude, still, their Lord is Christ, and no other. While good Christians make the best citizens, the best employees, and in fact, the best of everything, at least if they are True Christians, still, they are servants or slaves of no one irrespective of their position, except the Lord of Glory. Consequently, the greatest liberating force on the face of the Earth is never certain political philosophies, or anything else for that matter, save only the liberating Power of the Gospel of Jesus Christ.

(24) "BRETHREN, LET EVERY MAN, WHEREIN HE IS CALLED, THEREIN ABIDE WITH GOD."

Being the third time Paul says this (vss. 17, 20), it should be obvious that the Holy Spirit is attempting to impart very important information.

By Paul using the word *"Brethren,"* we know that he is speaking to Believers.

The phrase, *"Let every man, wherein he is called,"* refers to the condition in which we are when we are called by God. Once again, it does not speak of illegitimate vocations, but rather one's station in life.

In other words, the Holy Spirit is telling us, that it really doesn't matter if we are the poorest of the poor, or the richest of the rich. Wherever we are concerning status, place, or position, God can use us, and greatly so. This is what makes serving Christ so beautiful and wonderful. It is not limited to what status one occupies. In fact, even as we should know by now, these things matter little.

The phrase, *"Therein abide with God,"* presents a summary and reiteration of the Gospel contained in the whole paragraph.

The words *"With God"* literally mean, *"By the side of God, as in God's Sight."*

So, with this one word, the Holy Spirit through the Apostle, placed everybody in Christendom on the same level. Consequently, slaves were given just as much status in the Church as Masters. The poor were treated exactly as the rich. The uneducated were treated as the educated, and simply because all were now the property of The Lord Jesus Christ. This is the way Church ought to be, and the way it will be, if it is functioning in the sphere of Bible Christianity.

### RACE, PLACE, AND POSITION

If all races of people aren't equally welcome in a Church, that Church is not functioning in the New Testament pattern.

If the rich are given greater place and position than the poor, in fact if the poor are not welcome, the gathering ceases to be a Church.

NOTES

In fact, if all do not feel comfortable in a Church, and by that we mean given dignity, respect, and love, irrespective as to whom they may be, or what they may have once been, then something is wrong with that Church. As someone has said, all ground is level at the foot of the Cross. As well, anyone who has been Saved by the Precious Blood of Jesus, consequently bought with a price, then becomes His Property. As such, their very existence, whoever they may be, takes on a brand-new meaning. Considering to whom they belong, they are to be treated accordingly.

Consequently, Christianity alone, and I speak of that which is truly of Christ, smashes all racism and class distinction. Communism tried it and failed miserably, actually becoming the most class-conscious society in the world.

Democracy has succeeded up to a point, but only to a point. Legislation can never change an evil heart, so, of necessity, Democracy is limited in this respect, even though in a political sense it has made greater headway than all.

Only Christianity has fully addressed this problem even as we are now studying. As well, the inroads made by Democracy in a political sense, have been because of the tremendous influence of Bible Christianity.

(25) "NOW CONCERNING VIRGINS I HAVE NO COMMANDMENT OF THE LORD: YET I GIVE MY JUDGMENT, AS ONE THAT HATH OBTAINED MERCY OF THE LORD TO BE FAITHFUL."

The phrase, *"Now concerning virgins I have no Commandment of the Lord,"* could refer to one of two things:

1. There is nothing in the Law of Moses concerning this question, and neither did Jesus say anything about this during His earthly Ministry.

2. After he received the letter from Corinth concerning questions they had regarding Doctrine and other things, he took these things to the Lord, but did not receive any instruction respecting the particular question of *"virgins."*

I think the first is correct, because if not, the advice he is now about to give would not be inspired by the Holy Spirit. We know that is not correct, so he is meaning that the Old Testament or that the Lord did not say anything about this question.

The phrase, *"Yet I give my judgment, as one that hath obtained Mercy of the Lord to be faithful,"* tells us several things:

NOTES

1. First of all, the word *"virgins"* here, refer to young men and young ladies who had not yet married, and felt a call into the Ministry. Paul was not speaking of all Christian young men and young ladies, only those who felt a call to Ministry.

2. The manner in which Paul uses this statement concerning *"virgins,"* lends credence to the thought that he had never married. There has always been conjecture, as we have previously stated, regarding this. However, as stated, I feel that the manner in which he is addressing himself here, lends credence to the thought that he had never been married.

3. He is in effect addressing the sex drive in his statement, which as well, lends some credence to the thought that he had had a problem here somewhat with desire in this capacity, and had taken it to the Lord, with the Lord extending him *"Mercy"* in respect to Grace to overcome the desire, or else to take away the desire in this capacity altogether.

4. He had been *"faithful"* to his position of celibacy all his life.

(26) "I SUPPOSE THEREFORE THAT THIS IS GOOD FOR THE PRESENT DISTRESS, I SAY, THAT IT IS GOOD FOR A MAN SO TO BE."

The phrase, *"I suppose therefore that this is good for the present distress,"* is said hesitantly as is obvious. The hesitation is for two reasons:

1. There is nothing in the Word of God which says that Preachers should not have a wife. In fact, whatever instruction is given, lends credence to the very opposite. So this shoots down completely the vow of celibacy taken by Catholic Priests and Nuns.

2. Paul could only answer for himself, which he does. Concerning the other person's situation, they must seek the Lord for an answer concerning their own dilemma, which the Lord will give to them personally.

Concerning *"the present distress,"* notice that he used the word *"present."*

Nero was now in power, and in fact, the first five years of his reign would be somewhat uneventful, even producing some good Government. Even though he was of the worst sort regarding character and nature, the Empire was pretty much now being run by two powerful Roman Sages, who attempted to address Government with responsibility. Unfortunately, at about the time that Paul is writing this Letter to the Church at Corinth, he takes as his mistress a woman by the name of Poppaea Sabina. Under her influence he shook off all restraints, turned a deaf ear to his best advisers and plunged deeper into immorality and crime.

Even though she was married to another man, she was openly consorting with the Emperor, in fact starting him down the road to destruction, which would include the terrible persecution of the Christians. That persecution began with the great fire of Rome, which took place in July of A.D. 64.

So, Paul no doubt had a premonition from the Spirit of God of this which was coming, consequently speaking of the *"present distress."*

The phrase, *"I say, that it is good for a man so to be,"* simply means regarding this soon to come distress, which was already presently in the making by the Powers of Darkness, that a Preacher would be better unmarried. In fact, untold numbers of Preachers during this terrible time would pay with their lives. As should be obvious, if he had a wife and family, the hardships would be much worse.

(27) "ART THOU BOUND UNTO A WIFE? SEEK NOT TO BE LOOSED. ART THOU LOOSED FROM A WIFE? SEEK NOT A WIFE."

The question and answer, *"Art thou bound unto a wife? seek not to be loosed,"* as stated, refers to young men who are married, and are called into the Ministry. Once again let us emphasize, that Paul is not addressing his statement to all Christians, Preachers and otherwise, but Preachers only, and only for that present time, or any other similar time in the future.

The question and answer, *"Art thou loosed from a wife? seek not a wife,"* simply means that it might be better not to marry at this particular time, and once again speaking to young Preachers.

As well, the word *"loosed"* can mean *"divorced,"* and refers to Preachers whose wives have deserted them because of their stand for Christ.

So, Paul is addressing two groups, those who had not yet married, be they male or female who felt a call into the Ministry, and the men whose wives had deserted them because they (the men) had accepted Christ.

Once again, I feel he is speaking of Preachers and not just anyone!

NOTES

(28) "BUT AND IF THOU MARRY, THOU HAST NOT SINNED; AND IF A VIRGIN MARRY, SHE HATH NOT SINNED. NEVERTHELESS SUCH SHALL HAVE TROUBLE IN THE FLESH: BUT I SPARE YOU."

The phrase, *"But and if thou marry, thou hast not sinned,"* speaks of the men whose wives had deserted them because of accepting Christ, and preaching the Gospel. So, this tells us two things:

1. Even as we have already stated, if desertion is the case for the Cause of Christ, it is not a sin for that man (or woman) to remarry. Paul had already said, *"A brother or a sister is not under bondage in such cases"* (I Cor. 7:15).

2. As well, and despite his warning about the present distress, if the Preacher of the Gospel desired to marry again, he has not sinned. He needs to get the Mind of the Lord regarding the matter and do accordingly. Of course, this would pertain not only to Preachers, but for any Believer for that matter.

The phrase, *"And if a virgin marry, she hath not sinned,"* referred to young ladies who felt a Call of God to give themselves entirely to the Lord in His Service and Work. Paul is saying that she has not sinned or abrogated the Call, if she falls in love with a young man and they are married.

The word *"virgin"* as Paul here uses it, must be looked at in the entire context, which refers to both young men and young ladies — (vss. 25-28).

The phrase, *"Nevertheless such shall have trouble in the flesh,"* refers to the *"present distress"* which will cause more difficulties for Preachers of the Gospel or workers for the Lord, than if they were not married. Once again, Paul is speaking only of the present distress.

As well, and inasmuch as he mentions the pronoun *"she,"* he is saying that the young lady who feels a Call from God to full-time service in His Work, that being married will place added burdens on this dedication, as would be obvious. From the advice he will give in the following Scriptures, I think it is obvious that he is speaking only of those who feel a full-time Call to the Ministry, or else they are already involved full time in Ministry. To attempt to force all of these statements upon all Believers would make little sense.

The phrase, *"But I spare you,"* simply has reference to the fact that Paul is telling Preachers of the Gospel, or full-time workers for the Lord, that the marriage state, and he is speaking of these particular difficult times, is going to bring added burdens.

As well, all the instruction given regarding this matter, definitely applies in some cases to any and all times. In other words, there are some who the Lord desires to remain single, even as He did Paul. But again, the individual must find the Mind of the Lord in this matter regarding his own personal situation, and not be persuaded by others.

(29) "BUT THIS I SAY, BRETHREN, THE TIME IS SHORT: IT REMAINETH, THAT BOTH THEY THAT HAVE WIVES BE AS THOUGH THEY HAD NONE;"

The phrase, *"But this I say, Brethren, the time is short,"* has reference to two things:

1. The persecution of the Christians by Nero will shortly break upon the world of that day. It will be a dark time, with many paying with their lives.

2. All Believers are to understand that this life is short, even at its longest; consequently, as Believers we are to conduct ourselves wisely and responsibly concerning the Lord and His Work, making the very most of the little time we do have.

The phrase, *"It remaineth, that both they that have wives be as though they had none,"* refers to the fact, that the very object of the hastened end is that Christians should sit loose to earthly interests (Farrar). The Lord is to come first in all things, even with respect to our wives, the most precious thing a man can have other than Christ. Of course, the admonition would apply to the women regarding their husbands as well.

Even though these admonitions are very clear, I think most Christians pay little heed. Much of the time, the Lord and His Work are given short shift, with other things taking preeminence. One day all Believers will stand before the Lord at the Judgment Seat of Christ, and then what we did with our lives will be all-important, and we will realize that we should have done more and done better; however, it will then be too late to rectify the spiritual apathy presently held by so many.

(30) "AND THEY THAT WEEP, AS THOUGH THEY WEPT NOT; AND THEY THAT REJOICE, AS THOUGH THEY

REJOICED NOT; AND THEY THAT BUY, AS THOUGH THEY POSSESSED NOT;"

The phrase, *"And they that weep, as though they wept not,"* refers to the fact that earthly sorrow and joy and wealth are things which are merely transient and actually unreal, at least when compared with the awful, eternal, permanent realities which we shall soon have to face (Farrar).

What causes one to weep?

Strangely enough, great sorrow and its opposite, great joy, have a tendency to cause one to weep. Jesus wept at the tomb of Lazarus, but it was because of the great sorrow and heartache that sin had imposed upon the world, with death being its result. He Alone knew the terrible loss suffered by man as a result of the Fall in the Garden of Eden. In fact, that's why He came to this world and died on Calvary's Cross. One might say that He is setting the record straight, and one day soon it will be finished.

JESUS

Likewise, the Believer must understand, that the cause of all sorrow in the world is the fact of sin. To that problem, sin and its resultant weeping, Jesus is the only Answer.

Consequently, irrespective of the sorrow which produces weeping at the present, the Believer looks forward to the coming day when *"God shall wipe away all tears from their eyes; and there shall be no more death, neither sorrow, nor crying, neither shall there be anymore pain: for the former things are passed away"* (Rev. 21:4).

The phrase, *"And they that rejoice, as though they rejoiced not,"* speaks of the things of this world.

While at this very moment untold millions are weeping for sorrow, others are rejoicing at what they consider to be a positive turn of events. However, outside of Christ, nothing is actually positive. As I dictate these notes (3-23-98), the Academy Awards will be shown tonight over Television. Some few will rejoice as they receive these awards, and millions of others, I suppose, who look at these people as gods and goddesses, will rejoice with them. However, as stated, the rejoicing is fleeting and transient. While it may provide present riches and fame in the external sense, it does nothing to deal with the real problem of man, the problem of the wicked heart. So, tomorrow they will be weeping!

NOTES

The only *"rejoicing"* of lasting duration, is rejoicing in Christ. Hence, Paul said, *"Rejoice in the Lord alway: and again I say, Rejoice"* (Phil. 4:4).

The phrase, *"And they that buy, as though they possessed not,"* speaks to the idea that the possession is short-lived.

Possessions are either lost through business downturns, or for certain, death will claim the individual.

Someone asked the question regarding a very wealthy businessman who had died, *"How much did he leave?"*

The answer was quick, *"He left it all!"*

That's the reason Jesus told us, *"Lay not up for yourselves treasures upon Earth, where moth and rust doth corrupt, and where thieves break through and steal:*

*"But lay up for yourselves treasures in Heaven, where neither moth nor rust doth corrupt, and where thieves do not break through nor steal:*

*"For where your treasure is, there will your heart be also"* (Mat. 6:19-21).

(31) "AND THEY THAT USE THIS WORLD, AS NOT ABUSING IT: FOR THE FASHION OF THIS WORLD PASSETH AWAY."

The phrase, *"And they that use this world, as not abusing it,"* refers to the fact that Believers should use the world in the sense of using its resources to help them serve God, and to further His Cause; however, they should not be *"abusing it"* in the sense of selfishly becoming too attached to it (Rossier).

The phrase, *"For the fashion of this world passeth away,"* refers to the form or pattern of this world as the shifting scene of a theatre, or as a melting vapour (James 4:14).

THE WORLD

We must remember that the world represents the systematic expression of human sin in human cultures, and from that understand why the Believer is not to be of the world, though he is in the world (Jn. 17:14-18).

We are members of our society, yet the values we display and the structures we create in Church and home and occupation are to be distinctively Christian.

This understanding helps us sense the deadliness of worldliness. Worldliness is not a matter of engaging in those practices that some question. It is unthinkingly adopting the perspectives, values, and attitudes of our culture, without bringing them under the Judgment of God's Word. It is carrying on our lives as if we did not know Jesus. Hence, Paul under the guidance of the Holy Spirit, carefully addresses this very important issue (Mat. 16:26; Mk. 8:36; Lk. 9:25; I Cor. 5:10; II Cor. 7:10; I Jn. 2:15-16; 4:17).

### TRANSIENT

The word *"transient,"* as most know, simply means *"something which passes through quickly and is out of existence, or passing through with only a brief stay or sojourn."* This is what Paul is speaking of regarding the words *"passeth away."* Considering that, how can we as Believers attach too much significance to that which is merely transitorial? Everything the Believer does, should be done in the light of eternity, in other words, as to how it will impact our walk with God and His Work. Everything of the Lord is eternal, while all else is the very opposite.

As someone has well said, *"One life will soon be past, only what's done for Christ will last."*

(32) "BUT I WOULD HAVE YOU WITHOUT CAREFULNESS. HE THAT IS UNMARRIED CARETH FOR THE THINGS THAT BELONG TO THE LORD, HOW HE MAY PLEASE THE LORD:"

The phrase, *"But I would have you without carefulness,"* proclaims the very throbbings of the Heart of God.

Everything that affects His People is of commanding interest to Him. Nothing is too small for that wonderful Love. He would have His Children free from cares; and His Children's ambition should be to please Him (Williams).

The phrase, *"He that is unmarried careth for the things that belong to the Lord, how he may please the Lord,"* refers once again to Preachers of the Gospel, and especially considering the *"present distress."*

Exactly what does it mean to please the Lord?

Does it mean that all pleasure and delight should be off limits to Christians?

Considering how important *"pleasing the Lord"* actually is, I think a little more in-depth treatment of this very important subject would be satisfactory.

NOTES

### PLEASURE

At times Christians are suspicious of pleasure: if one enjoys something, it must be wrong. But the Bible has a different attitude.

Surely, human beings sometimes take pleasure in things that are wrong. But God has created a rich and beautiful world and given us the capacity to enjoy it. The Bible's rich vocabulary for pleasure, joy, and delight testify to the fact that God created men and women to experience the pleasure and joys of His World and His Presence.

### WORDS IN THE OLD TESTAMENT

A number of Hebrew words are associated with the idea of pleasure or of being pleased. Four of the words translated *"please," "pleasing,"* and *"pleasure"* are significant.

*"Tob"* is a very broad word in Hebrew, encompassing a sweeping range of concepts for which English has specific terms. These terms include the following: good, pleasant, glad, right, happy, righteous, and delightful. It is very seldom translated *"pleased"* or *"pleasant."*

The Hebrew word *"simhah"* means *"pleasure"* or *"gladness."* The basic idea is that of being glad or joyful with all of one's being.

### SOLOMON

In Ecclesiastes, Solomon describes his search for meaning in life apart from God. In one part he describes how he committed himself to pleasures of every kind (Eccl. 2:1-11). His pleasures included the much drinking of wine, enjoying sinful delights, accomplishing great projects, amassing wealth, gathering a harem — *"the delights of the heart of man."*

What was the result?

Solomon concludes: *"I denied myself nothing my eyes desired; I refused my heart no pleasure. My heart took delight in all my work, and this was the reward for all my labour.*

*"Yet when I surveyed all that my hands had done and what I toiled to achieve, everything was meaningless, a chasing after the wind; nothing was gained under the Sun"* (Eccl. 2:10-11).

Solomon's despairing conclusion testifies to the inability of pleasure alone to give life meaning. Apart from a relationship with God, which means a life that is pleasing to God, even life's good things prove to be only *"vanity."*

NOTES

*"Rason"* is another Hebrew word, which means *"pleasure."* It comes from a verb that means *"to be pleased with or favorable to."*

DESIRE AND DELIGHT

*"Hapes"* is another Hebrew word which, or one of its related words, occurs over a hundred times in the Old Testament, denoting the feeling of great delight or favor. This is a more emotional family of words than the others, suggesting strong emotional involvement. These words also may be translated *"desire"* and *"delight."*

These are also the words often found in more theologically significant Passages. God is not One Who *"takes pleasure in evil"* (Ps. 5:4). But neither does He take delight or pleasure in Sacrifices aside from a repentant heart (Ps. 51:16, 19).

Ezekiel makes it clear that God is forced by His Nature rather than by His desires to punish the wicked. *"Do I take any pleasure in the death of the wicked?"*, God asks. No, God's pleasure comes *"when they turn from their ways and live"* (Ezek. 18:23).

These words, among others, communicate the message that human beings, like God, are emotional beings. Our life in this world is enriched by joys and pleasures; and our character, like God's, is revealed by that which fills us with delight.

WORDS IN THE NEW TESTAMENT

A number of Greek words are translated *"pleasing"* or *"pleasure"* in the New Testament.

*"Hedone"* simply means *"pleasure," "something desirable."* It is used most often in an ethically questionable or bad sense. It is found only five times in the New Testament (Lk. 8:14; Tit. 3:3; James 4:1, 3; II Pet. 2:13). In each case, pleasure that appeals to man's sinful nature is in view.

Another Greek word *"eudokeia"* is found nine times in the New Testament, and indicates one's choice as one's *"pleasure,"* whether the choice was made by God or by a human being (Mat. 11:26; Lk. 10:21; Eph. 1:5, 9).

The same meaning of pleasure regarding one's choice expressed in that person's will or purpose is in the Greek verb (eudokeo), translated *"to be pleased"* a number of times (Mat. 3:17; 17:5; Mk. 1:11; Lk. 3:22; 12:32; Rom. 15:26-27; I Cor. 1:21; 10:5; Gal. 1:15; Col. 1:19; Heb. 10:6, 8, 38; II Pet. 1:17). Thus, a statement that the Churches to which Paul ministered were *"pleased"* to make a contribution to the poor (Rom. 15:26-27) indicates not only their state of mind but also their determined choice.

GOD WAS WELL PLEASED WITH JESUS

What does it mean when the New Testament reports that God spoke of Jesus as One with Whom He was *"well pleased"* (Mat. 3:17)?

It means, among other things, that Jesus was fulfilling the Messianic Role to which God had called Him. In contrast, God was not pleased with the Sacrifices and Offerings of the Old Testament System (Heb. 10:6, 8). If He had been pleased with them, Jesus would not have had to have come to this world and die on Calvary. The Old Testament System could not be established in His Purpose as a way to cleanse humanity from sin. In fact, the animal Sacrifices could only cover the sin and not take the sin away, which only Jesus could do (Jn. 1:29; Heb. 10:4).

ATTITUDE TOWARD LIFE

Another Greek word *"aresko"* is found some 17 times in the New Testament, and means *"to please," "to be pleasing."*

In Greek culture it speaks of the pleasure that a person derives from something. In Paul's writings the word is used to describe one's attitude toward life, even what we are now studying (Rom. 8:8; 15:1-3; I Cor. 7:32-34) A person seeks to please either himself or herself or else, like a servant, chooses to live to please God and others.

When the Bible, especially the New Testament, discusses pleasure and what pleases, it make a vital point. You and I may orient our lives to that which gives momentary pleasure to our old nature, but this will never satisfy.

Human beings have been created with a nature that cries out for a relationship with God and subjection to His Will. Only by commitment to what pleases the Lord can we find the enrichment of our lives that God intends us to have. Only by such a commitment will our joys outlast the fleeting days of life here and provide pleasures, true pleasures forevermore (Richards).

(33) "BUT HE THAT IS MARRIED CARETH FOR THE THINGS THAT ARE OF THE WORLD, HOW HE MAY PLEASE HIS WIFE."

The phrase, *"But he that is married careth for the things that are of the world,"* once again speaks of Preachers, and once again speaks of that particular time and the *"present distress."*

The *"things of the world"* do not speak of that which is unlawful, but rather the necessities of life, such as making a living for one's family, in other words, providing for them. Considering the terrible times which were about to break over the Roman world, at least regarding those who were followers of Christ, one can well understand the reason for Paul's advice. However, let us emphasize once again, that he is only dealing here with the Ministry, and not with the everyday functions of life respecting Believers, who are not in the Ministry. As well, and as previously stated, he was dealing only with the *"present distress,"* which in the last 2,000 years since he made these statements, there have also been other *"present distresses."* Irrespective, whether the Preacher or Worker for the Lord, should be married at that particular time, must be left up to the individual and what he or she feels is the Will of God for their lives.

The phrase, *"How he may please his wife,"* is a normal reaction for a Preacher of the Gospel, or any man for that matter.

The manner in those days in which Preachers had to travel, the long periods of time away from home at least for some of them, and especially the present dangers which were only going to become more acute, presents the reason for the counsel and advice of the Apostle. As well, that which the Holy Spirit says through him, lends even greater credence to the idea that we should understand just how transitorial is this present life. Especially considering how fundamental is the family unit, and how such is pleasing to the Lord, but yet the Holy Spirit used this as an example, that sometimes the Lord would desire that one forego these obvious pleasures, even as He did in the life and Ministry of the Apostle Paul. To be sure, He has not asked many to make this Sacrifice, but if He does, and He certainly has the right to do so, to be sure, He will make it up to the individual in other ways.

(34) "THERE IS DIFFERENCE ALSO BETWEEN A WIFE AND A VIRGIN. THE UNMARRIED WOMAN CARETH FOR THE THINGS OF THE LORD, THAT SHE MAY BE HOLY BOTH IN BODY AND IN SPIRIT: BUT SHE THAT IS MARRIED CARETH FOR THE THINGS OF THE WORLD, HOW SHE MAY PLEASE HER HUSBAND."

NOTES

The phrase, *"There is difference also between a wife and a virgin,"* concerns only the manner of availability for the Lord. However, this in no way is meant to imply that marriage is incompatible with the most absolute Saintliness.

The phrase, *"The unmarried woman careth for the things of the Lord, that she may be holy both in body and in spirit,"* once again pertains to a woman who feels that God has called her for Ministry of some nature. The avoidance of distraction, and the determination that are duty to God shall not be impaired by earth relationships, is what is here in view. Paul is not speaking to all Christian women, but only those who are called to Ministry, and more specifically, only those for which this would be the Will of God.

The word *"holy"* as it is used here, does not mean that the body of a married women is unholy. It means that the virgin's physical body is consecrated totally to the Lord, while the physical body of the married woman is consecrated both to the Lord and her husband.

The phrase, *"But she that is married careth for the things of the world, how she may please her husband,"* actually means that her interests are divided between the Lord and her husband, whereas that of the unmarried woman is that only of the Lord.

The word *"careth"* in the Greek is *"merimnao,"* and means *"to be anxious about."* Even though it does carry a note of worry, it does not necessarily imply a lack of Faith. Instead, such concern is natural and understandable, something appropriate to Love and to a sense of responsibility.

(35) "AND THIS I SPEAK FOR YOUR OWN PROFIT; NOT THAT I MAY CAST A SNARE UPON YOU, BUT FOR THAT WHICH IS COMELY, AND THAT YE MAY ATTEND UPON THE LORD WITHOUT DISTRACTION."

The phrase, *"And this I speak for your own profit; not that I may cast a snare upon you,"* means that his words are not binding, but are meant to serve as advice and counsel. Each individual is to seek the Lord respecting his own life and Ministry, feeling assured that the Lord will definitely answer and give direction, and then he is to follow that which the Lord says.

However, at times an answer from the Lord is not so direct or so clear. In that case, and to whom it applies, Paul's advice should be considered. That is all the Apostle is saying.

Anything that is done in the strict Will of the Lord is *always "for our profit."* As well, it *never* casts a *"snare,"* i.e., *"a trap."*

If there is in fact, a *"snare,"* one can be certain that it is not the Lord's doings, but our own doings. If the Lord would want a Preacher of the Gospel, be they male or female, to remain single for a period of time, or even for the rest of their life, one can be certain that the Lord will compensate in other ways, making that person's life pleasurable and fulfilled in Christ. However, if a person would impose such upon themselves, or have it imposed upon them by other men, such as the Catholic Church, it proves to be nothing but a *"snare,"* exactly as it has been and is for Catholic Priests. The Apostle is careful to delineate the fact that it is the Holy Spirit Who must do the leading, and Who will do the leading if men will only seek such Leading and Guidance.

The phrase, *"But for that which is comely,"* means that whatever the Will of the Lord is in individual matters of this nature, or of any nature for that matter, it will be right and obvious to all.

*"Comely"* in the Greek is *"euschemon,"* and means *"good, honorable and noble."*

## THE WILL OF THE LORD

Many Christians have an erroneous concept concerning the Will of God. Consequently, they are afraid to yield to Him, to pray and seek His Face, in other words, afraid of what He might require of them to do. Consequently, their consecration is tepid to say the least, with very little true relationship.

Satan plants some very distasteful things in their mind, which makes them believe that if they yield or consecrate to the Will of God, that they will have to live in a veritable prison the rest of their lives, something which they strongly dislike, etc. Nothing could be further from the Truth.

## THE WAY THAT GOD WORKS

Whatever the Lord asks of His Children, He will always do two things. They are as follows:

1. He will place in that person's heart a strong fondness for whatever it is He is asking, and then as they begin to obey Him, their fulfillment and joy will increase more and more. They will find that, the Will of God, and whatever it might be, is the most fulfilling, satisfying, rewarding, joyful thing there could ever be. Their life will have meaning, purpose, and direction because they are in the Will of God (Ps. 16:5-9; Rom. 8:14-15).

In fact, God has a Will, and a Perfect Will at that, for every single Believer. It is the Believer's task to find what that Will is, get in the very center of that which God wants and desires, and then the Believer will know his purpose and reason for living. As stated, it is the greatest life there is.

The idea that some Believers are living in a state of misery in their Work for the Lord, is a lie from Satan. Such does not exist. There are absolutely untold millions of people in the world who do not know the Lord, who are working at dead-end jobs, who have no reason and purpose for living, and in fact, are miserable. To tell the Truth, without God, and irrespective of how much money a person may have, or what position they may hold, misery is the lot of the ungodly.

The only miserable Christians, are those who are *not* in the Will of God, not those who are.

## MISERY

2. The word *"miserable"* which we have just used, is the second thing the Lord allows for those who do not want His Will, are not in His Will, and are actually running from His Will, whatever that may be. I speak of Christians. That Believer is miserable, and nothing will change the situation, until he finds the Will of God and gets in the direct center of that Will. That is the way it works, and it will not change.

The phrase, *"And that ye may attend upon the Lord without distraction,"* makes it probable that Paul had heard how Martha was *"anxious"* and distracted about much serving, while Mary sat at Jesus' Feet (Lk. 10:39-41).

This is not to mean that a Christian husband or wife, because they are a husband or wife, are distracted in their service for the Lord. Neither does it mean that all who are unmarried are necessarily not distracted in this occupation.

The idea is, that if it is the Will of God for the man or woman to remain single, that to do otherwise would be a *"distraction."*

*"Distraction"* in the Greek is *"aperispastos,"* and means *"to be cumbered,"* and in this case, to be *"without distraction or unincumbered."*

I think one could say without fear of contradiction, that anything that is not the direct Will of God, is a distraction, i.e., *"an encumbrance."*

(36) "BUT IF ANY MAN THINK THAT HE BEHAVETH HIMSELF UNCOMELY TOWARD HIS VIRGIN, IF SHE PASS THE FLOWER OF HER AGE, AND NEED SO REQUIRE, LET HIM DO WHAT HE WILL, HE SINNETH NOT: LET THEM MARRY."

The phrase, *"But if any man think that he behaveth himself uncomely toward his virgin,"* does *not* speak of a sweetheart as it here seems, but rather the Father of this young lady. Evidently, Paul had received a question about this situation, and we will see as the Holy Spirit guided Him, that he was far ahead of his time.

In the times of Paul, daughters were totally under the power of their fathers. The father could allow the daughter to marry or not to marry. If the father had devoted his daughter to perpetual virginity, which means that she would never marry, but then found out she had fallen in love with a young man, Paul said that the father should allow her to marry; in doing so, he would not commit sin.

In those days, if a Father so desired, he could dedicate his daughter to the Lord, in effect in the Service of the Lord, meaning that she would remain single all of her life. In our modern culture, it is difficult for us to understand such customs. However, the Holy Spirit through the Apostle, as we shall see here, will break down these customs, which in effect were not pleasing to the Lord.

While it was definitely pleasing to the Lord, for the Father to dedicate his daughter, and in fact all his children to the Lord, even as he should do so; however, to place such restrictions of an unmarried state on a child for life is not pleasing to the Lord. No parent actually had the right to do such, which the Holy Spirit here addresses through the Apostle.

The phrase, *"If she pass the flower of her age,"* pertained at that time to 20 years old, which the ancients regarded as the acme or the perfection of a woman's life.

The essence of the statement as given by Paul, is that this individual is no longer a child but a mature adult. As such, and to whatever her Father has dedicated her, she now must be allowed to make her own decision concerning marriage.

NOTES

The phrase, *"And need so require,"* means that she desires to get married instead of being a perpetual virgin.

The phrase, *"Let him do what he will, he sinneth not: let them marry,"* means that God does not hold the Father accountable respecting his dedicating her to the Service of the Lord when she was born, i.e., *"to remain unmarried all of her life."* He is to give his blessings to his daughter in marriage, that is if he can do so with all good conscience. Irrespective, whatever she decides to do, being an adult, he is not held responsible for her.

(37) "NEVERTHELESS HE THAT STANDETH STEDFAST IN HIS HEART, HAVING NO NECESSITY, BUT HATH POWER OVER HIS OWN WILL, AND HATH SO DECREED IN HIS HEART THAT HE WILL KEEP HIS VIRGIN, DOETH WELL."

The phrase, *"Nevertheless he that standeth stedfast in his heart, having no necessity,"* means that the girl did not desire to marry and, therefore, the Father could continue with his dedication respecting his daughter as Philip did concerning his daughters (Acts 21:8-9).

The phrase, *"But hath power over his own will, and hath so decreed in his heart that he will keep his virgin, doeth well,"* concerns his dedication of her to the Lord, which is her desire as well, with the understanding that he will bear the expense of caring for her all of his life.

Such being the case, and all agreeing respecting the situation, the Holy Spirit through the Apostle says that he *"doeth well."*

(38) "SO THEN HE THAT GIVETH HER IN MARRIAGE DOETH WELL; BUT HE THAT GIVETH HER NOT IN MARRIAGE DOETH BETTER."

The phrase, *"So then he that giveth her in marriage doeth well,"* means that he is not held responsible by the Lord respecting his dedication of her to the Work of the Lord, as a child. She desires to marry, and he should allow her to do so. The Lord never violates anyone's free moral agency. If the young woman does not desire to remain in perpetual virginity, but rather to have a husband, her wishes should be granted. In this matter, the Holy Spirit says of the Father, the same as He did of the opposite decision, *"He doeth well."*

The phrase, *"But he that giveth her not in marriage doeth better,"* pertains of course, to the wishes of the young lady, which is better all around if it so be, because the Work of the Lord will be better attended in such a case.

However, the words *"Doeth better,"* obviously do not speak of better in a moral sense, because, if one course be morally better than another, we are bound to take it; but *"better"* relative to the Work of God and the distress of that particular time.

(39) "THE WIFE IS BOUND BY THE LAW AS LONG AS HER HUSBAND LIVETH; BUT IF HER HUSBAND BE DEAD, SHE IS AT LIBERTY TO BE MARRIED TO WHOM SHE WILL; ONLY IN THE LORD."

The phrase, *"The wife is bound by the Law as long as her husband liveth,"* is evidently in answer to a question of the Corinthians about a woman whose husband was dead.

Paul does not go into any detail here concerning grounds for divorce and remarriage, inasmuch as that has already been addressed (vs. 15).

The phrase, *"But if her husband be dead, she is at liberty to be married to whom she will; only in the Lord,"* presents Paul giving the Christian Law on this, but laid down the restriction that she is to marry only a Christian.

## THE MARRIAGE BOND

The Greek word for *"binding"* or *"bond"* is *"deo."* It is an everyday word, used often in the New Testament and in the common speech of the New Testament era.

Like the Old Testament Hebrew word *"asar,"* which is translated by *"deo"* in the Septuagint, *"deo"* suggests the broadest range of meanings of *"to imprison"* and, thus, the notion of limiting one's freedom of action, as one might do in making an oath.

(A different word, however, *"anathema-tizo,"* is used of the oath mentioned in Acts 23:12, 14, 21 — its only other New Testament occurrence being in the account of Peter's denial, Mk. 14:71.)

## AS IT RELATES TO MARRIAGE

Two uses of *"deo"* in the New Testament have raised questions. In one instance it is linked with the marriage bond, and the question is whether, or in what situation, that bond is broken so that one may be free to remarry. The Passages in question are Romans 7:1-8 and I Corinthians, Chapter 7.

In Romans, Chapter 7, Paul notes that the marriage bond is broken when one party of the union dies. He argues that the Believer's relationship with Jesus is also a union and that in Jesus' Death and Resurrection the bond that obligates the individual to live by the Mosaic Law was also broken.

In I Corinthians 7:39, the Scripture of our subject, Paul restates the principle that death dissolves the marriage bond so that one is *"free to marry anyone she wishes, but he must belong to the Lord."*

## THE BOND BETWEEN BELIEVERS

The most controversial use of *"bind"* or *"bond"* is found in the Gospel of Matthew. Both Matthew 16:19 and 18:18 announce, *"Whatever you bind on Earth will be bound in Heaven, and whatever you loose on Earth will be loosed in Heaven."* In Matthew, Chapter 16 this is said to Peter and is associated with the *"Keys to the Kingdom of Heaven"* (Mat. 16:19). In Matthew, Chapter 18 the binding and loosing power is given to the Twelve, and by inference to all Believers. What is this power?

The Early Church Fathers believed that binding and loosing referred to a rarely mentioned but recognized Rabbinic authority — to expel persons from, or to receive them back into, a congregation. This understanding is supported by the flow of Matthew 18:15-18.

There Jesus establishes a process for correcting faults within the believing community. If we follow that process, and it is followed Scripturally, and a person still *"refuses to listen even to the Church,"* he or she is to be expelled from fellowship. It is at this point, as a culminating statement, that Jesus says such exclusion from fellowship (not exclusion from Salvation!) is binding in Heaven and on Earth.

God Himself has been at work in the process, and the one rejecting Scriptural correction steps out of fellowship with the Lord as well as with the Brethren on Earth.

## SCRIPTURAL!

However, it is to be understood that what is done must be Scriptural. The Word of God

NOTES

is always the Foundation for anything done in the Christian Community, or it ceases to be Christian.

Regrettably, there are some Religious Leaders who are actually appointed by man and not God, who feel that whatever they say and do, irrespective as to what it is, must be obeyed to the letter. Some of them even claim that if they demand something that is unscriptural, it must be obeyed without question, and they in turn will be responsible and not the person carrying out the demanded act.

However, let no one think that they are absolved of responsibility regarding an unscriptural act, irrespective as to who would demand such. While it is certainly true, that the one demanding such action will be responsible, however, the one obeying such foolishness will be responsible as well.

(Even though I have used the word *"foolishness,"* that of which we speak is far more serious, actually being sin.)

THE WORD OF ISAIAH QUOTED BY JESUS

The Hebrew word *"Habas,"* means *"to bind,"* or *"to wrap with a bandage."*

One of the greatest Prophetic Passages in the Old Testament portrays the Messiah's Announcement of His Mission — a Passage quoted by Jesus in the Synagogue at Nazareth (Isa. 61:1; Lk. 4:16-21): *"He has sent Me to bind up the brokenhearted, to proclaim freedom for the captives and release from darkness for the prisoners."*

Beautifully enough, the Ministry of the Messiah is not only to *"bind up the brokenhearted* (Habas) *but also to announce release for the prisoners for them that are bound,"* (Hebrew asar).

So, Jesus *"binds,"* but with a *"healing bandage,"* and at the same time unbinds, which means *"to announce release for the prisoners."*

Even though the word *"binding"* or *"bond"* is not used of Satan, still, the inference speaks of him graphically so respecting *"captives"* or *"prisoners."* In fact, almost all of the world falls under this terrible bondage of darkness, i.e., *"prisoners."*

By contrast, Jesus breaks these *"bonds"* and destroys this *"binding."* In fact, He Alone can do such a thing.

(40) "BUT SHE IS HAPPIER IF SHE SO ABIDE, AFTER MY JUDGMENT: AND I THINK ALSO THAT I HAVE THE SPIRIT OF GOD."

NOTES

The phrase, *"But she is happier if she so abide, after my judgment,"* refers to the woman whose husband is dead. The Holy Spirit through the Apostle proclaims the fact that she will be happier if she devotes the rest of her life to service for the Lord in some capacity.

Looking at this situation from present experience, how true this is. Many Christian women who suffer the misfortune of losing their husband, too often make a mistake in their second marriage, which does not turn out too well. Of course, this is certainly not the case all the time, and once again, the individual should seek the Face of the Lord about this matter, ascertaining His Will.

The phrase, *"And I think also that I have the Spirit of God,"* places Paul's advice out of the realm of mere human judgment, and into the realm of the Divine.

On another tack, the Corinthians boasted of their spiritual knowledge. The Apostle meets them with gentle irony on their own ground saying, *"I think that I also have the Spirit of God,"* thus conveying the reproof that he was conscious of having an intelligence which they only claimed.

As well, the contrast between the purity, refinement, sympathy, respect, and liberty of these marriage laws, versus the impurity, grossness, cruelty, and slavery of those of the Koran and of the Bedas, who claim to be holy, is most striking (Williams).

*"Spirit of Faith, come down, reveal the things of God;*
*"And make to us the Godhead known, and witness with the Blood.*
*"'Tis Thine the Blood to apply and give us eyes to see,*
*"Who did for every sinner die, hath surely died for me."*

*"No man can truly say that Jesus is the Lord,*
*"Unless Thou take the veil away, and breathe the Living Word.*
*"Then, only then we feel our interest in His Blood,*
*"And cry, with joy unspeakable, 'Thou art my Lord, my God!'"*

*"Oh that the world might know the all-atoning Lamb!*

*"Spirit of Faith, descend and show the virtue of His Name.*
*"The Grace which all may find, the Saving Power imparts;*
*"And testify to all mankind, and speak in every heart."*

## CHAPTER 8

(1) "NOW AS TOUCHING THINGS OFFERED UNTO IDOLS, WE KNOW THAT WE ALL HAVE KNOWLEDGE. KNOWLEDGE PUFFETH UP, BUT CHARITY EDIFIETH."

The phrase, *"Now as touching things offered unto idols,"* presents that which is also addressed in Romans, Chapter 14 and part of Chapter 15. Inasmuch as the Holy Spirit inspired the Apostle to write both accounts (Romans and I Corinthians), consequently, He (the Holy Spirit) considered this subject to be very important. It deals with the matter of Christian liberty. Even though meat sacrificed to idols serves as the specific example that Paul used, the principle established here would apply to many similar matters (Rossier).

Having answered their questions about marriage, he now deals with this very important subject. The denial of self, and Love to others, form the keynote of his reply.

For the sake of others Paul at times denied himself the enjoyment of particular types of food (I Cor. Chpt. 8), the sweet companionship of a wife (I Cor. Chpt. 9), and at times the relief of a salary (I Cor. Chpt. 9), and said that he kept under his body lest while inviting others to the Christian race he himself should fail of a prize; and he pointed to the fate of Israel in the desert (I Cor. Chpt. 10) as a warning to all who gratified their appetite for special food without consideration for the spiritual welfare of others.

He reasoned with these Corinthians that there should be no connection whatsoever between the Religious Feasts of the heathen and the weekly Fellowship Supper of the Christians; he urged that at that meal self should be denied and the food shared with the hungry; and he recalled how the Lord thus acted the last time that He supped with His Disciples (I Cor. Chpt. 11) (Williams).

NOTES

### OF PAUL AND LIBERTY

To which we have already alluded, Paul, despite the fact that the Holy Spirit through him had grandly proclaimed Christian Liberty, will still strongly advocate concern for weaker Christians, about which we will have more to say further later in this Chapter. In fact, Paul had to suffer cruel misrepresentation and bitter persecution as the consequence of this breadth of view (Acts 21:21-24); but that would not be likely to make him shrink from saying the Truth.

So, as usual, the Holy Spirit goes beyond the mere Letter of the Law, or even of Liberty, and deals with the hearts of Believers respecting why we do certain things, and what inspires the effort.

The majority of the Corinthians, being liberal in their views, held that it was a matter of perfect indifference to eat idol-offerings; and that, in acting upon this conviction, they contemptuously overrode the convictions of those who could not help thinking that when they did so they committed sin. Consequently, the practical decision of the question was one of immense importance.

If it were unlawful under any circumstances to eat idol-offerings, then the Gentile Convert was condemned to a life of Levitism (Legalism) almost as rigorous as that of the Jew. In fact, the distinction between clean and unclean meats formed an insuperable barrier between Jews and Gentiles.

### THE MANNER OF THE IDOL OFFERINGS

Heathen sacrifices to idol gods were very similar in some respects to the Jewish Sacrifices of old. They too used Lambs, Goats, Rams, and Bullocks. As the Jews, they would burn the fat and the entrails on the Altar. The part which remained, which was the major part of the animal, could be consumed by the people, or taken to the market to be sold to the public.

Some claim that the meat offered to idols was sold at a lower price than other meat in order to make the former more attractive to the public. Others have stated that it was sold at a higher price, with the idea in mind, that the spirit of the idol-god was in the meat, and would, therefore, be of benefit to the consumer. The market was, therefore, stocked with meat which had been connected with idol-sacrifices.

NOTES

## THE WISDOM OF THE HOLY SPIRIT THROUGH PAUL

It will be seen that Paul treats this subject with consummate wisdom and tenderness. His liberality of thought shows itself in this — that he sides with those who took the strong, the broad, the common-sense view, that sin is not a mechanical matter, that sin is not committed where no sin is intended.

He neither adopts the ascetic view (practicing strict self-denial), nor does he taunt the inquirers with the fact that the whole weight of their personal desires and interests would lead them to decide the question in their own favor.

On the other hand, he has too deep a sympathy with the weak to permit their scruples to be overruled with a violence which would wound their consciences. While he accepts the right principle of Christian freedom, he carefully guards against its abuse.

It might have been supposed that, as a Jew, and one who had been trained as a *"Pharisee of Pharisees,"* that Paul would have sided with those who forbade any participation in idol-offerings, pertaining to the eating of such meat.

However, Paul was ruled not at all by the former culture in which he had been brought up, but rather in a total sense by the Holy Spirit. Hence, he deals not with particulars, but rather with motives (Farrar).

## WHAT ABOUT THE JERUSALEM COUNCIL?

This same kind of issue was confronted in the Council in Jerusalem (Acts 15:29; 21:25). Why then did Paul not just apply the decision made on that occasion?

What we see in this Chapter in I Corinthians does not contradict what was decided in that Council, it actually explains the true intent of the decision. This amplification helps to show that the prohibition as handed down by James was limited in its scope. Besides, sometimes it was impossible to tell the difference between meat that was offered to idols and that which had not been. Of course, we speak of that which was sold in the marketplace.

*"That they abstain from pollutions of idols,"* is that which was handed down by James in Acts 15:20.

As the Holy Spirit gave this through James, it had little, if anything, to do with the question at hand — animals offered in sacrifice to idols, with their flesh then sold in the marketplace.

That to which the Holy Spirit was pointing, spoke of man's relationship to God, and that he must have no other gods. Almighty God is the Creator of all things, and He Alone is to be worshiped.

While some could stretch this prohibition offered by James to include the marketplace situation; however, to do so would destroy the real meaning and have a tendency to throw the Believer into Legalism, which is always a problem for Christians.

As we shall see, the real problem encountered here had little to do with the Jerusalem subject, but rather was more of a personal nature, exactly as it was in Romans, Chapter 14.

The phrase, *"We know that we all have knowledge,"* seems to present a touch of irony, which was probably brought on, that is if Paul meant it in that way, by a conceited remark which had occurred in the Letter from Corinth (Farrar).

Consequently, the Apostle immediately addresses the real core of the problem, which as we shall see, is knowledge without Love.

## OF WHAT TYPE OF KNOWLEDGE DOES PAUL SPEAK?

*"Knowledge"* in the Greek as used here by Paul is *"gnosis,"* and means *"be aware of, feel, know, perceive, be sure, understand, knowing."* So it is not of a wrong type of knowledge that Paul speaks, but actually the right kind, used in the wrong way.

Knowledge strictly is the apprehension by the mind of some fact or Truth in accordance with its real nature; in a personal relation the intellectual act is necessarily joined with the element of affection and will (choice, love, favor, or, conversely, repugnance, dislike, etc.).

Knowledge is distinguished from *"opinion"* by its greater certainty.

The mind is constituted with the capacity for knowledge, and the desire to possess and increase it. The character of knowledge varies with its object.

## THE MANNER OF KNOWLEDGE IN MAN

The senses give knowledge of outward appearances; the intellect connects and reasons about these appearances, and arrives at general Laws or Truths; Moral Truth is apprehended through the power inherently possessed by men of distinguishing right and wrong in the light of moral principle; spiritual qualities require for their apprehension spiritual sympathy (*"They are spiritually judged,"* I Cor. 2:14).

THE HIGHEST KNOWLEDGE OF ALL

The highest knowledge possible to man is the Knowledge of God, and while there is that in God's infinity which transcends man's power of comprehension (Job 11:7-9), God is knowable in the measure in which He has revealed Himself in Creation (Rom. 1:19-20, *"That which is known of God,"* etc.), and supremely in Jesus Christ, Who Alone perfectly knows the Father, and reveals Him to man (Mat. 11:27).

This Knowledge of God in Jesus Christ is *"Life Eternal"* (Jn. 17:3). Knowledge is affirmed of both God and man, but with the wide contrast that God's Knowledge is absolute, unerring, complete, intuitive, embracing all things, past, present, and future, and searching the inmost thoughts of the heart (Ps. 139:1-23); whereas man's is partial, imperfect, relative, gradually acquired, and largely mixed with error (*"Now we see in a mirror darkly . . . in part,"* I Cor. 13:12).

KNOWLEDGE AND THE SCRIPTURE

All these points about knowledge are amply brought out in the Scripture usage of the terms. A large part of the usage necessarily relates to natural knowledge (sometimes with a carnal connotation, as Genesis 4:1-17), but the greatest stress also is laid on the possession of moral and spiritual knowledge (Ps. 119:66; Prov. 1:4, 7, 22, 29; 8:10, etc.; Lk. 1:77; Rom. 15:14; II Pet. 1:5-6).

The highest knowledge, as said, is the Knowledge of God and Christ, and of God's Will (Hos. 6:6; Rom. 11:33; Eph. 1:17; 4:13; Phil. 1:9; 3:8; Col. 1:9-10).

The moral conditions of spiritual knowledge are continually insisted on (*"If any man willeth to do His Will, he shall know of the teaching, whether it is of God,"* Jn. 7:17).

INTELLECTUAL KNOWLEDGE

On the other hand, the pride of intellectual knowledge is condemned; it must be joined with Love (*"Knowledge puffeth up,"* I Cor. 8:1).

The stronger Greek term *"epignosis"* is used to denote the full and more perfect knowledge which is possessed in Christ, the conditions of which are Humility and Love. Of knowledge as connoting favor, choice, on the part of God, there are many examples (Ps. 1:6, *"Jehovah knoweth the Way of the Righteous"*; Gal. 4:9, *"Know God, or rather to be known by God"*; of Rom. 8:29, *"Whom He foreknew"*).

(The material on knowledge was derived from James Orr.)

The phrase, *"Knowledge puffeth up,"* presents a word which the Apostle has already used several times of the Corinthians (I Cor. 4:6, 18-19; 5:2).

The idea is, that if it is knowledge only which forms the basis from which we operate, arrogance will be the result.

The phrase, *"But charity edifieth,"* speaks of *"Love,"* and should have been translated accordingly. The fondness for variation which led King James' Translators to do so only obscures the identity of thought which prevails among all the Apostles respecting the absolute primacy of Love as the chief sphere and test of the Christian Life.

*"Edifieth"* in the Greek is *"oikodomei,"* and literally means *"a house-builder."* It has no quality to puff up (Satan being the first one to be puffed up) or tear down as does knowledge. It can only be constructive since it is of God (I Cor. Chpt. 13).

LOVE IS INTRODUCED IN THE BIBLE

Love to both God and man is fundamental to a true spiritual experience with the Lord, whether as expressed in the Old Testament or the New Testament. Jesus Himself declared that all the Law and the Prophets hang upon Love (Mat. 22:40; Mk. 12:28-34).

Paul, in his matchless ode on Love (I Cor. Chpt. 13), makes it the greatest of the Graces of the Christian life — greater than speaking with Tongues, or the Gift of Prophecy, or the possession of a Faith of superior excellence; for without Love all these Gifts and Graces, desirable and useful as they are in themselves, are as nothing, certainly of no permanent value in the sight of God.

Not that either Jesus or Paul underestimates the Faith from which all the Graces proceed, for this Grace is recognized as fundamental in all God's dealings with man and man's dealings with God (Jn. 6:28; Heb. 11:6).

NOTES

NOTES

However, both alike count that Faith as but idle and worthless belief that does not manifest itself in Love to both God and man. As Love is the highest expression of God and His relation to mankind, so it must be the highest expression of man's relation to his Maker and to his fellowman.

## THE LOVE OF GOD

First in the consideration of the subject of *"Love"* comes the Love of God — He Who is Love, and from Whom all Love is derived. The Love of God is that part of His Nature — indeed His whole Nature, for *"God is Love"* — which leads Him to express Himself in terms of endearment toward His Creatures, and actively to manifest that interest and affection in acts of loving care and self-sacrifice on behalf of the objects of His Love.

God is *"Love"* (I Jn. 4:8, 16) just as truly as He is *"Light"* (I Jn. 1:5), *"Truth"* (I Jn. 1:6), and *"Spirit"* (Jn. 4:24).

Spirit and Light are expressions of His essential Nature; Love is the expression of His Personality corresponding to His Nature. God not merely loves, but is Love; it is His Very Nature, and He imparts this Nature to be the sphere in which His Children dwell, for *"He that abideth in Love abideth in God, and God abideth in him"* (I Jn. 4:16).

Christianity is the only Faith that sets forth the Supreme Being as Love. In heathen religions he is set forth as an angry being and in constant need of appeasement.

## THE OBJECT OF GOD'S LOVE

Jesus is first and foremost, the object of God's Love (Mat. 3:17; 17:5; Lk. 20:13; Jn. 17:24).

The Son shares the Love of the Father in a unique sense; He is *"My chosen, in Whom My soul delighteth"* (Isa. 42:1).

There exists an Eternal Affection between the Son and the Father — the Son is the Original and Eternal Object of the Father's Love (Jn. 17:24). If God's Love is Eternal it must have an Eternal Object, hence, Christ is an Eternal Being.

## GOD AND THE BELIEVER

God loves the Believer in His Son with a special Love. Those who are united by Faith and Love to Jesus Christ are, in a different sense from those who are not thus united, the special objects of God's Love.

Said Jesus, Thou *"lovedst them, even as thou lovedst Me"* (Jn. 17:23). Christ is referring to the fact that, just as the Disciples had received the same treatment from the world that He had received, so they had received of the Father the same Love that He Himself had received.

They were not on the outskirts of God's Love, but in the very center of it. *"For the Father Himself loveth you, because you have loved Me"* (Jn. 16:27). Here the Greek word *"phileo"* is used for Love, indicating the Fatherly affection of God for the Believer in Christ, His Son. This is Love in a more intense form than that spoken of for the world (Jn. 3:16).

## GOD LOVES THE WORLD

This is a wonderful Truth when we realize what a world this is — a world of sin and corruption (Jn. 3:16; I Tim. 2:4; II Pet. 3:9).

This was a startling Truth for Nicodemus to learn, who conceived of God as loving only the Jewish Nation. To him, in his narrow exclusivism, the announcement of the fact that God loved the whole world of men was startling.

God loves the world of sinners lost and ruined by the Fall. Yet it is this world, *"weak," "ungodly," "without strength," "sinners"* (Rom. 5:6-8), *"dead in trespasses and sins"* (Eph. 2:1), and unrighteous, that God so loved that He gave His Only Begotten Son in order to redeem it.

The Genesis of man's Salvation lies in the Love and Mercy of God (Eph. 2:4). But Love is more than Mercy or Compassion; it is active and identifies itself with its object.

The Love of the Heavenly Father over the return of His wandering Children is beautifully set forth in the Parable of the Prodigal Son (Lk. Chpt. 15). Nor should the fact be overlooked that God loves not only the whole world, but each individual in it; it is a special, as well as, a general Love (Jn. 3:16, *"Whosoever"*; (Gal. 2:20, *"Loved Me, and gave Himself up for Me"*).

## THE MANIFESTATION OF THE LOVE OF GOD

God's Love is manifested by providing for the physical, mental, moral, and spiritual needs of His People (Isa. 48:14, 20-21; 62:9-12; 63:3, 12).

In these Scriptures God is seen manifesting His Power on behalf of His People in the time of their wilderness journey and their captivity. He led them, fed and clothed them, guided them, and protected them from all their enemies. His Love was again shown in feeling with His People, their sorrows and afflictions (Isa. 63:9); He suffered in their affliction, their interests were His; He was not their adversary but their Friend, even though it might have seemed to them as if He either had brought on them their suffering or did not care about it.

Nor did He ever forget them for a moment during all their trials. They thought He did; they said, *"God hath forgotten us," "He hath forgotten to be gracious"*; but no; a Mother might forget her child that she should not have compassion on it, but God would never forget His People.

How could He?

THE EXPRESSION OF LOVE

Had God not graven them (Israel) upon the Palms of His Hands (Isa. 49:15)?

Rather than His Love being absent in the chastisement of His People, the chastisement itself was often a proof of the Presence of the Divine Love, *"For whom the Lord loveth He chasteneth, and scourgeth every son whom He receiveth"* (Heb. 12:6-11).

Loving reproof and chastisement are necessary ofttimes for growth in Holiness and Righteousness. Our Redemption from sin is to be attributed to God's wondrous Love; *"Thou hast in Love to my soul delivered it from the pit of corruption; for Thou hast cast all my sins behind Thy back"* (Ps. 50:21; 90:8; Isa. 38:17). Ephesians 2:4-5 sets forth in a wonderful way how our entire Salvation springs forth from the Mercy and Love of God; *"But God, being rich in Mercy, for His great Love wherewith He loved us, even when we were dead through our trespasses, made us alive together with Christ,"* etc.

It is because of the Love of the Father that we are granted a place in the Heavenly Kingdom (Eph. 2:6-8). But the supreme manifestation of the Love of God, as set forth in the Scripture, is that expressed in the Gift of His Only-Begotten Son to die for the sin of the world (Jn. 3:16; Rom. 5:6-8; I Jn. 4:9), and through Whom the sinful and sinning but repentant sons of men are taken into the Family of God, and receive the adoption of sons (I Jn. 3:1; Gal. 4:4-6).

From this wonderful Love of God in Christ Jesus nothing in Heaven or Earth or Hell, created or uncreated or to be created, shall be able to separate us (Rom. 8:37).

NOTES

THE LOVE OF MAN

Whatever Love there is in man, whether it be toward God or toward His fellowman, has its source in God — *"Love is of God; and everyone that loveth is begotten of God, and knoweth God. He that loveth not knoweth not God; for God is Love"* (I Jn. 4:7); *"We love, because He first loved us"* (I Jn. 4:19).

Trench, in speaking of the Greek word *"agape,"* says it is a word born within the bosom of revealed Salvation. Heathen writers do not use it at all, their nearest approach to it being *"Philadelphia"* — the Love between those of the same blood.

Love in the heart of man is the offspring of the Love of God. Only the regenerated heart can truly Love as God Loves; to this higher form of Love the unregenerate can lay no claim (I Jn. 2:7-11; 3:10; 4:7, 11, 19, 21).

The regenerate (Saved) man is able to see his fellowman as God sees him, value him as God values him, not so much because of what he is by reason of his sin and unloveliness, but because of what, through Christ, he may become; he sees man's intrinsic worth and possibility in Christ (II Cor. 5:14-17).

This Love is also created in the heart of man by the Holy Spirit (Rom. 5:5), and is a Fruit of the Spirit (Gal. 5:22). It is also stimulated by the example of The Lord Jesus Christ, Who, more than anyone else, manifested to the world the spirit and nature of the True Love of God (Jn. 13:34; 15:12; Gal. 2:20; Eph. 5:25-27; I Jn. 4:9).

GOD MUST BE THE FIRST AND SUPREME OBJECT OF MAN'S LOVE

He must be loved with all the heart, mind, soul, and strength (Mat. 22:37; Mk. 12:29-34). In this last Passage the exhortation to supreme Love to God is connected with the Doctrine of the Unity of God (Deut. 6:4) — inasmuch as the Divine Being is One and indivisible, so must our Love to Him be undivided.

Our Love to God is shown in the keeping of His Commandments (Ex. 20:6; I Jn. 5:3; II Jn. vs. 6). Love is here set forth as more than a mere affection or sentiment; it is something that manifests itself, not only in obedience to known Divine Commands, but also in a protecting and defense of them, and a seeking to know more and more of the Will of God in order to express Love for God and further obedience (Deut. 10:12).

Those who Love God must hate evil and all forms of worldliness, as expressed in the avoidance of the lust of the eyes, the lust of the flesh and the pride of life (Ps. 97:10; I Jn. 2:14-17).

Whatever there may be in his surroundings that would draw the soul away from God and Righteousness, that the Child of God must avoid. Christ, being God, also claims the first place in our affections. He is to be chosen before Father or Mother, Parent or Child, brother or sister, or friend (Mat. 10:35-38; Lk. 14:26).

The word *"hate"* in these Passages does not mean to hate in the sense in which we use the word today. It is used in the sense in which Jacob is said to have *"hated"* Leah (Gen. 29:31), that is, he loved her less than Rachel; *"He loved also Rachel more than Leah"* (Gen. 29:30).

To Love Christ supremely is the test of true discipleship (Lk. 14:26), and is an unfailing mark of the Elect (I Pet. 1:8). We prove that we are really God's Children by thus loving His Son (Jn. 8:42). Absence of such Love means, finally, eternal separation (I Cor. 16:22).

MAN MUST LOVE HIS FELLOWMAN ALSO

Love for the brotherhood is a natural consequence of the Love of the Fatherhood; for *"In this the Children of God are manifest, and the children of the Devil: Whosoever doeth not Righteousness is not of God, neither he that loveth not his brother"* (I Jn. 3:10). For a man to say *"I Love God"* and yet hate his fellowman is to brand himself as a *"liar"* (I Jn. 4:20); *"He that Loveth not his brother whom he hath seen, cannot Love God Whom he hath not seen"* (I Jn. 4:20); He that Loveth God will Love his brother also (I Jn. 4:21).

The degree in which we are to Love our fellowman is *"as thyself"* (Mat. 22:39), according to the strict observance of the Law.

Christ set before His Followers a much higher example than that, however. According to the Teaching of Jesus we are to supersede this Standard: *"A New Commandment I give unto you, that ye Love one another; even as I have Loved you, that ye also Love one another"* (Jn. 13:34).

The exhibition of Love of this character toward our fellowman is the badge of True

NOTES

Discipleship. It may be called the sum total of our duty toward our fellowman, for *"Love worketh no ill to his neighbour: Love therefore is the fulfillment of the Law"*; *"For he that Loveth his neighbour hath fulfilled the Law"* (Rom. 13:8-10).

THE QUALITIES WHICH ARE TO BE SET FORTH

The qualities which should characterize the Love which we are to manifest toward our fellowmen are beautifully set forth in I Corinthians, Chapter 13. It is patient and without envy; it is not proud or self-elated, neither does it behave discourteously; it does not cherish evil, but keeps good account of the good; it rejoices not at the downfall of an enemy or competitor, but gladly hails his success; it is hopeful, trustful, and forbearing — for such there is no Law, for they need none; they have fulfilled the Law.

Nor should it be overlooked that our Lord commanded His Children to Love their enemies, those who spoke evil of them, and despitefully used them (Mat. 5:43-48). They were not to render evil for evil, but contrariwise, blessing. The Love of the Disciple of Christ must manifest itself in supplying the necessities, not of our friends only (I Jn. 3:16-18), but also of our enemies (Rom. 12:20).

WITHOUT HYPOCRISY

Our Love should be *"without hypocrisy"* (Rom. 12:9); there should be no pretense about it; it should not be a thing of mere word or term, but a real experience manifesting itself in Deed and Truth (I Jn. 3:18).

True Love will find its expression in service to man: *"Through Love be servants one to another"* (Gal. 5:13). What more wonderful illustration can be found of ministering Love than that set forth by our Lord in the Ministry of foot-washing found in John, Chapter 13? Love bears the infirmities of the weak, does not please itself, but seeks the welfare of others (Rom. 15:1-3; I Cor. 10:24; Gal. 6:2; Phil. 2:21); it surrenders things which may be innocent in themselves but which nevertheless may become a stumbling-block to others (Rom. 14:15-21); it gladly forgives injuries (Eph. 4:32), and gives the place of honor to another (Rom. 12:10).

What, then, is more vital than to possess such Love? It is the fulfillment of the Royal

Law (James 2:8), and is to be put above everything else (Col. 3:14); it is the binder that holds all the other Graces of the Christian life in place (Col. 3:14); by the possession of such Love *"we know that we have passed from Death unto Life"* (I Jn. 3:14), and it is the supreme test of our abiding in God and God in us (I Jn. 4:12-16).

(The statement on Love was provided by William Evans.)

(2) "AND IF ANY MAN THINK THAT HE KNOWETH ANY THING, HE KNOWETH NOTHING YET AS HE OUGHT TO KNOW."

Several very important things are said in this Verse. Some of them are as follows:

1. Even the Believer who has the greatest knowledge of the Word of God, whomever that may be, still knows very little, at least as far as the Great Plan of God is concerned. So, realizing that irrespective of our knowledge of the Word, that we have only scratched the surface, should humble us.

2. Irrespective as to how much we do know, we still don't know as much as we *"ought to know."*

The Word of God, totally unlike any other written material on the face of the Earth, is absolutely inexhaustible, because it is the Word of God. That means it is literally impossible for anyone to glean all the meanings out of any particular Verse of Scripture. It alone holds the answers to *"all things that pertain unto Life and Godliness, through the knowledge of Him that hath called us to Glory and Virtue"* (II Pet. 1:3). So, the Believer should make the Bible a lifelong study, an habitual study, and by that I refer to a daily basis. If one eats natural food each day, as one must do to survive, one must eat spiritual food as well, which Jesus put on the same par (Mat. 4:4).

3. The gist of what the Holy Spirit through the Apostle is saying, is that Love and Humility must accompany knowledge, even knowledge of the Word of God, and if not, pride will develop.

4. The phrase, *"And if any man think that he knoweth any thing,"* refers to the fact, that we never know as much about the Word of God, as we think we know.

The only One Who has ever had a Perfect Knowledge of the Word of God, which was accompanied by consummate Love and Humility, was The Lord Jesus Christ. When one studies the Gospels, one quickly realizes just how much He actually knew the Word.

NOTES

Most would shrug off that statement, thinking in their minds that it is of little consequence due to Who Jesus is. While that certainly does have a bearing on the subject, the Truth is, that Jesus had to learn the Word exactly as any other human being has to learn the Word. However, the difference is, that His Whole Being was consecrated to the Lord as no other human being ever even remotely was. In other words, He was the most perfect Receptacle of the Holy Spirit Who has ever lived, thereby being controlled by the Holy Spirit more so than any other.

However, He did have one great advance, and that was that He did not have a sin nature as the balance of humanity. Being Virgin born, He did not have the terrible clinging of the Fall inculcated in His Being, as we do.

(3) "BUT IF ANY MAN LOVE GOD, THE SAME IS KNOWN OF HIM."

In essence, the Apostle is saying that if we are to be *"known by others,"* it should not be for our knowledge, even though knowledge is very important, but rather for our Love for God. That is the reason the Prophet Jeremiah said a long time ago, *"Thus saith the Lord, Let not the wise man glory in his wisdom, neither let the mighty man glory in his might, Let not the rich man glory in his riches:*

*"But let him that glorieth glory in this, that he understandeth and knoweth Me, that I am the Lord which exercises Lovingkindness, Judgment, and Righteousness, in the Earth: For in these things I delight, saith the Lord"* (Jer. 9:23-24).

If a Believer does not have proper Love for God, his knowledge will be skewed as well. If Love for God grows commiserately with Knowledge of God (His Word), the knowledge will stay on track. Otherwise, it will tend to subvert the Believer, even as it did some of the Corinthians.

Some of them had become so puffed up in themselves, that they even thought the Apostle Paul was shallow in his Teaching of the Word. The absolute absurdity of such thinking should be obvious to all. But yet, this is what happens whenever consecration to the Lord is neglected, and training is given preeminence.

It all adds us to relationship. If one has the proper relationship with Christ, what one learns regarding the Word of God, will then be on track.

(4) "AS CONCERNING THEREFORE THE EATING OF THOSE THINGS THAT ARE OFFERED IN SACRIFICE UNTO IDOLS, WE KNOW THAT AN IDOL IS NOTHING IN THE WORLD, AND THAT THERE IS NONE OTHER GOD BUT ONE."

The phrase, *"As concerning therefore the eating of those things that are offered in sacrifice unto idols,"* now comes to the heart of the matter. This was the controversy in the Church.

HOW WAS IT A CONTROVERSY?

It was really a controversy in two ways: A. Erroneous thoughts and ideas held by some of the Believers; and, B. Christian Liberty carried too far in the actions of some.

I think one could say without fear of exaggeration, that all the Believers in the Church at Corinth, had been Saved out of rank Heathenism. In other words, all of them, or at least most of them, had formerly been idol-worshipers, with all its attendant evils.

For instance, fornication was practiced extensively relative to temple prostitutes, etc., plus they were taught extensively that the eating of meat offered to these idol gods would give one the spirit of such gods or goddesses. In other words, the entirety of the culture was built around the worship of these idols. In fact, the clothing of devotees was fashioned in a certain manner according to the particular god or gods worshiped. Such even pertained to the style of furniture in houses, etc.

So, when these people came to Christ, they left all of that behind with its attendant evil connotations.

Some of the Believers, now infused with the Divine Nature, and so turned off by their old life, which is exactly what should have been, went a little too far in their thinking, concluding that if they ate any of the meat sold in the marketplace, which had in fact been originally dedicated to particular idols, they would in essence, be committing sin. Others were claiming, and rightly so, even as Paul will here address, that there is no sin connected with such; however if someone thinks it is sin, to them it really is (Rom. 14:23). Consequently, those who were strong in the Faith, should not do anything to hinder those who are weak. This showed concern for others, even as our Lord has shown concern for us.

NOTES

As will be obvious, Paul goes beyond legalities, and looks at motives and the state of the heart.

The phrase, *"We know that an idol is nothing in the world,"* in effect has Paul saying that the eating of such meat contains no offense to the Lord or His Word.

He is as well saying, that Believers who make more of this than they should, are giving more credit to the Devil than he deserves.

But yet, though an idol has no being, and is really nothing at all, yet all who worship idols worship devils, for demons introduced such worship to man (I Cor. 10:20). But yet, as far as the idol itself is concerned, as should be obvious, it is no more than an absurdity made by man.

The phrase, *"And that there is none other God but One,"* speaks of the God of the Bible, and Who made all things (Gen. 1:1).

In fact, Israel was the only monotheistic Nation in the world, which means that she worshiped one God, while all the surrounding Nations worshiped many gods.

IDOLATRY

There is ever in the human mind a craving for visible forms to express religious conceptions, and this tendency does not disappear with the acceptance, or even with the constant recognition, of pure spiritual Truths.

Idolatry originally meant the worship of idols, or the worship of false gods by means of idols, but came to mean among the Old Testament Hebrews any worship of false gods, whether by images or otherwise, and finally the worship of Jehovah through visible symbols (Hos. 8:5-6; 10:5); and ultimately in the New Testament idolatry came to mean, not only the giving to any creature or human creation the honor or devotion which belonged to God Alone, but the giving to any human desire a precedence over God's Will (I Cor. 10:14; Gal. 5:20; Col. 3:5; I Pet. 4:3).

IDOL GODS

The neighboring gods of Phoenicia, Canaan, Moab — Baal, Melkart, Astarte, Chemosh, Moloch, etc. — were particularly attractive to Jerusalem, while the old Semitic Calf-Worship seriously affected the State Religion of the Northern Kingdom of Israel, which ultimately brought about its destruction.

NOTES

As early as the Assyrian and Babylonian periods (7th and 8th Centuries B.C.), various deities (so-called) from the Tigris and Euphrates region had intruded themselves — the worship of Tammuz later becoming the most popular and seductive of all (Ezek. 8:14) — with the worship of the Sun, Moon, Stars, and Signs of the Zodiac becoming so intensely fascinating that these were introduced even into the Temple itself (II Ki. 17:16; 21:3-7; 23:4-12; Jer. 19:13; Ezek. 8:16; Amos 5:26).

## ENTICEMENTS TO IDOLATRY

The special enticements to idolatry as offered by these various cults were found in their deification of natural forces (the Sun, Moon, etc.) and their appeal to primitive human desires, especially the sexual; also through associations produced by intermarriage and through the appeal to patriotism, when the help of some cruel deity was sought in time of war.

Baal and Astarte worship, which was especially attractive, was closely associated with fornication and drunkenness (I Ki. 14:23; Amos 2:7-8), and also appealed greatly to magic and soothsaying (Isa. 2:6; 3:3; 8:19).

## MANNER OF WORSHIP

Sacrifices to the idols were offered by fire (Hos. 4:13); libations were poured out (Isa. 57:6; Jer. 7:18); the firstfruits of the Earth and tithes were presented (Hos. 2:8); tables of food were set before them (Isa. 65:11); the worshipers kissed the idols or threw them kisses (I Ki. 19:18; Job 31:27; Hos. 13:2); stretched out their hands in adoration (Isa. 44:20); knelt or prostrated themselves before them and sometimes danced about the Altar, gashing themselves with knives (I Ki. 18:26-28).

## THE IDOL IS NOTHING

The Old Testament statements against idolatry, carried on chiefly by Prophets and Psalmists, recognize the same two Truths which Paul was later to affirm: that the idol was nothing, but that, nevertheless, there was a demonic spiritual force to be reckoned with, and that the idol, therefore, constituted a positive spiritual menace (Isa. 44:6-20; I Cor. 8:4; 10:19-20).

Thus, the idol is nothing at all: man made it (Isa. 2:8); its very composition and construction proclaim its futility (Isa. 40:18-20; 41:6-7; 44:9-20); its helpless bulk invites derision (Isa. 46:1-2); it has no life (Ps. 115:4-7).

As well, the Prophets derisively named them *"gillulim"* (Ezek. 6:4, and at least 38 other times in Ezekiel), which means *"dung pellets,"* or *"godlets."*

## THE PRINCIPLE INVOLVED

Though the idols within themselves were nothing, there were spiritual forces of evil involved, and the practice of idolatry brought men into deadly contact with these *"gods."* Isaiah, who is usually said to bring the ironic scorning of idols to its peak, is well aware of this spiritual evil.

He knows that there is only one God (Isa. 44:8), but even so no one can touch an idol, though it be *"nothing"* and come away unscathed. Man's contact with the false god infects him with a deadly spiritual blindness of heart and mind (Isa. 44:18).

Though what he worships is mere *"ashes,"* yet it is full of the poison of spiritual delusion (Isa. 44:20). Those who worship idols become like them (Ps. 115:8; Jer. 2:5; Hos. 9:10).

## DEMONIC POWER

Because of the reality of evil power behind the idol, it is an abomination to God (Deut. 7:25), a detested thing (Deut. 29:17), and it is the gravest sin, spiritual adultery, to follow idols (Deut. 31:16; Judg. 2:17; Hos. 1:2).

## ONE TRUE GOD

Nevertheless, there is only One God, and the contrast between the Lord and idols is to be drawn in terms of life, activity and government. The idol cannot predict and bring to pass, but God can (Isa. 41:26-27; 44:7); the idol is a helpless piece of flotsam on the river of history, only wise after the event and helpless in the face of it (Isa. 41:5-7; 46:1-2), but the Lord is the Master and Controller of history (Isa. 40:22-25; 41:1-2, 25; 43:14-15).

## THE NEW TESTAMENT

The New Testament reinforces and amplifies the Old Testament Teaching. Its recognition that idols are both nonentities and dangerous spiritual potencies has been noted above.

In addition, Romans, Chapter 1 expresses the Old Testament view that idolatry is a decline

NOTES

from True Spirituality, and not a stage on the way to a pure Knowledge of God.

This speaks to the Roman Catholic practice of the worship of images and the praying to Saints, etc. Such is not bringing them closer to God, as they think, but in reality has the opposite effect.

The New Testament recognizes, however, that the peril of idolatry exists, even where material idols are not fashioned: the association of idolatry with sexual sins in Galatians 5:19-20 ought to be linked with the equating of covetousness with idolatry (I Cor. 5:11; Eph. 5:5; Col. 3:5), for by covetousness Paul certainly includes and stresses sexual covetousness (I Cor. 10:7, 14; Eph. 4:19; 5:3; I Thess. 4:6).

John, having urged the finality and fullness of Revelation in Christ, warns that any deviation from the Word of God is idolatry (I Jn. 5:19-21). The idol is whatever claims that loyalty which belongs to God Alone (Isa. 42:8).

## MEATS OFFERED TO IDOLS

This situation regarding meats offered to idols in which Paul is here discussing, was of tremendous import in the world of his day.

In the ancient system of heathen sacrifice, which was the center not only of the religious life of the Graeco-Roman world in the First Century, but also of the domestic and social life, only part of the sacrifice was presented to the god in the temple. The sacrifice was followed by a cultic meal, when the remainder of the consecrated food was eaten either in the confines of the temple or at home. Sometimes the remaining food was sent to the market to be sold (I Cor. 10:25).

Evidence for the practice of a meal in the temple is found in the following discovered Papyrus, which has been regarded as a striking parallel to the reference in I Corinthians 10:27. It is as follows:

*"Chaeremon invites you to dinner at the table of the Lord Serapis* (the name of the deity) *in the Serapeum tomorrow the 15th at the 9th hour (3 p.m.)."*

## COMMONPLACE

An invitation to a meal of this character, whether in the temple or in a private house, would be commonplace in the social life of the city of Corinth, and would pose a thorny question for the Believer who was so invited. Other aspects of life in such a cosmopolitan center would be affected by the Christian's attitude to idol-meats.

Attendance at the public festivals, which opened with Pagan adoration and sacrifice would have to be considered. Membership of a trade guild and, therefore, one's commercial standing, and public-spiritedness were also involved, as such membership would entail sitting at *"a table in an idol's temple"* (I Cor. 8:10).

Even daily shopping in the market would present a problem to the thoughtful Christian in Corinth. As much of the meat would be passed on from the temple-officials to the Meat-Dealers and by them exposed for sale, the question arose:

Was the Christian housewife at liberty to purchase this meat which, coming from sacrificial animals which had to be free from blemish, might well be the best meat in the market?

Moreover, there were gratuitous banquets in the temple precincts which were a real boon to the poor. If I Corinthians 1:26 means that some of the Corinthian Church Members belonged to the poorer classes, which they no doubt did, the question of whether they were free or not to avail themselves of such meals, which some of them no doubt desperately needed, would have been a practical issue.

## DIFFERENT REACTIONS

Conviction in the Church was sharply divided. One group, in the name of Christian Liberty (I Cor. 6:12; 8:9; 10:23) and on the basis of a supposed superior knowledge (I Cor. 8:1-2), could see no harm in accepting an invitation to a cultic meal and no possible reason why food, formerly dedicated in the temple, should not be bought and eaten.

The justification for such an attitude was: A. That the meal in the temple precincts was just a social occasion. They claimed that it had no religious significance at all; and, B. They appeared to have stated that in any case the Pagan gods are nonentities. *"An idol has no real existence"* and *"there is no God but One"* was their plea of defense, Paul probably citing their own words (I Cor. 8:4).

On the other hand, the *"weak"* group (I Cor. 8:9; Rom. 15:1) viewed the situation differently. With abhorrence of the least suspicion of idolatry, they believed that the demons behind the idols still exerted malign influence on the food and *"contaminated"* it, thus rendering it unfit for consumption by Believers (Acts 10:14; I Cor. 8:7).

PAUL'S ANSWER

Paul begins his answer to the Church's inquiry by expressing agreement with the proposition. *"There is no God but One"* (I Cor. 8:4). But he immediately qualifies this explicit confession of his monotheism by reminding his readers that there are so-called gods and lords which exert demonic influence in the world. He concedes the point, however, that *"for us"* who acknowledge One God and One Lord, the power of these demons has been overcome by the Cross, so that the Corinthians ought no longer to be in bondage to them (Gal. 4:3, 8-9; Col. 2:15-16).

Not all the Corinthian Believers had found that total freedom in Christ, and their case must be remembered and their weak conscience not outraged by indiscreet action (I Cor. 8:7-13).

The Apostle has a more serious word to say on this matter, which he takes up after a digression in Chapter 9.

DEMON SPIRITS

Paul comes to grips with the menace of idolatry in I Corinthians 10:14. These Verses are an exposition of the inner meaning of the Lord's Table in the light of Communion in the Body and Blood of Christ (I Cor. 10:16); the unity of the Church as the Body of Christ (I Cor. 10:17); the spell cast by demons over their worshipers at idol-feasts which led actually to a compact with the demons (I Cor. 10:20); and the impossibility of a double allegiance represented by trying to share both the Table of the Lord and the table of demons (I Cor. 10:21-22).

ASSOCIATION

The Apostle in this section, therefore, takes a serious attitude to the implications of attendance at idolatrous banquets (I Cor. 10:14). He forbids absolutely the use of food and drink in an idol-temple (I Cor. 10:19-20; Rev. 2:14) on the ground no doubt that, as the Rabbis had said, *"As a dead body defiles by overshadowing, so also an idolatrous sacrifice causes defilement by overshadowing,"* i.e., by having been brought under a Pagan roof, and by this contact becomes ritually unclean.

NOTES

PERMITTED

But in regard to food which has formerly been offered in the temple and is afterward made available for purchase in the marketplace, Paul says that it is permitted on the basis of Psalm 24:1 (I Cor. 10:25).

Although such food has been dedicated in the temple and is exposed for sale in the meat market, it may be eaten by virtue of being God's Creation (I Tim. 4:4-5). This is a distinct departure from the Rabbinical ceremonial rules, but is a practical application of the Lord's Word in Mark 7:19, *"Thus He declared all foods clean"* (Acts 10:15).

THE LAW OF LOVE

The only qualification is that the *"Law of Love"* must be observed, and a Christian's own freedom to eat such food must be waived if the conscience of the *"weaker"* Believer is likely to be damaged and he is, therefore, caused to stumble (I Cor. 10:28-32), or if a Gentile is scandalized by this practice (I Cor. 10:32).

The situation envisaged by these Verses is a Christian's acceptance of an invitation to a meal in a private house (I Cor. 10:27). In such a circumstance the Believer is free to eat the food set before him, making no inquiries as to its *"past history,"* i.e., where it comes from or whether it has been dedicated in an idol shrine.

If, however, a Pagan, at the meal, draws attention to the food and says, *"This has been offered in sacrifice"* — then the food must be refused, not because it is *"infected"* or unfit for consumption, but because it *"places the eater in a false position, and confuses the conscience of others,"* notably his heathen neighbor.

(Bibliography. C. K. Barret, J. Hering, F. F. Bruce, H. Conzelmann.)

(5) "FOR THOUGH THERE BE THAT ARE CALLED GODS, WHETHER IN HEAVEN OR IN EARTH, (AS THERE BE GODS MANY, AND LORDS MANY,)"

The phrase, *"For though there be that are called gods,"* was probably lifted directly from their letter sent to him.

The heathen referred to all type of things as *"gods,"* but all the work of their own hands, which as stated, was ridiculed greatly by the Prophets of old.

The phrase, *"Whether in Heaven or in Earth,"* refers not only to images, but also to all the planetary bodies and all the other creation of God.

The phrase, *"As there be gods many, and lords many,"* is probably a reference to the cult of Caesar worship, i.e., the deification of Roman Emperors. The title *"Augustus,"* which they all had borne, was to Jewish ears *"the name of blasphemy,"* and because it implied that they (Emperors) were to be objects of reverence.

Indeed, the worship of the Caesars was, in that strange time of mingled atheism and superstition, almost the only viable cult that was left (Farrar).

(6) "BUT TO US THERE IS BUT ONE GOD, THE FATHER, OF WHOM ARE ALL THINGS, AND WE IN HIM; AND ONE LORD JESUS CHRIST, BY WHOM ARE ALL THINGS, AND WE BY HIM."

The phrase, *"But to us there is but one God,"* refers to *"one"* in unity and not necessarily *"one"* in number. Actually, it can refer to either.

There is but one God, but manifested in three Persons, *"God the Father," "God the Son,"* and *"God the Holy Spirit."* While the Members of the Triune Godhead are one in essence, they are not one in number. There are certain things which can be said about One which cannot be said about Another. For instance, Jesus Christ died on the Cross, but this did not refer to God the Father or God the Holy Spirit dying on the Cross. But They, in essence, were so in unity with Him that it could be said of Them that *"God was in Christ, reconciling the world unto Himself."* (This represents the Atonement as the work of the Blessed Trinity, and the result of love, not of wrath [II Cor. 5:19].)

The phrase, *"The Father,"* speaks of relationship which all Born-Again Believers have with God, which was made possible by The Lord Jesus Christ, and what He did at Calvary, the Resurrection, and the Exaltation.

GOD, THE FATHER

In the Christian experience God is conceived of as *"Father," "Our Father . . . in Heaven"* (Mat. 6:9, 14, 26), *"The God and Father of the Lord Jesus"* (II Cor. 11:31).

NOTES

The tenderness of relation and wealth of Love and Grace embraced in this profound designation are peculiar to Christ's Gospel.

IN THE OLD TESTAMENT

In the Old Economy of God He was revealed as Father to the chosen Nation (Ex. 4:22), and to the special representative of the Nation the King (II Sam. 7:14), while Fatherly Love is declared to be the image of His pity for those who fear Him (Ps. 103:13).

JESUS

In the Gospel of Jesus Alone is this Fatherhood revealed to be the very essence of the Godhead, and to have respect to the individual. Here, however, there is need for great discrimination.

To reach the heart of the Truth of the Divine Fatherhood it is necessary to begin, not with man, but with the Godhead Itself, in Whose eternal depths is found the spring of that Fatherly Love that reveals itself in time. It is first of all in relation to the Eternal Son — before all time — that the meaning of Fatherhood in God is made clear (Jn. 1:18).

In *"God the Father"* we have a Name pointing to that relation which the First Person in the adorable Trinity sustains to *"Son"* and *"Holy Spirit"* — also Divine (Mat. 28:19). From this Eternal Fountainhead flows the relations of God as Father: A. To the world by Creation; and, B. To Believers by Grace.

MAN

Man as created was designed by affinity of nature for Sonship to God. The realization of this — his true creature destiny — was frustrated by sin, and can now only be restored by Redemption. Hence, the place of Sonship in the Gospel, as an unspeakable privilege (I Jn. 3:1), obtained by Grace, through Regeneration (Jn. 1:12-13), and adoption (Rom. 8:14-19).

In this relation of nearness and privilege to the Father in the Kingdom of His Son (Col. 1:13), Believers are *"Sons of God"* in a sense true of no others. It is a relation, not of nature, but of Grace.

MORAL RULER AND JUDGE

Fatherhood is now the determinative fact in God's relation to Believers (Eph. 3:14). It is an error, nevertheless, to speak of Fatherhood as if the whole character of God was therein sufficiently expressed.

God is Father, but equally fundamental is His relation to His world as its Moral Ruler and Judge. From eternity to eternity the Holy God must pronounce Himself against sin (Rom. 1:18); and His Fatherly Grace cannot avert judgment where the heart remains hard and impenitent (Rom. 2:1-9) (James Ire).

(The Fatherhood of God only pertains to Believers and never of unbelievers, which can only be entered into by the Born-Again experience — Jn. 3:3.)

The phrase, *"Of Whom are all things,"* actually refers to God as the Creator of all things. It really speaks of the *"Kingdom of God"* which incorporates everything, including Satan, Fallen Angels, Demon Spirits, etc. Unfortunately, that section of God's Creation is in revolution against Him, which has caused all the heartache and problems for Earth regarding its known history. To be sure, God did not create Satan and Fallen Angels in this manner, but they became this way because of rebellion against Him.

THE CREATOR AND CREATION

The distinctive characteristic of Deity, as the Creator, is that He is the Cause of the existent Universe — cause of its being, not merely of its present arrangements.

The Doctrine of God being the Creator implies, that is to say, that He is the real and the exclusive Agent in the production of the world and all else for that matter. As someone has said, the thought of the Creator is the most fruitful of all our ideas. As Creator, He is the Unconditioned, and the All-conditioning, Being. The Universe is thus dependent upon Him, as its cause and care. He calls it, as Aquinas said, *"according to its whole substance,"* into being, without any presupposed basis.

His Power, as Creator, is different in kind from finite power. But the creative process is not a case of sheer Almightiness, merely creating something out of nothing, but an expression of God, as the Absolute Reason, under the forms of time and space, the Absolute Cause.

EVERYTHING IS WITHIN HIM

In all His Work, as Creator, there is no incitement from without, for there is nothing without, but it rather remains an eternal activity of self-manifestation on the part of God Who is Love.

God's free creative action is destined to realize particular ends and ideals, which are peculiar to Himself. In other words, He has a Divine Purpose and Plan for the entirety of His Creation. God being Who He is, must create with a purpose, which His directive agency will see at last fulfilled.

As Creator, He is distinct from the Universe, which is the produce of the free action of His Will. However, it must be understood, that His creative action was in no way necessary to His Own Blessedness or Perfection, which must be held as already complete in Himself.

To place Him otherwise, is to make Him subject to the Creation, when in reality, all Creation is subject to Him.

HIS PURPOSE

God's action, as Creator, does not lower our conception of His changelessness, regarding the purpose of His Creation. To assume that the will to create was a sudden or accidental thing, is to lower God to the level of His Creation. In other words, we make a mistake when we attempt to conceive of His Creative Thought or Purpose as subject to time as we know time. To understand God Who always was and always is, is plainly speaking, beyond human comprehension. So, even though time is certainly a factor with God, for He is the One Who created such, which proclaims a systematic order, still, God must never be subject to His Creation. His Creation must always be subject to Him. In other words, *"time"* such as days, weeks, years, does not restrain Him as it does human beings.

THE DIVINE WILL

The self-determined action of the Divine Will, then, is to be taken as the ultimate principle of all Creation. In other words, Creation did not come about as a result of *"need"* on the part of God or of *"necessity,"* but rather, as a result of His Absolute Personality. The Scripture says, *"Of Him, and through Him, and unto Him, are all things,"* which speaks of Christ (Rom. 11:36).

This creative action of God is mediated by Christ — by Whom *"were all things created, in the Heavens and upon the Earth, things visible and things invisible, whether thrones or*

NOTES

*dominions or principalities or powers; all things have been created through Him, and unto Him"* (Col. 1:16).

To say it another way, the One Who came down here to this mortal coil, died on Calvary, suffering the horrific indignities of evil men, rose from the dead on the third day, and sits today at the Right Hand of the Father, is in fact, the Creator of all things.

John said, *"All things were made by Him; and without Him was not any thing made that was made"* (Jn. 1:3).

His Name is Jesus.

The phrase, *"And we in Him,"* refers to the Truth that He is the End and Goal as well as the Author of our existence (Farrar).

This Blessed Union with Christ, goes back to I Corinthians 6:17, *"But he that is joined unto the Lord is one spirit."* As we have stated, this comes about by the *"Born Again"* experience (Jn. 3:3).

## JESUS CHRIST

The phrase, *"And One Lord Jesus Christ,"* presents the Second Person of the Divine Trinity. As well, He is *"Lord,"* and in fact the Only Lord, in contradistinction to all usurpers. In fact, Roman Emperors often took the title of *"Lord,"* and one of them — Domitian — insisted on the use of the expression. Actually, he insisted on being called *"Dominus Deusque Noster,"* which means *"Our Lord and God."* So, when Paul uses the word *"Lord"* referring to Jesus, the reason is twofold:

1. Jesus *is* God, i.e., *"Lord."* This means He is *"Lord"* of Heaven and Earth and all that is therein.

2. His statement is meant as well to combat the Caesar Cult of that time. In fact, untold numbers of Christians went to their death simply because they would not say *"Caesar is Lord,"* but rather *"Jesus is Lord."*

The phrase, *"By Whom are all things, and we by Him,"* refers to Christ as the Agent of Creation and Redemption (Jn. 1:3, 10; Heb. 1:2).

This means that He is our Saviour, the Giver of Eternal Life, the Baptizer with the Holy Spirit, the Healer of the sick, the Destroyer of every Satanic bondage, the Giver of all good things.

*"We by Him,"* or as it actually says, *"We through Him,"* is a way of saying that we belong to Christ because He is the Only One Who died for our sins (Rossier).

NOTES

## THE TRINITY

The term *"Trinity"* is not a Biblical term, but yet it expresses the Doctrine that there is One Only and True God, but in the Unity of the Godhead there are Three Coeternal and Coequal Persons, the same in essence and the same in substance, but distinct in subsistence.

The Doctrine of the Trinity lies in Scripture relative to its solution; when it is crystallized from its solvent it does not cease to be Scriptural, but only comes into clearer view.

Or, to speak without figure, the Doctrine of the Trinity is given to us in Scripture, not in formulated definition, but in fragmentary allusions; consequently, when we assemble all the parts or Scriptures on the subject, we are not passing from Scripture, but entering more thoroughly into the meaning of Scripture. While it may be true that in explaining the Trinity, we may state the Doctrine in technical terms, supplied by philosophical reflection, because that is the only way man can do such, but the Doctrine stated is a genuinely Scriptural Doctrine.

## THE DEEPEST THINGS OF GOD

In point of fact, the Doctrine of the Trinity is purely a revealed Doctrine. That is to say, it embodies a Truth which has never been discovered, and is indiscoverable, by natural reason.

With all his searching, man has not been able to find out for himself the deepest things of God. Exactly as Paul said, *"And if any man think that he knoweth any thing, he knoweth nothing yet as he ought to know"* (I Cor. 8:2).

As the Doctrine of the Trinity is indiscoverable by reason, so it is incapable of proof from reason.

One could probably say that there are no analogies to it in nature, not even in the spiritual nature of man, who is made in the Image of God.

In His Trinitarian mode of being, God is unique; and, as there is nothing in the Universe like Him in this respect, so there is nothing which can help us to comprehend Him in this fashion. So, the proof of the Trinity is solely in Scripture, as the proof must solely be in Scripture.

## PREPARATION IN THE OLD TESTAMENT

It is an old saying that what becomes patent in the New Testament was latent in the

Old Testament. Or as someone has said, the Old Testament is the New Testament concealed, while the New Testament is the Old Testament revealed.

It is important that the continuity of the Revelation of God contained in the two Testaments should not be overlooked or obscured. If we find some difficulty in perceiving for ourselves, in the Old Testament, definite points of attachment for the Revelation of the Trinity, we cannot help perceiving with great clearness in the New Testament abundant evidence that its writers felt no incongruity whatever between their Doctrine of the Trinity and the Old Testament conception of God.

The New Testament Writers certainly were not conscious of being *"setters forth of strange gods."* To their own apprehension they worshiped and proclaimed the God of Israel; and they laid no less stress than the Old Testament itself upon His Unity (Jn. 17:3; I Cor. 8:4; I Tim. 2:5).

They do not, then, place two new gods by the side of Jehovah, as alike with Him to be served and worshiped; they conceive Jehovah as Himself at once Father, Son, and Spirit. In presenting this One Jehovah as Father, Son, and Spirit, they as well do not betray any lurking feeling that they are making innovations. Without apparent misgiving they take over Old Testament Passages and apply them to the Father, Son, and Spirit indifferently.

Obviously they understand themselves, and wish to be understood, as setting forth in the Father, Son, and Spirit just the One God that the God of the Old Testament Revelation is; and they are as far as possible from recognizing any breach between themselves and the Fathers in presenting their enlarged conception of the Divine Being.

They may not amount to saying that they saw the Doctrine of the Trinity everywhere taught in the Old Testament. It certainly amounts to saying that they saw the Triune God Whom they worshiped in the God of the Old Testament Revelation, and felt no incongruity in speaking of their Triune God in the terms of the Old Testament Revelation.

The God of the Old Testament was their God, and their God was a Trinity, and their sense of the identity of the two was so complete that no question as to it was raised in their minds.

NOTES

SIMPLICITY AND ASSURANCE

The simplicity and assurance with which the New Testament Writers speak of God as a Trinity have, however, a further implication. If they betray no sense of novelty in so speaking of Him, this is undoubtedly in part because it was no longer a novelty so to speak of Him. It is clear, in other words, that, as we read the New Testament, we are not witnessing the birth of a new conception of God.

What we meet with in its pages is a firmly-established conception of God underlying and giving its tone to the whole fabric. It is not in a Text here and there that the New Testament bears its Testimony to the Doctrine of the Trinity. In fact, the whole Book is Trinitarian to the core; all its Teaching is built on the assumption of the Trinity; and its allusions to the Trinity are frequent, cursory, easy, and confident.

ALREADY MADE

It is with a view to the manner in which the Trinity inculcates the New Testament that *"the Doctrine of the Trinity is not so much heard as overheard in the statements of Scripture."* It would be more exact to say that it is not so much inculcated as presupposed.

The Doctrine of the Trinity does not appear in the New Testament in the making, but is already made. It takes its place in its pages, with an air almost of complaint, already *"in full completeness"* leaving no trace of its growth.

In fact, there is nothing more wonderful in the history of human thought than the silent and imperceptible way in which this Doctrine, to us so difficult, took its place without struggle — and without controversy — among accepted Christian Truths.

The New Testament is not a record of the development of the Doctrine or of its assimilation. It everywhere presupposes the Doctrine as the fixed possession of the Word of God.

JESUS CHRIST AND THE HOLY SPIRIT

The fundamental proof that God is a Trinity is supplied thus by the fundamental Revelation of the Trinity in fact: that is to say, in the Incarnation of God the Son and the outpouring of God the Holy Spirit.

In a word, Jesus Christ and the Holy Spirit are the fundamental proof of the Doctrine of the Trinity.

This is as much as to say that all the evidence of whatever kind, and whatever source derived, that Jesus Christ is God manifested in the flesh, and that the Holy Spirit is a Divine Person, is just so much evidence for the Doctrine of the Trinity; and that when we go to the New Testament for evidence of the Trinity we are to seek it, not merely in the scattered allusions to the Trinity as such, numerous and instructive as they are, but primarily in the whole mass of evidence which the New Testament provides of the Deity of Christ and the Divine Personality of the Holy Spirit. When we have said this, we have said in effect that the whole mass of the New Testament is evidence for the Trinity. For the New Testament is saturated with the evidence of the Deity of Christ and the Divine Personality of the Holy Spirit.

## THE UNITY OF THE GODHEAD

We may show that the New Testament everywhere insists on the Unity of the Godhead; that it constantly recognizes the Father as God, the Son as God, and the Spirit as God; and that it presents these Three to us as distinct Persons.

It is not necessary, however, to enlarge here on facts so obvious. We may content ourselves with simply observing that to the New Testament there is but One Only Living and True God; but that to it Jesus Christ and the Holy Spirit are Each God in the fullest sense of the term; and yet Father, Son, and Spirit stand over against Each Other as I, and Thou, and He. In this composite fact the New Testament gives us the Doctrine of the Trinity.

When we have said these three things, then — that there is but One God, that the Father and the Son and the Spirit are Each God, that the Father and the Son and the Spirit are Each a distinct Person — we have enunciated the Doctrine of the Trinity in its completeness.

## THE SCRIPTURE

The Three Persons already come into view as Divine Persons in the annunciation of the Birth of our Lord: *"The Holy Spirit shall come upon thee,"* said the Angel to Mary, *"and the Power of the Most High shall overshadow thee: wherefore also the Holy Thing which is to be born shall be called the Son of God"* (Lk. 1:35; Mat. 1:18).

Here the Holy Spirit is the active Agent in the production of an effect which is also ascribed to the Power of the Most High, and the Child thus brought into the world is given the great designation of *"Son of God."*

NOTES

The Three Persons are just as clearly brought before us in the account of Matthew 1:18, though the allusions to them are dispersed through a longer stretch of narrative, in the course of which the Deity of the Child is twice intimated (vs. 21): *"It is He that shall save His People from their sins."* Verse 23 says, *"They shall call His Name Immanuel; which is, being interpreted, God-with-us."*

In the Baptismal scene which finds record by all of the Evangelists at the opening of Jesus' Ministry (Mat. 3:16-17; Mk. 1:10-11; Lk. 3:21-22; Jn. 1:32-34), the Three Persons are thrown up to sight in a dramatic picture in which the Deity of Each is strongly emphasized. From the open Heavens the Spirit descends in visible form, and *"A Voice came out of the Heavens, Thou art My Son, the Beloved, in Whom I am well pleased."* Thus, care seems to have been taken to make the Advent of the Son of God into the world the Revelation also of the Triune God, that the minds of men might as smoothly as possible adjust themselves to the preconditions of the Divine Redemption which was in process of being wrought out.

## JESUS

With this as a starting-point, the Teaching of Jesus is Trinitarian throughout. He has much to say of God His Father, from Whom as His Son He is in some true sense distinct, and with Whom He is in some equally true sense One. And He has much to say of the Spirit, Who represents Him as He represents the Father, and by Whom He works as the Father works by Him.

It is not merely in the Gospel of John that such representations occur in the Teaching of Jesus.

In Matthew, Mark, and Luke, Jesus claims a Sonship to God which is unique (Mat. 11:27; 24:36; Mk. 13:32; Lk. 10:20); in the following Passages the title of *"Son of God"* is attributed to Him and accepted by Him: (Mat. 4:6; 8:29; 14:33; 27:40, 43, 54; Mk. 3:11; 12:6-8; 15:39; Lk. 4:41; 22:70; Jn. 1:34, 49; 9:35; 11:27), and which involves an absolute community between the Two in knowledge, say, and power. Both Matthew (11:27) and Luke (10:22) record His Great Declaration that He knows the Father and the

Father knows Him with perfect mutual knowledge: *"No one knoweth the Son, save the Father; neither doth any know the Father save the Son."*

In the Synoptics, too, Jesus speaks of employing the Spirit of God Himself for the performance of His Works, as if the activities of God were at His disposal: *"I by the Spirit of God"* — or as Luke has it, *"By the Finger of God"* — *"cast out demons"* (Mat. 12:28; Lk. 11:20; also the Promise of the Spirit in Mark 13:11; Luke 12:12).

## JOHN, THE GREATEST ADVOCATE OF ALL

In the discourses recorded in John, Jesus most copiously refers to the unity of Himself, as the Son, with the Father, and to the Mission of the Spirit from Himself as the Dispenser of the Divine Activities. Here He not only with great directness declares that He and the Father are One (One in unity) (Jn. 10:30; 17:11, 21-22, 25) also with a unity of interpenetration (*"The Father is in Me, and I in the Father"*) (Jn. 10:38; 16:10-11), so that to have seen Him was to have seen the Father (Jn. 14:9; 15:21).

As well, He removes all doubt as to the essential nature of His Oneness with the Father by explicitly asserting His Eternity (*"Before Abraham was born, I am,"* Jn. 8:58), also, His coeternity with God (*"Had with Thee before the world was* (Jn. 17:5)*"* (Jn. 6:62; 17:18).

## THE HOLY SPIRIT

Even though we have only scratched the surface regarding the examples which could be given respecting John, not to mention the Synoptics or the Writings of Paul and the other Apostles, the following is so strong respecting the Holy Spirit that it must be included.

This last feature is even more strongly emphasized in yet another Passage in which the Work of the Spirit in relation to the Son is presented as closely parallel with the Work of the Son in relation to the Father (Jn. 16:5).

*"But now I go unto Him that sent Me . . . nevertheless I tell you the Truth; it is expedient for you that I go away; for, if I go not away the Advocate will not come unto you: but if I go I will send Him unto you and He, after He is come, will convict the world . . . of Righteousness because I go to the Father and ye behold Me no more . . . I have yet many things to say unto you, but you cannot bear them now. Howbeit when He, the Spirit of Truth is come, He shall guide you into all the Truth; for He shall not speak from Himself; but what things soever He shall hear, He shall speak, and He shall declare unto you the things that are to come. He shall glorify Me: for He shall take of Mine and shall shew it unto you. All things whatsoever the Father hath are Mine: therefore said I that He taketh of Mine, and shall declare it unto you"* (Jn. Chpt. 16).

Here the Spirit is sent by the Son, and comes in order to complete and apply the Son's Work, receiving His Whole Commission from the Son — not, however, in derogation of the Father, because when we speak of the things of the Son, that is to speak of the things of the Father.

As we read we are kept in continual contact with the Three Persons Who act, each as a Distinct Person, and yet Who are in a deep, underlying sense, One.

There is but One God — there is never any question of that — and yet this Son Who has been sent into the world by God not only represents God but is God.

And this Spirit Whom the Son has in turn sent into the world is also Himself God. Nothing could be clearer, the Son and the Spirit are Distinct Persons.

## WORDS OF JESUS

The nearest approach to a formal announcement of the Doctrine of the Trinity which is recorded from our Lord's Lips or, perhaps we may say, which is to be found in the whole compass of the New Testament, has been preserved for us, not by John, but by one of the Synoptists. It too, however, is only incidentally introduced, and has for its main object something very different from formulating the Doctrine of the Trinity.

It is embodied in the Great Commission which the Resurrected Lord gave His Disciples to be their *"marching orders" "even unto the end of the world"*: *"Go ye therefore, and make Disciples of all Nations, Baptizing them in the Name of the Father, and of the Son and of the Holy Spirit"* (Mat. 28:19).

In seeking to estimate the significance of this great declaration, we must bear in mind the high solemnity of the utterance, by which we are required to give its full value to every word of it. Its phrasing is in any event, however, remarkable.

NOTES

NOTES

It does not say, *"In the Names* (plural) *of the Father and of the Son and of the Holy Spirit"*; nor yet (what might be taken to be equivalent to that), *"In the Name of the Father, and in the Name of the Son, and in the Name of the Holy Spirit,"* as if we had to deal with three separate Beings.

Nor, on the other hand, does it say, *"In the Name of the Father, Son and Holy Spirit,"* as if *"The Father, Son and Holy Spirit"* might be taken merely as three designations of a single person.

THE UNITY OF THE THREE

With stately impressiveness it asserts the unity of the Three by combining them all within the bounds of the single Name; and then throws up into emphasis the distinctness of Each by introducing them in turn with the repeated article: *"In the Name of the Father, and of the Son, and of the Holy Spirit."* These Three, the Father, and the Son, and the Holy Spirit, Each stand in some clear sense over against the others in Distinct Personality: these Three, the Father, and the Son, and the Holy Spirit, All unite in some profound sense in the common participation of the One Name.

THE NAME

Fully to comprehend the implication of this mode of statement, we must bear in mind, further, the significance of the term, *"The Name,"* and the associations laden with which it came to the recipients of this Commission. For the Hebrews did not think of the Name as we are accustomed to do, as a mere external symbol; but rather as the adequate expression of the innermost Being of its Bearer.

In His Name the Being of God finds expression; and the Name of God — *"This Glorious and Fearful Name, Jehovah thy God,"* (Deut. 28:58) — was accordingly a most sacred thing, being indeed virtually equivalent to God Himself.

It is not by accident, therefore, when we read (Isa. 30:27), *"Behold, the Name of Jehovah cometh"*; and the parallelisms are most instructive when we read (Isa. 59:19): *"So shall they fear the Name of Jehovah from the West, and His Glory from the rising of the Sun. When the enemy shall come in like a flood, the Spirit of the Lord shall lift up a Standard against him."*

So pregnant was the implication of the Name, that it was possible for the term to stand absolutely, without adjunction of the Name itself, as the sufficient representative of the majesty of Jehovah: it was a terrible thing to *"blaspheme the Name"* (Lev. 24:11).

Of course, we have only scratched the surface respecting the times that the Spirit of God in Authoring the Divine Text used the *"Name"* as the whole of all that God is. When, therefore, our Lord commanded His Disciples to Baptize those whom they brought to His obedience *"In the Name of . . . ,"* He was using language charged to them with high meaning. He could not have been understood otherwise than a substituting for the Name of Jehovah this other Name *"of the Father, and of the Son, and of the Holy Spirit"*; and this could not possibly have meant to His Disciples anything else than that Jehovah was now to be known to them by the New Name of the Father, and the Son, and the Holy Spirit.

THE NEW NAME

There is no alternative, therefore, to understanding Jesus here to be giving for His community a New Name to Jehovah, and that New Name to be the Threefold Name of *"The Father, and the Son, and the Holy Spirit."*

Nor is there room for doubt that by *"The Son"* in this Threefold Name, He meant just Himself with all the implications of Distinct Personality which this carries with it; and, of course, that further carries with it the equally Distinct Personality of *"The Father"* and *"The Holy Spirit,"* with Whom *"The Son"* is here associated, and from Whom alike *"The Son"* is here distinguished. This is a direct ascription to Jehovah, the God of Israel, of a Threefold Personality, and is therewith the direct enunciation of the Doctrine of the Trinity.

However, we are not witnessing here the birth of the Doctrine of the Trinity; that is presupposed. What we are witnessing is the authoritative announcement of the Trinity as the God of Christianity by its Founder, and one of the most solemn of His recorded Declarations.

Israel had worshiped the One Only True God under the Name of Jehovah; Christians are to worship the same One Only and True God under the Name of *"The Father, and the Son, and the Holy Spirit."* This is the distinguishing characteristic of Christians; and that is as much as to say that the Doctrine of the Trinity is, according to our Lord's Own apprehension of it, the distinctive mark of that which He founded, *"Christianity."*

THE REASON JESUS WORDED MATTHEW 28:19 AS HE DID . . .

To which we have already alluded, Jesus used the singular respecting the *"Name,"* and because there aren't three Gods, only One. The singular used here maintains the integrity of the Oneness of Jehovah.

However, He then referred to Three Distinct Personalities in using, *"Of the Father, and of the Son, and of the Holy Spirit."*

This proclaimed the Distinct Trinity of God, while at the same time preserving His Distinct Oneness.

Consequently, there is One God, but manifested in Three Persons, *"God the Father, God the Son, and God the Holy Spirit."*

(The Bibliography — F. C. Baur, G. Bull, *"A Defense of the Nicene Creed,"* Augustine, *"On the Holy Trinity,"* Calvin, *"Institutes of the Christian Religion,"* C. Hodge, *"Systematic Theology and Index,"* J. Pearson, *"An Exposition of the Creed,"* J. Owen, *"Vindication of the Doctrine of the Holy Trinity."*)

(7) "HOWBEIT THERE IS NOT IN EVERY MAN THAT KNOWLEDGE: FOR SOME WITH CONSCIENCE OF THE IDOL UNTO THIS HOUR EAT IT AS A THING OFFERED UNTO AN IDOL; AND THEIR CONSCIENCE BEING WEAK IS DEFILED."

The phrase, *"Howbeit there is not in every man that knowledge,"* refutes the claims of those whom Paul addressed in Verse 1. Many in the Church in Corinth were claiming superior knowledge, when in reality, they had very little true knowledge of the Lord and His Word.

Unfortunately this problem did not die with the Corinthians, being just as prevalent presently. Much of the present so-called Bible Knowledge, which deceives many Christians, is in fact, no Bible Knowledge at all. I speak of all the political happenings presently concerning Israel and a host of other things which could be named. While these things may or may not have relativity to Bible Prophecy, etc., still, they teach precious little about the Word of God. But yet, those who follow such, are deceived into thinking that this abundance of political information, or else mere speculation, is in fact True Bible Knowledge, which it is not.

NOTES

The Corinthians thought the same thing, as have untold millions of others down through the centuries. In fact, Paul combatted this thing constantly, hence him saying, *"For I determined not to know anything among you, save Jesus Christ, and Him Crucified"* (I Cor. 2:2).

PAUL

It is remarkable that Paul was greatly educated, both in the Old Testament and secular training as well, or so it seems. But yet, he never flaunted his education, and for the simple reason that it was of little consequence. In other words, it did not set captives free, but the Gospel of Jesus Christ does.

So, Paul is saying that some of the Believers at Corinth did not have the proper knowledge of the Word of God as they should have had; consequently, they held erroneous thoughts about some things.

The phrase, *"For some with conscience of the idol unto this hour eat it as a thing offered unto an idol,"* simply means that some could not dismiss from their minds the painful sense that, in eating the idol-sacrifice, they are participating in idol-worship.

The phrase, *"And their conscience being weak is defiled,"* refers to these Gentiles who until recently had been idolaters. To some of these, the eating of meat that had been offered to idols, was to them a semblance of apostasy.

The Truth was, that the thing which they were eating was, in its own essence, indifferent or clean, but since they could not help esteeming it unclean, they defied a conscientious doubt, and so their conduct not being of Faith, became sinful (Rom. 14:14, 23). Paul here admits that this weakness is the result of an imperfect enlightenment of Scripture; nevertheless, he proclaims, as we shall see, that their belief in this regard, although wrong, is entitled to forbearance and respect.

DEFILEMENT

*"Defiled"* in the Greek is *"molyno,"* and means *"to contaminate, or defile."* As water from a polluted well is unsafe, so the convictions of a polluted conscience are unsafe guidelines for Godly action. The cause of the pollution in this

Passage is one's acting against the dictates of conscience. Disregarding our sense of right and wrong corrupts us.

## ONLY THE PURE

Titus 1:15 also speaks of corrupted minds and consciences. Here the word translated *"defile"* is *"miaino,"* which also means *"stained"* or *"polluted."*

Here unbelievers' minds and consciences are the subject. Paul warns that only those who are pure can view life purely: *"To those who are corrupted and do not believe, nothing is pure."*

Without an experience of God's purifying, saving Work, mind and conscience will both be polluted. The product of the mind and conscience warped by inner sin must be impure.

## BITTERNESS

Hebrews 12:15 also uses the word *"miaino."* The Verse warns against bitterness, which *"grows up to cause trouble and defile many."* A bitter attitude has an impact on our relationship with other persons. Bitterness can pollute their lives as well as our own.

Keeping alert to recognize the Grace that God gives us to live Holy lives can free us from bitterness and keep our consciences clear (Heb. 12:14-15).

(For a more extended treatment of *"conscience"* please see our Commentary on Romans, Chapter 2.)

(8) "BUT MEAT COMMENDETH US NOT TO GOD: FOR NEITHER, IF WE EAT, ARE WE THE BETTER; NEITHER, IF WE EAT NOT, ARE WE THE WORSE."

The phrase, *"But meat commendeth us not to God,"* tells us several things:

1. First of all, eating meat or not eating meat has no spiritual content. Consequently, this destroys the vegetarian theory.

2. The Believer's *"standing"* before God is not affected by what he eats or does not eat, for meat does not commend the Believer to God.

3. If the Bible had been in the hands of the people during the Middle Ages, this Verse would have rendered impossible the idle superstition that to eat meat during Lent was one of the deadliest sins, or that there was any merit whatever in the Lenten Fast. This Verse says expressly, *"We lose nothing by not eating; we gain nothing by eating"* (Farrar).

NOTES

(Lent has to do with the Spring of the year, and is 40 weekdays from Ash Wednesday to Easter observed by Roman Catholics, when they are not supposed to eat certain types of meat, etc.)

The phrase, *"For neither, if we eat, are we the better; neither, if we eat not, are we the worse,"* completely shatters the old Levitical Law of Moses regarding dietary regulations.

In fact, all of these regulations had very little to do with anything which was truly spiritual, but rather was meant to serve as a symbol of physical purity, inasmuch as Israel was in effect to be the Womb of the Messiah. When He did come, all of this was fulfilled and set aside.

## FOOD

It appears that preflood civilization was vegetarian, but God allowed humanity to expand its diet after the Flood to include the flesh of animals (Gen. 9:3).

As we have stated, there are a number of religious regulations associated with food in the Old Testament era, but the Epistles of the New Testament make it clear that Christian Faith has nothing to do with what a person does or does not eat (Rom. 14:14; I Cor. 8:8). Instead, the Believer, recognizing God as the Source of all that he or she needs to maintain life, is released from anxiety and is free to put God's Kingdom first (Mat. 6:15-33).

(9) "BUT TAKE HEED LEST BY ANY MEANS THIS LIBERTY OF YOURS BECOME A STUMBLINGBLOCK TO THEM THAT ARE WEAK."

The Apostle admits the Truth of Christian Liberty, in fact is its greatest champion, but begs the Corinthians (and all others as well) to take heed lest this knowledge, if given too much liberty of action, should stumble others.

The Apostle could eat meat in an idol's temple because he knew that idols and idolatries in temples were all illusions, but he would not do so lest his indulgence of self should cause the moral destruction of his brother for whose Salvation Christ gave His Very Life.

Some of the Christians at Corinth tempted their Brethren to their condemnation instead of denying themselves in order to their Salvation.

So Love decided this question, and denied self, lest so far as it depended on the Believer himself, his action in eating might lead another to moral ruin. God would indeed guard His *"weak"* Child, but that would in no wise diminish the sin of him who led his brother to sin against his conscience (Williams).

We make men worse if by our example we teach them to act in contradiction of their conscience.

Evans said, *"Let your motto be forbearance, not privilege, and your watchword charity, not knowledge. Never flaunt your knowledge, seldom use your privilege."*

(10) "FOR IF ANY MAN SEE THEE WHICH HAST KNOWLEDGE SIT AT MEAT IN THE IDOL'S TEMPLE, SHALL NOT THE CONSCIENCE OF HIM WHICH IS WEAK BE EMBOLDENED TO EAT THOSE THINGS WHICH ARE OFFERED TO IDOLS;"

The phrase, *"For if any man see thee which hast knowledge sit at meat in the idol's temple,"* speaks of those who know and understand True Christian Liberty, but yet, lacked wisdom respecting the weakness of other Believers and Love respecting concern for their soul's Salvation.

### *"IDOLEUM"*

Even though my research does not discover the following, at least one Greek Scholar insinuates that Paul used the Jewish word *"idoleum"* for *"temple,"* in defining the heathen places of worship. If in fact he did use this word, it should have been a warning to them that even though Christian Liberty would allow such, still, discretion is always the better part of valor.

It was a word not used by Gentiles, but invented by Believers in the One God, to avoid the use of *"temple"* in connection with idols.

The Greeks spoke of the *"athenaeum,"* or *"apolloneum,"* or *"posideum"*; but Jews only of an *"idoleum"*— a word which (like other Jewish designations of heathen forms of worship) involved a bitter taunt. For the very word *"eidolon"* which referred to the idols in the temples, meant a shadowy, fleeting, unreal image (Farrar).

The phrase, *"Shall not the conscience of him which is weak be emboldened to eat those things which are offered to idols,"* contains the idea that such action on the part of the *"strong"* could very well fall out to the spiritual destruction of the one who is *"weak."* The idea is, that no Christian could be *"edified"* into a more dangerous course than that of defying and defiling his own tender conscience.

NOTES

What we are talking about here, which I trust we have amply portrayed, is far more than merely purchasing meat in the marketplace and eating it, which had once been used in offering up sacrifice to idol gods.

Some of these Corinthians had been so enmeshed in the sinful, wicked culture of idol worship before Conversion, that the enticement to be pulled back into this system could in fact be very strong, that is if the Believer was not careful. Whereas some Believers could be near such activity without it having any effect on them whatsoever, still, others were not that strong.

(11) "AND THROUGH THY KNOWLEDGE SHALL THE WEAK BROTHER PERISH, FOR WHOM CHRIST DIED?"

The beginning of the question, *"And through thy knowledge shall the weak brother perish, . . . ?"*, refers to a Believer losing out with God, ceasing to believe and thereby losing his soul.

*"Perish"* in the Greek is *"apollumi,"* and means *"to destroy, or be lost"* (Mat. 10:28; Mk. 8:35; Jn. 3:16; 6:12; 17:12; II Cor. 4:3). Farrar says, *"Paul could use no word which would more effectually point his warning."* Consequently, we are speaking here of something extremely serious.

Incidentally, this Verse, plus scores of others of similar nature completely refute the unscriptural Doctrine of Unconditional Eternal Security. This Doctrine teaches, as most know, that after a person is Saved, that irrespective of what they do, even though they may lose fellowship with God, they cannot lose their soul. As should be obvious, that is not what the Holy Spirit through Paul is here saying. In fact, He is saying the very opposite!

The conclusion of the question, *"For whom Christ died?"*, proclaims the tremendous worth of this soul.

The fact that he was *"weak"* constituted a fresh appeal to pity. It made him more emphatically one of *"Christ's little ones,"* and Christ had pronounced a heavy malediction on all who caused such to offend (Mat. 18:5-7).

*"Weak"* in the Greek is *"astheneo,"* and means *"to be feeble, strengthless."* It has to do with being weak in the Lord, as a result of being weak in the Word, which regrettably, characterizes many Believers presently as well.

The idea, as the Holy Spirit through Paul presents the case, is that these people, those weak in Christ, should be given every consideration respecting their spiritual condition. In other words, nothing must be done that will offend them, further weaken them, causing them to ultimately stumble and fall.

As well, the Truth is, that much of the time, these particular people do not really consider themselves to be *"weak,"* but rather the very opposite. In other words, they have the opinion that their particular scruples constitute Sanctification and Holiness. Consequently, those who are truly strong in the Lord, must not allow such an attitude to deter them from attempting to guard the direction of these people, whomever they may be.

## SPIRITUAL WEAKNESS

Spiritual weakness in any Believer can only be cured by a steady diet of the study of the Word of God, and Prayer. Both disciplines portray to the Believer what he really is, and then carries the power of making the Believer into what he should be. However, the study of the Word of God and Prayer, must be brought about in the heart and life of the Believer as it regards an habitual basis. In other words, it is not a matter of studying the Word and seeking the Face of the Lord only for a period of time, but rather it becomes a lifelong experience.

As one begins to study the Word, one will begin to develop more and more a hunger for the Word. As well, when one sets aside a certain amount of time each day for Prayer, one will find oneself eagerly looking forward to this particular time, and the resultant strength that comes from fellowship with the Lord. The sad fact is, most Believers little study the Word, and little pray, if at all.

## WHAT GOD CAN DO

Not only does growth in the Lord begin to occur, when these twin Graces are in fact, put into practice, but as well, the Believer is then brought into a position to where the Lord can do great things, actually touching every aspect of one's life.

There is nothing God cannot do. And when we get into the habit of taking everything to Him, seeking His Face diligently regarding every matter, whatever it may be, we find that our study of the Word builds Faith within our hearts, and then we truly begin to realize what the Lord can actually do. There is no problem He cannot handle. There is no difficulty which in fact, is difficult for Him. He can do all things. However, the knowledge of this, and even the practice of this, cannot come about, in fact is impossible to come about, unless we have a proper Prayer life and dedication to the study of the Word of God.

NOTES

## MISS OUT ON SO MUCH

Most Believers, and I exaggerate not, realize so little in their Christian experience as to Who and What the Lord actually is. In fact, much of the Gospel which presently abounds, is in fact, no Gospel at all. It mostly specializes only in what God can do for a person, instead of Who He is respecting His Person. Most Believers are taught how to get things from God, instead of really getting to know Him Personally. As stated, this can only come about by Prayer and study of the Word.

Most Believers miss out on all of this, simply because of not really getting to know Him. Consequently, they miss out on just about everything, not enjoying the so-called pleasures of the world, at the same time, even though a Believer, still not having the fullness of God. Yes, they are fully Saved, but that's not the idea. The idea is, that we get to know Him supremely in the realm of Fellowship and Communion. When this is done, it provides a fulfillment, development, purpose, fidelity, and peace, and as Peter said, *"joy unspeakable,"* which is the grandest thing that anyone could ever have. This is what one might say is *"real living"* (Jn. 10:10).

(12) "BUT WHEN YE SIN SO AGAINST THE BRETHREN, AND WOUND THEIR WEAK CONSCIENCE, YE SIN AGAINST CHRIST."

The phrase, *"But when ye sin so against the Brethren, and wound their weak conscience,"* here boldly proclaims that what the stronger Christian is actually doing, is sin, and sin in its worst force. Chrysostom said, *"What can be more ruthless than a man who strikes one who is sick?"* Is it not a cowardly exercise of liberty to strike the conscience of the defenseless? (Farrar).

*"Wound"* in the Greek is *"tupto,"* and means *"to strike or smite the heart."*

The phrase, *"Ye sin against Christ,"* in effect says, that Believers doing such to weak brothers, is at the same time striking Christ. It is impossible to strike those who are His, without at the same time striking Him. Consequently, that should sober us.

I think one could say without fear of contradiction, that this is one of the worst sins that anyone could ever commit, the doing of that which will hinder the spiritual progress of a fellow Believer in Christ. Such is unthinkable, and yet it goes on constantly.

## MODERN PENTECOSTAL DENOMINATIONS

The manner of treatment by the Leadership of some Pentecostal Denominations toward fellow Preachers who have had the misfortune of falling into sin, or whatever, is without a doubt, one of the most disgraceful, unscriptural, therefore, ungodly things that is being done today, and regrettably it is being done in the Name of Christ, which makes it all the more abominable. To be sure, some of these Brethren who have had the misfortune of failure, are not necessarily in that place because of spiritual weakness, even as David of old, but rather for other reasons, in some cases known only to God. Do not misunderstand, any wrongdoing on the part of any person is always the fault of that person. But at the same time, only the acutely self-righteous would feel morally qualified to point a finger.

These Preachers, whomever they may be, and who number into the untold thousands, are treated as second-class Christians, if allowed to maintain any type of spiritual status at all. Every effort by these self-righteous, self-appointed Leaders, is meant to dehumanize, demean, embarrass, and to further degrade the individual. In other words, this action is as un-Christlike as is possible to be.

## WHY?

The answer is very complex, but the real reason could probably be narrowed down to that which is twofold.

## GOVERNMENT?

First of all, most Pentecostal Denominations have an unscriptural form of Church Government, in fact, grossly unscriptural, which leavens everything else as well. That means, they are not following the Word of God in their Church Government, neither in their discipline. Whatever they do in this capacity, is man devised, with no Scriptural foundation, and to be frank, there's not even any attempt to follow the Word of God. In other words, the Bible regarding these matters, is not only not consulted, it is in fact, not even desired.

NOTES

## SELF-RIGHTEOUSNESS

The second reason pertains to self-righteousness, which of course is man-devised righteousness, which God will not accept. Consequently, self-righteousness cannot even remotely conceive of someone being unrighteous one moment, and due to Faith and Trust in Christ, being totally righteous the next moment. Such thinking is foreign to them.

To the self-righteous mind, one must *"pay"* for what one has done, with the self-righteous setting the price. That Jesus has already paid the price, is of no consequence to these people. While they pay lip service to such theology, it is lip service only, with their actions being diametrically opposed.

In fact, even though they would vigorously deny such, the Leadership of most Pentecostal Denominations actually practices *"penance,"* the same as Catholics. It is not called that, and as stated, they would deny such, but there is no other way it can be labeled.

If repentance before God is not enough, and to be frank it is not enough for these people, then we have to add something to repentance, which in effect is adding something to the Grace of God. Consequently, whatever *"penance"* they demand, whether it is two years without preaching, or six months without preaching, or whatever other type of foolishness they can think of, such in effect says, that what Christ did at Calvary is not enough, and something needs to be added to His *"Finished Work."* In other words, they make a mockery of the Grace of God.

What these people do is in fact a gross sin, even as Paul here states. However, most Christians do not think so, simply because most Christians think in a carnal way. And to the carnal mind, such *"punishment"* seems to be the thing to do, and in fact, to the world, it is the thing to do. However, what we are seeing here are the ways of the world brought over into the Church.

So, we have a departure from the Word of God, and acute self-righteousness. In fact, this is exactly what crucified Christ.

(13) "WHEREFORE, IF MEAT MAKE MY BROTHER TO OFFEND, I WILL EAT NO FLESH WHILE THE WORLD STANDETH, LEST I MAKE MY BROTHER TO OFFEND."

The phrase, *"Wherefore, if meat make my brother to offend,"* refers to doing something which would be a stumblingblock to a weaker Christian.

*"Offend"* in the Greek is *"skandalizo,"* which means *"to cast a snare before one so as to destroy him."*

The phrase, *"I will eat no flesh while the world standeth, lest I make my brother to offend,"* does not mean that Paul was a vegetarian relative to this situation, but that any time he was in the presence of weaker Christians who might stumble over his actions, that he at that time would refrain from such, whatever it might be.

THE LESSON LEARNED

If we pass over this lightly thinking that it applied only to eating meat offered to idols, consequently concluding that such does not pertain to us presently, because such presently does not exist, we are missing the point entirely.

First of all, the Holy Spirit through the Apostle is not addressing that which is obviously immoral or wrong, but rather things which within themselves are not sin or wrongdoing of any nature, but yet can cause people to stumble.

FOR EXAMPLE . . .

As a strong Christian, that is if the Lord would label me as such, there are some things I could do which within themselves are not wrong, but, nevertheless, which the doing of could cause spiritual difficulties for weaker Christians.

For instance, I am sure there are some movies in theaters which are clean and, therefore, would not be wrong to view. Nevertheless, I do not go to any movies shown in theaters (and watch very few over Television) for the simple reason that weaker Christians may observe such, and not having the strength or the wisdom to properly select and approve, could be hooked into going to see all types, which I think anyone would have to admit, is not the thing for Believers to do, especially considering the low, low level morally speaking, to which the movie industry has sunk.

NOTES

Another example might be proper:

I have never taken a drink of any type of alcoholic beverage in my life, and have no plans to do so. Nevertheless, from what little I know about alcohol and from what I know about the Word of God, I am sure that some people could drink a glass of wine each day without causing any spiritual problems, or problems to themselves or others. Nevertheless, by the Grace of God I will never do such, for the simple reason of the terrible destruction wrought by alcohol in the lives of untold millions, etc.

The Truth is, that this admonition given by the Holy Spirit through Paul is all but totally ignored in the modern climate in which we live. There are some few Christians who look at these things as I have mentioned, but not many. To be sure, the results are not good, with the greatest spiritual declension presently captivating the Church as it has never known before.

LOVE, NOT KNOWLEDGE, MUST BE THE GUIDE!

Even though I may know and understand my Christian experience according to the Word of God even as I should, thereby understanding the liberty given me in Christ. But still, the knowledge that I possess is not to be my guide respecting these matters, but rather Love.

By that I refer to fellow Believers, especially new Converts, who do not have the knowledge that I or others may have in the Word of God, and that before these people I must not flaunt my knowledge of Christian Liberty, but rather my Love for them and concern regarding their walk with the Lord. To Love one, is to never do anything which would hurt or hinder that person's progress in the Lord.

God knows that all of us have failed in this capacity far too much in one way or the other, but the Lord helps us that we learn from our failures, so that at least such will not be a total loss.

Even as Paul said, we must never forget that in the Lord this is *"my brother"* or *"my sister."* As such, I am to treat them accordingly.

BROTHER

The word *"brother"* dots both Testaments. It is prominent in the Bible, alerting us to the fact that the relationship of *"brother"* is very significant for any who venture out to live the life of Faith.

Consequently, considering as to how Paul has used this word, and how important it really is in reference to the Family of God, I think a little deeper study would be appropriate.

THE OLD TESTAMENT CONCEPT OF BROTHER

The Hebrew word for brother is *"ah."* It appears 630 times in the Old Testament, where it may be translated *"brother," "relative," "fellow countryman,"* or *"friend."*

Usually *"ah"* designates full brothers or half-brothers. The Old Testament family relationship was particularly strong, despite normal stress within families, as is portrayed in the Genesis stories of Jacob and Joseph.

The word *"ah"* is also sometimes used to designate all the people of Israel. The Israelites were brothers in the extended sense because they shared a common descent from the Patriarchs. They were also brothers in the sense of being fellow citizens, members of a distinct national community that was in fact a family. In this sense brother (*"ah"*) is often used in contrast to *"foreigner."*

DEEP FRIENDSHIP

A third major use of the term is illustrated in the relationship of deep friendship between David and Jonathan (II Sam. 1:26).

The word *"ah"* is also sometimes used in a polite or a political way. Thus, a stranger might be greeted as *"brother"* (Gen. 29:4). Archaeological finds suggest that in surrounding cultures *"brother"* was used to address persons of rank or occupation.

Finally, Nations linked by treaty or common heritage were thought of as brother Nations. The term was sometimes used by one ruler in addressing another (Num. 20:14; I Ki. 9:13).

The concept of brother in the Old Testament does more than acknowledge relationship. It also suggests a set of mutual responsibilities that were appropriate because of the special relationship. This is particularly seen in responsibilities of the people of Israel to one another.

BROTHERLY RESPONSIBILITIES

Every Israelite was bound to live by the Ten Commandments and thus to act lovingly to all mankind (Rom. 13:8-10). Yet within the community of Israel the brother relationship led God's people to treat fellow-countrymen with special concern, going beyond the duty owed to all persons.

That special concern did not make it right for the people to do injustice to foreigners. Aliens who had settled in Israel were to be treated with scrupulous fairness. Disputes were to be judged fairly, the people were told, *"Whether the case is between brother Israelites or between one of them and an alien. Do not show partiality in judging; hear both small and great alike"* (Deut. 1:16-17).

BEYOND FAIRNESS

But there was in the fact of brotherhood a call to go beyond fairness. For instance, every seven years the people of Israel were to cancel debts owed to one another: *"You may require payment from a foreigner, but you must cancel any debt your brother owes you"* (Deut. 15:1-3). Even when the time of canceling debts was near, God's people were told, *"Do not be hardhearted or tightfisted toward your poor brother. Rather be openhanded and freely lend him whatever he needs"* (Deut. 15:7-8). Grace, not fairness, is brotherhood's demand.

Similarly, if a brother Hebrew was sold into servitude, he or she was to be released in the seventh year and supplied liberally from the resources of the master (Deut. 15:12-15).

NO FINANCIAL INTEREST ON MONEY LOANED TO A BROTHER

Again, an Israelite might lend a foreigner money or food and expect repayment with interest. But the people were warned, *"Do not charge your brother interest, whether on money or food or anything else that may earn interest"* (Deut. 23:19-20). Even that which a poor person might give in pledge of a repayment was not to be kept if it would deprive the borrower of something he or she needed (Deut. 24:10-13).

There are other details of life that show that a special concern was to be exhibited in the national family. Tragically, history records no generation of Israelites that lived the life of Love that the Law of Moses describes. There were individuals who exemplified the ideal, but as a community, Israel never really caught the

NOTES

vision of the brotherhood that is possible for the people of God. Regrettably, it is pretty much the same in the modern Church.

## AS THE WORD *"BROTHER"* IS USED IN THE NEW TESTAMENT

In the Gospels and in Acts we find echoes of the Old Testament. The Greek word *"adelphos"* may mean *"brother," "neighbor,"* or *"kinsman"* and is used in these familiar ways.

(A different word, *"hetairos,"* used only by Matthew (11:16; 20:13; 22:12; 26:50), expresses the idea of *"friend"* or *"companion."*)

Near the end of his life Paul spoke to hostile crowds in Jerusalem and addressed them as *"brothers and fathers"* (Acts 22:1). They were brothers, *"Those of* (his) *own people, the people of Israel"* (Rom. 9:3).

## JESUS

Yet Jesus introduced the pivotal shift of meaning that shapes the concept as it developed within the Church. *"Who are My mother and brothers?",* Jesus asked.

*"My mother and brothers are those who hear God's Word and put it into practice"* (Lk. 8:21; Mat. 12:46-50; Mk. 3:32-34). Within the Nation a sharp distinction was being drawn. It was not one's race or nationality or country but one's response to God that was the criterion of relationship.

Jesus made the stunning announcement to the Pharisees that failure to believe in Him (and thus, in God Who sent Him) indicates that these religious men belonged to their *"father, the Devil* (Jn. 8:44)*"* (Jn. 8:31-47). By contrast, those who believe in Jesus are able to call God their Father. The image of family and the name *"brother"* were already becoming in Jesus' Ministry what the Epistles revealed them to be, i.e., indicative of intimate relationship, applied within the fellowship to those who belonged to God.

In most cases where we read *"brother"* or *"brothers"* in the Epistles, the meaning is simply *"fellow Christian(s)."*

The choice of the word *"brother,"* carrying with it the image of the family, is important theologically and practically. Within the family of brothers and sisters an exciting pattern of shared life emerges to define the way we Christians are to live with one another.

NOTES

## BROTHERLY RESPONSIBILITIES

The Writer of Hebrews admonishes: *"Keep on loving each other as brothers"* (Heb. 13:1). Peter states it in a fuller way: *"Now that you have . . . sincere Love for your brothers, Love one another deeply, from the heart"* (I Pet. 1:22).

The dynamic for this relationship is best explained by John. God's Own Love infuses the True Believer, expressing itself in deep caring for others in the Christian family. Thus, one who does not Love his brothers is still stumbling in the dark (I Jn. 2:9-11).

## LOVE

How do we Love our brothers? This is shown throughout the New Testament in nearly every Epistle and Gospel. Brotherly Love is expressed in confrontation and forgiveness (Mat. 18:15-35; Lk. 17:3), as well as by exclusion for disorderly conduct (II Thess. 3:6, 15). Brotherly Love is expressed by acceptance, by refraining from judging (Rom. 14:10-13), and by considering others while exercising one's own freedom (I Cor. 8:9-13).

No brother should be spoken against (James 4:11), wronged (I Thess. 4:6), or sued in a secular Court of Law (I Cor. 6:5). Rather, the needs of others in God's Family should be generously supplied when we are able to help (James 2:15-16; I Jn. 3:17).

Many Passages describe the way Christians are to live together in this new community that is also God's Family. All the Grace and Love urged in the Old Testament can now be known by Christians, in fellowships that are recognizable by their Love (Jn. 13:34-35).

## OTHER USES OF THE WORD *"BROTHER"*

A few New Testament Passages that use the word *"brother"* have raised questions. Let us consider some of them.

## THE BROTHERS OF JESUS

The Gospel of Matthew (13:55-56) makes reference to Jesus' brothers *"James, Joseph, Simon and Judas* (Jude)*"* and all *"His sisters."* Since these individuals are seen in company with Jesus' mother, Mary, it is obvious that they are the children of Mary and Joseph.

The Catholics argue that these *"brothers"* are half-brothers, children of Joseph before he married Mary, or that they are cousins. In Truth, putting all the material together concerning this subject, the language makes such impossible for it to be. There is no clear use of the Greek word *"adelphos"* in the New Testament in this sense of *"kinsman,"* as the Catholics claim. And there is no theological reason to suppose that Mary and Joseph should not have had children together after Jesus' Birth. The following proves such:

MARY

It is plainly stated in the Word of God that Jesus had four brothers and several sisters. One might refer to them as half-brothers and half-sisters. They were not cousins, as claimed by some (Mat. 13:55-56; Mk. 6:3).

THE FIRSTBORN

Jesus is called the *"Firstborn"* of Mary (Mat. 1:25; Lk. 2:7). This, within itself, tells us that she had other children. The Greek word for *"firstborn"* is *"prototokos."* It is used in Romans 8:29; Colossians 1:15-18; Hebrews 1:6, 11:28, and 12:23; and, Revelation 1:5. It, in essence, means *"the first of others."* If Mary did not have other children, the Greek word *"monogenes"* would have been used, which refers to an *"only son"* or *"only daughter"* (Lk. 7:12; 8:42; 9:38).

This word *"monogenes"* is used, in fact, of our Lord as *"The Only Begotten of the Father"* (Jn. 1:14, 18; 3:16, 18; I Jn. 4:9).

A PREDICTION

David prophesied of Christ, saying, *"I am become a Stranger unto My brethren and an Alien unto My mother's children"* (Ps. 69:8-9). This statement tells us that Mary had other children besides Christ.

HIS FAMILY

*"His mother and His brethren"* are mentioned as following Him to Capernaum (Mat. 12:46-50; Mk. 3:31-35; Lk. 8:19-21; Jn. 2:12).

UNBELIEF

*"His Brethren"* are said to not have believed on Christ until after the Resurrection (Jn. 7:3-10; Acts 1:14).

THE LORD'S BROTHER

James is called *"the Lord's Brother"* (Gal. 1:19).

NOTES

PAGAN CORRUPTION

The denial that Mary had other children, i.e., that she was a perpetual Virgin all of her life, would never have come up were it not for the Catholic Church insisting on this in order to raise Mary to the position of Co-redemptress with our Lord. All of this came from the Babylonian mysteries, as it pertained to the goddess of Paganism, who was supposed to be the mother of a Divine son and yet also a virgin.

In fact, Pope John Paul II has attempted to raise Mary to the level of Jesus, actually making her the co-Redemptress. In effect, the Catholics teach at present that one cannot be Saved, unless they go through Mary.

Even though the suggestion (co-Redemptress) was shelved, still, this demonic doctrine resides in the heart of this particular Pope, as well as untold millions of others.

Consequently, how can some Protestant Preachers claim that this Pope is a *"Godly man,"* as some have done, and how can they, even some who claim to be Spirit-filled, claim that Catholics are Saved?!

MARY

All types of objections are put up by the Catholic Church regarding Mary having other children, claiming that the brothers of Christ were rather cousins, the children of Mary and Cleophas. They even claim that Joseph might have had children by a former marriage.

But if Joseph had had children by a previous marriage, then Jesus could not be the legal heir to David's Throne, which by Law went to the firstborn.

Mary's lineage back to David was impeccable. While Joseph went back to David through Solomon, Mary's lineage went back to David through Nathan, another son of David; therefore, had the elders of Israel taken the time to have done so, they could have checked all of this in the Temple where all genealogies where kept. Actually, had the Davidic dynasty continued, Joseph would now be the king of Israel. So, Jesus being the *"firstborn"* of this family, means that His Kingship is established for the time when he will actually take the Throne.

REBELLION

Another use of *"brother"* is found in Prophetic Passages that announce a time when brother will battle brother, in one situation resulting from the divisive impact of the Message of Jesus (Isa. 9:19; Jer. 9:4; Ezek. 38:21; Mat. 10:21).

An historical example is the Old Testament incident in which the Levites, after one particularly evil lapse into rebellion by some of the Israelites, acted to destroy the rebels at God's Command (Ex. 32:19-29). Their loyalty to God surpassed even loyalty to family members, as all human relationships pale beside our responsibility to God.

How wonderful it is that an act of commitment to God gives you and me many brothers and sisters — an uncountable number — to Love and be Loved by them (Mat. 19:29).

(Inasmuch as we are now living in the time of the apostasy, the problems and difficulties of Christian brothers opposing other Christian brothers, and all because of the Message of The Lord Jesus Christ, is going to become more and more acute, in fact is prevalent presently. This situation will not grow better but rather worse. The Church is entering into the great *"falling away,"* and as such, the line has been drawn by the Holy Spirit, which will, and in fact does, separate the true from the false. In other words, all who call themselves *"brothers,"* actually aren't true brothers in the Lord. Nevertheless, the Lord knows those who are His.)

(Most of the material on *"brothers"* was supplied by Lawrence O. Richards.)

*"In Christ there is no East or West,*
*in Him no South or North;*
*"But one great fellowship of Love,*
*to show His Glories forth."*

*"In Him do true hearts everywhere this*
*sweet communion find;*
*"His service we do gladly share in Love*
*to all mankind."*

*"Join hands then, children of the Faith,*
*what-e'er your race may be:*
*"Each one who loves our Blessed Lord*
*shares in His Victory."*

*"In Christ now meet both East and West,*
*in Him meet South and North;*
*"All Blood-bought souls are in Him blest*
*thro' them His Love flows forth."*

*"This blessed bond begun on Earth,*
*will be more real in Heav'n,*
*"When we shall learn the glorious worth*
*of Him Whose Life was giv'n."*

NOTES

## CHAPTER 9

(1) "AM I NOT AN APOSTLE? AM I NOT FREE? HAVE I NOT SEEN JESUS CHRIST OUR LORD? ARE NOT YE MY WORK IN THE LORD?"

The question, *"Am I not an Apostle?"*, demands as the other three questions in this Verse, an affirmative answer.

While Paul does defend his Apostleship in this Chapter at least to a small degree, his main purpose is to show how he had abnegated his own rights, in order to be a proper example to others.

Being free and an Apostle, he could, if he had chosen, have claimed, as others had done, a right to be supported by the Churches to which he preached. He had thought it more for their good to waive this claim and, therefore, he had done so at the cost (as appears in many Passages: Acts 20:34; I Cor. 4:12; I Thess. 2:9) of bitter hardship to himself (Farrar).

And yet, even though this is his main thrust, still, he was having to continually defend his Apostleship. In other words, many in the Early Church, especially those of the Jewish persuasion claimed that he really was not an Apostle.

### PAUL THE APOSTLE

The reason for this hostility is much and varied. First of all, the Apostle claimed that the Lord had given him the New Covenant and as such, that it replaced the Old. Even though Jesus had plainly stated that He would do this (Mat. 9:16), still, it did not set well with many Jewish Believers. Irrespective that they were followers of Christ, and had accepted Him as Lord and Saviour, they continued to insist that all Believers, both Jews and Gentiles, must keep the Law of Moses as well as accepting Christ, in order to be Saved (Acts 15:1).

While this matter was supposedly settled at Jerusalem (Acts Chpt. 15), the decision handed down by James, although freeing the Gentiles from this yoke, did not do so with Jewish Believers. Consequently, the contention remained.

As Paul was so vocal in his denunciation of this direction, he naturally became their target.

So, one would have to conclude that the reason for this animosity and denial of his Apostleship, was because of jealousy; it didn't come through their committees, Jerusalem did not originate the idea, and Paul didn't ask their permission about anything (Gal. 1:1, 11-12).

## WHAT IS AN APOSTLE?

Concerning the great Plan of God for all time, including both Israel and the Church, Paul wrote, *"And are built upon the foundation of the Apostles and Prophets, Jesus Christ Himself being the Chief Cornerstone"* (Eph. 2:20).

Before Jesus came, this means that God used Prophets through whom His Word was given to the world.

The first one in the Bible spoken of as a Prophet is *"Enoch, the seventh from Adam"* (Jude vs. 14). Actually, he was not called a *"Prophet,"* but it did say that He *"prophesied"* concerning the Coming of the Lord. Abraham was the first one referred to directly as a *"Prophet"* (Gen. 20:7).

In Judges 6:8 it says, *"That the Lord sent a Prophet unto the children of Israel,"* but did not give his name. However, this was the first one spoken of in this fashion, being about 1200 years before Christ. Actually, it seems that Samuel was the first one to stand in the Office of the Prophet, to be followed by a long line of such Divinely-called men (I Sam. 3:20).

So, under the Old Economy of God, it was the Prophets who were given the Message which was to lead Israel, and in effect, who served as the spiritual guides of the people.

With the establishment of the Church on the Day of Pentecost, even though the Office or Calling of the Prophet remained in the Church, the Leadership of the Church passed to the Office of Apostles. To be sure, this was not leadership according to some elected office, but was rather the Government of God prescribing the manner in which the Church is to be led.

The Office or Calling of an Apostle refers to his Message. That which the Holy Spirit wants done, will always first of all be given through the Ministry of the Apostle. I speak of emphasis, direction, priority, etc. Of course, everything given by the Holy Spirit and faithfully delivered by Apostles, will always be directly according to the Word of God. It will never even in the slightest way violate the Word.

NOTES

As well, the Message given by the Holy Spirit to Apostles, as should be obvious, will affect the entirety of the Church all over the world, even though the particular Apostle so used may not even be known to most of the world. In fact, almost all of those who are truly Apostles, meaning they were called as such by the Holy Spirit, are not known as such to most of the Church. However, it should be obvious to the Church, regarding the thrust of certain ones, the obvious leadership, and above all, the Moving and Operation of the Holy Spirit regarding such Ministries.

If we are to use Paul as an example, and I surely think the Holy Spirit would desire that, we learn several things:

## THE MINISTRY OF THE APOSTLE

1. First of all, the New Covenant was given to an Apostle, i.e., *"the Apostle Paul."* It was not given to the Church at Jerusalem, or particular committees, or a hierarchy, which at that time actually did not exist in the Church. As well, we learn that even though there were quite a number of other Apostles, even the Apostles of our Lord, still, this great Message was given to just one man, the Apostle Paul.

Concerning the New Covenant, the Holy Spirit has not given anything else to add to this Covenant, and, in fact, will not give anything else to add to this Covenant. Being complete, such is not necessary. However, concerning its thrust and direction, the Holy Spirit is continuing to give Leading, Guidance, and Direction to Apostles, even unto this very hour.

2. We learn from the Book of Acts and the Epistles, that the thrust of the Gospel ever beyond its present borders, in other words World Evangelism, was priority with the Apostles. That is so obvious in the Book of Acts that it is irrefutable. So, the Holy Spirit is conveying the Message, that whatever direction is given to modern Apostles, it will not deviate from the Gospel of Jesus Christ being taken to the furthest corner of the globe. If World Evangelism ceases to be priority, or is given a secondary position, one can be certain that what is being done is not from a true Apostle of the Lord.

3. The Salvation of souls will always be paramount in these efforts. That is centerpiece in the Book of Acts and the Epistles. While it is certainly understood, that some Ministries may lean more heavily in other directions at times, and be proper in doing so; still, the Salvation of souls must always hold a prominent place in the effort of the Cause of Christ.

4. As well, the great Message of the Baptism with the Holy Spirit will hold a prominent place in the Ministry of Apostles. In fact, when the Holy Spirit began to fall at the turn of the century, in fulfillment of Joel's Prophecy concerning the Latter Rain (Joel Chpt. 2), the Lord called Apostles to herald and proclaim this Message. Even though emphasis was placed in this direction, as we have already stated, still, the Salvation of souls was not relegated to a side issue, but if anything, saw more people Saved. In other words, when the Holy Spirit has His proper Way in our efforts for the Cause of Christ, irrespective as to the necessary present emphasis, souls being Saved will always be priority, with many coming to Christ.

We see in the Book of Acts how that Believers being Baptized with the Holy Spirit was given much emphasis, and the True Apostle will follow accordingly.

5. Once again, with the Book of Acts being our Pattern, as the Holy Spirit definitely intended that it should be, we see that there were Deliverances, Healings, and Miracles which accompanied the Ministry of Apostles.

Given this Pattern in the Word of God, we are not to deviate at all from this laid down by the Holy Spirit, but are to follow accordingly. The True Apostle will have all of these earmarks, and if these earmarks are not present in one way or the other, what is happening is not truly the Ministry of an Apostle.

The thrust of the Church will always be guided by Apostles. God gives them the Message and they are compelled to preach the Message, whatever it may be. As stated, it will be quickly obvious as to whether the Message is genuine or not, according to the *"Fruit"* of the Message. As well, even as the True Apostle begins to deliver the Message, at the outset it may not even be obvious to him that the Lord is giving direction to the Church pertaining to a particular emphasis; nevertheless, it will become obvious very soon.

NOTES

## THE APOSTLE AND MODERN RELIGIOUS DENOMINATIONS

To be sure, Apostles have been resisted even from the beginning, even as Paul delineates in this 9th Chapter of I Corinthians. It should be obvious that Satan would do all within his power to hinder the True Government of God. Consequently, he does his best work not from outside the Church, but rather from inside the Church.

Not satisfied with God's Ways of Government, i.e., through the Apostles, he attempts to set up a pseudo-government, in which he has been very successful down through the nearly 2,000 years of history regarding the Church. Without going into detail, I speak of religious offices in the Church which are man-originated, man-devised, and man-instituted.

In fact, these offices, whatever they may be called, need not be unscriptural. They can come under the auspices of *"governments"* (I Cor. 12:28). However, these *"governments"* are to be administrative only, and are to never violate the Office of the Apostle.

The ideal is, that these administrative *"governments"* in the Church, should ascertain the manner in which the Spirit of God is moving, and to which He has given through His Apostles, and then seek with all their strength to carry out that which the Lord is doing. As stated, that is the ideal, but seldom the reality.

It is very difficult for men to occupy these administrative positions, and not seek to take upon themselves greater authority than their position is described Scripturally. Consequently, most Religious Denominations, are not guided the Biblical Way, which is the Holy Spirit functioning through called Apostles, but rather by committees and boards, etc. It is sad, most Religious Denominations, at least those who in their infancy were used greatly by God, were in fact, begun by the Holy Spirit through Apostles. To be frank, I think it would be impossible for these Organizations to have begun any other way, at least those which were once truly of God.

The sad reality is, that the Holy Spirit begins His thrust, which touches the world, and then gradually it is taken over by man, with the Ways of God gradually pushed aside, until ultimately it is totally man-controlled. The

Holy Spirit then starts all over again with more Apostles.

FREE!

The question, *"Am I not free?"*, presents that which is very interesting.

What did Paul mean by this question?

First of all he meant that he was a *"freeman,"* i.e., *"freedman,"* and made that way by the Lord. Of course, this refers to his Salvation made possible by the Precious Shed Blood of Jesus Christ, and his Faith in that Atonement. As such, he was set free from sin, the powers of darkness, and Satan's hold in every respect.

As well, it referred to Paul's freedom respecting his conduct, even as we are discussing. As being free in Christ, he has liberty; however, as he is plainly saying, he did not use that liberty in every case, even as he will further discuss.

Also, his freedom as an Apostle was never to be abrogated by outside forces of any nature. I speak of Roman power, or even that in the Church. In fact, both exerted great pressure, Rome with physical violence, and the Church with spiritual violence. Nevertheless, the Apostle never yielded at all, for to have done so, would have meant an abrogation of his Calling, which must never be violated.

A MINISTER OF THE GOSPEL

As a Preacher of the Gospel, and to be personal, one called for a special purpose, even though I greatly respect my Brethren and will submit to them in all cases, even as the Scripture demands, but never if it is a violation of the Word of God. In fact, True Scriptural submission is always horizontal instead of vertical. In other words, I am to submit to my Brethren in the Lord, and they are to submit to me, which is the case with all Believers (Eph. 5:21).

The question, *"Have I not seen Jesus Christ our Lord?"*, doubtless refers to the vision on the Road to Damascus (Acts 9:3, 17; 22:7-8), though he received other visions and revelations also (Acts 18:9; II Cor. 12:1). There is no record that he personally saw Christ during the Life of Jesus on Earth.

These words are possibly added to remind them that those who boasted of personal knowledge and relation with Jesus — perhaps the Christ party — had no exclusive prerogative (Farrar).

NOTES

This does not mean, even as some teach, that a person cannot have the Calling of an Apostle unless they have personally seen the Lord Jesus. We are plainly told by the Holy Spirit, that the governmental order of the Church is, *"Apostles, Prophets, Evangelists, Pastors and Teachers"* (Eph. 4:11). To be sure, these Designations and Callings continue unto this hour. In fact, a number who were referred to as Apostles in the Epistles, such as *"Andronicus"* (Rom. 16:7), *"Junia"* (Rom. 16:7), *"Apollos"* (I Cor. 4:6-9), *"Timothy"* (I Thess. 1:1; 2:6), *"Epaphroditus"* (Phil. 2:25), of these men, there is no record that they ever personally saw Jesus Christ, whether in His Earthly Ministry or even in a vision, etc. So, seeing Jesus is not a requirement to be an Apostle.

WHY DID PAUL MENTION THIS?

Of course, all the reasons we do not know; however, I think his primary reason for mentioning his vision of Jesus, was due to the fact that some, no doubt, were claiming that He was not an Apostle because He had not been a personal Disciple of Christ during His Earthly Ministry. It probably was very difficult for some to accept the fact that the Lord had given Paul the New Covenant, and not one of the Original Twelve; however, there is no record that any of the Twelve (Matthias having taken the place of Judas), ever contested Paul's claims in any way, but rather upheld him and respected him highly.

The question, *"Are not ye my work in the Lord?"*, tells us two things:

1. These very Corinthians were the Fruit of his Apostleship, which means, at least in this case, that if Paul truly was not an Apostle, and he was rather lying about his Calling, that the Holy Spirit would never have Anointed him to preach, which resulted in their Salvation. In fact, were he an impostor, he would have never come to Corinth to start with. Impostors and liars do not suffer for the Cause of Christ as Paul suffered. That is the proof of his Apostleship.

2. As well, the True Apostle will have souls Saved, irrespective as to the location of his Ministry.

(2) "IF I BE NOT AN APOSTLE UNTO OTHERS, YET DOUBTLESS I AM TO YOU: FOR THE SEAL OF MINE APOSTLESHIP ARE YE IN THE LORD."

The phrase, *"If I be not an Apostle unto others,"* concerns that of which we have stated, that some, if not many in the Early Church did not regard Paul's Apostleship. This at the first would have been exclusively among the Jews, and mostly from Jerusalem. However, some of these Jews from the Jerusalem Church, even as Paul will address in his second letter to the Corinthians, attempted constantly to prejudice the Gentile Converts against Paul, even those who were his own Converts. In fact, they had been quite successful among many of the Converts at Corinth, so much in fact, that for a period of time it looked as if the Church would be lost to Paul, and if lost to him, it would be lost totally (II Cor. Chpt. 7).

It is inconceivable that anyone would be successful in turning people against Paul, much less his own Converts, but the truth is, that they were successful in some cases, or nearly so.

We will study it much more as we go into Commentary respecting II Corinthians, but suffice to say, that such efforts, although in the Church, were as should be obvious, completely of Satan. In fact, Satan does his best work, as stated, in the Church. He does it through deception, and is successful for a variety of reasons.

SELFISH MOTIVES AND A PERSONAL AGENDA

Preachers used by the Evil One, just as in Paul's day, present men (or women) with selfish motives and a personal agenda. In other words, they are not following the Lord, even though they greatly claim to be doing so. Paul warned the Ephesians, *"For I know this, that after my departing shall grievous wolves enter in among you, not sparing the flock.*

*"Also of your own selves shall men arise, speaking perverse things, to draw away Disciples after them"* (Acts 20:29-30).

Believers are swayed in the wrong direction, because of not having a close walk with the Lord, which means that they have very little prayer life, if any, and as well, they spend very little time in the Word, if any at all. Consequently, they are prime targets for Satan, and for all obvious Scriptural reasons.

The phrase, *"Yet doubtless I am to you,"* means that there was absolutely no reason as to why the Corinthians should not understand his Calling as an Apostle.

NOTES

The phrase, *"For the seal of mine Apostleship are ye in the Lord,"* presents Paul using a figure which was undeniable.

*"Seal"* in the Greek is *"sphragis,"* which means *"a figure cut in stone and set in a ring by which letters of authority were stamped."* Paul used this terminology to prove to the Corinthians that their own conversion was proof of his Apostleship.

As we have previously stated, were he not who and what he said he was, he would never have endured the hardships suffered at Corinth to bring them the Gospel. Once again as stated, impostors do not do such a thing.

The fact that God Saved these Corinthians from the worst kind of spiritual darkness through Paul's Ministry, is the greatest *"seal"* of all, and which must be recognized by all. God does not anoint or bless sin, impostors, fakes, or selfish motives. Such should be obvious!

MY OWN PERSONAL EXPERIENCE

I find myself in the unenviable position of having to defend my Calling exactly as the Apostle Paul. With much of the Church denying that which God has called me to do, I can only offer the same proof as that of Paul.

I think I can say without any fear of exaggeration, that in any City in the world where the Telecast has aired, one will find souls Saved as a result of the Gospel we preach. These people number into the untold thousands, and have been delivered out of the worst type of spiritual darkness that one could ever begin to imagine. That is the *"Fruit"* of which I speak.

To be sure, that is the seal of Apostleship. The Lord does not anoint one to preach His Gospel, resulting in many people turning to Christ, and many being Baptized with the Holy Spirit, and many being delivered from all types of bondages of darkness, unless the Gospel that is preached is Scriptural. As well, the Messenger must be full of the Holy Spirit, as well as the Message being true. However, this does not mean that the Messenger is perfect.

In Truth there are no perfect Believers, nor even any perfect Preachers. There are only Believers and Preachers who are *"Forgetting those things which are behind, and reaching forth unto those things which are before,"* . . . consequently, *"pressing toward the mark for the prize of the High Calling of God in Christ Jesus"* (Phil. 3:13-14).

(3) "MINE ANSWER TO THEM THAT DO EXAMINE ME IS THIS,"

*"Answer"* in the Greek is *"apologia,"* and means *"clearing of self, defense."*

*"Examine"* in the Greek is *"anakrino,"* and means *"to scrutinize, investigate, determine."*

In effect, Paul is addressing those who were finding fault with him personally, and with what he taught regarding the Word of God. It was not that he felt obligated to do so respecting his own person, but he did feel an obligation because of the Work of God.

(4) "HAVE WE NOT POWER TO EAT AND DRINK?"

As an Apostle, and as the one who had brought these Corinthians the Gospel, which resulted in their Salvation, had he so desired, he was certainly in his rights by asking them for at least some financial help; however, he did not avail himself of that right, even though others did, when in reality they had little or no right at all.

It is amazing at the care taken by Paul in order that the Gospel not be hindered in any capacity. Regarding money, as we have already stated, he knew that the heathen Priests in these idol temples, were constantly demanding money of its devotees, and Paul wanted to portray the very opposite of that, which he did. No one could accuse Paul, at least honestly, of ever doing anything that would bring any type of reproach on the Gospel, or hindering it in any way. He went to extraordinary lengths, even depriving himself greatly, that his conscience may be clear in this capacity.

## THE APOSTLESHIP OF PAUL

The calling of the Apostle carries with it a special Message given to such an individual, which is meant for the edification of the Church. With Paul, this special Message pertained to *"Grace,"* in effect, *"the Cross."* In other words, Paul was the Apostle of Grace; or, one might say, the Apostle of the Cross.

It was to Paul that the meaning of the New Covenant was given, which was, in essence, the meaning of the Cross.

Prophets were the spiritual leaders in Old Testament times. While the Office of the Prophet remains under the New Covenant, the position of leadership has passed to the Calling and Office of the Apostle (Eph. 4:11). In fact, according to the account of the Early Church given in the Book of Acts, Apostles are the leaders of the Church. They are not in that position by popular ballot, but rather by the Call of God; they are identified by the Message they have.

NOTES

In truth, an Apostle can function in any of the fivefold Callings. It doesn't mean that Paul alone was an Apostle of Grace, for others had, in fact, the same emphasis on their Message. In the case of Paul, even though others may have preached the Message of Grace, and many did, still, the presentation of the Message by one who actually is an Apostle carried greater weight.

*"Power"* in the Greek is *"exousia,"* and means *"privilege, capacity, competency, right, and control."* The idea is, that he had the spiritual right, i.e., the Scriptural right, even as he gives in the 9th Verse.

(5) "HAVE WE NOT POWER TO LEAD ABOUT A SISTER, A WIFE, AS WELL AS OTHER APOSTLES, AND AS THE BRETHREN OF THE LORD, AND CEPHAS?"

The beginning of the question, *"Have we not power to lead about a sister, a wife, . . . ?"*, refers to the Scriptural right of having a flesh and blood sister travel with him at the expense of the Church, as evidently someone was doing. Paul is not advocating such, but only that there would be nothing wrong if he did. It would be the same for a *"wife,"* had he chosen to be married, which of course, he did not.

The continuing of the question, *"As well as other Apostles, . . . ?"*, portrays the fact that at least some of the other Apostles, whomever they may have been, were married men, with their wives traveling with them, etc.

In the 4th, 5th, and later centuries, as the Church further apostatized, some tampered with this Text, in the fruitless attempt to change its meaning. Little by little the Catholic effort was taking hold, which ultimately would triumph with *"Preachers"* called *"Priests"* which is totally unscriptural, along with the compelling doctrine of celibacy for the Priests and Nuns, etc.

The continuing of the question, *"And as the Brethren of the Lord, . . . ?"*, refers to the sons of Mary and Joseph, and at least speaks of James and Jude.

Such destroys the Catholic contention that Mary and Joseph had no other children other than Jesus, with the others named merely being His cousins, etc.

The conclusion of the question, *"And Cephas?"*, refers to Simon Peter, who the Scripture plainly says was married (Mat. 8:14).

(6) "OR I ONLY AND BARNABAS, HAVE NOT WE POWER TO FORBEAR WORKING?"

The beginning of the question, *"Or I only and Barnabas, . . . ?"*, presents Paul mentioning Barnabas after the quarrel (Acts Chpt. 15), which shows that the Apostle regarded him with Love and esteem. As well, Barnabas was an Apostle, by Divine Call, even as was Paul (Acts 13:2; Gal. 2:9).

The conclusion of the question, *"Have not we power to forbear working?"*, means to give up the manual labor by which he maintained himself. Even though Barnabas is no longer with Paul, it does seem that he continued in his separate Mission work the practice of independence which he had learned from Paul.

The idea is, that if Paul toiled at the dull, mechanical, despised, and ill-paid work of tent-making, he did so, not because it was, in the abstract, his duty to earn his own living, but because he chose this particular manner, especially here at Corinth, that his motives might be manifest to all (Farrar).

(7) "WHO GOETH A WARFARE ANY TIME AT HIS OWN CHARGES? WHO PLANTETH A VINEYARD, AND EATETH NOT OF THE FRUIT THEREOF? OR WHO FEEDETH THE FLOCK, AND EATETH NOT OF THE MILK OF THE FLOCK?"

The question, *"Who goeth a warfare any time at his own charges?"*, presents Paul giving the first of several reasons to prove the right of a Ministry to be supported by its congregation. The idea is, that a soldier would expect to receive *"rations"* and *"wages"* from the government which he is serving. A Minister of the Gospel should expect the same.

The question, *"Who planteth a vineyard, and eateth not of the fruit thereof?"*, presents another excellent illustration. Anyone who plants and gathers the harvest of a vineyard, surely will expect some return from that vineyard. The Preacher of the Gospel should expect the same, respecting his labor and effort.

The question, *"Or who feedeth a flock, and eateth not of the milk of the flock?"*, once again, draws an excellent analogy.

First of all, Paul uses examples which are understandable by all, and then he goes to the Scripture, respecting this particular situation of Preachers receiving pay or remuneration. He makes it abundantly clear that such is proper, but yet it is not so clear respecting his own involvement concerning Corinth.

NOTES

It is obvious that he received no pay while he was there, seemingly for the entire nearly two years, even though it seems that others did who followed him (vs. 12). So, why were the Corinthians complaining?

INSULT TO INJURY?

Exactly what happened we are not directly told; however, it seems like there is some credence to the idea that some in the Church at Corinth were admitting that they gladly paid some of the Preachers who followed Paul, but that Paul was not given anything because he wasn't worth anything. If that was the case, which I pray it was not, such would have added insult to injury.

It was bad enough for the man to labor in this city for nearly two years, actually being responsible for the planting of this Church, with most, if not all, the people in the Church his Converts, and then not give him anything in the way of financial remuneration. But yet, it seems as if he had purposed that he would not accept any money, and for the reasons previously given. Nevertheless, for some to insinuate that he was not worth any upkeep despite his tremendous labor, that is if such really happened, would have been the insult of insults. This we do know, whatever the reason for his statements, the Holy Spirit desired that he make them and in exactly the manner given.

(8) "SAY I THESE THINGS AS A MAN? OR SAITH NOT THE LAW THE SAME ALSO?"

The question, *"Say I these things as a man?"*, presents Paul making the case, that his statements are not merely his own thoughts, but are rather the Word of God.

The question, *"Or saith not the Law the same also?"*, refers to the Law of Moses, and is given in the next Verse, and is quoted from Deuteronomy 25:4.

(9) "FOR IT IS WRITTEN IN THE LAW OF MOSES, THOU SHALT NOT MUZZLE THE MOUTH OF THE OX THAT TREADETH OUT THE CORN. DOTH GOD TAKE CARE FOR OXEN?"

The phrase, *"For it is written in the Law of Moses,"* concerns that which is given next as being the Word of God, and the basis on which Paul is basing his argument.

The phrase, *"Thou shalt not muzzle the mouth of the ox that treadeth out the corn,"* presents basically what Jesus said in Luke 10:7

(I Cor. 9:9, 14). This is also a Testimony that Jesus and Jehovah are the One God (Williams).

The question, *"Doth God take care for oxen?"*, simply means that if the Lord would provide for a lowly beast, would He not do such for those who are doing far more important work, the taking of His Gospel to the world? The question demands an affirmative answer. The Lord takes care of oxen, and He takes care of His Ministers. Church Congregations should realize how privileged they are to be able to participate in the Plan of God for the furtherance of the Gospel, even as a farmer is proud to be able to feed the ox that helps work the corn, i.e., *"wheat or barley."*

(10) "OR SAITH HE IT ALTOGETHER FOR OUR SAKES? FOR OUR SAKES, NO DOUBT, THIS IS WRITTEN: THAT HE THAT PLOWETH SHOULD PLOW IN HOPE; AND THAT HE THAT THRESHETH IN HOPE SHOULD BE PARTAKER OF HIS HOPE."

The question, *"Or saith he it altogether for our sakes?"*, is once again meant to garner an affirmative answer.

The phrase, *"For our sakes, no doubt, this is written,"* proclaims by the Holy Spirit, that this is exactly why this Command was given in Deuteronomy 25:4. It wasn't really given for the sake of the poor beast, who must be cared for if it is to continue to work, but rather for those who labor on the Gospel Field, and those who should support them.

The phrase, *"That he that ploweth should plow in hope,"* presents Paul's large experience of life, and his insight into character, which sufficed to show him that despairing work must be ineffectual work. The hope of reward of some kind, is the engine of productivity and success. As a further example, even Faith in God, and especially Faith in God, promises reward.

The Scripture says, *"But without Faith it is impossible to please Him* (God)*: for he that cometh to God must believe that He* (God) *is, and that He is a rewarder of them that diligently seek Him"* (Heb. 11:6).

The phrase, *"And that he that thresheth in hope should be partaker of his hope,"* once again, expresses the same thing in a little different way.

As is obvious, Paul basis all of his analogies on the Scripture and rightly so. Consequently, there is absolutely no reason that anything should be misunderstood.

NOTES

(11) "IF WE HAVE SOWN UNTO YOU SPIRITUAL THINGS, IS IT A GREAT THING IF WE SHALL REAP YOUR CARNAL THINGS?"

The beginning of the question, *"If we have sown unto you spiritual things, . . . ?"*, presents the pronoun *"we"* shown both times in this Verse as emphatic, and, consequently, shows that the argument applies not only to all Preachers of the Gospel, but directly to Paul's own case (Farrar).

In fact, every single thing which was true and right that these Corinthians knew about the Gospel of Jesus Christ, which in fact had Saved their souls, which means it was the greatest thing that would ever happen to them in all of Eternity, all had been given and brought by the Apostle Paul. While the Holy Spirit definitely was the Author, still, it was Paul who was the instrument.

The conclusion of the question, *"Is it a great thing if we shall reap your carnal things?"*, refers here to money, or the equivalent thereof.

Of course, it would literally be impossible for the Corinthians to pay Paul for what he had brought to them. However, Paul is not asking that payment be made *"in-kind,"* for such would be impossible. He is merely saying that something should be given as a token of one's gratitude.

He will follow this same emphasis in his Second Epistle to the Corinthians, when he dealt with giving to a great degree, saying in one place, *"And to prove the sincerity of your Love"* (II Cor. 8:8).

In other words, it is not possible for the Believer to pay the Lord in-kind, or the equivalent in money, regarding what He has done for us in saving our soul. Consequently, what little we do regarding the giving of money to His Cause and Work, is merely done as a token which will hopefully express the sincerity of our Love for Him and the great Gift of Salvation which has been given unto us at great price. As it is humanly impossible for a person to repay the Lord, likewise, it was impossible for these Corinthians to repay Paul, or any Preacher for that matter who has been instrumental in bringing the Gospel to the lost soul. But at least, some gratitude should be shown, which in essence is what Paul is saying.

### PERSONAL OBSERVATION

Traveling in Evangelistic Work for many years, and being in many Churches all across America and around the world, I have noticed that Churches which generously care for their Pastor are always blessed wondrously by the Lord. On the other hand, I have noticed those who were tightfisted with their Pastor, and in every single case that I can remember, those Churches were deprived of the Blessings of the Lord.

It is not that one earns Blessings by the amount of money given, not at all! The idea is, that the Holy Spirit would not have gone to all of this trouble explaining this situation, even as He did through Paul, were it not very important to Him and to the Work of God.

If we think that these statements are merely the ramblings of a Preacher who is concerned about his Love Offering, we miss the point entirely. One of the reasons the Holy Spirit can make such a case of this issue, is simply because Paul had never received anything from the Corinthians, and in fact, had never asked for anything. So, what he said was not with prejudice, and neither was it self-serving. Consequently, the Holy Spirit could use him greatly in giving this Teaching respecting the Will of God in the matter of care for Ministers of the Gospel. In effect, the Holy Spirit is saying, as should be glaringly obvious, that if Churches take proper care of those who minister to them, that the Holy Spirit will see to the situation, that these people are cared for as well. This is the manner in which God has chosen to take care of His Business respecting the Church, and all of us would do well to heed these instructions properly.

(12) "IF OTHERS BE PARTAKERS OF THIS POWER OVER YOU, ARE NOT WE RATHER? NEVERTHELESS WE HAVE NOT USED THIS POWER; BUT SUFFER ALL THINGS LEST WE SHOULD HINDER THE GOSPEL OF CHRIST."

The phrase, *"If others be partakers of this power over you,"* presents a touch of indignation at the thought that these Corinthians submitted to the extremist and haughtiest exactions from other Teachers who had been loud in the statement of their own pretensions, while his own claims were shamefully disparaged (Farrar).

In fact, it seems as if these Teachers, whomever they may have been, were well paid, while Paul received nothing.

## POWER OVER YOU

The expression as used by Paul *"Power over you,"* presents a Truth of far greater magnitude than meets the eye.

NOTES

The Call of God on a Preacher's heart and life is a powerful thing. To be sure, there is a great chasm, spiritually speaking, between the Preacher and the Laity. The simple fact is that one has a distinct Call of God respecting the Office of the Apostle, Prophet, Evangelist, Pastor or Teacher, while the other (the Laity) doesn't. That does not make the Preacher of the Gospel any holier or any closer to God for that matter. However, it does give them an authority with God due to their Call, that is somewhat different than the Laity. Under the Holy Spirit, with Christ as the Chief Shepherd, still, the Undershepherds, Preachers of the Gospel, exercise a distinct *"power"* over the Laity, which is obvious, but which must be handled very delicately.

## WHAT JESUS SAID

Preachers exercising dominion over people is absolutely forbidden by the Lord. This is what He said:

*"Jesus called them unto Him, and said, Ye know that the princes of the Gentiles exercised dominion over them* (authority over people) *and they that are great* (Kings and Governors) *exercise authority upon them* (over the people)."

And then He said, *"But it shall not be so among you: but whosoever will be great among you, let him be your Minister* (the Preacher who executes the Command of the Lord as a servant to the people)."

And then, *"And whosoever will be chief among you, let him be your servant* (bondslave)" (Mat. 20:25-27).

So, the Lord forbids Ministers of the Gospel to exercise authority over people, while at the same time giving Preachers (or any Believer for that matter) great authority over the Powers of Darkness, i.e., Demon Spirits, etc. (Mk. 16:17-18; Lk. 10:19; Acts 1:8).

## THIS IS THE GREAT PROBLEM

Regrettably, many Preachers do not heed the Word of the Lord respecting this of which Jesus said, but do, in fact, exercise dominion (power) over the Laity in many and varied ways.

It is done in the realm of members of the Laity literally becoming servants to some Preachers. By that I mean they mow the yard for the Preacher, wash the dishes for his wife, etc. Such type spirit is not found by example anywhere in the Word of God.

The greatest problem of all, however, is for Preachers to take advantage of their position and to thereby, exploit the people. By that I mean this:

When a Preacher says *"God told me,"* that is certainly a legitimate statement, but at times, regrettably, not always true. However, people can be greatly controlled by such an attitude, which in fact, is used constantly.

For instance, many Preachers stand before congregations, whether in person, or by Radio or Television, or in print for that matter, saying, *"The Lord has told me that if you will give so much money, that certain great and wonderful things will come to you,"* or words to that effect. Once again, there is no example in the Word of God for such action. Let me give another example:

The Preacher says, *"If you will give a thousand dollars tonight, the Lord has told me that your home will be paid for at the end of this year."*

Has the Lord told the Preacher this of which has been said?

No!

There is nothing in the Word of God to substantiate such, and furthermore it appeals to greed and not Love. Pure and simple, the Preacher is exercising an authority (power) over people which is unlawful and illegitimate. As such, the people are fleeced, and all under the pretext of *"God said,"* when in reality, He has not said anything, and for the simple reason that God does not lie.

Incidentally, the illustration used is not hypothetical, but actually happened. Regrettably, such fraud, and fraud it is, is commonplace.

Actually, this is what Paul is speaking about. Preachers have *"power over you"* and they can use it in an unlawful manner.

Possibly even worse, some Preachers use this power to preach what people want to hear, instead of *"Thus saith the Lord."* They know that people will believe them, and they exercise this power unlawfully, preaching their false doctrine.

## A PERSONAL EXPERIENCE

I have been Preaching the Gospel over Radio and Television on a constant basis since January 1, 1969. Our first excursion into this medium was Radio. We went on with our Daily Program, Monday through Friday, called *"The Campmeeting Hour."* The Lord quickly began to bless, until in a short period of time we were on some 600 stations daily.

NOTES

A short time later, the Lord told me to go on Television, which we did.

Without going into detail, at a certain point in time, I began to more fully realize the veracity of the *"Power"* that God has given Preachers of the Gospel, which in a sense, even as Paul here says, is *"Power over people."* Two things developed in this of which I think may be of interest to you:

1. The Lord began to deal with me relative to the wrong use of this Power, i.e., *"exploitation."* In other words, He spoke to my heart, saying, *"If you ever use this Power, the Anointing, to exploit the people, I will take My Anointing from you."* He then said, *"You are to develop them, and to never exploit them."*

This Word was given to me so forcibly, that I can feel the impact of that which the Lord told me that day of so long ago, even unto this hour.

2. Not long after going on Radio, the Lord began to deal with my heart concerning some of our subject matter respecting Faith. In Truth He said to me, *"You are teaching Faith in a wrong manner, and it will not develop the people, but rather hinder them."*

To be frank, I am speaking of the *"Faith Message"* which is so prominent even now. However, that doesn't mean that all who preach and teach the Faith Message, are in fact teaching that which is wrong. I am only speaking of myself, and going back to that particular time of many years ago.

However, having said that, the Truth is, some parts of the Faith Message so-called, has been taken into heresy, and has caused great problems for many people. However, that is another subject.

## THE LORD SPOKE

Nevertheless, the Lord spoke to my heart, telling me that I was going to have to straighten up this situation over the Air. To be sure, I prayed about it very extensively, even fearful that I would lose the entirety of my audience. Irrespective, I felt in my heart that the Lord told me to publicly straighten out this situation, and irrespective as to the outcome, that I must do.

It wasn't easy going over the Air telling the people, that some of the things that I had taught them, I had come to believe now was not

Scriptural. I then related what I felt the Lord told me to relate. As I said, I didn't know what would happen to our audience, but miracle of miracles, it not only did not decrease, but rather increased.

The Preacher of the Gospel must ever be on guard lest he use this Power in an unlawful manner, actually exploiting Believers instead of developing them. As should be obvious, this is so very, very important.

The conclusion of the question, *"Are not we rather?"*, proclaims the fact that Paul has this Power as well, even as all Ministers do, at least to a certain degree — some more than others.

The phrase, *"Nevertheless we have not used this Power,"* in effect means, that Paul had not used this Power wrongfully.

The phrase, *"But suffer all things, lest we should hinder the Gospel of Christ,"* presents that which should ever be foremost in the heart and mind of the Preacher of the Gospel.

The Greek word for *"hindrance"* means *"cutting into, an impediment on a path."* If such were not possible for one to do, the Holy Spirit through the Apostle would not have caused these statements to be made.

In fact, Paul did take Offerings or a salary from other Churches (II Cor. 11:8), but not from the Corinthians, and for reasons which were indigenous to that particular area.

So, he is not saying that receiving an Offering is wrong, which actually the teaching of this Chapter portrays the opposite, but rather that the Preacher, and all Believers for that matter, be led by the Holy Spirit at all times and in all matters.

(13) "DO YE NOT KNOW THAT THEY WHICH MINISTER ABOUT HOLY THINGS LIVE OF THE THINGS OF THE TEMPLE? AND THEY WHICH WAIT AT THE ALTAR ARE PARTAKERS WITH THE ALTAR?"

The question, *"Do ye not know that they which minister about Holy Things live of the things of the Temple?"*, pertains to the Old Economy of God, which Paul is using as an example.

Paul is using all of this to proclaim the fact that it is ordained of God that Preachers should be supported by those to whom they preach the Gospel (Mat. 10:10; Lk. 10:7; Gal. 6:6; Heb. 7:1-11). As an example, the Apostle used the Temple of old and those who served in the Temple, whether those who ministered in Holy Things or those who waited on the Altar.

NOTES

The question, *"And they which wait at the Altar are partakers with the Altar?"*, pertained to certain portions of the Offerings (Sacrifices) which were allowed the Priests (Num. 18:8-13; Deut. 18:1).

(14) "EVEN SO HATH THE LORD ORDAINED THAT THEY WHICH PREACH THE GOSPEL SHOULD LIVE OF THE GOSPEL."

The phrase, *"Even so hath the Lord ordained,"* refers to one of the Discourses of Christ relative to this subject (Mat. 10:10; Lk. 10:7).

Oftentimes Paul will make such a reference to the Lord, and which pertains to that which Jesus said (I Cor. 7:10, 12, etc.).

The phrase, *"That they which preach the Gospel should live of the Gospel,"* proclaims the custom continuing which had begun under the old Levitical Order.

If one is to notice, Paul did not say *"to live of the Altar,"* and because Christians have no *"Altar"* except in the metaphorical sense in which the Cross is called an Altar (Heb. 13:10) (Farrar).

The idea is, as is obvious, that those who minister in spiritual things, should be supported financially by those to whom they minister.

(15) "BUT I HAVE USED NONE OF THESE THINGS: NEITHER HAVE I WRITTEN THESE THINGS, THAT IT SHOULD BE SO DONE UNTO ME: FOR IT WERE BETTER FOR ME TO DIE, THAN THAT ANY MAN SHOULD MAKE MY GLORYING VOID."

The phrase, *"But I have used none of these things,"* refers to him placing his care and concern for weaker Christians, above the rights that he had in the Gospel. The idea is, that he is appealing to his own abandonment of rights, in order to encourage them (the Corinthians) to waive, if need required, the claims of their Christian Liberty, because of their concern for others.

The phrase, *"Neither have I written these things, that it should be so done unto me,"* means that he is not saying the things he is saying concerning the giving of Offerings and the support of Ministers, in order that they may send him an Offering. That is not his idea at all. He is merely trying to portray a lesson to them, and a lesson it should quickly be added, which was not berthed from impure motives, but rather by the Holy Spirit.

The phrase, *"For it were better for me to die, than that any man should make my glorying void,"* in essence says that he would rather die than stoop to such a level as that. It may seem difficult for us to understand his violent language, but he had been falsely accused of so many things in Corinth, which actually would continue for some time, that he had to take this extreme posture (Rossier).

*"Glorying"* in the Greek is *"kauchema,"* and means *"boasting, whether in a good or bad sense."* Of course, it is in a good sense here. In other words, while Paul is boasting, it actually is in the Lord.

MONEY

When I was nine years old (1944) I asked the Lord to give me the talent to play the piano. To make the story brief, He did exactly that which I asked.

Along with that, He gave me some ability to sing, and I think above all, an ability to know and understand the flow of the Holy Spirit respecting music and its use in worship. In regard to that, the Lord has helped us to sell many recordings all over the world, actually to date April 1, 1998, some 15 million by count.

How I thank the Lord for that, giving Him all Praise and Glory for that which has been done, and which I believe, has been a blessing to many people.

BOASTING

In the same spirit as that of the Apostle Paul, in the Lord I will boast that the money received from the sale of this product, has not gone to enrich my family, but has rather gone to proclaim the great Gospel of Jesus Christ all over the world.

In fact, when I first went on Radio back in 1969, I felt that the Lord told me to give all the proceeds from the sale of our Recordings to His Work. To be sure, those sales were very small at that time, with the proceeds amounting to very little. Nevertheless, the Lord knew that would soon change.

Thankfully, after discussing this with Frances, and her always acquiescing to that which the Lord said, all the Recordings were taken out of my own name personally, and put in the name of the Ministry, which means that I no longer personally own them, and neither could I personally receive benefit from sales, etc. As stated, that was done back in 1969.

NOTES

In fact, the Board of Directors of the Organization has attempted several times to get us (my family) to take a small part of the sale of the Recordings, with such being placed in the minutes, but we have never done so, simply because the funds have always been greatly needed to take the Gospel around the world.

So, in the Lord I can boast that the sales of this product have not enriched our family. Even though it is told all over the world, with Satan instigating such, that Jimmy Swaggart is wealthy, that is only true in one sense — the things of the Lord. Respecting money, my family has a living and a home, and that is it. In fact, we have no investments, and as I write this, no savings and not even any retirement, except that owed us by the Ministry.

What people think is one thing, what the Lord knows is something else altogether. As well, Christians should be very careful as to what they hear and then believe. If they use the News Media as their source, it should be obvious that they are playing right into the hands of Satan. And regrettably, great segments of the Church seem to do little better in this regard, actually serving as a conduit for that which Satan desires. Such is sad but true.

The real problem in Paul's day was Christians believing the wrong thing, and which is the major problem presently.

(16) "FOR THOUGH I PREACH THE GOSPEL, I HAVE NOTHING TO GLORY OF: FOR NECESSITY IS LAID UPON ME; YEA, WOE IS UNTO ME, IF I PREACH NOT THE GOSPEL!"

The phrase, *"For though I preach the Gospel, I have nothing to glory of,"* sounds like a contradiction, considering that he has spoken of *"glorying"* in the previous statement (vs. 15). However, there is no contradiction.

Even though he did glory (boast) regarding his manner of life, and because he felt this is what the Holy Spirit desired, to the contrary, there was no glory in the Preaching of the Gospel. By that he means this:

The Preaching of the Gospel to Paul, and to all others who are truly called, was not a career choice, vocation, occupation, or advocation, but rather a Call from God. As well, if one is truly obedient to that Call, even though there is much joy involved in seeing God move and work in the Salvation of souls and the deliverance of mankind, still, the animosity aroused which the True Gospel always does, smothers any cause for *"glorying."* The anger and hostility to be sure, will little come from the world, but mostly from that which labels itself as the *"Church."*

Even this morning in prayer, my heart literally hurt as I grieved over Preachers who attempt to hurt our Ministry and to keep people from hearing the Gospel we preach. I do not speak of Modernists, but rather those who claim to be Pentecostal. Sadly, that of which I speak is not an isolated thing, but rather indicative of most of the Pentecostal and Charismatic Church World — the very ones who ought to know better. Many Preachers regrettably, do not want to do right, and if they can find an excuse not to do so, they willingly fall into the trap. Others regrettably, ignore what the Word of God says, seeking to please Denominational Heads. Regrettably, this group is quite large.

The phrase, *"For necessity is laid upon me,"* refers to the fact that the Preaching of the Gospel is not merely a choice on his part, but rather a Command from the Lord. In other words, Paul had no choice in the matter, and neither does any God-Called Preacher.

The phrase, *"Yea, woe is unto me, if I preach not the Gospel,"* proclaims an overwhelming moral compulsion, and he would have been miserable and even condemned, if he had tried to resist it.

## WHAT IS THE GOSPEL OF JESUS CHRIST?

*"Gospel"* in the Greek is either *"euaggelizo"* or *"euaggelion,"* both meaning *"glad, good tidings, Good News."* In its more pure sense of the word, it *"proclaims tidings of deliverance."* As well, it stands for the record of the Life of our *"Lord"* (Mk. 1:1), embracing all His Teachings, as in Acts 20:24.

But the word *"Gospel"* now has a peculiar use, and describes primarily the Message which Christianity announces. As stated, *"Good News"* is its significance. It means a Gift from God.

It is the proclamation of the forgiveness of sins and Sonship with God restored through Christ. It means remission of sins and reconciliation with God. The Gospel is not only a Message of Salvation, but also the instrument through which the Holy Spirit works (Rom. 1:16).

## THE GREEKS AND THE ROMANS

Up unto the time of Christ, the word *"gospel"* was frequently used in Grecian and Roman terminology. In other words, when something good happened, or something which was supposed to be good, it was referred to as the *"gospel."*

The Message of Christ, the greatest Good News the world had ever known, was automatically known as the *"Gospel."* This *"Good News"* being picked up and used extensively by the Early Church, little by little, the word *"Gospel"* came to define exclusively the Message of Jesus Christ. Otherwise, it came to be used less and less frequently.

The reason is obvious:

The only truly *"Good News"* in the world today, and in fact ever has been, is the Message of Jesus Christ. Consequently, when one now hears the word *"gospel,"* automatically it is understood, as the Gospel of Jesus Christ.

## THE GOSPEL AND THE LAW

The Gospel differs from the Law of Moses in being known entirely from Revelation. It is proclaimed in all its fullness in the Revelation given in the New Testament. It is also found, although obscurely, in the Old Testament. It begins with the Prophecy concerning *"the seed of the woman"* (Gen. 3:15), and the Promise concerning Abraham, in whom all the Nations should be blessed (Gen. 12:3; 15:5) and is also indicated in Acts 10:43 and in the argument in Romans, Chapter 4.

## THE MESSAGE OF CHRIST

In the New Testament the Gospel never means simply a Book, but rather the Message which Christ and His Apostles announced. In some places it is called *"The Gospel of God,"* as, for example, Romans 1:1; I Thessalonians 2:2, 9; and, I Timothy 1:11. In others it is called *"The Gospel of Christ"* (Mk. 1:1; Rom. 1:16; 15:19; I Cor. 9:12, 18; Gal. 1:7). In another it is called *"The Gospel of the Grace of God"* (Acts 20:24); in another *"The Gospel of Peace"* (Eph. 6:15); in another *"The Gospel of your Salvation"* (Eph. 1:13); and in yet another *"The Glorious Gospel"* (II Cor. 4:4).

The Gospel is Christ: He is the Subject of it, the Object of it, and the Light of it. It was preached by Him (Mat. 4:23; 11:5; Mk. 1:14; Lk. 4:18), by the Apostles (Acts 16:10; Rom. 1:15; 2:16; I Cor. 9:16), and by the Evangelists (Acts 8:25).

## THE SUBSTANCE OF ALL CHRISTIAN DOCTRINE

We must know the clear antithesis (contrast) between the Law of Moses and the Gospel. The distinction between the two is important because, as Luther indicates, it contains the substance of all Christian Doctrine.

*"By the Law,"* says he, *"nothing else is meant than God's Word and Command, directing what to do and what to leave undone, and requiring of us obedience of works. But the Gospel is such Doctrine of the Word of God that neither requires our works nor commands us to do anything, but announces the offered Grace of the forgiveness of sin and Eternal Salvation.*

*"Here we do nothing, but only receive what is offered through the Word."*

The Gospel, then, is the Message of God, the Teaching of Christianity, the Redemption in and by Jesus Christ, the Only Begotten Son of God, offered to all mankind.

## THE REMISSION OF SIN FOR CHRIST'S SAKE

The Gospel is bound up in the Life of Christ, His Biography and the record of His Works, and the proclamation of what He has to offer, all gathered into this single word, of which no better definition can be given than that of Melanchthon:

*"The Gospel is the gratuitous Promise of the remission of sin for Christ's sake."*

To hold tenaciously that in this Gospel we have a supernatural Revelation is in perfect consistency with the spirit of scientific inquiry. The Gospel, as the whole Message and Doctrine of Salvation, and as chiefly efficacious and effective for Contrition, Faith, Justification, Renewal, and Sanctification, deals with fact of revelation and experience (Bauslin).

## THE FOUR GOSPELS

By the Four Gospels, we mean, *"Matthew, Mark, Luke, and John."*

These Four Gospels were never questioned in the Church, in other words, as to their authenticity, etc. It is acknowledged that by the end of the Second Century, these Four Gospels, and none else, ascribed to the authors whose names they bear, were in universal circulation and undisputed use throughout the Church.

Three of the Gospels (Matthew, Mark, and Luke) are called the *"Synoptic Gospels,"* for the simple reason, that they are very similar in detail. No one could read these Gospels consecutively with attention, without being aware of the resemblances and differences in their contents. Each Writer sets forth his own account without reference to the other two, and, with the partial exception of Luke (1:1-4), does not tell his readers anything about the sources of his Gospel. Hence, they are called *"Synoptics."*

By the use of the word *"differences"* we are not meaning contradictions, but rather that one Writer will add to the same story something that another Writer does not mention.

## THE GOSPEL IN THE EARLY CHURCH

The Christian Church in its earlier form arose out of the teaching, example, and influence of the Apostles at Jerusalem. It was based on Apostolic Testimony as to the Life, Character, Teaching, Death, and Resurrection of Jesus Christ. That Testimony told the Church what Jesus had done, what He had taught, and of the belief of the Apostles as to What and Who He was, and What and Who He continued to be.

We read that the Early Church *"continued stedfastly in the Apostles' teaching and fellowship"* (Acts 2:42). The *"Teaching"* consisted of reminiscences of the Lord, of interpretations of the facts about Jesus and of agreements between these and the Old Testament.

## THE FIRST INSTRUCTION

The first instruction given to the Church was oral. Of this fact there can be no doubt. How long oral teaching continued we can't say, but it is likely that it continued as long as the Apostles dwelt together at Jerusalem.

To them an appeal could constantly be made. There was also the strictly Doctrinal Teaching concerning being Born-Again, the Baptism with the Holy Spirit, and Water Baptism, given to the Converts, and this Teaching would be given after the manner to which they had been accustomed in their earlier education.

It consisted mainly in committing accurately to memory, and in repetition from memory.

NOTES

Thus, there would be a strict tradition, concerning these things we have mentioned, and a looser tradition which consisted of as much as the people could carry with them from the Preaching of the Apostles at the daily or weekly assemblies.

No doubt, there was much coming and going from other areas outside of Jerusalem, and no doubt even from the far-flung reaches of the Roman Empire, who heard the Apostles in those early days. They would carry with them on their return to their homes some knowledge of the Life, Death, Resurrection, and Ascension of Jesus. To be sure, it may have been a meager Gospel that these carried with them to Antioch, to Rome, or to other cities. But that they did carry a Gospel with them is plain, for from their Testimony arose the Church at Antioch, where the Christians had without question a knowledge of the Gospel, which informed their Faith and guided their action.

## THE MAIN TOPIC

It is known from Acts, that at the beginning, the main topic of the Preaching of the Apostles was the Resurrection of the Lord. *"With great power gave the Apostles their witness of the Resurrection of the Lord Jesus"* (Acts 4:33).

It is evident, however, that the Apostolic witness would not be limited to the events of the Passion Week, or to the fact of the Resurrection. There would arise a thirst for information regarding the Life of Jesus, what He had done, what He had said, what manner of life He had lived, and what Teaching He had given.

Accounts of Him and of His Work would be given by the Apostles, and once these accounts were given, they would continue to be given in the same form. For example, tell a story to a child and he will demand that it be always given in the form in which he first knew it.

Hearers of a story are impatient of variations in the subsequent telling of it, which demands accuracy.

Memory is very tenacious and very conservative. It is clear that the first lessons of the Apostles were accounts of the Passion Week, and of the Resurrection. But it went backward to events and incidents in the Life of Jesus, and as we read the Synoptic Gospels, we soon see that the order was dictated by the events themselves. They are grouped together for no other reason than that they happened so.

NOTES

## A GEOGRAPHICAL THREAD

Most of the incidents concerning Jesus are hung on a geographical thread. In the Second Gospel, which seems to preserve most faithfully the traditional order, this is obvious to every attentive Reader; but in all the Three Gospels many of the Narratives go in well-established cycles.

To take only one illustration, where many might be instanced, the healing of the woman with the issue of blood is represented as occurring in the course of the walk to the house of Jairus (Mk. 5:21-43).

The only explanation is that this was the actual mode of its happening. Events happened, incidents arose, in the course of the journeys of Jesus and His Disciples, words were also spoken, and in the memories of the Disciples, when the journey was recalled, no doubt helped by the Holy Spirit, there arose also what had happened in the course of the journey.

In fact, as we follow the journey through Galilee, to the Coasts of Tyre and Sidon, through Samaria, down the Valley of the Jordan, through Jericho to Jerusalem, we find that the grouping of the material of the Gospels is determined by the facts. Most of what is recorded happened in the course of the journeys, and was borne in the memories of the Disciples in the order of its happening.

The order, then, is not arbitrary, nor is it the product of reflection; it is the outcome of the facts.

It is true that in pursuance of their several plans, Luke sometimes, Matthew frequently, deserts the order of Mark, but it is noteworthy that they never do so together. However, if they desert the order, it is never to mitigate against Mark. Luke sometimes deserts the order of Mark, and Matthew often does so; but in these cases Mark is always supported by the remaining Gospel. In other words, they never contradict each other, even though some will give information the other one did not give, or relate an incident not related necessarily by all, or maybe any of the others.

## THE HISTORIC SITUATION

When one studies the political geography of Israel during the time of Christ, he will find

NOTES

many confirmations of the historic situation in the Synoptic Gospels (Matthew, Mark, and Luke). For instance, the Birth of Jesus was in the time of Herod the Great, when the whole of Israel (Palestine) was under one Government. However, after the death of Herod, Israel was under several rulers.

Archelaus had possession of Judaea until the year A.D. 9 Galilee was under Herod Antipas until the year A.D. 37, and the tetrarchy of Philip had a distinct Government of its own.

About the year A.D. 40 Israel was again under one Government under Herod Agrippa. Now it is clear that the events of the Gospels happened while Herod Antipas ruled in Galilee and Peraea.

During the time of Christ Israel was divided into six districts. Judaea was on the South, with Samaria bordering it on the North. To Samaria's North was Galilee. In the extreme Northeast was Paneas, which was on the East side of Jordan. Immediately South of Paneas and, as well, East of the Jordan was Decapolis. Perea, which was on the East side of Jordan also, bordered Samaria and Judea from that direction, also jutting up into Decapolis. That was the Israel of Jesus' day.

It is clear that the events of the Gospels happened while Herod Antipas ruled in Galilee and Peraea, and while Pilate was Procurator (Governor) of Judaea.

In the itinerary recorded in Mark Chapter 5, the parts of Israel avoided are the dominions of Herod Antipas.

It is said in Mark 3:6, *"And the Pharisees went out, and straightway with the Herodians took counsel against Him, how they might destroy Him."* The significance of this alliance between the Pharisees and the Herodians should be noted. It is mentioned by Mark, but on it the Evangelist makes no remark. However, the conspiracy had a great effect on the Work of Jesus.

A little later we find Jesus little more in any of the Synagogues. He devotes Himself to the training of the Twelve, and is outside of the dominions of Herod Antipas (Galilee and Peraea).

It should not be forgotten that during these months Jesus is an Exile from His Own Land, and it was during that period of Exile that He began to prepare His Disciples of the decease He should accomplish at Jerusalem (Mat. 16:13).

## THE OLD TESTAMENT AND THE GOSPEL OF THE NEW TESTAMENT

It is always to be remembered that the Old Testament was the Bible of the early Christians. They accepted it as the Word of God, and as authoritative for the guidance of life and conduct. It is one thing to admit and assert this; it is another thing to say that the story of the Old Testament molded and directed the story of Jesus as it is in the Synoptic Gospels, and even the Gospel according to John.

In fact, it did do this, but not according to the Jews, and I speak of the Jews who would not accept Jesus as the Messiah. As a matter of fact, Christianity, when it accepted the Old Testament as the Word of God, interpreted it in a fashion which had not been accepted before. It interpreted it, even as it should have, in the Light of Jesus Christ.

## JESUS AND THE OLD TESTAMENT

Tendencies, facts, meanings, which had been in the Old Testament came into Light and the Old Testament of the Christian was an Old Testament which testified of Christ. That on which the Jews laid stress passed into the background, and that which they had neglected came into prominence.

This view is set forth by Paul: *"Unto this day, whensoever Moses is read, a veil lieth upon their heart"* (II Cor. 3:15). Or as it is put in Luke, *"O foolish men, and slow of heart to believe in all that the Prophets have spoken! Behooved it not the Christ to suffer these things, and to enter into His Glory?"* (Lk. 24:25-26).

In the Christian interpretation, stress was laid on meanings which Jewish Readers had neglected, and so the Church read the Old Testament in the New Light, and things formerly hidden leaped into view. So the Suffering Servant of Jehovah became for them the keystone of the Old Testament, and the Ritual Sacrifices and Ceremonies of the Old Testament obtained a new meaning, all as representative of Christ.

The story of Israel and of its Patriarchs, Lawgivers, Priests, Kings, and Prophets, became full of significance for the new experience, and its Psalms and Prophecies were searched because they testified of Christ.

## HOW TO FIND CHRIST IN THE OLD TESTAMENT

This Truth, and a Truth it is, once Christ is accepted, becomes so obvious, that it is undeniable.

The inference is that the Old Testament did not, as it was understood by the Jews, influence the conceptions which the Church had of Christ; rather the influence of Christ, His Commanding Personality, and His History gave a new meaning to the Old Testament, a meaning unknown previously.

The Epistle to the Hebrews might have as an alterative title, *"How to find Christ in the Old Testament."* So powerful was the impression made on the Disciples by the Personality of Jesus, by His Whole Demeanor, by His Teaching, His Life, Death and Resurrection, that they saw all things in the Light of it.

The difficulty we have in justifying the references to Prophecy concerning Christ, in the light of historical criticism, is a testimony to the fact that the Prophecy did not dictate the fact; it was the fact that dictated the accommodation of the Prophecy. In this relation also, the supreme fact is the Personality of Jesus.

In other words, the Prophecy did not prove Jesus, even though it certainly could have, but rather that the overwhelming evidence concerning Jesus was so obvious concerning Who and What He was, that that within itself proved the Prophecy. Consequently, it is undeniable.

## JESUS AS THE SOURCE OF THE GOSPEL

Turning from the conception of the Suffering Saviour in the Synoptics, we come to the aspect of Jesus as *"Teacher"* and for the want of a better word, *"Thinker,"* and here also we find abundant evidence of the Historical Character of the Gospel presentation. As the ethics of our Lord are examined, it is sufficient to say here that the conception of the ethical man and His conduct set forth in His Teaching is of unusual breadth, and when worked out in detail, yields an ideal of man in Himself, and in relation to others, which transcends all other ethical Teaching known to mankind. This, too, we must trace to His unique Personality, and not to the reflection of the Church. In fact, the Church did not give birth to Jesus, but rather Jesus gave birth to the Church (Mat. 16:18).

NOTES

A glance may be taken at Jesus under His more general aspect as Thinker. As Thinker, Jesus stands Alone.

## HIS AUTHORITY AND HIS MESSAGE

He speaks with such authority, that whoever understood what He was saying, was compelled to obey. The Synoptic Gospels, in this respect, are unique. Actually, there is nothing like them in literature.

Not even in the Bible is there anything to compare with them. Even in the other Books of the New Testament we do not find anything like the attitude of Jesus to the common things of life. The world's literature shows no parallel to the Parables of the Gospels.

Here, at any rate, we are on safe ground in saying that these are not due to the reflection of the Church, but rather that the Church is due to the reflection of His Message. The Gospels have an individual stamp which accredits them as the product of one mind. But a great deal more may be said on the characteristic features of the Thinking of Jesus.

## FROM THE COMMONPLACE TO THE COMPLEX

Jesus is the only Thinker Who goes straight from the common things of daily life and daily experience into the deepest mysteries of life. The deepest thoughts which man can think are suggested to Him by what everybody sees or does. It is not easy within reasonable limits to do justice to this feature of the Gospels. Jesus is at home amid the common things and common occupations of life, because He discerns the Father's Presence in them all.

What a series of pictures of the world, and of occupations of men, could be gathered from these Gospels! This feature of them was neglected until men under the teaching of Poets and Painters returned into sympathy with external Nature. We are only beginning to see what wealth, from this point of view, is in the Gospels.

For instance, Poetic sympathy with Nature is a comparatively modern attainment, yet it is already in the Gospels. Wind and weather, mountain and valley, seed time and harvest, Summer and Winter, sowing and reaping, buying and selling, all are there, transfigured into higher meanings, and made vocal of the mysteries of the Kingdom of Heaven. Other thinkers rise gradually, and by many steps, from common experience, into what they have to describe of the higher thought and wider generalizations through which they seek to interpret the mystery of life and of the universe. However, this Thinker called Jesus, needs no middle terms.

He sees, for instance, a woman preparing bread for the use of the family, and in this process perceives the mystery of the Kingdom of Heaven. Whenever He touches on these common things, immediately they are transfigured. They become luminous with the presence of the spiritual world, and Earth becomes full of Heaven, and every bush is aflame with God.

## THE BEARING AND ORIGIN OF THE GOSPELS

We note these things because they have a close bearing on the origin and character of the Gospels. In other words, they bear the stamp of a unique, a creative personality. Be the processes through which the materials of the Gospels have passed what they may, yet these have not obliterated nor blurred the essential characteristics of the Unique Personality of Christ.

When the comparisons of the similarities and what some may call differences as it pertains to the Gospels have been exhausted, the problem of their origin remains, and that problem can be solved only by the recognition of a Creative Personality Who alike by word and work was unlike any other that the world has ever seen.

## HOW DO WE REPRESENT A DIVINE BEING UNDER HUMAN CONDITIONS?

The Jesus of the Gospels is the Son of God. Stated in its highest form, the problem which the Evangelists had in hand was how to represent a Divine Being under human conditions, and to set Him forth in such a way that in that presentation there should be nothing unworthy of the Divine, and nothing inconsistent with the human conditions under which He worked and lived.

This was the greatest problem ever set to literature, and how the Evangelists presented and solved it is found in the Gospels. There it has been solved. Of course, it was the Holy Spirit Who guided them in that which they wrote, using their personalities, but at the same time, He Alone was the Author.

NOTES

As an example, Mark at the very beginning of his Gospel, presents Jesus not only as the Messiah of the Jewish people, but as well, the Miraculous Eternal Son of God, Whose Glory shown in the world . . . For the Faith of the community, which John shares, is that Jesus is the Miraculous Son of God, in Whom men believe, Whom men put wholly on the side of God.

The purpose of the Gospels, even as the reason for the Gospels, is to lead men to *"believe that Jesus is the Christ, the Son of God, that, believing, they may have Life in His Name"* (Jn. 20:31).

(Literature — E. A. Abbot, *"Gospels."* Rushbrooke, *"Common Tradition of the Synoptic Gospels."* Peake, *"Introduction to the New Testament."* J. M. Thomson, *"The Synoptic Gospels."* James Iverach, Compilation.)

(17) "FOR IF I DO THIS THING WILLINGLY, I HAVE A REWARD: BUT IF AGAINST MY WILL, A DISPENSATION OF THE GOSPEL IS COMMITTED UNTO ME."

The phrase, *"For if I do this thing willingly, I have a reward,"* refers to the fact of the one Called of God doing everything within his (or her) power to do exactly what the Lord wants done. It speaks of diligence, zeal, responsibility, concern, care, forthrightness, and all that could pertain to a task well done. In other words, when it comes to the Call of God we don't punch a clock. It is full time, and as well, the seeking of God's Face constantly, that we may always be a pliable and usable instrument by the Holy Spirit, i.e., a clear channel.

The phrase, *"But if against my will, a dispensation of the Gospel is committed unto me,"* refers to the Preacher, or anyone who names the Name of Christ, who does only what is his duty, and in fact, doesn't even quite do that.

*"Dispensation"* in the Greek is *"oikonomia,"* and means *"an administration or stewardship."* Paul's statement actually refers back to the *"Parable of the Talents"* as given by Jesus (Mat. 25:14-30).

The one who conducted himself in a negative way, even as the Parable proclaims, did not come out too well. I think Paul is basically saying the same thing. There is a great *"reward"* for those who diligently serve the Lord, but otherwise such a reward does not exist, with implications even of that which is very negative. The idea is, that if the one Called does not conduct himself (or herself) as he should, he is going to be called to account by the Lord at the Judgement Seat of Christ, paying the price accordingly.

(18) "WHAT IS MY REWARD THEN? VERILY THAT, WHEN I PREACH THE GOSPEL, I MAY MAKE THE GOSPEL OF CHRIST WITHOUT CHARGE, THAT I ABUSE NOT MY POWER IN THE GOSPEL."

The question, *"What is my reward then?"*, presents that which he considers to be a reward, but which has nothing to do with the *"reward"* spoken of in Verse 17. That *"reward"* will be given by the Lord at the *"Judgment Seat of Christ."* For someone such as Paul, one can well imagine as to what that reward will be.

However, the reward of which he now speaks in Verse 18, speaks of the satisfaction that he has and receives from the Lord respecting the privilege of taking the Gospel of Jesus Christ to all who may hear.

The phrase, *"Verily that, when I preach the Gospel, I may make the Gospel of Christ without charge,"* presents a tremendous statement.

First of all as just stated, this was his reward, at least as far as he was concerned, the privilege of taking the Gospel of Jesus Christ to others. However, and we again reiterate, this has nothing to do with the reward which will be his, when at long last he stands before the Lord, even as we all shall do.

Even though people are encouraged to give to God's Work, even as Paul has addressed in the major part of this Chapter, still, there must never be a price put on the Gospel in any capacity. As well, Preachers must never make Believers think that the Gospel is for sale in any case, i.e., that money buys favor with God, etc. So, what the Holy Spirit through the Apostle is here saying, involves far more than just the personal Ministry of Paul, but is rather meant to include all of the presentation of the Gospel and for all time. In other words, what is being said, is extremely important and very serious.

## AN EXAMPLE

Just the other day, I was told of a particular Church, actually a very small work, in a neighboring town to Baton Rouge. They do not have a Pastor at this small Church. In fact, several have applied, with the question always at the forefront, *"What do you pay?"*

To be sure, if that little Church accepts a Pastor of that nature, they are wasting their time. Of course, it is necessary that the Pastor be cared for; however, if he is going there for the money, or trying to find a good salary, that means he is a *"hireling."* Consequently, he will do the Work of God no good whatsoever. Regrettably, far too many fit that mode.

## WHAT SHOULD BE DONE

If the man of God, that is if he is truly a man of God, feels led of the Lord to go to a certain place, and the people desire that he come, he should trust the Lord for his support. To be sure, if the Lord has truly called him to that particular place, the Holy Spirit will see to it that he is supported, and more than likely, to a far greater degree than if he made demands.

However, even if the support does not come in, and he and his family have to sacrifice, even greatly, that would be far better, even as Paul here proclaims, than putting a *"charge"* on the Gospel. Money is to never be the object. If it is, it ceases to be the Gospel, and the Preacher ceases to be God-called.

The phrase, *"That I abuse not my power in the Gospel,"* presents the demand of the Holy Spirit.

*"Abuse"* in the Greek is, *"katachraomai,"* and means *"to misuse."* It is a misuse of the Power of the Gospel of Jesus Christ which comes with the Call.

The *"power"* given to the Preacher of the Gospel is meant to be used against demon spirits and every power of darkness. To be frank, the Power of God vested in Believers presents the only real opposing force against this terrible malady of destruction. So, if the Church is weak, there is very little opposition to that which steals, kills, and destroys (Jn. 10:10).

Regrettably, many Preachers use (misuse) this power against people instead, which it was never intended. And how is that done?

## ABUSE

1. As we have already stated, it is used oftentimes to extract money from people, by promising great things for them if they will give, etc. While it is certainly Scriptural that the Lord

will bless those who give bountifully, however, if the motivation of giving is simply receiving, it actually ceases to be a gift and becomes an investment — that which God will not honor (II Cor. 9:5).

2. The greatest misuse of all is the effort to *"control"* people, which is abominable in the sight of God. But yet, this is what most Denominations attempt to do, and pretty well succeed. They teach people to look exclusively to them, and not to God. In fact, the control factor presents Satan's greatest effort. It is done through religious means, which makes it acceptable.

The Head of the Church is Jesus Christ and not man. In fact, the Church belongs to Christ, and not man (Mat. 16:18).

If one is to notice, the entirety of the gist of Paul's admonitions, always direct the thrust toward Jesus Christ as the Head of the Church. In other words, Believers belong to Christ first of all, and as Undershepherds of the Gospel, we are to constantly point people to Him and never to ourselves or particular Denominations. Paul never overstepped that authority, never abrogated that authority, never abused that authority, which serves as an example to us.

One probably could say without any fear of contradiction, that there are more people today in Hell because of this one thing than anything else. They were controlled by religious forces, thereby believing a lie, and were damned (II Thess. 2:11-12; II Tim. 4:3-4). In fact, the *"deeds of the Nicolaitanes,"* which Jesus addressed in His Letter to the Church at Ephesus, and the *"Doctrine of Balaam"* addressed to the Church at Pergamos, fell under the auspices of *"control."* To say that these things were merely condemned by Christ, would be a gross understatement.

## IS THE HOLY SPIRIT IN CHARGE?

If the Holy Spirit is in charge, the Preacher or Denomination will never attempt to control the people. To give an example:

Having begun Family Worship Center in Baton Rouge, Louisiana, and according to the Will of God I might quickly add, in all of these years of pastoring these people, I have never sought to control them in any manner. I have never told them who they should hear regarding the Preaching of the Gospel, or anything else of that nature. And neither will I ever do so.

NOTES

It is my place as the Pastor of this Church, to teach the people from the Word of God well enough, that they will have the Word so lodged within their hearts, that they will automatically know what is right and what is wrong respecting what they hear. Consequently, they are treated as mature adults and not as children.

I have never told them where they could go or could not go, and would not even think of doing such a thing. In fact, it would be wrong to do such, even as we are here addressing.

Preachers who have controlling spirits, and that probably accounts for the majority, are definitely not controlled by the Holy Spirit.

(19) "FOR THOUGH I BE FREE FROM ALL MEN, YET HAVE I MADE MYSELF SERVANT UNTO ALL, THAT I MIGHT GAIN THE MORE."

The phrase, *"For though I be free from all men,"* pertains to one's true position in Christ. In other words, Christ is one's Lord and Master, not other men.

More specifically, even though this refers to all Believers, it is also proper to look at the situation as it refers to Preachers of the Gospel, for Paul, as is obvious, was a Preacher.

Even though Paul dearly loved, respected, and appreciated, in other words holding in very high regard, all the other Apostles, and especially the Apostles of the Lord, still, he did not answer to them, nor in fact, they to him. In other words, there was a horizontal submission, even as there should be in Christendom, and is designed thusly by the Holy Spirit (Eph. 5:21). In other words, Believers are to submit to each other, and those in Churches, even as they should be, are to submit themselves to the Pastor (Elder) (I Pet. 5:5). However, such submission in this case, and all cases for that matter, is to apply only as long as the situation is Scriptural. If it ceases to be Scriptural in any manner, submission is to end then and there.

## THE TRUTH!

Most Religious Denominations abrogate this Passage as given by Paul, which means that their Preachers are not *"free from all men,"* i.e., free to obey God. They would deny this, but what I am saying is true.

The Scriptural manner is, that each Church is the highest spiritual authority, and that nothing from the outside, be it secular or religious, must usurp the authority of the Local Church (Mat. 16:18; Acts 13:1; Rev. Chpts. 2-3). Regrettably, that is not true in most Denominational Circles, with the authority of the Local Church being set aside constantly by outside ecclesiastical forces.

For instance, Preachers are told where they can preach and can't preach, who can preach for them and who cannot preach for them, who they are to like and who they are not to like, etc. The idea among these Denominations is not the perpetration of the Word of God, but rather the perpetration of the Denomination.

From studying Paul as I have, I seriously doubt that he could have functioned in a Denominational Structure, nor even in some of the Charismatic Organizations. While he always, as stated, held in high regard his Brother in the Lord, never at any time would he tolerate anyone telling him what he could and could not do. To be sure, if what is suggested or even commanded is Scriptural, all should seek to obey that in every capacity. But if anything is demanded which is not Scriptural, it cannot be obeyed, in fact, it must not be obeyed. The criteria must always be the Word of God and the Word of God only, and not the Constitution and Bylaws of Denominations or Churches for that matter.

## THE SERVANT

The phrase, *"Yet have I made myself servant unto all,"* speaks of a voluntary submission, which is the Way of the Holy Spirit. Of course, involuntary submission, is not freedom but rather Law. However, even as we have already stated, Paul making himself a *"servant unto all,"* in no way meant that he would violate the Word of God in any capacity, that is if such were demanded by others.

What Paul is here doing, is exactly that which Jesus commanded in St. John Chapter 13. His Disciples and all others for that matter who followed Him, were to have the *"foot-washing spirit,"* which speaks of the servant spirit.

The actual rendering of this 19th Verse is, *"For being free from all men* (Gal. 1:10), *I enslaved myself to all."* In acting thus he obeyed his own principle, and really the principle of the Lord, of not abusing his liberty, but *"by Love serve one another"* (Gal. 5:13) (Farrar).

NOTES

The phrase, *"That I might gain the more,"* proclaims God's Way, which in essence, is the very opposite of man's way.

Men rule, the Lord serves! Religion captivates, the Lord sets free! Men demand, the Lord appeals! Men are prideful, the Lord is humble! Men hate, the Lord loves! Men seldom forgive, the Lord always forgives! Men forgive conditionally, the Lord forgives unconditionally!

We win people to the Lord, even as Paul here suggests, not by hitting them over the head with a Bible and telling them they are going to Hell if they don't change, which while certainly true, nevertheless, succeeds only in bringing out a contentious spirit. Rather, we win people to the Lord simply by loving them, and letting them know we love them. We do that by being their servant, it is just that simple!

(20) "AND UNTO THE JEWS I BECAME AS A JEW, THAT I MIGHT GAIN THE JEWS; TO THEM THAT ARE UNDER THE LAW, AS UNDER THE LAW, THAT I MIGHT GAIN THEM THAT ARE UNDER THE LAW;"

The phrase, *"And unto the Jews I became as a Jew, that I might gain the Jews,"* proclaims Paul here describing the innocent concessions and compliances which arise from the harmless and generous condescension of a loving spirit.

He never sank into the fear of man, which made Peter at Antioch unfaithful to his real principles. He did not allow men to form from his conduct any mistaken inference as to his essential views. In other words, he waived his personal predilections in matters of indifference which only affected *"the infinitely little"* (Farrar).

An example of him *"becoming as a Jew,"* could pertain to the vow of the Nazarite which he entered into, and is recorded in Acts 21:21-26. In fact, that is an excellent example of what he is speaking about.

The phrase, *"To them that are under the Law, as under the Law, that I might gain them that are under the Law,"* could pertain to him circumcising Timothy (Acts 16:3), which is a perfect example.

The idea is, that he followed the glorious example of the Lord Who laid aside the expression, but not the possession of Deity in order to become a human and give Himself as our Perfect Sacrifice (Phil. 2:5-8).

In fact, even though Paul seldom alludes to such directly, if one really studies his life and

Ministry, one finds that much of what he said and did actually pertained to the Life and Ministry of Christ. Of course, that should be obvious, but due to the fact that Paul is not so vocal concerning such, oftentimes it is overlooked.

## WHY DID HE NOT MAKE THIS EMULATION OF CHRIST MORE OBVIOUS?

First of all, I think he did not desire in any manner to take away from the original Twelve. Inasmuch as he was not actually there, respecting the Life and Ministry of Christ, and the Twelve were (plus the Seventy), this meant they were the authorities in this matter, and not himself. Therefore, it would be best that he speak of Christ in a more secondary way, exactly as he did.

Another reason may well have been the Judaizers. These individuals from Jerusalem, who were actually followers of Christ, but also of the Law of Moses, claimed that Paul among other things was not an Apostle, because he had not personally known the Lord. Of course, being an Apostle, or almost anything else for that matter, had little to do with that; but still, Paul did not want to leave any impression concerning Christ that was not absolutely one hundred percent.

In other words, to quote Jesus Personally and constantly, as he no doubt could have done, might have made it seem as if he was trying to claim personal knowledge which he really did not have. We find amazing wisdom in this man, which of course, could only have been given by the Holy Spirit.

(21) "TO THEM THAT ARE WITHOUT LAW, AS WITHOUT LAW, (BEING NOT WITHOUT LAW TO GOD, BUT UNDER THE LAW TO CHRIST,) THAT I MIGHT GAIN THEM THAT ARE WITHOUT LAW;"

The phrase, *"To them that are without Law, as without Law,"* refers to Gentiles. He is meaning that he never wilfully insulted their beliefs (Acts 19:37) nor shocked their prejudices, but on the contrary, judged them with perfect forbearance (Acts 17:30) and treated them with invariable courtesy (Farrar).

But yet in this, Paul never compromised the Gospel, while at the same time showing Love to all people, whomever they may have been. Still, his preaching at times made people very angry and because of the simple fact that the Gospel of Jesus Christ is very controversial. While at the same time, had those who grew very angry at Paul, truly knew Paul, they would have found an individual who was extremely agreeable, gracious, kind, and considerate. It should be understood, that almost everywhere he ministered, there were tremendous upheavals, even near riots at times. To be sure, such was not caused by a compromising Message.

The phrase, *"Being not without Law to God, but under the Law to Christ,"* speaks to the fact that despite Gentiles not being under the Law of Moses, which they were not, still were subject to the Law of God through Jesus Christ, as are all men.

To accept Christ, puts one under the *"Law of Christ,"* which satisfies the Mosaic Law as well, for Christ was the End of the Law. Irrespective, whether it be Jew or Gentile, all conclude in Christ, simply because He is the Saviour of man, the Redeemer of lost souls. To be sure, to be under *"the Law of the Spirit of Life in Christ Jesus,"* is the greatest privilege there could ever be for anyone (Rom. 8:2).

The phrase, *"That I might gain them that are without Law,"* pertains to two things:

1. One does not have to keep the Law of Moses to be Saved.
2. The Gospel is for all, both Jews and Gentiles, with all coming on the same basis — by Faith (Eph. 2:8-9).

(22) "TO THE WEAK BECAME I AS WEAK, THAT I MIGHT GAIN THE WEAK; I AM MADE ALL THINGS TO ALL MEN, THAT I MIGHT BY ALL MEANS SAVE SOME."

The phrase, *"To the weak became I as weak, that I might gain the weak,"* refers to Paul not availing himself of some of his Christian Liberties, simply because of the possibility of causing weak Christians to stumble.

The phrase, *"I am made all things to all men, that I might by all means save some,"* means that he did all within his power to be like those he tried to win, except to enter into sin with them.

## ERRONEOUS CONCLUSION

Some have used this Passage attempting to justify their actions respecting certain things of the world. In other words, this is one of the favorite verses of many in the Christian Music Industry, as they seek to imitate the Rockers, etc. They dress like them, act like them, conduct themselves like them, and attempt to style their songs and music like them, again, as stated, claiming they are obeying the Scripture that they might win them to the Lord.

First of all, I do not personally know of anyone who has been won to the Lord in this manner; therefore, to use that as an excuse is most feeble at best.

One cannot win the drunk to the Lord by drinking with him, or the gambler by gambling with him, or the drug addict by becoming an addict with him, and neither can unbelievers be won to the Lord by the Christian adopting their heathenistic, paganistic, sinful, ungodly ways.

## THE HOLY SPIRIT

First of all, people are won to the Lord by the Gospel being preached to them under the Anointing of the Holy Spirit, with the Holy Spirit then convicting them of their sin, and, thereby, awakening in them a need for Christ (Jn. 16:8-11).

Paul is merely speaking of showing kindness and graciousness to all people, whomever they may be. In no manner does he speak of sinning with them or compromising the Gospel in any way.

The Truth is, the devotees to Christian Contemporary Music so-called, do these things because they want to do these things. In their heart they want to be Rockers, etc. As well, they make a lot of money imitating the world, acting like the world, and functioning in the spirit of the world, while at the same time deceiving themselves into believing that all is well spiritually, when in fact, nothing is well.

(23) "AND THIS I DO FOR THE GOSPEL'S SAKE, THAT I MIGHT BE PARTAKER THEREOF WITH YOU."

The phrase, *"And this I do for the Gospel's sake,"* goes back to the first part of the 17th Verse. Such attitude and action, portray obviously so, that Paul is doing everything within his power to get others to Christ. His life, Calling, and Ministry, are not carried thusly out of necessity, or as mere duty, but in fact, are the very soul of his being. In other words, he lives, breathes, eats, and sleeps the Gospel of Jesus Christ. His constant attitude and action are the winning of souls. Not only constantly seeking God, he is constantly thinking in his mind how he can become agreeable to individuals, that

NOTES

they might in some way heed this of which he says.

The idea is, that if Jesus put such a value on souls that He would divest Himself of the expression of His Deity, taking upon Himself the weak robe of humanity, that surely he (Paul) must do all he can, to bring souls to Christ.

The worth of an object is the price that someone pays for that object. Considering what the Lord did in order to redeem humanity, which constituted God becoming Flesh and dying on a Cross at a place called Calvary, one can then understand, at least as far as is humanly possible, the worth of a soul. So, the idea is, if the Lord would do that, Paul surmises that whatever he sacrifices, irrespective of the cost to him, can little compare to that which the Lord did to save him and all others for that matter.

The phrase, *"That I might be partaker thereof with you,"* does not, as should be obvious, refer to Paul partaking of other's sins, etc. It does refer to him partaking as far as is possible, to the person's state, situation, difficulties, etc.

*"Partaker"* in the Greek is *"sugkoinonos,"* and means *"a co-participant, companion."* The word illustrates the deep humility of the Apostle.

## PAUL AND HUMILITY

Of all the qualities of this man, I think that the thing which stands out the most, even above his great Faith, Consecration, Dedication, or even his Zeal, is his humility. Actually, I think the closer that one gets to God, that this one attribute — humility — will become more and more obvious. If that is so, then the opposite would be the case for those who are little near to The Lord Jesus Christ.

## CHRIST AND HUMILITY

Of all the things Jesus said, the only thing He Personally said of Himself is the following, *"Take My yoke upon you, and learn of Me; for I am meek and lowly in heart: and ye shall find rest unto your souls"* (Mat. 11:29).

To think of the Lord of Glory being maltreated as He was, and worse yet, even by His Own, then one can perhaps get some understanding as to what true humility is really like.

Using Christ and Paul as examples, and above all Christ, one sees that humility is not only what we are, or rather seem to be, but as well, what we do, which is the fruit of what we are.

As someone has said, the importance of this virtue called humility springs from the fact that it is found as part of the Character of God. In Psalm 113:5-6, God is represented as being incomparably high and great, as should be obvious, and yet He humbles Himself to take note of the things which He has created, even down to the smallest of that Creation (Mat. 9:29-30).

## TRUE HUMILITY

The man or woman who is of note, whatever that may be, portrays what they really are, by how they treat a person when no one is watching, who is at the lowest rung of the social and economic ladder.

After studying Paul as I have, I believe that he would have been the same man toward the lowliest of the lowly, whomever that may have been, as he was toward the highest of the highest, whomever that may have been. In other words, he showed no partiality, but rather kindness to all.

(24) "KNOW YE NOT THAT THEY WHICH RUN IN A RACE RUN ALL, BUT ONE RECEIVETH THE PRIZE? SO RUN, THAT YE MAY OBTAIN."

The question, *"Know ye not that they which run in a race run all, but one receiveth the prize?"*, presents the Apostle using a well-known sporting event to serve as an illustration.

This of which he speaks were the triennial Isthmian games, which were the chief glory of the City of Corinth, and which at this period had even thrown the Olympic games into the shade. In the Greek, the words *"in a race,"* are rather *"in the Stadium."* Actually, the traces of this Stadium are still visible among the ruins of Corinth (Farrar).

The lesson being taught by Paul is that of self-denial. He speaks of those who train diligently for the particular races; however, even though all train, only one will win the prize, which is obvious.

The *"prize"* was merely a garland or wreath placed upon the head, along with whatever fame accompanied such. However, whatever, it was fleeting, and faded about as soon as the leaves on the wreath.

## PRESENT TIMES

Continuing to use the example of sports, even though modern athletes receive large sums of money, at least those who are proficient at their sport, still, whatever it is they are getting only lasts for a period of time, which is nothing in comparison to Eternity. The Truth is, nothing in this world can even remotely compare with the Eternal consequences of the human soul. But sadly, almost all preparations are made for the here and now, with almost nothing made for that which has a value so far beyond comprehension that it beggars description. That is why Jesus said, *"For what is a man profited, if he shall gain the whole world, and lose his own soul? Or what shall a man give in exchange for his soul?"* (Mat. 16:26).

The phrase, *"So run, that ye may obtain,"* presents two things:

1. First of all, the Holy Spirit through Paul is saying that Believers should allow the zeal and diligence of the training of Athletes to be an example concerning our Christian experience. However, the question is, how many Christians actually think as much of their Christian experience as athletes do of their efforts to excel in their sport?

Of course, only the Lord knows the answer to that, but from even preliminary observation, the answer would have to be *"precious few."*

What would take place in your life as a Believer, if in fact, you did begin to show the same diligence toward serving Christ, as an athlete does in his preparation?

I happen to somewhat know the answer to that question, because I have sought diligently to apply myself in this fashion, not meaning that one can earn something from the Lord by so doing, but rather that I may draw nearer and nearer to Him, and in every capacity. For me to attempt to explain the wonder and the joy of the nearness of Christ, His fulfillment within my life, the way He has changed and is changing things in my life which need to be changed, and above all filling my soul with His Presence, is truly as Peter said, *"Joy unspeakable and full of Glory"* (I Pet. 1:8).

It is truly a *"peace . . . , which passeth all understanding"* (Phil. 4:7).

2. Unlike the contestants in the world, every single runner in this race of Bible Christianity wins a prize. As well, it is not something that is merely transitorial, but rather Eternal. In other words, we are speaking of Eternal Life, a New Creation in Christ Jesus, the privilege of

NOTES

being in His Presence forever and forever. So, I would hope that it is understandable that the races run in this world, as famed as they may seem for the moment, are literally nothing in comparison to this race of serving God.

(25) "AND EVERY MAN THAT STRIVETH FOR THE MASTERY IS TEMPERATE IN ALL THINGS. NOW THEY DO IT TO OBTAIN A CORRUPTIBLE CROWN; BUT WE AN INCORRUPTIBLE."

The phrase, *"And every man that striveth for the mastery is temperate in all things,"* pertains to both the athlete (or whatever endeavor one may pursue in the world), as well as the Child of God. The fact is, millions in the world do *"strive for mastery,"* but only a precious few Christians do such, most being satisfied to just know they are Saved. In other words, precious little time and attention are given over to our lives lived for God, at least by most Christians.

*"Striveth"* in the Greek is *"agonizomai,"* and means *"to fight, to struggle, to contend with an adversary, to labor fervently."* Actually it is from this Greek word which we get our word *"agony or agonizing."*

*"Mastery"* refers to *"excelling to the place of victory."*

*"Temperate"* in the Greek is *"egkrateuomai,"* and means *"to exercise self-restraint."*

Now that the Believer is in Christ, actually a New Creature, the strength to be temperate is provided automatically, and this actually means exercising self-restraint in all things, i.e., *"appetite, passions, work, hobbies, in other words, any secular thing that we do in this world."* With the Lord, it is not possible for one to overdo the Christian life, but in fact, it is altogether possible, to overdo in all other things and situations.

## TEMPERANCE

Temperance can be described as *"self-control."* Actually, Solomon said, *"He that hath no rule over his own spirit is like a city that is broken down, and without walls"* (Prov. 25:28). In effect, it is the *"mastery"* of self. It can be described, therefore, as *"self-mastery,"* or *"self-restraint."* It is found in the verbal form, in Genesis 43:31, when Joseph exercised self-restraint respecting the presence of his Brethren, when they appeared before him.

Clement of Alexandria said: *"Not abstaining from all things* (lawful things), *but using sparingly such things as one has judged should be used."*

Chrysostom applies it to *"one mastering passion of tongue, hand and unbridled eyes."*

NOTES

## THE END DOING OF GOD'S WILL

The principle involved is that of the concentration of all man's powers and capabilities upon the one end of doing God's Will, in and through whatever Calling God appoints, and the renunciation of everything either wholly or to whatever degree necessary, however innocent or useful it may be in its proper place, that interferes with one's highest efficiency in this Calling.

Not limited to abstinence, it is rather the power and decision to abstain with reference to some fixed end, and the use of the impulses of the physical, as servants for the moral life (Rom. 6:19).

## BUT TO ALL

It does not refer to any one class of objects that meets us, but to all; to what concerns speech and judgment, as well as to what appeals to sense.

It is properly an inner spiritual virtue, working into the outward life, incapable of being counterfeited or replaced by any abstinence limited to that which is external.

## SOME THINGS ARE TO BE LAID ASIDE TOTALLY

Moderation which is another way to explain temperance, does not refer to immorality of any nature. Anything that is unlawful, one might say, to a Believer, must not be engaged in at all. So, temperance as used in the Bible, actually speaks of legitimate things, and as stated, but never the things of God. It is impossible to get too much of God, too much of His Work, too much of His Presence, too much of His Leading. In true terms, such does not exist.

While too much exercise in the physical sense can hurt a person, it is not possible for one to have too much exercise in the spiritual sense.

The phrase, *"Now they do it to obtain a corruptible crown,"* pertains, at least as Paul is here addressing the subject, to a laurel wreath placed on the head of the winner of the race, etc. In fact, these garlands or wreaths were so corruptible that they began to whither the moment they were made.

However, the spirit of the Text, has to do as well with every single achievement in which one may engage respecting all that is not of God, even though harmless within itself, even as this race to which Paul refers. Other than that which is of God, all things are corruptible, i.e., *"a transitorial stage."* In other words, irrespective as to how it may look at the present, it has no lasting power. So, for a man to put his eggs in that basket, is to automatically lose — but yet that is what most of the world does!

## AN EXAMPLE

When Billy Sunday, the famed Evangelist of the early 1900's, came to Christ, it was under most unusual circumstances.

He was a professional baseball player, with the team then called, if I remember correctly, the *"Chicago White Stockings."* He was reputed to be one of the fastest men to ever run the bases.

On a Saturday Night, he and three other friends, fellow team members, walked into a part of downtown Chicago. They stood on the street corner, listening to a Church Service taking place across the street, actually a Street Service.

To make the story brief, whenever the Message was concluded, and the Preacher began to give an Altar Call, the Spirit of God began to deal with Billy Sunday.

After a few moments, he turned to his fellow players and said, *"Boys, I'm going, what about you?"*

They looked at him somewhat peculiar, not really understanding what he was saying. *"Going to what?"*, they asked!

He turned and motioned toward the Preacher, signifying that he was responding to the Altar Call.

They shook their heads in the negative, even as he stepped off the curb, walked across the street, and in a few minutes time had given his heart and life to Jesus Christ.

## THE CORRUPTIBLE AND THE INCORRUPTIBLE

Of course, the world was greatly blessed by the Ministry of this one man, who saw untold thousands brought to a Saving Knowledge of Jesus Christ. What happened to the other three baseball players?

NOTES

In the Book which gave his life story, and several of his Messages, he went on to tell how those three men died a few years later from acute alcoholism. They all three died in the very prime of life, talents wasted, and the most horrible of all, their souls eternally lost.

That day when Sunday stepped off that curb to give his heart and life to Jesus Christ, there are very few in the world if any, who would have applauded him, instead telling him how foolish he was to do such a thing. In fact, that is exactly what his team members did and so did the newspapers, etc.

To them, to give up a great baseball career, to preach the Gospel, was unthinkable, as stated, in their minds, such a waste. However, the Truth was and is, that the very opposite of what they were thinking were actually the facts.

Anything for God is eternal, while all else is the very opposite.

The phrase, *"But we an incorruptible,"* speaks to the fact that all who follow Christ will win, and even above that, will win that which is eternal, i.e., Eternal Life, i.e., the privilege of being in the Presence of God forever. As well, if one wants a fuller description of this, one would do well to read Revelation, Chapters 21 and 22.

It is described in I Peter 5:4 as *"A Crown of Glory"*; in II Timothy 4:8, *"A Crown of Righteousness"*; in James 1:12 and Revelation 2:10, *"A Crown of Life."*

(26) "I THEREFORE SO RUN, NOT AS UNCERTAINLY, SO FIGHT I, NOT AS ONE THAT BEATETH THE AIR:"

The phrase, *"I therefore so run, not as uncertainly,"* speaks of this Christian race, with the eye fixed on a definite goal (II Tim. 1:12).

Paul speaks of himself as knowing and understanding the tremendous significance of this race, notwithstanding the difficulties, but yet knowing for certain what is ahead respecting the finished course.

If one is to notice, those who do not know God, have little understanding of the past, claiming mankind as the product of evolution, and no knowledge whatsoever of the future. In fact, such is a great void, a great unknown to them. If a person does not have the Bible view of things, he in fact has no view, or else a view which has no meaning. Consequently, he is ever trying to investigate his roots, and trying to figure out the future. So he turns to evolution for the past and star trek for the future, both products incidentally of fiction.

The phrase, *"So fight I, not as one that beateth the air,"* now presents the Apostle changing from the metaphor of running a race to that of boxing.

## BEATING THE AIR

*"Beating the air,"* in the case of the Believer, pertains to one not knowing and understanding what the Word of God says concerning this race. The idea is, that we fully know and understand our opponent. In this case, Paul is speaking literally of the physical body which must have its appetites and passions brought under control. Before Salvation, the physical body is king, and in every manner. This speaks of no preparation whatsoever for the soul and the spirit but all for the physical man. Hence, it is preened and petted, with the beautiful people of Hollywood so-called, setting the standard. Consequently, the works of the flesh are rampant.

However, upon the sinner coming to Christ, everything changes. The soul and the spirit are to be nourished by the Word of God and Prayer, which both speak of Communion with Christ, and Communion that is constant. The physical body although neutral, still is the danger point, because it is through the five senses that Satan carries out the sins of the heart. Therefore, if the Believer does not understand this, he will find himself failing the Lord, i.e., sinning, and then to stop the failure will take measures which are not Scriptural, fighting furiously, i.e., *"beating the air,"* but actually not landing a blow at all on the real opponent which is the *"Sin Nature."*

Many Believers not understanding the Sin Nature, as it is described in Romans, Chapters 6, 7, and 8, have tried to defeat the flesh (sins of the flesh) by the vehicle of the flesh (self-effort), and always fail. So, what does Paul mean by the word *"fight?"*

## THE GOOD FIGHT OF FAITH

The only *"fight"* that the Christian is to engage, is *"The good fight of Faith"* (I Tim. 6:12). And as well, as is stated, it is a *"good fight,"* because if fought properly, the Believer always wins.

NOTES

Consequently, the guarantee of victory, and victory every time at that, brings an unending joy to the soul.

## WHAT EXACTLY IS THE GOOD FIGHT OF FAITH?

Every attack by Satan against the Believer, and irrespective as to its nature whether physical, domestical, social, financial, material, or spiritual, is for the purpose of destroying the Believer's Faith, or at least severely weakening our Faith. That is Satan's objective, in other words, to cause us to quit believing God. Actually, the major difference between unbelief and belief is, that unbelief quits, while belief will not quit, despite the setbacks, difficulties, and even at times, failures. Faith keeps believing because that is what Faith is. As well, we fail, if in fact that has been the case, because we have not engaged this conflict properly, even as Paul is here addressing.

I think I can say without fear of exaggeration or contradiction, that precious few, if any, engage in this fight correctly to start with, and to be frank, sometimes the strict Biblical manner as designed by the Holy Spirit does not come easily or quickly. It didn't with Paul, even as the Seventh Chapter of Romans bears out. However, he persevered, even as we must, and the Lord gave him the great Truths of Romans, Chapters 6 and 8.

The idea is, respecting this fight of Faith, that we oppose Satan by the Power of the Holy Spirit (Rom. 8:1-2), and not by the flesh (anything which is not directly of God, irrespective of the good intentions), which is bound to fail (Rom. 8:3-4, 8).

The Believer who does not properly understand what Jesus has done for him at Calvary and the Resurrection, is bound to fail, even though he fights furiously. In fact, the harder he fights, the more he fails, simply because sin or the Sin Nature does not yield to the *"flesh"* but only the *"Holy Spirit."*

## THE DOUBLE CURSE AND THE DOUBLE CURE

So, what do we mean by all of this?

The physical body is the instrument by which the Sin Nature works. However, that does not mean that the body is evil, in fact, it is neutral. The Truth is, the physical body can be used for either Righteous acts or unrighteous acts. That is the reason Paul said, *"Neither yield ye your members* (members of your physical body) *as instruments of unrighteousness unto sin: but yield yourselves unto God, as those that are alive from the dead* (saved from sin), *and your members as instruments of Righteousness unto God"* (Rom. 6:13).

Paul also told us to *"Present our bodies a living sacrifice, holy, acceptable unto God, which is our reasonable service"* (Rom. 12:1).

So, it is not the body that is actually evil, but rather that it is the vehicle through which Satan works, that is if we allow him to do so, even as Paul is here addressing. So, how is the physical body brought under control?

THE DOUBLE CURSE

There is a double curse, so to speak, upon man, which refers to the: A. Sin debt hanging over his head (a debt owed to God), and as well, B. The grip of sin.

The manner in which Satan has a hold upon individuals is because of sin in their lives, i.e., original sin. Due to that sin debt hanging over unredeemed man, he has a grip on man, actually making slaves of mankind. In fact, that grip cannot be broken by education, proper environment, money, or any other method, at least as far as the world is concerned.

However, when Jesus died on Calvary, He paid the sin debt for every single human being who has ever lived and who shall live. All that remains is for the sinner to accept what Jesus did at Calvary (Jn. 3:16; Rom. 10:9-10, 13; Eph. 2:8-9; Rev. 22:17). Of course, if the sinner does not accept this of which the Lord has done, the sin debt remains, and the person will die eternally lost.

COMPLETELY BROKEN

When Jesus died and rose from the dead, the double curse of the sin debt and the sin grip were completely broken, with the new Believer now enjoying a spotless, perfect Righteousness granted to him by the Lord without works or merit, and because of his simple Faith in Christ (Rom. 8:1-2).

SO WHAT EXACTLY IS THE DOUBLE CURE?

The double cure is that Jesus: A. Paid the sin debt, which B. Automatically broke the grip of sin in the believing sinner. However, even though the sin debt is forever paid, and can never again be attributed to the Believer, it is possible for the sin grip to come back. Let us explain!

NOTES

The new Believer is now Born-Again, and in fact, a New Creature in Christ Jesus (II Cor. 5:17). However, that does not mean that Satan will never bother him again.

In fact, Satan comes back very soon probing for a weakness, enticing, and tempting the Believer, with all, after a while failing in one way or the other. Of course, when that happens, we always have recourse in Christ, asking His forgiveness, which He always does, and without reservation (I Jn. 1:9; 2:1). As well, there are no limitations on the number of times that God will forgive. Nevertheless, it is not God's Plan for the Believer to be constantly sinning, asking forgiveness, and then being forgiven. That is the road to disaster.

When the Believer fails he instantly knows it, simply because he is now the possessor of the Divine Nature which was imparted to him at Conversion. This new nature, or Divine Nature is what changes the Believer completely, actually making a New Creature out of him. All of this, is the Work of the Holy Spirit in the Believer (Jn. 3:3, 5-8). So, the moment the Believer fails, due to this Divine Nature in him, he automatically feels awful, and must quickly run to Jesus for forgiveness and mercy (I Jn. 2:1-2).

WHAT THEN?

At this particular stage, the Believer knows that the failure (whatever it may be) must stop. Therefore, he then begins to set things in motion which he thinks will solve his problem. To be sure, the things he sets in motion are normally good, such as fasting, prayer, greater study of the Word, more faithful Church attendance, to be anointed with oil and prayed for, etc., which within themselves always benefit the Believer and greatly so. However, he finds to his dismay that his sin problem (failure in a certain area) is not only not being stopped, but is rather getting worse. Consequently, he becomes very confused, not understanding why. In fact, he fights all the harder, but no lasting victory is forthcoming, and simply because he is *"beating the air."*

While all these things we have named are very good, and actually a necessity for spiritual growth, they are only good in their rightful place, and cannot take the place of what Jesus did at Calvary and the Resurrection. In fact, when the Believer does this, he turns these great Biblical qualities such as prayer, fasting, etc., into *"works."* In other words, by this method, whether he realizes it or not, he is attempting to earn a victory which has actually already been purchased for him by Christ. So, to do these things, as helpful as they may be in other areas, thinking that such will give us victory over sin (over the Sin Nature), we in effect are trying to add to the Finished Work of Christ, which is impossible. When this is done, and all of us have done it, the only thing we actually do is *"frustrate the Grace of God"* (Gal. 2:21). The Grace of God which works through the Holy Spirit cannot function, simply because we are trying to do this thing ourselves, i.e., bring about victory. We keep trying and we keep failing, even with the failures, as stated, getting worse and worse, despite our efforts, which not only frustrate the Grace of God, but frustrate us as well.

In fact, millions of Christians are in this very state, failing, and not really knowing why they are failing, and simply because they are fighting with every ounce of strength they have. However, they are not fighting the good fight of Faith, but as stated, rather, just *"beating the air."*

## THE ANSWER!

The Believer is in this condition, and please believe me these are not isolated cases, but actually affect the majority of Christendom, simply because he does not quite understand what Calvary is and what it did.

Most Believers put Calvary in the past. It was good and necessary for their Salvation, but they little understand that it also presently has everything to do, even on a daily basis, with their Sanctification, i.e., victory over sin, plus everything else. As stated, they understand the first part of the cure (Jesus paying the sin debt), but they little understand how the grip of sin is broken, and can remain broken. For this latter to be brought to bear, even on a daily basis, the Believer must evidence continued Faith in Christ, and the following is the way that it's done.

Paul outlined it in Romans 6:3 when he said, *"Know ye not* (and regrettably many don't know), *that so many of us as were Baptized into Jesus Christ were Baptized into His Death?"*

NOTES

Please understand, that this has nothing to do with Water Baptism, but actually means that when Jesus died on Calvary, that we were actually in Him experiencing His Death, even though we were not actually there. This is the reason that it must be by Faith. We must believe that we were in Him when He died. We must also know and understand, that all of this was done for us, in other words for sinners, and not for Himself.

So, the Believer must believe on a daily basis, a continued basis, that we were in Christ when He died, and as well, were buried with Him by Baptism into Death (Rom. 6:4).

When this happened, our *"old man was crucified with Him, that the body of sin* (Sin Nature) *might be destroyed, that henceforth we should not serve sin"* (Rom. 6:6).

The Believer must understand this, believe this, and know it for certain in his heart, mind, soul, and spirit.

As well, when *"Christ was raised up from the dead* (Resurrected) *by the Glory of the Father,"* we as well, were raised up with Him, and in fact, in Him, that *"We also should walk in newness of Life"* (Rom. 6:4).

This means that all the sin grip was broken, as well as the sin debt being paid. So at that time, we must *"reckon* (count or compute) *ourselves as being dead indeed unto sin, but alive unto God through Jesus Christ our Lord"* (Rom. 6:11).

In other words, this is something we should not look at as merely having happened when we got Saved, which it certainly did, but as well that it is applicable to us on a daily, ongoing basis.

Now that the Believer knows and understands this, he realizes that the sin debt is paid and the sin grip is broken. He then allows the Holy Spirit to energize all of this, by simply having Faith that the Holy Spirit will guarantee all that Christ has done, seeing that it is carried out in our life. We are to believe this each and every hour of each and every day, letting Him do the work, as He Alone can do.

## AT THIS POINT . . .

Knowing and understanding what Jesus has done for us, and allowing the Holy Spirit to guarantee the work within our lives, guarantees victory in every capacity. In other words, that thing we have fought so hard, and failed every time, now falls off without any struggle or fight whatsoever. The answer is simple, the Holy Spirit does it, and with Him it is easy. With us it is impossible, because the flesh is no match for the Powers of Darkness.

It is done without struggle, only by *"fighting the good fight of Faith."* Now we have perpetual victory, knowing and understanding that it is all in Christ, and that Calvary and the Resurrection were not only for our Salvation respecting the Born-Again experience, but are also the guarantee of our holy walk before God, even on a daily basis.

So, Calvary was important not only when we got Saved, but it is also very important on an ongoing basis, as I hope by now is obvious.

So, the Believer can *"fight"* wrongly, which means by the effort of the flesh, and find himself merely *"beating the air,"* which means he loses every time, or he can *"fight"* correctly, which means to *"fight the good fight of Faith,"* which pertains to leaning totally on Christ, and allowing the Holy Spirit to have His Way, and win every time. He cannot do both!

(27) "BUT I KEEP UNDER MY BODY, AND BRING IT INTO SUBJECTION: LEST THAT BY ANY MEANS, WHEN I HAVE PREACHED TO OTHERS, I MYSELF SHOULD BE A CASTAWAY."

The phrase, *"But I keep under my body, and bring it into subjection,"* presents Paul as keeping the body as a slave to the soul, not permitting the soul to be the slave of the body.

*"Keep"* in the Greek is *"hupopiazo,"* and means *"to hit under the eye, to buffet or disable."*

*"Subjection"* in the Greek is *"doulagogeo,"* and means *"to be a slave-driver."*

Even though the body is neutral, still, and as stated, it is through the body that Satan carries out his evil designs. Considering all that Paul has said about the human body, I think it would be best if we did a little more detailed study on this very important subject.

## THE OLD TESTAMENT

The two Hebrew words most often translated *"body"* are *"basar"* and *"beten."* The basic meaning of *"basar,"* usually translated *"flesh,"* is *"animal musculature."* The word is used often in this sense in discussions regarding the Old Testament Sacrifices.

*"Basar"* occurs about 270 times in the Old Testament, with its meaning extended to indicate the human body, living things, and life itself.

The Hebrew word *"beten"* is translated *"belly"* in the King James and indicates human inward parts. Often it means *"womb."*

Old Testament Passages use the word *"body"* in the full range of meanings the word expresses in English, from physical self even to the corpse.

## THE NEW TESTAMENT

The Greek word for body is *"soma."* It occurs almost 150 times in the New Testament, 92 of them in the 13 Epistles known to be Paul's.

The word *"ptoma,"* meaning *"body"* or *"corpse"* is found in Matthew 24:28; Mark 6:29; and, Revelation 11:8-9.

In the Gospels and non-Pauline Letters, *"soma"* is used much like *"basar"* in the Old Testament. This includes the sense of *"corpse"* (Mk. 15:43; Lk. 17:37; Heb. 13:11) and the concept of physical life (Mat. 10:28; Lk. 12:4).

*"Soma"* is also used to indicate the sphere in which we live out our life on Earth.

The Pauline Letters introduce a number of special theological uses of *"soma."* Some of these pick up and amplify concepts implicit in the Old Testament. Some uses are distinctly related to fresh revelations of the Gospel. These special uses are discussed in the following paragraphs.

## JESUS' BODY

Several times Paul emphasizes the fact that Jesus lived and died in the body. Paul reminded the Colossians, "(God) *has reconciled you by Christ's Physical Body through death to present you holy in His Sight"* (Col. 1:22).

This Teaching is vital because some people in New Testament times argued that Jesus *"came"* only in appearance. He seemed to be human, they said, but was not. However, it is vital to the Gospel that Jesus became human in fact, died in fact, and was raised in fact.

Thus, Paul and the Writer of Hebrews insist that *"We have been made holy through the Sacrifice of the Body of Jesus Christ once for all"* (I Cor. 10:16-17; 11:27, 29; Eph. 2:16; Heb. 10:10; I Pet. 2:24; 3:18; 4:1).

NOTES

## THE BODY OF SIN

Paul was deeply aware of the ruin the Fall had caused, even as we are now studying. Humanity is trapped, forced to live with a moral warp, pulled always toward sin and rebellion. This warp is not located in our physical nature alone.

*"Body"* is not used here in that sense, nor does Scripture separate the human being into isolated elements that we can label body, soul, and spirit.

Rather, the *"body of sin"* is the person himself in his bodily existence; that is, his life on Earth, warped and twisted by a sinful nature inherited from our first parents.

The *"body of sin"* calls our attention to man's nature as sinner and acknowledges the weakness that we must struggle with (Rom. 6:6; 7:24; 8:10).

## THE MORTAL BODY

This phrase also emphasizes the weakness inherent in human nature. But despite our weakness, Believers are told, *"Do not let sin reign in your mortal body so that you obey its evil desires"* (Rom. 6:12).

Victory is possible because now the Holy Spirit has come to empower us. *"If the Spirit of Him Who raised Jesus from the dead is living in you, He Who raised Christ from the dead will also give life to your mortal bodies through His Spirit. . . ."* (Rom. 8:11; Gal. 2:20).

## THE IMPORTANCE OF LIFE IN THE BODY

Against the backdrop of man's lost and hopeless condition, the news that God can render sin inoperative and bring life where there was only death is stunning indeed.

Our bodily life is the arena in which spiritual death has been experienced. Now our bodily life is to be the arena in which the new life that comes from Jesus must also be demonstrated.

Because we have been raised with Jesus, we are told, *"Do not let sin reign in your mortal body so that you will obey its evil desires"* (Rom. 6:12). Each of us is to offer our *"bodies as living sacrifices"* (Rom. 12:1), so that *"Christ will be exalted"* in our bodies (Phil. 1:20; I Cor. 6:16-20).

## THE EXPRESSION OF SIN AND THE EXPRESSION OF HOLINESS

Those who view spirituality as something related only to a person's inner life are in tragic error. It is in our bodily life on Earth that sin found expression; and it is in our bodily life on Earth with all of its relationships that Christ's Gift of Newness is also to find expression and in which Jesus is to be revealed (II Cor. 4:11).

Spirituality can never be isolated from the daily life you and I live in the world. A certain wise Christian used to say that the Christian should be natural in spiritual things, and spiritual in natural things.

## THE RESURRECTION BODY

Paul also speaks of a Resurrection Body (I Cor. 15:33-44; Phil. 3:21).

We will not be disembodied in the eternal state but will experience Eternal Life in a Resurrection Body that will be like Jesus' Own (I Jn. 3:1-2) (Richards).

The phrase, *"Lest that by any means, when I have preached to others, I myself should be a castaway,"* has been misinterpreted by some.

## OF SERVICE AND REWARDS

Some have interpreted Paul's statement as meaning that the Apostle feared that if he did not properly fulfill his Apostolic Office, he would be cast away by God into an eternity of suffering in the Lake of Fire. But there are three things that forbid this meaning.

1. The context is not one of Salvation, but of service and rewards. Salvation is a free gift with no strings tied to it. It was made possible by the infinite price that was paid at the Cross. Rewards are earned by service.

## CASTAWAY

2. The Words of Paul's Saviour are pertinent here, *"Him that cometh unto Me, I will in no wise cast out"* (Jn. 6:37).

The word *"castaway"* in our Corinthian Passage is an entirely different word from the two Greek words translated *"cast out,"* as used by Jesus, the latter being literally *"cast out into the outside."* The words *"in no wise"* are from a double negative in the Greek which does not make a positive assertion but means a most emphatic *"NOT."*

## APOSTOLIC SERVICE

3. The word *"castaway"* is from a word compounded of two parts of speech, a word meaning *"to put one's approval upon after one has tested something,"* and the Greek letter Alpha, which

when prefixed to a word makes the word mean the opposite to that which it originally meant.

The word means *"disapproval after having failed to meet the requirements."* Paul was speaking of his Apostolic service. He was careful as that should not meet the requirement of His Lord and that, therefore, he be disapproved, not as a Christian, for Salvation is not in view here, but as an Apostle, for his service was the thing that was being weighed in God's Balances.

Before Paul could be disapproved as to his standing in Christ, namely, as to his Salvation, his Lord would have to be disapproved. But He is God Himself, in His Holy Character unchangeable.

THE RACE

Paul was running a race. To win a crown, his service must be acceptable. Greek runners would compete for a prize, a crown of oak leaves. If they broke training, they would be disqualified, forbidden to race.

The Greek word translated *"castaway"* is this word *"disqualified,"* disapproved after having failed to meet the requirements. Paul served his Lord with an intense earnestness lest he be disqualified, forbidden to exercise his Ministry. Let us who are serving the Lord do our very best to please Him lest we be set aside and someone else put in our place (Wuest).

*"You have longed for sweet peace, and for Faith to increase, and have earnestly, fervently prayed;*
*"But you cannot have rest, or be perfectly blest, until all on the Altar is laid."*

*"Would you walk with the Lord in the Light of His Word, and have peace and content alway;*
*"You must do His sweet Will to be free from all ill; on the Altar your all you must lay."*

*"Oh, we never can know what the Lord will bestow of the blessings for which we have prayed,*
*"Till our body and soul He doth fully control, and our all on the Altar is laid."*

*"Who can tell all the Love He will send from above! Oh, how happy our hearts will be made!*
*"Oh, what fellowship sweet we shall share at His Feet, when our all on the Altar is laid."*

NOTES

CHAPTER 10

(1) "MOREOVER, BRETHREN, I WOULD NOT THAT YE SHOULD BE IGNORANT, HOW THAT ALL OUR FATHERS WERE UNDER THE CLOUD, AND ALL PASSED THROUGH THE SEA;"

The phrase, *"Moreover, Brethren, I would not that ye should be ignorant,"* presents an oft used phrase by the Apostle (Rom. 1:13; 11:25; I Cor. 12:1; II Cor. 1:8; I Thess. 4:1).

The word *"moreover"* means *"rather"* or *"for."*

In I Corinthians, Chapter 8, he warned mature Believers about the danger of offending new Converts. In I Corinthians, Chapter 10, he basically warns new Converts about the dangers facing them.

He teaches them historically that the possession of great privileges is no safeguard, and that the seductions, even of idolatry, must not be carelessly despised.

The *"ignorance"* to which he refers is not ignorance of the facts, but of the *"meaning"* of the facts.

Many Corinthians had, and many modern Believers have, the idea that they could sin all they desired and still maintain their claim on Christ. They felt that, inasmuch as they had been baptized in water and had taken the Lord's Supper, this guaranteed their Salvation, irrespective as to what they did. Paul here tells them that such is not the case (I Cor. 8:4-13; 10:16-33).

The phrase, *"How that all our fathers were under the cloud, and all passed through the sea,"* presents the Apostle showing the Corinthians that the Israelites of old also had their sacred ordinances, even similar to Christians. But yet, when they joined with idolaters, committing the sin of idolatry, they were judged, in a sense, by the Lord just like the heathen. The Lord doesn't save *"in sin,"* but rather *"from sin."*

The reason that the Corinthians, and likewise modern Christians, were going into false doctrine is because of a faulty understanding of the Cross. The only answer for sin is the Cross. If the Cross is misunderstood, the Believer will, in some way, go into sin, whether Israel of old, or modern Christians now (Rom. 6:1-14; 8:1-2, 11; Gal. 6:14).

Paul repeats the word *"all"* five times, because he wishes to show that, though *"all"* partook of Spiritual Blessings, most (vs. 5) fell irrespective of them.

He says, *"Our fathers,"* not only because he was himself a Jew, but also because the Patriarchs and the Israelites are spiritually the fathers of the Christian Church.

The *"cloud"* mentioned here by Paul, speaks of the Divine Presence. The Greek phraseology implies that they went under this cloud, i.e., *"Divine Presence,"* and remained under its shadow. The *"cloud"* is the *"pillar of cloud"* (Ex. 13:21), of which David says, *"He spread a cloud for a covering"* (Ps. 105:39). The idea of the *"cloud"* symbolizes the Baptism with the Holy Spirit.

The *"Passing through the Sea,"* symbolizes the Baptism in Water.

The emphasis is, as we shall see, that *"All"* experienced these great things from the Lord, but all did not respond in the same way to the Grace of God which had delivered them from Egypt. It is the same with modern Believers.

(2) "AND WERE ALL BAPTIZED UNTO MOSES IN THE CLOUD AND IN THE SEA;"

The phrase, *"And were all Baptized unto Moses,"* presents the Law-Giver as a Type of Christ. They identified with Moses as their Divinely-appointed Leader.

The phrase, *"In the cloud and in the Sea,"* once again symbolizes the Baptism with the Holy Spirit and Baptism in Water.

All of these people were Baptized, at least in a symbolic sense, which recorded the greatest Baptismal scene of all time, numbering some three million people or more. However, the terminology here also shows that Water Baptism is a symbolic act. If Baptismal Regeneration (the act of Water Baptism saves) were truly Scriptural, all these people would have been Saved. However, we will see that all were not Saved.

Just as now, Old Testament people were Saved by Grace through Faith as individuals, not in some corporate, ceremonial, ritualistic fashion as some teach (Rossier).

(3) "AND DID ALL EAT THE SAME SPIRITUAL MEAT;"

NOTES

By *"spiritual meat,"* Paul is speaking of the Manna, here a type of the *"Lord's Supper."*

(4) "AND DID ALL DRINK THE SAME SPIRITUAL DRINK: FOR THEY DRANK OF THAT SPIRITUAL ROCK THAT FOLLOWED THEM: AND THAT ROCK WAS CHRIST."

The phrase, *"And did all drink the same spiritual drink,"* refers to the Smitten Rock (Ex. 17:6; Num. 20:11; Ps. 78:15). Both the *"meat* (Manna)*"* and the *"drink"* were *"spiritual,"* because of its Source which was the Lord, and not because of its nature.

Whereas *"Moses"* was a Type of Christ in His High Priestly Work of Salvation, the *"Rock"* is a Type of Christ in His Role as Baptizer with the Holy Spirit (Mat. 3:11).

The phrase, *"For they drank of that Spiritual Rock that followed them,"* proclaims the fact that the *"Smitten Rock"* followed the Miracle of Manna from Heaven (Ex. Chpts. 16 and 17).

The words *"For they drank,"* say literally, *"They were drinking,"* implying a continuous gift.

Of the Rock following them, says literally, *"Of a spiritual following Rock."*

There is a Jewish legend, that says the original Smitten Rock at Rephidim (Ex. 17:6), followed them throughout their entire wilderness journey and supplied water for them.

The legend continues, by claiming that this Rock was round, some 15 feet high, and rolled itself up like a swarm of bees, and that, when the Tabernacle was pitched, this *"Rock"* came and settled in its vestibule, and began to flow when the Princes came to it and sang, *"Spring up, O well; sing ye unto it"* (Num. 21:17).

Is the legend true?

We do know as stated, that the Rock was first smitten at Rephidim (Ex. 17:6), and again at Kadesh (Num. 20:11), as the crow flies, a distance of approximately 200 miles, and then at Beer (Num. 21:16), which is another approximate 100 miles further on, actually very close to the border of Canaan.

The phrase, *"And that Rock was Christ,"* presents Paul speaking in a spiritual sense instead of the physical sense, i.e., *"The Rock typified Christ."*

So we know that Christ was following them or rather leading them, although unseen, except in the cloud by day and fire by night. Consequently, they experienced tremendous and mighty Miracles, as is always the case when Christ is present.

There is some small evidence that the Jewish legend is true, which certainly was possible; however, the evidence probably lends toward the spiritual view, that Christ met their needs wherever they were and in whatever manner was needed or desired. He could easily do such without a literal Rock following them around, although such definitely was possible.

(5) "BUT WITH MANY OF THEM GOD WAS NOT WELL PLEASED: FOR THEY WERE OVERTHROWN IN THE WILDERNESS."

The phrase, *"But with many of them God was not well pleased,"* presents a tremendous understatement. As well, it would probably be better translated *"Most of them,"* for all perished with the exception of Caleb and Joshua (Num. 26:64-65). In Hebrews 3:17 the Word used is *"They fell"* (Farrar).

## WERE ALL OF THESE PEOPLE SPIRITUALLY LOST WITH THE EXCEPTION OF JOSHUA AND CALEB?

No!

Some of them no doubt repented, which God always honors; nevertheless, a great many of them, as should be obvious, were eternally lost, and because they persisted in unbelief. In fact, Moses could not go in and because of failure; however, he definitely was not lost, but in fact, was one of the greatest men of God who ever lived.

## LAW AND GRACE

Even though the Scripture does not plainly say, I personally feel that Law and Grace had something to do with this.

The generation that came out of Egypt (minus those under 20 years old), was subject to the Law which was given at Sinai. The Law of Moses demands perfect performance, even as any Law does. Regrettably, no human being can live up to that type of performance, even Moses. In fact, only Jesus totally lived up to the Law in every respect. Consequently the Law did not inherit the Promised Land, even as it could not inherit the Promised Land. Joshua and Caleb were admitted as a result of their Faith, which is always the ingredient for receiving from God.

The generation which did in fact inherit the Promised Land, was a type of Grace. In fact, Joshua who led them in, was a Type of Christ, Who when He came, would actually be named Joshua (Joshua in the Hebrew and Jesus in the Greek).

So, I think that this of which I have mentioned, had something to do with those who perished in the wilderness. But still, those who sincerely repented, were certainly forgiven by the Lord, and even though they were not able to go into the Promised Land, were in fact Saved, as it regards their soul.

The phrase, *"For they were overthrown in the wilderness,"* actually refers to God purposely designing their destruction.

*"Overthrown"* in the Greek is *"katastronnumi,"* and means *"to strew down, to slay, to oppose."* The following Verses tell us why the Lord did this thing.

(6) "NOW THESE THINGS WERE OUR EXAMPLES, TO THE INTENT WE SHOULD NOT LUST AFTER EVIL THINGS, AS THEY ALSO LUSTED."

The phrase, *"Now these things were our examples,"* means that we are to learn from what happened then, and not make the same mistakes.

*"Examples"* in the Greek is *"tupos,"* and means, *"a die* (as struck), *a stamp or scar, a type, which should serve as a warning."*

There are many *"types"* in the Old Testament which are positive, such as the Sacrifices, which were Types of Jesus and what He did at Calvary; however, there are also negative types as here given, and meant to serve as examples. In other words, we must take a lesson from them.

The idea is, and as given by the Holy Spirit, that the punishments inflicted upon Israel will be inflicted upon Christians if they go back into sin after the example of those in the wilderness (Rom. 2:11-16; Heb. 4:1-11; 10:26-29).

The phrase, *"To the intent we should not lust after evil things, as they also lusted,"* proclaims the same results for modern Christians, as for the Israelites of old, that is, if modern Believers insist upon going into sin.

## A PURPOSED DESIGN

The idea is not failure, but rather a purposed design on the part of Believers to go into sin and to remain in sin.

*"Lust"* in the Greek is *"epithumetes,"* and means *"to set the heart upon, long for* (rightfully or otherwise, in this case otherwise), *covet and crave."* As stated, this was not something

they fell into, but something which they wanted and desired, and, therefore, went after it with a passion. The Psalmist said of them, *"But lusted exceedingly in the wilderness, and tempted God in the desert"* (Ps. 106:14). The account probably pertains to Numbers 11:4-15.

*"Evil things"* in the Greek is *"kakos,"* and means *"intrinsically worthless, depraved, injurious, bad, wicked."*

The five *"alls"* in Verse 1-4 emphasize the five downward moral steps of Verses 6-10 — the argument being that the very persons who enjoyed these five privileges were the very same who five times so deeply sinned.

The order of these examples is here moral; in Exodus, chronological. This is designed. The five successive steps are downward, and they may be recognized presently as well (Williams).

## LUKEWARMNESS TOWARD THE WORD OF GOD

1. The first step downward in the experience of the Believer who departs from the Truth, i.e., goes into Apostasy, is a lukewarmness toward the Word of God, and a desire (lust) for that which the world offers, i.e., magazines, newspapers, movies, etc. In fact, some of these things are not wrong within themselves, but only serve to show where the heart affection is (vs. 6).

## SUBSTITUTION

2. The substitution in the heart of a worldly religion — that accepted by the world — for Christ — for the heart must have a religion; so when Christ is dethroned there, an idol (a religion) is of necessity enthroned (vs. 7).

## FELLOWSHIP WITH THE WORLD

3. The third step always follows the second in this moral sphere. It is fellowship with the world. That is, spiritual adultery, for the world is Christ's great rival, for the affections of the heart, and when the rival is preferred the marriage bond is defiled (Num. 25:1-9).

Twenty-four thousand perished at that sad time, and here the Holy Spirit adds the terrible fact that 23,000 of them perished on one day alone (vs. 8).

## INFIDELITY

4. Infidelity is the fourth step (vs. 9).

NOTES

The first three downward steps lead surely to skepticism, which is the fourth step.

## THE WORLD

5. The fifth and last step is a resolution to throw Christ and the Bible aside and to go back altogether to the world (vs. 10). Israel said, *"Let us make a captain and return to Egypt"* (Num. 14:4) (Williams).

(7) "NEITHER BE YE IDOLATERS, AS WERE SOME OF THEM; AS IT IS WRITTEN, THE PEOPLE SAT DOWN TO EAT AND DRINK, AND ROSE UP TO PLAY."

The phrase, *"Neither be ye idolaters, as were some of them,"* presents Paul warning the Corinthians, plus all other Believers as well, and for all time. Idolaters are worshipers of man-made deities. So, the similarity between the Pagan feasts at Corinth and the sin of Israel must have been very evident (Rossier).

The idea is this: The Corinthians were arguing over eating meat offered to idols, etc. Some were flouting their Christian liberty, while others were offended by such. Paul addressed this situation, proclaiming the fact that what God had created was to be enjoyed, and that in fact, these idols were nothing, just the work of men's hands.

## IDOLATRY

Christian liberty can be taken too far, with the Believer caught in a snare of the Devil, in this case *"idolatry."* If such were not possible for a Believer to do, then the Holy Spirit through the Apostle would not have addressed himself accordingly.

The phrase, *"As it is written, the people sat down to eat and drink, and rose up to play,"* is taken from Exodus 32:6.

Had the Israelites of old been questioned regarding their worship of the Golden Calf, the worship of Moloch, Remphan, Baal-Peor, etc., they would probably have put forth sophisticated pleas in their own favor, saying that they were not worshiping idols, but only paying honor to cherubic emblems of Jehovah (Farrar).

*"Play"* in the Greek is *"paizo,"* and means *"to sport,"* used euphemistically for the worst concomitants of a sensual nature-worship (Ex. 32:3-6), which resembled the depraved and orgiastic worship of Aphrodite Pandemos at Corinth.

NOTES

## IDOLATRY AS PORTRAYED IN THE OLD TESTAMENT

The story of the experience of Israel, which ought to be extremely important to all Believers especially considering that their experiences are ultimately linked to our Salvation, could be told for the most part in terms of a tension between a spiritual conception of God and worship, the hallmark of the genuine Faith of Israel, and various pressures, such as idolatry, which attempted to debase and materialize Israel's consciousness of God and practice of true worship.

It is never found in the Old Testament, as ascending from idolatry to the pure worship of God, but rather the very opposite, a people possessing a pure worship and a spiritual theology, being lured aside by religious seductions, which almost always centered up in idolatry.

## NEVER IDOLS

If we consider the broad sweep of evidence for the worship of God as it regarded the Patriarchs, we find it to be an involvement of the Altar and of Prayer, but never of idols. There are certain events, all associated with Jacob, which might appear to show Patriarchal idolatry. For example, Rachel stole her Father's *"teraphim"* (Gen. 31:19). By itself, this, of course, need prove nothing more than that Jacob's wife had failed to free herself from her Mesopotamian religious environment. However, if these objects were of legal as well as religious significance, which they probably were, the possessor of them would hold the right of succession to the family property.

This accords well with the anxiety of Laban, who does not appear otherwise as a religious man, to recover them, and his care, when he fails to find them, to exclude Jacob from Mesopotamia by a carefully-worded treaty (Gen. 31:45).

## AGAIN WITH JACOB

Again, it is urged that Jacob's pillars (Gen. 28:18; 31:13, 45; 35:14, 20) are the same as the idolatrous stones with which Canaan was familiar. However, the interpretation is not inescapable. In other words, the pillar at Bethel is associated with Jacob's vow (Gen. 31:13), and could more easily belong to the category of memorial pillars, which actually had nothing to do with idols (Gen. 35:20; Josh. 24:27; I Sam. 7:12; II Sam. 18:18).

Finally, the evidence of Genesis 35:4, often used to show Patriarchal idolatry, actually points to the very opposite, the recognized incompatibility of idols with the God of Bethel.

Jacob must dispose of the unacceptable objects before he stands before God. That Jacob *"hid"* them is surely not to be construed as indicating that he feared to destroy them for reasons of superstitious reverence. Such thinking is to allow suspicion to govern proper exegesis if we do more than assume that this was the simplest, as well as the most effective, way of disposing of noncombustible objects. In other words, if they were made of metal, which they probably were, burying them was all he could do.

## THE MOSAIC PERIOD

The whole Narrative of the Golden Calf (Ex. Chpt. 32) reveals the extent of the contrast between the True Worship of God which stemmed from Mt. Sinai and the form of religion congenial to the unregenerate heart. The True Worship of God, which is in Spirit and in Truth, up beside any form of idol worship is incompatible. That of Sinai is emphatically without any type of symbolism or form, in other words, and again, in Spirit and in Truth.

Moses warned the people (Deut. 4:12) that the Revelation of God vouchsafed to them contained no *"form,"* lest they corrupt themselves with images. This is the essential Mosaic position, as recorded in the Ten Commandments (Ex. 20:4; 34:17).

The prohibition of sorts in Deuteronomy 4:12 was mostly in the realm of a warning. Actually, it is correct to speak of a similitude or *"form"* of the Lord, as Deuteronomy 4:12 and Numbers 12:8 have the same Hebrew word *"t'muna"* (*"form"*) in common. However, for Israel to carry this over into practice regarding a *"form,"* as it pertains to God, could only involve corruption of Truth and Life.

## THE SECOND COMMANDMENT

This is a striking Testimony to the nature of Israel's worship. In fact, the Second Commandment was unique in the world of its day, and the failure of archaeology to unearth a figure of *"Yahweh"* (while idols abounded in every other religion) shows its fundamental place in Israel's worship from Mosaic days.

It is a most significant thing that when Israel turned to idolatry, it was always necessary to borrow the outward trappings from the surrounding Pagan environment. In other words, there was absolutely nothing in the Law of Moses which gave vent to any form or idol as it related to Jehovah.

For instance, the Golden Calves made by Jeroboam (I Ki. 12:28) were well-known Canaanite symbols, in other words borrowed from those religions, and in the same way, whenever the Kings of Israel and Judah lapsed into idolatry, it was by means of borrowing from the surrounding Nations.

However, there was a tendency to corrupt the use of something which in itself was lawful, for instance the superstitious use of the Ephod (Judg. 8:27) and the Cult of the Serpent (II Ki. 18:4).

## THE MODERN PRACTICE OF IMAGE WORSHIP IN THE CATHOLIC CHURCH

Even though the following has been given in another of our Volumes, due to its significance it is repeated here.

The worship of Saints and Images is an integral part of the Roman Catholic Religion. Let us examine it as the Roman Catholic Church teaches and proclaims it — and then let us look at it in the light of the Word of God.

## THE TEACHING OF THE ROMAN CATHOLIC CHURCH TODAY

The Roman Catholic Church teaches that:

1. The Saints function as mediators between the faithful and God.

2. We should address prayers to the Saints and kneel before them to obtain their favor.

3. The Saints are pleased to see their images venerated and adorned with costly treasures, and they will recompense the faithful who are generous in their worship.

4. The images of the Blessed Virgin and the Lord Jesus Christ may be venerated under different names. This can give rise to competition between different images of the same person.

5. According to the Catholic position, *"Saints"* are individuals of the New Testament (or later martyrs or notable persons of *"The Church"*) who have died and subsequently been declared to be Saints by the Pope.

NOTES

## A GREAT PROBLEM

In this enlightened age it is difficult to realize that the majority of Catholics are unaware of the direct contradiction between a belief in an Omnipotent God and the worship of Saints as advocates and intercessors.

In a conversation between an Evangelical and several Roman Catholics, the following inquiry was raised:

*"Everyone accepts that the Saints are finite beings — not only on Earth but in Heaven as well. So how can finite beings hear the prayers of men who are on the Earth? If one would stop to think about this, it would seem impossible for a finite being to hear the prayers of not just two or three people, but those of multiplied thousands who are all praying at the same time.*

*"The only way they could hear so many thousands of prayers, and discern the heart attitudes of all of these people, is if they were both Omniscient and Omnipresent. In other words, each Saint would have to be God in order to accomplish this."*

When this question was put to the Roman Catholic Representatives, they did not know how to reply. Finally, after a whispered conference, one of them offered:

*"There is no difficulty. Even if the Saints can't hear our prayers, God can and He could reveal them to the Saints."*

Dare we anticipate the resulting conclusion in this dialogue?

This would then mean that we would be approaching the Saints through God — instead of God through the Saints.

The idea becomes more absurd the further we pursue it.

The very thought of individuals speaking to frail and finite humans — and expecting them to carry their ideas to God — is ludicrous. The Word of God states clearly that we can go directly to the Father, at any time, in the Name of the Lord Jesus Christ (Jn. 16:23).

## WHERE DID THE CATHOLIC WORSHIP OF SAINTS AND IMAGES ORIGINATE?

The Catholic System of Patron Saints is nothing more nor less than a continuation of ancient heathen beliefs in gods devoted to days, occupations, and the various needs of human life. Since the worship of Saints is really a perpetuation of these false gods, Romanism is patently guilty of worshiping other gods — a practice that is condemned repeatedly in Scripture.

By the Tenth Century some 25,000 Saints had been canonized by the Roman Catholic Church. Of course, by this time Rome had hopelessly insinuated Pagan religions into Christianity.

## SUBSTITUTE A CHRISTIAN-SOUNDING NAME

To make the Apostasy less obvious, the Leaders of the Roman Catholic Church substituted Christian-sounding names that were similar to the original Pagan names.

For example, the goddess Victoria of the Basses-Alps was renamed St. Victoirie. The Pagan god Osiris was renamed St. Onuphris. Apollo was renamed St. Apollinaris, and the heathen god Mars became St. Martine.

We are told that one of the best preserved of the ancient Temples in Rome is the Pantheon, which was originally dedicated to *"Jove and all the gods."* It was reconsecrated, however, by Pope Boniface IV to the *"Mother of God and all the Saints."* An edifice formerly consecrated to the Greek god Apollo now is displayed proudly at the Church of St. Apollinaris.

Where the ancient Temple of Mars in Rome once stood, we now find the Church of St. Martine. Rome simply adopted the heathen gods into the so-called Christian Church, renaming them as their worship continued uninterrupted.

Just as the Pagans worshiped idols or statues of their gods, so does the Roman Catholic Church utilize statues in their worship.

In many cases the same statue that was worshiped as a Pagan god was rechristened with the name of a Christian Saint, and worship continued. The statue of Jupiter, for example, was slightly changed and retitled *"Peter."*

Through the centuries more and more statues have been crafted (and venerated) until today there are Churches in Europe that contain as many as several thousand statues. However, whether in a great Cathedral, a small Chapel, or on the dashboard of an automobile, these are still idols and are absolutely forbidden by the Word of God.

NOTES

## NOT THE HINT OF SUCH IN SCRIPTURE OR IN THE EARLY CHURCH

It was not until the Fifth Century that pictures of Mary, Christ, and the Saints were made and used as objects of worship.

Scripture specifically condemns idol worship in countless places, as there is not a hint or a suggestion in the Word of God that the Early Church deviated from these age-old injunctions.

## THE VOICE OF THE ELDERS IN THE EARLY CHURCH

Irenaeus (about A.D. 130-202), a pupil of Polycarp (who sat at the feet of the Apostle John), said:

*"As the Church has received liberally from the Lord, so let it minister liberally, and not ask to do anything through the invocation of Angels, or through enchantments and other perverse rarities, but let prayers be addressed purely, clearly, and openly to the Lord, from Whom are all things, invoking the Name of our Lord Jesus Christ."*

Clement of Alexandria, a Greek Theologian (about A.D. 150-215), said:

*"It is the height of foolishness to pray as though to gods to those who are no gods at all, for there is but One Good God, to Him only do we and the Angels pray."*

In another place he said:

*"Every image or statue should be called an idol for it is nothing but vile and profane material, and for this reason and to remove idolatry by the roots, God has forbidden the use of any image or likeness of anything in Heaven or on Earth, and has also forbidden the making of such images, and for this reason we Christians have none of these material representations."*

Origen, Greek teacher and writer (about A.D. 185-254), said:

*"The Angels are greatly interested in your Salvation. They have been given as helpers to the Son of God, but all prayers to God, whether they are supplications or thanksgiving, should be raised to Him through Christ, the High Priest, Who is above all Angels . . . men do not know the Angels so it is unreasonable to address prayers to them instead of Christ Who is known of men. And even were we to know the Angels, we should not be allowed to address our prayers to anyone except to God, the Lord of all Creation, Who is sufficient for all, and we*

*come to Him through our Saviour, the Son of God."*

The same writer said in another place:

*"In the reproof of those who trust in the Saints, I would say, 'Cursed be the man that trusteth in man' (Jer. 17:5), and 'It is better to trust in the Lord than to put confidence in man' (Ps. 118:8). If it is necessary for us to have confidence in anyone, let us leave all others and trust in the Lord."*

Cyprian (martyred about A.D. 258), Bishop of Carthage (about A.D. 248-258) declared:

*"Why bow down before images? Lift up your eyes and heart to Heaven; that is the place where you should seek God."*

Athanasius, a Bishop at Alexandria and the father of Orthodoxy (about A.D. 300-373), said:

*"It is written, 'God (is) my Rock; in Him will I trust; He is my shield, and the Horn of my Salvation' (II Sam. 22:3), and 'The Lord also will be a Refuge for the oppressed, a Refuge in times of trouble' (Ps. 9:9). And how many similar words do we find in the Sacred Scriptures! Should anyone reply that these are Prophecies that apply to the Son, which may be true, then let them admit that the Saints do not venture to call any created being their help and refuge."*

Elsewhere Athanasius declared:

*"The invocation of idols is a sin, and anything that is sinful at the beginning can never be good later."*

## AUGUSTINE

Augustine, Bishop of Hippo (about A.D. 354-430), said:

*"Let not our religion be the worship of the dead, for if they lived a holy life, it is impossible to imagine that they desire such honors, rather they would wish that we should render our worship to Him through Whom we should be partakers with them of Salvation. Therefore we should honor them by imitating them — not by worshiping them.*

*"The only Image of Christ that we should make for ourselves is to keep before us His humility, patience and kindness, and endeavor to make our lives like His in all things. Those who go in search of Jesus and the Apostles in mural paintings, far from conforming to Scripture, fall into error."*

Jerome (about A.D. 343-420) who translated the Old Testament directly into Latin from Hebrew (the Vulgate Bible), quoted a letter from Epiphanius in which he stated the following:

*"In a part of the country that I visited I found a candle placed in the door of a Church over which was painted an Image of Christ and another of a Saint. I was displeased that, in this defiance of Holy Scripture, the image of a man should be hung up in the Church of Christ, and I cut the candle down, advising the Sacristan that it would be put to better use at the funeral of some poor person."*

NOTES

## THE USE OF IMAGES CONDEMNED BY MANY

The use of images was condemned by all in the Early Church and even condemned as late as the Synod of Elvira (A.D. 305), the Council of Frankfort (A.D. 794), and the Council of Rouen (A.D. 1445).

This later Assembly in its Seventh Canon condemned the practice of praying before images with names such as Our Lady of Piety, Our Lady of Help, or Our Lady of Consolation.

It said:

*"Such practices tend to lead to superstition, as though there were more power in some than in others."*

Desiderious Erasmus of Rotterdam (about A.D. 1466-1536), a Dutch Scholar held in high esteem by the Roman Catholic Church, was right when he said:

*"No one who bows before an image or looks at it intentionally is free from some kind of superstition; and not only so, but if he only prays before an image."*

## THE FOLLOWING ILLUSTRATIONS OF SUPERSTITION AND PRAYING TO SAINTS WERE COPIED FROM A ROMAN CATHOLIC PAPER PUBLISHED IN 1930.

1. Two Gossips were talking in confidential tones to each other at the end of the street. *"What troubles we've been through! You know all about it. But listen, I put great confidence in Our Lady of Purity and I've committed all our troubles to her."*

*"You don't mean to say,"* said the other, *"that you've gone to Our Lady of Purity? Why, I would never confide in her, that would be the last thing I would do."*

*"Why ever not?",* asked her companion.

*"Well, look. I always confide in the Mother of God of Sorrows. She has been through great affliction and understands my troubles. I wouldn't have the same confidence in Our Lady of Purity — she lacks experience!"*

2. A young woman entered a Church as an older woman with bowed shoulders and wrinkled skin was coming out.

*"Good morning, Grandmother. How early you are today."*

*"Yes, you are right. Seven months ago I promised the Virgin of Sorrows to take her a taper and I have at last taken it. But what a problem! I had to pass in front of the Virgin of the Rosary, and I was so afraid that she might notice that I was taking the taper to the other one. I hid it under my apron as I passed by, but even so I am afraid she may have seen it. What a trial! And we are too poor to afford one for each."*

## WHAT DOES THE BIBLE SAY?

*"Ye shall make no idols nor graven image, neither rear you up a standing image, neither shall ye set up any image of stone in your land, to bow down unto it: for I am the Lord your God"* (Lev. 26:1).

*"Be not deceived: neither fornicators, nor idolaters . . . shall inherit the Kingdom of God"* (I Cor. 6:9-10).

*"For there is One God, and One Mediator between God and men, The Man Christ Jesus"* (I Tim. 2:5).

*"Neither is there Salvation in any other: for there is none other name under Heaven given among men, whereby we must be Saved"* (Acts 4:12).

With regard to the worship of the Saints we read:

*"And as Peter was coming in, Cornelius met him, and fell down at his feet, and worshipped him.*

*"But Peter took him up, saying, Stand up; I myself also am a man"* (Acts 10:25-26).

*"And I John saw these things, and heard them. And when I had heard and seen, I fell down to worship before the feet of the Angel which shewed me these things.*

*"Then saith he unto me, See thou do it not: for I am thy fellowservant, and of thy Brethren the Prophets, and of them which keep the sayings of this Book: worship God"* (Rev. 22:8-9).

NOTES

## ALL TRUE CHRISTIANS ARE SAINTS

There is no indication in the Word of God that a person becomes a Saint after he dies. In fact, it is not the Pope who makes someone a Saint, it is God. In Scripture, Saints are always living people — never the dead.

For example, when Paul wrote to the Ephesians, his Letter was addressed *"To the Saints which are at Ephesus"* (Eph. 1:1).

Likewise, the Book of Philippians was written *"To all the Saints in Christ Jesus which are at Philippi"* (Phil. 1:1).

The early Christians in the Church at Rome were called *"Saints"* (Rom. 1:7; 16:15), as were the Christians who lived at Corinth (I Cor. 1:2; II Cor. 1:1).

Consequently, if a person wants a Saint to pray for him, he should find a Christian and ask him to join him in prayer, for all True Christians are Saints.

Anytime a person endeavors to contact people who have died, it is a form of spiritualism. The Bible repeatedly condemns any attempt to commune with the dead.

*"There shall not be found among you . . . an enchanter* (one who uses incantations), *or a witch, or a charmer, or a consulter with familiar spirits, or a wizard, or a necromancer* (one who entreats the spirits of the dead). *For all that do these things are an abomination unto the Lord"* (Deut. 18:10-12).

*"When they shall say unto you, Seek unto them that have familiar spirits, and unto wizards that peep, and that mutter: should not a people seek unto their God? For the living to the dead? . . . If they speak not according to this Word, it is because there is no Light in them"* (Isa. 8:19-20).

## WHAT ABOUT THE MIRACLES AND THE SHRINES?

I am sure, after reading this, that some will say, *"But what about the Miracles that have been performed by the Intercession of the Saints?"*

These consist of statues that weep (supposedly), form tears on faces, or produce (alleged) Miracles. The Virgin of Lourdes is the most publicized I suppose.

Actually, there is absolutely nothing in the Word of God that even hints at such a thing. God has never healed or performed Miracles or done any kind of good works through inanimate objects, except in the case of Paul's handkerchiefs and aprons, as described in Acts 19:12. And this one isolated case is not an example of worshiping or venerating an idol or image.

Any person visiting Lourdes presently, will be met by a carnival atmosphere. This is, of course, totally foreign to the Word of God and the Work of God. There are no true Miracles at Lourdes, no true Healings or cures or anything else of this nature. There may be emotional reactions, but that is as far as it goes with the following exception.

Satan, who causes sicknesses by demon oppression (Acts 10:38; Lk. 13:11-16) can take off what he puts on without opposing himself or casting himself out. When he can damn a soul by getting a person to deny the essentials of the Bible that will save the soul, then it is to his advantage to deceive by taking away sickness at times.

## SATAN IS THE MASTER OF DECEPTION

Many accept false religions that promise healing and other benefits. Satan cooperates with these religions which he himself has founded to deceive men. He can even bring about a withdrawal of the sickness if he so desires, from people without God being involved in the process. Such people naturally think they are in the true religion. They reject Christ and see no need of being saved from sin or of following the Word of God. They will be damned for doing so, Satan having won their souls.

One of the major works of Satan is the work of deception, and, in this vein, along with other efforts, he is leading much of the world astray.

Yes, we do believe in Miracles. We believe in Healing. We believe that God answers Prayer. But we believe that it must come about in a Biblical way.

Jesus said a long time ago:

*"Come unto Me* (Jesus Himself — not some Angel or dead Saint) . . . *and I will give you rest, Take My yoke upon you, and learn of Me* (not some Angel or dead Saint) . . . *and you shall find rest unto your souls"* (Mat. 11:28-29).

## THE WORD OF GOD

God uses living men and women to pray for the sick — and He does answer prayer when it is offered according to His Holy Word.

NOTES

*"Is any sick among you? Let him call for the Elders of the Church; and let them pray over him, anointing him with oil in the Name of the Lord:*

*"And the Prayer of Faith shall save the sick, and the Lord shall raise him up"* (James 5:14-15).

The worship of Saints and Images has absolutely no foundation in the Word of God. It is an excursion into superstition and paganism, which will further enfold its web of deceit around the follower of Roman Catholicism.

*"In that day ye shall ask Me nothing. Verily, verily, I say unto you, Whatsoever ye shall ask the Father in My Name, He will give it you.*

*"Hitherto have ye asked nothing in My Name: Ask, and ye shall receive, that your joy may be full . . . For the Father Himself loveth you, because you have loved Me, and have believed that I came out from God"* (Jn. 16:23-24, 27).

(8) "NEITHER LET US COMMIT FORNICATION, AS SOME OF THEM COMMITTED, AND FELL IN ONE DAY THREE AND TWENTY THOUSAND."

The phrase, *"Neither let us commit fornication, as some of them committed,"* once again is a warning against immorality.

The idol worship of Old Testament times, included sexual immorality, and during Paul's day it was the same. In fact, Temple Priestesses were nothing more than prostitutes. However, any and all types of fornication are sin irrespective as to whether it is involved with idol worship or not.

The phrase, *"And fell in one day three and twenty thousand,"* is derived from Numbers 25:1-9.

The account in Numbers records twenty-four thousand (Num. 25:9); however, the following could be the explanation:

Paul said the twenty-three thousand fell in one day, while the twenty-four thousand given in Numbers could include all who died over a period of two or three days, etc., or the twenty-four thousand could include the many leaders who were executed and their heads hung up before the Lord, while the twenty-three thousand were those who died as a result of the plague. This we do know:

The Jews in Paul's day had some information respecting the Old Testament regarding details, which we do not now have. For instance, Peter and John recorded David as having written the second Psalm, whereas the superscription of that Psalm gives no identification. So, they had information we do not now have (Acts Chpt. 4).

(9) "NEITHER LET US TEMPT CHRIST, AS SOME OF THEM ALSO TEMPTED, AND WERE DESTROYED OF SERPENTS."

The phrase, *"Neither let us tempt Christ, as some of them also tempted,"* presents Christ as identified with the Angel which went before the Israelites, whom they were specially warned not *"to provoke,"* because *"My Name is in Him"* (Ex. 23:20-21).

The word for *"tempt"* means *"tempt utterly," "tempt beyond endurance"* (Ex. 17:2, 7; Num. 14:22; 21:5-6) (Farrar).

The phrase, *"And were destroyed of serpents,"* refers to Numbers 21:5-9.

## WHAT DOES IT MEAN TO TEMPT CHRIST?

The Biblical idea of temptation is not primarily of seduction, as in modern usage, but of making trial of a person, or putting him to the test.

This is what Israel did regarding the Lord during their wilderness sojourn. They knew exactly what He had told them to do, but they pushed Him to the limit and even beyond, respecting disobedience, and disobedience of the worst kind. Their attitude and actions contained a sense of daring, as in *"we dare you,"* etc.

## A DEFIANT CHALLENGE

Not only Israel, but men test God by behavior which constitutes in effect a defiant challenge to Him to prove the Truth of His Words and the goodness and justice of His Ways (Ex. 17:2; Num. 14:22; Ps. 78:18, 41, 56; 95:9; 106:14; Mal. 3:15; Acts 5:9; 15:10).

The place named Massah was a permanent memorial of one such temptation (Ex. 17:7; Deut. 6:16). Thus, to goad God betrays extreme irreverence, and God Himself forbids it as would be obvious (Deut. 6:16; Mat. 4:7). In all distresses God's people should wait on Him in quiet patience, confident that in due time He will meet their need according to His Promise (Ps. 27:7-14; 37:7; 40; 130:5; Phil. 4:19).

(10) "NEITHER MURMUR YE, AS SOME OF THEM ALSO MURMURED, AND WERE DESTROYED OF THE DESTROYER."

NOTES

The phrase, *"Neither murmur ye, as some of them also murmured,"* proclaims one of Israel's greatest sins. In fact, of the ten plagues which came upon Israel as described in Numbers, nine of the ten were caused by murmuring or complaining. They are as follows:

1. Fire — For misuse of tongue (Num. 11:1-3).
2. Sickness — Misuse of tongue and lust for flesh (11:4-35).
3. Leprosy — Misuse of tongue and jealousy (Chpt. 12).
4. Death — Misuse of tongue and rebellion (14:28-35).
5. Sickness — Misuse of tongue and rebellion (13:31-33; 14:37).
6. Earthquake — Misuse of tongue and rebellion (16:1-3; 29-33).
7. Fire — Misuse of tongue and rebellion (16:1-3, 34-35).
8. Sickness — Misuse of tongue and rebellion (16:41-50).
9. Serpents — Misuse of tongue (21:5-9).
10. Sickness — Adultery and idolatry (25:1-9).

The Corinthians were at this time murmuring against Paul who was their Teacher and the Apostle of the Lord. To murmur against those who belong to the Lord, is to murmur against the Lord.

In essence, Paul is telling the Corinthians, and all others for that matter, that the lesson of the Old Testament should be sufficient, as to what the Lord thinks of such.

The phrase, *"And were destroyed of the destroyer,"* pertains to Numbers 16:41. Fourteen thousand seven hundred perished at that particular time.

All plagues and similar great catastrophes, as well as all individual deaths, were believed by the Jews to be the work of an Angel whom they called *"Sammael"* (Ex. 12:23; II Sam. 24:16; Job 33:22).

## IN FACT, WHO IS THE DESTROYER?

Immediately and instantly we know that it is God. While He may use any number of things, even Satan himself at times, still, God is the ultimate cause of judgment in whatever form it may take.

Of course, God in no way causes or tempts man to sin, to fail, or disobey in any manner, that always being of man's volition, notwithstanding the temptation afforded by Satan, etc. However, judgment upon sin, which must always come in one way or the other, unless security is sought in the Forgiveness and Grace of Jesus Christ, which is readily available to all who will come (I Jn. 1:9), is always from God. Even when the Lord uses Satan, which He often does, still, permission must be sought and received from God by the Evil One respecting whatever direction is to be taken (Job Chpt. 1). To not understand this, is to place God in the position of being submissive to Satan, which of course is preposterous! While Satan definitely *"steals, kills and destroys"* (Jn. 10:10), still, he can only do so by permission from the Lord.

## IS JUDGMENT SUSPENDED IN THIS DISPENSATION OF GRACE?

No!

In fact, Judgment is more pronounced now under the New Covenant of Grace, than it was under the Old Covenant. The Scripture plainly says, *"And the times of this ignorance* (under the Old Covenant) *God winked at; but now* (the day of Grace) *commandeth all men everywhere to repent"* (Acts 17:30).

The more *"Light"* that is given, the more that is required (Lk. 12:48). While Judgment was possibly more obvious in Old Testament times, and for reasons which we will not now address, still, the *"destroyer"* is ever present at this particular time, even as Paul is here warning.

Paul said, *"The Wrath of God is revealed from Heaven against all ungodliness and unrighteousness of men, who hold the Truth in unrighteousness"* (Rom. 1:18). That *"Wrath"* can be assuaged only by the Divine Protection of the Shed Blood of Jesus Christ availed by the sinner.

Tragically, most of the world denies Jesus Christ and what He did at Calvary and the Resurrection, consequently, cutting themselves off from any Divine Protection. As a result, diseases, plagues, inclement weather patterns, war, strife, criminal activity, etc., take their deadly toll on a constant basis. God can stop these things or allow them, and is constantly taking measures in one way or the other, which speaks of total and constant involvement.

Even for those who are Believers, the Lord will chastise if such is necessary (Heb. 12:5-11), with some even dying prematurely because of not properly *"discerning the Lord's Body"* (I Cor. 11:29). It certainly does *not* mean that all Christians who die at a young age fall into this category, but it definitely does pertain to some.

(11) "NOW ALL THESE THINGS HAPPENED UNTO THEM FOR ENSAMPLES: AND THEY ARE WRITTEN FOR OUR ADMONITION, UPON WHOM THE ENDS OF THE WORLD ARE COME."

The phrase, *"Now all these things happened unto them for ensamples,"* means exactly what it says, *"An example to modern Believers."*

*"Ensamples"* in the Greek is *"tupos,"* which means *"forewarning."* Warnings would not be needed if it was impossible for one to lose one's way with the Lord. We should consider this very carefully.

First of all, we know that the Holy Spirit through the Apostle is speaking to the Saints, because He uses the word *"Brethren"* (I Cor. 10:1). By the use of the word *"examples,"* and by particular examples being given, Paul is saying that what happened to Israel of old in these situations, can and will happen presently to modern Believers, that is, if they ignore the plain warnings of Scripture.

The phrase, *"And they are written for our admonition,"* once again pulls the word *"warning"* into the fore. *"Admonition"* in the Greek is *"nouthesia,"* and means *"to call attention to by implication or warning."*

The phrase, *"Upon whom the ends of the world are come,"* actually refers to the Church Age which began on the Day of Pentecost. The First Coming of Christ ushered in that period of time in which God will culminate His Redemptive activity before Jesus returns to set up His Millennial Reign on Earth. We should be sobered by understanding that we are presently living at the very conclusion of the Church Age, i.e., the time of which Paul speaks.

The phrase, *"Upon whom the ends of the world are come,"* would have been better translated, *"To whom the fulfillment of the ages has arrived."*

What has arrived?

That which has arrived is the last work or dispensation, i.e., the Church Age, i.e., the Redemptive Age, before the coming of the Kingdom Age. As stated, we are now living in the closing days of this very time.

NOTES

NOTES

## THE PEOPLE OF THE END

In these Texts as given by Paul, we have their Divinely-Ordained reason for being in Scripture. In these statements one captures a sense of Paul's view that both the historical events and the Scriptural Narrative are not simply history or isolated Texts in Scripture; rather, behind all these things lies the eternal purposes of the Living God, Who knows the end from the beginning, and Who, therefore, has Himself woven the examples into these earlier Texts for the sake of not only those who lived in Paul's day, but now as well.

Paul's statement sets the future in motion, and the new people of God, whether Jew or Gentile, bond or free, male or female, who are His by Grace alone, are the people of the End, *"Upon whom the ends of the ages have come"* and *"Toward whom all history has had its goal."* We have in these statements, the idea of the whole Old Testament pointing toward its fulfillment in God's New Covenant people. And that is why the Old Testament is our Book in particular — because it has Christ as its prime Actor and final Goal.

This does not mean that Israel, or its history, was not important in its own right, but that they stand at the beginning of the Promises of God that are now finding fulfillment at the end of the ages. Thus, all of these now exist in written form for *"our"* sakes, to warn *"us"* not to fail as they failed; for Christians stand at the end of history, at the time when God is bringing all the Divine Purposes into focus and fulfillment in Christ (Fee).

(12) "WHEREFORE LET HIM THAT THINKETH HE STANDETH TAKE HEED LEST HE FALL."

The phrase, *"Wherefore let him that thinketh he standeth,"* is addressed directly to the Corinthians, but to all other Believers as well.

Some of the Corinthians were smug in their *"knowledge,"* and were in danger of taking their Christian liberties too far, which in fact, millions have done.

*"Standeth"* in the Greek is *"histemi,"* and means *"to abide, continue or establish."*

## STANDING ON AN IMPROPER FOUNDATION

The Truth is, untold millions have built their spiritual house on a foundation of sand, instead of the solid Rock of Jesus Christ, and, consequently, will ultimately he destroyed (Mat. 7:26). I speak of improper doctrines, Church membership, Sacraments or Ordinances, good works, etc.

In fact, millions teach Baptismal Regeneration, in other words, that *"Water Baptism saves!"* Others teach that the Lord's Supper, or the Eucharist saves, as some do the keeping of the Seventh Day.

The truth is, Israel fell simply because they thought the Law could save, and, consequently, rejected Christ. If one stands on anything other than Christ, and I literally mean anything, one will be eternally lost.

To be frank, many Baptists think they are saved simply because they are Baptist. Consequently, even though they claim Christ as Saviour, for great numbers their *"standing"* is in the Baptist Church instead of Christ. The Church of Christ falls into the same category, along with certain elements of Pentecostals who think their particular Doctrines save them, etc.

Jesus Christ Alone is the Saviour, and nothing must be added to Him, and nothing must be taken from Him. If we stand on that *"Rock"* we shall never fall. All else as the song says, *"is sinking sand."*

The phrase, *"Take heed lest he fall,"* means to not merely fall from fellowship as some teach, but to fall from Eternal Salvation.

*"Fall"* in the Greek is *"pipto,"* and means *"to fall down."*

## TO FALL SPIRITUALLY

The idea of the word *"fall"* as it is used here by Paul, refers, as we shall see in this short study, to falling away from Christ. In other words, no one falls who continues to trust Christ, even though they may at times fail. As an example, Peter failed but he did not fall, while Judas failed and fell. Peter, despite his failure, continued to trust Christ, while Judas no longer trusted Him.

## WHAT DOES IT MEAN TO FALL FROM GRACE?

Paul said to the Galatians, *"Christ is become of no effect unto you, whosoever of you are justified by the Law* (seek to be justified by the Law)*; ye are fallen from Grace"* (Gal. 5:4).

In effect, this verse says, *"You who are trying to be justified by Law have been alienated from Christ; you have fallen away from Grace."*

This Passage and most of the Book of Galatians deal with the struggle in the Early Church to understand the Believer's relationship to Old Testament Law. Many zealous Jewish Christians felt that the Christian life was a matter of keeping the Law, and they brought this Doctrine to Gentile congregations.

Paul argues throughout his Letters that the key to vital Christian experience is to be found not in the Law but in Christ's living within the Believer (Gal. 2:20). We experience that relationship and know its vital power for Righteous living through Faith (Gal. 2:21). Paul points out several key issues.

Did Salvation come through the Law or through Faith (Gal. 3:1-2)? Why then expect God to abandon the Faith Principle when it comes to living as Saved men and women (Gal. 3:3)?

THE GREAT CONTRAST BETWEEN LAW AND FAITH

Then, in Galatians, Chapters 3 and 4, Paul explores the great contrasts between Law and Faith, which we will see when we arrive at Commentary on that particular Epistle.

To turn to Law as a pathway to spiritual growth is to reject the pathway of Grace. To struggle to keep the Law is to cut oneself off from Jesus, for it involves abandoning that daily Faith in Him by which Grace operates in our lives.

It is thus that Paul speaks of *"falling away from Grace."* The Christian life is a matter of Grace from first to last, and Grace is appropriated only by Faith — Faith in Christ. For the Christian to *"fall from Grace"* in this context indicates a turning from daily reliance on Jesus, which in turn results in being cut off from the victory and power which only He can give, which in effect, will conclude in the loss of one's soul, unless there is a return to Christ. It is absolutely impossible for one to live the Christian life by any method other than allowing Christ to live it through him.

THE CORINTHIANS AND THE GALATIANS

Paul uses the word *"fall"* in both cases, but with the Corinthians there being one danger, while with the Galatians there being another.

NOTES

The danger of the Corinthians was in turning their liberty into *"license,"* while with the Galatians it was the turning of their liberty into *"legalism."* Both lead to the same conclusion, *"a fall."* The idea is this:

LIBERTY AND LICENSE

The Corinthians were in danger of taking their liberty too far, thinking that nothing was wrong to them, which Paul condemns. To be frank, that problem has persisted even from the very beginning, and is no less prevalent at the present time.

Millions of modern Christians think they are Saved while continuing a life of sin. In other words, their particular Doctrines tell them that while sin may cause them to lose their fellowship with the Lord, they in fact cannot lose their Salvation, which of course Paul completely repudiates in this Tenth Chapter of I Corinthians. The True Believer cannot live a life of habitual sin. If he thinks so, the Truth is, that he has probably never been Saved to start with, or else he has fallen for the lie of Satan, even as the Corinthians were in danger of doing. Grace gives no one a license to sin, but rather gives liberty to live a Holy Life.

LIBERTY AND LEGALISM

The problem with the Galatians was Legalism, which refers to the keeping of laws or rules, which in some manner is supposed to bring about one's Sanctification or Holiness. This is what Paul was addressing in the Book of Galatians.

The Judaizers (those who claimed that one had to keep the Law of Moses as well as accept Christ in order to be Saved), had come into the Churches in Galatia spreading their Doctrine of Law-keeping.

Such a Doctrine always meets with a ready market. There is something in man, even those who are dedicated totally to Christ, which likes to think that one contributes something to one's Salvation. Consequently, keeping particular rules or laws, makes one *"feel"* holy, etc. The Truth is, such provides no Righteousness whatsoever, but rather self-righteousness. The little leaven ultimately leavens the whole, until one is no longer depending on Christ at all, but rather on his own law-keeping, whether the

Law of Moses, or laws of his own making, or the making of his Church, etc. Men love to make laws, and religious men love to make laws most of all.

So, we have these twin evils which plague the Believer in the form of *"license"* or *"legalism."* Both are deadly, leading to the same conclusion, and can actually cause one to lose one's soul.

## THE UNSCRIPTURAL DOCTRINE OF UNCONDITIONAL ETERNAL SECURITY

Is Salvation conditional or unconditional?

This question has been a cause of stormy debate among Biblical Interpreters for at least 16 centuries. It has divided the Christian world of Theology since the days of the Church Fathers. Christian Denominations today remain sharply divided over it. Doubtless the Reader will agree that the Truth on this question must be found on one side or the other. Truth is not a house divided against itself.

An impartial truth-seeker accepts facts as he finds them. He has no personal preference. I have no Doctrinal preference for any subject taught in the Bible. Let Truth be whatever it is about anything. If Salvation is unconditional, then I desire to believe it; but we must have proof for our beliefs.

The literature on this subject is immense and highly conflicting. How shall we decide between the two sides? Both claim to be right. What is Truth to one Interpreter is error to another. Denominational Teachers read a Bible Text and get different ideas from it. How can we decide what is Truth? What shall be the standard of evidence for our conclusion?

The following material on the subject of *"Unconditional Eternal Security"* is derived from the work of Guy Duty. Consequently, we are indebted to his research, scholarship, and above all, devotion to the Word of God in this great search for Truth, especially as it pertains to this particular Doctrine.

## PROVE ALL THINGS

A Bible Doctrine cannot be established merely by someone making a dogmatic statement. Doctrinal despots have done this for centuries. Even the Church Fathers were divided on conditional and unconditional Salvation. How can we know who was right? — assuming that one was right. We respect the Fathers but there was much in their writings that leave us on uncertain ground.

NOTES

The Apostle Paul said, *"Prove all things"* (I Thess. 5:21), and nothing is more important than to prove our Doctrines. So, there must be some way to prove them. If not, then we are adrift on a Sea of hopeless confusion, which means that Paul's statement is impossible of proof, which we know the Holy Spirit would not have done.

## CONDITIONAL OR UNCONDITIONAL

The point to be proved is whether Salvation is conditional or unconditional. I take the position that it is conditional, and will present an array of Biblical evidence to prove it. Using the eight worldwide adopted rules of interpretation, I will not only show that my interpretation satisfies all these rules but that the opposing interpretation violates them all.

With these rules of interpretation we shall see there is no contradiction in the Scriptures about Salvation, but that the whole Bible is bound together in a harmonious unit of Truth.

## RULES OF INTERPRETATION

This science is found in the writings of the foremost legal and Biblical authorities, both ancient and modern. They are found in the writings of Irenaeus, Master Interpreter among the Second-Century Church Fathers. They were used by the Master Expositors of the Middle Ages all the way to Luther and the Reformation Theologians who disproved Romish fallacies with them.

These rules were involved in the great doctrinal debates of the Theologians from the Council of Nice (A.D. 324) to the Council of Trent (1545-1563). It is impossible to determine the true meaning of a Bible Doctrine without them. There is nothing more important in all Biblical learning than to know how to correctly interpret that which the Holy Spirit through the Word of God teaches us.

## VIOLATION

The doctrinal errors of 19 centuries of Church history were violations of these principles. It is also true of all the false doctrines found in Christendom today. Think of any false doctrine you know about and see if it isn't true.

Christian Scientists, Jehovah's Witnesses, Unitarians, and others use these rules in the ordinary affairs of life but they will not apply them to the Scriptures. They would overthrow their Doctrines if they did. Calvinists and Seventh-Day Adventists use them when it is to their advantage to do so.

To be frank, these following rules which we will momentarily give, are used in one way or the other by all Law Courts in the Free World. If you should become involved in a Court case about the meaning of a Will, Contract, or Deed, the Court would use these rules to determine the meaning of the disputed document. In everyday reading and study, everyone uses these rules at times. You could not make sense from anything you read or write if you did not.

To be frank, exact rules are needed for an exact result. One cannot get a sure meaning with an uncertain rule. The Bible Student must not only study the Scriptures, he must decide how he will interpret them. Two persons can read the same Texts and get different ideas from them because they put different meanings upon the words.

## PROOF

A Doctrine is only as sure as the proof on which it is established, and it cannot be demonstrated as sure without these rules, which are the principles to which all logical inquiry appeals. It is by a violation of these rules that Eternal Security goes all the way from a false start to a false conclusion.

Many false doctrines are based on a single word or term. Teachers have taken a Biblical word or term and loaded it with a non-Biblical meaning. They then detached the word or term from all that the Bible teaches about it and built their Doctrine on it.

However, *"The whole Bible is a Context."* Consequently, no one has the right to speak as an authority on a Bible subject unless he knows all that the Bible teaches on that subject. When one applies the rules to all that the Bible teaches about a subject, he stands on proven ground. The Eternal Security Teachers have not done this with *"Predestination."*

## INTERPRETATION

Dr. G. Campbell Morgan is widely esteemed as *"one of the greatest Bible Expositors of the past century,"* and he said: *"We must be set free from the bondage of popular and traditional views in interpretation."*

Dr. R. A. Torrey worked with Dwight L. Moody and was the first head of Moody Bible Institute in Chicago. He wrote a valuable book on how to study the Bible, and said that if some Bible Teachers *"were practicing Law and should try in any Court of Justice to interpret laws, as they interpret the Bible, they would be laughed out of Court."*

Consequently, Augustine and Calvin, that is if Dr. Torrey was correct, would have been laughed out of Court concerning their interpretation of the Doctrine of *"Predestination."*

Solomon asked: *"Who knoweth the interpretation of a thing?"*, (Eccl. 8:1) and Peter said that no Scripture *"is of any private interpretation"* (II Pet. 1:20). No one knows the interpretation of Scripture if he has his own *"private* (personal)*"* interpretation.

For 19 centuries, many Interpreters have ignored the rules, forced their private beliefs upon the Scriptures, and claimed to have a Revelation from God. This is true of much doctrinal teaching in the world today.

Interpretation is more than knowing a set of rules, but the rules are necessary. The spiritual sense must be derived from the grammatical sense.

The following are the eight rules of interpretation:

1. RULE OF DEFINITION

Any study of Scripture . . . must begin with the study of words.

One then must define the terms and then keep to the terms defined.

In the final analysis, our theology finds its solid foundation only in the grammatical sense of Scripture. The Interpreter should . . . conscientiously abide by the plain meaning of the words.

The Bible Writers could not coin new words since they would not be understood, and were, therefore, forced to use those already in use. The content of meanings in these words is not to be determined by each individual Expositor . . . to do so would be a method of interpretation which can only conclude in error.

The Interpreter must confine the definitions strictly to their literal idiomatic (peculiar to a particular group) force; which, after all, will be found to form the best, and indeed the only safe and solid basis for proper theological deductions of any kind.

2. RULE OF USAGE

The whole Bible may be regarded as written for *"The Jew first,"* and its words and idioms ought to be rendered according to Hebrew usage.

Christ accepted the usage He found existing. He did not alter it.

Jesus of Nazareth Who was a Jew, spoke to and moved among Jews in Israel . . . He spoke first and directly to the Jews, and His Words must have been intelligible to them . . . It was absolutely necessary to view His Life and Teaching in all its surroundings of place, society and popular life.

This would form not only the frame in which to set the picture of Christ, but the very background of the picture itself.

In interpreting very many phrases and histories of the New Testament, it is not so much worth what we think of them from notions of our own . . . as in what sense these things were understood by the hearers and lookers on, according to the usual custom and dialect of the Nation.

3. RULE OF CONTEXT

Many a Passage of Scripture will not be understood at all without the help afforded by the context (other related Scriptures); for many a sentence derives all its point and force from the connection in which it stands.

Bible Words must be understood according to the requirements of the Context.

Every word one reads must be understood in the light of the words that come before and after it.

Bible Words when used out of context . . . can prove almost anything. Some Interpreters twist them . . . from a natural to a nonnatural sense. The meaning must be gathered from the context, i.e. what other Scriptures say on the same subject.

4. RULE OF HISTORICAL BACKGROUND

Even the general Reader must be aware that some knowledge of Jewish life and society at the time is required for the understanding of Gospel History.

The moment the Student has in his mind what was in the mind of the author or authors of the Biblical Books when these were written, he has interpreted the thought of Scripture . . . if he adds anything of his own, it is not proper interpretation.

NOTES

Theological interpretation and historical investigation can never be separated from each other . . . the strictest historical . . . scrutiny is an indispensable discipline to all Biblical Theology.

5. RULE OF LOGIC

Interpretation is merely logical reasoning.

The use of reason in the interpretation of Scripture is everywhere to be assumed. The Bible comes to us in the forms of human language, and appeals to our reason . . . it invites investigation, and . . . it is to be interpreted as we interpret any other Volume, by a rigid application of the same laws of language, and the same grammatical rules and analysis.

What is the control we use to weed out false theological speculation? Certainly the control is logic and evidence . . . Interpreters who have not had the sharpening experience of logic . . . may have improper notions of implication and evidence. Too frequently such a person uses a basis of appeal that is a notorious violation of the laws of logic and evidence.

It is one of the most firmly established principles of Law in England and in America that *"A Law means exactly what it says, and is to be interpreted and enforced exactly as it reads."* This is just as good a principle for interpreting the Bible as for interpreting Law.

Charles G. Finney, Lawyer and Theologian, is widely considered one of the greatest Theologians and most successful Revivalist since Apostolic times. He was often in sharp conflict with the Theologians of his day because they violated these rules of interpretation.

Finney said he interpreted a Bible Passage as he *"would have understood the same or like Passage in a Law Book."*

He stressed the need for definition and logic in Theology and said the Bible must be understood on *"fair principles of interpretation such as would be admitted in a Court of Justice."*

(Logic is the interrelation or sequence of facts or events when seen inevitable or predictable.)

6. RULE OF PRECEDENT

We must not violate the known usage of a word and invent another for which there is no precedent.

The professional ability of Lawyers in arguing a question of Law, and the Judges in deciding it, is thus chiefly occupied with a critical study of previous cases, in order to determine whether the previous cases really support some alleged Doctrine.

The first thing he (the Judge) does is to compare the case before him with precedents . . . back of precedents are the basic legal conceptions which are establishments of judicial reasoning, and farther back are the habits of life, the institutions of society, in which those conceptions had their origin . . . precedents have so covered the ground that they fixed the point of departure from which the labor of the Judge begins. Almost invariably, his first step is to examine and compare them. It is a process of search, comparison, and little more.

7. RULE OF UNITY

It is fundamental to a true interpretation of the Scripture, that the parts of a document, law, or instrument are to be construed with reference to the significance of the whole.

Where a transaction is carried out by means of several documents so that together they form part of a single whole, these documents are read together as one . . . (they are to be so read) that, such construction is to be preferred which will render them consistent. In other words, Scripture interprets Scripture, and a correct interpretation will not violate that principle. To say it another way, particular Scriptures on a particular Doctrine, will never contradict each other.

8. RULE OF INFERENCE

In the law of evidence, an inference is a fact reasonably implied from another fact. It is a logical consequence. It is a process of reasoning. It derives a conclusion from a given fact or premise. It is the deduction of one proposition from another proposition.

It is a conclusion drawn from evidence. An inferential fact or proposition, although not expressly stated, is sufficient to bind. This principle of interpretation is upheld by Law Courts.

For instance, Jesus proved the Resurrection of the dead to the unbelieving Sadducees by this rule (Mat. 21:31-32).

A proposition of fact is proved when its Truth is established by competent and satisfactory evidence. By confident evidence is meant such evidence as the nature of the thing to be proved admits.

By satisfactory evidence is meant that amount of proof which ordinarily satisfies an unprejudiced mind beyond reasonable doubt. Scripture facts are, therefore, proved when they are established by that kind and degree of evidence which would in the affairs of ordinary life satisfy the mind and conscience of a common man. Consequently the Rule of Interpretation can be summed up in eight words:

1. Definition; 2. Usage; 3. Context; 4. History; 5. Logic; 6. Precedent; 7. Unity; and, 8. Inference.

When we have this kind and degree of evidence it is unreasonable to require more.

NOTES

## VIEWS OF CHURCH FATHERS RESPECTING THE DOCTRINES OF ETERNAL SECURITY AND PREDESTINATION

It will be helpful to a right understanding of this question to know a few historical facts that lie in the background. The origin and history of a Doctrine are important to the proper understanding of the Doctrine. Many imminent names are connected with the history of Predestination and Eternal Security, but the foremost prominent are Augustine, Pelagius, Calvin, and Arminius.

### AUGUSTINE

Augustine was a Monk of the Fifth Century (354-430) in North Africa. He is generally considered at least as one of the greatest of the Church Fathers, and a Theological Master, who some even refer to as a genius. He was the dominant doctrinal authority of the Middle Ages, and his influence throughout the Christian world of Theology has been enormous. He generally controlled the leaders of the Church, and his influence extended for more than a thousand years.

Augustine's Doctrine of Predestination may be briefly expressed in the following quotations:

*"Before the creation of the world, God formed the resolution to redeem certain men in Christ and to apply to them His Grace. There is a 'good pleasure of His (God's) Will,' which has nothing to do with human merits, not even with such as were foreseen by God. On the contrary, the determination of God is the ground upon which the good will is imparted to this or that one . . . Predestination is the cause of Salvation. All Saving Ordinances are means for realizing it, and therefore really serve and*

*benefit only the predestinated — Only to the elect comes the effectual 'peculiar calling of the elect'. . . all, therefore, resting in the Hands of God, depends upon His Choice.*

*"Therefore, whoever has in the most provident ordering of God been foreknown, predestinated, called, justified . . . are now the sons of God and can by no means perish.*

*"The unpredestinated, or unforeknown, on the other hand, under all circumstances, fall into ruin, as parts of the masses which are lost. Even if they appear to be real Christians, called, justified, regenerated through Baptism, renewed — they will not be Saved, because they are not elected. No blame attaches to God; they are alone to blame, as they simply remain given over to their just fate.*

*"He who falls, falls by his own will; and he who stands, stands by the Will of God. In such God reveals His Justness, as in the elect His Mercy. No one is Saved unless God wills it."*

When Augustine was asked why God chooses some for Salvation and leaves other for damnation, he replied that it was God's mysterious Will, and that *"the creature must bow humbly before his Creator."*

## LOGICAL OBJECTIONS

When Augustine was confronted with logical objections that exposed the *"glaring defects"* in his system of interpretation on Predestination, he replied: *"The more difficult this is to understand, the more laudable is the Faith that believes it."*

We give due respect to Augustine, but a Doctrine is not true because it is adorned with a great name. Augustine, *"The Oracle of 13 centuries,"* was guilty of violating major rules of interpretation in his Predestination Teaching.

He had the serious weakness of other prejudiced Interpreters. He specialized on those parts of Scripture that seemed to favor his position, but he twisted or ignored other parts that went against him. He laid down rules for his opponents on other Doctrines, but he violated the same rules when teaching Predestination. He warned others about the dangers of distorting the Scriptures, but he was guilty of constantly doing the same on Predestination Scriptures. Historians friendly to Augustine wrote:

*"There is a multitude of inconsistencies and self-contradictory tendencies in his teaching (Predestination and Church, . . . Christ and Grace, Grace and Sacraments, the Knowledge of God and the Definition of God, Faith, and Love, etc.)."*

NOTES

Some Theologians followed the Augustinian ideas on Predestination but others saw through his fallacies. Others partly accepted his Theology and were called Semi-Augustinians. During the centuries of history of this hotly debated Doctrine, strong argumentation continued from both sides; but for many there was always something obscure, uncertain, and unclear about it. Confusion about the Doctrine never ceased — nor has it to our day. Multitudes today cannot accept Augustine's dictum: *"The more difficult this is to understand, the more laudable is the Faith that believes it,"* and rightly so!

## PELAGIUS

Augustine's chief opponent was a learned British Monk named Pelagius, who also lived during the Fifth Century. He opposed Augustine's Predestination and asserted the freedom of the human will to do good and evil.

He once led a Theological disputation in Rome where he refuted the Augustinian Doctrine of Predestination and asserted the freedom of the will. He argued that as God had commanded men to do what is good, he must, therefore, have the ability to do it; that is, man is free and it is, therefore, possible for him to decide for or against that which is good.

Freedom of the will consists in the possibility of committing sin or of abstaining from it. Man by nature is capable of good or evil but he must choose one or the other. Because of these views Pelagius was condemned and banished from Rome. Some Theologians went halfway with Pelagius and were called Semi-Pelagians.

## JOHN CALVIN

The Augustinian dispute continued for about 13 centuries to the time of a French Theologian named John Calvin (1509-1564). In Geneva, Calvin was a Pastor and Professor of Theology. He helped to establish a Theocratic Government there. Geneva was the center of the defense of Protestantism throughout Europe. Calvin gathered and systematized the reformed Theology of that period. Even his enemies admitted he was a brilliant Theologian.

Calvin got his inspiration on Predestination from Augustine. He developed Augustine's

Doctrine to a conclusion that is called, with other doctrinal points *"Calvinism."* Today, Calvin's Predestination is generally called *"Eternal Security."*

Calvin, like Augustine, defined Predestination as God's Eternal Decree by which God's Absolute Sovereign Will decided the eternal destiny of every individual. It was God's Absolute Predestinating Purpose that determined who would be Saved and who would be damned. Calvin admitted this was a *"horrible decree,"* but argued that it was based on God's Love and Justice.

Calvin taught, like Augustine, that *"Man therefore falls, God's Providence so ordaining, but he falls by his own fault."* He said that no cause for Salvation was to be sought other than the absolute and unconditional Will of God; and he said there was a deep mystery to this *"horrible decree."*

Calvin's writings on Predestination greatly intensified the dispute. It raged back and forth among the Theologians as it had for more than a thousand years. Synod after Synod debated the Doctrine but multitudes remain perplexed. Consequently, there is widespread perplexity about it to this day.

I quote from Calvin's Institutes Book Three, Chapter 21.

*"Predestination we call the decree of God, by which He has determined in Himself, what He would have to become of every individual of mankind. For they are not all created with a similar destiny: but Eternal Life is foreordained for some, and eternal damnation for others. Every man, therefore, being created for one or the other of these two ends, we say, he is predestinated either to life or death."*

## INCONSISTENT AND SELF-CONTRADICTORY STATEMENTS

Calvin's meaning here is forcefully evident. The facts of language are clear. But, as we shall see later, Calvin, like Augustine, made inconsistent and self-contradictory statements. It seems to me that sometimes they were on both sides of the question.

I do not see how anyone, especially those trained in precise analytical work, could get a clear and consistent picture of what they mean by Predestination according to the statements they make. If one studies their teachings thoroughly, analyzing them, one finds oneself in a foggy world of contradictory words and statements.

NOTES

In contrast, the Words of Scripture have a simplicity and clarity that even the *"wayfaring man, and the fool (uneducated) can understand." "If thou shalt confess with thy mouth the Lord Jesus, and shalt believe in thine heart that God hath raised him from the dead, thou halt be Saved"* (Rom. 10:9). *"Whosoever will, let him take the Water of Life freely"* (Rev. 22:17).

These words as found in Scripture are consistent, clear, understandable, and become confusing only if men intentionally confuse them.

Perhaps Augustine and Calvin didn't mean all that their opponents charged them with on Predestination, but their teachings are so obscure and contradictory that perhaps no one could be blamed for being confused about their meaning. Paul said: *"God is not the author of confusion"* (I Cor. 14:33). Who then is the author of this doctrinal confusion in Christianity today?

## EXPLAIN IT AWAY

It seems strange that Calvin, the Law Student, did not see the *"multitude of inconsistencies and self-contradictory tendencies"* in the Augustinian Theology he adopted.

Calvin, honest as he meant to be, found . . . the fatal facility of reading into Scripture what he wished to find there.

I am not quoting from Calvin's enemies but from a Historian friendly to him. Dean Farrar, an eminent Scholar, admitted that Calvin was one of the foremost interpreters of Scripture, but he also said:

*"Calvin had a manner in which he explains away every Passage which runs counter to his dogmatic prepossessions."*

Some of Calvin's friends couldn't go all the way with him on Predestination, even though they did believe in Unconditional Eternal Security, and were called semi-Calvinists. Full-fledged Calvinists were called Hyper-Calvinists. Many Calvinists today disagree about Predestination.

## ARMINIUS

As the Calvinist dispute continued, there appeared on the scene another important Theologian named Arminius (1560-1609). He was a

Dutch Pastor. At first he defended the views of Calvin, but further study caused him to adopt the beliefs of Calvin's opponents. He engaged in bitter arguments about Calvinism, rejecting the Augustinian-Calvinistic Doctrine of Absolute Predestination and taught Conditional Predestination. He was a powerful influence against Calvinism, and his influence extends even to our day.

During the many centuries dispute about the Doctrine, confusion was widespread. Perplexity never ceased, nor has it to our time. In an effort to settle the dispute, there was assembled (1618-1619) the famous Council of Dort, *"A Council which has no parallel in the history of Protestantism."*

The Dort Council was meant to be a general Council of all the Calvinist Churches to sit in judgment on Arminianism. The great majority of the representatives were Calvinists.

Present were 84 Theologians and 18 Secular Commissioners, whatever that is. Civil Governments sent delegates to represent their countries. Deputies were present from Switzerland, Nassau, Hesse, Bremen, Scotland, and England. The Council met in 154 formal sessions from November 1618 to May 1619. Arminius died before this Council was held. The Arminians were summoned before this Council and given a hearing, but biased from the start, the Council's decision was a foregone conclusion. The old prejudice and jealousy were fanned into hotter flames. The Arminian Doctrine of Conditional Predestination was examined and condemned. Arminius was branded a heretic. Two hundred Arminian Pastors were deprived of their Pastorates, and those who refused to be silenced were banished from their country.

## PERSECUTION

The Council Members were determined to crush the Arminian heresy, as they called it. Arminian Leaders were imprisoned. One was beheaded on the false charge of high treason. It was dangerous to oppose Calvinism, as Servetus, another Theologian, learned when Calvin and his associates at Geneva burned him at the stake as a heretic.

The Dort Council did not settle anything about the 1300 year-old dispute, as many of the important Church Councils from the Council

NOTES

of Nice A.D. 324, to the Council of Trent (1545-1563) also failed to settle doctrinal questions brought before them.

Much of this history is a sad record of dishonorable intrigue, power politics, world jugglery, and evasion of facts. The Calvinists at Dort did not answer the difficulties and objections that beset their Doctrines, nor have they to this day. What did *"Predestination"* mean? In these Councils attempt to get Scriptural definitions never ceased.

Professor Emil Brunner of Zurich, generally considered one of the world's leading Theologians said, that the best thing Christianity could do for the world would be to give it a dictionary of Biblical terms. Anyone who knows the doctrinal history of Predestination may very well agree.

The above historical sketch of the Predestination controversy should give you an idea of what it was all about. It is not necessary to take you through the long history of this complicated mass of confusion. However, a few quotations from a recent Calvinist Writer would probably be helpful.

## ARTHUR W. PINK

He wrote in his *"The Sovereignty of God"*:

*"God does not love everybody; if He did, He would love the Devil.* (p. 30) . . . *It is God Himself Who makes the difference between the elect and the non-elect* (p. 61) . . . *Faith in God's Gift, and apart from this Gift none would believe. The cause of His choice then lies within Himself and not in the objects of His choice. He chose the ones He did simply because He chose to choose them* (p. 71).

*"The New Birth is solely the Work of God the Spirit and man has no part in it. This from the very nature of the case. Birth altogether excludes the idea of any effort or work on the part of the one who is born. Personally we have no more to do with our spiritual birth than we had with our natural birth* (p. 88).

*"Again, Faith is God's Gift, and the purpose to give it only to some, involves the purpose not to give it to others. Without Faith there is no Salvation — 'He that believeth not shall be damned' — hence if there were some of Adam's descendants to whom He purposed not to give Faith, it must be because He ordained that they should be damned* (p. 101).

*"He (God) fits the non-elect into destruction by His foreordinating decrees. Should it be asked why God does this, the answer must be: to promote His Own Glory, i.e., the Glory of His Justice, Power and Wrath"* (p. 118).

On Page 119, Mr. Pink quotes Calvin:

*"There are vessels prepared for destruction, that is, given up and appointed to destruction; there are also vessels of wrath, that is, made and formed for this end, that they may be examples of God's vengeance and displeasure"* (His emphasis).

The next quotations come from his book, *"Shall Never Perish"*:

*"No man ever willed to be born into the human race, and equally impotent is he to will to separate himself from the human race . . . as it is impossible for man, by free action, to separate himself from the human race, so it is equally impossible for him, by a free act, to separate himself from God's Kingdom* (pp. 119-120).

*"Truly, once a son of mankind, always a son of mankind, and equally true, once a Child of God, always a Child of God. There is no possibility for a man, by his own will or action, to change either of these conditions . . . all who are Saved are secure for all eternity* (p. 120).

*"When one has of his own free will accepted Christ . . . he is given a new nature which makes it impossible for him to will to return to his former state* (p. 124).

*"It is taught in Ephesians 1:13-14, that after a person has believed (a finished act), he is sealed with the Holy Spirit until the Redemption of the purchased possession. This Passage once and for all rules out the argument that one must continue to believe. There is no need for continuous Faith on the part of the Saved person . . ."* (pp. 130-131).

QUESTIONS

So these questions are before us:

- Is it true that sinners are damned without freedom of will or choice?
- Is it true that the predestinated ones are *"Saved without regard to what they may or may not do?"*
- Is it true that *"if they sin, yet God so preserves His Holy Spirit in them that they can never fall entirely out of the state of Grace?"*
- Does the Bible teach that *"The unchangeableness of the Divine Decree excludes the possibility that a person could entirely fall away or be lost?"*
- Is Salvation conditional or unconditional?

In our study, let us not be Calvinists nor Arminians but Truth-seekers who accept nothing but proved facts. Paul said, as stated: *"Prove all things,"* and this includes Bible Doctrines. So let us accept only what is proved.

Our premise is this: Jesus said, *"Salvation is of the Jews."* It was of the Jews because it was founded on Jewish Covenants. These Covenants were conditional. Therefore, Salvation is conditional. *"Ye are Saved . . . if ye continue."*

SALVATION CONDITIONAL FROM THE BEGINNING

God's if-condition for Cain and Abel:

*"And in process of time it came to pass, that Cain brought of the fruit of the ground an Offering unto the Lord.*

*"And Abel, he also brought of the firstlings of his flock and of the fat thereof. And the Lord had respect unto Abel and to his Offering:*

*"But unto Cain and to his Offering He had not respect. And Cain was very wroth, and his countenance fell.*

*"And the Lord said unto Cain, Why art thou wroth? And why is thy countenance fallen?*

*"If thou doest well, shalt thou not be accepted? And if thou doest not well, sin* (a Sacrifice for sin in the form of a Lamb) *lieth at the door. And unto thee shall be his desire, and thou shalt rule over him"* (Gen. 4:3-7).

This simple illustration concerning Cain and Abel should be sufficient to convince an unprejudiced mind that acceptance with God is conditional. Here God clearly states the conditions to Cain.

Cain's Offering, the *"Fruit of the ground,"* was rejected by God. Abel's Offering, the *"Firstlings of his flock and of the fat thereof,"* was accepted. When God *"had respect"* unto Abel and his Offering, but did not have respect unto Cain and his Offering, Cain became angry and his countenance fell.

God tried to reason with angry Cain, that He did not have an unconditional preference for Abel. God's acceptance of Abel was because of his *"more excellent Sacrifice,"* in other words, that he obeyed what the Lord had previously said to do (Heb. 11:4). Cain could have done as Abel did, and he would have satisfied the conditional requirement for Offerings, and would have been accepted.

The Apostle John wrote:

*"Not as Cain, who was of that wicked one, and slew his Brother. And wherefore slew he him? Because his own works were evil, and his Brother's Righteous"* (I Jn. 3:12).

WE ARE TOLD WHY!

The Apostle told us here why Cain killed Abel. Cain was *"of that wicked one."* Cain's works were evil, but Abel's works were Righteous. Cain's Offering exhibited evil works. Abel's Offering exhibited Faith works. The world's first murder was caused by the hatred of evil worship for Righteous worship. Cain's unbelief was revealed in his *"evil works."* Abel's Faith was revealed in his *"Righteous works."*

Cain, the world's first Apostate, rejected God's *"if."* Evil Cain worshiped God but not *"by Faith,"* as Abel did, but by works which God would not accept.

All the world's religion today, as always, is divided into unbelief-worship and Faith-worship, i.e., *"The worship of God through Jesus Christ and what He did at Calvary and the Resurrection, are typified in the Sacrifices of old."*

Abel's Offering satisfied God's *"if,"* Cain's did not. That is the whole story. The Faith and Worth of Abel's Offering pleased God, and because it typified the Coming Redeemer, The Lord Jesus Christ. The unbelief and cheapness of Cain's Offering did not, because it typified the work of his own hands, in other words, claiming that he could save himself and, therefore, did not need a Redeemer.

*"By Faith Abel offered unto God a more excellent Sacrifice* (that which typified the Coming Christ) *than Cain, by which he obtained witness that he was Righteous* (because his Faith was in the Coming Redeemer instead of his own works), *God testifying* (a seal of approval) *of his* (Abel's) *gifts* (Sacrifice)*"* (Heb. 11:4).

By contrast, the Cain spirit of worship continues to our day. Jude said, *"Woe unto them! For they are gone in the way of Cain"* (vs. 11).

The *"Way of Cain"* is a system of religion. It can always be identified and marked by the fact that it has no part with God's if-condition for acceptable worship. It is Cain-worship — and it hates Abel-like worship. *"He that was born after the flesh* (Ishmael) *persecuted him* (Isaac) *that was born after the Spirit, even so it is now"* (Gal. 4:29). If Cain rejected God's if-condition so also the way-of-Cain religion rejects it today. Beware of any religion that rejects God's *"if."*

NOTES

THE READER MUST SEE

With these facts before us, can the Reader agree with the Calvinist Writers recently quoted?

If Abel had offered the same kind of Sacrifice as Cain, would he have been declared *"Righteous"* by God?

Would Cain have been rejected if he had obeyed God's *"if"* and had offered Faith-Gifts, like Abel?

Is not the same if-condition for acceptance worship required of us as for Cain and Abel?

I think the answer is obvious to all of these questions.

SALVATION CONDITIONAL IN THE ABRAHAMIC COVENANT

*"In the same day the Lord made a Covenant with Abram"* (Gen. 15:18).

*"As for Me, Behold, My Covenant is with thee"* (Gen. 17:4).

*"And I will establish My Covenant between Me and thee and thy seed after thee in their generations"* (Gen. 17:7).

It will be helpful if we first know what an ancient Covenant was. The Hebrew word for Covenant is *"berith,"* and the Greek word is *"diatheke."* The definition of Covenant in Hebrew and Greek is *"will"*— *"purpose"*— *"disposition."*

THE BIBLE COVENANT

A Bible Covenant was God's declaration of His *"Will-Purpose-Disposition"* toward those with whom He entered into Covenant. In making His gracious proposals to men, God, the Covenantor, expressed His Will and Purpose to His People, the Covenantees.

He pledged Himself that something is done, or would be done, for the Covenantees upon the performance by the Covenantees of such conditions as stated in the Covenant. We shall see many proofs as we proceed to show that God's Covenants were and are conditional.

There is much nonsense taught in Theology with the phrase, *"Sovereign Will of God."* The Eternal Security Teachers use it often. And some of them use it without explaining what they mean by it. The Bible does not use it. It is a term invented by men and loaded with the meaning about Predestination that the Bible does not bear. Other Doctrines are also taught by other Teachers with words and terms that the Bible does not use.

## CONDITIONS

God's Covenant with Abraham imposed a severe condition from the beginning.

*"Now the Lord had said unto Abram, Get thee out of thy country, and from thy kindred, and from thy Father's house, unto a land that I shew thee . . . So Abram departed, as the Lord had spoken unto him"* (Gen. 12:1-4).

The history of Israel begins with Abraham. In Scripture he is called the *"Father"* of the Jewish people. Proud Jews claimed that they were Abraham's children (Mat. 3:9). All God's dealings with Israel — past, present, and future — are founded in the Abrahamic Covenant. Salvation is also based on the Abrahamic Covenant — and this was a Conditional Covenant.

Other Bible Covenants also have their foundation in the Abrahamic Covenant. The Abrahamic Covenant is embodied in, and is called through, each succeeding Covenant. The New Covenant is based on the Abrahamic Covenant. God's Eternal Purpose of Salvation was conceived *"Before the foundation of the world"* (Mat. 25:34; Eph. 1:4), but this purpose is accomplished through the Abrahamic Covenant. Our Saviour was *"Slain before the foundation of the world"* (Rev. 13:8); but the Saviour said, *"Salvation is of the Jews"* (Jn. 4:22).

## OBEDIENCE — FIRST CONDITION

Paul stressed the fact that Christ is the Seed of Abraham (Gal. 3:16). The Abrahamic Covenant is the basis of many Messianic Prophecies. All Redemption is based on the Abrahamic Covenant, although conceived before the foundation of the world (Gen. 15:6). And it began with God's Call to Abraham.

*"By Faith Abraham, when he was called to go out into a place which he should after receive for an inheritance, obeyed; and he went out, not knowing whether he went"* (Heb. 11:8).

This was the first condition of the Abrahamic Covenant. And anyone able to recognize a fact when he sees it cannot deny that it was a condition. What God promised to do for Abraham was conditional upon his leaving his country, home, and kindred. He had to forsake all who would not go with him. If Abraham had not *"obeyed"* this condition, probably we would never have heard of him.

NOTES

Doubtless Abraham was fondly attached to his native home, and it may not have been easy for him to forsake the family ties and cherished affections. But *"by Faith"* he left all and went out to a life of testing as God's Covenant-partner. He was a wanderer in the Earth, living in tents in a *"strange country"* (Heb. 11:9).

Had he *"been mindful of that country"* he left, he could have returned (Heb. 11:15). There was no constraint, no coercion. Abraham acted with his own free will and choice. He obeyed God's Call, and it is nonsense to speak of obedience without free choice.

## CONDITIONAL PREDESTINATION

It should be evident even to the casual Reader that God's Predestinating Purpose in Abraham's life was related to, and conditional upon, a call to separation and obedience that required the acting of Faith. Predestination does not stand alone in the Scriptures. It is related to, and is conditional upon, other Truths. Here are a few examples:

*"Moreover whom He did Predestinate, them He also called: And whom He called, then he also Justified: and whom He Justified, them He also Glorified"* (Rom. 8:30).

This is the way it was with Abraham. His Calling and Justification were part of God's Predestinating Purpose. Between Abraham's Predestination and Glorification, he was *"Called"* and *"Justified."* God, in Predestinating Abraham's Glorification, also Predestinated the *means* for this. The Apostles gave much emphasis to this fact of God's *Call.*

We are *"Called to be Saints"* (I Cor. 1:2). *"God hath . . . called us . . . unto Holiness"* (I Thess. 4:7). We are *"Called"* to *"fight the good fight of Faith"* — *"Called"* to *"lay hold on Eternal Life"* (I Tim. 6:12). God has *"Called us with an Holy Calling"* (II Tim. 1:9). *"But as He which hath called you is Holy, so be ye Holy"* (I Pet. 1:15). These and other Texts give strong support to the fact that Predestination does not stand alone in the Scriptures, i.e., in other words, it is conditional. Certain things are Predestinated, if certain actions are carried forth. Those actions have to do with the individual in question.

NOTES

### A DANGEROUS DISTORTION OF GOD'S WORD

In the writings of the Eternal Security Teachers, you will not find Predestination used in relation to these conditional subjects. That would destroy their case for Unconditional Salvation if they did. In disconnecting Predestination from these Truths, they are guilty of a dangerous distortion of God's Word. And if we use the same method of interpretation on other Doctrines, we could destroy the meaning of other important Bible Truths as well. Some of the most dangerous errors in Christianity today are the results of this method of interpretation.

God called Abraham to forsake all. And Jesus said, *"Whosoever he be of you that forsaketh not all that he hath, he cannot be My Disciple"* (Lk. 14:33).

This forsaking all is the acting of Faith. It is the work of Faith, not the *"works of the Law."* Salvation is God's Grace and Love and Mercy to sinful mankind. It is not for man to boast or glory in the works of his Faith. The acts of his Faith are the fulfilling of God's Conditions for Salvation.

Abraham, by his Faith, fulfilled the conditions of God's Calling in his life, and Paul said that all who have Faith will also *"walk in the steps of that Faith of our Father Abraham"* (Rom. 4:12). The forsake-all condition was clearly stated by Jesus as a requirement to be His Disciple.

### TO WALK CONTINUALLY BEFORE GOD — SECOND CONDITION

We now consider the second condition in the Abrahamic Covenant.

*"I am the Almighty God; walk before Me, and be thou perfect.*

*"And I will make My Covenant between Me and thee, and will multiply thee exceedingly.*

*"And Abram fell on his face: and God talked with Him, saying,*

*"As for Me, Behold, My Covenant is with thee, and thou shalt be a Father of many Nations"* (Gen. 17:1-4).

The first condition required that Abraham leave his country and kindred. The second condition commanded him to *"walk"* (continually) before God. He left Chaldea by Faith, and by a continual act of Faith, he satisfied the Covenant condition of a continual walk before God. Men talk much about the Sovereign Will of God in relation to Salvation, but Divine Sovereignty imposed these Covenant conditions upon Abraham. Not to have obeyed these conditions would have been disobedience, unbelief, and an offense to Divine Sovereignty.

New Covenant Law has the same moral conditions as the Abrahamic Covenant. We must *"walk in the steps of that Faith of our Father Abraham."* This Truth has frequent emphasis in the New Covenant. God calls, but it is only those who freely accept the call who are predestinated for certain things. In fact, God has called the entirety of the earth for Salvation, but it is only those who accept who are saved (Jn. 3:16; Rev. 22:17).

### THE NEW COVENANT

In Romans 6:4, we *"walk in newness of life."* In Luke 1:6, God's Covenant members walk *"in all the Commandments and Ordinances of the Lord blameless."* In John 12:35, the New Covenantor commanded: *"Walk while you have the Light, lest darkness come upon you."* Our only security and protection against darkness is to walk in the Light.

What if some do not walk in the Light, as in fact, many have done?

In Galatians 6:16, Paul gave his blessing to those who *"walk according to this rule"* of New Testament Righteousness. In Ephesians 5:2, 8, we are commanded by the New Covenant Apostle to *"walk in Love"* and to *"walk as Children of Light."* Colossians 1:10 tells us to *"walk worthy of the Lord unto all pleasing."* From Galatians 5:16, we are told we must *"walk in the Spirit."*

I John 1:6 says that those who profess to be Saved and *"walk in darkness"* are liars. I John 2:6 declares: He who is Saved *"ought himself also to walk, even as He* (Jesus) *walked."* III John Verse 4 says that the True Children of God *"walk in Truth."* Those who are not of the Truth walk in *"lusts"* (I Pet. 4:3).

Paul gave us a test by which we can determine who is of God and who is not. He said we are to *"mark them which walk,"* and if they walk according to the *"ensample* (example)*"* Paul gave us, then they obey the New Covenant conditions and are Saved (Phil. 3:17).

Those who fail the walk-test are not Saved.

Is not the New Covenant opposed to the teaching that our Salvation does not depend on *"anything that we may or may not do?"*

## THE THIRD CONDITION, CIRCUMCISION — SEPARATION

In Genesis 17:9-14, the Covenantor added the third condition to the Abrahamic Covenant:

*"And God said unto Abraham, Thou shalt keep My Covenant therefore, thou, and thy seed after thee in their generations.*

*"This is My Covenant, which ye shall keep, between Me and you and thy seed after thee; every manchild among you shall be circumcised.*

*"And ye shall circumcise the flesh of your foreskin; and it shall be a token of the Covenant betwixt Me and you. . . .*

*"He that is born in thy house, and he that is bought with thy money, must needs be circumcised: and My Covenant shall be in your flesh for an everlasting Covenant.*

*"And the uncircumcised manchild whose flesh of his foreskin is not circumcised, that soul shall be cut off from his people; he hath broken My Covenant."*

Abraham and his family were placed under this Covenant condition. Those who did not obey the condition were *"cut off"* from the Covenant.

Covenant-breakers were not allowed to remain in the Covenant family. God told Abraham in Genesis 17:4, *"As for Me, Behold My Covenant is with thee. . . ."* The Pulpit Commentary comments on this: *"As for Me, is equivalent to 'So far as I am concerned' or 'I, for My part. . . .'"*

God had His part in the Covenant, and Abraham and his family had their part. God offered His Covenant to men, and for His part, as far as He was concerned, it was done. God recognizes His oath-bound Covenant responsibilities to perform and make good His Promises. The Covenantor fixed the conditions and pledged Himself to His Covenantees. If the Covenantees broke the Covenant conditions, they were cut off from the Covenant. They forfeited their Covenant rights.

Abraham lived by Faith and Obedience to the Covenant conditions. God required that he *"keep"* the Covenant, and no one could remain in the Covenant who did not likewise keep its conditions. There was no such security as once in the Covenant, always in the Covenant. In the Old Testament Covenants the death penalty was often inflicted for Covenant violations.

NOTES

## THE FOURTH CONDITION — TESTING

*"And it came to pass after these things, that God did tempt* (test) *Abraham, and said unto him, Abraham: And he said, Behold, here I am."*

*"And He said, Take now thy son, thine only son Isaac, whom thou lovest, and get thee into the land of Moriah; and offer him there for a Burnt Offering upon one of the mountains which I will tell thee of"* (Gen. 22:1-2, 10-12).

This was doubtless the greatest test of Abraham's life. Of course, we know that the Lord stayed his hand, and a Ram was substituted in the place of Isaac. However, it was Abraham who was tested.

Some Teachers deny free will and liberty of choice, and say it is all Sovereign Will. But if Abraham was not tested with his free will and choice, then, what was it that was tested that day on Moriah's Mount? Surely, God was not testing His Own Sovereign Will. Observe what God said about Abraham after the test:

*"By Myself have I sworn, saith the Lord, for because thou hast done this thing, and hast not withheld thy son, thine only son:"*

*"That in Blessing I will bless thee, and in multiplying I will multiply thy seed as the stars of the Heaven, and as the sand which is upon the Sea Shore; and thy seed shall possess the gate of his enemies;"*

*"And in thy seed shall all the Nations of the Earth be blessed; because thou hast obeyed My Voice"* (Gen. 22:16-18).

Now, dear Reader, with these facts before us, I ask you a fair question: When God said, *"Because thou hast done this thing . . . because thou hast obeyed My Voice,"* by all the laws of language and logic, does this not prove that God's Covenant dealings with Abraham were conditional? Would God have made the Promises to Abraham if he had not obeyed these conditions?

## FOREKNOWLEDGE

God had foreknowledge of Abraham, but this foreknowledge did not make him a predestinated puppet. This foreknowledge did not dispense with the Covenant conditions; it did not set aside the requirements for Faith and Obedience. The Covenant fulfillments did not come to Abraham by God's foreknowledge without Abraham's fulfillment of the conditions.

Three times God connected the Covenant fulfillments with — *"Because thou hast done this thing . . . because thou hast obeyed My Voice."* This is also indicated in Genesis 18:19, where God said He knew Abraham and what he would do:

*"For I know him, that he will command his children and his household after him, and they shall keep the Way of the Lord, to do Justice and Judgment; that the Lord may bring upon Abraham that which he hath spoken of him."*

This Text teaches that God chose Abraham to do His Will and to carry out His Purposes *"that"* the Covenant Blessings might come upon him. The Hebrew for *"that"* means, literally, *"to the end that," "in order that"* the Blessings might come upon him.

*"His habitual attention to, and faithful performance of, these duties, were a compliance with the conditions on which the Divine Promises had been made to him."*

## ON CONDITION

Dr. S. R. Driver (1846-1914), Regius Professor of Hebrew at Oxford, was one of the revisers of the English Translation of the Old Testament (1876-1884) and one of the top-ranking Old Testament Authorities of modern times.

Professor Driver wrote concerning the condition of the Abrahamic Covenant in Genesis 17:1-4; he said: *"Upon this condition . . . God grants His Covenant"* to Abraham. *"Walk before Me, and be thou blameless." "The condition Abraham is called upon to fulfill . . .* (is) *the duty of leading generally a Righteous and Holy Life . . . upon this condition . . . God grants His Covenant."* On the command that Abraham offer up Isaac, Professor Driver said: *"God tested Abraham to ascertain whether his Faith . . . was real."*

## JESUS AND THE PHARISEES

When Jesus was teaching in Israel, His sharpest rebukes went to a group of hypocritical Jews called Pharisees. They boasted that Abraham was their Father, and they considered themselves the predestinated heirs of Abraham's Eternal Kingdom. But Jesus exposed them with one test:

*"They answered and said unto Him, Abraham is our Father. Jesus saith unto them, If ye were Abraham's children, ye would do the works of Abraham"* (Jn. 8:39).

NOTES

Jesus with this Abrahamic works-test, exposed them as being of *"your father the Devil"* (Jn. 8:44). The true spiritual sons of Abraham will continually obey God's Covenant conditions, as Abraham did. Abraham did not have a one-act-of-Faith experience. Christ here made the New Covenant conditional by imposing similar conditions as those required of Abraham.

## THE NEW COVENANT AND THE ABRAHAMIC COVENANT

The New Covenant as stated, is founded on the Abrahamic Covenant. Salvation is of the Jews. Abraham is the *"Father of us all"* (Rom. 4:16). The Abrahamic Covenant was for Abraham and *"thy seed after thee in their generations."* This Covenant was not stripped of its conditions as it passed to Abraham's descendants. *It was not conditional for Abraham and unconditional for his seed.*

Not only Salvation but the Kingdom of God is founded on the Abrahamic Covenant. And membership in the Kingdom is conditional.

God gave Abraham an Everlasting Covenant and an Everlasting Kingdom *"because"* he obeyed God's Covenant conditions. God also gives us an Eternal Covenant of Life if we *"do the works of Abraham,"* regarding Faith. The Bible tells us more about Abraham's Faith than about the Faith of anyone. It is held up to our view as a model of Faith. It was a Faith that exhibited his works, and Jesus required the same works of Faith from those who claim Salvation in New Testament times.

The works of Abraham were continual. From Chaldea, where he was called to forsake all, to Moriah's Mount, where he was commanded to offer up his son Isaac, Abraham believed and obeyed.

God's Covenants carry a guaranteed security. They are instruments of certainty. They are Covenants of surety. But this Divine suretyship is denied to all who violate its conditions. So, it is not a question of what is in the Covenant, but who is in it. Again, these Covenants had no such security as *once in the Covenant, always in the Covenant,* unless one continued in the Covenant.

The facts of the Abrahamic Covenant force us to the conclusion that God's Covenant of

Salvation to Abraham was conditional. The leave-all condition, the walk-before-Me condition, and the offer-up-Isaac condition place it beyond all reasonable doubt. Salvation is of the Jews. The Abrahamic Covenant is the Foundation of Jewish Salvation, which is the same for the Gentiles.

## WORKS?

The Abrahamic Covenant is conditional.

The *"works"* of which we speak, are not works tendered as a means of merit or of earning one's Salvation, but rather that which is produced by Faith. If there is proper Faith, there will be Faith-works, which speak of Righteousness, Holiness, Sanctification, etc. In other words, Faith produces the work of Righteousness, Holiness, Sanctification, etc. Works do not produce Faith, but Faith does produce works.

Consequently, if these works are not produced in the life of a professing Believer, such is a sure sign that Faith is not present, which means that the individual is trusting in something other than Christ, i.e., *"Unconditional Eternal Security."*

There is definitely a Biblical Teaching which guarantees Eternal Security, but it is based on the conditions laid down by the Holy Spirit in the Word of God, and is extended to *"whosoever will"* (Rev. 22:17).

## PREDESTINATION!

As well, *"Predestination"* is a viable Biblical Doctrine, which for the most part simply means that certain things are predestined, providing that sinners do certain things (accept Christ), and Believers do certain things (continue to walk after the Lord).

The idea that God has predestined some for Heaven and some for Hell, irrespective of what they say, think, or do, is not taught anywhere in Scripture, and is actually an insult to the integrity and nature of God. For God to predestine anyone to Eternal Hell, with them having no choice in the matter whatsoever, presents a nature attributed to God, which is not taught in the Bible. God is Love, and there is no way that God could arbitrarily consign anyone to Eternal Darkness with them having no choice in the matter. Such is not only preposterous, but as stated, an insult to the Integrity, Love, Grace, and Glory of God. Such Teaching completely defies all the logic of Scripture, and above all the very Nature and Character of God Himself *"Who is longsuffering, not willing that any should perish but that all should come to repentance"* (II Pet. 3:9).

NOTES

That within itself shoots full of holes the error of *"Predestination"* as it is commonly taught, and as well, lays waste, the promoters of Unconditional Eternal Security. Repentance is demanded, and if not forthcoming, the soul will perish.

(13) "THERE HATH NO TEMPTATION TAKEN YOU BUT SUCH AS IS COMMON TO MAN: BUT GOD IS FAITHFUL, WHO WILL NOT SUFFER YOU TO BE TEMPTED ABOVE THAT YE ARE ABLE; BUT WILL WITH THE TEMPTATION ALSO MAKE A WAY TO ESCAPE, THAT YE MAY BE ABLE TO BEAR IT."

The phrase, *"There hath no temptation taken you but such as is common to man,"* proclaims two things to us:

1. The implication of the verse is that there will be *"temptations"*; consequently, it is not possible for the Believer to arrive at some certain place of victory where all temptations have come to an end. To be sure, that will happen, but only at the Resurrection (I Cor. 15:53, 54).

2. The phrase, *"But such as is common to man,"* refers to the limitations that God has placed upon Satan respecting that which he can or cannot do. To be sure, inasmuch as Satan is a fallen Angel, he most assuredly knows particular pressures and abilities to which man, even Godly men, could not favorably respond.

As well, the phrase refers to the fact that whatever a person is undergoing, as severe as it may seem to be, there are many others going through the same identical thing, i.e. *"common to man."*

*"Common"* in the Greek is *"anthropinos"* and means *"after the manner of men."*

## TEMPTATION

The Biblical idea of temptation is not primarily of seduction, as in modern usage, but of making trial of a person, or putting him to the test; which may be done for the benevolent purpose of proving or improving his quality, as well as the malicious aim of showing his weaknesses or trapping him into wrong action.

Actually, *"tempt"* or *"temptation"* means *"test,"* at least in its unrestricted sense. However, since the 17th Century, the word *"temptation"* has come to mean, and be limited to, testing with evil intent, which is done by Satan, and never by God. But yet God definitely *"tests"* His children, as we shall momentarily see. Such is not for His benefit, inasmuch as He already knows what is in us, but for our benefit.

THE PHARISEES AND CHRIST

Men test their fellow human beings, as one tests armor (I Kings 10:1; I Sam. 17:39), to explore and measure their capacities.

The Gospels tell of Jewish opponents, with resentful skepticism, *"testing"* Christ (trying Him out, we might say) to see if they could make Him prove, or try to prove, His Messiahship to them on their terms (Mk. 8:11). They also wanted to test, and in fact did test, His doctrine to see whether it was defective or unorthodox (Lk. 10:25); and to see if they could trap Him into self-incriminating assertions (Mk. 12:15).

THE LORD'S SUPPER

Men should test themselves before the Lord's Supper (I Cor. 11:28) and at other times as well (II Cor. 13:5), lest they become presumptuous and deluded about their spiritual state. The Christian needs to test his *"work"* (what he is making of his life), lest he go astray and forfeit his reward (Gal. 6:4). Sober self-knowledge, arising from disciplined self-scrutiny, is a basic element in Biblical Salvation.

THE MANNER IN WHICH GOD TESTS PEOPLE

God tests His people by putting them in situations which reveal the quality of their Faith and devotion, so that all can see what is in their hearts (Gen. 22:1; Ex. 16:4; 20:20; Deut. 8:2, 16; 13:3; Judg. 2:22; II Chron. 32:31). As stated, this is not that God may know, for He being Omniscient already knows, but that we may know, which is extremely important to the Child of God.

Thus, by making trial of Believers, the Lord purifies them, as metal is purified in the refiner's crucible (Ps. 66:10; 119:67, 71; Isa. 48:10; Zech. 13:9; I Pet. 1:6); He strengthens their patience and matures their Christian character (James 1:2, 12; I Pet. 5:10). As well, the Lord leads them into an enlarged assurance of His love for them (Gen. 22:15; Rom. 5:3).

NOTES

Through faithfulness in times of trial men become *"approved"* in God's sight (I Cor. 11:19; James 1:12).

SATAN AND TEMPTATION

Satan tests God's people by manipulating circumstances, within the limits that God allows him (Job 1:12; 2:6; I Cor. 10:13), in an attempt to make them desert God's Will. The New Testament knows Satan as *"the tempter"* (Mat. 4:3; I Thess. 3:5), the implacable foe of both God and men (I Pet. 5:8; Rev. Chpt. 12).

Christians must constantly be watchful regarding this danger of temptation (Mk. 14:38; II Cor. 2:11; Gal. 6:1) and active (Eph. 6:10; James 4:7; I Pet. 5:9) against the Devil, for he is always at work trying to make them fall; whether by crushing them under the weight of hardship or pain (Job 1:11; 2:7; Heb. 2:18; I Pet. 5:9; Rev. 2:10; 3:10), or by urging them to a wrong fulfillment of natural desires (Mat. 4:3; I Cor. 7:5).

As well, he attempts to make Believers complacent, careless, and self-assertive (Gal. 6:1; Eph. 4:27), or by misrepresenting God to them and engendering false ideas of His Truth and His Will (Gen. 3:1-5; Mat. 4:5; II Cor. 11:3, 14; Eph. 6:11).

Matthew 4:5 shows that Satan can even quote (and misapply) Scripture for this purpose. But God promises that a way of deliverance will always be open when He allows Satan to tempt Christians (I Cor. 10:13; II Cor. 12:7-10; II Pet. 2:9).

THE NEW TESTAMENT STRUCTURE

The New Testament presentation of temptation is reached by combining the manner in which God *"tests"* and the way in which Satan *"tempts."* The former is meant for improvement, while the latter is meant for destruction.

*"Trials"* can be both the work of God and the Devil (Lk. 22:28; Acts 20:19; James 1:2; I Pet. 1:6; II Pet. 2:9). They are testing situations in which the Servant of God faces new possibilities of both good and evil, and is exposed to various inducements to prefer the latter, i.e. *"evil."* From this standpoint, temptations are Satan's work; but Satan is God's tool as well as His foe (Job 1:11; 2:5), and it is ultimately God Himself Who leads His servants into temptation, or

rather allows them to be led into temptation (Mat. 4:1; 6:13), permitting Satan to try to seduce them for purposes of his own.

However, though temptations do not overtake men apart from God's Will, the actual prompting to do wrong is never of God, nor does it express His Command (James 1:12). The desire which impels men to sin is not God's, but one's own, and it is fatal to yield to it (James 1:14).

Christ taught His Disciples to ask God not to expose them, or rather allow them to be exposed, to temptation (Mat. 6:13), and to watch and pray lest they should *"enter into"* temptation, i.e. yield to its pressure, when at such times God saw fit to try them in this manner (Mat. 26:41).

Temptation is not sin, for Christ was tempted as we are, yet remained sinless (Mat. 4:1; Lk. 22:28; Heb. 4:15). Temptation becomes sin only when and as the suggestion of evil is accepted and yielded to.

## THE PROMISE

The phrase, *"But God is faithful, Who will not suffer you to be tempted above that ye are able,"* presents a most wonderful promise, as well as other great truths. They are as follows:

1. The Faithfulness of God is guaranteed the Believer respecting this all important part of one's Christian experience. God will not allow that over which we cannot persevere. As well, whatever we are undergoing, untold numbers of others have undergone, and in fact, are undergoing the same thing presently.

Considering what Paul has just said in the previous verses respecting his efforts in the running of this Christian race, and how terribly the children of Israel in the wilderness had failed to meet the requirements of God, one might be inclined to throw up every effort in despair. Consequently, Paul reminds us that these temptations are not superhuman, but such as other Believers down through the past ages have resisted, and, consequently, such as we can resist as well.

The Lord knows *"how to deliver the Godly out of temptations"* (II Pet. 2:9), and He will surely perform His side of the Covenant, and if we do our part, will establish and keep us from evil (II Thess. 3:3).

2. This phrase also tells us that Satan is constantly requesting greater latitude in the lives of Christians (Job Chpts. 1 and 2), but with the Lord promising that He will be the gauge of the temptation and not Satan. We have His Promise on that.

3. From this statement as well, we learn that Satan can do nothing unless he gets permission from the Lord, and that he has to follow to the letter that which God allows.

The phrase, *"But will with the temptation also make a way to escape, that ye may be able to bear it,"* presents another Promise which has served generations of Christians as a word of hope in times of difficulty.

However, addressing this phrase in the light of the previous verses, it is difficult to see how it fits into the scheme of the present argument, especially considering that Verse 14 follows Verses 1-12 so nicely. The best solution seems to be to regard it as functioning in two directions at once, both as a continuation of the warning in Verses 1-12 and, as well, as a word of assurance leading to the prohibition to *"flee idolatry"* in Verse 14.

There is no risk of falling, the Holy Spirit seems to say through Paul in response to Verse 12, as long as one is dealing with temptations which are not of one's own making. However, the Believer must *"flee from idolatry,"* because by implication there is no Divine aid when one is *"testing"* Christ in the way that Verse 9 brings out. The idea is that there is no pledge of victory whatever in the case of temptations into which one throws oneself, or by deliberation exposes oneself. However, these statements as given by Paul pose several questions:

## DOES GOD ALLOW THE SAME LEVEL OF TEMPTATION FOR ALL?

I think the answer is an unequivocal *"no!"*

For instance, the Lord would not have allowed the level of temptation with many, and maybe not with any, as He did with Job, at least at that particular time. Even in the course of this great test, the level increased according to certain particulars (Job Chpt. 2). As well, the Lord allowed a certain latitude with Simon Peter, which He no doubt would not have allowed with others (Lk. 22:31-34).

The level of test or temptation allowed is predicated on the Call of God on one's life, and the level of maturity. This is evidenced in God's dealings with Abraham, and in fact, all the

NOTES

Patriarch's and Faith worthies of the Old Testament. The New Testament falls into the same category. So, using these things as our guide, we know that the level of opposition allowed is predicated on several things.

## IS IT POSSIBLE THAT THE BELIEVER MAY NOT PROPERLY UNDERSTAND GOD'S WAY OF ESCAPE?

Yes, it is possible.

First of all, most Believers, I think I can say without exaggeration, in fact do not properly know or understand God's prescribed way of escape respecting the matter of temptation. Consequently, we institute our own ways, all the time thinking they are God's ways, when in reality they aren't.

For instance, I will use the problem of homosexuality, because that's about the worst sin I can think of at the present time.

There is Salvation for the Homosexual just as there is for anyone else; however, the Lord does not save us in our sin but rather from our sin. In other words, the drunkard quits his drinking, the gambler quits gambling, and the homosexual ceases his perverted lifestyle, etc.

However, with some, even after they come to Christ, the bent in that particular direction does not always leave immediately. I have had some come to me, asking what they should do in these times of temptation, etc.

Some twenty years ago (in the 1970's), I would have told them, and in fact did tell them, that they should pray more and study the Word more.

Of course, that advice is very good, which every Believer should do constantly, and will definitely draw one closer to God. In fact, without a proper prayer life and a proper dedication to the study of the Word of God, the Believer cannot grow in Christ. However, as true as that is, and as important as prayer and the study of the Word is, still, that will not handle the situation of which I speak.

## WHAT IS THE ANSWER?

The answer is found in the Sixth Chapter of Romans. Actually, the answer spans some three Chapters, 6, 7, and 8.

In the Sixth Chapter of Romans, we learn what Christ did for us at Calvary and the Resurrection. We learn that He provided a double cure for the double curse. The double curse was the terrible sin debt owed by man, and the grip of sin which Satan had on the sinner.

NOTES

When Jesus died and rose from the dead, the sin debt was forever paid, with the grip of sin broken, which constitutes the double cure. However, many Christians have been led to believe that Calvary is important only as it regards their Salvation, in other words when they got saved. They do not know or realize that Calvary is an ongoing part of our Christian experience, and what happened there must continue to be appropriated every day by Faith.

The grip of sin is broken at the time of Salvation, but of course, Satan does not stop there, continuing to probe, attempting to get the Believer to fail. In one way or the other, he always does. Having the Divine Nature within us, we are automatically repulsed by the failure and run to Christ for Mercy and forgiveness, which he always gives (I Jn. 1:9). However, at that time, instead of understanding that our victory rests in what Jesus did for us at Calvary and the Resurrection, and that we were actually in Him when all of this took place (Rom. 6:4-5), we too often attempt to get victory in the wrong way, which always fails, and actually makes the matter worse.

## THE HOLY SPIRIT

As I have stated, any person facing the powers of darkness must understand that it is the Holy Spirit Only Who can provide the victory that is needed, which is outlined in Romans, Chapter 8, and which He will only do according to our Faith respecting the great victory that Jesus won for us at Calvary and the Resurrection. In other words, He will not honor our wrong direction respecting efforts to overcome through our own machinations or personal strength. One cannot win a victory over the flesh by using the strength of the flesh. It simply cannot be done. However, what fools us is that we think we can pray it out, or fast it out, or some such thing, which definitely does help, but is not meant to be the solution in these situations.

Those things, as wonderful as they are in their own place, in effect tries to obtain victory, when in fact, victory has already been obtained through Jesus Christ.

So, to tell the former homosexual that he could pray his way out of those temptations is not the right answer. Such will surely help and strengthen him, but it will not provide the solution, simply because the solution has already been provided — in Jesus.

(Please see the Commentary on Chapters 6, 7, and 8 of Romans for a much greater treatment of this very important subject.)

*"Escape"* in the Greek is *"ekbasis"* and means *"an exit,"* in other words, Satan cannot bottle up the Christian.

DOES GOD GUARANTEE DELIVERANCE FROM ALL TEMPTATION?

He does, providing we trust Him, incorporating His *"Way."* However, He guarantees no deliverance at all, if we purposely place ourselves in the way of temptation.

Some sins are so incompatible with life in Christ that sure judgement, meaning loss of Salvation, is the inevitable result of persistence in them. These are not matters of being *"taken in,"* as it were, by temptation, thus falling into sin. These are deliberate acts, predicated on a false security, that put God to the test, as though daring Him to judge one of His *"eternally secure ones."* Such heady disobedience, Paul assures us, is headed for destruction.

But on the other side is the Faithful God, ready to aid those enduring trial, assuring them that there is a way out, and an end to it. And in the meantime, He is there to apportion the necessary ability to endure, appropriate to the trial (Fee).

In fact, untold millions sin with impunity because they have been told that while they may lose their fellowship with the Lord, they cannot lose their Salvation, irrespective of what they do. Of course, this is the grossly unscriptural doctrine of Unconditional Eternal Security, which has caused more people to be lost than one could ever begin to imagine.

There is no provision in the Word of God for Believers living in sin, only for victory over sin. In fact, John plainly states that those who habitually practice sin simply aren't saved (I Jn. 3:9).

(14) "WHEREFORE, MY DEARLY BELOVED, FLEE FROM IDOLATRY."

The phrase, *"Wherefore, my dearly beloved,"* is not meant as mere rhetoric or flattery, but rather portrays a deep-seated love for these Corinthians, that far surpassed any love from anyone else they would ever know, I think I can say without fear of exaggeration. It is somewhat ironical!

This is the man (Paul) who underwent untold hardships in obeying God to bring them the Gospel, resulting in their Salvation which is the greatest thing by far that would ever happen to anyone, with him continuing to seek the Face of God on their behalf, even though he is now in another field of endeavor. Along with this, he never received any type of financial remuneration for his services, rather resorting to the laborious task of tent-making repair, but yet it seems that this love and sacrifice were little returned by many of the Corinthian Believers, or even appreciated for that matter. Nevertheless, the Apostle did not allow that to deter his feelings for them, even though it must have hurt deeply.

The phrase, *"Flee from idolatry,"* is pure and simple, and proclaimed by the Holy Spirit at that.

The Apostle has addressed the matter of eating food offered to idols, stating that such contained no harm; however, he now warns them in no uncertain terms, that they must be very careful in regard to this question.

As previously stated, idol worship was of such magnitude in Corinth, and actually over the entirety of the Roman World, that every vestige of life and activity was saturated with this gross sin.

The trade unions, which were strong at that time, were heavily engaged into every type of idol worship, as could well be imagined. Almost anything that anyone did in respect to public life had some type of idol acknowledgement, whether the food that was eaten, blessings offered, sacrifices, etc. In other words, and as stated, society was shot through with this type of participation. So, Paul is warning them that they must be careful, even very careful, or they could be sucked back into that from which they had been brought out.

IDOLS AND IMAGES

It is stated in the Commandments: *"Do not make for yourself an idol in the form of anything in Heaven above or on the earth beneath or in the waters below. You shall not bow down to them or worship them"* (Ex. 20:4; Deut. 4:15-19).

The idol, or image, is anything that one may shape for use as an object of worship. The

NOTES

basic reason for this prohibition is that idols necessarily distort one's concept of God, Who is Spirit (Jn. 4:24) and Who must be worshipped in harmony with His Nature.

Human beings who worship idols are led from dependence on God to reliance on something that expresses their own religious thoughts and motivations, instead of that which is given in the Word of God. In Isaiah 2:8-22, the Prophet asserts that idolatry is an expression of human pride and arrogance.

He insists: *"Stop trusting in man, who has but a breath in his nostrils. Of what account is he?"*

A SIN WITH MORAL IMPLICATIONS

Although idolatry is essentially a spiritual sin, representing rejection of the True God, it is a sin that has moral implications. This is seen clearly in Romans 1:18-32. Here, Paul clearly rejects the theory that sees idolatry as *"primitive religion,"* which in time must naturally develop to *"higher"* forms.

Paul portrays mankind as having a knowledge of God but suppressing the truth by their wickedness (Rom. 1:18). People reject Creation's testimony to the Creator and, instead of worshipping and thanking Him, create images to worship.

This rejection of God cuts human beings off from a knowledge of their own immoral character and denies them a standard against which to measure choices. Consequently, they turn to all forms of immorality (Rom. 1:26-27) and sin (Rom. 1:28-31).

Deep within these God-rejecters is a sense of sin, but rejection of a knowledge of God renders them unable and unwilling to repent (Rom. 1:32).

THE OLD TESTAMENT

The process of alienation had its culminating expression in Canaan and in Canaanite religion. Yet it was in Canaan that God led Israel to settle.

The stern warnings against idolatry and the original inhabitants' practices linked with idolatry are found throughout the Old Testament. These passages, which use some ten different Hebrew terms for *"idol"* and *"image,"* are found in nearly every Bible Book up to the time of the Babylonian captivity. That exile purged

NOTES

Israel: after the exile, idolatry was no temptation to the Jewish people.

For a powerful satire on the futility of idolatry, see Isaiah 44:6-23.

THE NEW TESTAMENT

Idolatry was widespread in the world of the First Century. Paul, even as we are here studying, warned Believers to stay away from events featuring idol worship (I Cor. 10:14). Although the idol had no real existence (I Cor. 10:19; 12:2; Gal. 4:8; I Thess. 1:9) and idol worship accomplishes nothing (I Cor. 10:19), demonic beings are involved in pagan worship (I Cor. 10:20-22), and immorality was often interwoven with it (I Cor. 10:6-13).

The Gospel's impact on pagan culture was powerful. In Ephesus, riots were stimulated by silversmiths whose business — producing and selling miniatures of the goddess Artemis — was weakened by the conversion of many people to Christ. This is particularly significant because Ephesus was one of the religious centers of Asia, and the great temple there was on the itinerary of tourists and pilgrims alike.

WARNING

The condemnation of idolatry in the Old Testament and the New Testament warns us against trusting ourselves to anything but God Himself. In his powerful words, interpreting Israel's history, Hosea shows the spiritual power that worship has on a people: *"When I found Israel, it was like finding grapes in the desert; when I saw your fathers, it was like seeing the early fruit on the fig tree. But when they came to Baal Peor, they consecrated themselves to that shameful idol and became as vile as the thing they loved"* (Hos. 9:10).

The potential for fruitfulness was destroyed as God's Old Testament people became like that which they worshipped. How wonderful that we who believe can consecrate ourselves to the Living Lord! Worshipping the Lord, we can, like Him, become gracious and pure!

As well, idol worship does not pertain only to figures or figurines made out of particular materials, but is more so a spirit than anything else. In other words, anything that takes the place of God in our hearts and lives becomes an idol, whether sports, money, fame, religion, etc. In fact, religion is the greatest idol of all, actually being the cause of most people of the world being eternally lost.

So, the Believer should not think that idols and idol worship passed out of existence with the Roman Empire, etc. It is very much alive today, and in fact, always has been.

(15) "I SPEAK AS TO WISE MEN; JUDGE YE WHAT I SAY."

The phrase, *"I speak as to wise men,"* while it may contain a hint if irony, it more so attempts to address them on the level which they claim — that of being very wise or sensible people. Since they are sensible people by their own admission, he will, as in I Corinthians 11:13 and 14:20, appeal to them as such: *"judge for yourselves what I say,"* meaning in this case, *"what I am about to say."*

But he does not mean *"judge for yourselves"* as to its rightness or wrongness. They are to judge for themselves that Paul is right, and if they are as sensible as they say they are, they will immediately come to that conclusion. Consequently, he is saying, *"Since you are wise, you can see the necessity of refraining from any hint of idolatry."*

(16) "THE CUP OF BLESSING WHICH WE BLESS, IS IT NOT THE COMMUNION OF THE BLOOD OF CHRIST? THE BREAD WHICH WE BREAK, IS IT NOT THE COMMUNION OF THE BODY OF CHRIST?"

The question, *"The Cup of Blessing which we bless, is it not the Communion of the Blood of Christ?"*, presents the first of two Passages where the Apostle refers to the Lord's Supper (I Cor. 11:17-34). However, his main focus here is not the Lord's Supper, but rather the pagan meals (pagan worship) addressed in Verses 19-21. This passage serves as a presupposition for what he will say in those three verses.

On the basis of their (probably) common, and for Paul proper, understanding of the nature of their own sacred meal (The Lord's Supper), as well as a Biblical understanding of that of Israel which he will approach in Verse 18, he appeals to their common sense that they may not attend the pagan meals.

What he argues is that there is something inherent in the nature of the Lord's Supper that makes participation in the other absolutely incompatible. That something he describes is the fellowship and participation that one has with the Lord in the taking of the Lord's Supper, which certainly means that the Believer does not want to fellowship with devils, which was a part of the pagan meals (worship).

NOTES

### THE CUP OF BLESSING

*"Blessing"* in the Greek as used here is *"eulogia,"* and means *"adoration, consecration, benefit or largess, a matter of bounty."* Consequently, the blessing is twofold:

1. In taking the Lord's Supper, the Believer is to thank the Lord, grandly so, for what He has done in bringing the sinner out of darkness into the Light of the Gospel of Jesus Christ. The *"blessings"* afforded by the Lord to the Believer upon Faith, are absolutely inexhaustible. We are to thank Him for Salvation, the Baptism with the Holy Spirit, prosperity, and in effect, the privilege of being in the great Family of God. Considering what the Lord has done for all who come to Him, there is no limit to the necessity of our praises, nor is there an end to the Blessings.

2. What the Lord did at Calvary and the Resurrection, and at such great price, is that which affords all of this which we have in His vicarious, sacrificial, atoning Offering. In other words, everything comes through Calvary and the Resurrection. That's the reason this pivot point in history must be the centerpiece in our relationship with Christ. It must be our Message, the focal point of our worship, the reason for our victory, and the foundation of our Salvation. Consequently, that's why *"we bless"* this wondrous act of Mercy, the greatest in the history of mankind.

### THE COMMUNION OF THE BLOOD OF CHRIST

*"Communion"* in the Greek is *"Koinonia,"* and means *"partnership, participation, sharer, partaker and partner."*

One is not to think, as some teach, that the cup (grape juice) turns into the actual Blood of Christ and, therefore, affords Salvation. Neither the language or grammar, nor the example of Israel, allow such a meaning. Consequently, there is no Salvation in the Cup, nor is it intended to be; however, What and Who it symbolizes, the Lord Jesus Christ, i.e. His Death (shedding of His Blood) and Resurrection, does of course bring Salvation. However, the Believer is to ever understand that Salvation is never in Ordinances, Ceremonies, or Rituals, but rather in Christ particularly, and more directly, Faith in what He did which brought about our Redemption.

COMMUNION

The key is found in the word *"Communion."*

This *"Communion"* presents a unique relationship between Believers and the Lord. It makes the *"Body"* one in Christ, and Christ one with the *"Body,"* i.e. *"Church."*

There can be little doubt that Paul intends to emphasize the kind of bonding relationship of the worshippers with one another that the Lord's Supper expresses. In fact, Verse 17 seems to make this certain. It should be noted that the present sequence, Cup – Bread, is unique to the New Testament. The evidence from 11:23-25 makes it clear that the standard sequence, Bread – Cup, prevailed in the Churches during Paul's time, and prevails presently as well.

Why did Paul invert the order here?

The reason for this order seems to be that Paul has chosen to interpret the Bread in light of the present argument, concerning the idol feasts. It emphasizes the solidarity of the fellowship of Believers created by them all sharing *"the one loaf,"* whether at the Lord's Supper or the pagan feasts.

However, the distinctly spiritual nature of these feasts indicates that worship of Deity was involved, whether pagan or Christian and, therefore, that the participants most likely considered Him (or her, inasmuch as pagans worshipped female gods as well) also to be present in some way at the meal.

This is especially so in Judaism, in which the Israelites were expressly commanded to eat *"in the Presence of Jehovah."* We speak of the Passover, out of which came the Lord's Supper. So it is fellowship with the Lord and fellowship with each other.

RELATIONSHIP

It is this unique relationship between Believers and their Lord, celebrated at this meal, that makes impossible similar associations with other *"believers"* at the tables of demons.

This fellowship was a celebration of their common life in Christ, based on the New Covenant in His Blood that had previously bound them together in union with Christ by His Spirit (Fee).

NOTES

THE COMMUNION OF THE BODY OF CHRIST

The questions, *"The Bread which we break, is it not the Communion of the Body of Christ?"*, pertains to the incarnation, and more particularly, to His Perfect Body offered up in Sacrifice, which God accepted as payment for the terrible sin debt of man. Of course, the offering of His Body, necessitated the shedding of His Precious Blood, which actually represented His poured out life.

However, the statement also refers to the *"Body of Christ"* as the Church, the fellowship of Believers, all washed in the Blood of the Lamb.

Therein we discover the unity of the Church, for as the members share together the one loaf, they sit down as the one body of Christ.

As well, there are eschatological (end time) overtones, with the forward look to the advent in Glory.

However, as the *"Cup,"* Paul does not imply that the *"Bread"* turns into the actual Body of Christ, as some teach. As there is no Salvation in the Cup, likewise, there is no Salvation in the *"Bread."*

What is unique here is that Paul will go on to interpret the *"Bread"* in terms of the Church as *"His Body."* No where else in the New Testament is the *"Bread"* interpreted in this manner. Paul does so here probably because, in this context, the emphasis lies here.

(17) "FOR WE BEING MANY ARE ONE BREAD, AND ONE BODY: FOR WE ARE ALL PARTAKERS OF THAT ONE BREAD."

The phrase, *"For we being many are one Bread, and one Body,"* pertains to Jesus as the *"Bread"* with all Believers partaking of that *"Bread,"* and consequently, as a result, being *"One Body."*

Only those who have truly partaken of that Bread are truly born again (Jn. 3:3). This is what Jesus was addressing when He said, *"Except ye eat the Flesh of the Son of Man, and drink His Blood, ye have no life in you"* (Jn. 6:53).

The idea as He presented it was not literal and was not meant to be, as should be obvious. Whenever the sinner exhibits Faith in what Christ did at Calvary and the Resurrection, he is, in effect, partaking of that Sacrifice, actually in Christ in what Paul referred to as being *"baptized into His Death"* (Rom. 6:3).

The idea of this *"Communion"* or *"participation"* in the Body and Blood of Christ makes possible all Communion with Christ Personally, and as well, the Communion of Believers. Therefore, the participants in the Communion Service are One with Christ and with one another.

The phrase, *"For we are all partakers of that One Bread,"* speaks of Jesus Christ as being the only *"Bread of Life."* There is no other!

*"Partakers"* in the Greek is *"metecho,"* and means *"to share or participate, to occupy a particular position."* Consequently, the entirety of the Body of Christ partaking of Jesus, which numbers into tens of millions, constitutes the great group as *"One Body."*

## TRANSUBSTANTIATION AND CONSUBSTANTIATION

The Roman Catholic Church teaches that the Mass is an expiatory (sin-removing) sacrifice, in which the Son of God actually is sacrificed anew on the Cross. He literally descends (they say) into the Priest's hands during the act of transubstantiation, wherein the elements of the host (the wafer) literally are transformed into the Body, Blood, Soul, and Divinity of our Lord Jesus Christ. This was defined as such by the Council of Trent, although minor alterations were made in wording during the Second Vatican Council.

Furthermore, the Catholic Church teaches that if anyone denies that in the Sacrament of the Most Holy Eucharist are contained truly, really, and substantially, the Body and Blood together with the Soul and Divinity of our Lord Jesus Christ, and consequently the whole Christ; but saith that He is only therein as in a sign, or in figure, or virtue; let him be anathema.

In other words, if anyone fails to believe in the doctrine of Transubstantiation (the wafer and the wine literally turning into the Body and Blood of Jesus), he is lost.

Catholics are taught that when the Priest hovers over the wafer and says, *"This is My Body,"* it becomes the actual flesh of Christ. Likewise, after the Priest says the words, *"This is My Blood,"* the wine is said to become the actual blood of Jesus.

While it is true that Jesus actually did say, *"This is My Body . . . This is My Blood,"* it is obvious that He was speaking figuratively, just as He did when He said, *"I am the True Vine, and My Father is the Husbandman"* (Jn. 15:1).

NOTES

In other words, Catholics teach that the ceremony of the Mass actually contains Salvation.

Consubstantiation does not go quite as far as Catholic Transubstantiation, but is still gross error because it does claim that Christ in some manner, or in spirit, is brought into the Believer by the partaking of the Bread and the Wine. Once again, this particular doctrine teaches that Salvation is contained in the ceremony.

## GROSS ERROR

The Catholic Doctrine of Transubstantiation is, without question, one of the most absurd doctrines ever imposed upon a trusting public. The Roman Catholic Catechism of Christian Doctrine says:

*"The Holy Mass is one and the same sacrifice with that of the Cross inasmuch as Christ, Who offered Himself, a bleeding victim, on the Cross to His Heavenly Father, continues to offer Himself in the unbloody manner on the Altar, through the Ministry of His Priests."*

Roman Catholic errors are inevitably human innovations that were inserted into the Church during the early centuries.

In the First Century, as described in the New Testament, Holy Communion was a meal of fellowship eaten as a memorial to the Death of Christ and a symbol of unity among Christians — both with each other and with Christ.

In the Second Century, it began to shift toward a Ceremony, in which Christ was present in some undefined form. This was not yet the eventual Catholic Doctrine of *"Transubstantiation"* — which was a development of the Middle Ages — but it was a beginning in this unfortunate direction.

By the Third Century, the idea of sacrifice began to intrude, whereby Christ's Body and Blood were mysteriously produced by an ordained Priest for the gratification and benefit of both the living and the dead.

From the Third Century, Old Testament ideas of Priesthood were used by some to interpret the Eucharist as the *"Christian Sacrifice."* At first, the sacrifice was thought to consist of praises, but gradually it came to be held that an Offering was made to God to gain forgiveness of sins. By the Middle Ages, this had been developed to make the Eucharist a reoffering of Christ's Sacrifice on the Cross.

(The word *"Eucharist"* means *"gratitude or thanksgiving,"* and is contained in the partaking of the bread and the cup, which symbolizes the Body and Shed Blood of Christ. However, Catholicism has taken it further than symbolism, actually claiming that participation guarantees Salvation.)

There also arose magical ideas concerning the bread and wine. By the Fourth Century, it was held that either when the words of the Last Supper were repeated . . . or when the Holy Spirit was invoked on the bread and wine . . . a change took place. It was believed right to venerate the bread and wine as representing Jesus visibly.

THE DOCTRINE

The erroneous doctrine of Transubstantiation, which means that the bread and wine change to His literal Body and Blood, was first formulated by Paschasius Radbertus, Abbot of Corbey, at the beginning of the Ninth Century.

It was first named *"Transubstantiation"* by Hildebert of Tours in the early years of the Twelfth Century, and made an article of faith (official doctrine of the Catholic Church) by the Lateran Council in the beginning of the Thirteenth Century.

One has to wonder how that learned and educated men, supposedly in the Bible, could come to such erroneous, unscriptural conclusions?

The answer is that either they did not really know the Bible, which is no doubt the case, or else some few really did know the Bible, but chose to ignore its teaching.

Of course, we know that Scriptural error invariably stems from the Evil One, Satan. In this case, it was due, at least in part, to dabblings into the popular Eastern mystery religions, borrowing from Greek and Roman paganism and reverting, as well, to Old Testament, Mosaic customs — all of which demanded recurring Sacrificial Offerings attended by the Priesthood.

It is just one more tragic example of what happens when man's misguided intellect strays from the written Word of God.

IS TRANSUBSTANTIATION IDOLATRY?

The Catholic Catechism (the basic guidebook on Catholic Doctrine) defines *"idolatry"* as *"rendering to any creature the honor and adoration that are due to God Alone."* Consequently, they hang themselves by their own statement.

NOTES

I think a person would have to agree that what we have described in the preceding pages constitutes idolatry — the worshipping of a piece of bread that a person has become convinced is the Lord Jesus Christ.

This is not at all unlike the evil practice of Israel of old in the making of Golden Calves, or some such like idols, worshipping them, calling them *"Jehovah."* In fact, it is the same thing — idolatry.

The Lord's Supper is a symbol of the Broken Body and Shed Blood of the Lord Jesus Christ, in which our partaking is done in remembrance of Him and what He has done, and that we should do so until He comes. It is no more than that, and no less than that! (I Cor. 11:23-26)

(18) "BEHOLD ISRAEL AFTER THE FLESH: ARE NOT THEY WHICH EAT OF THE SACRIFICES PARTAKERS OF THE ALTAR?"

The phrase, *"Behold Israel after the flesh,"* is meant to portray the Law of Moses, which consisted of many Rituals, Ceremonies, and Sacrifices. The word *"flesh"* is used because the participants literally partook of the flesh of some of the Sacrifices, more particularly the Peace Offering (Lev. 7:11-27). By contrast, in the Lord's Supper no literal flesh is eaten, only a partaking of the Bread and the Cup, both a symbol of Christ.

The question, *"Are not they which eat of the Sacrifices partakers of the Altar?"*, would probably been better translated, *"Have they not Communion with the Altar?"*

The meaning is that by sharing in the Sacrifices (the Peace Offerings), the Jews stood in direct association with the Altar, the victims, and all that they symbolized (Deut. 14:22-26). As well, Paul is implying that the same thing is true of those who sympathetically partake of idol-offerings (Farrar).

The context indicates that Paul is referring to the meals described in Leviticus, Chapter 7 (the Peace Offering) and in Deuteronomy 14:22-27, and not to the Priest's share of the sacrifice alluded to in I Corinthians 9:13.

The language *"eat the sacrifices"* refers to the meal that followed the actual sacrifice of the whole Burnt Offering, which was the Peace Offering. The whole family on these occasions, and sometimes invited guests, together ate portions of the Sacrificed food.

Actually, the partaking of the Peace Offering by the worshippers of Old Testament times was what Jesus was speaking of in John 6:53, to which we have already alluded, and which the Jews should have understood. However, they had neglected the Word of God for so long, even as many presently, that they hardly knew what it said or meant anymore.

The probable reason that Paul uses this example is that it is more closely analogous to the pagan meals, which also involve sacrifice, followed by a meal in which the sacrificial food was eaten. However, in the Christian celebration of the Lord's Supper, no sacrifice is offered as in the Jewish worship Feasts of old, simply because the Sacrifice has already been offered in the Person of Christ.

The *"Altar"* of which Paul here speaks is the Brazen Altar, which sat in front of the Temple, with the Brazen Lavers in between it and the Temple. In other words, the *"Altar"* was first, because it must be first as it symbolizes the Crucifixion of Christ, and Him taking the sin penalty upon Himself which was death.

Even though Paul is not actually teaching here on the Altar, but only referring to it in passing to make a point, still the Bible Student will undoubtedly benefit from a deeper study on this all-important aspect of our Christian experience, which has its roots in the Jewish Sacrifices of old.

## THE ALTAR

The Altar played a central role in Israel's worship of God, as it also did in other ancient peoples' idolatrous worship. The regulations surrounding the Altar of Israel help us to better understand our own relationship with God through Jesus Christ.

## THE NATURE OF THE ALTAR

The essence of the Altar is revealed in its Hebrew name: *"misbeah."* The word comes from *"zabah,"* which means *"to sacrifice."* In other words, the Altar is *"the place of Sacrifice."*

God Himself instituted sacrifice in Eden when he used a covering of animal skins to clothe fallen Adam and Eve (Gen. 3:21). The first recorded instance of an Altar built to worship the Lord was the one Noah built after the Flood (Gen. 8:20), and each of the three Patriarchs followed this practice after meeting with the Lord (Gen. 12:7, 8; 26:25; 35:3, 7).

The Law of Moses (given about 1450 B.C.) contains detailed instructions about the construction of the Altar to be used by Israel and about the Sacrifices to be offered on it. Instructions about Sacrifice were given immediately after the moral and civil regulations of the Law were announced.

Once God's standards were inscripturated in the Law, every violation was sin and brought guilt. The Altar was a place where guilty people could come to bring the Sacrifices that would reestablish a harmonious relationship with the Lord.

## THE SIGNIFICANCE OF THE ALTAR

In early Genesis, the Altar seems to have been both a place of Sacrifice and a Memorial, reminding the worshiper of some special experience with the Lord. The Altar of Sacrifice that the Law instituted had a deeper significance.

God says of the Sacrificial animal: *"The life of the creature is in the blood, and I have given it to you to make Atonement for yourselves upon the Altar; it is the blood that makes Atonement for one's life"* (Lev. 17:11).

It was through this — the Altar and the covering of one's sins provided by the Atoning Sacrifice — that a sinner might approach a Holy God. The Altar, thus, was the point of contact with God; the place at which a sinning humanity might meet God in safety, with full assurance of forgiveness.

## ONE WORSHIP CENTER AND ONE ALTAR OF SACRIFICE

This significance is underlined in the design of the Tabernacle and the Temple. In each Worship Center, the plan called for an enclosed court. There was only one door to permit entry. It was immediately inside this door that the Altar of Sacrifice was located.

The lesson to Israel was clear: no one could approach apart from Sacrifice; that is, apart from the confession of sin and the Atoning Blood that the Sacrifice involved.

The Law also made it clear that there was to be only one Worship Center and one Altar of Sacrifice for God's Old Testament people. The Tabernacle served this purpose during the wilderness years; the Temple did so after it was completed in the rule of King Solomon.

The other people of the ancient Middle East had many altars and worshipped their gods and goddesses in local groves, temples, and on the top of hills. Israel was to destroy all such local worship centers. The pagan altars were to be broken down and the sacred stones and symbols smashed. Israel was not to worship God in pagan ways.

## GOD IS THE ONLY ONE

In the place of the many altars, there was to be only one, located in *"the place the Lord your God will choose"* to put His dwelling. Only to that place and only on that Altar were Burnt Offerings and Sacrifices to be brought (Deut. 12:1-7).

There were subsequent occasions, before the Jerusalem Temple was established about 959 B.C., when Offerings were made on temporary Altars (I Sam. 7:7-17; I Chron. 21:26).

There were even exceptions afterwards (I Kings 18:16-40). But God's insistence that there be only one Altar in Israel's worship is significant. The one Altar, like the one door opening into the Temple Court, showed Israel (and it shows us) that God is the Only One Who can establish the way humans are able to approach Him and that their approach can be made only through a Sacrifice God Himself ordains.

## TWO TYPES OF ALTARS

Israel's worship involved two Altars:

1. The great bronze Altar of Sacrifice, visible to all the people at the place of entry into the Temple.
2. The gold-overlaid Altar within the Holy Place, hidden from public view, where Incense was burned. The Inner Altar (Ex. 30:6; 40:5) is sometimes called the *"Altar before the Lord"* (Lev. 16:12).

The Incense that was burned on the Inner hidden Altar symbolizes prayer (Rev. 8:3).

## SYMBOLIC ALTARS

Not all Altars in Israel were intended to be used for Sacrifice. By long tradition, Altars were used as Memorials, reminders of some act of God or spiritually significant event. The Tribes who lived east of the Jordan River built an Altar by the riverside, *"not for Burnt Offerings or Sacrifices"* but as evidence of their common spiritual heritage with the other Tribes living in Canaan proper (Josh. Chpt. 22).

Gideon erected an Altar in Ophrah as a Memorial of the time God appeared to him (Judg.6:24).

Such Memorial Altars were carefully constructed on the pattern called for by Old Testament Law (Ex. 20:24-26).

NOTES

## THE NEW TESTAMENT REFERENCES TO ALTARS

The Greek word translated *"Altar"* is *"thysiaaterion,"* meaning *"place of Sacrifice."* Usually the Altar referred to in the Gospels is the Sacrificial Altar in the Jerusalem Temple of Jesus' day.

In I Corinthians 9:13, Paul argues by analogy for financial support of Christian Ministers. The Old Testament Priests who served the Altar were given a share of the animals they Sacrificed; this was for feeding their families.

As well, Paul points out in I Corinthians 10:18 that the worshipers also shared by eating the meat of some Sacrifices (Peace Offerings). This was considered participation in the Sacrifice. (Lev. Chpt. 7)

The young Believers at Corinth were warned that attendance at the Feasts linked with pagan worship constituted participation — and idolatry.

## THE BETTER SYSTEM

The whole argument of the Book of Hebrews is built by comparisons between the Old Testament system instituted by Law and the *"better system"* inaugurated by Jesus. Jesus' Priesthood is superior to that of the Levites who served the old Altar (Heb. 7:11-28). The earthly Worship Center was itself merely a copy of realities that exist in Heaven — and Jesus serves as Priest in that realm of ultimate reality (Heb. 9:1-24).

The Old Testament Tabernacle or Temple was never more than a shadow cast by reality, an illustration for the present time. The Sacrifices there could never really take away sin; so Jesus Himself became the Sacrifice on the real Altar (Heb. 9:9-14).

Jesus went outside the city of Jerusalem, beyond the walls within which the Temple and its Altar lay, to offer up his life on the Altar of Calvary.

Those who believe in Jesus must follow him outside the confines of the old system, abandoning its now-empty practices, and bear any disgrace that that may involve (Heb. 13:10-13).

## CALVARY AND FORGIVENESS

The Book of Revelation focuses on another aspect of the Altar. Blood Sacrifices were offered on the Altar to make Atonement for sin. The Sacrifice thus speaks not only of forgiveness but also of judgement.

Sacrifice shows that God cannot dismiss sin lightly. Death is the necessary consequence of sin. In the Old Testament and the New Testament, the Altar portrays God's willingness to accept the death of a substitute in place of the sinner. We discover that God Himself became the Sacrifice, as Christ at Calvary offered Himself in payment of the penalty justice demanded.

But what of those who reject the forgiveness offered on the basis of the Sacrificial Altar at Calvary? For them, the Altar carries only a message of doom.

In Revelation, we see burning coals, which had consumed the Sacrifice, hurled upon the Earth (Rev. 8:5) as the final judgement of humanity begins.

## BOTH TESTAMENTS

Under both the Old and the New Covenants, the Altar is a place of Sacrifice. The Old Testament describes in detail the Altar and its placement in the Tabernacle and the Temple.

The New Testament makes it clear that the pattern given in the Old Testament is intended to communicate spiritual Truths; it is a shadow, but one cast by spiritual reality.

Both the placement of the Altar and the fact that Israel was to offer Sacrifices on only one Altar picture for us this great Truth: There is only one way to approach Israel's God. It is the way of a Sacrifice that He Himself ordained, and that Sacrifice is God's Only Son, and our Saviour, The Lord Jesus Christ.

(19) "WHAT SAY I THEN? THAT THE IDOL IS ANY THING, OR THAT WHICH IS OFFERED IN SACRIFICE TO IDOLS IS ANY THING?"

The question, *"What say I then?"*, is meant to call to the attention of the Corinthians that they have failed to discern that, though an idol is not a god, still that does not mean that it does not represent supernatural powers, which it in fact does.

The questions, *"That the idol is any thing, or that which is offered in sacrifice to idols is any thing?"*, puts these things in their proper perspective.

The Corinthians had argued that eating idol food, meaning eating meals at the Temples, could not have any bearing on one's Christian life since there is only One God, which in turn means that an idol cannot have genuine reality. So, is Paul saying by his preceding argument *"that sacrificial food is anything"*? Of course not, is his intended response.

That we *"share in the Blood and Body of Christ"* does not thereby mean that there is genuine significance to the food eaten at pagan meals, as if it were actually sacrificed to a *"god."* Nor does it mean to imply that *"an idol is any thing."* On this point, they are agreed, an idol has no reality, in the sense that an idol does not in fact represent what might truly be called a *"god."*

However, to dismiss the situation that lightly, even as Paul now argues, is failing to see that which is behind these idols, even though they be nothing within themselves. I speak of the powers of darkness of which Paul will now become more explicit.

(20) "BUT I SAY, THAT THE THINGS WHICH THE GENTILES SACRIFICE, THEY SACRIFICE TO DEVILS, AND NOT TO GOD: AND I WOULD NOT THAT YE SHOULD HAVE FELLOWSHIP WITH DEVILS."

The phrase, *"But I say, that the things which the Gentiles sacrifice, they sacrifice to Devils, and not to God,"* proclaims in blunt terms the powers of darkness behind these idols, etc.

Correct, the idols within themselves are nothing, and as well, the sacrifices offered to them. However, that which energized the idol worship definitely was a reality, which were demon spirits. Consequently, the sacrifices of pagans are actually offered to demons, even though they do not realize such, and in reality, not to a Being Who might rightly be termed God.

However, for these people to understand what Paul was saying, he had to use Old Testament Revelation.

The manner in which he uses the phrase *"sacrifice to devils"* is taken from Deuteronomy

NOTES

32:17. It is the Song of Moses, and proclaims that Israel in the desert had rejected God their Rock for beings who were no gods, but rather were demons.

The phrase, *"And I would not that ye should have fellowship with Devils,"* presents Paul applying the stinger. He is in effect saying, *"I do not want you to be sharers or partners in demons."*

Since the Lord's Table or the Lord's Supper involves no sacrifice, inasmuch as Jesus has already been our Sacrifice, it took the additional illustration of Israel to give clarity to this present assertion.

Paul is contemporizing that the food eaten at the pagan meals had been sacrificed to demons; that means that those at the table are sharers in what had been sacrificed to demons in the same way that Israel shared in what had been sacrificed to God, respecting her participating in the eating of the Peace Offering.

Paul's point is simple: these pagan meals are in fact sacrifices to demons; the worship of demons is involved, even though these pagans were not aware of such.

One who is already bound to one's Lord and to one's fellow Believers through participation at the Lord's Table cannot, under any circumstances, nor would he desire under any circumstances, to also participate in the worship of demons. Paul will make the point even more explicit in the next verse (Fee).

## HOW DOES SUCH COMPARE WITH MODERN TIMES?

The lessons here taught by the Holy Spirit through the Apostle are so valuable, even for these modern times, and especially for these modern times, that if the lesson is unlearned, failure could definitely be in the offing.

For instance, when a Christian listens to music, he surely must understand that there are certain types of music which are actually generated by the Powers of Darkness. Consequently, to willfully lend one's ear, mind, and heart to such an offering, is to willfully open up oneself to the demon spirits which have inspired the music in the first place (negative inspiration).

The same can be said for many movies. That which is behind them are demon spirits, in which Christians should not desire to participate.

Gambling is another foray into vice which has its anchor in demon spirits, which speaks of superstition, witchcraft, magic, good luck charms, etc. In fact, the list is quite lengthy.

Consequently, the Christian should be very careful as to what he hears, attends, reads, or in which he participates. This is the analogy being drawn by Paul.

(21) "YE CANNOT DRINK THE CUP OF THE LORD, AND THE CUP OF DEVILS: YE CANNOT BE PARTAKERS OF THE LORD'S TABLE, AND OF THE TABLE OF DEVILS."

The phrase, *"Ye cannot drink the cup of the Lord, and the cup of devils,"* proclaims the two as being mutually exclusive. In other words, it is literally impossible to (you cannot) drink the cup of the Lord and the cup of demons at the same time.

As should be obvious, Paul does not merely *"not want"* them to be participants in the demonic, using the starkest kind of language, he asserts that they simply cannot do such a thing.

These words function as both warning and prohibition. They warn in terms of the following rhetorical questions (vs. 22); they prohibit in the sense of pointing out the absolute incompatibility of the two actions. One is not merely eating with friends at the pagan temple; one is engaged in idolatry, idolatry that involves the worship of demons (Fee).

The phrase, *"Ye cannot be partakers of the Lord's table, and of the table of devils,"* speaks of sharing at the Table of the Lord, and at the table of devils.

Those who eat at the Lord's Table, proclaiming His Death until He comes (I Cor. 11:26), are thereby also bound to one another through the death of the Lord that is thus celebrated. So also with pagans. Theirs is a sacred *"fellowship"* in honor of demons. Those who are bound to one another through Christ cannot also become *"fellows"* with those whose meals are consecrated to demons (Fee).

## THE LORD'S TABLE

This phrase, *"The Lord's Table,"* came to be one of the titles used for the *"Lord's Supper,"* i.e. *"Eucharist."*

However, the Christians at that time also had their fellowship feast. It was enjoyed on the first day of each week, and history records that the food consisted of meat, roast fowls, bread, juice, and other edibles. Christ was assumed to be the Host and those who attended were His

NOTES

guests; so it was called *"the Lord's Table"*; the other was called *"the table of devils,"* i.e. Satan's table, for he is the prince of the demons.

JEALOUSY

The Apostle argues that to gratify the appetite at both tables meant the association of demons with the Messiah, which is unthinkable. It placed them on an equality. Such action provoked Jehovah to jealousy, even as Verse 22 proclaims, and of the result of conflict with Him and His superior strength there could be no question. Holy jealousy is an activity of Divine Love.

The bread which they broke, and the cup for which they gave thanks are covering terms expressive of all the food that was upon the table. They symbolized the common spiritual life which animated all the guests, and the common brotherhood into which they had been brought, i.e. *"the family of God."*

FELLOWSHIP WITH CHRIST

But there was fellowship with Christ as well as with one another. The meal expressed a participation with Him, as foreshadowed by the participation of the worshiper in the Wilderness with the Altar. And just as in that case, the death of the Peace Offering was necessary in order to have the feast, so the fellowship meal at Corinth was based upon, and only possible because of the outpouring of Christ's Precious Blood.

Thus, the meal was a participation in the Body and Blood of the Lord, and outwardly expressed in shadow the inward reality of John 6:51-65.

THE SACRIFICE

The fact contrasted sharply with the table of demons, for none of them had sacrificed himself in order to provide a feast for his worshipers. But Christ did so, and in doing so, denied Himself; and upon this fact, the Apostle based his powerful appeal that they should imitate Him (Williams).

(22) "DO WE PROVOKE THE LORD TO JEALOUSY? ARE WE STRONGER THAN HE?"

The question, *"Do we provoke the Lord to jealousy?"* is answered when God's people abandon the Cross, which is the only answer for sin, and thereby foment other ways which allegedly lead to victory. All such will come under judgment.

NOTES

The expression, *"a jealous God,"* is used in the second Commandment which expressed reference to idolatry (Ex. 34:14-15).

In effect, Paul is saying, *"Will you continue eating at both meals, and thus arouse the Lord's jealousy, as Israel did in the desert?"* It seems that Paul is asking a rhetorical question, *"Are we trying to arouse the Lord's jealousy?"*

The term *"jealousy"* is a reflection of the Old Testament portrayal of God's Self-revelation (Ex. 20:5), which is related to His Holiness and Power, in which He is to be understood as so absolutely without equal that He will brook no rivals to His devotion.

In other words, Paul is saying here that it is possible for the Believer to conduct himself in such a rebellious manner, as to arouse the anger of God, which is something no one wants to do, that is if they are sane.

The question, *"Are we stronger than He?"*, proclaims the warning that God's *"jealousy"* cannot be challenged with impunity. Those who put God to the test by insisting on their right to do what Paul insists is idolatry are in effect taking God on, challenging Him by their actions, daring Him to act, in effect, tempting Him exactly as Israel did in the wilderness (I Cor. 10:9).

THE CORINTHIANS

The Believers at Corinth were arguing for the right to attend pagan feasts and were trying to *"build up"* others by having them attend as well. Paul says *"No."* Not only is the latter action totally unloving, and Christian behavior is based on love, not knowledge — but the action itself is totally incompatible with life in Christ as it is celebrated at the Lord's Table. Thus, he appeals, exhorts, and finally warns that such attendance is absolutely forbidden. But the matter is not completely finished. Not everything is absolute; there are still matters which need to be attended, even as Paul will address in the remainder of this Chapter.

CHRISTIAN FAITH

Without returning to Law, meaning Law as a means to right standing with God, the Christian

Faith has inherent within it something so radical that it absolutizes certain behavior.

Being members of one body in Christ makes it quite impossible to be involved in idolatrous practices. Fundamental allegiance is at stake. One cannot serve God and Mammon — or demons, whatever form they may take in our modern world.

Sitting at *"The Table"* and experiencing its benefits of Grace and Freedom does not give one license for religious or moral licentiousness. Rather, it binds us to one another in common fellowship around Christ and the New Covenant in such a way that our behavior in the new age is radicalized toward *"the Law to* (of) *Christ"* (I Cor. 9:21) (Fee).

Due to the way in which the word *"jealousy"* is used, perhaps a fuller investigation of the word would be helpful.

## JEALOUSY

One Hebrew word and one Greek word can both be translated either *"jealousy"* or *"zeal."* The distinction is not in the terms, instead it is found in the relationship of the person to the thing that is desired.

## JEALOUSY AND ENVY

The Hebrew root meaning *"jealousy"* portrays a very strong emotion, a passionate desire. The word is used in both a positive and a negative sense. In the negative, it is a desire for something that properly belongs to another (Gen. 30:1; 37:11).

When referring to the emotion itself, and not to the relationship between one person and another or between a person and an object, it is often translated *"envy"* (Prov. 3:31; 23:17).

The strong emotion represented by the word *"jealousy"* can be viewed positively as a high level of commitment when it describes the feeling of a person for something that is rightly his or her own. Here *"jealousy"* has the sense of intense love.

When applied to God, *"jealousy"* communicates the fierce intensity of His commitment to His people, even when they turn from Him.

## THE JEALOUS ZEAL OF GOD

In the Mosaic Law, special provision was made for testing the faithfulness of a wife if her spouse should begin to feel jealous (Num. Chpt. 5). Jealousy in marriage is an image used in the Old Testament to describe the relationship between God and His Covenant people, paralleling the relationship between husband and wife.

In giving the Mosaic Law, the Lord announced to the people of Israel that they must remain committed to Him and not turn to idolatry, and He gave this reason: *"I, the Lord your God, am a jealous God"* (Ex. 20:5). The jealousy of God is expressed in Old Testament history both in *"punishing"* and in *"showing love."*

In the Old Testament, God is said to be jealous for His people, for His land (Joel 2:18), and for Jerusalem and Zion (Zech. 1:14). While the anger of God is an expression of God's jealous wrath, the acts of judgement recorded in the Old Testament continue to be for the ultimate benefit of a people who must be brought back to a right relationship with God if they are to experience blessing.

## JEALOUSY IN THE NEW TESTAMENT

In New Testament passages where the Greek words are translated *"jealous,"* the tone is nearly always negative. For instance, the Jews were jealous of the Gentiles' response to the Gospel (Acts 5:17; 13:45; 17:5). In each case, this jealousy motivated hostile acts. It may be this link with sinful actions that is stressed in the New Testament.

Jealousy is often found linked with *"outbursts of anger"* (II Cor. 12:20; Gal. 5:20) and dissension (Rom. 13:13; I Cor. 3:3) in the New Testament's list of the behavior that springs from man's fallen nature.

Stephen refers to the Patriarchs' jealousy of Joseph (Acts 7:9), and Paul makes mention of Israel's attempt to provoke to jealousy (I Cor. 10:22), even as we are now studying.

Only in II Corinthians 11:2, where Paul speaks of his own jealousy over the Corinthians as being like God's jealousy (a fierce desire for what is best for them because they are his own), is the word used in a positive way.

## FEELINGS AND EMOTIONS

Neither God nor humans are cold, computer-like beings. Persons have emotions as well as intellect and will, and often these emotions are strong. Jealousy or zeal is one of the stronger emotions.

NOTES

God's jealousy, although it issues punishment as well as blessing, is viewed as something both righteous and good.

In general, human jealousy is viewed with suspicion. Our emotions are too often tainted by the sin that twists human personalities. But we can experience strong emotional commitments to what is good, as well as strong emotional desires for what is not our own.

It is good to remember that God's desire, as He works in our lives, is not to rob us of our emotions. Instead, He wants to capture and channel our capacity for intense commitment. He wants us to have a Godly jealousy for others and to be zealous for everything that is good (Richards).

(23) "ALL THINGS ARE LAWFUL FOR ME, BUT ALL THINGS ARE NOT EXPEDIENT: ALL THINGS ARE LAWFUL FOR ME, BUT ALL THINGS EDIFY NOT."

The phrase, *"All things are lawful for me, but all things are not expedient,"* addresses Christian liberty, but, as well, the manner in which it should be attended. Paul has shown, and continues to show, that Christian liberty must be modified by considerations of expediency and edification in accordance with the feelings of sympathy and charity. In other words, all *"rights"* must be looked at in the light of fellow Believers. How will such effect them?

The phrase, *"All things are lawful for me, but all things edify not,"* addressed the contention of the Corinthians that their Christian *"rights"* gave them the freedom to act as they saw fit. However, for Paul, it meant the *"right"* to become a slave of all; or as here, the *"right"* to *"benefit"* and *"build up"* others in the Body. Consequently, we see that which is Christlike versus that which springs from self-will.

Another translation of I Corinthians 10:23 considers the freedom God has won for us and observes, *"Everything is permissible,"* quickly adding, *"Not everything is constructive."*

The key Greek word is *"oikodomeo,"* which means *"to build up, to edify."* Although everything may be permitted to us who are Christians, not everything will help us advance spiritually. Mature use of freedom calls for us to choose those things that will help us grow, and others as well, and especially others.

NOTES

LAWFUL

The lawful (*"exesti,"* 32 times in the New Testament) is that which is permissible or permitted by Law. The word is used most often in the Gospels and Acts.

The Pharisees of Jesus' day had developed a vast network of interpretations of Old Testament Statutes and Commandments. The result was that these *"Commandments of Men"* (Mat. 15:9) condemned many perfectly neutral actions as unlawful. This is well illustrated in Matthew 12:1-14.

JESUS REJECTED LEGALISM

Jesus rejected Pharisaical legalism and met the issue head on. When those who wanted to accuse Jesus asked Him if it was legal to heal on the Sabbath, Jesus did not mince words, saying, *"It is lawful to do good on the Sabbath"* and He healed.

The Pharisees hated Jesus for cutting through their convoluted thinking to reestablish the original concern of Law: to show people how to love God and others.

Paul uses *"exesti"* in a distinctive way in I Corinthians 6:12 and 10:23. He says, *"All things are lawful for me, but...!"* His point is that, while Believers are not under the Old Testament Law — and thus technically all actions are lawful, there are still criteria by which one must evaluate his or her decisions (Richards).

(24) "LET NO MAN SEEK HIS OWN, BUT EVERY MAN ANOTHER'S WEALTH."

It should have been translated, *"Let no man seek his own, but every man another's good."*

This is the first appearance of this formula in Paul's letters, but it is so basic to his understanding of Christian ethics that it probably had long been part of the instructions he gave to the Churches. Both in Romans 15:1-2 and Philippians 2:4, he bases such a stance on the example of Christ, which is precisely how he approaches it at the end of the present argument (I Cor. 10:33-11:1).

For Paul, the death of Christ, in which He gave Himself *"for us,"* is not only God's offer of pardon for sinners, but also the only proper model of Discipleship. Hence, *"freedom"* does not mean *"to seek my own good"*; it means to be free in Christ in such a way that one can truly seek to benefit and build up another person (Fee).

NOTES

As possibly no other of Paul's statements, this of the 24th Verse epitomizes Christ perhaps greater than anything he has written. It is simple, clear, straightforward, to the point, and leaves absolutely no doubt as to its meaning.

This is so contrary to the ways of the world, so opposite of the religions of mankind, so different in spirit — this preference for others over oneself. To be frank, only the Love of God shed abroad in the hearts and lives of Believers can propel one towards such a destination. To be sure, most of the Corinthians did not have this type of love, and I am afraid that most Believers presently do not either.

However, the thrust of Paul's statement is that to prefer others is to prefer Christ.

(25) "WHATSOEVER IS SOLD IN THE SHAMBLES, THAT EAT, ASKING NO QUESTION FOR CONSCIENCE SAKE:"

The phrase, *"Whatsoever is sold in the shambles,"* refers to the marketplace or the meat market.

The phrase, *"That eat, asking no questions for conscience sake,"* means *"Do not trouble your conscience by scruples arising from needless investigation about the food"* (Farrar).

After giving a lesson on Christian liberty, which falls out to an extended concern for others, Paul now lays down guidelines.

All meat sold in the marketplace can be purchased and eaten without violating the Word of God in any manner; however, the Believers must be very careful regarding their association with the idol feasts, etc.

While the Holy Spirit, through the Apostle, has proclaimed loudly the concern that mature Believers ought to have for others, still one can only go so far in catering to erroneous beliefs. Consequently, as stated, Paul now draws the line.

His rule for everyday life in Corinth is a simple one: *"Eat anything sold in the marketplace without raising questions of conscience."* The reason for addressing this issue, even as we have previously stated, is that what was sold in the marketplace often contained meat butchered by the priests, much of it having been part of the pagan sacrifices. Since such meat was expressly forbidden to Jews, and since in their earliest days followers of *"the Way"* were considered a sect of the Jews, the whole issue of the Christians' relationship to the meat market, etc., was a thorny one.

## THAT WHICH THE HOLY SPIRIT IS TEACHING

If the reader only sees the surface situation presented here, he will miss the point entirely of what is being taught. While these particular problems do not effect modern Christians in any manner, still, the issue behind the scenes does affect all of us and greatly so. At least some of the lessons being taught are according to the following:

1. The Holy Spirit is to set the standard in our lives, which will always be according to the Word of God.
2. The Believer must ever understand that he is an example, or rather should be, of The Lord Jesus Christ to all of mankind. As such, he must ever be mindful of his conduct.
3. Christian liberty must never be taken as a license to sin, but rather the liberty to live a holy life.
4. Believers showing concern for other Believers must ever be the paramount conclusion.
5. The Believer must never partake of both the Lord's Table and the table of devils.
6. In looking at a situation as to whether it is right or wrong, one must look beyond the surface interest, ascertaining the source. Even though the idols were nothing, the source of those idols was demon spirits, with which no Believer would ever want to associate.
7. Even though mature Believers must ever be aware of weaker Believers, consequently doing nothing that would cause them difficulty, still one can only go so far in catering to personal beliefs which have no scriptural foundation.

(26) "FOR THE EARTH IS THE LORD'S, AND THE FULNESS THEREOF."

This passage is found in Psalms 24:1.

This is the passage used by the Jewish Rabbis to support the contention that a blessing must be said over every meal, and rightly so. However, what Paul does here contains some irony toward his Jewish heritage, whether intended or not.

The Rabbis saw the text as the reason for thanking God for their food; but the food they thus blessed had been thoroughly *"investigated"* before prayer. Paul now uses the text to justify eating all foods, even those forbidden by the

Jews, since God is the ultimate source of the food — even that sold in the marketplace (Fee).

Of course, positions such as this would not at all endear the Apostle to most Jewish Christians, with many at that time attempting to follow Christ and the Mosaic Law. Paul struck at this very hard, which he certainly should have, but which tended to raise great animosity against him. The pressure always has been and still is to compromise the Message. However, such is the bane of the Church, causing great spiritual declension.

### PAUL THE APOSTLE

The Apostle Paul was not an ordained minister in the ecclesiastically accepted sense. He did not receive his theological training in a denominational Seminary. He had no degrees, earned, honorary, or otherwise. He was not ordained by an official Council or Synod or Conference. He could produce no diploma from some great theological institution. He had not been licensed to preach by a committee of Elders, Bishops, or Presbyters. He belonged to no ministerial association.

There is no record that he was ever called *"Reverend"* or *"Doctor."* He never signed his name, Rev. Doctor Paul, D.D. Because of these facts, Paul was rejected by the religious legalists of his day.

He was not a product of their Seminary, had not been licensed or ordained by their church group, he was not a member of their association, and so they would exclude him.

Paul had received his Commission and his Message of Grace direct from Heaven. There has little been a place in organized religion for men like Paul, and for all the obvious reasons. The one word that characterizes organized religion is *"control."* Paul was not a man that could be controlled by other men, even though he definitely was controlled by the Holy Spirit. So, if religious men cannot control one, they seek to destroy one.

(27) "IF ANY OF THEM THAT BELIEVE NOT BID YOU TO A FEAST, AND YE BE DISPOSED TO GO; WHATSOEVER IS SET BEFORE YOU, EAT, ASKING NO QUESTION FOR CONSCIENCE SAKE."

The phrase, *"If any of them that believe not bid you to a feast, and ye be disposed to go,"* pertains to the homes of unbelievers and not to Temple feasts. I think one could say that Paul had absolutely forbidden attendance at Temple meals.

NOTES

The phrase, *"Whatsoever is set before you, eat, asking no question for conscience sake,"* is actually speaking of unbelievers who invite Believers to their homes for a meal, etc. The Believer on that occasion, is not to make inquiry respecting the source of the food, if it had pertained to idols or not, etc.

First of all, such an attitude would show extremely bad manners, and would project a *"holier than thou"* persona, which is definitely not Christlike.

Once again, by Paul using the word *"conscience,"* such refers to investigation. If the Believer does not know, concerning this particular question, there is nothing then for his conscience to address.

(28) "BUT IF ANY MAN SAY UNTO YOU, THIS IS OFFERED IN SACRIFICE UNTO IDOLS, EAT NOT FOR HIS SAKE THAT SHEWED IT, AND FOR CONSCIENCE SAKE: FOR THE EARTH IS THE LORD'S, AND THE FULNESS THEREOF;"

The phrase, *"But if any man say unto you, this is offered in sacrifice unto idols,"* refers strictly to information given by the host, but not solicited by the guest.

The phrase, *"Eat not for his sake that shewed it, and for conscience sake,"* speaks of the reason being that Christians are to make it plain that they will have no part in traffic with idols and demons. However, that stand is to be taken only if the information is revealed by the host.

To be factual, there is no harm in eating the meat either way it goes, but to set an example, the Believer is to decline if certain information is revealed regarding sacrifice to idols.

The phrase, *"For the earth is the Lord's, and the fulness thereof,"* sees Paul using this statement again, taken from Psalms 24:1.

The idea is that God made all the animals and plants, etc. Consequently, it is not wrong to partake of any animal regarding food, or any grain, plant or fruit, providing it is edible. As is obvious, and rightly so, Paul is moving away from the rudiments of the old Law of Moses, whether regarding sacrifices, ceremonies, rituals, or certain types of food, etc. It is not that the Law was bad, for it wasn't. In fact, it was holy because it was God's Law.

The reason is, the Law had served its purpose. It had done what it was intended to do, and now having been fulfilled by Christ, it is of no more consequence, at least respecting the Ceremonial, Civil, and Ritual. Of course, the moral Law, ensconced in the Ten Commandments minus the fourth, is still applicable because moral commandments can't change.

(29) "CONSCIENCE, I SAY, NOT THINE OWN, BUT OF THE OTHER: FOR WHY IS MY LIBERTY JUDGED OF ANOTHER MAN'S CONSCIENCE?"

The phrase, *"Conscience, I say, not thine own, but of the other,"* refers to the other Believer. The *"conscience"* of the strong Christian has already come to terms with the liberality of the Gospel, but yet, the strong Christian must consider the weaker ones as well, i.e. *"the conscience of the weaker ones."* Once again, Paul comes back to the necessity of the strong Christian being ever concerned about others.

The question, *"For why is my liberty judged of another man's conscience?"*, pertains to the fact that even though another person might think we are doing wrong, such does not furnish the smallest proof that wrong is actually being committed. In other words, I have Liberty in Christ, not because of what someone else thinks, but rather because of The Lord Jesus Christ.

Holiness is too often decided or defined by that other than the Bible, and I speak of social mores, prevailing opinion, conventional wisdom, rules, and regulations of some Church, or whatever others think. Such should never be the case!

However, Paul is also stating that liberty must never be used to satisfy the desires of our own person, but must always be measured according to others. In other words, don't do anything that would cause someone else to stumble.

(30) "FOR IF I BY GRACE BE A PARTAKER, WHY AM I EVIL SPOKEN OF FOR THAT FOR WHICH I GIVE THANKS?"

The phrase, *"For if I by Grace be a partaker,"* refers to this great Salvation we have in Christ, that was furnished us totally and completely by Grace, and not by works. In other words, I don't have what I have in Christ because I do not eat certain foods, do not go certain places, do not wear certain types of clothing, do not participate in certain things, but rather because of the Goodness and Grace of God. However, when many people read the words I have just written, they get it in their minds somehow that Grace provides a license to sin. No it doesn't! If a person is truly saved, they don't want to sin. To be frank, sin is repulsive to them.

NOTES

The idea is that all the things we receive from God are received totally by Grace, in other words God's unmerited favor, and not by works or good deeds we perform. In fact, the Grace of God bestowed upon the undeserving sinner gives us the power to live a holy life, instead of the opposite.

The question, *"Why am I evil spoken of for that for which I give thanks?"*, seems to say that he was criticized either way he went. If he did not eat of the particular meat in question, he was criticized by those who were proclaiming their liberty in Christ, and if he did eat, he was criticized by those who thought he was doing wrong by doing such.

The contention of his question is, even as the next verse proclaims, that whatever we do, we should *"do all to the Glory of God."* Everyone cannot be pleased; however, if we please God, we cannot go wrong.

## STUMBLINGBLOCK OR STEPPINGSTONE

Once again, most reading this Tenth Chapter of I Corinthians would wonder at its significance for modern day Christians. However, and as previously stated, if we are thinking only of the particular problem they had then, which was the eating or not eating of meat offered to idols, etc., we miss the point entirely.

Paul was dealing with something, or rather the Holy Spirit through him, that is incumbent upon every single generation, and in fact, every single Believer. Irrespective as to whether it is eating meat offered to idols, or in modern terminology, going to movies, etc., what line should the Christian draw respecting that which is legitimate or illegitimate.

As we have previously stated, there is not a single Commandment in the great Covenant of Grace. That comes as a shock to most modern Believers, but it is so. But yet, there are all types of things that Believers will not do, even as Paul is addressing in this Tenth Chapter.

## MORAL LAW

The idea is this: the Moral Law laid down in the Old Testament, and particularly enjoined in the Ten Commandments, minus the fourth, is still incumbent upon modern Believers, for the simple reason that Moral Truth or Law does not change, because it cannot change. So, if it was wrong to tell a lie, or steal, or commit adultery, etc., under the old Law, it's still wrong under Grace, and for all the obvious reasons and which Paul pointedly observes (I Cor. 10:5-11). And yet at the same time, the Believer must be very careful that he does not allow himself to be pushed back under Law, which is an ever present danger.

PAUL AND THE LAW

If there was anything which Paul was dead set against, and would not tolerate, it was being placed back under the Law of Moses from which he had been delivered by the Grace of God. That did not mean that the Law was bad, for it wasn't. Actually, it was the Law of God, and was given for specific reasons and performed its task exactly as intended.

It was meant to show man how sinful he was, and how absolutely helpless he was in view of his sinful condition, to obey God. There was no Salvation in the Law, no victory in the Law, simply because it was not intended to be. Even though there was Righteousness in the Law, still it was impossible to obtain, for the Law demanded perfect performance, which human beings could never do.

Paul now insists that he is living the life of victory in Christ, in which victory alone can be found. His life was no more governed by the demands of the Law, but the constraining power of the Love of Christ.

The reader must remember that he said, *"All things are lawful for me, but all things are not expedient* (not good for me)*: all things are lawful for me, but all things edify not* (do not help me, but rather hinder)*"* (I Cor. 10:23).

Four times in this one Epistle he makes the statement — *"All things are lawful for* (to) *me."* Paul says, *"As far as the Law is concerned, I am free."* Now don't misunderstand this statement.

Paul was not free to do as he pleased, but was rather free to please God. Please understand that, it is very important.

Under the Law of Moses, no one was free to please God simply because they did not have the power to do so, and as well, the Law did not provide such power. However, the Grace of God,

NOTES

which is given by Jesus Christ, now provides the power that is needed to live the life which is required. In fact, this law of love has no limitations. It does more than the law of Commandments ever required.

WHAT IS THIS LIBERTY?

1. Those who feel that what they are doing is not displeasing to God have the liberty to do so. But if it offends a weaker brother, the law of love should make us willing to sacrifice our liberty and refrain from anything that would cause another to stumble.

2. Those who do not agree with the liberties which some Christians enjoy should not sit in judgement or condemn them just because they do not see eye to eye. I am bold to assert that if the teaching of the Word in this matter was practiced, 95% of Church troubles could be solved without serious disagreement. There are two prongs to this weapon. They are both clearly stated in Romans 14:13:

*"Let us not therefore judge one another any more: but judge this rather, that no man put a stumblingblock or an occasion to fall in his Brother's way."*

How wonderful if these instructions could be followed by all of us. First let us refrain from sitting in judgement on a Brother's liberty in Christ. If you feel that your brother is doing things which you think are wrong, then don't do them, but don't condemn your brother. This, of course, never applies to those things which are already forbidden in the Bible, but I am referring whereon the Bible is silent and each one must decide for himself.

So, let us determine by God's Grace, *"I will not sit in judgement upon my Brother's honest convictions of conduct."* And now comes the other side of the story.

Neither are we who feel at liberty in things which we allow, to insist upon continuing them if we know it offends a disagreeing brother. To say, *"I see no wrong in this,"* and disregard what it does to another's conscience is to make your liberty a sin and a stumblingblock.

HOW FAR SHOULD WE GO?

Now I anticipate a question which must be answered. It is well and good to surrender our personal liberties for the sake of our testimony but how far must we carry this thing in order not to be an offense? To what extent must we sacrifice our liberty to please our neighbor and not injure their weak conscience?

For instance, some Christians object to the wearing of jewelry, gold rings and or ornaments. Others object to innocent amusements in which I personally see no wrong.

As well, there are those who object to a Christian lady wearing any type of make-up. Some object to articles of dress with which to adorn the temple of the Holy Spirit (our physical bodies).

As well, there are those who are offended by the use of coffee, or tea, or a hundred and one other things which could be mentioned.

To be frank, there are some of God's touchy Saints who, in their legal attitude, are so unreasonable in their condemnation of everything that they will find fault no matter what one does. There are some people whom no one can please. It is impossible to get along with them, try as you will.

As a Christian, we should ask ourselves some questions.

Are we under Law or under Grace? Is our conduct that which insists on our legal rights, or is it motivated by the law of love?

All we need ask in any case of doubt concerning the right or wrong of a thing is, *"Does it please God? Does it help or hinder my testimony? Is it what Jesus would do?"* To honestly make this the test of conduct would meet the demands of the Law, for *"love is the fulfilling of the law"* (Rom. 13:10).

WHAT PAUL IS SAYING . . .

It is clear that theoretically Paul sided with the views of the *"strong,"* but sympathetically with those of the *"weak."*

One might say that he disapproved of a defiant, ostentatious, insulting liberalism. On the other hand, he discouraged the miserable legalism, which exaggerated the importance of things external and indifferent.

Paul always tolerated the scruples of the weak, but would not suffer either weakness or strength to develop itself into a vexatious tyranny (Farrar).

Paul denied self, and in conduct imitated and obeyed his Master's symbolic action and command at the Last Supper, for He gave His Body and Blood for others (I Jn. 3:16), and Paul pressed the Corinthians to imitate him in his imitation of Christ (Williams).

NOTES

(31) "WHETHER THEREFORE YE EAT, OR DRINK, OR WHATSOEVER YE DO, DO ALL TO THE GLORY OF GOD."

The phrase, *"Whether therefore ye eat, or drink, or whatsoever ye do,"* covers every aspect of life and Godliness. In other words, it leaves nothing out, dealing with every aspect of our employment, domestic life, hobbies, conduct, or anything else that one could think. The idea is that the Believer belongs to Christ, and belongs to Christ totally.

As many Jews of old brought everything under the Sabbath, feeling free then to do basically whatever they desired on the remaining six days, many Christians have done the same thing with Sunday. God is pretty much forgotten the other six days. As the former was a Sabbath day religion, the latter is a Sunday religion. To be sure, such constitutes no relationship with Christ whatsoever!

The phrase, *"Do all to the Glory of God,"* presents itself as the criteria for all things.

The question that one should ask regarding everything that one does is, *"Does this bring Glory to God?"*

That pertains to what we eat, what we drink, where we go, what we read, what we say, and how we act in all matters. If we seriously consider that question, I think most of us would change some things in our lives.

WHAT DOES IT MEAN TO DO ALL TO THE GLORY OF GOD?

For instance, can a Believer drink a bottle of beer or a glass of wine occasionally, and do such for the Glory of God, knowing that alcohol is the cause of untold sorrow and heartache in the world?

Can a Believer frequent the movies, knowing that Hollywood is opposed to everything for which the Word of God stands, actually promoting the very opposite?

Can a Believer purchase and enjoy the music of the world, which makes no attempt to glorify God, but rather the very opposite?

As stated, as Believers, we have a great responsibility in this world as Ambassadors for Christ. So, as stated, everything we do should be done under the scrutiny of the question, *"Does this bring Glory to God?"*

NOTES

(32) "GIVE NONE OFFENCE, NEITHER TO THE JEWS, NOR TO THE GENTILES, NOR TO THE CHURCH OF GOD:"

The phrase, *"Give none offence,"* even though speaking of the matters at hand, still pertains to any and all things.

*"Offence"* in the Greek is *"aproskopos"* and means *"that which leads into sin."*

The phrase, *"Neither to the Jews, nor to the Gentiles, nor to the Church of God,"* means that one is not to purposely pursue a path that is to the detriment of another. To *"give offense,"* at least as Paul is here using the word, does not so much mean to *"hurt someone's feelings"* as to behave in such a way as to prevent someone from hearing the Gospel, or to alienate someone who is already a brother or sister.

Hence, *"freedom"* does not mean that one does whatever one wishes with no regard for others; nor do the limits on freedom suggested here mean that another's conscience dictates conduct. To the contrary, everything is for God's Glory and for the sake of the Gospel, that is, for the good of all, which from Paul's point of view means that they might be saved. That raises both concerns above mere *"rules of conduct."* Eating and drinking are irrelevant; the one who insists on the right to eat and drink is thereby making it significant. On the other hand, because it is irrelevant, one can use such freedom to restrain when necessary for the sake of the Gospel. This is what Paul is saying (Fee).

(33) "EVEN AS I PLEASE ALL MEN IN ALL THINGS, NOT SEEKING MINE OWN PROFIT, BUT THE PROFIT OF MANY, THAT THEY MAY BE SAVED."

The phrase, *"Even as I please all men in all things, not seeking mine own profit,"* proclaims the Apostle as offering himself as an example for the kind of conduct he is urging on others.

However, it should be noted that he is not speaking of *"pleasing people"* in the context of evangelism, in other words the preaching of the Gospel. In fact, concerning that, he said the very opposite, *"But as we were allowed of God to be put in trust with the Gospel, even so we speak; not as pleasing men, but God, which trieth our hearts"* (I Thess. 2:4). Actually, he said the same thing again in Galatians 1:10. In those passages, he refers to the kind of conduct that often characterized people pleasers or, in other words, preachers who curried the favor of others in order to gain their approval. So, Paul is not speaking here of preaching the Gospel, but rather that which pertains to his conduct.

His concern is not that he himself be pleasing to them, but that his conduct be such that he may not stand in the way of their being saved. This appeals to the example of Christ in His Suffering.

The phrase, *"But the profit of many, that they may be saved,"* echoes the language of I Corinthians 9:22.

In effect, Paul is repeating the language of Verses 23-24: *"Not seeking my own good but the good of many."* This is *"becoming all things to all people so that by all possible means I might save some."*

*"Christ Jesus has triumphed o'er Satan*
*and death, and now, praise His Name,*
*I am free.*
*"Al-though He has gone to the Father's*
*Right Hand, can others see Jesus*
*in me?"*

*"O will you give heed to this message*
*tonight, and to your commission*
*be true?*
*"Are you representing the Saviour*
*aright, can others see Jesus in you?"*

*"The harvest is plenteous, the fields they*
*are white, Alas! For the La-b'rers*
*are few.*
*"'Tis far better not to profess Jesus'*
*Name, if the world cannot see Him*
*in you."*

## CHAPTER 11

(1) "BE YE FOLLOWERS OF ME, EVEN AS I ALSO AM OF CHRIST."

Exactly what did Paul mean by this statement?

First of all, those who imitate Christ have a right to call upon others to imitate them. The point of comparison between Christ and Paul has already been clearly stated: Christ sought not His Own advantage but that of others. He came to seek and to save. Let this mind that was in Christ and then in Paul be also in us (Lenski).

NOTES

## AN APOSTLE

Apostleship afforded liberty in this respect as well; however, only in the sense that the Apostle follows Christ, as Paul certainly did.

In fact, as the Prophets were the spiritual guides of the people during Old Testament times (and I speak of True Prophets of God), likewise Apostles fill that role under the New Covenant (Eph. 2:20).

While there are those in the Church who can function in the realm of *"government"* and be scriptural in doing so, still it is to be only in the sense of administration and never in the sense of spiritual direction. Unfortunately, in too many religious denominations presently, the Scriptural role of the Apostle has been shunted aside, even forcibly so, and in its place, political direction instituted. I speak of those in the Church (Religious Denominations) elected by popular ballot, which never applies to an Apostle, who is always God-called (Eph. 4:11).

As a result, carnal direction comes into the Church, with the headship of Christ abrogated, meaning that the Holy Spirit can little function. Consequently, spiritual declension sets in, with such Religious Denominations less and less doing the Will of God and more and more carrying out their own will, i.e. perpetuation. Then it becomes merely an earthly organization, no different than other earthly organizations, albeit religious.

## FALSE APOSTLES

Paul urged the Corinthians to be imitators of him, even as he was an imitator of Christ, because there were, no doubt, false apostles coming into the Church, attempting to draw away Disciples after themselves, etc. In fact, this was a constant problem then, and is a constant problem presently.

The Lord calls certain ones for certain Ministries, with Satan attempting to counterfeit such callings. In fact, if he can get Believers to cease following God's appointed ones, whomever they may be, he will greatly succeed in weakening the Faith of such Christians, or even cause them to lose out entirely. That's at least one of the reasons that Paul strongly advised (even enjoined) the Corinthians to follow him.

He knew he had their spiritual welfare at heart, and as well, he knew that he had the mind of Christ, and he also knew that these interlopers were serving only their own selfish desires. In other words, they really could not care less about the people, only using them to further their ungodly ends.

To be frank, the modern prosperity message functions in the same capacity. Under the guise of leading people into a higher knowledge, in reality the people are used and abused for the selfish ends of the practitioners of this false message.

The people are told to give, and promised all type of financial rewards from the Lord for doing so. As such, it ceases to be giving and becomes an investment at best and a gamble at worst — neither of which will be acknowledged by God. In such a climate, the only ones who benefit are the Preachers.

However, it is a heady doctrine and attracts many followers, simply because it appeals to greed, which unfortunately finds a place in the hearts at times of even the Godliest.

It is believed by most Scholars, and rightly so, that the First Verse of this Eleventh Chapter should have been the last Verse of the previous Chapter. The language and argument are such that it seems clearly to conclude the message of I Corinthians Chapter 10, Verses 23 through 33. As stated, they are to follow (imitate) that example, in the same way that he has *"imitated"* Christ. The emphasis here is certainly on the example of Christ, which for Paul finds its primary focus in His Sacrifice on the Cross. Thus, the answer as given by Paul as the antidote to the behavior of the Corinthians, which they claimed to be predicated on wisdom and knowledge, is Christ crucified. It is hard to imagine a more telling way to end this long argument.

## PERSONAL FREEDOM

On this powerful note, the long section on *"idolatry"* comes to a conclusion. Behavior is not unimportant; but it is not regulated by law, at least not in Christ. However, some things are altogether incompatible with life in Christ and must be shunned (I Cor. 10:1-22); but other things are of no consequence whatsoever.

One is free with regard to these things; but the example of Christ must be predominant, and He *"pleased not Himself"* but willingly endured the insults of others that they might be saved (Rom. 15:3).

Despite this teaching by Paul, the issue of personal freedom in matters that are not clearly defined in the Bible, and the limitation of freedom for the sake of others, continue to haunt the Church. Usually the battle rages over what constitutes that which is right or wrong. Conservatives on these issues simply fail to reckon with how *"liberal"* Paul's own view really is. Hence, Paul is seldom heard for the sake of traditional regulations.

On the other hand, the assertion of freedom to the hurt of others is not the Biblical view either. However, in most contemporary settings, the *"offended"* are not unbelievers or new Christians, but those who tend to confuse their own regulations with the eternal Will of God (Fee). In other words, they tend to devise their own brand of personal Holiness, and then try to foster it off on others.

(2) "NOW I PRAISE YOU, BRETHREN, THAT YE REMEMBER ME IN ALL THINGS, AND KEEP THE ORDINANCES, AS I DELIVERED THEM TO YOU."

The phrase, *"Now I praise you, brethren, that ye remember me in all things,"* in effect refers to the letter they had sent to him respecting the particular questions addressed in this Epistle, plus others they did not address. Paul is thanking them for seeking his counsel.

His praising them has to do with the idea that, despite the efforts of Satan to disrupt this Assembly, and despite the fact that some in the Corinthian Church did not hold Paul as highly as they should, still the Holy Spirit maneuvered the situation in order that some in the Church would seek Paul's counsel on these very important matters. Thank the Lord they obeyed. Had they consulted others, which no doubt there was pressure from some quarters to do, the Church could have been, and probably would have been totally destroyed.

*"Praise"* in the Greek is *"epaineo,"* and means *"to commend or laud."* This is ironical, he praised them, but they little praised him.

The phrase, *"And keep the Ordinances, as I delivered them to you,"* no doubt refers to the whole body of Truth of the Gospel and not only the Lord's Supper and Water Baptism.

*"Ordinances"* in the Greek is *"paradosis,"* and means *"a handing down, doctrines, traditions"* (Mat.15:2-6; Mk. 7:3-13; Gal. 1:14; Col. 2:8; II Thess. 2:15; 3:6).

NOTES

To be a little more specific, an *"Ordinance"* or tradition is any bit of instruction, any principle, any rule of conduct which Paul handed over to the Corinthians when he was in their midst. The term is quite general and without technical ecclesiastical limitations. It includes points of Doctrine as well as points of practice; more over, these always go together, the latter growing out of the former.

Of course, Paul received this from the Lord (Gal. 1:12), which means these *"Ordinances"* were not man-originated or man-instituted.

(3) "BUT I WOULD HAVE YOU KNOW, THAT THE HEAD OF EVERY MAN IS CHRIST; AND THE HEAD OF THE WOMAN IS THE MAN; AND THE HEAD OF CHRIST IS GOD."

The phrase, *"But I would have you know,"* refers to the Divine Order in the moral government of the universe. The following probably addresses a question asked of Paul concerning the dress and role of women in the Church. As should be understood, all of this was uncharted territory.

The phrase, *"That the head of every man is Christ,"* refers to our Lord as the *"Representative Man,"* i.e. *"The Man Christ Jesus."*

*"Head"* in the Greek is *"kephale,"* and means *"authority or a sign of authority."*

It refers to the Angels being witnesses of the pre-eminent relationship as established by God in the creation of man as we will see in the Tenth Verse, with the spiritual significance regarding the position of Christ in relation to the Church.

The phrase, *"And the head of the woman is the man,"* pertains to the creation model. This, however, is merely an ordinance of earthly application. In the spiritual realm, *"there is neither male nor female"* (Gal. 3:28). In Christ, the distinctions of the sexes, relative to superiority, are done away.

It was, perhaps, an abuse of this principle which had led the Corinthian women to assert themselves in their rights more prominently than decorum warranted (Farrar).

If one is to notice, this, even as eating meat offered to idols, pertains to Christian liberty and the possibility of situations being taken too far.

The phrase, *"And the head of Christ is God,"* speaks here of two separate and distinct persons (I Tim. 2:5).

It refers to Christ as *"inferior to the Father as touching His Manhood,"* that His mediatorial Ministry involves a subordination of His co-equal Godhead. This too is the meaning of John 14:28, *"My Father is greater than I."*

Due to the significance of what the Holy Spirit is here saying concerning the role of women, perhaps a more detailed treatment of this very important subject would be in order.

## MALE AND FEMALE

It is clear that men and women do not have all roles in life in common in any society. But the problem for the Believer is this: Are male/female roles simply defined by one's culture, or are there limitations imposed by God in relation to gender?

In the following we will look at one aspect of this problem and explore Biblical testimony focused on the fact of maleness and femaleness.

## THE OLD TESTAMENT

The Hebrew word *"Adam"* generally means *"man,"* in the sense of mankind. Another word, *"is,"* designates any individual male, whereas *"zakar"* is often used when a sharp sexual distinction is made.

For instance, the male (zakar 83 times in the Old Testament) is the one that is to be circumcised (Gen. 34:15, 22, 24, 25); and the first male offspring of every animal was to be sacrificed to the Lord to commemorate the Passover (Ex. 12:5). Also, the first son of each family was to be purchased back from the Lord by a special offering (Ex. 13:12, 15).

As well, the Burnt Offering for sin had to be a male animal (Lev. 1:3), though a fellowship offering might be an animal of either sex (Lev. 3:1; Gen. 15:9).

A census was taken in Israel by counting every male of 20 years or more (Num. 1:20, 22). And genealogies were through the male line (Ezra 8:3-14).

## WOMAN

The Hebrew *"issah"* is usually translated *"woman"* or *"female."* It designates any individual woman.

*"Nqebah"* (22 times in the Old Testament) is often used in the same way that *"zakar"* is used, that is, when a clear sexual distinction is to be made. Thus, God is said to have created humanity *"male and female"* (Gen. 1:27; 5:2). In the Old Testament, the word for female is also used where differing time periods for ritual purification after the birth of male and female children is specified (Lev. 12:1-5).

NOTES

## GENESIS

In our search for Biblical perspective on male and female, we begin with the account of Creation. We see that God stated His intention to create humanity in His Own Image (Gen. 1:26). Immediately Scripture reports that *"in the Image of God He created him; male and female He created them"* (Gen. 1:27).

Adam searched animal creation for a suitable helper. Finally God took one of Adam's ribs to shape Eve. Awakening, Adam affirmed, *"This is now bone of my bones and flesh of my flesh"* (Gen. 2:23). Thus, the passage reinforces the essential identity ascribed to men and women as persons.

After the Fall, the Book of Genesis makes it plain that the wife is to be in subordination to her husband (*"He will rule over you,"* Gen. 3:16). Whatever this may imply for marriage, it does not suggest a wholesale inferiority of women to men.

## MALE ROLES IN THE OLD TESTAMENT

Hebrew society, like the other societies in the ancient world, was Patriarchal. Genealogies were reckoned through the male. The man was recognized as the civil and responsible head of the house. Civic responsibility for the community was also placed on male elders.

Although there is no Old Testament statement restricting this eldership to males, there are no Biblical examples of women who had been given this responsibility. This structure of society is reflected in, and — to the extent that existing patterns are sanctioned — is permitted by, Old Testament Commands and Statutes.

## THE PRIESTHOOD

The Old Testament Priesthood is a different matter. Only males from the Tribe of Levi and the family of Aaron were to officiate at public worship (Ex. 28:1-3; Num. 3:12-15). This pattern was specifically established by God, even though the whole people of Israel were holy (Num. 16:3).

But we should not conclude that this implies that women are inferior to men. Creation's design excludes men from bearing children, but this does not imply male inferiority. Old Testament Law does not permit women from any tribe, nor men from any other tribe than the tribe of Levi, to serve as Priests. But we cannot conclude from this that women are inferior, just as we do not consider men of the other Eleven Tribes inferior to the men of the Tribe of Levi.

### FEMALE ROLES IN THE OLD TESTAMENT

Old Testament society was Patriarchal in structure (a man who is father or founder), and men historically fill most roles of leadership and influence. It would be a mistake, however, to conclude that women were passive, or inferior, or necessarily discriminated against.

Proverbs Chapter 31 praises the noble wife and provides an insight into the opportunities for women to find personal fulfillment in ancient agrarian society. The passage shows that the *"nobel wife"* actually performed many of the roles of men in that culture. She supervised a staff of workers (Prov. 31:27). She served as buyer for her enterprises (Prov. 31:13). She sold what her staff produced (Prov. 31:18, 24) and she invested her profits (Prov. 31:16).

She had the freedom to give to help the needy (Prov. 31:20). She was respected for her wisdom and responsibility (Prov. 31:14-15, 26-31). This picture is striking, for it shows the woman of Old Testament times engaged in the functions of what today we call *"business."*

The Old Testament woman's activities were linked closely with her home and family, but she was not at all cast in what some think of when they suggest that women should *"keep house and take care of the children."* Women were viewed with far greater respect in Biblical times than that!

### OLD TESTAMENT LAW

It is true that Old Testament women did not share all the legal rights and civil responsibilities of men. But active wives, and women who were heads of households, were not restricted to *"women's work."*

In most cases, the Old Testament Civil Laws governing the rights of men and women reflect cultural patterns. They fall short of what many believe to be a deserved *"equality."*

NOTES

But it is important to remember that no culture in that day provided equality, with in fact, the Law of Moses providing the greatest equality of all.

In fact, injustices exist in every culture. And as well, Old Testament Law was not a perfect expression of God's ideal for the whole human race (Mat. 5:21-43). Old Testament Law was an accommodation, bringing Righteousness as close as possible to men and women who lived in a world in which all things were tainted and twisted by sin.

### THREE VALID CONCLUSIONS

There are three valid conclusions we can draw from the Old Testament:

1. Women and men were created in the Image and Likeness of God, both having worth as human beings.
2. Women and men are given, within the framework of their society, opportunities to use their full potential as human beings.
3. God ordained, in the specific case of the Priesthood, that only men (and men of a specific tribe and family) would fill at least one religious — social role.

### GREAT WOMEN OF THE OLD TESTAMENT

The Old Testament tells of a number of significant women. Some of these had roles within and some had roles outside of the framework of cultural expectations. Abigail (I Sam. Chpt. 25) and Ruth won commendation within cultural roles (Ex. Chpt. 15; II Ki. 22:11-13). Miriam (Ex. 15:20) and Huldah (II Ki. 22:14; II Chron. 34:22) and Deborah (Judg. 4:4) served in roles usually associated with men — all three were Prophetesses.

And Deborah was far more: she was a Prophetess who led Israel and functioned as a Judge, *"and the Israelites came to her to have their disputes decided"* (Judg. 4:5). In addition, Deborah communicated instructions to Barak in the Name of the Lord and then accompanied him on a military expedition that resulted in Israel's victory over their enemies (Judg. 4:6-10).

Deborah's role may have been inappropriate culturally. But is was not a role from which her womanhood excluded her per se. Just as clearly, the people of Israel recognized her Divine appointment and did not reject her leadership.

These and other women, such as Ruth and Esther, had important places in sacred history. In public office or private life, each demonstrated that spiritual significance is not a matter of gender. Significance and usefulness are determined rather by our being open to God and letting Him use us in the place and position He chooses.

## THE NEW TESTAMENT

The Greek word used to distinguish mankind from the gods and the animals is *"anthropos."* Generally all humanity is indicated when this word is used, but it can also refer to an individual man.

*"Aner"* is used also to indicate an individual man. But at times, it shifts in meaning to include mankind.

In the New Testament, *"aner"* is often used to distinguish man from woman. *"Gyne"* is the general word for woman, which also includes the meaning of *"wife."*

*"Arsen"* is another Greek word seldom used (only eight times in the New Testament) that emphasized maleness. It is found in three significant New Testament passages where it is contrasted with femaleness (*"thelys"*).

In Matthew 19:4 and Mark 10:6, *"arsen"* and *"thelys"* are used when Jesus, returning to the Genesis account of creation, says, *"God made them male and female."* Both *"arsen"* and *"thelys"* are found in Romans 1:26, 27, where Paul identifies homosexuality and lesbianism as unnatural and indecent perversions.

Finally, both words are found in Galatians 3:27, 28. There we find this statement: *"All of you who were baptized into Christ have clothed yourselves with Christ. There is neither Jew nor Greek, slave nor free, male nor female, for you are all one in Christ Jesus."*

## MEN AND WOMEN IN THE NEW TESTAMENT

In the Hellenistic world of New Testament times, a variety of attitudes toward women existed. Athens had a tradition of contempt for women; however, the Doric tradition gave women greater respect.

The Orient contributed a significant role for women in religious cults: they served as priestesses who might be called on to remain virgins or to become cult prostitutes. But it is clear in the Hellenic world (Grecian thought and culture), male and female were not equal.

It was not uncommon during the Greek era for girl babies to be exposed (put out on some garbage heap) at birth — a practice that differs from abortion only in that death was delayed until the fetus reached full term.

NOTES

## NEW TESTAMENT AND OLD TESTAMENT

Regarding Israel, women were shown more respect under the Old Law, even than under the Judaism of New Testament times. For instance, a Rabbi would not condescend to speak to women unless other men were present. Women were not allowed full access to the outer courts of Herod's temple in Jerusalem. Actually, for some three centuries before Jesus, women were isolated from men in the Synagogues.

One Rabbi announced, *"The woman does not read out of the Torah, for the sake of the honor of the congregation."* But any male member might be called on to read. Teaching the Law to women and even holding conversations with them were discouraged.

In A.D. 150, Rabbi Judah ben Elai announced: *"One must utter three doxologies every day: Praise God that He did not create me a heathen! Praise God that He did not create me a woman! Praise God that He did not create me an illiterate person!"*

However, Israel by this time was so far away from God, although very religious, that there was little resemblance whatsoever in the nation to that which God intended.

## JESUS

In view of the culture's view of women, it is striking to read in the Gospels that Jesus spoke naturally with women and taught them, despite the grossly unscriptural position of the religious leadership of Israel of that day (Lk. 10:38-42; Jn. 4:7-27).

He also used many illustrations drawn from the daily life of women. Mary Magdalene and Mary the mother of James and Joseph were among His closest followers (Mk. 15:40, 41). In fact, Mary Magdalene was given the privilege by the Holy Spirit of being the very first one to herald the great Message of the Resurrection of Christ (Jn. 20:18). In fact, Jesus showed no discrimination whatsoever between men and women.

## PAUL

It is even more striking, in view of Paul's training as a Rabbi, to note that he writes familiarly about seven women in Romans Chapter 16. And twice he named Priscilla before her husband, Aquila, perhaps acknowledging her significance in the Church that met in their home (Rom. 16:3; I Cor. 16:19; II Tim. 4:19).

All these attitudes and events, which we view as natural and normal from the perspective of modern attitudes, take on a stunning significance against the background of Biblical times. For those who read a bias against women in the New Testament, unfamiliarity with New Testament times has blinded them to the marks of acceptance and respect expressed on the Gospel pages and in Acts, as well as in the Epistles.

## I CORINTHIANS 11:2-16

There are a number of passages in the New Testament epistles that deal with the question of relationships between husband and wife and with the woman's role in the Church. But there is one passage that deals with male/female standing in the Church in itself. This passage is what we are presently studying, I Corinthians 11:2-16.

The women of Corinth became excited by the Gospel's affirmation of their spiritual equality with men in Christ. They determined, it seems, to show their equality by adopting a male hairstyle. Paul reacted strongly to this practice. He saw it as striking at the very heart of the Gospel Message.

## HEADSHIP RELATIONSHIP

Paul begins his discussion of this issue by stating that there is a headship relationship between Christ and man, man and woman, and God and Christ. He is simply noting the fact that God made humanity male and female.

With this as a basis, he proceeds to note that women, if they pray or prophesy, are to have their heads covered (to have long hair), whereas men are not to have their heads covered during Church Services.

Paul concludes with an argument for interdependence. Whatever the creation order, today men and women are not independent of each other. God has designed a universe in which each sex requires the other. Thus, it is

NOTES

proper for a woman to pray to God with her hair and dress proudly testifying to all the world that she is, in fact, a woman.

## WOMEN USED OF GOD IN THE NEW TESTAMENT ACCOUNT

The Gospels mention a number of women who were significant. One of them, Mary Magdalene, as stated, was especially honored by Jesus by being the one to whom He first appeared after the Resurrection (Mk. 16:9-11; Jn. 20:1-18).

Luke notes that some women — including Joanna, the wife of *"the manager of Herod's household"* (Lk. 8:3) — travelled with Jesus, ministering to Him out of their means. The closing of Romans refers to specific women who are identified by Paul as his *"fellow workers in Christ Jesus"* (Rom. 16:3) and as those who *"work hard in the Lord"* (Rom. 16:12).

Phoebe was commended to the Roman Church as a Deacon and maybe even the Pastor of the Church at Cenchrea (Rom. 16:1). Actually, the same term used of Phoebe was used of Male leaders in I Timothy 3:8-13.

We have already referred to Priscilla, who was mentioned before her husband Aquila, in some New Testament passages. These references, and more, bare witness to the importance in the life of the Early Church, where every member possessed a spiritual gift and was an essential member of the Body.

## IN CONCLUSION

God made human beings in His Own Image and gave the first couple the charge to exercise rule over His Creation (Gen. Chpts. 1-2).

The introduction of sin into the world distorted male/female relationships. Sacred history, including the Mosaic Law itself, testifies to the fact that God has historically made some definite distinctions between men and women. Even the Old Testament ideal, as expressed in the Law of Moses, which incidentally was God-given Law, failed to fully restore woman's worth and dignity, although Old Testament society provided women with greater opportunity for self-actualization than is generally realized.

## THE GOSPEL

With the Gospel, came the announcement that in Christ *"there is neither Jew nor Greek, slave nor free, male nor female, for you are all one in Christ Jesus"* (Gal. 3:28). This proclamation insists that there is spiritual equality in God's sight, despite cultural distinctions made in every society.

Yet Believers remain male and female, and at times in some parts of the world, slave and free. And each must live out his or her life within roles imposed by society as well as within the Believing community.

For the Church, the teaching of the Gospel is a challenge to become the kind of community that Scripture says we are — one that values persons apart from their social role. For the woman today, the teaching of the Gospel is a challenge to be comfortable with herself as a female.

A woman, because she is significant in Christ, can find worth and dignity by living life as a woman — without a need to act like a man.

(The dissertation on the role of male and female was derived from the scholarship of Lawrence O. Richards.)

(4) "EVERY MAN PRAYING OR PROPHESYING, HAVING HIS HEAD COVERED, DISHONOURETH HIS HEAD."

The phrase, *"Every man praying or prophesying,"* refers either to the Gift of Prophecy (I Cor. 12:10), or to Preaching the Gospel.

The phrase, *"Having his head covered, dishonoureth his head,"* means that every man praying or prophesying with a cap or turban on his head dishonoureth his Head, i.e. Christ. This was in direct contrast to the canons of Jews who did not permit a man to pray or prophesy unless his head was covered. It was called the *"tallith."*

Their idea was that man is unworthy to have an open face before God.

This was due to the fact that the Jews were having to continue to offer up Sacrifices, even on a daily basis, because Jesus had not yet come. Consequently, the sin debt, though covered by Atonement, was not actually taken away, as it would be when Jesus paid the price at Calvary's Cross.

Understanding that, the unworthiness of man to have an open face before God, portrayed that which was correct.

## THE PRICE THAT JESUS PAID

When Jesus died on Calvary, paying the sin debt, in effect for all men and for all time, He then became the *"Head"* or *"Covering"* for all of mankind, at least those who will believe (Jn. 3:16). As such, it says that the enmity between God and man has been removed, man has been reconciled to God, and Peace now reigns (II Cor. 5:17-19; Eph. 2:15, 16).

The uncovered head of man speaks of the freedom that one has in Christ, and the price that has been paid for man's Redemption. As stated, it is the opposite of the old Economy of God, and for the obvious reasons.

(5) "BUT EVERY WOMAN THAT PRAYETH OR PROPHESIETH WITH HER HEAD UNCOVERED DISHONOURETH HER HEAD: FOR THAT IS EVEN ALL ONE AS IF SHE WERE SHAVEN."

The phrase, *"But every woman that prayeth or prophesieth with her head uncovered dishonoureth her head,"* tells us several things:

1. This tells us that women did pray and preach in the Church (or wherever), which debunks the claim by some that women should not preach. In fact, Joel prophesied that the Holy Spirit would be poured out on women the same as men, and they would prophesy as well, etc. (Joel 2:28-32). Peter quoted him on the Day of Pentecost (Acts 2:16-21).

2. The dishonoring of her head speaks of her husband in particular, and man in general. In a complete sense, due to the fact that there is neither male nor female in Christ, Jesus is woman's Head as well as that of men.

3. The order given, *"the head of the woman is the man,"* maintains the creation model, which is very important.

4. *"Uncovered"* in the Greek is *"akatakaluptos,"* and means *"unveiled,"* with its opposite *"kalupto"* meaning *"to cover up."* It speaks of a woman not having short hair like a man, but rather having long hair, which Verse 15 says is her *"glory."*

Some have tried to contend from these verses that Paul was speaking of a woman being veiled like Moslem women, or at least wearing a hat, etc. Others have contended that he was only speaking of the custom of the times, which doesn't apply to us presently.

However, both of those contentions are wrong, inasmuch as the Holy Spirit would not have given something in this detail that only pertained to the custom of some particular time, etc.

Verse 15 plainly tells us what he is speaking about, that a woman should have long hair, consequently, not short like a man's.

NOTES

The phrase, *"For that is even all one as if she were shaven,"* speaks to the fact that some women in those days had their head shaved as a punishment for whoredom or adultery (Num. 5:18). Actually, this practice remained even up into the 1600's.

So, Paul is saying that if Christian women at Corinth, or anywhere else for that matter, took their Christian liberty too far, attempting to exert their Christian *"rights,"* that they conclude by looking like those women just mentioned. The manner in which Paul makes this statement, in effect says, *"Surely you don't want to give off that appearance?"*, as if she were shaven.

(6) "FOR IF THE WOMAN BE NOT COVERED, LET HER ALSO BE SHORN: BUT IF IT BE A SHAME FOR A WOMAN TO BE SHORN OR SHAVEN, LET HER BE COVERED."

The phrase, *"For if the woman be not covered, let her also be shorn,"* in effect says, *"If the woman wants to wear her hair short like a man, why not go all the way and be 'shorn,' i.e. shaven."*

The phrase, *"But if it be a shame for a woman to be shorn or shaven, let her be covered,"* refers to the fact that if she does not want to look like an adulteress, *"let her be covered,"* i.e. *"have long hair."*

Once again, Paul is going back to the principle of true Christian liberty, which must not be turned into license. Although there are no Commandments in Christianity, even though there were many in the Old Law, still our Christian freedom or liberty is not given to us to see how close to the world we can come, but rather in order that we may live a holy, righteous, and Godly life. So, to corrupt this *"Liberty"* is a travesty of the highest order!

(7) "FOR A MAN INDEED OUGHT NOT TO COVER HIS HEAD, FORASMUCH AS HE IS THE IMAGE AND GLORY OF GOD: BUT THE WOMAN IS THE GLORY OF THE MAN."

The phrase, *"For a man indeed ought not to cover his head, forasmuch as he is the Image and Glory of God,"* refers to Genesis 1:26-28, although the word *"glory"* does not appear in those Passages.

## HOW IS MAN THE IMAGE OF GOD?

In a few texts in Genesis 1:26, 27; 5:1-2; 9:6, man is said to have been created *"in"* or *"as"* the Image of God, *"according to His Likeness."* Though many interpreters have thought to locate the *"image"* of God in man's reason, creativity, speech, or spiritual nature, it is more likely that it is the whole of man, rather than some part or aspect of him, that is the Image of God.

The whole man, spirit, soul, and body, is the Image of God; man is the corporeal image of the incorporeal God. Man as the Image of God represents Him through his participation in the Divine Breath or Spirit (Gen. 2:7; no doubt the Spirit of God is included in the *"us"* of Gen. 1:26; also the reference is to the Spirit of God in Gen. 1:2).

Man's role as ruler of the earth is established by his creation as God's Image (Gen. 1:27). Elsewhere in the ancient Near East, it is usually the king who is said to be the Image of God, but in Genesis Chapter 1, it is mankind as a whole that is God's vizier and representative. Significantly, man is still spoken of as the Image of God after the Fall: the force of Genesis 9:6 depends on the belief that man represents God, so that an injury done to a man is an injury done to God Himself (James 3:9).

## IN THE NEW TESTAMENT

The New Testament teaching builds on the foundation laid in the Old Testament. There, man is described as made to be God's representative on earth and to act as God's vice-regent and steward of creation.

## I CORINTHIANS AND JAMES

The two Passages of I Corinthians 11:7 and James 3:9 re-echo this teaching, and both assert the continuance of man's position in the created order and as reflecting the Divine *"Glory,"* and that, despite human sinfulness. The emphasis in the New Testament, however, falls more on the person of Jesus Christ Who is called the *"Image of God"* (II Cor. 4:4; Col. 1:15).

Christ's rank as the *"Image"* of the Father derives from His unique relationship as preexistent. He is the Logos from all eternity (Jn. 1:1-18), and so He is able to reflect faithfully and fully the Glory of the Invisible God.

## JESUS

Hebrews 1:1-3 and Philippians 2:6-11 express parallel expressions which are used to clarify the unique relationship of Jesus Christ to God. *"Image"* (or its equivalent terms, *"form," "stamp,"*

NOTES

*"glory"*) does not suggest a mere likeness to God or a paradigm (example) of His Person.

Rather it connotes a sharing in the Divine Life and indeed of the Essence of God, so that the One Who is by nature invisible comes to visible expression in the figure of His Son.

THE ULTIMATE ADAM

Thus, Jesus is the *"ultimate Adam"* (I Cor. 15:45) Who stands at the head of a new humanity that draws its life from Him. So Jesus Christ is both the unique *"Image"* and the prototype of those who owe their knowledge of God and Life in God to Him (Rom. 8:29; I Cor. 15:49; II Cor. 3:18; I Jn. 3:2).

THE NEW MAN

The term *"Image of God"* is closely connected with *"the new man"* (Gal. 3:28; Eph. 4:24; Col. 3:10). This is a reminder that there are important social aspects to what the *"Image"* means as it is reproduced in human lives, both in the fellowship of the Church and in man's custodianship of nature (Ps. 8; Heb. 2:8).

There is also an End Time Dimension to be recognized. The fulfillment of God's Plan for humanity-in-Christ awaits the Second Coming when Christians' mortal existence will be transformed to a perfect likeness to our Lord (I Cor. 15:49; Phil. 3:20-21), and in this way the Image of God in man will be fully restored as it was before the Fall, and is meant to be.

(Bibliography: Morton Smith, *"The Image of God"*; J. Jervell; F. W. Eltester).

HOW IS MAN THE GLORY OF GOD?

*"Glory"* in the Hebrew is *"kabod,"* and contains the root idea of *"heaviness"* and so of *"weight"* or *"worthiness."* It is used of men to describe their wealth, splendour or reputation (though in the last sense this word is often rendered *"honour"*).

The Glory of Israel was not her armies but Jehovah (Jer. 2:11). Consequently, the most important concept is that of the Glory of Jehovah. This denoted the Revelation of God's Being, Nature, and Presence to mankind, sometimes with physical phenomena.

In the Pentateuch (first five Books of the Bible), the Glory of God went with His people out of Egypt and was shown in the Cloud which led them through the wilderness (Ex. 16:7, 10).

NOTES

The Cloud rested on Mt. Sinai, where Moses saw God's Glory (Ex. 24:15-18). No man could see God's Face and live, at least in all its Glory (Ex. 33:20), but some vision of His Glory was granted to Moses (Ex. 34:5-8).

MANIFESTATIONS

The Glory of God filled the Tabernacle (Ex. 40:35-36) and appeared especially at the hour of Sacrifice (Lev. 9:6, 23). These Passages seem all to be connected with a grand physical manifestation, that is if the Glory of God could be referred to in that manner. As well, there are also passages which suggest more the Character of the Lord which is to be made known throughout the earth (Num. 14:21-22).

The Historical Books tell of the Temple becoming the place where the Glory of God was especially to be located (I Kings 8:11; II Chron. 7:1-3).

In the Prophets there are both the physical conception of God's Glory as seen in the visions of Ezekiel (Ezek. 1:28) and also a more spiritualized doctrine (Isa. 40:4-5; 60:1-3). The Vision of Isaiah in the Temple seems to combine both ideas (Isa. 6:1-4).

There can be found, likewise, in the Psalms all the imagery of manifestation respecting God's Glory (Ps. 18:29) and also the idea of the future display of God's Character to the world (Ps. 57:11; 96:3).

IN THE NEW TESTAMENT

The Greek word for *"Glory"* is *"doxa,"* and means *"opinion"* or *"reputation."*

In certain places in the New Testament, *"doxa"* refers to human honour (Mat. 4:8; 6:29), but it's chief use is to describe the Revelation of the Character and the Presence of God in the Person and Work of Jesus Christ. He Alone is the perfect outshining of the Divine Glory (Heb. 1:3).

JESUS AND THE GLORY OF GOD

The Glory of God was seen by the Shepherds at the birth of Christ (when they viewed Him as a little baby) (Lk. 2:9, 14) and by His Disciples during His Incarnate Life (Jn. 1:14). Particularly was it revealed in His miracles (Jn. 2:11) and at His Transfiguration (Mat. 17:1-8; Mk. 9:2-8; Lk. 9:28-36).

This recalls the ascent of Moses to Sinai (Ex. 24:15) and of Elijah to Horeb (I Kings 19:8) and their Visions of the Glory of God. Now Christ both sees and reflects the Divine Glory, but no Tabernacle needs to be built because the Word of God has pitched His Tent in the human flesh of Jesus (Jn. 1:14); however, His Glory is to be more fully revealed at the Second Coming.

In the Fourth Gospel, it is the hour of dedication to death which is essentially the hour of glory (Jn. 7:39; 12:23-28, 13:31; 17:5; Heb. 2:9).

The Resurrection and Ascension are also seen as manifestations of the Glory of God in Christ (Lk. 24:26; Acts 3:13; 7:55; Rom. 6:4; I Tim. 3:16; I Pet. 1:21). But above all, and as stated, this Glory is to be revealed in all its fullness at the Second Coming (Mk. 8:38; 13:26).

### MAN AND THE GLORY OF GOD

Man, who was made as the Image and Glory of God for relationship with Him, even as we are now studying, has fallen short of his destiny (Rom. 3:23), but has, however, been fulfilled totally in Christ, the Second Adam (Heb. 2:6-9).

The Glory of God in the Face of Jesus Christ is still to be seen and reflected by the Church (II Cor. 4:3-6). It is the Glory of the New Covenant (II Cor. 3:7-11), and it is especially shared both now (I Pet. 4:14) and shall be hereafter (Rom. 8:18) by those who suffer with Christ.

The object of the Church is to see that the world acknowledges the Glory which is God's (Rom. 15:9) and is shown in His deeds (Acts 4:21), in His Disciples (I Cor. 6:20), and above all, in His Son, the Lord of Glory (Rom. 16:27).

The phrase, *"But the woman is the glory of the man,"* refers to the fact that Eve was not *"God's image and glory"* in the same sense as Adam was. Strictly, according to her creation, which also Redemption has not altered, as Paul said, she must be called *"man's glory."*

Paul does not add the other term, *"man's image,"* although he could do so. The higher and the more elucidating term *"glory"* includes *"image."* Her entire creation places her in direct and immediate relation to man. She was made for man; she was made to be his *"helpmeet."*

The reverse cannot be said. Adam expressed the Truth exactly: *"This is now bone of my bones, and flesh of my flesh. She shall be called Woman, because she was taken out of man."*

As we shall see, before Paul adds the obligation that rests upon her as far as expressed in this relation to man is concerned, he adds further explanations (Lenski).

NOTES

(8) "FOR THE MAN IS NOT OF THE WOMAN: BUT THE WOMAN OF THE MAN."

Adam was not in any way derived from woman, he was created directly by God. The opposite is the fact regarding woman.

Eve was derived from Adam: *"Bone of my bones, and flesh of my flesh."* This involves another difference, as the next Verse proclaims.

Once again, and continuously one might add, Paul holds up the creation model. This is not to be abrogated.

(9) "NEITHER WAS THE MAN CREATED FOR THE WOMAN; BUT THE WOMAN FOR THE MAN."

This Verse would probably have been better translated, *"For also man was not created on account of the woman, on the contrary, woman on account of the man."*

In the original, *"man"* is without the definite article, meaning any man, whomever he may be. God made *"a woman"* for Adam, but not *"a man"* for Eve. God could, indeed, have created both Man and Woman, Adam and Eve, in one undivided act.

Today many think and act as though God had really done so. But the fact is otherwise. Nor should we think and say that at this late date God's creative act, which lies far back in time, makes no difference. The facts of creation abide forever. They can be ignored without resultant loss or harm as little as can other facts of nature (Lenski).

At first blush, these sentences sound as if they indicate woman's subordination to man; nevertheless, Verses 11 and 12 make it clear that Paul did not intend for his statements to be taken in that manner. He is merely reinforcing the creation model, and that it must not be abrogated.

(10) "FOR THIS CAUSE OUGHT THE WOMAN TO HAVE POWER ON HER HEAD BECAUSE OF THE ANGELS."

The phrase, *"For this cause,"* refers again to the creation model that *"the woman* (is) *for the man."*

The phrase, *"Ought the woman to have power on her head,"* refers in the Greek (exousia) to authority.

Of what kind of power or authority is Paul speaking?

He is speaking of the authority on her head in the form of long hair, which is another way of verbalizing the concept of voluntary submission to the Plan of God, i.e. the creation model.

Submission to God in anything does not reduce one's power or authority, but rather has the very opposite effect. In fact, that has always been man's problem, not wanting to submit to God's Plan.

The phrase, *"Because of the Angels,"* has to do, as stated, with her submission to God's Plan as a constant reminder to the Fallen Angels, who rebelled against God's Plan in the revolution led by Lucifer, which took place long before Adam.

(11) "NEVERTHELESS NEITHER IS THE MAN WITHOUT THE WOMAN, NEITHER THE WOMAN WITHOUT THE MAN, IN THE LORD."

The phrase, *"Nevertheless neither is the man without the woman,"* in effect says by the word *"nevertheless," "let this not be overlooked."*

Whatever God arranged at creation when He made man the head, as far as being *"in the Lord"* is concerned, both are altogether equal. The man is not *"in the Lord"* in such a way that the woman is excluded, nor, of course, vice versa. Galatians 3:28 stands: *"Ye are all one in Christ Jesus."*

This one phrase by Paul debunks the idea that women cannot Preach the Gospel.

The phrase, *"Neither the woman without the man,"* destroys the modern feminists movements. These movements so-called, at least for the most part, claim that men are not needed. With artificial insemination, they can now bear children without men, or at least being directly involved with men.

All of this is of the spirit of Satan, which denies the mutual dependence originally created by God, and demanded of continuance.

The phrase, *"In the Lord,"* refers to the fact that this is the manner in which the Lord created the original model, and demands that it continue. Woman is not independent of man, nor is man independent of woman. As a race, man is not complete without woman; and woman is not complete without man. They form an indissoluble unity (Rossier).

(12) "FOR AS THE WOMAN IS OF THE MAN, EVEN SO IS THE MAN ALSO BY THE WOMAN; BUT ALL THINGS OF GOD."

NOTES

The phrase, *"For as the woman is of the man,"* refers to the fact that Eve was originally created from Adam (Gen. 2:21, 22).

The phrase, *"Even so is the man also by the woman,"* refers by or through the medium of natural birth.

All men, just as all women, are *"born of women,"* (Mat. 11:11), not excepting even Him Who became Incarnate by the Virgin Birth (Gal. 4:4).

Both Adam and Eve are exceptional, for neither was born. Yet Eve and all her descendants are classed together since they are all *"of"* Adam; he alone came immediately from the Hand of God. All other men have come through the medium of the woman, i.e. Eve and her daughters.

The phrase, *"But all things of God,"* puts everything on an even keel, meaning that men are no more important than women, or women than men. All things being *"of God,"* makes Him the all-important One, which the Holy Spirit through the Apostle explains.

(13) "JUDGE IN YOURSELVES: IS IT COMELY THAT A WOMAN PRAY UNTO GOD UNCOVERED?"

The phrase, *"Judge in yourselves,"* refers to the fact that if the Corinthians will use their common sense, they will see what he is saying is correct, and because it is obvious. Things are right not just because God does those things, but He does those things because they *are* right.

The question, *"Is it comely that a woman pray unto God uncovered?",* in effect refers back to Verse 5.

The Corinthians may judge this as far as it applies to them. They need to do no more than to ask the question regarding the propriety of the custom in vogue in their midst and in regard to what nature teaches them in support of this their custom. This alone will suffice.

As is obvious, Paul leaves out prophesying, apparently only in order to shorten the question, for this is the original question with which this entire situation deals (vs. 5).

(14) "DOTH NOT EVEN NATURE ITSELF TEACH YOU, THAT, IF A MAN HAVE LONG HAIR, IT IS A SHAME UNTO HIM?"

The beginning of the question, *"Doth not even nature itself teach you, . . .?",* presents an appeal to the *"way things are"* or *"the nature of things."*

Paul is not exactly appealing to nature, or to *"natural law,"* or to *"natural endowment,"* nor is Nature to be understood as a teacher. Rather, for Paul, it is a question of propriety, i.e. the true nature of a thing, which carries with it *"disgrace"* or *"glory."*

Thus, Paul is not arguing that men *must* wear their hair short, or that women *must* have long hair, as though *"nature"* meant some kind of *"created order."* Indeed, the very appeal to *"nature"* in this way suggests most strongly that the argument is by way of analogy (similarity), not of necessity.

The conclusion of the question, *"That, if a man have long hair, it is a shame unto him?"*, demands an affirmative answer.

When Paul writes *"nature itself,"* we understand, in view of what he has already said, that he has in mind nature as God has formed nature. Thus, nature is here placed over against mere taste or transient fashion or faulty ideas. Certain things comport with nature and with the way in which God has made us; they are proper for that reason. As well, certain things are unnatural and for that reason lack propriety.

Thus, when a man wears long hair, this is really not in accord with the nature of a man, even though at times it may be done.

JESUS AND LONG HAIR

Some may argue that Jesus had long hair, which is contradictory to what Paul is saying here; however, those who would make such a judgment are basing their reasoning on pictures of Jesus drawn by artists, who, in fact, did not know what He looked like, thereby, only painting something which came out of their imagination. In other words, no one knows what Jesus looked like.

The custom then was not long hair for a man, and in fact, had never been.

Understanding that what Paul is saying is inspired by the Holy Spirit, we have to come to the conclusion that Jesus, in fact, did not have long hair, and again, that such has never been the custom, at least on a general scale, concerning men.

(15) "BUT IF A WOMAN HAVE LONG HAIR, IT IS A GLORY TO HER: FOR HER HAIR IS GIVEN HER FOR A COVERING."

The phrase, *"But if a woman have long hair, it is a glory to her,"* is a way of saying that such manifests woman's voluntary submission to God's Will.

*"Glory"* in this instance, since it is the opposite of *"dishonor,"* must mean something like *"distinction"* or *"honor."* It gives her that womanly distinction.

The facts of creation and of nature stand unchanged. They should be recognized and accepted for what they are. To ignore them or to set them aside is always a mistake. In the end, these facts, as well as all the others, are bound to assert themselves. One of the most fundamental natural facts is this, that the sexes differ profoundly, far more so than is generally recognized.

A basic feature of this fact is that God gave the headship to the man and not to the woman. All attempts to abolish this headship and to place the sexes on the same level, at least in this capacity, must fail.

A perfect example of this is the effort of the Armed Forces of the United States to integrate men and women in all aspects of the service. While it is certainly true that women can serve in many capacities in the Armed Forces, in fact, just as readily in positions of Leadership as men. However, there are some aspects of the Armed Forces, and in whatever branch, which are not conducive at all to a woman, and if the issue is forced, irrespective of the effort, it is not possible to make what nature never intended in the first place.

On the front lines on fields of battle, and especially in hand-to-hand combat, such is no place for a woman. While she certainly has the intelligence, intuition, forethought, and ability to serve in these capacities, she simply does not have the physical strength to do so, at least as it regards most women.

The phrase, *"For her hair is given her for a covering,"* points to the idea in the Creation Model, that man is the head or covering of the woman, under Christ.

(16) "BUT IF ANY MAN SEEM TO BE CONTENTIOUS, WE HAVE NO SUCH CUSTOM, NEITHER THE CHURCHES OF GOD."

The phrase, *"But if any man seem to be contentious,"* refers to both men and women, and indicates that this is what some were doing. Most likely this referred to some women who were insisting on conducting themselves as a man, even with very short hair, in other words exhibiting too far their Christian freedom.

NOTES

The phrase, *"We have no such custom,"* could have been translated, *"We have no such practice."* The words *"such practice,"* therefore, must refer to that which the *"contentious"* are advocating, and which this argument by Paul has been combating.

This phrase does not mean, as some have advocated, that if some women insisted, they could wear their hair as they so desired and conduct themselves as they so desired. The Holy Spirit through the Apostle would not have given such a lengthy explanation, and then closed out the argument basically by saying, *"If you don't want to do what I've said, then do what you want to do."* Such thinking or action does not coincide with the guidance of the Holy Spirit. It rather means, *"heed what I have said."*

The phrase, *"Neither the Churches of God,"* means that if the Corinthians wanted to conduct themselves as the other Churches, they would follow the admonitions as laid down by Paul concerning this matter.

This is not the first time that Paul has tried to correct Corinthian behavior by appealing to what is taught or practiced in the other Churches. The pronoun *"we"* is meant to refer to all the Churches. Paul is again reminding the Corinthians of how much greater a Body it is to which he and they belong (I Cor. 1:2).

(17) "NOW IN THIS THAT I DECLARE UNTO YOU I PRAISE YOU NOT, THAT YE COME TOGETHER NOT FOR THE BETTER, BUT FOR THE WORSE."

The phrase, *"Now in this that I declare unto you I praise you not,"* refers back to the Second Verse where he did praise them. However, *"this"* of which he will now address is another matter altogether — the Lord's Supper.

The phrase, *"That ye come together not for the better, but for the worse,"* refers to Church Services. However, the Services at Corinth, or at least some of them, were being conducted in a manner which did not bring Glory to God, or edification for the people.

Without much study of the Word, or worship of God, their gathering was more social than anything else. Each would bring their own food and they would have a love feast, followed by the Lord's Supper.

These things had gotten out of hand, even as we shall see, with some even getting drunk, etc.

NOTES

As should be obvious, false teachers had evidently come into the Church, which led to such behavior. The services and gatherings certainly were not conducted in this manner when Paul planted the Church.

(18) "FOR FIRST OF ALL, WHEN YE COME TOGETHER IN THE CHURCH, I HEAR THAT THERE BE DIVISIONS AMONG YOU; AND I PARTLY BELIEVE IT."

The phrase, *"For first of all, when ye come together in the Church,"* speaks of their weekly gatherings (or ever how often), in order to worship the Lord. At least, that's what they were supposed to have been doing, but from the description here given, the Lord was little worshipped.

The phrase, *"I hear that there be divisions among you,"* presents something different from the *"quarrels"* and *"jealousy"* outlined in the First and Third Chapters. These *"divisions"* are spelled out along sociological lines. In the former divisions, there definitely were some anti-Paul sentiments in the quarreling, but in this there are only two groups, the *"have-nots"* and the *"haves,"* with no hint of a quarrel with Paul on this matter.

*"Divisions"* in the Greek is *"schisma,"* and means *"a split or gap, a rent or schism."*

## GOD'S WORK AND SATAN'S HINDRANCE

Someone has said that the Work of God is divided up into three sections. They are as follows:

1. VISION: For every Work of God done on earth, the Lord has called someone to perform that work, in essence giving them a *"Vision."* They feel it in their spirit, they see it in their spirit, exactly as Paul did when he was directed by the Holy Spirit to come to Corinth in order to plant this particular Church. To be frank, every God-called Preacher of the Gospel must have this *"Vision"* for anything he does for the Cause of Christ. The idea that Preachers are sent out by committees is pretty much foreign to the Word of God.

The manner is that God lays a burden on a person's heart for a certain place, a certain work, or a certain effort for the Cause of Christ. In other words, that man or woman has been *"Called"* to that particular work or ministry, i.e. *"they have a Vision."*

2. PROVISION: When the Lord gives the *"Vision,"* He also makes *"Provision."* He does this in many and varied ways.

The Lord provides the Faith for the Called individual regarding what is to be done (Rom. 12:3). He then as well begins to touch people in order that they be involved in the project, whatever that project may be, regarding their prayerful and financial support. In other words, the Lord makes *"Provision"* in every capacity.

3. DIVISION: Satan comes in at some point with *"Division."* He wants the *"Vision"* to die, hence, his effort being called *"Di-Vision."* He does this by attempting to hinder the people that God has called to support that particular *"Vision,"* or even attempts to hinder the Preacher, in any one of several ways.

If Satan can create a Division, exactly as he did here at Corinth, and as he does in so many places, unless the situation is properly addressed, even as Paul is here doing, it can destroy everything that has been done, i.e. destroy the Vision.

The phrase, *"And I partly believe it,"* lends credence to the idea that he is loathe to believe the worst, even on testimony that is good. We see that he discounts even credible reports.

His is the true Christian attitude, but regrettably only too few follow it.

Regrettably, many Christians are all too ready to believe the worst, which gives us an idea of the state of one's heart.

(19) "FOR THERE MUST BE ALSO HERESIES AMONG YOU, THAT THEY WHICH ARE APPROVED MAY BE MADE MANIFEST AMONG YOU."

The phrase, *"For there must be also heresies among you,"* presents the *"heresies"* as the cause of the *"divisions."*

HERESY

*"Heresy"* in the Greek is *"hairesis,"* and properly denotes *"choice."* However, it can refer to a philosophical school which the individual chooses to follow.

Similarly, the New Testament uses the word to denote a *"party"* with the suggestion of self-will or sectarian spirit; but it must be noted, at least in such a case, that none of the parties thus described is in a state of schism from its parent body. For instance, the Sadducees (Acts 5:17) and the Pharisees (Acts 15:5; 26:5) formed sects within the fold of Judaism.

When parties appear within the Church, they are called *"heresies,"* even as we are now studying, with Paul implying that, though bad, they have the good result of making it clear who are the true Christians. Such divisions are regarded as a work of the flesh (Gal. 5:20), and primarily as a breach of mutual love, so that the heretic, i.e. the man who stubbornly chooses to form or follow his own group, is to be rejected after two admonitions (warnings) (Titus 3:10).

However, all who are called *"heretics"* are not necessarily such. In fact, one could probably say that every single Religious Denomination presently active was referred to as *"heretics"* when they first began. While the label may definitely have been true in some cases, it was not true in all cases.

AS PRESENTLY DEFINED

Heresy can be presently defined (for proper clarification) as a departure from the Revealed Truth of the Word of God, or the enlargement of a Truth all out of proportion to its original intent.

In other words, when some in the Early Church were contending that Grace was of such magnitude that they could sin all they desired without concern, meaning that Grace would cover it irrespective as to what they did, Paul answered with the words, *"God forbid"* (Rom. 6:1, 2). In that case, the proponents of such had taken Grace, a viable, Revealed, Biblical, Doctrine and enlarged it all out of proportion to its original intent. Such then becomes *"heresy."*

Another example is Baptismal Regeneration, which pertains to the idea that Water Baptism saves. Water Baptism is a viable Christian Doctrine, but when taken to this extent, it becomes *"heresy."*

Some believe that one must speak in Tongues to be saved. Even though Tongues is a viable Christian Doctrine, it becomes heresy when taken to this extent. Eternal Security is another case in point, etc.

The phrase, *"That they which are approved may be made manifest among you,"* gives us a clue as to what type of heresies there may have been in the Church at Corinth.

The language of this Verse and others following suggests that the prosperous may have actually been comparing themselves to the poor, claiming that their prosperity was due to the fact that they were *"the approved ones"*

NOTES

before God. It is sad, but there are still among us today those who interpret their wealth as a sign that they are more spiritual than other people. Paul warned against such an unscriptural mind-set that equates wealth with godliness (I Tim. 6:5).

If, in fact, that was happening, such perfectly describes the modern *"Prosperity Message."* In this teaching, a person's faith is judged by the make or model of car he drives, cost of clothing, in other words, worldly trappings.

Actually, Paul was saying, *"That they which are truly approved may be made manifest among you,"* discounting the claims of the others.

## APPROVAL

As someone has said, one can have the approval of men or the approval of God, he cannot have both.

How do we win the approval of God? For that is actually the great question!

I think one can say, without fear of exaggeration, that every single person who has ever lived seeks approval in one way or the other. Children seek the approval of their parents, many, of their peers, or whatever the case. In this vast number, only a few actually seek the approval of God.

## THE GREEK WORDS AS USED IN THE NEW TESTAMENT

The occurrences of *"approved/approval"* in modern versions almost always signal the appearance in the original of a distinctive Greek word group.

*"Dokimos,"* a noun, is used in the New Testament in the sense of recognition of being officially approved and accepted. It is found in Romans 14:18; 16:10; I Corinthians 11:19; II Corinthians 10:18; 13:7; II Timothy 2:15; James 1:12.

The Greek word *"Dokimazo,"* a verb, implies putting to the test with a view to approving the genuine. That which has been tested is demonstrated to be genuine and trustworthy. This verb is used 23 times in the New Testament. Three times (Lk. 11:48; Acts 8:1; 22:20), Luke uses a compound word that expresses complete approval.

Another Greek word, *"syneudokeo,"* is used in only three places in the New Testament (Rom. 1:32; I Cor. 7:12, 13). In two of those verses, Paul says that if an unsaved spouse is *"willing"* to live with the partner who has become a Believer, no divorce should be initiated. Only in John 6:27 is the idea of approval not a rendering of some word in the *"dokimos"* word group. There the Greek word is *"sphragizo,"* and means *"seal,"* which correctly interpreted refers to one *"placing his seal of approval on a certain person or thing."*

NOTES

## TESTING

What seems important in the notion of approval is its linkage with testing. Approval is not lightly given, it is won.

Our character and our commitments emerge over time. It is only on evidence provided by experience and the passage of time that approval can be extended.

## THE APPROVAL OF PEOPLE

Time and experience provide the evidence on which one can be approved. But the criterion by which a person is evaluated is also important. The New Testament warns against trying to *"win the approval of men,"* even when these persons are fellow Believers (Gal. 1:10).

There are a number of reasons for this warning. Christ alone is our Master; it is He Whom we are to serve (Gal. 1:10).

As well, it is dangerous for us to even try to evaluate ourselves. Only God's evaluation and commendation counts (I Cor. 4:3-5; II Cor. 10:18).

As for the standards of unbelievers, Paul's pre-conversion approval of the stoning of Stephen shows how questionable their standards were (Acts 8:1; 22:20)! Clearly the warped consciences of the unsaved will often lead them to overlook serious sin or even to approve of those who today may be called *"beautiful people,"* whose lifestyles deny Righteousness (Rom. 1:32).

## THE APPROVAL OF GOD

Since the approval of God is so vital for us, what does the Bible say about winning it? Several New Testament Passages link God's approval to a subjective attitude and an objective standard.

The subjective attitude is one of commitment to serve Christ (Rom. 12:2; 14:18).

The objective standard is the Word of God, which of course, never changes. In Romans, Paul writes of Jewish reliance on the Law and of the fact that, through the Scriptures, the Hebrew people knew God's Will. They even approved of it as superior. But in fact, the Jews failed to do what they knew to be the Will of God (Rom. 2:17-29).

AN APPROVED WORKMAN

Paul warns Timothy against chattering on in theological dispute while drifting into ungodly behavior. An approved workman *"correctly handles the Word of Truth"* and demonstrates God's approval by turning away from wickedness (II Tim. 2:14-19).

Romans 12:1-2 sums it up:

We are to commit ourselves to be living sacrifices, dedicated to pleasing God. We must no longer conform to this world's patterns; our whole perspective on life is to be reshaped by God. Then we *"will be able to test and approve what God's Will is."*

Paul's point is a vital one. The Word of God — through which we come to know God's Will — must itself be put to the test by us. We put Scripture to the test by acting on what it says. When we do this, we experience God's good, pleasing, and perfect Will.

When we do God's Will, He will be able to approve of us as good workers who have no need to be ashamed.

(20) "WHEN YE COME TOGETHER THEREFORE INTO ONE PLACE, THIS IS NOT TO EAT THE LORD'S SUPPER."

The phrase, *"When ye come together therefore into one place,"* refers to the assembly of Believers. In those days, they did not have Church buildings because such was not allowed by Roman authorities, so they basically met in someone's home or in some other designated place. In fact, during times of persecution, they even met in caves, or deep in the forest, etc. Where, was not really that important. *"Why,"* was actually that which was significant, i.e. *"the worshipping of the Lord Jesus Christ."*

The phrase, *"This is not to eat the Lord's Supper,"* has reference to the fact that they may have called it such, but the way it was being done, was definitely not recognized by the Holy Spirit. It is not what we call it that makes it the genuine Eucharist, but the *way* it is observed.

It is called *"The Lord's Supper"* because it is derived from the *"Last Supper,"* when Jesus ate the Passover with His Disciples (Mat. 26:20-30; Mk. 14:22-26; Lk. 22:14-20; Jn. Chpt. 13).

NOTES

(21) "FOR IN EATING EVERY ONE TAKETH BEFORE OTHER HIS OWN SUPPER: AND ONE IS HUNGRY, AND ANOTHER IS DRUNKEN."

The phrase, *"For in eating every one taketh before other his own supper,"* had to do, as stated, with the love feasts, so-called, where in reality not much love was actually shown. Due to abuses, such as here, this practice soon died out.

The phrase, *"And one is hungry,"* gives us some description, although little is said, of what actually was taking place.

It seems that Believers were coming to these particular *"love feasts,"* which were supposed to be a time of fellowship, enjoyment, and sharing, with the Lord as the ever-present, but unseen Host. After this feast and fellowship, the entire body was supposed to take the Lord's Supper.

In the Early Church, all types of people were coming to Christ, some few very wealthy, and many very poor, some even slaves. To be frank, Christianity dealt the first major blow against class consciousness, etc. In fact, it is still the only great leveler of the human race. All must come to Christ on the same basis, whether rich, poor, great, or small, etc. In fact, the very action of Christ is, through the Holy Spirit, to develop love in our hearts for all people, irrespective as to their place, position, or station in life.

Of course, this is the ideal, and that which the Holy Spirit strongly desires and works toward. Unfortunately, the actual facts, as here, don't always measure up to that ideal.

THE CHURCH AT CORINTH

It seems that some few of the people in the Church were wealthy, consequently bringing very elaborate meals to the gatherings, and were not at all sharing with others who had very little if anything. In fact, from Paul's description by using the word *"hungry"* it meant just that, some had nothing. In fact, some were slaves.

Consequently, one could well imagine what type of attitude and spirit that such would foment, which meant that not very much love was actually being shown.

The phrase, *"And another is drunken,"* means exactly what it says.

*"Drunken"* in the Greek is *"methuo,"* and means *"intoxicated,"* which is unacceptable behavior.

As well, we should learn from this, and sadly so I might quickly add, that the Church of the Apostolic days was not totally pure. On the contrary, many of the heathen converts were unable at once to break the spell of their old habits, even as some presently.

THE SPECTACLE

So, the Holy Spirit paints a picture through the Apostle, of a Church which had great difficulties with the party spirit, with acts of immorality being condoned, and even in some cases it seems, being applauded, now joined by divisions and heresies and even drunkenness. But yet it was still a Church, and God was working in its midst, in order to bring victory out of this chaos.

As well, the condition in which we now find this Church in no way reflects on the foundation laid by the Apostle. To be frank, under the guidance of Paul, the people at Corinth had greater teaching and greater leadership and a greater example of spirituality than most today would ever think of having.

Consequently, this tells us that proper teaching, instruction, and even great spirituality which surely characterized Paul's Ministry, are no guarantee that the end result will be exactly as it ought to be.

And yet, as we shall see from Paul's Second Letter to the Corinthians, which we will study shortly, the Lord brought great victory out of this chaos. So, irrespective as to how bad the situation may presently seem, the Lord is able to do great and mighty things, even as he ultimately did at Corinth.

(22) "WHAT? HAVE YE NOT HOUSES TO EAT AND TO DRINK IN? OR DESPISE YE THE CHURCH OF GOD, AND SHAME THEM THAT HAVE NOT? WHAT SHALL I SAY TO YOU? SHALL I PRAISE YOU IN THIS? I PRAISE YOU NOT."

The one word question, *"What?",* is meant to render its force on what the Apostle is about to say regarding this situation. The one word, *"What"* in the form a question, shows the indignation of the Apostle, and rightly so!

NOTES

The question, *"Have ye not houses to eat and to drink in?",* is directed at the wealthy. The idea being that the wealthy had houses, in fact owned them, while the poor did not have the benefit of such.

Whatever fine foods they wanted to enjoy, and because they had the money to purchase such, they could do so in the privacy of their own homes, instead of greatly making a spectacle, embarrassing the poor, etc. In fact, Paul's words drip with sarcasm. The idea is this:

THE LOVE OF GOD?

He seems to be saying, *"If you have no regard for the plight of those who are not as fortunate as you, and you don't even have enough of the Love of God in your heart to share with them, at least take your gluttony and selfishness behind the walls of your own houses, and don't parade it before all of the Church"*

The beginning of the question, *"Or despise ye the Church of God, . . .?",* refers to the audacity of carrying on such selfishness in the very Assemblies where they were supposed to be worshipping the Lord.

The conclusion of the question, *"And shame them that have not?",* refers to the poor, even very poor, who had little if anything to bring to these feasts in the way of food, and were thereby *"shamed"* because of their lack in the presence of so much plenty.

Then after this particular *"love feast,"* they were all supposed to engage in taking the *"Lord's Supper,"* which within itself epitomized and symbolized the very opposite (unselfishness) of the selfishness here being portrayed by some.

Here in one of the most important matters of their faith that deals with the Sacred Supper, the Corinthians were woefully lacking. They had allowed themselves to drift far from Paul's teaching and example.

The question, *"What shall I say to you?",* presents the Apostle at being nonplussed and shocked over the state of things.

The question, *"Shall I praise you in this?",* probably is asked in response to his statement in I Corinthians 11:2, when he had in fact, praised the Corinthians. He now answers his own question.

The phrase, *"I praise you not,"* in effect says, *"I blame you."* He seems to ask himself: *"Do these people really realize what they are doing?"*

No *"Church"* can long endure as the people of God in which the old distinctions between bond and free (or Jew and Greek, or male and female) are allowed to persist. It is the business of the Holy Spirit to rectify these things. However, he can only do what we allow Him to do. In fact, He will never force the issue.

As a result, the Holy Spirit is no longer present in many Churches, simply because they persisted in a direction which is anathema to the Word of God. Even though such people still meet in congregations, in fact, calling themselves a Church, still, in the eyes of God it is no Church at all. In fact, looking at both Catholic and Protestant, most fall into the category of being no more than a man-devised institution, with the Lord present not at all.

(23) "FOR I HAVE RECEIVED OF THE LORD THAT WHICH ALSO I DELIVERED UNTO YOU, THAT THE LORD JESUS THE SAME NIGHT IN WHICH HE WAS BETRAYED TOOK BREAD:

The phrase, *"For I have received of the Lord that which also I delivered unto you,"* refers to that which he is about to give concerning the Lord's Supper, its order and significance, and which he received by Revelation. In fact, that which he gives is almost identical to the account given by Luke (Lk. 22:19, 20).

## THE MANNER IN WHICH IT WAS RECEIVED

We do know that the entirety of the New Covenant was given to Paul *"by the Revelation of Jesus Christ"* (Gal. 1:11, 12). However, that does not tell us exactly the manner in which it was done.

Every evidence seems to point to the fact that the Holy Spirit opened up the Old Testament to Paul, which then was the only Bible they had. In Truth, everything about the New Covenant is found in some manner in the Old Covenant, i.e. *"Old Testament."* However, until the Holy Spirit revealed these great Truths, even as Paul said in I Corinthians 2:10, they were not properly understood.

All of this was made possible by what Jesus did at Calvary and the Resurrection, removing the sin debt in order that the Holy Spirit could come into the hearts and lives of believing sinners. Because of what Jesus did, hence, *"the Revelation of Jesus Christ,"* these great Truths could now be made known. So, Paul saw the New Covenant in Revelation which had already been given by the Prophets of old.

NOTES

Respecting the *"Lord's Supper,"* he took what was already there, which no doubt Peter had discussed with him, and possibly even others, with the Lord telling him that this celebration of the New Covenant should continue in all Churches, and among all of God's people, until the Second Coming.

Paul now informs the Corinthians, that he had already delivered them the instructions regarding this very sacred occasion, and had no doubt practiced it with them many times while he was there. So, they were not in ignorance respecting their coarse treatment of this Covenant.

The phrase, *"That the Lord Jesus the same night in which he was betrayed took bread,"* recalls the sacred occasion.

As most Christians know, the Lord's Supper is an outgrowth of the Jewish Passover. In fact, Jesus, along with His Disciples, was keeping the Passover when He introduced the New Covenant, symbolized in what we refer to as the Lord's Supper.

## THE PASSOVER

The Passover was originated by God concerning the deliverance of the Children of Israel from Egyptian bondage. It is given in Exodus Chapter 12, with the Lord commanding the Jews to keep this sacred Feast forever. Consequently, it is still kept by Christians, the true Israel, in its new form.

At the time of Christ, the Passover time would have found thousands of people gathered in the Outer Temple Court in companies in order to slaughter the Passover lambs. Josephus said that as many as 250,000 were killed at the Passover when Christ was Crucified. Each family had to prepare its own animal, hence, the tremendous number.

## THE MANNER

The Priests stood in two rows; in one row each man had a golden basin, in the other, each man had a silver basin. The basin which caught the Blood of the expiring victim was passed from hand to hand in continuous exchange to the end of the line, where the last Priest tossed the blood in ritual manner on the Altar. As stated, this was done thousands of times.

All this was done to the singing of the Hallel (Ps. 113-118). The celebrating companies were generally family units, but other common ties were possible, such as that which bound our Lord to His Disciples.

THE ACTUAL EATING OF THE PASSOVER

After candlelight search for the forbidden leaven, and other careful preparations (Mk. 14:12-16), the Paschal supper proper was taken reclining. It included the symbolic elements of roasted lamb, unleavened bread, bitter herbs, some minor condiments, and four cups of grape juice at specified points.

The stipulated ritual hand-washings were carefully observed.

THE CUSTOM

The table was cleared before the second cup of juice, the story of the Egyptian Passover and Exodus then recounted in a dialogue between father and son (or some suitable substitutes).

The dishes of food were then brought back, part of the Hallel was sung, with the second cup of juice following. Then came the breaking of Bread.

In the Last Supper, it was probably at this point that Judas received the sop, and departed into the night to betray his Master (Jn. 13:30). On that fateful night, it may be assumed that the institution of the Lord's Supper or Eucharist was associated with the third cup of juice. The singing of the Hallel was completed with the fourth cup — doubtless the hymn of Matthew 26:30.

JESUS AND THE PASSOVER

It is assumed here that the Last Supper did coincide with the statutory Passover. In fact, Jesus ate the Passover with His Disciples early, because at the actual time it was being eaten, Jesus was dying or dead.

The symbolism, *"Christ our Passover,"* or *"Lamb of God,"* is familiar from New Testament usage. We have seen that the traditional lamb, if not provable in all instances, has widespread precedent.

For instance, it is laid down in Exodus 12:46 and Numbers 9:12 that no bone of the Passover victim is to be broken. This small detail is typologically fulfilled when it is reverently applied to the Crucified One (Jn. 19:36).

NOTES

After the destruction of the Jerusalem Temple in A.D. 70, any possibility of slaughtering a victim in ritual manner utterly ceased, and the Jewish Passover reverted to a mere family festival.

In Christian Faith, the Lord's Supper came to replace the Jewish Ordinance, just as Water Baptism came to replace Circumcision.

THE UNLEAVENED BREAD

The *"Bread"* which Jesus took that night so long ago was Unleavened Bread. It was to symbolize His Body offered as a spotless, uncorrupted, pure Sacrifice — the only thing which God would accept.

The normal word for bread in Hebrew is *"lehem."* A special term, *"massah,"* is used for Unleavened Bread — bread made without yeast or without waiting for the dough to rise.

Unleavened Bread (Massah) was often served to unexpected guests. On the night of Israel's deliverance from Egypt, *"Massah"* was eaten because of the hurried departure.

Throughout its generations, Israel was to commemorate that deliverance, and on the day of Passover the people were to eat Unleavened Bread (Ex. 12:8, 39). In fact, the *"days of Unleavened Bread"* included the Passover itself and the seven days that followed.

BREAD OF THE PRESENCE

In Israel's worship, fresh bread was baked each Sabbath and placed on a table within the Tabernacle or Temple. Twelve loaves were set before the Lord in two rows to represent the Tribes of Israel, worship being represented by Incense along each row. This Bread could be eaten later only, however, by members of the Priesthood.

Yet, I Samuel Chapter 21 tells of David, in sudden flight from Saul, demanding five of the consecrated loaves from the Priest at the Tabernacle.

Jesus later commented on the incident, when His Disciples were condemned by the Pharisees for plucking and eating ears of grain on the Sabbath.

Jesus reminded them of David's actions, claimed personal Lordship over the Sabbath, and announced that God has always valued Mercy over Sacrifice (Mat. 12:3-8). Law was intended to serve human need. But the rigid

Pharisees had twisted that intention and raised their questionable interpretations of Sabbath Law above the needs of human beings whom they, and Law, were supposed to serve.

EXPRESSIONS USING *"BREAD"*

A number of expressions in the New Testament use the word *"Bread."* Jesus reaffirmed an Old Testament confession, *"Man does not live on bread alone,"* when He was tempted by Satan (Mat. 4:4; Lk. 4:4; Deut. 8:3).

Human beings are more than animals trapped within the material universe and dominated by physical needs. They have a spiritual dimension. To live as true human beings, we must respond to the Word of God and not be driven by our physical urges.

In the prayer Jesus taught His Disciples, one familiar request is *"Give us today our daily Bread"* (Mat. 6:11; Lk. 11:3). The plea emphasizes constant dependence on God for everything we need to sustain us.

I AM THE LIVING BREAD

One of Jesus' great Discourses followed His miracle of feeding the five thousand with only five small barley loaves and two small fish.

The next day, eager crowds searched for Jesus. But when they found Him, He told them not to be so excited about food that spoils. There is a food that will sustain Eternal Life, He told them:

*"I am the Living Bread that came down from Heaven. If anyone eats of this Bread, he will live forever. This Bread is My Flesh, which I will give for the life of the world"* (Jn. 6:51).

The symbolism finds constant repetition in our practice of the Communion, even as we are now studying (I Cor. 11:23-28).

(24) "AND WHEN HE HAD GIVEN THANKS, HE BRAKE IT, AND SAID, TAKE, EAT: THIS IS MY BODY, WHICH IS BROKEN FOR YOU: THIS DO IN REMEMBRANCE OF ME."

The phrase, *"And when He had given thanks,"* portrays the ordinary Jewish meal beginning with the head of the house giving the traditional blessing over the bread, breaking it, and giving it to those at the table with him. Jesus, as the *"Teacher,"* played that role at the Last Supper, if not constantly with his Disciples.

At the Passover meal, the Blessing and distribution of the Bread came during the meal

NOTES

(Mk. 14:18; Lk. 22:17-19), immediately following the *"Passover liturgy,"* in which the reasons for this meal were expressed (a recital of the deliverance from Egypt). Hence, Jesus' action in Blessing and breaking the Bread at the Last Supper would have been in the natural course of things.

The remarkable thing that He did was to reinterpret the meaning of the Bread, as He was distributing it, in terms of His Own Death: *"This is My Body, which is for you."*

The phrase, *"He brake it,"* even though normally and commonly done at each Passover, still, represented His Body which would be broken at Calvary. This does not refer to His bones, for *"a bone of Him shall not be broken"* (Jn. 19:36).

It spoke of His Body being pierced and beaten and then given over in death, i.e. *"broken."*

It lies quite beyond both Jesus' intent and the framework within which He and the Disciples lived to imagine that some actual change took place, or was intended to take place in the Bread itself, as claim the Catholics regarding their doctrine of Transubstantiation. Such a view could only have arisen in the Church at a much later stage, in fact, as the Church began to apostatize.

The phrase, *"And said, "take, eat: this is My Body, which is broken for you,"* is meant to symbolize the death of Jesus on Calvary's Cross, and the believing sinner actually partaking of that Sacrifice by Faith.

HIS BODY

The use of the term *"body"* has elicited considerable discussion: does it mean *"Himself"* or His *"Flesh"?* Most likely, it means neither but refers to His actual Body, which was about to be given over in death. The analogy is with the Sacrificial victim (the Lamb), whose *"body (carcass)"* was placed on the Altar after the Blood had been poured out.

The phrase, *"which is broken for you,"* is unique to Paul and Luke, with Matthew and Mark not mentioning this phrase. And yet, it is absolutely certain that Jesus said these words. It links the Bread and the Cup together, both referring to Jesus' death.

Actually, the words *"for you"* are an adaptation of the language of Isaiah 53:12, where the Suffering Servant *"bore sin for many."* Thus, for Jesus Himself, this is almost certainly a prophetic, symbolic, action, by which He anticipated

His Death and interpreted it in Light of Isaiah Chapter 53 as in behalf of others. By giving them a share in *"His Body"* in this way, He invited His Disciples to participate in the meaning and benefits of that death, as in fact, He does with all Believers in our participation of the Lord's Supper (Fee).

The phrase, *"This do in remembrance of Me,"* as well was not mentioned by Matthew and Mark, but was recorded by Luke (Lk. 22:19).

Just as the Passover meal itself was such a *"remembrance"* to be kept forever in Israel, so Jesus is now reconstituting the *"memorial"* for the True Israel that will gather around the table in His Name to *"remember"* its own deliverance through Him. That is why He describes it as *"My remembrance."* It is not simply *"in memory of Him,"* but it is eaten as a *"memorial"* of the Salvation that He has affected through His Death and Resurrection.

By partaking of this meal (Supper), Believers *"proclaim"* Christ's Death until He comes, that is, we declare the good news of our Salvation that makes us all one. To participate unworthily means to come under judgement for the very reason that it fails to acknowledge the meal as a *"memorial"* of God's saving event (Fee).

## THE POWER OF THE WORD *"REMEMBER"* AS IT IS USED IN THE BIBLE

The past is rightly expected to shape our present. The Scripture suggests little about how human memory works. But it says much about what is to be remembered.

In view of what Jesus said about remembering the tremendous event of Calvary, perhaps it would be good to look at this word to a greater depth.

## HEBREW WORDS

The Hebrew words translated *"memory," "remember," "remembrance,"* etc., are related to *"zaker." "Zaker"* has a wide range of meanings, but most of these meanings focus on mental acts and can be grouped into three categories:

1. The mental acts themselves such as remembering, meditating on, paying attention to, and thinking about.

2. The mental acts and the behavior appropriate to these acts (thus, to *"remember the Covenant"* is to act in accordance with Covenant stipulations).

NOTES

3. Speaking to invoke memory or to recite from memory. The first two meanings are the ones that we find in the Old Testament.

## WHAT WE ARE TO REMEMBER

The Old Testament call to remember is more than an invitation to think about the past. Instead, it is a call to identify oneself with the past, and to let present life be shaped by it. Israel was to remember the Lord and His Commands (Num. 15:39, 40). Such remembering implies a perspective so shaped by God's Word that obedience results. Israel was also to remember their state of slavery in Egypt (Deut. 5:15; 15:15; 16:12; 24:18, 22) and all that God did to deliver them (Deut. 7:18; 8:2; 24:9).

Again, remembering suggests identification in such a way that one enters into the historic reality and recognizes oneself as a redeemed person. Failure to remember implies failure to take one's place among God's people and can be equated with disobedience (Ezek. 16:43-63).

Thus, the Old Testament stresses that memory should focus on Who God is and What He has done for Israel. Memory focused on the ways that the Lord has marked out and implies obedience to God's Will. To fail to remember means abandoning the Lord and His Righteous Path.

## CALLING ON GOD TO REMEMBER

The Old Testament contains appeals to God to remember the individual or nation (Neh. 13:14). God is asked to remember His *"Great Mercy"* (Ps. 25:6) and how the enemy has mocked Him (Ps. 74:18).

There is no suggestion that the Lord might have forgotten. Such appeals call on God to act. So when the Old Testament says that God *"remembered His Covenant"* (Ex. 2:24), it means that He acted in Covenant Faithfulness.

To say that God will *"now remember their wickedness"* (Jer. 14:10) is to say that He will now punish them.

## MEMORIALS

The idea that memory is linked to personal identification with God's historic acts or words is reflected in the Hebrew word *"zikkaron"* (*"a reminder"* or *"a remembrance"*).

It is used of objects or actions designed to help Israel identify with a particular reality or

Truth. Exodus 12:14 calls the annual festival of Passover a *"memorial day."* The ritual of that day reenacted God's great deliverance from Egypt and helped each individual sense his or her identity as one of the redeemed. The pile of stones set beside the River Jordan (Josh. 4:7) was to help later generations remember that God acted to part the river for His people.

Such memorial events or objects which enable the people to identify with God's historic acts or words, played a significant role in Faith development in Israel.

GREEK WORDS

Greek words translated *"remember," "recall,"* and *"remind"* include *"mimnesko"* (*"to recall, remember"*), *"mnemoneuo"* (*"to remember," "to mention"*), *"anamimnesko"* (*"to remind"*), and *"hypomimnesko"* (*"to remind"*). There are shades of difference, but in general these words should be considered as the basic Greek idea of *"remembering."*

The range of meaning suggested by this word group includes secular and religious meanings from the New Testament era. In common speech, *"to remember"* may be to recall (Lk. 22:61). *"To remember"* may, as in the Old Testament, mean to help (Lk. 1:54; Gal. 2:10).

To be mindful of the meaning of some truth or event may indicate that present choices are being shaped by it (I Cor. 4:17). In addition, there is the act of remembering in prayer (I Thess. 1:3; Phile. vs. 4) and teaching by reminding (II Pet. 1:12-15).

Most of our New Testament references are easily understood within the framework of these Old Testament uses. For instance, the Covenant Promise of full forgiveness reads, *"For I will forgive their wickedness and will remember their sins no more"* (Heb. 8:12). According to Biblical thought, this is best understood as God's Promise that forgiven sins are forever beyond punishment. What a wonderful thought that is!

New Testament admonitions to *"remember"* are usually calls to consider a Truth or event and to so identify with it that our choices are shaped by it.

REMEMBRANCE IN THE NEW TESTAMENT

One of the most significant and debated teachings in the New Testament relates to the Lord's Supper, which we are now studying. When Jesus instituted this Sacrament, He said, *"Do this in remembrance of Me"* (Lk. 22:19; I Cor. 11:24, 25). This *"remembrance"* in partaking of the Lord's Supper is to be continued until Jesus comes back.

The simplest and perhaps the best way to understand it is as an analogy to the Old Testament memorial (*"Zikkaron"*).

The Lord's Supper is a memorial, inviting us to identify ourselves with Jesus' Crucifixion. It is repeated, for each new generation of Believers must begin their spiritual life in and through the Blood shed on Calvary. As a Testimony to Faith and a call to focus our Hope in Jesus, the Communion Service affirms our identity with Jesus in His Death and in His Restored Life (Richards).

(25) "AFTER THE SAME MANNER ALSO HE TOOK THE CUP, WHEN HE HAD SUPPED, SAYING, THIS CUP IS THE NEW TESTAMENT IN MY BLOOD: THIS DO YE, AS OFT AS YE DRINK IT, IN REMEMBRANCE OF ME."

The phrase, *"After the same manner also He took the Cup,"* if one is to notice, does not mention the drink per se, but in all accounts of this event, uses the word *"Cup."*

I think there was a reason that the Holy Spirit had Jesus to address this in this manner. The argument has raged, and continues to do so unto this moment, as to whether the *"wine"* in the Cup was alcoholic or nonalcoholic. I contend that it was nonalcoholic, nonintoxicating, and offer the following proof:

THE BIBLE AND WINE

The Greek words for wine in the New Testament are *"Oinon," "Oinion," "Oine," "Oinos."* It means, *"the fruit of the Vine or grape-plant."* It is also used to denote various kinds of drinks or confections of other succulent fruits such as the date and lotus fruit, according to Liddell and Scott's Lexicon.

In fact, the Hebrew word in the Old Testament for wine is *"yain,"* and as well, was not confined to an intoxicating liquor made from fruits by alcoholic fermentation, but more frequently referred to a thick, nonintoxicating syrup, conserve or jam, produced by boiling to make them storable as articles of food, exactly as we do at the present day.

In other words, both the Greek and Hebrew words for wine can mean intoxicating beverage or nonintoxicating beverage, and to be frank, most often refers to the nonintoxicating kind. One has to ascertain from the associated texts as to which type it addresses.

The Greek word *"oinos"* does not always signify fermented, intoxicating drink, but grapes as fresh fruit, dried as raisins, or prepared as jam or preserved by boiling for storage, or as thick syrup for spreading upon bread as we do butter; and that syrup dissolved in water for a beverage at meals, as described in the Bible by Solomon and others. Actually, the mixing of the syrup with water ready for use at meals is alluded to in more than one of our Lord's Parables. The liquid was absolutely nonalcoholic and not intoxicating.

MANNER OF USE

Grape-juice was also prepared by heating it, as soon as possible, after it had been squeezed in the press, by boiling so as to prevent fermentation, and yet preserve its thin liquid form as a drink.

In fact, some of these methods of producing a nonintoxicating wine are still followed extensively in every grape-growing country of Southern Europe and Asia, as of old.

It should never be forgotten that when reading in the Bible of *"Wine,"* we are seldom dealing with the strongly intoxicating and loaded liquids to which that name is alone attached in the English language, but usually with beverages such as above described. They were as harmless and sober as our own teas, coffees, and cocoas.

Had they not been so, the ancient populations would have been perpetually in a more or less pronounced state of drunkenness, for they had none of our above-noted herb-made drinks to use as a part of their diet.

These facts should never be forgotten when we read of *"wine,"* for it was simple fruit syrup, except where especially stated to be of the intoxicating kind, which the latter Prophets always condemned.

REFERENCE IN MATTHEW

In Matthew 9:17, Jesus said: *"Neither do they pour new wine* (fresh grape-juice) *into old wine-skins; for if they did, the skins would burst, and the wine* (grape-juice) *be spilt, and the skins destroyed. On the contrary, they pour fresh juice into new skins, and both are safe together."*

NOTES

Only a determination to misread this metaphorical illustration of the subject which Jesus was discussing with the Disciples of John, can pervert this passage into a recommendation or sanction for habitual use of intoxicating liquors.

To keep the juice of the grape sweet and wholesome it needed to be especially prepared before being poured into new skins, where it would keep pure and benefit men as an article of diet, as a syrup or jam, such as the ancient writers upon agriculture and domestic economy inform us were in common daily use.

The interpretation put upon His Parable by the ignorant commentators of the Dark Ages that Jesus insisted upon the drinking of intoxicants, is little short of blasphemy, and it is a disgrace to our better informed age that writers should say that *"Christianity has given a sacred character to wine and its use."*

REFERENCES IN MARK

In Mark 15:20-24, it says: *"And when they had insulted Him they took off from Him the purple robe, and clad Him in His Own attire, and led Him out for Crucifixion. Then they seized a passer-by, who was coming up from the country — Simon the Cyrenian, the father of Alexander and Rufus — forcing him to accompany Jesus, to carry the Cross to Golgotha* (which means Skull-field)*, where they offered Him wine medicated with myrrh: but He refused to drink it. There they crucified Him, and divided His clothing among themselves, casting lots as to what part each should take."*

The question suggested in the above, to which no one seems to have found an answer, is: Why did Jesus refuse to drink the wine, medicated with a narcotic by the Centurion, out of a feeling of mercy to the victim, Whom he knew had been unjustly condemned to death upon a false accusation? He also knew that Pilate had been driven to condemn Him by terror for his own personal safety, after the Sadducean Priests had threatened to accuse him to the Emperor at Rome as a confederate with Christ to incite a revolt of the Jews against the empire, unless he did hand Jesus over to their will to be Crucified.

This narcotic liquor does not seem to have been offered to the two robbers who had been convicted of real crime and, therefore, we must conclude, as I have done, that this was an act of mercy from the Centurion who commanded the detachment of soldiers, especially to Jesus. Then why should Christ not have drunk it? He would know the kindness of heart of the soldier, and the nobility of soul that inspired the feeling of mercy. Then why did He not accept the act of mercy?

Many think the Lord refused the narcotic because He did not wish to diminish in the slightest degree the cruel tortures of the death He was about to suffer for mankind. However, that was not the reason.

## THE ETERNAL HIGH PRIEST

As to the bodily torments, He was only to suffer the same as the two miserable robbers, His companions in this method of death. Consequently, there must have been a far more powerful reason for His refusal than that commonly given.

What was it?

Upon that day, the day of His Crucifixion, Jesus the Messiah had entered upon His Office of the Eternal High Priest of mankind, and was about to Sacrifice the Paschal Lamb, His earthly body, upon the Cross. Paul, commenting upon the fact wrote: *"Do ye not know that a little ferment ferments the whole mass? Clean out the old ferment* (leaven)*, so that you may be a sweet mass, and thus you will be unfermented. For Christ, our Passover, was sacrificed for us, so that we might keep a Festival, not with an old ferment, neither in a ferment of filth and wickedness, but, on the contrary, with unfermented purity and truth"* (I Cor. 5:6-8).

By this we can perceive that the Crucifixion not only occurred during the Passover Week, but was done by Christ *"offering Himself,"* that is, His Body upon the Cross at the Passover to free mankind from sin, but He was also spiritually the High Priest fulfilling the duties of His Office of Sacrifice (Heb. 10:22-28).

## PROHIBITION

As the officiating High Priest was, by the Law given through Moses, prohibited from *"drinking intoxicating wine"* during the period of his ministration, before entering the Sanctuary, or while engaged in its duties, to refresh my readers' memory, I will give the

NOTES

whole passage from Leviticus, Chapter 10, Verses 8-11.

*"Then Moses spoke to Aaron and commanded: 'You or your sons with you shall not drink of wine or an intoxicant when you are going to the Sanctuary, so that you may not die. This is an everlasting institution for your posterity.*

*"For you shall distinguish between the Sacred and the common, and between sin and purity, so that you may teach the sons of Israel.'"*

These Divine Laws, and the statements of the Apostles, show why Jesus refused to drink of the drugged wine offered to Him by the pagan but merciful Centurion, or by his order; the wine was the rationed liquor served out to the Roman soldiers as part of their diet, and was fermented as well as drugged, and so was an intoxicant, and, consequently, forbidden to Christ as our High Priest, and also as an ordinary Israelite; and the whole nation was also prohibited during the seven days' preparation for the Passover from having any fermented thing in their dwellings or to drink fermented liquors — and Jesus came to *"fulfill the whole Law."*

He obeyed it absolutely, and refused both as Priest and as an Israelite to drink the intoxicant offered to Him. He did not abstain with the object of securing to Himself the utmost of bodily agony as some believe, nor is any such motive suggested in the Gospels.

In view of the fact as to what Jesus' death at Calvary meant, and that He was serving as our Great High Priest, consequently refusing all intoxicants, how could anyone think that it would be proper in celebrating this great event in thanksgiving and praise, to use an intoxicating wine to symbolize His Shed Blood?

## JOHN

In John Chapter 2, we are given the account of Jesus changing the water to wine.

Probably this is one of the most misunderstood and misrepresented Passages in the whole of the Gospels. To claim that this *"wine"* was of the intoxicating variety shows a complete misunderstanding of the Scriptures.

The misunderstanding has arisen from imposing upon the ancient Greek text, and ancient Jewish habits of food and drink, the modern conception that the word *"wine"* always means intoxicating liquor.

Amongst the old Orientals and the Romans, such an idea was not attached to *"wine"* as a universal conception. On the contrary, their *"best wines"* were not fermented at all.

The ordinary drink of the Romans, learned writers tells us, was juice of the grape, which they mixed with water, both hot and cold, and sometimes with spices. In fact, fermented wine was rare in early Roman times; was only used as an act of worship in the temples, and men under 30 years of age and women all their lives were forbidden to use it, except at the sacrifices.

Understanding this, it is certain that the *"wine"* created by Christ at Cana was of the nonintoxicating kind, which the ancient writers say was, *"the ordinary drink of the people"* in daily life.

PAUL

Paul said to Timothy: *"No longer drink water alone, but use with a little wine for the stomach, because of your frequent infirmities"* (I Tim. 5:23).

*"Stomach wine,"* or *"wine for the stomach,"* the old writers upon Greek medicine tell us, was grape-juice, prepared as a thick, unfermented syrup for use as a medicament for dyspeptic and weak persons, which was, consequently, what the Apostle told his friend to use.

WINE AND THE LORD'S SUPPER

Jesus described the wine that was being used at His Passover as the *"fruit of the vine,"* i.e. the offspring of the vine, or that which is borne of the vine.

Now the vine does not bear intoxicating drink. The fruit of the vine is not intoxicating as well. There is no alcohol in the fruit of the vine. It is pure, good, wholesome, and health-giving, a beautiful emblem of the life and strength-giving Grace of our Lord and Saviour Jesus Christ.

Intoxicating wine is the emblem of disease, sin, and death.

Considering the amount of wine that was to be drunk at the Passover, which pertained to every member of the family 12 years old and older, it is certain that, if the wine was intoxicating, the entire family would have been drunk at the end of the feast, even the boys and girls, and especially the boys and girls. How terrible to think of the mass of drunkenness in the Jewish families on the Passover night!

NOTES

It is revolting to think that our Lord and Saviour could countenance or sanction such a man-injuring and God-dishonoring system. No, the wine they drank was simple grape juice. It was simply *"the fruit of the vine."*

The actual method for the making of this *"wine"* was to cut up a quantity of raisins and place them in an earthen vessel, and add water to them, and allow them to simmer in the oven for a time, then separate the juice from the skins, then put it in the Passover vessel, and then use the wine (juice) for the Passover Service.

A FIT EMBLEM

Some theologians have taught, and alas still teach, that the contents of the Cup which our Lord said was His Blood, was of the same nature as the thing which the Scriptures had said was as the poison of serpents — as the adder's poison. My question is, *"How can such a death-producing thing be a fit emblem of the life-giving power of the Blood of Jesus Christ?"*

In conclusion, the historical account proves that alcoholic wine is not the *"fruit of the vine."* So, the wine associated with Jesus in any capacity was simply grape-juice.

The phrase, *"when He had supped, saying, This Cup is the New Testament in My Blood,"* presents the symbol of the Blood of Christ, because the Gospel Covenant was ratified by the shedding of His Blood.

The Jews had an absolute horror, at once spiritual and physical, of tasting blood. This was at least one of the reasons why the Synod of Jerusalem forbade even to the Gentiles the eating of *"things strangled"* (Acts Chpt. 15).

If the Apostles had not fully understood, which they certainly did, that our Lord was only using the ordinary language of Semitic imagery, and describing only a sacramental symbol, the words, *"This is My Blood,"* would have filled them with horror and repulsion. Consequently, the idea, as the Catholics teach, that the contents of the Cup turns into the literal Blood of Jesus upon imbibing its contents, is unscriptural and facetious indeed!

MARK'S VERSION

Mark's version is a little different, saying, *"This is My Blood of the New Testament* (Covenant), *which is shed for many"* (Mk. 14:24).

This is more directly parallel to the Bread in which that ingredient signified the Lord's *"Body."* Here the *"Cup"* signifies *"My Blood of the Covenant."* The language *"Blood of the Covenant"* is an allusion to Exodus 24:8, where blood, designated by this exact term, was sprinkled over the people to ratify the Covenant. To this phrase, Jesus also added a direct allusion to Isaiah 53:12, where the Lord's Servant *"poured out His Soul to death"* and thereby *"bore sin for many."*

PAUL

In Paul's version, the identification is made directly with the Covenant, in this case the *"New Covenant"* of Jeremiah 31:31, *"This Covenant is the New Covenant in My Blood."* However, that Passage also mentions the Covenant of Exodus Chapter 24, as stated, as that which is being replaced.

Therefore, in the one version (Mark's), the Old Covenant is referred to explicitly and the New implicitly, while in Paul's it is the reverse, the New being explicit (visible and clear) and the Old implicit (implied). In both versions, the point is the same, that the wine of the Cup signifies Jesus' Blood poured out in death, which ratified the New Covenant. Consequently, the Holy Spirit, in giving these two accounts, guaranteed the veracity of the New Covenant from both the viewpoint of the Old and the New.

THE BLOOD OF JESUS

The statement, *"This Cup is the New Testament in My Blood,"* is extremely important because it means that the Covenant, or Will, could not be ratified without the shedding of Jesus' Own Blood. In our society, we speak of a person's last will and testament which cannot be ratified until the person dies. This is what Jesus was talking about, and that is precisely why we refer to the Old and New Testaments. The New Testament was ratified by His Blood, just as the Old Testament was ratified by the shedding of the blood of innocent victims (lambs and goats) as types of the Perfect Sacrifice that one day would be given (Heb. 9:22) (Rossier).

The phrase, *"This do ye, as oft as ye drink it, in remembrance of Me,"* tells us several things:

1. *"This do ye,"* plainly tells us that this communion service is not optional. In other words, it is actually a Command. Believers are to regularly eat and drink the Supper.

2. *"As oft as ye drink it,"* does not specify any exact times. It can be taken daily, weekly, monthly, or reasonably as one desires.

3. *"In remembrance of Me,"* is repeated again by Paul, and for purpose. The reason for this *"Supper"* is Jesus, and more particularly what He did at Calvary and the Resurrection.

(26) "FOR AS OFTEN AS YE EAT THIS BREAD, AND DRINK THIS CUP, YE DO SHEW THE LORD'S DEATH TILL HE COME."

The phrase, *"For as often as ye eat this Bread, and drink this Cup,"* proclaims the second injunction that this Sacred Ceremony is to be continued.

The phrase, *"Ye do shew the Lord's death till He come,"* is meant to proclaim not only the Atoning Sacrifice necessary for our Salvation, but as well, as an ongoing cause of my continued victory in life. In other words, Calvary is not only for Salvation, but for continued victory after Salvation.

THE RATIFICATION

As we have stated, both the Old and New Covenants (Testaments) were connected with Blood. The former was sealed with the blood of animal sacrifice: *"Behold, the Blood of the Covenant, which the Lord hath made with you concerning all these words,"* (Ex. 24:4-8). This blood typified and promised the Blood of Christ, God's Own Son, the Seal of *"The New Testament"* by which we inherit all that this Blood has purchased and won for us.

The Old Covenant could be written in animal blood because it consisted of Promise; the New Covenant or Testament could be written only in the Blood of the Son because it conveys the complete fulfillment of the Promise, the actual purchase of our Redemption.

This is stressed by the strong statement given by Jesus which we may render: *"In connection with My Own Blood."* This very Blood together with the very Body from which it flowed are now given us in the Sacrament to certify us as heirs of this *"New Testament"* in Christ Jesus.

The word is *"Blood"* and not merely *"death,"* because a Sacrifice and a specific death, namely a Sacrificial death, are referred to. The idea is that there is no Sacrificial Body without

NOTES

Sacrificial Blood, and vice versa. Consequently, while the Sacrament consists of two acts and two elements, *"Body"* and *"Blood,"* these two are one and, consequently, inseparable.

The phrase, *"Till He come,"* speaks of the Second Coming, of which Paul did not know the date, and neither do we.

## THE THREE EMPHASES OF THE LORD'S SUPPER

In this short Verse, Paul explains and outlines the three emphases of the Lord's Supper, which of course, are extremely important. They are as follows:

1. It relates to the past because of the Death of Christ on the Cross. Calvary is the pivot point of all history. It is that to which all circumstances point, whether past, present, or future.

2. Calvary relates to the present in the sense that it serves as a vivid reminder of the continuous and Living Lordship of Christ. Every Believer draws daily from the victory of Calvary, which in fact, guarantees all present victorious living that is found only in what Christ did at Calvary and the Resurrection.

There Jesus paid the debt of sin, and as well, broke the grip of sin. However, even though the breaking of the *"grip"* is a past experience, in effect, a once for all experience, still it is something we have to appropriate every day, which the Believer does by Faith in Christ. So, Calvary relates not only to our Salvation experience which is in the past, but as well, relates to our present, ongoing, victorious, Christian experience.

3. It relates to the future as a constant reminder that Jesus one day will return to establish His Millennial Reign on earth. The Eucharist is a poignant proclamation of all three facts (Rossier).

## THE LORD'S SUPPER

The following is a compendium of this glorious participation in which we are privileged as Believers to engage. Hopefully, it will bring it more succinctly into focus.

The Lord's Supper or Holy Communion may be defined as the distinctive rite of Christian worship, instituted by the Lord Jesus on the eve of His Atoning Death. It consists of a spiritual partaking of bread and grape juice, which having been presented in memorial of Christ's inexhaustible Sacrifice, becomes a means of grace whereby we are inspired to increased Faith and faithfulness toward Him.

The following are the keynotes of this Ordinance:

## COMMEMORATION

*"This do in remembrance of Me."*

Every time a group of Christians gather to celebrate the Lord's Supper, they are remembering in a special manner the Atoning Death of Christ which freed them from their sins.

Why remember His Death above every event in His Life?

Because it was the crowning event in His Ministry and because we are saved not merely by His Life and Teachings — Divine though these are — but by His Atoning Sacrifice.

## INSTRUCTION

The Lord's Supper is a Sacred object lesson setting forth the two fundamentals of the Gospel:

1. The Incarnation: As we take the Bread, we hear John the Apostle saying, *"And the Word was made flesh, and dwelt among us"* (Jn. 1:14); we hear the Lord Himself declaring, *"For the Bread of God is He which cometh down from Heaven and giveth life unto the world"* (Jn. 6:33).

2. The Atonement: But the Blessings included in the Incarnation are imparted to us through the Death of Christ.

Bread and wine (grape juice) are in one way a picture of life, but in another way, a picture of death — the separation of body and life, the separation of flesh and blood.

The Bread tells us that the Bread of Life must be broken in death in order to be distributed among the spiritually hungry; the poured-out wine tells us that His Blood, which is His Life, must be shed in Death, which it was, in order that its cleansing and quickening power may be supplied to needy souls.

## INSPIRATION

The elements, especially the grape juice, reminds us that by Faith we may become partakers of Christ's nature, that is, have *"Communion"* with Him.

As we partake of the Bread and Wine of the Communion, we are reminded and assured that, by Faith, we may truly receive His Spirit and reflect His Character.

NOTES

### ASSURANCE

*"This Cup is the New Testament* (Covenant) *in My Blood."*

In ancient times, the most solemn form of agreement was the blood-covenant, which was sealed or signed with sacrificial Blood. The Covenant made with Israel at Mt. Sinai was a Blood Covenant.

After God has laid down His conditions, and the people have accepted them, Moses took a basin filled with Sacrificial Blood, which typified the Shed Blood of Christ, and sprinkled half of it upon the Altar of Sacrifice, signifying that God had bound Himself to His part of the agreement; he then sprinkled the rest of the Blood upon the people, thus binding them to keep their part of the contract (Ex. 24:3-8).

The New Covenant instituted by Christ is a Blood Covenant. God has accepted the Blood of Christ (Heb. 9:14-24) and has, therefore, bound Himself for Christ' Sake, to pardon and save all who come to Him. The Blood of Christ is the Divine guarantee that He will be gracious and merciful to the penitent.

Our part in this contract is to *believe* in the Atoning Death of Christ (Rom. 3:25, 26). Then we can testify to being sprinkled with the Blood of the New Covenant (I Pet. 1:2).

### RESPONSIBILITY

Who shall be admitted to or excluded from the Lord's Table?

Paul deals with the question of sacramental worthiness in I Corinthians 11:20-34. *"Whosoever shall eat this Bread, and drink this Cup of the Lord, unworthily, shall be guilty of* (an offense or sin against) *the Body and Blood of the Lord."*

Does this mean that only those who are worthy may approach the Lord's Table?

Then every one of us is excluded! For who among the children of men is worthy of the least of God's mercies? No, the Apostle is not speaking about the unworthiness of *persons,* but the unworthiness of *actions.* Thus, strange as it may sound, it is possible for an unworthy to partake worthily. And in a sense, only those who sincerely admit their unworthiness are in a right state to approach the Table; the self-righteous are never fit.

Further, it has been noticed that it is the deeply spiritual people who feel their unworthiness the most. Paul described himself as *"chief of sinners."*

The Apostle warns us against unworthy acts and an unworthy attitude in partaking of the Sacrament. How may one partake unworthily?

By doing anything that hinders us from clearly appreciating the meaning of the elements, and from approaching in a solemn, thoughtful, and reverent attitude. In the case of the Corinthians, the hinderance was a serious one, namely selfishness and drunkenness (Pearlman).

(27) "WHEREFORE WHOSOEVER SHALL EAT THIS BREAD, AND DRINK THIS CUP OF THE LORD, UNWORTHILY, SHALL BE GUILTY OF THE BODY AND BLOOD OF THE LORD."

The phrase, *"Wherefore whosoever shall eat this Bread, and drink this Cup of the Lord, unworthily,"* tells us plainly, even as we have already briefly addressed that such can be done. In fact, considering both Catholic and Protestant, the far greater majority who take the Lord's Supper fall into this category.

To which we have already alluded, as a point of reference, no Believer is worthy within himself, not in the slightest. Consequently, personal worthiness is not the idea. The idea of this statement as given by Paul, pertains to our purpose and reason for taking the Lord's Supper, which of course, has everything to do with how we understand this sacred event.

### SO HOW CAN ONE EAT AND DRINK UNWORTHILY?

1. If one thinks there is Salvation in the Ceremony, even as millions do, one is eating and drinking unworthily. Salvation comes by Faith in what the Supper represents, namely Christ offering up Himself on the Cross as a Sacrifice for lost humanity. For one to think or believe that the Ceremony contains Salvation within itself, in effect says that Christ did not need to come from Heaven in order to purchase man's Redemption, but rather that this Ceremony is sufficient for the task.

2. The self-righteous are never fit to take the Lord's Supper, which regrettably, pertains to a large segment of the modern Church. It is only those who know and feel their terrible state of personal unworthiness, thereby with a total necessity of looking to Christ, who in fact, are worthy to approach the Table. Their worthiness is in Christ, which is the only worthiness that God will recognize.

3. For one not to give the solemn respect and honor due this momentous occasion, even as did some of the Corinthians, and which Paul studiously addressed, portrays a gross unworthiness. To treat it with disdain, not only destroys its true meaning, but as well, places one in spiritual and physical jeopardy, as we will see in the following Scriptures.

4. If there is unconfessed, unrepentant, known sin in one's life, such constitutes gross unworthiness. One must remember that the Lord's Supper is not a Sacrifice, but only a symbol of the Sacrifice that has already been offered at Calvary's Cross. Consequently, the act of engaging in this sacred occasion, forgives or cleanses no sin. Confession, forgiveness, and cleansing must come before the Table is approached, and which can easily be done at any time. Consequently, there is no reason for anyone taking the Lord's Supper with unrepentant sin within one's life.

The phrase, *"Shall be guilty of the Body and Blood of the Lord,"* presents a tremendously serious offense.

*"Guilty"* in the Greek is *"enchos,"* and means *"in danger of judgement, subject to judgement."* Such a person draws on himself the penalty due to *"crucifying to himself the Son of God afresh,"* by *"putting Him to an open shame"* (Farrar). The idea is that the person is subject to the Judgement of God, which of necessity will be negative, even as the following verses proclaim.

## WHAT DOES IT MEAN TO BE GUILTY OF THE BODY AND BLOOD OF THE LORD?

It means to not properly understand or believe what Calvary and the Resurrection are all about.

Due to the Fall in the Garden of Eden, Adam and his offspring, which includes the whole of the human race, owed a debt to God, a sin debt if you will, that man was helpless to pay. To redeem fallen humanity, God would become man, taking upon Himself human flesh, thereby offering up His human body as a Perfect Sacrifice, which He did and which satisfied the claims of heavenly justice. As well, He arose from the dead on the third day, thereby ratifying what was done at Calvary.

Simple Faith in this great, wondrous, and momentous act, will guarantee the sinner the spotless, eternal Salvation called *"Eternal Life"* (Jn. 3:16).

NOTES

As prominently as Calvary figures in our Salvation experience, of which is total, as well, Calvary figures in our everyday walk before God, the living of a victorious, overcoming, Christian life. Even though such is a gross understatement, that is the reason it must never be forgotten.

## THE PASSOVER AS THE TYPE

At the Passover, Israel showed forth the death of the Paschal Lamb and confessed that they owed their redemption to its blood.

The true Paschal Lamb having been slain, all who are saved from eternal darkness owe their very lives and redemption to the pouring out of His Precious Blood at Calvary's Hill. This without a doubt, is the greatest event by far in the annals of human history, for in this the Crucifixion and Resurrection of our Lord, and that alone, is the Salvation of all who will believe (Rom. 10:9, 10, 13).

(28) "BUT LET A MAN EXAMINE HIMSELF, AND SO LET HIM EAT OF THAT BREAD, AND DRINK OF THAT CUP."

The phrase, *"But let a man examine himself,"* pertains to self-testing or introspection.

*"Examine"* in the Greek is *"dokimazo,"* and means *"to discern, to prove, to try."*

## EXACTLY WHAT TYPE OF EXAMINATION?

1. A Believer should examine himself (herself) to see if they are truly in the Faith. Are they trusting in Jesus for Salvation, or other things, such as the Church, etc.? As well, are they trusting in this Ceremony itself, or in what the Ceremony represents?

Our Faith must be totally in Christ and Christ Alone, and not in anything else.

2. We should examine ourselves regarding known, unconfessed sin within our lives.

3. We should examine ourselves in regard to the fact that we are saved not because of good things we have done, but because of the great thing He did at Calvary and the Resurrection.

4. We should examine ourselves regarding our attitude toward our brothers and sisters in the Lord. How are we treating them? Do we recognize them as fellow Brothers and Sisters in the Lord for whom Christ died?

The phrase, *"And so let him eat of that bread, and drink of that cup,"* refers to doing so after careful examination. As I hope we can see, this is no trifling matter.

(29) "FOR HE THAT EATETH AND DRINKETH UNWORTHILY, EATETH AND DRINKETH DAMNATION TO HIMSELF, NOT DISCERNING THE LORD'S BODY."

The phrase, *"For he that eateth and drinketh unworthily, eateth and drinketh damnation to himself,"* presents a serious situation indeed!

*"Damnation"* in the Greek is *"krima,"* and means *"the function or the effect, against a crime, i.e. judgement."* However, this *"damnation"* or *"judgement"* does not mean the loss of one's soul, but rather temporal penalties — temporal, but that which can go into much more serious difficulties, as we shall see. The *"judgement"* here mentioned by Paul can be easily removed by repentance, which in effect, is the pleading of the Holy Spirit through the Apostle.

### IN THAT CASE, SHOULD SOME NOT PARTAKE OF THE LORD'S SUPPER?

Not partaking is not the idea at all. In fact, the spirit of the text leads toward the idea that the same penalties will be suffered whether one takes the supper or not. The idea is that we examine ourselves and if we find things which are wrong, that we immediately repent, which alone addresses the situation properly. It is somewhat like Grace, in that this quality does not give one a license to sin, but rather liberty to live a holy life. So, the idea is not avoiding the Lord's Supper, but rather approaching it as we should.

The phrase, *"Not discerning the Lord's body,"* is a picturesque way of saying that the person is actually contributing to the death of Christ rather than benefitting from the results of it (Rossier).

Even though our sins put Christ on the Cross, the Cross was not brought about in order to a life of continued sin, but rather the opposite.

### WHAT DOES IT MEAN TO PROPERLY DISCERN THE LORD'S BODY?

First of all, the Lord does not demand that the Believer be a Scholar or Theologian in order to properly discern that of which is meant.

*"Discerning"* in the Greek is *"diakrino,"* and means *"to separate thoroughly."*

NOTES

The Believer simply must understand that Jesus took his place at Calvary's Cross, thereby affording him Salvation. It is obtained by Faith, simply believing what the Lord did (Eph. 2:8, 9).

The Christian must believe that every single victory in one's life, beginning at Salvation, is accrued to what Jesus did at Calvary and the Resurrection. He offered up His spotless, pure, unsullied Body as a Perfect Sacrifice for sin, spilling His Life's Blood, which paid, as stated, the sin debt.

As well, Satan was totally defeated at Calvary, because the hold of sin he had on the human race was taken away, consequently, breaking his grip. The Christian must believe that.

Even though all that I have just said could be summed up in the short statement, *"I believe that Jesus died for me, and in my believing that, I am saved."* But still, for those who are interested, and most definitely all should be, perhaps a greater treatment of this all-important subject would be helpful.

Properly discerning the Lord's Body can be summed up in one's understanding of the Atonement perhaps greater than anything else. So let's take a closer look at this greatest of all events in history.

### ATONEMENT IN THE OLD TESTAMENT

Why take time and space to describe Old Testament Sacrifices?

For the simple reason that in the word *"Sacrifice,"* we have the key to the meaning of the death of Christ. Many modern theories have been offered to explain that death, but any explanation that leaves out the atoning element is unscriptural, for nothing is more marked in the New Testament than the use of sacrificial terms to set forth the Death of Christ.

To describe Him as *"The Lamb of God,"* to say that His Blood cleanses from sin and purchases Redemption, to teach that He died for our sins — all this is to say that Jesus' death was a real Sacrifice for sin.

Since the Death of Jesus is described in language of Old Testament Sacrifice, a knowledge of sacrificial terms helps greatly in its interpretation. For Sacrifices (in addition to providing a ritual of worship for the Israelites) were prophetic signs (*"types"*) pointing to the Perfect Sacrifice which was to come, namely

The Lord Jesus Christ. Consequently, a clear understanding of the sign will lead to a better knowledge of that One Sacrifice.

Not only were these Sacrifices prophetic of Christ, but they also served to prepare God's people for the higher dispensation to be ushered in at Christ's coming. When the first Gospel Preachers declared that Jesus was the Lamb of God Whose Blood had purchased Redemption from sin, they did not have to define these terms to their countrymen, to whom these terms were already familiar.

We, however, who live thousands of years after these events, and who have not been brought up under the Mosaic Ritual must needs study the spelling book, so to speak, by which Israel learned to spell out the Great Message: Redemption through an Atoning Sacrifice. Such is the justification for this section on the origin, history, nature, and efficacy of the Old Testament Sacrifice.

THE ORIGIN OF SACRIFICE

The Atonement was no afterthought on the part of God. The Fall of man did not take Him by surprise, necessitating quick steps to remedy it.

Before the creation of the world, He, Who knows the end from the beginning, had made provision for man's Redemption. Just as a machine is conceived in the inventor's mind before it is built, so the Atonement was in the mind and purpose of God before its actual accomplishment.

This Truth is borne out by the Scriptures. Jesus is described as *"the Lamb slain from the foundation of the world"* (Rev. 13:8).

The Passover Lamb was *"foreordained"* several days before it was killed (Ex. 12:3, 6); so Christ, the Lamb without blemish and without spot, *"verily was foreordained before the foundation of the world, but was manifest in these last times for you"* (I Pet. 1:19, 20).

He purchased for man Eternal Life, which God *"promised before the world began"* (Tit. 1:2). That there should be a body of people sanctified by this Sacrifice was decreed *"before the foundation of the world"* (Eph. 1:4).

Peter told the Jews that although they had in their ignorance crucified Christ with wicked hands, they had nevertheless fulfilled the Eternal Plan of God, for He was *"delivered by the determinate counsel and foreknowledge of God"* (Acts 2:23).

Thus, it is evident that Christianity is not a new religion that began 1900 years ago, but is the historical manifestation of an eternal purpose.

ORDAINED IN HEAVEN, INSTITUTED ON EARTH

Since hundreds of years were to elapse before the consummation of the Sacrifice, what was sinful man to do in the meanwhile?

From the very beginning, God ordained an institution which should both foreshadow the Sacrifice and also become a means of Grace for the repentant and believing. We refer to animal sacrifice, one of the most ancient of human institutions.

The first mention of a slain animal occurs in the Third Chapter of Genesis. After our first parents sinned, they became conscious of physical nakedness — which was an outward indication of nakedness of conscience and naked to the Judgement of God.

Their efforts to cover themselves outwardly with leaves and inwardly with excuses were in vain. Then we read that the Lord God took the skins of animals and covered them. While the record does not state in so many words that this was a Sacrifice, yet in pondering the spiritual meaning of the act, one cannot avoid the conclusion that we have here a Revelation of Jehovah the Redeemer making provision for man's Redemption.

We see an innocent creature killed in order that the guilty might be covered; that is the primary purpose of Sacrifice — a Divinely provided covering for a guilty conscience. The first Book of the Bible pictures an innocent creature dying for the guilty, and the last Book of the Bible speaks of the spotless Lamb slain in order to loose the guilty from their sins (Rev. 5:6-10).

THE NATURE OF SACRIFICE

This original institution of Sacrifice very likely explains why sacrificial worship has been practiced in all ages and lands. Though perverted from the original pattern, heathen sacrifices are based upon two fundamental ideas, Worship and Atonement:

1. Man recognizes that he is under the power of a Deity Who has certain rights over him. As

NOTES

a recognition of these rights, and as a sign of his self-surrender, he offers a gift or a sacrifice.

2. Frequently, however, becoming conscious that sin has disturbed the relationship, he recognizes instinctively that the same God Who made him has the right to destroy him, unless something is done to repair the broken relationship. That the killing of a victim and the shedding of its blood would avert the Divine Wrath and secure the Divine Favor was one of the deepest and firmest of ancient beliefs.

But how did they learn all this?

Paul tells us that there was a time *"when they knew God"* (Rom. 1:21). Just as fallen man bears marks of his Divine origin, so even heathen sacrifices bear some marks of an original Divine Revelation, even though they affect no Atonement.

## SPIRITUAL BLINDNESS

After the Confusion of Tongues (Gen. 11:1-9), Noah's descendants scattered everywhere, carrying with them the true knowledge of God, for as yet there was no record of idolatry. What occurred in course of time is briefly described in Romans 1:19-32.

The nations turned from the pure worship of God and soon lost sight of His Glorious Godhead. Spiritual blindness resulted. Instead of seeing God through the heavenly bodies, which incidentally the Lord created, they began to worship these bodies as deities; instead of seeing the Creator through the trees and animals, they began to worship these as gods; instead of recognizing that man was made in the Image of God, they began to make a god in the image of man.

Thus, spiritual blindness led to idolatry. Idolatry was no mere intellectual matter; the worship of nature, which forms the basis of most heathen religions, led man to deify (make gods of) his own lusts, and moral corruption was the result.

Yet, despite this perversion, man's worship bore dim marks which indicated that there had been a time when he knew better. Behind the idolatries of Egypt, India, and China, one discovers a belief in one true God, the Eternal Spirit, Who made all things.

## ISRAEL

When spiritual darkness covered the nations, as moral corruption had covered the pre-Flood world, God made a new start with Abraham as He had previously done with Noah.

God's plan was to make Abraham the ancestor of a nation which should restore to the world the Light of the Knowledge and Glory of God. At Mt. Sinai, Israel was set apart from the nations to be a *"holy nation."*

In order to direct them in the life of holiness, God gave them a code of Laws governing their moral, national, and religious life. Among these were the Laws of Sacrifice (Lev. Chpts. 1-7), which taught the nation the right manner in which God should be approached and worshipped. The nations had a perverted worship; God restored to Israel the pure worship.

## THE SACRIFICES

The Mosaic Sacrifices were means whereby the Israelites rendered man's first obligation to his Maker, namely worship. They were offered with the object of attaining to Communion with God, and removing all obstacles to that Communion:

1. If the Israelite sinned and so disturbed the relationship between himself and God, he brought a *"Sin Offering"* — the Sacrifice of Atonement (Lev. Chpt. 4).

2. If he had wronged his neighbor, he brought a *"Trespass Offering"* — the Sacrifice of Restitution (Lev. 6:1-7).

3. Now that he was right with God and man and desired to reconsecrate himself, he offered a *"Burnt Offering"* — the Sacrifice of Worship (Lev. Chpt. 1).

4. He was now ready to enjoy happy Communion with God Who had pardoned and accepted him, so he presented a *"Peace Offering"* — the Sacrifice of Fellowship (Lev. Chpt. 3).

The purpose of these Bloody Sacrifices is fulfilled in Christ, the Perfect Sacrifice. His Death is described as a Death for sin, as a bearing of sin, hence, the *"Sin Offering"* (II Cor. 5:21).

As well, God made His Soul a *"Trespass Offering"* for sin (such is the literal rendering of Isaiah 53:10); He paid the debt we could not pay and blotted out the past which we could not undo.

As well, He is our *"Burnt Offering"* for His Death is set forth as an act of perfect self-giving (Eph. 5:2; Heb. 9:14).

Also, He is our *"Peace Offering"* for He Himself described His Death as a means of our sharing (having communion with) the Divine Life (Lev. 7:15, 20; Jn. 6:53-56).

## THE EFFICACY (POWER TO PRODUCE AN EFFECT) OF SACRIFICE

To what extent were the Old Testament Sacrifices efficacious?

Did they really secure pardon and cleansing?

What benefits did they secure for the offerer?

These questions are of real importance, for by comparing and contrasting the Levitical Sacrifices with Christ's Sacrifice, we shall be enabled to better perceive the efficacy and finality of the latter.

The subject is dealt with in the letter to the Hebrews. The writer is addressing a group of Hebrew Christians, who, discouraged by persecution, are tempted to return to Judaism and the sacrifices of the Temple. The realities they believe in are invisible; while the Temple with its gorgeous ritual seems so tangible and real.

To turn their thoughts from such a course of action, the writer makes a comparison between the Old and New Covenants, showing that the New is better than the Old, for the Old in imperfect and temporary while the New is perfect and eternal.

To return to the Temple with its Priesthood and Sacrifices would be forsaking substance for shadow, and perfection for imperfection. The argument is: the Old Covenant was good as far as it went, and for the purpose for which it was designed; but the New Covenant is better, much better.

## THE OLD TESTAMENT SACRIFICES WERE NECESSARY

Else would they not have been Divinely ordained. They were good in that they fulfilled a certain purpose in the Divine plan, namely, to be a means of Grace, that those of Jehovah's people who had sinned against Him might return to a State of Grace, be reconciled to Him, and continue to enjoy union with Him. When the Israelite had faithfully fulfilled the conditions, he could rest upon the Promise: *"And the Priest shall make an Atonement for him as concerning his sin, and it shall be forgiven him"* (Lev. 4:26).

As enlightened Israelites brought their Offerings, they were aware of two things:

NOTES

1. That repentance in itself was insufficient; a visible transaction must be gone through to indicate that the sin was put away (Heb. 9:22).

2. But on the other hand, he learned from the Prophets that the ritual without the right inner disposition of heart was a mere valueless formality. The act of Sacrifice must be the outward expression of the inner sacrifices of praise, prayer, righteousness, and obedience — the Sacrifices of *"a broken and contrite spirit"* (Ps. 4:5; 26:6; 50:12-14; 51:17; Prov. 21:3; Isa. 1:11-17; Amos 5:21-24; Mic. 6:6-8).

*"The sacrifice* (blood sacrifice) *of the wicked is an abomination to the Lord,"* declared Solomon (Prov. 15:8). The inspired writers made it clear that ritual *motions* without righteous *emotions* were unacceptable *devotions.*

## THE ONE SACRIFICE OF THE NEW TESTAMENT IS BETTER

While recognizing the Divine ordination of animal sacrifices, enlightened Israelites could not but feel that these were not a perfect means of Atonement, which they were not.

Consequently, all the Sacrificial Offerings of the Levitical Law, and even before, always pointed to the One Sacrifice which was ultimately to come, namely The Lord Jesus Christ.

## COULD NOT TAKE AWAY SIN

There was a wide disparity between an irrational, irresponsible creature and a man made in God's Image; and that the animal did not perform the Sacrifice either intelligently or voluntarily was evident; there was no fellowship between the offerer and the victim.

It was plain that an animal sacrifice could not on the one hand weigh in the balance against a human soul, nor on the other exercise any spiritual power on the inner man. There was nothing in the blood of an irrational creature which could effect the spiritual redemption of a soul; that could only be by the offering of a perfect human life.

The inspired writer truly voiced what must have been the conclusion of many Old Testament Believers when he said, *"For it is not possible that the blood of bulls and of goats should take away sins"* (Heb. 10:4).

At best, the Sacrifices were a temporary and imperfect means of covering sin until a more perfect redemption should come. The Law brought the people under conviction for sins (Rom. 3:20), which the Law was designed to do, and the Sacrifices rendered those sins powerless to provoke the Divine Wrath.

## NO SPIRITUAL VIRTUE WITHIN THEMSELVES

Animal sacrifices are described as *"carnal ordinances,"* that is, rites which removed bodily defilements, and atoned for the outward acts of sin (Heb. 9:10) but contained no spiritual virtue within themselves.

*"The blood of bulls and of goats . . . sanctifieth to the purifying of the flesh"* (Heb. 9:13); that is, they atoned for those outward defilements which cut off an Israelite from communion in the congregation of Israel.

For example, if a person defiled himself physically, he was considered unclean and cut off from the congregation of Israel (not allowed to worship) until he had purified himself and offered sacrifice (Lev. 5:1-6); or if he had materially wronged his neighbor, he was under condemnation until he had brought a Trespass Offering (Lev. 6:1-7).

In the first instance, the Sacrifice cleansed from physical defilement but did not cleanse the soul; in the second instance, the sacrifice made Atonement for the outward deed but did not change the heart. David himself recognized that he was in the grip of a depravity from which animal sacrifices could not free him (Ps. 51:16; I Sam. 3:14) and he prayed for that spiritual renewal which they were powerless to effect (Ps. 51:6-10).

## REPETITION

The repetition of the animal sacrifices points to their imperfection; they could not make the worshiper perfect (Heb. 10:1, 2), that is, give him a perfect standing or relationship with God upon which he might build his character.

Animal sacrifices could not give the sinner a *"once for all"* (Heb. 10:10) experience of spiritual transformation which should be the beginning of a new life.

## IMPERFECT PRIESTS

Animal sacrifices were offered by imperfect Priests, the imperfection of whose ministry was indicated by the fact that they could not enter at any time into the Holy of Holies, and were, therefore, unable to lead the worshiper directly into the Divine Presence.

NOTES

*"The Holy Spirit this signifying, that the way into the Holiest of all was not yet made manifest"* (Heb. 9:8).

The Priest had no sacrifice to offer whereby he might lead people into spiritual experience with God, and so make the worshiper *"perfect, as pertaining to the conscience"* (Heb. 9:9).

Had a spiritual Israelite been questioned concerning his hopes for Redemption, the same discernment which had revealed to him the imperfection of animal sacrifice would have led him to reply that the solution lay in the future, and that perfect Redemption was connected in some way with that perfect order to be ushered in at the coming of the Messiah.

Indeed, such a Revelation was granted to Jeremiah. That Prophet had despaired of the people ever being able to keep the Covenant of the Law; their sin was written with an iron pen (Jer. 17:1), their heart was deceitful and desperately wicked (Jer. 17:9); they could no more change their hearts than the Ethiopian could change his skin (Jer. 13:23); so calloused and depraved were they that they had passed the state where sacrifices could profit (Jer. 6:20); indeed, they had forgotten the prime purpose of these sacrifices.

From the human viewpoint, the people were hopeless, but God comforted Jeremiah with a Promise of the coming of an age when under a new, better Covenant the hearts of the people would be changed and when there should be a perfect remission of sins (Jer. 31:31-34). *"For I will forgive their iniquity, and I will remember their sin no more."*

In Hebrews 10:17, 18, we have the inspired interpretation of these last words, namely that a perfect redemption was to be accomplished by means of a perfect Sacrifice and that, therefore, the animal sacrifices were to pass away.

Compare Hebrews 10:6-10. Through this One Sacrifice, man has a *"once for all"* experience which gives him a perfect standing with God.

What the sacrifices of the Law could not do has been accomplished by the Perfect Sacrifice of Christ. *"And every Priest standeth daily ministering and offering oftentimes the same sacrifices, which can never take away sins: but This Man, after He had offered One*

*Sacrifice for sins forever, sat down on the right Hand of God"* (Heb. 10:11-12).

## IN ANTICIPATION OF THE FUTURE SACRIFICE

One more question remains to be considered. It is certain that people were truly justified before the Atoning Work of Christ. Abraham was justified by Faith (Rom. 4:23) and entered the Kingdom of God (Mat. 8:11; Lk. 16:22); Moses was glorified (Lk. 9:30-31); and Enoch and Elijah were translated.

There were, no doubt, large numbers of Godly Israelites who attained to the spirit stature of these worthies. Granted that animal sacrifices were inadequate, and that Christ's Sacrifice was the only perfect Sacrifice, on what basis were these Old Testament Saints justified?

They were saved in anticipation of the future Sacrifice, just as people today are saved in consideration of the accomplished Sacrifice. Proof of this is found in Hebrews 9:15 (compare also Rom. 3:25), which teaches that the Death of Christ was in some sense retroactive and retrospective; in other words, it has an efficacy in relation to the past.

Hebrews 9:15 suggests the following line of thought: the Old Covenant was powerless to provide a perfect Redemption. Christ closed this Covenant and opened the New Covenant with a Death which accomplished the *"Redemption of the transgressions that were under the First Testament."* That is, when God justified Old Testament Believers, He did so in anticipation of Christ's Work, *"on credit"* so to speak; Christ paid the full price on the Cross and wiped out the debt.

God gave Old Testament Saints a standing which the Old Covenant could not purchase and He did so in view of a coming Covenant which could effect this.

If it is to be asked whether the Old Testament Believers during their lifetime enjoyed the same benefits as those living under the New Testament, the answer must be in the negative. There was no permanent gift of the Holy Spirit (Jn. 7:39) to follow their Repentance and Faith; they did not enjoy the full Truth on immortality brought to Light by Christ (II Tim. 1:10), and in general they were limited by the imperfection of the Dispensation in which they lived.

NOTES

At best they had but a foretaste of good things to come.

## ATONEMENT IN THE NEW TESTAMENT

The Atonement which had been foreordained in eternity and typically foreshadowed in the Old Testament ritual was historically accomplished at the Crucifixion of Jesus, when God's Redemptive purpose was consummated.

*"It is finished!"* The writers of the Gospels describe the Sufferings and Death of Christ with a minuteness which has no parallel in their narratives of other events of His Life, and by referring to the fulfillment of Old Testament Prophesies indicate their sense of the importance of the event.

Some writers of the liberal school maintain that the Death of Christ was an accident and a tragedy. In their words, He began with bright hopes of success, they say, but found Himself enmeshed in a web of circumstances which led to the destruction which He had not foreseen and which He could not escape.

But what do the Gospels say about the matter?

According to their Testimony, Jesus knew from the beginning that Suffering and Death were part of His Divinely appointed destiny. In His declaration that the Son of man must suffer, that word *"must"* indicated Divine vocation and not unforeseen, inevitable fate.

## THE SUFFERING SERVANT

At His Baptism, He heard the words, *"Thou art My Beloved Son, in Whom I am well pleased."* These words were taken from two Prophesies, the first declaring Messiah's Sonship and Deity (Ps. 2:7), the Second describing Messiah's Ministry as the Servant of the Lord (Isa. 42:1).

Now the Servant mentioned in Isaiah 42:1 is the Suffering Servant of Isaiah Chapter 53. The conclusion is that even at His Baptism, Jesus was conscious of the fact that Suffering and Death were part of His Calling. His rejection of Satan's offers in the Wilderness implied a tragic issue to His Work, for he chose the hard way of rejection rather than the easy one of popularity.

The very fact of the Holy One standing with the rest of the people (Lk. 3:21) and submitting to Baptism was an act of identification with sinful humanity in order to bear the burden of their sins, even though He never sinned.

The Servant of the Lord, according to Isaiah Chapter 53, was to be *"numbered with the transgressors"* (Isa. 53:12). The Baptism of Jesus may be regarded as *"a great act of loving communion with our misery,"* for in that hour, He identified Himself with sinners, and thus, in a sense, His Work of Atonement began.

THE MEANING OF HIS DEATH

Many times during the course of His Ministry, the Lord referred to a hidden and figurative manner of His Coming Death (Mat. 5:10-12; 23:37; Mk. 2:19; 3:6, 20-30; 9:12-13); but at Caesarea Philippi He plainly told the Disciples that He must suffer and die. From that time on, He endeavored to brand upon their minds the fact that He must suffer, so that being forewarned they would not suffer shipwreck of Faith from the shock of the Crucifixion (Mk. 8:31; 9:31; 10:32).

He also explained to them the meaning of His Death. They were not to regard it as an unfortunate and unforeseen tragedy to which He must resign Himself, but as a Death with an Atoning Purpose. The Son of Man had come to *"give His life a Ransom for many."*

THE LAST SUPPER

At the Last Supper, which we are now studying, He gave instructions for the future commemoration of His Death as the supreme act of His Ministry. He ordained a rite which was to commemorate His Redemption of mankind from sin as the Passover commemorated Israel's Redemption from Egypt.

His Disciples, whose minds were as yet under the influence of Jewish ideas about the Messiah and Kingdom, were unable to grasp the necessity for His Death and could, with difficulty, be reconciled to the fact.

But after the Resurrection and the Ascension, and especially after the Day of Pentecost, they understood, and thereafter they affirm that the Death of Christ was a Divinely appointed means of Atonement. *"Christ died for our sins"* is their consistent testimony.

THE NECESSITY FOR THE ATONEMENT

The necessity for the Atonement follows from two facts: 1. God's Holiness; and, 2. Man's sinfulness. The reaction of God's Holiness against man's sinfulness is known as His Wrath, which may be averted by Atonement. Thus, the keynotes of our discussion will be as follows: Holiness, sinfulness, wrath, and Atonement.

NOTES

HOLINESS

God is Holy in nature, which means the He is Righteous in Character and in conduct. These attributes of His Character are manifest in His dealings with His creation. *"He loveth Righteousness and Judgment"* (Ps. 33:5). *"Justice and Judgment are the habitation of Thy Throne"* (Ps. 89:14).

God has constituted man and the world according to definite laws. His laws form the very foundation of human personality, being written upon man's heart or nature (Rom. 2:14-15) before being written on tables of stone.

These laws bind man to his Maker in a personal relationship, and form the basis of human responsibility. *"In Him we live, and move, and have our being"* (Acts 17:28), was spoken of mankind in general. Sin disturbs the relationship expressed in this Verse, and ultimately the impenitent sinner is cast eternally out of God's Presence. This is *"the second death."*

On many occasions, this relationship was reaffirmed, enlarged upon and interpreted under an arrangement known as a *"Covenant."*

For example, at Sinai, God reaffirmed the conditions under which He could have fellowship with man (the moral Law) and then enacted a series of regulations by which Israel might observe these conditions in the sphere of national and spiritual life. To keep the Covenant is to be in right relationship with God, or in Grace; for He Who is Righteous can have fellowship only with those who do right. *"Can two walk together, except they be agreed?"* (Amos 3:3). And to be in fellowship with God means Life. From beginning to end, the Scriptures declare this Truth, that obedience and life go together (Gen. 2:17; Rev. 22:14).

SINFULNESS

This relationship is marred by sin which is a disturbance of the personal relationship between God and man. It is violence done to the constitution, so to speak, under which God and man live, just as unfaithfulness does violence to the Covenant under which man and wife live (Jer. 3:20).

*"Your iniquities have separated between you and your God"* (Isa. 59:2).

To make amends for violated Law and to repair the broken relationship between God and man is the function of Atonement.

## WRATH

Sin is essentially an attack on God's Honor and Holiness. It is rebellion against God, for in willfully sinning, man chooses his own will rather than God's, and for the time being, becomes a law unto himself.

But should God permit His Honor to be attacked, He would then cease to be God. His Honor calls for the destruction of the one resisting Him; His Righteousness demands satisfaction of the violated Law; and His Holiness reacts against the sin, this reaction being described as *"Wrath."*

But this Divine reaction is not automatic; it does not always react instantly as would fire to a hand thrust into it. God's Wrath is governed by personal considerations: He is not hasty to destroy the work of His Hands. He pleads with man; He waits to be gracious. He delays judgement in the Hope that His Goodness shall lead man to repentance (Rom. 2:4; II Pet. 3:9).

But man misunderstands the Divine delays, and scoffs at the thought of Judgement. *"Because sentence against an evil work is not executed speedily, therefore the heart of the sons of men is fully set in them to do evil"* (Eccl. 8:11).

## WRATH AND RETRIBUTION

But though delayed, retribution must ultimately come, for in a world governed by Law there must be a reckoning. *"God is not mocked: for whatsoever a man soweth, that shall he also reap"* (Gal. 6:7). This Truth was demonstrated at Calvary where God declared *"His Righteousness for the remission of sins that are past, through the forbearance of God"* (Rom. 3:25).

One scholar translates: *"This was to demonstrate the justice of God in view of the fact that sins previously committed during the time of God's forbearance had been passed over."*

Another paraphrases the words as follows: *"He suspended judgement on sins of the former period, the period of His forbearance, with a view to the Revelation of His Justice under this Dispensation, when He, while remaining a Just Judge, can actually acquit the sinner who makes Faith in Jesus his plea."*

NOTES

In past ages, it seemed that God overlooked the sins of the nations; men sinned on, but they did not seem to reap the wages of sin. And the question arose, does God ignore sin?

But the Crucifixion revealed the awfulness of sin, and pictured the dread penalty upon it. The Cross of Christ declares that God never was, is not, and never can be, indifferent to man's sin. Comments one scholar: *"God gave proof of His anger against sin by now and then inflicting punishment on Israel and the Gentiles. But He did not inflict the full penalty: else the race would have perished. To a large extent, He passed over the sins of men. Now for a king to overlook crime, to forebear to punish, or even to delay punishment, is unjust. And God's Character was lowered in the eyes of some by His forbearance, which they misinterpreted as an indication that they would escape punishment. God gave Christ to die in order to demonstrate His Justice in view of the tolerance of past sins which seemed to obscure it."*

## ATONEMENT

Man has broken God's Laws and violated the principles of Righteousness; this knowledge is recorded in memory, and the conscience registers it as guilt. What can be done to remedy the past, and assure the future?

Is there an atonement for violated Law?

To this question, three answers have been given:

## POSSIBLE?

Some contend that Atonement is not possible. Life is governed, they say, by inexorable law which punishes violations with a machine-like remorselessness. As a man sows, so he must reap, and there is no escape. Sin abides.

The sinner can never escape from the past. His future is mortgaged to it and cannot be redeemed. This is the view expressed in the familiar poem:

*"The Moving Finger writes; and having*
*writ,*
*"Moves on; nor all your piety nor wit*
*"Shall lure it back to cancel half a line,*
*"Nor all your tears wash out a word of it."*

This theory makes man a slave to circumstances; he is powerless to do anything to effect his destiny. If its proponents acknowledge God at all, it is as a God Who is enslaved to His Own Laws, and Who cannot provide a way of escape for the sinful.

UNNECESSARY?

At the other extreme are those who teach that Atonement is unnecessary. God is too kind to punish the sinner, and to gracious to demand satisfaction for a broken Law. Therefore, Atonement, they say, is unnecessary and forgiveness can be taken for granted.

Said a physician to his patient, who had been speaking to him about the Gospel, *"I don't need an Atonement. When I do wrong I tell God I am sorry and that is sufficient."*

Some time later, his patient came to him and said, *"Doctor, I am well now. I am sorry that I fell sick, and I promise you that I will try never to fall sick again."*

At the same time, she hinted that there was no need of considering or even discussing the bill! We trust that the Doctor learned the lesson, namely, that mere repentance, at least within itself, does not pay the bill, nor repair the damage done by sin. There must also be an Atonement, which only Jesus could pay.

POSSIBLE AND NECESSARY

The New Testament teaches that Atonement is both possible and necessary: possible, because God is gracious as well as just; necessary, because God is just as well as gracious.

The two errors referred to are exaggerations of two truths concerning God's Character.

The first overemphasizes His Justice to the exclusion of His Grace; the second overemphasizes His Grace to the exclusion of His Justice.

The Atonement does justice to both aspects of His Character, for in the Death of Christ, God acts both justly and graciously. In dealing with sin, He must needs show His Grace, for He desires not the death of the sinner; yet in forgiving sin, He must needs reveal His Righteousness for the very stability of the universe depends upon the Sovereignty of God.

In the Atonement, God does justice to His Character as a Gracious God. His Righteousness called for this punishment of the sinner, but His Grace provided a plan for the pardon of the sinner. At the same time, He does justice to His Character as a Righteous God.

NOTES

God would not do justice to Himself if He displayed compassion to sinners in a way which made light of sin, and which ignored its tragic reality. People might think that God was indifferent or indulgent toward sin.

At Calvary, the sin penalty was paid and the Divine Law honored; God was thus enabled to be gracious without being unjust, and just without being ungracious.

THE NATURE OF THE ATONEMENT

*"Christ died"* expresses the historical fact of the Crucifixion: *"For our sins"* interprets the fact.

In what sense did Jesus die for our sins?

How is the fact explained in the New Testament?

The answer will be found in the following key words applied to the Death of Christ: Atonement, Propitiation, Substitution, Redemption, and Reconciliation.

1. ATONEMENT

The word *"Atonement"* in the Hebrew means literally *"to cover,"* and is variously translated in our authorized Version by the following words: *"make Atonement, purge, purge away, reconcile, make reconciliation, pacify, pardon, be merciful, put off."*

Atonement (in the original) includes the covering of both the sins (Lev. 5:18; Ps. 78:38; 79:9) and the sinner (Lev. 4:20). To atone for sin is to cover sin from God's sight so that it loses its power to provoke His Wrath. We quote from Dr. Alfred Cave:

*"The idea expressed by the Hebrew origin of the word translated 'Atone' was cover and covering, not in the sense of rendering invisible to Jehovah, but in the sense of engrossing His sight with something else of neutralizing sin, so to speak, of disarming it, of rendering it inert to arouse the righteous anger of God.*

*"To Atone for sin . . . was to throw, so to speak, a veil over sin so dazzling, that the veil, and not the sin, was visible, to place side by side with sin something so attractive as to completely engross the eye.*

*"The figure which the New Testament uses when it speaks of the 'new robe' (of Righteousness) the Old Testament uses when it speaks of 'Atonement.' When an 'Atonement' was made under the Law it was as though the Divine Eye,*

*which had been kindled at the sight of sin and foulness, was quieted by the garment thrown around it; or, to use a figure much too modern, yet equally appropriate, it was as if the sinner who had been exposed to the lightening of Divine Wrath had been suddenly wrapped round and insulated.*

*"Atonement meant so covering the sinner that his sin was invisible or non-existent in the sense that it could no longer come between him and his Maker. To use the words of a German theologian: 'When sinful souls approached the Altar of God, where dwelt His Holiness, their sinful nature came between them and God, and Atonement served the purpose of covering their sins, of canceling the charges on which they were arraigned.'"*

## THE BLOOD OF THE ATONEMENT

When the Blood was applied to the Altar by the Priest, the Israelite was assured that the Promise made to his forefathers would be realized for him. *"And when I see the Blood, I will pass over you"* (Ex. 12:13).

What were the effects of the Atonement or Covering?

The sin was blotted out (Jer. 18:23; Isa. 43:25; 44:22), removed, at least from the Eyes of God (Isa. 6:7), covered (Ps. 32:1), cast into the depths of the sea (Micah 7:19), cast behind God's back (Isa. 38:17), pardoned (Ps. 78:38). All these terms teach that the sin is covered so as to have all effects from it removed, put out of sight, invalidated, undone. Jehovah sees it no longer and it exerts no influence over Him.

Christ's Death was an Atoning Death because it was Death for the removing of sin (Heb. 2:17; 9:14; 26-28; 10:12-14). It was a Sacrificial Death or a Death having relation to sin.

What was that relation?

*"Who in His Own Self bare our sins in His Own Body on the Tree"* (I Pet. 2:24).

*"For He hath made Him to be sin for us, Who knew no sin; that we might be made the Righteousness of God in Him"* (II Cor. 5:21).

To Atone for sin is to bear sin and to bear it away, so that it is taken from the transgressor, who is then considered as justified from all unrighteousness, cleansed from defilement and sanctified to belong to God's people (I Cor. 6:9-11).

One Hebrew word used to describe cleansing means literally to *"un-sin."* By Christ's Atoning Death, sinners are *"un-sinned"* and then *"in-Christed"* (to coin a word). They die to sin in order to live for Christ.

NOTES

2. PROPITIATION

The word *"propitiation"* is believed to come from a Latin word *"prope"* meaning *"near."* Hence, the word means bringing together, making favorable, winning of reconciliation, to bring to an end.

A Sacrifice of propitiation brings man near to God, reconciles him to God by Atoning for his transgressions and winning Divine Favor and Grace. God in mercy accepts the propitiatory gift and restores the sinner to His love.

This is also the sense of the Greek word as used in the New Testament. To propitiate is to appease the righteous wrath of a Holy God by the offering of an Atoning Sacrifice. Christ is described as such a propitiation (Rom. 3:25; I Jn. 2:2; 4:10).

Sin keeps man at a distance from God; but Christ has so dealt with sin on man's behalf that its separative power is annulled; therefore, man may now *"draw nigh"* to God *"in His Name."* Access to God, the most sublime of privileges, has been purchased at a great price, the Blood of Christ.

Writes Dr. James Denney:

*"And just as in the ancient Tabernacle, every object used in worship had to be sprinkled with Atoning Blood, so all the parts of Christian worship, all our approaches to God, should consciously rest upon the Atonement.*

*"They should be felt to be a privilege beyond price; they should be penetrated with the sense of Christ's passion, and of the love with which He loved us when He suffered for sins once for all, the just for the unjust, that He might bring us to God."*

## PROPITIATION AND THE MERCY SEAT

The word *"propitiation"* in Romans 3:25 is the same word used to translate the word *"Mercy Seat"* in the Greek. In the Hebrew, *"Mercy Seat"* means literally *"covering,"* and in both Hebrew and Greek, the word conveys the thought of an Atoning Sacrifice.

The reference is to the Ark of the Covenant (Ex.25:10-22), which was composed of two parts:

1. The Ark, representing the Throne of Israel's Righteous Ruler, and containing the Tables of the Law as the expression of His Righteous Will.

2. The cover or lid, known as the *"Mercy Seat,"* is surmounted by Angelic figures know as the Cherubim. Two outstanding lessons were conveyed by this Sacred Vessel:

A. The Tables of Law taught that God was a Righteous God Who would not pass by sin and Who must enforce His Decrees and punish the wicked.

But how could a sinful nation live in His sight?

B. The Mercy Seat which covered the Law was the place where Blood was sprinkled once a year to make Atonement for the sins of the people. It was the place of the covering of sin, and taught the lesson that God Who is Righteous can consistently pardon sin because of an Atoning Sacrifice. By means of Atoning Blood, that which is a Throne of Judgement becomes a Throne of Grace.

PROPITIATION AND SACRIFICE

The Ark and Mercy Seat illustrate the problem solved by the Atonement. The problem and its solution are stated in Romans 3:25, 26, where we read that Christ was *"set forth to be a propitiation* (an Atoning Sacrifice) *through Faith in His Blood* (received by Faith), *to declare His Righteousness for the remission of sins that are past, through the forbearance of God* (to show that apparent delays in judgement do not mean that God winks at sin)*; to declare, I say, at this time, His Righteousness* (His way of making sinners righteous)*: that He might be just* (inflict the punishment for sin)*, and the Justifier* (remove the punishment due sin) *of him which believeth in Jesus."*

How can God at the same time both really inflict and really cancel the punishment for sin?

In the person of His Son, God Himself took the penalty, and thus cleared the way for the pardon of the guilty. His Law was honored and the sinner was saved. The sin was expatiated (put away) and God was propitiated (appeased).

Men can understand how God can be just in punishing and merciful in pardoning; but how God can be just in the act of justifying the guilty is a puzzle to them. Calvary solves the problem.

PROPITIATION, A REAL TRANSACTION

The fact should be emphasized that the propitiation was a real transaction, for there are some who teach that the Atonement was simply a demonstration of the love of God and of Christ, intended to move the sinner to repentance. That is indeed one of the effects of the Atonement (I Jn. 3:16) but it does not represent all the Atonement.

For example, we might jump into the river and drown in the sight of a poor person in order to convince him of our love; but that act would not pay his rent or his grocery bill!

The Atoning Work of Christ was a real transaction which removed a real obstacle between us and God, and which paid the debt we could not pay.

3. SUBSTITUTION

The Sacrifices of the Old Testament were substitutionary in nature; they were reckoned as doing on the Altar for the Israelite what he could not do for himself. The Altar represented God, and more particularly Jesus dying on Calvary; the Priest represented the sinner; the victim (the lamb) was the Israelite's substitute to be accepted on the sinner's behalf.

In like manner, Christ did for us on the Cross what we could not do for ourselves, and whatever our need we are accepted *"for His sake."* Whether we offer God our penitence, thanksgiving, or consecration, we do so *"in His name,"* for He is the Sacrifice through Whom we approach God the Father.

The thought of substitution is prominent in the Old Testament Sacrifices, where the Blood of the victim is regarded as covering or making Atonement for the soul of the offerer; and in that Chapter in which Old Testament Sacrifices reached their highest meaning (Isa. Chpt. 53), we read:

*"Surely He hath borne our griefs, and carried our sorrows . . . but He was wounded for our transgressions, He was bruised for our iniquities: the chastisement of our peace was upon Him; and with His stripes we are healed"* (Isa. 53:4-5).

All these expressions picture the Servant of Jehovah as bearing punishment due to others in order that He might *"justify many; for He shall bear their iniquities."*

Christ, being the Son of God, was able to offer a Sacrifice of infinite and eternal value. Having assumed human nature, He was able to identify Himself with mankind and so suffer their penalty.

NOTES

He dies in out stead; He took the penalty that was ours, in order that we might escape it. This explains the cry, *"My God, My God, Why hast Thou forsaken Me?"*

One Who sinless by nature and Who had never committed a sin in His life, became a Sin-Offering (taking the sinner's place). In the words of Paul:

*"He hath made Him to be sin* (sin-offering) *for us"* (II Cor. 5:21).

In the words of Peter:

He *"bare our sins in His Own Body on the tree"* (I Pet. 2:24).

4. REDEMPTION

The word *"redeem"* in both Old and New Testaments means to buy back by the paying of a price; to loose from bondage by the paying of a price; to buy in a market and to take from a market.

The idea is that we as sinners were slaves to Satan, and Jesus paid the debt that was owing, thereby setting us free. As well, He paid such a price that no one in all of eternity past, or eternity future, will ever be able to say that the price was insufficient.

The Lord Jesus is a Redeemer and His Atoning Work is described as a Redemption (Mat. 20:28; Gal. 3:13; 4:5; Titus 2:14; I Pet. 1:18; Rev. 5:9; 14:3-4).

The most interesting illustration of Redemption is found in the Old Testament Law of the Kinsman Redeemer (Lev. 25:47-49).

According to this Law, a man who had sold his property and sold himself into servitude because of debt could regain both his land and liberty at any time on the condition that he was redeemed by a man possessing the following qualifications:

1. He must be kin to the man.
2. The man must be willing to redeem or buy back.
3. The man must have the wherewithal to pay the price.

The Lord Jesus Christ measured up to all three qualifications: He became *kin* to us by taking our human nature; He was *willing* to give up all to redeem us (II Cor. 8:9), and being Divine, He was *able* to pay the price — His Own Precious Blood.

The fact of Redemption reminds us that Salvation is costly and, therefore, not to be lightly esteemed. When some Corinthian Believers became careless in their manner of living, Paul warned them, *"Ye are not your own. For ye are bought with a price: therefore glorify God in your body and in your spirit, which are God's"* (I Cor. 6:19, 20).

NOTES

## REDEMPTION AND THE SOUL OF MAN

Jesus said, *"For what is a man profited, if he shall gain the whole world, and lose his own soul? Or what shall a man give in exchange for his soul?"* (Mat. 16:26).

He meant that the soul, or real life, of man could be lost or ruined, and that when it was lost there could be no compensation for it, as there was no means of buying it back. Rich men may boast and trust in their wealth, but their power is limited. Says the Psalmist (Ps. 49:7-9), *"None of them can by any means redeem his brother, nor give to God a ransom for him:*

*"(For the Redemption of their soul is precious, and it ceaseth for ever:)*

*"That he should still live forever, and not see corruption."*

But since multitudes have already forfeited their souls by living in sin, and they cannot be redeemed by human means, what is to be done?

The Son of Man came into the world *"to give His Life a Ransom* (or Redemption) *for many"* (Mat. 20:28). The supreme object for which He came into the world was to lay down His Life as a Ransom Price that those to whom the forfeited (spiritual) lives belonged might obtain them again. The forfeited lives of many are liberated by the surrender of Christ's Life on our behalf.

## REDEMPTION FROM WHAT?

Peter tells his readers that they were *"redeemed . . . from your vain conversation* (literally, conduct, manner of life) *received by tradition* (that is, from the routine of custom)."

The word *"vain"* means empty and unsatisfying, literally, *"empty nothings."*

Life, before the Death of Christ, touches it as futile and vain; it is a groping or fumbling after something it can never find; and with all its strivings, it does not come into contact with reality; it has no abiding fruit.

*"What's the use of it all?"*, cries many a person.

From this bondage, Christ has redeemed us. When the Power of Christ's Atoning Death enters into any life, that life is no longer unsatisfying. It is no longer imprisoned within ruts of ancestral traditions or grooves of established custom.

The Christian's actions spring from a new life that has been stirred into being by the Power of Christ's Death. The Death of Christ, as a Death for sin, liberates and re-creates the soul.

RECONCILIATION

*"All things are of God, Who hath reconciled us to Himself by Jesus Christ, and hath given to us the Ministry of Reconciliation:*

*"To wit, that God was in Christ, reconciling the world unto Himself, not imputing their trespasses unto them; and hath committed unto us the Word of Reconciliation"* (II Cor. 5:18, 19).

When we were enemies, we were reconciled to God by the Death of His Son (Rom. 5:10). Men who were once alienated and enemies in mind through wicked works, yet now hath He reconciled in the Body of His Flesh through Death (Col. 1:21).

The Atonement is often misunderstood and misrepresented. Some imagine the Atonement to mean that God was angry at the sinner, and sullenly stood aloof until He was placated by His Son offering to pay the penalty; in other words, God had to be reconciled to the sinner.

This, however, is a corruption of the True Doctrine. Throughout the Scriptures, it is God the offended party Who takes the initiative in providing an Atonement for man. It is God Who clothes our first parents; it is the Lord Who ordains the Atoning Sacrifices; it is God the Father Who sends and gives His Son a Sacrifice for mankind.

God Himself is the Author of man's Redemption. Though His Majesty has been offended by man's sin, and His Holiness naturally must react against it, yet He is not willing that the sinner perish (Ezek. 33:11) but that he repent and be saved. Paul does not say that God was reconciled to man, but that God did something in order to reconcile man to Himself.

The act of Reconciliation is a finished work; it is a work that has been done in the interest of men so that in the sight of God the entire world is already reconciled. It remains for the Evangelist to proclaim it and the individual to receive it. Christ's Death has made the Reconciliation of all mankind to God possible; however, each individual must make it actual.

NOTES

This is the essence of the Gospel Message: the Death of Christ was a Finished Work of Reconciliation, achieved independently of us, at an infinite cost, and to which men are called by a Ministry of Reconciliation.

WHAT DOES SALVATION OR THE ATONEMENT ACTUALLY EFFECT IN ONE'S LIFE?

What does the Atoning Work of Christ's effect for men?

What does it produce in his experience?

Is the Believer the same as unbelievers, with the exception that he has Faith in Christ?

What really happens in the heart and life of a believing sinner upon accepting Christ?

PARDON OF TRANSGRESSIONS

Through His Atoning Work, Jesus Christ paid the debt we could not pay and secured remission of past sins. No longer does the sinful past hang like a dead weight upon the Christian, for his sins are blotted out, taken away, canceled, as well as the penalty of those sins, which is death (Jn. 1:29; Eph. 1:7; Heb. 9:22-28; Rev. 1:5).

He has begun life anew, confident that the sins of the past will never meet him at the judgement (Jn. 5:24).

FREEDOM FROM SIN

Through the Atonement, the Believer is not only freed from the guilt of past sins but also can be free from the power of sin. This subject is addressed by Paul in Romans Chapters 6-8.

Paul anticipates an objection which some of his Jewish opponents must have raised often, namely, that if people were saved by merely believing in Jesus, they would think lightly of sin, saying, *"If we continue in sin, Grace will abound"* (Rom. 6:1).

Paul repudiates the very thought and points out that he who truly believes on Christ has, by virtue of his Faith, made a clean-cut break with sin — a break so decisive as to be described as *"death."*

Living Faith in the Crucified Saviour results in the crucifixion of the old sinful nature. The man who believes with all the powers of his soul (and that is what real believing is) that Christ died for sins, has such a conviction of the awfulness of sin that he repudiates it with his entire being. The Cross means the doom of sin in his life.

However, the Tempter is busy and human nature is frail, hence, constant vigilance and daily crucifying of the sinful impulses (Rom. 6:11) are necessary.

And yet, the victory is assured. *"For sin shall not have dominion over you: for ye are not under the Law, but under Grace"* (Rom. 6:14).

That is, Law means something is to be done by the sinner; unable to pay the debt or do what the Law requires, he remains in the grip of sin. On the other hand, Grace means that something has been done for the sinner — the Finished Work of Calvary. As he *believes* what has been done for him, so he *receives* what has been done for him.

## THE DOUBLE CURE FOR THE DOUBLE CURSE

When Jesus died on Calvary, He effected a double cure by: A. Paying the sin debt; and, B. Breaking the grip of sin on the new Believer.

Man had a double curse on him, in that he had: A. A sin debt he could not pay; and, B. As a result of the sin debt, a grip of sin which he could not break. However, Jesus paid the debt and broke the grip.

To receive the benefits, the Believer must appropriate by Faith, each and every day of his life, the tremendous effects of Calvary, realizing that when Jesus died and rose again, that the sinner was actually in Him, as Christ became our Divine Substitute. It is Substitution and Identification.

He was *"Baptized into the Death of Christ,"* and *"buried with Him by Baptism into Death,"* and, when Christ was raised from the dead, literally raised with Him *"in newness of life"* (Rom. 6:3-8).

## THE HOLY SPIRIT

His faith has a powerful ally in the Person of the Holy Spirit, Who indwells him, helps him to crush the sinful impulses, helps him pray and gives him the assurance of his liberty and victory as a Child of God (Rom. Chpt. 8).

Indeed, Christ died to remove the obstacle of sin, so that the Spirit of God might come into

NOTES

human life (Gal. 3:13-14). Being saved by God's Mercy revealed in the Cross, the Believer receives an experience of cleansing and spiritual quickening (Titus 3:5-7).

Having died to the old life of sin, he is born again to a new life — born of the Spirit, thereby receiving Divine Life (Jn. 3:5). In other words, the Divine Nature was imparted to the believing sinner at the moment of conversion.

## DELIVERANCE FROM DEATH

Death has both a physical and spiritual meaning. In its physical meaning it denotes the cessation of physical life, consequent upon disease, natural decay or some violent cause. But it is more commonly used in the spiritual meaning, namely, as the penalty attached by God to human sin.

The Word expresses the spiritual condition of separation from and disfavor with God on account of sin. Dying out of favor with God, the impenitent remain separated from God in the other world, and the eternal separation which follows is known as the *"second death."*

The threat, *"In the day that thou eatest thereof thou shalt surely die"* (Gen. 2:17), as it was given in the Garden of Eden, would have failed in fulfillment if Death meant simply the physical act of death, for Adam and Eve continued after that date.

But the proclamation is profoundly true when we remember that the word *"death"* involved all the penal consequences of sin — separation from God, unrest, inclination toward evil, physical weakness, and finally physical death and consequences beyond death.

## CHRIST AND DEATH

When the Scriptures say that Christ died for our sins, they mean that Christ submitted not merely to physical death, but to death as the penalty for sin. He humbled Himself to the suffering of death *"that He by the Grace of God should taste death for every man"* (Heb. 2:9). Because of His Divine Nature, and the Divine Arrangement, He was able to effect this.

We may not understand the *"how"* of the matter, for evidently we are confronted with a Divine Mystery. But we accept many facts in this universe without understanding the *"how"* of them. No sensible person ever deprived himself of the blessings of electricity just because he does not fully understand what electricity is and why it should act as it does.

Neither does anyone deprive himself of the benefits of the Atonement just because he cannot reason it out as he would a problem of mathematics.

Since death is the penalty of sin (spiritual death), and Christ came to give Himself for our sins, He did so by dying. Concentrated into these few hours of death on the Cross was all the awful meaning of that death and the blackness of its penalty, and this explains the cry of abandonment, *"My God, My God, why hast Thou forsaken Me?"* (Mat. 27:46).

These are not the words of a martyr, for martyrs are frequently sustained by the consciousness of God's presence; they are the words of One performing an act which involved the divine separation, for Jesus was separated from the Father as He offered Himself for sin — Sin Offering. That act was sin-bearing (II Cor. 5:21).

While it is true that those who believe on Him will have to suffer physical death, unless they are alive at the time of the Rapture (Rom. 8:10), yet for them, the stigma or penalty is taken from death, and it becomes the door to a larger life. In this sense is Jesus' saying true, *"Whosoever liveth and believeth in Me shall never die"* (Jn. 11:26).

## THE GIFT OF LIFE ETERNAL

Christ died that we might not *"perish"* (the word being used in the Scriptural sense of spiritual ruin), *"but have Everlasting Life"* (Jn. 3:16; compare Rom. 6:23).

Eternal life means more than mere existence; it signifies life in favor and fellowship with God. Dead in trespasses and in sins, man is out of favor with God; through Christ's Sacrifice, the sin is Atoned for and he is in full fellowship with God. To be in favor and fellowship with God is Life Eternal, for it is Life with Him Who is eternal.

This Life is possessed now because Believers are in fellowship with God now; Eternal Life is also described as future (Rom. 6:22; Titus 1:2), because the future life will bring perfect fellowship with God. *"And they shall see His Face."*

## THE VICTORIOUS LIFE

The Cross is the dynamo which generates in the human heart that response which constitutes the Christian Life. *"I'll live for Him Who died for me,"* well states the dynamic of the Cross. The Christian life is the soul's reaction to the Love of Christ.

NOTES

The Cross of Christ inspires true repentance, which is repentance toward God. Sin may be followed by remorse, shame, and anger, but only where there is sorrow for having offended God is there real repentance.

This consciousness cannot be produced at will, for it is in the very nature of sin to darken the mind and harden the heart. The sinner needs a powerful motive for repentance — something to make him see and feel that his sin has deeply wronged and offended God.

The Cross of Christ supplies that motive, for it demonstrates the awfulness of sin, in that it caused the Death of the Son of God; it declares the terrible penalty of sin; but it also reveals the Love and Grace of God.

It has been well said that *"all true penitents are children of the Cross. Their penitence is not their own: it is the reaction toward God produced in their souls by this demonstration of what sin is to Him, and what His Love does to reach and win the sinful."*

## THE POWER OF THE CROSS

It is written of certain Saints, who had come through great tribulation, that they *"have washed their robes, and made them white in the Blood of the Lamb"* (Rev. 7:14). The reference is to the sanctifying power of the Death of Christ. They had resisted sin and were now pure.

Where did they secure the strength to overcome sin?

From the constraining power of the Love of Christ revealed at Calvary. The Power of the Cross descending into their hearts enabled them to overcome sin (Gal. 2:20).

*"They overcame him by the Blood of the Lamb, and by the Word of their Testimony; and they loved not their lives unto the death"* (Rev. 12:11).

The Love of Christ constrained them; and enabled them to overcome. The pressure upon them was great, but with the Blood of the Lamb as the motive behind them, they were unconquerable.

They dared not, with the Cross on which He died before their eyes, betray His Cause by cowardice, and love their lives more than He loved His. They must be His, as He had been theirs.

The victorious life includes victory over Satan. The New Testament declares that Christ conquered Satan on our behalf (Lk. 10:17-20; Jn. 12:30-32; Col. 2:15; Heb. 2:14-15; Rev. 12:11).

Christians have victory over the Devil as long as they have the *"Victor"* over the Devil!

(30) "FOR THIS CAUSE MANY ARE WEAK AND SICKLY AMONG YOU, AND MANY SLEEP."

The phrase, *"For this cause,"* refers to not properly *"discerning the Lord's Body."*

*"Cause"* in the Greek is *"dia,"* and means *"the channel of an act, by occasion of, by reason of."* The idea is that the sickness and death which are mentioned next were not causeless.

The phrase, *"Many are weak and sickly among you,"* tells us the cause, at least of some sickness.

*"Many"* in the Greek is *"polus,"* and means *"often."*

*"Weak"* in the Greek is *"astheneo,"* and means *"feeble, impotent, diseased."*

*"Sickly"* is *"arrhostos,"* and means *"infirm."*

This not at all means that all Believers who are sick are in that particular condition because of not properly *"discerning the Lord's Body,"* but it definitely does refer to some.

The phrase, *"And many sleep,"* refers to dying prematurely.

*"Many"* in this instance is *"hikanos,"* and is a little different from the previous word for *"many."* Here it means *"not a few, a considerable number."*

This *"judgement"* which Paul mentions is not eternal damnation, but rather an untimely physical death. Again, it does not mean that all who die prematurely fall into this category, but rather some, but more than one realizes.

## THE BODY OF CHRIST

Going back to the word *"discerning"* in the previous Verse, it is meant to distinguish something that is distinct and different. The Lord's Supper is not just any meal; it is *the* meal, in which at a common table Believers proclaim that through the death of Christ they are one body, the Body of Christ; and therefore, they are not just any group of sociologically divers people who could keep those differences intact at this table.

Here, they must *"discern/recognize as distinct"* the one Body of Christ, of which they all are parts and in which they all are gifts to one another. To fail to discern the Body in this way, can as well incur God's judgement.

NOTES

Paul is here stepping into the Prophetic role; by the Spirit, he has seen a Divine cause and effect between two otherwise independent realities: the present illnesses of many, which in some cases have led to death, and the actions of some at the Table of the Lord who are not properly discerning this meal, by harboring sin in one's life or a self-righteous attitude, which is probably the bigger culprit.

Again, we emphasize the point, that the idea is *not* that a Believer refuse to take the *"Supper"* due to present wrongs, for abstaining will not lessen the situation at all. The idea is that one make things right with God, which one can do very easily and quickly, if one will only be sincere.

(31) "FOR IF WE WOULD JUDGE OURSELVES, WE SHOULD NOT BE JUDGED."

The idea is that the Believer *"examine himself"* (vs. 28), and do so constantly, as to whether he has proper Faith respecting what Jesus did at the Cross. Jesus told us that if we were to follow Him, we must deny ourselves, and take up the Cross Daily (Lk. 9:23). If we refuse to do this, then we shall have to reap that which we sow. If we judge all sin by taking it to the Cross, pleading mercy from the Lord, and then, by the power of Christ through the Cross, put that sin away, we will not be chastened by God.

If one is to notice, Paul includes himself by using the pronoun *"we."* Apostle though he is, he, too, does not escape judgement if he does not carefully discern his own spiritual condition. The way of safety which he points out is the one and only way for all. None are excluded.

*"Judge"* as here used in the Greek is *"diakrino,"* and means *"to separate thoroughly."*

*"Judged"* is *"krino,"* and means *"to condemn, call into question, or to sentence."* The former is done by the Believer, while the latter is done by the Lord.

## SELF-INTROSPECTION

Most Believers, I think, have the habit of judging others quite severely, while they judge themselves quite leniently. We have a tendency to make excuse for ourselves, while allowing no latitude whatsoever for others. This attitude, that is if one functions accordingly, must be changed.

Examining others should be done with great leniency, while being harsh with ourselves. To be frank, if we properly look at ourselves, properly examine ourselves, we will be very lenient with all others, realizing that we have no moral right to judge others.

(32) "BUT WHEN WE ARE JUDGED, WE ARE CHASTENED OF THE LORD, THAT WE SHOULD NOT BE CONDEMNED WITH THE WORLD."

The phrase, *"But when we are judged,"* refers to refusing to judge ourselves and, therefore, being judged by the Lord.

The phrase, *"We are chastened of the Lord,"* is to be understood as *"Divine discipline,"* in which a loving God is correcting His children.

## A MISUNDERSTANDING

As noted throughout, these particular verses as given by Paul have had an unfortunate history of understanding in the Church. The very Table that is God's reminder and, therefore, His repeated Gift of Grace, the Table where we affirm again who and Whose we are, has been allowed to become a table of condemnation for the very people who most truly need the assurance of acceptance that this Table affords — the sinful, the weak, the weary.

It is not perfection here which the Holy Spirit demands, for if so, all of us fall down. Here by faith, one may once again receive the assurance that *"Christ receiveth sinners."* The idea is a proper attitude toward others and toward oneself.

Our attitude toward others must be one of understanding, love, and compassion. Toward ourselves, as being ever needful of what Christ affords at Calvary, as a result of knowing how unworthy we actually are.

## JUDGEMENT

On the other hand, any magical view of the Sacrament that allows the unrepentant to partake without properly *"discerning the Body"* makes the offer of Grace a place of Judgement. Grace *"received"* that is not recognized as such is not Grace at all; and Grace *"received"* that does not recognize the need to be gracious to others is to miss the point of the Table altogether (Fee).

## CHASTISEMENT

The Greek word for *"chastisement"* is *"paideia,"* and means *"to train up a child, to educate, to discipline."*

NOTES

In the New Testament, the Greek *"paideia"* is used with a variety similar to its corresponding to its Hebrew (musar) in the Old Testament. Examples of the fundamental idea, that of *"training"* are found in such passages as Acts 7:22; 22:3, where Moses and Paul are said to have been *"instructed,"* and II Timothy 3:16, where Scripture is said to be *"profitable . . . for instruction"* (Rom. 2:20; I Tim. 1:20; II Tim. 2:25; Titus 2:12).

A similar, but not identical, thought is found in Ephesians 6:4, *"Nurture them in the chastening and admonition of the Lord."*

But when *"paideia"* is described as a particular state, the mystery of suffering, which in the Old Testament is most fully treated in the Book of Job, at last finds its explanation.

## THE LORD AND THE BELIEVER

The Child of God realizes that he cannot be beneath God's Wrath, and hence, that the chastening which he endures is not destructive, but corrective (I Cor. 10:13; 11:32; II Cor. 6:9; Rev. 3:19).

In Hebrews 12:5-11, such consolation is afforded, not as in the above passages by incidental allusions, but by a full argument upon the basis of Proverbs 3:11. This, as is obvious, is an Old Testament Text that has depth and richness that can be understood and appropriated only by those who, through Christ, have learned to recognize the Omnipotent Ruler of Heaven and Earth as their loving and considerate Father.

## PUNISHMENT AND CHASTISEMENT

On the basis of this Passage, a distinction is often drawn between punishment and chastisement; the former, as an act of justice, revealing wrath, and the latter, as an act of Mercy, Love.

Since to Believers who are in Christ Jesus, there is no condemnation (Rom. 8:1), they can suffer no punishment, but only chastisement. Where there is guilt, there is punishment; but where guilt has been removed, there can be no punishment.

There being no degrees of justification, no one can be forgiven in part, with a partial guilt still set to his account for which he must yet give a reckoning, either here or hereafter.

If, then, all the Righteousness of Christ belongs to the Believer, and it certainly does, and no sin whatever remains to be forgiven, either in whole or in part, all of life's sorrows are remedial agencies against danger and are meant to train for the Kingdom of Heaven. In other words, God never condemns His Children, therefore, never punishes them; however, the Lord does chastise, and because He greatly loves us, and that it may be done for our profit, and never our loss.

The phrase, *"That we should not be condemned with the world,"* presents a necessity. In other words, the Lord chastises His children, in order that the problem may be corrected, whatever the problem may be, and will not, therefore, result in the loss of the soul, i.e. *"condemned with the world."*

This last statement in this Verse is a cogent reminder that it is possible to lose one's Salvation. The Bible does not teach unconditional, eternal security, but it does teach conditional, eternal security. As long as we abide in Christ, we are secure (I Jn. 5:11, 12) (Rossier).

(33) "WHEREFORE, MY BRETHREN, WHEN YE COME TOGETHER TO EAT, TARRY ONE FOR ANOTHER."

The phrase, *"Wherefore, my Brethren,"* proclaims the Apostle as addressing all of the Corinthians as *"Brethren,"* which of course, included the Sisters in the Lord as well, therefore, placing them in the Family of God. He is admonishing them to live up to their place, status, and position in Christ and not conduct themselves in an unChristlike manner.

The phrase, *"When ye come together to eat, tarry one for another,"* proclaims the idea that all must share and share alike. It was not so much what was done, but the spirit in which it was done, i.e. the rich not sharing with the poor, etc.

These particular *"love feasts"* faded out after awhile, even as they should have. Even though such is commendable occasionally, if carried out properly, even as Paul is here addressing, the frequency of its present action was of little value.

## THE FELLOWSHIP OF EATING AND DRINKING AS TAUGHT IN THE BIBLE

Considering this situation, I think it would be proper for us to look at the Word of God throughout its entirety respecting this part of fellowship among Saints. Eating and drinking were significant acts in the Biblical world. Besides satisfying physical needs, they were symbolic of both friendship and of participation.

Consequently, let's look at both the Old and New Testaments respecting this fellowship.

NOTES

## THE OLD TESTAMENT

The Hebrew word *"akal"* means *"to eat, consume, or devour."* One of its major Old Testament uses is to indicate times of hardship, during which resources and hope are consumed.

It also has the common meaning of eating food.

In addition, eating is associated with theologically significant concepts. Ritually, the worshiper of Old Testament times ate portions of some of the animals offered in Sacrifice. Participation in such a ritual meal was limited to true Believers. It was the mark of acceptance of, and acceptance by, the Lord.

As God said of the Passover meal, *"No foreigner is to eat of it. Any slave you have bought may eat of it after you have circumcised him but a temporary resident and a hired worker may not eat of it"* (Ex. 12:43-44).

The significance of the ritual meal in the Old Testament is seen in the Psalmist's commentary on a generation that rejected the Lord: *"They yoked themselves to the Baal of Peor and ate sacrifices offered to lifeless gods"* (Ps. 106:28). To participate in worship or a ritual meal was to yoke oneself either to idols or to the True God; i.e. to whoever the meal was dedicated, actually that which Paul addressed in I Corinthians Chapter 10.

## THE CLEAN AND THE UNCLEAN

In addition, Israel was given instructions concerning which mammals, birds, and fish might be eaten. They were limited to the flesh of *"clean"* animals.

This did not have a dietary or health purpose, but was a constant reminder to Israel that they were linked with Jehovah, and everything they did was to express their position as His special people.

This sense of association or fellowship that was expressed by eating affected interpersonal relationships in the Biblical world. Those who shared a meal entered into a closer relationship with each other, and such a meal implied real mutual obligations.

Against this background, Jesus warned those He taught during His earthly ministry: *"You will say, 'We ate and drank with you, and you taught in our streets,' but He will reply, 'I don't know you or where you came from. Away from Me all you evil doers!'"* (Lk. 13:26-27).

COMMITMENT

It is not the social obligation imposed by a shared meal, but the commitment symbolized by the ritual meal that stands for Saving Faith and for participation in all that Jesus brings to humanity.

The meaning of full participation is emphasized in other contexts. One who takes part in wickedness will be judged: he will *"eat the bread of wickedness"* (Prov. 4:17; Jer. 9:15; 23:15). On the other hand, one can participate in the rewarding aspects of work: *"You will eat of the fruit of your labor"* (Ps. 128:2).

THE NEW TESTAMENT

The New Testament word for eating is *"esthio."* Although Old Testament ritual requirements for eating clean animals are done away with in the New Testament, the link between food and participation is not. Partaking in the Lord's Supper, as we have been studying, continues as a symbolic affirmation of commitment to Jesus. And there is no room for Believers to take part in a feast offered in honor of an idol (I Cor. 10:14-22).

EATING AS FRIENDSHIP AND PARTICIPATION

The frequent meals shared by members of the Early Church (Acts 2:46; 11:3; I Cor. 5:11; 11:33) were indications of the deep fellowship that developed in the believing community. They were also symbolic of the commitment of Believers to one another and to the Lord.

Eating meets a basic need of all living creatures. But eating also meets other needs.

In human society, eating is an occasion for fellowship, and shared meals carry connotations of social obligation. Eating is also linked with worship in the Old Testament. The one who eats of a Sacrificial animal affirms his being yoked to God. In the Old Testament, only God's people were permitted to take part in ritual meals. And no true Believer would take part in a ritual meal provided in honor of an idol.

NOTES

In the New Testament, the Lord's Supper is a worship occasion. Only those who belong to Jesus share in it, for eating is an affirmation by the true Believer of his or her Faith commitment to Jesus as Saviour and Lord (Richards).

(34) "AND IF ANY MAN HUNGER, LET HIM EAT AT HOME; THAT YE COME NOT TOGETHER UNTO CONDEMNATION. AND THE REST WILL I SET IN ORDER WHEN I COME."

The phrase, *"And if any man hunger, let him eat at home,"* probably has reference to the fact that if the wealthy desired to satisfy their desire for the kinds of meals they were accustomed to eating at home, they should continue to do so at home, but not in the context of the gathered assembly, where some *"have nothing"* and are thereby humiliated (Fee.)

The phrase, *"That ye come not together unto condemnation,"* refers to the possibility of this agape or *"love feast"* being a detriment instead of a blessing. We should note these words very carefully:

It is awful for Church people to gather, supposedly in the Name of the Lord, but instead of receiving Blessings from the Lord, rather be condemned or judged, even causing many to be sick or even die prematurely. To be sure, if the worship is not Biblical, it will bring *"condemnation,"* i.e. *"judgement."*

When we realize that the far greater majority of Church Gatherings fall into this very category, then the matter becomes serious indeed!

Of course, this pertains to any type of Church service; however, addressing ourselves at the present only to these *"love feasts,"* it seems that such did not prove to be a permanent success. It was first transferred from the evening to the early morning *"before it was light"* (Pliny). Then it was separated from the Lord's Supper altogether, finally being totally abolished.

Justin Martyr, about A.D. 150, describes the Holy Communion without mention of the Agape, i.e. *"love feasts."*

The phrase, *"And the rest will I set in order when I come,"* does not give us a clue as to that of which he spoke. Maybe he had further instructions about the Communion Service; however, what the Holy Spirit wanted and desired is that which we are given in this Eleventh Chapter of I Corinthians.

*"Praise God from Whom all blessings flow;*
*"Praise Him all creatures here below;*
*"Praise Him above, ye heav'n-ly host:*
*"Praise Father, Son, and Holy Ghost."*

CHAPTER 12

(1) "NOW CONCERNING SPIRITUAL GIFTS, BRETHREN, I WOULD NOT HAVE YOU IGNORANT."

The phrase, *"Now concerning spiritual gifts, Brethren,"* in this case has to do with the nine Gifts of the Spirit outlined in Verses 8, 9 and 10. However, there are other types of gifts as well, listed in Romans Chapter 12. In fact, everything from God is a *"Gift,"* of which we will study momentarily. Actually, God has nothing for sale, with all that He has being offered as a *"Gift."* Nevertheless, we will confine our study at the present to the Gifts mentioned in this particular Chapter.

*"Spiritual"* in the Greek is *"pneumatikos,"* and literally means *"things of the Spirit."* So Paul is actually saying, *"Now concerning things of the Spirit...."*

The phrase, *"I would not have you ignorant,"* proclaims the Spirit of God, through Paul, saying that He didn't want the Church at Corinth to be ignorant concerning these Gifts. In fact, it would be the same for all Churches and all time, including the present.

Yet a gross ignorance does exist concerning these things. In some churches, if not most, people know nothing at all about them, not even that such Gifts exist. They have been taught that if they ever existed at all, they are no longer apropos for the present time. Others have some small knowledge of the Gifts, but not much.

The Truth is that, as long as the Church is in the world, it needs these Gifts in operation in the hearts and lives of Believers. That's the reason that the Apostle gave this teaching concerning this very important subject. The Holy Spirit does not want us to be ignorant concerning these things.

*"Ignorant"* in the Greek is *"agnoeo,"* and means *"not to know through lack of information or intelligence."*

NOTES

THE GENERAL NATURE OF THE GIFTS

The *"Gifts"* of the Spirit must be distinguished from the *"Gift"* of the Spirit. The former describes the supernatural abilities imparted by the Spirit for special ministry; the latter refers to the impartation of the Spirit to Believers as ministered by the ascended Christ (Acts 2:33).

Paul speaks of the Gifts of the Spirit (*"spirituals"* in the original Greek) in a threefold aspect:

1. *"Charismata"*: This pertains to a variety of Gifts bestowed by the One Spirit.

2. *"Diakonai"*: This refers to varieties of service rendered in the Cause of the One Lord.

3. *"Energemata"*: This speaks of the varieties of the power of the One God Who works all in all.

All these aspects are referred to as *"the Manifestation of the Spirit,"* which is given to men for the profit of all, and which we will study to a greater degree momentarily.

THE MAIN PURPOSE

What is the main purpose of the Gifts of the Spirit?

They are spiritual enablements for the purpose of building up the Church of God through the instruction of Believers and the winning of converts (Eph. 4:7-13). Paul enumerates nine of these Gifts as stated in Verses 8, 9, and 10, which may be classified as follows:

1. Three of the Gifts *say* something: Tongues, Interpretation of Tongues, and Prophecy.

2. Three of the Gifts *reveal* something: the Word of Wisdom, the Word of Knowledge, and Discerning of Spirits.

3. Three of the Gifts *do* something: Faith, the Working of Miracles, and Gifts of Healings.

Inasmuch as we are here dealing with the word *"Gift"* or *"Gifts,"* perhaps it would be profitable to go into greater detail respecting this of which the Scripture speaks.

GIFTS

Gift or Gifts are simple words. They imply the willingness and ability of one person to give something to another. Yet these words have rather deep, theological significance, particularly when used to describe the special endowments that Jesus gives to His people.

First of all, let's look at this word as it applies to the Old Testament.

NOTES

## THE OLD TESTAMENT

A number of Hebrew words are translated *"Gift."* But two word groups best express the underlying concept.

*"Minhah"* is a gift in the sense of an offering or tribute. In common use, it is a present (sometimes a bribe) that one person might give another.

Such Gifts are typically expressions of submission to, or attempts to gain the favor of, a powerful person.

The word is also used of Gifts given to God in recognition of His greatness or in the daily Grain Offerings prescribed by Law (Lev. Chpt. 2; 5:13; 6:14-23).

*"Natan"* is another Hebrew word with a variety of meanings. *"To give"* is primary among them. In fact, a number of words are derived from that one Hebrew word.

What is most significant about the use of these Hebrew words is the pattern visible within the culture. Gift giving was regarded as an act with definite social significance, for Gifts were viewed as an appropriate way for an inferior to express submission to, or to seek to win the favor of, a superior, even as we have already stated. A superior may deal generously with an inferior, but that behavior is not described in terms of giving Gifts.

## WHY THE OLD TESTAMENT IS SO IMPORTANT

The reader may wonder why it is so important to include Old Testament thought concerning New Testament Doctrines, etc.

It is very important in many and varied ways. The manner in which God dealt with Israel proclaims a pattern or foundation respecting His Way and His Word as it was given to the world. So, the pattern for all New Testament direction is found in Old Testament foundation.

To divorce the Old Testament from the New is a serious mistake indeed. In Truth, everything that Jesus did in His earthly Ministry was based on Old Testament Doctrine. As well, everything that Paul said and did came from the same Source.

## GIFT IN THE NEW TESTAMENT

The common word for giving in the Greek, *"didomi"* (found over 400 times in the New Testament), is used with all shades of meaning. There are also several words translated *"Gift."* Although these terms for Gifts are with-in the same family of words, each has a special emphasis.

The Greek word *"doron"* (found 19 times in the New Testament) is used very much in the Old Testament sense, and most frequently speaks of an Offering or Gift given by man to God. Only one time (Eph. 2:8) is God portrayed as the Giver, at least in this context, and in that reference we are shown that Salvation comes through Faith (*"Not from yourselves, it is the Gift of God"*) (Mat. 2:11; 5:23-24; 8:4; 15:5; 23:18-19; Mk. 7:11; Lk. 21:1, 4; Eph. 2:8; Heb. 5:1; 8:3-4; 9:9; 11:4; Rev. 11:10).

## GOD AS THE GIVER

Another Greek word, *"dorea,"* is used some 11 times in the New Testament, and wherever it is found, God is the Giver. God's Gifts in and through Jesus include Salvation, Righteousness, Enablement, and the Holy Spirit (Jn. 4:10; Acts 2:38; 8:20; 10:45; 11:17; Rom. 5:15, 17; II Cor. 9:15; Eph. 3:7; 4:7; Heb. 6:4).

*"Dorean"* is another word, and occurs only eight times. However, it is a significant word. It emphasizes the free character of the Gift, given spontaneously and without reference to human merit. Thus, *"we are justified freely by His Grace"* (Rom. 3:24) on the basis of what Jesus has done (Mat. 10:8; Jn. 15:25; Rom. 3:24; II Cor. 11:7; Rev. 21:6; 22:17). In Galatians 2:21 it means *"not without impact,"* and II Thessalonians 3:8 it means *"without payment."*

## THE ULTIMATE GIFT OF GOD

What is significant about the idea of Gift giving in the New Testament is the sudden and jolting reversal of the flow. Gifts are no longer presents offered by an inferior to a superior. God, the Ultimate Superior in the universe, is seen giving Gifts to humanity. His Gifts are freely and spontaneously offered, without reference to the merit of the one who receives and without the intention of later profiting from the transaction.

The impact of the New Testament Revelation is its demand that we see God in a new light: God is One Who is suddenly presented to us as *"Given."*

The teaching of the New Testament makes it clear that the Ultimate Gift of God is Jesus Himself. All other Gifts come to us through the

Son. Accepting Jesus, we step into the relationship with God that Paul describes in Romans 8:32, *"He Who did not spare His Own Son, but gave Him up for us all — how will He not also, along with Him, graciously give us all things?"*

CORBAN

Mark's Gospel (Mk. 7:11) uses this technical term where it is described as a Gift vowed to God (Mat. 15:5). The thing vowed was not actually transferred to the Temple treasury. All that was called for was the pronouncement of the vow, and others were thereupon barred from benefitting from the property or person so committed to God, or so it claimed.

The Rabbis of Jesus' day held that such a vow was always binding, even if it denied one's parents the resources required for their support.

Jesus condemned this interpretation.

His strong words about *"Corban"* need not imply that the practice was widespread. Instead they condemned the willingness of the religious leaders to set aside for a technicality God's command to honor parents. Jesus' complaint was that these interpreters of Israel's faith did *"many things like that"* (Mk. 7:13).

In other words, they were only interested in the letter of the Law and had little interest in the spirit of the Law.

SPIRITUAL GIFTS

The Greek word involved in this subject is *"Charisma."* It indicates a Grace Gift, one bestowed only by God to people in the New Testament.

In Romans, Paul speaks of *"the Gift that came by the Grace of Jesus, Eternal Life"* (Rom. 5:15; 6:23). But in most occurrences in the New Testament, *"Charisma"* is God's special endowment of Believers for service to the community of Faith.

This Greek word occurs 17 times in the New Testament (Rom. 1:11; 5:15-16; 6:23; 11:29; 12:6; I Cor. 1:7; 7:7; 12:4, 9, 28, 30, 31; II Cor. 1:11; etc.)

Because of the unusual character of some of the Spiritual Gifts identified in Scripture, the real significance of this Biblical Teaching has often been clouded.

BASIC PASSAGES ON SPIRITUAL GIFTS

The two major Passages are Romans Chapter 12 and I Corinthians Chapter 12.

NOTES

Romans Chapter 12 calls on Believers to look at life from God's perspective (Rom. 12:1-2). Immediately Paul moves to explain God's view of the individual Believer within the community (Rom. 12:3-8).

Individuals are to see themselves as members of a Body — parts of a living organism, within which each person has a distinct function. God has endowed each Believer with a Gift, an enablement that makes him or her able to contribute to others in the Body. Thus, the Church is an interdependent community, a living Body, within which each of us *"belongs to all the others"* (Rom. 12:5) and is to serve others.

In Romans 12:9-18, Paul describes the interpersonal relationships that members of the Body are to develop. Only loving and intimate personal relationships create a context for that loving service in which Spiritual Gifts operate.

I CORINTHIANS CHAPTER 12

The same themes are picked up in I Corinthians Chapter 12. There are different gifts (I Cor. 12:4), sovereignly distributed by God (I Cor. 12:7). Each Believer is (ideally) given a Gift to be used for the common good (I Cor. 12:7).

The Passage emphasizes the importance of each person to the Body, a corrective in a Church that tended to exalt some Gifts over others (I Cor. 12:14-26).

As in the discussion in Romans, Paul moves on to speak of the climate of love that is to mark the believing community (I Cor. Chpt. 13). It is in the context of interpersonal relationships shaped by Love that Spiritual Gifts function freely.

Peter sums up the personal impact of the Bible's teaching on Gifts: *"Each one should use whatever Gift he has received to serve others, faithfully administering God's Grace in its various forms"* (I Pet. 4:10).

THE FUNCTION OF SPIRITUAL GIFTS

The Grace Gifts of the New Testament are always seen within the context of the Christian community. Although Believers are called on to witness to, and to do good to, all people, the Passages that explore Spiritual Gifts are focused on the shared life of members of the Body of Christ. It is within the Body, that Spiritual Gifts function *"for the common"* (I Cor. 12:7).

According to Ephesians Chapter 4, the *"works of service"* of Christians are called for *"that the Body of Christ may be built up, until we all reach unity in the Faith and in the knowledge of the Son of God and become mature, attaining to the whole measure of the fullness of Christ"* (Eph. 4:12-13).

Vitalized by the Spiritual Life that flows from Jesus, the whole Body *"grows and builds itself up in love, as each part does its work"* (Eph. 4:16).

It is important that we see Spiritual Gifts as spiritual endowments that function within the Body, focused on the maturing of our fellow Christians and the Church as a whole. God surely works through His people to serve and witness to Him in the world. But Spiritual Gifts are in Scripture a family concern (within the Church).

QUESTIONS ABOUT SPIRITUAL GIFTS?

1. Do supernatural Gifts of the Spirit operate today?

Most definitely they do! Where the Spirit of God is truly present, there will be Gifts of the Spirit in operation.

2. Are all the spiritual gifts listed in the Bible?

It is best to take the various Gifts listed in Romans Chapter 12 and I Corinthians Chapter 12 as representative rather than as an exhaustive listing of God's endowments.

Any way in which we serve others and contribute to their lives must depend on the Holy Spirit's working through us and should be considered a *"Charisma."*

However, even though we are to look at these Gifts as representative, still, in the context of I Corinthians Chapter 12, I think the Nine Gifts of the Spirit listed denote *all* the Gifts of that particular category. Consequently, one would be unwise to add other Gifts, at least according to this particular capacity.

3. Where do Spiritual Gifts operate?

The context defined in the Bible is relational. Spiritual Gifts operate as we lovingly respond to others and seek to serve them. At times we mistakenly identify Spiritual Gifts with Church Offices or institutional roles. We should not assume that the Spiritual Gift of Teaching is summed up by functioning in a Sunday School classroom, etc. Actually, the two are not related at all.

NOTES

4. Can a person have more than one Spiritual Gift?

It is clear that Paul had more than one Gift (I Cor. 14:18; II Cor. 12:11-12).

As well, I believe that one can say without fear of contradiction, that each Believer has at least one Spiritual Gift. The problem is, many Believers are so little consecrated to the Lord, that they have no idea what that Gift is.

If one will truly seek the Lord in these matters, the Holy Spirit will most assuredly reveal to that person that which He has assigned.

Also, there is no reason to believe that any individual is necessarily limited to one Gift.

5. What is the difference between Spiritual Gifts and persons who are called God's Gifts to His Church?

Both I Corinthians Chapter 12 and Ephesians Chapter 4 speak of such gifted persons: Apostles, Evangelists, etc.

These persons were set aside in the Early Church, and continue so unto this hour, to a full-time Ministry relative to the particular Call.

They had to be gifted spiritually, and greatly so, to fulfill these Ministries. But the Offices of which we speak are not Gifts in the sense of *"Charisma."* In fact, each of these Callings (the Persons in these Callings) should have one or more of the Nine Gifts of the Spirit functioning within their lives and Ministries.

MISUSE

Having *"first of all"* (I Cor. 11:18) rebuked their un-Christlike and selfish conduct respecting the Lord's Supper, the Apostle now, in the second place, reproved the Corinthians' selfish action in respect to the *"Gifts"* which the Holy Spirit had given them for the profit of all. It seems they selfishly misused both the material and Spiritual Gifts of God.

Selfishness in the physical realm is deplorable but in the spiritual realm it is destructive. The gratification of physical self is degrading; the gratification of religious self is dishonoring. Such is man's heart. He will use even Spiritual Gifts as instruments of personal indulgence, and as a platform for personal importance.

THE HOLY SPIRIT

This Chapter states that there is only One Divine Spirit; that He has a treasury of Gifts; that He gives these Gifts to men; but not all to one man but distributively to many men; that each one is to use his *"Gift"* not for his own gratification or glory but for the profit of the entirety of the Body of Christ, and this because the Christian Assembly is comparable unto the human body, even as Paul will bring out in this Chapter (vss. 12-27).

As, therefore, the members in the body (physical body) mutually aid one another and do not desire selfish isolation and function, so the members of the Body of Christ should recognize their mutual relationship and dependence.

(2) "YE KNOW THAT YE WERE GENTILES, CARRIED AWAY UNTO THESE DUMB IDOLS, EVEN AS YE WERE LED."

The phrase, *"Ye know that ye were Gentiles,"* carries with it all the connotations of acute spiritual ignorance. The word *"Gentiles"* carries with it a history which does not include God, but rather gods of their own making.

GENTILES

The Hebrew word for *"Gentiles"* is *"goyim,"* and refers to all people of every nation, other than Jews. Actually, it was originally a general term for *"nations,"* but acquired a restricted sense by usage.

In the Old Testament the kinship of all nations is stressed in the tradition of Noah's descendants (Gen. Chpt. 10). In God's Covenant with Abraham his descendants are distinguished from other nations, but not in any narrowly exclusive sense (Gen. 12:2; 18:18; 22:18; 26:4).

Israel became conscious of being a nation uniquely distinct from others by being separated to God after the Exodus (Deut. 26:5), and the Covenant of Sinai (Ex. 19:6).

From then on this dedication dominated all her relations with other nations (Ex. 34:10; Lev. 18:24-25; Deut. 15:6).

THE TEMPTATION OF THE ISRAELITES

The Israelites were constantly tempted to compromise with the idolatry and immorality practiced by other nations (I Kings 14:24), so bringing God's judgement on themselves (II Kings 17:7; Ezek. 5:5). On their return from the Exile the danger was still more insidious because of the corruptness of the Jews who had remained in Canaan (Ezra 6:21).

This continual struggle against contamination from their neighbors led to such a hard and exclusive attitude toward other nations that by the time of Christ for a Jew to stigmatize his fellow as *"Gentile"* (Mat. 18:17) was a term of scorn equal in opprobrium to one cursed by God. Consequently, they earn for themselves from Tacitus the censure that *"they regard the rest of mankind with all the hatred of enemies."*

NOTES

THE PLACE OF THE GENTILES

Yet, the Gentiles were assigned a place in Prophecies of the Kingdom, merely as the vanquished who would enhance the Glory of Israel (Isa. 60:5-6), but of that necessary to be understood in its proper context, or as themselves seeking the Lord (Isa. 11:10), and offering worship (Mal. 1:11) when the Messiah should come to be their Light (Isa. 42:6), and to bring Salvation to the ends of the earth (Isa. 49:6).

In this tradition Simeon hailed Baby Jesus (Lk. 2:32), and Jesus began His Ministry (Mat. 12:18-21), and the Jews themselves could question whether He would go to the Gentiles (Jn. 7:35).

Although hesitant and astonished when Cornelius was converted (Acts 10:45; 11:18), the Church slowly accepted the equality of Jew and Gentile before God (Rom. 1:16; Col. 3:11), thus revealing the full scope of the Gospel and its glorious hope for all (Gal. 2:14: Rev. 21:24; 22:2).

The phrase, *"Carried away unto these dumb idols,"* presents these Christians before conversion, being led by superstition, witchcraft, astrology, in other words the powers of darkness, which really cannot say or do anything, at least that is true.

THE GREEKS AND THE ROMANS

The Greeks and Romans believed there were many divine spirits, but they little knew that in reality these were Satanic agents (demon spirits) who were permitted at times to incarnate themselves after a fashion, with the utterances of these afflicted victims accepted by the heathen as divine messages. A perfect case in point is the girl *"possessed with a spirit of divination"* delivered by Paul, and recorded in Acts Chapter 16.

Along with that of which we have just spoken, these *"spirits"* carried the Gentiles away unto the worship of idols, which themselves were dumb — but the demons who energized idolatry were not dumb.

The phrase, *"Even as ye were led,"* means that counsel and advice were sought from these idols concerning almost every decision of life.

MOST OF THE WORLD CONTINUES TO FOLLOW SUIT

Astrology is an excellent case in point (Isa. 47:13).

Many believe that the position of the stars at a person's birth influences his or her life. Consequently, by daily consulting the current position of the stars, believers in astrology expect to find guidance for the decisions they must make and to gain insight into their future.

What does the Bible say about these things?

ABSOLUTELY FORBIDDEN

The Word of God prohibits God's people from looking to any source but the Lord Himself for personal guidance. Deuteronomy Chapter 18 calls all such practices *"detestable"* and says, *"let no one be found among you . . . who practices divination or sorcery, interprets omens, engages in witchcraft, or casts spells, or who is a medium or spiritist or who consults the dead"* (Deut. 18:10-11).

The people of Israel were reminded that God Himself had spoken to them and had pledged to continue to speak through Prophets He would send (Deut. 18:14-20).

THE MANNER IN WHICH BELIEVERS ARE TO BE LED

There are a number of ways through which God is able to lead Believers today. These include the completed Word of God, the indwelling Holy Spirit, the insights of other Christians, circumstances, and the proper use of our renewed minds (Rom. 12:2).

These sources provide all the guidance we need. To turn to astrology or any other such medium, is to insult the Living Lord and to reject the guidance He has provided.

(3) "WHEREFORE I GIVE YOU TO UNDERSTAND, THAT NO MAN SPEAKING BY THE SPIRIT OF GOD CALLETH JESUS ACCURSED: AND THAT NO MAN CAN SAY THAT JESUS IS THE LORD, BUT BY THE HOLY SPIRIT."

The phrase, *"Wherefore I give you to understand,"* has the word *"wherefore"* linking the two facts together.

NOTES

First of all, Paul in essence is saying, *"Because it is true that you were once misled and cheated by your old religion, second, for that very reason I want you to know that in the Christian experience, everything is entirely different — and what a glorious difference it is."*

The phrase, *"That no man speaking by the Spirit of God calleth Jesus accursed,"* in effect tells us three things:

1. If a person is truly Born-Again, the Holy Spirit resides in that person. Consequently, that person will never speak lightly of Jesus, much less curse Him, but rather glorify Him, and more particularly, glorify Him at all times.

2. Some unbelievers were coming into the services at Corinth, who were either demon possessed or greatly influenced by demon spirits. As a result, when the Spirit of God would begin to move in the service, along with the Believers glorifying God and praising Jesus, some of these unbelievers would as well begin to prophesy, etc., but rather *"cursing Jesus."*

All of this being brand-new to the Corinthians, they lacked proper understanding as to what was happening. Consequently, Paul tells them that irrespective as to what these other Corinthians claimed, their cursing Jesus proved they were not of God.

THE ERRONEOUS JESUS DIED SPIRITUALLY DOCTRINE

3. There is an unscriptural heresy floating around the Charismatic world, proclaiming basically that Jesus had a sinful nature, that He supposedly died spiritually and took on the nature of Satan so that He could pay the penalty for our Salvation. They claim that He did this by dying and going to the burning side of Hell, as do all other unbelievers, and was *"Born-Again"* in Hell, consequently, becoming the *"Firstborn of many Brethren."* In effect, they are saying that Jesus is *"accursed."*

There is not a shred of Scriptural Truth in this doctrine, which in fact, strikes at the very heart of the Atonement, which is a serious sin indeed, even blasphemy!

In fact, the battle cries of error and truth have always been, *"Jesus is anathema* (cursed)*,"* or *"Jesus is Lord."* He cannot be both! (In fact, Jesus was cursed by God, *not* as a sinner, but as the penalty for our sins — Gal. 3:13-14.)

The phrase, *"And that no man can say that Jesus is the Lord, but by the Holy Spirit,"* tells us a variety of things:

1. It is the Holy Spirit Who reveals the Lordship of Christ to the Believer. The moment the believing sinner comes to Christ, the Divine Nature is imparted, which is actually the Person and Presence of the Holy Spirit, Who immediately begins to Glorify Christ (Jn. 16:14).

2. Anything and everything that one knows about Christ is revealed by the Holy Spirit. This means that the unsaved have no knowledge of Jesus Christ, at least in a spiritual sense, because it is impossible for the unsaved to have the Holy Spirit (Jn. 14:17).

3. The Baptism with the Holy Spirit, with the evidence of speaking with other tongues is closely associated with the Lordship of Christ. The reason being, that Jesus is the Baptizer with the Holy Spirit (Mat. 3:11).

As the Holy Spirit is allowed to have His way in the heart and life of the new Believer, He always works toward the Lordship of Christ, and as the Lordship becomes pronounced, the new Believer will then begin to hunger and thirst for the infilling of the Holy Spirit, referring to a Baptism of Power (Acts 1:4, 8).

If this *"light"* is rejected, the Lordship of Christ is rejected as well, with the spiritual advancement of the Believer placed on hold.

4. Regrettably, many Believers even after being Baptized with the Holy Spirit, little allow the Spirit of God to continue His work respecting the Lordship of Christ, which then greatly hinders what He then can do.

The Baptism with the Holy Spirit is potential in nature. In other words, the potential is there for all type of great and wonderful things, but is not guaranteed at all. It depends on the co-operation of the Believer with the Holy Spirit.

(4) "NOW THERE ARE DIVERSITIES OF GIFTS, BUT THE SAME SPIRIT."

The phrase, *"Now there are diversities of Gifts,"* obviously refers to differences, i.e., *"different types of Gifts."*

*"Diversities"* in the Greek is *"diairesis,"* it means *"difference, to separate, to distribute."*

DIFFERENT GIFTS

The idea, as held by the Holy Spirit, is to meet the needs of the Body of Christ, of which these nine Gifts address.

NOTES

As we have stated, the idea behind the word *"diversity"* is that of distribution. God does not intend that the Gifts operate through only a few persons. In fact, every Believer should have some manifestation of the Spirit, and there should operate in the Body every variety of Gift, and in fact will, if the Holy Spirit is allowed to have His way.

THE PROMISE GIVEN

It was to be expected that special spiritual enablement would be provided in order that the Church might carry out the Divine Mission committed to her by the Lord Jesus Christ. Jesus instructed His followers to go with the Gospel, but first to wait for enduement with power from on high (Lk. 24:47-49).

With the giving of *"The Great Commission,"* Jesus promised, *"These signs shall follow them that believe"*; such signs as: casting out demons, speaking with new tongues, and recovery of sickness by the laying on of hands. When Jesus announced His return to the Father, He promised His followers that He would send the Comforter Who would abide forever, Who would teach them all things, Who would bring all His sayings to their remembrance, Who would guide into all Truth, Who would convict of sin, righteousness and judgement and Who would testify of Him.

THE PROMISE FULFILLED

Then on the Day of Pentecost, the Promised Holy Spirit was poured out upon the waiting Church with visible and audible signs, and they began to speak in the Tongues predicted in The Great Commission. The Believers were filled with the Holy Spirit (Acts 2:2-4); they were so thoroughly enabled by the Spirit's Power that everywhere their Ministry is marked by the Supernatural.

The Apostles were not mere guardians of orthodoxy; they were Ambassadors of Christ equipped with Divine capabilities. They had a Divine work to do and they had Divine power with which to do it; thus, it must always be.

The Church's Mission is much more than propagating a new philosophy or calling to a new morality; it is delivering men from the Bondage of Satan; it is binding and loosing in the Name of Jesus (Mat. 16:19).

Philosophizing and moralizing can be done with mere human capabilities, and such is not unimportant, but delivering from bondage and bringing to Repentance and Faith, require an Anointing of the Holy Spirit (II Cor. 3:4-6).

Certainly, God accepts and honors all human talent dedicated to His service, but He enhances that dedicated talent with the Spirit's glow lifting it to a new level. God can and often does take natural capacities and transform them into spiritual operations (Ex. 35:29-35; Rom. 15:13-14; II Tim. 2:2; Titus 1:7-9).

The phrase, *"But the same Spirit,"* refers, of course, to the Holy Spirit. Notice the functions of the Trinity in Verses 4-6. As Paul did in another Epistle (Eph. 4:4-6), when he wanted to describe perfect unity he illustrated it with the Trinity.

Although they are three distinct Persons in One Divine Nature, They never disagree even though each One fulfills a different function in the Godhead (Rossier).

The two words *"same Spirit,"* were used by Paul for a purpose. Even though there are different Gifts, different Administrations, and different Operations, still, the Holy Spirit never contradicts Himself. If functioning properly, all the parts fit beautifully, making the whole.

## AN EXAMPLE

I will attempt to illustrate this by referring to what the Holy Spirit will not do, i.e. *"No contradiction of Himself,"* inasmuch as we have already noted that which He will do, i.e., *"The Godhead will never disagree."*

Years ago I was conducting a Meeting in a particular Church, in which the Lord helped us to see a great Moving and Operation of the Holy Spirit. Many people were saved and Baptized with the Holy Spirit. Even though what I am about to relate happened many times through the years, this one situation will serve, I think, as an excellent example.

## THE MOVING OF THE HOLY SPIRIT

If I remember correctly it was a Friday night. The building was packed to capacity, and the Lord anointed me greatly that night to preach the Gospel.

As I began to give the Altar Call, the convicting power of the Holy Spirit was there as well in a great way, with sinners being moved upon strongly to come to Christ.

NOTES

Right in the midst of the appeal for souls, and as stated, as the Lord was moving greatly, a lady burst out in Tongues very loudly.

Even though at times the Lord will move in an Altar Call relative to an utterance in Tongues with Interpretation, most of the time He won't. If He does, it will be obvious to all that it is the right thing, and will greatly help the service or whatever is taking place at the moment.

This lady was out of order, which was instantly obvious. After a few moments I very patiently requested that she stop, but if anything, she got louder.

The situation went from bad to worse, with me finally having to tell her if she did not stop, that I would have to have the ushers to remove her. Regrettably, by this time, the true Spirit of God had been so hindered, that the Altar Call for all practical purposes was ruined, exactly what Satan wanted.

## HE WILL NOT CONTRADICT HIMSELF

The Holy Spirit was anointing me to give this Altar Call, and doing so in a tremendous manner. Sinners were responding, and in that particular context, the Lord would not contradict himself in causing someone else to do something which would draw attention away from what was happening. As stated, the Holy Spirit does not do things in this manner, He does not contradict Himself.

Was this woman of the Devil?

She was not of the Devil, but she definitely was being used by the Devil. Actually, after the service I happened to see her in the lobby of the Church, and she was extremely indignant. I tried to patiently deal with her, and finally she blurted out, that she could not help herself, she had to do what she did.

Of course, that within itself is the tipoff, for *"the spirits of the Prophets are subject to the Prophets. For God is not the author of confusion,"* (I Cor. 14:32-33).

In other words, any time anyone claims that the Spirit of God is forcing them to do a certain thing, it is always wrong. While the Spirit may move, impress, stir, plead, etc., He will never force.

So, if it is the Holy Spirit Who is the author of these things, He will never contradict Himself, will never work at cross-purposes, but rather, all things will flow in perfect harmony. It is the *"same Spirit."*

This dear lady probably did what many have done. The Spirit of God was moving greatly in the service, in both convicting power upon the unsaved, and anointing me to give the Altar Call. Of course, every Saint of God in the building could sense and feel the Moving and Operation of the Holy Spirit. Unfortunately, during these times, some people, not being led by the Spirit but rather by self, think they have to respond to what they feel in some fashion, even as this lady. No! In most cases, and with few exceptions, the Believer feeling and sensing the Moving and Operation of the Holy Spirit, just means that He is working in the service, not necessarily that they should do something, etc.

There are places and times for utterances of Tongues and Interpretation, along with Prophesy, which we will study with great detail when we come to the 14th Chapter.

(5) "AND THERE ARE DIFFERENCES OF ADMINISTRATIONS, BUT THE SAME LORD."

The phrase, *"And there are differences of Administrations,"* places Christ as we shall see, in the position of deciding which Ministries go to which individuals.

It is important to notice the distinction between the gracious bestowments (Gifts) and the Ministries. The Holy Spirit is the One Who manifests Himself through individuals at various times and in miraculous ways, but He does so only under the auspices of The Lord Jesus Christ, Who is the Head of the Church.

Jesus is not only the Baptizer with the Holy Spirit (Mat. 3:11), but He is also the Possessor of the Anointing of the Holy Spirit (Lk. 4:18). As the Represented Man, He has the Holy Spirit beyond or above measure (Jn. 3:34). In this capacity, He is the One Who administers.

*"Administrations,"* in the Greek is *"diakonion,"* which means *"services, ministries, offices."* As stated, He is the One Who says who is to receive what Gift, with the Holy Spirit then carrying out in the life of the Believer that which is designated by the Lord.

The phrase, *"But the same Lord,"* pertains to Christ being in charge of all Administrations, and if so, there will never be contradictions or interruptions. Things become confused, only when Christ is not allowed His proper place, and the Holy Spirit His proper place.

NOTES

(6) "AND THERE ARE DIVERSITIES OF OPERATIONS, BUT IT IS THE SAME GOD WHICH WORKETH ALL IN ALL."

The phrase, *"And there are diversities of operations,"* refers to everything that is carried out, and that there are many different ways of this being done.

*"Operations"* in the Greek is *"energema,"* and means *"to be active, efficient, mighty in, show forth self, work effectually in, working."*

The phrase, *"But it is the same God which worketh all in all,"* has reference to the fact of God the Father Who energizes all things in all ways.

As is obvious in Verses 4-6, Paul refers to the three persons of the Godhead, but names the Persons in inverse order. He does this because he begins with the end result, which is the only way basically that the Believer can understand that of which the Lord does. It is the manner in which He carries out His work within our own personal hearts and lives.

In understanding the function of the Godhead, even though each One has particular tasks to perform, still all Three of the Persons are involved in all three of the relations. This is a necessity due to the unity and indivisibility of the Godhead.

(7) "BUT THE MANIFESTATION OF THE SPIRIT IS GIVEN TO EVERY MAN TO PROFIT WITHAL."

The phrase, *"But the manifestation of the Spirit,"* pertains to what the Gifts make manifest or reveal.

*"Manifestation"* in the Greek is *"phanerosis,"* which means *"to make visible."* If one truly has a Gift from the Lord, in some way that gift will be visibly manifested. In other words, what the Spirit does regarding these Gifts, will be obvious to all.

From this statement, some have concluded that Believers do not actually receive the Gifts, but rather the manifestation of the Gifts. However, that is not the idea of the Text. The idea is that these Gifts will manifest themselves regarding that which they are. If *"Healing,"* then people will be healed, etc.

The phrase, *"Is given to every man to profit withal,"* tells us several things:

1. Each Believer has his Gift, and every bestowal of a Gift is for the common good. *"To*

*each one"* or *"To every man"* singles out each person as an individual, and yet *"To each one"* also includes everyone, omitting none.

2. There is great *"spiritual profit"* and, in effect, profit in every way, when the Spirit of God begins to move and work in the midst of the Body of Christ. Of course, this is predicated on the Spirit being the Author and not self-will, i.e. *"the flesh."*

3. The Holy Spirit is no respecter of persons. His Gifts are available to all Believers, with the admonition given that we should *"desire Spiritual Gifts"* (I Cor. 14:1).

(8-10) "FOR TO ONE IS GIVEN BY THE SPIRIT THE WORD OF WISDOM; TO ANOTHER THE WORD OF KNOWLEDGE BY THE SAME SPIRIT;

"TO ANOTHER FAITH BY THE SAME SPIRIT; TO ANOTHER THE GIFTS OF HEALING BY THE SAME SPIRIT;

"TO ANOTHER THE WORKING OF MIRACLES; TO ANOTHER PROPHECY; TO ANOTHER DISCERNING OF SPIRITS; TO ANOTHER DIVERS KINDS OF TONGUES; TO ANOTHER THE INTERPRETATION OF TONGUES:"

The phrase, *"For to one is given by the Spirit,"* proclaims the Holy Spirit as being the One Who carries out the instructions of Christ relative to who gets what.

Man cannot bestow these gifts on other men, that alone being the prerogative of Christ through the Holy Spirit, with God the Father over all. Men can be taught by other men many things about the Gifts; however, the actual bestowal of the Gifts is never the prerogative of man, but always *"by the Spirit."*

## THE WORD OF WISDOM

By the Holy Spirit using the word *"one"* we learn that not all Believers have *"the Word of Wisdom,"* but only those whom the Lord selects. As well, the word *"one"* does not mean that only one person in the Church can have this Gift, but simply that it is given only to some.

First of all, let's see what this Gift is not.

It is *not* the Gift of Wisdom or the Gift of Knowledge, etc. That terminology is not correct. We must call them what the Bible calls them or we will become confused.

This Scripture is not talking about wisdom or knowledge in the general sense. The Holy Spirit is addressing Himself to just what it says — the Word of Wisdom and the Word of Knowledge.

NOTES

God has all knowledge. He knows everything, but He never reveals to anybody everything that He knows. He just gives them a word of what He knows. A word is just a fragmentary part of the whole. So, it is not the gift of wisdom, it is the *"Word of Wisdom."*

As well, the Word of Wisdom is not the benefit of many years of experience which older people have. Neither is it the ability to be able to apply knowledge, which some claim.

The Word of Wisdom is a Supernatural Revelation by the Spirit of God concerning the Divine Purpose in the Mind and Will of God. *It is a Revelation regarding the Plan and the Purpose in the Mind of God, concerning futuristic events.*

The difference between the two Gifts — the Word of Knowledge and the Word of Wisdom — is that the Revelation that the Word of Knowledge brings is always present tense or something that has happened in the past, whereas the Word of Wisdom always speaks of the future.

We divide these two Gifts and deal with them singularly; however, very often they operate together. For instance, when the Lord spoke to John on the Isle of Patmos, it was in the form of a vision. Jesus appeared to him and told him about the present condition of the seven Churches in Asia Minor. That was a manifestation of the Word of Knowledge. The present condition of those Churches was revealed to John.

Then the Lord went on to give him a Word of Wisdom. He told each one of the Churches what to do in the future, according to His plan and purpose for them.

## THE OLD TESTAMENT

We see these Gifts in operation all through the Old Testament. The Prophet particularly had these Gifts in operation as well as Prophecy in his life. He had to have them to be able to stand in the Office of the Prophet because he made predictions concerning the future and the simple Gift of Prophecy has no prediction in it. The prediction that he gave, even though it came by prophecy, was actually a Word of Wisdom. For example, we ride in an automobile, but we are not an automobile. Sometimes a Word of Wisdom is conveyed by Prophecy, but it really isn't Prophecy. It is a Word of Wisdom. The simple gift of Prophecy is, as Paul said in I Corinthians 14:3, *"He that prophesieth speaketh unto men to edification, exhortation, and comfort."* In the simple gift of Prophecy there is no prediction whatsoever.

In the Old Testament, Joseph received a Word of Wisdom through a dream which revealed to him God's Plan and Purpose for the future regarding his life. Of course, there are countless other examples as well.

Also, the Word of Wisdom can also come with Tongues and Interpretation. In fact, when any Revelation comes, it is always a Word of Wisdom, a Word of Knowledge, or discerning of spirits, because these are the only three Revelation Gifts.

## JAMES

In writing to the Church, James said that if any lack Wisdom, let him ask. . . . Yet Paul said in the verses of our text, *"To one is given the Word of Wisdom,"* to *one,* not to all. This infers that not everyone is going to have these manifestations. And he concludes by saying that it is only as the Spirit wills.

The Wisdom that James is addressing is the wisdom to deal wisely in the affairs of life, wisdom to know how to conduct oneself as a Christian. The Wisdom of which James spoke is not *"the Word of Wisdom,"* which is one of the nine Gifts of the Spirit. So, we must not confuse the two.

## A PERSONAL EXAMPLE

The Lord saved me and baptized me with the Holy Spirit when I was eight years old. That was in 1943.

Almost immediately, it being the summer months and not being in school, we began to have prayer meetings every day.

When the next summer came about (1944), again not being in school, we began the prayer meetings as we had done the year before. They were always conducted at our Church, or else at my Grandmother's house, or the house of my Aunt.

In these prayer meetings, the Lord would move mightily at times, with me on certain occasions actually going into a trance. When I would come out from under this type of thing, I would think that only a few minutes had passed, when at times it had been several hours.

NOTES

In the summer of 1944, the Lord began to speak through me, actually in both a Word of Knowledge and a Word of Wisdom. It concerned the Atomic Bomb. Of course, only a handful of people in the world in 1944 knew of this coming invention. Even at that time, a group of Scientists were working on this project in Manhattan, New York, and in Alamogordo, New Mexico. In fact, it was an extremely, closely guarded secret. The following is what the Lord said through me. I will not give the exact words, but as close as I can according to my memory.

*"A Bomb is being perfected at this time, that will be so powerful that the explosion of just one of these instruments will destroy an entire city. Tens of thousands will die in a moments time."*

Of course, this prophecy or Word of Wisdom was much more involved and actually continued for several days.

As a nine year old child, I had absolutely no knowledge of such an invention, and to be sure, most of the world knew nothing of such either. But yet the Holy Spirit did, and revealed it to me a year before it was actually dropped on two cities in Japan, ending World War II.

## WHY WOULD THE LORD DO THIS IN THIS MANNER?

I actually do not have the answer to that. As to why the Lord would give such information to a nine year old child, in a little obscure town in Louisiana, seems to have no rhyme or reason. But yet, the Lord does things in this manner quite often. Jesus said, *"I thank Thee, O Father, Lord of heaven and earth, that Thou hast hid these things from the wise and prudent, and hast revealed them unto babes: even so, Father; for so it seemed good in Thy sight"* (Lk. 10:21).

As we have stated, this was both a Word of Knowledge and a Word of Wisdom. The Bomb was under development at that particular time, which constituted the Word of Knowledge, and would be used in the near future, which was a Word of Wisdom.

## TO ANOTHER THE WORD OF KNOWLEDGE

God is all knowledge — He knows everything. But as we stated concerning *"the Word of Wisdom,"* the same applies to *"the Word of Knowledge."* The Lord just gives a word or a part of what He knows. A word is a fragmentary part of a sentence, so a *"Word of Knowledge"* would simply be a fragmentary part of knowledge.

The *"Word of Knowledge"* is a Supernatural Manifestation as are all of these Gifts. None of them are natural gifts, they are all supernatural Gifts. Consequently, this Gift does not refer to natural knowledge. Neither does it refer to education received in school or colleges, etc. *The Word of Knowledge is a Revelation regarding the Plan and Purpose in the Mind of God, concerning present or past events.*

Confusing this Gift with natural knowledge someone said, *"We don't need some of these lesser Gifts. We have the Gift of Knowledge,"* and the knowledge they were bragging about was intellectual knowledge, something they had gained themselves apart from the Holy Spirit and from the Word of God. This is not what this is talking about at all. In fact, there is no such thing as a gift of knowledge. There is the Gift of *"the Word of Knowledge."*

ANANIAS

The Bible is full of these examples. When Ananias went to pray for Paul as recorded in the Ninth Chapter of Acts, the Lord had already given him *"the Word of Knowledge"* concerning who Paul was and what Ananias should do regarding him. This was given through a vision. Actually, there is no proof that Ananias was either a Pastor or Evangelist, or a Minister at all. He wasn't even listed as being a Teacher. The Bible calls him a Disciple, which means he was a follower of Christ, and which also means that any Believer can have these Gifts, not just Preachers, etc.

Also, *"the Word of Knowledge"* may come through Tongues and Interpretation, or through the Gift of Prophecy or an Angel might come to deliver a *"Word of Knowledge."* God has many ways of doing things.

Also, this Gift of *"the Word of Knowledge"* is sometimes confused with a profound knowledge of the Bible. Some Preachers think they have *"the Word of Knowledge"* because they have studied the Bible very much.

While it is certainly true that God will help us to understand His Word, still that is not a Supernatural Gift. While this Gift of *"the Word of Knowledge"* does work in connection with the Bible, still knowledge of the Bible is not *"the Word of Knowledge."*

NOTES

Were that so, then we would not have to study the Word of God as we are admonished to do, even as Paul told Timothy.

As well, some have the mistaken idea that this Gift of *"the Word of Knowledge"* is the very real knowledge that comes by walking with God. However, even though one does gain a real knowledge of God by walking with Him and studying His Word, still that is something altogether different, than Supernatural Knowledge.

EXAMPLES

Even though there are scores of examples, the occasion of Jesus ministering to the woman at Jacob's Well portrays exactly that of which we mean.

When Jesus mentioned her husband, she said that she didn't have a husband. He said, in essence, *"You are right about that. You have had five husbands, and the man you are living with now isn't your husband."* Jesus knew this by an inward Revelation — a Word of Knowledge — and used this Gift to point her to Salvation.

It was in 1987. Two Baptists Preachers had been put in jail in the State of Nebraska because it was claimed they had violated some type of law respecting their Private Christian School. I don't remember the details at present, but I know they had been in jail for some weeks.

Along with two other Preachers, with whom I was little acquainted, and who weren't Pentecostal, I was called to Washington to meet with the Cabinet of President Reagan concerning this issue. In my mind I wondered why they had sent for me, or any of us Preachers for that matter. I wondered what we could do. I was to find out.

After arriving in Washington, I made my way to the Old Executive Office Building where this meeting was to be held along with the other two Preachers. Just before going into the meeting, Senator Orrin Hatch pulled me aside in a friendly fashion, and gave me some advice regarding this meeting, etc. He was a friend and I appreciated his kindness.

At the appointed time, we were ushered into a long meeting room with a long table in the middle surrounded by chairs. I was told where to sit with the other two Preachers at my left. To my right was Ed Meece, the Attorney

General of the United States. Across from me was Jim Baker, the Secretary of State. At the end of the table to my right was James McFarland, the Security Advisor to the President. Every other seat was filled with lawyers, with lawyers actually standing shoulder to shoulder all around the room, there to observe I suppose.

If I remember correctly, Mr. Baker spoke first, stating that the Administration would do anything within its power to get these Preachers out of jail, but would not do anything that was illegal or that which would embarrass the President.

William Ball, a noted Constitutional lawyer, who had argued several cases before the Supreme Court of the United States, spoke at length about the legalities of the situation. Also, I think the other two Preachers made some statement or the other, of which I cannot now recall. I said nothing!

THEN THE HOLY SPIRIT SPOKE

At a given point, Attorney General Meece spoke up in a very kind voice, once again reiterating the wishes of the President that something could be done to alleviate this situation, but seemingly they had not as yet found a way to effect the release of these Preachers.

While he was talking, all of a sudden the Spirit of God began to speak to me, giving me a *"Word of Knowledge"* concerning the situation. I knew it was the Lord, of that I had no doubt. Mr. Meece talked for four or five minutes I suppose, and when he came to the end of his statement, he then said, *"If anyone here knows anything we can do, we will do our best, whatever it may be, providing it does not embarrass the President."*

When he paused, the Spirit of God spoke to my heart and said, *"Now is the time, give them what I have just given to you."*

The room grew silent. I cleared my throat, and then began to speak. To be honest, there was fear in my heart. I found myself telling this room full of lawyers, plus a great part of the Cabinet of the President of the United States, how this thing should be done.

THE *"WORD"*

*"Isn't the President going to make a speech tonight which will be aired over the entirety of the nation?"*, I asked! *"Yes, he is,"* Mr. Baker said.

NOTES

*"Why not have the President mention the plight of these two Preachers in his speech, which will draw attention to the situation over the entirety of the nation, and will probably have the effect of bringing public opinion to bear upon those officials in Nebraska, who will then be shamed into releasing these men from Jail."*

That's what the Holy Spirit had told me to say. It was a *"Word of Knowledge."*

The room grew deathly quiet. All of a sudden, William Ball, at the end of the long table, jumped up, slammed his hand down on the table saying, *"Why didn't I think of that? Of course, it will work!"*, he exclaimed.

About that time, James McFarland spoke up, saying, *"I'm the one writing the speech for the President, and I know exactly how to insert this information."*

That night, the President made his speech to the nation. In the body of his address, he mentioned the plight of the two Baptist Preachers in Nebraska (or whatever State they were in), and what a shame it was that they were being held in jail all this time for trying to obey the Word of God and their conscience.

The next morning, the two Preachers were released from jail.

Looking back, it all seemed so simple. In fact, it was simple. But yet, not a single person in that room had thought about doing this, and neither did I. It was the Holy Spirit Who gave this *"Word of Knowledge"* to me, which was able to bring about the necessary results.

To be frank, I could give example after example in my own personal life and Ministry, but that which we have just given will suffice.

TO ANOTHER FAITH BY THE SAME SPIRIT

The Gift of *"Faith"* is supernaturally imparted to the Believer, enabling him (or her) to believe God for great things. This Gift will accompany a particular burden or call that the Lord has placed on a person's life, whether Layperson or Preacher. *It is "Great Faith," or "Special Faith," for a special thing, which is far and away beyond regular Faith of which we will speak momentarily.*

AN EXAMPLE

God called me for World Evangelism when I was a nine year old child. Of course, my understanding at that time was limited, but still, even from that moment I have had a general idea as to what my Ministry would be and what it would do. So, whenever the Lord helped us respecting Television, and giant Citywide Crusades in certain parts of the world, with literally tens of thousands responding to an invitation to accept Christ, this was not a surprise to me. In my spirit I had known it all along.

However, with this Call, the Lord gave me a *"Special Faith,"* or in other words, *"the Gift of Faith,"* enabling me to believe that I would be able to reach a great part of this world with the Gospel.

Countless times, I have had other Preachers to ridicule me about this very thing, insinuating that it was impossible to believe God for the entirety of the world, or at least reaching them with the Gospel. However, what seemed impossible to them, and in fact was impossible, was not impossible at all to me. I believed it for the simple reason that God had called me for this purpose and had given me the *"Faith"* to believe for this, despite the fact that it was of such magnitude.

As a result, the Lord has helped us to see hundreds of thousands of people brought to a saving knowledge of Jesus Christ. He has helped us to see tens of thousands Baptized with the Holy Spirit. He has helped us to see untold thousands delivered by the mighty Power of God from the worst types of bondage with which Satan imprisons people. Without this *"Special Faith,"* it would not have been possible for these things to have been brought about.

## DIFFERENT KINDS OF FAITH

There is such a thing as saving Faith, which is also a Gift, but not this Gift of the Spirit in question. Ephesians 2:8 says, *"For by Grace are ye saved through Faith; and that not of yourselves: it is the Gift of God."* However, as stated, even though this Faith is a Gift, it is not the Gift of the Spirit.

Also, there is the *"Fruit of the Spirit"* which is *"Faith,"* or rather *"Faithfulness,"* but which is not the *"Gift of Faith."*

Fruit is something that grows in the life of a Christian to establish him in spiritual character. But that is not the *"Gift of Faith."*

Thus, we learn that there are different kinds of Faith. Saving Faith comes before Salvation, Faith — or Faithfulness — the Fruit of the Spirit comes after Salvation. However, this manifestation of the Gift of Faith comes after the Baptism with the Holy Spirit (Acts Chpt. 2).

NOTES

## IS THE BAPTISM WITH THE HOLY SPIRIT NECESSARY FOR THESE GIFTS TO BE IMPARTED?

Yes, it is!

Without the Baptism with the Holy Spirit, which will always be received with the evidence of speaking with other Tongues (Acts 2:4), the Holy Spirit has little latitude in the Believer's life, although present. It is this Baptism which endues the Believer with Power from on High (Acts 1:8). Only then can these Gifts be given by the Spirit and manifested. That's at least one of the reasons that Jesus *"Commanded* (not suggested) *them* (His followers) *that they should not depart from Jerusalem, but wait* (for the Day of Pentecost) *for the Promise of the Father* (the Holy Spirit), *which saith He, Ye have heard of Me.*

*"For John truly baptized with water; but ye shall be baptized with the Holy Spirit not many days hence"* (Acts 1:4-5).

To be frank, without the Baptism with the Holy Spirit, there can be very little activity of the Spirit of any nature in the heart and life of the Believer. It is this experience which is subsequent to Salvation, which makes all the Attributes and Special Graces of the Holy Spirit possible.

And yet, the residence of the Holy Spirit is potential in nature, which means that Spirit-filled Believers have the potential for all of these things, although in fact, they may not have many of them or any of them, for that matter. The Holy Spirit never works apart from our cooperation. We must give Him the latitude and control in our lives, which He must have if He is to carry out His Work as He is instructed by the Father and the Son to do. We must never forget that He is in our hearts and lives to bring about the Will of God, and not our will.

As well, the Bible is full of examples of astounding things done which are a result of the *"Gift of Faith."* I speak of the Jericho Walls tumbling, and the fire losing its effect on the Hebrew children. I speak of Peter and Paul raising the dead, plus performing other outstanding miracles, which required this *"Gift of Faith."*

Incidentally, Old Testament Prophets had all nine Gifts of the Spirit, with the exception of *"Tongues"* and *"Interpretation of Tongues,"* which had not yet been given, although predicted (Isa. Chpt. 28; Joel Chpt. 2). (In that Dispensation, the Old Covenant, these Gifts were resident in only a few such Prophets, in other words, they were not available to all as now. This Dispensation of the Holy Spirit has changed all that, making the Gifts available to all Spirit-filled Believers.)

TO ANOTHER THE GIFTS OF HEALINGS BY THE SAME SPIRIT

*"Healing"* in the Greek is *"iama,"* and means *"a cure, make whole."* Incidentally, *"Healing"* is actually plural in the Greek text and should have been translated *"Healings"* or *"Gifts of Healings."*

*The "Gifts of Healings" are the Supernatural Healings of diseases and infirmities, without natural means of any source.* As we have stated several times, every one of these nine Gifts of the Spirit is supernatural. This means that this Gift has nothing to do with medical science or human learning, as helpful as those things may be in their own ways.

Luke, who was a Doctor, was with Paul on many of his Missionary journeys. He wrote the Acts of the Apostles as well as the Book that bears his name. He was with Paul when he was shipwrecked and they were on the Island of Malita.

Nothing is said at all to the effect that Luke ministered to the people with his medical knowledge, but the father-in-law of the chief man of the Island was sick and Paul entered in and laid his hands on him and he was healed. He was healed by Supernatural Power, and not by any efforts that Luke as a Doctor made.

Then they brought the sick from all over the Island, with Paul ministering to them, with many others being healed as well.

At the same time, we believe in Medical Science and thank God for what it can do. We are certainly not opposed to Doctors, Nurses, Hospitals, or medicine; however, we must not confuse Medical Science with the Gifts of Healings.

In fact, it is believed by many Preachers that the Gifts of Healings is that God has given Doctors and Medical Science to the world; however, that is Scripturally incorrect. If we follow that supposition, we would also have to say that God saves through Colleges. However, we know that is far from the Truth.

NOTES

As stated, I thank God for Doctors and Medical Science. As well, I thank God for medicine, and pray that Scientists in these fields of endeavor will be ever successful in developing antibiotics or different medicines which address many physical problems.

In fact, it is not wrong for a person to go to a Hospital, that is if such is necessary. The Lord has healed countless people in Hospitals, while they were under the care of Physicians. If it was wrong to take medicine, or to be in Hospitals, or to be under the care of Physicians, that is if such is needed, then it would be wrong for the Lord to heal anybody in these particular situations. It is not wrong, and to be frank, very seldom even shows a lack of Faith.

EXAMPLES

The Bible is full of healing of the sick in answer to prayer, and especially in the Ministry of Christ. The Early Church, as recorded in the Book of Acts, also experienced many and mighty healings.

The first recorded healing in Scripture is that of Abraham praying for Abimelech, and the Bible said, *"God healed Abimelech, and his wife, and his maidservants; and they bare children"* (Gen. 20:17).

When I was about 10 years old, the Lord beautifully and wondrously healed me in answer to Believing Prayer.

I do not actually know what the physical problem was, even though my parents took me to several Doctors, with them running all types of tests, but to no avail. They simply could not find what was wrong, even though I was losing weight steadily, and staying nauseated constantly.

In fact, at times I would go unconscious, which happened several times at School, with the School Principal telling my parents that if something was not done they would have to remove me from School. *"We don't want him dying on our hands"* was the answer and reason they gave.

In looking back, I know that Satan was trying to destroy me physically so that I would not be able to carry out the Work which God had called me to do.

NOTES

## HEALING CAME IMMEDIATELY, BUT ONLY AFTER BEING PRAYED FOR MANY TIMES

The time of my healing was an early Sunday Afternoon, actually about 1:00 p.m.

My Parents were taking the Pastor and his wife out to lunch after Service, and of course, I and my baby Sister were in the group. Before the meal, the Pastor stated that he had to go by the home of one of the Church Members, and pray for him due to the fact that he had been sick.

The scene, at least in parts, is indelibly imprinted upon my mind. I can see the small house and I faintly remember us praying for the Brother who was in bed. We then walked back to the front room, and were standing there all together, talking for a few moments. My Dad turned to our Pastor who was standing in the middle of the room with a bottle of oil in his hands, which he had just used in praying for the Brother in question.

I remember Dad saying to him, *"Brother Culbreth, anoint Jimmy with oil and let's pray for him."* He then went on to say, *"If the Lord does not heal him, we are going to have to take him out of School."*

I remember the Pastor smiling and walking toward me. He placed his finger over the end of the small bottle containing the oil and then touched my head in prayer. I don't remember what he said, but I do know, in a moments time, the Power of God hit that room. It went all through me just like hot oil. In fact, it was actually a hot sensation that went from the crown of my head to the sole of my feet, all the way through my body. I knew I was healed! I knew that I would never have any more trouble with that problem, whatever it was.

And that's exactly the way it was. From then until now, at the time of this writing, a period of over half a century, I have not suffered any lasting or sickness of this nature or any type from then until now. As Jeremiah the Prophet said, *"Heal me, O Lord, and I shall be healed; save me, and I shall be saved: for Thou art my Praise"* (Jer. 17:14). As stated, the Word of God is full of such (Num. 12:13; Deut. 32:39; II Kings 20:5, 8; Ps. 6:2; Isa. 19:22; 57:18-19; Jer. 30:17; Hos. 6:1; Mat. 8:7; 10:1, 8; 12:10; Mk. 3:2, 15; Lk. 4:18; 5:17; 7:3; 9:2; 10:9; Jn. 4:47; Acts 4:30).

## WHY DID THE LORD NOT HEAL ME THE FIRST TIME PRAYER WAS OFFERED?

The Truth is that the same Pastor, plus others, had prayed for me many times before this day of my Healing. He had anointed me with oil in the same manner all the previous times, and had believed God, but Healing did not come until the day in question.

Why?

That is a question I cannot answer, and I really don't think anyone else can either.

However, this I do know. God does all things well, and He has a purpose for everything He does. Sometimes that purpose pertains to us and sometimes it doesn't, but, nevertheless, all is for our good.

Quite possibly, the Lord does things in this way at times in order to test our Faith. Will we keep believing, or will we give up after the first time or two. True Faith will not quit. As well, Faith must always be tested, and Great Faith must be tested greatly.

## DID THIS PASTOR HAVE THE GIFTS OF HEALINGS?

No, I don't think he did! But yet people at times were healed just as I was. So, even though the results will be far greater for those who have the *"Gifts of Healings,"* still we are plainly told in the Word of God that *"These signs shall follow them that believe; . . . they shall lay hands on the sick, and they shall recover"* (Mk. 16:17, 18). So, any Believer can pray for the sick.

Someone has said that anytime one receives healing, it is the Gifts of Healings in operation. Actually, it is a Gift, as in one sense of the word, anything we receive from the Lord is a Gift generally speaking; but that wouldn't necessarily be this Gift in manifestation.

Everyone has the right to pray for the sick, that is if they are a Believer, even as we have already addressed, but Paul plainly tells us that not all have the *"Gifts of Healings,"* by him using the word *"another."*

Any person, be they Preacher or otherwise, who has the *"Gifts of Healings,"* will have far greater success in seeing people healed in the Name of Jesus than those who do not have this Gift, even though they, too, will see some healings.

As well, we may wonder why the word *"Gifts"* is in the plural, as well as *"Healings."*

In fact, the Scripture does not tell us as to why it is phrased in this way, but we do know there is a reason or the Holy Spirit would not have impressed Paul to label this Gift in this manner.

Kenneth Hagin has said, and I agree with him, *"I think there are Gifts of Healings because there are different kinds of diseases and one Gift wouldn't heal all kinds of different diseases."*

He went on to talk about certain Preachers seeing certain kinds of diseases healed in their ministry, with not too much success regarding other kinds.

Why?

I don't think anyone really has the answer, but this we do know: in the Ministry of Jesus, every manner of sickness and every manner of disease were healed because all the Gifts of Healings were in manifestation because He had the Spirit without measure.

Gifts of Healings are manifested through another to you. All healing is done by God, of course, but the difference is in the Channel.

## TO ANOTHER THE WORKING OF MIRACLES

*A "Miracle" is an intervention in the ordinary course of nature.* This of course, as all the other Gifts, is Supernatural.

In the realm of healing, many times *"Miracles"* are received, but they are not necessarily Working of Miracles, they are healing miracles. Everything that God does is miraculous in a sense, but it is not like turning common dust into insects just by a gesture, as happened in Egypt, or common water into wine just by speaking a word — that is the *"Working of Miracles."*

For instance, a conversion, being Born-Again, can be called a miracle because it is a supernatural act in the spiritual realm. However, in the true sense of the word, at least according to the standards of which we speak, that would not be labeled a miracle anymore than would a human birth. What we do call a Miracle is a supernatural act on a natural plane. Therefore, the New Birth is not a supernatural act on a natural plane at all, it is a supernatural act in the spiritual realm.

For instance, water turned into wine by the process of nature is a natural miracle. But water turned into wine just by speaking a Word, as Jesus did in John 2:1-11, is the meaning of the spiritual gift of the *"Working of Miracles."*

NOTES

To say it in greater detail, *"A Miracle, therefore, is a Supernatural intervention in the ordinary course of nature, a temporary suspension of the accustomed order, an interruption of the system of nature as we know it, operated by the force of the Spirit"* (Hagin).

Actually, the Working of Miracles was more prominent, or more in operation, in the Old Testament than in the New Testament, other than in the Ministry of Christ. Conversely, although people were healed and Gifts of Healings were in operation in the Old Testament, Gifts of Healings were more in operation in the New Testament than they were in the Old.

In fact, when the Red Sea was opened, two Gifts of the Spirit were in operation. The *"Working of Miracles"* divided the Sea, but what kept it divided? It took the Gift of Faith to do that. That was a continuing miracle. The people walked over dry-shod to the other side. The enemy attempted to do the same, but the waters came together and they were drowned in the depths of the Sea.

The difference between the Gift of Faith and the *"Working of Miracles"* is that the Gift of Faith *receives* a Miracle and the *"Working of Miracles" works* a Miracle.

## GOD'S POWER

The *"Working of Miracles"* is used to display God's power and magnificence. In Young's Concordance, the Greek word used here is called *"powers."* In other words, the *"Working of Miracles"* is called the *"Working of Powers."* It means, *"the explosions of Almightiness," "impelling, staggering wonders and astonishment."* The Greek could read, *"The working of impelling, staggering wonders or astonishments or the outworkings of explosions of Almightiness."*

## A PERSONAL EXAMPLE

Of that which I am about to relate, I am not sure if it could be labeled as a *"Miracle"* or not! I would have to leave that to the Lord. However, I personally believe that which was done was an intervention by the Lord into the ordinary course of nature.

We were in Winter Haven, Florida, for a Citywide Crusade which was conducted in an outdoor baseball stadium. It was not overly large, I suppose, seating several thousands of people at best.

On the Saturday of the Meeting, weather reports were coming in all day of a storm that was heading toward Winter Haven. Of course, I was constantly seeking the Lord all that day, that such would be averted, knowing that it would destroy the Service if in fact it did come as predicted.

When we began Service that night, the clouds were heavy over the city, with reports that this storm would hit at the very time we would be having Service. I suppose we were thirty minutes into the Service, when a State Trooper arrived and informed some of my Associates that we might best dismiss the people and cover our equipment because a veritable flood of rain was heading our way, and would arrive very shortly.

I deeply appreciated the kindness of this man, and did not take his suggestion lightly. Actually, I went before the people, told them what he had said, and that anyone who desired to leave could feel free to do so. However, I added, *"We are going to continue with the Service, and right now we're going to pray together, believing God that this storm will bypass Winter Haven, or at least this Stadium."*

That we did!

To carry on a Crusade of this nature requires a tremendous amount of equipment: Organ, Piano, all the Sound Equipment, etc. In other words, there was probably close to $100,000 worth of equipment exposed to the elements, which could be seriously damaged in the event of a rainstorm.

However, I felt that the Lord had told me to continue with the Service, and this is what we did.

## WHAT HAPPENED?

We found out after the Service that this rainstorm had come right up to Winter Haven, and then seemingly divided with one half going around one side of the city, with the other half around the other side, leaving the major part of the city dry, as well as the Stadium where we were conducting the meeting.

Now some may say that this would have happened in any case. Perhaps so! However, I personally believe the Lord heard our prayer, rewarded our Faith, and that what actually took place was caused by a direct intervention by the Lord. In other words, I believe that it was a Miracle.

NOTES

I could give illustrations of quite a number of incidents such as this, which took place through the years in our efforts for the Cause of Christ, which I think constituted *"Miracles."*

It is not proper for a Believer to claim things which God really has not done, and neither is it proper to discount what He actually has done.

The facts are, and the Truth is, that God is a God of Miracles, of which account is given in the very First Chapter of Genesis, and continues unto this hour. As stated, He is a *"Miracle Working God."*

## TO ANOTHER PROPHECY

Prophecy is the most important of the three gifts of Inspiration or Utterance, and of course the reason is that it takes the other two — Diverse kinds of Tongues and the Interpretation of Tongues — to equal this one, *". . . greater is he that prophesieth than he that speaketh with Tongues except he Interpret"* (I Cor. 14:5), inferring that to speak with Tongues and Interpret is equivalent to Prophecy.

*Prophecy is a supernatural utterance in a known tongue. Diverse kind of Tongues is Supernatural utterance in an unknown Tongue. Interpretation of Tongues is a Supernatural showing forth of that which has been said in Tongues.*

The Hebrew word *"to prophesy"* means *"to flow forth."* It also carries with it the thought *"to bubble forth like a fountain, to let drop, to lift up, to tumble forth, and to spring forth."* The Greek word that is translated *"Prophecy"* means *"to speak for another."* It means to speak for God or to be His spokesman.

In I Corinthians 14:1, we read, *"Follow after Charity* (love)*, and desire Spiritual Gifts, but rather that ye may Prophesy."* We are told to desire Spiritual Gifts, but especially that we might Prophesy. This doesn't mean that we are not to desire the others, but that we are to put this first.

## THE PROPHETIC OFFICE

The simple Gift of Prophecy should not be confused with the Prophetic Office, or the *"Office of the Prophet."* Concerning the Gift of Prophecy, Paul said, *"But he that prophesieth speaketh unto men to edification, and exhortation, and comfort"* (I Cor. 14:3). Thus, we can readily see that in the simple Gift of Prophecy there is no Revelation. Concerning the Office of the Prophet, however, we very often find Revelation coming forth even by Prophecy.

It is also interesting to note the difference between Prophecy in the Old Testament and Prophecy in the New Testament. In the Old Testament Prophecy is essentially foretelling, but in the New Testament this gift shifts strongly to forth-telling. So, one could say, that in the simple Gift of Prophecy as outlined here in I Corinthians Chapter 12, there is no foretelling whatsoever, but rather that which tendeth toward *"edification, exhortation, and comfort."*

PREACHING?

Some people think that to Prophesy means to preach; however, Prophecy is not preaching although sometimes there is an element of Prophecy in preaching when one is anointed by the Spirit and is inspired to say certain things.

To preach means to proclaim, to announce, to cry or to tell. The Scriptural purpose of the Gift of Prophecy is different from the purpose of preaching. Jesus didn't say that men would be saved by the foolishness of prophesying but by the foolishness of preaching (I Cor. 1:21). Supernatural Gifts are given to arrest people's attention, not to save them. Even on the Day of Pentecost when people were speaking in Tongues, nobody was saved until Peter preached to them.

As we have stated, the fact that one has the Gift of Prophecy doesn't mean that person is a Prophet. In fact, few are!

To constitute the Office of the Prophet, a person would have to have at least two of the Revelation Gifts operating in his Ministry plus the Gift of Prophecy. He would have to have the Word of Wisdom and/or the Word of Knowledge and the Gift of Discerning of Spirits plus Prophecy to be able to stand in that Office. Otherwise he would be a preacher in the same sense that others are preachers. Therefore, we should not confuse the Office of the Prophet with the simple gift of Prophecy. The fact is, we can all Prophesy, i.e., *"have that Gift,"* but we can't all be Prophets (Eph. 4:11).

THE MISUSE OF THIS GIFT

Another area of confusion regarding the Gift of Prophecy is caused by its misuse. If folks would use it as the Scripture teaches, it would be a Great Blessing. But some attempt to use this Gift, to tell others what to do, or to speak some word over them. While the Lord certainly does use people in this particular gift in the manner of giving others a word at particular times, still, it is seldom if ever done with the frequency that it is often used in many cases.

NOTES

Years ago I was in a meeting in Kansas City, Missouri. It was conducted in the Coliseum in that city.

After the Sunday afternoon Service, a man came up to me and asked if he could speak with me about a particular situation. This is what he related to me.

He had just recently uprooted his family from another city and moved to Kansas City. He didn't have a job, their situation was going from bad to worse, and he was greatly confused.

The cause for his confusion was that someone had prophesied over him in the city where he formerly lived, telling him he must quit his job, and move his entire family to Kansas City, which he did. However, everything had gone wrong since he had been there, and they were now on the edge of bankruptcy.

I asked him, *"Did the Lord tell you to do this thing, or did you do it strictly on the strength of this so-called prophecy?"*

He said, *"Brother Swaggart, the Lord did not say anything to me, but inasmuch as it was a prophecy, I felt it must be the Lord, so I obeyed." "However,"* he went on to say, *"If it is the Lord I don't understand what has happened, because I'm in the worst situation I've ever known."*

I went on to relate to him, as I have many others over the years, that if the Lord did not say that to him personally, he should have ignored this so-called Prophecy. At this particular stage, he should ask the Lord to forgive him for following that which was of the flesh and not of God, and help him to get things back together.

While the Lord may use the Gift of Prophecy to *verify* what He has already told someone else to do, He will never initiate direction of this sort. God is perfectly capable of telling anyone anything He wants, without having to go through an intermediary, i.e., someone else!

COUNTERFEITS!

As well, just because there are counterfeits, or that the Gift is misused at times, in fact, quite often, is no reason that we should back off from the reality of that which God has actually given. That is all the more reason that we need to produce the real. It is unfortunate that even Christians are misled at times about these things.

One fellow told a particular Preacher once, that before he went to work every morning he waited for the Lord to give him a word of Prophecy to know which tie to wear, etc.

To be frank, God is little interested in which tie one wears. This man was not hearing a word of Prophecy, in fact, he was opening himself up to deception by the Devil.

Whenever the true Gift of Prophecy is in evidence, people will be edified, and comforted. As well, they will be *"exhorted"* which means in the Greek *"a calling nearer to God."* Much that is referred to as the Gift of Prophecy doesn't bring anyone any comfort, but rather discomfort. While at times such might be found in the Office of the Prophet, it definitely is not found in the Gift of Prophecy.

In the 21st Chapter of Acts we have the Scriptural illustration of the Gift of Prophecy. It speaks of the four daughters of Philip the Evangelist. These girls, all virgins, the Scripture says *"did Prophesy"* (Acts 21:8-9).

Actually what they Prophesied, we are not told, but one can be sure, especially considering that it was the Holy Spirit who inspired Luke to write this, that it definitely edified and comforted the Believers who were present.

In fact, every Believer should covet to Prophecy, which will be to the Church *"edification, exhortation and comfort."*

## TO ANOTHER DISCERNING OF SPIRITS

This is one of the Gifts which reveal something, the other two being *"the Word of Wisdom,"* and the *"Word of Knowledge."*

*The "Discerning of Spirits" gives insight into the spirit world. It refers to the discerning of spirits both good and bad, and not just evil spirits as some teach. It is supernatural insight into the realm of spirits.* While the discerning of evil spirits is included, it is not that alone.

God let Moses look into the realm of spirits. He said, *"You can't look on My Face, but I am going to hide you in the cleft of the Rock and put My Hand over your face, and I'm going to pass by and let you see My Back."*

Moses was seeing into the spirit realm. He was able to discern the Similitude of God. All through the Word of God we see people who in vision form have also been able to see the Similitude of God. As He was revealed, they were seeing into the spirit world. That was a manifestation of Discerning of Spirits. Isaiah said, *"In the year that King Uzziah died I saw also the Lord sitting upon a Throne, high and lifted up"* (Isa. 6:1).

To discern means to see . . . in the spirit world there are Divine spirits and there are evil spirits. Also, we have the human spirit to deal with as well!

John on the Isle of Patmos is another example. He saw the Holy Spirit as Seven Spirits before the Throne of God. This simply meant that he was seeing into the spirit realm the seven aspects typifying perfection, of the Spirit of God. It also speaks of him seeing the Cherubims, Seraphims, and a host of Angels.

As well, Micaiah, the Prophet of God, was able to see into the spirit world, where he *"saw the Lord sitting on His Throne, and all the host of heaven standing by him on his right hand and on his left"* (I Ki. 22:19).

He also saw an evil spirit, which *"stood before the Lord . . ."* (I Ki. 22:21). Actually, it was a *"lying spirit,"* who was forced to appear before the Lord regarding certain matters. Micaiah saw all of this as it regarded wicked Ahab, etc. (I Ki. Chpt. 22).

## IT IS NOT DISCERNMENT

Some people say, *"I believe that I have the gift of discernment."* Actually there is no such thing as the gift of discernment mentioned in the Bible. It is the *"Discerning of Spirits."*

While it is true, that the ability to discern will be greatly strengthened upon coming to Christ, still, that is not this Gift. As well, we should be very careful that such discernment does not lead to a suspicious spirit, which many Christians, unfortunately, actually have.

Also, *"Discerning of Spirits"* is not a kind of spiritual thought reading. There are three kinds of spirits that we have to deal with: Divine, Satanic, and human. This is not psychological insight. It is not mental penetration. It is not power to discern the faults in others. In fact, such is absolutely forbidden in the Scriptures. Jesus said, *"Judge not that ye be not judged"* (Mat. 7:1).

One attribute of the Baptism with the Holy Spirit is to destroy this critical spirit and replace it with the sweet gift of gentle forbearance (leniency). The Gift of *"Discerning of Spirits"* is not fault finding. If those who think they have this particular gift would turn it on themselves for a few moments, they would never use it anymore. The *"Discerning of Spirits"* as well, is not discerning of character or faults, it is not even the discerning of people. It is called the *"Discerning of Spirits,"* because it concerns the spirit that might be manifested.

In Acts Chapter 16 we have the account of Paul dealing with the spirit of divination that possessed a girl. Paul dealt with the spirit involved, not the person. He spoke directly to the spirit, and cast it out. So, Discerning of Spirits is not a spiritual gift to uncover human failings. The Christian should walk in love, and love covers a multitude of sins.

## A PERSONAL EXAMPLE

The occasion of this happening was either in the latter part of 1953, or in the first part of 1954. Without going into much detail, and because I have given the full account in another one of our Commentaries, I will be brief.

The Lord gave me a dream one night in which I feel several of the Gifts of the Spirit were in operation. I speak of a *"Word of Knowledge,"* a *"Word of Wisdom,"* and the *"Discerning of Spirits."*

In the dream I saw a huge creature which stood over eight feet tall, and had the face of a man and the body of a bear. Its face carried the most evil design, and especially its eyes, that I had ever seen. It seemed like that every personification of evil was registered on the countenance of this evil spirit of darkness.

In the dream, it was descending on me, in which it was so powerful, that my strength literally drained from me, with me literally being unable to stand and thereby, falling to the floor.

Laying on the floor, so weak that I could not get up, and with nothing to defend myself, I screamed the words, *"In the Name of Jesus,"* even though my voice was only a little bit above a whisper despite my effort.

When I said that Name, even though in a weakened condition, still, the power of What and Who that Name was and is, seemed to hit this man/beast with mighty force. It began to clutch its head, screaming, and staggering around the room.

NOTES

I now began to get up, gathering strength, and said it again, *"In the Name of Jesus."* This time the blow to this thing was so hard, that it fell to the floor. And now, as the dream unfolded, instead of it towering over me, I was towering over it.

It continued to writhe on the floor, clutching its head and screaming, just like a snake which had received a death blow.

I opened my mouth the third time, saying again *"In the Name of Jesus,"* but without any effort at all on my part. It was like my voice had gained the strength of a hundred power. In other words, it boomed out over the room, and without any effort at all.

Then in the dream I heard the sound of a Mighty Rushing Wind, which swept through that room, sweeping the evil spirit outside. Irrespective of its great bulk, I saw it floating away in the air until it could no longer be seen.

I awakened that early morning hour, with the power of God all over me, speaking with other Tongues as the Spirit of God began to give utterance in me.

Concerning a *"Word of Knowledge,"* I believe the Lord told me at that time what it was, even though I did not then understand, but would come to understanding at a later date.

I believe it was also a *"Word of Wisdom"* because it had to do with the future.

As well, it was the *"Discerning of Spirits"* because the Lord was showing me the spirit of darkness which was opposing me and how it would be defeated. It is my belief that in this dream, the Lord was portraying to me the terrible opposition I would face and how it would be overcome. While wrongdoing is always and without exception, the fault of the individual involved, still, every Christian should know and understand, that these things are far more involved than meets the eye. In fact, this is spiritual warfare at its very highest, and should be treated accordingly.

I could say much more about what I believe this dream meant, which in fact, as stated, were Gifts of the Spirit in operation, even though conveyed through the medium of a dream, even as they often are. For instance, the Lord told Joseph to flee into Egypt with baby Jesus, for Herod was *"seeking the Young Child to destroy Him"* (Mat. 2:13).

This was a *"Word of Knowledge"* given to Joseph, as well as *"Discerning of Spirits,"* for the simple reason that the Lord conveyed to Joseph the murderous spirit which was in the heart of evil Herod.

### TO ANOTHER DIVERSE KINDS OF TONGUES

Diverse kinds of Tongues are Supernatural Utterance given by the Holy Spirit in languages never learned by the speaker, not understood by the mind of the speaker, or seldom understood by the hearer. Speaking with tongues has nothing whatsoever to do with linguistic ability, i.e., learning languages in schools, etc. It actually has nothing to do with the mind or the intellect of man. It is a vocal miracle.

Therefore, one reason we speak in Tongues is that Jesus said that this is one sign which should follow Believers (Mk. 16:17-20). It is the Scriptural evidence, the initial evidence, that one has been Baptized with the Holy Spirit (Acts 2:4).

### THE OLD COVENANT

Some would point to John the Baptist and state that he was full of the Holy Spirit but didn't speak with Tongues. That is true, but John the Baptist came under the auspices of the Old Covenant. No one under the Old Covenant spoke with Tongues, because the Holy Spirit did not then dwell within them (Jn. 14:17), and because Jesus had not then paid the sin debt.

We are not now living under the Old Covenant but rather the New. What happened back then was according to that Covenant, while what happens now is according to the New Covenant. The Believer should understand the Holy Spirit according to the dispensation in which we live. We are living in the time of the New Covenant, so we should have what the New Covenant affords.

We learn that in the Acts of the Apostles, which proclaims the New Covenant being carried out in practice. In Acts Chapters 2, 10, and 19, it says they spoke with Tongues, while inferring it elsewhere as well.

When Cornelius and his household were saved and baptized with the Holy Spirit, Peter told the leaders in Jerusalem, that he knew they had received the Holy Spirit, *"For they* (we) *heard them speak with Tongues, and magnify God"* (Acts 10:46).

NOTES

### THE DIFFERENCE

However, when Paul mentioned this Gift of the Spirit, *"diverse kind of tongues,"* he was not speaking of the Tongue or Tongues one will receive when initially baptized with the Holy Spirit, and continues to exercise in prayer and worship thereafter. He is rather speaking of this Gift which is meant to be Interpreted. In fact, there are millions who speak in Tongues every day of their lives, but do not have the Gift of Tongues, as it relates to this Gift of the Spirit. So, when one talks about *"the Gift of Tongues,"* one is actually meaning this Gift of the Spirit, and not the Tongues which all Spirit-filled Believers have.

This is confusing to many non-Pentecostal people. They do not understand the difference, thinking they are both one and the same. They aren't! For clarification allow us to say it again:

Every person who is Baptized with the Holy Spirit, speaks with other Tongues as the Spirit of God gives the Utterance. That in fact, is the initial physical evidence that one has received.

As well, Spirit-filled Believers will continue to pray and worship in Tongues the balance of their lives. But that within itself is not the Gift of Tongues as Paul is describing in this 12th Chapter of I Corinthians.

Even though all things from God are a Gift, at least in a general sense, that of which Paul is speaking about in this 10th Verse, pertains to Tongues which are supposed to be Interpreted. Whereas all Spirit-filled Believers speak in Tongues, only a few actually have this particular Gift, which we are now discussing. So, the two should not be confused.

### A PERSONAL EXAMPLE

I pray in Tongues almost every day of my life, and actually I think every single day. At times, this part of my praying will only last for a few moments, and at other times it will last longer. It is not meant to be interpreted, but is rather a part of worship. It is actually what Isaiah was speaking about whenever he mentioned that such would be a *"refreshing"* and a *"rest"* (Isa. 28:12). In fact, every single Spirit-filled Believer should function exactly in the manner in which I have just said.

However, the Lord seldom uses me relative to the Gift of Tongues, which as stated, is an Utterance that is given in a public setting of some nature, which is meant to be Interpreted. In fact, we have several Believers in Family Worship Center who are used in this Gift, and evidence it at certain times. It is always a Blessing to the entirety of the Body, when it is used according to the guidelines of the Holy Spirit. However, for it to be effective, the Gift of *"Interpretation of Tongues,"* must be in evidence as well, whether by the one who has the Gift of Tongues or by another.

## A QUESTION!

Why does the Lord bestow the Gifts of Tongues and Interpretation of Tongues, which joined together equal Prophecy, and not just Prophecy alone? In other words, why are Tongues and Interpretation necessary, when the Gift of Prophecy comes out to the same conclusion?

First of all, we know that the Lord does all things well, and that there is a great purpose for everything He does. So, to belittle anything which is given by the Lord, is to tread on dangerous ground, which only shows Spiritual and Scriptural ignorance.

The Scripture tells us this, *"Wherefore Tongues are for a sign, not to them that believe, but to them that believe not: but Prophesying serveth not for them that believe not, but for them which believe"* (I Cor. 14:22).

Those who *"believe,"* are referring to Christians, while those who *"believe not,"* are referring to non-Christians.

Tongues being a sign to unbelievers, portrays Supernatural power, which is meant to arrest the unbeliever with conviction, etc. In fact, most supernatural things done, are done as a sign to unbelievers, and especially *"Tongues."*

It is meant for them to see the Power of God, which, thereby, shows them that God is real.

Believers should not need such a sign, simply because they already know that God is real, and that His Power is in fact, Almighty.

Believers should not need *"signs,"* therefore, Prophecy is more powerful in their thinking, or should be.

The Key is in the word *"sign!"* That's why the Lord gave these two Gifts of Tongues and Interpretation of Tongues.

## AN EXAMPLE

A dear friend of mine, a Preacher of the Gospel, who incidentally is now with Jesus, spoke of he and his wife taking a young lady with them to a particular Campmeeting. The girl was unsaved.

At a particular time in the service, actually after the message had been preached, the Lord moved upon someone who had the Gift of Tongues to give out an Utterance. Someone else, or either the same person, Interpreted the Utterance, which went out over the congregation.

My friend went on to say how that the Spirit of God was moving mightily, even as he noticed the young girl under great conviction. When she heard the Tongues and Interpretation, she turned to them and with quavering voice said, *"That's God, isn't it!"*

They answered in the affirmative, and then asked her if she wanted to respond to the Altar Call, which she did. That night she was wondrously saved.

No doubt, such has happened uncounted numbers of times down through the centuries as *"Tongues"* served as a *"sign,"* to unbelievers.

## TO ANOTHER THE INTERPRETATION OF TONGUES

As we begin our study of this last of the Gifts, let us first define again the three vocal Gifts.

Prophecy is Supernatural Utterance in a known tongue. Diverse kind of Tongues are Supernatural Utterance in an unknown tongue (not known to the speaker, or for the most part to the hearers). *The Interpretation of Tongues is the Supernatural showing forth by the Spirit the meaning of an Utterance which has been given in other Tongues.* It is *not* translation of tongues; it is the *interpretation* of Tongues.

The Gift of Interpretation of Tongues is the least gift because it has to depend on another Gift in order to operate. It does not operate unless Tongues have been in operation already. The purpose of this Gift is to render the Gift of Tongues intelligible to the hearers so that the Church as well as the possessor of the Gift may know what has been said and may be edified thereby. Paul said, *". . . greater is he that Prophesieth than he that speaketh with Tongues, except he Interpret, that the Church may receive edifying"* (I Cor. 14:5).

## ITS MANNER

When someone gives out an Utterance in Tongues, which is meant to be interpreted, the

NOTES

person who is used in Interpretation, that is if different than the one giving out the Utterance, should immediately begin to be in tune with the Spirit, as the Lord may desire to use him (or her) in the operation of that Gift. Sometimes there will be several people in the service who have the Gift of Interpretation. In this case, all should be very susceptible to the Holy Spirit, and sensitive to His leading. However, the Lord will use one of the several, if in fact there are several, and that one should be ready and prepared, spiritually speaking.

As we have mentioned earlier, the Interpretation of Tongues is not a translation. Some may wonder at times, why the Interpretation will be somewhat shorter or longer than the length of the Tongues, etc. The reason is because, as stated, it is an Interpretation and not a translation. Consequently, at times it may be longer or shorter, depending on the language that was used in the initial Utterance.

According to I Corinthians 14:13, those who have the Gift of Tongues are instructed to pray as well, for the Gift of Interpretation. *"Wherefore let him that speaketh in an unknown tongue pray that he may Interpret."*

MORE INFORMATION

In I Corinthians 14:27, Paul said, *"If any man speak in an unknown Tongue, let it be by two, or at the most by three, and that by course; and let one Interpret."*

Some have asked the question, *"Does that refer to three Messages?"* Actually we do not find the expression *"Messages in Tongues"* anywhere in the Bible. This is just a phrase that man has coined to try to explain what is being done. A better term would be, and that which I have used, is *"Utterance in Tongues."* The 27th Verse is speaking of people, not Messages or Utterances. It says, *"If any man speak* (meaning man or woman) *. . . let it be by two or at the most by three . . ."* In this statement, the Holy Spirit through the Apostle does not actually say how much they should speak or not speak. He just said to let two or three speak and let it be by course. This implies that they shouldn't all speak at once. As well, it implies that an individual might speak more than once.

Notice that Paul said, *". . . Let one Interpret . . ."* There is nothing in the Scriptures that would do away with the thought that one may speak with Tongues and Interpret for himself. In fact, one of those who is giving the Utterance in Tongues might Interpret it. In fact, there may be more than one who could Interpret. Actually, Paul is admonishing us that we are not to have competitive Interpretations. There is nothing wrong with giving an Utterance in Tongues and Interpreting it oneself. Actually, as stated, I Corinthians 14:13, encourages such.

PRACTICAL ADVICE

In the 14th Chapter of this Book, Paul devotes this entire section to the Gifts of Prophecy, Tongues and Interpretation of Tongues. Evidently, he does this under the guidance of the Holy Spirit, because of the potential for confusion in these areas.

In fact, I have been in services, where two people would attempt to give the Interpretation at one time, or else two people at one time would attempt to give an Utterance in Tongues. This doesn't mean that the devil is behind this, it just means that people sometimes get things mixed up. If we will learn to stay in the Spirit, and follow the Spirit and walk according to the Word, and be very sensitive to what the Spirit wants and desires, everything will work out right, with no confusion, because God is not the Author of confusion.

Sometimes we just need good practical advice concerning these manifestations to help us maintain good order. More importantly, we are not to grieve the Spirit of God (Eph. 4:30). To be sure, He has been grieved at times in some of our Churches — grieved by wanting to manifest Himself and not being permitted to do so, or grieved by the way some folks do things and get things confused.

As a final point, we should stress concerning Tongues and Interpretation, that *"all things be done unto edifying"* (I Cor. 14:26). When it is in the Spirit — and here is one way to judge if that is correct — it will be edifying, inspiring, and blessed, which will be obvious to most.

(Much of the information respecting the Gifts of the Spirit, was derived from the teaching of Kenneth Hagin.)

Even though we have categorized the nine Gifts into three that *reveal* something, three that *do* something, and three that *say* something, still, that is not the manner in which they were grouped or given by the Holy Spirit. Paul, under the inspiration of the Holy Spirit, categorized these nine Gifts in three clusters, but in the following manner:

1. *"Word of Wisdom,"* and *"Word of Knowledge."* These two relate to ones understanding, in other words, they have something to do with the *"mind."*

2. *"Faith," "Gifts of Healings," "Working of Miracles," "Prophecy," "Discerning of Spirits."* These have to do with the *"will"* or to the exercise of power.

3. *"Kinds of Tongues," "Interpretation of Tongues."* This has to do with the *"emotions"* of the individual being used in these Gifts.

This does not mean, of course, that a particular person cannot be used by the Holy Spirit in all three of these groups. Paul himself would be a good example of a person who probably exercised all nine Gifts (Rossier).

(11) "BUT ALL THESE WORKETH THAT ONE AND THE SELFSAME SPIRIT, DIVIDING TO EVERY MAN SEVERALLY AS HE WILL."

The phrase, *"But all these worketh that one and the selfsame Spirit,"* refers to the fact that all the abilities and powers of the Gifts are produced and operated by the energy of the Spirit. Although the Gifts are many and varied in their form, the energy back of them and in them is the same: *"The One and same Spirit,"* He *"energizes"* all of them.

This is one of the vital points regarding the Gifts which Paul would have the Corinthians, and all others for that matter, to know. It will act as a strong corrective against false valuation of one Gift in comparison with another — all of them flow from one and the same Divine Energy.

Actually, in the balance of this Chapter, Paul is led by the Spirit to go into detail, as to the significance of all parts of the Body of Christ, which means that everything that God does, no matter how hidden or small some things seem to be, are still extremely important, and have their place in the Work and Kingdom of God.

The phrase, *"Dividing to every man severally as He will,"* refers to the fact that the Divine Spirit in His distribution, never ignores the make up, characteristic, age, position, and other particular features of a person. In other words, the Gift fits the man or woman.

NOTES

The phrase, *"As He will,"* refers to the Holy Spirit, and places the distribution within the discretion of the Spirit. While this shows that the Spirit is sovereign in the Bestowal of His Gifts, it leaves no room for the thought that this sovereignty is exercised with arbitrariness or partiality after the manner of self-willed earthly sovereigns.

*"As He will"* should remove all complaint on our part and thus, all envy, on the one hand, and all boasting, on the other. What a blessing it is for all of us that the distribution lies in the Spirit's hands, and that He allots the Gifts as He does, and as only He can do! (Lenski)

## THE MODERN CHURCH

It is regrettable, that this Chapter through Verse 11, along with the 14th Chapter are pretty well ignored in much of that today which goes under the guise of *"Church."* It is by and large rejected or explained away, as having ceased with the Apostles, etc.

Perhaps the greater tragedy for the Church is that it should have lost such touch with the Spirit of God in its ongoing life that it should settle for what is only ordinary and thus, feel the urgency to justify itself in this way. However, we have the promise of Verse 11, that the One and the same Spirit will do as He pleases, despite the boxes provided for Him by those who reject His Moving and Operation in this day and time.

Satan changes his methods. In Old Testament times, his plan was opposition to Truth, which was given by the Prophets which Satan contested by his false prophets.

Today, it is corruption of Truth. Satan imitates God in dispensational purpose and activity. As the Lord today speaks through the five fold Ministry (Eph. 4:11), which is always based on the Holy Scriptures, Satan speaks to the Church through his unholy scriptures. Hence, the multitudes of books now produced, professedly in support of the Bible, but in reality in opposition to it.

Confusion and corruption are his weapons. Catholicism, Mormonism, and other forms of corrupt Christianity, as well as so-called science falsely demonstrate his activity and coming (Williams).

(12) "FOR AS THE BODY IS ONE, AND HATH MANY MEMBERS, AND ALL THE

MEMBERS OF THAT ONE BODY, BEING MANY, ARE ONE BODY: SO ALSO IS CHRIST."

The phrase, *"For as the Body* (Church) *is one, and hath many members, and all the members of that one body, being many, are one Body,"* refers to the imagery of the Church as the *"Body of Christ."* The imagery itself was common in the ancient world, and was, therefore, probably well known to the Corinthians. It suits Paul's present concern perfectly.

The Body is one, yet the Body has many members. In saying that it is one, his concern is for its essential unity. But that does not mean uniformity. That was at least one of the errors of the Corinthians, to think that uniformity was a value, or that it represented true spirituality.

Paul's concern is for their unity; but there is no such thing as true unity without diversity. Hence, the need to strike that note so strongly, even as he does.

The phrase, *"So also is Christ,"* presents the Saviour as the Church, oneness in multiplicity.

*"Even as . . . so also"* presents the comparison. On the one hand the Church, on the other hand Christ.

Paul is emphasizing two points in this statement, *"Oneness and multiplicity."*

The idea is, that Christ and the Church form one Body, of which Christ is the Head; one Vine, of which Christians are the Branches (Jn. Chpt. 15); one Building, of which Christians are the Living Stones (Farrar).

(13) "FOR BY ONE SPIRIT ARE WE ALL BAPTIZED INTO ONE BODY, WHETHER WE BE JEWS OR GENTILES, WHETHER WE BE BOND OR FREE; AND HAVE BEEN ALL MADE TO DRINK INTO ONE SPIRIT."

The phrase, *"For by one Spirit are we all baptized into one Body,"* does not refer to Water Baptism, or the Baptism with the Holy Spirit as some think, but rather a Baptism into the Body of Christ which speaks of conversion, of which the Holy Spirit is the Agent. This refers to the Holy Spirit placing people into the Church from the outside (Rom. 8:9), and *not* Jesus baptizing us with the Holy Spirit after we are saved (Mat. 3:11).

## THE WORD, BAPTISM, AS IT IS HERE USED

The English word *"baptize"* is not the translation of the Greek word, but only its transliteration. Actually, the word, *"baptize"* is not a word native to the English language, and, therefore, has no meaning of its own.

In translation we bring the meaning of a word over into the second language, in transliteration, the spelling. Whatever it may rightly have in the Bible, must come from the Greek word of which it is the spelling in English. In this case, *"Baptize"* or *"Baptism."*

The Greek word is used in the New Testament in two ways. When man does the baptizing, a ceremony is in view. That is the ceremonial usage. When God does the baptizing, which is what is done in this 13th Verse, that which is in view is the exertion of God's Power. For the want of a better name, whereas we use the word *"ceremony"* as it relates to man doing the baptizing, we will use the word *"mechanical"* as it relates to God doing the baptizing.

Since we are not considering here the ceremonial usage, and for the reason that we are dealing with the act of God the Holy Spirit, we will look at the mechanical usage of the word *"Baptize."*

## *"PLACING IN"*

To be brief, the mechanical meaning of the word *"baptize"* is that of *"placing in."*

It carries the idea of a ship going under the water and not coming back to the surface. Consequently, we can give the following definition of the Greek word *"baptize"* in this manner: *"The introduction or placing of a person or thing* (in this case a person) *into a new environment or into union with something else so as to alter its condition or its relationship to its previous environment or condition."* The translation as stated is *"to place into,"* or *"to introduce into."*

## THE MYSTICAL BODY OF CHRIST

The *"Body"* of which Paul speaks in this Verse is clearly the Mystical Body of Christ of which Jesus is the Head and all Believers are members.

The personal Agent in this case who does the Baptizing into the Body of Christ at conversion is the Holy Spirit. He places or introduces the believing sinner into the Body of which the Lord Jesus is the Living Head. We could translate *"by means of the Personal Agency of one Spirit, we all were placed in one Body."* Thus, the meaning of the Greek word,

NOTES

*"to place"* or *"introduce into,"* gives us the purpose of the Baptism by means of the Spirit, namely, the introduction of a believing sinner into the Body of Christ, which is done by Faith on the part of the sinner.

## A CAREFUL DISTINCTION

This brings us to a careful distinction which we must make. That of which we are discussing is not the Baptism *with* the Spirit, it is rather the *"Baptism by the Spirit."* This Baptism does not bring the Spirit to us in the sense that God places the Spirit upon or in us. Rather, this Baptism brings the Believer into vital union with Jesus Christ. This means that the Baptism *by* the Spirit is not for power, for in this Baptism there is nothing applied to or given the Believer. He, the Believer, is placed into the Body of Christ. It is the Baptism by the Spirit, in the sense that God the Father does the baptizing through His Personal Agent, the Holy Spirit.

This Baptism is only for the purpose of uniting the believing sinner with the Head of the Body, Christ Jesus, and thus, making him a member of that Body.

So, the Believer, in reading I Corinthians 12:13, is not to confuse the issue thinking that Paul is speaking here of Water Baptism or being baptized with the Holy Spirit with the evidence of speaking with other Tongues. He is not referring to those things at all, but rather that the Holy Spirit is the Divine Agent Who Himself baptizes, the purpose of which Baptism is to place the believing sinner into vital union with Jesus Christ and thus, make him a member of the Body of which Christ is the Living Head. In other words, it speaks of Salvation. Of course, the believing sinner does not see any of this, even as his Faith brings it about, but he definitely feels the result of what is done.

The phrase, *"Whether we be Jews or Gentiles, whether we be bond or free,"* refers to the fact that all must now come in the same manner and same way, i.e. *"by and through Jesus Christ"* (Jn. 3:16).

This which Paul says speaks of social and national differences; however, they are all obliterated by union with Christ, which makes all equal members of one holy brotherhood (Gal. 3:28).

In effect, Paul is dealing with a problem which took place in the Corinthian Church, between the *"haves"* and the *"have-nots,"* referring to money and social standing, etc. All of this is blotted out in Christ, with the Jew being the same as the Gentile, and the Gentile the same as the Jew. As well, the slave is the same as the free man, and the free man as the slave. All are one in Christ.

In fact, the problem of class distinction has never really been properly addressed or solved except in Christ. Communism claimed to address this issue, but instead brought about the worst class distinction of all. It is only the Cross of Jesus Christ, and man's need, which properly erases all class and social distinctions.

The phrase, *"And have been all made to drink into one Spirit,"* refers to Jesus saying, *"If any man thirst, let him come unto Me, and drink.*

*"He that believeth on Me, as the Scripture hath said, out of his belly shall flow rivers of Living Water."*

John then added, *"But this spake He of the Spirit, which they that believe on Him should receive"* (Jn. 7:37-39). The Holy Spirit is the Agent Who effects the Work of Redemption carried out in our lives, and made possible by the Death, Burial, Resurrection, Ascension, and Exaltation of Christ.

Paul refers to this in Romans 8:15 as the *"Spirit of Adoption."* It is clear that he is referring to the Holy Spirit.

## THE SPIRIT OF ADOPTION

What does Paul mean by the phrase, *"Spirit of Adoption"*?

First of all, it is the Holy Spirit Who performs the act of adopting, and of course, we are speaking of the Salvation of a soul, and how it is brought about. He is, in that sense, the *"Spirit of Adoption."*

The Greek word translated *"adoption"* is made up actually of two words, a word meaning *"to place"* and the word *"son,"* its total meaning being *"to place as a son."*

Actually, it is a term of relation, expressing our sonship in respect of *"Standing."* It appears to be taken from the Roman custom with which Paul could not fail to be acquainted.

## THE ROMAN CUSTOM

Among the Jews there were cases of informal adoption, as in the instance of Mordecai and Esther (Esther 2:7). But Adoption in the sense of the legal transference of a child to a family to which it did not belong by birth had no place in Jewish Law.

In Roman Law, on the other hand, provision was made for the transaction known as *"adoption,"* the taking of a child who was not one's child by birth to be his son or the transference of a son who was now fatherless, as by the death of his proper father, to another father by solemn public act of the people, i.e. adoption.

Thus, among the Romans, a citizen might receive a child who was not his own by birth into his family and give him his name, but he could do so only by a formal act, attested by witnesses, and the son, thus adopted, had in all its entirety the position of a child by birth, with all the rights and all the obligations pertaining to that.

By *"adoption,"* therefore, Paul does not mean the bestowal of the full privileges of the family on those who are sons by nature, but the acceptance into the family of those who do not by nature belong to it, and the placing of those who are not sons originally and by right in the relation proper to those who are sons by birth. Hence, adoption is never spoken of concerning Christ, for He, Alone, is Son of God by nature. However, as it regards our sonship, we do not have the same position as Christ regarding our standing with God as His children. Our standing implies a new relation of Grace, founded on a Covenant relation to God and on the Work of Christ (Gal. 4:5). The word, *"adoption,"* seems to distinguish those who are made sons by an act of Grace by comparison with the Only-Begotten Son, The Lord Jesus Christ. However, this act of Grace is not one which makes only an outward difference in our position; it is accomplished in the giving of the Spirit (The Holy Spirit) which creates in us a new nature . . . We have not only the status, but also the *"heart of sons."*

## TWO WORDS

There are two words used in the Greek New Testament relative to the place of the Believer in God's family. One is *"teknon"* which means *"to bear, to give birth to."* Its proper translation is *"child"* or *"born one."* It speaks of a Child of God in his spiritual birth-relationship.

The other word is *"huios,"* the word used in the Greek word *"Adoption."* This word speaks of a Child of God in his legal relationship to God in His family.

NOTES

Under Roman Law, the only thing that stood in the way of a person adopting a child not his own, was the fact that the child did not come of his own flesh and blood. This obstacle was surmounted by the fact that the law gave him the right to make the child his own if he fulfilled the proper legal requirements.

But under the Divine Government of the universe, there were two things that stood in God's way of making human beings His children: A. The fact that they were not His children by birth; and, B. The fact that they were Lawbreakers. The first could easily have been remedied by Regeneration, but the thing that stood in the way of this act of Mercy on God's part was the fact that human beings are sinners, and God's justice demands that sin be paid for before Mercy can be righteously bestowed.

## GOD'S JUSTICE SATISFIED

To satisfy this requirement, Jesus died on the Cross, offering Himself in our stead as the Perfect Sacrifice which God would and did accept, thereby satisfying the legal claims of Heavenly justice.

As a result, to those who receive the Lord Jesus as their Savior as the One Who died in their stead on the Cross, thus satisfying the justice of God in view of man's sin, God gave the legal right to sinners to become His children. Regeneration is, therefore, dependent upon Justification, since an act of Mercy in a law court can only be justly based upon the fact of the law being satisfied in the punishment of the crime committed.

In human law courts, this is impossible, for the prisoner cannot be punished and be set free at the same time. And the judge certainly will not step down from the bench and take upon himself the penalty which he justly imposed upon the prisoner. But praise be to the Lord, it happened exactly that way in the Law Court of the universe. God, the Judge, stepped down from His judgment bench, and at Calvary paid the sinner's penalty, thus satisfying His justice and procuring for sinful man a legal right to receive the Mercy of God.

Thus, nothing stands in the way of a Just God regenerating a believing sinner and placing him as His son in His family. The Holy Spirit as the Spirit of Adoption regenerates the believing sinner and places him as a Child of God in a legal standing in God's family, having all the privileges and rights of God's Only-Begotten Son.

THINK OF IT!

Think of it, to occupy a place in God's family in which He loves us just as much as He loves His Only-Begotten Son.

Think of it, to have a place in God's family just as eternal and secure as His Only-Begotten Son.

Think of it, to have a place in God's family in which all the loveliness of God's Son is ours. The Spirit of Adoption is, therefore, the legal representative of God, so to speak, imparting to us the Divine Nature and placing us in the Family of God, doing all of this in accordance with the eternal and unchanging Laws of God.

(The material on the Spirit of Adoption was derived from Kenneth Wuest.)

(14) "FOR THE BODY IS NOT ONE MEMBER, BUT MANY."

Paul now introduces the human body with all its members, to illustrate the Body of Christ.

There is an old Roman fable concerning the human body which the orator, Menenius Agrippa, used to quiet the quarreling Roman citizens concerning a particular time of unrest. The fable went like this:

The other members of the body charged the stomach with being lazy and with allowing itself to be nourished, which the other members thought wrong. Thereupon, the hands refused to raise food to the mouth, the mouth refused to accept food, and the teeth refused to chew it. They would bring the stomach into line.

The result was that the entire body became emaciated and enfeebled and for the obvious reasons. Then these members at last saw their mistake.

It is regrettable that the Church has a much more difficult time seeing its mistake.

One member of the body does not suffer without the other members suffering likewise. The problem with the Church is that it has a tendency toward suicide.

If one of the members becomes sick, or is wounded, instead of trying to bring healing and help to that member, it oftentimes does the same thing as the members of the body tried to do to the stomach regarding the Roman fable. As a result, the entirety of the Body of Christ suffers terribly, and through its own fault.

NOTES

THE HUMAN BODY

Paul will now use the human body as an example of the Body of Christ, taking his cue from the Ministry of our Lord.

How simple the Parables of Jesus appear, and yet no human mind has ever produced comparisons that equal the Parables of the Lord in any way. Paul has been in the Master's school.

In the manner in which this example is used, we find that the earthly does not resemble the heavenly, but the heavenly *is* reflected in the earthly. Unless a man knows the heavenly, he cannot use the earthly as Jesus and Paul use it.

Paul thinks of the Spiritual Body of Christ throughout the scenario he now presents. But throughout, he views the spiritual body in the mirror of the human body. He addresses it in two ways:

1. The Body: its constitution — just how it comes to be what it is — Verse 18: *"Now hath God,"* etc.

2. The Members: their relation — just how this comes to be what it is — Verse 21: *"God tempered,"* etc.

The first fact settles all envious complaint, the second, all prideful disdain (Lenski).

The general idea of this illustration is that there is one body but many members. The one body is not one member; rather, it is composed of many constituent parts, meant to symbolize the Church.

Two things need to be emphasized:

1. It would appear at times that the Work of the Holy Spirit causes disunity among some. However, if that seems to be the case, it is not the Spirit's fault, but rather the pride and suspicion and distrust which prevail in many hearts and lives. When it comes to the Work of the Spirit, it is true that the Spirit does bring division, but it is division that is needed in order that the entirety of the body may function toward one paramount goal.

2. We tend to forget at times, that true unity (I said true unity) is the result of our common life in the Spirit, not our human machinations. It is our lack of the Spirit that has forced us to attempt unity on other grounds.

Paul saw the Holy Spirit as the key to everything in the Christian life. If that was the case then, and it definitely was, then it is the case now. But let the one who says that, not force his or her own brand of *"spiritual unity"* on the Church as simply another human machination. Our desperate need is for a Sovereign Work of the Spirit to do among us what all our *"program unity"* cannot do (Fee).

(15) "IF THE FOOT SHALL SAY, BECAUSE I AM NOT THE HAND, I AM NOT OF THE BODY; IS IT THEREFORE NOT OF THE BODY?"

The beginning of the question, *"If the foot shall say, Because I am not the hand, I am not of the body . . .?"*, presents Paul beginning his elaboration by the analogy of personifying some parts of the body.

The conclusion of the question is, *"Is it therefore not of the body?"*, presents these questions as self-answered. In other words, the answer is obvious.

(16) "AND IF THE EAR SHALL SAY, BECAUSE I AM NOT THE EYE, I AM NOT OF THE BODY; IS IT THEREFORE NOT OF THE BODY?"

The beginning of the question, *"And if the ear shall say, Because I am not the eye, I am not of the body . . .?"*, presents thus far a total of four body members, the foot, hand, ear, and eye.

The conclusion of the question is, *"Is it therefore not of the body?"*, once again demands a positive answer.

In both cases, these parts carry on comparable functions in the body; there is no hint that one is superior to the other. Consequently, the Apostle disallows the idea that any one of these members can deny their own place in the body, or that their place be denied by other members of the body. Just because they are different in their functions, does not make them any less necessary for the successful working of the entirety of the body.

The question, of course, is the intent of this picture. For example, there can be little question, at least as it regards the Body of Christ, that the disquieting desire on the part of some or even many to be something in the body other than what they are is a plague on our house. The idea to act in opposition to one another is, therefore, contrary to nature. As all the members agree together because it is in the best interest of the whole that each should be kept safe, so the Church should function accordingly. As the parts of the human body are made for mutual help, likewise, the same scenario plays out in the Body of Christ, or at least it is supposed to.

NOTES

(17) "IF THE WHOLE BODY WERE AN EYE, WHERE WERE THE HEARING? IF THE WHOLE WERE HEARING, WHERE WERE THE SMELLING?"

The question, *"If the whole body were an eye, where were the hearing?"*, proclaims Paul making the interchange of the sense organs, making it clear that his point is not the *"inferiority"* of one to the other. The point is the need for all members; otherwise, some function of the body would be missing.

## THE MANNER IN WHICH THE HOLY SPIRIT MAKES THIS COMPARISON

When Paul asked in this question, *"Where is the hearing,"* and the second, *"Where is the smelling?"*, he really employs an understatement. For if the whole body is converted into an eye, or into an ear, one may ask, *"Where are the all other members in the functions that a body requires in order to be a body?"*

But in many instances understatements are psychologically more effective than complete statements. They allow the reader or the hearer to supply what is left unsaid. And when he does this, the effect made on his mind is the greater.

When Paul speaks of the smelling without mention of the nose, our minds are led to think of all the other functions of the body, any one or all of which could be mentioned in this connection (Lenski).

The question, *"If the whole were hearing, where were the smelling?"*, again emphasizes the point.

The idea of this is, the Believer not fully recognizing or understanding his position in the Body of Christ as given to him by the Lord, not properly understanding his function, and thereby striving, in opposition to the will of God we must quickly add, to fill another role that was never intended, such will always bring dysfunction. Consequently, we have too much hearing and not enough seeing, or too much seeing and not enough hearing, or too much smelling and not enough seeing and hearing, etc.

The fact is the ear was not made to see, nor the eye to hear, nor the nose to hear or see, etc. Consequently, Believers not functioning in their assigned place and position given by the Holy Spirit even as we shall see, don't really function at all, actually becoming a hinderance.

(18) "BUT NOW HATH GOD SET THE MEMBERS EVERY ONE OF THEM IN THE BODY, AS IT HATH PLEASED HIM."

The phrase, *"But now hath God set the members every one of them in the body,"* continues to speak of the human body, but yet symbolizes the Body of Christ, i.e. *"the Church."* This plainly tells us that it is the Lord who appoints, allots, selects, designates, and places. Consequently, the question must be asked, *"Does envy, false humility, self-disparagement, or whatever may blind us, lead us to think that we can improve on God's ways?"*

FOR THE ENTIRETY OF THE WORK OF GOD

In fact, the great problem in the Church is man changing that which God has done to that which man wants to do.

The idea is that God lays out the blueprint, and man is supposed to follow that blueprint. However, he seeks to change what God has done, always to his detriment, and acute detriment at that!

For instance, as the Apostles in the Early Church one by one went home to be with the Lord, and finally those who knew them, little by little the Church began to go into apostasy. How could it do that?

It did it because it changed God's system of Church Government laid out in the Book of Acts and the Epistles, substituting its own government instead, which led to the Dark Ages. It is man changing God's order.

Salvation is another case in point. Cain wanted to offer the labor of his own hands, thereby, changing what God had directed as a Sin-Offering. Man continues to do the same thing presently, attempting to change God's method of Salvation.

So, continuing to use the human body as an analogy, we have a Church that cannot half see, hears but little, can little walk but rather stumbles along, and in fact, is barely alive.

The phrase, *"As it hath pleased Him,"* in effect plainly states it is not to please us.

NOTES

The reason is not arbitrary.

Salvation is all of the Lord because Salvation must be all of the Lord. The moment man touches it, it is polluted, defiled, and corrupt. So, God, pleasing Himself, is not the attitude of a dictator, etc., but rather, of a kind, gracious, benevolent Parent, Who knows better, just as earthly parents know better regarding their small children, or at least they certainly should!

(19) "AND IF THEY WERE ALL ONE MEMBER, WHERE WERE THE BODY?"

If the human body was one great eye, or one large ear, etc., it would no longer be a body, but rather a monstrosity.

Pleasing the Lord is the only thing that really matters. If this is done, all confusion and strife will cease.

Our problem is that we too often want to please ourselves, instead of God.

(20) "BUT NOW ARE THEY MANY MEMBERS, YET BUT ONE BODY."

Once again, we come back to the idea, actually the fact, that the Church, as the human body, is One Body, but with many members. Every member has its function and its significance.

(21) "AND THE EYE CANNOT SAY UNTO THE HAND, I HAVE NO NEED OF THEE: NOR AGAIN THE HEAD TO THE FEET, I HAVE NO NEED OF YOU."

The phrase, *"And the eye cannot say unto the hand, I have no need of thee,"* proclaims a mutual interdependence in the human body which typifies beautifully the interdependence in the Body of Christ (Rossier).

The phrase, *"Nor again the head to the feet, I have no need of you,"* presents exactly that which is being done in many Church circles.

Entire Religious Denominations numbering millions strong, in fact, say they have no need of Apostles, Prophets, or Evangelists. In their superior wisdom (superior only in their own eyes), they are in effect saying they know more than God.

All the Ministry Gifts are needed (Eph. 4:11), just as all the Gifts of the Spirit are needed (I Cor. 12:8-10). To disallow any or to place any calling in an inferior position, weakens the entirety of the Body.

I'll go back to the Roman fable:

The hands, mouth, and teeth, claiming that the stomach was lazy, refused to function any more, thereby depriving the stomach of food. The hands would not pass the food to the mouth, the mouth would not open, and the teeth would not chew.

While they succeeded in punishing the stomach, they seemed to little realize that it was the stomach that supplied them with strength and nourishment, which enabled them to carry out their functions. Consequently, even though they did succeed in punishing the stomach, they soon were unable to function as well!

All of us have need one of another. This means that our conduct toward our Brother and Sister in the Lord is not that merely of kindness or benevolence, but rather we should understand, that there is a true need on an individual basis, of each person, throughout the entirety of the Body of Christ.

(22) "NAY, MUCH MORE THOSE MEMBERS OF THE BODY, WHICH SEEM TO BE MORE FEEBLE, ARE NECESSARY:"

The phrase, *"Nay, much more those members of the body, which seem to be more feeble,"* refer, no doubt, to the inward parts which are covered. Consequently, the Lord has provided protection, as is obvious, for these particular parts of the human body.

The phrase, *"Are necessary,"* if anything, is a gross understatement.

Paul's point seems to be that such apparent weakness has no relationship to their real value and necessity to the body. One must be careful at this point not to allegorize and try to find people who are like this. This is not allegory, but analogy. Appearances deceive, Paul is saying. If one removed an organ because, in ignorance, they thought it was unnecessary, the body would cease to be whole, and actually would not function as it should.

For many years, Doctors thought that tonsils were not necessary; consequently, they advocated their removal as quickly as possible.

But in later years they came to realize that the tonsils were, in fact, very important. In fact, they serve as a trap for all types of disease germs, somewhat like a garbage disposal unit. When removed, there is no garbage disposal unit, with the human body, consequently, more easily becoming sick. Consequently, Doctors do not now advocate removing tonsils unless they are so infected there is no alternative or choice. When the Maker created the human body, He knew what He was doing, which means that every part has its place which, of course, completely debunks the mindless drivel of evolution.

NOTES

So, with the Church, all the parts are necessary, no matter what one may think.

(23) "AND THOSE MEMBERS OF THE BODY, WHICH WE THINK TO BE LESS HONOURABLE, UPON THESE WE BESTOW MORE ABUNDANT HONOUR; AND OUR UNCOMELY PARTS HAVE MORE ABUNDANT COMELINESS."

The phrase, *"And those members of the body, which we think to be less honourable, upon these we bestow more abundant honour,"* continues to speak of the internal organs.

For instance, I get on a treadmill almost every night (at least when we are at home) in order to exercise my heart. To be frank, just as Paul said, I bestow more attention to that one physical organ than I do anything else (No, I have nothing wrong with my heart, I'm just doing my best to see that it remains healthy.)

The phrase, *"And our uncomely parts have more abundant comeliness,"* refers to the privates of a human being which are always given *"abundant comeliness"* in reference to covering and dress.

As someone has said, a nation may exist without Astronomers and Philosophers, but the day laborer is absolutely essential to the existence of the people. One may look down on the cook and the washerwoman, but you do not dispense with them. Yet, in society, day laborers, etc., are seldom given the honor they deserve; so this illustration serves only the point of their necessity, even as it does the whole of the Church.

Paul groups the members that may be despised and thought unnecessary under three classes:

1. Such as are *"more feeble"*:

These seemingly weaker members seem so only to the prideful. They *"seem"* so but are really not so.

2. Such as are *"less honorable"*:

We just *"think"* these to be thus so, but they really aren't. In fact, the Scripture says we are to *"bestow more abundant honour"* upon those who fall into this category. This is the antidote for pride.

3. Such as are *"uncomely"*:

These are to be treated with the greatest grace of all.

There are reasons, as should be obvious for all of this:

A. Jesus died for these *"unseemly"* members of the Body of Christ.

B. Recognizing these *"unseemly"* members, honors Christ as the Head of the Church. In other words, He, Alone, is the Judge of who is what, because He, Alone, is qualified to judge.

C. These, whomever they may be, must be treated as members of the Body of Christ, simply because they are.

D. To recognize these people Scripturally, which we must do, addresses the pride factor which is so prone to show its ugly head.

## EXACTLY WHO ARE THESE PARTICULAR MEMBERS OF THE CHURCH OF WHOM PAUL SPEAKS?

First of all, the poorest of the poor would fall into this category. Due to their not being able to contribute very much in the way of financial resources toward the Church, the tendency is to not give these proper recognition and honor. However, we must never forget that most of the Church, at least on a worldwide basis, is made up of these poorest of the poor. As well, we make a terrible mistake in judgment if we measure people according to their financial resources. Many of these are the greatest prayer warriors in the Church which, of course, is the very strength of the Church.

As well, the uneducated would fall into this category. But again, education is never to be looked at as the barometer, despite the fact that it actually is in many, if not most, Church circles. Once again, this group has always made up the greater part of the Church and for the obvious reasons. Christ is their only hope, which in reality is the case for all, even though the rich and educated little know or understand that Truth.

However, the question should be asked, *"Educated in what?"*

Many of these people are uneducated regarding the criteria of the world, but not uneducated at all according to the Lord inasmuch as many of them are well educated in the Scriptures which, in fact, is the greatest education of all.

NOTES

Of course, the *"weak in the Faith"* would definitely fall into this category. Nevertheless, if that in fact is the case, as it often is, they are never to be discarded, but rather helped, strengthened, and encouraged, and that on a constant basis.

(24) "FOR OUR COMELY PARTS HAVE NO NEED: BUT GOD HATH TEMPERED THE BODY TOGETHER, HAVING GIVEN MORE ABUNDANT HONOUR TO THAT PART WHICH LACKED:"

The phrase, *"For our comely parts have no need,"* has reference to the need of strength, encouragement, help, etc. Inasmuch as these constitute the *"strong,"* these do not need the same attention as the others. Besides that, the Church is certainly not ashamed of these and, in fact, loves to display them. I speak of the rich, educated, talented, etc.

However, our love of display, at least in this case, does not show the Love of God. In fact, there is a Greek word for love, which pertains to this spirit. It is *"eros,"* and pertains to that which is rich, talented, useful, or in other words, makes the Church look good. However, if we love these people for these particular qualities, when those qualities are absent, the love is no longer there, which of course is the very opposite of the Christlike spirit.

In fact, this is the type of *"love"* on which the world turns and, regrettably, most of the Church. As long as the person is useful and makes our Church look good, they are not only welcome, but rather held up as great examples, etc. In fact, this is ungodly.

Even though this word, *"eros,"* is the type of love most engaged in the world, the Holy Spirit thought so little of it that it is not once used in the entirety of the New Testament. The Church is to have the *"agape"* kind of love which is that which springs from God, and God Alone!

## A PERSONAL EXAMPLE

Our Church, Family Worship Center, here in Baton Rouge, Louisiana, has almost from its inception run buses into the very worst parts of the city, bringing in little children to particular services. We do it every week.

There is no way that these kids, especially considering their station in life, can be of any benefit to the Church respecting monetary value or other things that one could name.

However, this is very special in the eyes of God, the care of these little ones and, consequently, it should be very special to us as well, and is, in our case.

I received a letter a short time ago from one of the Judges here in the city telling me that he wanted to use our Church as an example. What was he speaking about?

He went on to say as to how Family Worship Center is made up of people of every race, which is certainly true. He went on to say that this is the way it should be, and he is right.

I was taken somewhat aback at first, not understanding totally that of which he spoke for the simple reason that I thought, erroneously so I might quickly add, that all Churches open their doors to all people. However, that is not so, and for the very reason of which Paul addresses.

## TEMPERED

The phrase, *"But God has tempered the body together,"* speaks of the Lord creating the human body in such a way that some parts are given more dignity than others. And yet, every single part is necessary, with all parts functioning together, making the whole.

*"Tempered"* in the Greek is *"sugkerannumi"* and means *"to commingle, to combine, or assimilate."*

Once again, even though Paul is continuing to speak of the human body and its parts, still, it is meant to be a symbolism or analogy of the Church.

The manner in which this is done was designed by God, which means if man changes the order, which man repeatedly has done, he in effect is insulting God, providing an atmosphere in which the Holy Spirit will not, and in fact cannot, work.

The phrase, *"Having given more abundant honour to that part which lacked,"* presents the Holy Spirit using this three times, i.e *"more abundant."* Consequently, it is made prominent by these repetitions.

## WHAT DOES THE HOLY SPIRIT MEAN BY MORE ABUNDANT HONOUR, ETC.?

The *"honour"* of which the Holy spirit speaks actually has to do with the simple fact of the great number of these people, other than some particular recognition, etc. The Lord does not bestow *"honour"* on anyone because they are rich, poor, great, small, educated, uneducated, or because they are of a certain color. The simple idea is that the lack of some qualities in this particular group which makes up most of us, is made up by their sheer numbers. As well, the Grace of God demands that all be treated alike with no partiality shown or expected.

NOTES

(25) "THAT THERE SHOULD BE NO SCHISM IN THE BODY; BUT THAT THE MEMBERS SHOULD HAVE THE SAME CARE ONE FOR ANOTHER."

The phrase, *"That there should be no schism in the body,"* holds true for the physical body, but in the Church, much is yet to be desired.

*"Schism"* refers to disunion and disruption. The opposite of schism is unity and peace. It is God's purpose that the members may all have the same deep concern for each other, as He has for all.

The phrase, *"But that the members should have the same care one for another,"* refers to the fact that all should be treated alike, with one loved as much as the other is loved, irrespective of station, place, position, or circumstance in life.

This can only properly come about, as the leadership in the Church takes the initiative accordingly. If the pulpit proclaims degrees of respect and honor towards its members, most of those in the Pews, regrettably, will follow suit. However, if the pulpit shows equal love and appreciation for all, most in the Pews will function in the same spirit as well. We are to have equal concern for truly saved people.

(26) "AND WHETHER ONE MEMBER SUFFER, ALL THE MEMBERS SUFFER WITH IT; OR ONE MEMBER BE HONOURED, ALL THE MEMBERS REJOICE WITH IT."

The phrase, *"And whether one member suffer, all the members suffer with it,"* presents the way it ought to be. All the members suffer with the suffering member, not disjointedly but as a whole, since God intermingled them and made them an organism.

The phrase, *"Or one member be honored, all the members rejoice with it,"* once again, presents the ideal.

We readily see this is true with respect to the human body, but what about this fact in regard to the spiritual body where so many members are faulty?

THE IDEAL

The very purpose of Paul's illustrative analogy is by means of the facts concerning the human body to show, not what is true with regard to the spiritual body, but what ought to be true.

He also shows how unnatural and how wrong it is when it is not thus. This spiritual body ought to be as the human body is.

Paul's analogy vividly illustrates how unnatural, abnormal, unreasonable, and outrageous it is that the members of the spiritual Body of Christ act in contravention to the very constitution of their own body.

Once again, allow me to digress to the Roman fable, where the hands, mouth, and teeth sought to punish the stomach. They succeeded in doing this by refusing food, but in the end destroyed themselves. So is the Church! (vs. 14)

(27) "NOW YE ARE THE BODY OF CHRIST, AND MEMBERS IN PARTICULAR."

The phrase, *"Now ye are the Body of Christ,"* refers to the Church, and each Church being a sort of microcosm of the whole Church. This speaks of Christ's Own Body, which is made His Own by His indwelling.

The phrase, *"And members in particular,"* refers to every single individual in the Church who is truly Born-Again. In fact, to be *"Born-Again"* is the qualification for admittance (Jn. 3:3).

BODY OF CHRIST

This phrase has a threefold use in the New Testament. Consequently, to understand its true use, we must properly define its context or associating texts.

Let's look at its three meanings:

1. THE HUMAN BODY OF JESUS CHRIST

This speaks of the Incarnation of Christ, in that He had a flesh, blood, and bone body like all other human beings. Actually the denial that Jesus Christ came in the flesh is, according to John, *"of Antichrist"* (I Jn. 4:2-3).

The reality of Christ's Body is the proof of His True Manhood. That the Son should take a human body is a fact, essential for Salvation (Heb. 2:14) and specifically for Atonement (Heb. 10:20).

NOTES

The transformation (not relinquishment) of it at the Resurrection is a guarantee and prototype of the Resurrection Body for Believers (I Cor. Chpt. 15; Phil. 3:21).

2. THE BREAD

The Bread at the Last Supper over which Christ spoke the words, *"This is My Body,"* (Mat. 26:26; Mk. 14:22; Lk. 22:19; I Cor. 11:24) refers to symbolism.

The words have been interpreted historically as meaning both *"This represents My Sacrifice"* and also *"This is Myself."* Interpretation must be controlled by reference to the Person of Christ to His Sacrifice and to the Church, in that order.

3. THE CHURCH

The exact phrase is used by Paul even as we are now studying in I Corinthians 10:16 and 12:27 as a description of a group of Believers — *"one body in Christ"* (Rom. 12:5) and *"Body"* in Verses referring to a local Church or to the Universal Church (I Cor. 10:17; 12:12; Eph. 1:23; 2:16; 4:4, 12, 16; 5:23; Col. 1:18, 24; 2:19; 3:15).

It should be noted that the phrase is *"Body of Christ,"* not *"of Christians,"* and that it has visible, congregational, and also eschatological (end time) significance. In the Books of Romans and I Corinthians, it defines the unity existing between members of each local congregation; in Colossians and Ephesians, the whole Church is in view, with Christ as the Head.

The origin of Paul's image has been sought in the Old Testament idea that as each part receives its function from the whole, so the whole is weakened when any part fails. It also expresses the conviction that Christ is totally identified with all Christians.

The problem with correct interpretation is to establish the amount of metaphor in the phrase, *"Body of Christ."* If it is literal, the Church is viewed as an extension of the Incarnation.

However, the manner in which Paul uses the statement, with the probable Old Testament background, points rather to its being a metaphor (a likeness or example) instructing Church members that their existence and unity depend on Christ and that each member has power to promote or to imperil unity.

(28) "AND GOD HATH SET SOME IN THE CHURCH, FIRST APOSTLES, SECONDARILY PROPHETS, THIRDLY TEACHERS, AFTER THAT MIRACLES, THEN GIFTS OF

HEALINGS, HELPS, GOVERNMENTS, DIVERSITIES OF TONGUES."

The phrase, *"And God hath set some in the Church,"* refers to God the Father, but includes God the Holy Spirit and God the Son, as all have their respective place and position concerning the Church and all things for that matter. This does not mean that One is subordinate to the Other regarding essence, but it does refer to subordination concerning activity.

This means that God the Father is all-in-all (I Cor. 15:28).

God the Son is subordinate to God the Father as it regards the Incarnation, but not according to essence (that which identifies something as being what it is). In other words, God the Son is just as much God as God the Father.

However, due to God the Son having paid the price and accomplished the plan of Redemption, the Holy Spirit is subject to Him, even though He is, as well, of the same Essence, i.e. *"God"* (I Cor. 15:24-28; Jn. 16:13-15).

As well, God the Father, God the Son, and God the Holy Spirit have appointed, designed, planned, and instituted the various Ministries and Offices in the Church.

## GREATEST AREA OF CONFLICT

Man has ever attempted to change God's order, which has caused the greatest problems and difficulties in the Church, of all the many difficulties faced.

As we have said repeatedly, men love to lord it over other men, and religious men love to lord it over other religious men most of all. Jesus warned against this graphically so, by saying to His Disciples, *"But it shall not be so among you"* (Mat. 20:26).

The Early Church ultimately went into apostasy (beginning in the Second and Third Centuries), because of this very thing. It begins to abrogate the Headship of Christ, instituting its own offices instead, and then demanding that men honor these offices. Consequently, in the early 600's, after nearly two centuries of trying, a man was finally given the unscriptural title of *"Pope."*

During the years A.D. 390-461, Leo the first Bishop of Rome, used all his considerable powers to establish recognition for the Bishop of Rome as *"The Universal Bishop."* It was he who first made the claim that Peter had been the first Pope (some 400 years after this supposedly took place).

NOTES

The Eastern Branch of the Church emphatically denied these claims. Even the Counsel of Chalcedon (where Leo exercised great power) refused his request to certify his claims. His assertions of Papal Supremacy did, however, produce a profound affect in later years. The unscriptural office of *"Pope"* was finally realized after some 200 years of efforts in this direction.

## THE PROTESTANT CHURCH

However, the abrogation of the Headship of Christ is not paramount only in the Catholic Church; many Protestant Religious Denominations have an unscriptural form of Church Government as well. To be Truthful, some are very little different than the Catholic version, only with different names.

As it should be understood, *"Government"* is the single most important factor regarding any society, be it spiritual or otherwise. If the Government is wrong, nothing else much can go right. If it is right, the entire body experiences prosperity.

## PROPER CHURCH GOVERNMENT

The Book of Acts and the Epistles serve as the model for correct Church Government. It is very simple in its application:

1. God sets the various Ministries and Offices in the Church, and man is not to change that (Eph. 4:11).

2. The Local Church as the Book of Acts proclaims, is the highest spiritual authority, which means that no outside spiritual, religious, or governmental force is to override that institution. While there may be, and, in fact, will be outside administrators, such is to never flow over into the spiritual, overriding the decisions of the Local Church (Acts 13:1-3).

3. Churches are to be a fellowship and never subordinate to a religious hierarchy, which in fact, does not exist in the New Testament. To be sure, if the Holy Spirit had desired such, that would have been the time for it to be installed. The original Twelve Apostles who had personally spent some $3\frac{1}{2}$ years with Jesus as His especially Called Ones, would have made an excellent Hierarchy; however, there is not a hint in the Book of Acts that the Holy Spirit even remotely engaged such. While these men were

mightily used of God, they never functioned as a hierarchy.

As well, Jerusalem would have been the place for the Hierarchy to be established, inasmuch as it was the city chosen by God for the very center of His Work on earth.

As well, this was not done either, for the simple reason that it was now time for the Gospel to be a worldwide entity, and not be concentrated in one particular place. So, we find the Local Church, wherever it might be, as the highest spiritual authority, which is to never be abrogated by outside forces.

If this form of Government as instituted by the Holy Spirit is in the least interrupted or corrupted, it will always result in spiritual declension, just as it did with the ultimate apostatizing of the Early Church.

## APOSTLES

The phrase, *"First Apostles,"* is meant by the Holy Spirit to mean exactly what it says. In order of significance for the Church, there must first be God-Called Apostles. That refers not only to Paul's day, but unto the present, and will remain accordingly to the time of the Resurrection, which for all practical purposes will conclude the dispensation of the Church.

It is through Apostles even as the Book of Acts proclaims, as well as the Epistles, that the Holy Spirit guides the Church, but under the tutelage and headship of Christ.

The Apostle is the one who has the Message for the Church, or at least some part of the Message. It concerns leadership and guidance, all by the Holy Spirit, and ever according to the Word of God.

For instance, there are certain Apostles who are functional even at this present time, whom God has used, and is using, respecting Faith, Doctrine, Standards, and Emphasis — in whatever direction the Holy Spirit would desire. These men may or may not be known by the entirety of the Church, but, nevertheless, if they are faithful to their Calling, that which they Preach and proclaim, will affect the entirety of the Church in a positive way throughout the entirety of the world.

## THE OLD TESTAMENT AND THE NEW

Paul said, *"And are built upon the foundation of the Apostles and Prophets, Jesus Christ Himself being the Chief Cornerstone"* (Eph. 2:20).

NOTES

This *"foundation"* of which Paul speaks, proclaims Jesus as the *"Chief Cornerstone"* which refers to both the Old and New Testaments.

In the Old Economy, the Lord guided Israel through the Office and Ministry of the *"Prophets."*

Now, under the New Covenant, even though *"Prophets"* are still a part of the fivefold Ministry Offices (Eph. 4:11), leadership has shifted from that particular Office to the Office of the Apostle.

These men are God-called and not man-appointed, and can function in any of the fivefold Ministry Offices, and in fact, do just that.

## THE GREAT CONTROVERSY

Consequently, the Body of Christ is faced with two particular directions of Leadership:
A. Apostles, who are always God-Called; and,
B. The heads of Religious Denominations who are elected by popular ballot.

Almost without exception, God-Called Apostles are refused admittance in Religious Denominations, and much if not most of the time, are actively opposed. In fact, with some few exceptions, it is almost impossible, if not totally so, for an Apostle to function in a Denominational Structure. Denominational Leadership and for their own self-preservation purposes, seldom recognize these callings, and actually feel threatened by them. As a result, there is an antagonism which began even in the Early Church and continues unto the present.

Thankfully, as stated, there are some few exceptions to these things which I have said, and these exceptions have proven to be a tremendous benefit to the Cause of Christ all over the world, in fact, being greatly used of God. The Lord always has some who desire to follow Him exactly according to the Word of God and may, in fact, though elected by popular ballot, actually be a God-Called Apostle themselves. Such have existed, and in some rare cases, probably exist at present in different parts of the world.

## PROPHETS

The phrase, *"Secondarily Prophets,"* is meant to include Evangelists as well, even as Teachers are meant to include Pastors.

If one is to notice, Paul gave an example of each instead of listing all.

Prophets have the same function under the New Covenant as the Old, with one exception, in that Apostles have taken their place in the realm of Leadership. Otherwise, the Office is still the same. It pertains to *"foretelling,"* which has to do with a *"Word of Wisdom,"* a *"Word of Knowledge,"* and *"Discerning of Spirits."*

It also functions in the realm of *"forth-telling,"* which pertains to the Prophet being a *"Preacher of Righteousness."*

In the order of spiritual significance, the Holy Spirit relegates the Office of the Prophet as second to the Apostle which comes first.

TEACHERS

The phrase, *"Thirdly Teachers,"* includes Pastors as well, even as we have stated.

As someone has said, Preachers proclaim the Word, while Teachers explain the Word.

The phrase, *"After that Miracles,"* pertains to this particular Gift of the Spirit, *"The Working of Miracles."*

Of all the religions in the world, Christianity (which incidently is not a religion, but rather a relationship with Christ) alone can boast of Miracles. At least the segment of Christianity that believes in the Power and Working of the Holy Spirit at this present time. God is a Worker of Miracles, and He continues to do so unto this hour, at least for those who dare to believe Him. In fact, this is at least one of the reasons that Christianity, and I speak of true Christianity, is the most powerful force on the face of the earth.

The phrase, *"Then Gifts of Healings,"* pertains to another of the *"Gifts of the Spirit"* and which should be in operation in the modern Church, and is for those who dare to believe.

The Word, *"Helps,"* in the Greek is *"antilepsis,"* and means *"a support; help; succourer; an aid."* It refers to every kind of help God sets in the Church.

It cannot be limited to the work of Deacons and Deaconesses, as some teach, for there were other helps besides these (Rom. 16:3, 9; I Cor. 16:16; II Cor. 1:11, 24).

As well, it does not refer to persons only, but also to the various spiritual gifts which endue men with power to help.

*"Governments,"* in the Greek is *"kubernesis"* and means *"a steering; pilotage; a guiding."*

NOTES

It is used only here and refers to all the means of guidance that God has set in the Church. It has no reference to power to rule, but to men of extraordinary wisdom, knowledge, and discernment to guide the Church.

A perfect example is in the Old Economy of God, where it speaks of certain men who came to David, with the Scripture saying, *"And of the Children of Issachar, which were men that had understanding of the times, to know what Israel ought to do"* (I Chron. 12:32).

The phrase, *"Diversities of Tongues,"* speaks of the Gift of Tongues relative to particular Utterances which require Interpretation.

WHY DID THE HOLY SPIRIT THROUGH THE APOSTLE MENTION THESE MINISTRIES AND GIFTS IN THIS FASHION?

1. Everything the Holy Spirit does is for purpose and reason. Nothing is done in an haphazard way, but always with order and direction.

He mentioned Offices which pertain to particular Ministries, and in essence, includes all of them, with their correct order (Eph. 4:11).

2. He speaks of two of the Gifts of the Spirit which are probably, at least at the present time, the two most denied, claiming that such passed away with the original Apostles, etc.

3. He speaks of the function of Administration, which is definitely important, but yet which should not be taken beyond its parameters. The tragedy is, even as we have already stated, man seeks to make more out of *"helps"* and *"governments"* than the Holy Spirit intended, actually taking the place of *"Apostles"* and *"Prophets."* This is the area of greatest contention in the Church, and always has been.

4. He mentions *"Tongues"* which is also one of the great controversial areas in the modern Church.

So, taken in its proper prospective, I think we can see as to why the Holy Spirit gave this to Paul in the order He did.

(29) "ARE ALL APOSTLES? ARE ALL PROPHETS? ARE ALL TEACHERS? ARE ALL WORKERS OF MIRACLES?"

Each question is meant to solicit a negative answer. No! Every member in the Church is not an Apostle, but some few are. All are not Prophets, but some few are. Likewise, all aren't Teachers, but some few are. As well, all do not have the gift of *"working of miracles,"* but some few do.

(30) "HAVE ALL THE GIFTS OF HEALING? DO ALL SPEAK WITH TONGUES? DO ALL INTERPRET?"

Obviously, all do not have *"Gifts of Healing"* and all do not have the Gift of giving Utterances in Tongues, nor do all have the Gift of Interpretation of Tongues.

What the Holy Spirit, through the Apostle, is proclaiming, is that all people do not perform the same function in God's Church, any more than the human body has just one member.

Incidently, some have attempted to use the question, *"Do all speak with Tongues?"*, as proof that some can be Baptized with the Holy Spirit without Tongues, etc. However, this is not the subject that Paul is addressing whatsoever.

First of all, these mentioned, *"Workers of Miracles," "Gifts of Healing," "speaking with Tongues,"* and *"Interpretation"* all refer to Gifts of the Spirit (12:8-10).

Even though all Spirit-filled Believers do speak with other Tongues (Acts 2:4; 10:46; 19:6), even as we have previously addressed, all do not have the *"Gift of Tongues"* as it relates to one of the nine Gifts of the Spirit, even as Paul here addresses. Our non-Pentecostal friends get this confused at times.

(31) "BUT COVET EARNESTLY THE BEST GIFTS: AND YET SHEW I UNTO YOU A MORE EXCELLENT WAY."

The phrase, *"But covet earnestly the best Gifts,"* in essence speaks of that which the Holy Spirit wants a particular Believer to have. Several things are said here:

1. The *"Gifts"* are available to all. They have not passed away as some teach.

2. As Believers we are to *"covet"* these Gifts, which means to passionately desire such. This shows a strong interest in the Lord, and a strong interest in the things of the Lord.

3. *"Best Gifts"* as it is here used, does not mean that some of the Gifts are insignificant, but rather refers to the *"best"* for that particular Believer, which the Holy Spirit Alone knows.

The phrase, *"And yet shew I unto you a more excellent way,"* refers to the foundation of Love, of which Paul addresses in the next Chapter, and which must undergird all that we have and do in the Lord. In other words, whatever we do is to be motivated by unconditional love rather than by selfishness (Rossier).

NOTES

As well, this last phrase does not mean, as some teach, that the Gifts of the Spirit are of no consequence, but that we should rather desire the attribute or Gift of *"Love."*

The idea is, as stated, that love be a motivating force, and if not, even as Paul will say, our efforts will be as a *"sounding brass, or a tinkling cymbal."*

Inasmuch as Paul is here addressing the Church, perhaps a fuller exposition on this all-important *"Body of Christ"* would be appropriate.

## THE CHURCH

Plainly Jesus designed that there should be a society of His followers to give to mankind His Gospel and minister to mankind in His Spirit, to labor as He did for the increase of the Kingdom of God.

He fashioned no point by point organization for this society . . . He did a greater thing than give such — He gave Life. Jesus formed the society of His followers by calling them together about Himself. He communicated to it as far as He could while He was on earth His Own Life, His Spirit, and Purpose.

He promised to continue to the end of the world to impart His Life to His society, His Church. His great Gift to the Church, we may say, was Himself (Nichols).

## THE NATURE OF THE CHURCH

What is the Church? The question may be answered by considering:

1. The words describing that institution.
2. Words describing Christians.
3. Illustrations describing the Church.

## WORDS DESCRIBING THE CHURCH

The New Testament Greek word for Church is *"ecclesia,"* meaning *"an assembly of called-out ones."* The term is applied to:

1. The whole body of Christians in one city (Acts 11:22; 13:1).
2. A congregation (Rom. 16:5; I Cor. 14:19, 35).
3. The whole Body of Believers on earth (Eph. 5:32).

Our English word *"Church"* is derived from the Greek *"kuriake,"* meaning *"that which belongs to the Lord."* The Church, then, is a company of people called out from the world's system, even though remaining in the world, who profess and tender allegiance to the Lord Jesus Christ.

WORDS DESCRIBING CHRISTIANS

1. Brethren: The Church is a spiritual brotherhood or fellowship, in which all divisions that separate mankind have been abolished.

A. *"There is neither Jew nor Gentile"* — the deepest of all divisions based on religious isolation is overcome.

B. *"There is neither Greek nor Barbarian"* — the deepest of cultural divisions is overcome.

C. *"There is neither bond nor free"* — the deepest of social and economic divisions is overcome.

D. *"There is neither male nor female"* — the deepest of all human divisions is overcome.

2. Believers: Christians are called *"Believers"* because their characteristic Doctrine is Faith in the Lord Jesus.

3. Saints: They are called *"Saints"* (literally *"consecrated or holy ones"*) because they are separated from the world and dedicated to God.

4. The Elect: They are referred to as *"the Elect"* or *"the Chosen"* because God has chosen them for an important ministry and a glorious destiny.

5. Disciples: They are *"Disciples"* (literally *"learners"*) because under spiritual training with Christ-inspired instructors.

6. Christians: They are *"Christians"* because their spiritual experience centers around the Person of Christ.

7. Those of the Way: In the early days, they were often known as *"those of this way"* (Acts 9:2) because they lived according to a special way of life.

THE BODY OF CHRIST

The Lord Jesus Christ left this earth more than nineteen hundred years ago; but He is still in the world through the Person, Office, and Ministry of the Holy Spirit, Who makes His home through individual members of the Church which is His Body (I Cor. 3:16).

As Jesus lived His natural life on earth in an individual human body, so He lives His mystical life in a Body drawn from the human race in general. At the conclusion of the Gospels, we do not write, *"The End,"* but rather, *"To Be Continued,"* because the Life of Christ continues to be expressed through His Disciples as evidenced by the Book of Acts and by subsequent Church History. *"As My Father hath sent Me, even so send I you. He that receiveth you, receiveth Me."*

NOTES

THE VINE AND THE BRANCHES

Before He left this earth, Christ promised to assume this new Body. However, He used another illustration, *"I am the Vine, ye are the branches"* (Jn. 15:5). The Vine is incomplete without the branches; and the branches are nothing apart from the Life which flows from the Vine.

If Christ is to be known to the world, it must be through those who bear His name and share His Life. And to the extent that the Church has kept in touch with Christ her Head, has she shared His Life and experiences.

As Christ was anointed at the Jordan, so the Church was anointed at Pentecost. Jesus went about preaching the Gospel to the poor, healing the brokenhearted, and preaching deliverance to the captives; and the true Church has ever followed in His footsteps.

*"As He is, so are we in this world"* (I Jn. 4:17).

As Christ was denounced as a political menace and finally crucified, so His Church has in many instances, been crucified (figuratively speaking) by persecuting rulers. But, like her Lord, she has risen again and again! The life of Christ within her renders her indestructible.

This thought of the Church's identification with Christ must have been in the mind of Paul when he spoke about completing *"that which is behind* (remains) *of the afflictions of Christ in my flesh for His Body's sake, which is the Church"* (Col. 1:24).

AN ORGANISM

The use of the above illustration reminds us that the Church is an Organism, not merely an organization. An organization is a group of individuals voluntarily associated together for a certain purpose, such as a fraternal organization or trade union.

An organism is any living thing which develops by inherent life. Used figuratively, it means the sum total of related parts, in which the relationship of each part to part involves a relationship to the whole.

Thus, an automobile could be called an *"organization"* of certain mechanical parts; a human body is an *"organism"* because it is composed of many members and organs animated by a common life.

The human body is one, yet it is made up of millions of living cells, even as we have been studying; in like manner, the Body of Christ is one, though composed of millions of Born-Again souls.

As the human body is vitalized by the soul, so the Body of Christ is vitalized by the Holy Spirit. *"For by One Spirit are we all baptized into One Body"* (I Cor. 12:13).

## JESUS AND THE DIFFERENCE

Jesus, and Jesus Alone, of all the founders of the world's great religions (Christianity is really not a religion but rather a Relationship with Christ) brought to life a permanent organism, a permanent union of minds and souls, centering in Himself. Christians are not merely followers of Christ, but members of Christ, and of one another.

Buddha developed his society of the Awakened Ones (so-called), but the relation between them is merely external — the relation of teacher and pupil. It is his doctrine which unites them, not his life.

The same may be said of Zoroaster, of Socrates, or Mohammed, and the other religious geniuses of the race. But Christ is not only the Teacher, He is the Life of Christians.

What He founded was not merely a society which studied and propagated His ideas, but an organism which lived by His Life, a Body indwelt and guided by His Spirit (Dumphy).

## THE TEMPLE OF GOD

A Temple is a place in which God, Who dwells everywhere, localizes Himself in one particular place where His people may always find Him *"at home"* (Ex. 25:8; I Ki. 8:27).

As God dwelt in the Tabernacle and Temple, so He now lives by His Spirit in the Church, i.e. *"individual hearts and lives of Believers"* (I Cor. 3:16-17; Eph. 2:21-22). In this Spiritual Temple, Christians, as Priests, offer up Spiritual Sacrifices — Sacrifices of prayer, praise, and good works.

## THE FOUNDING OF THE CHURCH

Israel is described as a Church in that it was a nation called out from other nations to be the servant of God (Acts 7:38). When the Old Testament was translated into Greek, the word *"congregation"* (of Israel) was rendered *"Ekklesia"* or *"Church."* Israel, then, was the congregation or Church of Jehovah. After His rejection by the Jewish Church, which meant that the Kingdom was rejected, which subjected the world to continued rule by man, which meant more war and hatred, Christ of necessity founded a new Congregation or Church, a Divine Institution that should continue His Work on earth (Mat. 16:18). This is the *"Church"* which came into existence on the Day of Pentecost.

NOTES

## THE CHURCH OF JESUS CHRIST

The Church of Jesus Christ came into existence as such on the Day of Pentecost, when it was consecrated by the Anointing of the Spirit. Just as the Tabernacle was built and then consecrated by the descent of the Divine Glory (Ex. 40:34), so the first members of the Church were assembled in the Temple and consecrated as the Church by the descent of the Holy Spirit.

It is likely that the first Christians saw in this event the return of the Shekinah which had long departed from the Temple, and Whose absence was lamented by some of the Rabbis.

David gathered the materials for the building of the Temple, but the work was done by his successor, Solomon.

In like manner, Jesus had gathered the materials, so to speak, of His Church, during His earthly Ministry, but the edifice itself was reared by His Successor, the Holy Spirit. Actually, this work was done by the Spirit working through the Apostles, who laid the foundations and built the Church by their preaching, teaching, and organizing. Therefore, the Church is described as being *"built upon the foundation of the Apostles"* (Eph. 2:20).

## MEMBERSHIP IN THE CHURCH

The New Testament lays down the following conditions for membership: implicit Faith in the Gospel and a heartfelt trust in Christ as the only Divine Savior (Acts 16:31); submission to Water Baptism as a symbolic testimony to Faith in Christ, and verbal confession of Faith (Rom. 10:9-10), i.e. *"Born-Again"* (Jn. 3:3).

In the beginning (the Early Church) practically the entire membership of the Church was truly regenerate. *"And the Lord added to the Church daily such as should be saved"* (Acts 2:47).

Entering the Church was not a matter of joining an organization, but of becoming members of Christ through the Born-Again experience as a branch is grafted to a tree. In course of time, however, as the Church increased in numbers and popularity, Water Baptism and Church Membership, per se, took the place of conversion; the result was the influx into the Church of large numbers of people who were not Christian at heart.

And this has been more or less the condition of Christendom ever since. As in Old Testament times, there was an Israel within an Israel — Israelites in deed as well as Israelites in creed — so in the course of Church History, we see a Church within the Church — possessing Christians in the midst of professing Christians.

## THE VISIBLE AND INVISIBLE CHURCH

We must, therefore, distinguish between the Church invisible, which is composed of true Christians, irrespective of denominational affiliation, and the Church visible, consisting of all who profess to be Christians — the first being composed of those whose names are written in Heaven, the second comprising all those who have their names on earthly Church books.

This distinction is implied in Matthew 13:11, where the Lord speaks of *"the mysteries of the Kingdom of Heaven"* — which expression corresponds to the general designation, *"Christendom."*

The parables in that Chapter trace the spiritual history of Christendom between the first and second Advents of Christ, and in them we learn that there will be a mixture of good and bad in the Church until the Lord's Coming when the Church will be purified and a separation made between the genuine and the false (Mat. 13:36-43, 47-49).

Paul expresses the same Truth by comparing the Church to a house in which there are many vessels, some unto honor, and some unto dishonor (II Tim. 2:19-21).

## THE WORK OF THE CHURCH

1. It is the work of the Church to preach the Gospel to every creature (Mat. 28:19-20), and to expound the Plan of Salvation as taught in the Scriptures. Christ has made Salvation possible by providing it; the Church must make it actual by proclaiming it.

NOTES

2. The Church is to provide a means of Worship. Israel possessed a Divinely appointed system of Worship by which they approached God in all the needs and crises of life. The Church likewise must be a house of prayer for all people where God is honored in Worship, prayer, and testimony.

3. The Church is to provide spiritual fellowship. Man is a social being; he craves fellowship and exchange of friendship. He naturally assembles with those who share the same interests.

The Church provides a fellowship based on the Fatherhood of God and the Lordship of Christ. It is a Brotherhood of those who share a common spiritual experience.

The warmth of fellowship was one of the outstanding characteristics of the Early Church. In a world governed by the machinelike Roman Empire, where the individual was practically ignored, men longed for a fellowship where they might lose the feeling of loneliness and helplessness. In such a world, one of the strongest drawing features of the Church was the warmth and solidarity of fellowship — a fellowship where all earthly distinctions were obliterated and where men and women became Brothers and Sisters in Christ.

4. The Church is to hold up the moral standard. The Church is *"the light of the world,"* to banish moral ignorance; is the *"salt of the earth"* to preserve it from moral corruption.

The Church must teach men how to live as well as how to die. It must hold forth God's Plan for the regulation of all spheres of life and activity. Against the downward trends of society it must lift a warning voice; at all danger points it must plant a beacon light.

## THE ORDINANCES OF THE CHURCH

New Testament Christianity is not a ritualistic religion; at the heart of it is man's direct contact with God through the Spirit. Therefore, it does not lay down a hard and fast order of Worship, but leaves the Church in every age and land to adapt a method best suited for the expression of its life.

There are, however, two Ceremonies which are essential for proper fellowship and communion with the Lord (but not for Salvation) because Divinely ordained, namely Water Baptism and the Lord's Supper. Because of their

NOTES

sacred character they are sometimes described as *"Sacraments"*— literally *"Sacred Things"* or *"Oaths consecrated by a Sacred Rite"*; they are also referred to as *"Ordinances"* because they are *"Ceremonies ordained"* by the Lord Himself.

Water Baptism is the symbolic rite of entrance into the Christian Church, and symbolizes spiritual life begun; the Lord's Supper is symbolic of His Death and is the rite of Communion and signifies spiritual life continued.

The first, pictures Faith in Christ; the second, pictures fellowship with Christ. The first, is administered only once, for there can be but one beginning of the Spiritual Life; the second, is administered frequently, teaching that Spiritual-Life must be nourished.

## WATER BAPTISM

The word *"Baptize"* used in the formula means literally to dip or to immerse. This interpretation is confirmed by Greek Scholars and Church historians; even Scholars belonging to churches that baptize by sprinkling admit that immersion was the earliest mode. Moreover, there is good reason for believing that to the Jews of Apostolic times, the command to be *"Baptized"* would suggest immersion.

They were acquainted with *"Proselyte's Baptism"* which signified a heathen's conversion to Judaism.

The convert stood up to his neck in water while the Law was read to him, after which he plunged himself beneath the water as a sign that he was cleansed from the defilements of heathenism and had begun to live a new life of God's Covenant people. However, this practice was not commanded in the Law of Moses, but was added by men as a part of Jewish Ritual.

## SPRINKLING?

Whence, then, came the practice of sprinkling and pouring?

When the Church forsook the simplicity of the New Testament and became influenced by pagan ideas, it attached an unscriptural importance to Water Baptism, which came to be considered fully essential to Regeneration.

It was, therefore, administered to the sick and dying. Since immersion was out of the question in such cases, Baptism was administered by sprinkling. Later because of the convenience of the method, it was made general in some circles. Also, because of the importance of the Ordinance, pouring was permitted when there was insufficient water for immersion. Witness the following quotation from an ancient writing of the Second Century:

*"Now concerning Baptism, baptize thus: Having taught all of these things, Baptize ye into the Name of the Father and of the Son and of the Holy Spirit, in living* (running) *water. And if thou hast not living water, Baptize into other water: And if thou canst not in cold, then in warm. But if thou hast neither, pour water thrice upon the head in the Name of the Father, and of the Son, and of the Holy Spirit."*

However, the Scriptural original mode is by immersion, which is true to the symbolical meaning of Baptism, namely Death, Burial, and Resurrection, which is portrayed in the spiritual sense in Romans 6:1-4.

## THE FORMULA

*"Baptizing them in the Name of the Father, and of the Son, and of the Holy Spirit"* (Mat. 28:19). How do we reconcile this with Peter's command, *"Be Baptized every one of you in the Name of Jesus Christ"* (Acts 2:38).

These latter words do not represent a Baptismal formula, but were simply a statement that such persons who were baptized, acknowledged Jesus to be Lord and Christ. For example, the *"Didache,"* a Christian document of A.D. 100, speaks of Christian Baptism being in the Name of the Lord Jesus, but when it comes to describe the Rite in detail, the Trinitarian formula of Matthew 28:19 is prescribed.

When Paul speaks of Israel's being baptized in the Red Sea *"unto Moses"* he is not referring to a formula that was pronounced at the time; he simply means that because of the miraculous passage through the Red Sea the Israelites accepted Moses as the heaven-sent guide and teacher. In like manner, to be Baptized in the Name of Jesus means to commit one's self wholly and eternally to Him as a heaven-sent Savior, and acceptance of His Leadership dictates the acceptance of the formula given by Jesus Himself in Matthew Chapter 28.

The literal Greek rendering of Acts 2:38 is, *"be Baptized on the Name of Jesus Christ."* This means according to Thayer's Greek Lexicon, that the Jews were to *"repose their hope and confidence in His Messianic authority."*

Notice that the Trinitarian formula is descriptive of an experience. Those who are Baptized in the Name of the Triune God are thereby testifying that they have been plunged into spiritual communion with the Trinity; so that to them it may be said, *"The Grace of the Lord Jesus Christ and the Love of God and the Communion of the Holy Spirit is with you"* (II Cor. 13:14).

WHO ARE TO BE BAPTIZED?

All who sincerely repent of their sins and exercise a Living Faith in the Lord Jesus are eligible for Baptism.

In the Apostolic Church, the rite was accompanied by the following outward expressions:

1. Profession of Faith (Acts 8:37).
2. Prayer (Acts 22:16).
3. Vow of Consecration (I Pet. 3:21).

Since infants have no sins to repent of and cannot exercise Faith, they are logically excluded from Water Baptism. We are not thereby forbidding them to come to Christ (Mat. 19:13-14) for they may be dedicated to Him in a Public Service.

THE EFFICACY

Water Baptism in itself has no saving power; people are Baptized not in order to be saved but because they are saved. Therefore, we cannot say that the Rite is essential to Salvation. But we may insist that it is essential to full obedience.

As the election of the President of our land is made complete by his inauguration, so the convert's election to God's Grace and Glory is made complete by his public inauguration (water baptism) as a member of the Body of Christ.

THE MEANING

Water Baptism pictures the following ideas:

1. Salvation: Water Baptism is a Sacred Drama (if we may so speak), portraying the fundamentals of the Gospel. The lowering of the convert pictures Christ's Death accomplished; the submersion of the convert speaks of death ratified, or His Burial; the raising of the convert signifies Death conquered, or Christ's Resurrection.

2. Experience: The fact that the acts are performed with the convert shows that he has been spiritually identified with Christ. The immersion proclaims the message, *"Christ died for sin in order that this man might die to sin."*

NOTES

The raising of the convert conveys the following message: *"Christ rose from the dead in order that this man (or woman) might live a new life of Righteousness."*

3. Regeneration: The experience of the new birth has been described as a *"washing"* (literally *"bath"*) (Tit. 3:5), because thereby the sins and defilements of the old life are washed away.

As washing with water cleanses the body, so God in connection with the death of Christ and through the Holy Spirit, cleanses the soul. Water Baptism pictures this cleansing. *"Arise, and be Baptized, and wash away thy sins"* (that is as a sign of what has already been done) (Acts 22:16).

4. Testimony: *"For as many of you as have been Baptized into Christ have put on Christ"* (Gal. 3:27).

Even though this particular Verse does not speak of Water Baptism, but rather that which takes place at conversion, and comes about by Faith, still, Water Baptism signifies that the convert has by Faith *"put on"* Christ — the Character of Christ — so that men may see Christ in him as they see the uniform upon a soldier.

By the Rite of Baptism, the convert, figuratively speaking, publicly dons the uniform of the Kingdom of Christ.

THE LORD'S SUPPER

We have already given a dissertation on this particular Ordinance in Chapter 11; consequently, please refer to that Chapter.

THE WORSHIP OF THE CHURCH

From Paul's Epistles, we gather that there were two kinds of meetings for worship: one was in the nature of a prayer, praise, and preaching service; the other was a Worship Service known as the *"Love Feast"* (*"Agape"*).

The first was a public service; the second was a private service to which only Christians were admitted.

THE PUBLIC SERVICE

The public meeting *"was carried on by people as the Spirit moved them,"* writes Robert Hastings Nichols, and continues:

*"Prayers were offered and testimony and instruction given. There was singing of the Psalms and also of Christian Hymns which began to be written in the First Century. The Old*

*Testament Scriptures were read and expounded, and there was reading or recitation from memory of accounts of the Words and Deeds of Jesus. When Apostles sent to Churches letters such as we have in the Epistles of the New Testament, these were also read."*

At any time, this simple service might be broken into and superseded by the manifestation of the Spirit in the form of Prophecy, Tongues, and Interpretations or some inspired insight into the Scriptures. This feature of primitive worship is recognized by all careful students of Church History, regardless of their Church affiliation or school of thought. That this Spirit-inspired worship was a powerful means of touching the unconverted may be gathered from I Corinthians 14:24-25.

THE PRIVATE SERVICE

We read that the first Christians continued in *"breaking of bread"* (Acts 2:42).

Do these words describe an ordinary meal or the celebration of the Lord's Supper?

Perhaps both.

This is what may have occurred: at first the fellowship of the early Disciples was so close and vital that they had their meals in common. As they surrounded the table to ask God's Blessing upon the food, the memory of Christ's last Passover Meal would come to their minds, and the Blessing over the food would spontaneously enlarge itself into a service of Worship, so that in many cases it would be difficult to determine whether the Disciples were having a common meal or partaking of the Communion. Life and Worship were closely related in those days!

But very early, the two acts — Breaking of Bread and the Lord's Supper — were distinguished, so that the following was the order of service.

On a stated day, the Christians would assemble for a sacred fellowship meal known as the Love Feast, which was a joyful and sacred meal symbolizing brotherly love. Everyone brought provisions for the meal and these were to be shared by all alike.

In I Corinthians 11:21-22, Paul rebukes the selfishness of those who ate their food without sharing with the poor.

At the close of the Love Feast, the Lord's Supper was celebrated. In the Corinthian Church, some of the people became drunk (intoxicated) at the *"Agape"* and partook of the Sacrament in that unworthy condition.

Later in the First Century, the Lord's Supper was separated from the Agape or Love Feasts and celebrated on the Lord's Day morning.

Ultimately, the Love Feasts ceased altogether, and for various reasons, with, of course, the Lord's Supper continuing as it was meant to be.

THE GOVERNMENT OF THE CHURCH

It is clear that the Lord Jesus purposed that there should be a society of His followers to give mankind His Gospel and to represent Him in the world. However, He did not fashion an organization or Plan of Government, regarding a blueprint or constitution, etc. He gave no detailed Rule of Faith and practice. He did, however, ordain the two simple Rites of Baptism and Communion.

Yet He did not ignore organization, for His Promise of the coming Comforter implied that the Apostles should be led into all truth concerning these matters. And that's exactly what they did!

THE BOOK OF ACTS AS THE PATTERN

He ordained and presented Government by example, which is given to us in the Book of Acts, as we observe the Holy Spirit lay down the rule of the Government of God.

What He did for the Church was something higher than Organization, at least as we think of such — He imparted to it His very Life, making it, as previously stated, a living Organism. As a living body adapts itself to its environment, so the Living Body of Christ was to adapt itself to the environment furnished by the Holy Spirit. Of course, the Holy Spirit will not lead one contrary to the Teachings of Christ or to the Word of God in any manner. Any development contrary to Scriptural Principles is a corruption.

PLACE OF WORSHIP

During the days following Pentecost, the Believers worshipped privately in homes and kept the prayer times of the Temple (Acts 2:46). This was supplemented by Apostolic teaching and fellowship. As the Church grew in numbers, organization developed as the Holy Spirit

NOTES

placed emphasis in certain directions and areas. The possession of Spiritual Gifts singled out certain individuals for the Work of the Ministry. This was strictly the leading and guidance of the Holy Spirit.

DEMOCRATIC IN GOVERNMENT?

If the reader is to notice, the heading is followed by a question mark. One might call the Early Church democratic, but it would be in the form of a democracy fashioned by the Holy Spirit. The Gifts of the Spirit were available to all where any and all could be Divinely endowed with Gifts for Special Ministry, at least as the Holy Spirit directed. It is true that the Apostles and Elders presided at Business Meetings and at the appointing of Officers; but these things were done in cooperation with the congregation (Acts 6:3-6; 15:22; I Cor. 16:3; II Cor. 8:19; Phil. 2:25).

From Acts 14:23 and Titus 1:5, it might seem that Paul and Barnabas and Titus appointed Elders without consulting the congregation; however, upon further investigation, I think the record will show that they appointed them with the approval of the members of the Church concerned. So, it was democratic only in the manner that the Holy Spirit was allowed to have His way in all things, with the leaders and people working closely with Him concerning Direction.

HIERARCHY?

We see plainly that there is no warrant in the New Testament for the merging of the Churches into an Ecclesiastical machine governed by a Hierarchy.

Actually, the Early Church had no Centralized Government. Each local Church was self-governing and managed its own affairs in freedom.

Naturally, the Twelve were regarded with deference because of their relation to Christ and they exercised a certain authority (Acts Chpt. 15).

As well, Paul was used by the Lord mightily respecting oversight regarding the Gentile Churches; however, this authority was purely spiritual, and not an official authority such as that granted by an organization.

While each Local Church was independent of the other as far as jurisdiction was concerned, the New Testament Churches did enter into cooperative relationships with one another, in other words, a fellowship (Rom. 15:1, 26-27; II Cor. 8:19; Gal. 2:10; III Jn. vs. 8).

In the early centuries, the Local Churches, while they never lacked the sense that they all belonged to one body, were independent, self-governing communities, preserving relations with each other, not by any political organization embracing them all, but by fraternal fellowship through visits of particular Preachers, interchange of letters, and some indefinite giving and receiving assistance in the election and setting apart of Pastors.

THE MINISTRY OF THE CHURCH

Two kinds of Ministry are recognized in the Early Church:

1. The general and prophetic Ministry — general because exercised in relation to the Churches in general rather than to one Church in particular, and prophetic in that it was created by the possession of Spiritual Gifts.

2. The local and practical Ministry — local because confined to one Church, and practical because dealing with the administration of the Church.

THE GENERAL AND PROPHETIC MINISTRY

Please see commentary on Verse 28.

THE LOCAL AND PRACTICAL MINISTRY

The local ministry which was appointed by the Church on the basis of certain qualifications (I Tim. Chpt. 3) included:

1. Pastors: these went under the name not only of Pastors, but as well of Elders, Presbyters, Bishops, and Overseers. However, all of these titles refer to the Pastor of a *local Church* (Acts 20:28; Eph. 4:11).

In the Churches, there were usually several Preachers but one Senior Pastor to whom the other Preachers were to submit themselves (I Pet. 5:1-5).

2. Associated with the Pastors were a number of assistants called Deacons (Acts 6:1-4; Phil. 1:1; I Tim. 3:8-13) and Deaconesses (Rom. 16:1; Phil. 4:3), whose work appears to have been largely house-to-house visitation and practical ministry to the poor and needy (I Tim. 5:8-11).

The Deacons also assisted the Elders in the celebration of the Lord's Supper.

NOTES

(Most of the material regarding *"the Church"* was derived from the scholarship of Myer Pearlman.)

*"The Church's one Foundation is Jesus Christ her Lord;*
*"She is His new creation by water and the Word:*
*"From Heaven He came and sought her to be His holy bride;*
*"With His Own Blood He bought her, and for her life He died."*

*"Elect from every nation yet one o'er all the earth,*
*"Her charter of Salvation, One Lord, one Faith, one Birth;*
*"One Holy Name she blesses, partakes one holy food,*
*"And to one hope she presses, With every Grace endued."*

*"Though with a scornful wonder Men see her sore oppressed,*
*"By schisms rent asunder, By heresies distressed,*
*"Yet Saints their watch are keeping; their cry goes up — 'How long?'*
*"But soon the night of weeping shall be the morn of song."*

*"Yet she on earth hath union with God the Three in One,*
*"And mystic sweet communion with those whose rest is won.*
*"Oh, happy ones and holy! Lord, give us Grace that we,*
*"Like them, the meek and lowly, on high may dwell with Thee."*

## CHAPTER 13

(1) "THOUGH I SPEAK WITH THE TONGUES OF MEN AND OF ANGELS, AND HAVE NOT CHARITY, I AM BECOME AS SOUNDING BRASS, OR A TINKLING CYMBAL."

The phrase, *"Though I speak with the Tongues of men and of Angels,"* actually says in the Greek, *"If it were possible to speak with the tongues of men and of Angels . . ."*

NOTES

We do know that Paul *"spoke in Tongues"* often, because he said in Verse 18 of the next Chapter, *"I thank my God, I speak with Tongues more than ye all."* As well, as the context will show, he wasn't speaking of linguistic abilities (proficient in two or more languages), but rather to speaking with Tongues as a result of being Baptized with the Holy Spirit, even as he is addressing in I Corinthians Chapter 14.

Regarding the *"Tongue of Angels,"* we must not assume that Paul is writing only hypothetically. This would conflict with his evident purpose, namely to show that love must animate all even the highest Gifts. All else that Paul writes about Angels shows them to be real, and so their language is real as well. Also, by Paul using the plural *"Tongues"* in no way compels us to think that the Angels in Heaven speak a number of languages.

Actually, there is a possibility that Paul actually heard Angels speak, when *"he was caught up into paradise, and heard unspeakable words"* (II Cor. 12:4).

The phrase, *"And have not Charity,"* refers to *"Agape love,"* actually, *"the God Kind of Love,"* and should have been translated accordingly.

### THE ENVIRONMENT

That which Paul is expressing pertains to the environment in which the Gifts are exercised, and that such is just as important as the actual exercise of the Gifts.

Some people fail with respect to one of these aspects, and some to the other. That is, some people who are not Pentecostal reject the exercise of these Gifts altogether, while some Pentecostals exercise them without love. Either approach is a dreadful mistake, and it invariably leads to serious consequences (Rossier).

The manner in which this Chapter begins, indicates to us that Paul did not begin a new subject, but was describing the Scriptural motive that must underlie the functioning of Spiritual Gifts, and all else which occupies the Child of God for that matter.

### THE HEART OF THE APOSTLE

Gregory Nazianzen, one of the most celebrated orators of the early Church of the Fourth Century, writes in regard to this Chapter on love that here we may read what Paul said about Paul.

*"It is true; only a man in whose heart the Spirit of God has kindled a Faith like Paul's could evidence a love like Paul's and on the basis of his own experience of that love, recorded its glories in what may be called the 'Psalm of Love.'"*

Paul's own heart lies open before us in this Chapter. Here is the motive power, Faith working through Love, that sent him over Land and Sea to preach to others the unsearchable riches of Christ. Here is the inner power that sustained him amide all his labors, burdens, trials, sufferings, persecutions.

Here is what made him rise superior to hunger and hardship, false friends and bitter foes, bodily beatings and dangers of death.

We cannot understand this man save as we understand his Faith and its Fruit of Christian Love. All of his great joys and abilities, his high and holy office, his exalted position in the Work of God, his stupendous task and his astounding success — all of them are what they are and what they came to be because of the Love of Christ which abounded in Paul's heart.

This we must realize when he tells the Corinthians that besides his instruction on the Spiritual Gifts themselves, he now shows them the inner, Spiritual Power that must energize all of these Gifts if they are to be of real benefit to the Church.

## THE LOVE OF GOD

It is unfortunate that the King James translators used the word *"charity"* instead of *"love."*

The type of *"Love"* of which the Holy Spirit here speaks through the Apostle, would perhaps be properly explained by first of all going to Romans 12:9, where Paul said, *"Let love be without dissimulation."* The word *"love"* there as here, is from the same Greek work for *"love"* that we have in John 3:16; Romans 5:5 and I Corinthians Chapter 13. It is in its essence a self-sacrificial love, a love that puts self aside in an effort to help and bless others, yes, a love that goes to the point of suffering if that is necessary in order to bless others.

And for that highest kind of blessing, suffering is necessary, for *"we must bleed if we would bless."* This is the love of God, not love for God, but the love which God is and which He provides through the operation of the Holy Spirit as the Believer depends upon His Ministry, a love that will flow like rivers of water out from the Christian who is filled with the Spirit, refreshing the dry parched lives around him and making a desert-heart blossom like a rose. This is the love which God says should be without dissimulation.

NOTES

## DISSIMULATION

The word, *"dissimulation"* is from a Greek word which is made up of three parts, a verb which means *"to judge,"* a preposition which means *"under,"* and the Greek letter Alpha which when prefixed to a word gives it a meaning directly opposite to that which it had before.

It means *"to judge under,"* and has reference to one who gave off his judgement from under a mask or a cloak, thus appearing to be what he was not. This word comes over into our language in the work *"hypocrite,"* one who plays the part of a character which he is not, and does it to deceive. So, Paul is saying, *"Let love be without hypocrisy."*

## COUNTERFEIT LOVE

That is, do not try to counterfeit this love by seeming to love a Christian brother and yet not be willing to put that love into action. The same word is used in II Corinthians 6:6 and I Peter 1:22, where it is translated *"unfeigned."*

The world wears a mask. The love which it shows on the face is only external. That is feigned love. Ours should be, and in fact, must be unfeigned. If a Saint does not have a love which is unfeigned, the trouble is with his adjustment to the Holy Spirit Who is the One to provide that Saint with that love.

The Spirit-filled Saint does not have to play the hypocrite in the matter of love, for love shines right out of his eyes. It is on his face, in his actions.

## FOUR GREEK WORDS FOR LOVE

1. Stergein:

Stergein is used in the New Testament oftentimes with a prefix which negates the word. That is, makes it mean the opposite to what it meant in itself. It occurs in Romans 1:31 and II Timothy 3:3, and is translated in both instances by the words *"without natural affection."*

The word appears also in Romans 12:10 with the word *"philos* (love)," compounded with it, and is translated, *"kindly affection."*

Stergein designates the *"the quiet and abiding feeling within us, which resting on an object as near to us, recognizes that we are closely bound up with it and takes satisfaction in its recognition."*

It is a love that is *"a natural movement of the soul," "something almost like gravitation or some other force of blind nature."*

It is the love of parents for children and children for parents, of husband for wife and wife for husband, of close relations one for another.

It is found in the animal world in the love which the animal has for its offspring. It is a love of obligation, the term being used not in its moral sense, but in a natural sense. It is a necessity under the circumstances. This kind of love is the binding factor by which any natural or social unit is held together.

2. Eran or Eros:

This Greek word is thought so little of by the Holy Spirit that it is not found one single time in the New Testament. The word *"passion"* describes it. It is passion seeking satisfaction.

It is not intrinsically a base word. In its use it is found at the two extremes of low and high. It was used in pagan Greek writings of sex love.

It was used in Christian writings of Divine love, but I think misplaced.

Actually, the word refers to a very selfish type of love. For instance, the person is loved if the person is useful, i.e., rich, powerful, handsome, beautiful, talented, or hold place or position. In other words, the person is loved if they make certain people or situations look good. The moment they do not have that attraction, whatever that attraction may be, they're no longer *"loved."*

Actually, this is the type of love manifested most in the world, and, sadly, mostly in the Church as well.

Many people are not welcome in particular Churches, because the color of their skin is wrong, or their station in life does not meet certain standards.

However, such is not true Christianity, but rather a corrupted form.

The very ingredient of the Gospel, is that it reaches out to all, whatever race they may be, whatever their status in life may be, whatever their educational background. If it is not that way, it is not true Christianity, and can be described by this particular Greek word *"Eros."*

NOTES

3. Philein:

Philein is used 45 times in its various forms of verb and noun. This is an unimpassioned love, a friendly love. It is a love that is called out of one's heart as a response to the pleasure one takes in a person or object. It is based upon an inner community between the person loving and the person or object loved. That is, both have things in common with one another.

The one loving finds a reflection of his own nature in the person or thing loved. It is a love of liking, and affection for someone or something that is the outgoing of one's heart in delight to that which affords pleasure. The Greeks made much of friendship, and this word was used by them to designate this form of mutual attraction. *"Whatever in an object that is adapted to give pleasure, tends to call out this affection."*

It is connected with a sense of the agreeable and the object loved. The words which best express this kind of love are *"fondness, affection, liking."*

*"It shows the inclination which springs out of commerce with a person or is called out by qualities in an object which are agreeable to us."*

As an outgrowth of its meaning of fondness, it sometimes carries that sentiment over into an outward expression of the same, that of kissing.

4. Agapan or Agape:

Agapan is used in its verb, noun, and adjective forms about 320 times in the New Testament. It is a love called out of a person's heart by *"an awakened sense of value in an object which causes one to prize it."* It expresses a love of approbation and esteem. Its impulse comes from the idea of prizing. It is a love that recognizes the worthiness of the object loved. Thus, this love consists of the soul's sense of the value and preciousness of its object, and its response to its recognized worth in admiring affection.

In other words, it is the God kind of love.

In contrasting *"Phileo"* and *"Agape,"* we might say that the former is a love of pleasure, the latter a love of preciousness; the former a love of delight, the latter a love of esteem; the former a love called out of the heart by the apprehension of pleasurable qualities in the object loved, the latter a love called out of the heart by the apprehension of valuable qualities in the object loved; the former takes pleasure in, the latter ascribes value to; the former is a love of liking, the latter is a love of prizing.

As to the reason why *"philein"* or *"phileo"* occurs only 45 times in the New Testament in all forms, while *"agapan"* or *"agape"* is found 320 times in its various forms, the following can be said.

The principle reason for the more frequent use of *"agapan"* in the New Testament as over against the infrequent use of *"philein"* is that *"philein"* was a commonly used word for *"love"* in the classics, and *"agapan"* was used most infrequently, and when common Greek was spread over the world by the conquering armies of Alexander the Great, and remained in its simplified and modified form as the international language of the period between Alexander and Constantine, *"agapan"* suddenly sprang into the ascendancy.

Because it was the common word for *"love"* during these centuries, the New Testament writers naturally found it not only desirable but necessary to use it. It became the general word for love in the New Testament which most described the Love of God, and was sanctioned by the Holy Spirit.

## TAUGHT BY THE HOLY SPIRIT

But this does not mean that both words (Agape — Philein) are used indiscriminately, the one for the other, without any conscious sense of the differences between them. Whenever *"agapan"* is used, it means that the writer goes out of his way to use a word that was not in common use, and because he desired to convey a thought which *"philein"* did not contain. There was always a reason for such a selection although we may not always be able to see it.

The writers (I Cor. 2:13) claimed that their choice of words was taught them by the Holy Spirit. This being the case, we have an infallible use of the Greek words in their content of meaning and general usage in the Roman world at that period.

The Holy Spirit used *"agapan"* and *"philein"* advisedly in the places where they occur, and it is for us to find His reason and the Truth He wishes us to have from His use of the terms.

## THE UNDERSTANDING OF THE GOD KIND OF LOVE

In fact, even though the Greeks had the word *"agape"* it was seldom used at all. For instance, *"Agapan"* a form of *"Agape"* never was a common word in Classical Greek Literature, although it was in use from the beginning and occupied a distinctive place of its own. Its other form *"agapesis"* was rarely used. In fact, the form *"agape,"* so frequently found in the New Testament, did not occur in the Greek Classics at all.

This word *"agape"* conveyed the ideas of astonishment, wonder, admiration, and approbation when connected with the word *"agamai"* which meant *"to wonder at or admire."*

It was used in that particular form in Classical Literature in the same sentence with *"philein"* and had its distinctive sense, as stated, of *"a love of prizing"* as contrasted to *"philein," "a love of liking."* However, as stated, it was seldom ever used.

Consequently, the Holy Spirit used this word (Agape) to convey the new and higher conception of Divine Love which the New Testament presents.

The fact that the Greeks knew the word, but seldom used it due to having few, if any, examples to which it could be applied, made it the ideal receptacle into which the new moral and ethical content of Christianity could be poured.

## SELF-SACRIFICE

The Pagan Greeks knew nothing of the love of self-sacrifice for one's enemy which was exhibited at Calvary. Therefore, they had no word for that kind of love, simply because they did not need a word for that type of love, inasmuch as such was never exhibited, at least until Calvary. They knew nothing about the Divine analysis of this love which Paul gives us in this 13th Chapter of I Corinthians. So the New Testament writers seized upon this word as one that would express these exalted conceptions.

Therefore, the word *"agapan"* or *"agape,"* in the New Testament is to be understood in its meaning as given above, but also in the added meaning which has been poured into it by its use in the New Testament. The context of such passages as John 3:16; I Corinthians Chapter 13; I John 4:16; Romans 5:5 give us an adequate conception of its New Testament content of meaning.

## THE BIBLE STUDENT

I'm sure that the student can easily see the importance of knowing the Greek word which

NOTES

lies back of the English word *"love,"* as it pertains to the New Testament.

Some may wonder at the necessity of such detailed study. However, considering the tremendous significance of the Word of God, actually the single most important thing in the world by far, the true Lover of the Word of God has a hunger to know exactly what the Holy Spirit was saying, considering that it is the Holy Spirit Who gave these particular words (I Cor. 2:13), at least as far as a human being can grasp such.

The following are some examples which will help, I think, to explain these words to a greater degree.

## CALVARY

*"Agapan"* occurs in John 3:16. The love exhibited at Calvary was called out of the heart of God because of the preciousness of each lost soul, precious to God because He sees in lost humanity His Own Image even though that Image be marred by sin, precious to God because made of material which through Redemption can be transformed into the very Image of His Dear Son.

While it is a love based upon the estimation of the preciousness of the object loved, this from its Classical usage, it is also a love of self-sacrifice, complete self-sacrifice to the point of death to self, and that for one who bitterly hates the one who loves. This latter is its added New Testament meaning.

Include in that the constituent elements as analyzed by Paul in I Corinthians Chapter 13 where *"charity"* should be translated *"love,"* and we have the full content of this love which should always be kept in mind when interpreting Passages in the New Testament in which this word occurs, and where the love is shown either by God to man or by the Christian to others.

## HUSBANDS, LOVE YOUR WIVES

For instance, in interpreting *"Husbands, love your wives"* (Eph. 5:25), the love of John 3:16 and I Corinthians Chapter 13 is meant.

The husband already has a *"stergein"* and *"philein"* love for her. Consequently, these are saturated and thus elevated, purified, and ennobled by *"agapan,"* the God kind of Love.

However, Christian husbands are not left helpless in an attempt to obey this exhortation, for this very love is shed abroad in their hearts by the Holy Spirit (Rom. 5:5) and is one of His Fruits (Gal. 5:22).

When Saints are exhorted to love one another (I Jn. 4:11) it is with this *"agape"* kind of love.

## A LOVE OF LIKING

We now come to a consideration of the Greek word *"philein"* in the New Testament. We will examine a few representative passages.

The hypocrites love *"to pray standing in the Synagogues and in the corners of the streets"* (Mat. 6:5). *"Philein"* is used here rather than *"agapan"* because the inspired writer wishes to show that they take pleasure in that sort of thing, that it is part of their nature to desire to be seen of men. They love to do it.

*"Everyone that loveth and maketh a lie"* (Rev. 22:15) uses *"philein"* in order to show that there is *"a personal affinity with the false, inward kinship with it, leading to its outward practice."* As stated, *"philein"* is a love of liking, whether that which is Godly or un-Godly.

One likes someone because that person is like himself. The one loving in this way finds in the object loved a reflection of himself. Thus, the one who loves a lie, loves it because he finds in a lie that which is reflected in his own bosom. *"He that loveth his life shall lose it"* (Jn. 12:25).

It is a love that finds such pleasure in life that it becomes a fixed attitude in one's outlook, and nothing else comes into consideration in comparison with it. *"If the world hate you, you know that it hath hated Me first; if you were of the world, the world would love its own"* (Jn. 15:18-19). *"Philein"* is most appropriate here.

The words *"the world would love its own,"* speaks of an inner affinity. They speak of a community of nature between the world and its own. As stated, *"philein"* is a love of liking, and we like that which is like us.

But the world finds no community of nature in itself and the Christian, for the latter has been made a partaker of the Divine Nature (II Pet. 1:4), and for that reason the world hates the Christian.

## FRIENDSHIP

*"Philein"* is used of Jesus' love for Lazarus (Jn. 11:3, 36), the emphasis being upon the love

NOTES

of friendship which existed between the man Christ Jesus and His friend Lazarus.

It is the human heart of Jesus which we see here. *"Philein"* shows the personal intimacy of the affection existing between them. How wonderful, that, included in the self-humbling of God the Son in the Incarnation, there should be this capacity for human friendship.

Of course, our Lord Loved Lazarus with an *"agapan"* love also, for He died for Him on the Cross. But here the inspired writer wishes to present this particular kind of love. It fits the occasion and context.

The appeal of the Sisters was upon the basis of the mutual friendship existing between our Lord and Lazarus. When John speaks of Jesus' love for Martha, and Mary, and Lazarus, he uses *"agapan,"* the general term for love. They were very precious to Him. The non-use of *"philein"* is a good commentary upon the reserve which our Lord maintained toward womanhood. In other words, the word *"philein"* was not used of Jesus concerning Mary and Martha as it was with Lazarus, for the simple reason that such would not have been proper. He would love them with the God-kind of love (agape) but He did not express the same type of fondness for them as He did for Lazarus and for the obvious reasons. Neither is it proper for any man to express such for a woman other than his wife or blood kin; however, the Christian man can express the God kind of love toward the opposite gender, as he must, even as he does for his own gender.

## JESUS AND PETER

In the conversation between our Lord and Peter (Jn. 21:15-19), the Lord uses *"agapan"* twice and *"philein"* the third time, while Peter uses *"philein"* three times. Of the use of these two words for *"love"* in this passage, Warfield says, *"That anyone should doubt that the words are used here in distinctive senses would seem incredible prior to experience."* In other words, John used the exact word for *"love,"* which was used by Jesus at that time, and all other times for that matter respecting his writings, with Matthew, Mark and Luke following suit.

Our lord said to Peter twice, *"Simon, son of Jonas, doest thou have a love for Me that is called out of thine heart because I am precious to thee, a love of deep devotion that is sacrificial in its essence, a love that would make thee willing to die for Me?"*

Three times Peter said, *"Yea, Lord, Thou knowest that I am fond of Thee, Thou knowest that I have an affection for Thee that is called out of my heart because of the pleasure I take in Thee,"* i.e., or words to that effect.

## THE REASON FOR PETER'S ANSWERS

Jesus asked for a love of complete devotion. Peter offers Him a love of personal heart emotion. Jesus asked for a love of surrendering obedience. Peter offers Him a love of personal attachment.

Peter at the Crucifixion had denied His Lord even in the face of his statements, *"Though all men should be offended because of Thee, yet will I never be offended." "Though I should die with Thee, yet will I not deny Thee"* (Mat. 26:33, 35).

Peter had compared himself with the other Disciples. Now our Lord asked, *"Peter, doest thou have a personal devotion to Me to the point of self-sacrifice which is stronger than the personal devotion of these your fellow-Disciples?"*

Peter answers in deep humility, remembering his denial of his Lord, and without comparing his love for Jesus with that of the other Disciples.

The idea is that Peter did not want to make the mistake now that he had previously made respecting his denial. He had then boasted of his love, but found that it was not what he had thought. Now he purposely takes the low road, not claiming that which he had once claimed, and because he's not really sure of his own heart, at least to the point of making a bold declaration. We too should follow his example.

In our Lord's second question the comparison is omitted, and Peter has the opportunity to tell of his personal devotion to Jesus without comparing it with that of the other Disciples. But still, he only speaks of his personal friendly affection for Him, and for the reasons mentioned.

The third time Jesus questions Peter He uses *"philein,"* and asks with sharp directness and brevity whether Peter has any real affection for Him at all. Peter was grieved because Jesus used the lesser word *"philein,"* yet he still only asserts his fondness and friendly affection for his Master.

NOTES

NOTES

## THE FICKLENESS OF THE HUMAN HEART

Once again, one should not accept his answer as that of lack of consecration to Jesus, but rather the very opposite. Peter has now come to know and understand the fickleness of the human heart, and that even the best should walk softly in this capacity.

Then Jesus plainly tells Peter that someday he will indeed exhibit an *"agapan"* love for Him in that he will die a martyr's death for Him, for He tells him that he will die by Crucifixion for his testimony to his Saviour.

The idea is not that Peter does not have that type of love (agape) at the present time, and will gradually grow into such, but rather, that when such time does actually come for the supreme sacrifice demanded, that Peter need not fear, he will definitely conduct himself as he should at that time.

That must have been very comforting to the Apostle, with Peter's heart heavy with fear that he might repeat this terrible scenario again. Peter is now a changed man, which his actions portray, i.e., *"humility instead of boasting."* (Bibliography: Kenneth Wuest, Benjamin Warfield.)

The phrase, *"I am become as sounding brass, or a tinkling cymbal,"* does not refer to our modern musical instrument which we call by the same name. The cymbal that Paul wrote about here made nothing more than a clattering sound and was often used as a signal in battle (Rossier).

The idea is, that if *"love"* does not undergird all that we do for God, irrespective of the Gifts we may actually have, that which is done will be no more than noise.

## THE NATURE OF GIFTS

Many may have difficulty understanding these statements by Paul, considering that these Gifts are from the Holy Spirit. Consequently, most would think, that anyone who would be given such Gifts by the Spirit, would surely be a person of love.

That is true, but it needs qualification.

First of all, a *"Gift"* is a *"Gift,"* and as such, and due to its nature, irrespective of what the individual does with the Gift, the Gift remains. This is confusing to some people, but not if they will apply their understanding to Gifts as given by God, the same as gifts given by people to other people, etc.

If it is truly a gift, which means there are no strings attached, it belongs to the individual thereafter irrespective of what that person may do. While the use of the Gift may be greatly curtailed respecting the lack of consecration regarding some people, still it remains, and its use remains even in some form.

A perfect example is Balaam of old.

Many claim that he never was a true Prophet of God, but I think the evidence proves contrary. Balaam knew too much about God, too much about the worship of God, and too much about Prophesy, to have been an imposter all his life (Num. Chpts. 22-24). The Truth is, that some of the greatest prophesies ever given concerning Israel and more particularly, Israel's Messiah, the Lord Jesus Christ, came out of his mouth, despite his apostate condition at that time. So, the Gifts of God can continue to be used even though a person is not living right, and in fact, are done so at times. It is regrettable but true!

As well, there are some Believers, even many I'm afraid, who walk humbly before the Lord for a period of time, and then become lifted up in themselves because of Gifts, etc., and gradually begin to function without love as the proper motive. If such were not true, Paul would not have gone to the trouble to give all this instruction.

So, these things should not be a mystery, if understood properly. The ideal is, that one be greatly used by God, but remain humble and always be motivated by the Love of God.

(2) "AND THOUGH I HAVE THE GIFT OF PROPHECY, AND UNDERSTAND ALL MYSTERIES, AND ALL KNOWLEDGE; AND THOUGH I HAVE ALL FAITH, SO THAT I COULD REMOVE MOUNTAINS, AND HAVE NOT CHARITY, I AM NOTHING."

The phrase, *"And though I have the Gift of Prophecy, and understand all mysteries, and all Knowledge; and though I have all Faith, so that I could remove mountains,"* proves exactly what I have just said. Were it not possible for these *"Gifts"* to be had under these circumstances, Paul, as stated, would not have given this teaching.

As well, the manner in which he makes this statement, covers all bases, leaves nothing unsaid, and puts all in the same category.

The phrase, *"And have not charity* (love), *I am nothing,"* tells us in no uncertain terms how that God judges the situation. He doesn't look at the great things done, rather the motivation behind these things. As well, His conclusion is blunt and to the point, if one does not have Love, one is *"nothing."* This, as should be obvious, does not speak of diminished status, but rather no status at all!

*"Nothing"* in the Greek is *"ouden,"* and means *"not anything at all, nought."*

The Church too often places its recognition and seal of approval on the one who can move mountains, etc., and very little on *"love."* Consequently, it is judging the situation exactly opposite of the way it is judged by God. His criteria should be our criteria.

(3) "AND THOUGH I BESTOW ALL MY GOODS TO FEED THE POOR, AND THOUGH I GIVE MY BODY TO BE BURNED, AND HAVE NOT CHARITY, IT PROFITETH ME NOTHING."

The phrase, *"And though I bestow all my goods to feed the poor, and though I give my body to be burned,"* shifts the attention from Gifts of the Spirit, to Works for the Lord.

The phrase, *"And have not charity, it profiteth me nothing,"* proclaims the fact that if an individual follows the ultimate sacrifice of all his goods with the act of martyrdom, it will be completely meaningless unless motivated by unconditional love. As commendable as these acts may be, they bring a grade of zero unless God's love motivates them (Rossier).

The idea is, that God gave His all respecting the Redemption of mankind, which was motivated exclusively by love. Man had nothing that God needed, and in fact, due to the Fall, man was an enemy. Consequently, only love could motivate what God did, and if we are to be like God, our actions and conduct must be motivated in the same manner. Anything else is *"nothing,"* and the profit margin is the same.

The only manner in which true love can be ascertained or defined, is by beginning with God. If it begins with man, it is all tinted in some manner with selfishness. Love must begin with God if it is to end with God.

(4) "CHARITY SUFFERETH LONG, AND IS KIND; CHARITY ENVIETH NOT; CHARITY VAUNTETH NOT ITSELF, IS NOT PUFFED UP,"

The phrase, *"Charity* (love) *suffereth long,"* refers to Patience.

NOTES

PATIENCE

Paul is saying that *"love is patient."*

The New Testament contains many exhortations to be patient. But just what is patience?

The Greek word group which defines patience focuses our attention on restraint: that capacity for self-control despite circumstances that might arouse the passions or cause agitation.

In personal relationships, patience is forbearance, which means to bear long. This is not so much a trait as a way of life.

We keep on loving or forgiving despite provocation, as illustrated in Jesus' appointed stories in Matthew Chapter 18. Patience also has to do with our reaction to the troubles we experience in life.

Men may resist and antagonize God and thus arouse Him to anger. When He withholds His anger as He always does, He *"suffers long."* Mere things cannot arouse God; trials, tribulations, persecutions do not apply to God, with the exception as they applied to Jesus Christ, Who of course, is God. He underwent these things, consequently tempted in all points like as we are, that He might be the consummate patience. Thus, when Paul names the ability to suffer long as the first feature of love, we should note that this is a Godlike feature, consummate in Jesus Christ.

PATIENCE DEMANDED

The world is full of evil men, and even in our Brethren much evil meets us.

When this evil strikes us, and our natural reaction would be resentment, indignation, anger, bitter words, blows perhaps, then love steps in, *"suffers long,"* keeps calm, endures, and does this continually no matter how long the offense may persist — which of course, is beyond the capabilities of even the Godliest, without the help of the Holy Spirit.

The phrase, *"And is kind,"* represents the second side of the Divine attitude toward humankind, Patience being the first (Rom. 2:4).

On the one hand, God's loving forbearance is demonstrated by His holding back his wrath toward human rebellion; on the other hand, His kindness is found in the thousandfold expressions of His Mercy. Thus, Paul's description of love begins with this twofold description of

God, Who through Christ has shown Himself forbearing and kind toward those who deserve Divine Judgement. The obvious implication, of course, is that this is how His people are to be toward others.

DESCRIPTION

Paul does not describe love to us in the role of performing great, wonderful, and astounding deeds; he prefers to show us how the inner heart of love looks when it is placed among sinful men and weak and needy Brethren. He does not picture love in ideal surroundings of friendship and affection where each individual embraces and kisses the other, but in the hard surroundings of a bad world and a faulty Church where distressing influences bring out the positive power and value of love (Lenski).

These two positive expressions (Patience and Kindness) are followed by seven verbs that indicate how love does *not* behave, the first five which are taken right out of the Corinthian file. It is as though Paul were saying, *"You must have love; without it you are simply not behaving as Christians. And what is love? It is to behave in ways opposite to ourselves!"* (Fee).

The phrase, *"Charity envieth not,"* proclaims that love does not allow fellow Believers be in rivalry or competition, either for *"vaunted positions"* or to curry people's favor in order to gain adherents. Indeed, it seeks quite the opposite; how best do I serve these for whom Christ died, whatever my own desires?

In conjunction with *"strife," "envy"* denotes the *"rivalry"* expressed in the Corinthians' division over their teachers that is being carried on in the name of wisdom. More pointedly it probably reflects those who stand against Paul as his *"rivals"* for the affection of the community (Fee).

ENVY

The Greek word for *"envy"* is *"Phthonos,"* and is the bitter feeling roused by another's possession of what we want but do not have, whether material possession, popularity, or success.

Envy portrays the inner attitude of the heart which is not satisfied with God's provision, but desires that which belongs to others. It shows a lack of trust regarding God, a lack of dependence on His provision, and a lack of satisfaction regarding what He has provided.

NOTES

It is a person who desires to step out of the role designed for them by God, into that designed by God for another. While the envy is expressed toward another person and what they have, whatever that might be, it is more so directed toward God, whether the individual understands such or not.

When love sees another prosperous, rich, highly gifted, it is pleased and glad of his advantages. Love never detracts from the praise that is due another nor tries to make him seem less and self seem more by comparison.

The practice of the world is the opposite. Instead of being grievous, love is satisfied with its own portion and glad of another's greater portion (Lenski).

The phrase, *"Vaunteth not itself,"* refers to the fact that love is never a braggart. The very idea is foreign to its humble nature.

BOASTFUL BRAGGING

Behind boastful bragging there lies conceit, and an overestimation of one's own importance, abilities, or achievements.

*"Vaunteth"* suggests self-centered actions in which there is an inordinate desire to call attention to one's self.

Once again, the statement by Paul could very well reflect his *"rivals"* or *"opponents"* who in effect are leading the whole Church down the wrong paths. Over against Paul they think of themselves as having great *"wisdom"* (I Cor. 3:18) and *"knowledge"* (I Cor. 8:2), and especially as being *"spiritual"* (I Cor. 14:37).

The truth is, it is not possible to *"boast"* and love at the same time. The one action wants others to think highly of one's self, whether deserving or not; the other cares for none of that, but only for the good of the community as a whole (Fee).

The phrase, *"Is not puffed up,"* presents the next step, which naturally follows one's overestimation of oneself. From envy to boasting, from boasting to puffing oneself up is a natural sequence on the path of lovelessness. He that exalteth himself shall be abased; he that humbleth himself shall be exalted. Thus, in this case, the positive virtue is Christian humility and lowliness of mind.

In fact, Paul has mentioned being puffed up repeatedly in I Corinthians 4:6, 18, 19; 5:2; 8:1. Yet, if we conclude that Paul is speaking only of the Corinthians, we misunderstand the entirety of the Text. Even if Corinth had not existed, every line of this description would be true.

However, as it refers to the Corinthians, I think one can say that for Paul this was their greater sin, to be arrogant in the face of so much that is unholy and unloving and, therefore, un-Christian.

(5) "DOTH NOT BEHAVE ITSELF UNSEEMLY, SEEKETH NOT HER OWN, IS NOT EASILY PROVOKED, THINKETH NO EVIL;"

The phrase, *"Doth not behave itself unseemly,"* means that love is forgetful of self and thoughtful toward others.

Paul himself is a good example. No matter where he might find himself, among friends or foes, before people or before rulers and kings, he always knew how to act as became his station and the position into which he was placed.

Who taught this tentmaker such noble and beautiful manners, such perfect tact in all his bearing, that even the great in this world were compelled to respect him?

Paul was the very opposite of this attitude and spirit which causes pride to puff up the heart, which causes ill conduct naturally to follow. Tactlessness forgets its own place and fails to accord to others their proper dues of respect, honor, or consideration (Lenski).

The phrase, *"Seeketh not her own,"* presents that which is totally unworldly, therefore, unselfish. It does not believe that *"finding oneself"* is the highest good; it is not enamored with self-gain, self-justification, self-worth, etc. To the contrary, it seeks the good of one's neighbor — or enemy (Phil. 2:4) (Fee). True love, at least the God kind of love, is always unselfish.

How easily said, how hard to attain!

## SELFISHNESS

Selfishness lies at the root of a thousand evils and sins in the world and in the Church: between rich and poor, capital and labor, nation and nation, man and man, Christian and Christian.

Cure selfishness, and you plant a Garden of Eden.

As when one draws a beautiful face and makes one feature after another stand out until the eyes at long last light up the whole and give it complete expression, so in this portrait of love the inspired artist paints the eyes full of unselfishness, seeking in every glance not to their own but that which is another's. Yes, this is love: no envy, no boasting, no pride, no unseemliness because it is altogether unselfish. Not for self (negative), for others (positive) (Lenski).

NOTES

The phrase, *"Is not easily provoked,"* means that it is not embittered or enraged by abuse, wrong, insult, or injury.

While love treats others with kindness, consideration, unselfishness, it, in turn, receives much of the opposite.

Paul's life was full of such experience, especially from his Brethren in the flesh who ought to have especially loved him. He did not accuse them, Acts 28:19; he did the opposite: *"Bless them which persecute you"* (Rom. 12:14).

## NOT EASILY PROVOKED

The phrase, *"Is not easily provoked,"* literally means that it keeps no record of wrongs, does not reckon the evil. Love does not devise evil against someone else.

Just as God in Christ does not *"reckon our sins against us"* (II Cor. 5:19), so the one who loves does not take notice of the evil done against him/her in the sense that no records are kept, waiting for God or man to settle the score. Here Paul reflects the tradition of Jesus' Word on the Cross as found in Luke's Gospel (Lk. 23:34), where the Saviour extends forgiveness to those crucifying Him.

The Scripture does not say that Love is impossible of provocation, but that it is not *"easily provoked."* Even Jesus was provoked at the condition of the Temple, consequently, running out the money changers, etc. Certain things should provoke us, in fact, if not, showing that our direction is not Scriptural. However, the provocation should be in the sense of spiritual things, and not against our own person.

Jesus was not provoked by what they did to Him Personally, but He definitely was provoked by their ill-treatment of God's House, and the Pharisees perverting the Gospel (Mat. Chpt. 23).

The phrase, *"Thinketh no evil,"* means that love takes no account of the evil, i.e. *"the baseness or meanness which is inflicted upon us"*; not *"evil"* as it inheres in our own minds and hearts.

THINKETH NO EVIL

Love keeps no account book for the entry of wrongs on the debit side which are eventually to be balanced on the credit side with payments received when satisfaction is obtained for these wrongs.

Love forgets to charge any wrong done to itself. It is neither enraged at the moment, nor does it hold a grudge in vindictiveness afterward.

Chrysostom has well said: *"As a spark falls into the Sea and does not harm the Sea, so harm may be done to a loving soul and is soon quenched without disturbing the soul."*

This carries with it the spirit of the pardoning Act of God: he does not impute to us our guilt (Ps. 32:2; Rom. 4:8; II Cor. 5:19), but imputes to us Righteousness for Christ's sake (Rom. 4:6-11, 22-25; James 2:23).

JOSEPH AND HIS BROTHERS

Even though love *"thinketh no evil,"* it does not overlook the possibility of evil.

Whenever Joseph's Brothers came into his presence in Egypt, even though they did not recognize him, he did not immediately reveal himself to them, even though in fact he did recognize them. He tested them thoroughly. Were they the same men who sold him into captivity, and in fact wanted to kill him, or had they changed?

His testing them thoroughly did not show a lack of love, nor was it a case of him *"thinking evil"* against them. His later actions show that he had no thought of evil against them whatsoever, irrespective of what they had done. In his heart, he had long since forgiven them; however, unless there had been a real change within their lives, the good which he would show them, in fact, could not have been shown. Thankfully, they had changed (Gen. Chpts. 42-45).

Even though love *"thinketh no evil,"* seeketh no hurt or harm against another, still it does realize and recognize the potential of harm from an evil heart, and does what it can to take proper, Godly measures.

(6) "REJOICETH NOT IN INIQUITY, BUT REJOICETH IN THE TRUTH;"

The phrase, *"Rejoiceth not in iniquity,"* proclaims the fact that love absolutely rejects that most pernicious form of rejoicing over evil, gossiping about the misdeeds of others; it is not gladdened when someone else fails. Love stands on the side of the Gospel and looks for Mercy and Justice for all, including those with whom one disagrees.

NOTES

The phrase, *"But rejoiceth in the Truth,"* proclaims that which the Word of God identifies as Truth:

1. Jesus is Truth (Jn. 14:6).
2. The Holy Spirit is Truth (I Jn. 5:6).
3. The Word is Truth (Jn. 17:17).
4. The Anointing is Truth (I Jn. 2:27).

(7) "BEARETH ALL THINGS, BELIEVETH ALL THINGS, HOPETH ALL THINGS, ENDURETH ALL THINGS."

The phrase, *"Beareth all things,"* has reference to enduring and quietly suffering afflictions. Love never complains that it is made to endure and to suffer too much; its capacity for suffering is very great. Remember all that the Lord's Love suffered.

The phrase, *"Believeth all things,"* proclaims the spirit of taking the best and kindest views of all men and all circumstances, as long as it is possible to do so.

It is the opposite of the common spirit, which drags everything down to the lowest level and paints it with the darkest colors, thereby making the worst of it.

The phrase, *"Hopeth all things,"* proclaims the fact that *"hope"* is something more than the result of a sanguine temperament, but rather a Gift and a Grace.

It is the character of love to *"put up with everything."* In fact, there is nothing that love cannot face. Love always perseveres. It has a tenacity in the present, buoyed by its absolute confidence in the future, that enables it to live in every kind of circumstance and continually to pour itself out on behalf of others. Paul's own Ministry was a perfect example of such love (Fee).

Paul does not mean that love always believes the best about everything and everyone, despite facts to the contrary, but that love never ceases to have Faith; it never loses hope. This is why it can endure.

The life that is touched by the never-ceasing Love of God in Christ (Rom. 8:39) is, in turn, enabled by the Spirit to love others in the same way. It trusts God on behalf of the one loved, and hopes to the end that God will show Mercy on that person's behalf.

The phrase, *"Endureth all things,"* was exemplified in the Life of Christ in a manner that has never been equalled.

It is often pointed out that in this paragraph, Paul seems best to capture the Life and Ministry of Jesus. So much so that one could substitute His Name for the noun *"love"* and thereby describe love in a more personal way.

After doing so, however, one does not want to miss Paul's point, which ultimately is description for the purpose of exhortation. Perhaps that point could best be captured by putting one's own name in place of the noun *"love,"* and not neglecting thereafter to find a proper place for repentance and forgiveness (Fee).

(8) "CHARITY NEVER FAILETH: BUT WHETHER THERE BE PROPHECIES, THEY SHALL FAIL; WHETHER THERE BE TONGUES, THEY SHALL CEASE; WHETHER THERE BE KNOWLEDGE, IT SHALL VANISH AWAY."

The phrase, *"Charity* (love) *never faileth,"* sums up all of that which Paul has said.

## WHAT DOES IT MEAN, LOVE NEVER FAILETH?

This love has rightly been called *"the greatest thing in the world."* Paul does not describe love in its greatest works, sacrifices, martyrdoms, triumphs; he goes into the ordinary circumstance of life as we meet them day by day and shows us the picture of love as it must be under these general circumstances.

We find ready excuses when great things are made the goal of our attainment; Paul cuts off all such excuses. Be a true, everyday Christian in the exercise of love, then all great triumphs of love will take care of themselves. He who fails in the ordinary works of love will not even have an opportunity when the supreme moment for the performance of the extraordinary arrives (Lenski).

Love never fails, because love cannot fail.

Paul here proceeds to illustrate the value of love, from its *"permanency"* as compared with other valued endowments. It is valuable, and is to be sought, because it will always abide; may be always exercised; is adapted to all circumstances, and to all worlds in which we may be placed, or in which we may dwell.

The Greek word rendered *"faileth"* denotes, properly, to fall out of, to fall from or off; it may be applied to the stars of heaven falling, or to flowers that fall or fade, or to chains falling from the hands, etc.

NOTES

The expression properly means that love will continue in all eternity, and be exercised in heaven forever, because God is forever, and God is love.

The phrase, *"But whether there be prophecies, they shall fail,"* literally means that when the completeness of communication and knowledge comes, tongues will be no barrier and partial knowledge will be superseded by the perfect or complete. The partial knowledge will be superseded by perfect knowledge.

The Greek verbs used here by Paul are all future verbs, indicating that Prophecy, Tongues, and the Word of Knowledge have not yet ceased to function in the New Testament Church, and will not cease until the Resurrection.

The phrase, *"Whether there be Tongues, they shall cease,"* addresses itself in the same capacity.

The phrase, *"Whether there be knowledge, it shall vanish away,"* has reference to the Gifts of the Spirit outlined in Chapter 12, but which will not be needed after the Resurrection.

It should be quickly noted, that this Verse in no way has reference to the idea as projected by some that the Gift of Prophecy and the Gift of Tongues ceased with the Apostles, etc. If one is to notice, the same people who advocate such, seldom mention, if ever, that the *"Word of Knowledge,"* or *"knowledge"* in particular, ceased at that time as well. Of course, such thinking is silly!

Paul is merely speaking of many things, the Gifts of the Spirit included, which have a dispensational purpose and once that dispensation is finished, their purpose will have been ended. This is the Church Age; consequently, these Gifts continue to be needed. However, upon the occurrence of the Resurrection, those things will be brought to an end.

To the contrary, love is a quality which will never be brought to an end, and for the simple reason that Love is the very principle and nature of God.

As well, Paul is not repudiating the Gifts, as some teach, in favor of Love. He is merely being led by the Holy Spirit to pronounce the Truth that Love must be the foundation, the motivating factor in all things, or else these other things fall out to no value at all.

(9) "FOR WE KNOW IN PART, AND WE PROPHESY IN PART."

The phrase, *"For we know in part,"* pertains to the *"Word of Knowledge."*

Frankly, that's why the Gift is called *"the Word of Knowledge,"* insinuating, and strongly so, that the Believer is never given all the knowledge on that situation, but only a part, i.e. *"a word."*

The phrase, *"And we prophesy in part,"* in essence falls into the same category.

Even though Prophecy *"speaketh unto men to edification, and exhortation, and comfort,"* it by no means is all the edification, exhortation, and comfort for all time, but rather only a small portion.

(10) "BUT WHEN THAT WHICH IS PERFECT IS COME, THEN THAT WHICH IS IN PART SHALL BE DONE AWAY."

The phrase, *"But when that which is perfect is come,"* refers to the Coming of Christ, respecting the Resurrection.

*"Perfect"* in the Greek is *"teleios,"* and means *"completeness, of full age."* The word has no reference to the idea that Jesus is coming into completeness or full age, but rather speaks of the finish and completeness of this dispensation, with another beginning. Even though the meaning is broad, one could sum it up by referring exclusively to Christ. When He comes, Who is perfect, everything then will change and obviously so.

The phrase, *"Then that which is in part shall be done away,"* carries the same meaning going into the Resurrection Life, as did the conclusion of the Old Covenant, with the coming of the New.

All of the particulars of the Old Covenant were only *"in part"*; consequently, the blood of bulls and goats could not take away sin. However, when the *"Perfect"* came, i.e. The Lord Jesus Christ, all of these symbols of the Old Covenant, i.e. Sacrifices, Circumcision, Sabbath-keeping, etc., were *"done away."* Those things were not needed when Jesus came, and especially considering that He fulfilled them.

That analogy holds for that of which Paul here speaks as well. The New Covenant is far ahead of the Old Covenant, but even it is not perfect, and cannot be made complete until that which is *"Perfect"* comes, Who is Jesus. As His First Advent enhanced everything greatly, likewise, His Second Advent will do the same.

NOTES

### ERROR

This passage has nothing to do with the completion of the Canon of Scripture with John writing the Book of Revelation, as some claim. They claim that when the Perfect Word of God was finished, there was no more need for Gifts of the Spirit, etc. Such thinking is foolishness, which attempted exegesis holds no Textual validity whatsoever. This interpretation is totally contrary to the context in I Corinthians Chapters 12 through 14 which says nothing about the Canon of Scripture.

The grammar here reveals the meaning. One has to go back to the last Verse in I Corinthians Chapter 12 to find it in the statement *"the Gifts"* or *"the Gracious Bestowments."* These *"Gifts"* are in part because one day they no longer will be necessary — after the Coming of the Lord.

As well, and to carry the statement as Paul gives it all the way, this *"more excellent way,"* the way of Love, can only be experienced now to a limited extent, but one day it will be limitless when the Resurrection of the Church occurs (Rossier).

(11) "WHEN I WAS A CHILD, I SPAKE AS A CHILD, I UNDERSTOOD AS A CHILD, I THOUGHT AS A CHILD: BUT WHEN I BECAME A MAN, I PUT AWAY CHILDISH THINGS."

The phrase, *"When I was a child, I spake as a child, I understood as a child, I thought as a child,"* presents Paul comparing his childhood with his present state as an adult, respecting knowledge, information, understanding, and the general manner in which things were observed. As should be obvious, there is no comparison between the child and the adult.

The phrase, *"But when I became a man, I put away childish things,"* presents the obvious state.

The Apostle is comparing our status presently (before the Resurrection and the coming Glorified form), to a child. Compared to what is coming, our present state, irrespective of our spiritual maturity, can only be looked at as *"childish"* by comparison to that coming time.

He is likening full adulthood (a man), with its development far in excess of the child, as our coming state after the Resurrection.

The analogy as given by the Holy Spirit is excellent to say the least. Actually, the analogy itself is commonplace. The adult does not continue to *"talk"* or *"think"* or *"reason"* like a child. As well, Paul's point in context does not have to do with *"childishness"* or *"growing up,"* but with the difference between the present and the future. He is illustrating that there will come a time when the Gifts will pass away, and for the obvious reasons. They are not forever, only to help build up the Body — but only in the present, when such edification is needed. After Jesus comes, they will no longer be needed, as should be obvious.

As well, because of the use of the verb *"talk* (spake)*,"* which elsewhere is used with *"Tongues,"* some have attempted to see this as an analogy as referring to speaking in Tongues, which is now also considered *"childish"* behavior, which the Corinthians are now being urged to set aside in favor of love. Such a view flies full in the face of the argument itself, both here and in I Corinthians 12:4-11 and I Corinthians Chapter 14. In other words, that is *not* what Paul is speaking about. In fact, such an analogy can be labelled again as none other than *"silly!"*

(12) "FOR NOW WE SEE THROUGH A GLASS, DARKLY; BUT THEN FACE TO FACE: NOW I KNOW IN PART; BUT THEN SHALL I KNOW EVEN AS ALSO I AM KNOWN."

The phrase, *"For now we see through a glass, darkly,"* refers to a mirror of sorts.

The word *"darker"* in the Greek is *"ainigma,"* and means *"a dark saying, a riddle."* Trying to judge what the glorified life is going to be like is, to be frank, beyond our scope of comprehension. We can surmise, but that's about as far as we can go. The problem is realizing how absolutely wonderful it will be.

The idea of Paul's analogy is that the mirror is not very good (mirrors they had then were dim); consequently, the reflection, although present, is dim. It also refers to the light on the mirror, which is insufficient as much as the mirror itself.

NOTES

## THE MANNER OF THE SCRIPTURES

The Scriptures regularly employ earthly terms when they are speaking about Divine and supernatural realities. Think of the parables, the types, hundreds of comparisons, Paul's use of human illustrations in this very connection. All of these are riddles, more or less. We now see the Divine realities only as they are reflected in the mirror of the Word and not directly as they are in fact.

The way the Holy Spirit had Paul to say this proclaims that there is a medium or a means which intervenes between us and the object of our sight. The fact of the matter is that God Himself produced this medium.

He descends to us in the Word and speaks about heavenly realities in a human way, for the Word is couched in human expressions. Only in this way can we become cognizant of the Heavenly Truth. To speak totally in a heavenly way would defeat His purpose; and to show us Heavenly Realities directly without the mirror of the Word would simply blind and destroy us.

## GLASS IN PAUL'S DAY

The mirrors of the ancients were usually made of polished metal (Ex. 38:8; Job 37:18). However, by Paul's day, it is believed that a knowledge of glass, although imperfect, was had at that time. Pliny says that it was first discovered by accident.

A merchant vessel, laden with Nitre or Fossil Alkali, was driven ashore on the coast of Israel near the river Belus. The crew went in search of provisions, and accidentally supported the kettles on which they dressed their food upon pieces of the Fossil Alkali. The river sand, above which this operation was performed, was vitrified by its union with the alkali, and thus produced glass. It is believed that during Paul's time, that drinking vessels were made commonly of glass. Glass bottles for holding juice and flowers were in common use as well. This has been proved by the remains uncovered in the ruins of Pompeii.

Consequently, Paul could very well have been alluding to the imperfect and discolored glass which was then in extensive use, and which gave off a poor reflection. We have no reason to suppose that it was then as transparent as that which is now made. It was, doubtless, an imperfect and obscure medium and, therefore, well adapted to illustrate the nature of our knowledge here, compared with what it will be at the Resurrection and there after.

The phrase, *"But then face to face,"* proclaims by the word *"then"* that Paul is speaking of the coming Resurrection. *"Face to face"* is as when one looks upon an object openly, and not through an obscure and dark medium, as the mirror which Paul described.

The phrase, *"Now I know in part; but then shall I know even as also I am known,"* explains the *"face to face."*

Paul places himself in this same situation as now knowing only in part, the best for which any one presently can hope. However, the word *"then"* again projects the situation into the future, and speaks of the coming Resurrection and beyond, actually forever.

THE IMAGE

To be sure, it is not a distorted image that we have in Christ through the Spirit presently, but actually that which is incomplete. Our present *"Vision"* of God, as great as it is, is as nothing when compared to the real thing that is yet to be; it is like the difference between seeing a reflected image in a mirror, and an imperfect mirror at that, and seeing a person face to face.

The manner in which Paul uses the word *"know"* proclaims him delineating the difference between the *"knowing"* that is available through the Gifts of the Spirit and the final eschatological knowing (end time) that is complete.

The idea is that knowledge will then be perfect, i.e. complete. As well, it will be perfect for all, not just a select few, hence, *"even as also I am known."*

(13) "AND NOW ABIDETH FAITH, HOPE, CHARITY, THESE THREE; BUT THE GREATEST OF THESE IS CHARITY."

The phrase, *"And now abideth Faith, Hope, Charity* (Love),*"* present Paul adding *"Faith"* and *"Hope"* to *"Love,"* and that all three will abide forever.

Together these words embrace the whole of Christian existence, as Believers live out the Life of the Spirit in the present age, awaiting the Coming of the Lord. We have *"Faith"* toward God, that is, we trust Him to forgive and accept us through Christ. Even though now we do not see Him (or see, as it were, *"a reflection in a mirror"*), we trust in His Goodness and Mercy.

We also have *"Hope"* for the future, which has been guaranteed for us through Christ. Through His Resurrection and the Gift of the Holy Spirit, we have become a thoroughly future-oriented people. The present age is on its way out, therefore, we live in the present *"as if not."* We are on our way *"home,"* destined for an existence in the Presence of God that is *"face to face."*

We have *"Love"* one for another as we live this life of Faith and Hope in the context of a community of Brothers and Sisters of similar Faith and Hope. In the present life of the Church *"these three remain* (or continue)*: Faith, Hope, and Love,"* and in fact, will continue forever.

Some argue that Faith and Hope are not meant to be eternal, in view of the fact that *"Hope"* does not seem to be a meaningful concept once it has been realized, and to be sure, it will be realized at the Resurrection. However, *"Hope"* can be fully experienced now as a guarantee of the coming future, but not known exactly when, but then as a *"Hope"* totally and completely realized.

In fact, Faith falls into the same category, and in a sense, Love does as well.

To be sure, *"Faith," "Hope,"* and *"Love"* can only be fully realized when the object of this trinity is brought fully to view, namely The Lord Jesus Christ. However, Him being the object of Faith, Hope, and Love, in no way brings the three to an end, but only fully realizes their totality and potential.

EXPLANATIONS

In a certain way, Faith will cease and be turned into sight (II Cor. 5:7), namely inasmuch as the Word, the present medium for Faith, will be fulfilled when we at last see Christ as He is.

However, in another way Faith remains eternally, for our trust in the Triune God shall never cease. Through all eternity, Faith connects us with God and with Salvation. For this reason, Paul writes: *"And now remains Faith."*

This is equally true with regard to Hope. In Romans 8:24, etc., Hope as a sure expectation that is based on solid realities is compared with its coming consummation, the final possession and enjoyment of all for which we now hope.

However, that is quite different from what Paul says here about hope. Hope remains as the expectation of the ever-new unfolding of Glory in the future state. Heaven is not one everlasting monotony which, once attained, leaves nothing further to expect. The Angels sing ever-new Praises to God. So we, too, shall pass from one to another of the joys which God has prepared for us.

## ONCE AGAIN, THE GLASS DARKLY

It is naturally difficult for us to speak on this subject because of our present inferior knowledge. For one thing, eternity is not time, not even an endless stretch of time, but rather timelessness, as some might explain, the opposite of time (Rev. 10:6). Yet, we are fettered to conceptions of time even when we try to think in terms of eternity. So we can speak about heaven only in a poor, human way.

But the Glories of Heaven are inexhaustible, and we shall never get through exploring them. Thus, Paul writes, *"And now remains Hope."*

His sentence is so constructed that if Faith and Hope remained only until we enter heaven, as stated, Love, too, would remain only that long. It is impossible to drop Faith and Hope at the golden portal and to take only Love with us. Such a construction is made impossible in still another way, namely when Paul adds with strong emphasis: *"these three."*

He ties a band about these three as if, after naming them, he asks us to stop a moment and to contemplate these three which constitute one great unit, the supreme class of spiritual possessions, the class that endures eternally in contrast with the other class which endures only for time (Lenski).

The phrase, *"But the greatest of these is Charity* (Love)," presents the final surprise.

## THE GREATEST

Paul has combined Faith, Hope, and Love into one great unit possession that is marked by endless endurance and is distinguished from all other possessions. After all, Love must then share its throne with two others. We must then discount what was said about its high position. Is this the effect which Paul wishes to create?

With one stroke, all such thoughts are changed: *"Yet the greatest of these Love."*

In some translations, the word *"greater"* is used; however, in English this would be incorrect, we must say *"greatest."*

Paul simply makes this assertion and leaves us with the question as to how Love is the greatest of the trio. One thing is, of course, clear: Love is not greatest because it outlasts Faith and Hope, but because it outranks these two. But how does it outrank them?

NOTES

Love alone makes us like God. *"For Love is of God; and everyone that loveth is born of God, and knoweth God,"* (I Jn. 4:7).

*"If we love one another, God dwelleth in us, and His Love is perfected in us"* (I Jn. 4:12).

And then, *"God is Love; and he that dwelleth in Love dwelleth in God, and God in him"* (I Jn. 4:16).

## LOVE GIVES

What John says regarding our Love while we are in this earthly state may surely be used to cast a light upon our state above where it will be Love that brings us into the fullest union and communion with God. It is Faith's nature to receive, but Love gives; and giving is greater than receiving.

God's fullest purpose is attained in us when we are filled with Love. Hope also looks forward to receiving, but Love is full possession and completed joy. And for every joy which Hope receives in heaven, Love will be the response on our part. When we come to rest on the bosom of God, it will be by Love (Lenski).

## LOVE AS IT RELATES TO SOCIETY

Love is the great principle which binds the universe in harmony; which unites God to His creatures, and His creatures to Himself; and which binds and confederates all holy beings with each other.

It is, therefore, more important, because it pertains to society, to the Great Kingdom of which God is the Head, and because it enters into the very conception of a holy and happy organization.

Faith and Hope rather pertain to individuals; Love pertains to society, and is that without which the Kingdom of God cannot stand. Individuals may be saved by Faith and Hope; but the whole immense Kingdom of God depends on Love.

It is, therefore, of more importance than all other Graces and endowments; more important than Prophecy and Miracles, and the Gift of Tongues and Knowledge, because it will survive them all; more important than Faith and Hope, because although it may coexist with them, and though they all shall live forever, yet Love enters into the very nature of the Kingdom of God; binds society together; unites the Creator and the creature; and blends the interests of all the Redeemed, and of the Angels, and of God, into one (Barnes).

*"Oh Love that will not let me go,*
*"I rest my weary soul in thee.*
*"I give thee back the life I owe,*
*"That in thy ocean depths its flow*
*"May richer, fuller be."*

CHAPTER 14

(1) "FOLLOW AFTER CHARITY, AND DESIRE SPIRITUAL GIFTS, BUT RATHER THAT YE MAY PROPHESY."

The phrase, *"Follow after Charity* (Love)*,"* refers to the fact that *"Love" must* be the motivating factor concerning all that we do for God, and all that we are in God, and all that God does through us, hence, the Gifts. The Holy Spirit through the Apostle is adamant about this, which by now should be obvious.

If the Love of God does not permeate one's heart and life, which in turn will show itself toward fellow Believers, and even those in the world for that matter, whatever else the person does, and no matter how much the Church may acclaim his greatness, in the eyes of God he is nothing.

Once again, please allow us to emphasize what the Holy Spirit said at the beginning of the 13th Chapter of I Corinthians. God's Judgement Call does not rest upon the mighty feats of faith accomplishments, as wonderful as that may be, and as much as we ought to do these things, but rather on the motivation of Love in one's heart, or the lack of such.

As well, as Verse Two of Chapter 13 addresses Faith victories, Verse Three addresses the idea of good deeds being performed, even to the extent of the ultimate, but yet with the possibility of wrong motivation.

The Church gauges spirituality by Verse Two, while the world gauges spirituality by Verse Three (I Cor. Chpt. 13). While the Miracles and the Charity may definitely be motivated by Love, the fact of these two great things does not

NOTES

necessarily guarantee Love. So, there must be other telltale signs.

What may those signs be?

Even though the plural regarding *"signs"* is correct, it still can be summed up in the singular, *"sign."*

That sign is our love for humanity, which if we truly have, is the sign that we also love God.

However, we must be careful, even as we have already stated, not to accept in a blanket reception charitable deeds as that sign. Many people do these things for recognition, to gain approval, with some even hoping to earn Salvation. Such is never motivated by love, but rather by selfish motives.

The true Love of God, when truly residing in the heart of man, does not seek recognition, does not do things for men's approval, does not seek to earn anything, but simply does what is done because Love is truly present.

JESUS

Jesus addressed this thing very succinctly when He said, *"Take heed that ye do not your alms before men, to be seen of them: otherwise ye have no reward of your Father which is in heaven."*

He then said, *"Therefore when thou doest thine alms, do not sound a trumpet before thee, as the hypocrites do in the Synagogues and in the streets, that they may have glory of men. Verily I say unto you, they have their reward."*

And then, *"But when thou doest alms, let not thy left hand know what thy right hand doeth: That thine alms may be in secret: and thy Father which seeth in secret Himself shall reward thee openly"* (Mat. 6:1-4).

*"Follow"* in the Greek is *"dioko,"* and means *"to persecute, given to, press forward."*

The word *"persecute"* may seem strange regarding the meaning of *"follow,"* but it has to do with diligence, even to the point of violence.

The idea is that we properly understand what the Holy Spirit, through the Apostle, is saying regarding the gravity of pursuing *"Love."* In all practical applications, the individual cannot personally do anything that will bring about Love. This is strictly a Gift of God. However, the Believer can understand the significance of *"Love,"* and, therefore, ardently seek the Lord that his motives always be right, which in turn will be rewarded with Love — the Love of God.

SPIRITUAL GIFTS

The phrase, *"And desire Spiritual Gifts,"* completely repudiates the teaching that *"Gifts"* are of no significance, but rather Love. The idea is, as is overly obvious, that we be a proper vessel through which the Gifts of the Spirit can operate, which can only be if we are motivated by Love. It is not one or the other, but rather both.

*"Desire"* in the Greek is *"zeloo,"* and means *"to have warmth of feeling for, covet, be zealous."*

So, the Believer should desire, even strongly so, that the Holy Spirit would use him (or her) in these Gifts, for the simple reason that they are very much needed in the Church.

In the last few months at Family Worship Center, we have had a number of utterances in Tongues which were Interpreted, and a number of Prophecies, which have been of tremendous blessing to the entirety of the Body as a whole. As well, this given by the Holy Spirit has been a great encouragement to this Evangelist. I have relished what the Lord was saying, and, as a consequence, have been greatly strengthened, edified, and built up, as will be any Believer.

Also, we have seen other of the Gifts in operation, such as *"Gifts of Healings,"* along with the *"Word of Knowledge"* and the *"Word of Wisdom,"* etc. Actually I believe we have had all of the Gifts working within the Body, although some have not been quite as pronounced as I would like to see, but yet I definitely believe that this will improve as we are led even to a greater degree by the Holy Spirit.

I want all that God has for the Church, and for myself personally. I earnestly want Him to use me, and I thank Him so much that He has done so in the past and continues unto the present. But yet I am not satisfied, desiring to see an even greater manifestation of the Spirit within my own heart and life, in whatever capacity or direction He would desire. But above all, I want everything, even as we have repeatedly stated, to be motivated by the Love of God.

The phrase, *"But rather that ye may Prophesy,"* presents the greater of the Vocal Gifts.

Why did Paul say this?

By all means, he was not saying that the Gifts of Tongues and Interpretation of Tongues were not necessary. He was not saying that at all! Anything given by the Holy Spirit is necessary and must never be looked at in a slight manner. If God gave it, then it is important.

NOTES

Actually, this would fall under the same heading as Paul's description of the human body. Every part of the body is necessary, as should be obvious. Every one of the Gifts are necessary also, as ought to be obvious. So, what was Paul talking about?

THE EARLY CHURCH

All of these things of which we speak, at least for the most part, were brand-new, having only come about since the Day of Pentecost. While the Gifts were obvious in the Old Testament, with the exception of Tongues and Interpretation of Tongues, still they were not nearly as proliferated, actually only had or used by a few. But since the advent of the Holy Spirit on the Day of Pentecost, and due to what Jesus did at Calvary and the Resurrection, the Holy Spirit has much greater latitude in hearts and lives. Actually, He can now come in to abide within one's heart and life, whereas He was only with one in the Old Economy (Jn. 14:17). Actually, the difference in the Old Economy and the New, at least as far as the Holy Spirit is concerned, is monumental.

Of all the Gifts, *"Tongues"* was the most prominent and exotic. For someone to speak in Tongues out loud in the Assembly, created a greater sensation than any of the other Gifts, and for the obvious reasons. Consequently, more people wanted this Gift, thereby yielding to the Holy Spirit in this capacity more so than in other directions, which of course caused an imbalance.

As well, they had no regulation or order, it seems, as to how this Gift should be used; consequently, with a lack of order, which Paul will address in this very Chapter, at times, it seems there was confusion.

So, the Apostle is telling them, and us, that everyone should not desire the Gift of Tongues, but some that they may *"rather have the Gift of Prophecy."*

THE GIFT OF TONGUES

For clarification, and even at the risk of being overly repetitious, when we say *"Gift of Tongues,"* we are *not* addressing ourselves to speaking with Tongues which takes place when

NOTES

one is Baptized with the Holy Spirit (Acts Chpts. 2, 10, 19). Neither are we speaking of those who exercise their prayer language of speaking in Tongues in prayer and worship. Every Spirit-filled Believer does this constantly, and should do so, but that has nothing to do with this Gift of which we speak, the *"Gift of Tongues,"* one of the nine Gifts of the Spirit (I Cor. 12:8-10), which is an Utterance in Tongues given in a public meeting, which is meant to be Interpreted. This confuses many non-Pentecostal people. So, some attempt to make this First Verse mean something it does not mean.

For instance, Paul is *not* saying that we don't want the Gift of Tongues and Interpretation, but rather Prophecy, but that these Gifts must be balanced. He would not have given this long dissertation on the regulation of these Gifts, if they were of no significance, or not desired at all. Such would be silly, as should be obvious.

(2) "FOR HE THAT SPEAKETH IN AN UNKNOWN TONGUE SPEAKETH NOT UNTO MEN, BUT UNTO GOD: FOR NO MAN UNDERSTANDETH HIM; HOWBEIT IN THE SPIRIT HE SPEAKETH MYSTERIES."

The phrase, *"For he that speaketh in an unknown tongue speaketh not unto men, but unto God,"* tells us several things:

1. The word *"unknown"* was supplied by the translators, therefore, is not in the original text. It actually means, and rightly so, that it is unknown to the speaker, and most all the time to the listeners as well, but not unknown as far as a language is concerned.

In fact, *"Tongues"* are always a language known somewhere in the world. In other words, it is not babble, incoherent chatter, or gibberish.

To be frank, there are many languages in the world which are very peculiar, in fact, sounding very strange, but only to those who are not familiar with them.

2. The term, *"speaketh not unto men,"* means that if the Lord is speaking to men, He will speak to them in the language they understand. So, speaking with other Tongues is not meant to be understood by men, unless it is intended by the Holy Spirit to be Interpreted. That which is to be Interpreted, which Paul will address, falls into a narrow category.

The Corinthians not understanding this, were all blurting out in Tongues in the services it seems, with very little if any being Interpreted, which as would be obvious, created confusion. This is what Paul is addressing.

3. The phrase, *"But unto God,"* is meant to say that one can speak in Tongues silently, unless it's meant to be Interpreted, because it is only to God to Whom one is speaking.

In fact, I speak in Tongues almost, if not every single day of my life. It is in prayer and worship, and is not meant to be Interpreted. Consequently, it is between me and God, even as the Scripture here proclaims.

The phrase, *"For no man understandeth him,"* once again is obvious. What is being said is not meant to be understood by men, because it is not meant for others who may be listening, but is rather for the Lord.

In view of this, unless the Holy Spirit desires an Utterance to be given to the people, in which it will be Interpreted, the person should not normally speak where others can hear. He should speak to himself, etc.

The phrase, *"Howbeit in the Spirit he speaketh mysteries,"* is meant to be understood in this fashion.

*"Mysteries"* in the Greek is *"musterion,"* and means *"a secret."*

To be sure, Satan understands all languages, but he is not as God, Omniscient, i.e. *"all-knowing."* How much knowledge that Satan has we do not exactly know. We do know, as stated, that he is a creature and, therefore, although brilliant, still is more on the level of the knowledge of man than he is on the level of God.

Satan has to learn things exactly as we do, which he does through his many demon spirits, and other means. So the point is this:

Satan does not have the capacity to know and understand all of the people on the earth who are worshipping and praising God, with many of them worshipping in other Tongues. But yet, he definitely does have access to some through his spirits of darkness, etc. Even though he understands in these cases what is being said, still, the Holy Spirit codes that which is said, which the speaker does not know either, so that only God can understand.

## HOW CAN THAT HELP?

Some may wonder as to how worshipping or praying in Tongues could help a person, especially considering that they do not understand what they are saying. While that part is true, still, the Spirit of God flows into this Worship, which greatly helps the worshipper, even though he is not aware of what he is saying.

To give an example, on the Day of Pentecost when the Holy Spirit fell, and many began to speak in Tongues, there were quite a number of people present, in fact, having come in from all over the Roman Empire, who understood some of the languages spoken (Acts 2:7-12). The Scripture reports them as saying, *"We do hear them speak in our tongues the Wonderful Works of God"* (Acts 2:11).

I am certain that Satan was very much present that day upon the Great Advent of the Spirit, and even though he as well understood these words perfectly, they did not mean to him what they meant to God, of that one can be certain.

At this juncture I think it would be advisable to address ourselves to several aspects of the Holy Spirit, which will possibly be helpful to some of our readers.

NOTES

## THE BIBLE EVIDENCE OF THE BAPTISM WITH THE HOLY SPIRIT

The following are five recorded instances of people receiving the Holy Spirit in the Book of Acts:

1. *"And when the Day of Pentecost was fully come, they were all with one accord in one place. And suddenly there came a Sound from Heaven as of a Rushing Mighty Wind, and it filled all the house where they were sitting. And there appeared unto them Cloven Tongues like as of fire, and it sat upon each of them. And they were all filled with the Holy Spirit, and began to speak with other Tongues, as the Spirit gave them utterance"* (Acts 2:1-4).

2. *"Now when the Apostles which were at Jerusalem heard that Samaria had received the Word of God, they sent unto them Peter and John: Who, when they were come down, prayed for them, that they might receive the Holy Spirit: (For as yet He was fallen upon none of them: only they were baptized in the Name of the Lord Jesus.) Then laid they their hands on them, and they received the Holy Spirit. And when Simon saw that through laying on of the Apostles' hands the Holy Spirit was given, he offered them money"* (Acts 8:14-18).

3. *"And Ananias went his way, and entered into the house; and putting his hands on him said, Brother Saul, the Lord even Jesus, that appeared unto thee in the way as thou camest, hath sent me, that thou mightest receive thy sight, and be filled with the Holy Spirit"* (Acts 9:17).

4. *"While Peter yet spake these words, the Holy Spirit fell on all them which heard the Word. And they of the circumcision which believed were astonished, as many as came with Peter, because that on the Gentiles also was poured out the Gift of the Holy Spirit. For they heard them speak with Tongues, and magnify God"* (Acts 10:44-46).

5. *"And it came to pass, that, while Apollos was at Corinth, Paul having passed through the upper coasts came to Ephesus: and finding certain Disciples, He said unto them, Have you received the Holy Spirit since you believed? And they said unto him, We have not so much as heard whether there be any Holy Spirit. And he said unto them, unto what then were ye Baptized? And they said, Unto John's Baptism. Then said Paul, John verily baptized with the Baptism of Repentance, saying unto the people, that they should believe on Him which should come after him, that is, on Christ Jesus. When they heard this, they were Baptized in the Name of the Lord Jesus. And when Paul had laid his hands on them, the Holy Spirit came on them; and they spake with Tongues, and Prophesied. And all the men were about twelve"* (Acts 19:1-7).

The above records five instances of people receiving the Holy Spirit, covering a period of about 20 years, and involving from one to many individuals. Paul (Saul) was one; there were 120 on the Day of Pentecost who received, with an unknown number in Samaria who received, and then twelve in Ephesus.

Three times out of these five instances it is recorded that they spoke with Tongues when they received the Spirit. The other two passages really doesn't say whether they did or didn't, but infers that they did. Paul himself said, *"I thank my God, I speak with Tongues more than ye all"* (I Cor. 14:18). We know that he did not begin to speak with Tongues before he received the Holy Spirit, so it is logical to assume that he received the Holy Spirit just as everyone else did — with the evidence of speaking in other Tongues.

NOTES

## TWO OR THREE WITNESSES

The Bible says, *"In the mouth of two or three witnesses every word may be established"* (Mat. 18:16). We have three Scripture *"Witnesses,"* and that should be sufficient to cause any thinking person to believe that speaking with Tongues is the evidence or sign that one is filled with the Holy Spirit.

Bible students know that the Samaritans spoke with Tongues, for every one of the Early Church Fathers say that they did. One does not need to be a student of Church History, however, to realize this.

The Word says, *"When Simon saw that through laying on of the Apostles' hands the Holy Spirit was given, he offered them money"* (Acts 8:18).

There had to be some kind of sign or evidence that registered on Simon's physical senses for him to know that the Samaritans had received the Holy Spirit. It had to be more than merely the people being joyful, because in reading the first Verses in Acts Chapter 8 we find already *"there was great joy in the city"* (Acts 8:8). Likewise, the sign couldn't have been because of Devils being cast out or healings taking place, because these also had occurred previously, as mentioned in this same Chapter. As well, one cannot see the Holy Spirit with ones physical eyes for He is a Spirit. Therefore, there had to be some type of physical evidence that registered on Simon's physical senses for him to know that the Samaritans had received the Holy Spirit. It is only logical to assume that it is the same evidence that was registered elsewhere. It was the same sign or evidence that convinced the six Jewish Brethren who went with Peter to the house of Cornelius. These Brethren of the circumcision (Jews) were astonished because that on the Gentiles was poured out the Gift of the Holy Spirit. *"For they heard them speak with Tongues, and magnify God"* (Acts 10:46).

## IS IT NECESSARY TO SPEAK IN TONGUES?

If one wants the New Testament experience and wants to make sure that they have the same Holy Spirit that was given to the Apostles and the Early Church, then one wants to speak with other Tongues, exactly as the Bible says (Acts 2:4).

Why not?

If it is crystal clear in the Bible, and it is, that every one who receives the Holy Spirit speaks with other Tongues, then why would we not want that which is promised in the Word of God?

## IS ONE SUPPOSED TO SEEK TONGUES?

No!

In fact, the Scripture doesn't even actually say that one should seek the Holy Spirit. We are told to *ask* for the Holy Spirit (Lk. 11:13), and to *receive* (Acts 19:2).

It certainly is not wrong to seek the Lord, and actually we should do so constantly (Lk. 11:9-10). However, to seek something which has already been promised, and is in fact available, is not exactly proper as should be obvious.

## SEVEN STEPS TO RECEIVING THE HOLY SPIRIT

It must have been about 1971. The Spirit of the Lord had moved upon me greatly one particular night, actually awakening me. I got out of bed and went out to my prayer room. It must have been approximately 3:00 in the morning.

On January 1, 1969, I had gone on Radio daily, and because the Lord had spoken to my heart to do so. Almost immediately, He began to bless the program. It was only 15 minutes in length each day, but the Lord helped us to see great and mighty things.

Our meetings, as a result of the radio program, were getting bigger and bigger, and the Lord that early morning hour in prayer began to deal with my heart about something very special. This is what He told me:

## OUR MEETINGS

I was to set aside, the Lord told me that early morning hour, a particular service in each one of meetings which we were conducting around the country, for people to be baptized with the Holy Spirit. I was to preach on the Holy Spirit, call them forward, have hands laid on them, and believe for them to be filled with the Spirit.

As well, the Lord told me to begin teaching on the Holy Spirit over our daily Radio Program, which we did. I remember remonstrating to the Lord very strongly, that I was not qualified to do this. I was an Evangelist, not a Teacher.

I was right, I was not at all qualified, but the Holy Spirit spoke to my heart and told me that He would tell me what to do, which He did.

At that very time He added the Ministry of Teaching, even telling me how to go about carrying out this which He had commanded that I do.

OBEDIENCE

I immediately began to do exactly what He had instructed me to do, to teach on the Holy Spirit, which lasted for many months and probably one could say in one way or the other, several years.

We had a tremendous audience at that time, I suppose the largest audience in daily radio respecting the Gospel. Actually, we were on over 600 stations.

Me teaching on the Holy Spirit developed a hunger in the heart and lives of many people to receive from the Lord, which was the reason the Lord instructed me to set aside this particular service for people to be filled.

To make the story brief, in my first meeting which was actually in Ohio, I did exactly as the Lord told me, preaching on the Holy Spirit, and then called the people forward to be filled. Several hundreds responded.

To be factual, I did not really know how to deal with that number of people. The most I had ever seen filled in a single service I suppose, were ten or twelve. And now there were hundreds here to be filled and what could I do?

I did what I had always done, which worked fine with a few, but not at all with hundreds. I prayed with each one as best I could, and had others do the same, but there simply were not enough workers to go around, and to be frank, very few were filled.

I went back to the motel room that evening very discouraged, not really knowing what to do. I knew the Lord had spoken to my heart, but I also knew that what I was presently doing was not the right thing to do, at least if we were going to see hundreds of people Baptized with the Holy Spirit in a single service, which the Lord had told me would happen. Actually, He had told me that up to a thousand would be filled in a single service. Beautifully enough, I saw that fulfilled in our Sunday afternoon service at Madison Square Garden, in New York City (1985). Over a thousand people on that Sunday afternoon were wondrously Baptized with the Holy Spirit with the evidence of speaking with other Tongues, fulfilling exactly what the Lord told me would happen. Of course, in the aggregate, we saw literally thousands and probably tens of thousands filled over a period of time.

THAT WHICH THE LORD GAVE ME

My next meeting was in Toledo, Ohio, which lasted Friday through Sunday afternoon. On Saturday morning I was to speak at a Full Gospel Businessmen's Breakfast. This would have been about 1972.

I awakened early that morning before daylight, and the Lord spoke to my heart and said, *"I want you to preach on the Holy Spirit this morning, and I want you to pray for people to be filled with the Spirit."*

I'll never forget hearing those words in my heart, and with fear and trembling telling the Lord, that if I were to do this, He was going to have to tell me how to instruct the people to be filled with the Spirit, because what I had previously done was not working, at least if a large number of people were involved.

That which I am going to give was what the Lord gave me.

I preached on the Holy Spirit in that morning meeting, exactly as the Lord told me to do, and then called the people forward to be Baptized with the Holy Spirit. To be frank, I could hardly wait, because I knew what the Lord had given me would work.

There must have been pretty near 100 people who came forward that morning to be filled with the Holy Spirit. I then did what the Lord told me to do, briefly explaining to them how they were to receive. I then had them bow their heads while I prayed, and then asked others who were standing by them to lay hands on them.

Almost everyone that morning was baptized with the Holy Spirit with the evidence of speaking with other Tongues, with it happening all in a few minutes time.

I remember distinctly, one wonderful little Nazarene lady, a Grandmotherly type, who had come to many of my meetings at that particular time, had become aware of her need for the Holy Spirit, and had wanted to be filled. Over and over again she had asked the Lord to be filled, but seemingly to no avail. But that morning the Lord filled her, and I want you to know she didn't have to wonder as to what the Lord had done. She knew when she left that place that day, that she had been Baptized with the Holy Spirit. Her Christian experience, even along with the others, would never be the same again.

I mention her, because I had become embarrassed at her coming so many times to be filled and not receiving. I felt it was my fault, but I simply did not know what else to do. But that particular morning she was filled, and since that hour, as stated, we have seen literally thousands go through to this wonderful experience from Heaven.

Now let me give you the seven steps:

1. BORN AGAIN

The only (I said, only) requirement for one to be Baptized with the Holy Spirit, is to first be *"born again"* (Jn. 3:3).

Regrettably, many people ignorantly try to add requirements and qualifications which are not given in the Word of God. Those manufactured qualifications pertain to about anything that one could think. However, there is only one, as stated, that is, to be Born-Again.

Actually, even after people come to Christ, there are still problems in their lives which hinder their progress with the Lord. To be frank, that's one of the reasons they need the Holy Spirit. But to try to tell these people they've got to get rid of all of these things before they receive the Holy Spirit, whatever those things may be, is putting the cart before the horse.

For instance, my Grandmother was one of the Godliest women I ever knew. But yet, after she came to Christ, she had a real problem giving up cigarettes. In fact, she smoked cigarettes right up to the time that the Lord filled her with the Spirit. After that, she never touched another one, with the reasons being obvious. She now had the power that she did not previously have, to help her do the things that she could not do before being filled (Acts 1:8; Rom. Chpt. 8).

So, irrespective of whatever problems the Believer may have, other than unbelief, those things will not stop you from receiving the Holy Spirit. As stated, the only requirement is to be *"born again."*

2. SCRIPTURAL

The one who is asking for the Holy Spirit must settle it in his spirit once and for all, that

NOTES

this great Gift is for all Believers, and it is for all Believers at this particular time. He must get all doubt out of his heart, and every question which casts aspersions on the Word of God.

Jesus called the Holy Spirit the *"Promise of the Father"* (Acts 1:4). He also said, *"But ye shall be Baptized with the Holy Spirit . . ."* (Acts 1:5).

Satan will do everything within his power to bring doubt to the Believer, telling him this passed away with the Apostles, or that it was only for the Early Church, or that one gets everything when one is saved, etc. The list is endless, especially when one is making up their own doctrine and not following the Bible.

For the Believer to receive, the Believer must understand that the Baptism with the Holy Spirit is Scriptural, that it is for all, and that means every single, solitary Believer. Doubt has kept more from receiving than anything else. It is for you, and you must not allow Satan or any of Satan's tools (unbelieving Preachers, etc.) to talk you out of that which God has promised to you.

3. HAVE FAITH

Everything that everyone receives from the Lord is always by Faith. In other words, we are to believe what He has promised in His Word, and He has promised the Holy Spirit (Acts 1:4).

As I mentioned in the first step, if one is in a state of unbelief concerning the Baptism with the Holy Spirit, the Lord will not fill that person. The Scripture says, *"But without Faith it is impossible to please Him: for he that cometh to God must believe that He is, and that He is a rewarder of them that diligently seek Him"* (Heb. 11:6).

So, one must believe!

4. DO NOT FEAR

Some people have been erroneously taught, that if they ask the Lord for the Holy Spirit, that they're opening themselves up to the spirit world, and can receive demon spirits, etc. That is patently untrue.

The Scripture plainly tells us, *"If a son shall ask bread of any of you that is a father, will he give him a stone? Or if he ask a fish, will he for a fish give him a serpent? Or if he shall ask an egg, will he offer him a scorpion? If ye then, being evil, know how to give good gifts unto your children: how much more shall your Heavenly Father give the Holy Spirit to them that ask Him?"* (Lk. 11:11-13).

In other words, the Lord is telling us, that if we ask for the Holy Spirit, He will not allow us to receive anything else, except that for which we ask. In fact, and as is obvious, the Lord actually places a shield around those who ask for the Holy Spirit, which Satan is not allowed to enter.

Once again, we are speaking of those who are *"born again"* asking for the Holy Spirit, and not sinners. To be frank, if those who are unsaved would ask for such, it *is* possible for them to receive that which is not of the Lord. It is a different thing entirely when a sinner asks for such, but if a person is a Child of God, he is not going to receive an evil spirit.

5. WHAT TO EXPECT

Most Believers don't know what to expect relative to asking the Lord to Baptize them with the Holy Spirit. Consequently, they should be told what to expect. If we don't tell them, they won't know what is going on when the Spirit moves on them.

Tell the person that they are to expect the Holy Spirit to put supernatural words (Tongues) into their spirit, and then to move upon their vocal organs, etc.

Many Believers have the idea that the Lord will make them or force them to speak in Tongues, which He will not. He will give the Utterance, but that's all that He will do. It is left up to the Believer to speak out the words given to him by the Spirit within his heart.

To be frank, the Holy Spirit will not take you over and make you do anything. He will move upon the person, but they have to work in cooperation with Him. It is the Believer who speaks with other Tongues, not the Holy Spirit. Nowhere in the Bible do we find that the Holy Spirit speaks in Tongues Himself. Every Scripture reference tells us that it is people who do the speaking.

The Scripture says, *"They* (the people) *began to speak with other Tongues, as the Spirit gave them utterance"* (Acts 2:4). *"For they heard them speak with Tongues, and magnify God"* (Acts 10:46). *"And when Paul had laid his hands upon them, the Holy Spirit came on them; and they spake with Tongues, and Prophesied"* (Acts 19:6).

Notice in the Scriptures we have given, and many more we could give, that it is always the individual who speaks in Tongues, while the Holy Spirit is the One Who gives the Utterance.

NOTES

So, the Believer is to speak out the words that he hears down in his spirit, which are not English or any language he already knows. The words he speaks are those given by the Holy Spirit, but that is all the Spirit will do. It is up to the individual to go ahead and speak out what the Spirit is giving. If he doesn't do it, he cannot be filled.

Of course, this does not mean that one is to make up unintelligible words, etc. That is not the idea at all. However, whenever the person comes to receive the Holy Spirit, and they are sincere, and they yield before the Lord, the Holy Spirit will then begin to give the Utterance, which will be obvious in the person's heart.

As well, one may speak in Tongues for quite a length of time after being filled, or one may only speak a few words.

At Family Worship Center sometime ago, we were praying one particular night for people to be filled with the Spirit. A dear Baptist lady came forward to be filled, and when the service was over she, along with several others, confessed that the Lord had filled her with the Spirit. However, what she said was a little bit different than usual.

She went on to relate to me how that she had only spoken one word in Tongues. Thank the Lord that I had a little more experience at this particular time, and I encouraged her and agreed with her that she was filled.

On the way home that night with friends, the one word ceased to be enough, with the Holy Spirit all of a sudden right there in the automobile, beginning to flow through her as she began to speak out volumes, in fact, speaking in Tongues all the way home.

So, it is not how long one speaks, but just that there be some evidence even, as stated, just one word, which to be frank is rare, but sometimes does happen. Nevertheless, that person has genuinely been filled with the Holy Spirit.

6. YIELD

When the individual comes to be filled with the Spirit, they should be told to yield to the Spirit, which is absolutely necessary.

By yielding, I am meaning that in their heart they should say (not out loud), *"I am asking You Lord to fill me with the Holy Spirit, and I now receive."*

In fact, I encourage people not to pray out loud, and actually not even to themselves,

NOTES

other than what I have just said. The reason being, is that they cannot speak two languages at one time. If they are speaking English (or another language that they've learned in School or somewhere), they can only speak that and nothing else. And as stated, the Lord will not break in upon them and force them to speak in Tongues.

So, the person should open his (her) mouth and breathe in as deeply as possible, in their heart telling the Lord that they receive. Then he will begin to sense the words given him by the Holy Spirit which is not a language that he knows. He is to then speak those words, and continue to do so. That is what I mean by yielding.

The Scripture says, *"Unto Me men give ear, and waited, and kept silence at My counsel. After My Words they spake not again; and My speech dropped upon them."* As is obvious, the Scripture says they did not say anything but kept silence, and then the Lord said, *"My speech dropped upon them."*

It also says, *"And they waited for Me as for the Rain; and they opened their mouth wide as for the Latter Rain"* (Job 29:21-23). The latter rain, as every Bible student knows, is the outpouring of the Holy Spirit (Joel 2:23; Acts 2:16-18).

7. RECEIVE

The Candidate has to understand that God has already given the Spirit and that it is up to that person to receive the Gift now. It is a *"Gift,"* and, consequently, the only thing one can do respecting a gift, is to receive it.

Peter said in his Sermon on the Day of Pentecost, *"And ye shall receive the Gift of the Holy Spirit"* (Acts 2:38).

So, the Believer does not come before the Lord to tarry, at least as it regards receiving the Holy Spirit. While tarrying is wonderful and something that I do almost every day of my life, still, we are not told in Scripture to do that respecting receiving the Baptism with the Holy Spirit.

Many confuse the Scripture in Luke where Jesus said, *"And, behold, I send the Promise of My Father upon you: but tarry ye in the city of Jerusalem, until ye be endued with power from on high"* (Lk. 24:49).

While it is true that Jesus told His followers to *"tarry,"* it was only because the Holy Spirit had not yet come. On the Day of Pentecost, He came. Consequently, every other time that one reads in the Book of Acts about people receiving the Holy Spirit, there was no tarrying involved with them receiving *immediately.*

The Holy Spirit has already come as should be overly obvious, so there is no more need to tarry to receive Him.

To do so, constitutes works, and nullifies the *"Gift"* aspect of the Holy Spirit. So, even though tarrying is very good, it is good only for other particular types of things, not to be Baptized with the Holy Spirit.

So, the Believer must say, *"I am going to receive this Gift of God,"* which is all the Lord expects one to do, other than having faith and believing, etc. It is yours, promised by the Lord (Acts 1:4-5).

(3) "BUT HE THAT PROPHESIETH SPEAKETH UNTO MEN TO EDIFICATION, AND EXHORTATION, AND COMFORT."

The phrase, *"But he that Prophesieth,"* speaks of the sixth Gift of the Spirit, as listed by Paul (I Cor. 12:8-10).

As we have already stated in Commentary on the Twelfth Chapter, the Gift of Prophecy is entirely different than standing in the Office of the Prophet, which is one of the fivefold Ministry Gifts (Eph. 4:11). While it is true that all Prophets have the Gift of Prophecy, at the same time all who have the Gift of Prophecy are not Prophets. The Office of the Prophet pertains to foretelling (futuristic events) and forth-telling, as well as being a *"Preacher of Righteousness"* (II Pet. 2:5). Many who have the Gift of Prophecy, as here listed by Paul, are not Preachers.

Prophecy is supernatural utterance in a known tongue. The Hebrew word for *"to prophesy"* means *"to flow forth."* It also carries with it the thought *"to bubble forth like a fountain, to let drop, to lift up, to tumble forth, and to spring forth."* The Greek word that is translated *"Prophesy"* means to *"speak for another."* It means to speak for God or to be His spokesman.

The phrase, *"Speaketh unto men,"* presents that which is the opposite of the *"Gift of Tongues,"* which *"speaketh . . . unto God"* (I Cor. 14:2).

## EDIFICATION

The phrase, *"To edification,"* presents that which is needed by the Body, as should be obvious.

NOTES

*"Edification"* in the Greek is *"oikodome,"* and means *"architecture, a structure, a building, confirmation."* It speaks of something being built, in this case the Body of Christ.

Consequently, someone who gives forth words of condemnation and destruction are not functioning in the Gift of Prophecy. While it may be true, that such a person may be a Prophet of God, and definitely have a word from the Lord in this manner, still, it is not the Gift of Prophecy, which never condemns or functions negatively. Whenever the true Gift of Prophecy is in operation, the people will be exactly what the Holy Spirit through the Apostle says, *"edified."*

EXHORTATION

The phrase, *"And exhortation,"* falls into the same category.

*"Exhortation"* in the Greeks is, *"paraklesis,"* it means *"imploration — to implore, solace, comfort."*

The phrase, *"And comfort,"* completes the trio of edification.

COMFORT

*"Comfort"* in the Greek is, *"paramuthia"* it means *"consolation."*

Some people think that to Prophesy means to preach. All inspired Utterance is prophecy in some form or another, but prophecy isn't preaching. Sometimes there is an element of prophecy in preaching when one is anointed by the Spirit and is inspired to say things that come directly from the Holy Spirit.

To preach means to proclaim, to announce, to cry or to tell. The Scriptural purpose of the Gift of Prophecy is different from the purpose of Preaching. Jesus didn't say that men would be saved by the foolishness of prophesying but by the foolishness of preaching. Supernatural Gifts are given to arrest people's attention, not to save them. Even on the Day of Pentecost when people were speaking in Tongues, no one was saved until Peter preached to them.

Unfortunately, when most people think of the Gift of Prophecy, they think of prediction. However, the simple Gift of Prophecy, of which Paul here speaks, is not prediction but rather speaking unto men *"for edification, and exhortation, and comfort."*

As well, some Christians who lack knowledge of the Word, equate at times the *"Gift of Prophecy"* with that which is little more than unscriptural fortune-telling.

For instance, a book some years ago was written by a well-known Psychic, Jeanne Dixon, called *"The Gift of Prophecy."* While this woman did have psychic powers, such were no relation whatsoever to the Gift of Prophecy. In fact, what she had was from Satan.

When Jeanne Dixon was a little child, a gypsy fortune-teller told her that she had psychic powers. The Holy Spirit does not function in that capacity, and neither does He derive information from crystal balls, as did Ms. Dixon.

So, Christians should not confuse horoscopes, psychic phenomenon, or anything of that nature with the *"Gift of Prophecy,"* for such has no relationship whatsoever. The other of which I have mentioned is from Satan and the world of spirit darkness.

(4) "HE THAT SPEAKETH IN AN UNKNOWN TONGUE EDIFIETH HIMSELF; BUT HE THAT PROPHESIETH EDIFIETH THE CHURCH."

The phrase, *"He that speaketh in an unknown tongue edifieth himself,"* is not necessarily speaking of the *"Gift of Tongues"* or as the Scripture says, *"Divers* (Diverse) *kinds of Tongues"* (I Cor. 12:10).

Paul is speaking here, for the most part, of the *"Tongues"* which all Spirit-filled Believers have, and can exercise whenever they so desire. While most all in the Church at Corinth were Spirit-filled and, consequently, spoke with Tongues, and as the account here proclaims did so quite often, in fact, only a few in that Church actually had the Gift of *"Diverse kinds of Tongues,"* which is meant to be Interpreted.

The Tongues of which Paul is here speaking is not necessarily meant to be Interpreted, but is actually meant for edification of the speaker only.

Not understanding these things, the Corinthians were interrupting the Services with their own worship in Tongues, which edified the person doing the speaking, but as would be obvious, did not edify the listeners, for the simple reason that they could not understand what was being said. So, Paul is merely telling them that this Praise or Worship Tongue which all Spirit-filled Believers have, should be exercised at the right time (in private worship) and not so as to interfere with the Service.

The *"edifying himself"* is very important and we will address ourselves to that momentarily.

The phrase, *"But he that prophesieth edifieth the Church,"* refers to this Gift in operation, exactly as we studied in the previous Verse. The Gift of Prophecy is meant for the edification of the entirety of the Body, and not just for the speaker. However, this doesn't mean that personal edification is wrong, even as we shall see, but that it must not be done at the expense of others.

## HOW IMPORTANT IS SPEAKING IN TONGUES?

The following will constitute only a few reasons as to why speaking with other Tongues is important and is of benefit to the entirety of the Body of Christ:

1. Tongues as given to all Spirit-filled Believers are sent from God (I Cor. 14:21). Consequently, anything given by God is necessary, good, edifying, and extremely helpful.

2. Tongues are the initial physical evidence that one has been Baptized with Holy Spirit (Acts 2:4). While there are many other evidences, this is the primary, initial, physical evidence that one has been filled (Acts 10:45-46; 11:15-17).

3. This is one sign (tongues) which Jesus said would follow Believers (Mk. 16:17).

4. Speaking in Tongues *"edifies"* the speaker, even as Paul has here said. The word *"edifieth"* means to build oneself up. Instead of *"edified,"* perhaps *"charge"* would be the better word. We use the word *"charge"* in connection with charging a battery. Consequently, a more literal translation would be, *"He that speaketh in an unknown Tongue edifieth, or charges, or builds himself up like a battery."* As well, this isn't just for a few of God's children, it is for all.

One should notice that this is also mental and physical edification, which we will deal with in a moment, as well as *"spiritual edification."* Paul said, *"For if I pray in an unknown tongue, my spirit prayeth. . . .* (I cor. 14:14).

5. It is a prayer language. Paul said, and on which we have just commented, *"For he that speaketh in an unknown tongue speaketh not unto men, but unto God."* Here the Apostle, even as we have stated, is not speaking about diversities of Tongues or ministering Tongues in a public assembly. He is speaking about the individual Spirit-filled Believer employing the use of tongues in his prayer life. *"Howbeit in the Spirit he speaketh mysteries"* (I Cor. 14:2). Weymouth's translation says, *"He speaks Divine secrets."*

6. Speaking with Tongues is the supernatural way to magnify God. Acts 10:46 says concerning Cornelius and his household when they began to speak with Tongues, *"For they heard them speak with Tongues, and magnify God."*

7. Speaking in Tongues is also a physical edification. Isaiah prophesied about eight hundred years before Christ saying, *"For with stammering lips and another Tongue will He speak to this people."* He then said, *"This is the rest wherewith ye may cause the weary to rest"* (Isa. 28:11-12). Paul also quoted this very Scripture in the 21st Verse of Chapter 14, even as we shall see.

*"Weary"* in the Hebrew is *"ayeph"* and means *"languid, faint, thirsty."*

*"Rest"* in the Hebrew as it is first used in this Scripture is *"mnuchah"* and means *"a resting place."*

The second *"Rest"* used in this Scripture is *"nuwach"* and means *"to settle down."* It carries the idea of physical edification.

Hardly anyone would think of speaking with other Tongues in this capacity, but this is exactly what it means. Consequently, Spirit-filled Believers, no doubt, ward off many sicknesses and afflictions simply by praying and worshipping in Tongues.

8. It is a mental edification as well. Isaiah also said, *"And this is the Refreshing"* (Isa. 28:12).

*"Refreshing"* in the Hebrew is *"margeah"* and means *"to find ease, make to rest."* It carries the idea of something being tossed violently, such as a storm on the sea, and then quieting down or settling down. Consequently, it speaks of mental disturbance brought on by the cares of life being settled down or calmed.

Peter used this word, *"Refreshing,"* in Acts 3:19. In the Greek it is *"anapsuxis"* and means *"a recovery of breath, to relieve."*

In fact, speaking with other Tongues as the Spirit of God gives the utterance in one's private devotions and worship, is the greatest therapy there is. In fact, it is God's therapy which is guaranteed to work, versus man's therapy (psychological counseling) which does not work, and in fact, cannot work. Man deals only with external things because that's the best he can do. He may probe the mind the best he can, by getting the patient to talk, which is the best that can be done, which effects no healing or help.

The Lord deals with the very spirit of man, from which Tongues come, where rests the cause of mental disturbance.

By *"mental disturbance,"* we are not meaning mental sickness, but rather, the weight of the cares and frustrations of life.

### A PERSONAL EXAMPLE

The stress that Frances and I have labored under during the 1990's has been of monumental proportions. Without going into detail, suffice it to say that without what I am about to relate to you, I don't think it would have been possible for any human being to suffer such without being completely destroyed.

In October, 1991, the Lord spoke to my heart and told me to conduct two Prayer Meetings a day, which we have done. This would be with the exception of service times, etc.

I realize that to most Christians such would seem to be excessive; however, it is not possible for the Spirit of the Lord to be excessive in any manner. Actually, it is the very opposite.

We gather every morning (Monday - Friday) at 10 a.m. Generally, there are anywhere from five to fifty present. We gather as well at 6:30 p.m. each evening, with the exception of service nights.

We do not pray long, generally about an hour. I generally read a Verse of Scripture, comment on it for a few moments, take prayer requests, and then we go to prayer.

### PRAYER

These prayer times are definitely times during which we can petition the Lord for things we need, but most of all (to a far greater extent), it is a time for Communion with the Lord. Countless times I have come to one of the Prayer Meetings with a heavy heart, with problems which seemed to be unsolvable, and when I would leave, everything would be totally different. The Spirit of God would come down into my heart, move upon my very soul, even to such an extent that it's very difficult to even properly explain. Most of the time, the problems did not go away, but the strength to face these problems was definitely given, which is the important thing.

NOTES

I am not meaning that every single Prayer Meeting is like this. Sometimes, it's difficult to pray and there seems to be little done. But at other times, and very often I might quickly add, it is the very opposite, with a Moving of the Spirit that's absolutely phenomenal.

At the outset, the Lord spoke to my heart, telling me, *"Do not seek me so much for what I can do, but rather for Who I am."* I have never forgotten that, and most of my praying is worship and praise rather than petition.

However, the point I desire to make, is exactly that which Isaiah prophesied so long ago. Most of my praying is done in English, but at times the Spirit of God will move upon my heart, quite often in fact, and I will begin to worship the Lord in Tongues. At these times, I experience not only a spiritual edification, but also a physical and mental edification as well.

### WHAT OTHERS HAVE SAID

Most Christians, sad to say, little know or understand that of which I speak. Many have suggested that Frances and I were either ignorant of the disposition among most Christians against us, or else we were not facing reality, etc.

Oh, yes! We very well know of the animosity of which they speak, and as well, we are facing reality, actually in the only successful manner in which it can be faced, which is according to the Word of God. However, our demeanor, our nature, the victory we have within our hearts and lives, are given by the Lord. It is the *"Rest"* and *"Refreshing"* which Isaiah spoke about. It really does work; we have proved it.

It is regrettable that most of the modern Church have opted for humanistic psychology which in reality affords no help at all, rather than that given by the Lord, which is the only true help there really is, and which is *"joy unspeakable and full of Glory."* In fact, this is one of the reasons for the terrible animosity. We have let it be known in no uncertain terms that we are going to trust God. To a carnal church, this does not set well. It is the case of Cain and Abel all over again.

Abel trusted in the Promise of God which refers to the slain lamb which typified Christ. Cain trusted in the labor of his hands (the way of man), and was angry because God did not accept his offering; consequently, he killed Abel.

NOTES

I must remind the reader that it was Abel's Brother who did this. Consequently, the greatest hinderance to the Work of God has always been, regrettably, the Church. However, the Lord gives victory over that as well!

(5) "I WOULD THAT YE ALL SPAKE WITH TONGUES, BUT RATHER THAT YE PROPHESIED: FOR GREATER IS HE THAT PROPHESIETH THAN HE THAT SPEAKETH WITH TONGUES, EXCEPT HE INTERPRET, THAT THE CHURCH MAY RECEIVE EDIFYING."

The phrase, *"I would that ye all spake with Tongues,"* refers *not* to the Gift of Tongues, as that relates to the nine Gifts of the Spirit, but rather speaking with Tongues in one's worship and prayer language, which Paul discussed in the previous Verse.

The phrase, *"But rather that ye prophesied,"* now reverts to this particular Gift of the Spirit.

One could translate it in this manner, *"I want all of you to speak with other Tongues regarding your own private worship and devotion, but when it comes to the Gifts of Spirit, I would rather that more of you have the Gift of Prophecy than the Gift of Tongues and Interpretation of Tongues."* However, this is not meant to demean the latter Gift, but rather to put it in its proper perspective, even as we shall see.

The phrase, *"For greater is he that Prophesieth than he that speaketh with Tongues, except he Interpret,"* tells us the reason in the next phrase.

The phrase, *"That the Church may receive edifying,"* gives us the reason that Prophecy is the Greater Gift. It edifies the entirety of the Body of Christ (the Church), while Tongues edify only the individual, unless the utterance is Interpreted, which then equals Prophecy, and then also edifies the entirety of the Body.

## SOME EXPLANATION NEEDED

1. Paul is speaking about two things here, which tends to confuse some people. He is speaking of the prayer and worship Tongue which all Spirit-filled Believers have, but which is *not* one of the nine Gifts of the Spirit. However, he is also speaking of Tongues and Interpretation, which constitutes two of the Gifts. So, one has to distinguish that of which he speaks.

2. He is in effect telling the people that their speaking in Tongues in their own private worship and devotion should be to themselves and not in the Service where it will interrupt the proceedings. The speaker may be edified, and in fact is, but it does not help any of the other Believers, for the obvious reason that they cannot understand what is being said.

3. However, he leaves room for the twin Gifts of Tongues, which speaks of an Utterance which the Holy Spirit means to be Interpreted, which is then a blessing to the entire Church, and in its final consequence equals Prophecy.

4. The Gift of Prophecy is greater than the Gift of Tongues and Interpretation for the simple reason that the latter requires Interpretation and the former doesn't. The end result is the same, but at times, getting to that end result is not the same.

That's the reason that Paul will give more teaching on the Gift of Interpretation of Tongues, even as we shall see. However, in no way is the reader to think that the Apostle is demeaning Tongues and Interpretation. Quite the opposite! He is merely stating how they are to be used.

5. We learn from this Verse that the major thrust of the Gifts, and in whatever capacity, is to edify the Body of Christ, and not just a lone individual.

As one goes down through the Text, Paul is constantly delineating between one's prayer and worship language of Tongues, as opposed to Tongues and Interpretation as two of the Gifts of the Spirit. As repeatedly stated, all Spirit-filled Believers have their prayer and worship Tongue, but only a few would have the twin Gifts of Tongues and Interpretation.

(6) "NOW, BRETHREN, IF I COME UNTO YOU SPEAKING WITH TONGUES, WHAT SHALL I PROFIT YOU, EXCEPT I SHALL SPEAK TO YOU EITHER BY REVELATION, OR BY KNOWLEDGE, OR BY PROPHESYING, OR BY DOCTRINE?"

The phrase, *"Now, Brethren, if I come unto you speaking with Tongues, what shall I profit you,"* does not refer to the *"Gift of Tongues"* as one of the nine Gifts of the Spirit, which is meant to be Interpreted, but rather Believers praising and worshipping the Lord in Tongues out loud during the service which, as should be obvious, would be an interruption.

As previously stated, before now, it seems that the Corinthians, as well as probably most other Churches, had received very little teaching on this particular subject. Inasmuch as these Gifts were new to the Church, and that there were few regulations, if any, many people were worshipping in Tongues in the regular service, which no doubt edified the speaker, but did not edify the others, for the simple reason they did not know what was being said. One can imagine that confusion would be the result of such action.

The conclusion of the question, *"Except I shall speak to you either by Revelation, or by Knowledge, or by Prophesying, or by Doctrine?"*, pertains to the ways in which the Lord reveals Truth to His people.

## REVELATION

*"Revelation"* in the Greek is *"apokalupsis"* and means *"to take off the cover, disclose, reveal, to manifest."*

This pertains to the Holy Spirit opening up the Word to the Preacher of the Gospel, giving him light on particular Scriptures, or giving him a message specifically for that particular congregation at that particular place.

This requires great consecration on the part of the Preacher of the Gospel, in that he must seek the Face of the Lord in order that the Lord must speak to Him regarding what the Spirit wants. The Preacher is not to deliver his own mind, learning, or ability, but rather that such be used, in the realm of what the Lord wants said. As stated, this takes great consecration and study of the Word.

Unfortunately, most Preachers who will stand behind a pulpit this coming Sunday morning, or any other time, have little heard from the Lord, if at all, consequently, delivering their own mind to the people instead of the mind of the Lord, which will result in no benefit.

As well, Revelation can also pertain to the Spirit opening up the Word to the laity in their private worship and study.

## KNOWLEDGE

*"Knowledge"* in the Greek is *"gnosis"* and means *"a seeking to know, an enquiry, investigation, subjectively, of God's Knowledge."*

The manner in which Paul uses the Word gives it a twofold direction: A. A Word of Knowledge as one of the nine Gifts of the Spirit; and, B. Knowledge of the Word imparted by the Holy Spirit to the Preacher or Teacher, in order to be given to the people for their benefit and edification. As well, the Holy Spirit can give *"Knowledge"* directly to the laity in their worship and study. These things are not confined by any means to Preachers only.

Using myself as an example, time and again the Holy Spirit will impart to me information I have not previously had regarding segments of God's Word. At all times it is by *"Revelation"* showing us how these things work together, but with the Lord using various different means. By that I mean the following:

At times I will be studying what another Teacher has said on a particular subject, and even though he may not even be addressing the question at hand, at times I will read something he did say, which all of a sudden opens up that for which I am seeking, as the Holy Spirit takes the occasion to put it all together. In other words, He makes the pieces fit.

At other times, it will be by direct Revelation to my spirit, as a *"Word of Knowledge"* drops down into my heart. I am speaking of *"Knowledge"* concerning the Word of God, and its proper understanding. I then proceed to give what the Lord has given me to the people.

## PROPHESYING

*"Prophesying"* in the Greek is *"Propheteia"* and means *"foretelling and forth-telling, an inspired speaker."*

The word refers to the *"Gift of Prophecy,"* even as Paul has already explained, and, as well, it refers to this Gift at times being manifested in the midst of a Message being brought by a Preacher. It also can refer to the Office of the Prophet.

It pertains to a heavy Anointing of the Holy Spirit which takes the Preacher of the Gospel to a higher level of Anointing and which brings forth a truth which the Holy Spirit desires, which is quickened to the hearts of the people. Most of the time, such is not thought of as *"Prophecy,"* but that's exactly what it is.

Of course, this can only come about in the Ministry of a Preacher of the Gospel, who is heavily Anointed by the Holy Spirit. I'll give an example:

I have had this to happen countless times, even as late as ministering yesterday morning at Family Worship Center (May 10, 1998);

NOTES

however, the example I wish to use illustrates the point a little more succinctly.

THE FORMER SOVIET UNION

It was 1985, if I remember correctly. I was ministering in a Church in Minsk, Russia. It was a Sunday morning. The building was packed to capacity and the Lord especially Anointed me to preach that morning, even to the point of seeing my interpreter brought to Christ (He had been supplied by the Government, inasmuch as Russia, in those days, was still in the grip of Soviet Communism.).

At a particular point in the Message, the Lord heavily Anointed me, and I made this statement, which at the time, even though heavily accompanied by the Holy Spirit, seemed to be preposterous. This is what I said:

*"The Lord spoke these words through me, 'I am going to touch every single City, Town, and Village in the entirety of the Soviet Union with the Gospel of Jesus Christ.'"*

When it was said, there was a mighty move of the Spirit in the congregation. But yet, after the Service was over, I wondered in my mind as to how in the world such a thing could be done.

I remarked to Frances with some fear, *"I pray that was of the Lord, because in the natural such a thing is impossible."*

Well, it was of the Lord!

In 1989, I believe it was, we went on television in Riga, Latvia, which was then a part of the Soviet Union. The KGB checked into the matter closely I am told, even sending agents from Moscow, but miracle of miracles, the Program was not taken off the air. It was translated, of course, into Russian.

Actually, we began to translate into Russian on the strength of what the Lord had told us even before we had anywhere to air the program in that vast land.

In the latter part of 1989, the Lord opened up Television One in Moscow, which was the former Government Communist Channel, which covered every single City, Town, and Village in that vast land area, one-sixth of the world's land surface. In fact, we aired the Gospel over that vast network, which had several thousands of repeater stations, for nearly two years. Exactly as the Lord had said some four years earlier, every City, Town, and Village in the former Soviet Union was touched by the Gospel of Jesus Christ. As well, I would be remiss if I did not give Jim Woolsey the credit for helping to bring this to pass. It was his persistence, dedication, and above all, Faith in God, which made it possible for us to do this thing, which in fact, brought about a tremendous move of God in that vast land.

NOTES

Every Preacher of the Gospel should seek the Face of the Lord to such an extent, that the Holy Spirit can flow through him (or her) in order that he not only be Anointed to Preach, but as well, that this particular Gift of Prophecy can operate as the Spirit of God desires and when He desires.

DOCTRINE

Doctrine in the Greek is *"Didache"* and means *"instruction, teaching."*

Someone has said that Preaching proclaims the Gospel, while Teaching explains the Gospel. However, all Preaching should have some Teaching in the body of its delivery, and all Teaching should have some Preaching contained therein as well. Also, even though Teaching is altogether Doctrine, at least as a whole, all Preaching should contain at least some Doctrine.

As should be obvious, Paul is outlining the necessity of what Church is all about. While it definitely is to be a time of Refreshing and Blessing, it is not to be limited to such, but as well a place of Learning, which of course, can only be done in the language understood by all the people.

Inasmuch as Doctrine, which constitutes what one believes, is so very, very important, perhaps a little more information of this subject would be helpful.

THE NATURE OF DOCTRINE

Christian Doctrine (the word, *"Doctrine,"* as stated, means literally *"teaching or instruction."*) may be defined as the fundamental Truths of the Bible arranged in systematic form. This study is commonly called Theology, which means literally *"a treatise or reasoned discourse about God."* (The two terms will be used interchangeably in the following description.)

Theology or Doctrine may be described as the science that deals with our knowledge of God and His relations to man, according to His

Word. It treats of all things insofar as they are related to God and the Divine Purposes.

A SCIENCE?

Why do we describe Theology or Doctrine as a *"Science"*?

Science is the systematic and logical arrangement of certified facts. Theology is called a Science because it consists of facts relating to God and Divine things presented in an orderly and logical manner.

Some may ask the question, as to what is the difference between a Doctrine and a Dogma?

A Doctrine is God's Revelation of a Truth as found in the Scriptures; Dogma is man's statement of that Truth as set forth in a creed.

THE VALUE OF DOCTRINE

Doctrinal knowledge supplies the need for an authoritative and systematic statement of Truth.

There is a tendency in some quarters not only to minimize the value of Doctrine, but to dismiss it as outgrown and useless. However, as long as men think about the problems of existence, they will feel the need of an authoritative and systematically arranged answer to these problems. Doctrine will always be necessary as long as men ask, *"Where did I come from?"*, *"What am I?"*, or *"Where am I going?"*

It is often said, *"It does not matter what a man believes so long as he does right."*

This is one way of dismissing Doctrine as having no importance in relation to life. But every person has a theology, whether he knows it or not: man's actions are influenced by what he believes. For example, there would be a wide difference between the conduct of a ship's crew who knew that they were headed for a definite destination, and a crew who realized that they were drifting aimlessly without a definite course or destination.

Human life is a journey from time to eternity, and it matters much whether one believes that it is an aimless, meaningless journey, or one planned by man's Maker and directed to a heavenly destiny.

DOCTRINE IS NECESSARY FOR A FULL DEVELOPMENT OF CHRISTIAN CHARACTER

Strong beliefs make for strong character; clear-cut beliefs make for clear-cut convictions.

NOTES

Of course, a person's doctrinal belief is not exactly his personal experience with God, any more than the backbone is man's personality. But a good backbone is an essential part of a man's body, so a definite system of belief is an essential part of one's experience with God.

It has been well said that *"a man does not need to wear his backbone in front of him, but he must have a backbone, and a straight one, or he will be a flexible, if not a humpbacked, Christian."*

A French Unitarian Preacher once made the statement: *"Purity of heart and life is more important than correctness of opinion."*

To which another French Preacher answered: *"Healing is more important than the remedy; but without the remedy there would be no healing."*

Certainly it is more important to live the Christian life than to merely know Christian Doctrine, but there would be no Christian experience if there were no Christian Doctrine.

DOCTRINAL KNOWLEDGE IS A SAFEGUARD AGAINST ERROR

Scriptural references for that can be found in Matthew 22:29; Galatians 1:6-9; II Timothy 4:2-4.

It is often said that the stars came before the Science of Astronomy, and that flowers existed before Botany, and that life existed before Biology, and that God existed before Theology.

That is true. But men in their ignorance conceived superstitious notions about the stars, and the result was the false science of Astrology. Men conceived false ideas about plants, attributing virtues which they did not possess; and the result was witchcraft. Man, in his blindness, formed wrong conceptions of God, and the result was paganism with its superstitions and corruption.

But Astronomy came with true principles about heavenly bodies and so exposed the errors of Astrology; Botany came with the truth about plants and so banished the errors of witchcraft. In like manner, Bible Doctrine exposes false notions about God and His Ways.

*"Let no man think error in Doctrine a slight practical evil,"* declared D. C. Hodge, the noted Theologian. *"No road to perdition has ever been more thronged than that of False Doctrine. Error is a shield over the conscience, and a bandage over the eyes."*

## DOCTRINAL KNOWLEDGE IS A NECESSARY PART OF THE CHRISTIAN TEACHER'S EQUIPMENT

When a consignment of goods reaches a store, the goods are unpacked and placed in their proper compartments and receptacles, so that they may be handled in an orderly manner.

This is a rather homely illustration of one purpose of systematic study. The Bible indeed follows a central theme. But the various Truths relating to its great Theme are scattered throughout the various Books.

In order, therefore, to gain a comprehensive view of each Doctrine, and impart it to others, one must gather the references relating to it and place them in compartments (Topics) and in smaller receptacles (Sub-Topics).

## A SYSTEM OF DOCTRINE

According to what order shall the Topics be arranged?

No hard and fast rules may be laid down. There are many arrangements, each having its value. However, we shall try to follow an order based on God's Redemptive dealings with man:

1. The Doctrine of the Scriptures

From what Source shall we derive inerrant Truth about God?

Nature indeed reveals His Existence, Power, and Wisdom, but it tells of no way or pardon, provides no escape from sin and its consequences, supplies no incentive to Holiness, and contains no Revelation of the Future. We leave God's first Book — Nature — and go to God's other Book — the Bible, where we find God's Revelation concerning these matters.

On what grounds do we accept the Biblical view as being the right one?

The answer to this question leads to the study of the nature, inspiration, accuracy, and reliability of the Scriptures.

2. The Doctrine of God

We then seek to ascertain what the Scriptures teach about the greatest of all facts — the fact of God, His Nature, and Existence.

3. The Doctrine of Angels

From the Creator we naturally pass to a study of His creatures, and so we consider some of His Heavenly beings, Angels. This topic takes in also wicked angels, Satan and Demons.

4. The Doctrine of Man

NOTES

We do not dwell long on the subject of good and bad Angels, but come quickly to consider the Biblical view of man, for all Truths in the Scriptures cluster round two focal points — God and man.

Next in importance to the study of God is the study of man.

5. The Doctrine of Sin

The most tragic fact connected with man is sin and its consequences. The Scriptures tell us of its origin, nature, consequences, and cure.

6. The Doctrine of Christ

The study of man's sin is followed by a study of the Person and Work of Christ, man's Saviour.

7. The Doctrine of the Atonement

Under this heading, we consider the facts which throw light on the meaning of Christ's Supreme Work on man's behalf.

8. The Doctrine of Salvation

How is the Atonement applied to man's needs and made real in his experience? The facts supplying the answer are grouped under the Doctrine of Salvation.

9. The Doctrine of the Holy Spirit

How is Christ's work for man made real in man? This is discussed in the Doctrine of the nature and work of the Holy Spirit.

10. The Doctrine of the Church

Christ's Disciples obviously need some kind of organization for the purposes of worship, instruction, fellowship, and the propagation of the Gospel. The New Testament tells us about the nature and work of this Organization.

11. The Doctrine of Last Things

It is natural to direct one's gaze into the future and ask how everything — life, history, the world — will end, or evolve. All that has been revealed concerning the future is grouped under the heading of *"Last Things."*

Even though we will not at this time deal with all these subjects, I do think it would be profitable to deal with the veracity of the Word of God, inasmuch as that is actually to what Paul is referring.

## THE SCRIPTURES

*"Heaven and earth shall pass away, but My Words shall not pass away." "The grass withereth, and the flower fadeth: but the Word of our God shall stand for ever"* (Mat. 24:35; Isa. 40:8).

Destroy this volume, the Bible, as the enemies of human happiness have vainly endeavored to do, and you render us profoundly ignorant of our Creator, of the formation of the world which we inhabit, of the origin and progenitors of our race, of our future destination, and consign us through life to the dominion of fancy, doubt, and conjecture.

Destroy the Bible, and you deprive us of the Christian experience, with all the animating consolations, hopes, and prospects it affords which, in fact, has given the world every iota of freedom which it now enjoys, and leave us nothing but the choosing (miserable alternative!) between the cheerless gloom of infidelity and the monstrous shadows of paganism, with its worship of stars, trees, and demons.

Destroy the Bible, and you unpeople heaven, bar forever its doors against the wretched posterity of Adam, restore the king of terrors his fatal sting, bury hope in the same grave which receives our bodies, consign all who have died before us to eternal sleep or endless misery, and allow us to expect nothing at death but a similar fate.

In a word, destroy this Volume, and you take from us at once everything which prevents existence, becoming of all curses the greatest; you blot out the sun, dry up the oceans, and take away the atmosphere of the moral world, and degrade man to a situation from which he may look up with envy to that of the brutes that perish (Payson).

## THE NEED FOR THE SCRIPTURES

*"What is Truth?"*, asked Pilate, and his tone inferred that the search for it was vain and hopeless. If there be no authoritative guide to knowledge about God, man, and the world, then Pilate was right regarding his cynicism.

But there is no need to grope in doubt and skepticism, for there is a Book — *"the Holy Scriptures, which are able to make thee wise unto Salvation through Faith which is in Christ Jesus"* (II Tim. 3:15).

## SUCH A REVELATION IS TO BE DESIRED

The God Who created the universe must be a God of Wisdom, and a God of Wisdom will certainly have a purpose for His creatures. To neglect this purpose would be folly and to defy it would be sin.

But how may the Divine purpose be certainly known?

NOTES

History proves that mankind arrives at very different conclusions, and many people come to none. Experience shows that the problem cannot be solved by study alone. Some do not have the time, others, even if they have the desire, do not possess the ability: and even if successful, their conclusion would be reached slowly and doubtfully.

Wise men may build ladders of thought in the attempt to attain to heavenly Truth, but the tallest ladder will always prove to be too short.

*"The world by wisdom* (philosophy) *knew not God."* Truths that tell man how to pass from earth to heaven must be sent down from heaven to earth. In other words, man needs a Revelation.

## SUCH A REVELATION IS TO BE EXPECTED

In Nature, we have a Revelation of God that may be grasped by reason. But when man is bound by sin and burdened in soul, Nature and reason are powerless to give light and relief. Let the men of reason testify.

Said Kant, one of the greatest thinkers of all time, *"You do well to base your peace and piety on the Gospels, for in the Gospels Alone is the source of deep spiritual Truths, after reason has measured out its territory in vain."*

Another able philosopher, Hagel, when on his deathbed would have no book read to him but his Bible. He said that if he could prolong his life he would make this Book his study, for in it he found what reason could not discover.

If, as we believe, there be a good God, it is reasonable to expect that He will grant a personal Revelation of Himself to His creatures.

Writes David S. Clarke:

*"We cannot conceive that a natural father should forever conceal himself from his son, and never have communication with him. No more can we conceive of a good God Who would withhold knowledge of His Being and His Will from creatures created in His Own Image.*

*"God has made man capable and desirous of knowing the reality of things, and will He withhold a Revelation capable of satisfying that desire?*

*"Ancient Egyptian mythology tells of the fabled Sphinx who asked riddles of passers-by and killed them if they failed to answer. Such a loving and wise God would not permit man to*

*perish for lack of knowledge, baffled at the riddle of the Universe."*

SUCH A REVELATION WOULD BE WRITTEN

It is reasonable that God should embody His Message to a man in a Book. As Dr. Keyser says, *"Books are the best method of preserving Truth in its integrity and transmitting it from generation to generation.*

*"Memory and tradition are sometimes untrustworthy. Therefore God acted with the greatest Wisdom and also in the normal way in giving His Revelation to men in Book form. In no other way, so far as we can see, could He have imparted to mankind an infallible standard that would be available to all mankind and that would continue intact throughout the ages and from which all people could procure the same standard of Faith and Practice."*

It is reasonable to expect that God would inspire His servants to record Truths which could not have been discovered by human reason. And finally, it is reasonable to believe that God has providentially preserved the Manuscripts of the Bible Scriptures and led His Church to include in the Canon only those Books that had their origin in Divine Inspiration.

THE INSPIRATION OF THE SCRIPTURES

That an experience without inspired writings could be Divine is a conceivable possibility. As Professor Francis L. Patton observes:

*"If on simple, historical narrative alone, it can be proved that Jesus wrought Miracles, uttered Prophecies and proclaimed His Divinity — if it can be shown that He was crucified to redeem sinners, that He rose again from the dead and that He made the destiny of man to hinge on their acceptance of Him as their Saviour — then whether the records be inspired or no, woe unto him who neglects so great Salvation."*

We need not, however, discuss further this possibility, for we are not left in any doubt concerning the matter. *"All Scripture is given by Inspiration of God (literally, 'is God-breathed'),"* declares Paul (II Tim. 3:16).

*"For the Prophecy came not in old time by the will of man,"* Peter writes, *"but Holy men of God spake as they were moved by the Holy Spirit"* (II Pet. 1:21).

NOTES

WHAT IS INSPIRATION?

Inspiration is defined by Webster as *"the supernatural influence of the Spirit of God on the human mind, by which Prophets and Apostles and Sacred Writers were qualified to set forth Divine Truth without any mixture of error."*

According to one Theologian, it is the *"inexplicable power which the Divine Spirit exercised over the authors of the Scriptures, to guide them even in the employment of the words they were to use, and to preserve them from all error as well as from every omission."*

*"Inspiration, as defined by Paul in this passage (II Tim. 3:16), is the strong, conscious in-breathing of God into men, qualifying them to give utterance to Truth,"* writes Dr. William Evans.

It is God speaking through men, and both the Old and New Testaments are, therefore, as much the Word of God as though God spoke every word, and which He did.

The Scriptures are the result of Divine inbreathing, just as human speech is uttered by breathing through man's mouth. Peter's declaration may be said to intimate that the Holy Spirit was especially and miraculously present with and in the writers of Scriptures, revealing to them Truths which they did not know before, and guiding them alike in their recording of these Truths, and of the transactions of which they were eye and ear witnesses, so that they were enabled to present them with total accuracy to the minds of others.

THE SIMPLICITY OF THE GOSPEL

One might gather from the reading of various creeds of Christendom that Christianity is a rather complicated affair, bristling with theological puzzles and cumbered with abstruse definitions.

Such is not the case.

The Doctrines of the New Testament, as originally set forth, are simple, and may be simply defined. But as time passed, the Church was confronted with erroneous and defective views of Doctrines and was, therefore, obliged to hedge and protect them with definitions.

From this process of exact and detailed definition arose the Creeds. The Doctrinal statements played an important and necessary part in the life of the Church, and became a hindrance only when assent to them was substituted for a Living Faith.

The Doctrine of Inspiration, as set forth in the Word, is quite simple, but the advancing of erroneous and defective views has made it necessary to *"fence"* the Doctrine with full and detailed definitions. Against certain theories, it is necessary to contend that Inspiration of the Scriptures is:

1. DIVINE AND NOT MERELY HUMAN

The Modernist identifies the Inspiration of the Sacred writers with that spiritual insight and wisdom which is possessed by such men as Plato, Socrates, Browning, Shakespeare and other geniuses in the literary, philosophical, and religious world.

Inspiration is thus considered by such as purely natural. However, this theory empties the word Inspiration of all meaning, and is inconsistent with the unique and supernatural character of the Bible.

2. UNIQUE AND NOT COMMON

Some confuse Inspiration (that given by the Lord) with Illumination (the understanding of that given).

Illumination refers to the influence of the Holy Spirit, common to all Christians, which influence helps them to grasp the things of God (Mat. 16:17; I Cor. 2:4). They hold that such Illumination is an adequate explanation of the origin of the Bible. There is a faculty in man, so they teach, by which man can know God — a kind of eye of the soul. As the Godly men of old meditated upon God, the Divine Spirit quickened this faculty, giving it insight into the Divine Mysteries.

Such Illumination is promised to Believers and has been experienced by them. But it is not the same as Inspiration. We are told (I Pet. 1:10-12) that at times the Prophets received Truths by Inspiration and were denied Illumination for the comprehension of those same Truths. The Holy Spirit inspired their words, but did not see fit to grant the knowledge of the meaning of those words.

For instance, to use a far-out example, Caiaphas, who certainly was not of God, is yet described as being a vehicle for an inspired message (howbeit unconsciously), while as yet his mind was not on God. At the moment he was inspired, but not illumined (Jn. 11:49-52).

## TWO SPECIFIC DIFFERENCES

Note two specific differences between Illumination and Inspiration:

NOTES

A. As to duration, Illumination is, or can be, permanent. *"The path of the just is as the shining light, that shineth more and more unto the perfect day"* (Prov. 4:18).

The Anointing that the Believer has received of the Holy One abides in him, says John (I Jn. 2:20-27). On the other hand, Inspiration was intermittent; the Prophet could not prophesy at will, but was subject to the Will of the Spirit. *"For the Prophecy came not in old time by the will of man,"* declares Peter, *"But holy men of God spake as they were moved by the Holy Spirit"* (II Pet. 1:21).

The suddenness of Prophetic Inspiration is implied by the common expression, *"The Word of the Lord came to such an one."* A clear distinction is drawn between the true Prophets who speak only as the Word of the Lord comes to them and the false prophets who speak a message of their own devising (Jer. 14:14; 23:11, 16; Ezek. 13:2-3).

B. Illumination admits of degrees, Inspiration admits of none. People vary as to the degree of their Illumination (understanding), some possessing a greater degree of insight of others. But in the case of Inspiration, in the Bible sense, a person is either inspired or he is not.

3. LIVING AND NOT MECHANICAL

Inspiration does not mean dictation, even as I am doing with this dictaphone which I hold presently in my hand, in the sense that the writers were passive, their faculties having no part whatsoever in the recording of the material; although it is true that some portions of the Scriptures were dictated, for example, the Ten Commandments and the Lord's Prayer.

The very word Inspiration excludes mere mechanical action, and mechanical action excludes Inspiration. For example, I do not inspire my Secretary when I dictate letters to her. As well, God does not speak through man as one would speak through a megaphone; His Divine Spirit used their faculties, their education, their personalities, etc., so producing a perfectly Divine Message which bore the marks of their individuality.

It is the Word of the Lord and yet in a sense, the word of Moses, or of Isaiah, or of Paul. *"God has done nothing but by man; man has done nothing but by God. It is God speaking in man, God speaking by man, God speaking as man, God speaking for man."*

The fact of Divine and human co-operation and the producing of an inspired Message, is clear enough; but the *"how"* of the matter is beyond our observation.

The interaction of even mind and body is a mystery to the wisest man; how much more the interaction of the Spirit of God and the spirit of man!

4. COMPLETE AND NOT MERELY PARTIAL

According to the theory of partial Inspiration, the writers were preserved from error in matters necessary to Salvation, but not in subjects like history, science, chronology, and others. Therefore, according to this theory it would be more correct to say that *"the Bible contains the Word of God, rather than it is the Word of God."*

This theory plunges us into a morass of uncertainty, for who can unerringly judge of what is and what is not essential to Salvation? As well, the infallible authority to decide as to which part is the Word of God and which is not? And if the history of the Bible falls, then the Doctrine cannot be true as well, for Biblical Doctrine is founded upon Biblical History.

Finally, the Scriptures themselves claim full or plenary Inspiration. Christ and His Apostles apply the term *"Word of God"* to the entire Old Testament.

Consequently, every iota of the Word of God, its History, what little it says about Science, its Chronology and all else, is without error, i.e., *"The Word of God."*

5. VERBAL AND NOT MERELY CONCEPTUAL

According to another view, God inspired the thoughts but not the words of the writers. That is, God inspired the men, and left them to their own devices and judgement in the selection of words and expressions.

But the Scriptural emphasis is not necessarily upon inspired men, but rather on inspired words. *"God . . . spake in time past unto the fathers by the Prophets"* (Heb. 1:1).

*"Holy Men of God spake as they were moved by the Holy Spirit"* (II Pet. 1:21).

Moreover, it is difficult to separate word and thoughts; a thought is an internal word (*"Begin not to say within yourselves"*; *"The fool hath said in his heart"*); a word is a thought expressed.

Divinely inspired thoughts would naturally be expressed in Divinely inspired words. Paul tells us of *"Words . . . which the Holy Spirit teacheth"* (I Cor. 2:13). Finally, single words are sighted as the basis of weighty Doctrines (Mat. 22:42-45; Jn. 10:35; Gal. 3:16; Heb. 12:26-27).

NOTES

## THE DIFFERENCE BETWEEN REVELATION AND INSPIRATION

We should distinguish between Revelation and Inspiration. By Revelation we mean that act of God by which He discloses what man could not find out for himself; by Inspiration we mean that the writer is preserved from error in recording that Revelation.

For example, the Ten Commandments were revealed and Moses was inspired to record them in the Pentateuch (first five Books of the Bible).

Inspiration does not always imply Revelation; for example, Moses was inspired to record events which he himself had witnessed and which were, therefore, within the scope of his own knowledge.

Distinguish also between uninspired words and the inspired record. For example, many sayings of Satan are recorded in the Scriptures and we know that the Devil was *not* God-inspired when he said them; but the record of those Satanic utterances is inspired.

## THE VERIFICATION OF THE SCRIPTURES

In fact, the Bible is the only Book in the world, despite the claims of others, which is given by God, and in fact, can be verified to be the Word of God. It is about one third history, one third prophecy, and one third teaching. Of course, there is great Teaching even in its History as well as its Prophecy.

Also, of all the books claiming Inspiration, the Bible is the only one which contains Prophecy. The reasons are obvious. Prophecy demands Inspiration, or else it is quickly proven false. About half of the Prophecy in the Bible has already been fulfilled, with other Prophecy in the process of being fulfilled, with other shortly to be fulfilled:

1. THE SCRIPTURES CLAIM TO BE INSPIRED

The Old Testament claims to have been written under special inspiration of God. The term *"and God said,"* or its equivalent, is used over 2600 times. The History, Law, Psalms, and Prophesies, are said to have been written by men under special inspiration from God.

See for example: (Ex. 24:4; 34:28; Josh. 3:9; II Ki. 17:13; Ps. 78:1; Prov. 6:23; Isa. 34:16; 59:21; Zech. 7:12).

Christ Himself endorsed the Old Testament, quoted it and lived in harmony with its Teachings. He endorsed its Truth and Authority (Mat. 5:18; 23:1-2; 26:54; Lk. 18:31-33; 24:25, 44; Jn. 10:35), and so did the Apostles (Lk. 3:4; Acts 1:16; 3:18; Rom. 3:2; I Cor. 2:9-16; II Tim. 3:16; Heb. 1:1; II Pet. 1:21; 3:2).

Does the New Testament claim for itself a similar Inspiration?

In particular, the Inspiration of the Gospels is guaranteed by the Promise of Christ that the Spirit should bring to the minds of the Apostles all things which He had taught them, that the same Spirit should lead them into all Truth.

Everywhere the New Testament claims to give a fuller and clearer Revelation of God and that given in the Old Testament, and authoritatively declares the abrogation of the Old Laws. Therefore, if the Old Testament is inspired so must be the New.

In fact, Peter places the Writings of Paul on a level with those of the Old Testament (II Pet. 3:15-16), and Paul and the other Apostles claim to speak with a Divine Authority (I Cor. 2:13; 14:31; I Thess. 2:13; 4:2; II Pet. 3:2; I Jn. 1:5; Rev. 1:1).

2. THEY APPEAR TO BE INSPIRED

The Scriptures claim to be inspired, and an examination of them reveals the fact that their character supports their claim. The Bible comes into court with a good record.

As to authorship, it was written by men whose honesty and integrity cannot be questioned; as to contents, it contains the most sublime Revelation of God that the world knows; as to influence, it has brought Saving Light to nations and individuals, and it possesses a never-failing power to lead men to God and to transfigure their characters; as to Authority, it meets the need of a final court of appeal in things Spiritual, so that false cults find it necessary to quote its words in order to make an impression on the public.

To be specific, note:

A. Its accuracy. One finds a total absence of the absurdities found in other so-called sacred books. We do not read, for example, of the earth hatched out of an egg with a given number of years for incubation, resting on a tortoise, the land surrounded by seven seas of salt water, juice of sugar cane, spirituous liquors, clarified butter, sour milk, etc.

NOTES

Writes Dr. D. S. Clarke, *"There is a difference between the Bible and any other book that no man can fathom. The difference is caused by its origin."*

B. Its unity. Consisting of 66 Books, written by about 40 different authors, over a period of about 1600 years, and covering a variety of topics, it nevertheless carries a unity of theme and purpose that can be explained only by one Superintending Mind.

C. How many books can stand even two readings?

But the Bible can be read hundreds of times without its depths being exhausted, or it losing its interest for the reader. In fact, it is impossible.

D. Its remarkable circulation, being translated into hundreds of languages, and read in most countries of the world.

E. Its timelessness. It is one of the most ancient of books, and yet the most modern.

The human soul can never outgrow it. Bread is one of the most ancient of foods, and yet the most modern. As long as men are hungry they will want bread for the body; and as men yearn for God and things eternal they will want the Bible.

F. Its remarkable preservation in the face of persecution and the opposition of science, falsely called.

*"The hammers of opposition break, the Anvil of the Word of God remains."*

G. Its many fulfilled Prophesies, as stated, which guarantees the fulfillment of those not yet brought to completion.

3. THEY ARE FELT TO BE INSPIRED

*"But you don't believe that Book, do you?"* Said a Professor of a New York College to a Christian lady who had been attending Bible classes. *"Oh, yes,"* she answered, *"I happen to have a personal acquaintance with the Author."*

She had stated a most weighty reason for believing the Bible to be the Word of God, namely its appeal to our personal consciousness, speaking a tone which makes us feel that it comes from God.

The Roman Church asserts that the Divine origin of the Scriptures depends, in the final analysis, on the testimony of the Church, which is considered an infallible guide in all matters of all faith and practice.

*"As if the eternal and inviolable Truth of God depended on the judgement of God!"* Such stupidity makes the Bible answer to the whims of the Church, instead of the opposite. That's the reason for Catholic error, which is error in totality.

John Calvin wrote, and even though he was in error regarding some things, his statement respecting the Word of God bears repeating. He declared:

*"It is asserted that the Church decides what reverence is due to Scripture, and what books are to be included in the Sacred Canon . . . The question, 'How shall we know that they came from God, unless we are assured thereof by the decision of the Church?' is as foolish as the question, 'How shall we discern light from darkness, white from black, bitter from sweet?'*

*"The Witness of the Spirit is superior to all arguments. God in His Word is the only adequate Witness concerning Himself: and in like manner His Word will not find true credence in the hearts of men until it is sealed by the Witness of the Spirit. The same Spirit that spoke by the Prophets must enter our heart to convince us that they faithfully delivered the Message which He gave to them* (Isa. 59:21).

*"Let this then be a settled point, that those who are inwardly taught by the Holy Spirit place firm reliance on Scripture; and that Scripture is its own evidence, and may not lawfully be subjected to proofs and arguments, but obtains by the Testimony of the Spirit that confidence which it deserves."*

Since this is the case why adduce external evidence of the accuracy of the Scriptures and of their general reliability?

We do this first, *not in order* to believe that they are true, but *because* we believe that they *are* true; in the second place, it is natural and inspiring to be able to point to outward evidence of what we inwardly believe; finally, these proofs supply vehicles and containers, so to speak, wherewith we may convey our heart conviction in words, and so *"be ready always to give an answer to every man that asketh you a reason of the hope that is in you"* (I Pet. 3:15).

4. THEY PROVE TO BE INSPIRED

NOTES

Dr. Eugene Stock said:

*"When I was a boy, I read a story which showed me the different ways in which we can be sure that this Great Library of Sacred Books, which we call the Bible, is really the Word of God, His Revelation to mankind."*

*"The writer of the story had been explaining three different kinds of evidence — the Historical, the Internal, and the Experimental. Then he told how he once sent a boy to the Chemist to get some phosphorous. The boy brought back a little packet; was it phosphorous?*

*"The boy reported that he went to the shop and asked for phosphorous; that the Chemist went to his shelves, took some kind of stuff from a jar, put it in the little packet, and gave it to him, then he had brought it straight back.*

*"That was the Historical evidence that the packet had phosphorous in it. Then the gentleman opened the packet. The substance inside looked like phosphorous and smelled like phosphorous. That was the internal evidence."*

Then he put a light on it — *"See how it burns!"* That was the *experimental* evidence.

Intellectual defenses of the Bible have their place; but after all, the best argument is the practical one. The Bible has worked. It has influenced Civilization, transformed lives, brought light, inspiration and comfort to millions. And its Work continues.

In other words, the Bible speaks for itself and furnishes its own proof. It is the foundation on which every single life that's ever been changed, has in fact, been the cause of that change. It is the illumination of the world. It is the only Book on the face of the earth which tells man where he has been, where he is and where he is going.

Every other effort, irrespective as to its authors, pales into insignificance by comparison to the Bible, the Word of God.

(7) "AND EVEN THINGS WITHOUT LIFE GIVING SOUND, WHETHER PIPE OR HARP, EXCEPT THEY GIVE A DISTINCTION IN THE SOUNDS, HOW SHALL IT BE KNOWN WHAT IS PIPED OR HARPED?"

The beginning of the question, *"And even things without life giving sound, whether pipe or harp, except they give a distinction in the sounds, . . . ?"*, refers to musical instruments.

*"Distinction in the sounds,"* refers to a melody that is played.

Unless such is done, the musical instrument, be it *"pipe or harp,"* is only making noise.

The conclusion of the question, *"How shall it be known what is piped or harped?"*, in fact, cannot be known, unless a particular melody is played.

It doesn't matter how carefully crafted is the *"pipe or harp,"* it must be skillfully played, if the quality of the instrument is to be realized.

God is perfect and His Gifts are perfect, as well. However, far too often, the bearer of these Gifts, namely Believers, are not very skilled in their application. However, the fault is never in the Gifts, but in the individual.

Consequently, the Believer should seek the Lord earnestly, be consecrated to Him, and strongly desire that he function properly respecting these great Gifts, especially considering how beneficial they can be if properly utilized.

(8) "FOR IF THE TRUMPET GIVE AN UNCERTAIN SOUND, WHO SHALL PREPARE HIMSELF TO THE BATTLE?"

Paul was no doubt referring to the blowing of the Trumpets as given in the Law of Moses, concerning *"the calling of the Assembly,"* preparation for war, and regarding the Sacrifices, etc. (Num. 10:1-10). These Trumpets worked to blow in a certain way and at certain times. However, and even as the Apostle said, if they blew with an *"uncertain sound,"* their true purpose would be denied. In fact, it would be very critical, if an enemy was approaching and the Trumpet did not blow properly. There would be no preparation for battle, which could be disastrous indeed!

I greatly suspect that the Gifts far too often, fall into the category of an *"uncertain sound."* Just as there was nothing wrong with the Trumpet, but rather in the person blowing the instrument, likewise, there are no problems with the Gifts, only with the people who have the Gifts.

Placing the Gifts aside for a moment, the Truth is, far too much that is preached behind the pulpit, carries forth an *"uncertain sound."* The great matters which really count, *"a heaven to gain and a hell to shun,"* are little addressed, with other things placed in the forefront, things I might quickly add, which have little validity for anything.

(9) "SO LIKEWISE YE, EXCEPT YE UTTER BY THE TONGUE WORDS EASY TO BE UNDERSTOOD, HOW SHALL IT BE KNOWN WHAT IS SPOKEN? FOR YE SHALL SPEAK INTO THE AIR."

NOTES

The question, *"So likewise ye, except ye utter by the tongue words easy to be understood, how shall it be known what is spoken?"* Once again refers to some of the Believers in the Church who were blurting out in Tongues quite often, creating confusion. No one knew what they were saying, so even though they may have been blessed, no one else was blessed.

As should by now be obvious, Paul is not repudiating the speaking with other Tongues, but only its being done at the wrong time and the wrong place.

The phrase, *"For ye shall speak into the air,"* refers to the effort being unintelligible, therefore, of little significance, at least at that time, and concerning the entirety of the Church.

(10) "THERE ARE, IT MAY BE, SO MANY KINDS OF VOICES IN THE WORLD, AND NONE OF THEM IS WITHOUT SIGNIFICATION."

The phrase, *"There are, it may be, so many kinds of voices in the world,"* speaks of the many and varied languages which make up the entirety of mankind.

The phrase, *"And none of them is without signification,"* means that the language is important to the people who speak and understand that particular dialect, even though it may not be significant to others. So, Paul is not speaking disparagingly of other languages. That's not his idea, but that the language is important only if it is understood.

(11) "THEREFORE IF I KNOW NOT THE MEANING OF THE VOICE, I SHALL BE UNTO HIM THAT SPEAKETH A BARBARIAN, AND HE THAT SPEAKETH SHALL BE A BARBARIAN UNTO ME."

The phrase, *"Therefore if I know not the meaning of the voice, I shall be unto him that speaketh a barbarian,"* refers only to one who speaks a different or foreign language. Actually, the Greeks applied the word to all who did not use their tongue.

The Greeks were the most polished people of antiquity. They were the refined, the wise, as apposed to Barbarians. The word did not of necessity denote any rusticity of manners, or any want of refinement. Although, it is almost impossible for the Greeks to not have felt a

NOTES

superiority; however, this is *not* the manner in which Paul uses the word here.

The phrase, *"And he that speaketh shall be a barbarian unto me,"* simply refers to the fact, that the person could not be understood due to the foreign language.

(12) "EVEN SO YE, FORASMUCH AS YE ARE ZEALOUS OF SPIRITUAL GIFTS, SEEK THAT YE MAY EXCEL TO THE EDIFYING OF THE CHURCH."

The phrase, *"Even so ye, forasmuch as ye are zealous of Spiritual Gifts,"* tell us several things:

1. Paul is not criticizing their desire for such, inasmuch as he has already told them to *"desire Spiritual Gifts"* (I Cor. 14:1).

2. He is advocating to them that this of which he gives regarding *"Gifts,"* is from the Lord, and is to be heeded.

3. He is warning them about being lifted up in spiritual pride respecting the Gifts, which centered up in attention being drawn to the individual instead of the Lord.

The phrase, *"Seek that ye may excel to the edifying of the Church,"* presents the real foundation of all that is being said.

The edification of the entirety of the Body is that which is in view, and not the edification of particular individuals. This, the edification of the entirety of the Body, is one of the most valuable endowments of the Spirit, and should be earnestly desired.

This is the intention of the Holy Spirit, and it should be our intention as well. If it is not, we are not following the Lord. Consequently, what we do will *"become as sounding brass, or a tinkling cymbal."*

(13) "WHEREFORE LET HIM THAT SPEAKETH IN AN UNKNOWN TONGUE PRAY THAT HE MAY INTERPRET."

The phrase, *"Wherefore let him that speaketh in an unknown Tongue,"* refers to the idea that the Believer feels that God has given him the *"Gift of Tongues,"* i.e., *"one of the nine Gifts of the Spirit"* (I Cor. 12:8-10). This is the group to whom Paul is now speaking.

The phrase, *"Pray that he may Interpret,"* refers to the ninth Gift of the Spirit (I Cor. 12:8-10). The reason the Holy Spirit did this, is for the simple reason that the Gift of Tongues could then be utilized to its proper conclusion.

While it is true that many people have the Gift of Tongues and not the Gift of Interpretation of Tongues, and are used by the Lord in this capacity, however, if there is no one in the Service who has the Gift of Interpretation of Tongues, then the Gift of Tongues cannot be utilized to its proper conclusion. Consequently, the Holy Spirit through the Apostle tells all who have the *"Gift of Tongues,"* that they should seek the Lord, that the Gift of Interpretation would be given them as well. Then they are not depending upon someone else, which at times brings confusion otherwise.

### AN EXAMPLE

Years ago, I remember hearing a Preacher friend of mine, who is now with the Lord, and who was mightily used of God, give this illustration.

In the early days of his Ministry, he was pastoring a small church in New England. Two or three in the Church, if I remember correctly, he said had the *"Gift of Tongues."* As well, there was one lady who had the Gift of *"Interpretation of Tongues."* However, when she wasn't there, the Utterances being given, fell on deaf ears, simply because they were not interpreted.

He mentioned this once to an Evangelist, with the Evangelist telling him, *"Ask the Lord to give you the Gift of Interpretation, which will solve this problem."*

To make the story brief, that's exactly what my friend did, with the Lord answering his prayer. Then he wasn't dependent on a particular Lady being present, but, the times she was present, the Lord continued to use her along with my friend in this capacity of Interpretation.

So we learn from this, that one can have the *"Gift of Tongues"* without having the *"Gift of Interpretation of Tongues,"* or one could have the *"Gift of Interpretation of Tongues,"* and not have the *"Gift of Tongues."* However, the ideal is, even as the Apostle proclaims, that one person have both. Consequently, we are encouraged to pray for such.

(14) "FOR IF I PRAY IN AN UNKNOWN TONGUE, MY SPIRIT PRAYETH, BUT MY UNDERSTANDING IS UNFRUITFUL."

The phrase, *"For if I pray in an unknown Tongue, my spirit prayeth,"* refers to the manner in which the Holy Spirit unctions the Believer regarding speaking or praying in Tongues. It comes from a person's spirit, which is different than his mind, even as we shall see. In fact, the mind of man is the gateway to the spirit of man. They are *not* one and the same.

Paul is not here continuing to give dissertation on when the Gift should be used, etc., but is rather now explaining what happens when a person speaks in Tongues, wherever or whenever it is.

The phrase, *"But my understanding is unfruitful,"* concerns the mind of man. Even though the person is edified exactly as Paul has said (I Cor. 14:4), still, he has not understood anything that has been said. Once again, and I emphasize, this does not mean that it is not profitable, but is meant to portray the following:

The person who is doing the speaking, is edified and blessed, even though he does not understand what he says, for the simple reason that it is coming out of his spirit. However, if that same person takes up time in Church just by speaking in Tongues out loud for a period of time with no Interpretation, in fact, is not even meant to be interpreted, while he is blessed, the others in the Church will not be blessed. The reason is twofold:

A. They don't understand what's being said.

B. They're not the ones doing the speaking, so their spirit is not edified as that of the speaker! Consequently, they receive no benefit whatsoever.

(15) "WHAT IS IT THEN? I WILL PRAY WITH THE SPIRIT, AND I WILL PRAY WITH THE UNDERSTANDING ALSO: I WILL SING WITH THE SPIRIT, AND I WILL SING WITH THE UNDERSTANDING ALSO."

The question, *"What is it then?"*, is meant to put the proper face on that which Paul has been saying.

Up to this point, if one did not know better, one might think that Paul was opposed to speaking in tongues in any fashion. He is not!

What he is saying is this:

The phrase, *"I will pray with the spirit,"* means that he will pray in other Tongues, but in his own private devotions, where it will not waste the time of others. So, by this, he is telling us that he is not ridiculing or criticizing praying in Tongues, but that it be done at the right time in the right place.

The phrase, *"And I will pray with the understanding also,"* means that all of his praying will not be in Tongues, but some, if not most, will be in his language, which to him was Greek, whereas to us it is English. In other words, he would utilize both methods of prayer.

NOTES

The phrase, *"I will sing with the spirit,"* simply means that at times he would sing in Tongues, even as I have done many times, and some of you reading these words.

The phrase, *"And I will sing with the understanding also,"* does not necessarily refer to the Interpretation of someone singing in Tongues, with the Interpretation given by singing as well, although it certainly *can* refer to that.

The basic thought is that he would sing certain songs in Tongues at times, and again we speak of this being done in the proper manner. Also, he would sing the same songs at times in his own language.

Many times in Services, as the people would begin to sing, the Lord has flowed through me to sing the same song in Tongues, while the rest of the congregation was singing in English. This created no disturbance, and did not in any manner interfere with the worship of the people.

As well, when people are praising God in the Service, it is quite proper for anyone who desires to do so, to praise the Lord in Tongues. In fact, that is done often. However, that is far different than someone speaking in Tongues in a public service for a prolonged period of time, actually holding the balance of the congregation captive to what is presently being done, but not at all blessed.

It should be obvious as to what the Apostle is saying.

(16) "ELSE WHEN THOU SHALT BLESS WITH THE SPIRIT, HOW SHALL HE THAT OCCUPIETH THE ROOM OF THE UNLEARNED SAY AMEN AT THY GIVING OF THANKS, SEEING HE UNDERSTANDETH NOT WHAT THOU SAYEST?"

The beginning of the question, *"Else when thou shalt bless with the spirit, how shall he that occupieth the room of the unlearned say Amen at thy giving of thanks?"*, has the simple meaning of someone saying Grace at a meal. The word *"un-learned"* does not necessarily refer to someone who is unsaved, but simply to anyone who does not know the language that's being spoken, which is obvious.

The conclusion of the question, *"Seeing he understandeth not what thou sayest?"*, means simply that the individual has no idea as to what has been said over the food, consequently not knowing to what he is saying Amen.

Once again, Paul by using this little illustration, is not laying down a particular Doctrine, he is only using such as an example to prove his point.

(17) "FOR THOU VERILY GIVEST THANKS WELL, BUT THE OTHER IS NOT EDIFIED."

The phrase, *"For thou verily givest thanks well,"* means that it is accepted by the Lord as an offering of thanksgiving.

The phrase, *"But the other is not edified,"* means that while the speaker is edified, the others at the table aren't, for the reason that they did not understand what was being said.

The Apostle keeps coming back to the edification of others, and that all must be thought of in respect to everything that is done. It is the intention of the Spirit of God to edify the entirety of the Church and never to build up or laud a particular individual. In fact, if it is done properly, and I speak of that which the Lord does through individuals, everyone will be blessed, including the one being used, but in the proper manner.

(18) "I THANK MY GOD, I SPEAK WITH TONGUES MORE THAN YE ALL:"

So that others will not think that Paul is denigrating Tongues, he here plainly says as to how much he speaks or prays in Tongues, but as should be obvious, at the right time. So, he is not criticizing Tongues, not in the slightest, but rather, is regulating their use, even as the Holy Spirit guides him.

Actually, we do not see an explicit statement that Paul spoke in other Tongues when he was Baptized with the Holy Spirit following his conversion to Christ (Acts 9:17). Nevertheless, his own testimony here should be ample evidence that speaking in other Tongues was a common experience for him.

As well, this has nothing to do with linguistic ability, as some have claimed. While it is true that Paul knew at least two languages (Greek and Hebrew, that is not at all what the Text is saying. The lengths to which some will go, attempting to explain away the Word of God, are amazing to behold. Why not take the Scriptures exactly as they are given, comparing one with the other. The meaning then easily becomes clearer.

NOTES

Paul spoke very much in Tongues, especially in his own private worship and devotions, for the simple reason that he knew the value of such, how much strength it afforded, and how it built him up in the Spirit. Consequently, when he said, *"He that speaketh in an unknown tongue edifieth himself,"* he knew exactly that of which he spoke.

The Apostle needed that which speaking in Tongues brought and afforded, and to be sure, if the Apostle needed such, how much more do we need the same.

(19) "YET IN THE CHURCH I HAD RATHER SPEAK FIVE WORDS WITH MY UNDERSTANDING, THAT BY MY VOICE I MIGHT TEACH OTHERS ALSO, THAN TEN THOUSAND WORDS IN AN UNKNOWN TONGUE."

The phrase, *"Yet in the Church I had rather speak five words with my understanding,"* is speaking of public assemblies, where Believers gather together to worship the Lord.

The phrase, *"That by my voice I might teach others also,"* concerns the time in the public Assembly, when Truth is to be given to the public.

The phrase, *"Than ten thousand words in an unknown tongue,"* is not denigrating Tongues as some have claimed, but that it would do the people no good whatsoever for him, or any other Preacher, to stand behind a Pulpit, doing nothing but speaking in Tongues. During this time when the Message is to be preached, five words in a language that could be understood at that particular time, would do more good than ten thousand words in an language that cannot be understood.

It doesn't take a genius to figure that out, and actually presents the heart of what Paul is saying.

## WHEN TONGUES ARE IMPROPER

1. When there is a lack of love (I Cor. 13:1-3).
2. When in Church, and no interpreter is present (I Cor. 14:5, 27-28).
3. When it is time to give Truth to the public (I Cor. 14:6-13, 19, 23-25).
4. When saying Grace (I Cor. 14:16-17).
5. When people are present who would stumble over such action (I Cor. 14:23-25).
6. After two or three have given utterances

in tongues and they have been interpreted (I Cor. 14:27).

(20) "BRETHREN, BE NOT CHILDREN IN UNDERSTANDING: HOWBEIT IN MALICE BE YE CHILDREN, BUT IN UNDERSTANDING BE MEN."

The phrase, *"Brethren, be not children in understanding,"* means that they have the proper intelligence to understand what he is saying, consequently, there is no reason for it to be confused.

Paul is not saying here that only the spiritually immature, i.e., *"children,"* speak with other Tongues as some have claimed, as he is not meaning as some have claimed as well, that all who speak in Tongues are *"barbarians"* (I Cor. 14:11).

The phrase, *"Howbeit in malice be ye children,"* does not present a contradiction of what he has just said. Regarding *"understanding,"* he wants them to conduct themselves as adults; however, when it comes to *"malice"* (a desire to wish pain or distress to another), they are to have the spirit of children, which do not normally desire such.

The phrase, *"But in understanding be men,"* refers to conducting themselves with maturity.

### THREE STAGES OF HUMAN GROWTH

In this one Scripture Paul outlines the spiritual growth of Believers, by comparing particular stages of physical and mental growth. They are as follows:

1. The Greek word for *"children"* is *"paidon,"* and refers to *"a small child."* It refers to one just beginning to come into understanding.

Paul is saying that Believers, at least those who have been living for the Lord for any period of time, should not be that immature. Consequently, he refers to these Corinthians in that manner, which must have been a little stinging to them, considering that they concluded themselves to be above average respecting knowledge and wisdom.

2. *"Nepiazo"* is the next Greek word used for *"children,"* and means *"an infant or a baby."* A baby doesn't have *"malice"* toward anyone; consequently, Paul is saying that all Believers should, in this respect, be as an infant, who not only doesn't wish harm on anyone, but also is incapable of doing so.

3. The third Greek word is *"teleioi,"* and means *"men."* It refers to those of mature age, those who have some growth and understanding. So, the Apostle is saying that there is no excuse that Believers should not be mature in the Lord, that is if they've been living for the Lord anytime at all.

Consequently, this Verse could be translated, *"Do not be like little school children in understanding* (paidon)*; however, as it regards malice, be like infants* (nepiazo) *who cannot speak and who know nothing of sin, but as it regards understanding be men* (teleioi) *of maturity and growth."*

(21) "IN THE LAW IT IS WRITTEN, WITH MEN OF OTHER TONGUES AND OTHER LIPS WILL I SPEAK UNTO THIS PEOPLE; AND YET FOR ALL THAT WILL THEY NOT HEAR ME, SAITH THE LORD."

The phrase, *"In the Law it is written,"* refers to Isaiah 28:11-12.

The *"Law"* here refers to the *"Law of Moses,"* and refers, as used by the Jews, to the entirety of the Old Testament (Lk. 24:44; Jn. 10:34; 15:25).

The phrase, *"With men of other tongues and other lips will I speak unto this people,"* concerns a prophecy given by Isaiah nearly 800 years before Christ, and says that God intended to speak to men with stammering lips and other languages, i.e., *"Tongues."*

The phrase, *"And yet for all that will they not hear Me, saith the Lord,"* predicts that most in the world would not heed the Message given, nor as well, most in the Church. In fact, the Church world is probably split more over this issue than anything else.

However, *"Tongues"* alone would be an understatement. To be Pentecostal is an entirely different direction than most of the Church world, and is actually that which is given in the Word of God.

### WHAT DOES IT MEAN TO BE PENTECOSTAL?

First of all, it has nothing to do with a particular Church or religious Denomination. To be frank, to say that it is merely a Doctrine would be shortchanging that which is actually a Biblical Way of Life.

NOTES

What it means to be Pentecostal, which is Scriptural, was first given by the Prophet Joel, and then quoted by Peter on the Day of Pentecost. It involves an entire way of thinking, living, and the manner in which one looks at the Scriptures. As stated, I personally believe that the Scripture teaches that this is the only way of Christian life.

The Early Church characterized in the Book of Acts, was thoroughly Pentecostal. And if the Book of Acts, and the Epistles for that matter are examples, and they definitely are, then what I'm about to say will be very understandable. Otherwise, if what one believes does not coincide with the Book of Acts and the Epistles, then the following statements will be objectionable. To be Pentecostal refers to the following:

1. The Pentecostal Way is the way of fasting and prayer (Joel 2:15).
2. It is the Way of gladness and rejoicing (Joel 2:21).
3. It is the Way of the outpouring of the Holy Spirit all over the world, *"all flesh"* (Joel 2:28-29).
4. It is the Way of Signs and Wonders (Joel 2:30).
5. It is the Way of the soon Coming of the Lord (Joel 2:32).

(22) "WHEREFORE TONGUES ARE FOR A SIGN, NOT TO THEM THAT BELIEVE, BUT TO THEM THAT BELIEVE NOT: BUT PROPHESYING SERVETH NOT FOR THEM THAT BELIEVE NOT, BUT FOR THEM WHICH BELIEVE."

The phrase, *"Wherefore Tongues are for a Sign, not to them that believe, but to them that believe not,"* speaks to the thought that such is a reminder (literally a Sign) to unbelievers that they also will face the Judgement of God unless they repent of their sins. Believers, however, have already accepted the Sacrifice of Christ on their behalf, so their sins have already been forgiven; consequently, there is no need for such a *"sign"* on their part. The words, *"believe not,"* do not have so much to do with *"Tongues"* or whether it is of God, etc., as it does the Sacrifice of Christ at Calvary.

The idea of Verses 21 and 22 as it concerns Judgment and Tongues as a Sign, pertained to Isaiah's Prophecy of Judgment on backsliding Judah, and with it carrying over to the Dispensation of Grace, and including the whole world. Speaking in Tongues is a Sign to all unbelievers that they will face the Judgment of God unless they repent, just as this Prophecy of old was a Sign to Judah (Isa. 28:11-12).

The thought is, that the unbeliever know and understand that such a *"Sign"* of *"Tongues"* is from the Lord, and, therefore, Supernatural. As such, it is intended by the Holy Spirit to remind the unbeliever of their need for Christ. Unfortunately, much of the Church world has so repudiated this *"Sign,"* and the intentions of the Holy Spirit, that this of what the Lord has done, has been seriously weakened and hindered. Unfortunately, that holds true for almost all that Christ has done.

The phrase, *"But Prophesying serveth not for them that believe not, but for them which believe,"* is according to this manner for the obvious reasons.

Even though *"Prophesying"* is supernatural, the same as *"Tongues,"* still, it does not share the same meaning for the unbeliever. It must be remembered, that Tongues are for a *"Sign"* to the unbeliever, and not that instruction or that the Gospel may be imparted to them. The idea is, as stated, that the unbeliever will hear *"Tongues"* recognize it as God, and that it spells Judgment unless they repent.

So, this is at least one of the reasons that the Holy Spirit gives the Gift of Tongues along with Interpretation, as well as the Gift of Prophecy. Many may wonder as to why the Lord would give Tongues and Interpretation, when both combined seem to be a repetition of Prophecy. As stated, this is at least one of the reasons.

(23) "IF THEREFORE THE WHOLE CHURCH BE COME TOGETHER INTO ONE PLACE, AND ALL SPEAK WITH TONGUES, AND THERE COME IN THOSE THAT ARE UNLEARNED, OR UNBELIEVERS, WILL THEY NOT SAY THAT YE ARE MAD?"

The beginning of the question, *"If therefore the whole Church become together into one place, and all speak with Tongues, . . . ?"*, presents a situation which probably characterized, at least at times, what was going on in the Corinthian Assembly. The speaking in *"Tongues"* was not wrong, at least respective to the act itself, but the time and manner were definitely wrong. Paul now tells at least one of the reasons why.

The conclusion of the question, *"And there come in those that are unlearned, or unbelievers, will they not say that ye are mad?"*, tells us several things. They are as follows:

1. Speaking with *"Tongues"* can be done at any time one desires, as by now should be obvious.

2. Inasmuch as that is correct, then the Believer is responsible for its conduct respecting time and place. In other words, one cannot blame it on the Lord, as many attempt to do, claiming that the Lord made them do such, etc.

3. Believers have a great obligation to unbelievers, in order that foolish things not be done in the public services which could cause them to have a wrong opinion, i.e., *"Will they not say that ye are mad?"*

4. Even though *"Tongues"* are for a sign to unbelievers, even as Paul says in the previous Verse, still, all must be done at the right time and in the right place. If the Holy Spirit is followed, it will be done right with the Gift of Tongues used at the proper time, which can have the effect of putting the unbelievers under conviction, which will add to the Message which will be preached to them or has been preached. In other words, God has a correct order which should be obvious.

If such is not done, but rather the opposite, not only will the sinner not be convicted, but he may leave the service thinking that the Saints are crazy. So, we have a choice, God's Way which always brings the right results, or else man's way, or rather the way of self-will, which always is a detriment.

Untold numbers of Services have been hindered by individuals attempting to have their own way, instead of God's Way. How many times have earnest, seeking people left a service, incidentally, who did not know the Lord, and instead of being blessed, were rather confused by the entire proceedings, simply because, as we have stated, the Spirit of God was not followed, but rather stupidity and self-will!

Everything that God does is beautiful, wonderful, systematic, contains order, blesses, instructs, helps, and gives direction; however, pride, self-will, and the *"flesh"* far too often among God's people, seriously hinder that which the Lord desires to do. We all have possibly been guilty in one way or the other.

NOTES

We must not quench or grieve the Holy Spirit by refusing to allow Him to move, but at the same time, we must not get self involved in what the Holy Spirit wants to do, with it then being done improperly, and very much so! Consequently, very often we have a dichotomy presented in the Church: A. Those who don't want the moving of the Holy Spirit in any fashion; and, B. Those who claim to want the moving of the Holy Spirit, but will not allow the Holy Spirit to properly lead them because of self-will. Satan wins either way, which is exactly what Paul is here addressing.

(24) "BUT IF ALL PROPHESY, AND THERE COME IN ONE THAT BELIEVETH NOT, OR ONE UNLEARNED, HE IS CONVINCED OF ALL, HE IS JUDGED OF ALL:"

The phrase, *"But if all Prophesy, and there come in one that believeth not, or one unlearned,"* is not being said by Paul that all may come to the Service with a Prophecy, etc. That is not the idea at all. The Apostle is dealing with Prophecy which can be understood, by comparison with Tongues, which cannot be understood unless Interpreted.

Neither would it be proper, for every Church Member to give out different Prophesies in a particular Church Service. Even though what was said would be understandable, still it would be wrong because of the lack of order, which means the Holy Spirit would not be the Author of such, at least in that fashion.

The phrase, *"He is convinced of all, he is judged of all,"* presents that which is very simple in its application.

When the Lord does move upon Believers in the realm of *"Prophecy,"* what is being said is easily understood, because it's in the language of the people; consequently, the Holy Spirit can use it to convict the sinner of his perilous condition, or whatever the need may be. If one cannot understand what is being said, which is the case with speaking in Tongues and we're referring to Tongues without Interpretation, the *"unlearned, or unbelievers,"* cannot be helped at all, and neither can the Believers who are present, at least in such a situation.

(25) "AND THUS ARE THE SECRETS OF HIS HEART MADE MANIFEST; AND SO FALLING DOWN ON HIS FACE HE WILL WORSHIP GOD, AND REPORT THAT GOD IS IN YOU OF A TRUTH."

The phrase, *"And thus are the secrets of his heart made manifest,"* tells us plainly that the priority projected here by the Holy Spirit, is always the *"unlearned, or unbelievers,"* and how they can be reached with the Gospel, rather than the particular Blessing among the Believers. I'm afraid at times that we in the Church get it backwards.

The phrase, *"And so falling down on his face he will worship God, and report that God is in you of a Truth,"* proclaims the intended end result as generated by the Holy Spirit. In other words, this is what the Holy Spirit is striving for, and it should ever be primary in our hearts and minds as well.

Everything that God gives is done so in order to bring individuals to true repentance. This is that for which Jesus died (Jn. 3:16).

(*"Unlearned"* refers to those who are saved but not Spirit-filled, while *"Unbelievers"* refer to the unsaved.)

(26) "HOW IS IT THEN, BRETHREN? WHEN YE COME TOGETHER, EVERY ONE OF YOU HATH A PSALM, HATH A DOCTRINE, HATH A TONGUE, HATH A REVELATION, HATH AN INTERPRETATION. LET ALL THINGS BE DONE UNTO EDIFYING."

The question, *"How is it then, Brethren?"*, pertains to that which follows, and is not actually meant as a positive.

Some have concluded that Paul was saying these things in a positive tone, in other words boasting of the spirituality of the Corinthians, etc. However, the flavor of the entirety of these Passages, and especially the last sentence of this Verse, lends credence to the thought that he is being somewhat negative instead of positive.

What he is about to say is not meant to demean these particular Gifts, not at all! He is rather pleading for order, and for unselfish motivation.

The phrase, *"When ye come together,"* pertains to a Church Service as is obvious, where all come together to worship the Lord.

The phrase, *"Every one of you hath a Psalm, hath a Doctrine, hath a Tongue, hath a Revelation, hath an Interpretation,"* speaks of very good things, actually that which the Church needs so desperately, but yet being used in the wrong manner, and for the wrong purpose and reason.

NOTES

The emphasis is on the pronoun *"you,"* which lends credence to the idea that these particular people were coming to Church, not with the idea of the Spirit of God moving in order that sinners be brought to Christ, or other things of the Spirit be accomplished, but rather that they might be able to shine with their Tongue, Psalm, Revelation, etc. So, Paul's statement is not positive but rather negative, but in a narrowly defined channel.

On the other side of that coin, it is wonderful that the Holy Spirit was working in the hearts and lives of these people to that extent, and that the Lord was using them in this fashion. That is not to be demeaned, but rather encouraged, even as Paul will ultimately do. The idea in totality, is that all things be done to edify the entirety of the Body, and not just the person being used thusly, and that the Work of God be carried out, especially as it relates to the unsaved, etc.

The phrase, *"Let all things be done unto edifying,"* means exactly what it says. Everything done in the Church is to edify the entirety of the Body, and not to exhibit Gifts, which tend toward glorifying the person. What wonderful advice this is, as the Holy Spirit speaks through the Apostle. How timely and how wise it is.

(27) "IF ANY MAN SPEAK IN AN UNKNOWN TONGUE, LET IT BE BY TWO, OR AT THE MOST BY THREE, AND THAT BY COURSE; AND LET ONE INTERPRET."

The phrase, *"If any man speak in an unknown Tongue,"* proclaims the word *"unknown"* as inserted by the Translators, meaning it was not in the original Text.

Actually, there is no word here in the Greek for *"unknown."* This means that whatever language is spoken, it is known somewhere on the planet. The only way that a language is unknown is that the speaker does not know or understand the language which he speaks (I Cor. 14:2).

Paul is now addressing himself to the giving of Utterances in Tongues in a regular Service, and how it should be done. If in the previous Verses he was trying to stop the speaking with other Tongues as some claim, then what he says here would not make any sense.

No! At no time does he demean speaking in Tongues, or any of the other Gifts for that matter, only as he will later say, *"That all things be done decently and in order."* Actually, it is *"order,"* which characterizes the entirety of this Chapter, as given by the Holy Spirit through the Apostle.

PROPER EXPLANATION

As well, the Apostle is not speaking here of the number of Utterances which should be given in a single Service, but, rather of men (or women) who are giving the Utterances. We should not get the issue confused.

The phrase, *"Let it be by two, or at the most by three,"* once again is not speaking of Utterances but rather the individuals who are giving out the Utterances.

The reason I emphasize this, is because it is believed in most Pentecostal circles, that only two, or at the most three Utterances in Tongues can be given in a single Service. That is not exactly what is being said here.

As stated, it is speaking of the individuals who are giving the Utterances, and that at the most, there should be only three men or women used thusly in a single Service. It doesn't say anything about how many Utterances these two or three may give; therefore, it is not wise for us to place a limitation on the number. Still, it will be obvious to the Body, if the individual is not functioning in line with the Holy Spirit.

The word, *"And that by course,"* simply means that these two or three should not interrupt each other. If one feels that he has an Utterance that the Lord wants him to give at that particular time, and there is someone else being used accordingly, he should wait until it is certain that the first has concluded, i.e., *"by course."*

The phrase, *"And let one Interpret,"* tells us several things:

1. The speaking here done, is the Gift of Tongues, which is meant to be Interpreted.

2. This is not speaking of one worshipping in Tongues, as all Spirit-filled Believers do occasionally, and which should not be done during the order of the Service, at least out loud, and for all the obvious reasons. Paul has dealt with that in the 23rd Verse, and now he gives instruction as to how the Gift of Tongues ought to be used.

As we have said repeatedly, this confuses many non-Pentecostals, because they equate Tongues as used in prayer and worship, and the Gift of Tongues as one and the same. They aren't! Paul has just dealt with the worship aspect, and now he is addressing the Gift of Tongues (I Cor. 12:10).

3. The *"one"* Interpreting, does *not* mean that only one individual is to Interpret, irrespective as to whether the Utterances are given by two or three individuals, but rather that only *"one"* should Interpret at a time.

*"That by course,"* as it applies to the individuals giving their Utterances also applies to the ones Interpreting. As well, after each Utterance is given, the Interpretation should be given at that point in time.

(28) "BUT IF THERE BE NO INTERPRETER, LET HIM KEEP SILENCE IN THE CHURCH; AND LET HIM SPEAK TO HIMSELF, AND TO GOD."

The phrase, *"But if there be no Interpreter, let him keep silence in the Church,"* is given for the obvious reasons. What good does it do to give the Utterance if there is no one there to interpret the Utterance. The idea is this:

1. If the Assembly is small, and there is only one Interpreter in the Church, and that particular person is not present, the person or persons normally used to give the Utterance should not do so, for the simple reason that it would be pointless without the Interpretation.

Or if an Utterance is given, and no one Interprets the Utterance, nothing more should be given.

2. This is at least one of the reasons that Paul gave the counsel, *"let him that speaketh in an unknown Tongue pray that he may Interpret"* (I Cor. 14:13).

If one has both the Gift of Tongues, and the Gift of Interpretation of Tongues, the problem presented will in fact be solved.

The phrase, *"And let him speak to himself, and to God,"* means exactly what it says. If no Interpreter is present, or else the Lord doesn't give the Interpretation, the individual should not continue to give out an Utterance in Tongues.

3. The person can feel free to continue to speak in Tongues to himself and to the Lord, which means that it is not to be audible.

*"To himself,"* means under his breath, *"and to God,"* refers to the manner of Tongues in any case, whether praying to oneself, or giving an Utterance out loud. If its *"Tongues"* it is *"not unto men, but unto God"* (I Cor. 14:2).

(29) "LET THE PROPHETS SPEAK TWO OR THREE, AND LET THE OTHER JUDGE."

The phrase, *"Let the Prophets speak two or three,"* speaks not only of those who have the simple Gift of Prophecy, but also of those who stand in the Office of the Prophet, and or used in the realm of *"Word of Wisdom," "Word of Knowledge,"* and *"Discerning of Spirits."* In other words, Paul covers all things, setting it in order, giving the same instructions here as he did regarding the Utterances in Tongues, etc., i.e., *"two or three."*

As well, this completely shoots down the idea as some have misinterpreted Verse 24, that it is permissible for *"all to Prophesy,"* etc.

In fact, the Lord has nothing but that He has a systematic order for that which He does. It is up to us to find out what that order is, and then follow it closely.

The phrase, *"And let the other Judge,"* simply refers to the fact that everything should be judged according to its Scriptural validity. Unfortunately, there are things said and done in Church, which sound like the real thing; however, if it is not Scriptural it is to be dismissed out of hand.

The word *"other"* as Paul here uses it, does not speak of just one person, but of the entirety of the Body of Christ.

(30) "IF ANY THING BE REVEALED TO ANOTHER THAT SITTETH BY, LET THE FIRST HOLD HIS PEACE."

The phrase, *"If any thing be revealed to another that sitteth by,"* refers to someone who feels that the Lord is giving him a Revelation which should be given to the Church.

The phrase, *"Let the first hold his peace,"* refers to someone who has already given out a Prophecy, and that he should now allow the Lord to use someone else who feels they have a word as well. As they held their peace, while he spoke, now he (the first one) should hold his peace, as they speak that which God has given to them. Once again we are speaking of *"order."*

(31) "FOR YE MAY ALL PROPHESY ONE BY ONE, THAT ALL MAY LEARN, AND ALL MAY BE COMFORTED."

The phrase, *"For ye may all Prophesy one by one,"* must be understood in conjunction with the regulations given in Verses 29 and 30. Incidentally, both men and women were permitted to Prophesy (Acts 2:16-21; I Cor. 11:1-16).

NOTES

The phrase, *"That all may learn, and all may be comforted,"* goes back to the last sentence in Verse 26.

The idea is not that one person or just a few be blessed, but that *"all may learn, and all may be comforted."* The Holy Spirit ever has the entirety of the Body in mind, and that all members of the Body should work toward that goal, of blessing the entirety of its members and not just a select few.

(32) "AND THE SPIRITS OF THE PROPHETS ARE SUBJECT TO THE PROPHETS."

The phrase, *"And the spirits of the Prophets,"* does not refer to the Holy Spirit, but rather to our own human spirit.

The phrase, *"Are subject to the Prophets,"* means that even though these Gifts are conferred by the Holy Spirit, they are in fact conferred on free agents, with the Holy Spirit never interfering with that free agency.

For one to claim that the Holy Spirit is moving upon him is very easy; however, the Holy Spirit Himself is telling us through the Apostle that He (the Holy Spirit) never forces anyone to do anything; consequently, no one is to claim the moving of the Holy Spirit is the cause of acting disorderly or causing confusion. The Lord cannot be the Author of such.

Paul says these things on the heels of the instructions he has just given, for the simple reason that some would try to claim they had no choice but to do what they were doing, in other words, being forced by the Holy Spirit. So, the Holy Spirit tells us that He does not force anyone to do anything. As a man, though of the most splendid talents and commanding eloquence, has control over his own mind, and is not compelled to speak, so it was with those who are here called Prophets. The idea is, that one can speak or be silent at their own pleasure. Consequently, there is no excuse for disorder or confusion.

## THE SPIRIT OF GOD BY COMPARISON TO HEATHENISTIC WORSHIP

In this the Spirit of true inspiration differs essentially from the views of the heathen, who regarded themselves as driven by a wild, controlling influence, that compelled them to speak or do certain things, when they were unconscious of what they said or did.

Universally, in the heathen world, the priests and priestesses supposed or feigned that they were under an influence which was uncontrollable; which took away their powers of self-command, and which made them the mere organs or unconscious instruments of communicating the will of the gods.

The Scripture account of Inspiration is, however, a very different thing. In whatever way the mind was influenced, or whatever was the mode in which the Truth was conveyed, yet it was not such as to destroy the conscious powers of free agency, nor such as to destroy the individuality of the inspired person, or to annihilate what was peculiar in his mode of thinking, his style, or his customary manner of expression (Barnes).

(33) "FOR GOD IS NOT THE AUTHOR OF CONFUSION, BUT OF PEACE, AS IN ALL CHURCHES OF THE SAINTS."

The phrase, *"For God is not the Author of confusion,"* actually says, *"For God is not of confusion."* As we have already stated, He is a God of Order, Consistency, Decorum, and proper direction.

*"Confusion,"* in the Greek is *"akatastasia,"* and means *"instability, disorder, commotion, tumult."* It has to do not only with the manner of operation of the Gifts, but as well, for everything God does.

The phrase, *"But of Peace, as in all Churches of the Saints,"* refers to stability, certitude, a firm foundation, and that which is well ordered. In other words, when the Service has concluded, people are not left in a quandary wondering what has taken place, or what has been done. The Spiritual Trumpet has blown with a certain sound, meaning there were no disharmonizing notes.

*"Peace"* in the Greek is *"eirene,"* and means *"prosperity, rest, set at one again."*

And yet, God's *"Peace"* does not pertain to spiritual deadness, spiritual coldness, or necessarily to quietness. In fact, such is *not* the *"Peace of God."*

In fact, if the Holy Spirit has His Perfect Way, the Service at times, may be loud, boisterous, very active, with much loud praise, or it may be quiet, very little activity, at least in the physical sense, but yet both be of God. The Holy Spirit does not work the same at all times, but whatever way He does work, it will have a systemized order to that which is done, whether it be noisy or quiet. As well, it is the responsibility of the Preacher in charge of the Service, to lead the Service according to the direction the Holy Spirit is flowing. To do so, he must be very sensitive to what the Spirit wants done, ever seeking that course, which will not be denied providing there is a sincere desire for the Holy Spirit to have His way.

As well, this pertains to *"all Churches"* and not just to the Church at Corinth, and for all time one might quickly add.

(34) "LET YOUR WOMEN KEEP SILENCE IN THE CHURCHES: FOR IT IS NOT PERMITTED UNTO THEM TO SPEAK; BUT THEY ARE COMMANDED TO BE UNDER OBEDIENCE, AS ALSO SAITH THE LAW."

The phrase, *"Let your women keep silence in the Churches,"* refers to the manner of Services as conducted at that time. The women normally sat on one side, while the men sat on the other, in which some few churches still do.

With many things taking place which were unusual and different, even as Paul has been addressing, it was quite usual for the women to speak out in the Service, and ask their Husbands as to the meaning of certain things, etc. Paul is telling them, even as the next Verse proclaims, that they should not do this, interrupting the Service. Women were relatively uneducated in those days; therefore, it was not unusual for them to seek information wherever it could be found.

These two Verses make much more sense when the Bible student views them in the totality of the Chapter and in light of the immediate context. Unfortunately, they are taken out of context in many Church circles, and used by some male chauvinists to teach that God does not permit women to function in public Ministries. However, the context (related Verses) lends itself more to the subject of demeanor.

## PROPER INTERPRETATION

The Truth is, women were free to pray and prophesy (preach) in the Church (Joel 2:28-32; Acts 2:16-21; 21:9). Proper interpretation of Scripture is comparing Scripture with Scripture on the same subject. When that is done, the full meaning of what Paul is here saying, becomes more obvious.

NOTES

The phrase, *"For it is not permitted unto them to speak,"* refers to them calling out to their husbands across the Church, or wherever they were worshipping.

If the word *"speak"* is to be taken literally, then it would not be proper for a woman to pray in Church, prophesy in Church, preach in Church, teach in Church, or even sing in Church. Actually, it would not even be proper for the woman to say anything in any capacity, which we know is not the case.

In some Churches which teach that women are not supposed to Preach, etc., it is satisfactory for them to teach little children. However, if its wrong for one, it is wrong for the other. The Truth is, it's not wrong in either case.

The phrase, *"But they are commanded to be under obedience, as also saith the Law,"* refers back to Genesis 3:16 and the creation model.

The idea of Paul using the *"Law of Moses"* as an example, means that Genesis 3:16 was not in any way changed when the Law was given some 2,000 years later. Neither has it been changed yet, and will not be changed until the Resurrection.

The *"obedience"* of which Paul here speaks, refers to the command of the Lord concerning the man being the head of the woman (Gen. 3:16; I Cor. 11:3). This is the Creation model and is to be respected.

(35) "AND IF THEY WILL LEARN ANY THING, LET THEM ASK THEIR HUSBANDS AT HOME: FOR IT IS A SHAME FOR WOMEN TO SPEAK IN THE CHURCH."

The phrase, *"And if they will learn any thing, let them ask their husbands at home,"* tells us plainly as to what Paul was speaking about respecting women keeping silent in the Church. Once again, he is telling the women not to call out in the Church to their husbands sitting across the way asking about certain things, but wait until they get home and then ask. It has nothing to do with a woman preaching or praying in Church, etc.

The phrase, *"For it is a shame for women to speak in the Church,"* refers to that particular manner. If it is to be taken literally, then it would not be permissible for a woman to even open her mouth in Church in any capacity. However, Paul is not talking about silly things of that nature, and neither is he meaning that it is wrong for a woman to Preach, to sing, etc.

NOTES

Inasmuch as this is a very important subject, and a subject we might quickly add with diverse opinions, I think it would be wise to take a closer look.

## THE WOMAN'S ROLE IN THE CHURCH

This is not an issue that can be resolved by a study of words alone. We must look at the situations as it involves women and as given to us in the Word of God, in order to come to a Scriptural conclusion. As previously stated, the only sure way to interpret Scripture, is to compare Scripture with Scripture on the same subject. To build a Doctrine on one particular Scripture is not Scriptural within itself. The Word plainly tells us, *"In the mouth of two or three witnesses* (occasions or Scriptures) *shall every Word be established"* (II Cor. 13:1; Deut. 19:15; Mat. 18:16).

## THE SIGNIFICANCE OF WOMEN

Despite the reality of life in a male-dominated culture, women played a surprisingly significant role in the Early Church. The reason is undoubtedly that, in Christ, women as well as men are the recipients of Spiritual Gifts for Ministry.

Thus, the contribution of women to the total Ministry of the Body of Christ is basic to the health and growth of the whole congregation.

Specific lines of New Testament evidence show that an important place was given to women in the life of the Church. A few facts are worth noting.

## THE MANNER IN WHICH WOMEN ARE USED BY THE LORD

Women played a critical role in the establishment of several New Testament congregations (Acts 16:13-15, 40; 17:4, 12).

As well, women are identified by name and called *"fellow workers"* by Paul (especially Rom. Chpt. 16, where seven women are identified by name). The inclusion of women in a Ministry Team is a significant departure from Jewish practice. The naming of Priscilla before her husband Aquila is also extremely significant (Rom. 16:3).

Women are also seen participating through Prayer and Prophesy in Church meetings, even as we have recently studied (I Cor. 11:5). Although the Old Testament foretold a day when sons and daughters would prophesy as the Spirit was poured out on *"both men and women"* (Joel

2:28-32; Acts 2:17-18), the participation of women in Church Gatherings was totally different than Old Testament tradition, tradition I might quickly add which was most of the time man-devised and not from God.

### DEACONESS

Phoebe is identified in Romans 16:1 as a Deaconess, and other evidence suggests that women may have participated with men in the Diaconate (serving with them).

Despite the clarity of evidence in each of these areas, suggesting that women participated freely in the life of the Early Church and were recognized as significant contributors of Ministry, there are some areas that need further investigation.

### WOMEN IN CHURCH OFFICE

Most of the Offices mentioned in the New Testament were ordinarily filled by males. This seems especially true when one speaks of an Apostle. There is no record, of any woman being an Apostle, even though women do stand in the Office of the Prophet (Prophetess) (Ex. 15:20; Judg. 4:4; II Ki. 22:14; II Chron. 34:22; Neh. 6:14; Isa. 8:3; Lk. 2:36; Acts 21:9). The word *"Prophesy"* as used of the daughters of Philip in Acts 21:9, speaks of the Office of the Prophet and not the simple Gift of Prophecy. *"Prophesy"* as it is used here in the Greek, is *"propheteuo,"* and means *"to foretell events."* Actually, I think the New Testament bears out the fact of women serving in all the fivefold Ministry Offices, with the exception of *"Apostle."* As stated, there is no record of such in the New Testament. But at the same time, there is no Scripture that says that such could not be.

We have mentioned Phoebe, with Paul describing her as *"a servant of the Church which is at Cenchrea"* (Rom. 16:1).

*"Servant"* as it is here used in the Greek is *"diakonon,"* and means several things, one being the Pastor of a Church. So, there is a possibility that Phoebe was actually the Pastor of the Church at Cenchrea, and not merely a Deaconess.

It stands to reason, that if women stood in the Office of the Prophet, which they did, and these other Offices as well, that at the same time they would Preach, sing and testify the Gospel in any manner in which the Lord would desire to use them.

NOTES

As we have already stated, there were women Prophetesses in the Old Testament, of which the evidence is plentiful, and at least one woman serving as Judge in Israel, when that Office at that time was the highest in the land (Judg. Chpts. 4-5). Consequently, I hardly think that women would have a lesser role under the New Covenant which is a far better Covenant, but rather a greater role, which I believe is borne out.

### WOMEN IN THE WORSHIP SERVICE

The most controversial New Testament Passages regarding women have a common context; they deal with issues related to worship. However, to understand these Passages, we need to interpret them in the total context of a gathering in which women did take part, for Paul wrote about women Praying and Prophesying when the congregation gathered (I Cor. 11:5).

Within this framework of participation, the Passages and the most likely interpretations follow.

The most obvious Passage is that which we are now studying, I Corinthians 14:34-36. Women are to *"remain silent in the Churches"* to the extent that they *"are not allowed to speak."* Any questions should be held till they are at home and can *"ask their own husbands."* This very blunt instruction has been interpreted in several ways. Let's look at them:

1. Some claim this decisively rules out any female participation in the Worship Services, and especially of Preaching, etc. However, such a view violates what Paul said about women Praying and Prophesying in I Corinthians 11:5. Consequently, inasmuch as the Holy Spirit does not contradict Himself, we know this particular interpretation is wrong.

2. This statement concerning women was added by someone other than Paul, some claim. As well, that is as well foolish, because it says in essence, that the Holy Spirit was not powerful enough to safeguard the Text.

3. Some claim that this is but another example of Paul's inconsistence and reflects his culture-bound, antifeminine view. However, Paul did not have, as is overly obvious, an antifeminine view. As well, to claim that Paul is inconsistent, is to claim that the Holy Spirit is inconsistent, which is foolishness indeed!

Everything Paul wrote regarding the Scriptures, was inspired by the Holy Spirit, as well as all other Bible writers, which guarantees against error, contradiction, or inconsistency.

4. Some claim that Paul's statements in I Corinthians Chapter 11 are misunderstood, and women are not to speak in Church. My answer to that is, *"How can one misunderstand Paul's simple statement in I Corinthians 11:5, 'But every woman that Prayeth or Prophesieth . . .'?"*

5. The prohibition in I Corinthians 14:34-36 must be seen in the context of which it is given, as dealing with a specific problem in the Church, rather than reflecting a pattern in Church meetings as a whole.

This last option is most in keeping with the higher view of Scripture and with careful attention to the Text. In I Corinthians 14:26-40, Paul is dealing not only with disorderly meetings but also with the question of proper display of the Gifts. As is obvious, there was much confusion in the Church at Corinth, which precipitated some women evidently constantly asking their husbands the meaning of certain things. With men and women sitting on opposite sides of the Church, this would have created disorder, hence Paul saying, *"If they* (women) *will learn any thing let them ask their husbands at home"* (I Cor. 14:35).

PAUL'S ADMONITION IN I TIMOTHY

What did Paul mean by the statement, *"Let the woman learn in silence with all subjection. But I suffer not a woman to teach, nor to usurp authority over the man, but to be in silence"?* (I Tim. 2:11-12).

The Eleventh Verse of I Timothy Chapter 2, once again deals with the same question dealt with at Corinth. Women were not to call out to their husbands for Scriptural explanations during the service.

If one looks closely at Paul's statement respecting the right of the woman to teach, it plainly says, *"Nor to usurp authority over the man."*

The idea is, that the woman does not have power over the man. To do so, is to violate the Creation model. Women should not dictate to men, but they do have the right to exercise their privilege to Teach, Preach, Prophesy, Pray, and do other things under the authority of men.

NOTES

As should be obvious, the key is in not exercising authority over men. The Greek word for *"usurp"* is *"authenteo,"* and means *"to have power over it."* So, women are not to have power over men, at least as it regards the Work of God. But under the authority of men, they can do anything they feel the Lord has called them to do.

(36) "WHAT? CAME THE WORD OF GOD OUT FROM YOU? OR CAME IT UNTO YOU ONLY?"

The word *"What?",* although addressed as a question, is more so an exclamation. The idea seems to be, that Paul is ready to end this discussion respecting order in the Church, and he is going to do so in strong terms.

The question, *"Came the Word of God out from you?",* in effect asks the question as to whether these Corinthians actually thought that the Word of God originated with them? If they had not been conducting themselves in this attitude and spirit, the Apostle would not have asked such a question.

The question, *"Or came it unto you only?",* turns the scenario around, thereby projecting the idea that the Corinthians must seem to think that when God speaks, He speaks to them and to them alone.

Of course, all three questions are preposterous. They demand a negative answer, and a loud negative answer at that.

(37) "IF ANY MAN THINK HIMSELF TO BE A PROPHET, OR SPIRITUAL, LET HIM ACKNOWLEDGE THAT THE THINGS THAT I WRITE UNTO YOU ARE THE COMMANDMENTS OF THE LORD."

The phrase, *"If any man think himself to be a Prophet, or Spiritual,"* evidently is addressed to some in the Church who held their own position of Spirituality in higher regard, consequently giving direction to the Church that was the opposite of direction given by Paul.

The phrase, *"Let him acknowledge that the things that I write unto you are the Commandments of the Lord,"* in effect says that the judgement pronounced by the Corinthians on what Paul is writing, is really a judgement, not on Paul, and not on his writing, but on themselves. As well, if those who call themselves *"Prophets"* or *"Spiritual,"* fail to see the Divine Character of Paul's words, the proof is conclusive (evidential proof) that this person is no Prophet, that he really has no Spiritual Gift.

Paul proceeds exactly as Jesus did when He spoke with the Jews in John 8:47: *"He that is of God heareth the Words of God."* So, in effect, Paul is throwing down the gauntlet.

The idea is, that whoever these people are who claim to be *"Prophets,"* or *"Spiritual,"* must acknowledge that he (Paul) is an *"Apostle,"* which comes first in the Church (I Cor. 12:28).

He is not denying that those who oppose him are Prophets, nor that the Corinthians as a whole are Spiritual. He seems to be arguing that he is first of all an Apostle. As such, he has not only heard from the Lord, but he has the authority to say what is being said. As well, it must be heeded, that is, if the Corinthians, and all others for that matter, desire to follow the Lord. As is obvious, Paul claims Inspiration for this of which he says.

(38) "BUT IF ANY MAN BE IGNORANT, LET HIM BE IGNORANT."

*"Ignorant"* in the Greek is, *"agenoeo,"* and means *"not to know through lack of information or intelligence."* In this case, it would be through lack of intelligence, simply because the information is given by Paul.

In effect, Paul is pronouncing a Prophetic sentence of Judgement on those who fail to heed this letter.

He also is saying that if anyone affects to be ignorant of his authority, or whether he has the right to command, or if he affects to doubt whether he (Paul) is inspired, or whether he writes in accordance with the Will of God, he will do so at his own peril.

Paul is saying, *"I have stated my authority." "I have delivered the Commands of God." "And now, if anyone disregards them, and still doubts whether all this is said by Divine Authority, let him abide the consequences of rejecting the Law of God." "I have given full proof of my Divine Commission."*

In effect, this can be said for the entirety of the Word of God. If man refuses to accept what the Bible says, there is nothing more than can be said or done, the consequences are obvious.

(39) "WHEREFORE, BRETHREN, COVET TO PROPHESY, AND FORBID NOT TO SPEAK WITH TONGUES."

The phrase, *"Wherefore, Brethren, covet to Prophesy,"* closes out these instructions by once again extolling the veracity and weight of the Gift of Prophecy. He has given proper instructions regarding this excellent Gift, and in view of the things the Holy Spirit through him has said, its true worth should now be known and desired.

The phrase, *"And forbid not to speak with Tongues,"* proclaims the fact that all the instructions he has given are not meant to disallow Tongues, but rather to put them in their rightful order.

Tongues are permissible in the Assembly when accompanied by Interpretation, and may be experienced as much as one wishes in private.

So, where does that put the religious leaders who ignore this particular statement which is actually a *"Commandment of the Lord?"* In fact, in most Churches in America and around the world for that matter, *"Tongues"* are absolutely forbidden.

So, that means that these Churches are in effect under the Judgement of God. As well, it holds true for those who do believe in the Baptism with the Holy Spirit with the evidence of speaking with other Tongues, but ignore the regulations given for its use. I speak of the Gift being utilized, or any Gift for that matter, when not motivated by love.

(40) "LET ALL THINGS BE DONE DECENTLY AND IN ORDER."

The idea is, that all things be done in order, regularly, without confusion, discord or tumult. The word used here is, properly, a military term, and denotes the order and regularity with which an army is drawn up.

This is a general rule, which was to guide them. It was simple, and easily applied. There might be a thousand questions about the modes and forms of worship, and the customs in the Churches, and much difficulty might occur in many of these questions; but here was a simple and plain rule, which might be easily applied.

If they desire to follow Paul's admonitions, the Holy Spirit would in fact give them leading and guidance. Their good sense would tell them what becomes the Worship of God; and their desire to do the Will of God would restrain them from excesses and disorders.

This rule is still applicable, and is safe in guiding us in many things in regard to the worship of God. However, there are many things which cannot be subjected to rule, or exactly prescribed; there are many things which may and must be left to good judgement and good sense, which the Holy Spirit will always help and aid.

NOTES

*"O worship the King, all glorious above,*
*"O gratefully sing His power and*
*His love;*
*"Our Shield and Defender, the Ancient*
*of Days,*
*"Pavilioned in splendor, and girded with*
*praise."*

## CHAPTER 15

(1) "MOREOVER, BRETHREN, I DECLARE UNTO YOU THE GOSPEL WHICH I PREACHED UNTO YOU, WHICH ALSO YE HAVE RECEIVED, AND WHEREIN YE STAND;"

The phrase, *"Moreover, Brethren, I declare unto you the Gospel which I preached unto you,"* begins this Chapter, and proclaims the single most important portion of this Epistle, the Resurrection. It contains a connected, labored, and unanswerable argument for the Main Truth of Christianity, and, consequently, for Christianity itself.

### THE MOST IMPORTANT THING

Having an instinctive dread of death, the Resurrection is the most interesting to us as mortal beings than any other portion of this Epistle.

If the argument in this Chapter concerning this most important event is solid, then Christianity is true; and if true, then this Chapter unfolds to us the most elevated and glorious prospect which can be exhibited to dying, yet immortal man.

To be sure, it is true; however, it is evident, from Verse 12, that this important Doctrine of the Resurrection of the dead had been denied by some at Corinth, and it seems that this error had obtained a footing in the Church itself. On what grounds, or by what portion or party it was denied, is unknown. From II Timothy 2:18, we learn that it was held by some that the Resurrection was passed already, and, consequently, that there was nothing but a Spiritual Resurrection to come. To counteract these errors, and to put the Doctrine of the Resurrection of the dead on a firm foundation, and thus to furnish a demonstration of the Truth of Christianity, is the design of this Chapter.

NOTES

### MOREOVER

Paul, in essence, is saying, *"In addition to what I have said, or in that which I am now about to say, I make known the main and leading Truth of the Gospel."*

When he used the word *"declare,"* it does not mean that he was communicating to them a new Truth, but that he wished to remind them of a Truth he evidently had already given to them.

By using the word *"Gospel,"* Paul is declaring the Resurrection of all Believers to be a part of the glad announcement, or the good news about the Messiah, His Life, Sufferings, Death, and especially His Resurrection. In fact, as we shall see, Paul links the Resurrection of Christ to the Resurrection of Believers, and makes that his main subject. But he includes in the word *"Gospel,"* here, the Doctrine that Jesus died for sins, and was buried, as well as the Doctrine of His Resurrection (Barnes).

The phrase, *"Which also ye have received, and wherein ye stand,"* actually pertains to the New Covenant which was given to Paul. Neither Peter nor John, nor any of the other Apostles for that matter, were given this great Message called the *"Gospel."* Paul's writings proclaim the New Covenant, while the writings of the other Apostles complement that Covenant.

### THE RESURRECTION

Having rebuked the selfishness of the conduct of the Corinthians in several things, the Apostle now reproves their error in Doctrine as to the Resurrection of the body, at least for those who were being led astray by false teachers, for it was the Resurrection of the body that was in question.

And it was a fundamental question. It attacked the very foundation of the Christian Faith. For if the body be not raised then was Christ's body not raised? Then was the Resurrection not a fact? And if the Resurrection never occurred, then the Redemption of man which Christ came to accomplish, He failed to perform, for His Resurrection was the demonstration of the perfection and efficacy of His Atonement.

If Christ were not risen, sin was not put away; the Gospel was not true; the Corinthians, and all other Believers for that matter, had believed a fable; the Apostles were false witnesses; Christians were of all men most miserable; and their loved ones who had fallen asleep had eternally perished (Williams).

Consequently, that of which Paul here speaks is the single most important aspect of the Christian Faith. While Calvary certainly is the means by which man was Redeemed, still, had there not been a Resurrection, Calvary would have been in vain.

THE DOCTRINE OF THE RESURRECTION

One could say that this Chapter, and the 13th, on Christian Love, stand out, even among the writings of Paul, as pre-eminently beautiful and important, with I think this 15th Chapter standing at the Apex of all that the Holy Spirit said through this Apostle.

No human words ever written have brought such comfort to millions of mourners as the words of this Resurrection Chapter, which form a part, at least in some way, of the Burial Service of every true Christian community. It is the more deeply imprinted on the memory of men because it comes to us in the most solemn hours of bereavement, when we have most need of a Living Faith.

As Paul uses here the word *"Gospel,"* even though it refers to the entirety of the great Plan of Redemption, still, as he uses it here, it has special reference to the Resurrection, which is at least one of the most central and necessary Doctrines of the *"good tidings,"* and which always occupied a prominent place in the preaching of Paul (Acts 17:18; 23:6), as well as in that of all the Apostles (Acts 1:22; 4:2; I Pet. 3:21).

WHICH YOU HAVE RECEIVED

For the effects of the Gospel to be brought about in the heart and life of the individual, it must first be received and then maintained. In fact, the Corinthians had received this word, which was actually the means of their conversion; however, it was now being threatened by false teachers.

In essence, Paul is saying, *"I would remind you, however, that while that Truth may now be denied by you, it was once received by you, and you professed to believe in the fact that Christ rose from the dead, and that the Saints would also rise."*

NOTES

In effect, he is saying the Truth of the Resurrection is the Truth on which the Church is founded, and by which all Salvation and Hope have been produced, and which is actually the foundation of your faith. You were built up by this, and by this only can you stand as a Christian Church. This Doctrine is vital and fundamental. The Resurrection demonstrates that the Doctrines that Christ died *"for sins,"* and rose from the dead, are fundamental Truths of Christianity. They enter into its very nature; and without them there can be no true Salvation experience.

THE FOUNDATION

So there will be no misunderstanding, Paul, in effect, is saying by his use of the phrase, *"And wherein ye stand,"* that if one denies the Resurrection, one is denying the foundation principles of the Gospel, which then leaves it no Gospel at all.

There are certain fundamental Truths on which Christianity stands, actually in which one must believe in order to be saved. Those Truths are:

1. Jesus Christ, as the Son of God, died for sinners, thereby paying the penalty that we should have paid, but in fact, could not pay. To obtain the benefits of what Christ did at Calvary, the sinner must believe that *"Jesus died for me"* (Jn. 3:16; Rom. 10:9-10, 13; Rev. 22:17).

2. Jesus Christ rose from the dead on the third day, ascended to the Father in Heaven, and is there now exalted at the Father's Right Hand. In effect, one could say that the Resurrection ratified that which was accomplished at Calvary. As well, His Resurrection guarantees the Resurrection of every Saint of God who has ever lived.

There are many other Doctrines which enter into Christianity, but to be as brief as possible, if the great foundation Doctrines of the Bible, Calvary and the Resurrection, are denied in any manner, Salvation is forfeited.

Even though one may understand precious little of all that Jesus did in the Redemption of mankind, the Lord does require simple faith in these two foundation principles. In fact, the Holy Spirit has so reduced the great Fundamentals of the Faith to such a total simplicity, that when the Jailor asked Paul and Silas, *"Sirs, what must I do to be saved?"*, the Apostles answered, *"Believe on the Lord Jesus Christ, and thou shalt be saved, and thy house"* (Acts 16:30-31).

Were great scholarship required, most of us would have never qualified. Were money or wealth required, most of us as well would be left out. But simple Faith, and simple Faith alone, is the requirement, a requirement which anyone can meet (Eph. 2:8-9).

(2) "BY WHICH ALSO YE ARE SAVED, IF YE KEEP IN MEMORY WHAT I PREACHED UNTO YOU, UNLESS YE HAVE BELIEVED IN VAIN."

The phrase, *"By which also ye are saved,"* actually means that belief in the Resurrection is absolutely indispensable to one's Salvation.

## THE WHOLE OF FAITH

Concerning Salvation, man must understand that he is a sinner. He should act on the belief of this Truth, and repent.

There is a God. Man should believe it, and fear and love Him, and seek His favor. The Lord Jesus died to save man. To have Faith in Him is to believe that this is true, and to act accordingly; i.e. to trust Him, to rely on Him, to love Him, to feel that we have no merit, which we actually don't, and to cast our all upon Him.

There is a heaven and a hell. To believe this is to credit the account, and act as if it were true; to seek the one and avoid the other.

We are to die. To believe this is to act as if this were so; to be in readiness for it, and to expect it daily and hourly. In one word, Faith is feeling and acting as if there were a God, a Saviour, a heaven, a hell; as if we were sinners, and must die; as if we deserved Eternal Death, and were in danger of it; and in view of all, casting our eternal interest on the Mercy of God in Christ Jesus. To do this is to be *"Saved,"* i.e. *"to be a Christian"*; not to do it is to be an infidel.

The phrase, *"If ye keep in memory what I preached unto you,"* coincides with Paul's Epistle to the Hebrews, *"Therefore we ought to give the more earnest heed to the things which we have heard, lest at any time we should let them slip"* (Heb. 2:1).

*"Keep"* in the Greek is *"katecho,"* and means *"to hold fast, to retain, to possess, to have."*

*"Memory"* in the Greek is *"euprepeia,"* and means *"good suitableness, i.e. gracefulness — grace."* In effect, Paul is saying that our continued reliance on the Grace of God holds us fast in true Doctrine.

NOTES

## WHAT DOES IT MEAN, HOLDING TO THE GRACE OF GOD?

It means that whatever needs to be done in the spiritual sense concerning our Salvation and victory, cannot be brought about at all by our own abilities or strength, but only by the power of the Holy Spirit working within our lives. We are to understand that we do not deserve the help of the Spirit, in fact, we deserve nothing good from God, but upon Faith in Him, He freely gives us all that is needed to bring about this great Salvation. This is the Grace of God, which means unmerited favor.

When the Believer acts from self-will, or our motivation is wrong, as the 13th Chapter of I Corinthians brings out, such has a tendency to cause our *"memory"* to fail us respecting the great Doctrines of the Faith. Total dependence on the Grace of God keeps one's *"memory"* viable regarding the Word of God. In other words, when we study the Word, its true meaning comes to us, and because we are totally depending upon the Lord and not ourselves.

## BEING SAVED

The idea is that they were saved by this, or would be, if they faithfully retained or held the Doctrine as Paul delivered it; if they observed it, and still believed it, notwithstanding all the efforts of their enemies, and all the arts of false teaching to wrest it from them.

There is a doubt delicately suggested here, whether they did in fact still adhere to the Doctrine of the Resurrection, or whether they had not abandoned it in part for the opposite (Barnes).

The phrase, *"Unless ye have believed in vain,"* refers to believing at the first and then drawing back.

## WHAT DOES IT MEAN TO HAVE BELIEVED IN VAIN?

Two different concepts are reflected in uses of the word *"vain"* in Scripture. One idea is that of emptiness, of an entity without substance. The other idea is that of uselessness, of being without purpose or reward. We see both of these thoughts in both Testaments.

### *"VAIN"*

Four Hebrew words are translated *"vain."* They are *"saw," "rig," "hebel,"* and *"hinnam."*

The words *"saw"* and *"rig"* both mean *"emptiness."* The 53 times that *"saw"* appears in the Old Testament, it is used to designate that which is without substance or worth (Ex. 20:7; 23:1; Deut. 5:11, 20; Job 7:3; 11:11; Prov. 30:8; Isa. 1:13; etc.).

It describes the unreal. Thus, taking God's Name *"in vain"* (Ex. 20:7) is to treat God as unreality, to mention His Name without a true awareness of all that His Name represents.

*"Rig"* appears only 12 times in the Old Testament (Lev. 26:16, 20; Job 39:16; Ps. 2:1; 4:2; etc.).

*"Hebel"* and *"hinnam"* both mean *"vain." "Hebel"* literally means *"breath"* or *"vapor"* and thus, it can also mean *"without substance or reality."*

This word is used again and again in Ecclesiastes to depict the *"vanity"* or emptiness of a life lived apart from God, with meaning sought only within the confines of the material universe.

*"Hinnam"* has various meanings, with its *"for nothing"* emphasis both positive and negative. In Ezekiel 6:10, it is negative: *"in vain."*

### EMPTINESS

In essence, *"vain"* in English versions of the Old Testament means emptiness — a wandering in shadows without substance, a life lived without the possibility of satisfaction.

We may feel at times with the Psalmist: *"In vain have I kept my heart pure; in vain have I washed my hands in innocence"* (Ps. 73:13). Yet when life is oriented again to God, we recognize as fantasies those we formerly envied (Ps. 73:20), for God Himself is *"the Strength of my heart, and my portion for ever"* (Ps. 73:26).

### *"VAIN"* IN THE NEW TESTAMENT

In Greek, as in Hebrew, several words may be translated *"vain."* But the essential concept remains the same.

Matthew 15:9 and Mark 7:7 both quote from Isaiah Chapter 29, repeating God's accusation that His people worship Him *"in vain."* This quoted phrase follows the Septuagint. The Greek word here, *"maten"* (used only in these two Passages), indicates that Israel's worship was purposeless. God would not acknowledge those who approached Him according to made-up, human rules.

NOTES

### WITHOUT THE PROSPECT OF A REWARD

One of the seven New Testament occurrences of the Greek word *"eike"* for *"vain"* is I Corinthians 15:2, that which we are studying. This word focuses on result.

To the Believer *"in vain"* means to believe without the prospect of a reward. But Faith in Christ promises the reward of Resurrection.

Another Greek word, *"kenos,"* is rendered *"vain"* in four of its 18 New Testament occurrences (Acts 4:25; I Cor. 15:58; II Cor. 6:1; Gal. 2:2). The literal meaning is *"empty."*

Figuratively *"kenos"* can mean *"senseless," "worthless,"* or *"ineffective."* In Acts 4:25, Luke stresses with the Psalmist the senselessness of plotting something not in accord with God's purposes.

*"Kenodoxia"* is another Greek word translated *"vain,"* which means *"a passion for empty personal glory"* and appears in Philippians 2:3, where it is used there in sharp contrast with humility.

It is good to know, as we humble ourselves to follow Jesus, that our *"labor in the Lord is not in vain"* (I Cor. 15:58). In fact, in Christ there are no empty, meaningless lives (Richards).

### THE *"IF"* OF ETERNAL SECURITY

Going back to the phrase, *"Unless you have believed in vain,"* we must deal with the unscriptural Doctrine of Unconditional Eternal Security, which teaches that one cannot be lost after one is saved irrespective as to what one may do, which has probably caused more people to be eternally lost than maybe any other error propagated by the Evil One. Regrettably, it is believed by millions. As most error, it contains some Truth, but in the final analysis is an excellent tool which Satan has used very successfully.

While the Spirit of the Lord does not leave one easily, and while God is very Merciful and Gracious, still, the free moral agency of man is never abrogated by Salvation, but if anything, strengthened. While many may claim that after a person is saved, they will never desire to turn their back on God, perhaps it would be better to say it another way.

I greatly suspect that almost all involved in this error want the Lord, at least the things He gives such as Eternal Life, etc., but at the same time, some also want sin. So, they want sin, and I mean the practice of sin on a constant basis, and Salvation at the same time, which Eternal Security so-called tells them they can have. Such, to be sure, is a fool's hope.

## THE *"IF"* CONDITION OF PAUL

Before dealing with Paul's *"if"* in the Second Verse of this Chapter, it may help our purpose to consider first one of the most important conditional Passages in the New Testament concerning this Doctrine of Unconditional Eternal Security. Note the flow of Paul's thought:

*"Know ye not that they which run in a race run all, but one receiveth the prize? So run, that ye may obtain.*

*"And every man that striveth for the mastery is temperate in all things. Now they do it to obtain a corruptible crown; but we an incorruptible.*

*"I therefore so run, not as uncertainly; so fight I, not as one that beateth the air:*

*"But I keep under my body, and bring it into subjection: lest that by any means, when I have preached to others, I myself should be a castaway.*

*"Moreover, Brethren, I would not that you should be ignorant, how that all our fathers were under the Cloud, and all passed through the Sea;*

*"And were all baptized unto Moses in the Cloud and in the Sea;*

*"And did all eat the same spiritual meat;*

*"And did all drink the same spiritual drink: for they drank of that spiritual Rock that followed them: and that Rock was Christ.*

*"But with many of them God was not well pleased: for they were overthrown in the wilderness.*

*"Now these things were our examples, to the intent we should not lust after evil things, as they also lusted.*

*"Neither be ye idolaters, as were some of them; as it is written, The people sat down to eat and drink, and rose up to play.*

*"Neither let us commit fornication, as some of them committed, and fell in one day three and twenty thousand. . . .*

*"Now all these things happened unto them for ensamples: and they are written for our admonition, upon whom the ends of the world are come.*

*"Wherefore let him that thinketh he standeth take heed lest he fall"* (I Cor. 9:24-27; 10:1-12).

Do these Passages teach conditional Salvation? Eternal Security Teachers say they do not. Let us see if we can learn its true meaning.

First, it is necessary to see that these Scriptures are connected and that they contain a complete thought. If this can be proved, we shall win a major point for conditional Salvation.

## EXAMPLES USED BY PAUL

Paul began his train of thought with an illustration from the Olympic Games. Athletics was Paul's favorite illustration in his Epistles. He used it more than any other. He began with a footrace and referred to the strenuous training the athlete endured to win the prize, which was a *"corruptible crown."*

In Paul's day, the Olympic athlete subjected himself to ten months of severe training for the Games. If the athlete broke the rules of the contest, he was a *"castaway,"* which meant rejected.

Paul said that he, as God's athlete, did not run *"uncertainly"*; nor was he like one who *"beateth the air."* He said he kept his body under a severe discipline for fear that he be a castaway, like the athlete in his illustration.

Paul, even with the *"Gift"* of continence (I Cor. 7:7), and all the physical beatings and tortures he endures (II Cor. 11:23-27), spoke of his body as a strong power to be overcome and kept subdued. After all his preaching and labor for Christ, he feared being a castaway. It will help much if we can prove the meaning of *"castaway."* We quote the highest authoritative sources.

## THE RULES

On the meaning of *"castaway,"* which in the Greek is *"adokimos,"* Professor A. T. Robertson, who has been called *"the prince of modern Greek Grammarians,"* wrote:

*"It means not standing the test . . . Paul means rejected for the prize, not for the entrance into the race. He will fail if he breaks the rules of the game (Mat. 7:22) . . . Most writers take Paul to refer to the possibility of his rejection in his personal Salvation at the end of the race . . . At the end, he has serene confidence (II Tim. 4:7) with the race run and won.*

NOTES

*"It is a humbling thought for us all to see this wholesome fear instead of smug complacency in this greatest of all heralds of Christ."*

The new and highly authoritative *"A Greek-English Lexicon of the New Testament"* says on page 18: *"Not standing the test, then unqualified, worthless, base . . . disqualified (I Cor. 9:27): a man who is not tempted is unproved."*

The combined weight of leading New Testament Greek authorities support the view that Paul referred to his Salvation when he used the word *"castaway"* in I Corinthians 9:27.

## PROOF POSITIVE

Dean Alford, noted New Testament Scholar, wrote that Paul feared he might be rejected concerning the prize, and not from the contest altogether, as some commentators make it, *"For he was already in the contest."* Then Alford added:

*"An examination of the victorious combatants took place after the contest, and if it could be proved that they had contended unlawfully, or unfairly, they were deprived of the prize and driven with disgrace from the games.*

*"So the Apostle, if he had proclaimed the laws of the combat to others, and not observed them himself, however successful he might apparently be, would be personally rejected as unqualified in the great day."*

Vincent's Word Studies in the New Testament says: *"Rejected, as unworthy of the prize."*

Read again the Verses as we gave them at the beginning of this statement on Unconditional Eternal Security. See how Paul develops his thought. He told about running the race to obtain the prize. Then, referring to his Salvation, he told about his self-denial and rigid bodily discipline. He said he did this because he did not want the Great Judge to disqualify him in the end as a castaway, or as one unworthy of the prize.

The Olympic contestant was examined by the judges after the race before receiving the prize. This often happens today. A fighter's purse is held up, as was that of Mike Tyson in his last fight; winners are stripped of their medals, even as one was in one of the recent Olympics; and others have been banished for life from further participation in athletic contests because they broke the rules and kept breaking them even after repeated warnings.

NOTES

This is what Paul feared could happen to him if he ignored the checks of the Holy Spirit. He would not let the power of sin get its mastery over him. He did this by leaning exclusively on Christ, even as Romans Chapter 6 brings out.

Any uncertainty of reaching the goal for the prize was not distrust of God but distrust of himself. He was sure that God was able to keep that which he had committed unto Him, and in the surefooted certainty of God's Faithfulness, he moved with exerted effort toward the prize.

## EXAMPLES

Next, in the movement of Paul's thought, watch as he goes from *"castaway"* to *"moreover"*:

*". . . lest that by any means, when I have preached to others, I myself should be a castaway.*

*"Moreover, Brethren, I would not that you should be ignorant, how that all our fathers were under the Cloud, and all passed through the Sea"* (I Cor. 9:27; 10:1).

This connective, *"moreover,"* proves that there is here a unit of thought. Paul thus gives us *"ensamples* (examples)*"* of what he meant by the word *"castaway."*

Leading Greek authorities agree that the full meaning of castaway is expressed in the connective force of *"moreover."* The famous Baptist Scholar, Professor A. T. Robertson, wrote:

*"Moreover (for) Paul appeals to the experience of the Israelites in the wilderness in confirmation of his statement concerning himself in 9:26, and as a powerful warning to the Corinthians.*

*"Moreover (for) . . . introduces an illustration of rejection by God, and thus connects what follows with the close of the last chapter. It is possible that I may be rejected, for the Israelites were.*

*"Moreover (for) it serves to explain, make clear, illustrate a preceding thought or word: for, that is, namely; so that it begins an exposition of the thing just announced."*

The Expositors Greek Testament is an authoritative work by 17 distinguished Greek Scholars. In Volume 2, page 857, it says of this *"moreover"* in relation to *"castaway"*:

*"The Apostle has just confessed in warning others, his own fear of reprobation. That this is no idle fear the history of the Old Testament plainly proves.*

*"All the Israelite fathers were rescued from Egypt, and sealed with the ancient Sacraments,*

*and virtually partook of Christ in the wilderness; but, alas, how few of those first redeemed entered the Promised Land!"*

However, I must quickly add that failing to enter the Promised Land did not necessarily mean the loss of one's Salvation, for it is certainly possible that some of these people could have repented. In fact, Moses was not able to go into the Promised Land, because of failure. But Moses was not lost. However, at the same time, it is also certain that many of these people never did repent, and were, in fact, eternally lost.

FOR OUR ADMONITION

Paul said the Scriptures about Israel's *"examples"* were written *"for our admonition."* The Israelites were tested and rejected. This is the whole point of Paul's warning about *"castaway."*

There is much in the Bible about God's testing and proving His people. God proves that He might approve. That which is genuine passes the test, but the counterfeit breaks down under the test. The illustration of the testing of coins and metals in relation to Christians has considerable importance in the Bible. An example is I Peter 1:7. Christians may sometimes fail in a test, but it is the exception and not the rule. This was true of Abraham and David.

In fact, God proved the Israelites many times before rejecting them. He brought them to the bitter waters of Marah, *"and there He proved them."* They murmured against God and Moses.

When they desired the fleshpots of Egypt, God said he would *"prove them, whether they will walk in My Law, or no."*

Moses told them at Sinai: *"God is come to prove you."* He also told them that God led them for forty years in the wilderness *"to prove thee, to know what was in thine heart, whether thou wouldest keep His Commandments, or no"* (Ex. 15:25; 16:4; 20:20; Deut. 8:2; Judg. 2:22).

TESTING

Paul emphasized that the Israelites were tested through fleshly desires and pleasures. They *"lusted . . . sat down to eat and drink, and rose up to play"*; and they committed fornication. Satan has more success with these temptations than with anything else, except with worldly pride.

Paul told these Corinthians, *"Examine yourselves, whether ye be in the faith; prove your own selves. Know ye not your own selves, how that Jesus Christ is in you, except ye be reprobates (counterfeits)?"* (II Cor. 13:5).

NOTES

In *"examine"* and *"prove"* there is the idea of proving to determine whether persons are worthy to be accepted or not. Those that endure the proving are accepted as genuine, and those that do not are rejected as counterfeit.

This was true of Israelites in the wilderness provings. Those who failed the testings were rejected as counterfeits. Jeremiah said the Jews, in his time, were counterfeits. *"Reprobate* (counterfeit) *silver shall men call them, because the Lord hath rejected them"* (Jer. 6:30). They were castaways.

God tests everyone. All must be proved to determine if they are worthy to enter the Kingdom of God. Paul plainly told the Corinthians to test themselves — as metals are tested — to see whether they *"be in the Faith."* If they were reprobates, Christ was not in them, because Christ is not in counterfeits. Here are the opinions of two high ranking Greek authorities regarding Paul's Truth about reprobates:

REPROBATE

*"Unless indeed ye be reprobate . . . Paul challenged his opposers in Corinth to try themselves, to test themselves, whether they were 'in the Faith.' . . . Such tests can be made, unless, alas, they are 'reprobate' (adokmoi), the very adjective that Paul held up before himself as a dreadful outcome to be avoided (I Cor. 9:27).*

*". . . The falsehearted and those who belong to God only in semblance and in show . . . being proved or tempted, they will appear to be what they have always been."*

Some Calvinist writers make Paul's *"castaway"* to mean: *"To put on the shelf."*

Cracked pots were put on the shelf, and Paul did not want to be a cracked pot on the shelf.

These writers give no proof for this because they have none, and it is easy to refute: Paul's examples from Israel's apostate history were not cracked pots on the shelf. They were evil covenant breakers whose carcasses fell in the desert because they would not repent, and who shall never enter God's rest of Salvation.

Greek Professor Kenneth Wuest, of Moody Bible Institute, translated *"castaway"* like this: *"lest . . . I myself should be disqualified from further Christian service."* While this definition could certainly hold true in some cases, it does not in all.

I personally hold Kenneth Wuest, who incidentally is now with the Lord, in high regard, feeling from studying his work and material that he loved the Lord very much. However, he was an advocate of Unconditional Eternal Security, and in certain of his statements concerning this subject, I feel he was wrong. In fact, I think he violated his own ruling respecting proper interpretation.

In his own rule of definition concerning proper Scriptural interpretation, he said, *"The content of meaning in words is not to be determined by each individual expositor . . . to do so would be a method of interpretation that is a most vicious thing."*

ERROR

It surely is a most vicious thing. In fact, the false teaching in Christian Science, Jehovah's Witnesses, Unity, Higher Liberalism, and many others is the result of this most vicious thing.

For instance, *"Sin,"* as defined by Mary Baker Eddy of Christian Science, is in her words *"an illusion."*

Regarding Fosdick of Higher Liberalism, *"damnation"* is *"that old hell"* in which no intelligent person can believe.

*"Born again"* is stripped of all its glory by some. With others, *"everlasting life"* means what the words actually do mean, but *"everlasting punishment"* does not, they say. All such are dangerous distortions of Bible words.

Professor John H. Wigmore, one of America's famous legal authorities, wrote about this vicious method of interpretation in his textbook, *"Wigmore On Evidence."*

Professor Wigmore called some interpreters *"word magicians,"* and said that if these interpreters can make words mean what they want them to mean, then there is no need for rules of Interpretation. He then asked: *"What is the standard of Interpretation? In what sources is the standard to be found?"*

On page 523 of his book, he has the *"Rule Against Disturbing A Plain Meaning."* In other words, it must not be done.

LEGAL AUTHORITIES

We have quoted freely from legal authorities because, in this statement, we have based our arguments on God's Covenants, and Covenants are legal transactions. Therefore, the same interpretive laws that apply to other covenants also apply to God's Covenants.

NOTES

Search the history of false doctrines and you will find these word-magicians everywhere. To prove the meaning of *"castaway,"* we quoted several Greek works holding the highest authoritative positions for accuracy concerning the original language in which the New Testament was written. They are standard sources of evidence.

We proved the meaning by the *"Rule of Definition,"* and by the *"Rule of Context,"* and by the *"Rule of Usage."* Our interpretation satisfies all the rules. Professor Wuest's translation regarding *"castaway"* violates them all.

Dr. James Moffat, translator of *"Moffat's Translation of the Holy Bible,"* wrote this about *"castaway"* in I Corinthians 9:27:

*"Castaway conveys a serious idea . . . This is borne out by the following warning (I Cor. 10:1-11) . . . The latter illustration from Israel with the wilderness Sacraments broadens the range of the word 'disqualified.'*

*"To be disqualified is the opposite of securing one's share in the final Salvation . . . The whole context and illustration is about Salvation."*

THE *"IF"* OF I CORINTHIANS 15:2

*"Moreover, Brethren, I declare unto you the Gospel which I preached unto you, which also ye have received, and wherein ye stand;*

*"By which also ye are saved, <u>if</u> ye keep in memory what I preached unto you, unless ye have believed in vain"* (I Cor. 15:1-2).

Here *"if"* carries the same conditional force as all the other ifs we have seen. *"The Salvation of the readers depends on their holding fast the Word Preached."*

The Greek Text reads here: *". . . The Gospel . . . by which ye are being saved."*

The Expositors Greek Testament says: *"Saved (sozesthe) affirms a present, continuous Salvation"* (Rom. 8:24; Eph. 2:8).

Dr. Robertson, in his Word Pictures in the New Testament, wrote: *"Condition of first class . . . Paul holds this peril over them in their temptation to deny the Resurrection."*

BELIEVED IN VAIN

On this *"believed in vain,"* Dr. James Moffat wrote in his commentary on I Corinthians that

Paul said we are not saved *"by random impulse."* Paul calls it *"futile make-believe"*... *"light half-believers."*

These two conditional clauses, *"if you keep in memory what I have preached unto you,"* and *"unless you have believed in vain,"* have a sharp sting in them.

So, in this Scripture, we see another condition for Salvation: we must believe Bible Doctrines — as taught by Paul.

OTHER *"IFS"* AS GIVEN BY PAUL

It isn't necessary to deal with all Paul's *"ifs,"* but we will quote two or three more.

*"And you... hath He reconciled... to present you holy and unblamable and unreproveable in His sight: If ye continue in the Faith grounded and settled, and be not moved away from the Hope of the Gospel"* (Col. 1:21-23).

The Greek Text expresses a continuous process. The Colossians would be presented to the Lord in Holiness, provided they continued in the Faith.

That is the only way Holiness could be accomplished. Holiness, or Sanctification, is a major Bible Doctrine and is given much importance in relation to Salvation, as one can see in these Texts. The Holy Spirit is grieved that this Truth is largely neglected by Preachers and Christians today. Notice this *"present"* or *"present"* in other Texts:

*"For I am jealous over you with Godly Jealousy: for I have espoused you to one husband, that I may 'present' you as a chaste virgin to Christ"* (II Cor. 11:2).

*"Christ also loved the Church, and gave Himself for it; that He might sanctify and cleanse it with the washing of water by the Word, that He might 'present' it to Himself a Glorious Church"* (Eph. 5:25-27).

*"Whom we preach, warning every man, and teaching every man in all wisdom; that we may 'present' every man perfect in Christ Jesus"* (Col. 1:28).

*"Now unto Him that is able to keep you from falling, and to 'present' you faultless before the Presence of His Glory with exceeding joy"* (Jude vs. 24).

PREDESTINATION

Paul, in Ephesians 1:4-5, has Holiness connected with Predestination. Inasmuch as Predestination and Unconditional Eternal Security are twins, let us look at this Doctrine briefly.

*"According as He hath chosen us in Him before the foundation of the world, that we should be holy and without blame before Him in love:*

*"Having predestinated us unto the Adoption of Children by Jesus Christ to Himself, according to the good pleasure of His Will."*

These Texts do not say that God has predestined certain people to be saved, or lost for that matter, but that He has predestined that certain things happen to us, if we of our own free will accept Christ and follow Him. He has predestined then that we *"should be holy and without blame before Him in love."*

As well, in verse 5 just quoted, this also doesn't mean that the Lord has predestined certain people to be saved, but rather that He has *"predestined that we would be saved by being adopted into the Family of God by Jesus Christ."*

It is only the *manner* of Salvation which is predestined here, instead of those who would be in that Salvation. As repeatedly stated, that is *"whosever will"* (Rev. 22:17).

As well, all of this, even after one is saved, which we are here discussing, has conditional connections. We must not disconnect those conditions, regarding whatever it is of which the Lord is speaking.

As another example from athletics, it is predestined that certain schools will have a football team. However, who is to be on that team is not predestined but, in fact, who qualifies.

Even after one is chosen for the team, he is not necessarily allowed to remain unless he comes up to certain specifications.

Chosen to be holy and without blame was part of the predestinated plan. When God determined the end, He also determined the means to reach the end.

Paul's Jewish *"examples"* were chosen to be *"a peculiar people unto Himself"* (Deut. 14:2), but they became lustful and disobedient and did not reach the Promised Land — the Covenant objective — because they violated the conditions necessary to reach the objective, which was repentance and continued Faith. If they continued in the condition of refusing to repent and lacking in Faith, they were eternally lost.

NOTES

NOTES

## GOD'S CHOSEN PEOPLE

God has predestined that He would have a people, but who these people will be, is left up to their own volition (Jn. 3:16; Rev. 22:17). As well, he predestined that these people would come to Salvation as adopted children in Christ. Also, to those who willingly accept Him and now follow Him, they are chosen to be *"Holy and Blameless."* This is the *"good pleasure of His Will"* — His Sovereign Will.

These Predestination Truths stand in strong opposition to the Predestination teaching which says that God arbitrarily chose some to be saved while at the same time choosing others to be lost.

Paul told the Colossians the Sovereign Will and Purpose would be accomplished *"if ye continue in the Faith . . . and be not moved away from the Gospel."*

## CONTINUING IN THE DOCTRINE

In I Timothy 4:16, Paul proclaimed to Timothy a condition regarding his Salvation and the Salvation of others. He said:

*"Take heed unto thyself, and unto the Doctrine; continue in them: for in doing this thou shalt both save thyself, and them that hear thee."*

It was by continuing in the Doctrines of Christ and by doing them that Timothy and his hearers would be saved.

For another example, Jesus plainly said that *"Salvation is of the Jews"* (Jn. 4:22). However, that did not at all mean that all Jews were saved.

As well, Paul warned the Corinthians of Israelites (Jews) who had been saved, but because of unbelief lost their souls. It pertains to those who had been delivered out of Egypt and were in fact under the Blood Covenant of the Passover. The Scripture says of these people, and even as we have already addressed, *"The people sat down to eat and drink, and rose up to play"* (I Cor. 10:7). Consequently, they became *"castaways."*

Paul, a Jew, said he brought his body under subjection to God's conditions for Salvation. He also said, and even as we have studied, that the Jewish castaways are our *"examples,"* and the history of their lustings was written for *"our admonition."* We should not allow that *"admonition"* to go unheeded.

## BY FAITH

All sinners are saved by Faith, and all Believers maintain their Salvation on the same basis. However, Faith and Liberty as it concerns the Power of God and the Grace of God, are not given to us in order to continue in sin, but rather that we might live a life of Holiness before the Lord.

Even though no Believer is perfect, and there are failures in every Christian life; still, the effort of the Holy Spirit is ever toward victory in every capacity. He can do no less simply because His Nature, which is Divine, cannot brook or tolerate sin in any fashion. While the Grace of God is available to all, which guarantees His Mercy to sincere, seeking souls, still, the Attributes of God are never given to Believers in order that they may continue in sin. Paul's answer to that is *"God forbid"* (Rom. 6:1-2).

As long as the Believer trusts Christ, he cannot fall. However, trusting Christ which avails to us the Grace of God, does not give us a license to continue practicing sin. Using the old proverb, one cannot have his cake and eat it too.

If a Believer desires to stop believing, he has the prerogative to do that. When he came to Christ, he had the free will to believe and, therefore, to be saved, and after becoming a Christian, his free moral agency is no less, and if possible, even greater. In other words, he can quit believing if he so desires, even as some have done, and even as Paul addressed in Hebrews Chapters 6 and 10. If he quits believing, he loses his Salvation.

There are millions who are claiming to trust Christ, when in reality they are not trusting Christ at all, but rather a false doctrine called *"Unconditional Eternal Security."* If they were trusting Christ, they would be working in partnership with the Holy Spirit to get victory over anything in their lives which is detrimental to the Christian walk. Trusting Christ guarantees and demands that.

So, in effect, Paul says in this Second Verse of I Corinthians Chapter 15, that we are saved, if we keep practicing (keep in memory) the Gospel which has been preached unto us.

(3) "FOR I DELIVERED UNTO YOU FIRST OF ALL THAT WHICH I ALSO RECEIVED, HOW THAT CHRIST DIED FOR OUR SINS ACCORDING TO THE SCRIPTURES;"

The phrase, *"For I delivered unto you first of all that which I also received,"* literally means, *"Among the first things"*; however, the manner in which Paul is here using the phrase, it means *"first of all."* It does not occur elsewhere in the New Testament, but is found in Genesis 33:2; and II Samuel 5:8. That of which Paul speaks, and which he says was delivered to the Corinthians first of all, was the Resurrection which, of course, included Calvary (I Cor. 2:2). In fact, his summary of the Resurrection is absolutely remarkable and is as follows:

## THE RESURRECTION

1. It is the most complete summary found in the New Testament.
2. It refers to some incidents which are not mentioned in the Gospels.
3. It declares that the Death and Resurrection of Christ were a subject of ancient Prophecy.
4. It shows the force of the evidence on which the Apostles relied and the number of living eyewitnesses to whom they could appeal.
5. It is the earliest written testimony to the Resurrection, for it was penned within about 25 years of the event itself.
6. It shows that the evidence for the Resurrection as a literal, historical, objective fact, was sufficient to convince the powerful intellect of a hostile contemporary observer.
7. It embodies, and became the model for, a part of the earliest creed of the Church, which proclaims that the past Resurrection of Christ and the future Resurrection of His people are so completely bound up with each other — Christ's Resurrection being the presentation of the firstfruits and that of his people the completed harvest — that to give up belief in the latter logically demands giving up belief in the former, with consequent collapse of the Christian Faith. In other words, one cannot deny one without denying the other (Farrar — Bruce).

By using the word *"received"* Paul refers to the fact that he had received this Doctrine of the Resurrection, plus all other Doctrines of the Gospel from the Lord Jesus by Inspiration. He literally claims to be under Divine Guidance regarding these things which he says.

The phrase, *"How that Christ died for our sins according to the Scriptures,"* basically refers to Isaiah Chapter 53, but as well looks toward the entirety of the Levitical Law with all its Sacrifices, etc. Jesus' death was not just another death; it was to provide a propitiation for the sins of mankind (I Jn. 2:2).

NOTES

## THE ATONEMENT AND THE RESURRECTION

The Messiah, the Lord Jesus, died as an expiatory (to pay the penalty) offering on account of our sins. They caused His death; for them He shed His Blood; to make expiation for them, and to wipe them away, He expired on the Cross.

This passage is full proof that Christ did not die merely as a martyr, but that His Death was to make Atonement for sin. That He died as an Atoning Sacrifice or as a Vicarious Offering, is here declared by Paul to be among the first things that he taught; and the grand fundamental Truth on which the Church at Corinth had been founded, and by which it had been established, and by which they would be saved.

It follows that there can be no true Church, and no well-founded hope of Salvation, where the Doctrine is not held that Christ died for sin.

## WHAT IS THE GOSPEL?

The answer is found in Verses 3 and 4 of I Corinthians Chapter 15. It is the Atonement, which refers to what Jesus did at Calvary, and His Resurrection. These Doctrines are the two great foundation stones of the Gospel, and if either of them be denied then the Good News of the Gospel ceases to exist.

For if Christ did not die as an Atoning Sacrifice for sins, then sin has never been put away, nor God's eternal claims satisfied, and, consequently, there is no deliverance from its power and doom. And if the Resurrection be denied, then Christ failed to accomplish what He purposed to perform, for He came to put away sin by the Sacrifice of Himself as a Sin-Offering (Heb. 9:26), which also refers to the defeating of Death itself, which is the wages of sin.

These two great Foundation Doctrines based upon the Scriptures of the Old Testament; and those Writings being from God, their testimony silenced all discussion and controversy (Williams).

## ACCORDING TO THE SCRIPTURES

Of course, and as stated, Paul is speaking of the Old Testament. In fact, everything Paul taught, even the Foundation Doctrines of the

New Covenant, are found first in the Old Testament. By that I speak of the Prophecies given respecting this which the Lord would do in the future respecting Salvation (Ps. 16:10; 22:1; Isa. 52:14; Chpt. 53). One can also look at Daniel 9:26 and Zechariah 12:10.

That's the reason we constantly say, if the Believer does not know and understand the Old Testament, he really cannot properly understand the New. The Old is the foundation of the New, and all that is given in the New, is foretold in the Old.

At least one of the very reasons that foolish Doctrines are promoted, is because the Old Testament is little understood by the purveyors of these doctrines, whatever they may be.

## SCRIPTURE

The word for *"Scripture"* in Greek is *"graphe."* It simply means *"a writing"* or *"what has been written."*

But in the New Testament this term is used exclusively of Scripture and is used in such a way that quoting Scripture is understood to be the same as quoting God (Jn. 7:38, 42; Rom. 4:3; 9:17; 10:11; Gal. 4:30).

The nature of Scripture is explained by Paul when he writes that *"all Scripture is God-breathed and is useful for teaching, rebuking, correcting and training in Righteousness"* (II Tim. 3:16).

Without dictation or blocking out the individuality of the human writers, God the Spirit bore them along as they wrote, so that the product is *"the Holy Scripture,"* the Word of God.

Another important passage is II Peter 3:15. In the New Testament, *"graphe"* normally refers to the Old Testament Revelation or to an Old Testament Text, even as Paul here uses in this 15th Chapter of I Corinthians. But Peter writes of *"our dear Brother"* Paul's letters and identifies them with *"the other Scriptures."* Consequently, this reference and the evidence of Church history make it clear that the Writings that compose the New Testament were recognized very early as Scripture, i.e., *"the Word of God."*

(4) "AND THAT HE WAS BURIED, AND THAT HE ROSE AGAIN THE THIRD DAY ACCORDING TO THE SCRIPTURES:"

The phrase, *"And that He was buried,"* refers to the fact of His Death. Many claim He did not actually die, but only went unconscious and revived in the Tomb. However, we have a complete unbiased, unprejudicial testimony as to the proof of His Death.

NOTES

The Scripture tells us that Joseph of Arimathaea went to Pilate, the Roman Governor, requesting the Body of Jesus. The Bible says that *"Pilate marvelled if He were already dead."*

At that point, he *"called unto him the Centurion* (who officiated at the Crucifixion) *and asked him whether he had been any while dead."*

The Scripture says, *"And when he knew it of the Centurion, he gave the Body to Joseph"* (Mk. 15:43-45).

The phrase, *"And that He rose again the third day according to the Scriptures,"* is taken from Isaiah 53:12; Psalms 16:10; Jonah 1:17.

## THE MANNER OF PAUL'S STATEMENT

Paul wishes to emphasize the idea that Jesus is still risen. He is in essence proclaiming a past fact together with its present effect or result. Christ is now and continues to be in the condition of one who was raised from the dead.

The addition *"on the third day"* is positive in regard to the historic reality of the Resurrection. It fixes the exact time after the death and thus forms a natural transition to the appearances of the Risen Saviour.

Paul again adds *"according to the Scriptures,"* and this addition has the same force it had with reference to His Death, and is meant to have that same force. Both (His Death and Resurrection) are equally mentioned in Prophecy as Cardinal Acts in the Divine Plan of Salvation. As well, there is no indication in Verses 3 and 4 that Paul is reciting some type of fixed formula such as is found in the Apostles' Creed. In fact, there is no other case in which the wording used is like that which is employed here by Paul. The idea is, that the things said here by the Apostle, are not a recitation of things he had heard from other Apostles, etc., but rather that given to him directly by the Lord.

It is for sure that he had discussed these things with Peter, and perhaps others, but that which he writes, is not taken from that source, but rather by the Inspiration of the Holy Spirit.

Actually, the Apostle couples the Scriptures with more than 500 human witnesses as establishing the Resurrection. But he subordinates human testimony to the witness of the

Bible. The latter was conclusive because Divinely Inspired.

Modern religious teaching reverses this order. It puts human testimony first and Bible Testimony second, and for two reasons — to gratify man's high opinion of himself, and to belittle God's Word.

The Facts and Doctrines of the Gospel are always based upon the infallible Word of God. It alone decides everything. From it there is no appeal.

While human testimony may have been added, even as Paul here does, still, the testimony of the Bible comes first and is always decisive.

## THE THIRD DAY

The question is raised as to whether the phrase *"according to the Scriptures"* include only *"He has been raised"* or are also the time, *"on the third day."*

There is nothing in the Old Testament which specifically states that Christ would rise on the third day. Some have attempted to use Hosea 6:2 and possibly II Kings 20:5 as proof texts; however, neither can be used as proof, for neither of these Passages refer to Christ's Resurrection.

There was a myth among Persians and Jews that for three days the soul remains near the body and does not go to its place until the fourth day. Hence, it is claimed, Jesus rose from the dead after three full days and nights, in order to dispel all the claims of the Jews that He really was not dead.

While some Jews definitely did claim this, still, it is highly unlikely that the Lord would have remained dead three full days and nights, the reason only being the dispelling of this myth.

When the Jews demanded a sign of Jesus concerning his Messiahship, He said to them, *"There shall no sign be given to it, but the sign of the Prophet Jonas* (Jonah)*:*

*"For as Jonas* (Jonah) *was three days and three nights in the whale's belly; so shall the Son of man be three days and three nights in the heart of the earth"* (Mat. 12:39-40).

So, this proclaims the experience of Jonah as a foretelling of the length of time that Jesus would remain in the Tomb, but doesn't tell us as to why this length of time was required.

The only further answer that one could give is, that if the Lord had wanted us to know, He would have informed us. As well, there is a possibility that the reason is given in one of the *"types"* of the Old Testament, but that no Expositor has yet ferreted it out.

NOTES

1. THE IMPORTANCE OF THE RESURRECTION

The Corinthians, like other Greeks, were people of keen, restless minds, fond of philosophic speculation. That some of the members of the Corinthian Church partook of that spirit can be seen from the reading of the first two Chapters of this Epistle of I Corinthians. There, Paul declares the immeasurable superiority of Divine Revelation over human speculation.

With keen insight he foresaw that under the influence of the Greek spirit the Gospel might evaporate into a beautiful but powerless system of philosophy and ethics, somewhat as Judaism had done. In fact, that tendency was already apparent.

## GREEK MYTHOLOGY

Some of the members of the Church evidently were influenced by an old Greek doctrine of immortality which taught that at death the body perished forever but that the soul continued to live. Indeed, so ran this teaching, it was good that the body perish for it was a clog and hinderance to the soul.

It seems it was being taught by some false teacher in the Corinthian Assembly that, while soul or spirit lived after death, the body was gone forever and would know no Resurrection; that the only Resurrection was the spiritual resurrection of the soul from its death in trespasses and sins.

The Apostle challenged the claims of that teaching by saying, *"Now if Christ be preached that He rose from the dead, how say some among you that there is no Resurrection of the dead?"* (I Cor. 15:12). Taking this error as the starting point, Paul expounds the true doctrine and gives us this great Resurrection Chapter of the Bible, I Corinthians Chapter 15.

## THE BIBLICAL DOCTRINE OF MAN

As a basis for his argument, Paul takes the Biblical Doctrine of man, which in contradiction to the pagan doctrine, declares that the body is Sanctifiable (I Cor. 6:13-20), Redeemable, and included in man's Salvation. In the beginning God created man both spirit and body, and when spirit and body came together as a living unit, man became *"a living soul."*

Man was originally created immortal in the sense that he need not die, but mortal in the sense that he could die if he disobeyed God. Had man continued faithful, he would have developed to the fullest extent of the image of God. But man sinned, lost the right to the Tree of Life, and as a result began to die, the process culminating in the separation of spirit and body.

And the physical death was the outward expression of that spiritual death which is the consequence of sin.

REDEMPTION

Since man is spirit, soul, and body, Redemption must include the quickening of all three aspects of the human being; hence the need of Resurrection. And while man may become right with God and live spiritually (Eph. 2:1), yet his body dies as a result of his racial and sinful inheritance from Adam. But since the body is inherently part of his personality, his Salvation and his immortality are not complete until the body is raised and glorified. Such is the teaching of the New Testament (Rom. 13:11; I Cor. 15:53-54; Phil. 3:20-21).

THE REALITY OF SALVATION

Paul's argument in Verses 13-19 of this 15th Chapter is as follows: to teach that there is no Resurrection of the body is to strike a blow at the reality of Salvation and the hope of immortality. He develops his argument as follows:

If there is no Resurrection of the body, then Christ, Who took a human body, did not rise from the dead. If Christ, did not rise from the dead then Paul's preaching, as well as all others, is empty talk; worse, it is false and misleading. And if the preaching is vain, so also is the Faith and Hope of those who accept it.

If Christ did not actually rise from the dead, then there is no Salvation for sin; for how do we know that His Death was an atoning one — different from ordinary death — unless He rose from the dead?

And if the body of the Master did not rise, what hope is there for those who trust in Him? And if all this be true, then Sacrifice, self-denial, and suffering for the sake of Christ is in vain.

2. THE NATURE OF THE RESURRECTION

It is easy enough to state the fact of the Resurrection, but when we attempt to explain the how of the matter we find ourselves in deep waters, because we are dealing with mysterious supernatural laws beyond the grasp of our minds. We do know, however, that the Resurrection of the body will be characterized by:

A. Relationship: it will bear some relation to the old body — which fact Paul illustrates by the grain of wheat (I Cor. 15:36-37).

The grain is cast into the ground, dies, and the act of dissolution fertilizes the living germ within it, so that it develops into a beautiful new green plant. *"Only by the dissolution of the material particles in the seed is the germ of life* (which no microscope can detect) *made to operate."*

Who vitalizes the human body, making it capable of the glorious transformation into the Resurrection body?

The Holy Spirit! (I Cor. 6:19)

Speaking of the Resurrection, Paul utters the words in II Cor. 5:5, which one Greek Scholar has translated as follows: *"I am prepared for this change by God, Who has given me the Spirit as its pledge and installment."*

B. Reality: Many people have a false idea as to what Heaven will be like. They think it is some type of unsubstantial, vague kind of existence.

On the contrary, the life to come will be just as real as this present one — in fact, much more so. Glorified bodies will be real and tangible, and we shall know each other, converse with one another, and engage freely in heavenly activities. Jesus in His Resurrection body was real indeed to His Disciples; though Glorified, He was the very same Jesus, which tells us what the Resurrection body will be like.

C. Incorruption: *"Raised in incorruption and in power,"* the Resurrection body will be free from sickness, pain, weakness, and death (Rev. 21:4).

D. Glory: Our old bodies are perishable, subject to decay and weariness because they are *"natural"* (*"soulful"*) bodies, fitted to an imperfect existence in a very imperfect world; but the Resurrection body will be adapted to a glorious, immortal life in Heaven, i.e. spiritual bodies.

When Peter, the Great of Russia, worked as a mechanic in Holland in order to learn shipbuilding, he wore the humble garments of a mechanic although the titular leader of Russia. But on returning to his Palace, he was clothed in the resplendent bejeweled robes of royalty.

NOTES

Man's spirit originally inbreathed by God, now lives a humble existence in a perishable body (Phil. 3:21); but in the Resurrection it will be clothed with a glorious body, fitting it to see God face-to-face.

E. Agility: The glorified human body will then pass through space with lightning speed, even with the speed of thought as someone has said, due to the mighty energy quickening it.

F. Subtlety: I speak of the power of penetrating solid substances. In walking the earth in a glorified body we shall not be deterred by such a trifle as a wall or a mountain — we shall simply walk through it! (Jn. 20:26).

There are many things we do not, and cannot, yet know about the future life; *"it doth not yet appear what we shall be."* However, this we do know: *"Now are we the sons of God,"* and *"when He shall appear, we shall we like Him; for we shall see Him as He is"* (I Jn. 3:1-2).

## THE FUTURE LIFE AS TAUGHT IN THE OLD TESTAMENT

In studying Old Testament Teaching concerning the future life, it should be remembered that the Redemptive Work of Christ has exerted a mighty effect in relation to life and death. He *"hath abolished death, and hath brought life and immortality to light through the Gospel"* (II Tim. 1:10).

Christ brought fullness of light and assurance concerning the life to come. He also effected a certain deliverance for Old Testament Saints in the intermediate state, which resulted in an increase of blessedness for them.

But though the Old Testament Revelation concerning life after death is not so full as that of the New Testament, the Doctrine is undoubtedly taught.

## RELATIONSHIP TO GOD

The Old Testament Doctrine of immortality is based on man's relation to God. Man, made in the Image of God, is fitted for the knowledge of God, and for fellowship with Him. This implies that man is more than an animal; that he has a life which transcends time. He was created for life, not mortality. But sin brought death into the world and so frustrated man's destiny.

Death in its physical aspect, is the separation of body and soul. Death, however, does not imply the extinction of the soul. The Old Testament consistently teaches that man's personality survives death.

NOTES

## THE GRAVE

Man's body was laid in the grave while the soul passed into Sheol (translated *"hell," "the pit," "the grave"*), the abode of departed spirits. That Sheol was not Heaven as shown by the fact that it is described as being beneath (Prov. 15:24), downward (Ezek. 32:21), in the nether parts of the earth (Ezek. 32:18).

That it was not a place of bliss is evident from its description as a place of thanklessness (Ps. 6:5), cruelty (Song of Sol. 8:6), place of pain (Job 24:19), place of sorrow (Ps. 18:5), a place from which none seem to return (Job 7:9).

Sheol, unilluminated by the radiance of the Risen Christ, was a gloomy and forbidding place, and for this reason some of the Old Testament Saints *"shrank back from Sheol as a child shrinks from a darkened room."* See for example Psalms 88 and Isaiah Chapter 30.

## THAT WHICH JESUS DID

Sheol was inhabited by both the Righteous (Gen. 37:34-35; Job 14:13; Ps. 88:3) and the wicked (Job 24:19; Ps. 31:17; Prov. 5:3-5; 7:27), before Christ came.

From the incident of the Rich Man and Lazarus as told by Jesus, we learn that there were two parts in Sheol — a place of suffering for the wicked (Lk. 16:23-24) and another part for the Righteous, a place of rest and comfort (Lk. 16:25).

However, Old Testament Believers were not without hope. God's Holy One, the Messiah, would descend into Sheol; God's people would be redeemed from Sheol (Ps. 16:10; 49:15). This was fulfilled when Christ, after His Death, descended into the world of departed spirits (Mat. 12:40; Lk. 23:42-43), and delivered the Old Testament Saints from Sheol to the Upper Paradise (Eph. 4:8-10).

This last Scripture seems to indicate that a change took place in the world of spirits, and that the place where the Righteous await their Resurrection is now located in the heavenlies (Eph. 4:8; II Cor. 12:2).

Since then, the spirits of the Righteous at death go up to Glory and the spirits of the wicked at death go down to condemnation (Rev. 20:13-14).

NOTES

## OTHER EVIDENCES

Other evidences of the teaching of the future life in the Old Testament are the following:

1. The phrase *"gather to his fathers"* or *"people,"* used of Abraham, Moses, Aaron, and David, must refer to conscious existence after death and not to burial, for these men were not buried in their ancestral burying places.

2. The Translations of Enoch and Elijah prove certainly the existence of a future life of bliss in the Presence of God.

3. Christ's words in Matthew 22:32 represent a very strong statement of Jewish belief. Otherwise it would have had no force for the hearers.

4. The Doctrine of the Resurrection from the dead is plainly taught in the Old Testament (Job 19:26; Dan. 12:1-2). In that there isn't more information given, is because Jesus had not yet come to carry out the particulars which guarantee the coming Resurrection, such as paying the sin debt of man and serving as the Firstfruits of that which is to come concerning Resurrection.

5. When Jacob said, *"I will go down into the grave* (literally, *"Sheol")* *unto my son mourning"* (Gen. 37:35), he certainly could not have meant the literal grave, because the body of Joseph was supposed to have been devoured by a wild beast.

## WHAT THE NEW TESTAMENT TEACHES CONCERNING THE FUTURE LIFE

The New Testament recognizes a state beyond death in which the spiritual life is continued under new and better conditions. To enter into this life is the highest aim of man (Mk. 9:43).

By having Christ Himself, the Believer has already in this life made the transition from death to life (Jn. 3:36). However, this is only the beginning; its fullness belongs to another state of existence which commences with the *"Resurrection of Life"* (Jn. 5:29). There is a life to come (I Tim. 4:8); it is hidden now, but will be manifested when Christ our life appears (Col. 3:4), Who will award the Crown of Life promised to those who love Him (James 1:12).

Even the state of the righteous dead in Christ holds something better than our present life in Him (Phil. 1:21). But our fuller life, our land of Promise, our birthright as the sons of God, will only be disclosed at His Coming (Rom. 8:17; Gal. 4:7).

## NO INTERRUPTION

Physical death cannot interrupt the fellowship between the Christian and his Lord. *"I am the Resurrection, and the Life: He that believeth in Me, though he were dead, yet shall he live: and whosoever liveth and believeth in Me shall never die"* (Jn. 11:25-26).

With these words Jesus assured Martha and Mary that their brother had not really perished, but was safe. He as much as said: *"I loved your brother and had sweet fellowship with him; realizing Who I am, remembering My power, do you imagine for a moment that I will allow death to interrupt the fellowship which has been a delight to both of us?"*

There are many formal arguments for immortality, but more reassuring than cold logic is the knowledge that we are in fellowship with God and His Christ. Here is a Saint who for years had a delightful fellowship with the Son of God, has heard His Voice and felt His Presence. As he now lies upon his deathbed shall the Son of God say to him, *"We have walked together and held sweet converse, but now we must part and say an eternal farewell"?*

Unthinkable!

Those who are *"in Christ"* (I Thess. 4:14-17) cannot be separated from Him either by life or by death (Rom. 8:38-39).

The one who has consciously lived in the Presence of Christ, to be separated from Christ by death is impossible. For those bound by God's love to drop out of that love into nothingness or desolation is inconceivable.

Christ says to all Believers: *"Is Lazarus, is anyone, joined to Me? Has he attached himself trustfully to My Person?*

*"Then whatever I am, whatever power is in Me, will be operative in his life."*

In effect, the Lord is saying that all who are joined to Him by spiritual adoption, since He is the Resurrection and the Life, that same power must operate in Believers as well.

## THE DESTINY OF THE RIGHTEOUS

Inasmuch as we are speaking of the Resurrection, it is incumbent upon us to address ourselves, as well, to what this future life holds, namely the destiny of the Righteous.

The Righteous are destined to eternal life in the Presence of God. God created man to know, love, and serve Him in this present world and to enjoy Him forever in the world to come.

The Christian during his earthly life, experiences by Faith the Presence of the invisible God, but in the life to come this experience of Faith will become an actual reality. He will see God face-to-face — a Blessing described by some Theologians as the Beatific Vision.

Heaven is described by various names:

1. Paradise (literally, a Garden), reminding us of the happiness and blessedness of our first parents as they walked and talked with the Lord God (II Cor. 12:4; Rev. 2:7).

2. *"Father's house"* with its many mansions (Jn. 14:2), conveying the thought of home, rest, and fellowship.

3. A heavenly country to which we are traveling as Israel of old traveled to Canaan, the earthly Promised Land (Heb. 11:13-16).

4. A City, suggesting the idea of an organized society (Heb. 11:10; Rev. 21:2).

## THREE PHASES

The following three phases in the condition of departed Christians should be distinguished:

1. The intermediate state of rest while awaiting the Resurrection.

2. After the Resurrection follows judgment for works, i.e., *"The Judgement Seat of Christ"* (I Cor. 3:10-15; II Cor. 5:10).

3. At the close of the Millennium there descends from Heaven the New Jerusalem, the final home of the Blessed (Rev. Chpt. 21).

The New Jerusalem comes down from Heaven, is a part of Heaven, and is, therefore, Heaven in a real sense. Wherever God reveals Himself in a Personal Presence and unveiled Glory is Heaven; and such is true of the New Jerusalem (Rev. 22:3-4).

Why does this city come down out of Heaven?

God's ultimate purpose is to bring Heaven to earth (Deut. 11:21). In the dispensation of the fullness of time He will *"gather together in one all things in Christ, both which are in Heaven, and which are on earth"* (Eph. 1:10), and then God shall be *"all in all"* (I Cor. 15:28).

## THE NECESSITY FOR HEAVEN

The history of religions discloses the fact that the human soul instinctively believes that there is such a place. This instinct for Heaven has been implanted within the soul of man by God Himself, the Creator of human instincts. Arguments proving the existence of a future life are not formulated primarily that men may believe in it, but because of the fact that they do believe in it, and are desirous of bringing the mind into subjection to the deepest intuitions of the heart.

Then too, such a place is essential to fulfill the demands of justice. The sufferings of the Righteous upon earth and the prosperity of the wicked demand a future state where full justice is done. And the Bible teaches that such a place does exist.

Plato, the wisest of the Greeks, discussed the future life as a probability, and advised men to gather the best opinions on the subject, and embark upon them as a raft, and then sail perilously through life, *"unless one could more securely and less perilously sail on a stronger vessel or some Divine Word."*

The Divine Word of certainty which wise men have desired is found in the Scriptures, and the Scriptures alone, where the existence of a future life is taught, not as an opinion or theory, but as an absolute fact. Regrettably, Plato never learned of this, because he did not know the Scriptures.

## THE BLESSINGS OF HEAVEN

Human language at its best is inadequate to portray the realities of the life to come. In Revelation Chapters 21 and 22 the Spirit employs language which helps us to gain a slight conception of the beauties of that other world.

Revelation 21:23 and 22:5, tell us of its *"Light"* and *"Beauty."* Nevertheless, and even as Paul said, at the present time we only *"see through a glass darkly"* (I Cor. 13:12).

## FULLNESS OF KNOWLEDGE

The sentiment expressed by the wise Socrates when he said, *"One thing I know and that is that I know nothing,"* has been echoed by wise men ever since. Man is surrounded by mystery and hungers for knowledge. In Heaven this thirst for knowledge will be perfectly satisfied.

The mysteries of the Universe will be made plain; perplexing theological problems will shine as clear as day. The brightest kind of knowledge shall then be ours — the knowledge of God.

NOTES

Consequently, Paul says that we will then *"know as we are known"* (I Cor. 13:12).

REST

A conception of Heaven may be formed by contrasting it with the disadvantages of this present life. Think of all in this world that makes for weariness, pain, strife, and grief, and consider that Heaven is the place where such may not enter.

John, in his vision of Heaven, proclaimed that *"God shall wipe away all tears from their eyes; and there shall be no more death, neither sorrow, nor crying, neither shall there be any more pain: for the former things are passed away"* (Rev. 21:4).

SERVICE

There are many who have an incomplete idea of Heaven, thinking it is a place of inactivity, where the Saints spend their time strumming harps, etc. However, this is a misconception.

While the Redeemed will definitely play harps in Heaven, for Music will continue to be a part of the great Worship of God, still, there will be much work to be done.

The Scripture says, *"They serve Him day and night in His Temple . . . and His servants shall serve Him"* (Rev. 7:15; 22:3).

He who placed man in the first Paradise with instructions to keep and dress it will certainly not leave him inactive in the second Paradise.

JOY

The greatest conceivable earthly happiness, increased a millionfold but feebly expresses the enjoyment awaiting God's children in the realm of the blessed (Rev. 21:4).

If a powerful king, with limited means wished to build a palace for his bride, it would be everything that art, skill, and resources could provide. God loves us infinitely more than could any human being.

Having exhaustless resources and infinite skill, He can build a home which beauty is beyond the power or knowledge of human art or imagination. When He said, *"I go to prepare a place for you,"* He meant exactly what He said (Jn. 14:1-4).

STABILITY

Heaven's happiness will be forever. Indeed, permanence is necessary to complete happiness.

NOTES

Regardless of the wonderful beauty and blessedness of Heaven, the realization that it would come to an end would cause its joy to lose its perfection. For the mind would be continually weighed down by the knowledge that the end was inevitable, and such a frame of mind would prove a constant bar to perfect enjoyment.

Everyone craves permanence — permanent health, permanent peace, permanent prosperity. Instability and insecurity are feared by all. But the happiness of Heaven carries with it the Divine assurance that its joy will never end or diminish in intensity.

FRIENDSHIP

Man is by nature a social being. A solitary man is abnormal and exceptional.

If in this life social joys afford pleasure, how great must be the rapture of companionship in Heaven with those whom we love! In human relationships even those dearest to us have faults or objectionable traits which detract from their attractiveness.

In Heaven friends and relatives will be faultless. Social joys in this present life are accompanied by disappointments. Loved ones often become a cause of sorrow to us, friendships are broken, affections are blighted. But in Heaven there will be no misunderstandings, no strife — everyone will be good and beautiful, without shadow or defect, filled with heavenly wisdom and resplendent with a heavenly personality (I Thess. 4:13-18; Heb. 12:22-23).

FELLOWSHIP WITH CHRIST

*"Whom having not seen, ye loved; in Whom, though now you see Him not, yet believing, ye rejoice with joy unspeakable and full of glory"* (I Pet. 1:8).

In that day, we shall be like Him, for we shall see Him as He is; our bodies will be fashioned like unto His Glorious Body; we shall see His Face; and He Who shepherded His people through the vale of tears, will in Heaven lead them from joy to joy, from glory to glory, from Revelation to Revelation (Jn. 14:3; II Cor. 5:8; Phil. 1:23).

THE DESTINY OF THE WICKED

The destiny of the wicked is eternal separation from God, and the eternal suffering of His Wrath, known as the Second Death. Because of its terrible nature, it is a subject from which one naturally shrinks; yet it is one which must be faced, because it is a positive Truth of Divine Revelation.

Hence, the Christ of Gentleness and Love warned men against the sufferings of hell.

What He said concerning the hope of Heaven might well be applied to His teaching in regard to the existence of Hell — *"If it were not so, I would have told you"* (Jn. 14:2).

Hell is a place of: extreme suffering (Rev. 20:10), memory and remorse (Lk. 16:19-31), unsatisfied lustful desire (Lk. 16:24), contempt (Dan. 12:2), vile companionship (Rev. 21:8), hopelessness (Prov. 11:7; Mat. 25:41).

## FALSE VIEWS

As we have said elsewhere in this Volume, Satan's method of deception presently, and has been all through the New Covenant, is to pervert the Truth. What kind of lie he can get people to believe is of little consequence to him, just as long as they believe a lie.

The idea of a future Judgment does not sit well with man. In fact, the whole of humanity has been so psychologized that it in effect claims man's problems are external of himself, in other words, caused by others; therefore, the idea that man is responsible because he is the guilty party, meaning that his condition is the result of an evil heart, does not sit well. Consequently, it is rejected. Irrespective, there is coming a Judgment, and all who have not made Christ their eternal Saviour will be eternally lost (Rev. 20:11-15). The following are a few of the views of false Doctrine.

## UNIVERSALISM

This Doctrine teaches that everybody will finally be saved. It also goes under the heading of ultimate reconciliation.

That God is too loving to exclude anyone from Heaven seems to be their argument. This theory is disputed by such Scriptures as Romans 6:23; Luke 16:19-31; John 3:36, and others.

The Truth is that it is, in reality, a Mercy that God excludes the sinful from Heaven, for a defiled sinner would be just as miserable in Heaven as a Saint of God would be in hell.

## RESTORATIONISM

This perversion teaches that punishment in hell is not eternal, but a temporary experience for the purpose of purifying the sinner to fit him for Heaven. Purgatory is, in a sense, an offshoot of this pernicious Doctrine.

If this were the case, the fires of hell would have more power than the Blood of Christ. Besides, experience teaches that punishment in itself is not regenerative; it can restrain but cannot transform.

Teachers of this school contend that the word *"eternal"* in the Greek means *"age-long"* and not endless duration. But according to Matthew 25:41, if the punishment of the wicked has an end, so has the bliss of the Righteous.

Habit tends to fixedness. Character tends to final permanence. God will no more force a man to be saved in the future than He does in the present.

## SECOND PROBATIONISM

This perversion holds that all will have a second chance, or opportunity, to accept Salvation between Death and the Resurrection.

The Scriptures, however, teach that at death, man's destiny is fixed (Heb. 9:27).

Moreover, if people think they will have a second chance, how many will accept the first chance? And if they neglect the first chance, according to the laws of human nature, they will be weaker to accept the second.

## ANNIHILATIONISM

This Doctrine teaches that God will annihilate the wicked. Annihilationists point to II Thessalonians 1:9 and other Passages which state that the wicked shall be destroyed.

However, in Scriptural usage the word does not mean annihilation but rather ruin. And if the word *"destruction"* in this Verse really means annihilation, then the word *"eternal"* would be superfluous, for annihilation would be forever.

They cite also Scriptures which set forth death as the penalty of sin. But in these cases, the reference is to spiritual not physical death, and spiritual death means separation from God. God's promise of life to the obedient does not mean the gift of existence — for all men already have that. And if life as a reward does not mean the gift of bare existence, then death as a penalty does not mean the mere loss of existence (Pearlman).

(5) "AND THAT HE WAS SEEN OF CEPHAS, THEN OF THE TWELVE."

NOTES

The phrase, *"And that He was seen of Cephas,"* refers to Peter, and is found in Luke 24:34.

The phrase, *"Then of the Twelve,"* includes Matthias who was chosen to take the place of Judas (Mk. 16:14; Acts 1:26).

(6) "AFTER THAT, HE WAS SEEN OF ABOVE FIVE HUNDRED BRETHREN AT ONCE; OF WHOM THE GREATER PART REMAIN UNTO THIS PRESENT, BUT SOME ARE FALLEN ASLEEP."

The phrase, *"After that, He was seen of above five hundred Brethren at once,"* probably took place in Galilee, where the Lord Jesus had spent the greater part of His public Ministry, and where He had made most Disciples (Mat. 28:16).

The place, however, is not designated by Paul, or others for that matter, and, therefore, cannot be known exactly.

THIS GREAT APPEARANCE

There is a slight circumstance hinted at in Matthew 28:10, which may throw some light on this Passage. After His Resurrection, Jesus said to the women who were at the Sepulchre, *"Go tell My Brethren that they go into Galilee, and there shall they see Me."* And in Verse 16 it is said, *"The eleven Disciples went away into Galilee, and to a mountain where Jesus had appointed them."*

GALILEE

Jesus had spent most of His public life in Galilee. He had made most of His Disciples there. It was proper, therefore, that those Disciples, who would of course hear of His Death, should have some public confirmation of the fact that He had risen.

It is very probable also, that the Eleven who went down into Galilee after He rose would apprise the Brethren there of what had been said to them, that Jesus would meet them on a certain mountain; and it is morally certain that they who had followed Him in so great numbers in Galilee would be drawn together by the report that the Lord Jesus, Who had been put to death, was about to be seen there again alive.

Such is human nature, and such was the attachment of these Disciples to the Lord Jesus, that it is morally certain a large concourse would assemble on the slightest rumor that such an occurrence was to happen. Nothing more would be necessary anywhere to draw a concourse of people than a rumor that one who was dead would appear again; and in this instance, where they ardently loved Him, and when, perhaps, many believed that He would rise, they would naturally assemble in great numbers to see Him once more.

NOTES

One thing is proved by this, that the Lord Jesus had many more Disciples than is generally supposed. If there were five hundred who could be assembled at once in a single part of the land where He had preached, there is every reason to suppose that there were many more in other parts of Judea (Barnes).

EYEWITNESSES

The phrase, *"Of whom the greater part remain unto this present,"* appeals to a very large number of living witnesses. The evidence that these people would rather have died than lied, and that is the case, is of the highest evidential value. The idea is that these people can be appealed to and prove that they saw Him.

What more conclusive argument for the Truth of His Resurrection could there be than that of approximately five hundred persons who had seen Him, who had been intimately acquainted with Him in His Life, and who had become His followers? If the testimony of this number of people could not avail to prove His Resurrection, no number of witnesses could.

The phrase, *"But some are fallen asleep,"* presents this beautiful and common word for death found in the New Testament, at least as it applies to Believers (Mat. 27:52; Jn. 11:11; Acts 7:60).

The word denotes the calmness and peace with which Believers died, like sinking into a gentle sleep, and not of the existence after death as the soul and spirit go to be with Christ to await the Resurrection (Phil. 1:23).

SOUL-SLEEP

Some groups, such as the Seventh-Day Adventists as well as others, believe that the soul exists after death in an unconscious state until the Resurrection. This belief, known as *"soul-sleep,"* is shared by individuals in other groups.

It is true that the Bible describes death as a *"sleep,"* but it is referring to the manner of death (going to sleep) and not what happens after death.

Paul said, to which we have already alluded, *"For I am in a strait betwixt two, having a desire to depart, and to be with Christ; which is far better: nevertheless to abide in the flesh is more needful for you"* (Phil. 1:23-24).

THE CROSS OF CHRIST

Paul speaking of dying and going to be with Christ is all made possible by the Cross. Before Jesus died on the Cross, thereby atoning for all sin, past, present, and future, those who died during that time, even the Godliest, did not go to Heaven, but rather to Paradise.

Jesus mentioned this place in Luke 16:19-31. It is the illustration of the rich man and Lazarus. Even though it is speaking of the time before the Cross, still, it points to the fact that the soul does not sleep at death, but actually the soul and the spirit of the one who was a Believer, even before the Cross, instantly went to Paradise upon the event of death. All others went to Hell. This illustration given by Christ makes this abundantly clear. Consequently, several things are taught us as a result of the illustration of the rich man and Lazarus. They are as follows:

1. The rich man wasn't lost because he was rich, and Lazarus wasn't saved because he was a beggar. Lazarus did not allow his poverty to keep him from the Lord, and the rich man did not allow the blessings given to him to bring him to the Lord.

2. This illustration given by Christ completely blew to pieces the thinking of the Israel of that day, which taught that if one was rich, they most definitely were saved, and if they were poverty stricken, this meant they were under the curse of God, i.e., most probably lost. By this illustration, Jesus taught us that Salvation has nothing to do with material things or the lack thereof, but rather with Faith.

3. At the moment of death, the soul and the spirit either go to Paradise or to Hell.

4. If one knows the Lord, Angels come and take the soul to Paradise. More than likely, demons take the soul of the unredeemed individual to Hell.

5. Paradise, before the Cross, was in the heart of the Earth, but is now empty. After the Cross was a fact, Jesus delivered all of the Believers out of Paradise and took them with Him to Heaven (Eph. 4:8-10). Now when the Believer dies, as Paul said, the soul and the spirit instantly go to Heaven to be with the Lord.

6. The fire in Hell is literal and real.

7. The description given of all concerned proves that the soul and the spirit are conscious, can talk, can see, can feel, etc.

8. This illustration teaches that there is full consciousness after death, some of comfort and others of torment.

9. We are told in this illustration that the Word of God holds all the answers to eternity; if people will not accept that, they will accept nothing (Lk. 16:29).

NOTES

THE REASON FOR THE CHANGE

The reason that Believers before the Cross did not instantly go to Heaven, but were taken down into Paradise, is because the sin debt still remained with them. Paul plainly told us that the *"blood of bulls and goats could not take away sins"* (Heb. 10:4).

In truth, all of those Believers, at least in a sense, were held captive by Satan. While they were in Paradise, and thereby comforted, still, their deliverance from this place awaited the Cross. No doubt, the Evil One hoped to get them over into the burning side of Hell. He did not succeed because Jesus went to the Cross, thereby atoning for all sin, which settled the sin debt once and for all, with Jesus then legally entitled to deliver every soul in that place, which He did (Eph. 4:8-9).

Now that the Cross has atoned for all sin, the moment the Believer dies, as stated, such a person instantly goes to be with the Lord Jesus Christ. It was all made possible by the Cross, because the Cross alone addressed sin in every form, both as to its cause and its effect (Phil. 1:23).

Paul said, *"But this man* (this Priest, Christ Jesus)*, after He had offered one Sacrifice for sins forever* (speaks of the Cross)*, sat down on the Right Hand of God* (refers to the great contrast with the Priests under the Levitical system, who never sat down because their work was never completed; the Work of Christ was a *"Finished Work,"* and needed no repetition)*;*

*"For henceforth expecting till His enemies be made His footstool.* (These enemies are Satan and all the fallen angels and demon spirits, plus all who follow Satan.)

*"For by one Offering He has perfected forever them who are sanctified."* (Everything one needs is found in the Cross, and in the Cross alone [Heb. 10:12-14].)

While Christ is the Source, the Cross is the means!

(7) "AFTER THAT, HE WAS SEEN OF JAMES, THEN OF ALL THE APOSTLES."

The phrase, *"After that, He was seen of James,"* pertains to the half brother of Jesus (Gal. 1:19; Lk. 8:19).

James the son of Zebedee and brother of John had by this time been martyred, and James the son of Alphaeus was never much more than a name to the Church in general.

NO MENTION

Other than this occasion, there is no mention of this appearance. However, in one of the ancient writings, there is a legend that says that James had made a vow that he would neither eat nor drink till he had seen Jesus risen from the dead. It is said that Jesus appeared to him and said, *"My brother, eat thy bread, for the Son of Man is risen from the dead."*

Irrespective of that account, the Truth of this of which Paul speaks is strongly supported by the fact that James, like the rest of the Lord's *"Brothers," "did not believe"* in Christ before the Crucifixion, whereas after the Resurrection we find him and the rest of *"the Lord's Brothers"* ardently convinced (Acts 1:14) (Farrar).

This James, the half brother of our Lord, also the author of the Epistle that bears his name, was Pastor of the Church in Jerusalem. When Paul went there, after his return from Arabia, he had an interview with James (Gal. 1:19), *"But other of the Apostles saw I none, save James the Lord's Brother."* As well, it is highly probable that Paul would state to him the vision which he had of the Lord Jesus on his way to Damascus, and that James also would state to Paul the fact that *he* had seen Him also after He rose.

This may be the reason why Paul here mentions the fact, because he had it from the lips of James himself.

The phrase, *"Then of all the Apostles,"* probably refers to those other than the original Twelve. As to who they were, Paul does not say.

Even though all who were witnesses of His Resurrection were definitely not designated as Apostles, still all who were commissioned to Ministry probably were. This one thing is certain, these, whomever they may have been, would definitely have had a special Message, i.e. which would have qualified them to be an Apostle.

(8) "AND LAST OF ALL HE WAS SEEN OF ME ALSO, AS OF ONE BORN OUT OF DUE TIME."

The phrase, *"And last of all He was seen of me also,"* refers to after all the other times in which He appeared to men. As well, it was after He had ascended to Heaven. However, this Passage proves that the Apostle Paul saw the same Lord Jesus, the same body which had been seen by the others or else his assertion would be no proof that He was risen from the dead. In fact, what he saw was not even a Revelation that He had risen; it was a real vision of the ascended Redeemer, who actually spoke with Him (Acts 9:3-6, 17). As is known, this was on the way to Damascus.

The phrase, *"As of one born out of due time,"* does *not* refer, as some think, to the unfitness of the time when he saw the Lord Jesus or that he was that much younger than the Apostles, for he probably wasn't, but rather of one that was exceedingly unworthy. He was meaning that he was not worth regard; that he was unfit to be employed in the service of the Lord Jesus; that he had the same relation to that which was worthy of the Apostolic Office which an abortion has to a living child. The expression seems to be proverbial, and to denote anything that is vile, offensive, loathsome, or unworthy (Num. 12:12).

The phrase, *"One born out of due time,"* actually refers to a dead fetus.

PAUL'S THINKING

The dead fetus is naturally expelled from the womb because it is dead. When Christ appeared to Paul on the road to Damascus, Paul was utterly devoid of spiritual life, a violent persecutor of Christ and of Christ's followers.

In fact, it is thought that the vile name, *"the dead fetus,"* is that which was applied to Paul by his enemies. Paul is thought to take up this ugly term in a manner to admit its truth as applying to himself, yet also in part to offer a correction.

This is not to mean that Paul is thinking of his enemies in this statement. To be frank, we never have difficulty knowing when Paul deals with his slanderers. In such cases, he is very clear.

Paul himself applies this term to himself and at once tells us in what sense it is to be understood.

He uses it in the sense that he alone among the Apostles is *the* unworthy one who came to be placed among their number.

By Paul using the words, *"of me also,"* he presents a tone of deep humility. It is expressive of Paul's feeling that as a nonbeliever he had no right whatsoever to be thus distinguished by the Lord.

NOTES

It has also been suggested that the Corinthians themselves had used the term (one born out of due time) to describe Paul as one who, because of his personal appearance, is something of a *"freak"* in comparison with other Apostles, especially Apollos and Peter. Others have suggested that the term is a play on Paul's name — Paulus, *"the little one."* Hence, they dismissed him as a *"dwarf."*

Of course, there is no proof regarding these accusations, but Verses 9 and 10 do lend at least some small credence to their possibility.

As we have seen throughout, this tension between him and them (Corinthians) over their activities — and supposed theological justification for them — has also brought about the anti-Pauline sentiment that is in part responsible for their divisions as well as their attitude toward him and his Apostleship.

What they see as weakness and, therefore, as evidence of a lesser standing, if in fact they did, he sees as the true evidence that his Apostleship is from the Lord, i.e. *"that only the Grace of God could qualify such a one."*

APPEARANCE

Inasmuch as Paul is addressing himself to the appearances of Christ after the Resurrection, perhaps this would be a good time to look more closely at the word *"appearance"* as it applies to this and all similar occurrences.

Perhaps we might go into more detail than desired by most, still inasmuch as we are speaking of extremely important *"appearances,"* I think the following will be helpful.

We human beings are limited in our view of the universe in which we live. We meet the world through our senses. Sight, smell, hearing, taste, and touch are the avenues that provide us with information, but they do not always enable us to grasp the reality of what we experience.

Words about appearance relate to such sensory perceptions. The Passages in which they are found help us to examine a number of things about God's relationship to this world in which we live.

THE HEBREW WORDS

The Hebrew words usually translated by a word in the *"appear"* group are *"raah* (to see, look at, inspect)*"* and its derivatives *"ri* (looking, appearance)*"* and *"mareh* (sight, appearance).*"* The verb literally means *"seeing with the eyes"* but it has multiple extended and metaphorical uses.

NOTES

These include special uses such as *"seeing"* God's Word (a metaphor for believing acceptance) and *"seeing"* as the act of a Prophet who receives Revelations from God (a Seer).

GOD'S APPEARANCES TO PEOPLE

A number of times the Old Testament speaks of the fact that God has appeared to human beings. He appeared to the Patriarchs (Gen. 12:7; 17:1; 18:1; 26:2, 24; 35:1, 9; 48:3; Ex. 6:3), to Moses in Egypt (Ex. 4:1), a number of times during the Exodus (Ex. 3:2, 16; 4:5; Lev. 9:4, 6, 23; Num. 14:10; 16:19), and less frequently afterward (Judg. 6:12; 13:3, 10; I Sam. 3:21; II Chron. 1:7; 3:1; 7:12).

These Passages do not always tell us how God appeared, and they do not suggest that God was seen in His essential Being. Moses heard a voice speaking from a burning bush. All the people of Israel saw the Glory of God as blazing brightness over the Tabernacle (Num. 14:10). God appeared as the Angel of the Lord both to Gideon and to the wife of Manoah (Judg. 6:12; 13:3).

The significant thing about such Passages is that in some way God acted so that He could be perceived and experienced by human beings, who are limited to sensory capacities that function only in the physical universe. God acted to make Himself known, and in the encounter God also communicated information about Himself.

PEOPLE'S APPEARANCES BEFORE GOD

The Old Testament often refers to such. For instance, during the three annual Festivals, all the men of Israel were required to appear before the Lord (Ex. 23:17; 34:23-24).

When Korah and his followers violated God's Commands, Moses told them to *"appear before the Lord"* on the following day (Num. 16:16). Moses referred to all the people appearing before the Lord during the Feast of Tabernacles (Deut. 31:11).

In each case, the phrase is related to the Worship Center at which God promised to be uniquely present (Deut. 12:7).

When God's Old Testament people wished to worship or to appeal to God, it was to the Tabernacle, and later to the Temple, that they

NOTES

came. Coming to these structures for some specific purpose is always implied in the Old Testament when people *"appeared before God."*

## DESCRIPTION IN PROPHETIC VISIONS

In reading the accounts of Old Testament Prophets, at least as it concerns their Visions, at times it appears that they struggled to communicate what they had seen in these Visions.

Ezekiel saw an immense cloud surrounded by brilliant light, and *"what looked like four living creatures"* (Ezek. 1:5). He attempted to describe them, saying, *"The appearance of the living creatures was like burning coals of fire or like torches"* (Ezek. 1:13).

Joel describes what may be a locust army or a demonic horde and says, *"They have the appearance of horses; they gallop along like cavalry"* (Joel 2:4).

The point in these and similar Prophetic Visions is that what the Prophets actually saw was actually difficult for them to describe, even though the Holy Spirit was inspiring them. In seeking to communicate some image of the vision, the Prophets had to find words that could form a link between what they saw and what their readers may have experienced and to thus could relate.

An excellent example is the Apostle Paul who addressed his *"Visions and Revelations"* but really did not even attempt to portray what he had seen, simply saying, *"And heard unspeakable words, which it is not lawful for a man to utter"* (II Cor. 12:4).

Consequently, even though we must attempt to interpret Prophetic descriptions, we must be careful in doing so. About the best that one can say is that our efforts are approximations, even as the Prophets attempted to frame their report in images that would enable readers to understand at least somewhat, and thereby catch a glimpse of the reality of what they experienced.

## APPEARANCES VERSUS REALITY

In gathering data, we humans are limited to our senses. What we sense this limited way is open to further misinterpretation.

Jacob expresses this concern to his mother as to the plot to deceive the near-blind Isaac. Jacob feared that his masquerade might be discovered and he *"would appear to be tricking him"* (Gen. 27:12). In this case, the conclusion would be justified: the two actually were attempting to trick Isaac.

When Samuel was sent by God to anoint the next king of Israel (I Sam. Chpt. 16), he was impressed by the physique of Eliab, and he thought, *"Surely the Lord's anointed stands here"* (I Sam. 16:6).

But God corrected Samuel. He told him, *"Do not consider his appearance or his height."* God explained that *"The Lord does not look at the things men look at. Men look at the outward appearance, but the Lord looks at the heart"* (I Sam. 16:7). Appearances may be deceiving. Only God, Who sees beyond them, is able to consistently know reality.

## REVELATION

This is a vital reason why Revelation is essential to Faith. What we experience in this world is open to misinterpretation. Even God's mighty acts would be open to misunderstanding if their true meanings were left to those who saw and experienced them.

But God does not leave us confused or uncertain. In His Word, God, through the Prophets and Apostles, explains and interprets what His people experienced. God has spoken in the Scriptures to communicate in Words the shape of a reality our senses can little grasp, if at all.

## APPEARING, AS FULFILLMENT OF PROPHECY

The Old Testament looks back to God's appearances in history to find the anchor for Faith. But the Old Testament also looks forward. The Prophets spoke of what was to happen in the future, and *"appear"* in its ultimate fulfillment.

The point is that what has been foretold actually will be visible to human beings (at least some of them) when it happens in our world of time and space. Thus, Daniel describes world empires that would arise (Dan. 7:23; 11:2-4).

But the Prophets also speak of God once again becoming plainly visible through His Own unmistakable acts. God will appear as His Glory is seen in a restored and righteous Israel (Isa. Chpt. 60). Likewise, He will appear in the judgments preceding and during the restoration (Hos. Chpt. 6; Zech. Chpt. 9; Mal. 3:1-4). Just how complete the appearance of God to people has been and will be is unveiled in the New Testament.

## THE NEW TESTAMENT

Although the range of Greek words translated *"appear"* seems wide respecting the New Testament, still the words retain the traditional emphasis of the Old Testament. All are linked with sight and the notion of becoming visible in an optical or spiritual sense.

What is in view in the New Testament, as in the Old Testament, is human perception of events in the real world. Thus, Angels appear to people (Mat. 1:20; Acts 11:13) and individuals appear before a tribunal for an audience (Acts 5:27; 19:30).

Among the Greek words commonly translated by forms of *"appear"* is *"phaino."* The word means *"to shine or gleam," "to manifest,"* and thus, *"to show."* It is commonly used in the general sense of being visible. Typical uses of *"phaino"* are found in Matthew 1:20; 13:26; Mark 16:9; James 4:14.

## GOD'S REVELATION OF HIMSELF IN JESUS

*"Phaneroo"* is extremely common in the New Testament and in early Christian writings. It is another Greek word which basically means *"to make visible,"* as of Jesus in I Timothy 3:16 (*"He appeared* [was made visible] *in a body"*). John explains that in Jesus' Incarnation, *"the life appeared,"* and he goes on to say that *"we have seen it and testified to it"* (I Jn. 1:2). *"Phaneroo"* is often used of God's Revelation of Himself in Jesus.

Another Greek word, *"Epiphaneia,"* has a distinct and special theological use in the New Testament. It is used only to refer to the future appearance of Jesus in His Second Coming.

## REALITY

In several places, the New Testament deals with the problem of appearances versus reality. Jesus called the rigidly religious Pharisees and teachers of the Mosaic Law who criticized Him hypocrites: *"You are like whitewashed tombs, which look beautiful on the outside but on the inside are full of dead men's bones and everything unclean. In the same way, on the outside you appear to people as righteous but on the inside you are full of hypocrisy and wickedness"* (Mat. 23:27-28).

NOTES

The contrast between what things seem outwardly to be and what they are within is picked up in the Epistles. *"God does not judge by external appearance,"* Paul writes in Galatians 2:6. The Greek phrase is literally *"by the face* (prosopon) *of man."* This word is used in similar phrases in II Corinthians 10:1, 7 and also in Luke 12:56, which speaks of the religious leaders being able to interpret *"the appearance* (face) *of the earth and the sky"* but not being able to interpret the meaning of Jesus' appearance in Israel (Mat. 16:3). In each case, what is visible to the eye is emphasized, along with the fact that some observers are unable to interpret correctly what they see.

## THE CHRISTIAN AND APPEARANCES

A man made the statement the other day that people in Washington D.C. often judge things as they appear to be instead of how they actually are. Scripture warns us that Christians, too, are susceptible to mistaking appearances for reality.

In Colosse, the young Church was attracted to a teaching that called for an ascetic approach to life. To be spiritual, the Colossians were told by false teachers that one must be rigorous in choosing what he eats and drinks, must cut himself off from all pleasures, and must keep a strict religious calendar.

Paul attacks this ascetic perversion of spirituality based on human commands and teachings and not on God's Word: *"Such regulations indeed have an appearance of wisdom* (literally, *'passes for wisdom'*), *... but they lack any value in restraining sensual indulgence"* (Col. 2:23).

These merely human notions of how one grows in his or her relationship with God actually feed the sinful aspects of our personality and have no value for true spiritual growth. But yet, it's a lesson which we do not learn easily.

How do we avoid the traps set by appearances?

Paul's comment to the Colossians is the key. We are to avoid notions *"based on human commands and teachings"* (Col. 2:22). We are to turn instead to the reliable Word of God and let God's inspired writings open our eyes to a reality that lies beyond what we can see or even imagine.

## JESUS' INCARNATION AS AN APPEARANCE

There are two senses in which the New Testament speaks of Jesus' Incarnation as an appearance. The first is reflected in Titus 2:11 (*"The Grace of God that brings Salvation has appeared to all men"*) and 3:4 (*"The Kindness and Love of God our Saviour appeared"*).

These Passages look at the Incarnation as an event with timeless impact. When the Son of God became a man, He made visible in a fresh, totally compelling way the Grace, Kindness, and Love of God of which all the Scriptures testify. As Paul writes in II Timothy 1:9-10, *"Grace was given us in Christ Jesus before the beginning of time, but it has now been revealed through the appearing of our Saviour, Christ Jesus, Who has destroyed death and has brought life and immortality to light through the Gospel."*

THE CORRECT APPEARANCE

The second sense in which Jesus' Incarnation is spoken of as an appearance is found in Philippians 2:8 (Jesus being *"found in appearance as a man"*) and I Timothy 3:16 (*"He appeared in a body"*).

Some have wrongly argued that these Passages deny the true humanity of Jesus, saying that they imply that Jesus only *"seemed"* to be a man. The familiar *"epiphaneo"* is used in I Timothy 3:16; a different word, however, in Philippians 2:8 (*"schema"* rendered *"appearance"*) lays stress on outward appearance. Both Passages emphasize the fact that the Eternal Son of God became visible to humanity in human form, appearing to us as one of us. The rest of Scripture makes it clear that His appearance was in full harmony with reality. In the Incarnation, Jesus truly is both totally God and fully human.

APPEARANCE OF JESUS:
THE SECOND COMING

The news that Jesus had to go away stunned the Disciples. But Jesus immediately reassured them, *"Do not let your hearts be troubled. Trust in God; trust also in Me. In My Father's House are many mansions; if it were not so I would have told you. I am going there to prepare a place for you. And if I go and prepare a place for you, I will come back and take you to be with Me that you also may be where I am"* (Jn. 14:1-3).

These words of promise have brought comfort to generations of Believers since the First Century. Jesus lives. He is preparing for us. And when the time is right, He will return for those who trust Him.

NOTES

The promise of Jesus' return is found in the Early Church's proclamation of the Gospel (Acts 3:19-21), and the Epistles are aglow with excitement at the prospect of His appearing.

COMING TO BE PRESENT WITH US

One of the Greek words associated with Jesus' Second Coming is *"parousia."* The word means *"presence"* or *"coming"* and emphasizes both the idea of *"being there"* and the idea of *"having come."*

Paul uses the word in its everyday sense when he observes that some of the Corinthians say of him, *"His letters are weighty and forceful, but in person ('his bodily presence') he is unimpressive"* (II Cor. 10:10).

*"Parousia"* is sometimes used in a technical sense as the term for an official visit or the arrival of a person of high rank. But even then, the word does not normally emphasize the person's arrival but the fact of that person's physical presence with those to whom he or she has come (I Cor. 16:17; II Cor. 7:6-7; Phil. 2:12).

IN PERSON

When *"parousia"* is used to describe the return of Jesus, our thoughts are directed to the fact that He will return in person and that His being with us will have a transforming impact on our lives.

*"Parousia"* is found four times in the Olivet Discourse (Mat. 24:3, 27, 37, 39). The context makes it clear that Jesus' initial appearing is intended, for the Disciples asked how they could recognize the sign of His Coming. Jesus explains that He will appear suddenly, unexpectedly, and with devastating impact on those who do not believe (Mat. 24:39).

Yet the emphasis in the total passage (Mat. Chpts. 24-25) is not on the meaning of the Second Coming but on the fact that, until Jesus does come, we are to watch, committing ourselves to serve our absent Lord.

The New Testament's basic passage on Resurrection is I Corinthians Chapter 15, even as we are now studying. *"When He comes"* (I Cor. 15:23), His appearance in person will initiate our own Resurrection and mark the beginning of History's end at least as we know such. Jesus, our resurrected Lord, being here, He *"must reign"* and must destroy every competing authority. No enemy can stand in the overpowering Presence of the Glorified Son of God.

THE JOY OF HIS PRESENCE

I Thessalonians three times refers to Jesus' Coming as a *"parousia."* Paul speaks of the joy he will know when he sees his dear converts standing in Jesus' Presence when Jesus is again present with us (I Thess. 2:19).

He asks God to strengthen the converts so they will be blameless and holy at that time (I Thess. 3:13). But it is in I Thessalonians 4:13-18 that Paul unveils more of the exciting meaning for us of Jesus' return.

Paul describes the Resurrection of the believing dead and the transformation of those who are still alive when the Trumpet of God announces the return of Jesus. Caught up and transformed to meet the Lord in the air, *"we will be with the Lord forever"* to experience the joy of His Presence.

THE DESTRUCTION OF THE ENEMY

II Thessalonians corrects misunderstanding of the Thessalonian Church, which was confused by the teaching of some that Jesus had already come (II Thess. 2:1, 2). Paul explains that Jesus will not appear in person until the Antichrist (called the *"lawless one"* here) has been clearly identified by his actions (II Thess. 2:3-12).

Then Jesus will return and, *"by the splendor of His Coming* (the splendor of Jesus personally being here)*"* will destroy this satanically energized enemy.

JAMES AND PATIENCE

James views Jesus' return in a different perspective. He observes the injustice and oppression experienced by God's people and calls for patience. When Jesus is personally present (James 5:7-8), the oppressed will experience a rich harvest of reward.

GLOWS WITH HOPE

Peter speaks of the *"parousia"* three times in his Epistles. he recalls his experience on the Mount of Transfiguration (Mat. Chpt. 17; Mk. Chpt. 9; Lk. Chpt. 9), where he witnessed Jesus shining in the unveiled Glory that will be seen at His Coming.

NOTES

Peter exposes the foolishness of those who hold that the physical universe and its laws are all there is to reality and of those who deride the promise of a personal appearance by Jesus (II Pet. 3:4).

For unbelievers, Jesus' Promised Presence holds out no hope, for they can expect only the certainty of cataclysmic judgment (II Pet. 3:5-7).

For us who believe, however, the prospect of Jesus' return glows with Hope. We are moved to live close to Him, *"so that when He appears we may be confident and unashamed before Him at His Coming"* (I Jn. 2:28; II Pet. 3:11-13).

*"Parousia,"* then: emphasizes the fact that when Jesus appears again, He will come in person to be with us; and, it focuses our attention on the impact that Jesus' return will have on Believers. We will be transformed at His Coming, to share the Glory of His Resurrection and to participate in the joy that comes when the world is at last set right.

COMING TO INTERVENE IN HISTORY

The Greek word *"epiphaneia"* means quite simply *"appearing,"* or *"appearance."* As a spiritual term, it indicates a visible manifestation of a hidden Deity, either in Person or by some great act through which His Presence is revealed.

Jesus will come in a star-burst of power, burning His Image on the retinas of faithless, blinded humanity. The Kindness and Love of God have already appeared (Tit. 2:11; 3:4), but our *"Blessed Hope"* is focused on the day when Jesus Himself will appear in glory to all (Tit. 2:13) (Second Coming).

Titus makes the point that our experience of Saving Grace has taught us to reject ungodliness and worldly passions, for we have been redeemed from wickedness that we might be purified as God's own people (Tit. 2:11-14). Having recognized the Glory of God in Jesus' First Coming, we have also seen the warped and twisted shape of a sin-filled world. But to those without Faith, only the personal intervention of Jesus at His return will expose the corruption.

THE OVERTHROW OF WICKEDNESS

In II Thessalonians 2:8, Paul combines *"epiphaneia"* and *"parousia"* in a most instructive way. He writes of the Antichrist whom Jesus will overthrow and destroy *"by the splendor* (*"epiphaneia"* — flaming, visible manifestation of power) *of His Coming* (Parousia — Personal Presence)." The Presence of Jesus, which means comfort and joy to us, means the overthrow of the evil personage who typifies the sinful world system i.e., *"the Antichrist."*

In II Timothy, Paul, again, contrasts the Glory visible to the eyes of Faith and the Glory that will be unmistakable at Christ's Coming. The eyes of Faith recognize the birth of life and immortality in Jesus' First Coming (II Tim. 1:10).

When Jesus and His Kingdom appear at last, in unmistakable power, all will be subject to judgment (II Tim. 4:1). There will be a crown for those who have seen beyond this world's illusions and who long for Jesus' appearing as something that will shatter the empty hopes of humanity and evaporate the empty values by which this world operates.

A DISRUPTING INTERVENTION

*"Epiphaneia,"* then, emphasizes the fact that Jesus' return will constitute a disrupting intervention in a world that remains blind to God's Grace.

Shattered by His appearance, the world's system of today will be replaced by the long-awaited kingdom of Righteousness and evil will be judged. For the Believer, *"epiphaneia"* contains a challenge. We are to look at the ways of the world in which we live and to utter a decisive *"No!"* to human society's values. We are to commit ourselves simply to doing good while we long for Jesus to return to intervene and at last restore the tangled world to its intended beauty.

COMING TO UNVEIL REALITY

The last word linked closely with Jesus' appearance at His Second Coming is *"apokalypsis."* It means *"to disclose or bring to light."*

In the Bible, *"apokalypsis"* is used particularly to mean the disclosure of supernatural secrets — the unveiling of Truths that people (unaided) could not have discovered but that the Holy Spirit shared with us through Scripture (I Cor. 2:10).

Associated with Jesus' Second Coming, *"apokalypsis"* highlights the fact that while information about Jesus has been shared with humanity and recorded in the Bible, it is Jesus Himself Who will be disclosed when He comes again. Then all preceding Revelation about Him will be unmistakably confirmed.

NOTES

The coming of Jesus as God's final, culminating disclosure will vindicate every Promise and Affirmation of the Word of God.

HUMANITY WILL BE CAUGHT UNAWARE

Luke 17:22-35 describes the shock of that day when Jesus is suddenly revealed, visible to all mankind in His Second Coming. As at the devastation of Sodom, humanity will again be caught unaware, engrossed in daily affairs.

Again in II Thessalonians, the disclosure of Jesus to all mankind is associated with judgment (II Thess. 1:7). Jesus will be seen then in blazing fire, accompanied by His powerful Angels, punishing with *"everlasting destruction"* those who have refused to respond favorably to the Gospel. Romans 8:19 makes it clear that we, too, will one day be disclosed as Children of God.

Thus, we will share in Jesus' Glory (I Pet. 5:1), while He will be *"glorified in His Holy People"* and *"marveled at among all those who have believed"* (II Thess. 1:10).

THE GLORY OF OUR PERSONAL RELATIONSHIP WITH THE LORD

Written against the background of the sufferings we experience in the present world, I Peter also stresses the fact that Jesus' return will display to all people the Glory of a personal relationship with the Lord.

The trial of our faith will result *"in praise, glory, and honor when Jesus Christ is revealed"* (I Pet. 1:7). Today we may know *"an inexpressible and glorious joy"* (I Pet. 1:8). Then all that we experience subjectively will have its objective manifestation.

Knowing this, we rest the full weight of our hope on the return of Jesus and long for *"the Grace to be given* (us) *when Jesus Christ is revealed"* (I Pet. 1:13). If we participate today in Jesus' sufferings, we will *"be overjoyed when His Glory is revealed"* (I Pet. 4:13).

THAT WHICH WILL HAPPEN

*"Apokalypsis,"* then, emphasizes the following facts:

1. Jesus' return will be witnessed by all, His glory at last unmistakable.

2. For the unsaved, this unveiling of Jesus initiates the day of vengeance; for Believers, Jesus' unveiling means that the moment of fulfilled hope has come.

3. For God, Jesus' final disclosure as Lord means full vindication of His Gospel and His warnings to humanity. Jesus will come. Every eye will see Him. Every knee will bow before Him. And every tongue will confess that Jesus Christ is Lord, to the Glory of God the Father (Phil. 2:10-11).

THE SECOND COMING OF JESUS

The Second Coming of Jesus is a rich and complex New Testament theme. Like Jesus' First Coming, it does not take place as a single act, but stretches over a span of time as God's many purposes are worked out at time's end. However, New Testament words associated with Jesus' reappearance help us to see what that return means for us and for others.

The most wonderful Truth for Believers is that Jesus will come in Person for them (the Rapture). In the Resurrection, we will be transformed, enabled at last to share fully in joyful fellowship with God forever.

UNBELIEVERS

For unbelievers, Jesus' appearing will constitute a jarring intervention. All mankind's values and hopes, settled as they are on the narrow confines of this life, will be exposed as empty and meaningless. The glory of our Personally Present Lord will dispel the illusions that captivates humanity and mankind will come face-to-face with reality at last.

By yearning for this intervention, Believers can escape the passions that move the lost, and they can learn to say a final yes to Jesus, which at the same time says no to evil.

GOD'S FINAL AND ULTIMATE SELF-DISCLOSURE

Finally, the return of Jesus is God's final and ultimate Self-disclosure. All that God has shown us in the Words of Scripture will be experienced then by all mankind. Both the delayed judgments and the delayed rewards will be given out, and God will become all in all.

As we meditate on Jesus' appearance, we find our own lives are enriched. Our present sufferings seem increasingly unimportant in view of the glory to come. We toss aside the playthings of the world, with childhood's toys, and we build our lives on those solid realities that, when Jesus comes, will remain (Richards).

NOTES

(9) "FOR I AM THE LEAST OF THE APOSTLES, THAT AM NOT MEET TO BE CALLED AN APOSTLE, BECAUSE I PERSECUTED THE CHURCH OF GOD."

The phrase, *"For I am the least of the Apostles,"* presents not mock modesty but rather the most deep humility.

Paul knew the special Gifts which he had received from God. He was well aware that to him had been entrusted the ten talents rather than the one talent. He could appeal, consequently, to far vaster results than had been achieved by the work of any other Apostle.

He knew his own importance as *"a chosen vessel,"* a special instrument in God's hands to work out exceptional results. But in himself he always felt, and did not shrink from confessing, that he was *"nothing."* (II Cor. 12:11).

In Ephesians 3:8, he goes further, and calls himself, *"less than the least of all Saints,"* though even there he claims to have been the special Apostle of the Gentiles (Farrar).

HIS FEELINGS

Paul's feelings were not on account of any defect in his commission or any want of qualification respecting his consecration before the Lord, but rather on account of the great crime of his life, the fact that he had been a persecutor of the followers of Christ. He could never forget that; as a man who had been profane and a scoffer, when he becomes converted, can never forget the deep guilt of his former life. The effect will be to produce humility, and a deep sense of unworthiness, ever afterward.

And yet, a person *is* what they are in Christ, and nothing else. It all pertains to Christ and one's position in Christ, and not what one was before Christ, or not what others think at present concerning one's position in Christ. Fortunately what others think does not count. It's what God knows!

WHAT IS IN PAUL'S MIND

Of course, only the great Apostle himself fully knew; however, I think he is actually speaking of the original Twelve and not all Apostles in general, concerning him being the least of the Apostles.

The Twelve (Matthias having taken the place of Judas) were Apostles who had been duly selected and appointed by the Lord followed by a course of training and preparation. And to them, the Lord appeared after His Resurrection.

Paul, before conversion, was a persecutor of the Church, a vile, dead thing spiritually, fit only to be carried out and buried from sight. Yet to *him,* while being such, the risen Lord also appeared — he, the abortion, placed at the side of these living men, treated, honored, dignified like them by the Lord! (Lenski).

I think that such constituted such an act of Grace, such a work of Grace, such a magnitude of Grace for that matter, that Paul, even though the great Apostle of Grace, still could not accept the magnitude of it all.

Why?

How?

And yet, when honestly and truthfully looking at ourselves, and considering that which the Lord has done for us in His Mercy and Grace, I think all must come to the same conclusion as Paul, *"I am the least . . ."*

The phrase, *"That am not meet to be called an Apostle,"* in effect says, *"I am not fit or worthy to be regarded as a follower of the Lord Jesus, or as appointed to defend His Cause, or to bear His Name among the Gentiles."*

I think it is obvious that the Apostle had a deep sense of his unworthiness, which, incidentally, is the total opposite of much of the modern Faith Message. The memory of his former life ever tended to keep him humble.

PAUL'S ANSWER

There were many in the Early Church of that time, who were not at all sympathetic toward Paul. While this would *not* have included any of the original Twelve, it was in fact, the feeling among many. Understanding that the beginning years of the Church were made up almost exclusively of Jews, and that many of them did not take lightly the idea of laying aside Judaism, even as Paul demanded, and as well, that they looked at him as some type of interloper, especially considering that he had been a persecutor of the Church, consequently, there was jealousy it seems, respecting his proclaimed position. Some even denied that he was an Apostle. In other words, he was not a part of the inner circle, and as well, his independent spirit seemed to rub some the wrong way.

His answer to these charges and jealousies, whatever they may have been, portrays the total Spirit of Christ *"Who, when He was reviled, reviled not again"* (I Pet. 2:23).

NOTES

While he did affirm that he *is* an Apostle, he answered the charges by viewing himself even in a lesser way than did his detractors. He would take the situation a step further, saying that he does *"not even deserve to be called an Apostle"*; however, his reason for his feelings would be totally different than theirs. His reason has to do with his former way of life: *"because I persecuted the Church of God."*

WHAT THIS TELLS US ABOUT THE MAN

As we have already stated, what a person is in Christ *is* what that person is. Irrespective as to what others may think, be it good or bad, such thinking does not add to or take away from that particular individual. What a man is in Christ is what the man is, and in reality, is the only thing that is actually important. When it is all said and done, the praises or slurs of men will fall away, with Christ Alone being left as the eternal Judge.

Did it hurt the Apostle for remarks of negative nature to be made about him? For many to deny his place and position in the Body of Christ and the Work of God?

Of course, it did! As long as we are human, those things will sting; however, they have an affect on a person only as that person allows such to have an affect. Otherwise, it is of no consequence.

Paul's answer shows that he knew fully and totally what and who he was in Christ; therefore, instead of defending himself against the slurs, insults, and unkindnesses, he depreciates himself even further, but as stated, for a different reason.

BUT YET, WHAT DID THE LORD THINK OF ALL OF THIS?

While Paul brushed aside the insults, still, one can be absolutely certain that the Lord did not do such concerning His attitude and judgment respecting the situation. To speak disparagingly of that which belongs to Christ, is to speak disparagingly of Christ. To touch one who belongs to the Lord, is to touch the Lord and if it is negative, is not wise to say the least!

There have been few men in history, if any in fact, who have been used by the Lord as was Paul. The Lord entrusted him with the New Covenant, which is the single most important happening in History. In respect to this, he wrote almost half of the New Testament. He, under Christ, is literally the founder of the Church.

Understanding this, what does the reader think the Lord thought about those who named the Name of Christ, and yet opposed Paul?

I have always had a fear in my heart, of opposing that which is truly of God, or of accepting that which is really not of the Lord. Either way presents a lose/lose position.

The phrase, *"Because I persecuted the Church of God,"* presents such being graphically described in Acts Chapter 9. This was the one sin for which, though he knew that God had forgiven him (I Tim. 1:13), yet still bothered him, and for the obvious reasons.

Regarding the language used in Acts Chapter 9, this persecution by Paul as leveled against the Church, was probably more deadly than usually supposed, involving not only torture, but actual bloodshed (Acts 8:3; 9:1). I speak of bloodshed other than the martyrdom of Stephen.

The poet said:

*"Saints, did I say? With your remembered faces;*
*"Dear men and women whom I sought and slew?*
*"Oh, when I meet you in the heavenly places,*
*"How will I weep to Stephen and to you!"*

DECEPTION

While a persecutor, Paul thought he was doing God a favor; for him this was *"zeal"* for the Lord and *"advancement"* in Judaism. But on this side of his encounter with the Risen Lord, he saw himself for what he really was, the chief of sinners (I Tim. 1:15) and persecutor of the Church of God.

Out of this encounter, which without a doubt is one of the most remarkable in history, comes the basis of his theology of Grace. Even though he greatly found the teaching of Grace in the Old Testament, in which he was helped by the Holy Spirit, still, I feel his personal experience with Christ, played just as much a part in his theology as did all else. Since God was gracious to him, God's enemy, in this way, he came eventually to realize this is the way God is toward all, Jew and Gentile alike, making no distinctions. Since all alike are sinful, all alike are potential recipients of God's Grace.

NOTES

In like manner he views his Apostleship. It is a matter of Grace, and Grace alone. Since his detractors have not given him his authority, they can neither take it from him nor deny it to him. It has been given him by a Gracious Act of God, which point he will make in the next Verse (Fee).

THE EFFECT

The Apostle always aimed at a moral as well as a mental effect in his writings. Hence, he magnified the Grace that saved him — a persecutor, an abortion, a man not worthy to be the least of the Apostles, and yet that Grace energized him so effectually that he accomplished more than all the Apostles put together.

In Romans 11:13 and in II Corinthians 6:4, he magnified not himself but the ministry which Grace committed to him (Williams).

It is evident, however, that deeply as Paul might feel his unworthiness and his unfitness to be called an *"Apostle,"* yet that did not render him an incompetent witness of what he had seen. In fact, he *was* unworthy; but he had no doubt that he had seen the Lord Jesus; and amidst all the expressions of his deep sense of his unfitness for his Office, he never intimates the slightest doubt that he had seen the Saviour and that the Saviour had changed him totally and completely.

He felt himself fully qualified to testify to that; and with unwavering firmness he did testify to it to the end of his life.

HUMILITY

Humility does not disqualify a man to give testimony, but rather furnishes an additional qualification, hence, the Holy Spirit having the Apostle to answer as he did. His detractors denigrated him, but he answered as stated, by denigrating himself even to a greater degree. Consequently, there is no man to whom we listen more attentively, or whose words we more readily believe, than the modest and humble man, the man who has had abundant opportunities to observe that of which he testifies, and yet who is deeply humble. Such a man was the Apostle Paul; and he evidently felt that, much as he felt his unworthiness, and ready as he was to confess it, yet he also at the same time boldly proclaims that the word he gives is from the Lord, i.e., *"The Word of God."* Here we witness true humility and true meekness. It understands who and what it is without Christ, but at the same time what it is in Christ. Consequently, it can boldly proclaim.

(10) "BUT BY THE GRACE OF GOD I AM WHAT I AM: AND HIS GRACE WHICH WAS BESTOWED UPON ME WAS NOT IN VAIN; BUT I LABOURED MORE ABUNDANTLY THAN THEY ALL: YET NOT I, BUT THE GRACE OF GOD WHICH WAS WITH ME."

The phrase, *"But by the Grace of God I am what I am,"* concerns the Favor or Mercy of God. What I have is to be traced to Him and not to any native tendency to goodness, or any native inclination to His service, or to any merit of my own.

All my hopes of Heaven; all my zeal; all my success; all my piety; all my Apostolic endowments, are to be traced to Him.

THE WHY OF PAUL'S STATEMENT

Nothing is more common to the writings of Paul than a disposition to trace all that he had to the mere Mercy and Grace of God. And nothing is a more certain indication of true piety than such a disposition.

At least one of the reasons that Paul here introduces this particular subject seems to be this:

He had incidentally, and undesignedly, introduced a comparison in one respect between himself and the other Apostles. He had not had the advantages which they had. Most of all, he was overwhelmed with the recollection that he had been a persecutor.

He seemed to feel that there was a peculiar obligation resting on him to make by diligence for the want of their advantages of an early personal conversation with the Lord Jesus, and to express his gratitude that so great a sinner had been made an Apostle (Barnes).

NOT IN VAIN

The phrase, *"And His Grace which was bestowed upon me was not in vain,"* tells us something about Grace and the Work of God.

In these statements, Paul makes this point:

God's Grace in his case *"was not without effect."* That is, it did not become something given *"in vain."*

Most likely this sentence points in two directions. On the one hand, it points back to Verse 2 with that Scripture implying that Grace can in fact, be given in vain, and forward to Verse 14, where it seems there is considerable danger that if the Corinthians persisted in their present folly, God's Grace to them will have turned out to be *"in vain."*

NOTES

WHAT DOES IT MEAN FOR THE GRACE OF GOD TO BE BESTOWED IN VAIN?

*"Vain"* in the Greek is *"kenos"* and means *"literally empty."*

Arising out of the basic act of Pardon and legal acquittal (Rom. 8:31), which characterizes the act of Grace as it refers to Salvation, Paul understands the whole movement of the Christian Life from beginning to end as Grace (Jn. 1:16; Rom. 5:2; II Cor. 6:1-9). It is guaranteed by being anchored in the Purpose of God (Rom. 8:28).

Human weakness, not self-determination, is its sphere of activity (II Cor. 12:9). In effect, the Grace of God makes the new man what he is (I Cor. 15:10), which is exactly what we are studying. It might even be said that he remains as dependent upon Grace as a diabetic is upon insulin.

So, the Grace of God is not only that which actually brings about our Salvation, but as well, the Grace of God thereafter, enables us to live the life we should live in Christ, and be what we ought to be for Christ.

THE DEFINITION OF GRACE

The common definition is *"unmerited favor."* To perhaps better explain *"Grace,"* one possibly could say that *"Grace is the Goodness of God extended to undeserving Saints."* God has no more Grace presently than He did 3,000 years ago. In fact, God cannot change. It is the Cross which has made it possible for Grace to be extended to individuals in an uninterrupted flow, and without measurement. As we've said repeatedly, Christ is the Source, but the Cross is the means.

The following possibly may help explain that.

THE GOSPELS AND GRACE

The word *"Grace"* was never used by our Lord except on four occasions in the ordinary sense of *"thanks"* (Lk. 6:32-34; 17:19). In fact, it is entirely absent from both Matthew and Mark. Luke alone of the three synoptists mentioned it

NOTES

on four other occasions, three of which have the sense of favor (1:28, 30; 2:52). The fact that Jesus never used the term *"charis,"* which is the Greek word for *"grace,"* in any other way than that of *"thanks"* is significant for two reasons:

1. Some erroneously claim that the Early Church attempted to force meaning into the statements of Christ, which actually was not there. The Early Church took the words of Christ literally, at least as far as possible, as they were neither adding nor subtracting.

2. It makes evident that Jesus could not have used a word to convey what Paul, for example, afterwards sought to express by the Greek word *"charis,"* for the reason that His Own Death and Resurrection were the facts which were to give to the concept its real meaning.

As stated, Christ is the Source, while the Cross is the means.

## JESUS AND GRACE

When Jesus spoke, the people did not simply marvel at the charming way in which He spoke, or at its fascinating effects. Jesus indicated that His Presence in the world was to have a result wider and deeper than any nationalistic aid to the people of Israel. This was more than a hint of the Gospel as *"Grace for all."* While Luke, of all the synoptic writers, was impressed by the gracious manner of Christ's teaching, he wishes his readers also to be aware of the gracious matter of His teaching. The words of our Lord caused many to marvel because they came as *"words of Grace about Grace."*

Throughout the Gospels in several ways, the category of Grace was demonstrated in Christ's acts and teaching. He came to fulfill a Divine commission. The recurrent phrase, *"I am come"* (Mat. 9:13; 10:34; Lk. 12:51), accentuates this acceptance. He had come as the Father's Beloved Son to seek and to save that which was lost. That is Grace!

By His attitude, Jesus demonstrated what is meant by Grace. He sought out the sinful. This is a new note of the Gospel. Judaism taught that God was ready to be Gracious, but was inclined to leave the first step with the sinner. The distinctive thing with Jesus was His taking of the deliberate initiative on God's behalf. That is Grace! The whole tendency of His teaching was in the same direction.

There are Passages in His recorded proclamations, the logical drift of which is that Salvation is a matter of God's free generosity. In the illustration concerning the rich young ruler (Mk. 10:17-31), for example, the astonished Disciples ask, *"Then who can be saved?"* They are answered that the ultimate right to enter the Kingdom of God and be saved lies with God. Christ enunciates the Gospel of Grace in contrast with the Gospel of Law and Works.

Several critical writers introduce the term *"Grace"* at this point to bring out the essential meaning of Christ's reply. A place in His Kingdom is not gotten by anything given up for God. It is given by the Father, and the Father's Giving is the Father's Grace.

*What are we to get?"* asked the Disciples, with the Parable of the Laborers in the Vineyard in mind (Mat. 20:1-8). They are reminded of the folly of bargaining with God. The final principle of God's dealing with men is a matter of Grace. The Parable of the Pharisee and the Publican shows clearly that *"Grace is Grace"* because, though wholly concerned with moral goodness, it does not at all depend upon how moral we are.

## THE CROSS AND GRACE

The symbolism of the Last Supper makes clear that Jesus wished to indicate that the Divine purpose of Grace was focused in His Cross. The Blood of the Cross inaugurated a New Covenant and was essential to God as a means and medium of His saving work. It was not a post factum explanation of what had happened. From the beginning, the Life and Work of Christ was read in the category of Grace. The story of the Cross was not given as an account of how the Life of Jesus ended, but as revealing the basis upon which God's Grace is assured and secured.

Two broad facts are clear from the record of the Gospels. On the one hand, it is evident that the saving initiative is with God; and, on the other hand, any plea to human merit is ruled out. While Jesus is not the source of the term *"Charis,"* which describes these two facts, His Own Person is the Source of the *"Grace"* of which the whole New Testament speaks. It was the Apostle Paul who took these twin ideas and included them under the one pregnant term *"Charis."*

## PAUL AND GRACE

While all the shades of meaning noted earlier are to be found in the New Testament, not all of them together convey the richness which the term acquired in the theology of Paul. For him, *"Grace"* was nothing less than the unsought and unbought saving activity of God which made him a debtor forever. The Damascus Road encounter with the Risen Jesus brought to focus the two basic ideas which unite in the word *"Charis"*— that the saving initiative is with God and human merit is of no avail.

By *"Grace,"* then, is meant that Salvation is from first to last a Gift of God, all made possible by the Cross. God's saving relation to man has its beginning and ending in His Own eternal purpose as the counterfoil of history. He loves because He would love; saves because He would save. God acts in Grace; acts without waiting for a sign or a nod from us. This is Grace!

## THE EPISTLES OF PAUL

The idea of the absoluteness of Grace in man's Salvation is especially indicated by the fact that Paul never begins or ends his letters without a reference to Grace. By beginning as he does, Paul is suggesting the supremacy of Grace as the source from which flow all the blessings of the new order into which God's unmerited favor has brought the redeemed soul. Everything rests on God's free Grace in Christ. In so using it, the Apostle was virtually authenticating his position as an Apostle to whom the Grace of God had come in such abundance.

At the beginning, Paul always associates *"Grace"* and *"Peace,"* while, in his salutations, the close connection of the two concepts is not always immediately seen. The Apostle seldom concludes without some reference to *"Peace."* The two words, *"Grace"* and *"Peace,"* seem always to be associated in his mind; the term *"Peace"* comes somewhere in the context (II Cor. 13:11-13; Eph. 6:23-24; I Thess. 5:23-28; II Thess. 3:16-18).

As the first word of greeting and the last word of salutation, *"Grace"* sums up for the Apostle the totality of the blessings which come from God through Christ. *"Grace"* is the Source; *"Peace"* the stream. *"Grace"* denotes the Love of God manifested in the form of pardon toward sinful men; *"Peace,"* the feeling of profound calm or inward quiet which is communicated to the heart by the possession of reconciliation.

## THE DISPENSATION OF GRACE

Since the Cross, we have the privilege of living in the Dispensation of Grace. While Christ is the Source of all Grace, the Cross is the means by which such Grace is given unto us. In fact, it is impossible for Grace to be imparted to anyone without the benefit of the Cross. Even the Grace which was dispensed in Old Testament times was dispensed, as one might say, on credit, thereby looking forward to the Cross which was to come. Then it was a Prophetic Jesus, while now it is an Historical Jesus.

Being Prophetic, and thereby in the future, Grace was necessarily limited in Old Testament times. But yet, every single good thing we read about in the Old Testament, every miracle, every goodness of God shown to His people, always and without exception, all were through the principle of Grace. The Cross opened it up, as if floodgates were opened, with mercy drops no longer falling, but rather showers pouring down upon God's people.

Because we are living in the Dispensation of Grace, millions of Christians think that Grace is automatic, meaning that it just simply comes to us because we are living in the Dispensation of Grace. Nothing could be further from the truth.

## FRUSTRATING THE GRACE OF GOD

Paul said, *"I am crucified with Christ* (the foundation of all victory; Paul here takes us back to Romans 6:3-5)*: nevertheless I live* (have new life)*; and yet not I* (not by my own strength and ability)*, but Christ lives in me* (by virtue of my dying with Him on the Cross and being raised with Him in newness of life)*: and the life which I now live in the flesh* (my daily walk before God) *I live by the Faith of the Son of God* (the Cross is ever the object of my Faith)*, Who loved me and gave Himself for me* (which is the only way that I could be saved).

*"I do not frustrate the Grace of God* (if we make anything other than the Cross of Christ the object of our Faith, we frustrate the Grace of God, which means we stop its action, and the Holy Spirit, Who is the Dispenser of Grace, will no longer help us)*: for if Righteousness come by the Law* (any type of Law)*, then Christ is dead in vain."* (If I can successfully live for the Lord by any means other than Faith in Christ and the Cross, then the Death of Christ was a waste [Gal. 2:20-21].)

As I think has already been made obvious, if the Believer places his faith in anything other than Christ and the Cross, and I mean anything, we *"frustrate the Grace of God,"* which means that we stop its work and action. Such a position, a position, I might quickly add, in which the majority of modern Christendom finds itself, leads to untold trouble. Virtually the entirety of modern Christendom is frustrating the Grace of God. They are doing it because they do not understand the Cross, as it regards Sanctification; therefore, they try to live for God in all the wrong ways, thereby frustrating the Grace of God.

FALLING FROM GRACE

Paul also said, *"Behold* (Mark my words!) *I Paul say unto you* (presents the Apostle's authority regarding the Message he brings), *that if you be circumcised, Christ shall profit you nothing.* (If the Believer goes back into Law, and Law of any kind, what Christ did at the Cross on our behalf will profit us nothing. One cannot have it two ways.)

*"For I testify again to every man who is circumcised* (some of the Galatian Gentiles were being pressured by false teachers to embrace the Law of Moses, which meant they would have to forsake Christ and the Cross, for it's not possible to wed the two; as well, it's not possible to wed any Law to Grace), *that he is a debtor to do the whole Law* (which, of course, is impossible; besides, the Law contained no Salvation).

*"Christ is become of no effect unto you* (this is a chilling statement, and refers to anyone who makes anything other than Christ and the Cross the object of his faith), *whosoever of you are justified by the Law* (seek to be justified by the Law); *you are fallen from Grace"* (fallen from the position of Grace, which means the Believer is trusting in something other than the Cross; it actually means *"to apostatize"* [Gal. 5:2-4]).

Even after having the Grace of God extended to man, if at some point he desires to walk in disobedience, he is a free moral agent and can do so. However, if such is the case, the Grace of God is given to that individual in vain.

The phrase, *"But I laboured more abundantly than they all,"* proclaims that which Grace enabled Paul to do.

PAUL'S LABORS AND THE GRACE OF GOD

Only when the fruits of this labor are made the chief point, can Paul turn about and ascribe everything he has done to the Grace of God. To be sure, it was Grace that prompted him to work strenuously, but one may often work with tireless zeal and yet bring forth only meager results. We are not able to say just how much effort the other Apostles put forth; it must have been a great deal. No one is able to make a comparison with Paul on this point. For Paul to do so would not be seemly; it would sound too much like self-praise, which is far from Paul's mind.

It would also convey the criticism that the other Apostles should have worked harder than they did and thus have been equal to Paul. All this disappears when the point of Paul's statement is perceived, namely that he is thinking about the result of his labor.

As a matter of mere fact, these results are outstanding. Witness the record of the Book of Acts and the evidence in Paul's Epistles.

Paul intends as is obvious, to say a great deal when he compares results he has achieved with those of the other Apostles. Exactly how much?

Does he intend to say that he accomplished more than any one of the other Apostles or more than all of them together?

The words as they stand express the latter thought.

The phrase, *"Yet not I, but the Grace of God which was with me,"* presents the Apostle truthfully saying what he does regarding the results attained by him, but he does not dream taking any credit to himself.

GRACE ALONE ACHIEVED ALL THESE RESULTS

Now follows the main statement, *"yet not I; on the contrary the Grace of God with me."*

This contrast of *"I"* with *"the Grace of God"* is conclusive evidence that Paul thinks chiefly of the results of his labor. It is literally true: Grace alone achieved all these results.

Paul is not merely ascribing them to Grace with a sort of humble generosity on his part. When he thinks of what he originally was and then looks at these results, he finds only one explanation: *"not I — but God's Grace."*

This doesn't mean that Grace alone performed these great things, for Paul, too, was by no means inactive. In fact, Grace and Paul are in association, even as the Work of Grace must follow the same principle with all. While the laborer must say, *"Thy pound hath gained ten pounds!"* This laborer is not the slothful servant who folded his hands and did nothing.

NOTES

Consequently, it would be a mistake to picture God's Grace and Paul's effort as two horses together drawing a wagon, for the two are not coordinate.

Paul's effort is, in the last analysis, due to God's Grace, and it is put forth only as long as the Holy Spirit rules, guides, and leads him.

PAUL'S PURPOSE

Verses 9 and 10 are a digression. But is not Paul's purpose to defend himself and his office against opponents in Corinth? To attach such a defense to a statement concerning Christ's appearance to him on the way to Damascus would be strange indeed. Moreover, these two Verses do not constitute a defense. Paul is moved to add this digression as an expression of his inmost feeling to the greatness of the Grace of God vouchsafed to him. When he thinks back to that great moment near Damascus and to all for which God has since used him he is overwhelmed with humble, shamefaced gratitude, and joy; he must worship and magnify the Grace that wrought it all by using him.

Thus, in Pauline theology, even though his labor is a response to Grace, it is more properly seen as the effect of Grace. All is of Grace; nothing is deserved. Neither, therefore, can he lay claim to his own Ministry, nor can others truly reject it, even though they may attempt to do so. It is God's activity in him on their behalf.

Although God's Gracious Gift of Apostleship was the result of Divine initiative, and Divine initiative alone, hence all of Grace, nonetheless it requires Paul's response, just as it requires our response, i.e., *"proper response."* If not, the Grace of God will be given to us in *"vain"* (Fee).

(11) "THEREFORE WHETHER IT WERE I OR THEY, SO WE PREACH, AND SO YE BELIEVED."

The phrase, *"Therefore whether it were I or they, so we preach,"* has reference to the fact that the Leaders of the Early Church, which of course, included the Apostles of the Lord, no matter to which of these notable heralds they listen, they will always hear the identical testimony and proclamation: *"The Lord is risen; He is risen indeed!"* There was no difference on this all important point.

The idea is, the Message of the Resurrection is what they had been preaching, what they were preaching, and what they would continue to preach right along.

NOTES

*"We are preaching,"* means *"as long as we preach at all, no matter whether men refuse to believe or are willing to believe, we do not stop preaching, neither do we stop preaching this Message."*

The phrase, *"And so ye believed,"* refers to the fact that preaching is intended to engender believing, and that believing is the normal response to preaching.

Voices in Corinth are questioning the Resurrection in general. If they are right, then Christ is not risen, and all this testimony adduced by Paul is false. Then the Corinthians must change what they have believed until this moment, which of course, puts an entirely different perspective on everything.

THE VERY CENTER OF THE CHRISTIAN FAITH

The Holy Spirit now emphasizes the very center of the Christian Faith, which of course, is the Resurrection. It is not that the Resurrection was more important than Calvary, for it isn't. The idea is, that without the Resurrection, Calvary is to no avail. In other words, the Resurrection ratified Calvary.

The manner in which Paul addresses this subject, enables the Corinthians, even the doubters among them, to give their undisturbed attention to the central fact on which their Faith rests and in their inmost hearts to reaffirm the Faith they have held to the present moment. No deflecting thought has had an opportunity to disturb this reaffirmation. Paul has not left, and will not leave any room whatsoever for side excursions. They must reaffirm their faith in Christ's Resurrection and do so in totality, exactly as Paul has always preached this Gospel to them, and exactly as all of the Apostles preached, or else deny the totality of Christianity.

The effect produced must have been very strong when Paul's words were first read in Corinth.

THE PREACHING OF THE GOSPEL

The manner in which God has chosen to present to the world the proclamation of the greatest Story ever told is through the medium of men and women Preaching the Gospel. *"To preach"* means *"to make proclamation as a herald."* A *"herald"* is a public messenger who lifts up his voice and claims public attention to some definite news he has to announce. Then the Christian preaching (I Cor. 1:21) is the public proclamation of the *"Good News"* to the world, for the meaning of the word *"Gospel"* is *"Good News."*

## A DIFFERENCE

Yet there is a difference between the proclamation of a town crier, or in modern terminology one who delivers the news by Television, Radio, etc., and the preaching of the Gospel. A herald may be more or less indifferent to the news he proclaims. The Christian Preacher, on the contrary, is a man who himself has been *"laid hold on by Christ Jesus"* (Phil. 3:12), and who personally believes in the Good News he announces to others.

Another difference is that of preaching and teaching.

The New Testament writers draw a clear distinction between *"to preach"* and *"preaching"* on the one hand, and *"to teach"* and *"teaching"* on the other. Preaching is the proclamation of the Gospel to men who have not yet accepted it. Teaching is an instruction or exhortation on various aspects of the Word of God addressed to Believers already established in the Faith. As someone has said, preaching proclaims the Gospel, while teaching explains the Gospel.

The difference between preaching and teaching explains the fact, at first sight astonishing, that the Old Testament scarcely used the term *"preaching"* to describe the mission of the Prophets. In fact, their commission was to exhort the elect people to remain faithful to their God.

It may well be compared with the charge of the New Testament Preacher; however, these Prophets of Old Testament times were not bringing news; they were asking rather for a better and stricter obedience to the given Law.

In two cases only, the terms *"preaching"* and *"to preach"* have in the Prophets their present meaning. First, in the Book of Jonah (3:2), the Prophet must *"preach the Message"* of God to non-Jews, in this instance, the Ninevites.

Second, the terms *"to evangelize"* and *"to preach"* are used by Isaiah (61:1-2) and Luke (4:18-21) to announce the Good News of the coming Salvation, which of course, would be brought by Jesus Christ.

NOTES

## THAT WHICH SHOULD BE PREACHED

In Matthew, Mark, and Luke, we see Jesus *"preaching the Gospel of God"* (Mk. 1:14).

In the Pauline letters, we commonly read of *"preaching Christ."* In the Book of Acts, both forms of expression are used. The Apostles preach *"Jesus"* (Acts 17:18) or *"Christ"* (Acts 8:5), and they preach the *"Kingdom of God"* (Acts 28:31).

These differed expressions are by no means opposed to one another. They only mark the development of the Message in line with the development of the history of Salvation from the days of Jesus to the Apostolic age.

## THE PREACHING OF JESUS

By His proclamation that *"the time is fulfilled, and the Kingdom of God is at hand; repent, and believe the Gospel"* (Mk. 1:15), Jesus did not simply continue the Ministry of John the Baptist. He rather accomplished it, and appeared as that *"Greater One"* the Baptist had announced.

The belief in the Gospel (Good News) which Jesus requires is loyalty to Him as the Representative of the Kingdom, as the King and Messiah. Since the days of Jesus' Ministry and later, since Jesus' Death and Resurrection, the Kingdom begins to be realized in Jesus, although it is true that the Kingdom itself, materially speaking, is yet to come.

Thus, after Jesus' days, the Kingdom of God is still to be announced. Yet the preaching of the Kingdom necessarily becomes likewise the preaching of Jesus or Christ, Who has brought the Kingdom nearer by His Words and Mighty Works of Salvation.

## APOSTOLIC PREACHING

The preaching of the Apostles, in effect, began with Peter on the Day of Pentecost (Acts 2:14-40). As well, Peter and the other Apostles continued preaching in Jerusalem after Pentecost (Acts 3:12-26; 5:29-32), with them then spreading out to other parts (Acts Chpts. 8 and 10).

That of which they preached could have probably been summarized as follows:

God has realized the Promises of the Old Testament and brought Salvation to His people

(Acts 2:16-21, 23; 3:18, 24; 10:43). This has taken place through the Ministry, Death, and Resurrection of Jesus (Acts 2:22-24; 3:13-15; 10:37-39).

Jesus has been exalted as *"Lord and Christ"* (Acts 2:36). The Holy Spirit in the Church is the Sign of Christ's Present Power and Glory (Acts 2:33; 5:32). However, Salvation will not reach its consummation until the return of Christ to judge the living and the dead (Acts 3:21; 10:42).

The Apostles were chosen by God as witnesses of the Ministry of Jesus and above all of His Resurrection, even as Paul here is addressing (Acts 2:32; 3:15; 10:40-41; I Cor. 15:4-7). They addressed to their hearers an appeal for Repentance and offered to the Believers forgiveness of sins and the Gift of the Holy Spirit (Acts 2:38-39; 3:25-26; 5:31; 10:43).

In short, the primitive preaching of the Apostles is a proclamation of the Work of Salvation made by God in Christ and a Call to believe and to be Saved.

THE PREACHING OF PAUL

Paul's preaching does not essentially differ from the Preaching of the Apostles and others, as he himself testifies, which refers to the Text of our study, I Corinthians 15:11.

However, his Messages recorded in the Book of Acts (Acts 13:16-41; 14:15-17; 17:22-31) in effect, reveal, besides some minor differences, an important new element.

As the Apostle to the Gentiles, addressing pagan audiences, Paul adds to the Preaching of Christ an appeal for Faith in the Living God Who made the heavens and the earth (Acts 14:15; 17:24; I Thess. 1:9).

PREACHING AND TEACHING

Jesus preached the Gospel openly to the crowds, but He reserved His Teaching for His Disciples, thus revealing to them His most profound thoughts and particularly the mystery of His Own Person (Mk. 8:31-32).

Likewise, the Apostles gave teaching to those who had already accepted the preaching, i.e. *"accepted Christ"* (Acts 2:42; Col. 1:28). In fact, the far greater part of the New Testament Epistles is not preaching but teaching.

The Teaching develops the fullness of the Gospel Message in order that the Believers may become mature in Christ.

NOTES

For instance, Paul in effect, is preaching when he writes: *"Do ye not know that the unrighteous will not inherit the Kingdom of God?"* (I Cor. 6:9-10), but then he reverts back to teaching as he explains what a correct Christian Life actually is (I Cor. Chpts. 5 and 6).

(Bibliography: C.H. Dodd, *"The Apostolic Preaching and Its Development"*; F.W. Gorsheide, *"The Pauline Epistles; A Synopsis of Early Christian Preaching"*; F.V. Filson.)

WHAT DOES IT MEAN TO BELIEVE?

In this 11th Verse, to which we address our commentary, Paul spoke of the Corinthians who had believed the Message he had delivered, which was the Message of the Crucified, Risen, Ascended, and Exalted Lord, and were, therefore, saved, i.e. *"became Believers."*

Over and over again as we study the Epistles, we find that faith in Jesus does not actually come through an observation of miracles, signs, wonders, etc. Faith is born as we learn about Jesus, find out what He said, and put our trust in Him. We then go on to deeper Faith, and an active reliance on the Power and Presence of God.

And as we trust, our life opens up to all sorts of possibilities. Miracles follow Faith. Believing, we experience God at work in our lives.

So, in the strict sense of the word, miracles are not the cause of Faith, but rather the result of Faith.

BELIEVING AND EVIDENCE

In Christian Faith, knowing and believing are linked. We respond to testimony about Jesus with our intellect as well as with our heart. For instance, John's Gospel looks at two kinds of testimony. They are the Testimony of Jesus' Miracles and the Testimony of Jesus' Words.

At times, these two lines of Testimony enhance each other. Thus, the Twelve, who were already committed to Jesus, saw the miracle at Cana (Jn. 2:11) and found their belief in Jesus strengthened.

It is not unusual to find that many of the observers of Jesus' Works were moved to some kind of belief. The Testimony of His Miracles was compelling (Jn. 7:31; 11:45; 12:11). Yet others who saw the same signs chose not to believe, rejecting Jesus *against* the evidence of the Lord's Works (Jn. 10:38; 14:11).

In John, we see that the Testimony provided by miracles and signs forces observers to take Jesus seriously. But signs and miracles alone did not bring about saving Faith.

## SUPERFICIAL BELIEF

John distinguishes between two types of *"believing."* His Gospel was written, he told his readers, *"That you may believe that Jesus is the Christ, the Son of God, and that by believing you may have Life in His Name"* (Jn. 20:31).

Yet when John describes the response of the crowds to the Testimony of Jesus' Miracles, it is clear that those who *"believed"* did so in a way that fell short of life-giving belief in Jesus as the Son of God.

John 2:22-23 tells of many who saw His Signs and *"believed in Him."* But later, after that same crowd of shallow Disciples heard Jesus speak about Himself as the Bread of Life (Jn. Chpt. 6), they complained: *"This is a hard teaching. Who can accept it?"* (Jn. 6:60). John observes that *"from this time many of His Disciples turned back and no longer followed Him"* (Jn. 6:66).

Superficial faith came in response to the miraculous, and it died when Jesus communicated the Divine content of His Message.

## NICODEMUS!

Just so Nicodemus, a religious leader, confessed, *"We know You are a Teacher Who has come from God. For no one could perform the miraculous signs you are doing if God were not with him"* (Jn. 3:2). Yet when these leaders heard the Message that Jesus spoke (Jn. 7:16-17), they refused to go on to the belief that involves commitment to Jesus as Lord (Jn. 7:45-47).

Wonder at Jesus' Powers and even agreement that God must have sent Him falls far short of Saving Faith.

Only when he recognizes Jesus as the Son of God and commits himself completely to Him, which he ultimately did, does a person believe in the fullest, saving sense. The commitment involves accepting His Words and making them the framework of one's life, which of course, includes Calvary and the price paid for our sins.

## BELIEF AND LIFE

Over and over in his writings, John links Faith with Life, and unbelief with death. The one who believes in Jesus has Eternal Life. The one who does not believe is already condemned to eternal death.

NOTES

The intimate connection between life and believing is as marked in John's Gospel and Epistles as is the connection between Faith and Righteousness in the writings of Paul.

In giving the account, John proclaims Jesus explaining to Nicodemus that all people must be *"born again."* This concept should not have surprised this religious leader: the Old Testament speaks of a *"New Covenant"* under which the forgiven are given a new heart (Jer. Chpt. 31).

Jesus explained to Nicodemus that the new Life God had promised from ancient times comes from the *"One and only Son"* Whom God gave so *"that whoever believes in Him should not perish but have Eternal Life"* (Jn. 3:16).

Jesus spoke very plainly. The Son came to save. No One who believes in the Son is condemned. Whoever does not believe continues in his present state of condemnation. Believing in Jesus is the one and only doorway to Eternal Life.

## HEARING AND BELIEVING

Jesus again announced that Life is available through the Son: *"Whoever hears My Word and believes Him Who sent Me has Eternal Life and will not be condemned; he has crossed over from death to Life"* (Jn. 5:24).

In John Chapter 8, the Apostle explores the link between the Testimony of the miraculous and the Testimony of the Message. Jesus teaches clearly that He and the Father are inseparably One. Thus, belief in Jesus is the critical issue for every hearer: *"If you do not believe that I am the One I claim to be, you will indeed die in your sins"* (Jn. 8:24).

The Miracles of Jesus cannot be argued away. But when Jesus spoke the Truth, the religious leaders attacked Him. Unlike Abraham, who heard God speak and responded with belief in the Lord, this generation did not respond to the Word of Truth.

When the physical descendants of Abraham rejected the fresh Word of God that came through Jesus, they proved themselves to be of a different spiritual family, for Abraham believed God, and these men refused to believe God's Son.

## BELIEVING FROM A DIFFERENT PERSPECTIVE

John Chapter 11 proclaims the story of the raising of Lazarus. While many accepted the Testimony of this Miracle and accepted Jesus' Word about Himself, the story itself looks at believing from a slightly different perspective.

Mary and Martha, the sisters of Lazarus, did believe in Jesus. They believed that Jesus as the Source of Life would raise Lazarus *"at the last day"* (Jn. 11:24), for Jesus was the Christ and the Son of God (Jn. 11:27). But although Saving Faith was present, the women still failed to understand the life-giving power of Jesus, power that enabled Him to raise their brother then and there, recalling him to Life even though he had been dead for four days.

We may have Saving Faith in Jesus and yet limit His Power, even as millions do presently. Millions simply do not believe that Jesus heals today, or performs miracles, even though they do believe Him for Salvation. However, these people are limiting themselves by their lack of faith in this respect.

While it will not result in the loss of their soul, still it greatly shortchanges that which the Lord can do, but for which He requires Faith.

When we put our trust in Jesus, the Son of God, we enter a relationship with One Who is Lord and Whose ability to act in our world is without limitations — except for our unbelief.

## AN ACTIVE, CONTINUING TRUST IN JESUS

John sees believing as an active, continuing trust in Jesus. The act of believing draws an individual across the dividing line between death and Eternal Life. That act of Faith is described by John as receiving Jesus (Jn. 1:12) and as coming to Him (Jn. 6:35), as well as loving Him (I Jn. 4:19).

## COUNTERFEIT BELIEF

There is counterfeit belief, which exists as a limited trust in Jesus. Counterfeit belief acknowledges that there is something special about Jesus but refuses to accept Scripture's full Testimony about Him. Saving Faith goes beyond limited belief. It recognizes Jesus as the Son of God and trusts completely in him as He is unveiled in God's Word. Saving Faith demonstrates belief by acting on the Words Jesus has spoken (Jn. 8:31-32).

In making a Faith commitment, a person considers the evidence and accepts God's Testimony about Who Jesus is. The one who does not believe may be impressed with the evidence but will hold back from entrusting himself or herself to Jesus.

Yet it is only by believing, as a total commitment of oneself to the Lord, that Life can be found. How vital, then, that we consider the Testimony of Scripture, accept it, and believe on the One Who speaks Words of promise there.

NOTES

## PAUL, AND THE ROLE OF FAITH IN ONE'S LIFE

Paul's task as World Evangelism Strategist and Preacher and Teacher of the young Churches was not simply to present the Gospel. To Paul fell the task of giving Testimony — and explanation. In Paul's two great theological expositions, there is a clear explanation of the nature and role of Faith in the Christian Life. There the relationship between Faith and Salvation, Faith and Righteousness, and Faith and Fellowship with God is made clear.

In his introduction to the Book of Romans, Paul announces his concern with Faith: *"I am not ashamed of the Gospel, because it is the Power of God for the Salvation of everyone who believes: first for the Jew, then for the Gentile. For in the Gospel a Righteousness from God is revealed, a Righteousness that is by Faith from first to last"* (Rom. 1:16-17).

We find *"Faith"* words clustered in Romans and in Galatians. So in order to understand the Faith that brings us Salvation and Righteousness, it is best to look at the Chapters in which these clusters appear.

## THE ROLE OF FAITH

In the first three Chapters of Romans, Paul demonstrates the fact that all humanity is lost, without a shred of Righteousness that would permit God to accept any individual.

*"Therefore no one will be declared Righteous in His (God's) sight by observing the Law"* (Rom. 3:20). Yet God has determined to bring mankind a Salvation that necessarily involves that sinners become Righteous in His sight.

This, Paul explains, is accomplished in the Death of Christ, which was a Sacrifice of

Atonement. Through *"Faith in His Blood,"* the individual who believes is declared Righteous. Thus, Salvation and Righteousness come through Faith in Jesus; and through Faith, Salvation, and Righteousness are available to all.

THE NATURE OF FAITH

But what is that *"Faith"* that provides the Believer with Salvation and cloaks him with Righteousness? In this Chapter in which *"Faith"* and *"Believe"* are found no fewer that 15 times, Paul argues that Faith is the same thing today that it was when it was exercised by Old Testament Saints such as Abraham and David. And Faith always has the same result.

Abraham and David won forgiveness by Faith (Rom. 4:1-8); and for us today, forgiveness is also found by Faith.

In Romans Chapter 4, we see that to believe means simply to count on God's Promise. We accept the Word of the God Who spoke, and we accept that God Himself.

Paul shows that the God Who spoke with Promise to Abraham is the same God Who, in Jesus, speaks with Promise to us: the God *"in Whom he* (Abraham) *believed — the God Who gives life to the dead and calls things which are not as though they were"* (Rom. 4:17).

THE POWER OF FAITH

Verses 18-25 of Chapter 4 of Romans are critical to Paul's definition of Faith. Here he analyzes Abraham's Faith. Abraham faced the fact of his and Sarah's advanced age.

He knew that conceiving a child was impossible. But Abraham *"did not waver through unbelief regarding the Promise of God."* Instead, he was *"fully persuaded that God had Power to do what He had promised."*

And so Paul concludes, *"This is why 'it was credited to him as Righteousness.'"*

Abraham heard the Promise. He looked beyond the impossibility of its fulfillment and considered God. Abraham, confident that God would keep His Promise, expected that what God announced would come to pass.

The Promise Abraham believed was the Promise the he would father a child. The Promise held out today in the Gospel in which we are to believe is the Promise that God, Who has raised Jesus up for our sins and raised Him to life again for our Justification (Rom. 4:25), will save us because of Jesus. We look beyond the possibility that the natural person sees. We consider God. And we too are confident that what God has announced will come to pass.

Believing, we receive the Gifts of Salvation and Righteousness.

NOTES

THE WORD OF FAITH

Paul saw the enthusiasm of his fellow Israelites for God. He admitted their zeal but pointed out that their attempt to establish their own righteousness by works was a refusal to submit to God's Righteousness.

God's Righteousness comes to man through faith (Rom. 10:5-8), specifically a Faith that confesses Jesus as Lord and believes that God has raised Him from the dead. It is only through accepting this Promise by Faith that a person will be saved (Rom. 10:9-13).

Throughout history, God has given Promises to humanity. Throughout history, Faith has been a trusting response, a confidence in the God Who has promised. *"Consequently,"* Paul says, *"Faith comes from hearing the Message, and the Message is heard through the Word of Christ"* (Rom. 10:17).

FAITH AND FELLOWSHIP

Paul teaches that Faith is a believing response to God's Word of Promise. The Believer trusts God to act as He has said He would, and so he commits himself to the Lord. Paul reminds the Galatians that Abraham received Righteousness as a Gift through this kind of Faith. Righteousness is ours as well through Faith.

But then Paul goes on to argue that our relationship with the Lord is also maintained by Faith. We are not to attempt to live in fellowship with God by trying to keep the Law of Moses, or some religion devised by man. Paul reminds us, *"The Righteous will live by Faith"* (Gal. 3:11; Hab. 2:4).

Law is based on a contrary principle: reliance on human activity. It is not based on Promise. Since we must relate to God through His Promise rather than through His Works, we must continue on in our relationship with the Lord by Faith. We must hear the Words of Scripture as Promised, and we must rely on them as Promised.

### LIVING BY FAITH

In personal Testimony, Paul says, *"I have been crucified with Christ and I no longer live, but Christ lives in me. The life I live in the body, I live by Faith in the Son of God, Who loved me and gave Himself for me"* (Gal. 2:20).

The life of Faith is ours as we continue to count on God's Words to us. We hear them as Promised and believe that God will do in us all that He has spoken.

As we live by Faith, the Righteousness of which the Bible speaks as being ours in God's sight gradually infuses our life and character, and we become Righteous persons in fact and in deed.

### FAITH ACCORDING TO JAMES

Paul's task in Romans and Galatians was to explain the nature and role of Faith. James had a simpler mission. James wrote to Believers who were members of the First Church at Jerusalem. He did not try to explain Faith or its role in Christianity. He simply wrote as a Pastor, concerned that Believers conduct themselves in ways that harmonized with their confession of Christ.

To James, a person with a Living Faith will find guidance in prayer (James 1:2-7), will act on the Divine Promise rather than simply hear it (James 1:19-25), will have compassion for the powerless (James 1:26-27), will control his or her tongue (James 3:1-12), will adopt God's peaceable wisdom rather than the contentious wisdom of the world (James 3:13-18), will turn from any worldly motives, which conflict with Godliness (James 4:1-6), will find patience in suffering (James 5:7-11), and will find relief in Prayer (James 5:13-18).

### NO CONFLICT WITH PAUL

Nestled among the practical Pastoral matters is a discussion of Faith (James 2:14-26) that some have felt conflicts with Paul. But when we look at James' concerns and see how he develops his argument, we see that there is no conflict.

James makes his concern clear from the start. He asks what good is it *"if a man claims to have Faith but has no deeds?"* (James 2:14). James, then, is examining a *"Faith"* that fails to produce good and loving conduct.

NOTES

In his argument, James establishes the fact that Faith as mere *"belief about"* God is empty: *"Even the demons believe* (that there is one God) — *and shudder"* (James 2:19).

Looking into history, James shows that the Believers the Old Testament recognizes as examples of Faith are those whose Faith found some expression in action.

Abraham's *"Faith and his actions were working together, and his Faith was made complete by what he did"* (James 2:22).

In the same way, Rahab can be considered Righteous, not because of some mere claim to belief, but because she acted on her conviction that the Lord is God — she hid the Israelite spies.

By each illustration, James shows that one's claim to *"have Faith"* is justified (demonstrated valid) *"by what he does."*

Biblical Faith is a dynamic transforming force. It brings the Believer into living relationship with God. Infused by the Holy Spirit, the Believer's attitudes, values, and conduct change, to come more and more into harmony with the Lord.

### TRUSTING RELIANCE ON JESUS

You and I have committed ourselves to a God Who is known through the Gospel Message. Trust and its content cannot be isolated from each other. Nor are the wonderful products of Faith in the heart and life of the Christian ever found in isolation from trusting reliance on Jesus as Living Lord.

Along with statements about Faith that dot the New Testament, the Scriptures have one other grand exposition — Hebrews Chapter 11. Faith, the writer says, is *"being sure of what we hope for and certain of what we do not see"* (Heb. 11:1). It is Faith that lets us look beyond the visible and realize that *"the universe was formed at God's Command"* (Heb. 11:3). Faith moves us to a realm inaccessible to the senses and not open to ordinary means of verification.

In Faith, there must be that inner assurance that God does exist and the He rewards those who seek Him, and this assurance makes possible the Believer's response to Promise. Faith never rests in a Doctrine but always in a person and in the trustworthiness of that person (Heb. 11:6).

Then the writer of Hebrews goes on to show what Faith produces in the lives of those who do believe. Over and over we are shown that the obedient, who hear the Promise and act on it, experience the reality of the unseen God (Heb. 11:4-40). In each case, there is both that trusting of oneself to God's Message, as Romans emphasizes, and — what is so important as well to James — the evidence of trust in obedient action, which falls out to good works, etc.

IT HAS ALWAYS BEEN FAITH

The Old Testament picture of Faith as a personal, trusting response to God Who speaks Words of Promise is reflected in the New Testament. The New Testament explains in depth the role God has given to Faith.

Although the basis on which God is free to forgive human beings in every era is the Sacrifice of Jesus on Calvary, the object of Faith has differed from age to age. For in different ages, God has spoken different Words of Promise, but yet always with Jesus somehow in view.

To Abraham, there was the Promise of a son and multiplied descendants. To those under Law, there was the Promise of Blessing to accompany obedience. To us, there is the Promise of cleansing and acceptance through Jesus.

In each age, Faith is man's response to the Promise. In each age, Faith is trusting oneself to the God Who has spoken. In each age, Faith is accepted by God in place of a Righteousness that no human being could produce.

THROUGH FAITH

In the New Testament, we see with unmistakable clarity that it is through Faith that God gives Salvation and Righteousness. It is in the New Testament that we see with unmistakable clarity that Faith is a personal response to God and a complete commitment of ourselves to Him.

There also we see that Faith calls for a continuing relationship of response to Jesus' Word. It is in the New Testament that we see with unmistakable clarity that Faith transforms human beings, bringing us a Life that is Eternal and can be experienced now.

Through Faith we come into a relationship with God in which He commits Himself not simply to declare us righteous, but also to make us truly good persons.

Trusting God is the heart and soul of the Faith that centers in our Lord Jesus Christ (Richards).

NOTES

(12) "NOW IF CHRIST BE PREACHED THAT HE ROSE FROM THE DEAD, HOW SAY SOME AMONG YOU THAT THERE IS NO RESURRECTION OF THE DEAD?"

The beginning of the question, *"Now if Christ be preached that He rose from the dead . . .?"*, presents the foundation and all that pertains to that foundation, concerning the great Doctrine of the Resurrection. Paul having provided direct evidence of the Resurrection of Jesus Christ, proceeds here to demonstrate that the dead would rise by showing how it followed from the fact that the Lord Jesus had risen, and as well, showing what consequences would follow from denying that Truth. The whole argument of the Resurrection is based on the fact that the Lord Jesus had risen. If that was admitted, and it certainly must be, he shows that it must follow that His people would also rise.

THE HOLY SPIRIT

The word *"preached"* as it is used here, and as we have so stated, refers to preaching that is to be believed, in other words, preaching with power. If Jesus had not risen, there would be no Power, for the simple reason that the Holy Spirit Who provides the Power could not have come in this fashion unless Jesus had, in fact, risen from the dead and gone back to Heaven, thereby sending the Holy Spirit. Jesus Himself had said, *"Nevertheless I tell you the Truth; It is expedient for you that I go away* (ascension to Heaven after the Resurrection)*: for if I go not away, the Comforter will not come unto you; but if I depart, I will send Him unto you"* (Jn. 16:7).

So, the very fact that Believers now have the Holy Spirit living within them, thereby carrying out all of His Great Works and the Work of God in general, is proof positive that Jesus rose from the dead.

The conclusion of the question, *"How say some among you that there is no Resurrection of the dead?"*, presents an exclamated surprise. In other words, it is easy to feel the surprise expressed in Paul's question: *"How say some among you?"* etc.

We learn from this statement that *"some"* in the Corinthian Church were actually repudiating the Doctrine of the Resurrection. Who the pronoun *"some"* referred to, we have no means of knowing.

Since the Corinthians were Greeks they would be inclined to philosophic ideas and reasonings. They possibly could have been a few educated members of the congregation who revived some of the views that were advocated by certain pagan Greek philosophers.

Again, it may well have been false teachers who had come in from the outside which had nothing to do with Greek philosophy. However, the manner in which Paul addresses himself in the balance of this Chapter lends, I think, some credence to the thought that this erroneous reasoning probably came from the Greek myths.

THE PENCHANT FOR DOUBT

Human reason always finds objection to all the great Doctrines of the Bible, and especially the Doctrine of the Resurrection, and in one way or another attempts to show that it cannot be true. Paul sees at once what others at first apparently fail to see: the Resurrection in general cannot be denied without ultimately advancing to a denial also of Christ's Resurrection. As we have stated, both stand or fall together.

What the denial of the latter implies is no less than destruction of the entire faith of the congregation, i.e. the abolition of the Gospel and all its parts. This terrible result is the weapon which Paul uses to crush the incipient error in Corinth and to establish and to safeguard the Truth (Lenski).

It was probably held by these doubters that the Resurrection was impossible. To all this, Paul answers by demonstrating a fact, i.e. eyewitnesses, and showing that such an event had occurred, and that, consequently, all the difficulties were met.

PROOF POSITIVE

Facts are unanswerable demonstrations; and when a fact is established, all the obstacles and difficulties in the way must be admitted to be overcome. Actually, this is the foundation of all philosophy. Consequently, Paul meets these detractors on their own ground.

In accordance with the principles that the Greek Philosophers claimed to use, Paul established the fact that Jesus had been raised, and thus, met at once all the objections which could be urged against the Doctrine.

NOTES

Paul could have gone into great detail respecting spiritual admonitions, but if one is to notice, he went straight to practical applications, which anyone can understand, as he produced the eyewitnesses to the Resurrection of Christ. He established this fact at once, argued from that, and thus, met all the difficulties at once.

THE DOCTRINE OF THE RESURRECTION

As a result, the Doctrine of the Resurrection does not rest on a mere spiritual subtility; it does not depend on human reasoning; it does not depend on analogy; it rests just as the Sciences of Astronomy, Chemistry, Anatomy, Botany, and natural philosophy do, on well ascertained facts; and it is now a well understood principle of all true Science, that no difficulty, no obstacle, no subtility, no embarrassment about being able to see how it is, is to be allowed to destroy the conviction in the mind which the facts are fitted to produce (Barnes).

FALSE IDEAS OF THE DAY

Inasmuch as these people were probably Gentiles, they could have been persuaded by the philosophy of the Epicurean, who disbelieved in a future life altogether.

Or it could have been the Stoics, who held that the future life was only an impersonal absorption into the Divine, which in effect, says nothing. Both these schools of philosophers *"jeered"* at the very notion of a bodily Resurrection (Acts 17:32).

In II Timothy 2:18, Paul mentioned Hymenaeus and Philetus, who erred, saying *"that the Resurrection was passed already."*

These teachers were incipient Gnostics, who spiritualized the Resurrection, or rather said that the term was only applicable to the rising from the death of sin to the life of righteousness (Farrar).

PHILOSOPHIES OF THE WORLD

As someone has well said, no man or woman can truly be said to be educated unless that man or woman is educated in the Bible. However, the Bible cannot be studied, understood, or learned as other material is absorbed.

While the Bible is definitely a Book containing History as well as Law, Social Direction as well as some Science, which of course, can be understood in the same manner in which such material is placed in other books. However, the Bible is also a Spiritual Book in that it is the Word of God, containing the Plan of God, and is spiritually discerned. In other words, man cannot learn the Bible as he would learn other subjects. He must first be acquainted with the Author in the realm of Salvation, with the Holy Spirit then coming into the Believer's heart and life, Who then reveals Truth to the Believer (I Cor. 2:9-16).

There is a Bible view of all things, and we might quickly add that this view never contradicts true Science. In fact, the Bible provides the foundation and framework for all true Science. So what am I saying?

I am saying that all false philosophies of which the world is filled, which in fact are inspired by Satan, cannot be absorbed by any person, without it affecting that person in a negative way. In other words, the individual has studied and learned a lie, and to be sure, that lie has a telling affect on the mind from there on. That's the reason the Holy Spirit, through the Apostle, said, *"Be not conformed to this world: but be ye transformed by the renewing of your mind, that you may prove what is that good, and acceptable, and perfect Will of God"* (Rom. 12:2).

The Believer must understand that there is no view, at least that is correct, other than the Bible View, and that pertains to all things. In other words, one can believe the Bible which is Truth, or one can believe the vain (empty) philosophies which are untrue. He cannot believe both! As well, to attempt to wed the two presents an impossible exercise. It cannot be done because a lie and Truth do not mix.

The Believer's every thought must be, *"What does the Bible say?"* Whatever it says is Law and Gospel, and should be the criteria on which all stands. The Corinthians were not following this principle, but were either not believing the Bible or else did not sufficiently know the Bible, which is probably the case.

PRESENT SITUATIONS

I marvel presently as I hear Preachers advocating certain things, which are so blatantly unscriptural, and yet they do not seem to know what they are saying.

I think the problem in the hearts of many is that the Bible is the Rule only for some matters, and is not applied to all matters. Or else, they are so unacquainted with the Word of God, that they really do not know what it says regarding particulars.

NOTES

To be sure, the Word of God addresses every single thing that we do and believe, even as Peter said, *"According as His Divine Power hath given unto us all things that pertain unto Life and Godliness, through the knowledge of Him that hath called us to Glory and Virtue"* (II Pet. 1:3).

(13) "BUT IF THERE BE NO RESURRECTION OF THE DEAD, THEN IS CHRIST NOT RISEN:"

If the whole subject is held to be impossible and absurd, then it must follow that Christ is not risen, since there were the same difficulties in the way of raising Him up which will exist in any case.

He was dead; and was buried. He had lain in the grave three days. His human soul had left the body. His frame had become cold and stiff. The blood had ceased to circulate, and the lungs to heave.

In His case, there was the same difficulty in raising Him up to life that there is in any other; and if it is held to be impossible and absurd that the dead should rise, then it must follow that Christ has not been raised.

THE ARGUMENT

This is the first consequence which Paul states as resulting from the denial of this Doctrine of Resurrection, and this is inevitable. Paul thus shows them that the denial of the Doctrine, or the maintaining the general proposition *"that the dead would not rise,"* lead also to the denial of the fact that the Lord Jesus had risen, and consequently, to the denial of Christianity altogether, and as well, the annihilation of all their hopes.

There was, and is, such a close connection between Christ and His people, that the Resurrection of the Lord Jesus makes their Resurrection certain (Barnes).

Inasmuch as Christ was like us when He died, actually *"flesh of our flesh, bone of our bone,"* and in this respect altogether one with us, although in Person He was the Son of God, still it cannot be argued that He was a different and higher Being and, therefore, exempt from the rule that the dead are not raised (Lenski).

NOTES

Paul will now proceed to show the further logical consequences of their position, which he takes up in the rest of the paragraph.

(14) "AND IF CHRIST BE NOT RISEN, THEN IS OUR PREACHING VAIN, AND YOUR FAITH IS ALSO VAIN."

The phrase, *"And if Christ be not risen,"* presents a shattering blow to the whole of Christianity, that is if it were true.

The phrase, *"Then is our preaching vain, and your Faith is also vain,"* refers to *"empty nothings,"* for that is what *"vain"* or *"vanity"* means.

The argument here is addressed to all their feelings, their hopes, and their belief. It is drawn from all their convictions that the system was true.

FALSE AND DECEPTIVE?

Could they be prepared to admit a Doctrine which involved the consequences of their Salvation, and had affected their minds and won their hearts, was in fact untrue? If they were not prepared for this, then it followed that they should not abandon or doubt the Doctrine of the Resurrection of the dead (Barnes).

In effect, the Apostle is saying that if Christ has not been raised from the dead, which is the Firstfruits of all Believers who ultimately will be raised, then all preaching is a lie. The Truth is conveyed by preaching, and so, what they had heard contains no credence.

PREACHING AND FAITH

If one is to notice, Preaching and Faith are linked together, for the simple reason that Preaching presents the Word of God, and Faith comes by hearing the Word of God (Rom. 10:17). Consequently, I don't think the Corinthians exactly knew what they were saying.

As well, I wonder if the reader knows as well?

FAITH

Does the reader know and understand, that one's Faith is actually all that one really has. Everything else is transient. It is here and then gone. So, when it is all said and done, irrespective as to *who* the person may be, or *what* the person may be, his Faith is all he has, and if he doesn't have any Faith, he doesn't have anything. I speak of Faith in God and His Word.

One might could say, that all have Faith in something or someone; however, it is only Faith in God which will stand the test and is actually eternal (I Cor. 13:13).

Oncoming death strips one of everything. Money then is of no consequence. Education, at least in the things of the world matter little. Place and position are of no consequence. Then, it is only one's Faith in God which really matters.

ESSENTIAL DOCTRINES

Glaringly so, the Apostle proclaims to the Church, that there are some particular Doctrines regarding the Word of God which must be believed, in order for one to be saved. Resurrection, of course, is one of those Foundational Doctrines.

If one does not believe in the Resurrection, then one has no more use for Faith in God in any capacity. What's the point! If Jesus wasn't raised from the dead, which insures the coming Resurrection of all the sainted dead, then the whole thing is no more than a joke.

THE RESURRECTION AND THE RAPTURE

Many in the modern Church, even those who claim to be Spirit-filled, deny the coming Rapture of the Body of Christ (I Thess. 4:13-18). What they do not seem to realize, is that the Resurrection and the Rapture are one and the same. So, to not believe in the Rapture, is not to believe in the Resurrection as well.

Probably one could say, that the claims of such ones to disavow the Rapture, are simply a lack of knowledge of the Word of God. Nevertheless, honest ignorance, that is if ignorance could ever be described as such, brings the same results as willful rejection of Light — destruction.

(15) "YEA, AND WE ARE FOUND FALSE WITNESSES OF GOD; BECAUSE WE HAVE TESTIFIED OF GOD THAT HE RAISED UP CHRIST: WHOM HE RAISED NOT UP, IF SO BE THAT THE DEAD RISE NOT."

The phrase, *"Yea, and we are found false witnesses of God,"* presents a serious implication indeed!

FALSE WITNESS

If it is to be found that we have affirmed that which is not true of God; or have said that He has done that which He has not done, nothing could be regarded as a greater crime than this, whatever might be the immediate subject under consideration.

To bear false witness of a man, or to say that a man has done what he has not done, is regarded as a grievous crime. How much more so to bear false testimony of God!

The idea is, that God never testifies through false witnesses. Such is a monstrous thought concerning those who testify falsely about Him.

The phrase, *"Because we have testified of God that He raised Christ: Whom He raised not up, if so be that the dead rise not,"* means, if correct, they would have been just plain lying witnesses. This is the plain proposition which all of those must accept who today deny the reality of the Bodily Resurrection of Christ. In fact, they can maintain their denial only by making all of the witnesses who beheld the risen Saviour (from Peter downward to Paul) liars.

Besides, they make liars also of the ancient Prophets who bore a witness that God Himself had told them, namely, that He would raise up the Messiah Whom He never intended to raise up. Yet this blasphemous denial is today made from many pulpits which claim the Christian Name.

While they may tone down their statement by saying that the Prophets were subjective liars who did not actually know that they were lying; but a well-intentioned liar is often much worse than a conscious liar.

## THREE POINTS

Three points have been noted that deserve attention:

1. The identity of the category into which Paul places Christ's Bodily Resurrection and our own bodily Resurrection — the Resurrection of Believers dependant upon the Resurrection of Christ.

2. The Sacredness of the Apostolic Testimony regarding the former — the Resurrection of Christ.

3. Paul's fanatical self-delusion if the appearance of Christ to Him is, indeed, a psychological hallucination which makes his own spiritual transformation and his entire Gospel rest on this delusion and on the pitiful mental weakness that made such a delusion possible — in other words, Paul was crazy, as well as all the other witnesses.

NOTES

Can one imagine the verdict of humanistic psychology, that is if such pap had existed then! And then to think that much of modern Christianity has embraced this subtlety of Satan, is almost beyond comprehension.

## TO TESTIFY AGAINST GOD

*"Of God,"* should have been translated *"against God,"* for that is what it means.

If in fact there is no Resurrection, our evidence has been against Him. We have affirmed that which is not true; and this is against God. It is implied here, that it would be a crime to testify that God had raised up the Lord Jesus if He had not done it; or that it would be affirming that of God which would be against His Character, or which it would be improper for Him to do. This would be so:

1. Because it would be wrong to bear *any* false witness of God, or to affirm that He had done what He had not, in fact, done.

2. Because *if* the Lord Jesus had not been raised up, it would prove that He was an imposter, since He had declared that He would be raised up; and to affirm of God that He had raised up an impostor would be *against* Him, and would be highly dishonorable to Him, therefore, taking His Name in vain.

3. If it was denied that Christ was raised, it would prove that all the Apostles were false witnesses of the worse character — false witnesses against God.

4. This the Apostle seems to have presumed the Corinthians could not believe. They had too much evidence that the Apostles spoke the Truth; they had proclaimed their uniform respect for God, and desire to bear witness of Him and in His favor; they had two conclusive evidences that the Apostles were inspired by Christ, with some even having the power of working miracles. They were too fully convinced of their honesty, truth, and piety, ever to believe that the Apostles could be false witnesses against God.

These Apostles had ample opportunity to know whether God did raise up the Lord Jesus; and they were witnesses who had no inducement to bear a false witness in any case (Barnes).

## THAT WHICH IS SO SERIOUS, SO MANY TAKE SO LIGHTLY

Paul's argument is, at least as it related to the Corinthians, that they really had not thought through this course on which they had embarked. To deny the Resurrection, is to deny everything which pertains to God — in fact, all of it being a farce. However, the Corinthians were not saying this and Paul knew they were not saying this. He was attempting to show them, which he did in a powerful way, where this error was leading.

Tragically, most Christians, it seems, do not think through many of the erroneous directions which they take.

To use myself as an unworthy example, the Lord has helped us to see untold thousands brought to a saving knowledge of Jesus Christ. By the Grace of God, we have seen people delivered of every type of sinful bondage which darkness could concoct, that which could be referred to as none other than miracles of Redemption.

And yet I have seen some of these people, some incidentally who were saved under my Ministry, turn against me, even claiming that I am not of God, but actually of Satan. They seem not to understand, if that is so, they have believed a false Gospel, for that's all an imposter can preach, which means they are not really saved. If I was of God then, and I definitely was, then I am of God now, and in fact, I definitely am.

All error always leads to impossible conclusions. That's what makes false doctrines so devilish, and why they should be detectable.

Whatever one believes, one must ascertain that it is Biblical in its foundation, in its institution, and in its application.

Second, one must follow that Doctrine through all the way to its total conclusion to see where it leads. This the Corinthians evidently were not doing, and which most presently are not doing as well!

(16) "FOR IF THE DEAD RISE NOT, THEN IS NOT CHRIST RAISED:"

This Verse is a repetition of Verse 13, to emphasize the argument that the Christian Faith in the Resurrection rests not on philosophic theory, but on an historic fact (Farrar).

The Holy Spirit has Paul to repeat this statement, in order to signify its great importance. It was a great and momentous Truth which would bear repetition, that if there were no Resurrection as some held, then it would follow that the Lord Jesus was not raised up.

NOTES

## REPETITION, BUT FOR PURPOSE

One series of deductions has been concluded. A second series must be unfolded in order to display still more fully the fateful consequences that lie hidden in the Corinthian error. This second series corroborates the first.

By thus bringing the argument back to the position of the Corinthians with regard to the Resurrection of the dead, Paul seems to be implying that ultimately the false witness against God is to be laid not at the Apostles' feet, but, rather, at the feet of those who deny the Resurrection.

(17) "AND IF CHRIST BE NOT RAISED, YOUR FAITH IS VAIN; YE ARE YET IN YOUR SINS."

The phrase, *"And if Christ be not raised, your Faith is vain,"* presents the second phase of Paul's argument.

The deduction concerning Faith has been made already in part in connection with the preaching mentioned in Verse 14, where both the preaching and the Faith are said to be *"empty."* But more must be said. So Paul takes up this deduction independently and expands it and also follows it with two further deductions along the same line in Verses 18 and 19.

## EMPTY AND USELESS

In Verse 14 Paul says *"Your Faith is 'empty',"* hollow, without a reality on which to rest.

Here he says: Your Faith is *"useless,"* idle, it gets you nothing. The King James translation uses the word *"vain"* to translate both Greek words, which in fact, obscures the important difference.

Only because Faith is regarded as *"useless"* can Paul add the next phrase.

The phrase, *"Ye are yet in your sins,"* presents a situation of calamitous proportions.

## THE MOST HORRIBLE THOUGHT OF ALL

Faith is to benefit us, bring us something, namely the greatest of all treasures, the forgiveness of sins. If it in fact, brings us nothing, it is *"useless."*

On the other hand, Faith is *"empty"* when the Word to which it clings is untrue, unreal. Though it cling ever so firmly it grasps only an empty shadow, a delusive lie. The two ideas are clearly distinct, yet they are also closely related, for a Faith that is empty and rests on empty air is for that very reason also of no use whatever.

WHAT DOES IT MEAN TO BE YET IN YOUR SINS?

To be in our sins, in that deadliest sphere where all of our sins surround us and accuse us before God even as so many deadly wolves about to tear us to pieces, is the most horrible thought of all.

Make the Savior what you please, if He failed to rise from the dead, He in fact, is useless, for He cannot free us from our sins, the one thing for which we need a Savior. If there is no Resurrection, there is also no Redemption, no Reconciliation with God, no Justification, no Life, no Salvation.

If Christ is still dead, then every Believer is still dead in trespasses and sins. As long as Christ, our Surety, is not released, it is certain that our debt is not paid, we are still liable, no matter how much we may trust in some supposed payment or in some release without payment.

Christ's Resurrection is the proof positive that His Sacrifice was, indeed, sufficient and fully accepted by God. Therefore, Christ, even as Paul said, was raised for our Justification (Rom. 4:25).

To reject His Resurrection is to reject the efficacy of His Sacrifice, and the death which He died is just as useless as our Faith in such a dead Christ (Lenski).

THE ARGUMENT EXPRESSED

The argument in this Verse consists in an appeal to the experience in Christ of the Corinthians and their hopes. It may be thus expressed:

1. You have reason to believe that your sins are forgiven. You cherish that belief on evidence that is satisfactory to you. But if Christ is not raised, that cannot be true. He was an impostor, and sins cannot be forgiven by Him. As you are not, and cannot be prepared to admit that your sins are not forgiven, you cannot as well, admit a Doctrine which involves that.

2. You have evidence that you are not under the dominion of sin. You have repented of it; have forsaken it, and are leading a holy life. You know that, and cannot be induced to doubt this fact.

But all that is to be traced to the Doctrine that the Lord Jesus rose from the dead. It is only by believing that, and the Doctrines which are connected with it, that the power of sin in the heart has been destroyed. And as you *cannot* doubt that under the influence of *that Truth* you have been enabled to break off from your sins, so you cannot admit a Doctrine which would involve it as a consequence that you are yet under the condemnation and the dominion of sin. You must believe, therefore, that the Lord Jesus rose; and that, if He rose, others will also.

3. This argument is good also now, insomuch as it now touches every Christian.

Through the belief of a risen Savior, the dominion of sin has been broken, and, every Christian is, therefore, in an important sense a witness of the Resurrection of the Lord Jesus, a living proof that a system which can work so great changes, and produce such evidence that sins are forgiven as are furnished in the conversion of sinners, stands as the greatest evidence of all, that Jesus Christ was raised from the dead.

(18) "THEN THEY ALSO WHICH ARE FALLEN ASLEEP IN CHRIST ARE PERISHED."

When Paul wrote this letter near Easter of the year 57, or as some claim, the year 59, some of the Corinthians had already died, believing and trusting in Christ to the end.

To fall asleep in Christ is the beautiful Scriptural expression to designate the Christian's death. As previously stated, it does not necessarily refer to the state of the spirit, soul, and body, but rather to the *manner* of death. It is the same as going to sleep. In fact, it is only the body that sleeps, while the soul and spirit instantly go to be with Jesus, to await the coming Resurrection, when a Glorified body will be given and reunited with the soul and the spirit (I Thess. 4:13-18).

This very designation (asleep in Christ) is already a denial of the Corinthian error, a clear testimony to the Heavenly hope of the Resurrection of the dead at the last day according to the promise of Christ.

DID PERISH

One word reveals the tragedy like a blow: *"did perish."*

When these Believers, and all others for that matter, closed their eyes in death, at that moment they perished completely and forever with body and with soul. We also say that they are lost or damned. The sense is the same.

In this crushing way Paul brings home to his readers what the denial of the Resurrection really involves. He who persists in this denial writes over every Believer's tomb: *"Lost!"* Or, what amounts to the same: *"Damned!"*

Nothing more heart-rending could be said. The entire hereafter is shrouded in the blackest night. This blackness has swallowed up those who have passed beyond and waits to swallow up those whose life is now swiftly passing away. And this some foolish Corinthians, whether they realized it or not, were putting in place of the Light and the Hope that shines beyond the grave for every Believer.

Some false cults have claimed that the verb *"to perish"* actually means *"to be annihilated,"* to be deprived of existence. This has been taken to mean that no hell or hellfire exists for the wicked.

But in sacred language the word *"perish"* or *"perishing"* refers to one losing their salvation in contradistinction to being saved by obtaining Salvation.

The actual meaning is, that he who perishes is forever separated from God, heaven, and Eternal Life. His body and his soul share the fate of Satan in the eternal torment of hell (Lenski).

PAUL'S APPEAL TO THE CORINTHIANS

In effect, Paul is saying, *"Can you believe it possible that the good men who have believed in the Lord Jesus are destroyed? Can you believe that your best friends, your kindred, and your fellow Christians who have died, have gone down to perdition? Can you believe that they will sink to woe with the impenitent, and the polluted, and abandoned? If you cannot, then it must follow that they are saved. And then it will follow that you cannot embrace a Doctrine which involves this consequence."*

To believe that there is no Resurrection, is to believe that all go to the same place at death whatever that may be, the Godly and the ungodly, the filthy and the clean, the righteous and the unrighteous, the saved and the unsaved!

It means that the Apostle Paul will spend eternity with Adolf Hitler, for according to this pernicious Doctrine, if there is truly no Resurrection, that's exactly what will happen. The most Godly, the most Righteous, will be

NOTES

in the same condition as the most filthy, the most ungodly!

That's what I meant, and its what Paul means, by not thinking through these Doctrines which we sometimes embrace.

Can it be believed that God will destroy those who are living to His honor; who are pure in heart, and lovely in life, and who have been made such by the Christian experience? If it cannot, then every man knows that Christianity is not false, and that infidelity is not true (Barnes).

(19) "IF IN THIS LIFE ONLY WE HAVE HOPE IN CHRIST, WE ARE OF ALL MEN MOST MISERABLE."

It is overly obvious that Paul's thinking is futuristic. He understood both the Death and Resurrection of Christ and the subsequent Gift of the Spirit as eschatological realities. That is, he recognized that in those events, God has set in motion the events of the End in such a way that they must of Divine necessity be brought to consummation. The absolutely crucial matter in this view is the Resurrection of Jesus from the dead.

THE BIBLE AND ENDTIME EVENTS

The fact that the Resurrection had already taken place referring to Christ, within history meant that the End had been set inexorably in motion: the Resurrection of Christ absolutely guaranteed for Paul the Resurrection of all who are *"in Christ."*

For Paul, Christ's Resurrection and Ascension mean that Christ now rules; but it is also clear that despite His rule, the enemy is still at work since people still die.

Thus, for Paul there is a Divine necessity to the Resurrection of the dead since that alone is the evidence of the final overthrow, death itself. Christ's Resurrection, therefore, also set in motion the defeat of death, the final form of which the overpowering of its stranglehold on humanity is in the form of Resurrection. When that occurs, that is, when the final enemy is thus defeated through Resurrection, and I speak of the Resurrection of the Saints, then God becomes *"all in all."*

THE CHRISTIAN AND ENDTIME EVENTS

The Bible is very clear concerning the future. In fact, to not understand the future as the Bible relates that future is to really not understand the Bible at all.

We quickly learn from its pages that not only is the present in view referring to Salvation, of course, which is an absolute necessity, but as well, Salvation points forward to something, in other words, the total benefits of Salvation.

As Paul so graphically describes the coming Resurrection of the Saints in this Chapter, we at the present time realize that this event is even at the door. I speak of the Rapture of the Church, which in fact, is the Resurrection (I Thess. 4:13-18).

Immediately after the Rapture of the Church, the man of sin will appear, as Satan makes his final effort to take over this world and defeat Christ (II Thess. Chpt. 2).

Of all the attempts that Satan has made in the past to thwart the Plan of God, the coming Great Tribulation will be his greatest effort of all. Of all the efforts he has made to destroy the Jews, this will be his final solution. He knows that if he can destroy the Jew, to whom the Promises of God have been made, then the Word of God falls to the ground, and in effect, Satan has won. That's the reason that Jeremiah referred to this event as *"the time of Jacob's trouble."* However, he then said, *"But he shall be saved out of it"* (Jer. 30:7).

At the conclusion of the Great Tribulation period to which Jesus referred to as well (Mat. 24:21), the Second Coming of the Lord will take place (Rev. Chpt. 19). At that time, Israel will fully accept Christ as Lord, Saviour, and Messiah, which she failed to do upon His First Advent, and which she must do in order for the Kingdom to be fully installed. The Prophet Zechariah tells of this coming time (Zech. Chpts. 12-14). Satan will then be locked away (Rev. 20:1-3).

Jesus will rule and reign for a thousand years, of which Isaiah grandly portrayed as well as other Prophets (Isa. 9:6-7; 11:3-12; 12:1-6; 14:1-8; etc.). During this time, all the Resurrected Saints will reign with Christ, along with a restored Israel.

However, at the conclusion of this period, *"Satan shall be loosed out of his prison,"* when he will make one final attempt of destruction, which will be short-lived. He will then be *"cast into the lake of fire and brimstone . . . and shall be tormented day and night for ever and ever"* (Rev. 20:7-10).

NOTES

Then the heavens and the earth will be cleansed with the New Jerusalem which John saw, coming down from heaven to earth, as God literally changes the location of His Headquarters (II Pet. 3:13; Rev. 21:1). John then said, *"And there shall be no more curse: but the Throne of God and of the Lamb shall be in it; and His servants shall serve Him and they shall see His Face; and His Name shall be in their foreheads . . . and they shall reign for ever and ever"* (Rev. 22:3-5).

## AN IMPROPER VIEW?

Believers who have an improper, unscriptural view of coming events, also have an improper, unscriptural view of present events. Regrettably, this is very obvious in the modern Church.

I think the modern Church knows less about the coming Resurrection (Rapture) than it ever has in its history. It is almost exclusively *"here and now,"* hence, its unscriptural message, which for the most part reduces the great Plan of God down to the low level of money, i.e. *"the prosperity message."* What blasphemy!

The Truth is the Rapture of the Church could take place at any moment.

The Greek word that Paul used in the translation *"caught up"* (I Thess. 4:17) is *"harpazo."* It actually has five meanings to it, with one of those meanings being *"to snatch out and away."* This tells us that the Rapture will occur so suddenly that it will take the Church by surprise.

How soon will this be?

It cannot be far off for the simple reason that the Church has already entered into the Great Apostasy (the falling away from Truth), which Jesus foretold in His Message to the Church at Laodicea, which actually symbolizes this particular time (Rev. 3:14-22).

## RESURRECTION

The Doctrine of the Resurrection (Rapture) is pivotal in the Christian Faith. Paul wrote, even as we are now studying, *"If in this life only we have hope in Christ, we are of all men most miserable."* What, then, is the shape of the Believer's Hope?

The New Testament speaks decisively. It is not simply the continuation of existence. It is Resurrection, with all that Resurrection implies!

## RESURRECTION IN THE OLD TESTAMENT

There is no sharply defined Doctrine of the Resurrection in the Old Testament as it is in the New, except in shadow.

There are Passages that can be interpreted to speak of deliverance in this life with a hint at a deliverance that extends beyond this life (Job 14:14; Ps. 17:15; 49:7-20; 73:23-26).

Some Passages seem to promise Resurrection more specifically. These are found especially in the Prophets. For instance, Isaiah wrote, *"He will swallow up death forever"* (Isa. 25:8) and *"Your dead will live; their bodies will rise. You who dwell in the dust, wake up and shout for joy"* (Isa. 26:19). The clearest statement of all is found in this statement: *"Multitudes who sleep in the dust of the earth will awake: some to Everlasting Life, others to shame and everlasting contempt"* (Dan. 12:2).

## THE GOD OF THE LIVING

There are also Passages that suggest, rather than explicitly teach, a Resurrection. Jesus' interpreted God's claim in Exodus Chapter 3 (to be the God of Abraham, Isaac, and Jacob) to imply unending existence: *"He is not the God of the dead, but of the living"* (Mat. 22:32).

Both Enoch and Elijah were taken directly to be with the Lord without passing through death (Gen. 5:24; II Kings 2:11). Their snatching away suggests the continuation of life beyond our world, though the method by which they left the world is so dramatically different.

While the Doctrine of Resurrection is not plainly developed in the Old Testament, it is certainly fair to say that the emergence of the New Testament's clear teaching comes as no surprise. The Pharisees, who held to the Doctrine of Resurrection, and the Sadducees, who denied it, might argue about the Old Testament's implications for the Resurrection, but Jesus justly condemned the denial of the Sadducees, saying, *"You are in error because you do not know the Scriptures or the Power of God"* (Mat. 22:29; Mk. 12:27; Lk. 20:38).

## RESTORATION OF EARTHLY LIFE

Both the Old Testament and New Testament report incidents in which individuals are restored to earthly life. Among them are the restoration of two women's sons (I Kings 17:17-24; II Kings 4:18-37), Jesus' raising of the daughter of Jairus (Mat. 9:18-26; Mk. 5:22-43; Lk. 8:41-56), and most spectacularly, the raising of Lazarus four days after his burial (Jn. Chpt. 11).

Each of these incidents demonstrates clearly that God has power over death. But none of them involved Resurrection, although it did prove that He will be able to raise the dead in the coming Resurrection.

Resurrection, as we discover it in the New Testament, is to an endless life in a transformed state of being.

## THE RESURRECTION OF JESUS

The significance of Jesus' Resurrection is beyond imagination, even as Paul outlines in this 15th Chapter of I Corinthians. Just a few of the New Testament Scriptures associated with Resurrection show the central place that His Resurrection must play in our Faith.

## PROOF

Paul points out that Jesus *"through the Spirit of Holiness was declared with power to be the Son of God by His Resurrection from the dead"* (Rom. 1:4). Consequently, the Resurrection is proof of all of Christ's claims and a solid foundation for our Faith.

It is also true that Jesus is called the *"Firstfruits of those who have fallen asleep"* (I Cor. 15:20). His Resurrection is the guarantee that the death that grips the human race because of Adam has been conquered and that life is now our destiny.

## PERMANENT PRIESTHOOD

Jesus' Resurrection to endless life guarantees that *"because Jesus lives forever, He has a permanent Priesthood. Therefore, He is able to save completely those who come to God through Him, because He always lives to intercede for them"* (Heb. 7:24-25).

## COMPLETED WORK

Jesus' Resurrection presents the completed work of Redemption in the heart and life of the Believer, as it refers to dominion over sin.

While believing sinners are baptized into the death of Jesus Christ, which guarantees the sin debt being paid, we are also raised with Him in *"newness of life,"* which guarantees the

NOTES

breaking of sin's grip, making immobile that monster (Rom. 6:1-14).

So, while Calvary destroyed the old man with all his passions, the Resurrection guaranteed the new man with total victory over those passions.

Paul wrote, *"Forasmuch then as the children are partakers of flesh and blood* (human body), *He* (Jesus) *also Himself likewise took part of the same* (Incarnation)*; that through death He might destroy him that had the power of death, that is, the Devil;*

*"And deliver them* (newness of Life) *who through fear of death were all their lifetime subject to bondage* (bondage of sin broken)*"* (Heb. 2:14-15).

So, the Resurrection of Jesus along with Calvary figure prominently, in fact is the totality, of our present walk of victory in this world.

KEY

Finally, Jesus' Resurrection is the key to fulfillment of all the Old Testament and New Testament Promises about the future. God's purposes will be achieved only when Jesus returns.

This helps us to understand why the Resurrection of Jesus was a keystone in Apostolic proclamation of the Gospel (Acts 2:24-36; 3:15-26; 4:10; 5:30; 10:40; 13:34, 37; 17:18-32).

(20) "BUT NOW IS CHRIST RISEN FROM THE DEAD, AND BECOME THE FIRSTFRUITS OF THEM THAT SLEPT."

The phrase, *"But now is Christ risen from the dead,"* presents the Apostle pursuing the Corinthian error to its last, desperate conclusion. He strikes at the claim of no Resurrection, at least as it regards the Church, by means of the tremendous, undeniable, and admitted fact that Jesus Christ did rise from the dead. Even the Corinthian doubters knew and admitted this fact. However, something had blinded their eyes so that they failed to see that this one fact destroyed their entire proposition regarding the Resurrection.

DRAMATIC TURN

With a sudden, dramatic turn, which is as effective as all of the reasoning by deduction which Paul employs, he hurls the great Easter fact at the Corinthian error.

But Paul does far more than merely introduce the fact of Christ's Resurrection as it took place on Easter morning. That fact, which is merged with our coming Resurrection, transports Paul's mind to the end of the age, to the final triumphant consummation when *"God shall be all in all."*

Only when Christ's Resurrection is thus seen in its glorious connection with the final consummation is its full significance properly apprehended.

NOW

There is peculiar force in the word *"now"* as Paul here uses it. The meaning may be thus expressed:

*"I have shown the consequences which would follow from the supposition that Christ was not raised up. I have shown how it would destroy all our hopes, plunge us into grief, annihilate our Faith, make our preaching vain, and involve us in the belief that our pious friends have perished, and that we are yet in our sins.*

*"I have shown how it would produce the deepest disappointment and misery. But, all this was mere supposition. There is no reason to apprehend any such consequences, or to be thus alarmed. 'Christ is risen.'*

*"Of that there is no doubt. That is not to be called in question. It is established by unimpeachable testimony; and consequently our hopes are not vain, our Faith is not useless, our loved ones in Christ have not perished, and we shall not be disappointed."*

The phrase, *"And became the firstfruits of them that slept,"* refers to Jesus Himself being the actual Resurrection, and as well, the first part of the Resurrection, with the balance yet to come.

FIRSTFRUITS

By the using of the term *"Firstfruits,"* Paul is alluding to the ceremony that occurred on the day following the Passover when the first sheaf of the new Barley crop was presented in the Temple as an offering to God (Lev. 23:9-11). This happened every year on the day that later became our Easter, the Day of Jesus' Resurrection.

The first sheaf of ripe grain (Barley) was required to be offered to the Lord, and waved before Him by the Priest, as expressing a sense of gratitude, and the recognition of the fact that God had a right to all that he had. The word, therefore, comes to have two senses, or two ideas:

NOTES

1. That which is first, the beginning, or that which has the priority of time.

2. That which is a part and portion of the whole which is to follow, and which is the earnest or pledge of that; as the first sheaf of ripe grain was not only the first in order of time, it was also the earnest or pledge of the entire harvest which was soon to succeed. In allusion to this, Paul uses the word *"Firstfruits"* here.

It was not merely or mainly that Christ was the first in order of time that rose from the dead — for the daughter of Jairus and the widow's son and Lazarus had been raised before Him — but it was that He was Chief in regard to the dignity, value, and importance of His rising; He was connected with all that should rise, as the first sheaf of the harvest was with the crop; as our Representative Man, He was a part of the mighty harvest of the Resurrection, and His rising was a portion and guarantee of that great rising, as the sheaf was a portion of the harvest itself.

He is so connected with us all, and our rising so depends on His, that His Resurrection was a demonstration that we shall also rise.

NEVER TO DIE AGAIN

The three of which we have just mentioned who were raised from the dead, died again, as is obvious. However, He is the first of those who were raised so as not to die again; consequently, nor will those whom He will raise up in the Resurrection die anymore. He is, therefore, the first of those that thus rise, and a portion of that great hosts which shall be raised to die no more.

The first sheaf of the harvest was consecrated to God, and then all the harvest was regarded as consecrated to Him.

As well, by the Resurrection of the Lord Jesus, all those of whom He speaks are regarded as the harvest of old, as sacred to God. As the grain in the old economy belonged to Him, likewise, every Believer belongs to Him, Who is the *"Firstfruits"* (Barnes).

(21) "FOR SINCE BY MAN CAME DEATH, BY MAN CAME ALSO THE RESURRECTION OF THE DEAD."

The phrase, *"For since by man came death,"* refers to Adam and the Fall in the Garden of Eden. Physical death came by Adam, which resulted in spiritual, and thereby eternal, death (Rom. 5:12-21).

NOTES

DEATH

This passage may be regarded as proof that death would not have entered the world had it not been for transgressions; or, in other words, if man had not sinned, he would have remained eternal on the earth, or would, as some surmise, have been translated to heaven, as Enoch and Elijah were, without seeing death.

The Apostle here, by using the word *"man"* undoubtedly, as stated, refers to Adam; but the particular and specific idea which he intends to insist on is that as death came by human nature, or by a human being, by a man, so it was important and proper that immortality, or freedom from death, should come in the same way, by One Who was a man. Man introduced death; therefore, man would also have to recover from death. The evil was introduced by one man; the recovery would be by another.

LIFE

The phrase, *"By man came also the Resurrection of the dead,"* refers to the Lord Jesus Christ. However, even though Deity, still He accomplished this thing as the Son of God in human nature.

The Resurrection came by Him, because He first rose — first of those who should not again die; because He proclaimed the Doctrine, and raised it on a firm foundation; and because by His power the dead will be raised up. Thus, He came to counteract the evils of the Fall, and to restore man to more than his primeval dignity and honor.

The Resurrection through Christ is with the assurance that all who are raised up by Him shall never die again.

LIKE HIM

But it is not only the fact of the Resurrection of the dead in general that is here affirmed, but the Resurrection of certain persons out from among the dead in virtue of their living union with Christ as a man.

He, as a Man, went down into death to deliver man from the power of death; and God, in taking Him up from among the dead, made a public exhibition in Man of complete victory over all the power of the enemy. Death could not hold Him; so He, as Man, arose from among all the other dead — thus declaring Deliverance and Redemption — and became the Firstfruits of all who sleep.

Had Christ not won this victory, His people must always have remained in the dark prison house of death. But they are associated with Him in Resurrection.

Like Him, they come out not only from death but from among the dead. They are one — if they do not rise then He never rose. If Resurrection is denied to them it is denied to Him.

But His Resurrection is established; and, therefore, the Believer's Faith does not rest on a fable, nor can it be overthrown nor its Redemption results frustrated.

VICTORY IN THIS LIFE AS WELL

God will indeed by His power bring men out of death when He commits all judgment to the Son. However, that is future. As well, the Death and Resurrection of Christ brings about presently a glorious victory to those who believe upon Him, which brings us out of the state where sin and its consequences reign, and into a realm into which neither death nor judgment can enter. If these Doctrines are fables, then those who believe them are of all men most to be pitied. (Williams)

(22) "FOR AS IN ADAM ALL DIE, EVEN SO IN CHRIST SHALL ALL BE MADE ALIVE."

The phrase, *"For as in Adam all die,"* refers to Adam's Fall in the Garden of Eden, which brought about instant spiritual death (separation from God), and ultimately physical death, and in fact, death over everything.

In the original Greek, it is *"the Adam"* signifying this specific man, and as well, it is *"the Christ."*

WHAT PAUL IS ACTUALLY SAYING

Paul does not say that *"in the person of Adam"* all died, i.e., when death struck him, etc., meaning that death ended there. Therefore, it could be translated, *"For as in the Adam all go on dying,"* which means *"a continuous process of dying."* In other words, the force of that death continues unto this hour, and in fact, deepens with time. To say it another way, from the moment of Adam's Fall, all have continued to fall, with the process increasingly worsening. The idea is, that Adam's one sin was the death of all of us.

NOTES

In Romans, Paul stresses the historic fact that occurred in the tragedy of Eden, in Corinthians the continuous fact that deepens from Eden, and continues to deepen until this hour.

HOW COULD ALL DIE IN ADAM?

When God made the Angels, every evidence is that He made them all at one time and fully mature. In other words, there have never been any baby angels. However, when He created man, He in fact created only a pair, and gave them the power of procreation, i.e., to bring sons and daughters (offspring) into the world.

In fact, this was such a privilege, such an honor, at least before the Fall, that had they not fallen, they would have in fact brought sons and daughters of God into the world (Lk. 3:38).

As it is, and due to the Fall, Adam and Eve were only able to bring children into the world in the likeness of *"Adam"* instead of the likeness of God (Gen. 5:1-5). Consequently, this is the cause of all sin, sickness, suffering, war, hate, greed, selfishness, brutality, murder, etc.

THE REPRESENTATIVE MAN

Adam having this power (the power of procreation), means that he was the representative man for all of humanity. In other words, whatever he did, would affect every single child that would ever be born, and because in actuality all were then in his loins. So, when he sinned, he sinned for all. As well, the penalty for spiritual death which passed to him instantly upon the Fall, also, passed to all who would follow him (Gen. 3:19). It affected all, involved all in the certainty of death.

The sentence that was passed upon the woman (Gen. 3:16) made it certain that all women would be subjected to the same condition of suffering to which Eve was subjected; and the sentence that was passed on man (Gen. 3:17), — that he should cultivate the ground in sorrow all the days of his life, that it should bring forth thistles and thorns to him (Gen. 3:18), that he should eat bread in the sweat of his brow (Gen. 3:19) — made it certain that this would be the condition of all men as well as of Adam.

It was a blow to the head of the human family, and they were subjected to the same train of evils as he was himself. In like manner, they were subjected to death.

WHAT TYPE OF DEATH?

First of all, as stated, it was spiritual death, which meant separation from God. In other words, the life cord to the Creator was broken, which meant that man is now left on his own, but even worse than that, he is fatally and hopelessly perverted, spoiled, twisted, and ruined, at least within himself. Physical death followed spiritual death, even as it must.

However, Paul in this passage is not actually speaking of spiritual death, but in reality of physical death. He is discussing the Resurrection, which pertains to the Sainted dead.

Nothing is more important in interpreting the Bible than to ascertain the specific point in the argument of a writer to be defended or illustrated, and then to confine the interpretation to that.

The argument of the Apostle here is ample to prove that all men are subjected to temporal death by the sin of Adam; and that this evil is counteracted fully by the Resurrection of Christ and the Resurrection through Him. Consequently, to this point this Scripture should be limited. It speaks of the Resurrection of those who died in Adam, at least those who have accepted Christ.

If one is to notice, the Text says *"in Adam,"* which means more than just the mere result of something, but that when he sinned, we sinned as well. That is what is meant by *"original sin."* As a result, the fountain was polluted, perverted, became unclean, and can only produce that which is perverted and unclean, etc. Hence, all being born in sin, for the simple reason we all were *"in Adam."*

IN CHRIST

The phrase, *"Even so in Christ shall all be made alive,"* refers to Christ as the Representative Man as well, Who would do what the first representative man, Adam, failed to do.

*"In Christ,"* refers to every facet of the Life, Ministry, and Sacrifice which was part of the Redeemer. It is far more extensive than most realize.

REPRESENTATIVE MAN

As the Representative Man, literally, God becoming flesh, Jesus was born of the Virgin Mary, for the simple reason that this is what had to be. Had He been born as a result of the union of Joseph and Mary, He would have been born in original sin as all others.

NOTES

Due to the fact that Joseph was not the father of Jesus, but rather God Himself, Jesus was born without sin, i.e., *"the original sin,"* and, therefore, was and is the Son of God.

In fact, Mary only furnished a house for Jesus for some nine months. Jesus did not have the traits of either Mary or Joseph, as all other children do to one extent or the other, regarding their parents. In other words, Mary's egg was not joined to Joseph's sperm, as conception normally occurs. In fact, Mary's egg was not germinated at all, the conception of Jesus being by the Holy Spirit. It was a miraculous conception, brought about by the Power of God, i.e., *"a decree."* In other words, the Power of God brought it about, which meant there was nothing in this physical, but all in the spiritual.

As a result, when a believing sinner is *"born again"* the terrible stain and blight of original sin, is instantly removed. Faith in Christ guarantees that, which is an absolute necessity if God is to accept any person.

That's what John was speaking about when he said, *"Behold the Lamb of God* (Jesus), *which taketh away the sin of the world* (original sin)," (Jn. 1:29).

SINLESS LIFE

For thirty-three and one-half years, Jesus walked absolutely perfect before God and man, never failing, never sinning, thereby keeping in totality the prescribed Law of God, i.e., *"The Law of Moses."* Consequently, acceptance of Christ also means that a perfect, sinless life is granted to the believing sinner.

It sounds like a contradiction in terms when perfection is attributed to the believing sinner.

In fact, it would be a contradiction if eyes were upon the believing sinner, but those Eyes, which are the Eyes of God, are rather on Christ our Representative Man. God grants that Faith in Christ on the part of the believing sinner guarantees such a person, which includes us all, the perfection of all that Christ is.

So, due to my Faith in Him, I am now a *"Lawkeeper,"* instead of a *"Lawbreaker."*

IN HIM AT CALVARY AND THE RESURRECTION

When Jesus died on Calvary, in the mind of God, every believing sinner literally was in

Christ, actually baptized into His Death, when He died (Rom. 6:3).

Consequently, regarding His Resurrection, being in Him when He died, we are now raised in Him, *"in newness of Life"* (Rom. 6:4).

WITH HIM AT THE RIGHT HAND OF GOD

This union is so complete regarding the believing sinner and Christ, that inasmuch as God *"hath raised us up together* (His Resurrection, and our being in Him)*,"* He has also *"made us sit together in heavenly places in Christ Jesus"* (Eph. 2:6).

So, *"in Christ,"* carries with it a far reaching glory and power. That's why Paul said, *"Now if we be dead with Christ, we believe that we shall also live with Him"* (Rom. 6:8).

ALL BE MADE ALIVE

Some claim that the word *"all"* here refers to both Believers and unbelievers, Believers raised to everlasting life, with unbelievers raised to everlasting damnation, but irrespective, all being made alive.

However, Paul is not speaking here of unbelievers, but rather Believers. In fact, he says, *"in Christ,"* which refers to the Salvation experience.

So, Paul is not instructing the Corinthians in regard to all men, he is speaking only about Believers and throughout his discussion, as we have stated, does not mention unbelievers. None are in connection with Christ except by true Faith alone.

Paul is not a philosopher-theologian, but a fact-theologian to the very core. So true is this regarding Paul, that he is governed, not even by abstract ideas or abstract forms of thinking, but by simple actualities and realities, in fact, exactly as Jesus approached things.

Therefore, claiming that the word *"all"* as here given refers to all of humanity, is taking Paul's statement further than he intended. While it is true that even the unbelieving dead will ultimately be raised, even to eternal damnation, which will take place at the Second Resurrection of Death, still, that is not what Paul is referring to at this time (Rev. 20:5-6, 14).

*"Alive"* as here used, is in the Greek *"zoopoieo,"* and means *"to give life, to quicken"* which refers to the Resurrection.

(23) "BUT EVERY MAN IN HIS OWN ORDER: CHRIST THE FIRSTFRUITS; AFTERWARD THEY THAT ARE CHRIST'S AT HIS COMING."

NOTES

The phrase, *"But every man in his own order,"* refers to the Resurrection, and speaks only of Believers, as proved by Christ being the *"Firstfruits"* of which He is only to Believers.

*"Order"* in the Greek is *"tagma,"* and means *"a rank or company."*

WHAT DOES PAUL MEAN BY THE WORD *"ORDER"?*

Paul is speaking of the *"order"* of the Resurrection, in other words, in the manner in which it will be carried out. It is as follows:

CHRIST AS THE FIRSTFRUITS

Christ being raised from the dead, was the *"Firstfruits"* in this *"order."*

Some claim that all the Old Testament Saints were Resurrected with Him; however, even though they did experience a form of Resurrection, by Christ delivering them from the prison house of Paradise below (Lk. Chpt. 16), with the spirit/soul of all being taken to Heaven, there is no Scriptural clue that they experienced Resurrection as we are here addressing. In other words, they were not then given a glorified body.

Before Jesus paid the sin debt at Calvary, Satan maintained a claim on all of the Old Testament Saints, for the simple reason that even though the sin debt was covered by Atonement, it was not removed. That happened only when Jesus paid the price at Calvary.

As a result, all of these people, including the Prophets of old, were taken down into Paradise and actually held captive by Satan. While they were not in the burning side of the pit, still, if Jesus had not been Resurrected, their fate, plus that of all others for that matter, would have been the same as all lost sinners — hellfire. However, Jesus did deliver them, even as Paul mentions in Ephesians 4:8-9.

Resurrection demands the final form, which is Glorified bodies, which will take place at the Rapture. There is no record that Old Testament Saints received glorified forms, but certainly shall do so, even as all New Testament Saints at the Coming Resurrection.

Now, due to what Jesus did in paying the terrible sin debt, when a Believer dies, his soul/spirit instantly goes to Heaven, where the souls/spirits of all the Saints even back to Adam are now waiting (Phil. 1:23). The Resurrection will conclude that wait.

THE MAIN BODY OF RESURRECTION

The second group in this *"order"* of Resurrection pertains to the main body of Resurrection which could take place at any time, and which we refer to as the *"Rapture of the Church."* This includes everyone in Christ, dead or alive (Lk. 21:34-36; Jn. 14:1-3; I Cor. 15:23, 51, 54; II Cor. 5:1-8; Eph. 5:27; Phil. 3:11, 20-21; Col. 3:4; I Thess. 2:19; 3:13; 4:16-17; 5:9, 23; II Thess. 2:1, 7; James 5:7-8; I Pet. 5:4; I Jn. 2:28, 3:2).

THE MAN CHILD

The *"man child"* is the 144,000 Jews who will be saved in the first three and one half years of the coming Great Tribulation (Rev. 7:1-8). They will be caught up, or raptured, in the middle of the Great Tribulation, or about three and one half years before the Second Coming (Isa. 66:7-8; Dan. 12:1; Rev. 12:5; 14:1-5).

The idea is, in order to complete the analogy of the harvest, even which Paul uses by referring to Jesus as the *"Firstfruits"* one has to consider the gleanings which were left in the fields for the poor to garner, after the main harvest.

Figuratively, they are groups that the Lord will take to be with Him after the bulk of the harvest is received before the coming seven year Tribulation begins on Earth. These gleanings are the 144,000, plus the next two groups.

TRIBULATION SAINTS

The Scripture tells us that many people will be saved during the Great Tribulation, perhaps even millions (Rev. 6:9-11).

The disappearance of every single Believer on the face of the Earth will cause quite a stir, as should be obvious. There will be millions who will then know that they had better get right with God, and, in fact, will do so. While most will not repent, some most definitely will.

Joel predicted, and Simon Peter further quoted him, that many would be saved, during the Great Tribulation Period (Acts 2:16-21). As a side issue, this means the Holy Spirit will not be taken out of the world at the Rapture, as some claim, because it is impossible for one to be saved without the administration of the Holy Spirit.

NOTES

THE TWO WITNESSES

The Rapture of the two witnesses, Enoch and Elijah, who in fact have never yet died, and will come back to this Earth during the Great Tribulation, and will actually minister in person in Jerusalem, where they will be finally killed by the Antichrist (Rev. 11:7-11).

They, too, will be Resurrected in time for the Marriage Supper, and will come back with Christ at the Second Coming, as will all Saints for all time, and all with Glorified Bodies.

So, that is the *"order"* of which Paul speaks.

The phrase, *"Christ the Firstfruits,"* refers to Christ being first in this *"order"* which as well is a pledge that all Believers shall rise.

The phrase, *"Afterward they that are Christ's at His Coming,"* pertains to all Believers guaranteed of Resurrection and because of the Resurrection of Christ. He must necessarily be the *"Firstfruits"* in order that all may follow.

AT HIS COMING

This pertains to the Rapture of the Church (I Thess. 4:13-18), and not the Second Coming (Rev. Chpt. 19).

While the Rapture (or Resurrection) is definitely a Coming, it is not the Second Coming, which will actually take place seven or more years after the Rapture.

WHAT IS THE DIFFERENCE IN THE RAPTURE AND THE SECOND COMING?

We mean by the Rapture (Resurrection) of the Church, the catching up of all true Believers in Christ to meet the Lord in the air. This event is simply and clearly predicted in Luke 21:34-36; John 14:1-3; I Corinthians 15:23, 51-58; Philippians 3:20-21; Colossians 3:4; I Thessalonians 4:13-17.

If one carefully reads I Thessalonians 4:16-17, there is no room for misunderstanding. So it is obvious that if one does not believe in the Rapture (Resurrection) it is because he does not believe the Bible. In fact, if one believes in the Resurrection, one must believe in the Rapture, for they are one and the same.

THE COMING OF THE LORD

The Rapture of the Church is called the *"Coming of the Lord"* but never the Second Coming of Christ. At the Rapture, Christ does not appear visibly to those on the Earth, but

He comes in the air above the Earth to catch up or Rapture the dead and living Saints who rise together to meet Him in the air.

There are many different ideas about these two Comings of Christ, which have made it difficult to distinguish one Coming from the other. There are so many Scriptures that have been misapplied to the one or the other Coming that one might readily see why many have found themselves involved in difficulties from which they are unable to clear themselves.

The Rapture is purely a New Testament Doctrine and was first revealed to Paul as a special revelation (I Cor. 15:51-58), while the Second Coming of Christ is not only a New Testament Doctrine, but is one of the chief themes of the Old Testament as well.

## THE OLD TESTAMENT AND THE CHURCH

The Old Testament Prophets never saw the New Testament Church, much less the Rapture of the Church. The Rapture should never be called the Second Coming or Second Advent of Christ, for He does not come to the Earth at that time. Also, it should never be referred to as one stage or phase of the Second Coming of Christ for the two will be separated by at least seven years, and possibly longer.

The Rapture is a distinct Coming in itself, not to the Earth, but in the air where Christ meets the Saints and then takes them back to Heaven to present them blameless before God (Jn. 14:1-3; I Thess. 3:13; 4:16-17).

## THE DIFFERENCE IN THE TWO COMINGS

1. The Rapture takes place several years before the literal Advent of Christ to the Earth.

2. The Saints are in Heaven before God, from the time of the Rapture to their coming again with Christ to reign as kings and priests (Zech. 14:5; Jude vs. 14; Rev. 19:14). This seems clear from the facts that the Saints are judged, are given their rewards, and partake of the Marriage Supper in Heaven, immediately before the Second Coming (II Cor. 5:9-10; Rev. 19:1-10).

3. At the Rapture Christ comes *for* the Saints (I Thess. 4:16-17); at the Second Coming, He comes back to Earth *with* the Saints (Jude vs. 14; Zech. 14:5).

4. At the Rapture, the Lord comes from Heaven as far as the air above the Earth, and the Saints will be caught up to meet Him in the air. At the Second Coming, the Saints are already in Heaven, and will come back with the Lord to the Earth together.

5. The Rapture (Resurrection) takes place *before* the coming Great Tribulation, whereas the Second Advent takes place *after* the coming Great Tribulation.

6. The Rapture could occur at any moment. The Second Advent cannot occur until certain things happen such as the rise of the Antichrist, etc. (II Thess. Chpt. 2).

(24) "THEN COMETH THE END, WHEN HE SHALL HAVE DELIVERED UP THE KINGDOM TO GOD, EVEN THE FATHER; WHEN HE SHALL HAVE PUT DOWN ALL RULE AND ALL AUTHORITY AND POWER."

The phrase, *"Then cometh the end,"* does not refer to the time immediately following the Rapture or even the Second Coming, but when all satanic rule, authority, and power will have been put down, which will take place at the conclusion of the Millennial Reign (Rev. Chpt. 20). The final conclusion will actually be Satan loosed out of his prison for a short period of time, which will take place at the end of the Millennial Reign, when the Lord will make short order of this last attempt by the Evil One, with him being *"cast into the lake of fire and brimstone . . . and shall be tormented day and night for ever and ever"* (Rev. 20:7-10).

The phrase, *"When He shall have delivered up the Kingdom to God, even the Father,"* tells us what happens when the *"end"* comes.

## END OF WHAT?

The phrase, *"When He shall have put down all rule and all authority and power,"* refers to every last vestige of evil and wickedness under the auspices of Satan and his minions, which actually began with Satan's rebellion against God and is described by both Isaiah and Ezekiel (Isa. 14:12-15; Ezek. 28:11-19). This began long before the episode in the Garden of Eden.

As a result of this rebellion, in which a third of the angels threw in their lot with Lucifer (Rev. 12:4), untold sorrow and heartache have come to the Earth, with possibly much more elsewhere.

## JESUS THE VICTOR

It is Jesus Who will *"deliver up the Kingdom to God,"* a Kingdom incidentally, that will

NOTES

then be free of all Satanic *"rule," "authority,"* and *"power."*

Jesus defeated Satan at Calvary and the Resurrection.

The idea is, that the Lord Jesus has received or been entrusted with an important power or office as Mediator; that He has executed the purpose implied in that trust or commission; and, that He is now rendering that to God (or will in that day) the Office and Authority which He had received at God's Hands.

As the work has been accomplished which had been contemplated in His Design; as there would be no further necessity for mediation when Redemption should have been made, and His Church recovered from sin and brought to Glory, there would be no further need for that peculiar arrangement which had been implied in the Work of Redemption, and, of course, all the entrustment of Power involved in that which will now be restored to the Hands of God.

THE GOVERNMENT OF GOD

The idea is that He will deliver up the Kingdom as the Governors of Provinces render again or deliver up their commission and authority to the Caesars who appointed them. There is no absurdity in this view.

For if the world was to be redeemed, it was necessary that the Redeemer be entrusted with power sufficient for His Work. When this Work is done, and there is no further need of that particular exercise of power, then it would be proper that it should be restored, or that the Government of God should be administered as it was before the Work of Redemption became necessary and was undertaken.

This does not mean that the Second Person of the Trinity will surrender all power, or cease to exercise Government. It will be that power only which He had as Mediator; whatever part in the Administration of the Government of the universe He shared as Divine before the Incarnation, He will still share, with the additional glory and honor of having redeemed a world by His Death and Resurrection.

THE KINGDOM

This word means properly dominion, reign, the exercise of kingly power.

In the New Testament, it means commonly the reign of the Messiah or the dominion which

NOTES

God would exercise through the Messiah; the reign of God over men by the Laws and Institutions of the Messiah.

At this time, all the enemies of God will have been subdued, and done so by Jesus Christ. His power shall have asserted. The Authority of God shall have been established, and the Kingdom or the Dominion shall be in the Hands of God Himself; and Jesus shall reign, not in the peculiar form which existed in the Work of Mediation, but absolutely, and as He did over obedient minds before the Incarnation.

TO GOD

This refers to God as God; to the Divinity.

The Mediator, the Lord Jesus Christ, shall have given up this peculiar power and rule and He shall then exercise the power and authority of God as God, but yet retaining His Glorified Manhood.

The word *"Father,"* as applied to God in the Scriptures, is used in two senses: To designate the Father, the First Person of the Trinity as distinguished from the Son; and in a broader, wider sense, to denote God as sustaining the relation of a Father to His creatures, i.e., Creation — as the Father of all.

It is in the latter sense, perhaps, that the word *"Father"* is here used — not to denote that the Second Person of the Trinity is to surrender all power into the hands of the First, or that He is to cease to exercise Dominion and Control; but that the power is to be yielded into the hands of God as God, i.e., as the universal Father, as the Divinity, without being exercised in any peculiar and special manner by the different Persons of the Godhead, as had been done in the Work of Redemption.

At the close of the Work of Redemption, this peculiar arrangement will cease; and God, as the universal Father and Ruler of all, will exercise the Government of the world, and in fact, of all His creation.

(25) "FOR HE MUST REIGN, TILL HE HATH PUT ALL ENEMIES UNDER HIS FEET."

The phrase, *"For He must reign,"* refers to the one thousand year reign of Christ on Earth after He returns. Resurrected Believers will have the honor of assisting Him in that process (Rev. 2:26-27; 3:21).

## THE MANHOOD OF CHRIST

The Mediatorial Reign of Christ as King over all the Earth is that spoken of in Verses 24-28. Psalms 2, 8, 45, and 110, with many other Scriptures predicting that Reign.

Christ as the Glorified Man, is now seated on the Father's Throne waiting until His enemies be placed as a footstool for His Feet. He will then rise up from His Father's Throne, ascend His Own Mediatorial and Kingly Throne, and there reign until He has overthrown every power, including death, which disputes the supremacy of God.

He will then hand that perfected Kingdom with Himself as Son of God in His Humanity — His Title by merit distinct from His Sonship with God in Being and Essence — and retaining His Manhood, He will in that Manhood eternally exist in perfect union and obedience with God, just as He existed upon Earth in His First Advent in the same perfection of Being and Obedience.

These communications establish the heart of the Believer in a peace that is unshakable and in a joy that is unspeakable, because Christ's eternal Manhood secures the eternal existence and bliss of all human beings who are united to Him as human beings.

The phrase, *"Till He hath put all enemies under His Feet,"* refers to the position of a conqueror.

## KING OF KINGS

We now learn that a Divine necessity lies back of all this: Christ's rule as King must extend that far, i.e., *"the subjugation of all evil powers."* He would not be truly a King and rule as a King if at the end, when He transfers the Kingdom, any enemies remained active.

If even a single enemy were left who might use any measure of power, Christ would not be the King that God intended Him to be.

The Text denotes *"completeness." "All His enemies"* defines who is meant by *"all rule."*

*"Under His Feet"* brings out the full force of *"shall have abolished."*

The meaning is, that the power of Satan shall be broken so utterly and forever that they shall not again arise from the ground or stir a finger against the King. In other words, the victory is complete; the victory is total; the victory is eternal.

NOTES

(26) "THE LAST ENEMY THAT SHALL BE DESTROYED IS DEATH."

We learn several things from this passage:

Death is the result or wages of sin (Rom. 6:23). I think from I Corinthians 15:55 and Revelation 20:14, that one can say that Death is personified. In other words, Death is a person, or rather a fallen Angel. If in fact, it is proper to refer to Death in that fashion, we would have to assume that this Angel was not made in this fashion in the beginning, but became the Angel of Death after he threw in his lot with Satan in the revolution against God.

## THE CONCEPTION OF SIN AND DEATH

According to Genesis 2:17, God gave to man, created in His Own Image, the command not to eat of the tree of knowledge of good and evil, and added thereto the warning, *"In the day that thou eatest thereof thou shalt surely die."*

Though not exclusively, reference is certainly made here in the first place to bodily death. Yet because death by no means came upon Adam and Eve on the day of their transgression, but took place hundreds of years later, the expression, *"In the day that,"* must be conceived in a wider sense actually referring to spiritual death, which within itself ultimately brought on physical death.

Genesis 2:17 places a close connection between man's death and his transgression of God's Commandment, thereby attaching to death a spiritual and ethical significance, and on the other hand, makes the life of man dependent on his obedience to God.

This spiritual — ethical nature of life and death is not only decidedly and clearly expressed in Genesis Chapter 2, but it is the fundamental thought of the whole of Scripture and forms an essential element in the Revelations of Salvation.

## DEATH, THE OPPOSITE OF CHRIST

In Christ is all Life, as in Satan is all death.

At the present time, death covers everything, casting its pall over all the living, to the extent that even its seeds permeate that which is alive.

Its reason, as stated, is sin, and due to the Fall, it festers upon everything, because everything is covered by sin.

The Medical profession does not really understand why the human body ages. They say, and rightly so, that the physical organs are so marvelously constructed, that they should in fact last forever. However, they age and ultimately die, and why?

SPIRITUAL

The reason that the Medical profession is stymied, is because the problem is not physical, but rather spiritual. So, it doesn't matter how many wonder drugs or antibiotics are developed, the ultimate arrival of death may be prolonged a short time, but never stopped, at least in this fashion.

Its only Conqueror is the Lord and in reality, the Life of God.

ENEMY

Death is an enemy: It is a foe, a hinderance to all that is good.

By the efforts of Medical science, men know that something is wrong respecting life and death. Something so marvelous and wonderful as the human being should not die. Death is an enemy to all life, to all hopes, to all dreams, to all fulfillment, to all completion. It breaks up homes, relationships, marriages, loves, affections, friendships, etc. It stops the creative process, the development process, the end result of all that is good, etc.

It is man's greatest enemy, and in fact, his greatest enemy to all that he does and is.

It is said that shortly before Albert Einstein died, he said, *"If I only had five more years."*

This brilliant man was on the verge of unlocking other secrets of the universe, but time ran out, cut short by the monster called *"death."* Truly it is an *"enemy."*

DESTROYED

Death shall be *"destroyed." "Destroyed"* in the Greek is *"katargeo,"* and means *"to abolish, to nullify,"* and so to render something inoperative or ineffectual. The power that death has to quiet human beings will be forever nullified.

This great Verse (I Cor. 15:26) proclaims Christ's ultimate victory. It makes a declaration that is absolutely astounding!

As we have stated, men attempt to hold back death by various remedies, and rightly so; however, Jesus, having already taken the fear out of death, will then remove it completely.

NOTES

The same word (destroyed) is also found in II Timothy 1:10. Jesus has already rendered spiritual death inoperative in those who turn to Him, which means that we can experience now the life and immortality we have in Him (Heb. 2:14).

LAST

Why is it the last enemy to be destroyed?

During the coming one thousand year Reign of Christ, all evil and iniquity will be addressed in a practical sense, even as it has already been addressed in a spiritual sense, i.e., *"Calvary and the Resurrection of Christ."* As a result, Satan along with all his fallen Angels and demon spirits, will be locked away in the *"bottomless pit,"* at the beginning of this great Reign (Rev. 20:1-3); consequently, the difference that will make will be literally astounding within itself. The Tempter's power is broken! He has no more latitude to steal, kill, and destroy (Jn. 10:10). The demon powers which infest the entirety of the world at present, and especially nations which do not know Jesus Christ, will be no more.

But yet, such is the nature of the incurable human heart that many millions at this time (the Kingdom Age), although forced to obey the Lord, still, will oppose Him in their hearts; however, they will not be allowed to take away the peace of that time, and if they persist, some will be executed.

Because of that, during the coming Millennial Reign, even though death's power will have been removed, he still will be present. In fact, Isaiah said, *"There shall be no more thence an infant of days nor an old man that hath not filled his days: for the child shall die an hundred years old; but the sinner being an hundred years old shall be accursed"* (Isa. 65:20).

This does not mean that individuals will still be children at a hundred years old, but that at a hundred years old, a man's life will only be beginning, even as the life of a child presently.

As well, the Prophet is saying that anyone who does not accept Christ in this coming age, at least by the time he is a hundred years old, he will be *"accursed,"* meaning that he is in serious straits.

TWO CLASSES OF PEOPLE

Actually, during this coming time there will be two classes of people in the world: The

NOTES

Glorified Saints, which will comprise every Believer who has ever lived; and a second group that could be referred to as the natural people, who will have come over from the Great Tribulation at the Second Coming, and as well those who are born during this time.

All will be given opportunity to accept Christ, and many will; however, Revelation 20:8 tells us that many won't.

At that time, the natural people will stop aging and death, by partaking of the product of the trees which will grow beside the river flowing out from the Temple in Jerusalem (Ezek. 47:12). The Scripture says, *"And the leaf thereof for medicine."*

So, even though *"death"* will remain active during the coming Millennial Reign, it will be on a very limited scale. He is allowed to remain during this time, simply because there will be many in the world who will not accept Christ. Consequently, it is proper that the Mediatorial Work of Christ should continue until this great work of total redemption is effected.

During this time, the enmity of the human heart shall be subdued by the triumphs of the Gospel. The scepter of Satan will be broken and wrested from him. The false systems of religion that had tyrannized over men will be destroyed.

The Gospel shall spread everywhere, and the world will then serve God with many accepting Christ as Saviour, but even those who do not will not be allowed to take away, as stated, the *"peace"* of that coming time.

Consequently, when that time ends, the only enemy left, will be death, and he will then be destroyed.

(27) "FOR HE HATH PUT ALL THINGS UNDER HIS FEET. BUT WHEN HE SAITH ALL THINGS ARE PUT UNDER HIM, IT IS MANIFEST THAT HE IS EXCEPTED, WHICH DID PUT ALL THINGS UNDER HIM."

The phrase, *"For He hath put all things under His Feet,"* refers to God the Father putting all things under the Feet of Jesus. He has made all things subject to Him, or has appointed Him to be Head over all things (Mat. 28:18; Jn. 17:2; Eph. 1:20-22).

## PARADISE LOST, PARADISE REGAINED

The words *"hath put all things under His Feet,"* are found in Psalms 8:6, and are applicable to man, and are designed to show the dignity and dominion of man. However, through sin, man lost dominion over the powers of Earth so that only vestiges of that dominion remain.

In the end, every man succumbs, and his body yields, to death. However, God did not leave man in this helpless situation, but joined Himself to us, actually making us His Brethren (Heb. 2:11-14). In fact, He died that *"through death"* and His *"propitiation"* He would *"bring many sons unto Glory."*

It is thus that Christ, our Brother, has all things placed under His Feet, namely for our sakes, in order to restore us to our original high and glorious position.

And this, of necessity, includes among *"all things"* death, which was made subject to Christ our Redeemer, in order that He *"might deliver all them who through the fear of death were all their lifetime subject to bondage"* (Heb. 2:15).

## DOMINION AND DEATH

Nothing exhibits sinful man's loss of dominion as does *"death."* A thousand tiny and great forces in nature are busy killing our race. Already while Christ was on Earth, death had to obey Him and to yield up its prey at His Command (the daughter of Jairus, the widow's son, and Lazarus).

Death received its own deathblow when Christ arose from the tomb. And at the end, even as we have been studying, death shall be abolished forever.

The phrase, *"But when He saith all things are put under Him, it is manifest that He is excepted, which did put all things under Him,"* has reference to the fact that *"all things"* do not include God the Father being made subject to Jesus. God is excepted, as should be obvious.

## THE REASON FOR PAUL'S STATEMENT

Anything the Holy Spirit says is always done for a purpose. Consequently, the following are at least some of the reasons that Paul made this statement:

1. Paul said this to avoid the possibility of misconstruction of the phrase, *"All things,"* as if it meant that God would be included, and would be subdued to Him; as, among the heathen, Jupiter is fabled to have expelled his father Saturn from his throne and from heaven.

2. It might be to prevent the supposition, from what Paul had said of the extent of the

Son's Dominion, that He was in any respect superior to the Father. It is implied by this exception here, that when the necessity for the peculiar Mediatorial Kingdom of the Son should cease, there will be a resuming of the Authority and Dominion of the Father, in the manner in which it subsisted before the Incarnation.

3. The expression may also be regarded as intensive or emphatic; as denoting, in the most absolute sense, that there was nothing in the universe but God, which was not subject to Him. God was the only exception; and His Dominion, therefore, was absolute over all other beings and things.

4. In fact, the very cause of all the problems with mankind is that Lucifer had rebelled against God's Dominion, and has brought man into this rebellion; consequently, the Holy Spirit through the Apostle wants no misunderstanding concerning the totality of God the Father.

As is obvious in the Text, it is God Who purposely gave certain Dominion to Christ, while Satan attempted to take it by force. Such proclaims the true way of God, versus the false way of Satan. In other words, Jesus did not take this *"Dominion,"* it was given to Him freely by the Father.

(28) "AND WHEN ALL THINGS SHALL BE SUBDUED UNTO HIM, THEN SHALL THE SON ALSO HIMSELF BE SUBJECT UNTO HIM THAT PUT ALL THINGS UNDER HIM, THAT GOD MAY BE ALL IN ALL."

The phrase, *"And when all things shall be subdued unto Him,"* implies that in Paul's day, this total Dominion had not yet been exercised, and in fact, has not done so unto this present hour, but the Lord in effect is carrying forward the plans for the subjugation of all things to God, which will happen shortly.

The pronoun *"Him"* refers to Jesus, Who in fact, is the One Who will carry forth this great victory.

We must never forget, that *"all things shall be subdued unto Him,"* and not Mohammed, Buddha, Confucius, or any other fake luminary. Jesus is the One to Whom the world must answer, and in fact, to Whom Satan and his minions must answer as well. Paul's point is that in raising Christ from the dead God has set in motion a chain of events that must culminate in the final destruction of death, which is the wages of sin, and thus, of God being once again, as eternity past, *"all in all."*

NOTES

In Paul's view the consummation of Redemption includes the whole sphere of creation as well (Rom. 8:19-22; Col. 1:15-20). Nothing lies outside God's Redemptive purposes in Christ, in Whom all things finally will be *"united"* (Eph. 1:9-10).

Therefore, at the death of death the final rupture in the universe will be healed and God alone will rule over all beings, banishing those who have rejected His offer of life and lovingly governing all those who by grace have entered into God's *"rest"* (Fee).

The phrase, *"Then shall the Son also Himself be subject unto Him that put all things under Him,"* refers to the Incarnation.

Up to the moment of this glorious consummation of which Paul speaks, an economic division of functions presently exists between the Three Persons of the Godhead in regard to this sinful world and its Salvation. In this very paragraph the Father does certain things, and the Son does other things. While nothing is said about the Holy Spirit, other Passages tell us about His part of the Work.

In this economic division the Incarnate Son rules as King and Lord. He thus stands in the foreground for His Church. When the consummation is reached, this position shall cease, in the very nature of the case it must then cease, for its final objective has been attained.

## THE INCARNATE SON

When God, the Second Person of the Godhead took upon Himself humanity, which He had to do in order that the price be paid for man's Redemption, which Paul explains in Philippians 2:5-11. While never ceasing to be God, and losing none of His supremacy of Deity, still, He did lose much of its expression. He now resides in Glorified Form, but still in the human state, but still God. Nevertheless, He experienced a *"loss"* in the Incarnation one might say, in order to redeem man, which will remain with Him forever. It is in this manner that He is *"subject unto Him* (God the Father) *Who hath put all things under Him* (under the Son)*."*

If one is to notice, the Holy Spirit through Paul uses the appellative *"Son"* denoting the Incarnation, and that of which we speak.

However, let us emphasize strongly, this in no way means that He is any less God.

HIS RULE

Christ, the Son of God, in His Divine Nature, as God, shall never cease to reign. As Mediator, He may resign His commission and His peculiar office, having made an Atonement, having recovered His people, at lease those who will believe, yet as One with the Father, as the *"Father of the everlasting age,"* He shall not cease to reign (Isa. 9:6).

As we have already stated, the subjection of which Paul here speaks does not mean that the second person in the Trinity, as such, should be subject to the First; but it means the Incarnate Son, the Mediator, — the Man Who was born and was raised from the dead, and to Whom this wide dominion had been given, should resign that dominion, and for the simple reason that the task is completed, with that part of the Government of God now being reassumed by the Divinity as God. And yet, the Second Person of the Godhead will retain His Glorified Human Form forever, which He willingly makes subject to the Father.

The phrase, *"That God may be all in all,"* does not teach *"Ultimate Reconciliation,"* as some claim.

This evil doctrine, which is somewhat derived from this Verse, claims that all people will ultimately be saved, even going back to the very beginning, plus Satan, his demon hoards and fallen angels, etc.

ALL IN ALL

But the fact that God shall be all in all is not the doctrine of Ultimate Reconciliation or restoration of all things, i.e., that even the ungodly and the devil shall at last be restored and brought into communion with God. The Scriptures know only the opposite of this doctrine, which Paul also declares in the paragraph before us. Such a non-biblical view cannot be substantiated by the simple word *"all in all."*

What Paul says is plain: after all things are at last subjected to Christ, and He Himself subjects Himself to God, then God shall be supreme, *"all in all,"* in one perfect harmony with not a hand or a voice in the whole universe raised against Him.

NOTES

Christ has disposed of the wicked and the Devils. Their rule, authority, and power are abolished so that no trace of them is left. All of these enemies are under Christ's Feet so that none of them can ever show themselves again or do anything.

They are judged, undone, in hell. The new heavens and the new earth shall know them not. This is the absolute opposite of Ultimate Reconciliation (Lenski).

Such a doctrine destroys the free moral agency of man and as well, makes the Atonement unnecessary or ineffectual at best. If men reject God, which in fact most do, how can they at the same time accept God!

THE LAKE OF FIRE

Revelation 20:15 says, *"And whosoever was not found written in the Book of Life was cast into the Lake of Fire."*

Concerning that place, it says *"And shall be tormented day and night for ever and ever"* (Rev. 20:10).

To be sure, such is not the Will of God, for He is not willing that any should perish, but it definitely is the Justice of God, and Justice demanded at that. If such were not to be, the opposition of God against sin, then the Righteousness of God becomes a joke and falls to the ground.

(29) "ELSE WHAT SHALL THEY DO WHICH ARE BAPTIZED FOR THE DEAD, IF THE DEAD RISE NOT AT ALL? WHY ARE THEY THEN BAPTIZED FOR THE DEAD?"

The question, *"Else what shall they do which are baptized for the dead, if the dead rise not at all?",* proclaims the Apostle referring once again to the Resurrection. In other words, he is saying, *"It is a fruitless point to baptize for the dead, which is unscriptural anyway, if there is no Resurrection as some are teaching."*

IS THERE SUCH A THING AS BAPTISM FOR THE DEAD?

No! nor is Paul advocating such here. Commentators and expositors have argued over this one Verse for centuries, I suppose ever since it has been written.

Some claim that due to Paul's statement here, that Baptism (Water Baptism) for the dead is valid. Others claim that this proves that Baptismal Regeneration, i.e., Water Baptism saves.

Of course, none of that is true, which as well, flies totally in the face of all that Paul teaches.

Others claim that this practice of baptizing for the dead was being carried on in the Church at Corinth; however, that is erroneous as well.

To be sure, if such was being done in the Church at Corinth, Paul would definitely addressed it in detail instead of just casual mention. So, why did he mention this at all?

THEN, AS NOW

Then, as now, erroneous doctrine was rampant everywhere. No doubt, some people outside the Church at Corinth were practicing *"baptizing for the dead,"* meaning that a friend or loved one could be baptized in water on behalf of someone who had previously died but was not saved, and such would insure their Salvation. Paul, no doubt, had heard of this, as well as all types of other false doctrines, and now casually mentions this fact without going into any detail. Quite possibly, those who were teaching such error, were also teaching that there is no Resurrection of the dead.

So the Apostle puts the two together, *"baptizing for the dead"* and *"no Resurrection,"* and uses it as a point to emphasize the inconsistency of such a position. Again, there is no proof whatsoever that the erroneous doctrine of *"baptizing for the dead"* was any way practiced in the Church at Corinth.

The question, *"Why are they then baptized for the dead?"*, proclaims the foolishness of doing such a thing, if there is no such thing as a Resurrection. In effect, both questions of this Scripture are the same — the portrayal of the inconsistency of such action.

FALSE DOCTRINE AND
THE CROSS OF CHRIST

Possibly one could say, and with no glee, that the Church is probably in worse condition spiritually than it has been at any time since the Reformation. False doctrine abounds on every hand. Three particular forms of apostasy are:

1. The Purpose Driven Life doctrine.
2. The Government of Twelve doctrine.
3. The Word of Faith doctrine.

The Word of Faith doctrine openly repudiates the Cross, claiming that it was the greatest defeat in human history. It is referred to as *"past miseries."* In fact, in Word of Faith Churches, no mention of the Cross is made, and no song containing words regarding the Blood, the Cross, or Calvary are used, because such are, they claim, defeatist. The end result of this gospel, so-called, is money; regrettably, it has infected almost every facet of Church life.

NOTES

However, the greatest thrust of all is the *"Purpose Driven Life"* doctrine. It should be a tip-off when almost every Denomination has accepted this false direction, and to a degree never previously known.

The Government of Twelve, while much less known than the Purpose Driven Life, still, has invaded many Churches.

For lack of space, let us say that the real reason these particular doctrines are not of God, and are gross error, is because they make something the object of faith other than the Cross. In both cases, to be frank, it is *"works,"* which constitutes law.

Paul addressed that plainly by saying, *"If Righteousness come by the Law, then Christ is dead in vain"* (Gal. 2:21).

To be sure, these particular doctrines aren't the only systems of error in the Church presently. There are many others, but these three are presently the most prominent!

(30) "AND WHY STAND WE IN JEOPARDY EVERY HOUR?"

Gordon Fee said, and I agree with him, that much of the reason for the erroneous doctrine (no Resurrection) which seemed to characterize the Corinthian Assembly, was because of their opposition to Paul. Fee went on to say that their opposition was based in part on conflicting views of what it means to be an Apostle, which had inherent in it their taking a less than enthusiastic view of his weaknesses and sufferings as one called to this Office.

HOW COULD THEY BE
OPPOSED TO PAUL?

That is an excellent question, especially considering that these people had been saved under his Ministry, and without him, they probably would not have had an opportunity to accept Christ at all, consequently, dying eternally lost. If one is to remember, Paul had said to them, *"For though ye have ten thousand instructors in Christ, yet have ye not many fathers: for in Christ Jesus I have begotten you through the Gospel"* (I Cor. 4:15).

All the reasons, of course, we cannot know, and yet, the following is more than likely the greatest reason of all:

When Satan attempts to turn a person away from the true Gospel, most of the time he will manufacture in the heart of that person, opposition to the one who is delivering the True Message. They will begin to find fault with that particular Preacher, even though he has been their source of blessing, even as these found fault with Paul.

In their minds, finding some fault, real or imagined, justifies their position concerning doctrine. Most of the time, the Preacher in question will have no idea whatsoever as to why they are turning on him, and to be frank, neither does his detractors.

However, the method of attacking the Preacher of the Gospel in a personal manner is one of Satan's chief means of weaving his web.

PAUL'S METHOD

What Paul seems to do in the next three Verses is to capitalize on his weaknesses once more (I Cor. 2:1-5; 4:10-13; 15:9-10), this time, however, agreeing that if they are right on the one count (there is no Resurrection), then they are surely also right on the other (his Apostleship is of no profit whatsoever). But of course, they are not right on the former (I Cor. 20-28), and his Apostleship has everything to do with their being saved.

(How anyone could oppose the Apostle Paul is hard to understand, but I think the facts are clear that some did, even some who had been saved under his Ministry.)

HIS LIFE AND CONSTANT JEOPARDY

His point, of course, is that he is indeed crazy to put his life in constant jeopardy for the sake of others, even as he had done for these Corinthians, if neither he nor they have hope in the Resurrection. But even more, this sentence also indicates the absolutely central and crucial role that Christ's Resurrection played in Paul's life. One must remember throughout, that to deny the Resurrection of the dead meant to deny the Resurrection of Christ (I Cor. 15:12-19), which meant for Paul the denial of the Christian Life altogether. Thus, everything Christians do as Christians — and especially the labors of an Apostle — are an absurdity if there is no Resurrection (Fee).

Paul, using the term *"every hour"* as it referred to *"jeopardy,"* in no way overstated the case. The Jews were constantly trying to kill him. As well, they were constantly attempting to bring in the Roman authorities so as to place them against Paul, which they had done at Corinth, and now would do at Ephesus (Acts Chpt. 19). In fact, it was only by the Power of God that he escaped death in either place.

If Satan could knock out this man, he could cripple the New Covenant extensively, and seriously hinder World Evangelism. Consequently, the Evil One concentrated much of his energy on Paul.

(I have mentioned Corinth and Ephesus regarding this opposition, simply because Paul had planted the Churches at both Corinth and Ephesus, and, in fact, was in Ephesus when he was writing I Corinthians. However, he suffered the same opposition everywhere else as well.)

(31) "I PROTEST BY YOUR REJOICING WHICH I HAVE IN CHRIST JESUS OUR LORD, I DIE DAILY."

The phrase, *"I protest by your rejoicing which I have in Christ Jesus our Lord,"* is translated somewhat strangely.

The meaning of the phrase is probably, *"I protest, or solemnly declare by my glorying or exultation which I have on your account; by all my ground of glorying in you; by all the confident boasting and expectation which I have of your Salvation."*

Conversely, many of the Corinthians did not too much glory in Paul as they well might; many of them gloried in other leaders (I Cor. 1:12), etc.

Paul is proud of his successful work among the Corinthians. He glories in it. Yet Paul would never take undue credit to himself. He is only the Lord's instrument while he is doing His Work, and when that work shows marked success as it did at Corinth (despite the problems), Paul returns all the credit to Christ.

RESURRECTION TITLE

The very manner in which Paul addresses the Saviour, *"Jesus, our Lord,"* proclaims the idea of Resurrection. Without the Resurrection we should have no *"Christ Jesus, our Lord"* to commission Paul, to accomplish great things through Paul, to make the Corinthians Paul's glory, pride, and joy.

The word *"glorying* (rejoicing)" is, indeed, subjective, something that Paul does; but this subjective act rests on objective fact, namely on the Corinthian Church with all of its spiritual

NOTES

realities. And this fact rests on one that is still greater: *"Christ Jesus, our Lord,"* in and by Whose Living Power all that exists in Corinth is wrought.

ANOTHER TRUTH

This manner used by the Apostle to address the Corinthians, tells us something else as well.

As is fully obvious, the problems at Corinth were many. As well, and even as we have addressed, some of the Corinthians were denigrating this Apostle of all Apostles, irrespective of the fact that they had found Jesus under his Ministry. Still, Paul looked beyond all of this, and gloried in what the Lord had done in the Salvation of these many souls.

He did not discount the fact that problems existed. Neither did he discount the fact of their attitude toward him personally. These things no doubt hurt, and hurt deeply. But still, he ever sees the big picture, and knows that Satan will not take best.

Just this morning in prayer (5/25/98), as I began to seek the Lord, the problems were monumental, to be frank, not totally unlike these of which Paul mentions. In attempting to address these things, I seemingly made no progress whatsoever.

And then the Holy Spirit gently whispered to my heart, *"Forget the problems, and begin to thank the Lord for all the wonderful things He has done."*

I instantly began to do that, and the Spirit of God came down in such a wonderful way, literally bathing my person in that which I needed so much, a touch from Heaven. Did the problems leave? Not really! But me thanking and praising the Lord for all the wonderful things He had done, and was doing, gave me an assurance in my heart that these other things would be handled as well.

We must not allow the difficulties of the moment to hide the big picture. The big picture is that the Lord will triumph. His Way will be brought to pass. Satan will not take best. Despite the fact that many have ridiculed the Church at Corinth, from then until now, Paul *"gloried at what the Lord had done"* in this pagan city, and to be sure, one can guarantee oneself that many Corinthians made it into the portals of Glory.

Hallelujah!

NOTES

I DIE DAILY

The phrase, *"I die daily,"* refers to the constant strain and hardships of the life which Paul lived. He faced trouble and problems every day of his life, even the possibility of death. He wasn't necessarily meaning here that we have to die to sin daily, as many teach, but rather was speaking of physical hardships.

Paul's Gospel was that we become dead to the sin nature once and for all, then stay dead to the sin nature (Rom. 6:1-14; Gal. 2:20).

He is saying that he is constantly in danger of his life, and that his sufferings each day are equal to the pains of death.

He could well be referring to the perils and trials which even then were taking place at Ephesus. His object was to impress their minds with the firmness of his belief in the certainty of the Resurrection. On no account would he subject himself to constant danger, which ultimately did take his life, if he was not certain of a Resurrection. On this account he suffered much, and as well, all the hopes of all Believers rests also on this Doctrine.

(32) "IF AFTER THE MANNER OF MEN I HAVE FOUGHT WITH BEASTS AT EPHESUS, WHAT ADVANTAGETH IT ME, IF THE DEAD RISE NOT? LET US EAT AND DRINK; FOR TO MORROW WE DIE."

The question, *"If after the manner of men I have fought with beasts at Ephesus, what advantageth it me, if the dead rise not?"*, is not meant to be taken literally. If so, he would have mentioned it in II Corinthians Chapter 11 as one of his deadliest perils, and it would have been recorded by Luke in his full account of Paul's life at Ephesus, or wherever.

Actually, a Roman citizen was legally exempt from this mode of punishment (Farrar).

Paul is actually saying two things in this question:

1. *"I am risking my life daily, just as surely as those who fight the wild beasts in the arenas. As well, as surely as these gladiators will sooner or later be killed, so will I."*

I think Paul knew he was sentenced to martyrdom, although he did not at this stage know the time.

2. What does all this advantage him, if there is no Resurrection? He's risking his life for nothing, in fact, inviting certain death.

His only advantage is not in this world, nor anything it offers, but rather in the coming

Resurrection. Consequently, he does not put so much stock in this present life, in fact, risking it constantly, trusting in the Lord to keep him.

This exemplifies exactly what Jesus was speaking about when He said, *"He that findeth his life* (refuses to give it to Christ) *shall lose it: and he that loseth his life for My Sake shall find it"* (Mat. 10:39).

The phrase, *"Let us eat and drink; for to morrow we die,"* is quoted by Paul from Isa. 22:13.

THE FUTILITY OF LIFE AS SEEN BY SOME

When Isaiah uttered these Words nearly 800 years before Christ, they referred to the Jews when besieged by Sennacherib and the army of the Assyrians.

The Prophet says, that instead of weeping and fasting and humiliation, as became them in such circumstances, they had given themselves up to feasting and revelry, and that their language was, *"Let us eat and drink; for to morrow we shall die"*; that is, there is no use in offering resistance or in calling upon God. We must die; and we may as well enjoy life as long as it lasts and give ourselves up to unrestrained indulgence.

Paul does not quote these words as having any original reference to the subject of the Resurrection, but as language appropriately expressing the idea that if there is no future state; if no Resurrection of the dead; if no happy result of toils and sufferings in the future world, it is vain and foolish to subject ourselves to trials and privations here. We should rather make the most of whatever this present life is, enjoy all the comfort we can, and make pleasure our chief good, rather than looking for happiness in a future state.

This seems to be the language of the great masses of the world. They look to no future state. They have no prospect, no desire of Heaven; and they, therefore, seek for happiness here, and give themselves up to restrained indulgence in this life. Only the followers of Christ have a hope of a wonderful and glorious future.

THE OPPOSITE OF MUCH OF THE PRESENT GOSPEL

The Holy Spirit through the Apostle is plainly telling us that this life is not *"where it is."* That which is worthwhile is found in the coming Resurrection. But yet, much of the modern Gospel zeroes in on the here and now, instead of the there and then. Consequently, there is not much desire for the Coming of the Lord, or the Rapture of the Church. In fact, the latter is denied in many, if not most, religious circles.

The end of Faith presently, at least in the manner in which it is taught, is money and material things. However, the end of true Faith, which in reality will never end, is that which is coming in the Resurrection. If we miss that, we have missed the entire application of the Gospel. That's why Paul said, on which we have already commented, *"If in this life only we have hope in Christ, we are of all men most miserable"* (I Cor. 15:19).

(33) "BE NOT DECEIVED: EVIL COMMUNICATIONS CORRUPT GOOD MANNERS."

The phrase, *"Be not deceived,"* proclaims an exertation by the Apostle respecting the false doctrine that was being delivered to the Corinthians by false teachers. The statement actually says, *"Do not go on being deceived!"*, for in all candor many of the Corinthians had already been deceived.

The phrase, *"Evil communications corrupt good manners,"* is derived from Menander, a celebrated comic poet of Athens, educated under Theophrastus. His writings were replete with elegance, refined wit, and judicious observations, but yet immoral. He is said to have drowned himself in the 52nd year of his age, 293 B.C., because the compositions of his rival, Philemon, obtained more applause than his own.

However, this in no way proves that Paul was familiar with classic literature of that age.

The line just quoted is such which may have been carved on the gate of any Greek town, as well as two other quotations he gave (Acts. 17:28; Tit. 1:12). It is very unlikely he would have deliberately quoted from the immoral play of a corrupt comedian like Menander.

More accurately, the proverb means, *"evil occasions corrupt excellent morals."*

DECEPTION

It is implied in this statement that there were some false teachers who were endeavoring to corrupt the minds of the Corinthians from the simplicity of the Gospel. The sentiment of the passage is that the intercourse of evil-minded men, or that the close friendship and conversation of those who hold erroneous opinions, or who are impure in their lives, tends to corrupt the morals, the heart, the sentiments of others. The particular to which Paul here applies it, is the subject of the Resurrection.

If Believers, whether Corinthians or otherwise, begin to listen to false teachers, sooner or later they will be corrupted.

The word *"communications"* is used here by Paul to designate *"associations"* or *"company,"* with the meaning that such will have a definite influence.

Paul intends to say in the present connection that association with deceivers who are full of skeptical ideas is bound to react hurtfully to the hearts of Christians. Instead of letting the Divine Truth mold their manner of living, they let the false and insidious ideas of their associates mislead them. Even one bad apple spreads rot among many others.

He who rejects the Resurrection cannot live and act like one who truly believes this Divine reality.

Our *"associations"* and *"company"* we keep, pretty well decides the direction in which we are headed. Consequently, all should be very careful as to the Preachers they hear over Television, Radio, or any place for that matter. That is why Jesus said, *"Who hath ears to hear, let him hear"* (Mat. 13:9).

The idea is that we be very careful as to what we hear, closing our ears to that which is false and opening them wide to that which is Truth.

(34) "AWAKE TO RIGHTEOUSNESS, AND SIN NOT; FOR SOME HAVE NOT THE KNOWLEDGE OF GOD: I SPEAK THIS TO YOUR SHAME."

The phrase, *"Awake to Righteousness,"* in effect says, *"come to your senses"* or *"awake at once from a drunken sleep."*

The manner in which Paul uses the statement intimates that the doubters in Corinth (doubters of the Resurrection), imagined that they were thinking soberly, as most, if not all people in such circumstances do, and that they assailed the Believers in the Doctrine as people who were being carried away by foolish and fanatical notions because they actually believed such an impossible doctrine as the Resurrection.

ERROR

Such is the way of all skeptics who have departed from the Word of God and who charge true Believers with blind acceptance of *"Dogmas."* Against this pseudo-soberness and pseudo-saneness, Paul launches his statement.

NOTES

The Pharisees claimed, *"We see!"* (Jn. 9:41), and proceeded with mighty assurance *"to justify themselves"* (Lk. 16:15); but the Judgment of God declared them wickedly and willfully blind and cast them out.

So Paul commands the Corinthians to be sober in the true way that God approves. He is rightly sober who sees and believes the Divine realities as God reveals them, and who does all his thinking so that every thought accords with these realities. And this man does not wait for the Divine verdict that he is rightly sober; that verdict is recorded in a thousand places in the Scriptures.

RIGHTEOUSNESS?

Why did Paul use the word *"Righteousness"*?

As the next short phrase will bear out, departure from the Word of God always leads to sin, hence, *"unrighteousness."* Such is inevitable.

As well, there is a narcotic type effect to deception which is false doctrine. To be frank, it takes the Power of God to break such a spell. The reason is spiritually obvious:

False doctrine regarding the Word of God, is not nearly a problem of the intellect, but rather a problem of the spirit. As such, it blinds people, even as it is designed by Satan to do, i.e., spiritual blindness. That's the reason it is very dangerous, even as Paul addressed in the previous Verse to listen to false teachers. They hook an individual with things that sound right, and in fact, are right. However, the right things they say only makes them more dangerous, because the right things have opened up the heart of the listener to receive the false.

The phrase, *"And sin not,"* literally means, *"And do not go on missing the mark."* There is, then, a kind of thinking and reasoning that seems to be sanely sober and is yet wholly wrong because it goes on missing the mark, namely the true mark set by God for all our thinking, which refers to His Word, and a true and righteous dividing of that Word.

In fact, this is the worst kind of sinning, for it affects not only our conduct but corrupts the very heart, the source of all conduct.

SIN

It is implied here, that, if they suffer themselves to embrace a Doctrine which is a denial of the Resurrection, the effect will be that they will fall into sin; or that a denial of that Doctrine (or any Bible Doctrine) leads to a life of self-indulgence and transgression. This truth is everywhere seen; and against this effect, Paul sought to guard them.

Consequently, he did not regard the denial of the Doctrine of the Resurrection as a harmless speculation, but as leading to most dangerous consequences in regard to their manner of life and conduct (Barnes).

The phrase, *"For some hath not the Knowledge of God,"* in effect says, *"For some are ignorant of God."* However, it is a willful ignorance, simply because the Truth has already been presented to them by Paul. Consequently, they are to blame for this ignorance which they carry around with them and which they try to sell to others as knowledge.

WHAT IS THE KNOWLEDGE OF GOD?

The *"Knowledge of God"* is, of course, the Word of God, but more particularly, the rightful dividing of that Word (II Tim. 2:15).

Regrettably, most Christians, I think I can say with little fear of exaggeration, have little of the *"Knowledge of God,"* simply because they little study the Word of God. As well, many study the Word with the attitude and spirit of attempting to force the Word into their thinking or Doctrine instead of allowing the Word to mold their Doctrine.

I like what one Preacher said, *"I have no preconceived ideas as to what the Word teaches, and in fact, I don't really care what it teaches one way or the other. I just want to know what it does teach, and then follow it the best I can with the help of the Holy Spirit."*

The problem with our daily walk before God, and lack of victory, is that we have an improper understanding of some certain part of the Word, which always falls out to defeat in one manner or the other. The same holds true for entire Religious Denominations. They make up their own rules which have no Biblical foundation, thereby departing from the Word of God, which always ultimately spells spiritual doom.

The attitude of every single Believer always must be, *"What does the Bible say?"* It is not what my Church says, or particular Denomination, or even the Preacher for that matter. While the Lord has definitely set in the Church, *"Apostles, Prophets, Evangelists, Pastors, and Teachers,"* and for the edifying of the Body of Christ, still, every Believer should know the Word of God well enough that he will know if what he is being taught is Truth. The Believer must not allow others to do his thinking for him. Untold numbers are in Hell at this very moment because of that very thing.

NOTES

UNDERSTANDING THE BIBLE

Many Christians do not bother to read the Bible, using for an excuse that they are unable to understand what it is proclaiming. That is a *"cop-out!"* They are not studying the Bible simply because they do not desire to study the Bible.

I don't care who a person is, or how little education he may have, if he will ask the Lord to help him understand the Word of God, it is absolutely certain that the Holy Spirit will do exactly that (Lk. 11:9-13).

The phrase, *"I speak this to your shame,"* actually says, *"I am speaking to shame you. The objective of all I am saying is to excite your shame — not as in some previous instances, 'to spare you.'"*

False doctrine never aids true moral conduct, but works to corrupt that conduct. Whatever eats at the root (Doctrine and Faith) damages or destroys the fruit (love and Christian Virtues) (Mat. 7:16-17).

Paul was addressing the Church at Corinth and speaking in this manner because they had been given abundant opportunities to know the Truth. It was a subject of deep disgrace that there were some in the Church who denied the Doctrine of the Resurrection of the dead.

SHAME

*"Shame"* in the Greek is *"entropay"* and means *"confusion."*

The emphasis here is on the Word of God, even with the individual having the Word of God, but departing from that Word. Such will bring *"shame"* to an individual or to the entirety of a Religious Denomination.

Actually, this statement as given by Paul concerning *"shame,"* would apply to most Religious Denominations presently. Many have left the Word of God, following after cunningly devised fables or science, falsely called. Consequently, the Lord labels *"shame"* on those particular Denominations or even individuals for that matter, even though the world may applaud them or even the Church.

When people do not know the Word of God, or else they have departed from the Word of God which is more often the case, spiritual discernment is then lost, with that person or an entire Denomination, not knowing what is of God and what is not of God.

That which goes under the guise of *"Christian Television,"* is an excellent case in point. While some little is actually of God, therefore accomplishing a great work for the Lord, the far greater majority is the opposite. In other words, it is a *"shame."*

I speak of Preachers *"selling"* the Gospel by telling the people, *"If you will give $100* (or whatever)*, the Lord will send you back $1,000 or $10,000, etc."* The word *"shame"* aptly describes such blasphemy.

Others preach with no Anointing of the Holy Spirit whatsoever, for the simple reason that they do not have Him, or else He has departed. It is instantly recognizable, at least by those who know the Lord, and again, the word *"shame"* aptly describes such.

Another Preacher says that one must be Baptized in water to be saved, or some such other foolishness, which once again, earns the label of *"shame."*

To be as truthful as one knows how, all of us in some way have brought *"shame"* to the Work of God; however, even though that is bad enough, to refuse to repent and come back to God's Way, is far worse.

(35) "BUT SOME MAN WILL SAY, HOW ARE THE DEAD RAISED UP? AND WITH WHAT BODY DO THEY COME?"

The question, *"But some man will say, How are the dead raised up?"*, presents Paul moving from the mighty *fact* of the Resurrection to the wonderful *manner* of the Resurrection. Yet in the discussion of the change which our bodies will undergo in the Resurrection, the basic question is still the reality of the Resurrection itself.

This teaching concerning the change is intended to remove the main objection of the skeptics in regard to the possibility and actuality of the Resurrection.

NOTES

The skeptics asked the very question which Paul now puts forward. They can conceive of the human body only in its mundane form as we see it in this life. Bodies of this kind, and which are overly obvious, are unfit for Heavenly existence. So the skeptics conclude: There is no Resurrection.

HOW ARE THE DEAD RAISED UP?

This question is one which would likely be made by the subtle and doubting Greeks. The Apostle, indeed, does not draw it out at length, or state it fully, but it may be regarded probably as substantially the same as that which has been made in all ages.

How is it possible that the dead should be raised? They return to their native dust. They become entirely disorganized. Their dust may be scattered; how shall it be recollected?

Paul will answer this, as we shall see.

The question, *"And with what body do they come?"*, refers to the form, shape, size, etc. What are we to suppose as concerning this?

WITH WHAT BODY DO THEY COME?

Are we to suppose that the aged will be raised as aged, and the young as young, and that infancy will be raised in the same state, and remain such forever?

Are we to suppose that the bodies will be gross, material, needing support and nourishment, or, that there will be a new type of body?

All these questions and numerous others have been asked in regard to the bodies at the Resurrection.

The objection is that of some who do not know the Power of God, or do not believe in the Power of God.

The Resurrection of the body was a difficulty alike to Sadducees and Gentiles. Paul meets this difficulty by natural analogies, which are intended to show that the Resurrection-body, though identical with the mortal body as far as the preservation of personal identity is concerned, is yet a Glorified Body, so that the objections urged on the ground that it is impossible to preserve the same material particles which have passed into dust, are beside the point.

Paul gives no sanction to the coarse physical conceptions of the Resurrection which described the human being as rising in that manner.

*"How"* is a question which, of course, admits to no answer. Exactly how the Lord will do this, we cannot now know. But to deny that He will, is to deny His Power, which Jesus told the Sadducees (Mat. 22:23-33).

Paul answers these questions by analogy, implying that the Resurrection-body is the same body, not so much by way of material identity as of glorious individuality (Farrar).

(36) "THOU FOOL, THAT WHICH THOU SOWEST IS NOT QUICKENED, EXCEPT IT DIE."

The phrase, *"Thou fool,"* could be translated *"Oh, foolish man,"* or *"Fool thou art!"*

The Greek word for *"fool"* is *"aphron,"* and means *"Oh unreasonable!"*

Some evidently were attempting to make a joke of the Resurrection and to turn the laugh upon simple Believers by stating that the dead body will be patched together again from the dust, once more to begin its round of life in eating and drinking, digesting and eliminating, sleeping and working, begetting, etc.

Paul is simply saying, *"What a fool to think of the Resurrection in so pitiful a way!"*

The person who thinks such foolishness is a person who has failed to take God into account.

The phrase, *"That which thou sowest is not quickened, except it die,"* in effect says that this foolish man refutes himself every time he sows seed. Regarding the seed, he then reckons with a dying which results in a quickening to a new and wonderful life; in Truth, this strange quickening, he knows, cannot occur unless the dying precedes. Compare Christ's similar analogy in John 12:24 — dying grain and resulting fruit, the first being necessary for the second, and the second wholly dependent on the first.

## NATURE TEACHES

Using this analogy, we find that nature teaches that to have a harvest there must be a prior death. The *"bare grain"* figures a dead body. The grain dies in the ground and a most wonderful resurrection follows. So is it, and so will it be in respect to man.

In our effort to apply an analogy or a comparison, we should not go beyond the point of the comparison. Here it is decomposition and yet new life. As stated, the first is necessary for the second, the second dependent on the first.

NOTES

The analogy is not between the germ in the seed and something similar to it in our dead buried bodies, for nothing similar to this germ is found in our dead and buried bodies. As well, the analogy is not between the bulk of the seed and the bulk of the dead body so that both bulks act alike. For the bulk of the former decomposes and remains decomposed, and only the germ shoots up into a plant, while our very dead and buried bodies rise from their graves and leave nothing behind.

The germ of the plant develops, produces new kernels as fruit, and these repeat the process indefinitely. Not so our bodies when they rise.

The fact concerning the Resurrection is not that a germ which is hidden in our dead bodies comes forth while our dead bodies themselves remain dust and ashes. So what exactly does happen?

Paul tells us in the following Verses.

(37) "AND THAT WHICH THOU SOWEST, THOU SOWEST NOT THAT BODY THAT SHALL BE, BUT BARE GRAIN, IT MAY CHANCE OF WHEAT, OR OF SOME OTHER GRAIN:"

The phrase, *"And that which thou sowest, thou sowest not that body that shall be,"* in essence says, *"The seed is a grain of wheat. One does not plant what the ultimate product will become, but one plants 'a naked grain.' Then the seed dies and new life rises from it. The seed does not merely take a different form, but a totally new plant comes from it."*

In the same way, God will not just dress up the dead human corpse, but He will bring an entirely new body out of it, even though it still will be recognized as the same person (Rossier).

The phrase, *"But bare grain, it may chance of wheat, or of some other grain,"* simply means that in the bare grain itself, one can little tell exactly how the finished product will be.

## BARE GRAIN

All conceptions of the Resurrection to the effect that the bodies of the dead shall return to their former coarse existence are eliminated by Paul's analogy. All skeptical objections that seek to ridicule the Doctrine on this score evidence an ignorance of what the Doctrine actually is.

Much has been said about the words *"bare grain,"* which Paul applies to the kernel of grain.

The matter is quite simple, for Paul himself places a *"bare grain"* in contrast with the plant that grows out of it so that we understand exactly what he means.

As stated, he is saying that the *"bare grain"* presents little clue as we hold it in our hands, or even put it in the ground as to exactly what the finished product will be. Unless the person knows exactly what type of seed it is, he has no idea if it will be wheat, *"or of some other grain."*

By that statement he is *not* claiming that some Resurrection bodies will be different than others, but simply that as one cannot look at a seed or its grain and surmise the finished product, likewise, we cannot look at our present physical bodies and, thereby, tell what the coming Glorified Body will be. That is all he is saying, and we should not take it further than what he is saying.

(38) "BUT GOD GIVETH IT A BODY AS IT HATH PLEASED HIM, AND TO EVERY SEED HIS OWN BODY."

The phrase, *"But God giveth it a body as it hath pleased Him,"* presents God as the Divine Order.

A LESSON IN BIOLOGY?

Paul is not delivering a biological lecture as such. He is constructing a simple analogy which all his readers are able to understand whether they are scientific Biologists or not. A dying results in a quickening and a new life — we see it in the seed in which we plant.

God's creative act is back of what we see and not a will or an arrangement of ours. What goes into the ground is a bare seed, what comes out is a beautiful plant. God is responsible for this marvel: *"God gives it a body."*

Paul does not stop with the so-called *"laws of nature"* or at a halfway station. He goes back to God Who created all the processes of nature. This he does in beautiful harmony with the purpose of his analogy, for the Resurrection of our dead bodies is also an act of God.

AFTER HIS KIND

More than this: God does what we see Him doing with the kernel of grain *"even as He did will,"* when, at creation, He ordained that each plant should yield seed *"after his kind"* (Gen. 1:11).

NOTES

*"And it was so,"* and due to that original Divine volition it has been so ever since. Each kind of seed grows its own body; each is true to its nature. Even though we now speak of such in learned botanical terms, Paul as guided by the Holy Spirit, is content to draw attention to the great creative fact as such.

Because many Botanists often study only the botany of the case they lose sight of God and the Law which He ordained at creation. They eliminate God and creation and substitute their speculative *"evolution."*

HIS OWN BODY

The phrase, *"And to every seed his own body,"* thwarts every evolutionary speculation.

A seed of wheat produces a plant of wheat and no other species of plant; and so does every other kind of seed. In the resultant plant every seed gets a body of its own, always the one God originally designed for it, the one God now gives it.

The vast world of nature demonstrates this in endless succession. *"Great Oaks from little acorns grow"* and not great Elms, or Beeches, nor little currants or raspberry bushes.

The simple analogy is thus made secure against misunderstanding: seed and body go into the ground — new living forms result; but in both cases with a marvelous change that is due entirely to God's Almighty Will and Power (Lenski).

This also means that every person will have his own body, whatever the color is, and not that of another. In other words, the Glorified Body will have the same features it now has, minus any imperfections.

This means that men will continue to be men and women will continue to be women.

The glorified body will probably bring every age to 33. This was the age of Christ when He was resurrected, and John said that in the Resurrection we shall be like Him (I Jn. 3:2).

(39) "ALL FLESH IS NOT THE SAME FLESH: BUT THERE IS ONE KIND OF FLESH OF MEN, ANOTHER FLESH OF BEASTS, ANOTHER OF FISHES, AND ANOTHER OF BIRDS."

The phrase, *"All flesh is not the same flesh,"* is another way of saying that all unorganized matter is not the same kind of matter, a point that definitely contradicts the theory of evolution (Rossier).

## WITH WHAT BODIES DO THEY COME?

This Verse is designed to answer the question *"With what bodies do they come?"* The argument here is, that there are many kinds of bodies; that all are not alike; that while they are bodies, yet they partake of different qualities, forms, and properties; and that, therefore, it is not absurd to suppose that God may transform the human body into a different form and cause it to be raised up with somewhat different properties in the future world.

The phrase, *"But there is one kind of flesh of men, another flesh of beasts, another of fishes, and another of birds,"* refers to all being *"flesh,"* but of different types.

The idea here is, that although all the bodies of animals may be composed essentially of the same elements, yet God has produced a wonderful variety in their organization, strength, beauty, color, and places of abode, as the air, earth, and water.

It is not necessary, therefore, to suppose that the body that shall be raised shall be precisely like that which we have here.

The idea of this Verse is the proclamation of the fact, that God is not limited to one type of flesh. He is able to do whatever is desired. In creation God was not restricted to one kind of flesh; how then can he then be restricted in the Resurrection?

The human body which we bury shall rise again, but, although it remains the very same body, it will appear wonderfully different in the Resurrection. We see this in the case of Christ: the identical body, now dead, now risen; now laid limp and lifeless into the tomb now comes forth Glorified.

## ANIMALS

Even though this Verse does not lend itself to the wonder of the animal kingdom, as do some of the last Chapters of Job, for that is not Paul's purpose inasmuch as he is dealing with the Resurrection; still, insofar as animals are mentioned here, perhaps a more detailed study regarding this subject would be beneficial.

What is our relationship with other forms of life that share our planet? How does Scripture view animal life? Insights come from both the Old Testament and the New Testament.

NOTES

## HEBREW AND GREEK WORDS FOR ANIMALS

It has been estimated that there are over three thousand Biblical references to animals. Many are two specific kinds: Dogs, Ponies, Donkeys, Sheep, Lions, Camels, etc. But there are also generic terms, usually translated *"animal"* or *"beasts"* in both Old Testament and New Testament.

The Hebrew word *"behemah"* means four-footed animals as distinct from birds. These animals may be wild or domesticated: the term refers collectively to the animal kingdom.

The Hebrew word *"hayyah"* means *"living thing"* and is normally used referring to wild in contrast to domestic ones.

The Greek word *"therion"* is used to translate this Hebrew term. Revelation uses *"therion"* some thirty-eight times (of forty-six New Testament occurrences) to identify the fierce, ruthless, beastly powers that will be ranged against God at history's end.

The Hebrew word *"miqneh* (larger cattle)*"* and *"soneh* (smaller cattle, sheep, and goats)*"* identify domestic animals. The New Testament uses the Greek word *"ktenos"* for domestic animals. The Hebrew word *"beir"* is typically translated *"beast"* but is a generic term for cattle, and does imply brutishness.

A survey of the Hebrew and Greek words tells us that the people of Bible times made a number of distinctions among creatures of the animal kingdom. But the words themselves tell us nothing of theological questions often raised today. For answers, we must see how these words are used in Scripture in what is taught there about the creatures who share our world.

## THE PLACE OF ANIMALS AND THE CREATED ORDER

The creation story told in early Genesis presents God as the originator of both human and animal life. The story, however, makes several important distinctions.

Animals and man were created on different *"days."* Human Beings were created in a unique way and in God's Own Image and Likeness. Humanity was given dominion, to *"rule over the fish of the Sea and the birds of the Air, over the livestock, and over all the creatures that move over the ground"* (Gen. 1:26).

The right to rule, however, is not the right to exploit. But the superiority of humanity is clearly taught. It is also important to note that nowhere in the Bible is the human race classed among the animals.

Within the Creation framework that is provided by Scripture, animals are viewed as valuable property (Ex. Chpts. 21-22; Lev. Chpt. 27). They are used for food, for sacrifice, and are classified as *"clean"* or *"unclean,"* depending on their suitability for these uses.

Israel was warned not to make an idol in any shape — including that of an animal (Deut. 4:16-17). As well, one who has sexual intercourse with animals is considered worthy of death (Ex. 22:19; Lev. 18:23).

### THE CREATION ORDER IS COMPLETELY FOREIGN TO EVOLUTION

The Biblical picture of Creation and the concept of animal life as created within fixed boundaries of role and purpose are completely foreign to the evolutionary notion that higher orders of animal life developed from lower orders.

Genesis says that God commanded the land to produce animals *"according to their kinds . . . each according to its kind"* (Gen.1:24). The Hebrew word *"min"* (*"kind"*) occurs thirty-one times in the Old Testament. It suggests that the form (whether of animal or vegetation) has its own generic group in which it was placed by the Creator.

However, the Biblical data does not enable us to match *"kind"* with any of the modern biological classifications (such as genus species, family, or order). It seems that *"men"* is used at one time or another in each of these senses, but it is very clear that *"men"* is never used in the sense of kingdom, phylum, or class.

God has structured His universe with order and regularity. In this order of universe, animal life has its own place — and will stay in that place.

### DISTINCTIONS BETWEEN HUMANS AND ANIMALS

When Solomon in his search for life's meaning limited himself to what he could observe in the material universe, he was puzzled at the relationship between humanity and the animals. Ecclesiastes 3:18-21 reports his thoughts:

NOTES

*"I also thought, As for men, God tests them so that they may see that they are like the animals . . . the same fate awaits them both. As one dies, so dies the other. All have the same breath; man has no advantage over the animal . . . All go to the same place; all come from dust, and to dust all return. Who knows if the spirit of man rises upward and if the spirit of the animal goes down into the Earth?"*

The fact that these thoughts are located in Ecclesiastes — a Bible Book that records the struggles of the human mind to understand the meaning of life — tells us that Solomon's conclusions are not necessarily correct. In fact, the rest of Scripture assures us that Solomon was not correct and that there are vital differences between humanity and the animal creation.

### DIFFERENCE IN IMAGE

This the first and most basic difference. In creating the world, God made living creatures after a model that existed in His own imagination (Gen. 1:24-25). The Passage goes on to point out that the animal kingdom is now destined to reproduce *"according to its kind."* But the same Passage says that man was created in God's Image.

The model after which humanity was shaped was God Himself. Those capacities that mark God as a Person, with emotion, intellect, will, self-consciousness, etc., were given uniquely to mankind. This basic difference sets human beings completely off from the animals, over whom they are to rule (Gen. 1:26-27).

### DIFFERENCE IN DESTINY

The Bible teaches that each human being will retain his personal, self-conscious existence after death. It is significant that in the key passage on Resurrection, Paul points to the fact that human and animal creations are different, even as we are now studying (I Cor. 15:39).

It is the human body and human flesh that will be raised to imperishability (I Cor. 15:42-49) in a Resurrection intended to restore the original Image of God and all its fullness, unmarred by the sin inherited from Adam after the Fall (I Cor. 15:45-58). No such hope is ever suggested for animals.

### DIFFERENCE IN MIND

When God brought His Judgment of temporary insanity on Nebuchadnezzar, the curse stated: *"Let his mind be changed from that of a man and let him be given the mind of an animal, till seven times* (years) *pass by for him"* (Dan. 4:16).

Given the mind of an animal Nebuchadnezzer apparently lost all self-awareness; he lived with the wild donkeys and ate grass until the day God restored his sanity (Dan. 4:34; 5:21).

There are several other passages in the Bible that help us better define the differences in mind that Daniel identified. The Psalmist Asaph describes his depression when he was torn with envy at the prosperity of the wicked.

In his despairing state, Asaph looked only at external circumstances, and felt self-pity at the apparent uselessness of his own commitment to Holiness. Asaph recovered perspective when he gained God's perspective: *"I entered the Sanctuary of God; then I understood their final destiny"* (Ps. 73:17).

Later, looking back at his time of depressions, Asaph said, *"I was senseless and ignorant; I was a brute beast before You"* (Ps. 73:22). Asaph's expression here is important. He had looked at the present with no perspective either on God or on the future. His evaluations had been based only on immediate experience. But he recovered his perspective when he considered God.

NO AWARENESS OF THE SPIRITUAL UNIVERSE

The animal mind (brute beast) is locked into present experience and must react to the present without awareness of the spiritual universe and without ability to project from the present to the future.

An animal may learn from past experience; but it cannot draw from information beyond experience, nor can it reason from information to the end of a chain of probable cause-and-effect events.

A similar point is made by both Peter and Jude. They describe false teachers as being like *"brute beasts, creatures of instinct"* (II Pet. 2:12) who *"understand by instinct, like unreasoning animals"* (Jude vs. 10).

The animal mind is capable of understanding. But its understanding is of a different order from that of human understanding. Animal experiences are interpreted by instinct, and animals lack the capacity to reason from experience to a deeper understanding of the past or of the future.

NOTES

While man and beast depend on God and are under His care (Ps. 36:6), the animal creation is of a distinctly different order from that of humanity.

NO ETERNAL DESTINY

Animals share with human beings the world that God has created, and they have been placed under humanity's rule. Animals have a different place and role in the creation order from those of human beings, for they are distinctly different in original image, in destiny, and in nature, as shown by differences in the mind.

There is no evidence in Scripture, which is the final authority, to indicate that animals (even the most loved of pets) will share in our Resurrection or have an eternal destiny. There is no evidence in Scripture that animals, which are recognized as sentient beings, have *"rights"* that correspond to human rights. Yet, there is evidence that God does have concern for the living beings in the animal creation (Jonah 4:11; Mat. 6:25-26).

We are called, by the responsibility of rule, to share God's concern for the animals. In other words, they are to be treated with kindness, as far as possible.

(Bibliography: Richards.)

(40) "THERE ARE ALSO CELESTIAL BODIES, AND BODIES TERRESTRIAL: BUT THE GLORY OF THE CELESTIAL IS ONE, AND THE GLORY OF THE TERRESTRIAL IS ANOTHER."

The phrase, *"There are also celestial bodies, and bodies terrestrial,"* refers to heavenly bodies, such as the Sun, Moon, and Stars, as well as earthly bodies, which refer human beings, animals, trees, plants, etc.

*"Celestial"* in the Greek is *"epouranios,"* and refers to that which is *"heavenly,"* i.e., *"in the heavens."*

*"Terrestrial,"* in the Greek is *"epigeious,"* and pertains to the Earth, i.e., *"earthly."*

The sense is there is a great variety of bodies. Actually, Paul is presenting two entire classes of bodies. Consequently, we can see how they differ.

Can it be deemed strange if there should be a difference between our bodies when on earth and when in heaven? Do we not, in fact, see a vast difference between what strikes our eye here on Earth and in the sky? And why should we deem it strange that between bodies adapted to live here and bodies adapted to live in heaven there should be a difference, like that which is seen between the objects which appear on Earth and those which appear in the sky?

The phrase, *"But the glory of the celestial is one, and the glory of the terrestrial is another,"* refers to the fact that the beauty, dignity, and magnificence of the heavenly differ much from those on earth. That is one thing; the beauty of earthly objects is another and a different thing.

Beautiful as may be the human frame; beautiful as may be the plumage of birds; beautiful as may be the flowers, the topaz, or the diamond, yet they differ from the heavenly bodies, and are not to be compared with them.

Why should we deem it strange that there may be a similar difference between the physical body as adapted to the residence here and as adapted to its residence in heaven? This the Truth which the Holy Spirit is bringing out through the Apostle.

(41) "THERE IS ONE GLORY OF THE SUN, AND ANOTHER GLORY OF THE MOON, AND ANOTHER GLORY OF THE STARS: FOR ONE STAR DIFFERETH FROM ANOTHER STAR IN GLORY."

The phrase, *"There is one glory of the Sun, and another glory of the Moon, and another glory of the Stars,"* presents Paul simply drawing attention to the many differences that appear in bodily forms.

God never finds Himself restricted when variety in forms is concerned. So He knows what He will do with our bodies when He calls them forth from the grave, how beautiful and how glorious He will make them appear in the Resurrection.

Paul is establishing the fact that the Lord will have no difficulty raising the human body, and giving it an eternal frame. He calls attention to creation to prove his point, referring to all that God has done referring to variety and glory, whether heavenly or earthly.

Also, Paul is *not* writing about the differences that will appear between the Saints and the fact that some will shine in greater glory than others, which is taught by some. That is not his subject.

The phrase, *"For one star differeth from another star in glory,"* tells us that each of the stars, which number into the literal trillions we are told, each has its own particular glory, which is different than the others. In fact, the Psalmist said, *"He* (God) *telleth the number of the Stars; He calleth them all by their names"* (Ps. 147:4).

NOTES

### THE GREATNESS OF OUR GOD

Astronomers claim there are over 40,000,000,000,000,000,000,000 (40 sextillion) Stars which are Suns to other Planets. God knows the exact number of them for He made them (Isa. 45:18).

We are told there are over 500,000 words in the unabridged Webster Dictionary. If God has every star named, which He does, then there are enough such names to fill about 80,000,000,000,000,000 (80 quadrillion) books that size. It would be hard to estimate how many more it would take to record all the other words God uses concerning the whole of His vast universe.

No wonder the Psalmist says in the next Verse, *"Great is our Lord, and of great power: His understanding is infinite"* (Ps. 147:5).

Actually, some few stars are named in Scripture: *"Orion"* (Job 9:9; 38:31; Amos 5:8). *"Arcturus"* (Job 9:9; 38:32), *"Pleiades"* (Job 9:9; 38:31), and *"Mazzaroth"* (Job 38:32).

(42) "SO ALSO IS THE RESURRECTION OF THE DEAD. IT IS SOWN IN CORRUPTION; IT IS RAISED IN INCORRUPTION:"

The phrase, *"So also is the Resurrection of the dead,"* refers to the grain that is sown and the different degrees of splendor and magnificence in the bodies in the sky and on the Earth. The idea is, that there will be a difference between the body here and the body in the Resurrection.

The phrase, *"It is sown in corruption,"* refers to the grave, a place where it shall corrupt, in a form tending to putrefaction, disorganization, and dust.

The phrase, *"It is raised in incorruption,"* refers to the Glorified Form and the type of Body which God will provide.

In the previous Verses (I Cor. 15:36-41), Paul had reasoned from analogy, and had demonstrated that it was possible that the dead should rise, or that there was no greater difficulty attending it than actually occurred in the events which were, in fact, constantly taking place all around us.

He here states positively what will be, and affirms that it is not only possible, but that such a Resurrection will actually occur.

NOTES

INCORRUPTION

*"Incorruption"* in the Greek is *"aphtharsia"* and means *"immortal."*

This means that it will be no more liable to decay, sickness, disorganization, and putrefaction. This is one characteristic of the body that shall be raised, that it shall no more be liable as here, to wasting sickness, disease, and to the loathsome corruption of the grave.

That God can form a body of that kind, no one can doubt; that He actually will, the Apostle positively affirms. That such will be the bodies of the Saints is one of the most cheering prospects that can be presented to those who are here wasted away by sickness, and who look with dread and horror on the loathsome putrefaction of the tomb. (Barnes).

(43) "IT IS SOWN IN DISHONOUR; IT IS RAISED IN GLORY: IT IS SOWN IN WEAKNESS; IT IS RAISED IN POWER."

The phrase, *"It is sown in dishonour,"* refers to the awful and intolerable indignity of *"dust to dust."* It refers to the grave.

The phrase, *"It is raised in glory,"* refers to the same body. In other words, the identical body that is first buried is afterward raised. To think of two bodies, one that is buried and remains buried, and a second that is raised out of the grave is unwarranted.

Now the manner in which God will do this, is unknown presently. But that He can is understood, and that He will is here stated.

THE DEAD BODY

The dead body is buried *"in dishonor,"* it is raised *"in glory."*

We, indeed, try to honor the dead whom we bury by clothing them in their best, giving them a fine casket, flowers, our attending presence, etc. All of this is well; it means much if we have the sure hope of a Blessed Resurrection with reference to the dead.

What it means when this hope is absent we need not say. Yet the body itself is enveloped *"in dishonor"*— we soon hurry it from sight. In a little while its decomposition would cause us to shrink in horror.

In the Resurrection this identical body appears in Glory. This does not mean that honor and glory are merely heaped upon it from the outside, but the body itself is made glorious, it is like that of Christ at the time of the Transfiguration, Radiant, and Shining. We have never seen this heavenly condition and are powerless to describe it adequately.

The phrase, *"It is sown in weakness; it is raised in power,"* presents a tremendous understatement.

WEAKNESS AND POWER

To say that only the strength to resist decay is gone is too narrow a view. Helpless lies the dead body, wholly a prey to natures elements. At the time of the Resurrection this identical body appears *"in power,"* filled with ability to do all that its new state requires.

This is not power as we know it now in our living bodies, but transcendent power, beyond all that our minds can now conceive.

The next Verse gives us a stronger indication as to what the Resurrection Body will be.

(44) "IT IS SOWN A NATURAL BODY; IT IS RAISED A SPIRITUAL BODY. THERE IS A NATURAL BODY, AND THERE IS A SPIRITUAL BODY."

The phrase, *"It is sown a natural body; it is raised a spiritual body,"* refers to the former as having been energized by *"blood,"* for *"the life of the flesh is in the Blood"* (Lev. 17:11), while the latter is energized by the Holy Spirit.

The *"natural body"* is what we now have and the *"spiritual body"* is what we will then have.

*"Spiritual body"* in the Greek is *"pneumatikos,"* which means *"the resurrected body will be of immortal substance."* It does not mean that the Glorified Body will have no material substance. In fact, the resurrected bodies will still be flesh and bone, though not flesh and blood, even as we have said (Lk. 24:39; Phil. 3:21).

Concerning this, John said, *"It does not yet appear what we shall be, but we know that, when He shall appear, we shall be like Him; for we shall see Him as He is"* (I Jn. 3:2).

The phrase, *"There is a natural body, and there is a spiritual body,"* refers to that which already is.

Of course, it is obvious as to the *"natural body,"* because of what we presently are. However, to understand the *"spiritual body,"* we have to understand the Glorified Body of our Lord, along with the bodies of Angels, etc.

NATURAL AND SPIRITUAL

The word *"natural"* is from the word which

the Greeks use to designate the soul of man.

The word *"spiritual"* is from a word which speaks of the spirit of man. A human being is composed of three parts:

1. With his physical body he has world consciousness. His five sense located in this body receive sense impressions from the outside world.

2. With his soul he has self-consciousness. He knows that he is a personality.

3. With his spirit, he has God-consciousness. He is enabled to know that there is a God, and to worship that God when that spirit, dead because of sin, is made alive by the operation of the Holy Spirit.

## THE NATURAL BODY

The body as it exists before death is a natural or *"soul-body."* That is, it is so constituted that most of its activities are concerned with the individual's experience on Earth, in his adjustments to his fellowman, his work, his play, himself.

The human spirit functions at the same time, enabling man to adjust himself to the spiritual environment which surrounds him. If he is a pagan, he worships idols and participates in the ceremonies of the idol's temple.

If his human spirit is quickened by the Holy Spirit as part of the Saving Work of God, he is then enabled to worship God and to participate in the service of the Lord Jesus. But this constitutes a lesser part of his life than that occupied by the activities of the soul.

The type of spiritual life determines the quality of the soul life. Thus the body we have now is a natural body, one in which the spiritual life is not absent, and where it occupies not a lesser place but less of one's time and energy, and where the soul life is most prominent in the sense of the latter two specifications.

## THE SPIRITUAL BODY

The Resurrection Body will be a Spiritual Body.

By that we do not mean that it will be composed of some intangible, vapory, illusive substance. It will be a body in which the spiritual life of man will predominate. That is, the individual will be occupied for the most part with the things of God, His Worship, His Fellowship, His Service, while to a far less degree will one be occupied with the soul life, if at all.

NOTES

In other words, the tables will be turned. As the Psalm, *"Eternity's too short to sing Thy praise."*

This body dominated by the spirit, will be the same body, as to identity which we have now, but changed as to composition and life principle.

As stated, it will be a body of flesh and bones that can be felt by the physical sense of touch as we have that sense today, for the Disciples handled our Lord's Resurrection Body with a view to investigating as to whether or not it was a body of flesh and bones as He claimed to have (Lk. 24:39; I Jn. 1:1).

As stated, the Resurrection Body will have no blood, and since the life of the body today is in the blood, it follows that a new life principle must animate that body. That Life Principle is the Holy Spirit.

Our Resurrection bodies will be like our Lord's (Phil. 3:20-21).

(45) "AND SO IT IS WRITTEN, THE FIRST MAN ADAM WAS MADE A LIVING SOUL; THE LAST ADAM WAS MADE A QUICKENING SPIRIT."

The phrase, *"And so it is written,"* is derived from Genesis 2:7.

The phrase, *"The first man Adam was made a living soul,"* continues the discussion by explaining the *"natural body."*

We might expect Paul to pass by the existence of *"the natural body"* as being a truth that is quite self-evident to all. Of course, it is self-evident; but Paul is concerned that his readers should know just what he means by *"the natural body,"* for unless they do they will not understand what he means by *"the spiritual body."* And they may doubt its existence and be inclined to reject the Resurrection despite what he has stated thus far. Therefore, Paul points his readers to Genesis 2:7 — *"Thus also it has been written,"* meaning *"it has been written and it is still on record."*

## THE FIRST MAN ADAM

When God breathed His breath into the body of inert Earth which He had formed, the first man became a living soul. All of Adam's descendants are like him in this vital feature: In the body of everyone of us there is a living soul. From Adam onward every human being has an animated body of this kind.

Paul uses this statement as he did concerning Adam becoming a living soul, because this is the very way in which the Scriptures themselves speak in Genesis 2:7. However, under the guidance of the Holy Spirit, Paul added the word *"first"* and identified the *"man"* as *"Adam."* It is designed thusly to lead to the second phrase, where Paul's concern lies.

THE CREATION

Even to which we have already alluded, the manner in which God created Adam and Eve, giving them the power of procreation, i.e., the ability to bring offspring into the world, also made the first Adam the representative head for all who would follow. Consequently, when he sinned and fell, his sin and Fall, passed down to every single human being who would ever live, because in fact, all were in his loins.

THE LAST ADAM

The phrase, *"The Last Adam was made a quickening spirit,"* is used in this manner for purpose.

The one stands at the head of all those who have an existence represented by the words, *"a living soul"*; the Other of all those who shall have a spiritual body in heaven. Jesus is called *"The Last Adam"*; meaning that there shall be no other after Him who shall affect the destiny of man in the same way, or who shall stand at the head of the race in a manner similar to what had been done by Him and the first father of the human family, namely the first Adam.

They sustain peculiar relations to the race; and in this respect they were *"The first"* and *"The last"* in this peculiar economy.

The name *"Adam"* is not elsewhere given to the Messiah, though a comparison is several times instituted between Him and Adam. The idea is this:

The first Adam failed; consequently, all of humanity failed as well, because all were in his loins. The *"Last Adam"* The Lord Jesus Christ, did not fail, and in fact, redeemed all that had been lost, so that all who had been lost in the first Adam could now be saved in the Last Adam.

That's the reason that Jesus had to be born of the Virgin Mary. Had he been born according to natural procreation, in other words, that Joseph, or any other man for that matter had been His father, He would have been born with original sin like all other sons of Adam. However, the Virgin Birth bypassed this terrible situation, and still allowed Christ to fit the Type.

NOTES

By that I mean that the original Adam was not born as the result of natural procreation, for the simple fact that He was the first, and was, therefore, created by God. So, the Last Adam, The Lord Jesus Christ, in becoming man, as He had to do in order to redeem humanity, did not take undue advantage by the manner of His birth, i.e. *"the Virgin Birth."*

It was absolutely necessary that God become man in order to redeem man, hence, the Incarnation. In other words, Angels could not redeem fallen man, because Angels are of another race, i.e., another creation. Likewise, God could not redeem man as God, because God cannot die, which was necessary if man was to be redeemed. So, God would become man, in effect the Last Adam, to redeem what the first Adam had lost.

A QUICKENING SPIRIT

If it is true that the first Adam is a living soul, then it must be equally true that the Last Adam is the opposite, a Life-Giving Spirit.

If Adam had not sinned, Christ would never have come; the living soul of Adam would never had needed rescue by the Life-Giving Spirit of Christ.

The first Adam due to the Fall, left us on this low level and necessitated the Coming of The Last Adam because sin and death had entered the world. This tragic fact underlies the entire 15th Chapter of I Corinthians.

It is even true that before the Incarnation, throughout the Old Testament, Christ was the Mediator of Spiritual Life, because everything in the Tabernacle, Temple, and the entirety of the Law of Moses pointed to Christ. In that he began His Work, but because, having begun, He gloriously finished this Work which is related in the four Gospels, and especially by the Apostle Paul.

In His Resurrection and His Glorification Christ literally and historically became *"The Last Adam, a Life-Giving Spirit."*

Consequently, we should consider the Resurrection and the Enthronement at God's Right Hand together: *"Wherefore God highly exalted Him and gave Him the Name which is above every name"* (Phil. 2:9).

One form of that Supreme Name is *"The Last Adam, a Life-Giving Spirit."*

Jesus still has His human body and will have it forever, which is now *"the Body of His glory"* (Phil. 3:21).

A LIFE-GIVING SPIRIT

When Paul writes that He became *"a Life-Giving Spirit"* he does not mean that Christ discarded His Body and that He now exists in heaven only as a spirit. *"Life-Giving Spirit"* designates Christ in relation to us: He is the fountain of spiritual life for us. That spiritual life flows, not from His Body, although it has become a Spiritual Body, and the Body of His Glory, to our body; but from the Spirit that dwells in His Glorious body to our spirit that dwells in our body and thus, quickens us spiritually and gives us life.

In all of this it is the human spirit of Christ that gives us life. In that human spirit of His Person is the Eternal Son of God (in humiliation as well as in exaltation). Yet not the mere union of the person of the Son with the human spirit, soul, and body makes Him for us the fountain of life, but the expiating work which He accomplished for us does, and I speak of Calvary and the Resurrection. As the one who died for us and rose again He now brings back life and immortality to us.

REGENERATION

This giving of life to us begins in Regeneration, which we receive upon accepting Christ. This begins in us the work of the Last Adam Who is a Life-Giving Spirit.

The consummation of this work will be the Resurrection and the Glorification of our bodies which shall then again be joined to our souls and our spirits and be made spiritual bodies. (I Cor. 15:22).

*"Who shall fashion anew the body of our humiliation, conformed to the body of His Glory, according to the working whereby He is able even to subject all things to Himself."* (Phil. 3:21; Col. 3:4; I Thess. 4:16-17).

In this life the ordinary animation of our physical body continues even though we are spiritually reborn, but in the Resurrection the spirit takes complete control of the body which has been gloriously refashioned so as to respond fully to that control.

NOTES

Here our spirit rules the animated body only partially, with the soul ruling mostly, and the spirit not at all referring to the unsaved. Then (in the Resurrection) the spirit shall rule the body perfectly as itself being a truly spiritual subject.

WHAT PAUL MEANT BY THE QUICKENING SPIRIT OF CHRIST

*"Quickening"* in the Greek is *"zoopoieo,"* and means *"to vitalize, make alive, give life."*

So, the idea is that the spirit of Christ, even His human spirit, is a vivifying spirit; a spirit giving aura or imparting life. Not a being having mere vital functions, or its animated nature, even as all other human beings have, but a Being Who has the power of imparting Life.

This is not a quotation from any part of the Scriptures per se, but seems to be used by Paul as conveying the substance of what was revealed respecting the Messiah in the Old Testament.

No doubt, it was a reference as Paul uses it, to what the Savior Himself taught, that He was the Source of Life; that He had the power of imparting life, and that He gave life to all whom He pleased.

He said, *"For as the Father hath Life in Himself; so hath He given to the Son to have Life in Himself"* (Jn. 5:26).

He also said, *"For as the Father raiseth up the dead, and quickeneth them; even so the Son quickeneth whom He will"* (Jn. 5:21).

SPIRIT

The word *"Spirit,"* as used by Paul as it applies to Christ is in contradistinction from *"a living being,"* as applied to Adam, and seems to be used in the sense of Spirit of Life, as raising the bodies of His people from the dead, and imparting life to them.

Jesus was constituted not as having life merely, but as endowed with the power of imparting life; as endowed with that spiritual or its vital energy which was needful to impart life.

All life is the product of creation or its a production of *"Spirit,"* as applied to God the Father, God the Son, and God the Holy Spirit. Spirit is the Source of all vitality. God is a Spirit, and God is the Source of all Life. And the idea here is, that Christ had such a spiritual existence, such power in His Spirit; that He was, and is, the Source of all Life to His people.

The word *"Spirit"* is applied to His Exalted spiritual nature, in distinction from his human nature (Rom. 1:4; I Tim. 3:16; I Pet. 3:18).

The Apostle does not here affirm that Christ had not a human nature, or a vital existence as a man; but that His main characteristics in contradistinction from Adam, was He was endowed with an elevated spiritual nature, which was capable of imparting vital existence to the dead (Barnes). And yet, His exalted spiritual nature, was definitely a part in some manner of His human nature, which was necessary concerning Him being a Man, The Man, Christ Jesus.

(46) "HOWBEIT THAT WAS NOT FIRST WHICH IS SPIRITUAL, BUT THAT WHICH IS NATURAL; AND AFTERWARD THAT WHICH IS SPIRITUAL."

The phrase *"Howbeit that was not first which is spiritual, but that which is natural,"* proclaims the order which was and is.

What is briefly and pointedly summarized here is more fully developed in the following Verses: first Adam, then Christ; first those who belong to Adam, then those who belong to Christ. Paul has no philosophy of the matter, he records simply the historical facts (Lenski).

He is doing this in order to nail down the Doctrine of the Resurrection.

## THE TENDENCY OF ERROR

Because Paul places the negative first by saying that the spiritual is not first, that seems to be an indication that some of his readers were inclined to philosophize instead of adhering simply to the facts.

They possibly were inclined to think that the spiritual ought to precede the natural. They may then take the next step and argue that the spiritual, being the original, ought alone to remain. Thus, they repudiate the natural and arrive at the rejection of the Bodily Resurrection. Paul eliminates all such deductions by this simple statement of fact and by its further explanation in the following Verses.

As well, some have referred to this Verse as the law of creation which proceeds from the lower to the higher in a kind of evolution. A misleading philosophy is then built up on this law.

However, this is error pure and simple. Paul would subvert his entire Gospel if he made the natural bring forth or produce the spiritual, which it simply cannot do. Furthermore, Paul

NOTES

is not recording a law or *"a principal of universal application."* He is merely stating the order as it is.

There is a reason that the Lord designed this order in this fashion.

We must reckon with the physical or natural side of this present life in the Spirit. It is somewhat like a training ground.

## THE NATURAL

This answers somewhat the reason as to why the Lord allows the sin nature to remain in the Believer after coming to Christ. Even though it is disconnected so to speak, still, its potential for great harm is there, and in fact, it has caused many Believers much difficulty and problems.

Why the struggle between the flesh and the spirit, many would ask? Why is it so difficult to walk after the Spirit?

These things are necessary for our Sanctification. They are not pleasant, but it is the order in which the Lord has designed, and always for our good.

Man's problem has always been that of pride. It's what caused the Fall, and it is what characterizes the results of the Fall. There is only one way that pride can be defeated, and that's by enough difficulties coming our way, that we will have to constantly look to the Lord for leading and guidance, help and strength. Otherwise, pride rears its ugly head, and does so very speedily.

The phrase, *"And afterward that which is spiritual,"* refers to that which is coming in the Resurrection. Then the *"natural"* will be laid aside, its time being over.

The idea is, that there is a tendency towards perfection, and that God observes the proper order by which that which is most glorious shall be secured. However, such perfection can only be secured in God's Way. Any other manner of approach tends toward the very opposite.

(47) "THE FIRST MAN IS OF THE EARTH, EARTHY: THE SECOND MAN IS THE LORD FROM HEAVEN."

The phrase, *"The first man is of the earth, earthy,"* tells us some things about Adam.

## THE FIRST MAN

Formed as Adam was, with a soul and a spirit breathed into him even before a volition of his

NOTES

own existed, it became his task to make his spirit the master of his entire being, we may say to spiritualize his soul and his body.

As well, God gave him the necessary ability to achieve this great purpose of his being. By a volition which was in harmony with his own spirit and with the help of God Who bestowed that spirit upon him, Adam could and should have risen to the intended heighth and have obtained the state of glory that was awaiting him. Adam failed. His spirit abdicated its mastery.

Consequently, in him and in his descendants the spirit (human spirit) no longer rules; the control has gone to his animated body. As a result, man is now *"earthy"* even in his thinking and his willing. His spirit is enslaved, reduced to the low level of only the consciousness of his personal being, with only conscience left as *"the spirit-remnant."* In other words, man has become materialized, i.e., materialistic instead of spiritual.

The phrase, *"The Second Man is the Lord from heaven,"* presents Paul now using the word *"second"* instead of *"last"* as he did in Verses 45, but with both meaning the same, referring to Christ.

Paul characterizes the first man (Adam) with respect to his body (his physical being) and the Second Man (Christ) with respect to His person (Who and What He really is).

The one is derived from the earth, the other is derived from heaven. The origin is twice mentioned, but these origins are opposites. Therefore, He Who is *"out of heaven"* cannot be derived from him who is *"out of the earth,"* nor can Christ be the source of Adam.

However, this last statement seems to be a contradiction. Aren't the soul and the spirit of Adam not also of heavenly origin, breathed into his body by the Creator Himself? And is the human body of Christ, born of the Virgin Mary not a descendant of Adam, *"out of the earth"* just as much as Adam's body?

Both observations are quite true. The first man has a heavenly side, the Second Man an earthly side, both being necessary.

As well, Christ retained his earthly body, but transformed it, and elevated it to the Glory of the Trinity, which was the Will of God for the first Adam, but in which he failed.

## THE DIFFERENCE

Nevertheless, Paul's statement stands: despite the similarities, similarities we must quickly add which were absolutely necessary, there is still an absolute difference in origin as well as in being between Adam and Christ.

Adam began with the dust of earth. God formed that dust into a body that was composed of earth. Then, without knowledge, consent, or activity of this body, God breathed His Breath into it. Thus, Adam became a living soul or living being.

The complete opposite is true regarding Christ. The Person of the Son of God existed from all eternity. By that Person's own volition and power a human body was conceived in the womb of the Virgin, in which this Person became Incarnate, not for the purpose of His own existence, but for the purpose of redeeming our fallen race. Thus, Adam is *"out of the earth, earthy"*; Christ *"out of heaven."*

From the very beginning of His Earthly Being, by His human spirit in which the Holy Spirit ruled, Christ controlled perfectly His Body, as well as His Soul. He is Lord not only of all who follow Him, but as well of Himself. By His Own free will He humbled Himself in order to work out our Salvation. Thus, while He was on earth He did not appear in Glory.

However, Paul is not concerned about that fact at this time; he looks at *"The Second Man"* in the Exaltation of His Resurrection and His Ascension, when He Who is *"out of heaven"* is fully revealed as such by His return to heaven.

Consequently, Paul compares and contrasts Adam as the one who began in Eden, with Christ in His Resurrection, Ascension, and Exaltation.

He is not contrasting the two respecting Christ's earthly Life and Ministry, but rather what He accomplished with Him now being back in heaven. Consequently, he is looking at what happened in Adam (the fall and death) and what happened in Christ (Victory and Eternal Life).

(48) "AS IS THE EARTHY, SUCH ARE THEY ALSO THAT ARE EARTHY: AND AS IS THE HEAVENLY, SUCH ARE THEY ALSO THAT ARE HEAVENLY."

The phrase, *"As is the earthy, such are they also that are earthy,"* presents the case that Adam is earthy, and all others who are earthy are like him. All of us are by nature the children of Adam. As such our distinguishing mark is the fact that we are earthy. Ours is a body of earth that is controlled by the soul; consequently, the body is thrust out of control. It is the body and its present condition to which Paul points with the term *"earthy."*

The phrase, *"And as is the heavenly, such are they also that are heavenly"* presents the other side which is Christ, *"The Second Man."* He is *"The Heavenly One,"* and all others who are *"the heavenly ones"* are like Him.

Even though Paul does not state how this heavenly quality is obtained, we know that it is by Grace through Regeneration (Jn. 3:3).

THAT WHICH SHALL BE

Yet Paul is careful not to say that, as Christ is *"from Heaven,"* or *"out of heaven,"* so those who are like Him also *"out of heaven."* For that would make these the equals of Christ which, of course, is falsehood.

Paul is speaking only about bodies and about their characteristic, bodies in which the spirit rules as it should, *"heavenly"* in this sense.

Paul is thus thinking, not of the beginning of this condition as we experience it presently on earth, but of the completion and consummation in the Resurrection. Grace and regeneration being the change; the Resurrection consummates it (Phil. 3:21).

A CALL TO THE HEAVENLY

The question remains as to whether our sharing of the *"heavenly"* existence has not already begun, that is, whether our corresponding to the Man of Heaven refers only to the Resurrection Body that we are to assume at that time, or whether Paul is here intending also a broader sense, including behavioral implications, involved in our sharing in His likeness now?

That is exactly what Paul is doing. The text bears it out.

The Corinthians and all other Believers for that matter, are being urged to conform to the life of the *"Man of Heaven"* considering that we now share His Character and Behavior. As in Verses 33, 34, and 58, the concerns over the denial of the Resurrection and over unchristian behavior merge. The implication is that not only are they (some of the Corinthians) not fully Spirit led now, but they will not be fully Spirit led at all if they do not *presently* also *"bear the Likeness of Man of Heaven."*

NOTES

We are being urged to become what we actually are by Grace; but as Verses 50-57 make plain, what we presently are by Grace will not be fully realized until this mortal puts on immortality and the final defeat of death is realized.

ERROR

The problem is that some of the Corinthians believed that they had already assumed the heavenly existence that was to be, an existence in the Spirit that discounted earthly existence both in its physical and in its behavioral expressions. What Paul is doing once again, is to refute both notions.

They (we) have been reborn — but still bear the likeness of the man of earth, i.e. *"Adam."* Because of that we are destined to die. But in Christ's Resurrection and our being *"in Him"* we have also begun to bear the Likeness of the Man of Heaven. The urgency is that we truly do so now, at least as far, as it is possible, as we await the consummation (Resurrection) when we shall do so fully.

This of which Paul says, strikes at the erroneous doctrine held by some, that at Salvation, the spirit is saved but not the soul and the body. Others contend, that the spirit and soul are saved, but not the body.

Consequently, some teach that when a Christian sins, it is not his spirit that is sinning, but rather his soul and body, or with some, only the body.

However, none of that is true, with Paul making it plain that the two images (the earthy and the heavenly) are present in all Believers, and will be until the coming Resurrection. Consequently, he said, *"And the Very God of Peace sanctify you wholly; and I pray God your whole spirit and soul and body be preserved blameless unto the Coming of our Lord Jesus Christ"* (I Thess. 5:23).

When the believing sinner comes to Christ, he is saved *"spirit and soul and body,"* as well, when the Believer sins, his *"whole spirit and soul and body"* is blamed, i.e., *"sins,"* which the Text bears out.

This doctrine is taught and believed by some, because they misunderstand the relationship of the spirit and the soul to the body, and many desire to absolve themselves of responsibility regarding sin.

(49) "AND AS WE HAVE BORNE THE IMAGE OF THE EARTHY, WE SHALL ALSO BEAR THE IMAGE OF THE HEAVENLY."

The phrase, *"And as we have borne the image of the earthy,"* refers to the fact that as our first father, we are frail, decaying, dying; as we are so closely connected with Him as to be like Him. This does not necessarily refer, mainly, to one bearing His moral character, although all unsaved do, but to the fact that we are, like Him, subject to sickness, frailty, sorrow, and death.

In fact, even though we have been redeemed, still, we continue to bear the image of the earthy, and will do so until the Coming Resurrection.

The phrase, *"We shall also bear the image of the Heavenly,"* refers to The Lord Jesus Christ, Who was from Heaven, and Who is in Heaven.

As we are so closely connected with Adam as to resemble him, so by the Divine arrangement, and by Faith in the Lord Jesus, we are so closely connected with Him that we shall resemble Him in Heaven. And as He is now free from frailty, sickness, pain, sorrow, and death, and as He has a pure and Spiritual Body, adapted to a residence in Heaven, so shall we be in that future world.

## PAUL HERE ANSWERS THE GREAT QUESTION

This is Paul's final triumphant response to the questions of Verse 35, *"Is it possible for the dead to be raised? With what kind of body will they come?"*

The argument here is, that the connection which is formed between the Believer and the Savior is as close as that which subsisted between him (Believer) and Adam; and as that connection with Adam involved the certainty that we would be subjected to pain, sin, sickness, and death, so the connection with Christ involves the certainty that we will be like Him, free from sin, sickness, pain, and death, and, like Him, will have a body that is pure, incorruptible, and immortal at the Resurrection.

As stated in Commentary on the previous Verse, as Believers, we now bear two images. The image of mortality we now bear in our bodies is, indeed, one that is derived from the earthy one, namely Adam; and the image of Righteousness we now bear is also truly derived from the Heavenly One, namely Christ. However, the latter Image, is not yet fully developed, and will not be until the Coming Resurrection.

What our bodies will look like and with what heavenly powers and functions they will be endowed at that time, like unto Christ's Glorious Body, we may now surmise but cannot now properly describe.

NOTES

## IMAGE AND LIKENESS

These are theological words in both the Old Testament and the New Testament. In the Old Testament they are used to make important statements about the nature of man.

In the New Testament they are used to make important statements about Jesus and about the destiny of those whose lives have been renewed through Faith in Him.

## MANKIND IN GOD'S IMAGE AND LIKENESS

Two Hebrew Words are used in Old Testament Passages that assert that man was made *"in the Image and Likeness of God"* (Gen. 1:26-27; 5:1-3; 9:6).

The Hebrew word *"selem"* means *"image," "representation."* It is used five times in the Old Testament (the Passages cited above) in reference to people. Most of its uses are to designate an idol shaped in the form of a person or an animal.

Another Hebrew word *"Dmut"* translated *"likeness,"* is a word of comparison. It is used to attempt to explain something by referring to something else that it is like. Although God makes it very clear that there is no way we can understand Him by comparing Him to a person or thing (Isa. 40:18), we can, however, understand the nature of man by comparing human beings with the Lord (Gen. 1:26).

Only some Biblical statements about human nature use *"selem"* and *"dmut"* together (Gen. 1:26; 5:1-3). It is best to understand these words as necessarily linked in this theological statement. Man is a likeness-Image of God.

## THE INNER NATURE OF HUMAN BEINGS

The creation story makes it clear that the likeness-image is not a physical form, that is, that God does not have a physical body. Material for creation was taken from the earth. It is the inner nature of human beings that reflects something vital in the nature of God. Thus, Bible Scholars generally agree that the likeness is rooted in all that is required to make a human being a person: and our intellectual, emotional, and moral likeness to God, Who has revealed Himself to us as a Personal Being.

It is this likeness-image that sets human beings apart from the animal creation, and it is transmitted through the process of reproduction to succeeding generations (Gen. 5:1-3). It is this likeness-image of God that makes each human life so precious that nothing of however great value can possibly be offered in compensation for the taking of another's life (Gen. 9:5-6).

Both Genesis Chapter 1 and Psalms 8 make it clear that with the likeness-image, God gave humanity a place of unique responsibility in the universe. Moved by one wonder at God's Gift of personal capacity to humanity, the Psalmist writes: *"What is man that you are mindful of him, the son of man that you cared for him? You made him a little lower than the Angels and crowned him with glory and honor. You made him ruler over the works of Your hand; You put all things under his feet"* (Ps. 8:4-6).

CHRIST IN GOD'S IMAGE

The New Testament teaches that Jesus perfectly expressed the Image of God. The Greek word for image is *"eikon,"* which means *"representation."*

In Classical Greek thought, the *"eikon"* had a share in the reality it expressed. This word is used several times to speak of Jesus' relationship with God. Paul calls Jesus *"the Image of God"* (II Cor. 4:4) and the *"Image of the Invisible God"* (Col. 1:15).

The word expresses the relationship of a coin to its die; that is, it is not speaking of mere comparison but rather an exact expression of the thing of which the coin is molded. In Hebrews 1:3 Jesus is described as the *"exact representation of His* (God's) *Being"* (*"Charakter"* being the Greek word here — its only use in the New Testament — for its *"exact representation"*).

God is so perfectly expressed in Jesus that when Philip asked to be shown the Father, Jesus could say, *"Anyone who has seen Me has seen the Father"* (Jn. 14:9).

CHRIST IN THE LIKENESS OF MANKIND

The New Testament word group expressing likeness is *"homoioo."* It is often used in statements making comparisons, such as Jesus' frequent statements beginning *"The Kingdom of Heaven is like. . . ."* This word of comparison suggests similarity of kind, and resemblance.

NOTES

Several times the New Testament affirms that in the Incarnation, Jesus was made *"like His brothers"* (Heb. 2:17) and *"in the likeness of sinful man"* (Rom. 8:3) or *"in human likeness"* (Phil. 2:7).

Although the New Testament never speaks of Jesus as being in the image of man, we should not conclude that He simply seemed to be human; for He is never said to be in the likeness of God, for He is fully God.

THE FULL DEITY OF CHRIST

In the Bible we find the full Deity and true humanity of Jesus (Jn. 1:1-14; Heb. Chpts. 1-2).

We should note the delicacy of the distinctions. Jesus in His Person perfectly represented God as He truly is. However, Jesus could not perfectly represent man as he is, for humanity is tainted by sin.

Jesus' human nature was untainted by sin. Thus, Jesus is in the image of humanity as it will be renewed when the drama of redemption is complete.

RENEWAL OF THE IMAGE AND LIKENESS

Even as sinners, human beings bear something of the image and likeness of God. The Fall has not robbed us of personhood, though sin makes each person a sad mockery of the beauty that might have been ours.

Yet the Gospel brings the bright Promise of full restoration. The Believer has *"put on the new self, which is being renewed in knowledge in the Image of its Creator"* (Col. 3:10).

God's Spirit even now is at work within us, and we *"are being transformed into His Likeness with ever-increasing glory"* (II Cor. 3:18). When Resurrection comes, as it certainly shall, we will know our destiny and be *"conformed to the likeness of His Son"* (Rom. 8:29; I Cor. 15:49-54). And John adds, *"When He appears, we shall be like Him, for we shall see Him as He is"* (I Jn. 3:2).

(50) "NOW THIS I SAY, BRETHREN, THAT FLESH AND BLOOD CANNOT INHERIT THE KINGDOM OF GOD; NEITHER DOTH CORRUPTION INHERIT INCORRUPTION."

The phrase, *"Now this I say, Brethren,"* makes the statement that follows emphatic; and *"I say"* together with *"Brethren"* lend a personal touch.

The phrase, *"That flesh and blood cannot inherit the Kingdom of God,"* pertains to our present physical bodies as they are now. Presently *"the life of the flesh is in the blood"* (Lev. 17:11).

In the coming Resurrection even though the body will continue to be physical, i.e. *"flesh and bone,"* there will be no blood, or at least the Scripture does not mention such but insinuates the opposite. Jesus said, concerning His Resurrected Body, *"Behold My Hands and My Feet, that it is I Myself: handle Me, and see; for a spirit hath not flesh and bones, as you see Me have"* (Lk. 24:39).

The life force presently being in the blood, we learn that in some mysterious way the seed of sin which came about at the Fall, bringing with it the wages of death, has in some manner something to do with the blood. To be sure it is not physical, but yet, it affects the physical, and does so through the blood which affects the entirety of the human body.

The Resurrection Body will not have *"blood"* but will be rather energized, it seems, by the Holy Spirit (Jn. 14:17).

Even though the Holy Spirit is literally *"in"* the Believer, presently, still, at the moment it is a body of flesh and blood, which greatly limits Him. It is not that He is limited, for the Holy Spirit is God, and He cannot be limited; however, the material in which and with which He works, is definitely limited, which limits what He can do.

THE KINGDOM OF GOD

*"God's Kingdom"* is, of course, identical with Christ's Kingdom, for there is only one Kingdom. Christ reigns in this Kingdom until He delivers it up to God the Father.

To inherit God's Kingdom means much more than merely to receive a place in that Kingdom as one of its subjects. Already in this life we ourselves are royal (I Pet. 2:9), actual kings who reign (Rev. 1:6; 5:10; 20:6), and in the life to come Crowns await us, (II Tim. 4:8; James 1:12; I Pet. 5:4; Rev. 2:10; 3:11), and a great Coronation Day when we, the sons of *"The King"* shall have authority over five cities, yea, over ten, shall sit with The King in His Throne (Rev. 3:21) shall reign with Him forever (II Tim. 2:12).

When Paul speaks of inheriting the Kingdom he places us in the midst of these realities. Now it is impossible for *"flesh and blood,"* as such refers to our bodies, and as they exist in this life, to receive this royal inheritance. Our present physical nature is totally unfit to exercise these supreme prerogatives that are here implied.

NOTES

A tremendous transformation must take place before our inheritance can be completely turned over to us. The fact that this change shall, indeed, take place is the positive implication that lies back of Paul's negative statement regarding the impossibility of ordinary flesh and blood inheriting the Kingdom.

The phrase, *"Neither doth corruption inherit incorruption,"* actually says the same thing as the first phrase.

*"Flesh and blood"* come under *"corruption"* while *"The Kingdom of God"* comes under *"incorruption."*

THE IMPOSSIBILITY

Paul records the fact: *"Corruption does not inherit incorruption"*— it never does. Whereas he first asserts the impossibility: *"cannot,"* He now seals this impossibility by stating the fact: *"does not."*

The idea is, that because corruption does not inherit incorruption, never does, therefore, flesh and blood cannot inherit God's Kingdom.

The corruption or ruination, in plain words are decay and rot. Flesh and blood do not remain flesh and blood upon the occasion of death, but break up. Their organic existence is destroyed; the organism disintegrates; only dust and ashes are left, which disappear among the elements.

How can a body of such a nature, as long as it remains thus, inherit incorruption?

The latter, incorruption, denotes indestructibility and changelessness of nature and a form as well as of substance. Incorruption equals immortality.

God's Kingdom always remains just as it is, in timeless existence, in eternal immutability, in changeless perfection like God Himself.

Corruption is found in our flesh and blood because of sins; God's Kingdom is incorrupt because sin is excluded from its very nature. This Kingdom cannot breakdown or disintegrate. Only when sin together with its affects are completely removed from our bodies, which will take place in the Resurrection, do our bodies then attain incorruption, and thus, are able to inherit God's Kingdom — all because of what Jesus did at Calvary and the Resurrection.

(51) "BEHOLD, I SHEW YOU A MYSTERY; WE SHALL NOT ALL SLEEP, BUT WE SHALL BE CHANGED."

The phrase, *"Behold, I shew you a mystery,"* does not refer to something that is unintelligible, but that which had been heretofore unknown. In other words he is saying, *"I now communicate to you a Truth which has not been brought into the discussion, and in regard to which no communication has been made to you."* On this subject there had been no previous Revelation.

Though the Pharisees held that the dead would rise, yet they do not seem to have made any statement in regard to the living who would remain when the dead should rise.

As well, this subject does not seem to have occupied the attention of the other Apostles, nor it seems had there been any direct communication on it from the Lord Jesus Himself.

Paul then here says, that he was about to communicate a great Truth, which till then had been unknown, and to resolve a great inquiry on which there had as yet been no Revelation.

The phrase, *"We shall not all sleep,"* has reference to the fact that at the time of the Resurrection (Rapture), there will be many Believers then alive as would be obvious. *"We"* in effect, says *"We Christians."* It includes all Believers who have ever lived, on up to the time of the Rapture, with by far the great majority, as would be obvious, having already died, i.e. *"sleep."*

The phrase, *"But we shall all be changed,"* refers to all Believers whether they are dead or whether they are alive when the Resurrection takes place; Paul is speaking about our bodies. These bodies, he says, *"shall be made other,"* which is translated *"shall be changed"* or altered. Just what shall be done with them, Paul in a moment tells us in detail.

This entire Chapter thus far certainly shows that the dead bodies in the grave must undergo a great change before they, too, are able to enter heaven. The same is true regarding the bodies of all Believers who are still alive at that time as *"flesh and blood."*

## THE NATURE OF THE RESURRECTION

Greek philosophy tried in vain to pierce the unseen world, both that of the present and the future. The Bible, since it is God's Word, does for the human race that which the philosophers and brightest minds of Athens were not able to do. It pierces into the future life, and tells us what the Believer's physical body will be like at that time.

NOTES

Salvation has in it, not only a provision for the Standing of a person before God's Holy Law, and a provision for his present life on earth in relation to sin and righteousness, but it also provides for his physical body after death.

## JUSTIFICATION

The first provision we know as Justification, the act of God removing the guilt and penalty of sin from the believing sinner, and bestowing a positive Righteousness in which the Christian stands uncondemned, guiltless, and Righteous before God's Law for time and eternity. This is a judicial matter, for in fact, that's what Justification actually means, a legal act, with God declaring the sinner *"not guilty."* It is all done because of the sinner's Faith in Jesus Christ, and what He did at Calvary and the Resurrection.

## SANCTIFICATION

The second provision is known as Sanctification, the act of God breaking the power of indwelling sin and implanting the Divine Nature, also giving the Believer the Holy Spirit as a permanent indweller, which act is followed by a continuous process in which sin is eliminated from the life of the Christian and Righteousness produced in its place by the Holy Spirit, as the Believer cooperates with Him in this work.

## GLORIFICATION

The third provision is Glorification, the act of God transforming the physical body of the Believer for the eternity which is to come. Of this we wish to speak now.

There are three changes which will take place in the physical body of the Believer at the Resurrection. The first has to do with the activities of the body and of the person who possesses it. In I Corinthians 15:44, Paul informs us that our present body as constituted, is a natural body, and the future body, a spiritual one.

This natural body is dominated by the soul which is the *"seat of feelings and desires."*

Thus, a physical body that is a natural body, is one which is adapted to a life in which the activities of the will, the emotions, and the reason predominate in the sense that these occupy the large part of the person's world, the things of time and place, the things of human life as it is lived on this earth. In other words, the human being is *"soulish,"* even though he has a spirit.

## THE SPIRITUAL BODY

The body the Believer will have at the Resurrection is a spiritual body. The Greek word is *"pneumatic."* Thayer defines this word as *"that part of man which is akin to God, and serves as His instrument or organ."* It is that part of man which gives him God-consciousness. In this sense the animal creation does not have *"pneuman"* or spirit.

With the physical body, man has world-consciousness, with the soul he has self-consciousness, and with the spirit he has God-consciousness. With the spirit (his human spirit) man has to do with the things of God. He worships God by means of his human spirit, that is, when that spirit is energized by the Holy Spirit, otherwise it is impossible. He serves God in the same way.

## THE PRESENT AND THE FUTURE BODY

The present body is so constituted that it is the efficient organ of the soul. The future physical body, however, will be so adjusted that it will be the efficient organ of the spirit (human spirit). In this present life most of our time and activity has to do with the things of time and space, making a living, with the creative arts, with recreation, with the material world.

The human spirit, however, should be the determining factor as to the character of the soul-life. Yet it is in active use but a small part of the time, when we worship God, study the Bible, Pray, serve God in some distinctive service in which we are giving out the Word of God to those who do not know Him (the human spirit in the unsaved have no connection with God at all, and is, therefore, unused.)

But in the future life, conditions will be changed. Then the soul-life as we know it now, will be a thing of the past. We will be occupied entirely with God and His Worship and Service. Our bodies will then be adjusted to the new life. They will be changed so they will be efficient instruments of the human spirit. Just what the nature of this change will be the Bible does not exactly say.

## AN INCORRUPTIBLE BODY

The second change which will take place in the physical body at the Resurrection, is that it will be an incorruptible one, and thus, an immortal one. Paul says: *"This corruptible must put on incorruption, and this mortal must put on immortality"* (I Cor. 15:53).

NOTES

This present body has death in it, disease, and decay. It becomes tired and exhausted. It may even have deformities. Parts of it may have been taken away through an accident or operation.

The future physical body will have no death in it, no weakness, deformity, or disease. The parts that have been removed, if so, will be restored. What a blessed state that will be, to have a body which can never die, in which there will be no indwelling sinful nature, which will never become weary or exhausted, in which there will never be any pain.

## A DIFFERENT LIFE PRINCIPLE

The third change will have to do with the composition of the body. Our present bodies are made of flesh, blood, and bones. As we have already stated, its life principle is in the blood. Moses knew this latter fact and stated it over 3,000 years before Medical Science discovered it. He said in Leviticus 17:11, *"The life of the flesh is in the blood."*

In our future physical body there will be a different life principle. The body will be devoid of blood, a body of flesh and bones. Paul, in Philippians 3:21, speaks of the Lord Jesus *"Who shall change our vile body, that it may be fashioned like unto His Glorious Body, according to the working whereby He is able even to subdue all things unto Himself."*

An expanded translation here would give us the following: *"Who shall change our humiliated body* (that is, humiliated by the presence of sin and death)*, conforming it as to its outward expression to the body of His Glory, according to the energy whereby He is able to marshall all things under Himself."* Our future body will be like that which our Lord possesses now.

He tells something about His present physical body in His word in Luke 24:39. He said, *"Behold My hands and My feet, that it is I Myself. Handle me with a view to investigation and see; because a spirit does not have flesh and bones as you with critical, understanding sight see that I have."*

## THE LORD'S GLORIFIED HUMAN BODY

These words tell us some interesting things about our Lord's Body. There were the marks of the nails of the Crucifixion still in His Hands and Feet, left there even though His Resurrection Body was perfect, for purposes of identification. The Body our Lord had after His Resurrection was the same Body He had previous to the Cross, and in which He died.

We will possess the same body in the future life that we have now, except changed. Since that is true, we will have the same facial expression, however, with all the sin wrinkles ironed out. Since that is true, we will know each other in the future life.

A SOLID PHYSICAL BODY

Second, our Lord's Body was a solid, physical body. The Disciples handled His Body with their hands, depending upon what their sense of touch would tell them as to its reality and composition.

John says in his first Epistle, *"That which we handled with a view to investigation"* (I Jn. 1:1). He uses the same Greek word Luke uses to report our Lord's Words. It was, therefore, a Body that would respond to the sense of touch, a Body made of solid material. Our bodies will be like that.

FLESH AND BONES

Third, it was a Body made up of flesh and bones, but changed in composition.

Our future bodies will be made of flesh and bones, the same flesh and bones we have now, but changed as well, as to composition.

A BODY WITHOUT BLOOD

Fourth, it was a Body without Blood. If our Lord's Resurrection Body had had Blood, he would have mentioned that fact when He spoke of flesh and bones. His Precious Blood had all run out from a heart pierced by the spear of the Roman soldier. It paid the penalty for your sins and mine.

Peter tells us that we Christians were redeemed with the Precious Blood of Christ. Since our Lord's Resurrection Body did not have any Blood in it, it must have had a new life principle animating it. Our future bodies will also have a new life principle in them. It will be the Holy Spirit.

NEW POWERS

Fifth, our Lord in His physical body of flesh and bones went through the stone wall of the building in which the Disciples were meeting. The doors of the room were closed.

This tells us that we will be capable of the same thing also. He had new powers of locomotion. He could make Himself visible or invisible at will. He was here one minute and in another place the next. So will it be with us in the future life. Believers will travel with the speed of thought.

A NEW COVERING

Finally, our Lord's Resurrection Body needed no clothing for a covering, but had a covering that was produced from within. Our Lord's Body after the Resurrection was not covered with clothing. The only clothes He had at the time of His Death were taken away from Him. His grave clothes, He left in the Sepulchre of Joseph. He emerged through the stone walls of the Resurrection tomb clad in a new covering for His Body that was produced from within.

Paul said, *"Who shall change our vile body, that it may be fashioned like unto His Glorious Body"* (Phil. 3:21).

All this is given us in the Greek word Paul uses in the above Scripture, translated *"fashioned."* It is the word *"morphe,"* which refers to an outward expression which is not put on from without, but one that comes from within and which is a true representation of one's inner nature.

This, in the case of our Lord, was a Glory Covering, an enswathement of Glory which covered His Resurrection Body. On the Mount of Transfiguration, our Lord's Face and clothing shown with a radiance that came from within. A radiance similar to this, was the covering of His Body after the Resurrection.

ALWAYS GOD'S PLAN

It has always been God's Plan for His creatures to cover themselves with a covering produced from within. Adam and Eve covered their bodies with an enswathement of Glory which was produced from within their beings. When they sinned, they lost the power to produce such a covering from within. To cover their naked bodies which now had sin and death in them, they made clothing for themselves.

Birds cover themselves with beautiful plumage which is produced from within. Animals

NOTES

cover themselves with fur or a thicker type covering which is produced from within. Thus, in the life to come, Believers will cover their bodies with an enswathement of Glory, a Light covering which will be produced from within.

NOTES

### THAT WHICH WILL BE

Now, to gather together our information regarding the future body of the Believer.

It will be a body adapted to a Spiritual Life in which all one's time and activity have to do with God, His worship, and service.

It will be a body that will be incorruptible and immortal.

It will be a body of flesh and bones, but no blood.

This body will have a New Life Principle animating it.

It will be a body, the Covering of which will be produced from within.

(52) "IN A MOMENT, IN THE TWINKLING OF AN EYE, AT THE LAST TRUMP: FOR THE TRUMPET SHALL SOUND, AND THE DEAD SHALL BE RAISED INCORRUPTIBLE, AND WE SHALL BE CHANGED."

The phrase, *"In a moment, in the twinkling of an eye,"* proclaims how long it will take for this change to take place.

The repetition of the phrase, *"In a moment, in the twinkling of an eye,"* emphasizes the instaneousness.

*"Moment"* in the Greek is *"atomo,"* and means *"a point of time which cannot be cut or divided."* It is a single instant, immediately.

*"Twinkling"* in the Greek is *"hripe,"* and means the *"glance of an eye."* This is an expression denoting the least conceivable duration of time.

The phrase, *"At the last trump,"* does *not* denote by the use of the word *"last"* that there will be successive trumpet blasts, but is a word denoting that this is the consummation or close of things. In other words, it will end the economy of this world; it will be connected with the last state of things.

Some have taught that the word *"last"* refers to two trumpet blasts, with the first raising the Sainted dead, and the second (last) occasioning the change of those who are then alive to immortality. However, that is incorrect.

Even though the dead in Christ will rise first (I Thess. 4:16), still, the being *"caught up"* to be with the Lord, will occasion both groups, those who had been dead and those alive, going at the same time (I Thess. 4:17).

*"Last"* in the Greek is *"eschatos"* and means *"final, last, latter end, uttermost."* There will be just one Trumpet blast.

### THE SEVEN TRUMPETS OF REVELATION

The *"Trumpet"* here of which Paul speaks is the *"Trump of God"* (I Thess. 4:16), which will take place at the time of the Rapture (Resurrection). Some people confuse these Trumpets, thinking that the Seventh Trumpet of Revelation 11:15-13:18 is the same of the *"Trump of God"* of I Thessalonians 4:16. They aren't the same at all.

The first one, which will signal the Rapture, is the *"Trump of God"* (I Thess. 4:16). The other is the *"Trumpet of the Seventh Angel"* (Rev. 11:15), which will herald great judgment coming upon the Earth. One may very well refer to the first as a *"Trump of Blessing"* and to the other as a *"Trump of Woe."*

One is before the beginning of Daniel's Seventieth Week (II Thess. 2:7-8; Dan. 9:27; Rev. 4:1), the other is in the middle of the seven year Tribulation period (Rev. 11:15-12:6); one is before the Saints arrive into Heaven, the other is after the Saints are already in Heaven (Rev. 11:15-12:5); one is before the Seven Seals and first six Trumpets (Rev. Chpts. 6-9), the other is after them (Rev. 11:15).

Consequently, we do not need to confuse this Trumpet and Rapture with the Seventh Trumpet and Rapture of the Man child (144,000 Jews).

The phrase, *"For the Trumpet shall sound,"* has to do with I Thessalonians 4:16, where it tells us three things will happen at the Rapture. They are as follows:

1. Jesus will come back with a shout.
2. The Archangel, evidently Michael, will join his *"voice"* with the *"shout"* of the Lord. Exactly what that *"voice"* will be we are not told, whether an adjoining shout, or something said.
3. The Trump of God will sound, even as Paul here says, which evidently God will blow Himself. Inasmuch as it is God Who will blow this Trumpet, such signifies the tremendous importance of that which is to be done. In fact, as the Day of Pentecost signaled the beginning of the Church,

the Resurrection will signal the end of the Church, at least as far as its earthly sojourn is concerned.

The phrase, *"And the dead shall be raised incorruptible,"* is the equivalent to saying that this corruptible must become incorruptible, and this mortal must become immortal.

## INCORRUPTIBLE

The fact that they shall be raised we know from the preceding statements; however, it is now stated in so many words. The future tense has the effect of a Glorious Promise: they shall be raised, there is no doubt about the coming fact.

The emphasis is, however, on the adjective *"incorruptible."* We have had full preparation for it in Verse 50. *"The dead"* are the dead bodies in the grave; souls do not arise and are not raised. Bodies as they are now, due to the Fall, are corruptible. So, when they are brought forth, it will not be in their old form as *"flesh and blood,"* but without even a trace of corruption and the decay that held them for so long a time.

It means that at the instant of the Resurrection they shall be without corruption — the same bodies but in a new state.

## HUMAN REASON

The secret revealed in these Verses is actually the great subject of the entirety of this Chapter. Human reason never could have discovered this secret.

The power that will raise the sleeping Saints will change the living Believers, and altogether, in bodies of Glory (Phil. 3:21), they will be caught up into the clouds to meet the Lord in the air and so ever be with Him (I Thess. 4:17).

The time of this Rapture, as stated, is to synchronize with *"the last Trump,"* i.e. *"the Trump of God."*

That Trump first sounded in human history in Exodus 19:16. It will sound for the last time at the Resurrection of the Saints.

The phrase, *"And we shall be changed,"* refers to *"all,"* both Old Testament Saints and New Testament Saints, in other words, every Believer who has ever lived from the time of Adam to the time of the Trump.

## CHANGED

Let's look at this word *"changed"* as it is used in the Bible, and especially as it relates to the Resurrection.

NOTES

Change threatens many of us, and we struggle to keep things the same. But change is built into the very structure of the universe. *"That which is seen,"* Paul writes in II Corinthians 4:18, *"is temporary, but what is unseen is eternal."*

Anything that you and I can touch or see or feel can and will change. Only the God beyond the universe is stable and unchanging.

The theme of Change and temporality is seen often in Scripture. The Psalmist looks at the earth and heavens God has created and says, *"They will perish, but You remain; they will all wear out like a garment. Like clothing You will change them and they will be discarded. But You remain the same, and Your years will never end"* (Ps. 102:26-27).

The fact of change is not viewed in Scripture as threatening. It contains a warning for us, but it offers hope.

## THE GREAT CHANGE THAT IS COMING

The warning is implied in Passages such as James 1:9-11. We cannot rest our confidence in anything in this brief life, lived as it is on the shifting sands of history (Heb. 12:25-29). Yet at the same time, the fact of change provides a ground for hope. We are not trapped by our past, unable to change. In fact, we *"are being transformed into His (Jesus') Likeness with ever-increasing Glory, which comes from the Lord, Who is the Spirit"* (II Cor. 3:18).

And, ultimately, *"we will all be changed — in a flash, in the twinkling of an eye, at the last Trumpet. For the Trumpet will sound, the dead will be raised imperishable, and we will be changed"* (I Cor. 15:51-52).

Change, then, is viewed by Scripture as imbedded in the very nature of the created universe. It will always be part of the human experience. Yet, the Believer can still hope even though in an uncertain world. By God's Will, we even now experience an interchange, a growth toward Godliness. And we will experience the ultimate change in the Resurrection.

We are confident of this, for we have God's Promise *"I the Lord do not change"* (Mal. 3:6), in other words, He will not change His Mind regarding the great *"change"* He has promised us, and which will come shortly.

(53) "FOR THIS CORRUPTIBLE MUST PUT ON INCORRUPTION, AND THIS MORTAL MUST PUT ON IMMORTALITY."

The phrase, *"For this corruptible must put on incorruption,"* denotes all forms of necessity regarding the coming Resurrection.

NOT A LAW BUT A REVELATION

In the present instance there is a temptation to take *"must"* in the absolute sense, as though Paul is referring to an abstract law or principle which is operative in the entire world as such.

This has been defined as the triumph of the Eternal-Divine over all things perishable, earthly, that are dominated by sin and death. However, if Paul intended *"must"* to be understood in this sense, he himself would be a philosopher like these who read such into what he has said. Paul plays no such role.

He merely reports what the Lord has revealed to him. This *"must"* simply and beautifully states what God has ordered and arranged in His Plan for our Restoration.

INCORRUPTION

In Verse 50, Paul states what cannot and, in fact, does not take place: *"Corruption does not inherit incorruption."* Now, with the same form of parallelism, he states what must and will take place. But he could not say: *"Corruption must put on incorruption; mortality must put on immortality."*

Instead of using the mere words *"corruption"* and *"mortality"* he feels constrained to use concrete terms: *"this corruptible," "this mortal."*

We must not forget that the Holy Spirit actually chose these words for the Apostle to use.

These are concrete terms and denote the body itself which has been wrecked or is in the process of being wrecked by the power of corruption and of death. This present body, although it is now in so sad a condition, can both inherit and put on the new form and the quality of incorruption and immortality. In other words, corruption and mortality can be, and according to God's arrangement, will be driven out by incorruption and immortality.

By Paul using the word *"this,"* it is possible that he was pointing to his own body.

Paul has twice said: *"We shall be changed."* We now see what he means: our bodies shall be clothed with incorruption and immortality.

*"Incorruption"* is the new heavenly condition and form which ever remain perfect. Every trace of sin and of its effects are gone, and in their place there is the Glory, Beauty, and Power of an imperishable life, *"an inheritance incorruptible and undefiled, and that fadeth not away reserved in heaven for you"* (I Pet. 1:4).

NOTES

The phrase, *"And this mortal must put on immortality,"* proclaims the second condition and a corresponding form that are free from the power of death and from any deterioration or change which death works.

*"Incorruption"* does away altogether with sin and the possibility of sin.

*"Immortality"* does away altogether with the fruit or wages of sin, which is death.

So, as man experienced the double curse (the sin debt and the grip of sin), and was delivered by the double cure (the payment of the sin debt and the breaking of the sin grip), he is likewise given a double change (incorruption and immortality).

PUT ON

Paul uses the figurative *"put on"* to express the instantaneous act, with it being repeated for the sake of emphasis.

This does not, of course, mean that corruption and mortality shall merely be covered up and hidden from view by having a mantle of incorruptibility and immortality cast over them in order merely to hide what is underneath. These two are opposites that exclude each other to such an extent that whoever puts on the new garment must first lay off the old. It is like being clothed with the garment of Christ's Righteousness, which means laying off the garment of sin and guilt and the filthy rags of our own self-righteousness.

Sadly, in this life, and despite our greatest efforts, it seems that sin and guilt keep appearing again and again and must again and again be removed by daily contrition and repentance; however, when we put on *"incorruption"* and *"immortality,"* corruption and death are gone forever.

NOT POSSIBLE TO CONVEY
THE TOTAL REALITY

These figures which Paul uses, and which the Holy Spirit desired that he use, can convey only a part of the great reality. All of them (incorruption, immortality, etc.) understate even when they are made as strong as possible.

The Truth is that what the Lord is going to do in the coming Resurrection will be of such moment, such magnitude, such glory and power, that there is no way that mere words can properly express this great happening, even though the strongest words be used.

(54) "SO WHEN THIS CORRUPTIBLE SHALL HAVE PUT ON INCORRUPTION, AND THIS MORTAL SHALL HAVE PUT ON IMMORTALITY, THEN SHALL BE BROUGHT TO PASS THE SAYING THAT IS WRITTEN, DEATH IS SWALLOWED UP IN VICTORY."

The phrase, *"So when this corruptible shall have put on incorruption,"* presents something that is grand and glorious, as if though Paul is ringing out the chords of a triumphal song. He makes them literally ring in our ears.

*"When"* does not tell us the date, but does guarantee that God has actually fixed a date that it will happen, and happen it shall!

The phrase, *"And this mortal shall have put on immortality,"* proclaims the second Verse of this grand and glorious song which is now sung by Faith, but will then be sung in reality.

The phrase, *"Then shall be brought to pass the saying that is written, Death is swallowed up in victory,"* is quoted by Paul from Isaiah 25:8. So, nearly 800 years before Christ, Isaiah wrote: *"He* (Jehovah) *swallows up death forever."*

*"Swallowed"* or *"swallow up"* is extremely powerful in the Greek and expresses complete destruction. Luther said: *"The Scriptures announce how one death* (Christ's) *devoured the other* (ours)." *"And death shall be no more"* (Rev. 21:4).

## DEATH

The way the Apostle uses the word *"death,"* it could be translated *"the death,"* which refers to the destructive power that is in us at birth and finally lays our bodies into the grave.

*"In victory"* proclaims the manner in which *"death"* will be swallowed up.

Read Isaiah's Triumphant Song. Death is not merely destroyed, so that it cannot do further harm, while all the harm which it has wrought on God's children remains.

The tornado is not merely checked so that no additional homes are wrecked while those that were wrecked still lie in ruin. The destruction of death is far more intense:

Death and all of its apparent victories are undone for God's Children. What looks like a victory for death and like a defeat for us when our bodies die and decay shall be utterly reversed so that death dies in absolute defeat, and our bodies live again in absolute victory.

Yes, more!

For these bodies will be restored, not merely again to be *"flesh and blood,"* but henceforth to be *"incorruptible," "immortal," "spiritual"* (I Cor. 15:44), *"heavenly"* (I Cor. 15:49).

(55) "O DEATH, WHERE IS THY STING? O GRAVE, WHERE IS THY VICTORY?"

The question, *"O death, where is thy sting?"*, proclaims Paul exulting in this great coming victory, that is a complete and final triumph over this great enemy of the happiness of man, and that man would die no more. It is a triumphant view which burst upon the soul as it contemplates the fact that the work of the Second Adam has repaired the ruins of the first (Glory to God) and that man is redeemed; his body will be raised; not another human being shall die, and the work of death shall be ended.

However, it is more!

Death is not only at an end; it shall not only cease, but its evils shall be repaired; and the glory and honor shall encompass the body of man, such as would have been unknown had there been no death. Where sin abounded, Grace did much more abound.

## WHERE IS THY STING?

No commentary can add to the beauty and force of the language in this Verse; and the best way to see its beauty and to enjoy it, is to sit down and think of death; of what death has been, and has done; of the billions who have died; of the earth strewed with the dead, and *"arched with graves"*; of our own death for that matter; the certainty that we must die, and our parents, and brothers, and sisters, and children, and friends; that all, all must die; — and then to experience the Truth, in its full-orbed splendor, to rise upon us, that the time will come when death shall be at an end! Who, in such contemplation, can refrain from the language of triumph, and from hymns of praise?

The word which is here rendered *"sting,"* refers to a rod or staff with an iron point, for goading oxen, and then a sting properly, as of a scorpion. It denotes here a venomous thing, applied to death personified, as if death employed it to destroy life, as the sting of a bee or a scorpion is used.

The idea is derived from the venomous sting of serpents, and is deadly.

ITS DEFEAT

The language here concerning death and its sting is that of exultation, proclaiming such being taken away and destroyed. The *"sting"* or *"stinger"* is gone, it has simply been removed.

Paul sees death forever conquered and sings a song of triumph over the vanquished foe. *"Thy victory is crushed by the victory of another."*

Death's victory seems assured, so assured that the world is full of skeptics regarding even the possibility of a bodily Resurrection. Among these skeptics there are found even *"Christian"* Preachers and Theologians.

They look at the dead bones in countless graves, all of this dying from which even God's people are not exempt. Is death not supreme in victory, they surely ask?

The reality is otherwise.

Death is only an instrument in God's Hands and, having done its temporary work, is thrown aside; Resurrection steps in and by its supreme victory reverses all of that which seemed a victory for death.

The question, *"O grave, where is thy victory?"*, announces its defeat.

*"Grave"* in the Greek is *"Hades,"* and means *"state of departed souls, hell."* Consequently, the word should have been translated *"hell"* instead of *"grave."*

HELL

According to the Jews, and as taught by Jesus (Lk. 16:19-31), hell is a vast subterranean receptacle, or abode, where the souls of the dead existed. It was dark, deep, still, awful. The descent to it was through the grave; and the spirits of all the dead were supposed to be assembled there; the righteous occupying the upper regions, and the wicked the lower; however, this has now been changed somewhat since the Death and Resurrection of Christ.

While the bodies of all the dead still enter the grave, the souls of the righteous pass at once into the hands of the Father and of Christ (Acts 7:59; Phil. 1:23; etc.), while those of the wicked are cast into Hades or hell.

Those now in hell, and those who will go to hell, will be released only to stand at the Great White Throne Judgment, where they will be then consigned to the *"lake of fire"* and be tormented forever and forever (Rev. 20:11-15).

NOTES

WHAT JESUS SAID

Jesus said in John 8:51, *"Verily, verily, I say unto you, if a man keep My saying, he shall never see death."*

Our Lord here presents the Christian view of death.

The assertion in the Greek is very strong. The idea is, *"shall absolutely not see death."* Then the statement is made stronger by the addition of a phrase which in other places in the New Testament is translated *"forever."* Thus, *"If any man keep My saying, he shall absolutely not see death, never."*

TO SEE

The key to the interpretation of the Verse is found in the meaning of the word *"see."* There are six words in the Greek language which mean *"to see"*:

The first refers simply to the act of physical sight (Mat. 12:22).

The second refers to physical sight that is accompanied by mental discernment (I Jn. 1:1).

The third means *"to look upon, contemplate, view attentively."* Used for instance, of a civilian watching a military parade (I Jn. 1:1, *"Looked upon"*).

The fourth means *"to scrutinize with the purpose of bringing about the betterment of the person so observed"* (Heb. 2:6, *"visitest,"* Acts 20:28, *"overseers"*).

The fifth word means *"to fix one's eyes upon," "to fix one's mind upon one as an example"* (Acts 3:4, *"fastening his eyes upon him with John"*). Even Peter and John judged these beggars as to their worthiness to receive alms.

The sixth word is the one used in John 8:51. It is used, primarily, not of an indifferent spectator, but of one who looks at a thing with interest and for a purpose. It expresses a fixed contemplation and a full acquaintance.

PHYSICAL DEATH

Now, the death spoken of here by Jesus is physical death, for the Jews speak of Abraham as being dead, and our Lord does not correct them by saying that He was speaking of spiritual death. He, therefore, says that when a Christian is being put to sleep (I Thess. 4:14), as he is dying, he will not look at Death with interest and for a purpose. He will be an indifferent spectator of Death, for he will have his eyes fixed on Jesus.

The terrors of that awful thing called death, are not experienced by the one who puts his Faith in the Lord Jesus. His attention will not be focused on death, nor will he feel its bitterness. This is what Paul means when he says (I Cor. 15:55), *"O death, where is thy sting?"*

But those that go out of this life rejecting Him, have before them all the terrors of death.

Oh, reader, are you sure that you are trusting in the Precious Blood of Jesus poured out in the substitutionary Atonement on the Cross for you personally?

We read in Hebrews 2:9 that Jesus tasted death for every man. That is, He not only died, but He experienced all the terror and bitterness of death in order that those who place their trust in Him as Saviour will not experience the terror and bitterness of it all.

So, the *"sting"* of which Paul spoke, and the *"grave"* which he mentioned, not only speaks of that coming day when all such darkness will be vanished, but as well, tells us that as far as the Believer is concerned, the *"sting"* and *"terror"* have been removed even now.

Regarding the two questions asked by Paul in this Verse, he is quoting from Hosea 13:14, but not verbatim.

(56) "THE STING OF DEATH IS SIN; AND THE STRENGTH OF SIN IS THE LAW."

The phrase, *"The sting of death is sin,"* could be translated, *"The sting of the death is the sin."*

This simply means that there would be no death without sin. In fact, the Apostle here personifies death as if it were a living being, which in fact it is (Rev. 20:14-15). It makes use of sin to inflict its penalty, its mortal agony. The idea is that sin is the cause of death. It introduced it; it makes it certain; it is the cause of the pain, distress, agony, and horror which attends it. Had there been no sin, men would not have died. If there were no sin, death would not be attended with horror or alarm, in fact, death would not be at all.

## ORIGINAL SIN

The fact, therefore, that men die is proof that they are sinners. Actually, all, due to Adam's Fall, are born in sin, i.e. *"original sin,"* i.e. *"the sin."*

NOTES

Sin means *"missing the mark,"* i.e. which is set by the Divine Law.

In fact, even the smallest sin had in it the power to kill. Men try to play with *"the sting of death"* and hope to avoid its fatal stroke. That game is impossible; the thing cannot be done, at least in that manner.

The phrase, *"And the strength of sin is the Law,"* refers to the Law of Moses.

That Body of Legislation, given exclusively by God, defined sin, stressed its penalty (death), and showed man, even God's chosen, the Jews, that man was so full of sin due to the Fall, so depraved, so without Righteousness, at least on his own, that he could not within himself, keep even the smallest Laws demanded by God.

## WHAT DID PAUL MEAN BY THE STRENGTH OF SIN BEING THE LAW?

How could the Law of God, which the Law of Moses actually was, and which was Righteous and Holy, be the strength of sin?

As we have stated, the Law as given by God told man what he must do, how he must live, how he must look to God and how he must treat his fellowman. However, even though that Law was Righteous and Holy, by its very nature of being Law, excited the sinful nature in man, which in fact it was designed to do. It was designed to show man how helpless he was to keep even the most simple Laws of God, at least within his own power. That is why the Law was the *"strength of sin."* It defined what sin actually was, and it showed man that he was a sinner, and portrayed his helplessness.

Men have an awful time admitting what they really are. And religious men most of all have a terrible time admitting the Truth.

Whereas man could deny his condition before the Law, after that Legislation, he could not deny what he was, at least not honestly, for the record was clear. He was and is a Lawbreaker.

Sin is always connected with God's Law, for His Law sets the mark, and by missing the mark the sin obtains its fatal reaction. The Law never submits or consents to be violated, for if it did, it could not be Law.

It always reacts against the violator, as all Law must. For the Law is not merely so many words of a code, it is the Divine Will itself. To challenge that Will is to declare war against God. In this way, the Law is the power of the sin.

Take away God's Will and Law, and all right and all wrong, all sin and all Righteousness disappear. But this means to take away God Himself — and us also.

In fact, sin does not try to thrust the Law and God aside as if they do not exist and could thus be treated with impunity. In this way, Law becomes the death power of the sin. It reacts instantly, makes itself and God back of it felt, with invincible power to strike and kill.

Thank God that Jesus perfectly kept all the Moral Law of God which we could not do, and upon Faith in Him, we are changed from the status of Lawbreaker to that of *"Law-keeper."* However, that is only through Jesus and Faith in what He did for us at Calvary and the Resurrection.

(57) "BUT THANKS BE TO GOD, WHICH GIVETH US THE VICTORY THROUGH OUR LORD JESUS CHRIST."

The phrase, *"But thanks be to God,"* is similar to Romans 7:25, or at least the first phrase of that Verse. In both cases, Paul is thanking God for giving us something which we did not deserve, and in fact, could not deserve, and in no way could have obtained within our own strength and ability.

GOD

The emphasis is on *"God,"* Who is, therefore, placed first and is also in contrast to the forces of sin and death. As someone has said, in Verse 56, Paul looks down, in Verse 57 he looks up. The Author of the miraculous change which Paul describes is the Triune God; hence, all our thanks belong to Him.

The phrase, *"Which giveth us the Victory,"* means that our future victory over death is as certain as though we had it now.

As well, the way the Greek is used by the Apostle, it also defines the very nature of God. In other words, it is His nature — His Very Nature — to give the victory to us. It actually says, *"He that keeps giving."*

It describes God by telling us about His continuous giving by a grand act of Grace. It does not speak only about what God will do at a future time, but about what He does now and does continually. In other words, the *"victory"* is bestowed upon us now, hour by hour. We obtain it from God in ever-increasing measure.

This wonderful giving deserves the deepest thanks on our part.

NOTES

The phrase, *"Through our Lord Jesus Christ,"* tells us how this *"victory"* has come about.

VICTORY

*"Victory"* denotes enemies and battle, but it is not a battle that we have won, for it is not possible for us to have won. This stupendous victory was won by Jesus Christ, and is being freely given to us.

Consequently, this phrase names the Victor, names Him as the Medium through Whom the victory gift becomes ours. *"Our Lord Jesus Christ"* is His full Personal and official Name in which *"Our Lord"* voices faith, confession, and adoration on the Believer's part.

Consequently, it is fitting that this Glorious Resurrection Chapter should end with the Name of Him Who is the Resurrection and the Life for all of us.

As we have previously stated, that victory was won at Calvary and the Resurrection.

Apart from the Atonement and Priesthood of the Lord Jesus Christ, there neither is, nor can be, a victory over sin, which is the sting of death.

(58) "THEREFORE, MY BELOVED BRETHREN, BE YE STEDFAST, UNMOVEABLE, ALWAYS ABOUNDING IN THE WORK OF THE LORD, FORASMUCH AS YE KNOW THAT YOUR LABOUR IS NOT IN VAIN IN THE LORD."

The phrase, *"Therefore, my beloved Brethren,"* proclaims the Apostle voicing his own tender love for the Corinthians. This is a love of full understanding and of highest spiritual purpose, which is deeper than mere fondness or affection. However, the Apostle at the same time, and as we shall see, appeals to the Corinthians to show themselves worthy of being addressed by such a title.

Paul begins this Verse by using the word *"Therefore,"* which reaches back over the entire Chapter. Even if we connect this conjunction with Verse 57 only, in particular with God's giving us the victory, the result is practically the same, for the entire Chapter comes to a climax in this victory gift.

This *"therefore"* bases the practical on the Doctrinal.

DOCTRINE

The word shows how true Doctrine results in Godly Life. Doctrine is a statement of the Divine facts.

When these facts are apprehended, they automatically shape the life. Take away the Doctrine with its substance of Divine Facts, and the life drifts and is blown about by every wind of (false) Doctrine (Eph. 4:14), which ignores or denies the facts.

The True Doctrine is, in its very nature, one, ever will be one and the same; false doctrine is always manifold, its very nature is division, nonunity. With the facts in our possession, we have something to live for; when these facts are absent from our hearts, what have we to live for?

The phrase, *"Be ye stedfast,"* actually says, *"Continue to be stedfast."*

Paul presupposes that the Corinthians *are* stedfast; by no means that they are unsteady and are to achieve steadfastness.

STEDFAST

*"Stedfast"* in the Greek means *"sitting, established in a seat, and thus fixed, settled, firm, solid."*

It thus refers to our own inner Faith and Conviction. Having a victory so great and vital, our first obligation is to be firmly and fully settled in it and thus to realize for ourselves its greatness and its glory, its preciousness and its power, and to abide in it with happiness and thankfulness to God.

So many are inwardly unstable, or like water or sand, never settled down solidly in the Gospel and its glorious Faith. They allow their hearts to be fixed elsewhere; and as empty as the other ideas are, so empty is their attachment to them.

UNMOVEABLE

*"Unmoveable"* means in the Greek *"be not shifted from your position."*

This refers to outward solicitation and attack. Foes are always ready to assail our Faith. Some strike at it with open denial, some with subtle error that leads us to compromise our Faith and our Confession, and some come with immoral temptation. They seek to turn us, who are Victors in Christ into slaves of men.

Paul bids us stand *"unmoveable against all of them."*

The phrase, *"Always abounding in the Work of the Lord,"* means we are not called to idleness and mere enjoyment, but to diligent effort *"in the Work of the Lord."*

NOTES

If Christ is not risen, and no transformation awaits us, then we should have no real work in life. Creature enjoyments would be our all. But now a thousand voices call upon us to be busy and tireless. Paul is an excellent example in following his own admonition.

THE WORK OF THE LORD

Paul significantly calls this *"the Work of the Lord."* This is the Work of the Gospel, the Work of filling our own hearts and our lives with the Truth, the power, and the Light of the Gospel and the hearts and the lives of as many others as possible.

This is the work of the Church in taking the Gospel of Jesus Christ to the entirety of the world. Its nature is spiritual throughout.

This significant phrase *"of the Lord"* should correct the so-called *"Church Work"* of many who busy themselves with worldly tasks in the Churches, with mere humanitarian *"social service"* and a hundred other things with which the Lord and the Gospel are not concerned.

*"Always"* adds another point. It appeals to both youth and age. It refers to the fact whenever many work with us, and work is a joy, and as well, when we plod on alone with heavy hearts, when we have already done much, and when it seems as though others have done scarcely anything. We *"always"* continue.

With this labor for the Lord, the laborer will not stand there with empty hands. This is the case with all who work for money, honor, and mere temporalities; when they are through working, their hands are empty.

The phrase, *"Forasmuch as ye know that your labour is not in vain in the Lord,"* proclaims a glorious promise. Because our labor is in connection with the Lord, therefore, it is highly productive. All of the harvest and all of the reward come from Him (Mat. 20:8; 28:20; Lk. 19:17). Without Him, all of our love's labor is lost.

FOR THE MOST PART INVISIBLE

The Lord's Work is mostly Spiritual, and its results are, therefore, for the greater part invisible to our eyes.

We cannot measure Faith, love, or virtues in the hearts of God's people.

In the case of secular work, the result is easily measured. A bricklayer lays so many bricks in so many hours and receives so much pay. A merchant sells so much in his store and makes so much profit. But it is not so in this Work of the Lord. We cannot actually count or take inventory. The results are too intangible. The Lord Alone sees and knows.

At times, we feel as though our efforts are in vain, therefore, becoming discouraged, consequently, to cease the strong effort, or to stop altogether. Hence, this Apostolic assurance: *"Having realized that our labor is not empty in the Lord."* This deep conviction sustains our spirit to continue to the end with joyful confidence (Jn. 4:36).

As we look at the last Word or Title in this 15th Chapter, we see it is the title *"Lord."* It is fitting that it ends thusly!

*"As the heart, about to falter, in its trembling agony,*
*"Panteth for the brooks of water, so my soul doth pant for Thee.*
*"Yea, a thirst for Thee I cry; God of Life, O when shall I come again to stand before Thee*
*"In Thy Temple, and adore Thee?"*

*"Bitter tears of lamentation are my food by night and day;*
*"In my deep humiliation where is now thy God? they say.*
*"Yea, my soul doth melt in me, when I bring to memory,*
*"How of yore I did assemble with the joyful in Thy Temple."*

*"But the Lord will send Salvation, and by day His love provides;*
*"He shall be my exultation, and my song at eventide.*
*"On His praise in the night I will ponder with delight,*
*"And in prayer, transcending distance, seek the God of my existence."*

*"O my soul, why are thou grieving, why disquieted in me?*
*"Hope in God, thy faith retrieving; let Him still thy refuge be.*
*"I shall yet extol His Grace for the comfort of His face;*
*"He has ever turned my sorrow into gladness on the morrow. And in Him I hope to be."*

NOTES

## CHAPTER 16

(1) "NOW CONCERNING THE COLLECTION FOR THE SAINTS, AS I HAVE GIVEN ORDER TO THE CHURCHES OF GALATIA, EVEN SO DO YE."

The phrase, *"Now concerning the collection for the Saints,"* refers specifically to Jerusalem. This *"collection"* or rather gathering of money for the poor Saints at Jerusalem occupies a goodly number of mentions, plus two whole Chapters in II Corinthians. They're found in Acts 11:29-30; 24:17; I Corinthians 16:1-4; II Corinthians Chapters 8 and 9; and, Galatians 2:10.

### THE OCCASION FOR THESE COLLECTIONS

There was a real and genuine need in Jerusalem to which we will address momentarily, but first we should mention that Paul it seems, used this effort to bring unity between Gentile and Jewish Christianity. The Law/Grace issue loomed large for most of the Ministry of Paul, and hopefully to mend this threatened breach, he hopes to prove his love for Jerusalem and the Jewish segment of the Church in this manner. However, for Paul I think it went deeper than that, for if the Gentiles had shared in the Jews' Spiritual Blessings, which they had, they in a manner, owed it to the Jews to share with them their Material Blessings (Rom. 15:27).

### THE SAINTS IN JERUSALEM

The major reason for the financial difficulties regarding the Church in Jerusalem, concerned the tremendous number of Jews who had given their hearts and lives to Christ since the Day of Pentecost, which number was actually into the thousands. While this is wonderful almost beyond belief, and which portrayed a tremendous Moving and Operation of the Holy Spirit, at the same time it brought about hardship in view of the fact that almost all, if not all of those who had given their hearts to the Lord were instantly excommunicated from the Synagogue in Jerusalem.

The Religious Leadership of Israel hating Christ, especially considering that they had crucified Him, were in no mood to show mercy and kindness to His followers. Consequently, the venom and anger were severe to say the least.

Excommunication from the Synagogue in the everyday life of Israel, was an extremely serious matter. Actually there were three types of excommunication, which we will not now address, but to be sure, the most brutal excommunication was carried out on the followers of Christ.

This type of excommunication meant that the victims were cut off from all social and religious contact in the Israel of that day, with the exception of the Temple; however, even that became a source of contention. Inasmuch as almost everything centered around the Synagogue, this meant that their Children could no longer attend school (school was conducted in the Synagogues), that is if they had Children in school. It also meant that they were instantly cut off from employment, unless their employer in fact was a Believer. Unless they owned their own home, most were instantly evicted, in fact, barred from almost everything.

As well, they were cut off from their immediate families, being treated as though they were dead, and their names not allowed to be mentioned ever again. In fact, when they died, no member of the family would even attend the funeral. As stated, the excommunication was just about complete in every detail.

While all families may not in fact have been that harsh, still, the Religious Leaders of Israel were adamant in their demands that every measure be taken that was possible against these people, consequently, making it as hard for them as they could. As a result, thousands were out of work, with no ways or means to provide for their families.

DIRE NEED AND NOT COMMUNISM

This is the meaning of the statement in Acts Chapter 2 where it says, *"And all that believed were together, and had all things common; and sold their possessions and goods, and parted them to all men, as every man had need"* (Acts 2:44-45).

This was not the undertaking of a different form of government, even that of Socialism or Communism as some have suggested, but rather the fact that thousands had been excommunicated from the Synagogue, which

NOTES

meant as stated, that most opportunities were cut off regarding making a living for one's family. Consequently, everyone shared, even as the Scripture proclaims, attempting to meet this need.

To be sure, the need did not exhaust itself in a matter of weeks or months, but lengthened throughout the years of the account of the Book of Acts. Consequently, Paul is attempting to be of help by receiving Offerings in all Churches throughout much of the Roman Empire. The need was great, and he was attempting to do what could be done to help alleviate the situation.

RELIGION IS A CRUEL BUSINESS

Of course, when I say *"religion,"* I am speaking of that which is man-devised and man-instituted. In other words, it is not of God. Sadly and regrettably, such makes up a great part of what is referred to as *"Christianity."* Ideally, Christianity, at least the Bible version, is not a religion at all, but rather a relationship, and a relationship with a Man, The Man, Christ Jesus.

True Christianity allows the Lord to be the Head of the Church, consequently, defending His Church. Religion does the very opposite! It always feels threatened, and, therefore, feels it has to defend its interests.

Judaism had long since drifted from the True Word of God, now little more than an ethical system. Consequently, feeling very threatened, it felt it had to protect itself; therefore, its leaders took extreme measures against those who were followers of Christ. Unfortunately, such did not die with Judaism of old.

Religion is the same presently. It will kill the Lord in the Name of the Lord!

I realize that's quite a statement, but it is true. The Bible is pushed aside, with man's rules taking its place. Consequently, deceived and deceiving, there is nothing that they will not do to protect their interests. That's the reason why religious wars are the worst of all.

Somehow, people think if their cause is righteous, this gives them a license to do almost anything. They seldom see the hypocrisy and contradiction of their efforts. All they see is their religion; consequently, they must protect their religion.

The earth has been soaked with blood countless times because of this very thing.

Never mind that the Saints in Jerusalem and elsewhere in Judaea, never lifted a hand in protest or violence against these persecutors. Their simply being followers of Christ was enough to warrant the opposition.

The phrase, *"As I have given order to the Churches of Galatia, even so do ye,"* refers to this matter as the responsibility of all the Churches.

Elsewhere Paul speaks of this collection in terms that are full of Spiritual content. He uses words like *"Fellowship," "Service," "Grace," "Blessing,"* and *"Divine Service,"* especially in Chapters 8 and 9 of II Corinthians.

All of this together suggests that the *"collection"* was not some mere matter of money, but was for Paul, and being led by the Holy Spirit, an active response to the Grace of God that not only ministered to the needs of God's people, but also became a kind of ministry to God Himself, which resulted in thanksgiving toward God and a bond of fellowship between *"God's people"* across the Empire.

## THE CHURCHES OF GALATIA

Galatia was a province in Asia Minor. It occupied the region now known as central Turkey.

In 64 B.C., Galatia became a client of the Romans. After the death of Amyntas, its last king, it was given full status as a Roman province. This took place in 25 B.C.

The new province of Galatia of which Paul mentions, included not only the old ethnic territory but also parts of Pontus, Phrygia, Lycaonia, Pisidia, all somewhat familiar names in the Book of Acts. The cities of Antioch, Iconium, Lystra and Derbe were in this Province (Acts Chpts. 13-14).

Paul used the Galatians as an example of giving to the Corinthians, and the Corinthians to the Macedonians, and the Macedonians as an example to all (II Cor. 8:1-5; 9:1-2).

The fact that the destination of the collection is not mentioned in this Scripture, and only indirectly in Verse 3, implies that they well knew for whom it was intended. The same holds true for the fact that Paul here offers so little information about the collection itself — its purpose, for whom, and its spiritual significance. Quite possibly the Corinthians had asked Paul about the matter of the collection in the letter which they had written to him, and Paul now makes his reply.

NOTES

## EVERYDAY LIFE

The sudden step from the vast mysteries and wondrous marvels of Chapter 15, to the small daily interests and duties of the Christian's everyday life, makes vivid the wonders of the power and the tenderness of the love perpetually in exercise in ministering to and protecting the feeblest member of the flock of God. So that power and love at once here legislate for the daily bread of hungry people.

(2) "UPON THE FIRST DAY OF THE WEEK LET EVERY ONE OF YOU LAY BY HIM IN STORE, AS GOD HATH PROSPERED HIM, THAT THERE BE NO GATHERINGS WHEN I COME."

The phrase, *"Upon the first day of the week,"* of course, speaks of Sunday. This is the day that early Christians observed as their day of rest and worship (Jn. 20:1, 19, 26; Acts 20:7).

## TEN REASONS WHY CHRISTIANS KEEP SUNDAY

1. To commemorate the Resurrection and the Finished Work of Christ in His Victory over death, hell and the grave (Mat. 28:1; Mark 16:9; Jn. 20:1).

2. The Risen Lord's manifestations to His Disciples were on Sunday (Mat. 28:1; Mark 16:9; Jn. 20:1, 19, 26).

3. Christ ignored completely the old Jewish Sabbath. The first day is the prominent day after the Resurrection (Mat. 28:1; Mark 16:9; Jn. 20:1, 19, 26).

4. The outpouring of the Holy Spirit came on Sunday. Pentecost was the first day after seven Jewish Sabbaths (Lev. 23:15-21; Acts 2:1). Thus, both Christ and the Holy Spirit manifested themselves to the Church on this day, completely ignoring the Jewish Sabbath.

5. Christ or no Apostle commanded to keep the old Jewish Sabbath or any other day, but did command all men not to be bound by any particular day (Rom. 14:5-6; Gal. 4:9-11; Col. 2:14-17). Sin is sin whenever committed. It is transgression of the Law that constitutes sin (I Jn. 3:4), not the day in which it is done. Anything sinful on Saturday or Sunday is sinful on every other day. If it is not sinful on Monday, Tuesday, etc., it is not sinful on Sunday.

6. Although no set day is commanded to be the Sabbath (day of rest) in the New Covenant, as in the Old Covenant which was abolished,

they did keep Sunday as their day of worship (Mat. 28:1; Mark 16:9; Jn. 20:1, 19, 26; Acts 20:7; I Cor. 16:2; Rev. 1:10).

7. Typology of the Old Covenant made Sunday a day of worship:

A. The Jewish Sabbath was a changeable Sabbath, changing at Pentecost every year to one day later until each day of the week was observed every seven years. Pentecost was the first day after the Sabbath (Lev. 23:15-21).

B. The Feast of Firstfruits came on Sunday, typifying the Resurrection (Lev. 23:9-14; Mat. 28:1; Jn. 20:1).

C. The Feasts of Unleaven Bread and Tabernacles also were observed at least one Sunday and perhaps two, being seven and eight days long (Lev. 23:6-36).

8. God honored Sunday by giving the Law on that day (Ex. 12:2-18; 19:1, 3, 11; Lev. 23:3-6).

9. God again honored Sunday when giving the Book of Revelation on that day (Rev. 1:10).

10. Constantine and the Pope did not change the Sabbath in A.D. 321 and 364, as some claim.

## SUNDAY AND THE EARLY CHURCH

As should be obvious from I Corinthians 16:2 and Acts 20:7, Sunday was the day set aside for worship by the Early Church, for two reasons:

1. This was the day Jesus rose from the dead.

2. The old Jewish Sabbath of Saturday was a part of the Mosaic Law, and was meant to symbolize the *"Rest"* which would come in Christ, even as all the Feasts Days and Sacrifices symbolized Christ. When He came, there was no more need for the symbolism, as should be obvious.

## THE CROSS OF CHRIST

The early Christians were loyal Jews. They worshipped daily in the Temple at Jerusalem (Acts 2:46; 5:42). They attended Services in the Synagogue (Acts 9:20; 13:14; 14:1; 17:1-2, 10; 18:4). They revered the Law of Moses (21:20). The Jewish Christians undoubtedly continued to observe the Sabbath.

When Gentiles were brought into the Christian community, a problem arose with regard to their relation to the Jewish Law. There were those who insisted that it was necessary for them to submit to the rite of Circumcision and keep the Law of Moses, which would, of course, include the Sabbath Command (Acts 15:1, 5; Gal. 2:3-5). Others, of whom Paul became the leader, affirmed that it was not necessary for the Gentile converts to accept the religion of Judaism. Paul argued that since they had received the Spirit without observing Jewish Law, they were not obligated to adopt Jewish ceremonies in order to live righteously (Gal. 3:2-3; Acts 15:7-10).

## BONDAGE

The Apostle Paul regarded the Law as a yoke of bondage from which the Christian had been set free (Gal. 5:1). In his *"revolt against external Law,"* Paul made no distinction between moral and ceremonial law. It was all a part of the Old Covenant, which was done away in Christ (II Cor. 3:14). The Sabbath is definitely included in *"the bond which stood against us with its legal demands,"* which, Paul declares, God canceled and set aside, *"nailing it to His Cross"* (Col. 2:14). It is mentioned along with festivals and new moons, all of which are declared to be *"only a shadow of what is to come"* (Col. 2:16-17). To *"observe days and months and seasons and years"* is to be slaves to *"the weak and beggarly elemental spirits"* (Gal. 4:9-10; Col. 2:20). The observance of days is a characteristic of *"the man who is weak in faith"* (Rom. 14:1-5).

Paul provides no grounds for imposing the Hebrew Sabbath on the Christian. The Christian is free from the burden of the Law. The Spirit of Christ enables him to fulfill God's Will apart from external observance of the Law's demands. Paul, in Hebrews, speaks of the Hebrew Sabbath only as a type of *"God's Rest,"* which is the inheritance of all the people of God (Heb. 4:1-10). He does not tell his readers to keep the Sabbath, but rather urges them to *"strive to enter that Rest"* (Heb. 4:11).

## JESUS FULFILLED EVERY ASPECT OF THE LEVITICAL LAW

Even as we have already stated, Jesus addressed every aspect of the Levitical Law in His Life and Living, and above all, in His Death on Calvary. In His Life and Living, He kept the Law perfectly and in every respect. In other words, He never failed in thought, word, or deed. Also, it must be understood that He did these things totally as our substitute, i.e., *"The Second Man."*

Having kept the Law perfectly in His Life and Living, it now remained that the curse of the

NOTES

broken Law must be addressed. In other words, every human being who has ever lived, and who is alive presently, and who will be born, at least in this age, have broken the Law. The penalty is death (Rom. 6:23). The only way the Law could be assuaged, at least in the mind of God, to whom the debt was owed, was that a Perfect Sacrifice be offered — a human sacrifice. Because of original sin, man could not supply the sacrifice. In other words, since the Fall, every human being who has been born, has been born in the likeness of Adam, thereby a product of the Fall, which speaks of original sin. So, no human being was eligible to offer this sacrifice; consequently, if Salvation had been left up to man, man would have been doomed. But God didn't leave it up to man. He provided the Perfect Sacrifice. God became man, took upon Himself the habiliments of human flesh, but without its sin, in order that the price be paid. That price was the Cross of Calvary. There every debt was paid, which satisfied the Righteousness of a Thrice-Holy God, opening the door for man to be saved.

The phrase, *"Let every one of you lay by him in store,"* refers to an Offering being given by each family, each Sunday when they gathered to worship the Lord. It did not mean that they were forced to give on this particular day each week, even as the next phrase proclaims, but that this was to be the basic time for their giving, which would be systematic even as it should be.

The phrase, *"As God hath prospered him,"* proclaims that they were to give as they were in turn paid for their secular work whatever that may have been, whether it was once a week or once every two weeks, etc.

GIVING TO THE LORD

If one is to notice, Paul said *"Every one of you,"* which included both rich and poor. Each person was to esteem it his duty and his privilege to give to the Work of the Lord. It was not to be confined to the rich only, but was the common duty of all. The poor, as well as the rich, were expected to contribute according to their ability.

LAY BY HIM IN STORE

The Believer is to designate a certain portion of his income for the Work of the Lord. He is to do it not for the sake of display, but as a matter of principle, and because it is the Will of the Lord.

NOTES

As well, Paul intended that they should be systematic in their giving, and that they should give from principle, not merely under the impulse of feeling. The idea is, the Lord has prospered us, and we owe it to Him as a debt of gratitude. And according to our prosperity and success, we should honestly devote our property to God.

THE DOCTRINE OF TITHING

Many Christians are somewhat confused about the Doctrine of Tithing. Some claim it is a part of the Mosaic Law, and, consequently, is not binding on Christians presently.

Let's see what the Bible actually says about Tithing and Giving to God.

TITHING BEFORE THE LAW OF MOSES

We find Tithing practiced some 430 years before the Law of Moses was given.

The Scripture says that Abraham paid Tithes to Melchizedek, who was a type of Christ. Melchizedek said of him, *"And blessed be the Most High God, which hath delivered thine enemies into thine hand. And he* (Abraham) *gave him* (Melchizedek) *Tithes of all"* (Gen. 14:20). This is the first example of paying Tithe given in the Bible. Consequently, the Lord must have instructed Abraham to do such, and in fact there is some thought that the phrase, *"Firstlings of his flock"* concerning Abel, had to do with Tithe (Gen. 4:4).

So, this is a Doctrine that began near or at the dawn of time, and was given by God and for a purpose.

Tithe and Offerings is the manner in which God has chosen to finance His Work. However, and as should be obvious, there is no selfish motive or purpose relative to God, inasmuch as He needs nothing.

Tithes and Offerings were designed by the Lord for the principle purpose of blessing His people. His Word is abundant concerning Blessings and Prosperity for those who will give to His Cause and Work (Mat. 18:18; Lk. 6:38; Jn. 15:7; II Cor. 9:6-9; etc.).

TITHING UNDER THE LAW OF MOSES

It was commanded (Lev. 27:30; Mal. 3:10).

Actually under the Law of Moses there were three Tithes demanded, which amounted to 23 1/3 percent. They are as follows:

1. The first Tithe (or 10%) was designated for the Levites and Priests (Lev. Chpt. 27; Num. Chpt. 18; Deut. 14:27).

2. A second Tithe was demanded by the Lord to be used by the individual himself and his household to cover expenses at the national Feasts, so there would be no excuse for not going (Deut. 12:11, 21; 14:22-26).

3. There was a third Tithe which was to be used for the poor, and was to be paid every three years. Consequently, it amounted to three and a third percent per year.

Consequently, this was not a burden in any degree; God more than made up for it in His Blessings of Prosperity on the crops and stock of the whole nation.

Spread out over the three year period the yearly tax for the poor would amount to three and a third per cent of the nation's increase. It was not to be taken to the place of Worship, as the other two Tithes, but distributed locally as needed throughout the three years it covered.

TITHING IN THE NEW TESTAMENT

The greatest treatment on *Giving"* is given by the Apostle Paul in the Eighth and Nineth Chapters of II Corinthians. Relative to Giving, nothing is ignored or omitted in these two Chapters. The Holy Spirit covered everything.

Even though the word *"tithing"* is not mentioned, this is done for a reason. Under the New Covenant, Believers are to give to an even greater extent than Tithing. While Tithing may be used as a base of our giving, Paul said, *"He who sows bountifully shall reap also bountifully"* (II Cor. 9:6).

He then told us not to give *"grudgingly, or of necessity: for God loves a cheerful giver"* (II Cor. 9:7).

Paul actually said that we should give to *"prove the sincerity of our love"* (II Cor. 8:8). That, and that alone, is the highest motive for giving, i.e., *"tithing."*

PROSPER

By Paul using the phrase *"as God hath prospered him,"* tells us that the Lord will definitely prosper those who give to His Work, and give because they love Him (II Cor. 8:8).

Consequently, Believers should expect the Lord to prosper them, should expect Him to bless them, should expect Him to do these things He has promised, and to be certain, He shall.

NOTES

The phrase, *"That there be no gatherings when I come,"* refers to their systematic giving.

If all were encouraged to give each week, or at least at an appointed week or whatever it might be, such pertains to systematic giving, which is what the Holy Spirit desires. If they gave nothing until Paul came, then attempting to raise a large offering at one time, such would be improper, for the simple reason that it would not teach people to give to God. If one is giving systematically, which is what this phrase teaches, one will give as they should, and one will realize the Sacredness and blessing of Giving. For those who give only when they feel like giving, the truth is, not much giving is done, and besides, such disorder is not according to the Word of God.

(3) "AND WHEN I COME, WHOMSOEVER YE SHALL APPROVE BY YOUR LETTERS, THEM WILL I SEND TO BRING YOUR LIBERALITY UNTO JERUSALEM."

The phrase, *"And when I come,"* is now the second clear reference to his own proposed visit (I Cor. 4:18-21). He will spell out the details in the next paragraph (I Cor. 16:5-9).

The phrase, *"Whomsoever ye shall approve by your letters,"* means that the congregation at Corinth was to select one or more persons to take these funds to Jerusalem. They were to have a letter of introduction respecting who they were, from what Church, and the amount of money, etc.

PAUL'S PURPOSE

It is significant that Paul had determined to send along representatives of the congregations, probably from key Churches in larger geographical areas, or possibly from each Church, to accompany the Gifts. There were no doubt, a number of reasons for this.

First of all, there would be safety in numbers, especially considering that they were carrying a considerable sum — all in coins!

As well, it would be a practical way of assuring the various Churches of the basic integrity of the entire enterprise.

On the other hand, surely for Paul the personal representation would be as important as the Gifts themselves in his greater concern for the unity for the Church. He no doubt, desired to bring the Corinthians and others, into personal contact with their Brethren in Jerusalem. The men selected would return and would report in detail regarding Jerusalem and the conditions that were prevalent in the mother congregation. Paul is, no doubt, concerned about such contacts and their effect in strengthening the feeling of the oneness of the Church in general.

In all of this, we see that this entire project goes far beyond being a grand piece of charity to the needy, even though it definitely was that. It is connected with Paul personally as an Apostle to the Gentiles and with all his successful work among the Gentiles. Through all of these Churches that had been founded by him Paul is now reaching out to the Mother Church in order to cement all of them together the more.

In this, he is no doubt attempting to show the Jerusalem Brethren who were altogether Jews, that he in no way intends for the Law/Grace controversy to divide them. Of course, concerning the prevalent conditions in Jerusalem, of that Paul was greatly concerned. But at the same time, his orchestration of the giving toward this cause and great need, portrayed him putting wings to his prayers so to speak and some feet to his concern. This one thing is certain, Paul made every effort to court Jerusalem and for all the obvious reasons; however, other than the actual help extended to those in need, there is no record that the theological problems were ameliorated to any degree.

In fact, due to the Jewish sector of the Church attempting to hold onto the Law of Moses, the Church as a whole, as time went by, became more and more Gentile, and less and less Jewish.

The phrase, *"Them will I send to bring your liberality unto Jerusalem,"* referred to those chosen by the Churches.

There is indication that Paul, at least at this time, was not intending to make the journey with them, but which seems to have been changed according to II Corinthians 8:16-23. Actually, Acts Chapters 20 and 21 bear it out I think, that Paul delivered these funds himself, accompanied by these representatives, of whom some of them may have been named in Acts 20:4.

(4) "AND IF IT BE MEET THAT I GO ALSO, THEY SHALL GO WITH ME."

NOTES

As stated, it seems that at this stage of planning, Paul is uncertain as to whether he will also go to Jerusalem with this Gift. However, by the time he wrote II Corinthians he had decided to go and as stated, have the brothers accompany him (II Cor. 1:16; Rom. 15:25).

THAT WHICH FOLLOWED

What happens next with regard to this collection is taken up in II Corinthians and Romans. But two points may be noted:

First, the evidence of Romans 15:26-27 makes it clear that the collection from this Church was finally received, and *"they were pleased"* to do it, according to Paul.

Second, according to II Corinthians 8:10-11 the Church had made a good beginning, but had failed to follow through with it. Hence, Titus was dispatched — twice — to help them bring it to completion.

Their reluctance in the meantime is almost certainly the result of the crisis brought about by Paul's sudden, *"painful"* visit noted in II Corinthians 2:1, which also caused the (second) change of travel plans explained in II Corinthians 1:15-2:13 and 7:2-16.

Most likely the proposed return portion of that visit is when he intended to pick up the collection; but the visit had been so painful that he went on to Ephesus from Macedonia instead, and in his place dispatched Titus with a letter. All of this had to do with the many problems in the Church at Corinth, with Satan attempting to turn the people against Paul and subvert the Church.

On their meeting again in Macedonia, Titus reported to him that things were basically better between him and the Church in general, but the matter of the collection was still on hold. Hence in II Corinthians he sends Titus and three others, part of whose purpose is to get the collection ready for Paul's arrival. The evidence of Romans Chapter 15 is that, despite these setbacks, the Corinthian contribution was finally collected (Fee).

(5) "NOW I WILL COME UNTO YOU, WHEN I SHALL PASS THROUGH MACEDONIA: FOR I DO PASS THROUGH MACEDONIA."

The phrase, *"Now I will come unto you,"* refers to plans for a proposed visit. He mentions this again in II Corinthians 1:15-16.

It seems that he originally planned to go directly by Sea from Ephesus where he is presently, to Corinth, then to visit Macedonia and to return to Corinth, and then to proceed to Jerusalem (Acts 19:21). In a letter now lost, Paul probably so informed the Corinthians. For the reason stated in II Corinthians 1:23, etc., he changed his plan and now informs the Corinthians regarding that change.

The phrase, *"When I shall pass through Macedonia: for I do pass through Macedonia,"* presents Paul visiting the Churches in this area, which, incidently, was greatly beneficial for the congregations.

He now plans to go by land from Ephesus, passing through Macedonia and then through Greece to Corinth. This new plan he eventually carried out as we see from II Corinthians 2:13 and from Acts 20:1-2.

Paul was later severely censured by his detractors for altering his plans, and in II Corinthians he makes an extended reply to the charge of fickleness.

To quote again, *"For I do pass through Macedonia,"* proclaims his intention respecting his new plan to not linger in Macedonia, but to pass through it as rapidly as maybe possible and to stop at each of the Churches only a short while (Lenski).

Some of the Churches in this area included Philippi, Thessalonica, and Berea. They seemed by and large to have maintained his ways, but it had been several years since he had visited them; however, the situation at Corinth is so critical that he feels he must spend more time at that particular Church, and less in the Churches in Macedonia.

## A GREAT CONCERN

In all of this, we see the true Shepherd heart. The Apostle is greatly burdened respecting the false doctrine held by some of the Corinthians, and no doubt placed there by false teachers.

The Churches so founded by Paul, were for the most part pastored by someone raised up in the local Assembly, after Paul left to go to other fields of endeavor. As should be understood, there were not many Preachers in those days.

Even though the Lord definitely placed the Call to Ministry on some, who would then lead the Church (wherever it may have been); still, these people whomever they may be, were not very versed in the Word of God, which caused problems which immaturity always brings about. Consequently, such situations made for excellent pickings for false teachers, even as the Apostle would warn as recorded in Acts 20:28-31.

These false teachers would attempt to undermine Paul, even as he will address in his Second Letter to the Corinthians, by either insisting that the Law of Moses must be kept as well as accepting Jesus, in order for one to be saved, or else to enrich themselves in a material way. This problem it seems, persisted on a continuing basis. So, the Apostle labored constantly not only to take the Gospel to unevangelized regions, but as well, to keep the various Churches already established on the right track. To be sure, the task was not easy.

Almost always, these false teachers attempted to turn the local congregations against Paul as a person. In other words, they denigrated his Calling, Ministry, and even his very person. It is almost inconceivable, to comprehend how that these Believers (or at least some of them), could be made to turn against the very one who had brought them the Gospel, in fact, one of the Godliest men who ever lived. But yet, it seems these detractors were successful in some cases.

## IN FACT, HOW COULD SUCH A THING HAPPEN?

Unfortunately, this is not a problem which arose and died in Paul's day, but continues unto this hour. Whenever Believers get cold in the Lord, in essence weakening their relationship with Christ, they become vulnerable to Satan's suggestions. Almost exclusively, he uses false teachers or preachers to bring this about. Unfortunately, these methods work all too well.

The only defense against this, is for the Believer to stay close to Christ, which can be done only by a healthy prayer life and devotion to the Word. Many times, even as at Corinth, such individuals take on an air of spiritual superiority. In other words, they think spiritually they have gone beyond the true man of God, even as some at Corinth did regarding Paul. It is almost beyond belief, that anyone could think they had more knowledge of the Word and Ways of God than Paul, but yet this is exactly what happened.

NOTES

The truth is, these individuals were immature in Christ, even as their modern counterparts. In other words, they were that of which they accused the Apostle, shallow.

Normally the manner in which Satan works in this capacity, is through the realm of flattery and attention. The false teachers flatter them, while at the same time subtlety suggesting (and sometimes not so subtle), the deficiencies of the true man of God, even Paul. Due to pride, these people fall for the flattery and subtlety are led astray.

(6) "AND IT MAY BE THAT I WILL ABIDE, YEA, AND WINTER WITH YOU, THAT YE MAY BRING ME ON MY JOURNEY WHITHERSOEVER I GO."

The phrase, *"And it may be that I will abide, yea, and winter with you,"* concerns an amount of time for a particular purpose. He no doubt feared that it would take some time for him to square away the breakdown in relationships between him and them, in other words, to undo the damage done by these false teachers.

It is spring when Paul writes this letter at Ephesus. He hopes to reach Corinth at the beginning of the coming winter and to spend the entire winter in Corinth. He actually spent three months there as recorded in Acts 20:2-3. However, from the manner in which he makes the statement, he refrains from making his promise absolute, possibly foreseeing contingencies arising which could detain him.

The phrase, *"That ye may bring me on my journey whithersoever I go,"* refers to the Corinthians helping the Apostle with his needs whatever they may be at the time. Such could include many things, even money.

## REACHING OUT

Here is a touch of the friendly spirit of Paul reaching out to the Corinthians. He intends to favor them with a stay of notable length and with an acceptance of their kindly service when he at last proceeds on his journey. I think it is obvious that Paul at this time is unsettled in his spirit regarding exactly what he is going to do concerning direction. It pertained to him possibly going to Jerusalem and as well to Rome. In fact, he would find great difficulties in both places, with Jerusalem attempting to take his life, and with Rome imprisoning him.

NOTES

In Acts 19:21 Luke informs us that Paul eventually decided on going to Jerusalem. This journey as it was afterward made by Paul and his several companions is described at length by Luke in Acts Chapters 20-28.

At this time, the Apostle needed kindness and graciousness more than anything else, but instead finds himself having to defend his ministry to the Corinthians.

The moral of this is, that Believers must do all within their power to ease the burden of the journey of fellow Believers, instead of making it harder. Unfortunately, the latter is too often the case, instead of the former. This is undoubtedly one of the reasons that Paul would later say, *"Bear ye one another's burdens, and so fulfill the Law of Christ"* (Gal. 6:2).

(7) "FOR I WILL NOT SEE YOU NOW BY THE WAY; BUT I TRUST TO TARRY A WHILE WITH YOU, IF THE LORD PERMIT."

The phrase, *"For I will not see you now by the way,"* refers to him not being able to come immediately, as it seems he had originally proposed. As previously stated, we learn from II Corinthians 1:15-16, that it had been Paul's intention to sail from Ephesus to Corinth, then after a brief stay, to proceed to Macedonia, and on his return to come again for a longer stay at Corinth on his way to Judaea. It seems in an Epistle, now lost (I Cor. 5:9), he announced to them this intention. He changed his plan because, in the present disgraceful state of disorganization into which the Church had fallen, he felt that he could not visit them without being compelled to exercise a severity which, he hoped, might be made unnecessary by writing to them and delaying his intended visit. Nothing but his usual kindness and desire to spare them prevented him from stating all this more fully (II Cor. 1:23; 2:1). Unfortunately, mistaking the kindness of his purpose, the Corinthians accused him of levity. He defends himself from this charge in the Second Epistle, and carried out the plan which he here announces (II Cor. 2:13; 8:1; 9:2, 4; 12:14; 13:1).

The phrase, *"But I trust to tarry a while with you, if the Lord permit,"* presents the Apostle intending to carry out the work in Macedonia as quickly as possible, and thus, to be free to remain in Corinth for some time. From his statement, it seems that his most important work is to be done in the latter place, and he intends to allow ample time for it.

In all of Paul's movements and work, he always eagerly sought the Lord's directions and permission, hence the phrase, *"if the Lord permit."*

LEADING BY THE LORD

The Believer must ever understand, that the Lord is involved totally and completely in his life and in every aspect. In fact, we belong to the Lord in every capacity, hence, Paul saying, *"For ye are bought with a price"* (I Cor. 6:20). Of course, the price of which he speaks, concerns Jesus purchasing us from Satan by the shedding of His Own Precious Blood. As a result, the Believer is to seek the Lord constantly for guidance and direction, never allowing anything to interfere with this process.

Sometimes it is easy to find the Mind of the Lord, and sometimes not, even as Paul here suggests. Nevertheless, we are to keep seeking until certain direction is given, which it most certainly shall.

The sadness is, many Christians do not seek the Will of the Lord regarding His direction in their lives, but rather make their own plans. Plans made by men ultimately fail, while plans made by God always succeed.

(8) "BUT I WILL TARRY AT EPHESUS UNTIL PENTECOST."

Paul is writing a short time before the Jewish Passover and intends to leave Ephesus after a period of about two months, after the Jewish Feast of Pentecost.

This mention of *"Pentecost"* is not evidence that a Christian Festival by this name was celebrated at this early date at Ephesus or at Corinth. If this were the case, other evidence would be needed to establish the fact, which, of course, does not exist.

In the present connection *"Pentecost"* is used merely to indicate a specific date or time. On the other hand, such a casual mention of it in this way may suggest that the Church very early saw Christian significance to this Feast; however, only as a result of the birth of the Church on the Day of Pentecost, but not in any way to keep this Feast as the Jews of old under the Mosaic Law.

Consequently, Paul's tentative plan apparently included spending the spring at Ephesus, the summer in Macedonia, the following winter in Corinth, and the next Pentecost in Jerusalem, which it seems he did (Pentecost occurred 50 days after the Passover).

NOTES

(9) "FOR A GREAT DOOR AND EFFECTUAL IS OPENED UNTO ME, AND THERE ARE MANY ADVERSARIES."

The phrase, *"For a great door and effectual is opened unto me,"* presents the word *"door"* as figurative for opportunity to advance the Work of the Gospel. Consequently, *"a great door"* is a great opportunity.

*"An effectual door"* is one that is not merely looked at but is made use of effectually. Acts 19:19-20 could very well describe the great opportunity to which Paul refers, but he could be speaking of other areas as well.

The phrase, *"And there are many adversaries,"* speaks of those who opposed his ministry, something that seemed to be a way of life for this Godly man.

These were, doubtless in part, Jews who excited opposition to him, and even Pagans as here at Ephesus.

*"Adversaries"* in the Greek is *"antikeimai,"* and means *"to lie opposite, to be adverse, to be contrary, to oppose."*

OPPOSITION

We must always understand that such a Work of Grace, as manifested in the Ministry of Paul, and especially the setting open of a great and effectual door, is often the occasion of increased opposition to the Gospel. It is no uncommon thing that the adversaries of Christ should be excited at such times.

Such opposition always is evidence that the Holy Spirit is working. It is proof that the enemies of God are alarmed, and that the Kingdom of Christ is advancing.

The Preacher of the Gospel should never wish to make enemies to the Gospel, nor seek to excite them to make opposition, but such opposition, as stated, is often the evidence that the Spirit of God is moving and working, resulting in the Salvation of souls, along with Believers being baptized with the Holy Spirit, sick bodies healed, and people delivered by the Power of God.

And so, such opposition is often a sign that God is moving and doing great things. Satan is not angered until his kingdom is invaded, and to be sure, his kingdom cannot be invaded unless the Holy Spirit is truly working and moving.

NOTES

### ADVERSARIES?

Even though Paul did experience opposition from Pagan Rome, by far the greatest opposition came from those who claimed Christ, or at least claimed to know God as the unbelieving Jews. However, opposition from unbelieving Jews and the Pagans was expected. The greater damage was done by those who claimed Christ, therefore, having access to the Churches. In fact, Satan raises his greatest adversaries from this source. In other words, the greatest hinderance to the Church is the Church.

### ADVERSARIES AT THE PRESENT TIME

Using our own Ministry as an example, there are many doors presently opened for us to air the Telecast regarding the presentation of the Gospel, but as Paul said, there are many adversaries.

In fact, God has signally called us for this very task; consequently, that is the reason we see so many souls saved, thereby being brought to Christ. In fact, the Lord has helped us to literally see hundreds of thousands brought to a saving knowledge of Jesus Christ. In this, every manner of bondage has been broken, presenting some of the greatest testimonies of Grace that one could ever hear.

Considering this, one would think that the entirety of the Church as a whole, would be pleased and glad respecting this great number of souls being saved. Tragically, that is not the case. In fact, the opposition is so intense attempting to keep us off Television, that I literally stand amazed at the lengths some Preachers will go to in order to carry out their devious designs.

Why?

I personally think it is the same now as in the times of Paul. They don't like the Message we preach, irrespective that it brings tremendous numbers to Christ, or the Anointing of the Holy Spirit on that Message. The reason is their agenda, both then and now.

If the agenda is to get people saved, lives changed, Believers baptized with the Holy Spirit, sick bodies truly healed by the Power of God, and people delivered from the worst type of bondages, their attitude and spirit would be of a different nature. However, if the agenda is something else, and irrespective of what the something else is, they will act accordingly — with opposition.

### REASONS OR EXCUSES

In Paul's day, the reasons or excuses would have been according to the following:

Many were jealous of Paul, especially considering that the Lord gave him the New Covenant, and not them, or whomever they may have desired. In other words, they didn't like God's choice.

Others simply did not believe his Message of Grace, and desired to add the Law of Moses to that Message. Consequently, they took great umbrage at Paul disallowing their efforts.

And then again, others were strictly after monetary gain. Peter made mention of them by saying, *"And through covetousness shall they with feigned words make merchandise of you"* (II Pet. 2:3). Satan follows the same course presently as then.

We expect opposition from the world, i.e., the News Media, etc., but to be opposed by those who claim to be preaching the same Gospel is something else altogether again. That is by far the greatest hinderance, i.e., *"adversaries."*

My prayer is that the Lord ever help me, that I not find myself opposing that which is actually of Him, or conversely accepting that which is really not of Him. The end results are the same in either direction — spiritual wreckage.

(10) "NOW IF TIMOTHEUS COME, SEE THAT HE MAY BE WITH YOU WITHOUT FEAR: FOR HE WORKETH THE WORK OF THE LORD, AS I ALSO DO."

The phrase, *"Now if Timotheus come,"* refers to Timothy. It seems that Paul had already sent Timothy (I Cor. 4:17), with Erastus (Acts 19:22), to go to Corinth by way of Macedonia and prepare for his visit. But possibly he had countermanded these directions when he postponed his own visit.

If this indeed had happened, due to the uncertainty of ancient travelling, he could not be certain whether his counterorder would reach Timothy or not.

We have no way of knowing, unless II Corinthians 1:19 is an indication. We do know that Paul ultimately sent Titus (II Cor. 2:13).

### PAUL'S REASON

Just what news Paul had received from Corinth when he gave Timothy his commission

NOTES

we do not know. The duty assigned to this young man shows that the Corinthians were to be reminded of Paul's teaching regarding the true wisdom of Christ as opposed to all spurious wisdom.

Since Timothy's mission is mentioned by Paul in connection with the first part of his letter (this Epistle of I Corinthians), is it fair to conclude that Paul had already heard from *"those of Chloe"* (I Cor. 1:11-12) the news regarding factual contentions in Corinth, when he sent Timothy, and that it was Timothy's task to endeavor to correct these disturbances?

Then, it seems, the letter from the Corinthians to Paul arrived together with all the additional news which we see reflected in Paul's letter of reply. Timothy was already on his way, but via Macedonia, so that he would stop at the various Churches along his route, which would delay his arrival at Corinth for some time.

The letter which Paul is writing will be taken to Corinth by the direct sea route, and Paul expects it to reach Corinth before Timothy's arrival, that is, if he did actually arrive there at all.

All that Paul has heard about Corinth after he had sent Timothy away makes him anxious regarding the reception which his messenger will receive. So he here tells the Corinthians what treatment they are to accord Timothy upon his arrival.

The phrase, *"See that he may be with you without fear,"* probably speaks of the youthfulness of Timothy more than anything else.

## TIMOTHY

That Timothy was by nature a timid person is an unfounded supposition. He must have been both brave and competent in order to carry out missions such as the present one and afterward to be placed in charge of the entire work in the Province of Asia.

Regarding the additional news as had been brought to him concerning Corinth, the mission of this young man as the development of events now reveals, will be harder to execute than Paul had supposed when he had first dispatched Timothy. Some of the more haughty and puffed-up members may imagine that this young man from Lystra, whom they all know well, need not be treated with much respect because of his youth. They may even attempt to show arrogance and thus try to intimidate Timothy. For this reason Paul writes pointedly: *"See to it that he be with you without fear"*: i.e., let no one intimidate him and make him afraid. Afterward, when Timothy was the Pastor at Ephesus, Paul wrote to him: *"Let no man despise thy youth"* (I Tim. 4:12).

The phrase, *"For he worketh the Work of the Lord, as I also do,"* means that inasmuch as Timothy's work is identical with Paul's, he is to be treated accordingly. The Apostle puts the two on the same level and insists that the Corinthians do likewise. From this we may deduce that Timothy had the Calling of an Apostle as Paul.

(11) "LET NO MAN THEREFORE DESPISE HIM: BUT CONDUCT HIM FORTH IN PEACE, THAT HE MAY COME UNTO ME: FOR I LOOK FOR HIM WITH THE BRETHREN."

The phrase, *"Let no man therefore despise him,"* refers to his youth and inexperience. Considering the situation in the Church at Corinth, Paul feared that some might be disposed to look upon him with contempt, especially considering their high judgment of themselves.

The manner in which the Apostle phrases the sentence means that he does not harbor concern in regard to the congregation as such, but rather to only one, or at most, a few in the congregation.

## THE MANNER OF CONDUCT

Concerning these people at Corinth, or at least some of them, I wonder what their thoughts would have been had they viewed the situation as it should have been viewed? By that I mean the following:

Paul has been chosen by the Holy Spirit to give the world the New Covenant, for which Jesus died, and, in effect, to establish the Church. In fact, even though the other Apostles, even the original Twelve, contributed greatly to this effort as should be obvious, still, it was Paul who was given the responsibility of the Master Builder (I Cor. 3:10). As well, there were probably few people on the face of the earth of that time, if any, who were closer to the Lord than this man.

So, considering all these things, we must come to the conclusion that anyone who opposed Paul was in fact sinning against the Lord, and in fact, grievously so. Unless they repented, and there is evidence in the Seventh Chapter of II Corinthians that they did, they will have to answer for this at the Judgment Seat of Christ.

How many presently fall into the same category? They are truly saved, but are so carnally minded, that they're actually doing more to hurt the Cause of Christ than they are to help that great Cause.

How so much all of us should earnestly seek the Lord, attempting to walk as close to Him as possible, in order that we do not oppose that which is actually of Him. In my mind, very little could be more awful than such a position.

The phrase, *"But conduct him forth in peace, that he may come unto me,"* has reference to the fact that when his work is done, the Corinthians are to send him forward on his journey back to Ephesus and to Paul, or to wherever Paul would direct him.

## PEACE

The expression *"to send forward in peace"* is not derived from the statement or formula: *"Go in peace!"* The idea of the words *"in peace"* is meant to contrast to the preceding injunctions not to intimidate and not to despise Timothy. Paul wants Timothy's mission to proceed and to end in a peaceful way so that, when he leaves, no trouble or strife are to be left behind.

The Apostle writes that he is expecting him, i.e., is anxious to receive his report, especially that part of it which deals with Corinth while Paul does not say that he wishes that Timothy might hurry back as soon as possible, the fact that he is expecting Timothy implies that the Corinthians are not to detain him unduly in Corinth. As soon as his mission has ended, he is to be sent forward to Paul (Lenski).

The phrase, *"For I look for him with the Brethren,"* pertains to those who went with Timothy, whomever they may have been.

(12) "AS TOUCHING OUR BROTHER APOLLOS, I GREATLY DESIRED HIM TO COME UNTO YOU WITH THE BRETHREN: BUT HIS WILL WAS NOT AT ALL TO COME AT THIS TIME; BUT HE WILL COME WHEN HE SHALL HAVE CONVENIENT TIME."

The phrase, *"As touching our brother Apollos,"* Paul is probably now referring back to the letter brought to him by the Corinthians. Quite possible they had requested in the letter that Paul send Apollos to them since they were anxious to have him come.

NOTES

Apollos had labored in Corinth for quite a while and had done so very successfully. We do not know just when he left the city.

The phrase, *"I greatly desired him to come unto you with the Brethren,"* probably refers to the ones who brought the letter from Corinth to Paul in Ephesus.

The phrase, *"I greatly desired,"* or *"I urged him"* gives the impression that Paul did this at once after receiving the letter from Corinth, and also that at the moment of Paul's writing, Apollos is temporarily absent from Ephesus. This would also explain why at the conclusion of this letter Paul has no greetings from Apollos to the Corinthians.

## PAUL AND APOLLOS

If we are to remember back to the first Chapter of this Epistle, Paul mentioned several parties which had been formed in the Church at Corinth after particular Preachers, Apollos being one of those Preachers. However, there is absolutely no proof whatsoever that Apollos had anything to do with the carryings on of those in Corinth who would pit him against Paul. Actually, there is every evidence that he deplored this action, this being the very reason he would not now go to Corinth.

Consequently, we have no intimation whatsoever that Paul and Apollos are not on the most friendliest terms, for Paul could then not have urged him as he did.

There quite possibly were at Corinth persons malignant enough to have suggested that Paul had refused their requests; that he would not send Apollos to them out of jealousy of Apollos' superiority and of the party which assumed his name. Evidently, Paul anticipated this sneer.

However, his nature was much too noble to feel the least jealousy. Both he and Apollos here show themselves in the purest light (Farrar).

The phrase, *"But his will was not at all to come at this time,"* does not here refer to *"the Will of God,"* but rather his own human will.

Here it means that Apollos had decided not to come at present, obviously because his name had been abused for purposes of party faction (I Cor. 3:5). Endeavoring to make him the head of a party, on this account Apollos might have been unwilling to return among them.

However, some Expositors insist that these things mentioned had nothing to do with the attitude of Apollos, but that he was overly busy elsewhere, and simply could not spare the time, at least at the present period. However, I personally think the evidence mitigates against that direction.

The phrase, *"But he will come when he shall have convenient time,"* rather says, *"When a good opportunity offers itself to him."* Whether Apollos ever revisited Corinth or not we do not know (Farrar).

When Paul writes this, Apollos, as stated, is already absent from Ephesus in order to do other things.

THE CHURCH BELONGS TO CHRIST

There can be little question that for Paul, several of the issues spoken to in this letter in various ways pose threats to his Apostolic Authority regarding the Church at Corinth. At times he takes up this challenge in vigorous ways (I Cor. 4:18-21; Chpt. 9) that one could get the impression that he, as so often happens in the Church, had so identified the Gospel and the Church with his own Ministry that a threat to the one (his Ministry) is a threat to the other (the Gospel). At times this seems to be precisely what he says. But in I Corinthians 3:5-23, and again in I Corinthians 4:1-13, he puts all of this into proper perspective.

The Gospel is God's thing, and His Alone, and so too, therefore, is the Church. The Church, he argues strenuously, belongs neither to himself, nor to Apollos, nor to them (Corinth). The Church belongs to God through Christ, and all of its Ministers, including the founders (Early Church Apostles), are merely servants.

This final word about Apollos is living evidence that Paul is as good as his word. If the Church at Corinth were Paul's, the last person in the world he would want to return would be Apollos. Indeed, the real pressure would be to keep him away for some time while things cooled off. But not so Paul.

Apollos watered what Paul had planted (I Cor. 3:6); and *"all things are theirs in Christ Jesus"* including Apollos (I Cor. 3:21-22).

So, for the sake of the growth of the Church he can urge Apollos to return (whether he did or not), despite some of the inherent difficulties that would entail. Here is another piece of clear evidence along with Philippians 1:12-18, of the incredible bigness of the Apostle to the Gentiles — far greater than that of many of his detractors, one is wont to add (Fee).

NOTES

MODERN CIRCUMSTANCES

These things which we have just said, are a far cry from many in the modern Church. One of the greatest harms to the Work of God presently, and in fact always has been, is improper (unscriptural) Church Government. A part of this improper government pertains to the very issue here mentioned. Certain Denominations, or rather the leaders in these Denominations, conduct themselves as if they own the Church. Setting themselves up as Spiritual Authorities, despite the fact that they occupy a man-devised office, they demand obedience, even to the extent of that which is unscriptural. Consequently, it becomes very obvious, very quickly, as to who is leading such a Church. This we do know, it is certainly not the Holy Spirit, for He will not function under such circumstances.

Paul's example must be an example to all of us, that is if we desire to follow the Word of God. The Church belongs to Christ. As well, the Ministers, at least those who are God-called, belong to Him. Also, Church Government is His domain as well, and which He has given proper instructions in Acts and the Epistles even as we are now studying.

There were no dictatorial airs about Paul. Even though he at times warned, he never really threatened. He didn't have to, because Jesus was the Head of the Church, and the Lord working mightily in the midst of such Government, as He always does, is perfectly capable of guiding His Work through the Office, Person, and Agency of the Holy Spirit.

Paul always conducted himself as a servant, and never as a lord dictator, which Jesus warned against (Mat. 20:20-28).

(13) "WATCH YE, STAND FAST IN THE FAITH, QUIT YOU LIKE MEN, BE STRONG."

The phrase, *"Watch ye,"* is in effect a military command. The word used here means, to keep awake, to be vigilant, etc.; it is a military metaphor derived from the duty of those who are stationed as sentinels to guard a camp, or to observe the motions of an enemy. The term is frequently used in the New Testament, and the duty frequently enjoined (Mat. 24:41-42; 25:13; Mk. 13:35; Lk. 21:36; Acts 20:31; I Thess. 5:6; II Tim. 4:5).

AGAINST EVILS

This sense here is, that they were to watch, or to be vigilant, against all the evils of which Paul had admonished them — the evils of dissension, of erroneous doctrines, of disorder, of false teachers, etc.

They were to watch lest their souls should be ruined, and their Salvation endangered; lest the enemies of the Truth and of Holiness would steal silently upon them, and with surprise.

They were to watch with the same vigilance that is required of a Sentinel who guards a camp, lest an enemy should come suddenly upon them, and surprise the camp with the army locked in sleep.

The phrase, *"Stand fast in the Faith,"* refers back to the word *"watch."*

They are to watch lest their Faith be eroded by false doctrine and, therefore, comprised.

HOLDING FAST THE FAITH

They were to be firm in holding and defending the Truths of the Gospel. They were not to yield to any foe, but maintain the Truth, and adhere to confidence in the Lord and to the Doctrines of the Gospel with unwavering constancy.

They were to be firm in maintaining what they believed to be true, and to hold on to their personal confidence in God, notwithstanding all the arts, insinuations, and teachings of seducers and the friends of false doctrine.

Every attack by Satan against a Child of God, and in whatever direction it takes, is for but one purpose, and that is to destroy or at least weaken one's Faith in God.

Of what type of Faith are we speaking?

Unfortunately, when many Pentecostals or Charismatics think of Faith, they think of believing God for something, etc. While such is certainly included, this is not the type of Faith of which Paul speaks.

He is speaking of the great Doctrines which make up our Christian experience, such as Salvation by Grace, the Price Jesus paid at Calvary, the Baptism with the Holy Spirit, a victorious, overcoming Christian life, the Resurrection, etc.

NOTES

So, the watchfulness demanded by the Holy Spirit through Him, pertains to many things, but most of all to our *"Faith in God."*

STRANGE DOCTRINES

Even though Apostasy has always existed, even as it did in Paul's day, it is in fact, more entrenched now than ever before. Actually I think that one can say that this is the age of Apostasy. Consequently, the situation regarding seducers and false doctrine, are not going to get better but rather worse. As a result, the Believer is going to have to be anchored firmly in the Faith, or else he will be pulled astray.

Even at this present time, ridiculous things are taking place in Churches, and being labeled as a Moving of the Holy Spirit, when actually there is no Scriptural ground for such. As well, these type of things are only going to increase, and because of the great Apostasy.

So, if the warning given by Paul was apropos then, how much more is it apropos now!

*"Examine yourselves, whether ye be in the Faith; prove your own selves. Know ye not your own selves, how that Jesus Christ is in you, except you be reprobates?"* (II Cor. 13:5).

The phrase, *"Quit you like men,"* means, to render one manly or brave; to show one's self a man; that is, not to be a coward, or timid, or alarmed at enemies, but to be bold and brave.

It means to maintain one's ground at all costs, to resist, to press forward, to strike a deadly blow.

It as well, as does the entire framework of this Scripture, speaks of a continuous action. In other words, we are not to do such for a while and then stop, but rather on a constant basis until Jesus comes.

The phrase, *"Be strong,"* means to be firm, fixed, steadfast.

In effect, Paul is urging them to remain steadfast in the Gospel he preached, and to do so courageously in the face of the errors and behavioral aberrations that are rife among them.

In fact, the greatest thrust of these admonishments is to stand strong against false doctrine, which means that the Believer must know firmly where he stands regarding the Word of God, and what it says about any and every subject. The tragedy is, many Christians are Scripturally illiterate. In other words, they don't know the Word of God.

Too much time is spent on things of little or no consequence, with the Word of God taking short shift, if any shift at all. One is easy prey for Satan, if one stands timidly on the Word, i.e., *"does not properly know the Word."*

(14) "LET ALL YOUR THINGS BE DONE WITH CHARITY."

Once again, the Apostle goes back to Chapter 13 of I Corinthians. It is repeated on account of its great importance, and because it is a summing up of all that he has said in this Epistle.

Love is to regulate all that is done. This is a simple rule, and if this is observed, everything will be done well.

LOVE

When Paul writes *"all your affairs"* (*"all your things"*), he includes the entire work of the Corinthian congregation, different features of which he has discussed in this Letter. All of this work centers in Faith and, thus, requires watchfulness, firmness, manliness, and strength. But it also requires Love, this supreme Fruit of Faith.

Paul's Letter has already shown the vital need of Love; he has also described this Love at length; the Corinthians have also been made to feel their deficiency of Love. So Paul makes the last admonition the indispensableness of Love.

We may translate: *"all your Affairs, let them be connected with love!"* Everything in the Corinthian Congregation is to be and is to move in that sphere; nothing is to be outside of it.

This *"love"* is the love of full comprehension and of spiritual purpose; thus, love is the final word. It is to continue and is never to be absent.

It, too, will grow the more it is practiced (Lenski).

(15) "I BESEECH YOU, BRETHREN, (YE KNOW THE HOUSE OF STEPHANAS, THAT IT IS THE FIRSTFRUITS OF ACHAIA, AND THAT THEY HAVE ADDICTED THEMSELVES TO THE MINISTRY OF THE SAINTS,)"

The phrase, *"I beseech you, Brethren,"* portrays a favorite phrase of the Apostle. But yet it shows more than that.

It shows kindness, graciousness, patience, and Christlikeness. It also portrays the fact that Paul knows, therefore, honors, and proclaims Christ as the Head of the Church. Consequently, Paul never places himself in a dictatorial position. He always reminds himself that irrespective of what particular Believers have done, that still they belong to the Lord, and as such are very special in His sight, and must be in Paul's sight as well. How so much we all could learn from such a spirit and attitude.

NOTES

The phrase, *"Ye know the house of Stephanas,"* refers to the entire family of Stephanas, as the Greeks always say, *"house"* for family.

In kindly fashion Paul requests the Corinthians to honor Stephanas and his family because of their eminent service to the Church. Paul himself baptized this family (I Cor. 1:16).

PAUL'S REASON

These statements as made by Paul are not to be explained simply on formal grounds, in other words, that Paul is simply saying something nice. As we shall see, the Apostle gives the reason that Stephanas and his household should be recognized in a very favorable light.

This strong commendation of Stephanas implies that he had been loyal to Paul in the present tensions within the Corinthian Church. Furthermore the language of Verse 16, as we shall see, makes certain that he is a leader in the Church. Very likely he is also a source of further information about the condition of the Church, quite apart from the letter that he delivered to Paul.

The phrase, *"That it is the Firstfruits of Achaia,"* means that in all of Greece the family of Stephanas was the first to come to Faith as a consequence of the Ministry of Paul.

*"Achaia"* in its largest sense, comprehends the whole of Greece. Achaia proper, however, was a province of which Corinth was the Capital. It embraced that part of Greece lying between Thessaly and the southern part of the Peloponnesus.

Some have concluded from the way Paul addresses himself, that this house was not the Firstfruits of Corinth, but rather elsewhere in Greece. While such may very well have been the case, it is not necessarily certain. Irrespective, this was the first family won to Christ in Greece.

The phrase, *"And that they have addicted themselves to the Ministry of the Saints,"* presents the second reason that Paul is honoring this family, them being the Firstfruits as the first reason.

The word *"ministry"* in the Greek as used here is *"diakonia,"* and means *"to give attendance as a servant, to run errands, or attend other duties menial or otherwise."*

*"Addicted"* in the Greek is *"tasso,"* and means *"one determined to minister,"* in other words, their Calling.

SERVICE

*"For service"* (Ministry), permits us regarding the way it is used, to include any and all kinds of service. This says a great deal with regard to this family.

The idea is, that they have been performing such type of service long before Paul here mentions the fact.

As well, we may conclude that the family of Stephanas had means and some prominence which enabled them to do much for *"the Saints."* Yet on the other hand, even down to this present day, experience proves that families of slender means at times, often distinguish themselves in this manner above many others who are financially much more able.

What service was rendered we can only surmise, for Paul offers no intimation.

However, that is the manner in which the Holy Spirit works. Things are not to be done for Him, i.e., *"for the Saints,"* in order for show, but rather the very opposite. Jesus said if such is done for *"show"* one already has their reward (Mat. 6:1-4), and, consequently, will not be rewarded by the Lord.

(16) "THAT YE SUBMIT YOURSELVES UNTO SUCH, AND TO EVERY ONE THAT HELPETH WITH US, AND LABOURETH."

The phrase, *"That ye submit yourselves unto such,"* in effect says, *"let Stephanas and those like him, be the ones you follow, instead of those who boast of their great knowledge, spirituality, etc."* The idea is, that the practical Christianity of this man is what true Christianity is all about, and not hollow boasts of one's spirituality, etc.

SUBMIT

The verb *"submit"* is used only here in the New Testament to refer to the relationship of a Christian community to those who labor among them. Both the context and the similar passage in I Thessalonians 5:12-13 suggest rather that it means *"submission in the sense of a voluntary yielding in love,"* much the same as in Ephesians 5:21, where all are urged to be *"subject to one another out of reverence for Christ."*

NOTES

The phrase, *"And to every one that helpeth with us, and laboureth,"* portrays the fact that such respect or *"submission"* is not gender or socioeconomic status, but Ministry.

As stated, he is telling these Corinthians that it is these types of Believers who should be followed, instead of those who were constantly boasting of their great spirituality, etc.

Paul does not imply that the Corinthians are reluctant to pay proper reference to Stephanas and to the others in the congregation who are like him. He is here, at the end of his Letter, not voicing a covert criticism. That would be neither tactful nor wise.

What moves Paul to add this request is the perfect example it provides. The *"Love"* which he has preached so strongly to them in this letter, is portrayed in the Christianity of this particular family. Consequently, even in a practical sense which all true Christianity really is, this is the example that should be followed.

PRACTICAL CHRISTIANITY

By the term *"practical Christianity"* I am referring to that which portrays itself in actions and deeds, but not for the applause of men, but because of the Love of God. The Holy Spirit dealt with this by saying through the Apostle John, *"But whoso hath this world's good, and seeth his brother have need, and shutteth up his bowels of compassion from his, how dwelleth the Love of God in him?"*

He then said, *"My little children, let us not love in word, neither in tongue; but in deed and in truth"* (I Jn. 3:17-18).

Christianity which professes, but never gives anything to help take the Gospel to the world, never tries to bring anyone to Christ, and as well exhibits no Goodness of Christ, are poor examples of the Faith.

So, Paul takes this opportunity to point to that which should be the example and who should be followed, i.e., *"to every one that helpeth with us, and laboureth."*

(17) "I AM GLAD OF THE COMING OF STEPHANAS AND FORTUNATUS AND ACHAICUS: FOR THAT WHICH WAS LACKING ON YOUR PART THEY HAVE SUPPLIED."

The phrase, *"I am glad of the coming of Stephanas and Fortunatus and Achaicus,"* refers to them coming to Paul at Ephesus.

These persons are not referred to anywhere else in the New Testament. It appears that Fortunatus survived Paul, for he was subsequently the messenger of the Church at Corinth to that at Rome, and bore back to the Corinthians the Epistle which Clement of Rome sent to them.

THAT WORTH NOTING

After the fact, several things here are easy to ascertain, and should be noted:

First of all, the kindness evidenced by these men toward Paul, is inscribed in the Word of God, which is the greatest and highest honor that could ever be afforded anyone. It also tells us, that all such kindnesses are recorded by the Lord, even though they are not placed directly in the Word of God as here.

Second, the ones who aided and helped Paul, who, of course, are chosen by the Lord, are named, whereas those who opposed Paul are not named, and thankfully so.

Third, it is very obvious as to what the Holy Spirit thought of these men, in that they were helping Paul instead of opposing him. This should be a lesson for all of us.

When by the Grace of God I reach the portals of Glory, I want to meet these men, and so will millions of others. We should allow all of this to be a lesson to us in that everything we do, every decision made, every word spoken, are noted by the Holy Spirit. Consequently, and as previously stated, we should make it very certain and sure that we do not oppose that which is of the Lord, or accept that which is really not of God.

The phrase, *"For that which was lacking on your part they have supplied,"* could refer to one of two things, or both.

Love thinks no evil but, on the contrary, believes in, and counts upon, the affection of others. Hence, the Apostle says that the money given to him by the three Brethren from Corinth not only refreshed him but refreshed the Corinthians — that is, in his affection for them he was sure that they would be glad to hear of his receiving this relief, possibly from the personal funds of these three or at least one of them, possibly Stephanas.

Other Expositors say that the language *"lacking on your part"* actually says *"the lack of you,"* i.e., the Corinthians themselves.

NOTES

The idea is, that Paul would liked to have had the Corinthians where he could talk with them instead of being obliged to write to them from a distance. The object lacked is *"you,"* the persons of the Corinthians.

This lack, the three messengers from Corinth *"filled"* for Paul, literally, *"filled up"* like a vessel that is otherwise not full enough. Paul can talk with them, and ask them many things about the Corinthians, and hear all that they had to communicate.

That is what causes Paul to rejoice. Here we again meet a kindly touch on the part of Paul.

To be frank, this is probably the correct interpretation of the phrase. He would rather have had all the members of the Church at Corinth before him so he could speak with them, but, lacking that, these three will make up the part of all the others.

(18) "FOR THEY HAVE REFRESHED MY SPIRIT AND YOURS: THEREFORE ACKNOWLEDGE YE THEM THAT ARE SUCH."

The phrase, *"For they have refreshed my spirit and yours,"* sheds more light on the previous Verse.

LOVE THINKS NO EVIL

Paul himself explains what he means by this lack as voiced in the previous Verse, and how it is being made good. *"They eased my own spirit and yours."*

If Paul and the Corinthians could have met, both his mind and theirs would have been put at ease regarding all the questions that had arisen. Through the presence of these three representatives this was in fact actually accomplished in a way. By their presence these three furnished easement to Paul's spirit and at the same time, by enabling the congregation to confer with Paul through them, furnished a like easement to their spirit.

This is again a tender touch. Paul thinks not only of himself but also of the Corinthians. Despite opposition to him by some, he credits them irrespective with gracious feelings that are just like his own. That's what we mean by *"love that thinks no evil."*

Even though he has had to say some hard things in his Letter to them, even warning them, still, he does so with the attitude and conscious that they are going to receive his words in good faith, and that his love for them is going to be rewarded in kind. In other words, they will love him, even those who are now contrary to him. The Seventh Chapter of II Corinthians bears out that Paul's Faith did not go unrewarded. Again, what a beautiful example.

Paul had every right to form suspicions of some in the Church at Corinth, especially considering what they were doing; however, he would not allow himself to believe that they would continue on this path, but rather that they would be brought back to the right direction.

The phrase, *"Therefore acknowledge ye them that are such,"* refers to the three mentioned in the previous Verse, and that what they say will be correct and right.

In effect, he is asking the Church to receive them kindly on their return, and regard with deference and respect the counsel which they might offer, and the message which they might bear from him (Barnes).

(19) "THE CHURCHES OF ASIA SALUTE YOU. AQUILA AND PRISCILLA SALUTE YOU MUCH IN THE LORD, WITH THE CHURCH THAT IS IN THEIR HOUSE."

The phrase, *"The Churches of Asia salute you,"* usually denotes Asia Minor in general, of which Ephesus was the Center and Capital. However, Paul was no doubt also speaking of Smyrna, Laodicea, Philadelphia, etc.

## FELLOWSHIP OF CHURCHES

Such greetings as these become another way that Paul keeps the Churches aware of, and thus in relationship to, one another. The greetings in this case are threefold; from: A. All the Churches of Asia; B. Aquila and Priscilla and the Church that meets in their house; and, C. All the Brothers presently with him.

There were no Denominations as such in the time of the Early Church, and in effect no Headquarters, at least as we think of such presently. Each Church was autonomous (having the right or power of self-government), but were joined together by like Faith and a common bond of Fellowship. In other words, even though Apostles such as Paul could give advice and council, there was no outside authority which could force the Church into a particular mode of conduct, even as right as such conduct may be. Consequently, each particular Church constituted the highest Spiritual Authority. However, even though that was true of each Church, it as well had its limitations, simply because Christ was the Head of the Church.

If the Church did not function properly, the Message of Jesus through the Holy Spirit is, *"Remember therefore from whence thou art fallen, and repent, and do the first works; or else I will come unto thee quickly, and will remove thy candlestick out of his place, except thou repent"* (Rev. 2:5).

To be frank, had the Holy Spirit desired a Headquarters Church, Jerusalem certainly would have been the place, and for all the obvious reasons. Nevertheless, even though Jerusalem did play a very important part in the Early Church which should be obvious, still, it was not looked at, nor treated as superior.

Consequently, modern Denominations exerting spiritual authority over Churches, or else attempting to do so, is not pleasing to the Lord, and is actually the result of a man-devised form of government, which is not of God.

## ADMINISTRATION

Actually, there is nothing unbiblical about forming a Denomination, or even having a Headquarters as such, for administration is definitely needed in all things. However, it should begin and end with administration, with no idea of supposed Spiritual Authority, which in fact does not exist, at least Scripturally. If such functions according to the Word of God, proper administration as should be obvious, can be of tremendous boon and blessing to the Kingdom of God. Otherwise, it usurps authority over the Headship of Christ as the Head of the Church.

## CHURCH GOVERNMENT

Proper Church Government, and I speak of that which is Scriptural as outlined in the Book of Acts and the Epistles, is perhaps the single most important function of the Kingdom of God on Earth. I think I do not exaggerate when I make this statement.

The Early Church ultimately apostatized (over a period of time), because of this very reason. Men attempted to institute forms of Government which were not Biblical, and which gradually abrogated the Headship of Christ, which necessitated the Holy Spirit removing Himself from the effort. In other words, without the Holy Spirit the Church is simply a human institution. As a result, it does nothing for God, although it may be admired greatly by the world.

For the Holy Spirit to function as He must, we must adhere to the Word of God in all things. To be sure, no one can boast of perfection, for such does not exist. But when one deliberately takes the Government of the Church out of the hands of Christ, thereby abrogating the office the Holy Spirit respecting His involvement in the Church, spiritual disaster is always the result.

The phrase, *"Aquila and Priscilla salute you much in the Lord,"* proclaims this couple who were well known at Corinth. They had no small share in founding the Churches both of Corinth and Ephesus. Being Paul's partners in trade, he spent much time with them. For all that is known of them, see Acts 18:1-2, 26 and Romans 16:3-5.

PRISCILLA AND AQUILA

Priscilla as is obvious, was the wife of Aquila. Paul had first found them at Corinth. Aquila was a Jew born in Pontus, who had resided at Rome, and who had left Rome, and come to Corinth, when Claudius expelled the Jews from Rome.

It is believed that they were converted under the preaching of Paul, but there is no concrete evidence of such.

Paul lived with them, due to all of them making their living, at least at times, by repairing tents. Consequently, they had the advantage of his private instruction (Acts 18:3).

At the death of Claudius, or whenever the decree for the expulsion of the Jews was repealed, it is probable that they returned to Rome. However, they are now with Paul at Ephesus.

The phrase, *"With the Church that is in their house,"* either speaks of the meeting place for the Church at Ephesus, or one of the meeting places. In fact, most all Churches in those days were located in houses.

Not long after this, taking advantage of relaxations toward Jews by Rome, they seemed to be back in that imperial city (Rom. 16:3).

(20) "ALL THE BRETHREN GREET YOU. GREET YE ONE ANOTHER WITH AN HOLY KISS."

The phrase, *"All the Brethren greet you,"* once more ties all the Churches together in a bond of fellowship.

NOTES

Paul is speaking not only of the *"Brethren"* at Ephesus, but as well, all the Churches of Asia, etc.

The reason he mentions *"Asia"* is because he is writing from that area. It does not imply that these were the only Churches in fellowship, for such was not the case. It is merely an acknowledgment from where Paul is located at that particular time.

The phrase, *"Greet ye one another with an holy kiss,"* presents that which was simply the culture for that day and time, but which now is a handshake or to embrace.

The salutations of the Churches and the friends from afar signified that all of these Brethren are in fraternal accord with the Corinthians, one with them in Faith and in Love. Then the Corinthians, too, must be in the same fraternal accord with each other. Their own mutual Salutation is to express this accord and to serve as a response to the Salutations from afar.

As the song says:

*"I'm so glad I'm a part of the family of*
*God, changed by His power, washed*
*in His Blood."*

(21) "THE SALUTATION OF ME PAUL WITH MINE OWN HAND."

Paul had dictated his letter up to this point, and some capable amanuensis (scribe) did the writing. Now Paul himself takes the pen and, as we may say, himself signs the letter.

When Paul did actually write a letter himself, his words seem to have been large and straggling (Gal. 6:11). But this was an age in which documents were frequently falsified by designing persons, and this seems to have happened as well to Paul. It concerned the Thessalonians.

After warning them not to be frightened *"by Epistles as from us"* (II Thess. 2:2), he adds, at the close of the letter, that henceforth he intends to authenticate every letter from henceforth by an autograph Salutation, in other words to sign his own name (Rom. 16:22; Col. 4:18; II Thess. 3:17).

(22) "IF ANY MAN LOVE NOT THE LORD JESUS CHRIST, LET HIM BE ANATHEMA MARANATHA."

The phrase, *"If any man love not the Lord Jesus Christ,"* places the entirety of the Gospel and God's Plan for man in its proper perspective.

*"Lord Jesus Christ"* is the Resurrection Name of our Lord. It signifies a Finished Work.

This one Verse, even as we shall study, puts the entirety of the world on notice and for all time. To be blunt, it is Jesus Christ or Hell. There is no alternative, no side motions, no other way. Jesus Christ and more particularly, *"The Lord Jesus Christ"* is the only Way. To think of Him as merely a good man is not enough. To recognize His miracle working powers is not enough. Even to believe that He is Virgin Born, which He is, is not enough. The title as given by Paul tells what we must believe:

1. *"Lord"*: This speaks of Deity, Jesus Christ is God.

2. *"Jesus"*: Jesus is Saviour, and the only Savior, for that's what this Name means.

3. *"Christ"*: He was and is the Jewish Messiah, but not for Israel only but for the whole world, for *"Christ"* means *"Messiah"* or *"Anointed."*

Anointed for what?

Anointed to *"preach the Gospel to the poor, heal the broken hearted, preach deliverance to the captives, recovering of sight to the blind, to set at liberty them that are bruised, and to preach the acceptable year of the Lord"* (Lk. 4:18-19). This is the portrayal of the Redemption of humanity. However, it would take Calvary and the Resurrection to actually perform the task.

## TO LOVE JESUS

Paul uses the Greek word *"Phileo"* in speaking here of love for Jesus.

It is a love which consists of the heart kindled by the perception of that in the object which affords us pleasure. It is the response of the humans spirit to what appeals to it as pleasurable.

The Greeks made much of friendship. The word was used to speak of a friendly affection. It is a love called out of one in response to a feeling of pleasure or delight which one experiences from an apprehension of qualities and another that furnished such pleasure or delight.

*"Agapao"* (*"Agape"*) on the other hand, speaks of a love which is awakened by a sense of value in the object loved, and an apprehension of its preciousness.

*"Phileo"* is found in Revelation 22:15; Matthew 6:5; 10:37; 23:6; Luke 20:46; John 11:3-36; I Corinthians 16:22.

NOTES

Those who find pleasure in a *lie* and thus love it, will go to a lost eternity. Hypocrites find pleasure in ostentatious prayer and thus love it. Those who take more delight in Father or Mother than in God, love them better and for that reason.

## DELIGHT IN HIM

Our Lord found delight in the response of the heart of Lazarus to His Own and thus loved him. God has a love of delight in those who's love for Jesus is based upon their delight in Him. *"Phileo"* like *"Agapao"* has its quality determined by the character of the one who loves and of the object loved.

*"Agapao"* is a love springing from a sense of the preciousness of the object loved, while *"Phileo"* as Paul here uses the word, arises from a sense of pleasure found in the object loved. When used in a good meaning, both (*"Agape"* and *"Phileo"*) are legitimate, but the first (Agape) is the nobler word.

In John Chapter 21, our Lord uses *"Agapao"* in Verses fifteen and sixteen, *"Phileo"* in seventeen. Peter uses *"Phileo"* three times.

Our Lord uses the noblest in the Greek language the first two times and changes to Peter's word the third time, but assures Peter that His coming Martyrdom speaks of the fact that his future love for his Lord will be based not only upon his delight in his Lord but upon his apprehension of His preciousness.

*"Phileo"* is used in John 16:27. The Saints have a love for the Lord Jesus which springs from their joy in Him, a love of delight. The Father has a love of delight in the Saints, for He finds in each Saint the One in whom He takes delight, The Lord Jesus, and because the Saints find their delight in Him also (Wuest).

The phrase, *"Let him be Anathema Maranatha,"* in effect says, *"let him be accursed."* More than anything else, this is directed against the Jews and Heathen who delighted to call Jesus accursed.

## ANATHEMA

Regrettably, most Jews hated, and still hate, the Lord Jesus Christ, and expressed this hatred by referring to Him as *"Anathema,"* which means *"one accursed, one so abominable as not fit to live on Earth."*

The great tragedy of the Jews, even as

expressed by Paul in Romans, Chapters Nine through Eleven, is the fact that they did not know their own Messiah when He came.

The idea of the entirety of this Verse is, that he who does not believe in the Lord Jesus and love Him, will be, and ought to be, devoted to destruction, or accursed of God. It expresses what ought to done; it expresses a Truth in regard to God's dealings, not the desire of the Apostle.

No matter what any man's endowments might be; no matter what might be his wealth, his standing, or his talent; no matter if he were regarded as a ruler in the Church, or as the head of a party; yet, if he have not true love for the Lord Jesus, he cannot be saved. This sentiment is in accordance with the declaration of the Scripture everywhere.

MARANATHA

Maranatha means *"the Lord comes"*; i.e., *"will come."*

The idea is, that there is no earthly power to punish a want of love for the Savior; though the State could not, and ought not to punish it; and though the Church could not exclude all who do not love the Lord Jesus from its bosom, yet they will not escape. For the Lord Himself will come to take vengeance on His enemies, and no one shall escape. Though, therefore, those who did not love the Lord Jesus could not be punished by men, and in fact, should not be punished by men, yet they could not and shall not escape Diving Condemnation. The Lord will come to execute vengeance Himself, and they shall not escape.

How important, then, to ask whether we have that love? Whether we are attached to the Lord Jesus in such a manner as to secure His approbation? Whether we so love Him as to be prepared to hail His coming with joy, and to be received into His Everlasting Kingdom.

AN ALTAR CALL

In the close of the notes on this Epistle, I will ask anyone who shall read these pages, whether he has this love? And I may press it upon on the attention of each one, though I may never see his face in the flesh, as the great inquiry which is to determine his everlasting destiny.

The solemn declaration stands here, that if he does not love the Lord Jesus, he will be, and he ought to be, devoted to destruction. The Lord Jesus will soon return to make investigation, and to judge the world, there will be no escape; and no tongue can express the awful horrors of an eternal curse, pronounced by the lips of the Son of God, especially considering, that Jesus has paid such a price for our Redemption, and all we have to do is accept. A living relationship with Jesus is the only thing that can prevent an eternity in hell (Barnes).

NOTES

(23) "THE GRACE OF OUR LORD JESUS CHRIST BE WITH YOU."

All Paul's letters conclude with the Grace-benediction. It is *"Grace,"* the favor of God that is theirs through *"The Lord Jesus,"* that he wishes for them. Thus the Letter begins with a salutation *"Grace to you"* and concludes the same way. Grace is the beginning and the end of the Christian Gospel; it is the single word that most fully expresses what God has done and will do for His people in Christ Jesus.

GRACE

In its most simplistic explanation, Grace is the unmerited favor of the Lord and all the gifts that flow from that favor. To the sinner this Grace extends unmerited pardon, and all, although Believers, still come short of the Glory of God on a daily basis. Consequently, we ask for this pardoning Grace every time we pray the Lord's Prayer, or a similarity thereof.

But every other Gift, that we receive from the Lord likewise flows from this Grace *"without any merit or worthiness on our part."* The Source of this Grace is *"The Lord Jesus Christ,"* who is named according to His Person (Jesus), His Work (Christ), and His Saving Relation to us (Lord) (Lenski).

(24) "MY LOVE BE WITH YOU ALL IN CHRIST JESUS. AMEN."

This Letter is somewhat peculiar because Paul adds another word after the formal benediction which assures the Corinthians of his love to them.

Paul probably adds this note, simply because he has had to write some very strong things in the body of the Letter. Now he desires to show them that it is not from the realm of personal satisfaction that these things were said, but because of his love for them. He does not merely write about love, he exercises it to the full.

NOTES

### THE LAST WORD IS AND MUST BE *"CHRIST JESUS."*

The Apostle's great heart swells once more. Whatever other emotions he has shown in writing this Letter, Love, is the deepest, richest of them all. And it embraces all the Corinthians, even those who distress his heart as well as those who delight his heart.

Back of everyone of his admonitions to them stands his heart of love. The last word is and must be *"Christ Jesus."* He and He Alone is the sphere in which Paul's love lives, moves, and has its being. Into that sphere of love Paul, like a magnet, draws all who come into contact with it (Lenski).

*"Rescue the perishing, care for the dying,*
*"Snatch them in pity from sin and the grave;*
*"Weep o'er the erring one lift up the fallen,*
*"Tell them of Jesus so Mighty to save."*

*"Though they are slighting Him, still, He is waiting,*
*"Waiting the penitent child to receive;*
*"Plead with them earnestly, plead with them gently,*
*"He will forgive if they only believe."*

*"Down in the human heart, crushed by the tempter,*
*"Feelings lie buried that Grace can restore;*
*"Touched by a loving heart, awakened by kindest,*
*"Chords that were broken will vibrate once more."*

*"Rescue the perishing, duty demands it;*
*"Strength for thy labor the Lord will provide.*
*"Back to the narrow way patiently win them;*
*"Tell the poor wanderer a Savior has died."*

It is June 10th, 1998, 9:13 a.m. as I conclude the notes on I Corinthians. I believe the Lord truly and surely has helped us to open up this Epistle, at least somewhat, that it will prayerfully be a blessing to you. This I do know, these great questions as addressed by the Apostle of old, have personally taken me deeper into the Word of God. If I have been able to properly convey on paper that which I have felt in my heart, then I know this effort, by the Grace of God will be of help and blessing to you. I pray that it shall.

As I conclude the commentary on this particular Epistle, it is now a little bit over six years since I began this task, and actually I should say well over fifty years, because what little I have learned in all of this time becomes a part of this which hopefully the Lord has helped me to give to you. If our efforts glorify Christ, then they have been worthwhile. If not, then the effort has been wasted. If there is any help or good in these pages, the Glory goes to the Lord in totality.

## BIBLIOGRAPHY

Strong's Exhaustive Concordance of the Bible.

Zondervan Pictorial Encyclopedia of the Bible.

Williams' Commentary on the Bible.

Word Studies in the Greek New Testament, Kenneth Wuest.

The Bible Dictionary.

The Interlinear Greek-English New Testament.

The International Standard Bible Encyclopedia.

The Dictionary of Paul and his Letters.

The Expository Dictionary of Bible Words, Richards.

Josephus, The Essential Writings.

Ellicott's Commentary on the Whole Bible.

Vine's Expository Dictionary of the New Testament Words.

Webster's New Collegiate Dictionary.

# INDEX

The index is listed according to subjects. The treatment may include a complete dissertation or no more than a paragraph. But hopefully it will provide some help.

As well, even though extended treatment of a subject may not be carried in this Commentary, one of the other Commentaries may well include the desired material.